# ILLUSTRATED ATLAS
## OF AMERICAN HISTORY

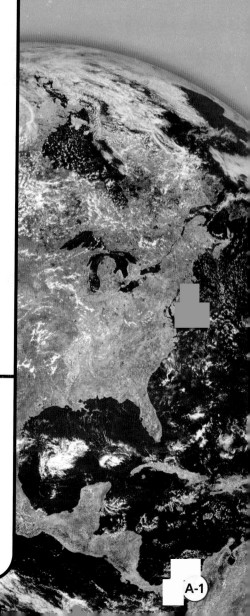

## Table of Contents

## Introduction

This illustrated atlas contains dramatic maps and vibrant pictures and graphs to bring your study of American history to life. You can use these pages to compare regions or to make connections between past and present. The atlas has been placed at the front of your textbook, so you will have it as a ready reference throughout the year.

*Get up-to-date information about any country in the world. Use the World Desk Reference Online to learn about the world today, practice critical thinking skills, and get updated statistics and data.*

# UNITED STATES
## POLITICAL

Golden Gate Bridge, San Francisco, California

115°W    110°W    105°W    100°W

Seattle

Spokane

Olympia  **Washington**

Great Falls

Minot    Grand Forks

Helena  **Montana**  **North Dakota**

Portland    Bismarck

Salem

Billings

Eugene  **South Dakota**

**Oregon**

Boise  **Idaho**    Rapid City    Pierre

**Wyoming**    Sioux Falls

Pocatello

Casper

Ogden    Cheyenne

Reno  *Great*  Salt Lake

San Francisco  Carson City  *Salt Lake*  City    **Kansas**

Sacramento    Denver

Oakland  **Nevada**  **Utah**  **Colorado**    Wichita

San Jose

Colorado
Springs

**California**

Las
Vegas    **Oklahoma**

125°W    Santa Fe    Oklahoma
City

Los Angeles    Albuquerque

Long Beach

*PACIFIC*    **New Mexico**

*OCEAN*    San Diego

30°N

Las
Cruces    Fort Worth

El Paso

115°W    110°W  **Texas**    Austin

120°W    San
Antonio

160°W    155°W    180° 70°N 170°W    160°W  150°W
**RUSSIA**    140°W

Honolulu  **Hawaii**    130°W

*PACIFIC OCEAN*    Arctic Circle

20°N    **Alaska**

0 km    100    60°N    Fairbanks    **CANADA**

0 miles    100

Mercator Projection    Anchorage    **MEXICO**

160°E    170°E    *Bering*    *Gulf of*    Juneau

50°N    *Sea*    *Alaska*

*PACIFIC*    0 km    400

*OCEAN*    0 miles    400

Albers Conic Equal-Area Projection

105°W    100°W

A-2

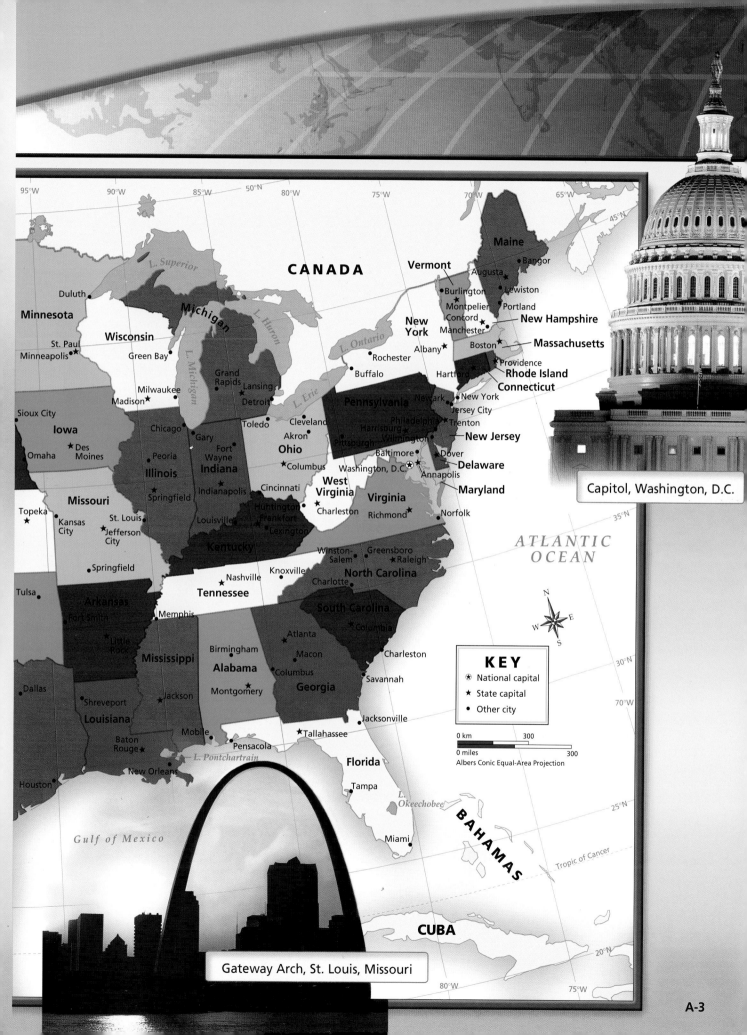

Minnesota
Duluth
St. Paul
Minneapolis

Wisconsin
Green Bay
Milwaukee
Madison

Michigan
Grand Rapids
Lansing
Detroit

CANADA

L. Superior
L. Michigan
L. Huron
L. Ontario
L. Erie

Vermont
Burlington
Montpelier
Concord
Manchester

Maine
Bangor
Augusta
Lewiston
Portland

New Hampshire

New York
Albany
Rochester
Buffalo

Boston
Providence
Hartford

Massachusetts

Rhode Island
Connecticut

Sioux City
Iowa
Des Moines
Omaha

Chicago
Gary
Peoria
Illinois
Springfield
Indianapolis

Fort Wayne
Indiana

Toledo
Cleveland
Akron
Ohio
Columbus

Pennsylvania
Harrisburg
Pittsburgh
Newark
New York
Jersey City
Trenton
Philadelphia
Wilmington
Baltimore

New Jersey

Dover
Delaware

Topeka
Missouri
Kansas City
Jefferson City
St. Louis
Springfield

Cincinnati
West Virginia
Louisville
Frankfort
Huntington
Lexington
Kentucky

Charleston

Washington, D.C.
Annapolis
Maryland

Virginia
Richmond
Norfolk

Tulsa

Arkansas
Fort Smith
Little Rock

Memphis

Nashville
Tennessee

Knoxville
Winston-Salem
Greensboro
Raleigh
Charlotte

North Carolina

ATLANTIC OCEAN

Dallas
Shreveport
Louisiana
Baton Rouge
New Orleans
Houston

Mississippi
Jackson

Birmingham
Alabama
Montgomery
Columbus
Mobile
Pensacola

Atlanta
Macon
Columbus
Georgia
Savannah

South Carolina
Columbia
Charleston

Jacksonville

Tallahassee

Florida
Tampa

L. Pontchartrain

Gulf of Mexico

L. Okeechobee

Miami

BAHAMAS

CUBA

**Capitol, Washington, D.C.**

**KEY**
- ⊛ National capital
- ★ State capital
- • Other city

0 km     300
0 miles     300
Albers Conic Equal-Area Projection

Tropic of Cancer

**Gateway Arch, St. Louis, Missouri**

95°W 90°W 85°W 50°N 80°W 75°W 70°W 65°W 45°N 35°N 30°N 70°W 25°N 20°N 75°W 80°W

# UNITED STATES
## PHYSICAL

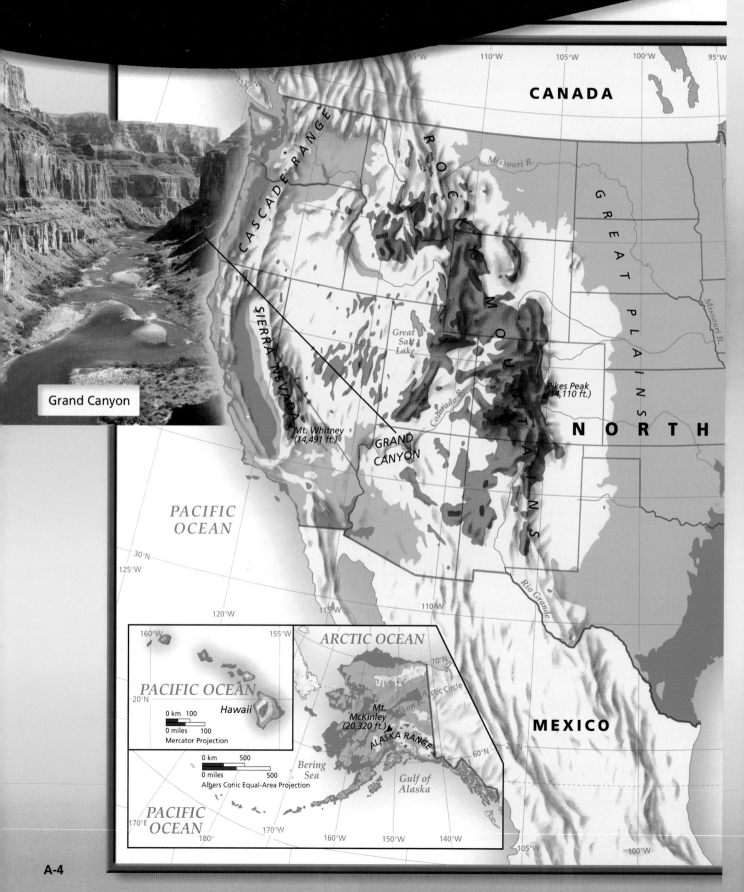

Grand Canyon

CANADA

125°W  5°W  110°W  105°W  100°W  95°W

CASCADE RANGE

R O C K Y

Missouri R.

G R E A T

SIERRA NEVADA

Great Salt Lake

M O U N T A I N S

P L A I N S

Colorado R.

Missouri R.

Pikes Peak
(14,110 ft.)

Mt. Whitney
(14,491 ft.)

GRAND
CANYON

N O R T H

PACIFIC
OCEAN

30°N
125°W

120°W

115°W

110°W

Rio Grande

MEXICO

ARCTIC OCEAN

160°W  155°W

PACIFIC OCEAN

20°N

Hawaii

70°N

Arctic Circle

0 km  100
0 miles  100
Mercator Projection

Mt.
McKinley
(20,320 ft.)

Yukon R.

0 km  500
0 miles  500
Albers Conic Equal-Area Projection

ALASKA RANGE

Bering
Sea

60°N

105°W

100°W

Gulf of
Alaska

2  N

PACIFIC
OCEAN

170°E

180°

170°W

160°W

150°W

140°W

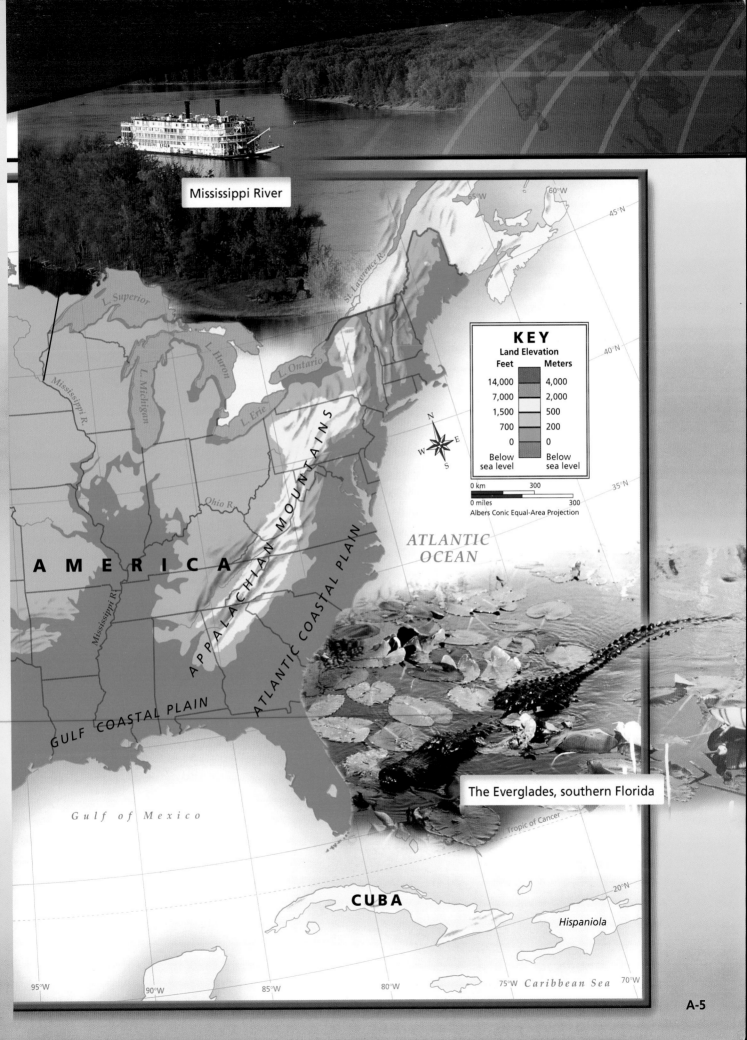

Mississippi River

# KEY

## Land Elevation

| Feet | Meters |
|------|--------|
| 14,000 | 4,000 |
| 7,000 | 2,000 |
| 1,500 | 500 |
| 700 | 200 |
| 0 | 0 |
| Below sea level | Below sea level |

N
W E
S

0 km 300
0 miles 300
Albers Conic Equal-Area Projection

*L. Superior*

*L. Huron*

*L. Michigan*

*L. Ontario*

*L. Erie*

*Mississippi R.*

*St. Lawrence R.*

*Ohio R.*

A M E R I C A

A P P A L A C H I A N   M O U N T A I N S

*Mississippi R.*

ATLANTIC COASTAL PLAIN

GULF COASTAL PLAIN

*ATLANTIC OCEAN*

The Everglades, southern Florida

*Gulf of Mexico*

Tropic of Cancer

CUBA

*Hispaniola*

*Caribbean Sea*

65°W
60°W
45°N
40°N
35°N
20°N

95°W
90°W
85°W
80°W
75°W
70°W

# UNITED STATES
## RESOURCES & THE ECONOMY

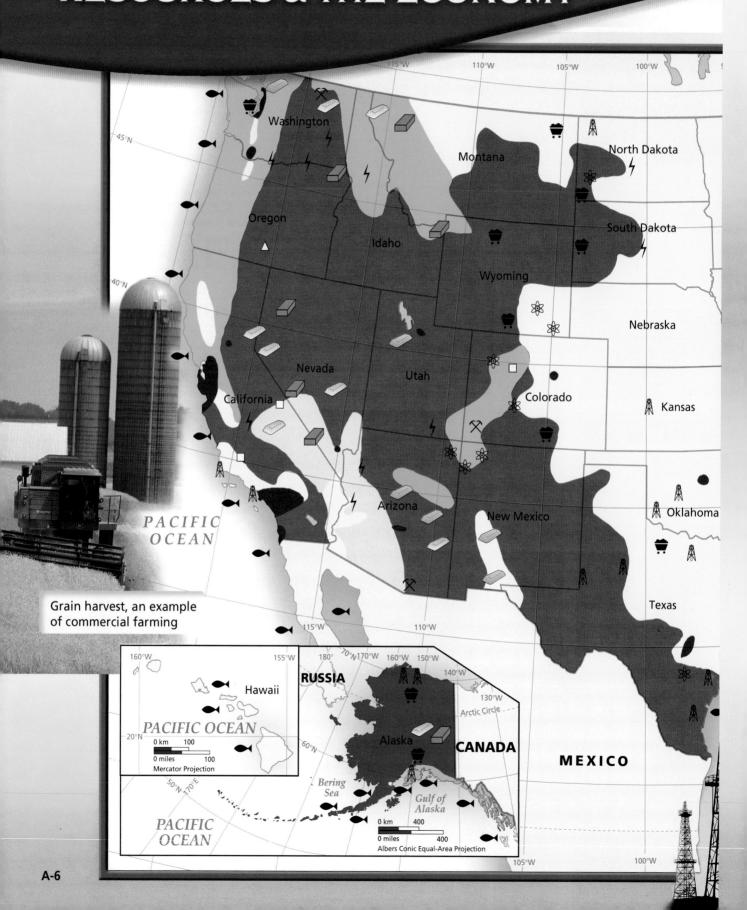

Grain harvest, an example of commercial farming

CANADA

Minnesota

L. Superior

Michigan

L. Huron

L. Michigan

Wisconsin

L. Ontario

New York

L. Erie

Iowa

Illinois

Indiana

Ohio

Pennsylvania

West Virginia

Vermont

Maine

New Hampshire

Massachusetts

Rhode Island

Connecticut

New Jersey

Delaware

Maryland

Virginia

Missouri

Kentucky

North Carolina

ATLANTIC OCEAN

Tennessee

Arkansas

South Carolina

Mississippi

Alabama

Georgia

0 km            300

0 miles          300

Albers Conic Equal-Area Projection

N

W         E

S

Louisiana

Florida

Gulf of Mexico

**Medical research, a key service industry in the U.S. economy**

**KEY**

| | | | |
|---|---|---|---|
| ▮ | Hunting and gathering | 𝌡 | Iron |
| ▮ | Forestry | ▱ | Copper |
| ▮ | Livestock raising | ⛏ | Bauxite |
| ▯ | Commercial farming | ▭ | Gold |
| ▮ | Manufacturing and trade | ▱ | Silver |
| 🐟 | Commercial fishing | ● | Phosphates |
| ▯ | Little or no activity | ⚛ | Uranium |
| ⛏ | Coal | ✕ | Lead |
| 🛢 | Petroleum | △ | Nickel |
| ⚡ | Hydroelectric power | □ | Tungsten |

**Oil wells pump petroleum, an important natural resource**

95°W   90°W   85°W   50°N   80°W   75°W   70°W   65°W

20°N

75°W

# THE WORLD: POLITICAL

100°W 80°W 60°W

*Greenland (Den.)*

*Alaska (U.S.)*

60°N

**CANADA**

**NORTH AMERICA**

Ottawa ✪

**UNITED STATES**

40°N

Washington, DC ✪

*Bermuda (U.K.)*

**ATLANTIC OCEAN**

Tropic of Cancer

*Hawaii (U.S.)*

*Gulf of Mexico*

**MEXICO**

20°N

Mexico City ✪

*Caribbean Sea*

**GUYANA**

Paramaribo ✪

Georgetown ✪ Cayenne ✪

Bogotá ✪

**VENEZUELA**

**COLOMBIA**

*French Guiana (Fr.)*

**SURINAME**

*Galápagos Is. (Ecuador)*

Quito ✪

Equator 0°

**ECUADOR**

**SOUTH AMERICA**

**SAMOA**

**PERU**

**BRAZIL**

*American Samoa (U.S.)*

*French Polynesia (Fr.)*

Lima ✪

**PACIFIC OCEAN**

**TONGA**

*Cook Is. (N.Z.)*

**BOLIVIA**

La Paz ✪

Brasília ✪

20°S

*Pitcairn I. (U.K.)*

**PARAGUAY**

Tropic of Capricorn

*Easter Is. (Chile)*

Asunción ✪

**CHILE**

Santiago ✪

Buenos Aires ✪

**URUGUAY**

Montevideo ✪

International Date Line

40°S

**ARGENTINA**

*Falkland Is. (U.K.)*

60°S

**SOUTHERN OCEAN**

Antarctic Circle

**ANTARCTICA**

## Central America and the Caribbean

0 km 300
0 miles 300
Azimuthal Projection

30°N

**UNITED STATES**

*Gulf of Mexico*

N
W ✦ E
S

Nassau ✪

B A H A M A S

Tropic of Cancer

Havana ✪

20°N

**CUBA**

**MEXICO**

Kingston ✪

**DOMINICAN REPUBLIC**

Port-au-Prince ✪

**HAITI**

*Br. Virgin Is. (U.K.)*

*Puerto Rico (U.S.)*

**ANTIGUA AND BARBUDA**

Belmopan ✪

Santo Domingo ✪

*Virgin Islands (U.S.)*

*Guadeloupe (Fr.)*

**JAMAICA**

**ST. KITTS AND NEVIS**

**BELIZE**

*Caribbean Sea*

**DOMINICA**

**GUATEMALA**

**HONDURAS**

*Martinique (Fr.)*

Guatemala ✪

Tegucigalpa ✪

**ST. LUCIA**

San Salvador ✪

*Neth. Antilles (Neth.)*

**NICARAGUA**

**ST. VINCENT AND THE GRENADINES**

**BARBADOS**

*Aruba (Neth.)*

**EL SALVADOR**

Managua ✪

**GRENADA**

10°N

**COSTA RICA**

San José ✪

Caracas ✪

Port-of-Spain ✪

**TRINIDAD AND TOBAGO**

**PACIFIC OCEAN**

Panamá ✪

60°W

**ATLANTIC OCEAN**

**PANAMA**

**COLOMBIA**

**VENEZUELA**

**GUYANA**

80°W 70°W

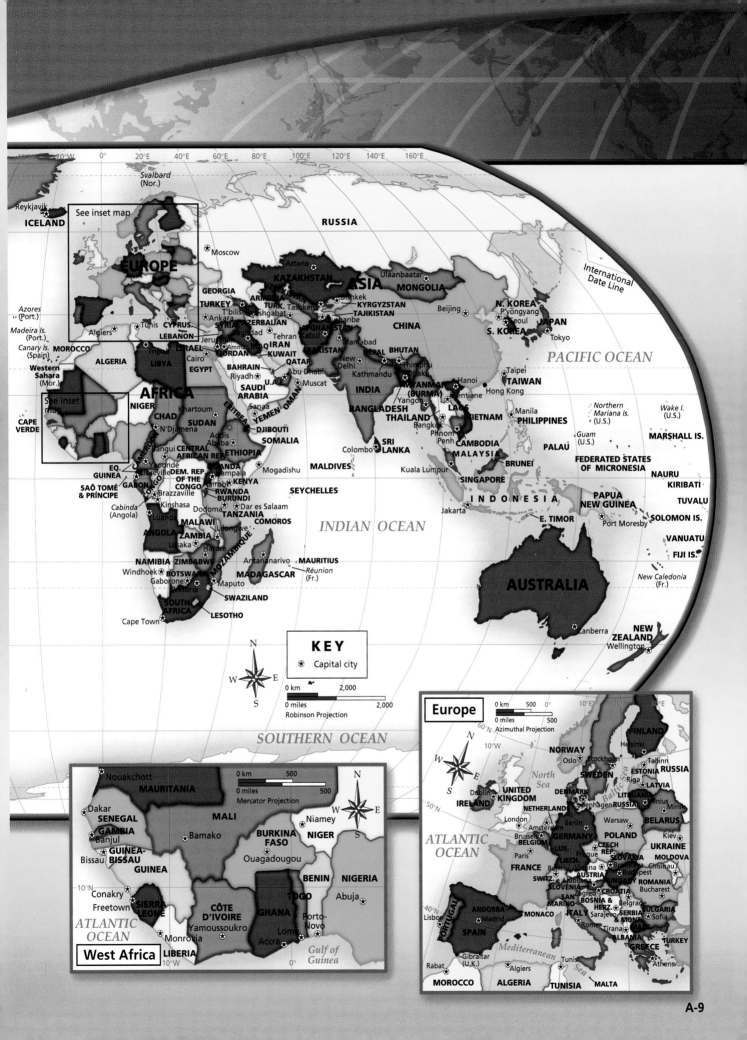

ICELAND
Reykjavik

Svalbard
(Nor.)

EUROPE
See inset map

Moscow

RUSSIA

ASIA

KAZAKHSTAN
Astana

MONGOLIA
Ulaanbaatar

Azores
(Port.)

GEORGIA
TURKEY
ARMENIA
Ankara
AZERBAIJAN
SYRIA
CYPRUS
LEBANON
ISRAEL
Jerusalem
Tripoli
JORDAN
Cairo

TURK.
T'bilisi
Ashgabat
Tashkent
Baghdad
Tehran
Amman
IRAQ
KUWAIT
Riyadh
Abu Dhabi
U.A.E.

KYRGYZSTAN
Bishkek
TAJIKISTAN
Dushanbe
AFGHANISTAN
Kabul
Islamabad
PAKISTAN

Beijing

N. KOREA
P'yongyang
Seoul
S. KOREA

JAPAN

Tokyo

PACIFIC OCEAN

Madeira Is.
(Port.)
Canary Is.
(Spain)
MOROCCO
Algiers
Tunis

ALGERIA
Western
Sahara
(Mor.)

LIBYA
EGYPT

BAHRAIN
QATAR

SAUDI
ARABIA

IRAN

CHINA

NEPAL
BHUTAN
New
Delhi
Kathmandu
Thimphu
Dhaka

Taipei
TAIWAN
Hong Kong

CAPE
VERDE

AFRICA

NIGER
CHAD
SUDAN

ERITREA
Khartoum
N'Djamena

DJIBOUTI

Sanaa
YEMEN
OMAN
Muscat

INDIA

BANGLADESH

MYANMAR
(BURMA)
Yangon

Hanoi

Vientiane
LAOS
VIETNAM

PHILIPPINES

Manila

Northern
Mariana Is.
(U.S.)

Wake I.
(U.S.)

MARSHALL IS.

See inset
map

CAMEROON
EQ.
GUINEA
SAŌ TOMÉ
& PRÍNCIPE
GABON

Pangui
CENTRAL
AFRICAN REP.
Yaoundé
Libreville

ETHIOPIA
Addis
Ababa

SOMALIA

Mogadishu

MALDIVES

SRI
LANKA
Colombo

THAILAND
Bangkok

Phnom
Penh
CAMBODIA
MALAYSIA

Kuala Lumpur

SINGAPORE

BRUNEI

PALAU

Guam
(U.S.)

FEDERATED STATES
OF MICRONESIA

NAURU
KIRIBATI

Cabinda
(Angola)

CONGO
Brazzaville
Kinshasa
DEM. REP.
OF THE
CONGO
Luanda

UGANDA
Kampala
Nairobi
KENYA
RWANDA
BURUNDI
Dodoma
TANZANIA
Dar es Salaam

SEYCHELLES

INDONESIA

Jakarta

PAPUA
NEW GUINEA

TUVALU

SOLOMON IS.

ANGOLA
ZAMBIA
Lusaka
MALAWI
Lilongwe
Harare

COMOROS

INDIAN OCEAN

Port Moresby

VANUATU

FIJI IS.

NAMIBIA
Windhoek
BOTSWANA
Gaborone
ZIMBABWE
MOZAMBIQUE
Pretoria
Maputo
SWAZILAND
LESOTHO
Cape Town
SOUTH
AFRICA

Antananarivo
MADAGASCAR

MAURITIUS
Réunion
(Fr.)

AUSTRALIA

New Caledonia
(Fr.)

Canberra

NEW
ZEALAND
Wellington

International
Date Line

**KEY**

⊛ Capital city

N
W        E
S

| 0 km | 2,000 |
| 0 miles | 2,000 |

Robinson Projection

SOUTHERN OCEAN

---

**West Africa**

Nouakchott
MAURITANIA

| 0 km | 500 |
| 0 miles | 500 |

Mercator Projection

N
W        E
S

Dakar
SENEGAL
GAMBIA
Banjul
GUINEA-
BISSAU
Bissau
GUINEA
Conakry
Freetown
SIERRA
LEONE
Monrovia
LIBERIA

MALI
Bamako

Niamey
NIGER

BURKINA
FASO
Ouagadougou

BENIN

NIGERIA
Abuja

CÔTE
D'IVOIRE
Yamoussoukro

TOGO
GHANA
Accra
Lomé
Porto-
Novo

Gulf of
Guinea

ATLANTIC
OCEAN

10°N

10°W
0°

---

**Europe**

| 0 km | 500 |
| 0 miles | 500 |

Azimuthal Projection

N
W        E
S

NORWAY
Oslo

Stockholm
SWEDEN

FINLAND
Helsinki

Tallinn
ESTONIA
RUSSIA
Riga
LATVIA
LITHUANIA
Vilnius
Minsk

North
Sea

Baltic
Sea

Dublin
IRELAND
UNITED
KINGDOM

DENMARK
Copenhagen
NETHERLANDS
London
Amsterdam
Berlin
BELGIUM
Brussels
GERMANY
LUX.
CZECH
REP.
Prague
Paris
LIECH.
FRANCE
SWITZ.
Bern
Vienna
AUSTRIA
SLOVENIA
Ljubljana
Zagreb
CROATIA
SAN
MARINO
ITALY
Rome

RUSSIA
Warsaw
POLAND
Kiev
UKRAINE
SLOVAKIA
Bratislava
Chisinau
MOLDOVA
Budapest
HUNGARY
ROMANIA
Bucharest
Belgrade
SERBIA
& MONT.
BOSNIA &
HERZ.
Sarajevo
BULGARIA
Sofia
Tirana
ALBANIA
GREECE
Athens

BELARUS

ATLANTIC
OCEAN

PORTUGAL
Lisbon
ANDORRA
Madrid
SPAIN
MONACO

Gibraltar
(U.K.)
Rabat

Mediterranean
Sea

Algiers
Tunis

TURKEY

MOROCCO
ALGERIA
TUNISIA
MALTA

# THE UNITED STATES
## A DIVERSE NATION

POLLING PLACE

投票站 CASILLA ELECTORAL
投票所 LUGAR NG BOTOHAN
투표소 PHÒNG PHIẾU

Sign at a California polling place

ASIA

CANADA

UNITED

### Asian Migration
According to the 2000 census, 10.2 million Asian Americans make up 3.6 percent of the total U.S. population. Asian immigrants include people from China, Japan, Korea, the Philippines, as well as those from countries in Southeast Asia and South Asia.

N
W E
S

0 km          3,000
0 miles          3,000
Mercator Projection

PACIFIC OCEAN

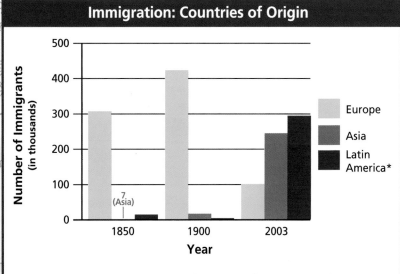

## Immigration: Countries of Origin

Number of Immigrants (in thousands)

500
400
300
200
100
0

7 (Asia)

1850    1900    2003

**Year**

Europe
Asia
Latin America*

*Latin America includes the Caribbean, Mexico, and the countries of Central America and South America.

Sources: *Historical Statistics of the United States* and *Statistical Yearbook of the Immigration and Naturalization Service*

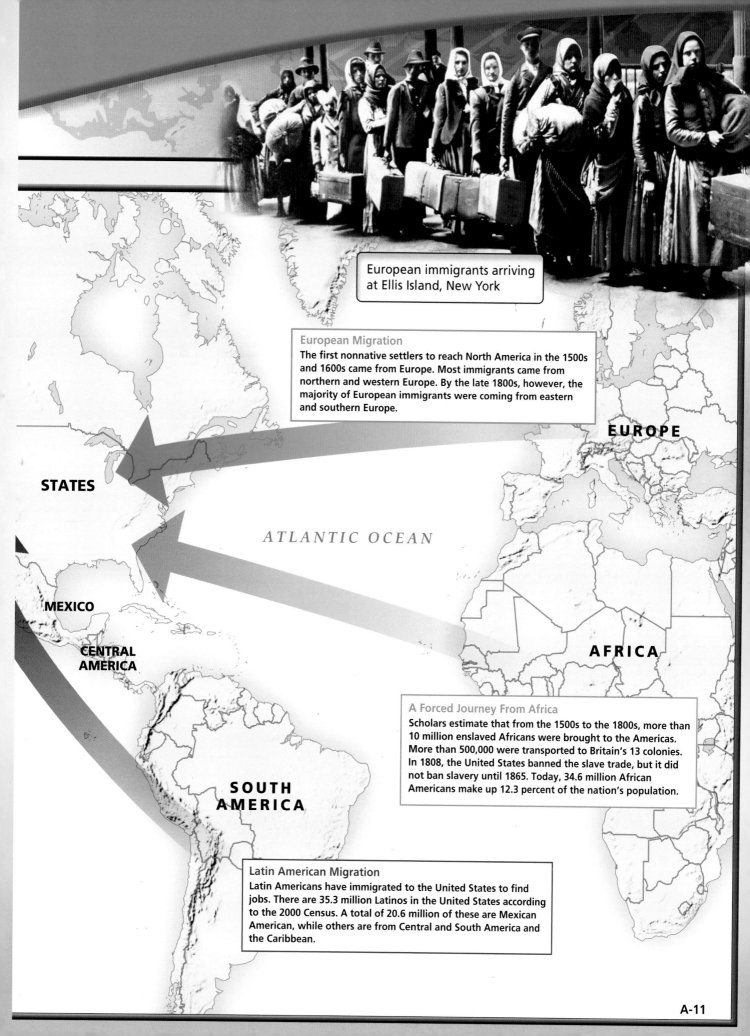

European immigrants arriving at Ellis Island, New York

**European Migration**

The first nonnative settlers to reach North America in the 1500s and 1600s came from Europe. Most immigrants came from northern and western Europe. By the late 1800s, however, the majority of European immigrants were coming from eastern and southern Europe.

EUROPE

STATES

ATLANTIC OCEAN

MEXICO

CENTRAL
AMERICA

AFRICA

**A Forced Journey From Africa**

Scholars estimate that from the 1500s to the 1800s, more than 10 million enslaved Africans were brought to the Americas. More than 500,000 were transported to Britain's 13 colonies. In 1808, the United States banned the slave trade, but it did not ban slavery until 1865. Today, 34.6 million African Americans make up 12.3 percent of the nation's population.

SOUTH
AMERICA

**Latin American Migration**

Latin Americans have immigrated to the United States to find jobs. There are 35.3 million Latinos in the United States according to the 2000 Census. A total of 20.6 million of these are Mexican American, while others are from Central and South America and the Caribbean.

# UNITED STATES
## TERRITORIAL EXPANSION
## TO 1853

Mandan Village, like the one visited by Lewis and Clark during their exploration of the Louisiana Territory

A covered wagon, the mode of transportation for people moving west in the 1800s

The Alamo, site of a key battle in the war for Texas independence; Texas became part of the Mexican Cession

*PACIFIC OCEAN*

**OREGON COUNTRY**
(Agreement with Britain, 1846)

(Ceded by Britain, 1818)

**LOUISIANA PURCHASE**
(Purchased from France, 1803)

**MEXICAN CESSION**
(Treaty of Guadalupe-Hidalgo, 1848)

**TEXAS ANNEXATION**
(Annexed by Congress, 1845)

**GADSDEN PURCHASE**
(Purchased from Mexico, 1853)

**MEXICO**

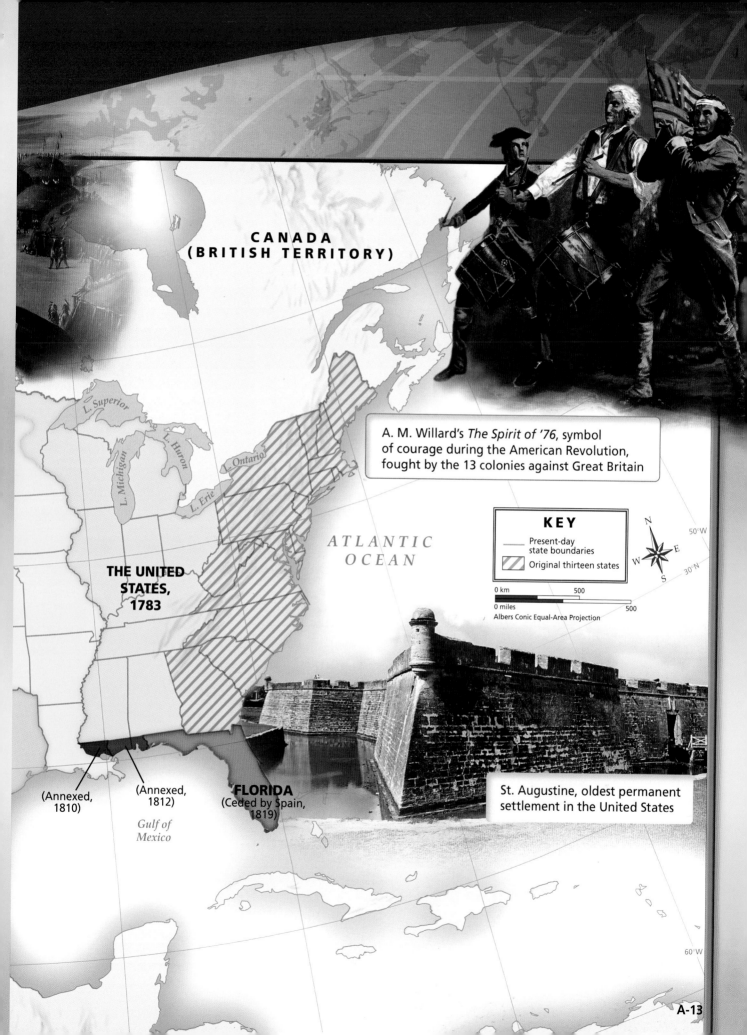

CANADA
(BRITISH TERRITORY)

L. Superior

L. Michigan

L. Huron

L. Ontario

L. Erie

THE UNITED
STATES,
1783

ATLANTIC
OCEAN

A. M. Willard's *The Spirit of '76*, symbol of courage during the American Revolution, fought by the 13 colonies against Great Britain

**KEY**

Present-day state boundaries

Original thirteen states

0 km 500

0 miles 500

Albers Conic Equal-Area Projection

50°W

30°N

60°W

N W E S

(Annexed, 1810)

(Annexed, 1812)

**FLORIDA**
(Ceded by Spain, 1819)

*Gulf of Mexico*

St. Augustine, oldest permanent settlement in the United States

# UNITED STATES
## POPULATION DENSITY

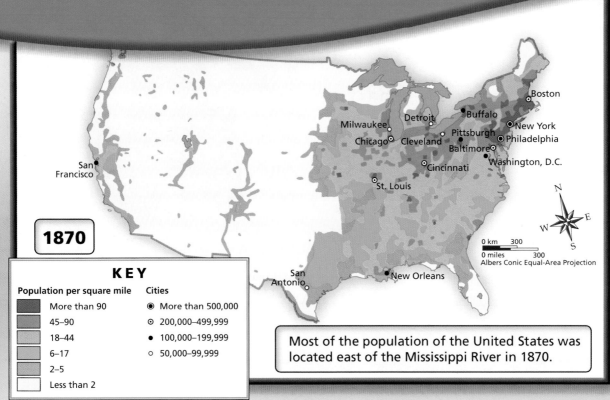

**1870**

### KEY

**Population per square mile**

- More than 90
- 45–90
- 18–44
- 6–17
- 2–5
- Less than 2

**Cities**

- ◉ More than 500,000
- ◎ 200,000–499,999
- ● 100,000–199,999
- ○ 50,000–99,999

Most of the population of the United States was located east of the Mississippi River in 1870.

By 1960, the Midwest and the West had become more populated. A number of large cities had grown in these regions.

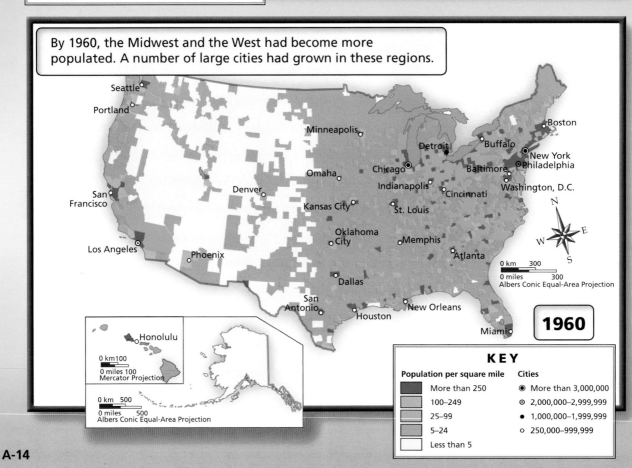

**1960**

### KEY

**Population per square mile**

- More than 250
- 100–249
- 25–99
- 5–24
- Less than 5

**Cities**

- ◉ More than 3,000,000
- ◎ 2,000,000–2,999,999
- ● 1,000,000–1,999,999
- ○ 250,000–999,999

In the 1880s, Anaheim, California, outside of Los Angeles was rural. By the twenty-first century Los Angeles, as well as surrounding cities like Anaheim, were modern bustling cities connected by freeways.

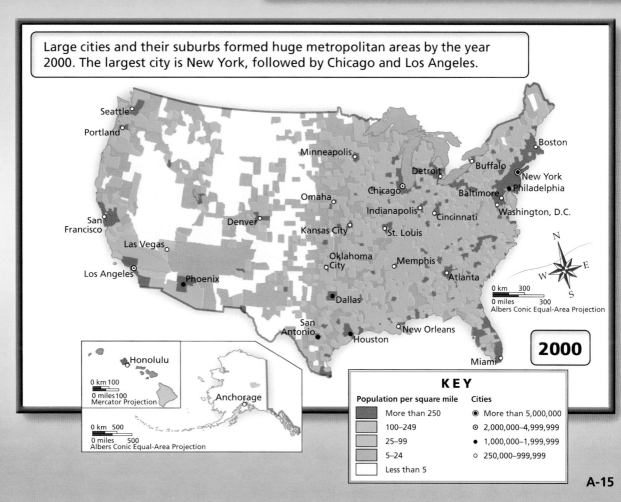

Large cities and their suburbs formed huge metropolitan areas by the year 2000. The largest city is New York, followed by Chicago and Los Angeles.

Seattle
Portland
Minneapolis
Boston
Detroit
Buffalo
Chicago
New York
Omaha
Philadelphia
Indianapolis
Cincinnati
Baltimore
San
Francisco
Denver
Kansas City
St. Louis
Washington, D.C.
Las Vegas
Los Angeles
Oklahoma City
Memphis
Atlanta
Phoenix
Dallas
San Antonio
Houston
New Orleans
Miami

0 km 300
0 miles 300
Albers Conic Equal-Area Projection

2000

Honolulu
0 km 100
0 miles 100
Mercator Projection

Anchorage
0 km 500
0 miles 500
Albers Conic Equal-Area Projection

**KEY**

Population per square mile | Cities
--- | ---
More than 250 | ◉ More than 5,000,000
100–249 | ◎ 2,000,000–4,999,999
25–99 | ● 1,000,000–1,999,999
5–24 | ○ 250,000–999,999
Less than 5 |

# SYMBOLS OF OUR NATION

Today's American flag has thirteen red and white stripes representing the original thirteen states. Fifty white stars stand for the current number of states. The first official flag had thirteen stars and was approved in 1777.

Thirteen white stars

American bald eagle

Scroll reading *E Pluribus Unum* ("Out of Many, One")

Olive branch (symbol of peace)

Thirteen arrows (symbol of war)

The Great Seal of the United States was designed after the American Revolution to represent the new nation, and the values of its founders. The Great Seal appears on the back of the one-dollar bill of the United States.

Prentice Hall

# AMERICA

## HISTORY OF OUR NATION

PEARSON

Prentice Hall

Upper Saddle River, New Jersey
Boston, Massachusetts

*Authors*

James West Davidson
Michael B. Stoff

THE LANDING OF THE PILGRIMS :1620    MABELLE L. HOLMES

Acknowledgments appear on page 1067, which constitutes an extension of this copyright page.

**Copyright © 2007 by Pearson Education, Inc., publishing as Pearson Prentice Hall, Boston, Massachusetts 02116.** All rights reserved. Printed in the United States of America. This publication is protected by copyright, and permission should be obtained from the publisher prior to any prohibited reproduction, storage in a retrieval system, or transmission in any form or by any means, electronic, mechanical, photocopying, recording, or likewise. For information regarding permission(s), write to: Rights and Permissions Department, One Lake Street, Upper Saddle River, New Jersey 07458.

**Discovery School®** is a registered trademark of Discovery Communications, Inc.
**MapMaster®** is a registered trademark of Pearson Education, Inc.

**Pearson Prentice Hall™** is a trademark of Pearson Education, Inc.
**Pearson®** is a registered trademark of Pearson plc.
**Prentice Hall®** is a registered trademark of Pearson Education, Inc.

ISBN 0-13-130735-5

1 2 3 4 5 6 7 8 9 10    09  08  07  06  05

# Authors

## James West Davidson

Dr. James Davidson is coauthor of *After the Fact: The Art of Historical Detection* and *Nation of Nations: A Narrative History of the American Republic.* Dr. Davidson has taught at both the college and high school levels. He has also consulted on curriculum design for American history courses. Dr. Davidson is an avid canoeist and hiker. His published works on these subjects include *Great Heart,* the true story of a 1903 canoe trip in the Canadian wilderness.

## Michael B. Stoff

Dr. Michael Stoff received his Ph.D. from Yale University and teaches history at the University of Texas at Austin. He is the author of *Oil, War, and American Security: The Search for a National Policy on Foreign Oil, 1941–1947,* coauthor of *Nation of Nations: A Narrative History of the American Republic,* and coeditor of *The Manhattan Project: A Documentary Introduction to the Atomic Age.* Dr. Stoff has won numerous grants, fellowships, and teaching awards.

# Senior Program Consultants

## Albert M. Camarillo

Dr. Albert Camarillo received his Ph.D. in U.S. history from the University of California at Los Angeles. He has been teaching history at Stanford University since 1975. Dr. Camarillo has published six books, including *Chicanos in a Changing Society: From Mexican Pueblos to American Barrios* and *California: A History of Mexican Americans.* His awards for research and writing include a National Endowment for the Humanities Fellowship and a Rockefeller Foundation Fellowship. Dr. Camarillo is the Miriam and Peter Haas Centennial Professor in Public Service.

## Diane Hart

Diane Hart is a writer and consultant in history and social studies. She earned bachelor's and master's degrees in history from Stanford University and was a Woodrow Wilson Fellow. As a former teacher at the elementary, secondary, and college levels, Ms. Hart remains deeply involved in social studies education through her active participation in both the National and California Councils for the Social Studies. She has written a number of textbooks for middle school students.

# Senior Reading Consultants

## Kate Kinsella

Kate Kinsella, Ed.D., is a faculty member in the Department of Secondary Education at San Francisco State University. A specialist in secondary language acquisition and adolescent literacy, she teaches coursework addressing language and literacy development across the secondary curricula. Dr. Kinsella earned her M.A. in TESOL from San Francisco State University and her Ed.D. in Second Language Acquisition from the University of San Francisco.

## Kevin Feldman

Kevin Feldman, Ed.D., is the Director of Reading and Early Intervention with the Sonoma County Office of Education (SCOE) and an independent educational consultant. At the SCOE, he develops, organizes, and monitors programs related to K–12 literacy. Dr. Feldman has an M.A. from the University of California, Riverside, in Special Education, Learning Disabilities, and Instructional Design. He earned his Ed.D. in Curriculum and Instruction from the University of San Francisco.

## Academic Reviewers

**William R. Childs, Ph.D.**
Associate Professor of History
Ohio State University
Columbus, Ohio

**Theodore DeLaney, Ph.D.**
Associate Professor of History
Washington & Lee University
Lexington, Virginia

**Wanda A. Hendricks, Ph.D.**
Associate Professor of History
University of South Carolina
Columbia, South Carolina

**Emma Lapsansky, Ph.D.**
Professor of History and Curator of Special
    Collections
Haverford College
Haverford, Pennsylvania

**Brendan McConville, Ph.D.**
Professor of History
Boston University
Boston, Massachusetts

**Gordon Newby, Ph.D.**
Chair, Department of Middle Eastern
    and South Asian Studies
Emory University
Atlanta, Georgia

**Judy A. Ridner, Ph.D.**
Assistant Professor of History
Muhlenberg College
Allentown, Pennsylvania

## Teacher Reviewers

**Peggy Althof**
Social Studies Facilitation, K–12
D-11 Public Schools
Colorado Springs, Colorado

**Lon Van Bronkhorst**
K–12 Social Studies Curriculum Supervisor
Grand Rapids Public Schools
Grand Rapids, Michigan

**Katherine A. Deforge**
Chair, Social Studies Department
Marcellus Central Schools
Marcellus, New York

**Roceal N. Duke**
Social Studies Content Specialist (retired)
District of Columbia Public Schools
Washington, D.C.

**Dee Ann Holt**
Chair, Social Studies Department
Horace Mann Arts and Science
    Magnet Middle School
Little Rock, Arkansas

**Deborah J. Miller**
Detroit Public Schools
Detroit, Michigan

**Carol Schneider**
Curriculum Coordinator
Rock Point Community School
Rock Point, Arizona

**Dr. Leigh Tanner**
Division of Instructional Support
Pittsburgh Public Schools
Pittsburgh, Pennsylvania

## Partnership School Consultants

**Melanie Alston**
Hackensack Middle School
Hackensack, New Jersey

**Matthew Facella**
Hackensack Middle School
Hackensack, New Jersey

**Karina Koepke**
Hackensack Middle School
Hackensack, New Jersey

**Richard Yannarelli**
Principal
Hackensack Middle School
Hackensack, New Jersey

## Content Consultants

**Michal Howden**
Social Studies Consultant
Zionsville, Indiana

**Kathy Lewis-Stewart**
Social Studies Consultant
Fort Worth, Texas

**Joseph Wieczorek**
Social Studies Consultant
Nottingham, Maryland

# Table of Contents

## Explore the past through the power of technology.

**MAP★MASTER®**
Skills Activity

Develop geographic literacy through dynamic map skills instruction. Learn map skills, and interact with every map online and on CD-ROM.

**Discovery School Video**

Visit the times and places you are studying in American history with a high-impact video program created to enhance your experience of this textbook by our partner Discovery School.

PRENTICE HALL
**StudentEXPRESS™**
Learn · Study · Succeed

Activate your learning with a suite of tools online and on CD-ROM:
• Interactive Textbook
• Reading and Notetaking Study Guide
• Social Studies Skills Tutor
• Web Resources

**History Interactive**

Launch into an interactive adventure online—using special graphics in this textbook as jumping-off points—to extend your understanding of American history.

# Unit 1 Beginnings of American History. . 1

**Surrender at Yorktown**

# Table of Contents

The signing of the Constitution

The Lewis and
Clark expedition

# Table of Contents

San Francisco, 1850s

# Unit 5 Civil War and Reunion . . . . . . . 476

The Civil War: African
American soldiers

# Table of Contents

The Brooklyn Bridge

# Unit 7    A New Role in the World . . . . . 674

Duke Ellington and his band

# Table of Contents

D-Day, June 6, 1941

# Unit 9  Moving Toward the Future. . . . 868

A father and daughter commemorate 9/11

# Special Features

## History Reading Skills

Enhance your ability to read and understand textbooks through reading skills instruction.

## Skills for Life

Build skills that will help you analyze American history content.

## Writing Workshop

Develop your writing skills through step-by-step writing instruction and practice.

# LIFE AT THE TIME

Learn more about how people lived at different places and times in history.

# GEOGRAPHY AND HISTORY

Discover the role geography has played in American history.

# Literature

Experience American history through works of literature.

# Links Across Time

Expand your understanding of American history by connecting the past and the present.

# Links to . . .

Make connections between American history and civics, government, economics, science, geography, and the arts.

# Special Features (continued)

## Biography Quest

Search for answers to mysteries about key people in American history.

**Sitting Bull**

## MAP MASTER® Skills Activity

Increase your understanding of American history by studying maps.

## Illustrated Atlas of American History

**Understand your world by comparing maps of the United States today with historical maps.**

## Charts, Graphs, and Diagrams

## Political Cartoons

## In-Text Sources

**Gain insights by examining documents, eyewitness accounts, and other sources.**

# Special Features (continued)

## Primary Sources

# Tools to help you along the way...

## Taking Notes

In history, there's a lot to read about and a lot to understand. Taking good notes is one way to help you remember key ideas and to see the big picture. This program has two ways to help you.

You can keep your notes in the *Interactive Reading and Notetaking Study Guide*. Or you can go online to take your notes. Either way, you will be able to record what you are learning. And, by the end of the year, you'll have created a perfect study tool.

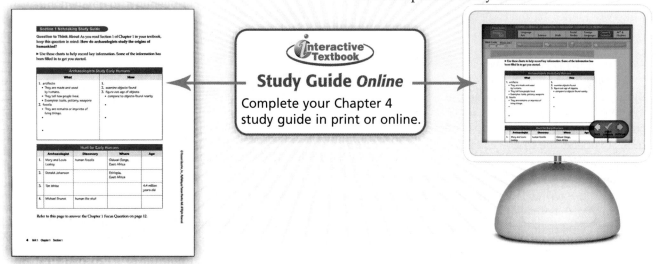

**Study Guide** *Online*

Complete your Chapter 4 study guide in print or online.

## Monitor Your Progress

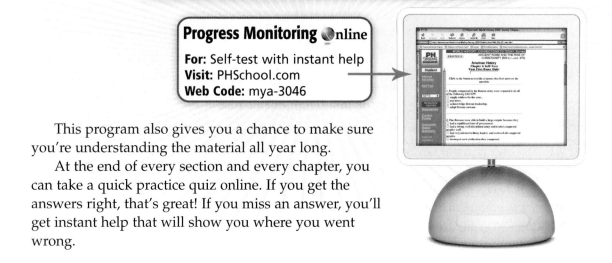

**Progress Monitoring** *Online*

**For:** Self-test with instant help
**Visit:** PHSchool.com
**Web Code:** mya-3046

This program also gives you a chance to make sure you're understanding the material all year long.

At the end of every section and every chapter, you can take a quick practice quiz online. If you get the answers right, that's great! If you miss an answer, you'll get instant help that will show you where you went wrong.

# Historian's Toolkit

## Introduction: Studying Our Past

The nation was at war with itself, the North fighting against the South. In July 1863, more than 50,000 soldiers had died at a horrible battle in Gettysburg, Pennsylvania. A few months later, President Abraham Lincoln visited Gettysburg to dedicate the battlefield as a cemetery. Lincoln spoke of the soldiers who had given their lives to keep the nation together:

**❝The world will little note, nor long remember what we say here, but it can never forget what they did here.❞**

—Abraham Lincoln, Gettysburg Address

Lincoln was partly right. The world still remembers the soldiers who died during the Civil War. But we also remember what Lincoln said and what he did for the cause of freedom. As you study American history this year, you will be asked to remember all those who came before us—soldiers and Presidents, explorers and inventors, religious leaders and business leaders, the people who wrote our Constitution, and the people who fought to end slavery.

Helping us remember the past is the job of the historian. Historians explore important questions in order to find out how people lived and why they made the decisions they did. Historians also try to understand how history affects our lives today.

On the next few pages, you will learn to think like a historian. You will also get to try out some of the tools historians use. Your Historian's Toolkit can make your study of American history easier and more rewarding.

**Union soldier**

# Historical Evidence

Historians use many types of evidence to learn about the past. This evidence can be divided into primary sources and secondary sources.

**Primary Sources** A primary source is firsthand information about people or events. Primary sources include official documents, such as laws and public speeches, as well as eyewitness accounts, such as diaries, letters, and autobiographies. Primary sources may also include visual evidence, such as news photographs or videotapes.

Another type of primary source is an artifact. This is an item left behind by people in the past. This might take the form of a statue, a tool, or an everyday object.

Primary sources are valuable because they are created at the time when an event occurs. But this does not necessarily make them "true." Primary sources are created by people, and they may reflect the points of view of the people who created them. The person might not have been aware of certain facts, might have been trying to impress someone, or may even have been lying. So primary sources must be evaluated carefully and considered in relation to other sources on the subject.

**Secondary Sources** Historians also use secondary sources. These are sources created by someone who did not actually witness events. This textbook, for example, is a secondary source. The authors gathered information from many sources to reach an understanding of what happened and why it happened. Then, they wrote their interpretation of the events. Other secondary sources include news articles and biographies.

## Types of Historical Sources

| Type of Source | Description | Examples |
|---|---|---|
| **Primary Sources**  | • Provide direct evidence about an event<br>• Have a limited viewpoint<br>• May be reliable or unreliable<br>• Include objects left behind by people | • Official documents<br>• Letters and diaries<br>• Speeches and interviews<br>• Autobiographies<br>• Photographs<br>• Artifacts<br>  • Tools and weapons<br>  • Statues and other art |
| **Secondary Sources**  | • Consist of secondhand information about an event<br>• Use primary sources to create a broader picture<br>• May be reliable or unreliable | • History books<br>• Biographies<br>• Encyclopedias and other reference works<br>• Internet Web sites |

AMERICA
HISTORY OF OUR NATION

# Using Historical Sources

Everyone who wants to know about history starts by asking questions. You might be familiar with the types of questions found in your textbook or asked by your teacher. But historians ask questions the way a detective would. Each answer is a clue that leads to another question. The questions and answers bring the historian to an understanding of events in the past.

Consider this situation. Patricia was going through some very old books she found in her great-grandmother's trunk in the attic. Between the pages of one book, she found an old letter on thin, yellowing paper. A copy of the letter is shown here at right.

While reading the letter, Patricia asked herself many questions. Some of her questions are shown at right. Trying to find the answers to the questions is the same sort of thinking that historians use to find out about the past.

June 12, 1849

Dear Sean,

Everyone was happy to get your last letter. After surviving such a long, difficult journey, it must have been wonderful to arrive at last in New York.

Things in our village are not as bad as when you left. But many children and old people are still starving, and too many people have no place to live. You were wise to go to America.

Please tell me more about your plans. After traveling for so long, why would you want to begin a new journey? Where is this place called California? And why are you so sure you can get rich there?

I miss you. I only hope I live long enough to join you someday.

Your loving brother,
Michael

Where did Sean come from? Why was the trip so hard?

What has happened to cause these problems?

How does Sean plan to get rich?

Patricia may follow several steps to find the answers to her questions.

- **Start with what is known.** Patricia knows that her ancestors came to the United States from Ireland many years ago. She thinks this letter might explain why.

- **Read and observe.** Patricia can look for further information in primary and secondary sources. She might look at a map to see where Ireland is and how far it is from New York to California.

- **Speculate.** To help get started, Patricia might make some guesses, called hypotheses, about the answers to her questions.

- **Evaluate evidence.** As Patricia finds more information, she will test her hypotheses against the information that turns up. She can always change her hypotheses as she learns more.

- **Draw conclusions.** Patricia states what she believes are the final answers to her questions.

To start her search, though, Patricia will need to practice her skills of reading like a historian and using maps. The information on the following pages will help you review some of these skills.

# Read Informational Texts

Reading a magazine, an Internet page, or a textbook is not the same as reading a novel. The purpose of reading nonfiction texts is to acquire new information. On page HT 7, you'll read about some ⊙ **History Reading Skills** that you'll practice as you read this textbook. Here, we'll focus on a few skills that will help you read nonfiction with a more critical eye.

## Analyze the Author's Purpose

Different types of materials are written with different purposes in mind. For example, a textbook is written to teach students information about a subject. The purpose of a technical manual is to teach someone how to use something, such as a computer. A newspaper editorial might be written to persuade the reader to accept a particular point of view. An author's purpose influences how the material is presented. Sometimes, an author states his or her purpose directly. More often, the purpose is only suggested, and you must use clues to identify the author's purpose.

## Distinguish Between Facts and Opinions

Active reading enables you to distinguish between facts and opinions when reading informational texts. Facts can be proved or disproved, but opinions reflect someone's own point of view.

Because newspaper editorials usually offer opinions on current events and issues, you should watch for bias and faulty logic when reading them. For example, the newspaper editorial at right shows factual statements in blue and opinions in red. Highly charged words are underlined. They reveal the writer's bias.

More than 5,000 people voted last week in favor of building a new shopping center, but the opposition won out. The margin of victory is irrelevant. Those radical voters who opposed the center are obviously self-serving elitists who do not care about anyone but themselves.

This month's unemployment figure for our area is 10 percent, which represents an increase of about 5 percent over the figure for this time last year. These figures mean that unemployment is worsening. But the people who voted against the mall probably do not care about creating new jobs.

## Identify Evidence

Before you accept a writer's conclusion, you need to make sure that the writer has based the conclusion on enough evidence and on the right kind of evidence. A writer may present a series of facts to support a claim, but the facts may not tell the whole story. For example, the writer of the newspaper editorial on the previous page claims that the new shopping center would create more jobs. But what evidence is offered? Is it possible that the shopping center might have put many small local stores out of business? This would increase unemployment rather than decreasing it.

## Evaluate Credibility

Whenever you read informational texts, you need to assess the credibility of the writer. In other words, you have to decide whether the writer is believable. This is especially true of sites you may visit on the Internet. All Internet sources are not equally reliable. Here are some questions to ask yourself when evaluating the credibility of a Web site:

☐ Is the Web site created by a respected organization, a discussion group, or an individual?

☐ Does the Web site creator include his or her name as well as credentials and the sources he or she used to write the material?

☐ Is the information on the site balanced or biased?

☐ Can you verify the information using two other sources?

☐ Is there a date telling when the Web site was created or last updated?

# How to Read History

## Build Vocabulary

One of the most important tools in reading informational texts is to make sure you understand the key vocabulary used by the writer. This textbook uses two devices to help you understand important vocabulary terms.

### Key Terms

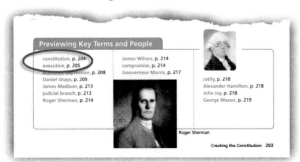

**1** Key social studies terms for each chapter are introduced in the chapter opener.

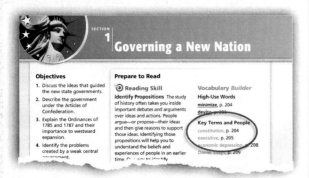

**2** They are then listed at the beginning of the section in which they will be used.

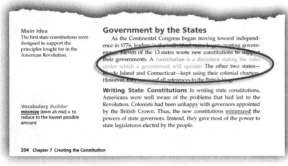

**3** Notice that they are always shown in blue type. Their definitions are also in blue.

### High-Use Academic Words

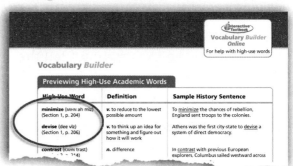

**4** High-Use Academic Words appear on the chapter opener in a chart. The chart gives a sample history sentence using each high-use word.

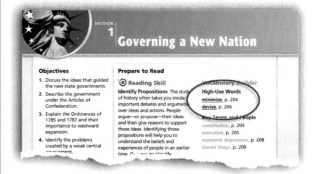

**5** The high-use words are then listed at the beginning of the section in which they will appear.

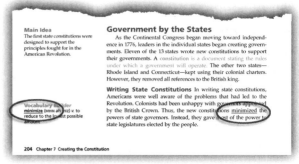

**6** High-use words are underlined in the text and defined in the margin.

# History Reading Skills

The History Reading Skills described on this page are important in helping you read and understand the information in this book. Each chapter uses a primary or secondary source to teach a reading skill. As you learn to use these skills, you will find that you can apply them to other books you read.

**Clarify Meaning** You can better understand what you read by using summaries and outlines and by taking notes to help identify main ideas and supporting details. **Chapters 1, 2, 21, 22.**

**Compare and Contrast** When you compare, you examine the similarities between things. When you contrast, you look at the differences. **Chapters 3, 28.**

**Use Context** Learn to use context clues to help you understand the meaning of unfamiliar words and words with more than one meaning. **Chapters 4, 17, 24.**

**Word Analysis** Discover how to analyze words to determine their meanings. **Chapters 6, 8, 18.**

**Understand Sequence** A sequence is the order in which a series of events occurs. Noting the sequence of important events can help you understand and remember the events. **Chapters 9, 15.**

**Analyze Cause and Effect** Every event in history has causes and creates effects. You will learn how to identify causes, which are what make events happen, and effects, which are what happen as a result of an event. **Chapters 10, 14, 23, 25.**

**Draw Conclusions** You will learn how to use details from primary and secondary sources to draw conclusions. **Chapters 5, 12, 26, 29.**

**Evaluate Information** As you read history, it is important to evaluate how writers' support their propositions, or the ideas they put forth. To do so, it is important to know how to identify and explain central issues and frame good research questions. **Chapters 7, 11, 13, 16, 19, 20, 27.**

**MAP★MASTER**

## CONTENTS

**Go Online**
PHSchool.com  The maps in this textbook can be found online at **PHSchool.com,** along with map-skills practice.

# Geography and History

Historical information is not presented only in written sources. Maps are often a key to understanding what happened and why.

Do you remember when Patricia was asking questions about the letter she found? (See page HT 3.) In addition to using primary and secondary sources, Patricia could have used maps to locate Ireland and to trace Sean's route from New York to California.

In order to get the most out of maps as sources, you need to make sure that your geography map skills are strong. On the next few pages, you can review some of the basic tools historians use to understand maps and geography.

The pictures above show two different geographical regions of the United States. The Midwest (above, left) has fertile plains suitable for farming. The rocky coasts of New England (right) are home to a large fishing industry.

# Five Themes of Geography

Studying the history and geography of the United States is a huge task. You can make that task easier by thinking of geography in terms of five themes. The five themes below are tools you can use to organize geographic information and to answer questions about the influence of geography and human history.

## Location

1 The exact location of a country or city is expressed in terms of longitude and latitude. Relative location defines where a place is in relation to other places. For example, the exact location of the city of Chicago, Illinois, is 42° north (latitude) and 88° west (longitude). Its relative location could be described as "on the shore of Lake Michigan" or "821 miles north of New Orleans."

## Place

2 Location answers the question, "Where is it?" Place answers the question, "What is it like there?" You can identify a place by such features as its landforms, its climate, its plants and animals, or the people who live there. Much of the history of the southeastern United States was shaped by the fact that it had a mild climate and fertile land suitable for large-scale farming of crops such as cotton.

## Regions

3 Regions are areas that share common features. Regions may be defined by geography or culture. For example, New York is one of the Middle Atlantic states because it is located on the Atlantic Ocean. In colonial days, it was one of the Middle Colonies. And in the early 1800s, New York was one of the "free states" because slavery was banned there.

## Movement

4 Much of history has to do with the movement of people, goods, and ideas from place to place. In Patricia's letter, we saw two examples of movement: the movement of immigrants to the United States from other countries and the movement of Americans from the East to the West. Both played a key role in the history and growth of the United States.

## Interaction

5 Human-environment interaction has two parts. The first part has to do with the way an environment affects people. For example, people in the harsh deserts of North Africa developed very different ways of life from those living in the rich farmlands of Italy. The second part of interaction concerns the way people affect their environment. Even in ancient times, people found ways to bring water from rivers to farms or to build roads across mountains.

### Practice Geography Skills

Look at the photographs on page HT 8 and read the caption. How do these pictures illustrate the themes of place, region, and interaction?

## How to Use a Map

Mapmakers provide several clues to help in understanding the information on a map. Maps provide different clues, depending on their purpose or scale. However, most maps have several clues in common.

**Locator**
Many maps are shown with locator maps or globes. They show where on Earth the area of the map is located.

**Title**
Maps have titles. The title tells you the subject of the map.

**Key**
Often a map has a key, or legend. The key shows the meaning of the symbols and colors used on the map.

**Compass rose**
Many maps show direction by displaying a compass rose with the directions north, east, south, and west. The letters N, E, S, and W are placed to indicate these directions.

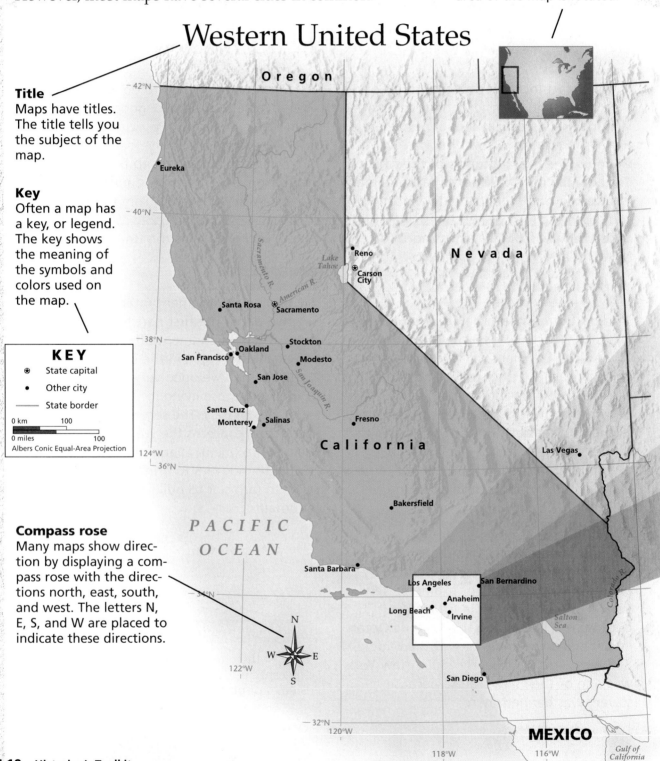

Western United States

**KEY**
⊛ State capital
• Other city
— State border

0 km 100
0 miles 100
Albers Conic Equal-Area Projection

# Maps of Different Scales

Maps are drawn to different scales, depending on their purpose. Here are three maps drawn to very different scales. Keep in mind that maps showing large areas have smaller scales. Maps showing small areas have larger scales.

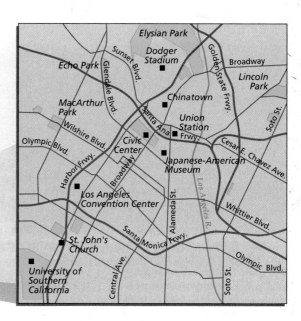

## ▲ Downtown Los Angeles

Find the gray square on the map of Greater Los Angeles. This square represents the area shown on the map above. This map moves you closer into the center of Los Angeles. Like a zoom on a computer or a camera, this map shows a smaller area, but in greater detail. It has the largest scale. You can use this map to explore downtown Los Angeles.

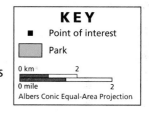

**KEY**
■ Point of interest
▨ Park

0 km ————— 2
0 mile ————— 2
Albers Conic Equal-Area Projection

## ▲ Greater Los Angeles

Find the light gray square on the main map of California (left). This square represents the area shown on the map above. It shows Los Angeles in relation to nearby cities, towns, and the Pacific Ocean. It also shows some features near the city, such as the airport and major roadways.

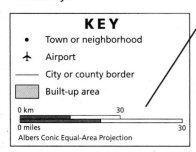

**KEY**
• Town or neighborhood
✈ Airport
— City or county border
▨ Built-up area

0 km ————— 30
0 miles ————— 30
Albers Conic Equal-Area Projection

## Scale bar
A scale bar helps you find the actual distances between points shown on the map. Most scale bars show distances in both miles and kilometers.

## Practice Geography Skills
- What part of a map explains the colors used on the map?
- How does the scale bar change depending on the scale of the map?

## Political Maps

Historians use many different types of maps. On the next four pages, you will see four maps that relate to American history. Each map shows a different area in a different way and for a different purpose.

One of the most familiar types of map is the political map. Political maps show political divisions, such as borders between countries or states. Colors on a political map help make the differences clear. Political maps also show the location of cities. This map shows the United States in 1790, at the time George Washington was President.

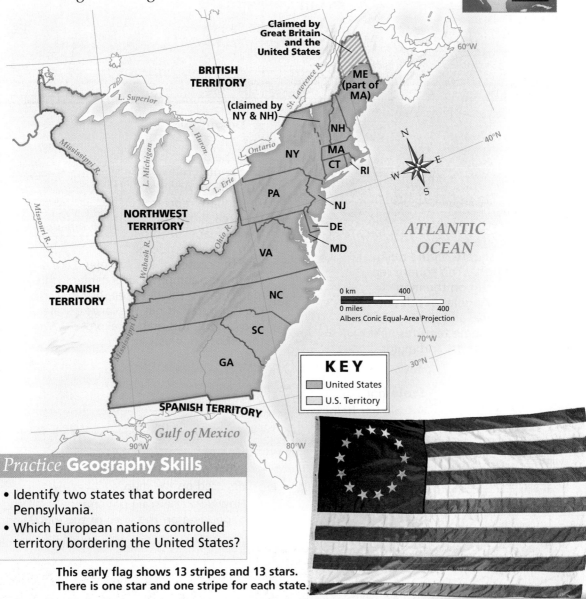

*Practice* **Geography Skills**

- Identify two states that bordered Pennsylvania.
- Which European nations controlled territory bordering the United States?

This early flag shows 13 stripes and 13 stars. There is one star and one stripe for each state.

# Physical Maps

Physical maps show the major physical features of a region, such as seas, rivers, and mountains. The larger the scale of a physical map, the more detail it can show. For example, the map below shows the rivers that run through the American Southwest. If you compare this map to the physical map in the Atlas at the front of this textbook, you will notice that there are several rivers shown on this map that are not shown on the Atlas map.

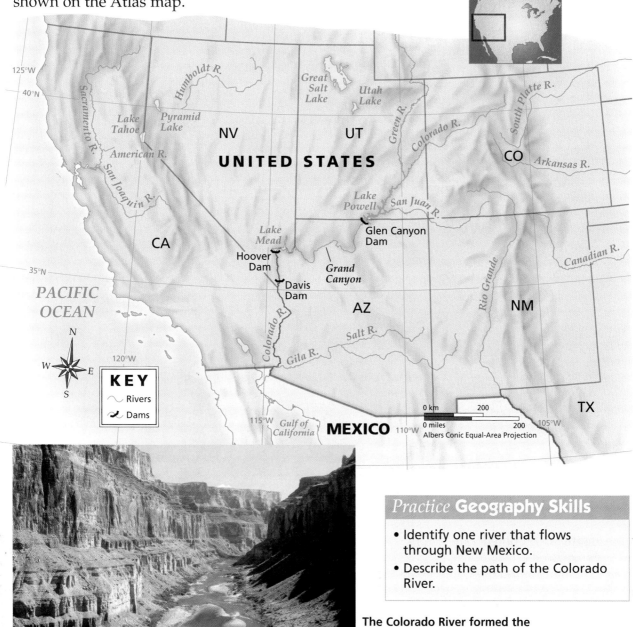

## Practice Geography Skills

- Identify one river that flows through New Mexico.
- Describe the path of the Colorado River.

**The Colorado River formed the Grand Canyon in Arizona.**

## Special-Purpose Maps
### Battle Maps

In addition to political maps and physical maps, there are different types of special-purpose maps. These range from road maps to weather maps to election maps. Some special-purpose maps use arrows to show the movement of people and goods from place to place. The map below shows the battles and troop movements that led up to the Battle of Gettysburg in July 1863.

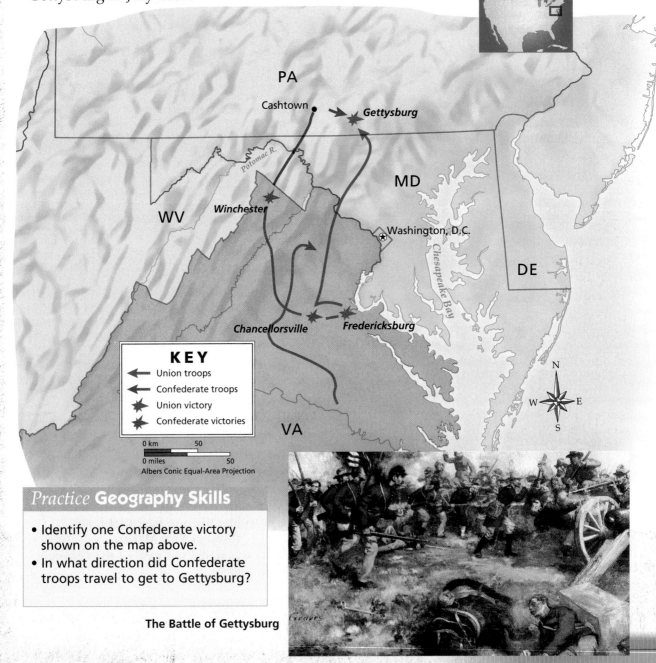

**KEY**
← Union troops
← Confederate troops
★ Union victory
✦ Confederate victories

0 km          50
0 miles          50
Albers Conic Equal-Area Projection

### Practice **Geography Skills**

- Identify one Confederate victory shown on the map above.
- In what direction did Confederate troops travel to get to Gettysburg?

**The Battle of Gettysburg**

# Election Maps

Have you ever seen a newspaper or watched television during a presidential election? If you have, then you have probably seen an election map. Election maps show all of the states voting in the election. Different colors are used to show which candidates won the vote in which states. The map below shows the election of 1912, when three major candidates were running for President.

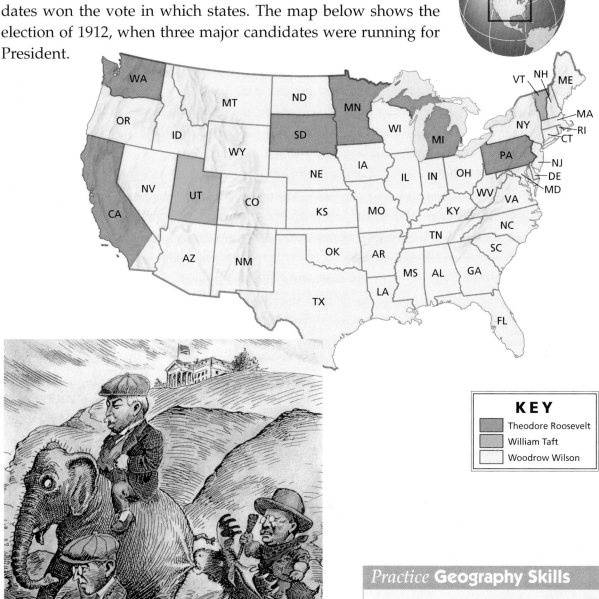

**KEY**

- Theodore Roosevelt
- William Taft
- Woodrow Wilson

## Practice Geography Skills

- Which candidate won in California? In Illinois?
- How many states did Taft win?

Cartoon showing Wilson, Taft, and Roosevelt running for President in 1912

# Read Visual Information

In this textbook, the information you need to know is presented in written form. Often, however, key information is also summarized in chart form. Charts organize facts and ideas in a visual way that makes them easier to understand.

The next four pages review some of the basic types of visuals you will find in this textbook. Building your ability to analyze visuals will help you get the most out of the information provided.

## Timelines

Every chapter in this textbook begins with a timeline. You have used timelines before, but the ones in this book have a few special features. Most of them are made up of two parts:

- **U.S. Events** This is the main part of the timeline. It shows the events that are described in that chapter that took place within the United States.

- **World Events** This part of the timeline shows events that took place in other parts of the world during the same time period. These events are often included because they related to what was going on in the United States.

Timelines make it easier to understand the sequence of events over time. The timelines in this textbook will help you explain how major events are related to one another in time.

*Practice* **Chart Skills**

- How many years after gold was discovered in California was gold discovered in Australia?
- Which world event was probably related to one of the U.S. events?

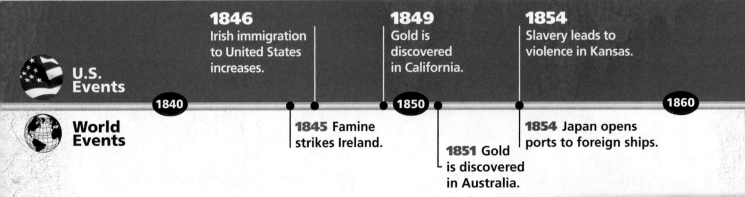

**1846**
Irish immigration to United States increases.

**1849**
Gold is discovered in California.

**1854**
Slavery leads to violence in Kansas.

**U.S. Events**

1840

**World Events**

1850

1860

**1845** Famine strikes Ireland.

**1851** Gold is discovered in Australia.

**1854** Japan opens ports to foreign ships.

# Build Chart Skills

## Tables

Tables provide a simple way to organize a large amount of information graphically. A table is arranged in a grid pattern. Columns run vertically, from top to bottom. Rows run horizontally, from left to right.

This sample table summarizes some basic facts about four major wars you will learn about this year. The four wars are listed in the column at the far left, at the beginning of each row. The categories of information given about each war are listed at the top of each column.

Tables can be very large. You may have seen computer spreadsheets that include dozens of columns and rows. Yet, all tables follow the same basic grid pattern shown below.

### Four American Wars

| War | Dates | Opponents | Results |
|-----|-------|-----------|---------|
| American Revolution | 1775–1781 | American colonists vs. Britain | • Colonists win.<br>• United States wins independence. |
| War of 1812 | 1812–1814 | United States vs. Britain | • No clear winner emerges.<br>• Increased sense of national pride felt. |
| Mexican-American War | 1846–1848 | United States vs. Mexico | • United States wins.<br>• United States gains new territory in the West. |
| Civil War | 1861–1865 | North vs. South | • North wins.<br>• Union is preserved.<br>• Slavery ends. |

### *Practice* Chart Skills

- What were the results of the Mexican-American War?
- In which two wars did Americans fight the same opponent?

# Build Chart Skills

## Pie Charts

Some charts and graphs in this book show statistical information, that is, information based on exact numbers. Pie charts show statistical information in terms of percentages. The circle, or pie, represents 100 percent of a group. Each wedge of the pie represents one subgroup of the whole. The bigger the wedge is, the larger the group. This pie chart shows how the population of southern states was divided in the year 1850, when slavery was still legal in the South.

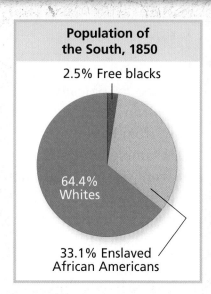

**Population of the South, 1850**

2.5% Free blacks

64.4% Whites

33.1% Enslaved African Americans

## Line Graphs and Bar Graphs

Line graphs and bar graphs show statistical information as it changes over time. The horizontal, or side to side, axis usually tells you the time period covered by the graph. The vertical, or up and down, axis tells you what is being measured. By lining up the points on the graph with the horizontal and vertical axes, you can see how many or how much of something there was at a given time.

On a line graph, the points are connected. On a bar graph, each year is represented by a bar. The line graph (below left) and the bar graph (below right) show the same information: the number of patents, or licenses for new inventions, issued by the U.S. government.

### *Practice* **Chart Skills**

- What percentage of southern society in 1850 was made up of enslaved African Americans?
- About how many patents were issued in 1860? In 1880?

## U.S. Patents, 1860–1900

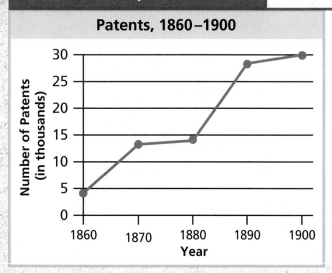

**Patents, 1860–1900**

Number of Patents (in thousands)

Year

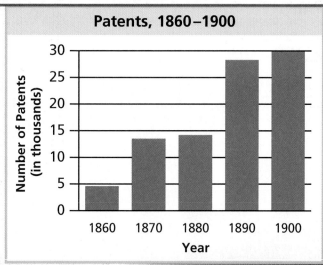

**Patents, 1860–1900**

Number of Patents (in thousands)

Year

# Build Political Cartoon Skills

This textbook also includes a number of political cartoons. Political cartoons are drawings that comment on events and issues through both visual imagery and words. Cartoonists often use symbols and exaggeration to make their points. Learning to analyze cartoons can help you better understand viewpoints on current and historical events.

The first step in analyzing a political cartoon is to identify common symbols. A symbol is an object that represents something besides itself. For example, an eagle or the figure of Uncle Sam may be used to represent the United States. Sometimes, symbols are labeled to make their meaning clear.

Look at the details in the drawing. (In this textbook, we help you focus on certain details by calling them out.) Also, look at the words being spoken by the people in the cartoon. Finally, use both words and pictures to identify the main point the cartoonist is making.

The cartoon below comments on one of the main responsibilities of American citizens: voting.

## Practice Chart Skills

- Why is the pan labeled "Non-Voters" lower than the pan labeled "Voters"? What does this mean?
- What is the cartoonist's view of people who do not vote?

The cartoon starts with one person who decides not to vote.

The label shows what the scale symbolizes.

You have learned how to use historians' tools to learn about the past. The next step is to write about what you have discovered. Historians share their findings in a variety of ways, including expository essays, narratives, research papers, and persuasive essays or speeches.

At the end of each unit in this textbook, you will find a Writing Workshop. Each Writing Workshop presents detailed instruction about one type of writing. You will have a chance to practice each type.

## Expository Essays

An expository essay is a piece of writing that explains something in detail.

### 1 Select and Narrow Your Topic

Define exactly what you want your essay to do. Do you want to describe a process? Compare and contrast two ideas? Explain the causes and effects of a historical event or development? Explore possible solutions to a problem? You cannot plan your essay until you know what you are trying to do in it.

### 2 Gather Evidence

Create a graphic organizer that identifies details to include in your essay, such as the one shown below.

### 3 Write a First Draft

Write a topic sentence, and then organize the essay based on what you are trying to do. If your essay describes a process, write about the steps of the process in order. If your essay explores solutions to a problem, state the problem, and then describe different possible solutions.

### 4 Revise and Proofread

Make sure that all the details support your topic sentence.

| Problem | Suggested Solutions | Evaluation of Solution |
|---|---|---|
| The Articles of Confederation left the nation weak because they did not provide for a central authority. | Leave the Articles alone, and persuade other countries and Americans to respect the new nation. | Not practical—what would make more established governments and local rebels accept a weak authority? |
| | Get rid of the Articles, and create an entirely new plan. | Possible, but it would be a huge task to start all over again. |

If you were writing a problem-solution essay, you might create a chart like this to help you organize your ideas.

## Narrative Essays

History is like a story. It has characters, both leaders and everyday people. It has a setting where events take place. It even has a plot, in which events unfold, conflicts arise, and resolutions occur.

### ① Select and Narrow Your Topic

In this textbook, you will be asked to write narratives about the past. You might be asked to imagine a setting and describe how it affects what is happening. You might be asked to take the point of view of one of history's characters. Or you might be asked to explain the conflict or resolution of a historical situation. First, you must understand what you are being asked to do or who you are asked to be.

Suppose you are asked to imagine you are a pioneer traveling from Missouri to Oregon by wagon train in the 1840s. You can use your imagination and your knowledge of history to create a narrative. For example, how do you feel about the long journey? Would you miss the home you had left behind? Do you think the trip is worth the trouble? Identifying your viewpoint will help you plan your narrative.

### ② Gather Details

Brainstorm a list of details you would like to include in your narrative.

### ③ Write a First Draft

Start by writing a simple opening sentence that conveys the main idea of your essay. Continue by writing a colorful story that has interesting details. Write a conclusion that sums up the main points presented in your essay.

### ④ Revise and Proofread

Check to make sure you have not begun too many sentences with the word *I*. Replace general words with more colorful ones.

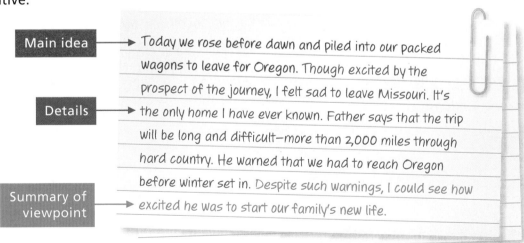

**Main idea** → Today we rose before dawn and piled into our packed wagons to leave for Oregon. Though excited by the prospect of the journey, I felt sad to leave Missouri. It's

**Details** → the only home I have ever known. Father says that the trip will be long and difficult—more than 2,000 miles through hard country. He warned that we had to reach Oregon before winter set in. Despite such warnings, I could see how

**Summary of viewpoint** → excited he was to start our family's new life.

# Write Like a Historian

## Research Papers

Research papers present information that you have found about a topic.

### 1 Select and Narrow Your Topic

Choose a topic that interests you. Make sure that your topic is not too broad. For example, instead of writing a report on Native Americans, you might write a report about the Cherokees who were forced to move west in 1837 on a journey known as the Trail of Tears.

### 2 Acquire Information

Locate several sources of information about the topic from the library or on the Internet. Be sure to evaluate the source. Is it reliable? How does the information compare to what you have found in other sources?

For each resource, create a source index card. Then, take notes using an index card for each detail or subtopic. On the card, note which source the information was taken from. Use quotation marks when you copy exact words from a source.

### 3 Make an Outline

Use an outline to decide how to organize your research paper. Sort your index cards in the same order.

### 4 Write a First Draft

Write an introduction, a body, and a conclusion. If you are preparing your first draft by hand, leave plenty of space between lines so you can go back and add details that you may have left out.

### 5 Revise and Proofread

Be sure to include transition words between sentences and paragraphs. Here are some examples:

- To describe a process: *first, next, then*
- To show a contrast: *however, although, despite*
- To point out a reason: *since, because, if*
- To signal a conclusion: *therefore, as a result, so*

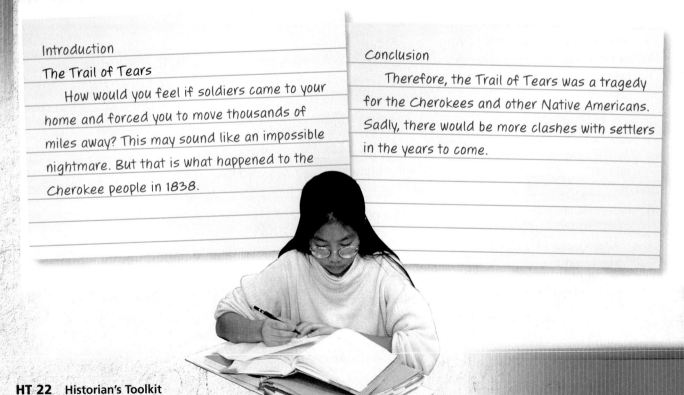

Introduction

The Trail of Tears

How would you feel if soldiers came to your home and forced you to move thousands of miles away? This may sound like an impossible nightmare. But that is what happened to the Cherokee people in 1838.

Conclusion

Therefore, the Trail of Tears was a tragedy for the Cherokees and other Native Americans. Sadly, there would be more clashes with settlers in the years to come.

## Persuasive Essays

A persuasive essay is a piece of writing that supports a position or opinion.

**❶ Select and Narrow Your Topic**

Choose a historical topic that has at least two sides or two interpretations. Choose a side. Decide which argument will best persuade your audience to agree with your point of view.

**❷ Gather Evidence**

Create a chart that states your position at the top, and then lists the pros and cons for your position in two columns below. Predict and address the strongest arguments against your viewpoint.

**❸ Write a First Draft**

Write a strong thesis statement that clearly states your position. Continue by presenting the strongest arguments in favor of your position and acknowledging and refuting opposing arguments.

**❹ Revise and Proofread**

Check to make sure you have made a logical argument and that you have not oversimplified the argument.

## Practice Your Writing

In this textbook, you will have many opportunities to practice your writing skills. The chart below shows how you can build writing skills in each section, chapter, and unit of this textbook.

| **Check Your Progress: Writing** (end of every section) | **Review and Assessment: Writing** (end of every chapter) | **Writing Workshop** (end of every unit) |
|---|---|---|
| Helps you build writing skills you will need to complete the unit-level Writing Workshop. | Helps you practice the skills from Check Your Progress and build toward the unit-level Writing Workshop. | Helps you learn and practice the steps needed to write a type of essay—expository, research, or persuasive. |
| *Examples:* <br> • Identify causes. <br> • Identify effects. <br> • Use a cause-and-effect chart to organize information. | *Example:* <br> • Write a paragraph describing one cause and one effect of an event. | *Example:* <br> • Expository Composition: Causes and Effects |

# Unit 1

## Think Like a Historian

As you read this unit, think about this question: *How did the colonists, with strong roots in the past, develop their own way of life?*

**Across the Atlantic** Sailing three small ships across the Atlantic in uncharted waters, Christopher Columbus opened the Americas to regular contact with the people of Europe.

# 1492

**Slave Trade** By the late 1600s, a steady stream of ships carried enslaved Africans to the Americas. Most enslaved Africans were forced to work on plantations in the West Indies and in South America. Slavery grew in North America after the plantation system took hold in the South.

# LATE 1600s

# Beginnings of American History

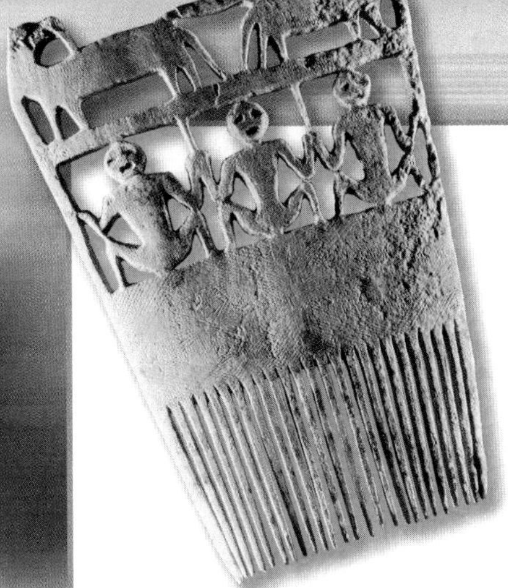

**The Five Nations** The Iroquois of the Eastern Woodlands formed the League of the Iroquois to keep the peace among their peoples. The figures on this comb represent the five nations in the League.

## 1500s

**The Pilgrim Community** Seeking freedom to practice their religion, Pilgrims founded the colony of Plymouth. In time, the idea of religious freedom for all would become a cornerstone of American democracy.

## 1620

**English Colonies Flourish** The English founded 13 colonies along the Atlantic coast of North America. People in the New England, Middle, and Southern colonies developed distinct ways of life. Some children attended school, where they learned reading, writing, and arithmetic.

## 1750

# Chapter Preview

For centuries, the Americas were geographically isolated from other parts of the world. Native Americans developed varied ways of life. At the same time, different cultures were developing in Africa, Asia, and Europe.

Prehistory      1000      1200

**World Events**

**20,000–30,000 years ago** First people come to the Americas.

**1095** Pope calls for crusades to begin.

Hundreds of years ago, Native Americans built these cliff dwellings at Mesa Verde in present-day Colorado.

| 1200 | | 1400 | | 1600 |
|---|---|---|---|---|
| **1200s** African empire of Mali rises. | **1300s** Renaissance begins in Europe. | **1400s** Aztecs conquer most of Mexico. | **1500s** Iroquois League is formed. | |

## History Reading Skill  Read Actively

### How did early Native Americans work together?

In this chapter, you will practice active reading. Read the following description of how the Iroquois people joined together. The side notes suggest ways to read actively.

**Introduction**  About 1570, five Iroquois nations formed the League of the Iroquois. According to Iroquois tradition, a leader named Hiawatha helped found the League. Chief Elias Johnson relates the story of Hiawatha in this selection.

> Before reading, check features such as an introduction and vocabulary list.

**Vocabulary**  Before you read the selection, find the meaning of these words in a dictionary: *assembly, tremble, hordes.*

The council met. Hiawatha entered the assembly with even more than ordinary attention. Every eye was fixed upon him  when he began to address the council in the following words.

"Friends and Brothers: You being members of many tribes, you have come from a great distance. The voice of war has aroused you up. . . . You tremble for your safety. Believe me, I am with you. . . . To oppose those hordes of northern tribes, singly and alone, would prove certain destruction. . . . We must unite ourselves into one common  band of brothers, we must have one voice. . . . This will give us strength."

> Connect to your own knowledge about ways that working together creates strength.

—from *Cry of the Thunderbird: The American Indian's Own Story*

**READING REVIEW**
Why did Hiawatha suggest forming the League?

> Ask questions or use review questions to set a purpose for reading. Then, read to answer those questions.

### Read Actively
- Preview each section. Read introductory material, headings, and marginal notes. Scan illustrations and graphic material.
- Notice the text organization, and use it to plan a specific reading approach, such as comparing and contrasting.
- Formulate questions based on your preview. Review the questions that appear within the section or at the end of the section. Then, read to find answers to your questions.
- Connect what you read to your prior knowledge or personal experience.

### Document-Based Questions
1. How can you tell that the other members of the council respected Hiawatha?
2. What was the goal of the League of the Iroquois?
3. According to Hiawatha, why should the Five Nations band together?

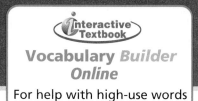

# Vocabulary *Builder*

## Previewing High-Use Academic Words

| High-Use Word | Definition | Sample History Sentence |
|---|---|---|
| **deprive** (dee PRĪV) (Section 1, p. 7) | *v.* to take away | People who were enslaved were <u>deprived</u> of their freedom. |
| **reside** (ree ZĪD) (Section 1, p. 8) | *v.* to live; to make one's home in | The people who <u>reside</u> in a city or state make up its population. |
| **currency** (KUH rehn see) (Section 2, p. 11) | *n.* items used as money | The dollar is the basic unit of <u>currency</u> in the United States. |
| **distinct** (dihs TIHNKT) (Section 2, p. 12) | *adj.* clearly different in quality | There are <u>distinct</u> differences between the climate of Alaska and the climate of Florida. |
| **transmit** (trans MIHT) (Section 3, p. 16) | *v.* to pass along; to send | Traders <u>transmitted</u> goods and ideas from one place to another. |
| **sphere** (sfeer) (Section 3, p. 17) | *n.* rounded shape | Some early people believed Earth was flat rather than shaped like a <u>sphere</u>. |
| **participate** (pahr TIHS uh payt) (Section 4, p. 24) | *v.* to take part in | Adult American citizens have the right to <u>participate</u> in elections. |
| **precise** (pree SĪS) (Section 4, p. 27) | *adj.* exact; accurate | Early people were able to create <u>precise</u> calendars based on the sun. |

## Previewing Key Terms and People

Vasco da Gama

Kayak

# The Earliest Americans

## Objectives

1. Understand how people may have first reached the Americas.

2. Find out how people learned to farm.

3. Explore the civilizations of the Mayas, Aztecs, and Incas.

## Prepare to Read

### ⊙ Reading Skill

**Preview Before Reading** The first step in active reading is to preview the text. Read the Prepare to Read information. Scan all the headings and side-margin notes. Read the captions and look at the illustrations. Finally, read the questions that appear at the section's end.

### Vocabulary *Builder*

**High-Use Words**
**deprive**, p. 7
**reside**, p. 8

**Key Terms**
glacier, p. 6
irrigate, p. 7
surplus, p. 7
civilization, p. 8

☆ **Background Knowledge** Tens of thousands of years ago, no humans lived in North America or South America. In this section, you will learn how the first humans may have come to the Americas.

**Main Idea**
The first people in the Americas came from Asia and eventually learned to farm.

## The First Americans

Scientists have various ideas about how people came to the Americas. Some think that people may have come from Asia in large canoes. However, most think that the first humans arrived by land.

**The Land Bridge Theory** Between 10,000 and 100,000 years ago, much of the world was covered by glaciers, or thick sheets of ice. As more and more of the world's water froze, the level of the oceans dropped. Areas that once were covered by shallow water became dry land. One of these areas stretched between Siberia and Alaska. It became a bridge of land many miles wide. The area now lies under a narrow waterway called the Bering Strait.

The land bridge may have appeared and disappeared several times. However, many scientists believe that people first came to North America between 20,000 and 30,000 years ago. They were hunters, possibly following the coast of Siberia as they hunted prehistoric mammals such as the woolly mammoth. Over thousands of years, hunting bands moved over the land. They eventually spread across North America and South America.

**Other Theories** Not everyone agrees with the land-bridge theory. Some scientists think that people may first have crossed the arctic waters by boat and traveled southward along the Pacific coast. This idea is known as the coastal-route theory.

Woolly mammoth

Many Native Americans also dispute both the land-bridge theory and the coastal-route theory. Each group has its own tradition explaining how they settled in the lands they did. These traditions appear in their creation stories.

**Learning to Farm** For centuries, early humans could fill most of their needs by hunting. Game animals provided food, furs for clothing, and bones for tools.

In time, many of the larger animals began to disappear. <u>Deprived</u> of their main source of food, hunters had to change their ways of life. In many places, hunters became gatherers. They traveled from place to place, searching for wild plants and small game.

Some 8,000 years ago, gatherers in Mexico began growing food plants, including squash and lima beans. The discovery of farming transformed life. No longer did families have to wander in search of food. In dry regions, farmers developed methods of irrigation. Irrigation is a method to water crops by channeling water from rivers or streams. Farmers also learned how to raise animals such as cattle, pigs, and llamas.

With a more dependable food supply, the population grew more rapidly. Once Native Americans produced surplus, or extra, food, they traded with others. Some farming communities grew into cities. The cities became centers of government and religious life.

✓**Checkpoint** How do scientists think people first reached the Americas?

**Vocabulary** *Builder*
<u>deprive</u> (dee PRĬV) *v.* to take away

**Preview Before Reading**
Preview the matter on the following pages under the heading "Three Civilizations." What do the subheadings, images, and captions tell you?

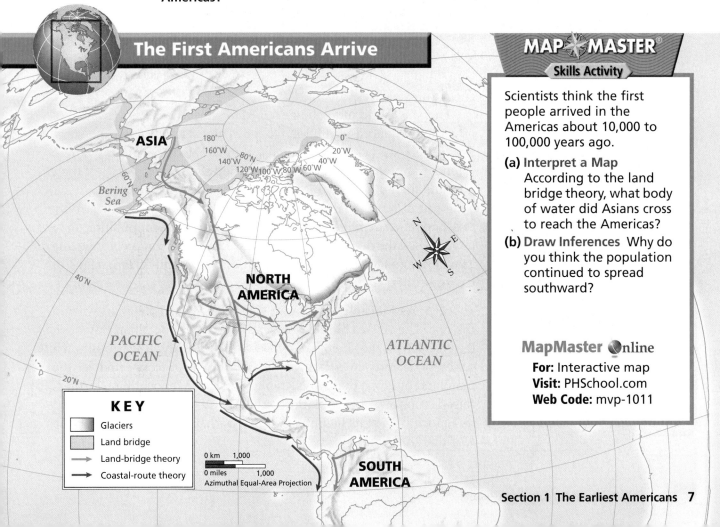

**The First Americans Arrive**

ASIA

180°
160°W
140°W    80°N          0°
120°W 100°W 80°W 60°W   20°W
                       40°W

Bering
Sea

60°N

NORTH
AMERICA

40°N

PACIFIC
OCEAN

ATLANTIC
OCEAN

20°N

**KEY**
Glaciers
Land bridge
→ Land-bridge theory
➡ Coastal-route theory

0 km    1,000
0 miles    1,000
Azimuthal Equal-Area Projection

SOUTH
AMERICA

**MAP MASTER®**
**Skills Activity**

Scientists think the first people arrived in the Americas about 10,000 to 100,000 years ago.

**(a) Interpret a Map** According to the land bridge theory, what body of water did Asians cross to reach the Americas?

**(b) Draw Inferences** Why do you think the population continued to spread southward?

**MapMaster ◯nline**
**For:** Interactive map
**Visit:** PHSchool.com
**Web Code:** mvp-1011

**Tenochtitlán** The Aztecs built their capital city of Tenochtitlán on a group of islands in the middle of a lake. The center of the city was dominated by a huge temple (inset). **Critical Thinking:** *Draw Conclusions* *How does this picture support the idea that the Aztec society was highly organized?*

**Main Idea**
The Mayas, Aztecs, and Incas developed advanced civilizations in Central and South America.

**Vocabulary** *Builder*
<u>reside</u> (ree zīD) *v.* to live; to make one's home in

# Three Civilizations

With the development of cities came the beginnings of civilization. A **civilization** is an advanced culture in which people have developed cities, science, and industries. Over the centuries, several civilizations rose and declined in the Americas. The largest were the civilizations of the Mayas, the Aztecs, and the Incas.

**Mayas** Between A.D. 250 and A.D. 900, the Mayas built cities in what is now Mexico and Central America. These splendid cities contained large public plazas lined with pyramids, temples, ball courts, and palaces.

The Mayas did more, however. They developed arts, a system of government, and a written language. They also observed the stars. From their study of the heavens, they created the most accurate calendar known until modern times. They also carved stories of their past and their gods into the stones of their buildings.

Around A.D. 900, the Mayas began to abandon their cities. Why this happened remains a mystery. Disease or overpopulation may have caused the decline. Although the Mayan civilization is gone, the Mayan language still forms the root of more than 20 languages of Central America.

**Aztecs** As Mayan civilization declined, a new civilization was on the rise. The Aztecs built a great capital city, Tenochtitlán (tay noch tee TLAHN), on the site of present-day Mexico City. It was built on a series of islands in a large lake. The city was connected to the mainland by stone roadways. In many parts of Tenochtitlán, farmers raised crops on floating platforms. More than 200,000 people <u>resided</u> in Tenochtitlán at its height, making it perhaps the largest city in the world at that time.

The center of the city was a sacred place with dozens of temples that honored the Aztec gods. This was appropriate because religion dominated Aztec life. To the Aztecs, prosperity depended on the good will of the gods. Like a number of other ancient peoples, the Aztecs practiced human sacrifice as an offering to their gods.

During the 1400s, Aztec armies brought half of modern-day Mexico under their control. The Aztecs proved to be effective but harsh rulers. Conquered tribes were forced to send treasure, food, and prisoners to the Aztec capital. The Aztecs forced the people they conquered to pay high taxes. Resentful subjects would eventually turn on the Aztecs when the empire most needed allies.

**Incas** In the 1400s, the largest empire was not in Europe or Asia. It was in South America. The vast empire of the Incas stretched down the coast of South America along the Andes, across the Atacama desert, and reached the fringes of the Amazon rain forest.

At the center of the empire was the Inca capital, Cuzco (KOOS koh). Cuzco was linked to other cities and towns by a great network of roads. A Spaniard who traveled the main Inca highway called it "the finest road to be seen in the world."

The Incas constructed buildings of huge stones carefully shaped to fit together. Their engineers built walls to hold soil in their fields, canals to carry water, and bridges over deep canyons. The Incas produced fine weavings and metalwork. Inca rulers wore gold and silver jewelry, and their palaces contained plates of gold.

☑ **Checkpoint**  **Where were the Aztec and Inca civilizations located?**

☆ **Looking Back and Ahead**  Most Native Americans did not live in large cities like Tenochtitlán or Cuzco. In the next section, you will learn about the ways of life of people north of Mexico.

Figure of an Inca ruler or priest

---

**Section 1** | **Check Your Progress**

**Progress Monitoring** ⦿nline
**For:** Self-test with instant help
**Visit:** PHSchool.com
**Web Code:** mva-1011

**Comprehension and Critical Thinking**

**1. (a) List** Name one skill that people had to learn in order to grow crops.
**(b) Identify Benefits** What benefits could farmers get from learning to raise animals?

**2. (a) Define** What is a civilization?
**(b) Apply Information** How did the Mayas and Aztecs fit that definition?

**Reading Skill**

**3. Preview Before Reading** Preview Section 2. Read its headings, study its images and captions, and review its questions. Tell what you think Section 2 will be about. Use the headings to identify the text organization. How can you use this information to plan your reading?

**Vocabulary** *Builder*

Answer the following questions in complete sentences that show your understanding of the key terms.

**4.** How did the growth of glaciers affect water levels in the ocean?
**5.** Why was learning about irrigation important for farmers?
**6.** What are the advantages of having a surplus of crops?

**Writing**

**7.** Outline a paragraph in response to the following question: How did early civilizations use industry and science to improve their way of life? Then, list four or five supporting details. Next, write a concluding sentence.

# Cultures of North America

## Objectives

1. Learn about the earliest peoples of North America.

2. Discover what different groups of Native Americans had in common.

3. Explore the impact of geography on Native American cultures.

## Prepare to Read

### Reading Skill

**Apply Prior Knowledge** You can prepare for reading by building on and connecting to what you already know. This can be information from an earlier section, chapter, or other reading. It can also be prior knowledge from your own life experience. Applying this knowledge while you are reading helps you interact with and engage in the text. This, in turn, will help you understand and remember what you have read.

### Vocabulary *Builder*

**High-Use Words**
<u>currency</u>, p. 11
<u>distinct</u>, p. 12

**Key Terms**
culture, p. 10
culture area, p. 11
kayak, p. 12
potlatch, p. 12
adobe, p. 12
clan, p. 15
sachem, p. 15

⭐ **Background Knowledge** In the last section, you explored civilizations in Central America and South America. In this section, you will read about the peoples who settled farther north.

## First Cultures of North America

In North America, as elsewhere, groups of people developed unique cultures, or ways of life. Around 3,000 years ago, various groups began to emerge in an area stretching from the Appalachian Mountains to the Mississippi Valley. We call these people Mound Builders because they constructed large piles of earth. Many mounds were burial places, but some served as foundations for public buildings. One group of Mound Builders, the Mississippians, built the first cities in North America. As many as 40,000 people may have lived in the largest Mississippian city, Cahokia, in present-day Illinois.

A far different culture, which we call the Anasazi, emerged in southern Utah, Colorado, northern Arizona, and New Mexico. They built large cliff dwellings, probably to defend against attacks by outsiders such as the Navajos or even the Aztecs. Their largest community housed about 1,000 people. The Anasazis were skilled in making baskets, pottery, and jewelry. They also engaged in trade. Mysteriously, by 1300, the Anasazis had abandoned their cliff dwellings.

### Main Idea
Early cultures developed in the Southwest and the Mississippi Valley.

Anasazi pottery

From about 300 B.C. to A.D. 1450, highly skilled farmers called the Hohokam dug irrigation canals in the deserts of present-day Arizona. Trade brought them in contact with people who lived on the Gulf of California. The Hohokam traded for seashells, which they used to create jewelry and religious objects.

**✓Checkpoint** **For what purposes were mounds built?**

## Ways of Life

Scholars classify Native Americans into several culture areas, regions in which groups of people have a similar way of life. Though these cultures were very different from one another, many shared some basic traits.

**Meeting Basic Needs** Early Native American societies developed a variety of ways to meet their needs. In many areas, women collected roots, wild seeds, nuts, acorns, and berries. Men hunted for game and fished. Wild game was plentiful in regions like the Pacific Coast and the Eastern Woodlands.

In many culture areas, agriculture allowed people to grow and store food. Native Americans learned to grow crops suited to the climate in which they lived. They used pointed sticks for digging. Bones or shells served as hoes. Some used fertilizer, such as dead fish, to make the soil more productive. Where Native Americans lived by farming, their population was much larger than in nonfarming areas.

Trade was a common activity in all the North American cultures. In some areas, items such as seashells or beads were used as currency. Shells, flint for making fires, copper, and salt were all important trade items.

**Shared Beliefs** Many Native Americans felt a close relationship to the natural world. They believed that spirits dwelled in nature and that these spirits were part of their daily lives.

Traditions reflected these beliefs. For example, the Indians of the Southeast held the Green Corn Ceremony in late summer. The ritual, which could last for more than a week, was a form of natural and spiritual renewal at the end of the growing season. The Pueblo Indians revered spirits known as kachinas. To teach their children about these benevolent spirits, the Pueblos carved kachina dolls.

Native Americans also had a strong oral tradition. Storytellers memorized history and beliefs and then recited them. In this way, their tradition was passed on from generation to generation.

**✓Checkpoint** **How did North American cultures meet their needs?**

**Main Idea**
Many of the varied cultures of North America shared some basic features.

**Vocabulary** *Builder*
**currency** (KUH rehn see) *n.* items used as money

**Native American Farmers**
Early farmers made and used stone tools such as the digging stick and axe shown to the left. **Critical Thinking:** *Clarify Problems Based on this picture, what difficulties might these farmers face?*

**Main Idea**
Culture groups of North America adapted their ways of life to their environment.

**Vocabulary** *Builder*
distinct (dihs TIHNKT) *adj.* clearly different in quality

# Native Americans of North America

Well before 10,000 B.C., Native Americans had spread across the North American continent. They had adapted to the various climates and living conditions of the lands in which they settled. By A.D. 1500, when the first Europeans reached the Americas, the Native Americans living in North America were a richly diverse group of people with distinct ways of life.

**Far North** The people of the Arctic lived in a vast and harsh land, some of it covered with ice all year long. The people survived on fish, shellfish, and birds. They also hunted marine mammals, such as whales, seals, and walruses, from **kayaks**, small boats made from skins. In the summer, they fished on the rivers and hunted caribou.

South of the Arctic lay the dense forests of the subarctic region. With a climate too cold for farming, subarctic peoples relied on animals and plants of the forest for food. Most hunted caribou, moose, bear, and smaller animals.

**Northwest** Many Native Americans lived in the region of the Pacific Northwest, the land that stretches from southern Alaska to northern California. Deer and bears roamed forests rich with roots and berries. Rivers swarmed with salmon. With so much food available, people here were able to live in large, permanent settlements even though they were not farmers.

In many societies of the Northwest, high-ranking people practiced a custom called the potlatch. A **potlatch** was a ceremony at which the hosts showered their guests with gifts such as woven cloth, baskets, canoes, and furs. A family's status was judged by how much wealth it could give away.

**Far West** The people of the Far West lived in different geographic regions. Winters could be very cold in the forests and grasslands of the north. On the other hand, southern parts could be desertlike. In California, with its warm summers and mild winters, food was abundant. People there ate small game, fish, and berries.

Housing differed, depending on the area. Some Native Americans lived in pit houses, which were dug into the ground. Others lived in cone-shaped houses covered with bark. In the north, houses were made of wooden planks.

**Southwest** The area that is now Arizona, New Mexico, and the southern parts of Utah and Colorado was dry most of the year. But in late July and August, thunderstorms drenched the desert. All the groups in this area did some farming, although certain groups also followed and hunted animals. Farming peoples had to learn to collect and store the rain for the dry times.

The Pueblo people such as the Hopis and Zunis had stable towns that lasted for hundreds of years. To protect themselves from attack, they built large apartment houses made of **adobe**, or sun-dried brick.

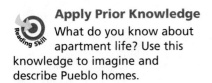

**Apply Prior Knowledge**
What do you know about apartment life? Use this knowledge to imagine and describe Pueblo homes.

# Homes of Native Americans

Native Americans lived in several distinct culture areas. In each region, geography and climate helped shape the people's way of life.
**Critical Thinking: *Apply Information*** *Look at the map and the pictures. Identify the group that lived in tepees.*

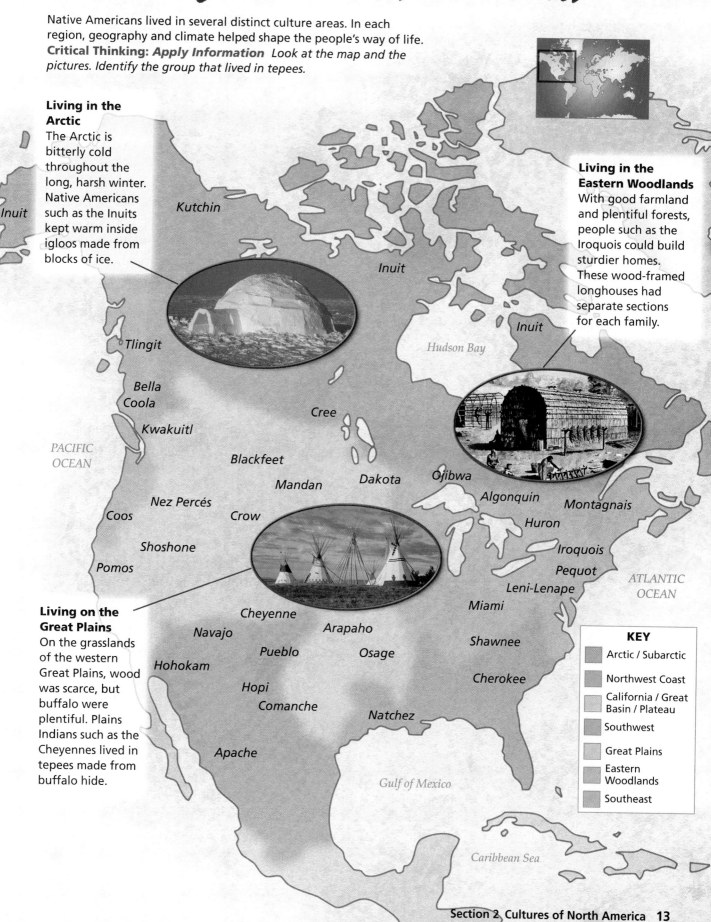

**Living in the Arctic**
The Arctic is bitterly cold throughout the long, harsh winter. Native Americans such as the Inuits kept warm inside igloos made from blocks of ice.

**Living in the Eastern Woodlands**
With good farmland and plentiful forests, people such as the Iroquois could build sturdier homes. These wood-framed longhouses had separate sections for each family.

**Living on the Great Plains**
On the grasslands of the western Great Plains, wood was scarce, but buffalo were plentiful. Plains Indians such as the Cheyennes lived in tepees made from buffalo hide.

Inuit

Kutchin

Inuit

Inuit

Hudson Bay

Tlingit

Bella Coola

Kwakuitl

Cree

PACIFIC OCEAN

Blackfeet

Mandan

Dakota

Ojibwa

Algonquin

Montagnais

Nez Percés

Crow

Huron

Coos

Shoshone

Iroquois

Pomos

Pequot

ATLANTIC OCEAN

Leni-Lenape

Cheyenne

Arapaho

Miami

Navajo

Pueblo

Osage

Shawnee

Hohokam

Cherokee

Hopi

Comanche

Natchez

Apache

Gulf of Mexico

Caribbean Sea

**KEY**
- Arctic / Subarctic
- Northwest Coast
- California / Great Basin / Plateau
- Southwest
- Great Plains
- Eastern Woodlands
- Southeast

## The Iroquois Constitution

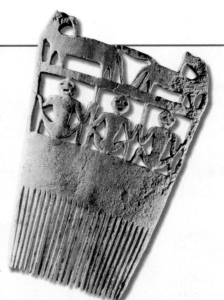

"Whenever the Confederate Lords shall assemble for the purpose of holding a council, the Onondaga Lords shall open it by expressing their gratitude to their cousin Lords and greeting them, and they shall make an address and offer thanks to the earth where men dwell, to the streams of water . . . to the forest trees for their usefulness, to the animals that serve as food and give their pelts for clothing . . . and to the Great Creator who dwells in the heavens above."

—Iroquois Constitution

The figures on this Seneca comb represent the five Iroquois nations.

### Reading Primary Sources
#### Skills Activity

The constitution of the Iroquois League was at first a spoken rather than a written document. The excerpt above describes how members of the Iroquois League were to begin a meeting.

**(a) Apply Information** What attitude toward nature does this selection reflect?

**(b) Draw Conclusions** Why do you think members of the Iroquois League wanted to begin each meeting with a set ritual?

**Great Plains** The Great Plains is a vast region stretching between the Mississippi River and the Rocky Mountains. The people of the eastern Plains lived mainly by farming. Women planted corn, beans, and squash in river valleys. Many people lived in earth lodges. These buildings had log frames and were covered with soil.

Much of the western Great Plains was too dry and too matted with grass to be farmed. The treeless land provided few building materials. In the west, some people lived in tepees made of animal skins. Other Plains people dug round pits near their fields for shelter.

Hunting parties followed buffalo across the plains. The Plains people depended on the buffalo for many things. They ate the meat and used the hides to make tepees, robes, and shields. Buffalo bones were made into tools.

**Eastern Woodlands** Hundreds of years ago, most of what is now the eastern United States was covered by forests of maples, birches, pines, and beeches. The earliest woodlands people lived by hunting, fishing, and foraging for nuts and berries. By about A.D. 1000, a number of woodlands people had taken up farming.

Two groups dominated the Eastern Woodlands. One group spoke Algonquian (al GOHN kee un) languages. The Algonquian people were scattered through southern Canada, the Great Lakes area, and along the Atlantic coast to Virginia. The other groups, speaking Iroquoian (IHR uh kwoy an) languages, lived in what is now New York.

The Iroquois were made up of five distinct nations. Each nation was made up of **clans**, or groups of families that were related to one another. Because membership in a clan was passed from a mother to her children, women had great influence in Iroquois society. They owned all the property that belonged to a clan. Women also chose the clan's **sachem**, or tribal chief.

During the 1500s, the five Iroquois nations went through a period of constant warfare. Finally, Iroquois leaders convinced their people to make peace. They formed a union called the League of the Iroquois. It established a council to make laws to keep the peace. Each tribe was still free to deal with its own affairs.

**Southeast** The climate in the Southeast was mild, but the summers were steamy and hot. The land and climate supported farming. People such as the Cherokees and Creeks built houses on wooden frames, covered with straw mats. They then plastered the houses with mud clay to keep the interiors cool and dry.

The Natchez people of the Gulf Coast created a complex society. At the top stood the ruler, called the Great Sun, and the nobles. At the bottom were commoners, known as Stinkards. By law, all nobles—including the Great Sun himself—had to marry Stinkards. In this way, membership in each class kept changing.

Cherokee mask

✓**Checkpoint** **In what culture areas was hunting the main way of life?**

⭐ **Looking Back and Ahead** In this section, you learned about Native American cultures. In the next sections, you will explore cultures that developed on the other side of the world.

---

Section 2 | **Check Your Progress**

**Progress Monitoring** Online
**For:** Self-test with instant help
**Visit:** PHSchool.com
**Web Code:** mva-1012

**Comprehension and Critical Thinking**

**1. (a) Recall** What role did nature play in many Native American religious beliefs?
**(b) Draw Inferences** How does that emphasis on nature reflect the everyday life of the people?

**2. (a) Identify** Identify two culture areas where farming was the main way of life.
**(b) Analyze Cause and Effect** Why do you think farming did not develop extensively in the Arctic and the subarctic regions?

**Reading Skill**

**3. Apply Prior Knowledge** Reread the first paragraph under the heading "Native Americans of North America." How is your culture group different from others? How is it the same? Use this knowledge to describe how Native American cultures were the same and different.

**Vocabulary** *Builder*

Fill in the blank in each question with a key term from this section.

**4.** The _____ of a people includes its customs, beliefs, and ways of making a living.
**5.** The _____ provided leadership in Iroquois communities.
**6.** Members of the same _____ shared a common ancestor.

**Writing**

**7.** Create a chart that shows how three different groups of Native Americans adapted to the regions in which they lived. Use the following column headings: Region, Way of Life, Diet, Shelter.

# Trade Networks of Asia and Africa

## Objectives

1. Learn about the role played by Muslims in world trade.

2. Discover how great trading states rose in East Africa and West Africa.

3. Find out how China dominated an important trade route across Asia.

## Prepare to Read

### Reading Skill

**Ask Questions** Asking questions when you read will help you organize your reading plan and get involved with the text. You can use your questions, for example, to set a reading purpose—answering the questions. Two ways to generate questions are to restate headings and to study the review questions at the end of the section.

### Vocabulary *Builder*

**High-Use Words**

transmit, p. 16

sphere, p. 17

**Key Terms and People**

Muhammad, p. 16

Mansa Musa, p. 18

navigation, p. 19

Zheng He, p. 19

⭐ **Background Knowledge** In the previous section, you learned how important trade was to Native Americans. In this section, you will learn how trade helped link together the people of Asia, Africa, and Europe.

## The Muslim Link in Trade

**Main Idea**
The Muslim world linked traders across three continents.

From earliest times, trade linked groups who lived at great distances from one another. As trade developed, merchants established regular trade routes. These merchants carried their culture with them as they traveled.

By the 1500s, a complex trade network linked Europe, Africa, and Asia. Much of this trade passed through the Arabian Peninsula in the Middle East. Ships from China and India brought their cargoes of spices, silks, and gems to ports on the Red Sea. The precious cargoes were then taken overland to markets throughout the Middle East.

**Rise of Islam** The growth in trade was also linked to the rise of the religion of Islam. Islam emerged on the Arabian Peninsula in the 600s. Its founder was the prophet Muhammad. Muhammad taught that there is one true God. Followers of Islam, called Muslims, believed that the Quran (ku RAHN), the sacred book of Islam, contained the exact word of God as revealed to Muhammad.

**Vocabulary *Builder***
transmit (trans MIHT) *v.* to pass along; to send

Islam was underlinedtransmitted rapidly through conquest and trade. Arab armies swept across North Africa and into Spain. Muslim merchants also spread their religion far into Africa, and from Persia to India. Millions of people across three continents became Muslims.

**Advances in Learning** Arab scholars made remarkable contributions to mathematics, medicine, and astronomy. They helped develop algebra and later passed it along to Europe. Arab astronomers measured the size of Earth, supporting the Greek belief that Earth was a <u>sphere.</u> Arabs also made important advances in technology. They built ships with large, triangular sails that allowed captains to use the wind even if it changed direction.

☑ **Checkpoint**  **How did Islam spread?**

## The African Link in Trade

Africa has a long history of trade, going back as far as 3100 B.C., when the great civilization of Egypt arose. Egyptian traders sailed throughout the eastern Mediterranean Sea and the Red Sea to bring home cedar logs, silver, and horses. Following routes south from Egypt, they traded for ivory, spices, copper, and cattle.

**East African Trade Centers** About A.D. 1000, trade centers began to appear in eastern Africa. The most powerful was Zimbabwe (zim BAH bway), which became the center of a flourishing empire in the 1400s. Zimbabwe lay on the trade route between the east coast and the interior of Africa. Traders passing through Zimbabwe had to pay taxes on their goods.

Trade brought prosperity to a number of cities along the east coast of Africa. Kilwa, the chief trading center, attracted merchant ships from as far away as China. Kilwa traders did a brisk trade with the African interior, exchanging cloth, pottery, and manufactured goods for gold, ivory, and furs. An active slave trade also developed between East Africa and Asia across the Indian Ocean.

**Vocabulary** *Builder*
<u>sphere</u> (sfeer) *n.* rounded shape

**Main Idea**
Complex trade networks developed in both East Africa and West Africa.

**Ask Questions**
*Reading Skill* Preview the headings on the next two pages. Turn them into questions that you would expect to find the answers to as you read.

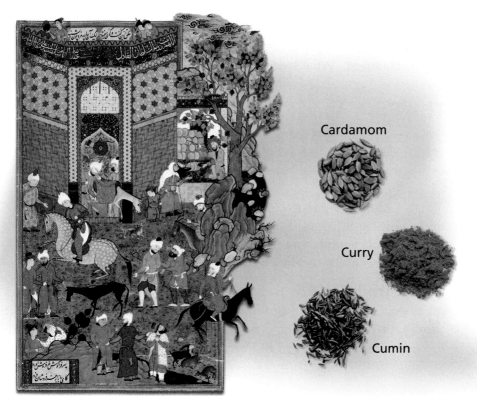

Cardamom

Curry

Cumin

**Merchants in the Middle East**
At outdoor bazaars, Muslim merchants bought and sold goods from around the world. Probably the most valuable goods sold at this Persian bazaar were spices from Southeast Asia, such as the ones shown here. **Critical Thinking:** *Link Past and Present* *How is this bazaar similar to a modern shopping area? How is it different?*

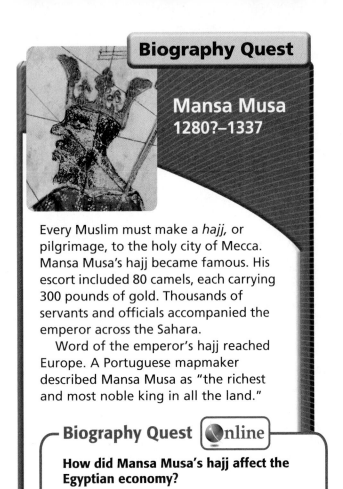

**West African Trade Centers** Trade networks also linked the Middle East and West Africa. Desert nomads guided caravans, or groups of camels and their cargo, across the vast Sahara, the largest desert in the world.

Ghana was the first major center of trade in West Africa. The kingdom was located between the sources of salt in the desert and the gold fields farther south. By the ninth century, the demand for gold had grown in the Middle East. On the other hand, people in West Africa needed salt in their diet to prevent dehydration in the hot tropical climate. As the trade in gold and salt increased, the rulers of Ghana became rich.

Shifting trade routes and disruptions caused by war gradually led Ghana to weaken. In the 1200s, the kingdom was absorbed into the empire of Mali. Mali reached its height under the Muslim ruler Mansa Musa. As Mali prospered, its great city of Timbuktu became a center of learning. Merchants from Mali traded throughout the region for kola nuts, food, and, of course, gold.

In the 1400s, Mali had a number of weak rulers. When nomads captured Timbuktu in 1433, the empire had been in decline for some time. It would soon be replaced by Songhai.

The rulers of Songhai captured Timbuktu in 1468. Songhai rulers restored the city as a center of Islamic learning. Trade across the Sahara expanded, which brought wealth to the Songhai Empire. Salt, gold, and captives for sale as slaves passed through Songhai on the way to Muslim markets in the north.

☑**Checkpoint**   **What trading kingdoms arose in West Africa?**

**Main Idea**
China dominated the trade routes that linked East Asia to the Middle East.

## The East Asian Link in Trade

As early as 221 B.C., a strong ruler had unified China into a single empire. Later rulers added to the empire until it covered a large part of the continent of Asia. Highways, canals, and a postal system linked China together.

As China's empire expanded, so did its trade. China established trade links with India, Korea, Japan, the Middle East, and Africa. China's trade centers grew into cities. By the 1200s, Hangzhou (HAN JOW) was one of the world's largest cities.

**World Traders** China had a higher level of technology than any other civilization of the time. Around 1050, the Chinese invented printing with movable type. This was about 400 years before this technology was developed in Europe.

The Chinese made great advances in navigation. Navigation is the science of locating the position and plotting the course of ships. The Chinese invented the magnetic compass, which made it possible for ships to sail out of sight of land and still find their way home.

By the 1300s Chinese ships were sailing trade routes that stretched from Japan to East Africa. The Chinese explorer Zheng He made several voyages with a fleet of more than 300 giant ships. The fleet visited 30 nations throughout Asia and Africa, trading silks and pottery for spices, gems, medicinal herbs, and ivory.

**Spice Trade and the Silk Road** Chinese silks, bronze goods, pottery, and spices flowed west from China along a route known as the Silk Road. The Silk Road was one of the great trade routes of ancient times. It was not really a single road but a series of routes that stretched about 5,000 miles from Xi'an (SHE AHN) in China to Persia.

Merchants on the Silk Road brought silk and other goods from China across Asia for sale in Middle Eastern and European markets. Along the way they traded in the Middle East for products like cloves, nutmeg, and peppercorns from the Spice Islands in Southeast Asia. The Silk Road declined in importance when alternative sea routes were discovered.

✓**Checkpoint** What was the Silk Road?

⭐ **Looking Back and Ahead** The trade links between Asia and Africa developed at a time when much of Europe was isolated. In the next section, you will learn about the development of Europe. You will also see how Europe began to look toward the riches of Asia.

This Chinese figurine is made of jade, a precious trade item.

---

**Section 3 | Check Your Progress**

**Progress Monitoring** Online
**For:** Self-test with instant help
**Visit:** PHSchool.com
**Web Code:** mva-1013

**Comprehension and Critical Thinking**

**1. (a) Recall** What role did the Muslim world play in trade?
**(b) Interpret Maps** Locate the Arabian Peninsula on a world map. Why was its location ideal for a trading center?

**2. (a) Recall** Why were gold and salt important in West African trade?
**(b) Contrast** How did trade in East Africa differ from trade in West Africa?

**Reading Skill**

**3. Ask Questions** Look at the questions you asked, and look at the section review questions. Did the reading answer those questions? How did previewing help you set purposes and increase your understanding?

**Vocabulary** *Builder*

**4.** Write two definitions for the key term navigation—one a formal definition for a teacher, the other an informal definition for a younger child.

**Writing**

**5.** Consider the following thesis statement: The trading network between Asia, Africa, and Europe began a useful exchange of ideas and products. Write one or two paragraphs to develop that thesis.

# Global Trade in the Fifteenth Century

For centuries, merchants and traders used land and sea routes to travel between Europe, Africa, and Asia. Before the first European voyages to the Americas, a global trading network linked the major civilizations of three continents. Gold and salt moved east from Africa while silk and spices moved west from China and India. Use the map below to trace the patterns of global trade.

Ivory

Gold

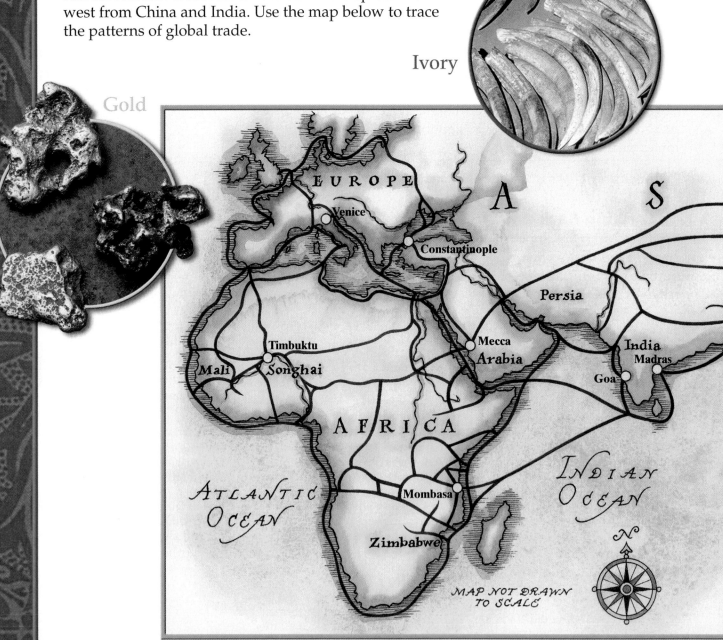

**History** *Interactive*
**Explore Global Trade**
**Visit:** PHSchool.com
**Web Code:** mvl-1013

## Gold, Salt, and Ivory

Trade centers in East and West Africa saw heavy traffic in gold, salt, and ivory. African gold was highly valued in the Middle East.

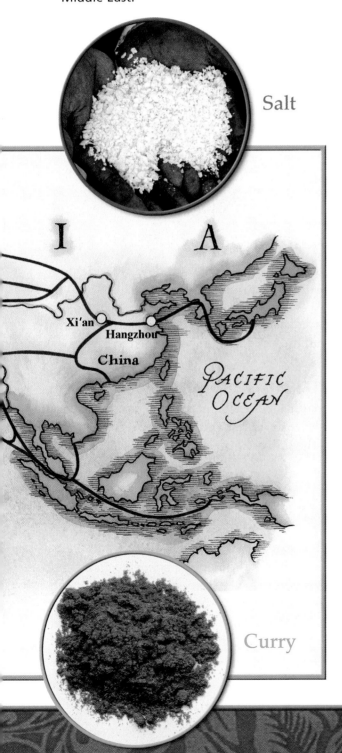

Salt

China

Xi'an

Hangzhou

*PACIFIC OCEAN*

Curry

*Understand Effects:*

## The Network Expands

When Christopher Columbus sailed west from Spain in 1492, he opened up a new era in global trade. Prior to Columbus's voyage, the Americas were isolated from the flow of goods and ideas that connected Europe, Africa, and Asia. After 1492, the old trade networks expanded across an ocean to a new world of resources.

▲ Trade flourished throughout Asia. Ships from China and India unloaded their cargoes in Arabian ports for overland transport to African or European markets.

### *Analyze* GEOGRAPHY AND HISTORY

Worldwide trade allowed for the exchange of goods and ideas across continents. Write a paragraph describing how West African gold might travel to China.

# The European Heritage

## Objectives

1. Understand the importance of the Judeo-Christian tradition.

2. Learn how Greece and Rome shaped ideas about government and law.

3. Discover the impact of the Crusades and the Renaissance on Europe.

4. Find out why Europeans began to look beyond their borders.

## Prepare to Read

 **Reading Skill**

**Use Graphics to Construct Meaning** Textbooks include information beyond the main text that can be useful to your understanding. Nontext material includes maps, tables, charts, photos, and illustrations. In addition, these materials often have accompanying text such as captions or titles. Use this material to gain understanding when you preview, and then refer to it for details as you read.

### Vocabulary *Builder*

**High-Use Words**
participate, p. 24
precise, p. 27

**Key Terms and People**
monotheism, p. 22
Jesus, p. 23
salvation, p. 23
direct democracy, p. 24
republic, p. 25
feudalism, p. 25
Martin Luther, p. 26
Henry the Navigator, p. 27
Vasco da Gama, p. 27

⭐ **Background Knowledge** In the previous section, you learned how trade influenced civilizations in Asia and Africa. In this section, you will read about how civilization developed in Europe.

## The Judeo-Christian Tradition

European beliefs and values were shaped by two religions of the ancient Middle East: Judaism and Christianity. The influence of these two religions is known as the Judeo-Christian tradition.

**Judaism** Around 1700 B.C. a system of beliefs called Judaism arose among the Israelites, a nomadic people of the Middle East. Judaism was the first major world religion to teach monotheism, the idea that there is only one God.

The Israelites credited Moses with bringing God's laws to them. Those laws included the Ten Commandments, a set of religious and moral rules. Jews believed that every Jew must obey the Ten Commandments and other religious and moral laws.

Other early religions regarded rulers as gods. Judaism held that even the most powerful ruler had to obey God's laws. This belief formed the basis for the later view that no person, no matter how powerful or wealthy, is above the law.

**Main Idea**
Judaism and Christianity became the foundation of religious beliefs in Europe.

**Use Graphics to Construct Meaning**
Preview the pictures in this section. What do they suggest to you about the content of the text?

**Christianity** About 2,000 years ago, a Jewish teacher named Jesus of Nazareth began to preach in the region around the Sea of Galilee. Jesus attracted a following. Many believed that he was the Messiah, the Savior chosen by God.

The Gospels, which recount the life of Jesus, tell how crowds flocked to hear Jesus teach and perform miracles. Local officials, however, saw Jesus as a political threat. The Roman rulers of Jerusalem arrested, tried, and crucified Jesus. Followers of Jesus said that he rose from the dead three days later.

The life and teachings of Jesus inspired a new religion, Christianity. Christianity is based on the belief that Jesus was indeed the Messiah, sent by God to save the world. Christians teach that Jesus was, in fact, God in human form.

The teachings of Jesus emphasized love, mercy, and forgiveness. Jesus also taught that all people have an equal chance for salvation, or everlasting life. These beliefs appealed to many people, especially the poor and oppressed. This helped Christianity spread from the Middle East across Europe.

As Christianity spread, the Romans at first viewed it as a threat. Christians were subject to arrest and death. Later, emperors accepted Christianity and made it the official religion of the Roman Empire. As a result, it eventually became the dominant religion of all of Europe.

✓**Checkpoint** **What does Christianity teach about Jesus?**

## The Ten Commandments

"[I.] I am the Lord your God, who brought you out of the land of Egypt, out of the house of bondage. You shall have no other gods before me. . . .
[III.] You shall not take the name of the Lord your God in vain; . . .
[V.] Honor your father and your mother, that your days may be long in the land which the Lord your God gives you.
[VI.] You shall not kill. . . .
[VIII.] You shall not steal."

—Book of Exodus, Revised Standard Version

Painting showing Moses with the Ten Commandments

### Reading Primary Sources
#### Skills Activity

According to the Bible, God gave the Ten Commandments to the Hebrew leader Moses. Five of the Commandments are given above.

**(a) Apply Information** How does this selection reflect the Judeo-Christian idea of monotheism?

**(b) Draw Conclusions** How do the Ten Commandments say we should treat other people?

**Vocabulary** *Builder*
**participate** (pahr TIHS uh payt) *v.* to take part

# Greek and Roman Traditions

Judaism and Christianity shaped European religious and moral thinking. At the same time, the ancient civilizations of Greece and Rome shaped European political traditions. Greek and Roman ideas would later deeply influence the Founders of the United States.

**Athenian Democracy** In the fifth century B.C., the Greek city-state of Athens experienced a sudden explosion of learning and creativity. Perhaps its most remarkable achievement was the birth of democracy.

Athens was a direct democracy. **Direct democracy** is a form of government in which an assembly of ordinary citizens makes decisions. This differs from the modern American form of government, in which citizens elect representatives to make laws. Any adult male citizen could participate in the Athenian Assembly. The Athenian leader Pericles described the Athenian idea of democracy:

> **❝**Our constitution is named a democracy, because it is in the hands not of the few but of the many. . . . We decide or debate, carefully and in person, all matters of policy.**❞**
> —Pericles, from *The History of the Peloponnesian War* (Thucydides)

Still, Athenian democracy had limitations. Women, slaves, and foreign-born people could not participate in government.

Athenians believed that a democracy depended on well-rounded, educated citizens. In Athenian schools, boys studied many areas of knowledge, from history and grammar to poetry and music. Because Athenian citizens were expected to voice their opinions in the Assembly, schools also trained students in public speaking.

**Roman Government and Law** While democracy was developing in ancient Greece, a few small villages in central Italy were growing into the city of Rome. Over time, the Romans developed new traditions in law and government.

**Education in Athens**
This Greek vase painting shows an Athenian school. At the center, a teacher checks a student's writing tablet. **Critical Thinking: Interpret Art** *Identify one other subject that the students at this school are learning.*

# Links Across Time

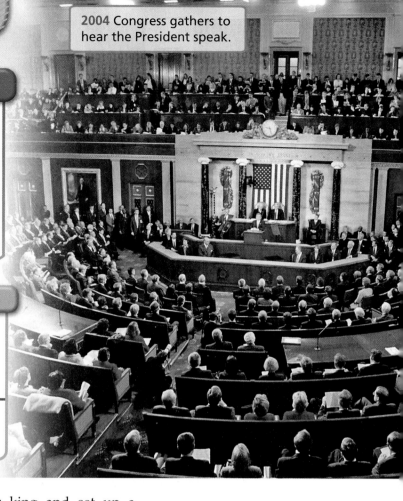

2004 Congress gathers to hear the President speak.

## Republican Government

**509 B.C.** The Roman Republic was established. The elected Senate became the chief governing and law-making body of Rome.

**1787** The Founders of the United States admired the Roman Republic. When they wrote the Constitution, they gave lawmaking power to an elected Congress similar to the Roman Senate. But they divided Congress into two separate houses, the Senate and the House of Representatives.

## Link to Today  Online

**Congress Today** Today, as in the past, the men and women of Congress make laws that affect the lives of all Americans.

**For:** Congress in the news
**Visit:** PHSchool.com
**Web Code:** mvc-1014

In 509 B.C., the Romans overthrew their king and set up a republic. A **republic** is a form of government in which people choose representatives to govern them. In the Roman Republic, an elected senate and assembly made the laws.

Rome's code of laws defined the rights of citizens. According to the code, everybody was equal under the law. People accused of crimes were considered innocent until proven guilty. These principles form the framework of the American system of justice.

Long years of civil war led to the collapse of the Roman republic. In 27 B.C., a noble named Octavian declared himself emperor. The Roman Empire would last for almost 500 years. During this time, Roman ideas about law and government spread over a wide area.

✓**Checkpoint** **How did citizens participate in Greek and Roman government?**

# New Horizons

After a period of decline, the Roman Empire fell to invaders in A.D. 476. Europe fragmented into many small states. The 1,000-year period after the fall of Rome is known as the Middle Ages.

**The Middle Ages** By the ninth century, feudalism had arisen in Europe. **Feudalism** is a system in which a ruler grants parts of his land to lords. In exchange, lords owed the king military service and financial assistance. In turn, lords granted land to lesser lords.

**Main Idea**
The Crusades and the Renaissance inspired Europeans to look beyond their own world.

**Copying a Manuscript**

In Europe during the Middle Ages, learning was in the hands of the Church. Monks like this one spent hours and hours each day carefully copying books by hand. **Critical Thinking: *Make Predictions*** *How might the invention of mechanical printing affect learning in Europe?*

The Roman Catholic Church had great power in the Middle Ages. Daily life revolved around the rituals of the Catholic Church. The Catholic Church was also the center of learning. Outside of members of the clergy, few people, even among the nobility, were able to read and write.

**The Crusades** In 1095, the leader of the Roman Catholic Church, Pope Urban II, declared a crusade, or holy war. Its object was to win back control of the region known as the Holy Land, the land where Jesus had lived and taught. There were nine crusades over the next 200 years. In the end, they failed to win permanent control of the Holy Land.

Still, the Crusades had important long-term effects. They put Europeans in closer contact with the more advanced Muslim civilization. Europeans were attracted by the rich goods they saw in the Holy Land. They tasted strange foods and spices, such as oranges, pepper, and ginger. They also learned about advanced technology used for navigation. In time, the Crusades would help inspire Europeans to look overseas for trade.

**The Renaissance** Beginning in the 1300s, there was a rebirth of learning that is known as the Renaissance. European scholars rediscovered the classical texts of ancient Greece and Rome. Artists reflected a new interest in subjects that had influenced ancient thinkers.

Science and invention flourished. One invention, in particular, had a great impact on society. In the mid-fifteenth century, Johann Gutenberg invented a printing press. Using movable type, the printing press enabled a printer to produce a large number of identical books in a short time. As books became more available, the ability to read became more widespread.

During the late Middle Ages, powerful nation-states emerged in Europe. Italian cities had long controlled trade on the Mediterranean. The new nations—Spain, Portugal, France, and England—would shift the important trade routes to the Atlantic Ocean.

**The Reformation** Since the late Roman Empire, most Europeans had belonged to the Roman Catholic Church. Not all were happy with Catholicism, however. In 1517, a German monk named Martin Luther demanded that the Roman Catholic Church reform.

When his demands were rejected, Luther rebelled against the Catholic Church authority. Followers of Luther were called Protestants, because they were protesting certain Catholic Church practices. The movement Luther led is called the Protestant Reformation. Over time, Luther's movement split, and many Protestant churches emerged. The Reformation also plunged Europe into a long series of wars between Catholic and Protestant forces.

☑**Checkpoint** **What was the Renaissance?**

# An Age of Exploration Begins

**Main Idea**
Portugal led the way in European exploration.

The Renaissance, the rise of nations, and the expansion of trade set the stage for an era of exploration. The person who provided the leadership for this new era was a brother of the king of Portugal, known to history as Prince Henry the Navigator. A deeply religious man, Henry hoped not only to expand Portuguese power but also to spread Christianity to new lands.

In the 1400s, Henry set up a center for exploration at Sagres (SAH greesh) in southern Portugal. He brought mathematicians, geographers, and sea captains to this center to teach his crews everything they needed to know about navigation and mapmaking.

At Sagres, sailors learned how to use the magnetic compass to find their direction at sea. They also learned how to use an instrument called the astrolabe to determine their <u>precise</u> latitude, or distance from the equator.

**Vocabulary** *Builder*
<u>precise</u> (pree sĭs) *adj.* exact; accurate

Using their new skills, Portuguese sailors began sailing southward along the western coast of Africa. By 1498, the Portuguese sailor Vasco da Gama passed the southern tip of Africa and continued north and east to India. Da Gama's course became an important trade route and helped boost Portuguese wealth and power. Later, Portuguese sailors pressed on to the East Indies, the source of trade in spices.

**✓Checkpoint** **What was Prince Henry's goal?**

⭐ **Looking Back and Ahead** By the time Vasco da Gama reached India, Prince Henry was long dead. However, his work opened the way for European sailors to reach far-flung corners of the globe. In the next chapter, you would see how these sailors linked the long-separated worlds of the east and west.

## Section 4 | Check Your Progress

**Progress Monitoring** ⦿nline
**For:** Self-test with instant help
**Visit:** PHSchool.com
**Web Code:** mva-1014

### Comprehension and Critical Thinking

**1. (a) Recall** What role did citizens play in Athens?
**(b) Contrast** How did Athenian democracy differ from the Roman Republic?

**2. (a) Recall** How did Europeans make greater contact with the outside world?
**(b) Identify Benefits** How might Europeans of that time benefit from increased trade?

### ↻ Reading Skill

**3. Use Graphics to Construct Meaning** How did previewing visual material in this section help you read more actively? How did this material add detail to your understanding of European civilization?

### Vocabulary *Builder*

Answer the following questions in complete sentences that show your understanding of the key terms.
**4.** How did monotheism differ from other early beliefs?

**5.** Why were nobles important in feudalism?
**6.** How are leaders chosen in a republic?

### Writing

**7.** Some of the events covered in this section include the Crusades, feudalism, and the Renaissance. What do you think life was like in Europe before these events happened? How did life in Europe change after these events? Answer the questions in one or two paragraphs.

History books are full of information. Although you cannot remember every fact, you can learn to identify the main ideas and note the details that explain and support them. The following passage is a description such as you might find in a textbook.

Native Americans developed a variety of ways to meet their basic needs for food, clothing, and shelter. In some culture areas, tribes hunted animals and gathered the nuts and fruits that grew in the wild. Other tribes depended on the sea for food. They made boats out of animal skins or carved canoes out of trees. From their boats and canoes, they speared fish or hunted marine animals such as seals, walruses, and whales.

Whether hunting, fishing, farming, or gathering wild plants, Native Americans had a great respect for the natural world. Their prayers and ceremonies were designed to maintain a balance between people and the forces of nature. They believed that they must adapt their ways to the natural world in order to survive and prosper.

## Learn the Skill

*Use these steps to learn how to identify main ideas and supporting details.*

1. **Find the main idea.** The main idea is what the passage is about. Often, the main idea is stated in the first sentence of a paragraph. However, it can occur in other parts of a paragraph as well.

2. **Restate the main idea.** To be sure you understand the ideas expressed in paragraph, restate the main idea in your own words.

3. **Look for details.** Details might include facts, reasons, explanations, examples, and descriptions that tell more about the main idea.

4. **Make connections.** Note how the details support and expand the main idea.

## Practice the Skill

*Answer the following questions based on the paragraph above.*

1. **Find the main idea.** (a) What is the main-idea sentence in the first paragraph? (b) What is the main-idea sentence in the second paragraph?

2. **Restate the main idea.** Restate the main idea of each paragraph in your own words.

3. **Look for details.** Identify a detail that supports the main idea in each paragraph.

4. **Make connections.** (a) How do the details in the first paragraph help explain its main idea? (b) How do the details in the second paragraph help explain its main idea?

## Apply the Skill

*See the Review and Assessment at the end of this chapter.*

**Study Guide *Online***
Complete your Chapter 1
study guide in print or online.

## Chapter Summary

### Section 1
### The Earliest Americans

- Most scientists believe that early people came to the Americas from Asia by way of a land bridge.
- As people learned to farm, they formed permanent settlements.
- The Mayas, Aztecs, and Incas built civilizations in Central America and South America.

### Section 2
### Cultures of North America

- The Mound Builders were among the earliest cultures of North America.
- People of North America developed varied ways of life, depending upon the environments in which they lived.
- The League of the Iroquois created a pact between warring nations in the Eastern Woodlands.

### Section 3
### Trade Networks of Asia and Africa

- The Muslim world linked Asia to Africa and Europe through trade.
- Various trading states emerged in both East Africa and West Africa.
- China dominated East Asian trade along the Silk Road.

### Section 4
### The European Heritage

- Judaism and Christianity formed the foundation for European religious beliefs.
- Greece and Rome shaped ideas about democratic government.
- After the Middle Ages, Europeans began to look beyond their boundaries.

## Key Concepts

These notes will help you prepare for questions about key concepts.

### Culture Groups of North America

**Far North**
- Cold climate
- Hunting and fishing

**Northwest**
- Rich forests
- Permanent settlements

**Far West**
- Climates vary from desert to mild

**Southwest**
- Hot, dry climate
- Pueblo people built large settlements

**Great Plains**
- Farming in east
- Buffalo hunting in west

**Eastern Woodlands**
- Forests and farming supplied needs
- Iroquois formed league to make peace

**Southeast**
- Mild climate, hot summers
- Farming communities

### Traditions That Came to the Americas From Europe

**Judeo-Christian Tradition**
- Ideas on justice and morality
- No ruler is above God's law
- Emphasis on love, mercy, and forgiveness

**Greek and Roman Civilizations**
- Concept of democracy
- Republican system of government
- Roman law in which everyone is equal before the law

## Vocabulary *Builder*

### Key Terms

1. Draw a table with eight rows and three columns. In the first column, list the following key terms: glacier, irrigate, culture, clan, navigation, monotheism, direct democracy, republic. In the next column, write the definition of each word. In the last column, make a small illustration that shows the meaning of the word.

## Comprehension and Critical Thinking

2. **(a) Recall** Describe the land-bridge theory that scientists have developed to explain how people first came to the Americas.
**(b) Clarify Problems** Some scholars have different ideas about how people first came to the Americas. Why do you think we are not sure about this event?

3. **(a) Describe** How did the Aztecs build a large empire?
**(b) Compare** What features did the Aztec civilization have in common with civilization of the Incas?
**(c) Contrast** How did the civilization of the Aztecs differ from other societies of North America?

4. **(a) Recall** What was the purpose of the League of the Iroquois?
**(b) Identify Costs and Benefits** What did each Iroquois Nation give up by joining the League? What did they gain?
**(c) Draw Conclusions** Why do you think the Iroquois League succeeded?

5. **(a) Describe** How did trade goods move between West Africa and the Middle East?
**(b) Apply Information** Describe two ways that goods from China might have reached the trading states of East Africa.
**(c) Make Generalizations** Based on your reading, write a one-sentence generalization about the importance of trade routes in Asia and Africa.

6. **(a) Summarize** Which Greco-Roman traditions influenced the shaping of government in the United States?
**(b) Link Past and Present** How do these Greco-Roman ideas directly impact political life in the United States today?

7. **(a) Define** What were the Crusades?
**(b) Analyze Cause and Effect** What were the long-range effects of the Crusades?
**(c) Draw Conclusions** Do you think the Crusades were a failure or a success? Explain.

## History Reading Skill

8. **Read Actively** Apply what you learned about active reading to the next chapter. Preview the headings and prereading material. Scan the graphic material. Generate two questions to help you guide your reading.

## Writing

9. **Write a paragraph on the following topic:** Historical events led to increasing contacts between people in different parts of the world. **Your paragraph should:**
   - begin with a thesis statement that explains the critical events and ideas that started the move toward increasing contacts;
   - support these events or ideas with facts and examples.

10. **Write a Narrative:**
You are a sailor who studied with the navigator Prince Henry. Write a paragraph explaining why you attended Prince Henry's school, what you learned, and your goals after leaving the school.

## Skills for Life

### Identify the Main Idea

Reread the text following the subheading "Far West" in Section 2, then answer the following questions.

11. What is the main-idea sentence of each paragraph?

12. Summarize the main idea of the two paragraphs in your own words.

13. What details support the main-idea sentence of the first paragraph?

# Test Yourself

1. **Native American religious beliefs were based on**

   A the Ten Commandments.

   B the Quran.

   C reverence for nature.

   D the teachings of the Mound Builders.

2. **The Roman Senate was most similar to**

   A the Athenian assembly.

   B the U.S. Congress.

   C the feudal system.

   D the Aztec government.

   Refer to the map at right to answer Question 3.

3. **What do the three civilizations shown on the map have in common?**

   A They were all located in South America.

   B They all traded with the Iroquois.

   C They all disappeared for unknown reasons.

   D They were all very organized societies.

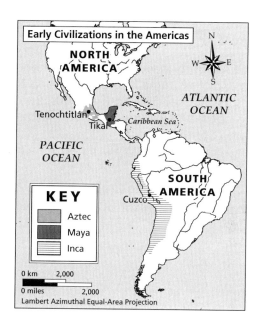

Early Civilizations in the Americas

NORTH AMERICA

ATLANTIC OCEAN

Tenochtitlán

Tikal

Caribbean Sea

PACIFIC OCEAN

SOUTH AMERICA

Cuzco

**KEY**
- Aztec
- Maya
- Inca

0 km 2,000
0 miles 2,000
Lambert Azimuthal Equal-Area Projection

# Document-Based Questions

**Task:** Look Documents 1 and 2, and answer their accompanying questions. Then, use the documents and your knowledge of history to complete the following writing assignment:

> Write a paragraph describing the influence of geography on the Tlingit society.

**Document 1:** This photograph shows the land where the people of the Pacific Northwest, such as the Tlingit and Nootka, lived. *Based on this picture, what resources did the Pacific Northwest people have for building homes and finding food?*

**Document 2:** In this excerpt from an oral history, a Tlingit boy describes the traditional life of his people. *Why did the Tlingit expect young people to work?*

"Land ownership is one of the biggest laws in the Tlingit culture. You did not fish or hunt on somebody else's land without their permission. If you did and you were caught, your equipment would be broken and you would have to leave. . . .

The Tlingit people subsisted in seasonal rounds. . . . They hunted black and brown bear with spear and deadfall. For wolf, coyote, and fox they used snares. They used traps to get mink, weasel, and land otter. With bow and arrow, they hunted the mountain goat. They fished Halibut, King salmon, Silver salmon, and Humpy salmon. . . .

The jobs of young children long ago depended on the mental and physical capabilities. They had to do whatever they could. They had to pick berries, gather roots and plants, and clean fish. The older they got the harder the tasks became. This is how they learned."

# Chapter Preview

During the 1400s, two worlds collided when European explorers came into contact with Native Americans. From the 1500s to the 1700s, European nations competed to explore and build settlements in North and South America.

## ☑ What You Will Learn

The search for a water route to Asia led to the European discovery of two continents and the exchange of resources between the Eastern and the Western hemispheres.

The Spanish established an extensive empire in the Americas and created a colonial society with a rigid class structure.

European economic and religious conflicts quickly spilled over into North America, leading France, Holland, and England to finance explorations there.

Prosperous French and Dutch colonies in North America often interacted with Native Americans.

**1001**
Vikings reach North America.

**1492**
Columbus lands in the West Indies.

**U.S. Events**

1000

1400

1500

**World Events**

With its long coastline facing the Atlantic Ocean, Portugal funded many journeys of exploration during the 1500s. This monument in Lisbon, Portugal, pays tribute to brave Portuguese explorers.

**1539**
De Soto begins exploration of what is today the southeastern United States.

**1626**
New Netherland is settled by the Dutch.

**1673**
Marquette and Joliet explore the Mississippi River.

**1500**

**1517** Protestant Reformation begins in Germany.

**1588** English defeat the Spanish Armada.

**1600**

**1608** French establish settlement in Quebec.

**1700**

**History Reading Skill** Identify Main Ideas and Details

## What did European explorers find in the Americas?

Read the following account by the explorer Christopher Columbus about his first voyage to the Americas. The side notes suggest ways to identify main ideas and their supporting details.

On August 3, 1492, Christopher Columbus, hoping to find a sea route to Asia, set sail from the Spanish port of Palos with three ships and about 90 men. Read the following account about his arrival, three months later, on the island he named San Salvador.

**Primary Source**

Presently, many people of the island assembled. . . . I wanted us to form a great friendship, for I knew they were a people who could be more easily freed and converted to our holy faith by love than by force.

> This is the main idea of the paragraph. The main idea gives all the details and information in the text.

. . .They afterwards came to the ship's boats where they were bringing us parrots, cotton threads in skeins, darts, and many other things. And we exchanged them for other things that we gave them. In time, they took all, and gave what they had with good will. It appeared to me to be a race of people very poor in everything.

> These details give more information about the main idea.

. . .They should be good servants and intelligent, for I saw that they quickly took in what was said to them. I believe that they would easily be made Christians as it appeared to me that they had not religion.

> The details of this paragraph reflect an implied main idea. Columbus believes it will be easy to rule these people.

—Adapted from *The Journal of Christopher Columbus*, 1893

## Identify Main Ideas and Details

- Main ideas express the most important ideas in a text. Supporting details give more information about the main ideas.
- Some main ideas are directly stated. Other main ideas are implied and must be figured out by determining what idea fits with all the details.

## Document-Based Questions

1. What impresses Columbus most about the people he meets?
2. Why do you think Columbus wanted to make the people he meets Christians?

# Vocabulary *Builder*

**Vocabulary *Builder***
*Online*

For help with high-use words

## Previewing High-Use Academic Words

| High-Use Word | Definition | Sample History Sentence |
|---|---|---|
| **myth** (mihth) (Section 1, p. 37) | *n.* traditional story of unknown authorship | The ancient Greeks developed many <u>myths</u> to explain the world around them. |
| **negative** (NEHG ah tihv) (Section 1, p. 41) | *adj.* opposite to something regarded as positive | The arrival of Europeans in the Americas had some <u>negative</u> results for the Native Americans. |
| **factor** (FAK tor) (Section 2, p. 45) | *n.* important element of something | A major <u>factor</u> in pushing Spain to explore a sea route to Asia was the control of the land route by Italy. |
| **rigid** (RIH jihd) (Section 2, p. 48) | *adj.* not bending; not flexible | European feudalism was a <u>rigid</u> social system that prevented people from rising in society. |
| **restore** (ree STOR) (Section 3, p. 50) | *v.* to give back something taken away | Roman senators hoped to <u>restore</u> a republic by assassinating Julius Caesar. |
| **province** (PRAHV ahns) (Section 3, p. 51) | *n.* territorial district of a country | Quebec and Alberta are <u>provinces</u> of Canada. |
| **decline** (dee KLĪN) (Section 4, p. 54) | *v.* to lessen in force, health, strength, or value | England's defeat of Spain's navy in 1588 signaled the <u>decline</u> of Spain's power. |
| **motive** (MOH tihv) (Section 4, p. 55) | *n.* inner drive that causes a person to do something | Most Spanish soldiers' <u>motive</u> for coming to the Americas was to gain wealth. |

## Previewing Key Terms and People

# The Age of Exploration

## Objectives

1. Explain what happened to the Vikings who explored Newfoundland.

2. Describe the voyages of Christopher Columbus.

3. Describe the expeditions of such Spanish explorers as Vasco Núñez de Balboa and Ferdinand Magellan.

4. Explain the importance of the Columbian Exchange.

## Prepare to Read

### ⟳ Reading Skill

**Identify Stated Main Ideas** Each section in this textbook begins with a paragraph headed **Background Knowledge** that presents information you learned earlier. Then, throughout each section, important ideas are organized by major red headings that look like this: **First Visitors From Europe.** The main idea is also stated in the margin alongside each major heading.

### Vocabulary *Builder*

**High-Use Words**

<u>myth</u>, p. 37

<u>negative</u>, p. 41

**Key Terms and People**

Christopher Columbus, p. 36

Vasco Núñez de Balboa, p. 39

Ferdinand Magellan, p. 40

strait, p. 40

circumnavigate, p. 40

⭐ **Background Knowledge** In a previous chapter, you learned about changes in Africa, Asia, and Europe that led to increased trade and cultural ties among these lands. While those changes were taking place, cultures in the Americas were unaffected. In this section, you will learn about the first European contacts with the Americas and how those encounters changed both the Americas and Europe.

**Main Idea**

Spain agrees to finance Christopher Columbus's voyage to find a sea route to Asia.

Viking adventurers preparing to land

## First Visitors From Europe

If you had been in school 50 years ago and your teacher asked "Who discovered America?" you would probably have answered, "Christopher Columbus." But was Columbus really the first?

In a previous chapter, you have read that ancestors of today's Native Americans crossed into the Americas from Asia thousands of years ago. There are also many theories about people from Europe, Asia, and Africa who may have visited the Americas prior to Columbus.

So far, we only have evidence of the arrival of a European people known as the Vikings. The Vikings were a seagoing people who originally lived in the part of northern Europe known as Scandinavia.

In 1963, scientists found the remains of an early Viking settlement in Newfoundland. The findings supported the truth of old Viking stories. According to one story, a Viking named Leif Erikson and 35 others sailed from a colony on Greenland, in 1001, to investigate reports of land farther west. They explored the region and spent the winter in a place they named Vinland.

**The Voyages of Columbus** Vinland existed only in <u>myths</u> for the next 500 years. Whether Christopher Columbus ever heard the stories is not known. However, Columbus believed he could reach Asia and the East by sailing west across the Atlantic Ocean. He never suspected that a huge landmass was blocking the way.

Christopher Columbus grew up near Genoa, an important port on the west coast of Italy. In the 1470s, he settled in Portugal, which was Europe's leading seafaring nation. Columbus sailed on Portuguese ships, studied maps and charts, and learned about the world beyond Europe. From all this he developed his idea for a voyage to Asia.

Portugal's king showed little interest in Columbus's plan. The king hoped to reach Asia by following the route Bartholomeu Dias and other Portuguese explorers were pioneering around southern Africa. He also believed the world was larger than Columbus had calculated. Thus, in his view, the voyage would be much longer than Columbus expected. For these reasons, Portugal refused to finance such a trip.

Columbus did not give up. He moved to Spain and set his plan before King Ferdinand and Queen Isabella. They liked Columbus's plan. But it took six years before they finally agreed to provide ships for the voyage.

**Setting Sail** In August 1492, about 90 men—most of them Spaniards—prepared to make the voyage. Columbus's ships—the *Niña*, the *Pinta*, and the *Santa Maria*—were tiny, between 55 and 90 feet long. Sailing with the wind, they covered up to 170 miles per day.

Columbus predicted that they would reach Asia in 21 days. After a month at sea, there was no sight of land. The crew became restless and spoke of mutiny, or soldiers and sailors rebelling against their officers. Columbus held firm against the threat.

Finally, on October 12, a sailor spotted land. Coming ashore in a small boat, Columbus claimed the island for Spain. Curious islanders soon gathered on the beach. Believing he was in the Asian islands known as the Indies, Columbus called these people Indians. The next day he wrote in his journal, "I intend to go see if I can find the island of Japan."

Columbus then sailed southwest to a large island. At first he thought it was Japan. Actually, Columbus was on the island of Cuba. His guides next pointed Columbus west to the island of Hispaniola. Columbus set sail to return to Spain in January 1493.

**Vocabulary** *Builder*
<u>myth</u> (mihth) *n.* traditional story of unknown authorship

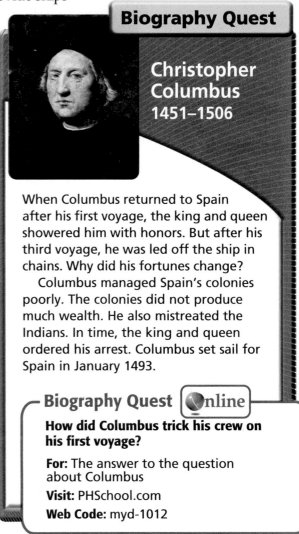

**Biography Quest**

**Christopher Columbus**
**1451–1506**

When Columbus returned to Spain after his first voyage, the king and queen showered him with honors. But after his third voyage, he was led off the ship in chains. Why did his fortunes change?

Columbus managed Spain's colonies poorly. The colonies did not produce much wealth. He also mistreated the Indians. In time, the king and queen ordered his arrest. Columbus set sail for Spain in January 1493.

**Biography Quest** (online)

**How did Columbus trick his crew on his first voyage?**

**For:** The answer to the question about Columbus
**Visit:** PHSchool.com
**Web Code:** myd-1012

# Early Voyages of Exploration, 1492–1609

During the 1400s and 1500s, a number of daring explorers started the exploration to find a sea route to Asia.
**Critical Thinking:**
*Draw Conclusions*
How did technology contribute to the age of exploration?

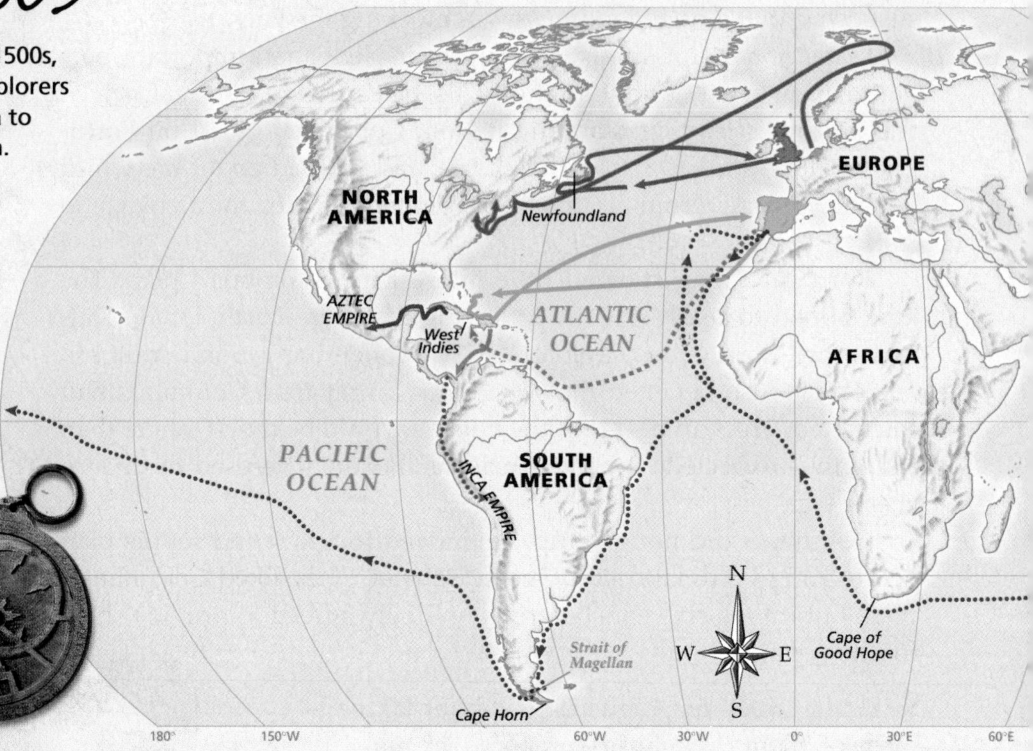

**The Mariner's Astrolabe**
Sailors used the mariner's astrolabe to determine latitude, longitude, and time of day. ▶

NORTH AMERICA

Newfoundland

EUROPE

AZTEC EMPIRE

West Indies

ATLANTIC OCEAN

AFRICA

PACIFIC OCEAN

SOUTH AMERICA

INCA EMPIRE

Strait of Magellan

Cape Horn

Cape of Good Hope

N W E S

180° 150°W 60°W 30°W 0° 30°E 60°E

---

**Identify Stated Main Ideas**
What important idea from the first paragraph following the subheading "Spain Backs More Voyages" is discussed throughout the passage?

**Spain Backs More Voyages** In Spain, Columbus reported that there were huge amounts of gold in the land he referred to as the West Indies. The grateful monarchs made him governor of all he had claimed for Spain.

In September 1493, he sailed again for the West Indies. This time he commanded 17 ships filled with 1,500 soldiers, settlers, and priests. The Spanish planned to colonize and rule the land they thought was the West Indies. They also intended to convert the people there to Christianity.

On this second voyage, Columbus discovered other islands, including Puerto Rico. He found that the men he had left behind on Hispaniola had been killed by Indians. Not discouraged, Columbus built another settlement nearby and enslaved the local Indians to dig for gold. Within a few months, 12 of his ships returned to Spain, their cargo holds filled with some yellow metal.

On his third expedition in 1498, Columbus reached the northern coast of South America and decided it was the Asian mainland. Spain permitted him to try to prove his claims in a fourth voyage, in 1502.

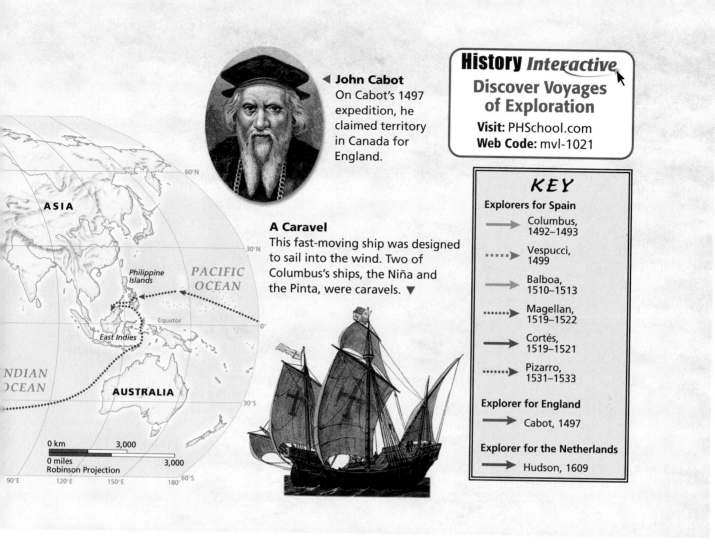

**◄ John Cabot**
On Cabot's 1497 expedition, he claimed territory in Canada for England.

**History** *Interactive*
**Discover Voyages of Exploration**
**Visit:** PHSchool.com
**Web Code:** mvl-1021

**A Caravel**
This fast-moving ship was designed to sail into the wind. Two of Columbus's ships, the Niña and the Pinta, were caravels. ▼

**KEY**

**Explorers for Spain**

→ Columbus, 1492–1493

┅► Vespucci, 1499

→ Balboa, 1510–1513

┅► Magellan, 1519–1522

→ Cortés, 1519–1521

┅► Pizarro, 1531–1533

**Explorer for England**

→ Cabot, 1497

**Explorer for the Netherlands**

→ Hudson, 1609

---

He returned to Spain two years later with his beliefs unchanged. Columbus died in 1506, still convinced that he had reached Asia.

☑**Checkpoint** **Why were Spain's monarchs interested in the proposal Columbus made to them?**

# The Continuing Search for Asia

Many explorers followed the route charted by Columbus. Another Italian explorer, Amerigo Vespucci, made two trips to the new lands. His trips convinced Vespucci that the lands he saw were not part of Asia. Upon his return to Europe, he wrote a letter describing a "new world . . . more densely peopled and full of animals than our Europe or Asia or Africa." A German mapmaker labeled the region "the land of Amerigo" on his maps. The name was soon shortened to "America."

Meanwhile, the Spanish continued to explore and colonize. In 1510, Vasco Núñez de Balboa, a Spanish colonist, explored the Caribbean coast of what is now Panama. Hacking his way across the jungle, he became the first European to set eyes on the Pacific Ocean.

**Main Idea**
The survivors of Magellan's voyage across the Pacific were the first sailors to sail all the way around the globe.

## The Columbian Exchange

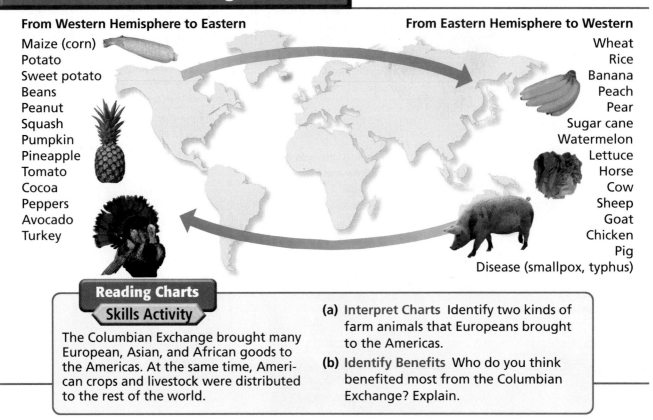

**From Western Hemisphere to Eastern**

Maize (corn)
Potato
Sweet potato
Beans
Peanut
Squash
Pumpkin
Pineapple
Tomato
Cocoa
Peppers
Avocado
Turkey

**From Eastern Hemisphere to Western**

Wheat
Rice
Banana
Peach
Pear
Sugar cane
Watermelon
Lettuce
Horse
Cow
Sheep
Goat
Chicken
Pig
Disease (smallpox, typhus)

### Reading Charts
### Skills Activity

The Columbian Exchange brought many European, Asian, and African goods to the Americas. At the same time, American crops and livestock were distributed to the rest of the world.

**(a) Interpret Charts** Identify two kinds of farm animals that Europeans brought to the Americas.

**(b) Identify Benefits** Who do you think benefited most from the Columbian Exchange? Explain.

The discovery that another ocean lay west of the Americas did not end the search for a water route to Asia. In September 1519, Portuguese explorer Ferdinand Magellan set out to find an Atlantic-Pacific passage.

For more than a year, the small fleet slowly moved down the South American coast looking for a strait, a narrow passage that connects two large bodies of water. As it pushed farther south than earlier expeditions, it encountered penguins and other animals that no European had ever seen before. Finally, near the southern tip of present-day Argentina, Magellan found a narrow passage. After 38 days of battling winds, tides, and currents, his ships exited what today is called the Strait of Magellan. They now entered the large ocean Balboa had seen nine or ten years earlier. Although Magellan did not realize it, Asia was still thousands of miles away.

Magellan finally reached the Philippine Islands. There, he and several others were killed in a battle with Filipinos. The survivors fled in two of the ships. One ship finally reached Spain, in September 1522. Three years after they had begun, the 18 men aboard became first to circumnavigate, or travel around, the entire Earth.

✓**Checkpoint** What were the contributions of Balboa and Magellan as explorers?

# The Columbian Exchange

These early Spanish voyages set the stage for a great exchange between the Western and the Eastern hemispheres. The next century began what is now known as the Columbian Exchange, a transfer of people, products, and ideas between the hemispheres.

Many of the changes brought about by the Columbian Exchange were positive. Europeans introduced cows, hogs, and other domestic animals to the Western Hemisphere. Many food plants, such as wheat and oats, also arrived on the ships that brought the Europeans.

The exchange also had <u>negative</u> effects on the Americas. Europeans brought germs to which Native Americans had no immunity, or natural resistance. Smallpox, chickenpox, measles, and other contagious diseases killed Native Americans by the thousands.

The impact of the Americas on Europe was no less important. Europeans in the Americas found plants and animals they had never seen before either. For example, the Americas introduced llamas, turkeys, squirrels, and muskrats to the rest of the world. More important, however, were the crops that Native Americans taught the Europeans to cultivate. Today, plants that once were found only in the Americas account for nearly one third of the world's food supply.

☑ **Checkpoint** **What impact did the Columbian Exchange have on Europe?**

☆ **Looking Back and Ahead** The voyages of Columbus marked the beginning of a new historical era. The foothold he established in the Caribbean would expand into a vast empire. By 1600, Spain would control much of North and South America and would be one of the world's richest nations.

**Main Idea**
The Spanish voyages of discovery brought about a huge global exchange of goods and ideas.

**Vocabulary Builder**
<u>negative</u> (NEHG ah tihv) *adj.* opposite to something regarded as positive

---

**Section 1 | Check Your Progress**

**Progress Monitoring** Online
**For:** Self-test with instant help
**Visit:** PHSchool.com
**Web Code:** mva-1021

## Comprehension and Critical Thinking

**1. (a) Recall** Who were the Vikings?
**(b) Apply Information** What problems might there be with using Viking myths as historical sources?

**2. (a) Recall** What is the Columbian Exchange?
**(b) Support a Point of View** Did the Columbian Exchange bring more changes to the Americas or to Europe? Explain your view.

## Reading Skill

**3. Identify Stated Main Ideas** Read the text under the heading "The Columbian Exchange." Identify the stated main idea and explain how the paragraphs support that idea.

## Vocabulary Builder

Fill in the blanks with the correct key terms.

**4.** Magellan's ships sailed through a _____ in order to reach the Pacific Ocean.
**5.** The few survivors of Magellan's crew were the first to _____ Earth.

## Writing

**6.** Create a timeline showing early explorations in the Americas. Choose three entries that you think are most significant. For each choice, write one or two sentences explaining why you made that choice.

# Danger at Sea

When Europeans began to make voyages of discovery, they had no idea what they would find. Some of the dangers that they feared did not really exist. Other dangers were all too real. But the more they traveled, the more their views of the world changed.

◀ **Fearsome Sea Monsters**

Popular tales warned that the oceans were filled with dragons, sea serpents, and other monsters. Happily, these dangers turned out to be imaginary.

▲ Storms at Sea

One real danger was bad weather. A violent storm could send a ship and its whole crew to the bottom of the ocean.

## ▼ Getting Lost

Another real fear was that a ship might get lost in the vast, endless ocean. Fortunately, improved navigational tools, like the sextant and more accurate maps, made this danger less likely.

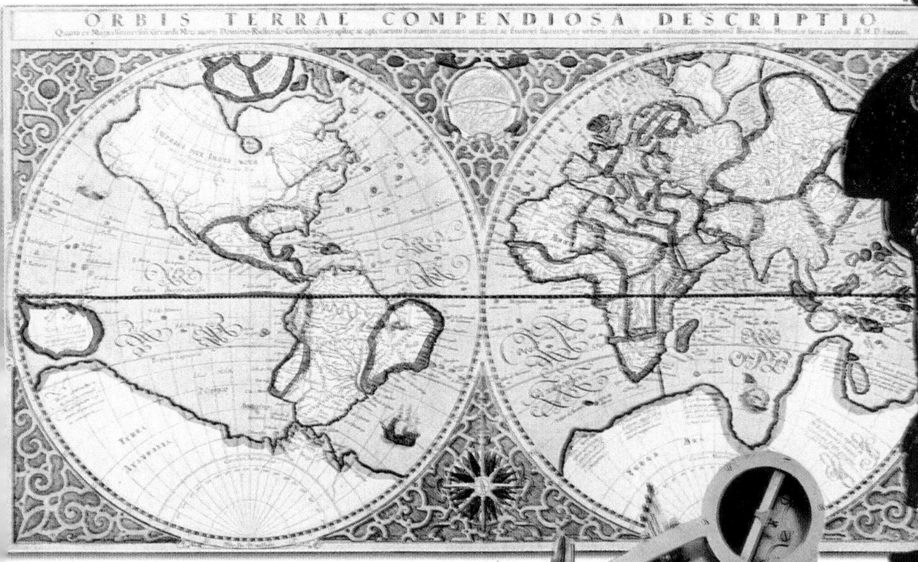

Sextant

## Piracy ▲

When ships began to carry treasure to Europe, a new danger emerged: piracy. Pirates would attack merchant ships, steal the cargo, and often, murder the crew. Some pirates, such as Captain Kidd (shown above), became legendary for their boldness.

## ▼ Starvation

Running low on supplies at sea meant disaster. One Spanish sailor described what happened when his ship ran out of food.

*"We . . . ate only old biscuit reduced to powder, full of grubs and stinking from the dirt which rats had made on it. We drank water that was yellow and stinking."*

—Antonio Pigafetta, *Journal*

### Analyze LIFE AT THE TIME

Imagine you are a European sailor about to go on an ocean voyage. Write a letter explaining your view of the world and why you are going on the voyage in spite of the dangers.

# Spain's Empire in the Americas

## Objectives

1. Describe how the Spanish were able to defeat the empires of the Aztecs and Incas.

2. Identify Spanish explorations in areas that later became part of the United States.

3. Explain how society was organized in Spain's empire in the Americas.

## Prepare to Read

### Reading Skill

**Identify Supporting Details**
Text includes details to support a main idea. These details might be examples, reasons, facts, or descriptions. They enable readers to understand a main idea by helping them to picture it or to make sense of its argument or to believe its accuracy. As you read Section 2, look for details that support the main ideas.

### Vocabulary *Builder*

**High-Use Words**

<u>factor</u>, p. 45

<u>rigid</u>, p. 48

**Key Terms and People**

conquistador, p. 44

Hernando Cortés, p. 44

Moctezuma, p. 44

plantation, p. 47

*encomienda*, p. 47

Bartolomé de Las Casas, p. 47

mission, p. 47

*peninsulare*, p. 48

⭐ **Background Knowledge** Even though Columbus never realized that he had reached a region previously unknown to Europeans, his voyages gave Spain a head start on its European rivals in colonizing the Americas. In this section, you will learn how Spain explored and colonized the lands it claimed.

## Spanish Conquistadors

**Main Idea**
The conquests of Cortés and Pizarro helped establish a huge Spanish Empire in the Americas.

By the early 1500s, the Spanish had a firm foothold in the Americas. From Spain's island colonies in the Caribbean, soldier-adventurers called conquistadors set out to explore and conquer a world unknown to them. They hoped for riches and glory for themselves and for Spain.

**Cortés and Pizarro** In 1519, conquistador Hernando Cortés sailed from Cuba to Mexico with more than 500 soldiers. The first Native Americans he met presented him with gifts of gold.

On November 8, 1519, Cortés marched into the Aztec capital city of Tenochtitlán. As the Spaniards moved closer to Tenochtitlán, many Native Americans joined them. Conquered by the Aztecs, they hated the Aztec's brutal rule.

The Aztec leader Moctezuma (mokt uh ZOO muh) (also spelled *Montezuma*) met with Cortés and tried to get him to leave by offering him gold. The gold had the opposite effect. Cortés took Moctezuma hostage and claimed all of Mexico for Spain. However, the Aztecs soon rebelled and forced the Spaniards to flee.

About a year later, Cortés returned with a larger force, recaptured Tenochtitlán, and then destroyed it. In its place he built Mexico City, the capital of the Spanish colony of New Spain.

Cortés used the same methods to subdue the Aztecs in South America that another conquistador, Francisco Pizarro, used. Pizarro landed on the coast of Peru in 1531 to search for the Incas, who were said to have much gold. In September 1532, he led about 170 soldiers through the jungle into the heart of the Inca Empire. Pizarro then took the Inca ruler Atahualpa (ah tuh WAHL puh) prisoner. Although the Inca people paid a huge ransom to free their ruler, Pizarro executed him anyway. By November 1533, the Spanish had defeated the leaderless Incas and captured their capital city of Cuzco.

**Why the Spanish Were Victorious** How could a few hundred Spanish soldiers defeat Native American armies many times their size? Several <u>factors</u> explain the Spaniards' success. First among these was technology. The Indians' weapons simply were no match for the armor, muskets, and cannons of the Europeans. In addition, many of the Spaniards rode horses, which the Native Americans had never before seen. Finally, the Native Americans were divided among themselves. In Peru, a civil war had just ended. In Mexico, many Native Americans hated the Aztecs.

☑**Checkpoint** Why were a few Spanish conquistadors able to defeat the larger armies of the Aztecs and Incas?

**Spanish Conquistadors**
The Spanish soldiers were outnumbered by the Aztecs and the Incas, yet they were able to easily defeat these empires.
**Critical Thinking:** *Explain Problems* Some Native Americans sided with the Spanish against the Aztecs and the Incas. What problems might this have caused between the groups after the battle?

**Discovery SCHOOL**

**Explore More Video**
To learn more about Spanish exploration in the Americas, view the video.

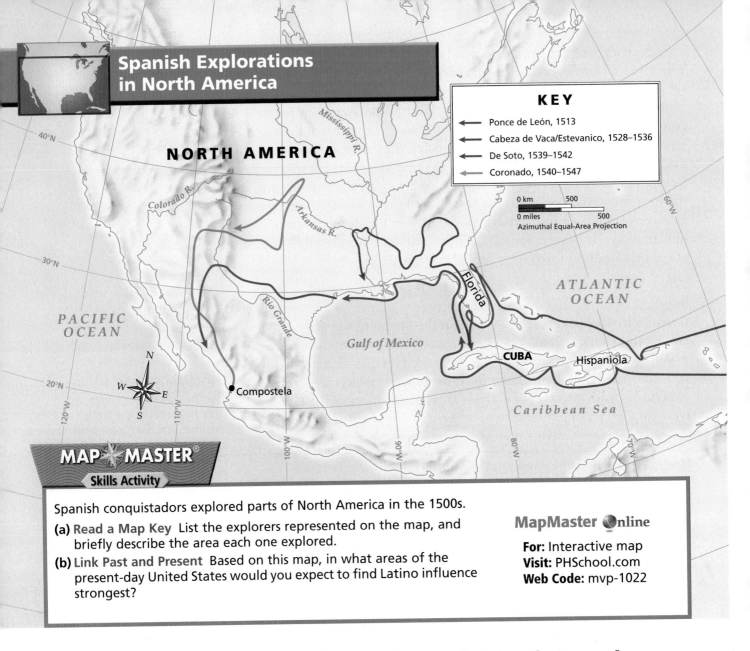

## Spanish Explorations in North America

**NORTH AMERICA**

**KEY**

→ Ponce de León, 1513
→ Cabeza de Vaca/Estevanico, 1528–1536
→ De Soto, 1539–1542
→ Coronado, 1540–1547

0 km    500
0 miles    500
Azimuthal Equal-Area Projection

Mississippi R.

Colorado R.

Arkansas R.

Rio Grande

PACIFIC OCEAN

Gulf of Mexico

Florida

ATLANTIC OCEAN

CUBA    Hispaniola

Caribbean Sea

● Compostela

40°N  30°N  20°N
120°W  110°W  100°W  90°W  80°W  70°W  60°W

**MAP★MASTER®**

**Skills Activity**

Spanish conquistadors explored parts of North America in the 1500s.

**(a) Read a Map Key** List the explorers represented on the map, and briefly describe the area each one explored.

**(b) Link Past and Present** Based on this map, in what areas of the present-day United States would you expect to find Latino influence strongest?

**MapMaster ●nline**

**For:** Interactive map
**Visit:** PHSchool.com
**Web Code:** mvp-1022

---

**Main Idea**
Spanish explorers believed that the area of what is today the United States contained cities of gold.

# Spanish Explorers in North America

The Spanish did not limit themselves to the exploration of what we now call Latin America. In 1513, Juan Ponce de León sailed north from Puerto Rico to investigate reports of a large island. He found beautiful flowers there, so he named the place *La Florida*. Ponce de León became the first Spaniard to set foot in what is now the United States.

Exploration along Florida's west coast began in 1528, when about 400 Spaniards landed near the present-day city of St. Petersburg. Finding none of the gold they had hoped for, they marched into northern Florida. There, under attack by Native Americans, they built five crude boats and set out to sea. About 80 survivors led by Álvar Núñez Cabeza de Vaca eventually landed at present-day Galveston Island on the Texas coast.

Starvation and disease reduced their number to 15 before Indians enslaved them. Finally, only four—including Cabeza de Vaca and Estevanico, an African slave—remained alive. After six years in captivity, they escaped and spent two more years finding their way to Mexico City. In 1536, eight years after landing in Florida, the four survivors of the 400-man expedition returned to Spanish lands.

In Mexico City, the men related stories they had heard from Native Americans about seven great cities filled with gold far to the north. Officials asked the survivors to head an expedition to find these cities. However, only Estevanico was willing to go. In 1539, he led a group into what is now western New Mexico. When Estevanico was killed by Indians, the others returned to Mexico City.

The conquistador Francisco Coronado (koh roh NAH doh) set out with about 1,100 Spaniards and Native Americans to find the golden city. Although he never found the city, he did explore much of what is now New Mexico, Arizona, Texas, and Kansas.

While Coronado was trekking through the southwest, Hernando de Soto was searching for riches in today's southeastern United States. De Soto traveled as far north as the Carolinas and as far west as Oklahoma. He died in what is now Louisiana, in 1542, having found the Mississippi River but no cities of gold.

Native Americans received harsh treatment from Spaniards.

☑Checkpoint   **What regions in the present-day United States did Spaniards explore?**

# Colonizing Spanish America

At first, Spain let the conquistadors govern the lands they had conquered. However, this was not successful. In order to control its new empire, Spain created a formal system of government to rule its colonies.

**Harsh Life for Native Americans** Within Spain's vast empire, there was little place for Native Americans except as a source of labor. Government officials granted settlers huge tracts of land to start mines, ranches, and plantations—large farms worked by laborers who live on the property. To help Spanish colonists find needed workers, the Spanish government granted *encomiendas* (ehn KOH mee ehn dahz). These were land grants that included the right to demand labor or taxes from Native Americans. The Spanish forced Native Americans to work in the gold and silver mines. Many died when the tunnels caved in. Some Spaniards protested this cruel treatment. The priest Bartolomé de Las Casas traveled through New Spain working for reform. Largely due to Las Casas's efforts, the government of Spain ordered reform of the *encomienda* system in the mid-1500s.

Like other Europeans in the Americas, the Spanish believed they had a duty to convert Native Americans to Christianity. They set up missions, religious settlements, run by Catholic priests and friars. San Francisco, San Diego, San Antonio, and a number of other U.S. cities got their start as Spanish missions in the 1700s.

**Main Idea**
The priest Bartolomé de Las Casas spoke out against the cruelty of the *encomienda* system.

**The Trade in Humans** As the death toll for Native Americans continued to rise, Spanish colonists looked across the Atlantic Ocean for a new source of labor.

In 1517, Spain brought about 4,000 Africans to the Caribbean islands and forced them to work there. By the middle of the 1500s, the Spaniards were shipping about 2,000 enslaved Africans each year to Hispaniola alone. You will read about the growing slave trade in another chapter.

**Society in the Spanish Colonies** A rigid social system based on birthplace and blood developed in the Spanish colonies. At the top of the social structure were the *peninsulares,* Spanish colonists who had been born in Spain. Almost all government officials came from this class. Colonists born in America of two Spanish parents were called *Creoles.* Generally, Creoles also held important positions. Many of the wealthiest merchants and plantation owners were Creoles.

People of mixed parentage were lower on the social ladder. *Mestizos,* people of Spanish and Indian blood, could achieve economic success as ranchers, farmers, or merchants. But entrance into the upper levels of society was impossible for them. Below mestizos were *mulattos*—people of Spanish and African heritage. Native Americans and African Americans were held at the bottom of society. This rigid class system helped Spain keep control of its empire in the Americas for more than 300 years.

☑Checkpoint **How were Native Americans treated under the *encomienda* system?**

☆ **Looking Back and Ahead** The resentment and tensions caused by the rigid class system eventually provided the seeds for revolutions in the early 1800s that ended Spain's American empire.

**Vocabulary *Builder***
rigid (RIH jihd) *adj.* not bending; not flexible

**Identifying Supporting Details**
Identify two details in these two paragraphs that support the following main idea: *Spain created a formal system of government in America to rule the vast regions it claimed.* Explain how the details support the main idea.

---

Section 2 | **Check Your Progress**

**Progress Monitoring ⬤nline**
**For:** Self-test with instant help
**Visit:** PHSchool.com
**Web Code:** mva-1022

**Comprehension and Critical Thinking**

1. **(a) Identify** What parts of the North American continent did Spanish conquistadors explore?
**(b) Apply Information** How did the conquistadors help establish the Spanish Empire in the Americas?

2. **(a) Identify** What was the lasting accomplishment of Bartolomé de Las Casas?
**(b) Summarize** How would you describe the lives of Native Americans in New Spain?

**Reading Skill**

3. **Identify Supporting Details** Read the text following the subheading "Society in the Spanish Colonies." Identify three details that support its main idea: A rigid social system, based on birthplace and blood, developed in Spain's colonies over time. Explain how the details support the main idea.

**Vocabulary *Builder***

4. Write two definitions for each of the following key terms: conquistador, plantation, mission,

*peninsulare.* First, write a formal definition for your teacher. Second, write a casual definition in everyday English for a classmate.

**Writing**

5. **(a)** Prepare an outline you would use to write an essay describing the effects of Spanish colonization in the Americas.

6. **(b)** Then, write several sentences describing the views of Bartolomé de Las Casas and a conquistador about Spanish rule in the Americas.

## Objectives

1. Describe the religious and economic conflicts in Europe during the Reformation.

2. Explain why European powers continued to search for a new route to Asia.

3. Describe the outcome of the search by explorers John Cabot and Henry Hudson for a northwest passage around the Americas.

## Prepare to Read

### 🎯 Reading Skill

**Identify Implied Main Ideas** Sometimes a portion of text does not state the main idea directly. However, the text still has a main idea. This idea is implied, or suggested, by the many details contained in the text. You can identify this idea by reading all the details and developing an idea that fits all of them. State the idea to yourself in a sentence, then reread the text and confirm that the details do support it.

### Vocabulary *Builder*

**High-Use Words**

<u>restore</u>, p. 50

<u>province</u>, p. 51

**Key Terms and People**

mercantilism, p. 50

John Cabot, p. 51

northwest passage, p. 51

Henry Hudson, p. 52

☆ **Background Knowledge** Europe in 1500 was in the midst of a great cultural change—the Renaissance. New ideas changed how Europeans thought about their world. Some people, such as Martin Luther, a German priest, boldly called for changes in the Roman Catholic Church. A new movement, the Protestant Reformation began. In this section, you will learn how religious conflict fueled other conflicts that would lead to struggles in the Americas.

## Conflicts in Europe

As the appeal of the Reformation increased, the split between the Catholics and the Protestants increased religious and economic tensions between countries in Europe.

**Religious Conflicts** By 1530, the rulers of Sweden, Denmark, and several European states had split with the Roman Catholic Church and set up Protestant churches in their countries. Elsewhere in Europe, the teachings and writings of Swiss thinker John Calvin had a great influence on the development of Protestant churches in France, Switzerland, Scotland, and the Netherlands.

English Protestants found a supporter in King Henry VIII. Henry was married to Catherine of Aragon, the daughter of King Ferdinand and Queen Isabella of Spain. When Catherine did not produce a male heir to the English throne, Henry sought to divorce her and remarry.

**Main Idea**

Religious and economic conflicts in Europe increased tensions among the major powers on the continent.

King Henry VIII

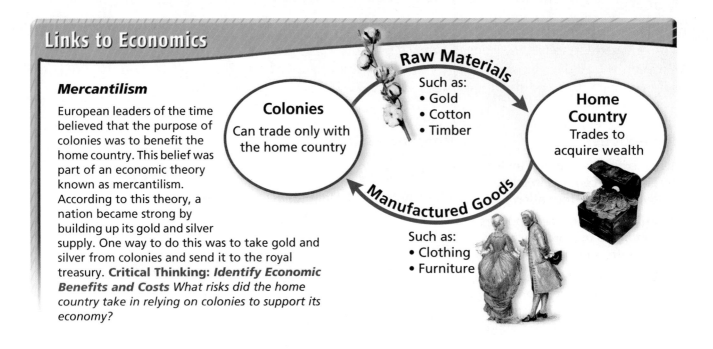

### Mercantilism

European leaders of the time believed that the purpose of colonies was to benefit the home country. This belief was part of an economic theory known as mercantilism. According to this theory, a nation became strong by building up its gold and silver supply. One way to do this was to take gold and silver from colonies and send it to the royal treasury. **Critical Thinking:** *Identify Economic Benefits and Costs What risks did the home country take in relying on colonies to support its economy?*

**Colonies**
Can trade only with the home country

**Raw Materials**
Such as:
• Gold
• Cotton
• Timber

**Home Country**
Trades to acquire wealth

**Manufactured Goods**
Such as:
• Clothing
• Furniture

---

**Identify Implied Main Ideas**
What is the implied main idea of the text you have read so far in this section?

**Vocabulary** *Builder*
restore (ree STOR) *v.* to give back something taken away

Because Catholic law does not permit divorce, Henry asked the pope to annul, or cancel, his marriage. This had occurred before. Popes had annulled royal marriages. The pope's refusal to grant the divorce caused Henry to break with the Roman Catholic Church in 1533. He set up a Protestant church and named it the Church of England.

**Economic Conflicts** Religious tensions created by the Reformation inflamed rivalries that already existed among the nations of Europe. Wars were common and alliances often shifted. This uncertainty made European rulers believe they could not depend on one another to protect their country's security.

For example, Spain was unwilling to depend on Italian or Portuguese traders. As a result, the Spanish monarchs eagerly supported Columbus's search for a new route to Asia. The Spanish thought that if they could start colonies there, goods from those colonies would make Spain wealthy and powerful. Most importantly, the Spanish hoped Asian colonies would provide gold. Nearly every European nation sought gold to pay for its wars and help strengthen their armies. In fact, Spain required one fifth of all gold that Spaniards found to be sent to the king. This requirement was part of a system widely followed at the time, called mercantilism (MER kuhn tihl ihz uhm). The system of mercantilism held that colonies existed to make the home country wealthy and powerful.

**The Spanish Armada** England's King Henry VIII died in 1547. He was succeeded by his son Edward, who ruled only a short time before he died, too. The throne then passed to Mary I, who made plans to restore the Roman Catholic Church in England. However, Mary died in 1558 and Elizabeth I, a Protestant, took the throne.

The rule of the Protestant Queen Elizabeth I renewed the rivalry with Roman Catholic Spain. Spain's King Phillip II hoped to make England a Catholic nation again. Relations were also strained by English raids on Spanish ships at sea. Many of these ships carried gold from the Americas. The Spanish also resented English assistance to rebels trying to win independence in the Spanish <u>province</u> of Holland.

**Vocabulary** *Builder*
**province** (PRAHV ahns) *n.* territorial district of a country

In 1588, Phillip assembled a fleet of 130 warships known as the Spanish Armada. Phillip hoped to force Elizabeth from the throne. A fleet of English ships met the Spanish off the coast of France. The smaller and faster English ships sank many of the Spanish ships. Barely half of the Spanish Armada returned to Spain.

The defeat of the Spanish Armada changed the balance of power in Europe. Spain was weakened and so was its control of the seas. This enabled countries like England and France to found colonies in the Americas. Europe's religious and economic conflicts were not settled by the defeat of the Armada, however. As England and France founded colonies, these conflicts spread to the Americas.

☑**Checkpoint** **How did economic concerns among European nations lead to conflicts?**

## Asia Continues to Beckon

Columbus's return from his first voyage interested another Italian explorer, John Cabot. Cabot decided that a more northern route to Asia would be shorter and easier.

**Main Idea**
Northern voyages of discovery failed to locate a northwest passage through or around North America.

**The Northern Voyages** Neither Spain nor Portugal had any interest in Cabot's ideas. However, the English were interested enough to finance a voyage of exploration. Cabot left England with one ship, in May 1497. He crossed the North Atlantic and explored the region around Newfoundland. On a second voyage in 1498, Cabot may have explored the North American coast as far south as Chesapeake Bay. However, we cannot be sure. His ships disappeared without a trace.

Europeans soon realized that the lands Cabot had reached were not Asia, but a land they had never seen. England, France, and Holland all financed voyages of exploration to North America. These voyages focused on finding a **northwest passage,** a sea route from the Atlantic to the Pacific that passed through or around North America.

In 1524, another Italian explorer, Giovanni da Verrazano (vehr rah TSAH noh), searched for such a passage for King Francis I of France. Verrazano explored the Atlantic coastal region from North Carolina to Newfoundland. In doing so, he discovered the mouth of the Hudson River and New York Bay. French explorer Jacques Cartier (kar tee YAY) made three trips to North America for France. In searching for a northwest passage, he discovered the St. Lawrence River and explored it as far as present-day Montreal.

Queen Elizabeth I

With his son and a few loyal crew members, Henry Hudson was set adrift, by mutineers, in Hudson Bay. They died a lonely death somewhere on the bay.

English explorer Henry Hudson made four voyages in search of a northwest passage. Two voyages in the Arctic Ocean, during 1607 and 1608, were unsuccessful, and Hudson's English backers gave up on him. However, the Dutch grew interested in his activities and financed a third expedition in 1609. Crossing the Atlantic, Hudson reached what is now New York and explored up the river that today bears his name.

Hudson's discoveries on his third voyage convinced the English to sponsor a fourth voyage in 1610. Hudson again sailed into the Arctic, looking for a passage to the Pacific. He reached as far as Hudson Bay, which also is named for him, before the icy waters forced a halt to the voyage. In the spring of 1611, Hudson's crew, unhappy about spending the winter in this harsh land, grew desperate. They mutinied and set the explorer, his teenage son, and seven loyal crew members adrift in a small boat. The mutineers returned to England. Like John Cabot, Hudson was never heard from again.

☑ **Checkpoint** **Why did explorers continue to look for routes to Asia?**

☆ **Looking Back and Ahead** Hudson's last voyage marked the end of serious efforts to find a northwest passage. Europe's attention shifted to the lands that the voyagers had explored. In these lands, explorers reported, were vast amounts of timber, fish, and other resources. Europeans began to think of North America not as an obstacle blocking their way to Asia but as a land to be exploited for profit.

---

Section 3 | **Check Your Progress**

**Progress Monitoring** ⬤nline
**For:** Self-test with instant help
**Visit:** PHSchool.com
**Web Code:** mva-1023

**Comprehension and Critical Thinking**

1. **(a) Recall** How did the Reformation lead to religious conflict in Europe?
   **(b) Apply Information** Why do you think the religious tensions that developed during the Reformation among European nations spread to the Americas?

2. **(a) Summarize** How did the defeat of the Spanish Armada change the political balance of power among European countries?

   **(b) Analyze Cause and Effect** How did the shift in the political balance of power affect the exploration of North America?

**☺ Reading Skill**

3. **Identify Implied Main Ideas** Find the implied main ideas of the text under the heading "Asia Continues to Beckon." Then, combine this main idea with the main idea you identified under the heading "Conflicts in Europe" to state a single main idea for both of these portions of text.

**Vocabulary *Builder***

Complete each of the following sentences so that the second part further explains the first part and clearly shows your understanding of the key term.

4. Spain's economy was based on the system of mercantilism, under which ____.

5. European explorers searched for a northwest passage, ____.

**Writing**

6. Why do you think Spain and Portugal refused to support John Cabot's proposed voyage? Write a paragraph explaining your views.

## Objectives

1. Describe how the French colony of New France spread into the interior of North America.
2. Explain how the Dutch established a thriving colony along the Hudson River.
3. Explain the influence of these settlements on the Native Americans of the region.

## Prepare to Read

### ⏵ Reading Skill

**Combine Main Ideas to Construct Meaning** Several main ideas are developed in each section in this textbook. Use the red heads to identify the bigger main ideas. The blue heads introduce text that further develops the main ideas. As you read Section 4, identify the main ideas and the ways in which the information helps you to understand these ideas.

### Vocabulary *Builder*

**High-Use Words**

<u>decline</u>, p. 54

<u>motive</u>, p. 55

### Key Terms and People

Samuel de Champlain, p. 53

*coureur de bois,* p. 54

Jacques Marquette, p. 55

alliance, p. 57

---

☆ **Background Knowledge** By the early 1600s, England, France, and the Netherlands had each sponsored explorations of North America. Each had staked claims to lands there. In this section, you will learn about the colonies begun by the French and Dutch and how Native American peoples were affected by these colonies.

## New France

The French began to settle colonies in the early 1600s. In 1603, Samuel de Champlain made the first of 11 voyages to explore and map the lands along the St. Lawrence River. In 1608, Champlain established a settlement on the banks of the St. Lawrence, which he named Quebec. From this base he ventured east, in 1609, and explored the large lake on the border of present-day Vermont and New York that bears his name. His activities gave the French an influence in the region that lasted 150 years.

**Life in New France** New France, as the French colony was called, developed in quite different ways than New Spain. As you know, the Spanish sought gold, silver, and other precious minerals. The French, on the other hand, profited from fish and furs. The Spanish forced Native Americans into harsh labor. The French traded with Native Americans for the animal skins so highly valued in Europe. Beaver skins sent to Europe and made into hats were a profitable item.

**Main Idea**
The major French settlements in North America were based on fur trade with Native Americans.

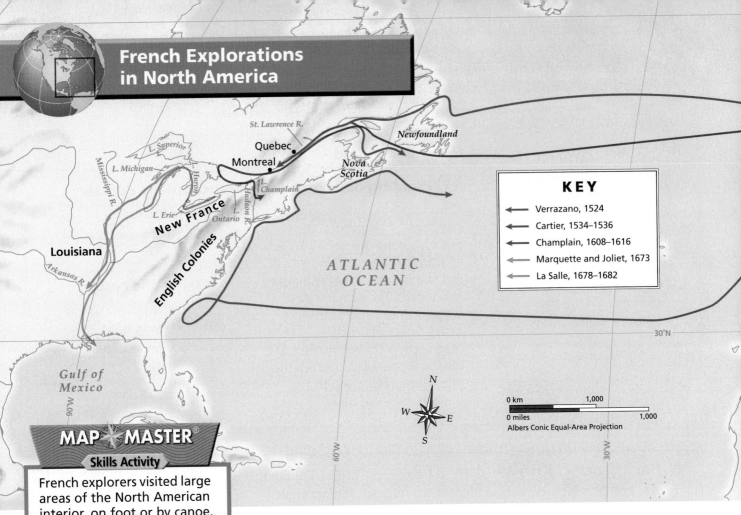

## French Explorations in North America

**KEY**
- Verrazano, 1524
- Cartier, 1534–1536
- Champlain, 1608–1616
- Marquette and Joliet, 1673
- La Salle, 1678–1682

St. Lawrence R.
Quebec
Montreal
Newfoundland
Nova Scotia
L. Superior
L. Michigan
L. Huron
L. Erie
L. Ontario
L. Champlain
Mississippi R.
New France
Louisiana
Arkansas R.
English Colonies
Hudson R.
ATLANTIC OCEAN
Gulf of Mexico
30°N
60°W
90°W
30°W

0 km 1,000
0 miles 1,000
Albers Conic Equal-Area Projection

## MAP★MASTER®

### Skills Activity

French explorers visited large areas of the North American interior, on foot or by canoe.

**(a) Read a Distance Scale** Find the route taken by La Salle. About how many miles did he travel from Montreal to the mouth of the Mississippi River?

**(b) Make Predictions** What kinds of rivalries do you think the French explorations started?

**MapMaster Online**

**For:** Interactive map
**Visit:** PHSchool.com
**Web Code:** mvp-1024

**Vocabulary Builder**
**decline** (dee KLĪN) *v.* to lessen in force, health, strength, or value

This pattern was set during Champlain's first days in the Americas. He established the colony's first settlement—a trading post—in what is today Nova Scotia, in 1604. As he continued to explore the region, he convinced local Indians to bring pelts to the trading posts established by the French. Trading posts such as Quebec City and Montreal became busy centers of commerce.

Brave employees of the fur companies paddled large canoes into the wilderness to find and acquire pelts from Native Americans. *Coureurs de bois*, the French term for "runners of the woods," were independent traders who lived among the Indians. Many of them married Indian women and started families.

Not until the late 1600s did French colonists begin to farm in large numbers. One reason for this change was that the market for furs in Europe was in <u>decline</u>. Another reason was the disruption that Indian wars brought to the fur trade. Still another was the 3,000 French settlers—including many single young women—that King Louis XIV sent to New France in the 1660s. After the new settlers arrived, the population began to expand. New France had about 5,000 colonists by 1672.

**Exploring the Mississippi** The same economic and religious motives that established New France also inspired its expansion. By 1670, French missionary Jacques Marquette had founded two missions along the Great Lakes, in present-day Michigan. Meanwhile, French traders explored the Great Lakes area looking for new sources of furs.

In 1673, Father Marquette and Louis Joliet, a French Canadian trader, paddled their canoes along the shores of Lake Michigan to what is now Green Bay, Wisconsin. They made their way west until they reached the Mississippi River. For the next month they followed the river downstream, thinking that it might be the long-sought northwest passage. In July, the group reached Mississippi's junction with the Arkansas River. Convinced that the Mississippi flowed into the Gulf of Mexico and not into the Pacific Ocean, they returned home.

Although Marquette and Joliet did not find a northwest passage, they provided the French with a water route into the heart of North America. The river's exploration was completed in 1682 by René Robert Cavelier, also known as La Salle. Reaching the river's mouth at the Gulf of Mexico, La Salle claimed the entire Mississippi Valley for France. He named the region Louisiana, in honor of King Louis XIV.

☑**Checkpoint** What was the goal of the voyage of Marquette and Joliet on the Mississippi?

**Vocabulary** *Builder*
<u>motive</u> (MOH tihv) *n.* inner drive that causes a person to do something

**Combine Main Ideas to Construct Meaning** Identify three main ideas from the paragraphs following the subheading "Life in New France." Then, state the big idea of these paragraphs.

**Exploring the Mississippi**
This drawing shows Father Marquette and Louis Joliet traveling the unknown waters of the Mississippi River. **Critical Thinking:** *Draw Conclusions How would settling the Mississippi Valley benefit New France?*

The New York Stock Exchange today

## Wall Street

**Late 1600s** Built in 1653, a wall at lower end of Manhattan protected Dutch settlers from outside attacks. Gradually, the path by the wall became an important place for merchants and traders.

**1792** The New York Stock Exchange began in lower Manhattan where a group of New York businessmen met daily to buy and sell stocks. Today, Wall Street is part of the thriving commerce of New York City.

## Link to Today

**Wall Street Today** How has the role of Wall Street changed in today's financial market? Go online to find out more about Wall Street today.

**For:** Wall Street in the news
**Visit:** PHSchool.com
**Web Code:** mvc-1024

**Main Idea**
Dutch settlements along the Hudson River valley became a barrier to westward expansion of the English colonies.

# New Netherland

Dutch land claims in North America were based on Henry Hudson's exploration of the Hudson River. In 1610, Dutch traders arrived in the Hudson River valley and began a busy trade with Native Americans. The trade was so profitable that the Dutch West India Company decided to establish a permanent colony in what the Dutch called New Netherland.

In 1624, about 300 settlers arrived from the Netherlands. Most of them settled at Fort Orange, a fur-trading post that was later renamed Albany. In 1626, another group settled at the mouth of the Hudson River. The colony's governor, Peter Minuit, purchased the island from nearby Indians. The colonists named their new home New Amsterdam. The town grew steadily as new colonists arrived. By 1653, it had a population of about 800.

New Netherland was a barrier to the English. It kept English settlers from moving westward. In 1664, English forces seized New Netherland. The new territory was renamed New York, after the king's brother, the Duke of York.

**✓Checkpoint** **Why did the Dutch establish settlements along the Hudson River?**

# The Impact on Native Americans

As you have read, Native Americans provided fur pelts to French and Dutch traders. The Europeans gave Native Americans manufactured goods, such as cloth, iron pots and tools, and guns. Ultimately, however, the fur trade had a grave effect on Native Americans.

The French and the Dutch each made alliances with Native American peoples. An **alliance** is an agreement between parties that benefits them both. Long before the Hurons became trading partners with the French, the Iroquois and the Hurons were enemies. The Hurons became partners with the French, and the Dutch had an agreement with the Iroquois. The Iroquois, using guns from the Dutch, began to attack the Hurons. The attacks were devastating to the Hurons.

Even worse were the diseases caused by contact with Europeans. Furthermore, the overtrapping of animals weakened the food chain on which Native Americans depended. As the fur-bearing animals disappeared, the Native Americans' value to the colonists decreased. Instead, Native American land became more valuable to the colonists.

☑**Checkpoint** **How did the French and Dutch settlements affect Native Americans?**

⭐ **Looking Back and Ahead** England did not stand by as France and Holland carved out colonies in North America. As English colonies spread over the Atlantic shores of North America, their competition with New France and New Netherland grew.

**Main Idea**
The French and Dutch tried to establish peaceful relations with Native Americans, but their presence had a major impact on the Native Americans' future.

Dutch traders with Iroquois

**Progress Monitoring ●nline**
**For:** Self-test with instant help
**Visit:** PHSchool.com
**Web Code:** mva-1024

Section 4 | **Check Your Progress**

## Comprehension and Critical Thinking

**1. (a) Describe** How did the colonists in New France support themselves?
**(b) Compare and Contrast** How did the economic activities of New France compare with those of New Spain?

**2. (a) Identify** Name two Dutch settlements in the Americas.
**(b) Apply Information** How did the geographic location of these settlements contribute to their success?

## 🔁 Reading Skill

**3. Combine Main Ideas to Construct Meaning** What is the big idea of Section 4? What smaller main ideas work together to support this big idea?

## Vocabulary *Builder*

Answer the following questions in complete sentences that show your understanding of the key terms.

**4.** Who were the *coureurs de bois,* and how did they contribute to the economic success of New France?

**5.** What were the consequences of the Dutch alliance with the Iroquois for the Hurons?

## Writing

**6.** In Section 2, you read about Bartolomé de Las Casas's observations concerning relations between the Spaniards and the Native Americans. Write similar eyewitness accounts of relations between Native Americans and **(a)** the French and **(b)** the Dutch in the Americas.

When you study history, you generally read about events in the sequence, or order, in which they happened. One way to understand the sequence of historical events is by creating a timeline. A timeline identifies major events and the dates that each took place. You should read a horizontal timeline from left to right. Reading a timeline helps you judge how events could be related in time.

## Exploring the Americas

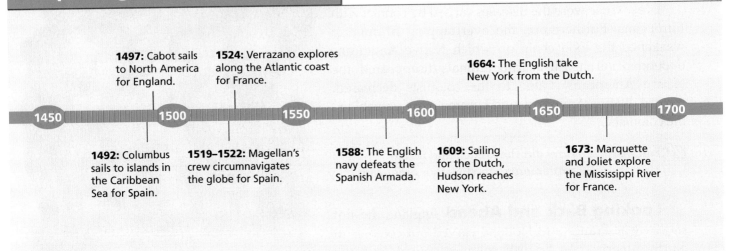

**1497:** Cabot sails to North America for England.

**1524:** Verrazano explores along the Atlantic coast for France.

**1664:** The English take New York from the Dutch.

1450 · 1500 · 1550 · 1600 · 1650 · 1700

**1492:** Columbus sails to islands in the Caribbean Sea for Spain.

**1519–1522:** Magellan's crew circumnavigates the globe for Spain.

**1588:** The English navy defeats the Spanish Armada.

**1609:** Sailing for the Dutch, Hudson reaches New York.

**1673:** Marquette and Joliet explore the Mississippi River for France.

## Learn the Skill

*Use these steps to understand sequence.*

**1** **Identify the time period covered in the timeline.** Look for the beginning date and the ending date.

**2** **Figure out the intervals between each date on the timeline.** Timelines are always divided into time periods of equal length, such as 10, 50, or 100 years.

**3** **Add additional events.** Include other important historical events on the timeline, based on your reading of the text.

**4** **Draw conclusions.** Use the timeline to draw conclusions about the events that took place during a particular period in history. Framing questions based on the timeline can help you draw sound conclusions.

## Practice the Skill

*Answer the following questions about the timeline on this page.*

**1** **Identify the time period covered in the timeline.** (a) What is the date of the first event? (b) What is the date of the last event?

**2** **Figure out the intervals between each date on the timeline.** How many years are there between each major date on the timeline?

**3** **Add additional events.** What other events might you add to this timeline? Why?

**4** **Draw conclusions.** How does the timeline show conflict among European nations during this period?

## Apply the Skill

*See the Review and Assessment at the end of this chapter.*

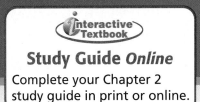

# Chapter Summary

## Section 1
### The Age of Exploration

- The Vikings set up a colony in Newfoundland.
- Christopher Columbus, seeking a sea route to Asia, reached the West Indies in 1492 instead.
- European explorers continued to explore and colonize the Americas.
- The Columbian Exchange resulted in the transfer of products, people, and ideas between Europe and the Americas.

## Section 2
### Spain's Empire in the Americas

- Spanish conquistadors conquered Native American civilizations in the Americas.
- As the Spanish Empire grew, Native American workers were harshly treated.
- A strict class system developed in Spain's American colonies.

## Section 3
### Europeans Compete in North America

- During the Reformation, the authority of the Roman Catholic Church was challenged.
- The defeat of the Spanish Armada undermined Spanish control of the seas.
- European explorers continued to seek a northwest passage to Asia.

## Section 4
### France and the Netherlands in North America

- Colonists in New France established a fur trade with Native Americans.
- The Dutch established permanent settlements in what is now the northeastern United States.
- The French and Dutch settlements had a negative impact on Native American life.

# Key Concepts

These notes will help you prepare for questions about key concepts.

## European Exploration and Settlement of the Americas

**Reasons for Exploration**
- Rivalries among European nations sparked a search for an alternate route to Asia.
- Spain backed voyages of exploration to find a western sea route to Asia.
- English, French, and Dutch explorers searched for a northwest passage from the Atlantic to the Pacific that would pass through or around North America.

## Results of Exploration
- Christopher Columbus discovered land in the West Indies in 1492.
- Balboa discovered the Pacific Ocean in 1513; Magellan's crew sailed around the world from 1519 to 1522.
- Spanish conquistadors extended Spain's empire in the Americas, from South America into North America.
- During the seventeenth century, the English, French, and Dutch established settlements in the Americas.

## Europe's Impact on the Americas

**Positive Effects**
- The Columbian Exchange brought many new animals and plants to America.
- French and Dutch fur traders gave Native Americans goods, including cloth and iron tools and pots.

**Negative Effects**
- Europeans brought diseases to the Americas that killed many Native Americans.

## Vocabulary *Builder*

### Key Terms

Complete each of the following sentences so that the second part further explains the first part and clearly shows your understanding of the key term.

**1.** Hernando Cortés and Francisco Pizarro were Spanish conquistadors_____.

**2.** Because Spain's empire in the Americas needed workers, the government issued *encomiendas*_____.

**3.** In the 1500s and 1600s, many European nations practiced mercantilism_____.

**4.** During a time of war, it may help to form an alliance_____.

## Comprehension and Critical Thinking

**5. (a) Recall** What discoveries did Balboa and Magellan make on their voyages?
**(b) Apply Information** How did the achievements of those explorers change the way in which people viewed their world?

**6. (a) Identify** What were some of the products exchanged between Europe and the Americas as a result of the Columbian Exchange?
**(b) Link Past and Present** What kinds of cultural and economic exchanges occur between nations today?

**7. (a) Recall** How did the Spanish government bring order to new Spanish settlements being developed in Spanish colonies?
**(b) Apply Information** How does the image below show how religion was used to bring order to the settlements?

**8. (a) List** List three ways that French and Dutch colonists affected the lives of Native Americans.
**(b) Explain Problems** Why do you think England felt it was a problem when they learned of the presence of French settlements in the valleys of the Ohio and the Mississippi rivers?

**9. (a) Recall** What role did gold play in the economy of Europe during the 1500s?
**(b) Identify Costs** How did mercantilism affect the growth of colonies in the Americas?

## ⟳ History Reading Skill

**10. Identify Main Ideas and Details** Identify the main idea of Section 2. Find details to support the main idea.

## Writing

**11. Write two paragraphs:**
Discuss the causes and effects of European exploration in the Americas.

**Your paragraphs should:**
* begin with a thesis statement that expresses a main idea about the beginning of European exploration in the Americas;
* support the main idea with facts, examples, and other information about the era;
* use chronological order as much as possible.

**12. Write a Persuasive Speech:**
The year is 1510. You are an adventurer eager to continue the attempt to find a route to Asia. Prepare a speech you will give to persuade a monarch that spending money on this voyage is a wise decision.

## Skills for Life

**Understand Sequence**
Use the chapter timeline on pages 32–33 to answer the following questions.

**13.** What time period is covered in the timeline?

**14.** Into what time intervals is the timeline divided?

**15. (a)** When did the French establish Quebec?
**(b)** How many years later did Marquette and Joliet explore the Mississippi?

**16.** What additional events might you add to the timeline? Why?

**17.** What trend does this timeline show? Explain.

## Test Yourself

1. Which of the following people was the first Spaniard to set foot in what is now the United States?

   A Christopher Columbus

   B Juan Ponce de León

   C Francisco Pizarro

   D Francisco Coronado

2. How did Europe's attitude toward North America change after Henry Hudson's last voyage?

   A Efforts to find a northwest passage continued.

   B French and Dutch fur traders set up more trading posts.

   C Efforts began to profit from the lands explored.

   D Most countries no longer gained from the system of mercantilism.

3. In return for the fur pelts, what goods did the Europeans trade with Native Americans?

   A tobacco

   B food crops

   C cloth and tools

   D pots and silk

4. Unlike the Spaniards, French claims in North America were largely for

   A settling farm communities.

   B economic gains.

   C establishing missions and forts.

   D establishing lumber trade posts.

## Document-Based Questions

**Task:** Look at Documents 1 and 2, and answer their accompanying questions. Then, use the documents and your knowledge of history to complete the following writing assignment:

   Write a two-paragraph essay describing positive and negative effects of the Columbian Exchange.

**Document 1:** The Columbian Exchange involved hundreds of items that enriched people's lives. But one item was deadly—European disease. Bernal Díaz del Castillo, who traveled with Hernando Cortés, describes the scene in the Aztec capital of Tenochtitlán in 1521. *What conditions did the Spanish encounter in Tenochtitlán?*

"All the houses and stockades in the lake were full of corpses. . . . It was the same in the streets and courts. . . . We could not walk without treading on the bodies and heads of dead Indians. . . . . Indeed, the stench was so bad that no one could endure it . . . and even Cortés was ill from the odors which assailed his nostrils."

**Document 2:** The arrival of Columbus set off a tragic chain of events for the people of the Americas. Study the graph to see how the population of central Mexico declined after the European arrival. *What happened to the population between 1500 and 1560?*

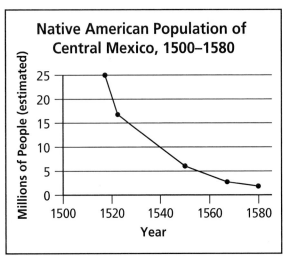

**Native American Population of Central Mexico, 1500–1580**

Source: Nicolás Sánchez-Albornoz, *The Population of Latin America*

CHAPTER 3

# Colonies Take Root

## 1587–1752

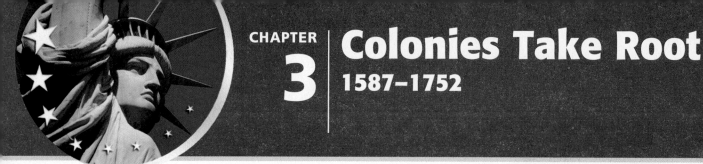

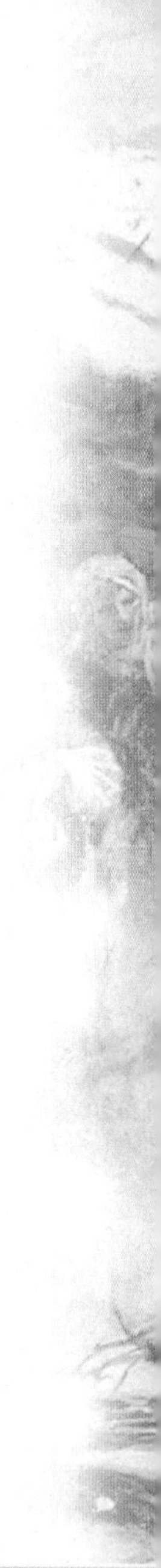

## Chapter Preview

As the wealth and power of Spain's empire in the Americas grew, so too did England's push to build a successful empire in North America. English colonists came seeking wealth, religious freedom, and better living conditions. In this chapter, you will learn how the English started their colonies.

| Section | ☑ What You Will Learn |
|---|---|
| **Section 1**<br>**The First English Settlements**<br>Pages 66–70 | After two failed efforts in the 1580s, the English started colonies in North America in the 1600s. |
| **Section 2**<br>**The New England Colonies**<br>Pages 71–76 | The religious beliefs of Puritans influenced the New England Colonies. |
| **Section 3**<br>**The Middle Colonies**<br>Pages 77–81 | The Middle Colonies attracted a wide range of settlers and offered a haven of religious tolerance. |
| **Section 4**<br>**The Southern Colonies**<br>Pages 84–89 | The Southern Colonies developed rich coastal plantations based on slavery, whereas backcountry farmers struggled to survive. |
| **Section 5**<br>**Spanish Colonies on the Borderlands**<br>Pages 90–93 | Lands from Florida to California formed the vast Spanish Empire in the Americas. |

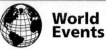

**U.S. Events**

**1565** Spain builds first permanent European settlement in North America.

**1607** English start colony at Jamestown, Virginia.

**1620** Pilgrims sign the Mayflower Compact and settle at Plymouth Bay.

1550 — 1600 — 1650

**World Events**

**1558** Elizabeth I becomes queen of England.

**1602** Dutch start East India Company.

**1640s** The English fight a civil war.

This painting shows thankful Pilgrims arriving in Plymouth, Massachusetts, in 1621.

**Discovery SCHOOL**

**Quick View Video**
View the chapter video for a quick preview of the main ideas.

**1664**
The English take over New Amsterdam from the Dutch.

**1682**
William Penn founds the colony of Pennsylvania.

**1732**
Georgia is founded by James Oglethorpe.

1650

1700

1750

**1689** William and Mary sign the English Bill of Rights.

**1712** Thomas Newcomen's steam engine is put to use in British coal mines.

**History Reading Skill** Compare and Contrast

**What was New York City like in the late 1600s?**

In this chapter, you will learn how to compare and contrast.

> In the 1690s Englishman John Miller lived in New York, where he was the city's only Episcopal minister. He wrote the following description of the city after leaving New York in 1695. Note the spelling differences.

**Primary Source**

> The number of the inhabitants in this Province are about 3000 families whereof almost one halfe are naturally Dutch, a great part English, and the rest French. . . . As to their Religion they are very much divided. . . .
>
>   As to their wealth & disposition, thereto ye Dutch are rich & sparing, the English neither very rich nor too great husbands, the French are poor. . . .
>
>   The Air of this Province is very good & much like that of the best parts of France. . . . The weather is indeed hotter in summer than one would wish. . . .
>
>   He that is not pleased with these advantages may if he please to take a little pains in clearing . . . have good land or pastures. . . . Indeed not all alike for ye land toward the South is generally a sandy soile & not very fruitfull . . . but to the Northward & in the Indian Country the Land is much better. . . .
>
> — John Miller, *New York Considered and Improved, 1695*

*The author compares the three population groups without ever stating that he is making a comparison.*

*The author compares the air of New York to that of France.*

*The word like signals the comparison.*

*The words not all alike signal the contrast.*

*The author contrasts land in the South with that of the North.*

## Compare and Contrast

- Look for similarities and differences between people, places, and ideas.
- Remember that some comparisons and contrasts are directly stated in the text, whereas others are unstated.
- One way to find unstated comparisons and contrasts is to connect information from different parts of the text.
- Signal words such as *like* or *unlike* and *similarly* or *in contrast* indicate comparisons and contrasts.

## Document-Based Questions

1. Who is the author of this source?
2. How did he gain his knowledge of New York?
3. What evidence in the text might support the assumption that the author has visited the European continent?

# Vocabulary *Builder*

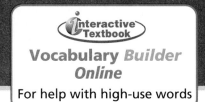
## Previewing High-Use Academic Words

| High-Use Word | Definition | Sample History Sentence |
|---|---|---|
| **impose** (ihm POHZ) (Section 1, p. 66) | *v.* to place a burden on something or someone | Manufacturers wanted the government to <u>impose</u> a high tax on imports. |
| **sustain** (suh STAYN) (Section 1, p. 68) | *v.* to support; to keep going | The colonists were unable at first to grow enough food to <u>sustain</u> themselves. |
| **specify** (SPEHS ih fī) (Section 2, p. 73) | *v.* to point out in detail | The government will <u>specify</u> the exact procedures for registering land. |
| **restrict** (ree STRIHKT) (Section 2, p. 75) | *v.* to place limitations on something or somebody | Some laws <u>restrict</u> undesirable activities. |
| **fundamental** (fuhn duh MEHN tahl) (Section 3, p. 78) | *adj.* most important part | Religious freedom was a <u>fundamental</u> goal of many settlers in colonial America. |
| **accumulate** (uh KYOOM yoo layt) (Section 3, p. 81) | *v.* to increase in amount over time | A person who invests wisely may <u>accumulate</u> great wealth. |
| **proprietor** (proh PRĪ ah tor) (Section 4, p. 86) | *n.* owner of a business or a colony | Lord Baltimore was the <u>proprietor</u> of Maryland in colonial times. |
| **contrast** (KAHN trast) (Section 4, p. 89) | *n.* difference shown between things when compared | The lives of women and men in colonial times provided many <u>contrasts</u>. |
| **function** (FUHNK shuhn) (Section 5, p. 91) | *n.* purpose; proper use | The <u>function</u> of government is to serve the people. |
| **convert** (kuhn VERT) (Section 5, p. 91) | *v.* to change from one religion to another | European missionaries sought to <u>convert</u> Native Americans to Christianity. |

## Previewing Key Terms and People

# The First English Settlements

## Objectives

1. Explain why England wanted to establish colonies in North America.

2. Describe the experience of the settlers who founded the first permanent English colony in Jamestown.

3. Explain how the Pilgrims managed to survive their first years in the Plymouth Colony.

## Prepare to Read

### Reading Skill

**Identify Contrasts** As you read about early English settlements in North America, think how each of these settlements was unique. How was each different from the other early settlements? For example, you might look at the purpose of the settlements, the conditions each endured, and the composition of the settlers themselves.

### Vocabulary *Builder*

**High-Use Words**

impose, p. 66

sustain, p. 68

### Key Terms and People

charter, p. 67

John Smith, p. 67

representative government, p. 69

pilgrim, p. 69

Squanto, p. 70

⭐ **Background Knowledge** While Spain, France, and Holland sought colonies in the Americas, England did not remain idle. In this section, you will learn about the first English settlements in North America.

## England Seeks Colonies

### Main Idea
During the age of exploration, England joined the other European powers in seeking colonies in the Americas.

### Vocabulary *Builder*
**impose** (ihm POHZ) *v.* to place a burden on something or someone

Like most of Europe in the age of exploration, England was a monarchy. However, in England, the power of the king or queen was limited by law and by a lawmaking body called Parliament.

Ever since the 1200s, English law had limited the king's power to punish people without trial. The law guaranteed the right to trial by jury. Other provisions limited the king's power to impose new taxes. The king could set new taxes only with Parliament's consent. Still, the king's powers were much greater than those of Parliament.

England began to establish colonies in North America in the late 1500s. Colonies would provide new markets for English products and important raw materials for English industries.

Two of the earliest English efforts to establish colonies took place during the 1580s. Both were set up on a small island off the coast of what today is North Carolina. The first colony at Roanoke Island was established in 1585, but it was abandoned a year later. The second colony is one of the great mysteries of American history. It was set up in 1587. The next year, England found itself at war with Spain. No ship was able to visit the Roanoke colony until 1590. By then, the colony was abandoned. It had disappeared without a trace.

☑**Checkpoint** What benefits did England hope to get from establishing colonies in North America?

# Founding Jamestown

In 1607, a group of wealthy people made a new attempt to establish an English colony in North America. Eager to gain a share of the wealth of the Americas, they formed the Virginia Company of London. Some of the founders hoped to discover gold or silver. Others expected the colonists to trade with the Indians for furs, which could then be sold in Europe at a profit. Lumber also could be cut from North America's vast forests. Farmers could plant vineyards to grow grapes or mulberry trees to produce silk. England needed all of these products.

England's King James I backed the project. The king granted the merchants a charter to establish a colony called Virginia. A charter is a document issued by a government that grants specific rights to a person or company. It gave the Virginia Company authority over a large portion of North America's Atlantic coastline.

The first colonists arrived in Virginia in the spring of 1607. About 100 men sailed into Chesapeake Bay and built a fort they called Jamestown. It would prove to be England's first permanent settlement in North America.

Jamestown barely survived its first year. It was located on a swampy peninsula where insects thrived in warm weather. During the first summer, many colonists caught diseases, such as malaria, and died.

The colony had another serious problem. Many of the colonists had no intention of doing the hard farmwork needed to grow crops. Those men who came to the colony were not farmers. They were skilled in other trades. They spent their time looking for gold, expecting to get the food they needed from the Native Americans. The colonists found no gold. The local people, led by a chief named Powhatan, supplied some food to the colony. But it was not enough. By the spring of 1608, only 38 of the original colonists were still alive.

## John Smith Takes Charge

Conditions in Jamestown were extremely bad, in part because the colony was poorly led. Then, in the fall of 1608, John Smith was sent out from London to lead the colony. Smith lost no time taking command. He drew up tough, new rules. The most important rule was "He who works not, eats not."

Under Smith's firm leadership, the Jamestown colonists cut timber, put up new

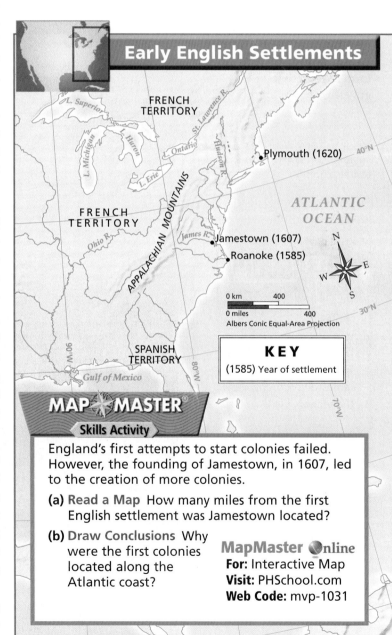

## Early English Settlements

FRENCH TERRITORY

FRENCH TERRITORY

L. Superior

L. Michigan

L. Huron

Ontario

L. Erie

Hudson R.

St. Lawrence R.

APPALACHIAN MOUNTAINS

Ohio R.

James R.

Gulf of Mexico

SPANISH TERRITORY

Plymouth (1620)

ATLANTIC OCEAN

Jamestown (1607)

Roanoke (1585)

40°N

30°N

80°W

70°W

90°W

N S E W

0 km 400
0 miles 400
Albers Conic Equal-Area Projection

**KEY**
(1585) Year of settlement

### MAP MASTER
**Skills Activity**

England's first attempts to start colonies failed. However, the founding of Jamestown, in 1607, led to the creation of more colonies.

**(a) Read a Map** How many miles from the first English settlement was Jamestown located?

**(b) Draw Conclusions** Why were the first colonies located along the Atlantic coast?

**MapMaster Online**
**For:** Interactive Map
**Visit:** PHSchool.com
**Web Code:** mvp-1031

buildings, and planted crops. Meanwhile, hundreds of new colonists arrived. They included the first English women to settle in Jamestown. To get more food, Smith raided Native American villages. This angered Powhatan, who feared the English intended "to invade my people and possess my country."

**The "Starving Time"**  In the fall of 1609, John Smith returned to England after being injured in an explosion. With Smith gone, conditions in Jamestown quickly worsened. So did relations with the Native Americans. Powhatan decided the time had come to drive the English away. First, he refused to supply them with food. The English settlers quickly ran out of food. The terrible winter of 1609–1610 is called the "starving time." By the spring of 1610, only 60 colonists were still alive.

✓**Checkpoint**  **Why did settlers in Jamestown have difficulties at first?**

**Main Idea**
The Virginia colonists set up a form of representative government and introduced slavery.

**Vocabulary** *Builder*
<u>sustain</u> (suh STAYN) *v.* to support; to keep going

## Jamestown Prospers

During the hard times, the Virginia Company did not give up. It continued to send new colonists and offered free land to keep old colonists from leaving. Most important, it sent new leaders from England to restore order in the colony.

These measures would not have succeeded if the colonists had not found a dependable source of income to <u>sustain</u> the colony. What they found was tobacco, a crop native to the Americas. By the 1580s, smoking tobacco had become popular in several European countries, including England.

**Explore More Video**
To learn more about the Jamestown Colony, view the video.

**The House of Burgesses**  On July 30, 1619, the 22 elected members of the House of Burgesses first met together at the Jamestown church. That hot day marked the beginning of representative government in what is now the United States.
**Critical Thinking:** *Link Past and Present  How would a lawmaking body today be similar? What differences would you expect to see?*

The governor calls the meeting to order.

Soldiers stand guard.

The secretary records what is said at the meeting.

Farmers in Jamestown and nearby settlements in Virginia began planting tobacco in 1612. By the early 1620s, Virginia farmers were selling all the tobacco they could grow. Their success drew new colonists from England.

**The House of Burgesses** During these years, Virginia developed a tradition of representative government—the form of government in which voters elect people to make laws for them. In 1619, Virginia's lawmaking body, the House of Burgesses, was elected and met for the first time. The House of Burgesses could pass laws and set taxes. However, it shared power with Virginia's appointed governor, who could veto its acts. The House of Burgesses marked the start of representative government in North America.

**Africans Come to Virginia** In the summer of 1619, a Dutch ship arrived in Virginia from the West Indies. On board were 20 Africans, who had been captured and taken from their homeland. The Africans were sold to the Virginia colonists as slaves. However, that did not necessarily mean they would be enslaved for the rest of their lives. In the early days of the colony, enslaved people had a chance to earn their freedom after working a certain number of years. Some enslaved Africans were able to do this. Permanent slavery for Africans was not established in Virginia until the last part of the 1600s.

African American artist Romare Bearden presents the forced journey enslaved Africans made to the Americas in his painting *Roots Odyssey.*

✓**Checkpoint** **What were the responsibilities of the House of Burgesses?**

# The Plymouth Colony

In England during the 1500s, people could be punished for their religious beliefs. In the 1530s, when King Henry VIII declared himself head of the Church of England, everyone was expected to follow the ways of the Church of England.

About the time Jamestown was founded, a group of people in eastern England left their homes and settled in Holland. They wanted to separate from the Church of England and practice Christianity in their own way. These people, called Separatists, were often persecuted or treated badly because of their religion.

Between 1607 and 1609, several groups of Separatists settled in Holland. Although they were allowed to worship as they pleased, they still were not happy. In 1620, one group of Separatists decided to leave Holland and settle in Virginia. They are the people we know today as the Pilgrims. A pilgrim is a person who takes a religious journey.

**The Mayflower Compact** In September 1620, about 100 Pilgrims sailed for Virginia aboard a ship called the *Mayflower.* After a long voyage, they arrived safely in North America. However, storms had blown them off course, and they landed far to the north in what today is Massachusetts. They called their new home Plymouth, after a port city in England.

**Main Idea**

The Pilgrims founded the Plymouth Colony in order to practice their religion freely.

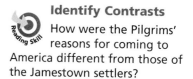

**Identify Contrasts**

How were the Pilgrims' reasons for coming to America different from those of the Jamestown settlers?

Squanto

Because they had landed outside Virginia, the Pilgrims believed they were not bound by the rules of the Virginia Company. But they needed rules of some sort. Before going ashore, 41 adult men signed the Mayflower Compact. It called for a government that would make and follow "just and equal laws." Officeholders would be elected by the colony's adult males.

Thus, a year after the creation of Virginia's House of Burgesses, the Pilgrims had taken a second step toward self-government in the Americas. The Mayflower Compact was the first document in which American colonists claimed a right to govern themselves.

**The First Thanksgiving** The Pilgrims had a very difficult first winter in Plymouth. They had arrived too late to plant crops and did not have enough food. During the winter of 1620–1621, half the colonists died from hunger or disease.

Conditions improved in the spring of 1621. As had happened at Jamestown, help from local Native Americans sustained the Pilgrims. A local chief gave the Pilgrims some food. Another Native American, named Squanto, brought the Pilgrims seeds of native plants—corn, beans, and pumpkins—and showed them how to plant them. He also taught the settlers how to catch eels from nearby rivers.

In the fall of 1621, the Pilgrims set aside a day to give thanks for their good fortune. Today's Thanksgiving holiday celebrates that occasion.

☑ **Checkpoint** Why was the Mayflower Compact important?

☆ **Looking Back and Ahead** The early settlers faced many challenges before they were able to claim success. In the next section, you will read how English settlers established additional colonies in New England.

---

Section 1 | **Check Your Progress**

**Progress Monitoring** ⬤nline
**For:** Self-test with instant help
**Visit:** PHSchool.com
**Web Code:** mva-1031

**Comprehension and Critical Thinking**

1. **(a) Recall** What actions did John Smith take to help Jamestown?
**(b) Identify Alternatives** What other methods do you think Smith could have used to save the colony?

2. **(a) Identify** Who were the Pilgrims?
**(b) Analyze Cause and Effect** How did the Pilgrims' experiences in England affect the government they established in the Plymouth Colony?

**Reading Skill**

3. **Identify Contrasts** How did the government of the Jamestown settlers differ from that of the Plymouth settlers?

**Vocabulary** *Builder*
Fill in the blanks with the correct key terms.

4. The English king gave the merchants of the Virginia Company a _____ to establish a colony called Virginia.

5. English colonies in North America established a form of _____ based on elections.

**Writing**

6. Imagine that you are preparing a news report about the founding of Jamestown Colony. Make notes providing background information about this development. Your notes should include the economic benefits of colonialism and the particular details about how Jamestown Colony was founded.

# The New England Colonies

## Objectives

1. Describe the geography and climate of the New England Colonies.

2. Describe the Puritan settlement in Massachusetts.

3. Identify the new settlements that developed in New England as a result of Puritan religious practices.

4. Explain the changes that took place in the New England Colonies in the 1600s.

## Prepare to Read

### Reading Skill

**Make Comparisons** Despite differences, the New England colonies were alike in many ways. Look for these similarities in this section. For example, how was the climate similar in various colonies? You might also look at the shared reasons colonists had for coming to North America and at the ways that similar government structures evolved throughout New England.

## Vocabulary *Builder*

### High-Use Words

<u>specify</u>, p. 73

<u>restrict</u>, p. 75

### Key Terms and People

John Winthrop, p. 72

toleration, p. 73

Roger Williams, p. 73

Anne Hutchinson, p. 74

Thomas Hooker, p. 74

John Wheelright, p. 75

town meeting, p. 75

Metacom, p. 76

⭐ **Background Knowledge** As you learned in the previous section, Plymouth Colony survived its first winter and began to grow slowly. Meanwhile, new colonies were growing up in this region, which is present-day New England. In this section, you will learn about the challenges the new colonies faced.

## Geography of New England

New England is in the northeastern corner of the United States. Massachusetts, Connecticut, and Rhode Island make up southern New England. New Hampshire, Vermont, and Maine make up the northern part.

Much of New England is made up of hills and low mountains. Large areas are covered by forests. The soil is thin and rocky, which makes farming difficult. There are narrow plains located along the Atlantic coast. The Connecticut River, the region's longest river, flows from New Hampshire and Vermont through Massachusetts and Connecticut before reaching the sea. Just off New England's long, jagged coastline are some of the richest fishing grounds in the world.

Winters in New England tend to be long and snowy. Summers are shorter and warm. This helped the early colonists in the region, who caught fewer diseases and lived longer than the colonists in Virginia.

**Main Idea**
Farming is difficult in New England, but the region has resources like forests and rich fishing grounds.

New Englanders pursue a whale

✓ **Checkpoint** Why would colonists in New England have turned to fishing rather than to farming?

**Make Comparisons**
Compare the reasons that England's Puritans went to North America with the reasons that the Pilgrims left England. How are they similar?

## Puritans in Massachusetts Bay

Similar to the Pilgrims, a group known as the Puritans had disagreements with the Church of England. Rather than split off from the established church, they wanted to reform, or change, it. In the early 1600s, the Puritans were influential in England. Many were important professionals such as merchants, landowners, or lawyers.

The 1620s brought hard times for England's Puritans. King Charles I opposed their movement and persecuted them. Hundreds of Puritan ministers were forced to give up their positions.

**The Puritans Leave England** A number of Puritans eventually decided to leave England and make the hazardous voyage to North America. In 1630, about 900 Puritans set off in 11 ships. They had formed the Massachusetts Bay Company, which received a charter to establish settlements in what are now Massachusetts and New Hampshire. The Puritans were led by John Winthrop, a respected landowner and lawyer.

In founding their own colony, Puritan leaders believed that their way of life would provide an example to others. As Winthrop said in a sermon during their voyage:

> **“**Now the only way . . . is . . . to walk humbly with our God. . . . We must consider that we shall be as a City upon a Hill. The eyes of all people are upon us.**”**
> —John Winthrop, "A Model of Christian Charity," 1630

# The Salem Witch Trials

Today, the Salem witch trials show how quickly false accusations can be accepted as true. **Critical Thinking:** *Draw Conclusions Do you think this kind of judgment is possible today? Explain.*

◀ **The Accusers**
Clergymen such as Cotton Mather of Boston helped to feed the hysteria by asserting that the Devil was luring Salem's people into witchcraft.

◀ **The Accused**
An accused woman is strapped to a dunking stool, a common form of punishment.

**The Massachusetts Bay Colony** The Puritans established several settlements in their colony. The main town was Boston, which was located on an excellent harbor. By 1643, about 20,000 people lived in the Massachusetts Bay Colony.

By the mid-1630s, Massachusetts Bay had an elected assembly, the General Court. Each town sent representatives to the assembly. But voting was limited to adult male members of the Puritan church. Both the General Court and the colony's governor were elected each year.

The Puritans had founded their colony so they could worship as they chose. However, they did not give non-Puritans the same right. The Puritans did not believe in religious toleration—recognition that other people have the right to different opinions.

✓**Checkpoint** **Why did the Puritans go to North America?**

## New Colonies

Disagreements about religion led to the founding of other colonies in New England. A key dispute involved Roger Williams, minister of a church in the town of Salem. Williams believed the Puritans should split entirely from the Church of England. He also criticized colonists who had seized Native American lands. Williams specified that colonists should pay Native Americans for their land.

Williams was forced to leave Massachusetts Bay in 1635. He moved south, to what today is Rhode Island, where he bought land from Native Americans. In 1636, he founded the town of Providence.

**Main Idea**
Religious disputes led some people to spread out and start new colonies in New England.

**Vocabulary** *Builder*
specify (SPEHS ah fī) *v.* to point out in detail

▼ **On Trial**
In 1692, hysteria about witches swept through Salem, Massachusetts. A special court tried dozens of women and men accused of witchcraft.

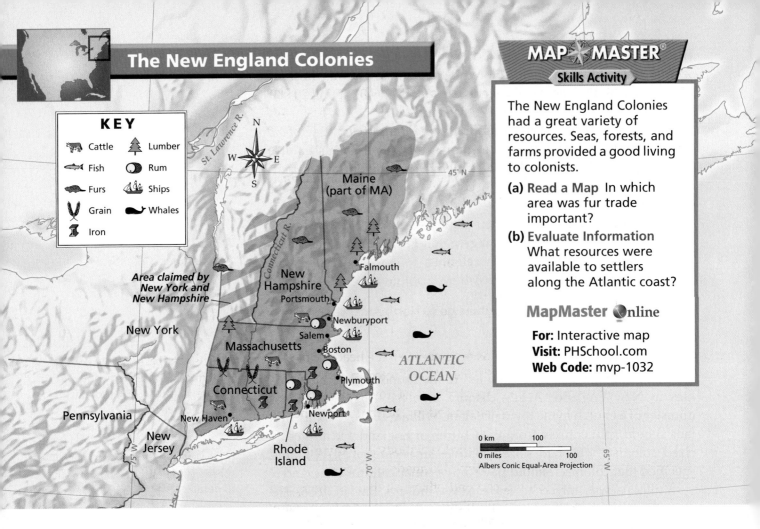

## The New England Colonies

MAP MASTER®
Skills Activity

The New England Colonies had a great variety of resources. Seas, forests, and farms provided a good living to colonists.

**(a) Read a Map** In which area was fur trade important?

**(b) Evaluate Information** What resources were available to settlers along the Atlantic coast?

**MapMaster Online**

**For:** Interactive map
**Visit:** PHSchool.com
**Web Code:** mvp-1032

**KEY**

- Cattle
- Fish
- Furs
- Grain
- Iron
- Lumber
- Rum
- Ships
- Whales

Area claimed by New York and New Hampshire

New York

Pennsylvania

New Jersey

Maine (part of MA)

New Hampshire

Portsmouth

Falmouth

Newburyport

Salem

Boston

Massachusetts

Plymouth

Connecticut

New Haven

Newport

Rhode Island

ATLANTIC OCEAN

St. Lawrence R.

Connecticut R.

45° N

70° W

75° W

65° W

0 km 100
0 miles 100
Albers Conic Equal-Area Projection

In 1644, the colonists in Rhode Island received a charter from the king to govern themselves. In doing so, they made an important contribution to religious toleration. They decided that Rhode Island would have no established church. People of all faiths could worship as they saw fit. Among the people who found religious freedom in Rhode Island were followers of the Jewish faith.

**Anne Hutchinson's Dissent** A Boston woman, Anne Hutchinson, questioned some of the Puritan teachings. She was put on trial in 1638 and was expelled from Massachusetts. Hutchinson established a settlement on an island that is now a part of Rhode Island. In 1642, she traveled farther south, in what is today New York State.

**Settling Connecticut** Thomas Hooker, a minister, disagreed with the Puritan leaders. He left Massachusetts with about 100 followers in 1636 and settled in what today is Connecticut. There, he founded the town of Hartford. Hundreds of Puritans followed, and soon Connecticut had several new settlements.

In 1639, the colonists drew up the Fundamental Orders of Connecticut, which established a new government with an elected legislature and governor. In 1662, Connecticut received an official charter from the king granting it self-government.

John Wheelright also was forced to leave Massachusetts. He got into trouble because he agreed with some of Anne Hutchinson's views. In 1638, Wheelright and some followers moved to New Hampshire, where they founded the town of Exeter. For a time, Massachusetts tried to control New Hampshire. Finally, in 1680, a charter from the king made New Hampshire a separate colony.

☑ **Checkpoint** **Why did Roger Williams and Anne Hutchinson leave the Massachusetts Bay Colony?**

## Growth and Change

The Puritans believed that towns and churches should manage their own affairs. They also believed that people should work hard and live in strong and stable families.

Each Puritan town governed itself by setting up a town meeting—an assembly of townspeople that decides local issues. Membership in town meetings was <u>restricted</u> to male heads of households. Town meetings set local taxes and elected people to run the towns. New England became a region of towns and villages where neighbors knew one another and participated together in government.

New England families earned their livelihoods in many different ways. Farmers grew crops, but they also made leather goods and other products. Fishers caught cod and other fish that were shipped to customers in Europe. A shipbuilding industry provided many jobs. By the 1660s, more than 300 ships from New England were fishing off the coast or moving products across the Atlantic Ocean.

**Main Idea**
As the number of colonists in New England grew, the region went through many changes.

**Vocabulary *Builder***
**restrict** (ree STRIHKT) *v.* to place limitations on something or somebody

## Links to Civics

### The Town Meeting

The New England town meeting was a place to argue important town issues. Questions such as "What roads should be built?" and "How much should the schoolmaster be paid?" were discussed. Town meetings gave New Englanders an opportunity to speak their minds. This early experience encouraged the growth of democratic ideas in New England. Sometimes, as shown here, the exchanges became quite heated. **Critical Thinking: *Interpret Paintings*** *How would you describe the attitude of the artist toward the townspeople he portrays?*

Metacom, known to the English as "King Philip"

**King Philip's War** By the 1670s, the Native American population was decreasing, mainly because large numbers of Native Americans had died from diseases that they caught from Europeans. By 1670, there were only 12,000 Native Americans in New England, one tenth of their population 100 years earlier.

In 1675, a major conflict erupted. Opponents of the English were led by Metacom, the chief of the Wampanoag, who was also known by his English name, King Philip. His goal was to stop Puritan expansion. Other Native American groups, from Maine to Rhode Island, joined the war, some siding with the settlers. The fighting lasted a year and cost thousands of lives. Metacom and his allies destroyed 12 English towns. The uprising ended in 1676 when Metacom was captured and killed. The war's end left the English colonies free to expand.

**Puritan Influence Declines** By the 1670s, the outlook of New Englanders was changing. There was a new generation of people born in North America. The new generation had lost some of their parents' religious fervor, as people concentrated on running farms and businesses. In growing towns like Boston, successful merchants were becoming the new community leaders. The English colonies of New England were doing well. But the stern religious rules of the original founders now had less influence over the people who lived there.

☑Checkpoint  **Why did Metacom declare war on the English colonists?**

⭐ **Looking Back and Ahead** As English colonies spread through New England, other colonies were being established to the west and south.

---

Section 2 | **Check Your Progress**

**Progress Monitoring** Online
**For:** Self-test with instant help
**Visit:** PHSchool.com
**Web Code:** mva-1032

**Comprehension and Critical Thinking**

1. **(a) Summarize** What was the geography and climate of New England?
   **(b) Identify Economic Costs** How did geography affect the New England economy?

2. **(a) Recall** Why did Puritans establish the Massachusetts Bay Colony?

**(b) Analyze Cause and Effect** How did the lack of religious toleration affect politics in the Massachusetts Bay Colony?

🔁 **Reading Skill**

3. **Make Comparisons** Compare the way the English government treated the Puritans with the way the Puritans treated Anne Hutchinson. How are they similar?

**Vocabulary** *Builder*

4. Write two definitions for each key term: toleration, town meeting. First, write a formal definition for your teacher. Second, write a casual definition in everyday English for a classmate.

**Writing**

5. Create a concept web. Label the main oval "Religion." Then, add entries that show how religion played a major role in the settling of the New England Colonies. Add as many secondary ovals as necessary.

# The Middle Colonies

## Objectives

1. Describe the geography and climate of the Middle Colonies.

2. Describe the early history of New York and New Jersey.

3. Explain how Pennsylvania and Delaware were founded.

4. Explain how the Middle Colonies changed in the 1600s and early 1700s.

## Prepare to Read

### Reading Skill

**Identify Signal Words** Signal words help readers spot comparisons and contrasts. For example, when we say, "Kentucky is warm. New York is *also* warm," the word *also* suggests that the two states and climates are similar. If the text reads, "Kentucky is warm. *Instead*, New York is cool," the word *instead* suggests that the two states and climates are different. Look for comparison and contrast signal words as you read this section.

### Vocabulary *Builder*

**High-Use Words**

fundamental, p. 78
accumulate, p. 81

**Key Terms and People**

proprietary colony, p. 78
royal colony, p. 78
William Penn, p. 78
backcountry, p. 81

⭐ **Background Knowledge** While the New England colonies were growing, important developments were taking place in the region south of New England. In this section, you will learn about this region, which became known as the Middle Colonies.

## Geography of the Middle Colonies

Four states made up the Middle Colonies: New York, Pennsylvania, New Jersey, and Delaware. New York, now the largest of these states, also is the farthest north. The scenic Hudson River flows south through eastern New York before reaching the sea at New York City. Long Island, the easternmost piece of New York, extends into the Atlantic Ocean for more than 100 miles. Today, New York City is the most populous city in the country.

Pennsylvania is the region's second-largest state. The southeastern section is a lowland. Philadelphia, Pennsylvania's largest city, is located there, on the Delaware River.

Most of New Jersey is a lowland along the Atlantic coast. Delaware, the region's smallest state, is on the coast directly south of New Jersey.

Middle Colony farmers had an easier time than farmers in New England. The climate was warmer, with a longer growing season. The fertile soil was well suited for crops like wheat, fruits, and vegetables.

☑**Checkpoint** **What conditions in the Middle Colonies favored farming?**

**Main Idea**
With a warmer climate and more fertile soil than New England, the Middle Colonies became a farming region.

**Identify Signal Words**
What signal words suggest a contrast between the Middle Colonies and the New England Colonies? What contrast is suggested?

# New York and New Jersey

New York began as the Dutch colony of New Netherland. By 1660, it was an economic success. Farmers in the Hudson River valley were prosperous. The colony was the base for a profitable fur trade between the Dutch and Native Americans. The Dutch also made money trading with merchants in the British colonies. This trade violated Britain's mercantile laws and angered the government.

One of New Netherland's major problems was its small Dutch population. Many of the colonists came from Sweden, France, and Portugal. There also were some English Puritans who had settled on Long Island. These people often were hostile to Dutch rule.

Tension also existed between England and Holland. New Netherland separated England's northern colonies from its colonies farther south. Furthermore, England and Holland were rivals at trade.

**New Netherland Becomes New York** In 1664, England's King Charles II granted the right to all the Dutch lands in North America to his brother James. All that James had to do was conquer the territory. James sent a few warships to do the job, and the Dutch surrendered immediately. The colony was renamed New York, after James, the Duke of York. New Amsterdam, its capital, became New York City. The colony grew slowly. At the end of the 1600s, New York City was still a village on the southern end of Manhattan.

**New Jersey** New Jersey was established in 1665, when part of southern New York was split off to form a new colony. Like New York and several other English colonies, New Jersey at first was a proprietary colony—a colony created by a grant of land from a monarch to an individual or family. In 1702, New Jersey received a new charter as a royal colony—a colony controlled directly by the English king. New York had become a royal colony in 1685.

☑**Checkpoint** How did New Jersey become a separate colony?

Main Idea
Pennsylvania and Delaware were founded by Quakers, who believed in religious toleration.

Vocabulary *Builder*
fundamental (fuhn duh MEHN tahl) *adj.* most important part

# Pennsylvania and Delaware

In the 1640s and 1650s, the Quakers were one of a number of new religious groups in England. Their ideas set them apart from most groups, including the Puritans.

The Quakers believed that all people had a direct link, or "inner light," with God. Groups of Quakers, therefore, did not need ministers. Another fundamental Quaker belief was that all people were equal in God's eyes. Thus, they were among the first in England to speak out against slavery. Women were considered equal to men in spiritual matters and often were leaders in Quaker meetings.

By the 1660s, there were thousands of Quakers in England. Many of them refused to pay taxes to support the Church of England. Because of their views, they often suffered from persecution. One Quaker leader was William Penn, a wealthy man who personally knew King Charles II. Penn wanted to find a place for Quakers to live where they would be safe from persecution. He used his connections to get a charter from the king for a new colony in North America. In 1681, he received an area almost as large as England itself, mainly in what is now Pennsylvania.

**Penn's "Holy Experiment"** Penn arrived in his colony in 1682. To attract settlers, he printed pamphlets in several languages and distributed them in England and on the European continent. Soon, new settlers began arriving from many places—England, Scotland, Wales, and Ireland. Still others came from Germany, Holland, and Switzerland.

Penn considered his colony to be a "holy experiment." His goal was to create a colony in which people from different religious backgrounds could live peacefully. In 1682, Penn wrote his Frame of Government for Pennsylvania. It granted the colony an elected assembly. It also provided for freedom of religion.

Penn tried to deal fairly with Native Americans. He did not allow colonists to settle on land until the Native Americans sold it to them. Relations between settlers and Native Americans in Pennsylvania were far from perfect. However, during Penn's lifetime they were much better in Pennsylvania than in other colonies.

## Links to Art

***Penn's Treaty With the Indians*** by Edward Hicks
Edward Hicks, a Quaker preacher, first painted signs and coaches before he became an artist. In this painting Hicks wanted to show a peaceful meeting between settlers and Native Americans. **Critical Thinking: Detect Points of View** *How might this picture have been different if a Native American artist had painted it?*

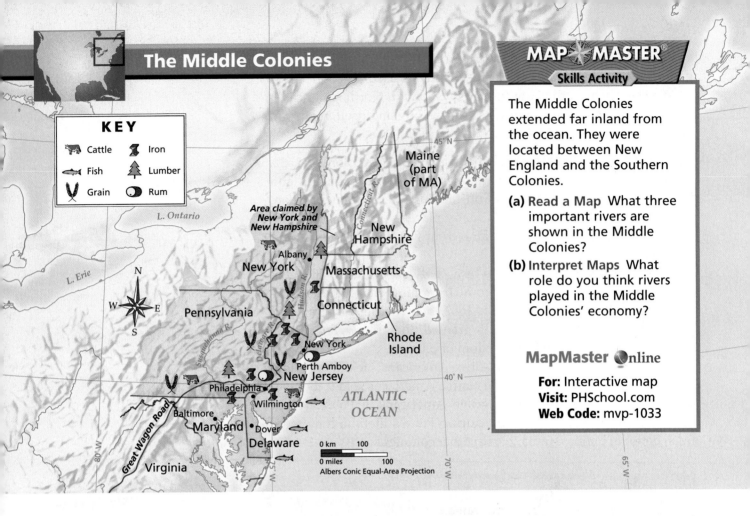

**KEY**

| | |
|---|---|
| Cattle | Iron |
| Fish | Lumber |
| Grain | Rum |

L. Ontario

L. Erie

Area claimed by
New York and
New Hampshire

Maine
(part
of MA)

New
Hampshire

Albany

New York

Massachusetts

Connecticut

Pennsylvania

Hudson R.

Susquehanna R.

Delaware R.

New York

Rhode
Island

Perth Amboy

New Jersey

Philadelphia

Wilmington

ATLANTIC
OCEAN

Great Wagon Road

Baltimore

Maryland    Dover

Delaware

Virginia

45° N

40° N

80° W

75° W

70° W

65° W

0 km    100

0 miles    100

Albers Conic Equal-Area Projection

**MAP MASTER®**
**Skills Activity**

The Middle Colonies extended far inland from the ocean. They were located between New England and the Southern Colonies.

**(a) Read a Map** What three important rivers are shown in the Middle Colonies?

**(b) Interpret Maps** What role do you think rivers played in the Middle Colonies' economy?

**MapMaster Online**

**For:** Interactive map
**Visit:** PHSchool.com
**Web Code:** mvp-1033

**Delaware: A Separate Colony** People from Sweden were the first European settlers in Delaware. The Dutch took control of the territory in the 1650s, but they lost it to the English when they lost New York.

Penn's charter for Pennsylvania included Delaware. Because Delaware settlers did not want to send delegates to a distant assembly in Philadelphia, Penn gave the area its own representative assembly. In 1704, Delaware became a separate colony.

☑**Checkpoint** Why did Penn call Pennsylvania "a holy experiment"?

**Main Idea**

People from many European countries settled in the Middle Colonies during the 1600s and early 1700s.

## Growth and Change

By the early 1700s, more than 20,000 colonists lived in Pennsylvania. Fertile soil and hard work made its farms productive. Farmers grew more than they could use and sold the balance. The top cash crop, wheat, was sold to customers in New England and abroad. Because of all its wheat, Pennsylvania was called America's breadbasket. New Jersey also produced large amounts of wheat.

Manufacturing was just beginning in the Middle Colonies during the 1700s. The largest manufacturers produced iron, flour, and paper. Meanwhile, artisans in towns worked as shoemakers, carpenters, masons, weavers, and in many other trades. Among the most important artisans were coopers, who made the barrels used to ship and store flour and other foods.

**The Backcountry** The western section of Pennsylvania was part of a region called the backcountry. The backcountry was a frontier region extending through several colonies, from Pennsylvania to Georgia.

Many of the people who settled in the backcountry were not English. Thousands were Scotch-Irish. Originally from Scotland, they had settled in Ireland before coming to North America. Large numbers of German immigrants began arriving early in the 1700s. The word these German newcomers used to describe themselves was *Deutsch*, for "German." Americans thought they were saying "Dutch." As a result, German immigrants in Pennsylvania were called the Pennsylvania Dutch.

By the middle of the 1700s, many settlers were pushing south and west along a route that led from Pennsylvania to Georgia. Because they often traveled in covered wagons, the route was called the Great Wagon Road. These backcountry settlers often fought with Native Americans.

**Diverse and Thriving Colonies** By 1750, the non-English immigrants had made the Middle Colonies the most diverse part of English North America. Philadelphia and New York were accumulating people at such a rate that they had become the largest cities and busiest ports in the colonies. All of the colonies had thriving economies.

**Vocabulary** *Builder*
accumulate (uh KYOOM yoo layt)
*v.* to increase in amount over time

☑Checkpoint **How was Pennsylvania a breadbasket?**

☆ **Looking Back and Ahead** Both the New England and Middle Colonies had many small family farms. In the next section, you will read that parts of the Southern Colonies developed a plantation economy that was far different.

---

Section 3 | **Check Your Progress**

**Progress Monitoring** ⏻nline
**For:** Self-test with instant help
**Visit:** PHSchool.com
**Web Code:** mva-1033

**Comprehension and Critical Thinking**

1. **(a) Recall** What was the geography and climate of the Middle Colonies?
   **(b) Identify Economic Benefits** What advantages did the geography and climate give to people living in the Middle Colonies?

2. **(a) Summarize** What were William Penn's goals for his colony?
   **(b) Compare** How did Penn's "holy experiment" differ from the Puritans' "city on a hill"?

⏻ **Reading Skill**

3. **Identify Signal Words** What word in the sentence that follows suggests a comparison? What similarity is being identified?
   **Sentence:** Both Pennsylvania and New Jersey produced a lot of wheat.

**Vocabulary** *Builder*

Answer the following questions in complete sentences that show your understanding of the key terms.

4. How was New Jersey different after it became a royal colony in 1702?

5. Why did so many people settle in the backcountry?

**Writing**

6. Imagine that you are a Pennsylvania farmer. Write a letter to a fellow farmer in New England telling him about your life in your new home. Then, write a letter that the New England farmer might send back describing his life in New England.

# Landscapes of the 13 Colonies

The physical geography of the 13 British colonies differed widely from region to region. While farmers in New England had difficulty planting crops in thin and rocky soil, farmers in the Middle and Southern colonies had better luck with more fertile soil and warmer climates.

KEY
- NEW ENGLAND COLONIES
- MIDDLE COLONIES
- SOUTHERN COLONIES
- CLAIMED BY NH and NY

## Three Regions

Although farming was an important economic activity throughout the colonies, poor soil forced people in New England to concentrate on the sea for economic survival. For the colonists to the south, better geography yielded more favorable soils and longer growing seasons.

▲ **New England** farmers had to break up rocks in the soil to clear land for crops. Because this was difficult work with only a small chance for financial success, many New Englanders relied upon fishing off the New England coast to provide for their families.

◄ Farmers in the **Middle Colonies** of Pennsylvania and New Jersey had an easier time growing crops. Better soil and a warmer climate in this region rendered huge wheat fields that gave Pennsylvania the nickname America's breadbasket.

◄ The **Southern Colonies** shared a lowland area called the Tidewater. Farmers there grew crops such as sugar, tobacco, and rice (pictured left). These crops thrived in the region's hot, humid environment. Because the Tidewater crops were grown on great stretches of land and required a great deal of labor, large farms, called plantations, developed in the South.

---

### *Understand Effects:*
# Slavery in the Southern Colonies

Because the climate of the Southern Colonies supported long growing seasons, plantation owners purchased enslaved people and used their labor to harvest rice and sugar crops. As the plantation system grew to dominate the economy of the Southern Colonies, slavery spread throughout the region.

---

### *Analyze* GEOGRAPHY AND HISTORY

Colonists in each of the three major regions of the 13 colonies learned to adapt to their environments. Write a paragraph describing how physical geography affected the output of food in the colonies.

# The Southern Colonies

## Objectives

1. Describe the geography and climate of the Southern Colonies.

2. Describe the early history of Virginia.

3. Explain how Maryland, the Carolinas, and Georgia were founded.

4. Identify the factors that produced the Tidewater and backcountry ways of life.

## Prepare to Read

### Reading Skill

**Compare and Contrast** As you read about the Southern Colonies in this section, think about how they are the same and different from one another. What physical features do they share? What human features? In what ways are the communities and places different? Comparing and contrasting will help you better understand the colonies.

### Vocabulary *Builder*

**High-Use Words**

proprietor, p. 86

contrast, p. 89

**Key Terms and People**

Nathaniel Bacon, p. 85

Lord Baltimore, p. 86

James Oglethorpe, p. 87

debtor, p. 87

plantation, p. 87

---

⭐ **Background Knowledge** In the previous section, you learned how the Middle Colonies had diverse populations and economies. The Southern Colonies were much less diverse, as you will see in this section.

## Geography of the Southern Colonies

**Main Idea**

With a warm climate suited to crops requiring many workers, the Southern Colonies came to depend on slavery.

During the 1760s, Charles Mason and Jeremiah Dixon were hired to settle a boundary dispute between Maryland and Pennsylvania. They conducted a survey—a careful measuring of an area with scientific instruments using the techniques of mathematics—that took four years to complete. The boundary they drew is known as the Mason-Dixon line. This line on a map marked much more than the boundary between two colonies. After the American Revolution, it was the dividing line between the northern states where slavery was abolished and the southern states where slavery persisted.

Five colonies were located south of the Mason-Dixon line: Maryland, Virginia, North Carolina, South Carolina, and Georgia. They shared a coastal area called the Tidewater, a flat lowland that includes many swampy areas. On its west, the Tidewater blends into a region of rolling hills called the Piedmont.

The climate of these states is warm and humid. Hot summers provide a long growing season that colonial farmers used to raise crops such as tobacco and rice. Both crops required many workers in the fields and thus were partly responsible for helping to spur the early development of slavery.

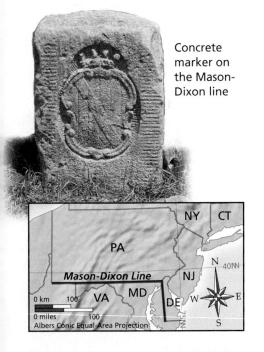

Concrete marker on the Mason-Dixon line

✔**Checkpoint** What conditions in the Southern Colonies favored the development of a plantation economy?

# Virginia Grows

Virginia's population grew gradually during the 1600s. New settlers arriving from Europe made up for the fact that disease and difficult living conditions kept the death rate high. After 1650, the death rate fell, and the population increased more quickly. In 1640, about 10,000 settlers lived in Virginia. By 1670, the number had reached 40,000.

The makeup of Virginia's population also changed. By the 1670s, there were more children because fewer were dying at a young age. The percentage of women in the population rose as well.

**Conflicts With Native Americans** As Virginia's white population grew, the Native American population shrank. Disease and violence took their toll. In 1607, there had been about 8,000 Native Americans in Virginia. By 1675, only about 2,000 Native Americans were left.

Farmers took over more land to plant tobacco. This led to trouble with the Native Americans. There were two violent confrontations— one in 1622 and the other in 1644. Although the Native Americans killed hundreds of colonists, they were defeated both times. After 1644, the Native Americans living near the coast had to accept English rule.

**Bacon's Rebellion** There was more trouble to come. Beginning in the 1660s, wealthy Virginia tobacco planters bought most of the good farmland near the coast. That left no land for poorer colonists who wanted to start their own farms. Most of these colonists were young men who were forced to work the land for wealthier farmers. The young men also were angry because without property, they could not vote.

Many poor colonists moved inland to find good farmland. Fighting broke out with Native Americans, and people were killed on both sides. Farmers on the frontier demanded that the governor take strong measures against the Native Americans. However, the governor hesitated. He hoped to avoid an all-out war with the Native Americans, partly because he benefited from his fur trade with them.

Nathaniel Bacon became the leader of the frontier settlers. In 1675, he organized a force of 1,000 westerners and began attacking and killing Native Americans. The governor declared that Bacon and his men were rebels. Bacon reacted by attacking Jamestown, burning it to the ground, and forcing the governor to run away.

The revolt, known as Bacon's Rebellion, collapsed when Bacon became sick and died. The governor hanged 23 of Bacon's followers. Still, he could not stop English settlers from moving onto Native American lands.

✓ **Checkpoint** **What was the main cause of Bacon's Rebellion?**

**Bacon's Rebellion**
Nathaniel Bacon (center) is shown here taking part in the burning of Jamestown during his 1675 rebellion. **Critical Thinking:** *Explain Problems How did the interests of frontier settlers differ from those of colonists in towns and on plantations?*

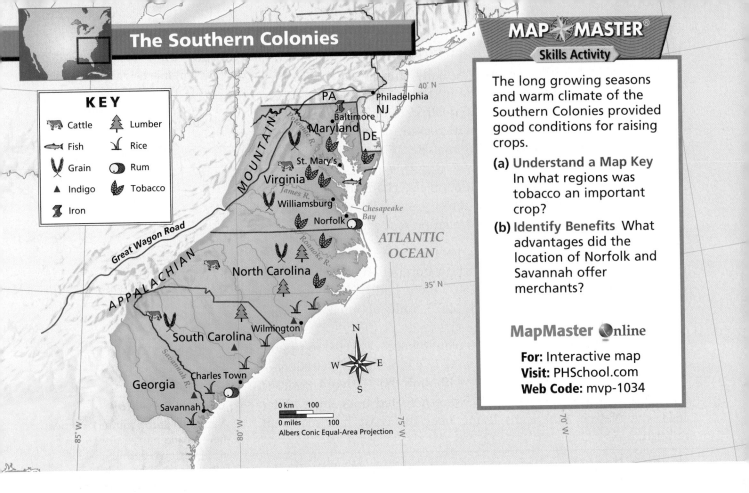

## The Southern Colonies

### MAP✦MASTER
#### Skills Activity

**KEY**
- Cattle
- Fish
- Grain
- Indigo
- Iron
- Lumber
- Rice
- Rum
- Tobacco

The long growing seasons and warm climate of the Southern Colonies provided good conditions for raising crops.

**(a) Understand a Map Key** In what regions was tobacco an important crop?

**(b) Identify Benefits** What advantages did the location of Norfolk and Savannah offer merchants?

**MapMaster ◉nline**

**For:** Interactive map
**Visit:** PHSchool.com
**Web Code:** mvp-1034

---

**Main Idea**
Religious toleration among Christians was a key feature of the Maryland Colony.

**Vocabulary *Builder***
**proprietor** (proh PRĪ ah tor) *n.* owner of a business or a colony

**Compare and Contrast**
Compare and contrast the population growth, agriculture, and political tensions of Maryland with those of Virginia.

**Main Idea**
Large plantations took hold in South Carolina, whereas North Carolina and Georgia tended to have small farms.

## Religious Toleration in Maryland

In 1632, King Charles I granted a charter for a new colony to George Calvert, an English Catholic. Catholics suffered great discrimination in England. Calvert aimed to set up a colony where Catholics could live safely. His colony, Maryland, lay across Chesapeake Bay from Virginia.

The first settlers included both Catholics and Protestants. They grew tobacco and harvested the sea life of Chesapeake Bay. When George Calvert died, his son, Cecil Calvert, Lord Baltimore, became proprietor. As the charter required, there was a representative assembly similar to the House of Burgesses in Virginia.

Soon there was tension between Protestants and Catholics. Fearing that Catholics might lose their rights, Lord Baltimore got the assembly to pass the Act of Toleration, in 1649. It welcomed all Christians and gave adult male Christians the right to vote and hold office. Although the Toleration Act did not protect people who were not Christian, it was still an important step toward religious toleration in North America.

✔**Checkpoint** Who benefited from Maryland's toleration?

## Colonies in the Carolinas and Georgia

By the 1660s, a few settlers from Virginia had moved south beyond the colony's borders. In 1663, King Charles II granted a charter for a new colony to be established there, in the area called Carolina.

The northern part of Carolina developed slowly. It lacked harbors and rivers on which ships could travel easily. Settlers lived on small farms, raising and exporting tobacco. Some produced lumber for shipbuilding.

The southern part of Carolina grew more quickly. Sugar grew well in the swampy lowlands. Many planters came from Barbados in the West Indies. They brought enslaved people to grow sugar. Soon the colonists were using slave labor to grow another crop, rice. It became the area's most important crop.

As rice production spread, Carolina's main city, Charles Town (today's Charleston), eventually became the biggest city in the Southern Colonies. By then, Carolina had become two colonies: North Carolina and South Carolina.

**Georgia** The last of England's 13 colonies, Georgia was founded for two reasons. First, the English feared that Spain was about to expand its Florida colony northward. An English colony south of Carolina would keep the Spanish bottled up in Florida. Second, a group of wealthy Englishmen led by James Oglethorpe wanted a colony where there would be protection for English debtors— people who owe money. Under English laws, the government could imprison debtors until they paid what they owed.

Georgia's founders wanted Georgia to be a colony of small farms, not large plantations. Therefore, slavery was banned. However, this restriction was unpopular with settlers and did not last. By the 1750s, slavery was legal in Georgia.

☑**Checkpoint** **Why did Oglethorpe and the other founders establish the colony of Georgia?**

## Change in the Southern Colonies

During the 1700s, the Southern Colonies developed two distinct ways of life. People along the coast lived very differently from people who settled inland on the frontier.

**The Tidewater Region** The most important feature of life along the coast in the Southern Colonies was the plantation, a large farm especially in a hot country where crops such as cotton, sugar, and rice are grown. This led to an economy dominated by plantations in the Tidewater region. The plantation system began in Virginia and Maryland when settlers started growing tobacco. It spread southward when planters found other crops they could export profitably to Europe.

**Main Idea**
The Tidewater region and the backcountry developed two different ways of life.

## Founding of the 13 Colonies

| Colony / Date Founded | Leader(s) | Reason(s) Founded |
|---|---|---|
| **New England Colonies** | | |
| ■ Massachusetts<br>Plymouth / 1620<br>Massachusetts Bay / 1630 | William Bradford<br>John Winthrop | Religious freedom<br>Religious freedom |
| ■ New Hampshire / 1622 | Ferdinando Gorges<br>John Mason | Profit from trade and fishing |
| ■ Connecticut / 1636 | Thomas Hooker | Expand trade; religious and political freedom |
| ■ Rhode Island / 1636 | Roger Williams | Religious freedom |
| **Middle Colonies** | | |
| ■ New York / 1624 | Peter Minuit | Expand trade |
| ■ Delaware / 1638 | Swedish settlers | Expand trade |
| ■ New Jersey / 1664 | John Berkeley<br>George Carteret | Expand trade; religious and political freedom |
| ■ Pennsylvania / 1682 | William Penn | Profit from land sales; religious and political freedom |
| **Southern Colonies** | | |
| ■ Virginia / 1607 | John Smith | Trade and farming |
| Maryland / 1634 | Lord Baltimore | Profit from land sales; religious and political freedom |
| ■ The Carolinas / 1663<br>North Carolina / 1712<br>South Carolina / 1719 | Group of eight proprietors | Trade and farming |
| ■ Georgia / 1733 | James Oglethorpe | Profit; home for debtors; buffer against Spanish Florida |

### Reading Charts
#### Skills Activity

By 1733, England had established 13 colonies on the Atlantic coast of North America. These colonies were founded for a variety of reasons.

**(a) Interpret a Chart** Identify one Middle Colony and one Southern Colony founded for religious reasons.

**(b) Understand Sequence** How many English colonies were there by 1700?

The Tidewater region in South Carolina and Georgia was well suited for rice. However, rice-growing required large numbers of workers laboring in hot, humid, unhealthy conditions. This was one reason rice-farming helped promote the spread of slavery. In time, the enslaved population outnumbered the free population of South Carolina.

The plantation system did not just create a society of slaveholders and enslaved people in the Tidewater. It also divided the white community into a small group of wealthy people and a much larger group with little or no property, most of whom were poor and lived in the backcountry South.

**The Backcountry** The backcountry was cut off from the coast by poor roads and long distances. Families usually lived on isolated farms. They often did not legally own the land they farmed. Many families lived in simple one-room shacks. Few families had servants or enslaved people to help them with their work. Women and girls worked in the fields with the men and boys.

In the backcountry, people cared less about rank. Life in the backcountry provided a sharp <u>contrast</u> to life near the coast. As a result, backcountry people believed that the colonial governments on the coast did not care about them. They thought that colonial government cared only about protecting the wealth of the Tidewater plantation owners.

**Vocabulary** *Builder*
<u>contrast</u> (KAHN trast) *n.* difference shown between things when compared

☑**Checkpoint**  **How did people live in the backcountry?**

⭐ **Looking Back and Ahead**  As you have seen, the English colonies developed along distinct regional lines. But Spain, too, was competing for influence in North America. It had started its own colonies long before the English arrived.

---

**Section 4 | Check Your Progress**

**Progress Monitoring** 🌐nline
**For:** Self-test with instant help
**Visit:** PHSchool.com
**Web Code:** mva-1034

**Comprehension and Critical Thinking**

1. (a) **Summarize** How did the geography of the Southern Colonies affect the kinds of crops that were grown there?
(b) **Draw Conclusions** Why did the struggle for rich farmland affect the colonists in Virginia?

2. (a) **Recall** Why did Lord Baltimore want Maryland's Act of Toleration?
(b) **Compare** How would you compare the motives of Lord Baltimore in founding the colony of Maryland with those of James Oglethorpe in founding Georgia?

**Reading Skill**

3. **Compare and Contrast** Compare and contrast the Tidewater and the backcountry regions of the Southern Colonies.

**Vocabulary** *Builder*

Read each sentence. If the sentence is true, write YES. If the sentence is not true, write NO and explain why.
4. Debtors could not be imprisoned under English law.
5. There were many plantations where crops such as wheat, fruits, and vegetables were grown.

**Writing**

6. List the different groups of people living in the Southern Colonies between 1620 and the 1700s. Write two or three sentences about each group.

# Spanish Colonies on the Borderlands

## Objectives

1. Describe Spain's colony in Florida.
2. Explain how Spain established settlements throughout much of North America.
3. Describe the significance of the Spanish missions.

## Prepare to Read

### Reading Skill

**Compare and Contrast Across Sections** The colonies discussed in Sections 1 through 4 were settled primarily by people from the British Isles. Section 5 discusses Spain's colonies in North America. Recall information from Sections 1 through 4 in order to compare and contrast the English colonies with those of Spain. Examine the text in Section 5 to ask: How are these similar to or different from the colonies discussed in Sections 1 through 4?

### Vocabulary *Builder*

**High-Use Words**

**function**, p. 91
**convert**, p. 91

**Key Terms and People**

borderland, p. 91
Junípero Serra, p. 92
presidio, p. 92
pueblo, p. 93

⭐ **Background Knowledge** While the English colonies were forming along the coast, Spanish colonies in the Americas were already hundreds of years old. Spain had planted colonies in the Caribbean, Mexico, and South America. Spain's first colonies in the area that is today the United States were established on the peninsula of Florida.

**Main Idea**
Spain established a colony in Florida decades before English settlers arrived in North America.

Fort at St. Augustine

## Spanish Florida

Spanish explorers reached Florida early in the 1500s. In 1565, fearing that France might take over the area, Spain built a fort called St. Augustine in northern Florida. It was the first permanent European settlement in what is now the United States.

As English colonies spread southward, Spanish control was threatened. To weaken the English colonies, in 1693, the Spanish announced that enslaved Africans who escaped to Florida would be protected. They would be given land if they helped to defend the colony. During the 1700s, hundreds of enslaved African Americans fled to Florida.

Spain's Florida colony grew slowly. By 1763, there were only three major Spanish settlements there. All were centered around forts, and all were in the north. The Spanish had little control over the rest of Florida.

✓**Checkpoint** Why did the Spanish colonize Florida?

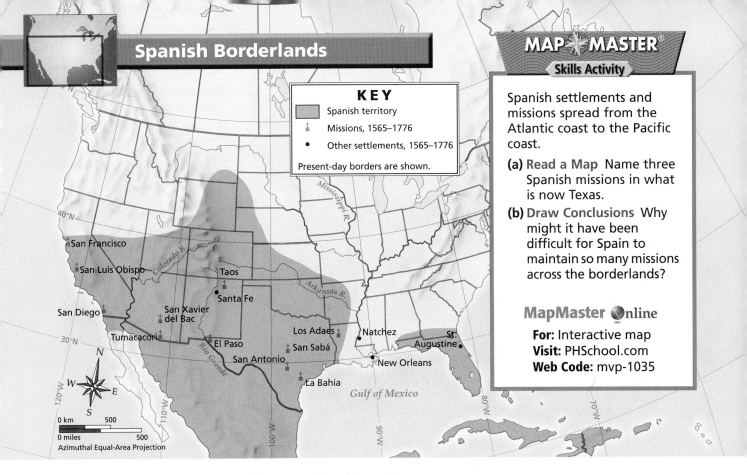

## Spanish Borderlands

**MAP MASTER®**
**Skills Activity**

Spanish settlements and missions spread from the Atlantic coast to the Pacific coast.

**(a) Read a Map** Name three Spanish missions in what is now Texas.

**(b) Draw Conclusions** Why might it have been difficult for Spain to maintain so many missions across the borderlands?

**MapMaster** ●**nline**
**For:** Interactive map
**Visit:** PHSchool.com
**Web Code:** mvp-1035

**KEY**
Spanish territory
Missions, 1565–1776
Other settlements, 1565–1776
Present-day borders are shown.

# Settling the Spanish Borderlands

Spain's most important colonies were in Mexico and South America. Its territories north of Mexico were called the borderlands, meaning lands along a frontier. The main <u>function</u> of the Spanish borderlands was to protect Mexico from other European powers.

The borderlands began in the east with Florida. Farther west, they included most of Texas, New Mexico, Arizona, Colorado, Utah, Nevada, and California. This vast area differs greatly from place to place with humid lowlands in Texas and deserts and mountains in New Mexico, Arizona, and Utah. Colorado has highlands and mountains, while California has deserts in its southeast corner.

**Juan de Oñate in New Mexico** The first Spanish explorers did not start permanent settlements. Then, in 1598, Juan de Oñate (WAN day ohn YAH tay) led an expedition into New Mexico. He aimed to find gold, <u>convert</u> Native Americans to Christianity, and establish a permanent colony. Oñate never found gold, but in 1598 he established Spain's first permanent settlement in the region at Santa Fe.

Oñate brought more than 300 horses. At their settlements, the Spanish used Native Americans to look after the horses. When some Native Americans ran away from the Spanish, they spread the skill of horseback riding from one Native American group to another. This skill forever changed the lives of the Native Americans of the region.

The Native Americans suffered under Spanish rule. In 1680, several groups in New Mexico rebelled and drove the Spanish from the region. After that defeat, the Spanish did not return for more than 10 years.

**Main Idea**
Spain controlled much of North America during the 1600s and early 1700s.

**Vocabulary Builder**
<u>function</u> (FUHNK shuhn) *n.* purpose; proper use; official duty

**Vocabulary Builder**
<u>convert</u> (kuhn VERT) *v.* to change from one religion to another

## A Mission: Then and Now

**History *Interactive***

**Explore an Arizona Mission**
Visit: PHSchool.com
Web Code: myp-6152

**A Mission: Then and Now**
The Tumacácori Mission in southern Arizona was founded in 1691 and rebuilt in 1800. It looks much as it did when Henry Cheever Pratt portrayed it in 1855 (at left). The mission is now a National Historical Park. **Critical Thinking: *Draw Conclusions*** *Why are abandoned missions like this one considered important to the history of the U.S. Southwest?*

**Missions in Texas and Arizona** Roman Catholic missionaries played a key role in colonizing the borderlands. To win Native Americans to Christianity, they established missions—religious settlements that aim to spread a religion into a new area. At the missions, priests taught about Catholicism and made Native Americans work by set rules. The missionary who led the way in spreading Spanish influence in what today is Arizona and Texas was Father Eusebio Francisco Kino.

At first, the Spanish had little success. The only early mission that took root in Texas was about 150 miles north of the Rio Grande. Although the mission failed to convert many Native Americans, it did attract Spanish colonists. This mission became the city of San Antonio.

**Missions Along the California Coast** Spain's California missions were especially important. Spain began colonizing California in 1769. A missionary named Junípero Serra (hoo NEE peh roh SEHR rah) played an important role in that effort. His first mission, just north of today's Mexican-American border, eventually became the city of San Diego. Serra later established other missions, including those located in what is now San Francisco and Los Angeles. Altogether, the Spanish founded almost 20 missions in California between 1769 and 1800.

**Presidios and Pueblos** Along with missionaries, Spain sent soldiers. They set up presidios—military posts—to defend the missions.

**Compare and Contrast Across Sections**
Compare and contrast the role of religion in the Spanish settlements with that in the Southern Colonies and New England.

The Spanish also established what they called pueblos—civilian towns. The pueblos were centers of farming and trade. In the middle of the town was a plaza, or public square. Here, townspeople and farmers came to do business or to worship at the church. Church, shops, and homes lined the four sides of the plaza.

☑**Checkpoint** **What role did missionaries play in Spain's expanding North American empire?**

## Life in Spanish Missions

Thousands of Native Americans labored at Spanish missions. They farmed, built churches, and learned a wide range of crafts. The Native Americans were not overworked by Spanish standards of the time. They worked from five to eight hours per day and five or six days per week. They did not work on Sundays or religious holidays.

However, the Native Americans did not have control over their lives. The missionaries punished them harshly if the Native Americans violated mission rules. Native Americans were imprisoned and often kept in shackles or whipped while tied to whipping posts.

Native Americans often rebelled against such treatment. Meanwhile, their population fell as thousands died because of poor living conditions and European diseases.

☑**Checkpoint** **Why did some Native Americans rebel against rules set by missionaries?**

⭐ **Looking Back and Ahead** Spain had now built a vast empire in the Americas. But the 13 English colonies were destined to grow, too. New frictions would develop within the English Empire as it grew.

**Main Idea**
Spain established missions to convert Native Americans and to teach them farming and crafts skills.

Section 5 | **Check Your Progress**

**Progress Monitoring** Online
**For:** Self-test with instant help
**Visit:** PHSchool.com
**Web Code:** mva-1035

**Comprehension and Critical Thinking**

1. (a) **Identify** Where is Saint Augustine located?
(b) **Draw Conclusions** Why do you think the colony failed to attract settlers?

2. (a) **Summarize** Why were the borderlands important to Spain?
(b) **Apply Information** How did the importance of the borderlands influence the way Spain ruled this region?

3. (a) **Recall** How did Junípero Serra help establish Spain's presence in the Americas?
(b) **Link Past and Present** In what way have the early Spanish missions influenced today's Americans?

🔊 **Reading Skill**

4. **Compare and Contrast Across Sections** Compare and contrast the experiences of Native Americans in Spanish settlements and in English colonies.

**Vocabulary** *Builder*

5. Draw a table with two rows and three columns. In the first column, list the following key terms from this section: presidio, pueblo. In the next column, write a definition of each word. In the last column, make a small illustration that shows the meaning of each word.

**Writing**

6. Review the table you created in Vocabulary Builder. Add a column to the table. Write two or three sentences for each key term. Explain how it relates to the settlement of Spanish colonies in the Americas.

Historians use primary sources to find out information about the past from people who lived during that period. A primary source is firsthand information about people or historical events. The following primary source describes events that took place near the Jamestown Colony in 1608.

This selection is from John Smith's book *A Generall Historie of Virginia, New-England, and the Summer Isles*, published in 1624. It describes his capture by Native Americans and his rescue by Pocahontas, the daughter of the Indian chief Powhatan. Using the writing style of this period of history, Smith refers to himself in the third person, using "he" or "him" instead of "I" or "me."

**Primary Source**

". . . Finding he was beset with 200 savages, two of them he slew still defending himself with the aid of a savage, his guide, . . . yet he was shot in his thigh a little, and had many arrows that stuck in his clothese; but no great hurt, til at last they took him prisoner.

Six or seven weeks those barbarians kept him prisoner, . . . yet he . . . diverted them from surprising the fort . . . [gained] his own liberty, and got himself and his company such estimation among them that those savages admired him more than their own *quiyouckosuchs* [gods]. . . .

1608 At last they brought him to . . . Powhatan, their emperor. . . . Having feasted him after their best barbarous manner they could, a long consultation was held, but the conclusion was: two great stones were brought before Powhatan; then as many as could laid hands on him, dragged him to them, and thereon laid his head, and being ready with their clubs to beat out his brains, Pocahontas, the king's dearest daughter, . . . got his head in her arms, and laid her own upon his to save him from death."

## Learn the Skill

*Use these steps to read a primary source.*

❶ **Identify the source.** Ask questions that help you identify the writer or speaker.

❷ **Identify the author's purpose for writing.** Often, eyewitnesses might want to inform or persuade the reader to share their views.

❸ **Recognize the author's point of view.** Distinguish between facts and the author's opinion.

❹ **Evaluate whether the source is reliable.** Consider who wrote the primary source and the information presented. Compare this information with what you know about the subject.

## Practice the Skill

*Answer the following questions about the primary source on this page.*

❶ **Identify the source.** (a) Who wrote this excerpt? (b) When did the events occur?

❷ **Identify the author's purpose for writing.** Why did the author write this source?

❸ **Recognize the author's point of view.** What is the author's opinion of Native Americans?

❹ **Evaluate whether the source is reliable.** Is this a reliable source for learning about the history of the Jamestown Colony? Explain.

## Apply the Skill

*See the Review and Assessment at the end of this chapter.*

## Chapter Summary

### Section 1
**The First English Settlements**

- The English colony at Jamestown is founded in 1607.
- English Pilgrims seeking religious freedom settled the Plymouth Colony.

### Section 2
**The New England Colonies**

- Puritans seeking religious freedom settled the Massachusetts Bay Colony in 1630.
- People unhappy with the Puritans' religious intolerance founded Rhode Island, Connecticut, and New Hampshire.

### Section 3
**The Middle Colonies**

- After the English takeover, New Netherlands was renamed New York.
- Pennsylvania was founded in 1681 by a Quaker, William Penn.

### Section 4
**The Southern Colonies**

- Maryland was founded as a colony where Catholics could worship freely.
- Large plantations marked the Tidewater region, and small farms dominated the backcountry.

### Section 5
**Spanish Colonies on the Borderlands**

- Spain had large colonies in the Caribbean, Mexico, and South America.
- Spanish missions sought to convert Native Americans to Christianity.
- Spain established presidios and pueblos throughout the borderlands.

## Key Concepts

These notes will help you prepare for questions about key concepts.

### Why English Colonies Were Founded

- Religious and Political Freedom: Plymouth; Massachusetts Bay; Rhode Island; Connecticut; New Hampshire; New Jersey; Pennsylvania; Maryland; the Carolinas; Georgia
- Economic Reasons (trade; farming): Virginia; the Carolinas; Georgia
- Other Reasons (conquest; political division): New York; New Jersey; Delaware

### Why Spanish Colonies Were Founded

- Political Reasons (establish/maintain empire): Florida; Spanish borderlands

### Principles of Government in English Colonies

- Elected assemblies
- Right to vote restricted to certain groups of colonists
- Colonial governors
- Town meetings in each Puritan town

### How Spain Controlled Colonies in the Americas

- In Florida: forts; settlements
- In borderlands: religious missions; military presidios; pueblos

## Vocabulary *Builder*

### Key Terms

Answer the following questions in complete sentences that show your understanding of the key terms.

1. How did the charter of the Virginia Company help the colonization of the Americas?

2. What problems resulted because Puritans did not believe in religious toleration?

3. What groups settled in the backcountry?

4. How did town meetings affect the governing of New England colonies?

5. Why was New Jersey a royal colony?

## Comprehension and Critical Thinking

6. **(a) Recall** What was the Mayflower Compact?
**(b) Apply Information** Why do you think the Mayflower Compact is an important part of our country's history?

7. **(a) Identify** Who were the Puritans and the Pilgrims?
**(b) Compare and Contrast** How would you compare and contrast the Pilgrims and Puritans?
**(c) Synthesize** Do you think Puritans and Pilgrims would worship together in America? Explain.

8. **(a) Summarize** How does the Edward Hicks painting below show the nature of William Penn's dealings with Native Americans?
**(b) Contrast** How would you contrast the way colonists in Pennsylvania and in Massachusetts got along with Native Americans?

9. **(a) Identify** How was land farmed in the Tidewater region and in the Virginia backcountry?
**(b) Draw Conclusions** Would a farmer living in the Tidewater or in the backcountry be more likely to support the Virginia government? Explain.

### History Reading Skill

10. **Compare and Contrast** Choose any two colonies from among those discussed in Chapter 3. Make a list of three important features of the colonies. Then, compare and contrast these features in the two colonies you have chosen.

## Writing

11. **Write two paragraphs on the following topic:** Describe the factors that led to the establishment of English and Spanish colonies in the Americas.

12. **Write a Dialogue:**
Write a conversation that Roger Williams might have had with William Penn. Include issues about how their colonies were settled.

## Skills for Life

### Read a Primary Source

Use the primary source below by William Bradford, governor of the Plymouth Colony, to answer the questions that follow.

> [1621] "[What] was most sad and lamentable was that in two or three months' time, half of their company died, . . . being infected with the scurvy and other diseases. . . . [I]n the time of most distress, there were but six or seven sound persons who . . . spared no pains night or day, but with abundance of toil and hazard to their own health fetched them wood, made them fires . . . made their beds . . . and all this willingly . . . without any grudging in the least."
>
> —from the book *Of Plymouth Plantation, 1620–1647*, by William Bradford

13. Who wrote these observations?

14. Why did the author write this source?

15. How does the author show his feeling about the people who cared for the sick colonists?

16. Do you think the author gives an accurate view of the events? Why?

# Test Yourself

1. **Which of the following established the right of American colonists to govern themselves?**

   **A** mercantilism

   **B** pueblo

   **C** proprietary colony

   **D** Mayflower Compact

2. **The followers of Nathaniel Bacon**

   **A** supported the governor of Virginia.

   **B** had a profitable fur trade with the Native Americans.

   **C** were poor farmers seeking good farmland.

   **D** were fully represented in the House of Burgesses.

3. **What geographical feature helped New England colonists?**

   **A** long growing seasons

   **B** mountains

   **C** natural harbors

   **D** fertile soil

**Refer to the passage below to answer Question 4.**

> Roger Williams said that **"**God Land will be as great a God with us English as God Gold was with the Spanish.**"**

4. **Which event can be judged as a result of the colonists' push for land in the Americas?**

   **A** Spanish missions in Florida

   **B** King Philip's War

   **C** the settlement of Pennsylvania

   **D** the establishment of presidios

# Document-Based Questions

**Task:** Look at Documents 1 and 2, and answer their accompanying questions. Then, use the documents and your knowledge of history to complete this writing assignment:

> Write a short essay explaining why these two documents were important in the development of democratic government in America.

**Document 1:** The Ordinance for Virginia, dated July 24, 1619, called for the creation of an assembly chosen by and made up of colonists. The House of Burgesses, as the assembly is known, marked the beginning of representative government in America. *What powers did the Burgesses have?*

> **"**And this General Assembly shall have free Power . . . to make, ordain, and enact such general Laws and Orders, for the Behoof [good] of the said Colony, and the good government thereof. . . .**"**

**Document 2:** In 1620, the Pilgrims arrived in America. While still aboard the *Mayflower,* they drew up and signed the Mayflower Compact. *What powers did the Mayflower Compact give the Plymouth settlers?*

> **"**We . . . combine ourselves together into a civil Body Politick, . . . [to] enact, constitute, and frame, such just and equal Laws, Ordinances, Acts, Constitutions and Offices, from time to time, as shall be thought most meet and convenient for the general Good of the Colony; unto which we promise all due Submission and Obedience.**"**

## Chapter Preview

Government and daily life in England's 13 North American colonies were shaped by European ideas. Still, by the mid-1700s, the colonies had developed their own ideas and traditions.

☑ **What You Will Learn**

English ideas about government, individual rights, and trade deeply affected colonial life.

Although colonial society was divided into different social and economic classes, it was far less rigid than European society of the time.

By the 1700s, slavery had become a part of American life, serving the economic interests of both northern traders and southern planters.

Religion played a key role in colonial life, while the European Enlightenment influenced scientific and political thought.

**U.S. Events**

**1647**
Massachusetts requires large towns to have public schools.

**1663**
First major slave revolt occurs in Gloucester, Virginia.

**1700s**
Triangular slave trade brings increasing numbers of enslaved Africans to the colonies.

**1650**

**1675**

**1700**

**World Events**

**1650s** Parliament passes Navigation Acts.

**1689** English Bill of Rights is issued.

This needlework depicts the fine clothing and refined manners of wealthy colonists. Most members of colonial society did not enjoy such an elegant lifestyle.

**Quick View Video**
View the chapter video for a quick preview of the main ideas.

**1730s**
The Great Awakening sweeps through the colonies.

**1735**
The Zenger case marks a step toward freedom of the press.

**1750**
Georgia becomes last of colonies to permit slavery.

1700

1725

1750

**1700s** The Enlightenment influences European intellectual thought.

**1748** Montesquieu's *The Spirit of the Laws* argues for separation of powers.

## History Reading Skill  Determine Meaning From Context

### How was life in the colonies dangerous?

In this chapter, you will practice using context to determine word meaning. Read the following description of early life in colonial Virginia. The side notes show you how to use context to determine word meaning.

> As you have read, Bacon's Rebellion broke out in 1676 due to a conflict between frontier settlers and the government in colonial Virginia. Below is an excerpt of a report of the incident.
>
> In these frightful times the most exposed small families withdrew into our houses, which we fortified with palisades and redoubts. . . . No man stirred out of doors unarmed. Indians were sighted . . . . I rarely heard of any houses burnt, . . . or other injury done, besides murders. . . .
>
> Frequent complaints of bloodshed were sent to Sir William Berkeley, the governor . . . . [The people] grew impatient at the many slaughters of their neighbors. They rose for their own defense, choosing Mr. Bacon for their leader.
>
> During these delays, with people often slain, the officers and 300 men, led by Mr. Bacon, met. They discussed the danger of going on without a commission on the one part, and the continual murder of their neighbors on the other part. . . . This day ended and no commission came. So they marched into the wilderness in quest of these Indians. . . . [T]he Governor sent his proclamation, denouncing all rebels who should not return within a limited time. Most obeyed.
>
> —*Beginning, Progress and Conclusion of Bacon's Rebellion in Virginia.*

*Palisades* and *redoubts* are nouns; they must be things used to fortify or protect a home.

The familiar word part *fort* suggests that *fortified* means "made strong, like a fort." A preceding clue, *frightful times,* confirms that meaning.

Personal knowledge can help. Artists get *commissions*, army officers get *commissions*; both are payments.

Read on for information. A description of why someone would be denounced follows. *Denouncing* means "criticizing or condemning, usually in public."

Unfamiliar word

### Determine Meaning From Context

- Clues such as familiar base words and parts of speech can suggest a word's meaning.
- Surrounding sentences may include examples or descriptions of an unfamiliar word, as well as familiar related words or synonyms.
- Consider how the word is used today.
- Ask: What does the word do?

### Document-Based Questions

1. Who might have been the author of these paragraphs?
2. Does the author seem to think Bacon's actions were justified?
3. How might a Native American's report on the same events differ from this text?

# Vocabulary *Builder*

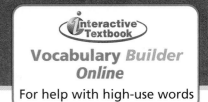

**Vocabulary *Builder***
*Online*
For help with high-use words

## Previewing High-Use Academic Words

| High-Use Word | Definition | Sample History Sentence |
|---|---|---|
| **levy** (LEHV ee) (Section 1, p. 102) | *v.* to impose (a tax, for example); to force to be paid | In the federal government, Congress holds the power to <u>levy</u> taxes. |
| **retain** (ree TAYN) (Section 1, p. 103) | *v.* to keep | The British government <u>retained</u> final say in colonial affairs. |
| **domestic** (doh MEHS tihk) (Section 2, p. 108) | *adj.* having to do with the home or household; pertaining to a country's internal affairs | The children busied themselves with <u>domestic</u> duties such as sweeping the floor and cooking dinner. |
| **prospect** (PRAHS pehkt) (Section 2, p. 110) | *n.* expectation; something to look forward to happening | The <u>prospect</u> of a brighter future drew many immigrants to America. |
| **maximum** (MAK sah mahm) (Section 3, p. 113) | *adj.* largest; highest; greatest | Business people seek to make the <u>maximum</u> possible profit on their investments. |
| **revolt** (ree VOHLT) (Section 3, p. 116) | *v.* to rebel; to participate in an uprising | Slave owners feared that angry slaves might <u>revolt</u> against their enslavement. |
| **finance** (FĪ nans) (Section 4, p. 120) | *v.* to supply with money; to manage monetary situations | People often seek a bank loan to <u>finance</u> the purchase of a home. |
| **reinforce** (ree ihn FORS) (Section 4, p. 122) | *v.* to make stronger; to strengthen; to make more effective | The army <u>reinforced</u> its defenses in anticipation of an attack. |

## Previewing Key Terms and People

Benjamin Franklin

# Governing the Colonies

## Objectives

1. Explain how English political traditions influenced the 13 colonies.

2. Describe the responsibilities of early colonial governments.

3. Identify John Peter Zenger's role in establishing freedom of the press.

4. Understand how the Navigation Acts affected the colonies' economy.

## Prepare to Read

### Reading Skill

**Use Word Clues to Analyze Meaning** When you encounter an unfamiliar word, look for clues within the word itself. For example, to understand the term *notable*, the familiar word *note* is helpful. If *note* means "to notice or remember," then *notable* may mean "worth remembering or noticing." Also, consider whether the word seems to be a verb, an adjective, or a noun.

### Vocabulary *Builder*

**High-Use Words**

**levy,** p. 102

**retain,** p. 103

**Key Terms**

legislature, p. 103

bill of rights, p. 103

habeas corpus, p. 104

freedom of the press, p. 105

libel, p. 105

**Main Idea**
As English subjects, colonists believed they had political rights and protections.

**Vocabulary *Builder***
**levy** (LEHV ee) *v.* to impose (a tax, for example); to force to be paid

⭐ **Background Knowledge** In the previous chapter, you learned that the New England, the Middle, and the Southern colonies developed in unique ways. However, all three regions shared a common heritage. In this section, we will see how English ideas about government and trade took root in the colonies.

## The English Parliamentary Tradition

The English colonists brought with them the idea that they had political rights. This idea was rooted in English history.

**Magna Carta** In 1215, English nobles forced King John to sign the Magna Carta, the Latin name meaning "great charter." The Magna Carta was the first document to place restrictions on an English ruler's power. It limited the monarch's right to levy taxes without consulting the nobles. It also protected the right to own private property and guaranteed the right to trial by jury:

> **❝**31. Neither we nor our [officials] shall take, for our castles or for any other work of ours, wood which is not ours, against the will of the owner of that wood....
>
> 39. No free man shall be taken or imprisoned . . . except by the lawful judgment of his peers, or by the law of the land.**❞**
>
> —Magna Carta

The rights listed in the Magna Carta were at first limited to nobles. Over time, the rights were extended to all English citizens.

**Parliament** Under the Magna Carta, nobles formed a Great Council to advise the king. This body developed into the English Parliament (PAHR luh mehnt). Parliament was a two-house legislature. A legislature is a group of people who have the power to make laws. The House of Lords was made up of nobles, most of whom inherited their titles. Members of the House of Commons were elected. Only a few rich men and landowners had the right to vote for the House of Commons.

Parliament's greatest power was the right to approve new taxes. No monarch could raise taxes without the consent of Parliament. This "power of the purse" gave Parliament a degree of control over the monarch.

In the 1640s, power struggles between King Charles I and Parliament led to the English Civil War. Parliamentary forces eventually won the war, executed the king, and briefly ruled England by itself. In 1660, the monarchy was restored. Still, Parliament <u>retained</u> its traditional rights.

**Vocabulary** *Builder*
<u>retain</u> (ree TAYN) *v.* to keep

**English Bill of Rights** An event in 1688 further boosted parliamentary power. Parliament removed King James II from the throne and invited his daughter Mary and her husband William to rule. This was called the Glorious Revolution. In 1689, King William and Queen Mary signed the English Bill of Rights. A bill of rights is a written list of freedoms that a government promises to protect.

## English Bill of Rights

William and Mary

These selections from the English Bill of Rights deal with the powers of Parliament:

4. **"** That levying money for or to the use of the crown . . . without grant of Parliament . . . is illegal; . . .
6. That the raising or keeping a standing army within the kingdom in time of peace, unless it be with the consent of Parliament, is against the law; . . .
8. That election of members of Parliament ought to be free;
9. That the freedom of speech and debates or proceedings in Parliament ought not to be impeached [challenged] or questioned in any court or place out of Parliament. **"**

—English Bill of Rights

### Reading Primary Sources
#### Skills Activity

The English Bill of Rights was issued under William and Mary in 1689. It guaranteed the powers of Parliament and the basic rights of English citizens.

**(a) Interpret a Primary Source**
Summarize item 4 in your own words.

**(b) Draw Conclusions** Why do you think Parliament included item 9 in the Bill of Rights?

The English Bill of Rights restated many of the rights granted by the Magna Carta, such as trial by jury. It upheld habeas corpus, the principle that a person cannot be held in prison without being charged with a specific crime. Finally, the Bill of Rights required that Parliament meet regularly and declared that no monarch could levy taxes or raise an army without the consent of Parliament.

☑Checkpoint  **How was the power of English monarchs limited?**

## Colonial Self-Government

**Main Idea**
White male settlers in the American colonies gained limited rights of self-government.

The legal rights that Englishmen had won over the centuries led the colonists to expect a voice in their government. The ideas of limited monarchy and representative government were dear to them. In their new land, colonists wanted to take part in governing themselves.

**Colonial Legislatures** As you have read, from 1619 the Virginia Company allowed the House of Burgesses to make laws for the Jamestown Colony. The House of Burgesses became the first legislature in British North America. Massachusetts colonists also set up a legislature called the General Court in 1629. Five years later, Massachusetts colonists gained the right to elect delegates to the General Court.

On the other hand, the British government gave William Penn outright ownership of Pennsylvania. The governor and a large council made laws that an assembly could only approve or reject. But the Pennsylvania colonists wanted to draw up laws themselves. In 1701, they forced Penn to agree that only the General Assembly could make laws. The king could overturn laws passed by the General Assembly, but neither Penn nor his council had any part in lawmaking.

By 1760, every British colony in North America had a legislature of some kind. However, the legislatures still clashed at times with the colonial governors appointed by the king.

**The Right to Vote** In many ways, the colonies offered settlers greater political rights than they would have had in England. From 50 to 75 percent of white males in the American colonies could vote. This was a far greater percentage than in England.

Still, the right to vote did not extend to everyone in the colonies. English women—even those who owned property—could not vote in any colony. Neither could the Native Americans who still lived on land claimed by the colonists. Finally, no Africans, whether free or enslaved, could vote.

## Links Across Time

### Making State Laws

**1619** The House of Burgesses became the first colonial legislature. For the next 155 years, the Burgesses helped govern the affairs of the Virginia Colony.
**1776** After the United States declared independence from Britain, Virginia replaced the House of Burgesses with the General Assembly. The other states also set up state legislatures to make laws.

### Link to Today

**State Legislatures Today** There are 50 separate state legislatures operating in the United States. What issues do these lawmakers face?

**For:** State legislatures in the news
**Visit:** PHSchool.com
**Web Code:** mvc-1041

☑Checkpoint  **Which groups of people were permitted to vote in colonial elections? Which were not permitted to vote?**

There are two Sorts of Monarchies; an absolute and a limited one. In the first, the Liberty of the Press can never be maintained ...

# Freedom of the Press

The colonists expected to enjoy the traditional rights of English subjects. A notable court case in 1735 helped establish another important right. This was freedom of the press, the right of journalists to publish the truth without restriction or penalty.

John Peter Zenger, publisher of the *New York Weekly Journal*, was arrested for printing a series of articles that criticized the governor. Zenger was charged with libel, or the publishing of statements that damage a person's reputation. Under modern American law, statements must be untrue in order to be considered libel. However, English law at the time punished writings that criticized the government—even if the statements were true.

At Zenger's trial, Zenger's lawyer, Andrew Hamilton, admitted that Zenger had printed the statements against the governor. However, Hamilton argued that the articles Zenger published were based on fact and, therefore, should not be considered libel. Hamilton told the jury:

> **"**By your verdict, you will have laid a noble foundation for securing to ourselves, our descendants, and our neighbors, the liberty both of exposing and opposing tyrannical power by speaking and writing truth.**"**
>
> —Andrew Hamilton, in A Brief Narrative of the Case and Trial of John Peter Zenger

The jurors agreed. They found that Zenger was not guilty of libel.

The Zenger case later helped establish a fundamental principle. A democracy depends on well-informed citizens. Therefore, the press has a right and responsibility to keep the public informed of the truth. Today, freedom of the press is recognized as a basic American liberty.

☑ **Checkpoint** Why was the Zenger case important?

**Main Idea**
The Zenger trial of 1735 helped to establish the principle that the press can seek and report the truth.

**Use Word Clues to Analyze Meaning**
Use the familiar base word part *tyrant* as a clue to the meaning of *tyrannical*.

**Main Idea**
England's Navigation Acts had a mixed effect, and many colonists came to resent the acts.

# Regulating Trade

As you have read, under the theory of mercantilism, colonies existed in order to serve the economic needs of their parent country. They were a source of raw materials and a place to sell the home country's goods.

In 1651, the English Parliament passed the first of several Navigation Acts to support mercantilism. By these laws: (1) Shipments from Europe to English colonies had to go through England first. (2) Any imports to England from the colonies had to come in ships built and owned by British subjects. (3) The colonies could sell key products, such as tobacco and sugar, only to England. This helped create jobs for English workers.

In many ways, the Navigation Acts benefited the colonies. Colonial traders had a sure market for their goods in England. Also, the law contributed to a booming shipbuilding industry in New England.

Still, as colonial trade expanded, many colonists came to resent the Navigation Acts. In their view, the laws favored English merchants. Colonists felt that they could make more money if they were free to sell to foreign markets themselves. Some colonists got around the Navigation Acts by smuggling—that is, by importing and exporting goods illegally.

A Boston merchant counts up the profits from shipping.

✓**Checkpoint**  Why did many colonists resent the Navigation Acts?

☆ **Looking Back and Ahead**  As the 13 colonies grew, colonists established lawmaking bodies and developed the economy. In the early days, England's monarchy and Parliament influenced the decisions the colonies made. Yet, the colonies were far from England, and colonists were developing their own ideas. In the next section, you will look at the structure of colonial society.

---

**Section 1 | Check Your Progress**

**Progress Monitoring** ⦿nline
**For:** Self-test with instant help
**Visit:** PHSchool.com
**Web Code:** mva-1041

## Comprehension and Critical Thinking

**1. (a) Identify** What political rights had England's citizens won by 1688?
**(b) Apply Information** Why do you think those living in the 13 colonies believed they were entitled to those rights?

**2. (a) Recall** What were the Navigation Acts?
**(b) Identify Economic Costs and Benefits** How did the Navigation Acts affect the colonial economy?

## 🔲 Reading Skill

**3. Use Word Clues to Analyze Meaning** Use its part of speech to help you analyze the meaning of *boomed* in this sentence: As a result of a law that allowed colonists to build their own ships, the shipbuilding industry in New England *boomed*.

## Vocabulary *Builder*

Complete each of the following sentences so that the second part further explains the first part and clearly shows your understanding of the key term.

**4.** Based on English traditions, colonial legislatures _____.
**5.** The English Bill of Rights protected the rights of individuals, including habeas corpus, _____.
**6.** John Peter Zenger was accused of libel, _____.

## Writing

**7.** List at least two examples from colonial society to support this main idea: English colonists believed they should have the same freedoms as English citizens.

# Colonial Society

## Objectives

1. Learn about life on a colonial farm.

2. Describe the roles of men, women, and children in colonial America.

3. List the class differences that existed in colonial society.

## Prepare to Read

### 🔊 Reading Skill

**Use Sentence Clues to Analyze Meaning** To find a word's meaning, you may examine other words within the same sentence for clues. For example, you may find familiar descriptive words near the unfamiliar word or find details that suggest a possible meaning. Ask: How is the unfamiliar word connected to a familiar word in the sentence? How is the word described?

### Vocabulary *Builder*

**High-Use Words**

**domestic**, p. 108

**prospect**, p. 110

**Key Terms**

extended family, p. 107

apprentice, p. 110

gentry, p. 110

middle class, p. 111

indentured servant, p. 111

⭐ **Background Knowledge** In this section, we will see how a common culture united American colonists despite their differences.

## The Family in Colonial Times

The family played an important role in colonial America. Many people lived with their extended families. An **extended family** is a family that includes, in addition to the parents and their children, other members such as grandparents, aunts, uncles, and cousins.

**On a Farm** Most colonists lived on farms, where a large family was considered an advantage. Many hands were needed to operate a farm. Usually, farms were widely separated, often by dense forests. This made it necessary for families to be closely knit and self-sufficient. On a farm, each member of the family had many responsibilities. Family members helped plant, cultivate, and harvest crops. There were always fences to mend, animals to tend, and wood to chop.

By today's standards, farmhouses were not very comfortable. Most were made of wood and had few rooms. People sat on stools or benches and slept on planks. Some houses had mattresses of corncobs. There were few utensils, and they were crudely made. In the New England and the Middle colonies winters were cold, and the only source of heat in each house might be a fireplace in the kitchen room. On cold winter nights, the family might huddle around the fire telling stories and shelling nuts.

### Main Idea

Colonial Americans lived mainly on farms, often in large extended families.

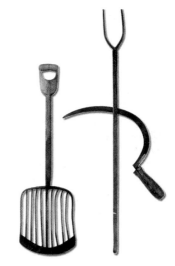

Tools on colonial farms included hay forks, sickles, and potato shovels.

**In a Town** In the colonies' few cities and towns, it was easier for single people to sustain themselves. However, family ties were still held in the highest regard. In Puritan New England, single men and women were expected to live with a family as a servant or a boarder.

☑**Checkpoint** **Why was a large family useful on a farm?**

**Main Idea**
In colonial society, men, women, and children had clearly defined roles.

## Men, Women, and Children

The lives of men and women differed. Even on the frontier, where families had to labor together to survive, men and women generally took on different roles. A North Carolina settler wrote:

> **❝**Men are generally of all trades, and women the like within their spheres. . . . Men are generally carpenters, joiners, wheelwrights, coopers, butchers, tanners, shoemakers, tallow-chandlers, watermen, and what not; women soap-makers, starch-makers, dyers, etc. He or she that cannot do all these things, or has not slaves that can, over and above all the common occupations of both sexes, will have but a bad time of it.**❞**
>
> —John Urmstone, letter, July 7, 1711

A husband and father controlled a family's income and property. Other family members were expected to accept his authority. In addition to fulfilling their home duties, men represented their families in public life as voters and, sometimes, as officeholders.

**Roles of Women** In colonial America, most women were expected to marry men chosen by their parents. In choosing, parents considered a man's property, his religion, and their own family interests. Romantic love was not considered the most important reason for marriage. Furthermore, when a woman married, her property and any money she might earn became her husband's. A woman often bore her husband many children. She was expected to be his faithful helper in every way.

**Vocabulary** *Builder*
domestic (doh MEHS tihk) *adj.* having to do with the home or household; pertaining to a country's internal affairs

Besides childcare, a woman had many <u>domestic</u> responsibilities. She cooked, did the laundry, and spun yarn into cloth that she made into family clothing. Outside, she took care of the garden, milked the cows, tended the chickens, churned butter, and preserved food. If the family had money, she might have help from servants.

Sometimes, however, the line blurred between women's work and men's work. On the western frontier, a woman might help plow or pitch hay. If she lived in a town, she might keep a shop or an inn, or work as a baker, a printer, or even an undertaker. Her husband or sons might help make cloth, if needed.

Women had little or no role in public life. They could not hold office or vote. On the western and southern frontiers, however, the rules were sometimes bent. For example, Mary Musgrove Matthews, a woman of English and Creek ancestry, advised Georgia governor James Oglethorpe on Indian affairs.

# COLONIAL WOMEN

Most women in colonial homes were required to handle a wide variety of tasks. In addition to domestic chores, women often worked in the fields along with the men. **Critical Thinking: *Compare and Contrast*** *How might a woman's responsibilities differ if she lived in a town? How might they be similar?*

**History *Interactive***

**Explore the Lives of Colonial Women**

**Visit:** PHSchool.com
**Web Code:** mvl-1042

▲ **Running the Household**
Women were responsible for running the household and caring for the children. Women were not permitted to vote and were not expected to take part in public affairs.

▲ **Making Clothes**
Women's duties included making most of the clothes worn by their families. Among the gentry, women might wear fancier dresses sewed by professional seamstresses.

◀ **Preparing a Meal**
In colonial times, preparing meals from scratch took a great deal of time and effort.

▲ **Milking the Cows**
Families that owned cows had fresh milk to use and sell.

Children's dolls were made from cornhusks or from more elaborate materials.

**Young People** If they survived infancy, colonial children had about seven years before they were required to work. In these years, they could pass the time playing. Children played many games that are still familiar. Marbles, hopscotch, leapfrog, and jump rope were all popular.

The toys colonial children played with were usually homemade. Girls enjoyed dolls made of cornhusks and scraps of cloth, while boys built houses of corncobs. Sometimes, a spinning top would be fashioned out of a bit of leftover wood and string. Children whose families were well-to-do had fine dolls and toy soldiers that were made in Europe.

By the age of seven, most children had work to do. They might do household or farm chores, or, if they were poor, they might become servants in other families. On farms, children were expected to fetch water and wood and to help in the kitchen and in the fields. Older children had greater responsibilities. Boys were expected to work the fields with their fathers, while girls labored beside their mothers learning how to run a house. Parents believed that tasks like these prepared children for adult life.

Boys who were learning trades, such as making shoes or building furniture, began as apprentices. An apprentice is someone who learns a trade by working for someone in that trade for a certain period of time. The apprentice would live in the home of a master artisan. At the end of his apprenticeship, the young man was prepared to work independently.

☑**Checkpoint**  How did the jobs of boys and girls differ?

## Social Classes

Many European colonists came to America hoping to build a better life than they could have in Europe. In England and other European countries, land was the main measure of wealth. Land in Europe, however, was in the hands of a relative few. America appeared to have land in abundance, offering immigrants the chance to own land. The possibility of owning land played a large part in the appeal of life in America.

In Europe, a person's <u>prospects</u> were determined by birth. Those who were born wealthy generally stayed wealthy. Those who were born poor had little opportunity to improve their station in life. By contrast, in colonial America there was more social equality among settlers—at least among white settlers. Still, there were many class distinctions.

**The Gentry** A group known as the gentry were the upper class of colonial society. The gentry included wealthy planters, merchants, ministers, royal officials, and successful lawyers. Prosperous artisans, like goldsmiths, were often considered gentry as well. The gentry were few in number, but they were the most powerful people. For example, in Virginia, some 50 plantation-owning families held most of the land and power.

**Main Idea**
Colonial society was divided into distinct classes, with a small group of gentry at the top.

**Vocabulary** *Builder*
**prospect** (PRAHS pehkt) *n.*
expectation; something to look forward to happening

In New York, wealthy Dutch estate owners lived in luxury. Their homes featured gold mirrors, clocks, richly carved furniture, and jewels. These things were far beyond the means of ordinary colonists.

Because many official jobs paid no salary, few but the gentry could afford to hold office. They felt that serving the community in public office was both their duty and their right, and most people agreed.

**The Middle Class** The great majority of colonists from Europe were what colonists called "the middling sort." Neither rich nor extremely poor, this middle class was made up of small planters, independent farmers, and artisans. Middle-class men could vote, and a few held office. This middle class was mostly white, but some of its members were of African descent. About 1 percent of African Americans were free during the colonial period.

The growth of the middle class gave the poor something to hope for and work for. The poor who were free might never be rich, but they could always maintain the hope that some day they would be middle class. In this way, the colonies were different from England and the rest of Europe. Not only could people move around the land, they could acquire property and move up the social scale.

**Indentured Servants** Lower on colonial America's social scale, and just above enslaved Africans, were farmhands and indentured servants. An indentured servant signed a contract to work from 4 to 10 years in the colonies for anyone who would pay for his or her ocean passage to the Americas. In the 1600s, most indentured servants came from England. In the 1700s, a growing number came from Ireland and Germany.

**Use Sentence Clues to Analyze Meaning** Who belonged to the middle class in colonial times? What does *middle class* mean?

**Life Among the Gentry**
The gentry lived a more comfortable life than most colonists. Servants attended to many of their needs. **Critical Thinking: Compare and Contrast** *How do the comforts of the family in this picture compare to those of a middle-class family today?*

An indentured servant assists a colonial bricklayer.

During the time of service, indentured servants had few, if any, rights. They were bound to obey their masters, who could work them almost to death. Those who disobeyed or tried to run away risked being whipped or having time added to the service.

At the end of a term, an indentured servant received a set of clothes, tools, and 50 acres of land. About 1 indentured servant in 10 became a prosperous landowner. Another 1 in 10 became an artisan. The others either returned home to Europe or joined a class of landless, poor whites. The hardships they endured drove many poor whites to resent wealthy landowners.

**Free African Americans** Free people of African ancestry were never a large portion of the colonial population. By the time the first census was taken in 1790, there were nearly 60,000 free people of African ancestry, compared with more than 757,000 enslaved.

Free African Americans were allowed to own property, even in the South. This permitted them to become slaveholders. Some free blacks purchased relatives who were enslaved and set them free. Still, the lives of free African Americans were restricted. Most African American property owners were not allowed to vote or sit on juries.

☑ **Checkpoint**  **How might one become a member of the middle class?**

⭐ **Looking Back and Ahead** Life in America offered more opportunities than did life in England. This was especially true for the poor and middle class. However, if indentured servants occupied the lowest level of white society in the English colonies, one group was even more disadvantaged. In the next section, you will look in detail at the enslaved Africans who were brought to America against their will.

---

Section 2 | **Check Your Progress**

**Progress Monitoring** Online
**For:** Self-test with instant help
**Visit:** PHSchool.com
**Web Code:** mva-1042

**Comprehension and Critical Thinking**

1. (a) **Summarize** Describe the responsibilities that children in colonial times were expected to meet.
(b) **Link Past and Present** How do these responsibilities differ from those of children today?
(c) **Draw Conclusions** How might you explain this difference?

2. (a) **Recall** Identify the social classes in colonial society.

(b) **Apply Information** Which two groups had the most privileges and opportunities? Which two groups had the least?

🔵 **Reading Skill**

3. **Use Sentence Clues to Analyze Meaning** Use sentence clues to analyze the meaning of *prospects* in the following sentence: In many countries, a person's *prospects* for success in life are determined by birth.

**Vocabulary** *Builder*

4. Write two definitions for each key term: extended family, apprentice, gentry, middle class, indentured servant. First, write a formal definition for your teacher. Second, write a casual definition for a classmate.

**Writing**

5. Write a paragraph describing the importance of work in colonial society.

# Slavery in the Colonies

## Objectives

1. Describe the conditions under which enslaved Africans came to the Americas.
2. Explain why slavery became part of the colonial economy.
3. Identify the restrictions placed on enslaved Africans in the colonies.
4. Describe how African culture influenced American culture.

## Prepare to Read

### Reading Skill

**Use Paragraph Clues to Analyze Meaning** When you encounter an unfamiliar word, read the nearby sentences for clues. You may find clues in examples or descriptions. Sometimes a nearby sentence includes a contrast clue to what the word *does not* mean.

### Vocabulary *Builder*

**High-Use Words**

**maximum**, p. 113
**revolt**, p. 116

**Key Terms**

triangular trade, p. 115
racism, p. 116
slave code, p. 116

⭐ **Background Knowledge** In a previous chapter, you learned how Spanish settlers first brought Africans to the Americas as a source of slave labor. In this section, you will learn about the development of slavery in the English colonies.

## The Atlantic Slave Trade

Some scholars estimate that more than 10 million enslaved Africans were transported to the Americas between the 1500s and the 1800s. The Spanish and Portuguese brought the first Africans to the Americas. The British, Dutch, and French also entered the slave trade. In time, English colonists—especially from New England—were actively shipping enslaved Africans across the Atlantic.

Slave traders set up posts along the West African coast. Africans who lived along the coast made raids into the interior, seeking captives to sell to the Europeans. Bound at the leg and neck, captives were forced to march as far as 300 miles to the coast. Half of these captives died along the way.

**Middle Passage** Once they arrived at the coasts, captives were traded for guns and other goods. They were then loaded onto slave ships and transported across the Atlantic on a brutal voyage that became known as the Middle Passage.

To increase their profits, some slave-ship captains crammed the maximum number of captives on board. As many as 350 people might be bound together in a tiny space below deck, without light or air. Other captains provided better conditions, in the hope that more captives would survive in good health and fetch a higher price.

**Main Idea**
The Atlantic slave trade became a key part of the colonial economy.

**Vocabulary *Builder***
**maximum** (MAK sah mahm) *adj.*
largest; highest; greatest

# The Atlantic Slave Trade

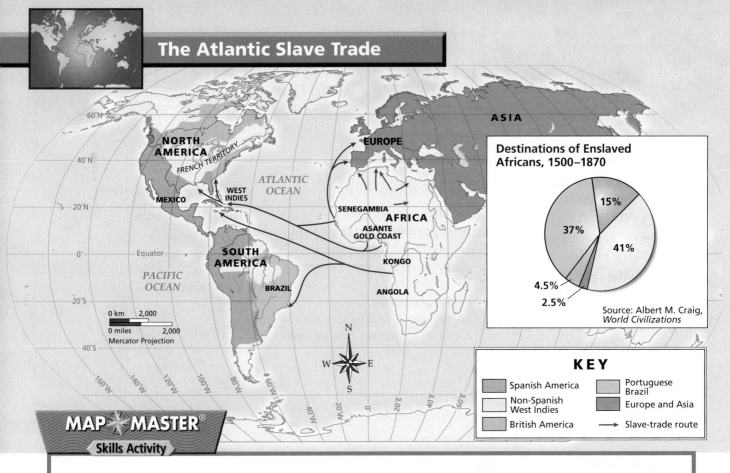

**Destinations of Enslaved Africans, 1500–1870**

15%
37%
41%
4.5%
2.5%

Source: Albert M. Craig, *World Civilizations*

**KEY**

- Spanish America
- Non-Spanish West Indies
- British America
- Portuguese Brazil
- Europe and Asia
- → Slave-trade route

## MAP MASTER®
### Skills Activity

The slave trade linked the Americas with Europe and western Africa.

**(a) Evaluate Information** How did British trade in slaves compare to that of the Spanish and Portuguese?

**(b) Identify Costs** Did the slave trade help or hurt western Africa? Explain your reasoning.

**MapMaster Online**

**For:** Interactive map
**Visit:** PHSchool.com
**Web Code:** mvp-1043

---

**Use Paragraph Clues to Analyze Meaning**
Use the quoted paragraph's description and examples of *inconceivable* to analyze the word's meaning.

Olaudah Equiano told of being captured in western Africa when he was a boy. He later described the conditions aboard a slave ship:

> "The closeness of the place, and the heat of the climate, added to the number in the ship, which was so crowded that each had scarcely room to turn himself, almost suffocated us.... The shrieks of the women, and the groans of the dying, rendered the whole a scene of horror almost inconceivable."
>
> —The Interesting Narrative of the Life of Olaudah Equiano

As a result of such conditions, from 15 to 20 percent of enslaved Africans died or committed suicide during the Middle Passage.

Once slave ships reached the Americas, healthy men, women, and children were put on the auction block. They might be sold one by one or in groups. Family members were often separated at this stage. The vast majority of those sold ended up on plantations in the Spanish colonies, Brazil, or the Caribbean. (See the pie chart above.) But for some 500,000 enslaved Africans, their final destination was British North America.

**Triangular Trade** By about 1700, slave traders in the British colonies had developed a regular routine, known as the triangular trade. The triangular trade was a three-way trade between the colonies, the islands of the Caribbean, and Africa.

On the first leg of the three-leg voyage, ships from New England carried fish, lumber, and other goods to the Caribbean islands, or West Indies. There, Yankee traders bought sugar and molasses, a dark syrup made from sugar cane. The ships then sailed back to New England, where colonists used the molasses and sugar to make rum.

On the second leg, ships carried rum, guns, and other goods from New England to West Africa. There, merchants traded the goods for enslaved Africans. On the final leg, ships carried their human cargo to the West Indies for sale. With the profits from selling enslaved Africans, traders bought more molasses.

Many New England merchants grew wealthy from the triangular trade. In doing so, they often disobeyed the Navigation Acts, which required them to buy only from English colonies. Because demand for molasses was so high, traders also made purchases from the West Indies. They then smuggled their cargoes into New England.

An advertisement for a colonial slave auction

✓Checkpoint  **What was the Middle Passage?**

## Slavery in the Colonies

Slavery had existed since ancient times. However, in many cultures, slavery was not for life. In some early Christian societies, for example, slaves were freed if they became Christians. In many African societies, people captured in war were often enslaved for only a few years. Then, they were freed and became full members of the community. In the Americas, however, a harsher system of slavery developed over time.

**Slavery Takes Root** The first Africans who reached Jamestown may have been treated as servants. But by the late 1600s, ships were bringing growing numbers of enslaved Africans.

Why did slavery take root? One reason was the plantation system. The profits that could be made from tobacco and rice led planters to import thousands of enslaved Africans to work the fields. The southern economy came to depend on slavery.

For planters, slaves were preferable to servants. Indentured servants were temporary. Once their terms were over, they could go. Also, as conditions improved in England, fewer servants came to America.

**Enslaved for Life** As the need for cheap labor grew, colonies made slavery permanent. In 1639, Maryland passed a law stating that baptism did not lead to liberty. This meant people could be enslaved for life. In 1663, a Virginia court held that any child born to a slave was a slave too.

**Main Idea**
The southern economy came to depend on the labor of enslaved Africans.

**Slave Labor** Preparing tobacco was one of the tasks performed by enslaved workers at a Virginia plantation in the 1700s. **Critical Thinking:** *Draw Conclusions* *How did the cultivation of crops such as tobacco and rice encourage the growth of slavery in North America?*

Early on, there were attempts to stop slavery. In 1652, Rhode Island passed the first antislavery law. However, it did not survive long, because Rhode Island shippers made high profits from the slave trade. Georgia had a ban on slavery until the 1750s and then lifted it. Slavery became legal in all the colonies.

Not every African in America was a slave, but slavery came to be restricted to people of African descent. Thus, slavery was linked to racism. **Racism** is the belief that one race is superior or inferior to another. Most English colonists believed themselves superior to Africans. Also, some colonists believed that they were helping Africans by introducing them to Christianity and European ways.

**Resistance to Slavery** As the number of enslaved people grew, whites began to worry that they would <u>revolt</u>. The first serious slave revolt took place in 1663, in Gloucester, Virginia. The rebels were betrayed, probably by an indentured servant, and the uprising failed. Soon, other revolts occurred in Connecticut and Virginia.

Fearing more trouble, colonial authorities wrote **slave codes**, or strict laws that restricted the rights and activities of slaves. Under the codes, enslaved people could not meet in large numbers, own weapons, or leave a plantation without permission. It also became illegal to teach enslaved people to read and write. Masters who killed enslaved people could not be tried for murder. Slave codes gave masters more control over enslaved Africans. It also made it harder for escaped slaves to survive.

The new laws did not stop resistance. In 1739, an enslaved Angolan named Jemmy led a revolt in South Carolina. He and his followers killed more than 20 whites before they were defeated. Revolts continued to flare up until slavery itself ended in 1865.

**Vocabulary** *Builder*
<u>revolt</u> (ree VOHLT) *v.* to rebel; to participate in an uprising

☑**Checkpoint** **What was the purpose of slave codes?**

# African Cultural Influences

The lives of enslaved Africans differed greatly from colony to colony. Only 10 percent of the enslaved population lived north of Maryland. In cities of the North, they were often hired out to work as blacksmiths or house servants. On small farms, they might work alongside the owner. Over time, they might buy their freedom.

Even in the South, the lives of enslaved Africans varied. On rice plantations in South Carolina, Africans saw few white colonists. As a result, more than any other enslaved Africans, these workers kept the customs of West Africa. They reproduced the African grass baskets used to sift rice. They spoke Gullah, a special dialect that was created on the west coast of Africa during slave times. This dialect blended English and several African languages. Even today, some residents of the coastal South speak Gullah.

Enslaved Africans in colonies, such as Virginia and Maryland, were less isolated from white society. Still, many African customs survived. Craftsworkers in cities used African styles to create fine quilts, furniture, carved walking sticks, and other objects. The rhythm of drums used for communication by Africans found its way into American music. The banjo came from Africa as well. African folk tales became a part of American culture.

☑Checkpoint  **What cultural influences did Africans bring to America?**

⭐ **Looking Back and Ahead** In this section, we have seen how millions of Africans were transported to the colonies against their will. In the next section, we shall see how education and religion developed in colonial America.

**Main Idea**
African culture contributed to music, crafts, and other aspects of American life.

African-style banjo from the 1700s

---

Section 3 | **Check Your Progress**

**Progress Monitoring** ●nline
**For:** Self-test with instant help
**Visit:** PHSchool.com
**Web Code:** mva-1043

## Comprehension and Critical Thinking

**1. (a) Recall** Why did fewer indentured servants come to America in the 1700s?
**(b) Analyze Cause and Effect** How did the plantation system and the lack of indentured servants affect the status of Africans in America?

**2. (a) Identify** Why did the Gullah dialect develop in South Carolina?
**(b) Compare and Contrast** In general, how did the experience of enslaved Africans in the North differ from that of enslaved Africans in the South?

## Reading Skill

**3. Use Paragraph Clues to Analyze Meaning** Some paragraphs give you examples and descriptions of unfamiliar words. Reread the second paragraph under the heading "African Cultural Influences." Use paragraph clues to explain the meaning of *dialect* in that context. Explain the clues you used.

## Vocabulary *Builder*

Answer the following questions in complete sentences that show your understanding of the key terms.
**4.** What was triangular trade?

**5.** How did racism affect the status of Africans in America?
**6.** Why did white colonists create slave codes?

## Writing

**7.** Create an outline for an essay that discusses the geographic and economic factors that resulted in some colonies using slave labor more than other colonies.

## Objectives

1. Describe the education colonial children received.

2. Summarize the development of poetry and literature in colonial America.

3. Explain how the Great Awakening affected the colonies.

4. Explain how the colonies were affected by the spread of new ideas.

## Prepare to Read

### Reading Skill

**Use Context to Determine Meanings** When the clues you have tried do not work, broaden the context. Where else might you have encountered this word? Do you remember it from films or books? Was it defined in previous sections? Can you find examples of it elsewhere? Finally, imagine yourself in a situation like the one in which the word appears.

### Vocabulary *Builder*

**High-Use Words**

finance, p. 120

reinforce, p. 122

**Key Terms and People**

public school, p. 118

dame school, p. 119

Anne Bradstreet, p. 120

Phillis Wheatley, p. 120

Benjamin Franklin, p. 120

Jonathan Edwards, p. 121

natural rights, p. 122

divine right, p. 122

separation of powers, p. 123

⭐ **Background Knowledge** As you have read, the Puritans set up a government based on religion. In this section, you will see the impact of Puritan ideas on education. You will also read about a religious movement that swept the colonies.

## The Importance of Education

To Puritans, education went hand in hand with religion. In early New England, everyone was expected to read the Bible.

**Main Idea**
Schools and colleges in the early colonies were influenced by religion, and the majority of students were white males.

**Puritan Beginnings** The Puritans passed laws to promote education. They required parents to teach their children and servants to read. Another law required every town with at least 50 families to start an elementary school. Every town with 100 families had to have a grammar school for older students.

These Massachusetts laws were the beginning of public schools in America. A public school is a school supported by taxes. Puritan schools were very different from the public schools of today, however. Puritan schools were run with both private and public money. In addition, Puritan education laws were not completely compulsory. Some towns paid a fine rather than set up a school. Laws that required all children to attend school did not begin until the late 1800s.

### Reading Skill
**Use Context to Determine Meaning**
Use the clues in the surrounding sentences and your own knowledge about education today to determine the meaning of the word *compulsory*.

**Colonial Schools** Another difference between colonial schools and modern public schools is that colonial schools included instruction in religion. Most schools in the 1600s were under religious sponsorship. Schools in New Netherland (later New York) were run by the Dutch Reformed Church. Pennsylvania schools were run by the Quakers.

In addition to religion, colonial elementary schools taught basic skills such as reading, writing, and arithmetic. Many students learned lessons from a hornbook, a paddle-shaped board with a printed lesson on top, protected by a transparent piece of animal horn. The hornbook might have the ABCs, the Roman numerals, and the Lord's Prayer so that children could copy and memorize them. A reading book called the *New England Primer,* first published in the 1680s, became widely used.

In the South, people were separated by great distances, so there were few schools. Members of the gentry often hired private tutors to instruct their children. Children from poorer families often received no formal education at all.

Some colonial elementary schools admitted girls. Others taught them only in summers or when boys were not in school. Girls might also attend **dame schools**, schools that women opened in their homes to teach girls and boys to read and write.

## Education for African Americans

Most colonial schools were restricted to white children. However, in New York, an Anglican church group ran a school for free African Americans, as well as for Native Americans and poor whites.

Some Quaker and Anglican missionaries taught enslaved people to read. After slave codes in the South outlawed this, some enslaved people passed along their learning in secret. Still others taught themselves from stolen or borrowed books.

**Colonial Education**

Young children were often educated in dame schools, such as the one shown. **Critical Thinking: Evaluate Information** *Look at the page from the* New England Primer, *below. What kinds of lessons does it include?*

Now the Child being entered in his Letters and Spelling, let him learn these and such like Sentences by Heart, whereby he will be both instructed in his Duty, and encouraged in his Learning.

*The Dutiful Child's Promises.*

I Will fear GOD, and honour the KING.
I will honour my Father & Mother.
I will Obey my Superiours.
I will Submit to my Elders.
I will Love my Friends.
I will hate no Man.
I will forgive my Enemies, and pray to God for them.
I will as much as in me lies keep all God's Holy Commandments.

Hornbook ▶

▲ Page from the *New England Primer*

**Upper Levels** After elementary school, some boys went on to grammar school. Grammar schools were similar to modern high schools. They prepared boys for college. Students learned Greek and Latin, as well as geography, mathematics, and English composition.

The first American colleges were founded largely to educate men for the ministry. The Puritan general council <u>financed</u> what became Harvard College. Opening in 1638, Harvard was the first college in the English colonies. In 1693, colonists in Virginia founded the College of William and Mary, the first college in the South.

☑**Checkpoint** **How did education differ for girls and boys?**

## Roots of American Literature

The earliest forms of colonial literature were sermons and histories. Books such as John Smith's *General History of Virginia* and William Bradford's *Of Plymouth Plantation* provided lively accounts of life in the first colonies.

**Poetry** The first colonial poet was Anne Bradstreet. Her book *The Tenth Muse, Lately Sprung Up in America* was first published in 1650, in England. It was not published in Boston until after her death. Bradstreet's poems, such as "Upon the Burning of Our House" and "To My Dear and Loving Husband," expressed the joys and hardships of life in Puritan New England.

A later poet, Phillis Wheatley, was an enslaved African in Boston. Her first poem was published in the 1760s, when she was about 14. Her works were in a scholarly style that was then popular in Europe.

**Ben Franklin** Perhaps the best-loved colonial writer was Benjamin Franklin. At age 17, Ben moved from Boston to Philadelphia and started a newspaper, the *Pennsylvania Gazette.* It became the most widely read newspaper in the colonies.

Franklin's most popular work was *Poor Richard's Almanack,* published every year from 1733 to 1753. The *Almanack* was full of pithy sayings that usually had a moral. These included "Eat to live, not live to eat" and "God helps them who help themselves." Franklin also published a vivid autobiography.

Franklin was far more than a writer. He was a businessman, community leader, scientist, inventor, and diplomat. He founded a library and a fire department, made discoveries about electricity, and invented such useful items as bifocal eyeglasses and a stove. As you will see, he also became one of the founders of the United States.

☑**Checkpoint** **How did Ben Franklin contribute to American literature?**

**Vocabulary** *Builder*
<u>finance</u> (fī nans) *v.* to supply with money; to manage monetary situations

**Main Idea**
Colonial literature featured sermons, histories, and poetry as well as writings for a popular audience.

### Biography Quest

**Phillis Wheatley**
**1753?–1784**

When she was eight, Phillis Wheatley was captured by slave traders in Africa and sent to Boston. But she was luckier than most enslaved Africans. The family she worked for educated her and gave her time to write.

Wheatley won fame as a poet and later gained her freedom. Sadly, her last years were full of hardship. She is recognized today as America's first poet of African descent.

**Biography Quest** 🌐**nline**

**How did Wheatley meet George Washington?**

**For:** The answer to the question about Wheatley

**Visit:** PHSchool.com

**Web Code:** mvd-1044

# The Great Awakening

From the start, religion played a key role in the 13 English colonies. In Plymouth and Massachusetts Bay, religious leaders set extensive rules on moral and religious matters. Even in colonies that were founded primarily for economic reasons, such as Jamestown, early laws required colonists to attend church regularly.

By the 1700s, rules on religion had become less strict in many of the colonies. The Puritan tradition gradually declined in New England. Still, churches remained centers of faith and community life in all of the colonies.

**Religious Revival** An emotion-packed Christian movement swept through the colonies in the 1730s and 1740s. This period of religious revival is called the Great Awakening. The Great Awakening began as a reaction against what some Christians saw as a decline of religious zeal in the colonies. Leaders such as Massachusetts preacher Jonathan Edwards called on people to examine their lives and commit themselves to God. In a famous sermon, Edwards warned sinners what would happen to them after they died unless they changed their ways and sought forgiveness:

> **"**The God that holds you over the pit of hell, much as one holds a spider, or some loathesome insect, over a fire, abhors you, and is dreadfully provoked; his wrath towards you burns like fire; he looks upon you as worthy of nothing else, but to be cast into the fire.**"**
>
> —Jonathan Edwards, Sinners in the Hands of an Angry God

Forceful preachers quickly spread the Great Awakening throughout the colonies. George Whitefield, an English minister, made several tours of the colonies. His listeners often wept with emotion. After a Whitefield visit to Philadelphia, Benjamin Franklin observed that "one could not walk thro' the Town in an Evening without Hearing Psalms sung in different Families of every Street."

**Impact of the Great Awakening** The Great Awakening led to the rise of many new churches. Methodists and Baptists, which had been small sects or groups, grew quickly. The Presbyterian, Dutch Reformed, and Congregationalist churches split between those who followed the new movement and those who did not. In time, the growth of new churches led to more tolerance of religious differences in the colonies.

**Main Idea**
The Great Awakening led to the rise of new churches and strengthened democratic ideas.

**Religious Awakening**
Traveling preachers, such as English evangelist George Whitefield (below), provoked a broad religious revival in the 1730s and 1740s. **Critical Thinking: *Draw Conclusions*** *Why might the Great Awakening have unsettled many prominent church leaders of the time?*

## Divine Right Versus Natural Rights

| | Divine Right | Natural Rights |
|---|---|---|
| Where does the right to govern come from? | From God to the ruler | From the people |
| Where do people's rights come from? | From the ruler | From God to the people |
| What happens if a government violates people's rights? | People must obey ruler | People can change their government |

### Reading Charts
#### Skills Activity

Did the right to rule come from the will of God or from the people? The answer to this question would alter the course of history in nations around the world.

(a) **Read a Chart** Which column represents the views of John Locke?

(b) **Draw Conclusions** Which of those views would be most attractive to the American colonists? Explain.

**Vocabulary** *Builder*
reinforce (ree ihn FORS) v. to make stronger; to strengthen; to make more effective

The Great Awakening was one of the first national movements in the colonies. It reinforced democratic ideas. People thought that if they could decide on their own how to worship God, they could decide how to govern themselves.

☑**Checkpoint** How did the Great Awakening affect American society?

**Main Idea**
The ideas of the Enlightenment in Europe had a far-reaching influence on American political thought.

## The Enlightenment

Starting in the late 1600s, a group of European thinkers came to believe that all problems could be solved by human reason. They ushered in a new intellectual movement that became known as the Enlightenment. Enlightenment thinkers looked for "natural laws" that governed politics, society, and economics. The Enlightenment reached its height in France in the mid-1700s. However, some of its key ideas came from an Englishman, John Locke.

**Locke** In 1690, Locke published *Two Treatises on Government*. In this influential work, Locke argued that people have certain natural rights, that is, rights that belong to every human being from birth. These rights include life, liberty, and property. According to Locke, these rights are inalienable, meaning that they cannot be taken away.

Locke challenged the idea of divine right. Divine right is the belief that monarchs get their authority to rule directly from God. According to this belief, any rights that people have come to them from the monarch. By contrast, Locke stated that natural rights came from God. He argued that people formed governments in order to protect their rights. They give up some individual freedoms but only to safeguard the rights of the community.

Locke's reasoning led to a startling conclusion. Because government exists to protect the rights of the people, if a monarch violates those rights, the people have a right to overthrow the monarch. This idea would later shape the founding of the United States.

**Montesquieu** A French thinker, the Baron de Montesquieu (MON tehs kyoo), also influenced American ideas. In his 1748 book *The Spirit of the Laws*, Montesquieu argued that the powers of government should be clearly defined and limited. Furthermore, he favored separation of powers, or division of the power of government into separate branches. Separation of powers, he said, protects the rights of the people because it keeps any individual or group from gaining too much power.

Montesquieu suggested that government should be divided into three branches: a legislative branch to make laws, an executive branch to enforce the laws, and a judicial branch to make judgments based on the law. He wrote:

Montesquieu

> **"**There would be an end to everything, were the same man or the same body . . . to exercise those three powers, that of enacting laws, that of executing the public resolutions, and of trying the causes of individuals.**"**
>
> —Baron de Montesquieu, *The Spirit of the Laws*

As you will see, this division of power would become the basis of government in the United States.

☑**Checkpoint** **What was the goal of Enlightenment thinkers?**

⭐ **Looking Back and Ahead** By the 1770s, educated colonists had come to accept the idea that they were born with certain natural rights. As you will see in the next chapter, this belief would set the stage for conflict with the English king and Parliament.

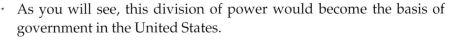

**Section 4 | Check Your Progress**

Progress Monitoring Online
**For:** Self-test with instant help
**Visit:** PHSchool.com
**Web Code:** mva-1044

**Comprehension and Critical Thinking**

1. **(a) Recall** What role did religion play in colonial schools?
**(b) Support Generalizations** Find at least two facts to support the following generalization: Education was important to the colonists.

2. **(a) Describe** What was the Great Awakening?

**(b) Analyze Cause and Effect** What was one effect of the Great Awakening?

**Reading Skill**

3. **Use Context to Determine Meaning** Reread the quotation by Jonathan Edwards in this section. Use context to determine the meaning of *abhors*. Explain the clues you used.

**Vocabulary** *Builder*

4. Write two definitions for each key term: public school, dame school, natural rights, separation of powers. First, write a formal definition for your teacher. Second, write a definition in everyday English for a classmate.

**Writing**

5. Write two to three closing sentences for an essay on the Enlightenment. Focus particularly on the impact of this movement.

# How I Became a Printer
## by Benjamin Franklin

## Prepare to Read

### Introduction

It took Benjamin Franklin 17 years to finish his *Autobiography,* and it was not published until after his death. Today, it is recognized as a classic of early American literature. The book covers only the first 51 years of Franklin's long life, so it does not tell of his later role in the founding of the United States.

### Reading Skill

**Analyze Autobiographical Approach** Writers of autobiographies often convey their attitudes and beliefs as they are conveying a story. As you read, look for clues about Franklin's attitude toward the government. Do you think Franklin approves of the Assembly's actions against James?

### Vocabulary *Builder*

As you read this literature selection, look for the following underlined words:

**chandler** (CHAND ler) *n.* person who makes or sells candles, soap, and other items made from the fat of animals

**tedious** (TEE dee uhs) *adj.* boring

**censure** (SEHN sher) *v.* to condemn or criticize

**admonish** (ad MAHN ihsh) *v.* warn

 **Background**

Tithing (TĪTH ing) is the practice of giving one tenth of one's earnings to the church annually. Here, Franklin jokingly implies that his father wished to follow this same tradition by giving the tenth of his children, Benjamin, rather than a tenth of his earnings.

I was put to the grammar-school at eight years of age, my father intending to devote me, as the tithe of his sons, to the service of the Church. My early readiness in learning to read (which must have been very early, as I do not remember when I could not read), and the opinion of all his friends, that I should certainly make a good scholar, encouraged him in this purpose of his. . . . But my father, in the mean time, from the view of the expense of a college education, which having so large a family he could not well afford . . . took me from the grammar-school, and sent me to a school for writing and arithmetic. . . . At ten years old I was taken home to assist my father in his business, which was that of tallow-<u>chandler</u> and soapboiler. . . . Accordingly, I was employed in cutting wick for the candles, filling the dipping mold and the molds for cast candles, attending the shop, going of errands etc.

I disliked the trade, and had a strong inclination for the sea, but my father declared against it. However, living near the water, I was much in and about it, learned early to swim well, and to manage boats; and when in a boat or a canoe with other boys, I was commonly allowed to govern, especially in any case of difficulty; and upon other occasions I was generally a leader among the boys. . . .

From a child I was fond of reading, and all the little money that came into my hands was ever laid out in books. . . .

This bookish inclination at length determined my father to make me a printer, though he had already one son (James) of that profession. In 1717 my brother James returned from England with a press and letters to set up his business in Boston. I . . . signed the indenture when I was yet by twelve years old. I was to serve as an apprentice till I was twenty-one years of age, only I was to be allowed journeyman's wages during the last year. In a little time I made great proficiency in the business, and became a useful hand to my brother.

Though a brother, he considered himself as my master, and me as his apprentice, and accordingly, expected the same services from me as he would from another, while I thought he demeaned me too much in some he required of me, who from a brother expected more indulgence. Our disputes were often brought before our father, and I fancy I was either generally in the right, or else a better pleader, because the judgment was generally in my favor. But my brother was passionate, and had often beaten me, which I took extremely amiss; and thinking my apprenticeship very <u>tedious</u>, I was continually wishing for some opportunity of shortening it, which at length offered in a manner unexpected.

One of the pieces in our newspaper on some political point, which I have now forgotten, gave offense to the Assembly. He [James] was taken up, <u>censured</u>, and imprisoned for one month, by the speaker's warrant, I suppose, because he would not discover [reveal] his author. I too was taken up and examined before the council; but, though I did not give them any satisfaction, they contented themselves with <u>admonishing</u> me, and dismissed me. . . .

During my brother's confinement, which I resented a good deal, notwithstanding our private differences, I had the management of the paper; and I made bold to give our rulers some rubs in it, which my brother took very kindly. . . . My brother's discharge was accompanied with an order of the House (a very odd one), that "James Franklin should no longer print the paper called the New England Courant."

There was a consultation held in our printing-house among his friends, . . . it was finally concluded on as a better way, to let it be printed for the future under the name of BENJAMIN FRANKLIN; . . . the contrivance was that my old indenture should be returned to me, with full discharge on the back of it, to be shown on occasion, but to secure to him the benefit of my service, I was to sign new indentures for the remainder of the term, which were to be kept private. A very flimsy scheme it was; however, it was immediately executed, and the paper went on accordingly, under my name for several months.

**Ben Franklin (center)**

From *The Autobiography of Benjamin Franklin,*
by Benjamin Franklin. © 2003. Yale University Press.

 **Analyze Autobiographical Approach**

Throughout the story, Franklin conveys his feelings about his brother. When his brother is imprisoned, Franklin takes action by giving the Assembly "some rubs in." Do you think he does this more out of family loyalty or because he supports a free press?

☑ **Checkpoint** **What plan did Franklin's brother approve to keep publishing the newspaper after his confinement?**

*Analyze* **LITERATURE**

Benjamin Franklin disliked being his brother's apprentice. Imagine that you are Franklin. Write a letter to the *New England Courant* expressing your opinion about the fairness or unfairness of being made an apprentice at the age of 12.

If you liked this passage, you might want to read *The Printer's Apprentice* by Stephen Krensky, illustrated by Madeline Sorel. Yearling. 1996.

A Venn diagram is a graphic organizer that shows similarities and differences. You can use a Venn diagram to compare and contrast information about any two items, including time periods, historical events, people, and ideas. Aspects of the two items that are different appear outside the shared area where the circles intersect. Aspects that are similar are listed within the shared area.

Copy and complete the Venn diagram below to compare and contrast information about colonial women and women today. Use information that follows the subheading "Roles of Women" in Chapter 4, Section 2, and your own knowledge about contemporary American women.

### Colonial Women

- Did not hold political office or vote
- Parents often chose husbands
- Usually could not own property

### Both

- Can have personal opinions about politics
- Work very hard inside and outside the home

### American Women Today

- Can hold political office and vote
- Can choose their own husbands
- Able to own property

## Learn the Skill

*Use these steps to create a Venn diagram.*

**1** **Identify the subject.** Decide what items you will compare and contrast on the Venn diagram. Write a title summarizing the subject of the organizer.

**2** **Identify the differences.** Write the differences between the items being compared in each circle under the appropriate heading.

**3** **Identify the similarities.** Write the similarities between the items being compared in the intersecting circle under the heading "Both."

**4** **Draw a conclusion about the subject.** Use the information on the Venn diagram to write a sentence summarizing the conclusions.

## Practice the Skill

*Answer the following questions about the Venn diagram on this page.*

**1** **Identify the subject.** What is a good title for the Venn diagram on this page?

**2** **Identify the differences.** What is a difference between colonial woman and American women today?

**3** **Identify the similarities.** What is a similarity between colonial women and American women today?

**4** **Draw a conclusion about the subject.** Based on the information in the Venn diagram, what is one conclusion you can draw about colonial women and American women today?

## Apply the Skill

*See the Review and Assessment at the end of this chapter.*

# Test Yourself

1. **The colonies offered the right to vote to**

   A Native Americans.

   B African Americans.

   C white male property owners.

   D any colonist born in England.

2. **One reason that colonists disliked the Navigation Acts was that the laws**

   A prevented colonial merchants from selling their goods in England.

   B led to a decline in the shipbuilding industry.

   C created manufacturing jobs in England.

   D cut colonial merchants off from profitable foreign markets.

3. **What was one result of the Great Awakening in the 13 colonies?**

   A It reinforced the principle of freedom of the press.

   B It led to the decline of the Puritan Church in New England.

   C It led to the formation of new churches.

   D It encouraged colonists to accept royal authority.

4. **According to John Locke, natural rights**

   A cannot be taken away.

   B are granted by the king or queen.

   C apply only to English citizens.

   D apply only to the gentry.

# Document-Based Questions

**Task:** Look at Documents 1 and 2, and answer their accompanying questions. Then, use the documents and your knowledge of history to complete the following writing assignment:

> Write an essay about the treatment of enslaved Africans on the journey to America. How does Document 1 support Equiano's statements about conditions during the journey?

**Document 1:** These diagrams show the loading plan of a slave ship during the Middle Passage from Africa to the Americas. *Based on this picture, describe the way enslaved Africans were treated on the journey.*

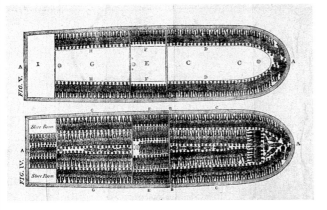

**Document 2:** Olaudah Equiano, an African who survived the voyage, wrote this description of his experiences. *What were two causes of suffering on the ship?*

"The closeness of the place and the heat of the climate, added to the number in the ship, which was so crowded that each had scarcely room to turn himself, almost suffocated us. . . . The air soon became unfit for respiration . . . and brought on a sickness among the slaves, of which many died. The shrieks of the women, and the groans of the dying, rendered the whole a scene of horror almost inconceivable. Happily perhaps for myself I was soon reduced so low here that it was thought necessary to keep me almost always on deck; and from my extreme youth I was not put in fetters. In this situation I expected every hour to share the fate of my companions, some of whom were almost daily brought upon deck at the point of death, which I began to hope would soon put an end to my miseries. Often did I think many of the inhabitants of the deep much more happy than myself; I envied them the freedom they enjoyed, and as often wished I could change my condition for theirs.

Every circumstance . . . served only to render my state more painful, and heighten my . . . opinion of the cruelty of the whites. One day they had taken a number of fishes, and when they had killed and satisfied themselves with as many as they thought fit . . . they tossed the remaining fish into the sea again, although we begged and prayed for some."

# Writing Workshop

## Expository Essay
## Historical Overview

### ▶ Introduction

In a historical overview, you survey a particular period or development from history. You present a central idea about the period or development, supporting that idea with facts about that time. A historical overview should have the following characteristics:

- a historical period or development that can be surveyed from beginning to end
- a thesis statement that presents a main idea about that period
- facts and incidences that support the main idea
- interesting descriptions of details and incidents
- an informative tone

**Assignment** On the following pages, you will learn how to write a historical overview. You will get step-by-step instructions. Each step will include an example from a sample overview about the Age of Exploration.

Read the instructions and the examples. Then, follow each step to plan and write an essay of 500–700 words.

> **Write a historical overview of one region of the 13 colonies from the mid-1600s to the mid-1700s.**

### ▶ Prewriting

**Define the scope of the overview.** In writing a historical overview, you start with a well-defined idea of what happened before, during, and after the period you are writing about. It helps to make a timeline showing the major events to be covered.

> For a review of the steps in the writing process, see the **Historian's Toolkit, *Write Like a Historian.***

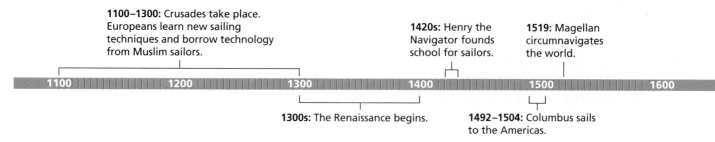

**1100–1300:** Crusades take place. Europeans learn new sailing techniques and borrow technology from Muslim sailors.

**1420s:** Henry the Navigator founds school for sailors.

**1519:** Magellan circumnavigates the world.

1100    1200    1300    1400    1500    1600

**1300s:** The Renaissance begins.

**1492–1504:** Columbus sails to the Americas.

**Brainstorm about the "big picture."** Focus on the "big picture" rather than on the details of the period. Your goal is to communicate an important central idea about the whole period to your audience.

**Write a thesis statement.** A thesis statement expresses the main idea of your essay in a sentence or two.

**List supporting information.** The body of your essay will support and develop your thesis statement with facts, events, and other information. You may have more information than you need. Be sure to choose facts, individuals, and incidents that are most relevant to the idea you are presenting.

> **Sample thesis statement:**
> The age of exploration created a demand in Europe for new goods to consume and new lands to conquer; it opened the way for centuries of colonialism.

## ▶ Drafting

**Choose an organization.** Now you need to decide the best order in which to present your information. You have several choices for organizing your historical overview.

One approach is to use chronological order. The advantage of chronological order is that it is easy to stick to and easy for your readers to follow.

You could also modify chronological order by focusing on certain topics, showing how each of these developed during the period.

**Introduce your thesis and give background information.** Draft an introductory paragraph. Briefly describe the period or development you will be covering, explain why it is important, and lead up to your thesis statement. You could place your thesis statement anywhere in your first paragraph; particularly strong locations are the opening and the closing sentences of the introduction. You may also want to use a quotation or brief incident to catch your readers' interest.

**Cover the main developments.** Write the body of your essay, following the organization you chose and using your prewriting notes. The body of your essay consists of several paragraphs that support your main idea with facts. You may also need to give your readers some background information about the events you are writing about. For example, it might be helpful to know that Native Americans had never been exposed to diseases that the European settlers brought to the New World.

**Pull it together with a strong conclusion.** In your final paragraph, restate your main idea and summarize the main support for it. Finish in a powerful way, indicating what lessons this period can teach us or making some other important point.

# Writing Workshop *continued*

## ▶ Student Model

Read the following model of a historical overview. Notice how it includes the characteristics you have learned about.

### Spanish Exploration of the Americas

During the Renaissance, Europeans became interested in finding new trade routes to Asia. First, the Portuguese sailed east around Africa to Asia and traded goods for gold. Then, Spain's rulers decided to finance voyages to discover a western water route to Asia. These voyages resulted in the exploration of the Americas and the establishment of Spain's empire there.

In 1492, the Italian sea captain Christopher Columbus set sail from Spain. His goal was to reach the East Indies by sailing west across the Atlantic Ocean. Instead, Columbus landed on an island in the Caribbean. Convinced that he had reached Asia, Columbus made three more voyages.

Columbus's discoveries encouraged other Spanish explorers to travel west. In 1513, Juan Ponce de León explored the coasts of Florida. The same year, Vasco Núñez de Balboa crossed the Isthmus of Panama and reached the Pacific Ocean.

Then, in 1519, Ferdinand Magellan set out from Spain with five ships and about 250 crew members. His expedition sailed around the southern tip of South America and started across the Pacific Ocean. Three years later, in 1522, the survivors finally reached Spain after sailing around the world. Magellan never lived to see it, but his sailors had sailed west and finally found the all-water route for Spain.

Spain's search for the western route to Asia started in 1492 and ended successfully in 1522. During this period, Spanish explorers discovered new lands, learned more about Earth's true size, and established Spain's empire in the Americas.

---

**The introductory paragraph describes the historical period and explains its importance.**

**The thesis statement expresses the main idea of the essay.**

**Is this composition organized by chronological order or by the development of certain key topics?**

**The body of the essay supports the main idea with facts.**

**A strong conclusion restates the main idea and summarizes the main points that support it.**

# ▶ Revising

After completing your draft, read it again carefully to find ways to make your writing better. Here are some questions to ask yourself.

## Revise to strengthen your thesis and support
- Does the thesis state your main idea clearly?
- Does each paragraph include reasons and facts that support that main idea?
- Does the essay provide interesting details and descriptions?

## Revise to meet written English-language conventions
- Are all sentences complete, with a subject and a verb?
- Are all the words spelled correctly? Use a spell-checker or a dictionary to make sure.
- Are all proper nouns capitalized, including names of people and places?
- Did you use proper punctuation? Check punctuation within sentences as well as at the ends of sentences.

# ▶ Rubric for Self-Assessment

*Evaluate your historical overview using the following rating scale:*

| | Score 4 | Score 3 | Score 2 | Score 1 |
|---|---|---|---|---|
| **Organization** | Supports the thesis with a series of logically ordered paragraphs; uses some type of chronological order | Uses a reasonably clear organization to present the supporting information | Chooses an organization not suited to the topic | Shows lack of organizational strategy |
| **Presentation** | Supports the main idea effectively with relevant facts and incidents; links all information to the main idea | Supports the main idea adequately with several facts, details, or examples; links most information to the main idea | Does not support the main idea adequately; does not link supporting information to the main idea; includes irrelevant information | Does not provide facts, details, or examples to support the main idea |
| **Use of Language** | Varies sentence structure and vocabulary successfully; includes no or very few mechanical errors | Uses some variety in sentence structure and vocabulary; includes few mechanical errors | Uses the same types of sentences without varying them; does not vary vocabulary; includes many mechanical errors | Writes incomplete sentences; uses language poorly; sounds confused; includes many mechanical errors |

# Unit 2

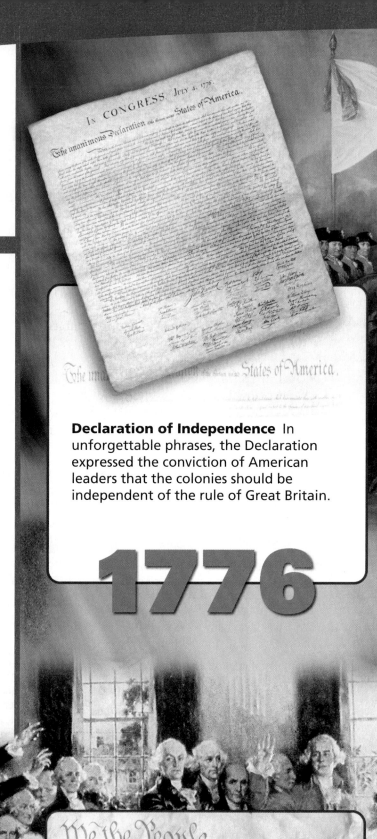

**Declaration of Independence** In unforgettable phrases, the Declaration expressed the conviction of American leaders that the colonies should be independent of the rule of Great Britain.

# 1776

**Writing the Constitution** All through the hot summer of 1787, delegates from the states debated the new shape of the U.S. government. The Constitution created a framework for the government of the United States we enjoy today.

# 1787

# Forming a New Nation

**The Final Battle** Trapped by American and French forces, the British were forced to surrender at the Battle of Yorktown. The British defeat marked the end of the fighting in the American Revolution.

## 1781

**A Bill of Rights** The Bill of Rights was intended to prevent the kind of abuses Americans had suffered under English rule. One of the rights protected was the right of the people peaceably to assemble.

## 1791

## Chapter Preview

As the 13 colonies became increasingly independent throughout the 1700s, it became harder for Britain to control them. The colonists resisted Parliament's and King George III's efforts to control the economy and government of the colonies. Tensions continued to rise, finally erupting in war between Britain and its 13 colonies in 1775.

☑ **What You Will Learn**

A struggle on the western frontier draws France and Britain into a worldwide struggle.

Efforts to solve Britain's financial problems raise the anger of people in the colonies.

By 1775, many Americans were so enraged by British tax policies that they were ready to break away from Britain.

In the first days of the war, both sides expected the struggle to be short. They never expected to fight for seven years.

**1740s**
English move into Ohio Valley.

**1754**
French and Indian War begins.

**1759**
British capture Quebec.

**U.S. Events**

1740 · 1750 · 1760

**World Events**

**1748** Britain and France fight to control trade in India.

**1756** Seven Years' War breaks out in Europe between France and Britain.

**Quick View Video**
View the chapter video for a quick preview of the main ideas.

The first shots of the American Revolution were fired on the green at Lexington, April 19, 1775. No one knows who fired the very first shot, but the battle ended with British troops in full retreat toward Boston.

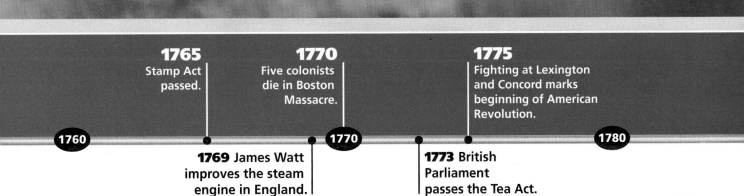

**1765** Stamp Act passed.

**1770** Five colonists die in Boston Massacre.

**1775** Fighting at Lexington and Concord marks beginning of American Revolution.

1760

**1769** James Watt improves the steam engine in England.

1770

**1773** British Parliament passes the Tea Act.

1780

**History Reading Skill** Draw Inferences and Conclusions

## What conflicts arose between colonists during the American Revolution era?

In this chapter, you will learn how to draw inferences and conclusions. Read the following account of struggle between colonists loyal to England and those seeking independence. The side notes show you how to draw inferences and conclusions.

During the period when many American colonists fought to win independence from Britain, other colonists remained loyal to Britain and its king. Patriot colonists and Loyalist colonists argued passionately. On some occasions, as you will read below, the arguments became violent.

**Primary Source**

> You can infer that the writer sympathizes with Malcolm.

The most shocking cruelty was exercised a few nights ago upon a poor old man, one Malcolm. A quarrel was picked with him. . . . He was stripped naked on one of the severest cold night this winter. His body was covered all over with tar, then with feathers. . . .

> You can infer that Malcolm is a Loyalist and his attackers are Patriots.

> Details that support the inference: He is loyal to the king and governors. He calls those attacking him "traitors."

The unhappy wretch they say behaved with the greatest bravery. When under torture they demanded of him to curse his masters, the king [King George of Britain], governors, etc., which they could not make him do. He still cried, "Curse all traitors.". . .

They are angry with him, particularly because he was with Governor Tyron [of New York]. . . . The Governor has declared that [Malcolm] was of great service to him in that affair, by his courageous spirit encountering the greatest dangers.

—Ann Hulton, *Letters of a Loyalist: Lady Ann Hulton*

## Draw Inferences and Conclusions

- An inference is an idea suggested, but not stated, in the text. Support inferences with details in the text.
- Draw a conclusion by analyzing what you have read and forming an opinion about what it means.

- Add information from previous readings or from personal experience to complete an inference or conclusion.

## Document-Based Questions

1. Who wrote this letter?
2. How might the letter have been different if written by a Patriot?

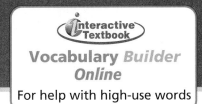

**Interactive Textbook**

**Vocabulary** *Builder* **Online**

For help with high-use words

# Vocabulary *Builder*

## Previewing High-Use Academic Words

| High-Use Word | Definition | Sample History Sentence |
|---|---|---|
| **collide** (koh LĪD) (Section 1, p. 140) | *v.* to come into violent conflict | French and British ambitions collided in the Ohio River valley in the 1750s. |
| **resolve** (ree SAHLV) (Section 1, p. 143) | *n.* strong determination to succeed in doing something | The goal of gaining land for Spain strengthened Columbus's resolve to find a sea route to Asia. |
| **minimum** (MIHN ah muhm) (Section 2, p. 146) | *n.* smallest quantity possible | With the end of the French and Indian War, colonists expected a minimum rise in taxes to the British. |
| **emotional** (ee MOH shuhn ahl) (Section 2, p. 147) | *adj.* appealing to the emotions, or feelings, of people | After the French and Indian War, colonial soldiers returned to an emotional homecoming. |
| **prior** (PRĪ or) (Section 3, p. 150) | *adj.* preceding in time; earlier; former | Prior to the arrival of Cortés, the Aztecs ruled over a mighty empire. |
| **react** (ree AKT) (Section 3, p. 152) | *v.* to act in return | The French reacted strongly to Washington's expedition into the Ohio River valley. |
| **crisis** (KRĪ sihs) (Section 4, p. 156) | *n.* time of great danger or trouble | The crisis was eased when the British Parliament repealed the Stamp Act. |
| **restore** (ree STOR) (Section 4, p. 158) | *v.* to bring back to a normal state; to put back; to reestablish | By the end of 1763, the French knew there was little opportunity to restore its empire in North America. |

## Previewing Key Terms and People

John Adams

George Washington, p. 140
militia, p. 140
alliance, p. 141

cede, p. 144
duty, p. 146
boycott, p. 147
petition, p. 147
writ of assistance, p. 148
John Adams, p. 149
Samuel Adams, p. 149
monopoly, p. 151
repeal, p. 152
minuteman, p. 152

blockade, p. 161
mercenary, p. 161

George Washington

**The Road to Revolution  139**

# Trouble on the Frontier

## Objectives

1. Identify the reasons why fighting broke out between France and Britain in North America.

2. Describe the early defeat of the British by the French at the beginning of the French and Indian War.

3. Explain how the British gained victory, and explain the results of the French and Indian War.

## Prepare to Read

### ◉ Reading Skill

**Make Inferences** When ideas are not actually stated, readers must infer these ideas by analyzing the details and evidence in the text. As you read about the choices and views of both the Americans and the British in colonial times, think about the inferences you can make from their actions.

### Vocabulary *Builder*

**High-Use Words**

collide, p. 140

resolve, p. 143

**Key Terms and People**

George Washington, p. 140

militia, p. 140

alliance, p. 141

cede, p. 144

---

⭐ **Background Knowledge** Between 1650 and 1750, American colonists developed a large degree of self-government. Americans were proud of their hard-won rights and intensely loyal to the British monarch. In this section, you will learn how this loyalty was strained by a conflict on the North American frontier.

## Competing Empires

**Main Idea**
A struggle over control of the Ohio River valley led to conflict between England and France.

**Vocabulary** *Builder*
**collide** (koh LĪD) *v.* to come into violent conflict

By the middle of the 1700s, France and Britain each controlled large areas of North America which bordered on each other for thousands of miles. Each country feared the other and sought to increase the area it controlled. These ambitions collided on the frontier and eventually led to war.

Native Americans lived on most of the territory claimed by France and Britain. There were few French settlers. Therefore, they did not threaten to seize Native American lands. However, the need of British settlers for farmland led to conflict with the Native Americans. By the 1740s, British settlers were pushing into the Ohio River valley lands claimed by the French. The pressure soon led to trouble.

**The French and Indian War Begins** In 1753, the French began building forts to back their claim to the land between Lake Erie and the Ohio River. This news alarmed the Virginia Colony, which also claimed the Ohio River valley. The governor of Virginia decided to send soldiers to order the French to leave. He chose a 21-year-old surveyor in the Virginia militia, George Washington, as the leader. The militia is a force made up of civilians trained as soldiers but not part of the regular army. Washington made the dangerous journey, returning home to tell the governor that the French had rejected his warning.

The next year, Washington traveled west again with orders to build a fort where the Allegheny and the Monongahela (muh non goh HEEL uh) rivers meet to form the Ohio River.

Washington arrived too late. The French were there already, building their own fort, which they called Fort Duquesne (du KANE). Washington marched south for about 50 miles and built a small fort of his own. He called it Fort Necessity.

Later, Washington's troops attacked and defeated a small French force. However, a larger French army arrived and forced Washington to surrender Fort Necessity. The French allowed Washington and his men to return home to Virginia with the message that they would never give up the Ohio River valley.

**The Albany Congress** Expecting war to break out soon, the British government called a meeting of colonial leaders. It took place in Albany, New York. The British wanted the colonies to agree to cooperate in defending themselves against the French. The British also invited the Iroquois tribes to the meeting. They hoped to form an alliance with the Iroquois against the French. An alliance is an agreement between countries to help each other against other countries.

The Iroquois refused to make an alliance, in part because they expected the French to defeat the British in a war. The colonial leaders tried to work out a plan to defend themselves. Benjamin Franklin of Pennsylvania believed the colonies had to succeed. To make that point, his newspaper, the *Philadelphia Gazette*, published a picture of a snake chopped into pieces with the warning "Join, or Die."

**Make Inferences**
How did Virginia's governor view George Washington? Give one detail that supports your inference.

## Join, or Die

JOIN, or DIE.

**Reading Political Cartoons**

**Skills Activity**

Benjamin Franklin's 1754 cartoon was a plea for unity in defending the colonies during the French and Indian War.

(a) **Distinguish Relevant Information** Identify the eight sets of initials that label the eight pieces of the snake.

(b) **Draw Conclusions** What point is Franklin making about the importance of colonial unity?

Franklin drew up a plan, called the Albany Plan of Union. It called for a council of representatives elected by the colonial assemblies. The council would have authority over western settlements, relations with Native Americans, and other urgent matters. It also could organize armies and collect taxes to pay its expenses.

The Albany Congress approved Franklin's plan, but the colonial assemblies rejected it. The colonies wanted to control their own taxes and armies. Franklin complained that "everyone cries, union is necessary," but they behave like "weak noodles" when the time comes to take action.

✓ **Checkpoint** **Why were the British concerned about French activity in the Ohio River valley?**

**Main Idea**

The first years of the French and Indian War were marked by a series of military disasters for the British.

## Early British Defeats

Soon after Washington's return, the British government decided it had to push the French out of the Ohio River valley. In 1755, it sent General Edward Braddock to Virginia with orders to capture Fort Duquesne. Braddock arrived with a large force of regular British troops and Virginia militia. Colonel George Washington joined Braddock's force as a volunteer.

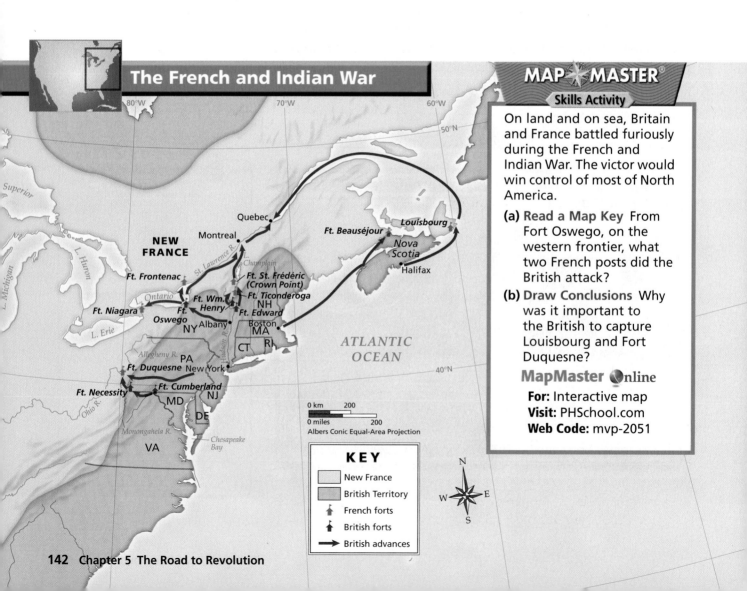

### The French and Indian War

**MAP MASTER**

**Skills Activity**

On land and on sea, Britain and France battled furiously during the French and Indian War. The victor would win control of most of North America.

**(a) Read a Map Key** From Fort Oswego, on the western frontier, what two French posts did the British attack?

**(b) Draw Conclusions** Why was it important to the British to capture Louisbourg and Fort Duquesne?

**MapMaster** ⬤nline

**For:** Interactive map
**Visit:** PHSchool.com
**Web Code:** mvp-2051

**KEY**

- New France
- British Territory
- ⬆ French forts
- ⬆ British forts
- ➜ British advances

**Disaster at Fort Duquesne** General Braddock understood military tactics used in Europe, where armies fought in formation on open fields. But he knew nothing about fighting in North America, where conditions were very different. Braddock did not respect colonial soldiers. He did not listen to warnings that soldiers marching down a narrow road through a dense forest in red uniforms were perfect targets for an enemy fighting from behind trees and bushes. When Benjamin Franklin warned him about the danger of ambushes, Braddock said they were no threat to his well-trained troops.

As Braddock's force neared Fort Duquesne in early July, it was ambushed by French troops and their Native American allies. More than half of Braddock's men were killed or wounded, with the general himself among the dead.

General Edward Braddock

**More British Defeats** The British had other setbacks during 1755. An army led by the governor of Massachusetts failed to take Fort Niagara on Lake Ontario. Further east, an army of British colonists and Native Americans was ambushed and suffered heavy losses near Lake George. These defeats may have strengthened Iroquois leaders' <u>resolve</u> not to ally with Britain.

In May 1756, Britain declared war on France, marking the official beginning of the Seven Years' War between the two countries. Shortly thereafter, French troops led by General Louis de Montcalm captured and destroyed Britain's Fort Oswego on Lake Ontario. In 1757, Montcalm captured Fort William Henry on Lake George.

**Vocabulary** *Builder*
<u>resolve</u> (ree SAHLV) *n.* strong determination to succeed in doing something

☑**Checkpoint** **What fatal errors did General Edward Braddock make?**

# The British Turn the Tide

The situation improved for Britain during 1757 when William Pitt became prime minister. Pitt sought top generals who had genuine military talent. He chose James Wolfe, who was only 30 years old when he became one of Britain's top generals.

With Pitt's generals in command, the war entered a new phase. In the summer of 1758, Britain scored its first major victory in the war. It captured the fort at Louisbourg. In the fall, the British took Fort Duquesne. The British renamed the post Fort Pitt, in William Pitt's honor. It later became the city of Pittsburgh.

These and other victories led the Iroquois to side with the British. More victories in 1759 set the stage for the British attack on Quebec and the key battle of the war.

Quebec, the capital of New France, was located on a high cliff, overlooking the St. Lawrence River. General Montcalm commanded the French defenders, and General Wolfe led the British attack. At first, the British made little progress. Then, they found an unguarded trail that allowed them to climb the cliffs, protecting the city at night without being discovered. In September 1757, approximately 4,000 British soldiers defeated 4,500 French soldiers on the plains in

**Main Idea**
New leadership allowed the British to win a series of important victories and led to the French surrender.

The British attack Quebec.

front of the city. More than 2,000 soldiers were killed or wounded in the battle, including both Wolfe and Montcalm.

After losing Quebec, France could no longer defend the rest of its North American territory. Montreal, the other major French city in Canada, fell in 1760. In February 1763, Britain and France signed the Treaty of Paris. France lost almost all of its North American possessions. France ceded, or surrendered, French Canada to Great Britain. Great Britain also gained all other French territory east of the Mississippi, with the exception of New Orleans. Britain also received Spanish Florida. New Orleans, along with all French territory west of the Mississippi, went to Spain.

Native Americans also lost a great deal. Without French help, the Native Americans could not stop British settlers from moving on their lands.

☑Checkpoint **What was the outcome of the Battle of Quebec?**

☆ **Looking Back and Ahead** The defeat of the French left the British in control of a vast area in North America. However, whatever sense of triumph British leaders felt at the war's outcome was soon replaced by a nagging realization. The victory had substituted one set of problems for another.

---

Section 1 | **Check Your Progress**

**Progress Monitoring** ⬤nline
**For:** Self-test with instant help
**Visit:** PHSchool.com
**Web Code:** mva-2051

**Comprehension and Critical Thinking**

1. **(a) Summarize** How did the French and Indian War affect the 13 colonies?
   **(b) Detect Points of View** How did most colonists feel about helping the British? Explain.

2. **(a) Recall** How did the war go for the British before 1757? After 1757?
   **(b) Make Predictions** How might the outcome influence relations between the British and the American colonists?

⟳ **Reading Skill**

3. **Make Inferences** Think about how the Iroquois felt about the Ohio River valley. Why do you think the Iroquois may have preferred to be neutral in the conflict between France and England? What can you infer about how the Iroquois felt about European conflicts in North America?

**Vocabulary *Builder***

4. Write two definitions for each key term: militia, alliance. First, write a formal definition for your teacher. Second, write a definition in everyday English for a classmate.

**Writing**

5. Write two or three sentences identifying the problems facing the Albany Congress. Were these problems solved? Explain your answer in three or four sentences.

# The Colonists Resist Tighter Control

## Objectives

1. Explain the conflict between Native Americans and British settlers in 1763.

2. Describe how the colonists responded to British tax laws.

3. Describe what happened during the Boston Massacre.

## Prepare to Read

### Reading Skill

**Support Inferences With Details** Inferences must be based on information. This information may be details stated in the text. First, make the logical inference, then read the text and identify support for your inference. If you cannot support the inference, adjust it until the evidence will support it.

### Vocabulary *Builder*

**High-Use Words**

<u>minimum</u>, p. 146
<u>emotional</u>, p. 147

**Key Terms and People**

duty, p. 146
boycott, p. 147
petition, p. 147
writ of assistance, p. 148
John Adams, p. 149
Samuel Adams, p. 149

⭐ **Background Knowledge** By defeating France, Britain solved one problem. However, the outcome of the war created another problem. In this section, you will learn how financial problems led Britain to pass measures that angered American colonists.

## Conflict With Native Americans

By 1763, Britain controlled almost all of North America east of the Mississippi River. This enormous territory promised endless room for settlement. However, Native Americans living west of the Appalachian Mountains were desperately trying to keep their lands. Fighting between Native Americans and white settlers began as soon as the French and Indian War ended.

**Pontiac's War** In the last days of the French and Indian War, the leader of the Ottawa nation, Pontiac, formed an alliance of western Native Americans. In May 1763, Pontiac and his allies attacked British forts and settlements throughout the area. Nearly half a dozen western British forts were destroyed and at least 2,000 backcountry settlers were killed. British settlers reacted with equal viciousness. They killed Native Americans who had not attacked them.

The British finally defeated Pontiac's forces in early August at a battle near Fort Pitt. Pontiac continued to fight for another year, but by the fall of 1764, the war was over.

**The Proclamation of 1763** Britain wanted to avoid further wars with Native Americans on the frontier. Therefore, the British government issued the Proclamation of 1763. It banned colonial settlement west of a line drawn along the Appalachian Mountains. Settlers were told they had to move to a location east of that line.

**Main Idea**

Colonists moving westward into the Ohio River valley spurred a reaction by Native Americans led by Pontiac.

### Support Inferences With Details

Use details from the text to support this inference: Chief Pontiac thought that keeping his people's lands and way of life was more important than anything else.

## Effects of the French and Indian War

THE FRENCH AND INDIAN WAR

- France loses its North American possessions.
- Britain is left with a large debt.
- Colonists develop a sense of unity.
- Colonists begin settling in the Ohio River valley.
- Native Americans resist colonists settling in the Ohio River valley.

The struggle between France and Great Britain to establish an empire in the Americas ended in 1763. The results brought political, social, and economic change to North America.

(a) **Read a Chart** Which nation faced huge expenses after the war?

(b) **Apply Information** How do you think the war impacted relations between Britain and the colonies?

The Proclamation of 1763 angered many colonists who believed they had the right to reside wherever they wanted. The proclamation was widely ignored and proved impossible for the British to enforce.

☑**Checkpoint** What were the terms of the Proclamation of 1763?

**Main Idea**
Conflict arose when the British government attempted to impose taxes on the colonists.

**Vocabulary** *Builder*
**minimum** (MIHN ah muhm) *n.* smallest quantity possible

## British Rule Leads to Conflict

The colonists were proud of their contribution toward winning the French and Indian War. Tens of thousands of men had served as soldiers, and many had died in the war. Massachusetts alone lost more than 1,500 men. The colonists expected Britain to be grateful for their assistance. At best, they expected only a <u>minimum</u> rise in taxes.

Although ties between the colonies had begun to grow before the war, the 13 colonies still were divided in many ways. But the people of those colonies also saw themselves as different from people living in Britain. In 1763, the colonists still considered themselves loyal British subjects. Increasingly, however, they identified more with one another than with Britain.

The British saw things differently. The French and Indian War left Britain deeply in debt. Furthermore, these expenses continued. The British government had to keep troops in North America to make sure France did not try to regain its lost territory and to protect settlers against Native American attacks. British leaders believed the colonists should pay part of the debt.

**The Sugar Act** The British effort to impose new taxes on the colonies began in 1764 when Parliament passed the Sugar Act, which put a duty—or import tax—on several products, including molasses. It also called for harsh punishment of smugglers. Colonial merchants, who sometimes traded in smuggled goods, protested.

**The Quarering Act** One year later, Parliament passed the Quartering Act. The purpose of the Quartering Act was to save money. To enforce the Proclamation of 1763, Britain kept about 10,000 soldiers in the colonies. The act required colonists to quarter, or house, British troops and provide them with food and other supplies. The colonists protested angrily. Once again, the colonists complained that Parliament was violating their rights.

☑**Checkpoint** **Why did the British impose new taxes on the American colonists?**

## The Stamp Act

An even more unpopular law was the Stamp Act, passed by Parliament in early 1765. The Stamp Act required that all colonists buy special tax stamps for all kinds of products and activities. The stamps had to be placed on newspapers, wills, licenses, insurance policies, land titles, contracts, and other documents.

Protests against the Stamp Act were widespread. Virginia's House of Burgesses passed several resolutions declaring that it alone had the right to tax the people of Virginia. Patrick Henry, one of the youngest members of that body, made an <u>emotional</u> speech attacking the law. Henry ended his speech with a reference to the murder of Julius Caesar in ancient Rome. When Henry said that some good American would do the same to King George III, cries of treason were hurled against him. Henry replied, "If this be treason, make the most of it."

Other colonial assemblies followed Virginia's example. Merchants in New York, Boston, and Philadelphia organized a boycott—an organized campaign to refuse to buy certain products— of British goods. The protests spread to every colony.

In October, delegates from nine colonies met in New York for the Stamp Act Congress. They sent a petition—a written request to a government. Addressed to the king and Parliament, this petition demanded the end of both the Sugar Act and Stamp Act.

The protests worked. In 1766, Parliament repealed the Stamp Act. However, at the same time it passed the Declaratory Act, which said Parliament had total authority over the colonies. That set the stage for further trouble between Britain and her colonies.

☑**Checkpoint** **Why did colonists object to the Stamp Act?**

**Main Idea**
Protests over the Stamp Act spread throughout the colonies and led the British to repeal the act.

**Vocabulary** *Builder*
<u>emotional</u> (ee MOH shuhn ahl) *adj.* appealing to the emotions, or feelings, of people

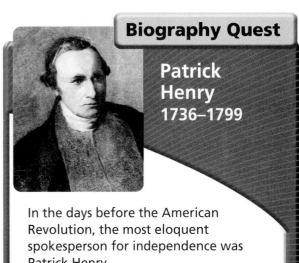

**Biography Quest**

**Patrick Henry**
**1736–1799**

In the days before the American Revolution, the most eloquent spokesperson for independence was Patrick Henry.

Henry gave his famous speech in 1775. He urged Virginians to take up arms in their defense. "I know not what course others may take," he roared, "but as for me, give me liberty or give me death!" He later went on to serve six terms as governor of Virginia.

**Biography Quest**

**How did a salary dispute make Henry famous?**

**For:** The answer to the question about Patrick Henry
**Visit:** PHSchool.com
**Web Code:** mvd-2052

**Massacre!** An American view of the Boston Massacre shows an organized unit of British troops firing directly into a group of colonists. But, in fact, more than 400 colonists surrounded the troops, cursing them and throwing sticks, rocks, and ice at them. **Critical Thinking: *Detect Points of View*** *How does the artist show the tension at the scene of the Boston Massacre?*

**Main Idea**
Attempts to enforce writs of assistance and the Boston Massacre infuriated many colonists.

## Protests Spread

British officials sought a means of taxing the colonists in a way that would not anger them. Under the Townshend Acts of 1767, Britain would no longer tax products or activities inside the colonies. It would only tax products brought into the colonies.

**Writs of Assistance** The Townshend Acts set up a system to enforce the new import duties. To help customs officers find illegal goods, they were allowed to use writs of assistance—court orders that allowed officials to make searches without saying for what they were searching. Many colonists saw these writs and the searches they allowed as yet another violation of their rights.

Charles Townshend, the official in charge of the British treasury, also wanted to weaken the colonial assemblies. When the New York assembly refused to supply money to house and feed soldiers under the Quartering Act, Parliament suspended the assembly. The colonists again reacted by boycotting British goods.

**The Boston Massacre** Once again, the protests worked. The boycott hurt British merchants and manufacturers, who put pressure on Parliament. On March 5, 1770, Parliament repealed all the Townshend duties—except the one on tea. That tax was left in force to demonstrate Parliament's right to tax the colonies.

Parliament had not acted in time. On March 5, 1770, in Boston, an angry crowd of workers and sailors surrounded a small group of soldiers. They shouted at the soldiers and threw snowballs and rocks at them. The frightened soldiers fired into the crowd, killing five and wounding six.

Governor Thomas Hutchinson tried to calm things down by having the nine soldiers involved in the shooting arrested and tried for murder. John Adams, a well-known Massachusetts lawyer, defended them. Adams also was a leading defender of colonial rights against recent British policies. Yet, he took the unpopular case because he believed that in a free country every person accused of a crime had the right to a lawyer and a fair trial. Only two soldiers were convicted of the crime. Their punishment was having their thumbs branded.

**Committees of Correspondence** As tensions grew, colonial leaders saw the need to keep in closer contact with people in other colonies. After the Boston Massacre, Samuel Adams, a cousin of John Adams, established what he called a Committee of Correspondence. The aim was to keep colonists informed of British actions. Soon, committees were sprouting in other colonies. The committees wrote letters and pamphlets to spread the alarm whenever Britain tried to enforce unpopular acts of Parliament. In this way, the committees helped unite the colonists against Britain.

Samuel Adams

☑**Checkpoint** How did colonists react to the Townshend Acts?

⭐ **Looking Back and Ahead** When colonists heard that the Townshend Acts had been repealed, they were overjoyed. But the dispute over taxes was not settled. Before long, colonists would face other crises that would lead to armed resistance.

**Section 2 | Check Your Progress**

> **Progress Monitoring Online**
> **For:** Self-test with instant help
> **Visit:** PHSchool.com
> **Web Code:** mva-2052

**Comprehension and Critical Thinking**

1. **(a) Recall** What was the Proclamation of 1763?
   **(b) Apply Information** Why did the British feel the Proclamation was critical in their relationship with the Native Americans?

2. **(a) Describe** What happened during the Boston Massacre?
   **(b) Detect Points of View** Why do you think the colonists described this event as a "massacre"?

↩ **Reading Skill**

3. **Support Inferences With Details** Read the text following the subheading "Committees of Correspondence." Give a detail from the text to support the following inference: The colonists believed that the strength of unity would help them.

**Vocabulary Builder**

Answer the following questions in complete sentences that show your understanding of the key terms.

4. How did the American boycott affect Great Britain economically?

5. What did the delegates to the Stamp Act Congress hope to achieve by sending a petition to the British king and Parliament?

6. Why did colonists object to writs of assistance?

**Writing**

7. As a member of Parliament, you vote against repealing the Stamp Act. Brainstorm one or two possible solutions that you think would work better.

# From Protest to Rebellion

## Objectives

1. Identify the causes of the Boston Tea Party.
2. Explain how the colonists protested the Intolerable Acts.
3. Describe the events of April 19, 1775, at Lexington and Concord.

## Prepare to Read

### Reading Skill

**Draw Logical Conclusions**
Reaching conclusions means analyzing what you have read and forming an opinion about what it means. As with inferences, you can add your own personal knowledge to the information to draw a conclusion. Always ask yourself: Does this conclusion make sense?

### Vocabulary *Builder*

**High-Use Words**

**prior**, p. 150
**react**, p. 152

**Key Terms**

monopoly, p. 151
repeal, p. 152
minuteman, p. 152

⭐ **Background Knowledge** The British policy of taxation had angered American colonists in all the colonies. But the anger stopped short of armed resistance to the British. This section describes how the conflict deepened until the colonists turned to armed rebellion.

## A Dispute Over Tea

**Main Idea**
Opposition to the British tax on tea led to a dramatic confrontation in Boston Harbor.

During the early 1770s, the protests in the colonies against British policies quieted down. However, that did not mean the colonists were satisfied with the British government. Although most of the Townshend duties had been repealed, the one on tea remained. Many colonists drank tea. With every cup they drank, they were paying a tax that Parliament had placed on them without their consent.

**The Tea Act** In 1773, the British Parliament passed the Tea Act. It was intended to help the British East India Company, one of Britain's most important companies. For many years, the company had made money growing tea in India and selling it in Britain and in the colonies. However, the colonial boycott of tea seriously hurt the company.

**Vocabulary *Builder***
**prior** (PRĪ or) *adj.* preceding in time; earlier; former

The Tea Act actually lowered the price of tea by allowing the East India Company to ship tea directly to the colonies. Prior to the Tea Act, the tea first had to be shipped to Britain. Frederick North, the prime minister of England, felt the colonists should not object to the Tea Act since the price of tea was lowered. However, some colonists reacted angrily to the part of the act that gave the East India

Company a monopoly on selling British tea in the colonies. A **monopoly** is total control of a market for a certain product.

The monopoly hurt colonial merchants. Many of them sold Dutch tea that was smuggled into the colonies. Now, they would not be able to compete with the lower-priced East India Company Tea. Many colonial leaders also argued that even though the price of tea was lowered, colonists still had to pay the tax on tea.

**The Boston Tea Party** A group of colonists called the Sons of Liberty soon organized in port cities to stop the East India Company tea from being unloaded. They threatened ship captains who were bringing in the tea and colonial tea merchants who said they would buy it. No tea was unloaded in New York, Philadelphia, or other ports. However, in Boston, Governor Thomas Hutchinson decided to make sure that the tea would be unloaded. He refused to give the arriving tea ships papers that would allow them to return to England. So, when the first tea ships from Britain arrived, Hutchinson ordered the cargo to be unloaded.

For more than two weeks, feelings were tense in Boston. Finally, on the night of December 16, 1773, a large crowd gathered in the harbor. Suddenly, a large group of men disguised as Native Americans boarded the tea ship. During the next three hours, they threw 342 cases of tea into the harbor. As the crowd cheered and shouted, the raiders destroyed 90,000 pounds of tea worth thousands of dollars.

☑️**Checkpoint** **How did Boston colonists show their opposition to the Tea Act?**

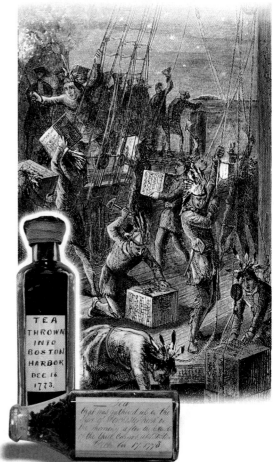

**Boston Tea Party**
Members of the Sons of Liberty protested the Tea Act by dumping chests of tea into Boston Harbor.
**Critical Thinking:** *Apply Information* *Why do you think the colonists chose to disguise themselves as Native Americans?*

# The Intolerable Acts

The Boston Tea Party outraged the British government. King George III called for tough action to make examples of the people of Boston and Massachusetts.

In response, Parliament passed four laws. These laws were so harsh that colonists called them the Intolerable Acts. The first act closed the port of Boston. Two others increased the powers of the royal governor, abolished the upper house of the Massachusetts legislature, and cut the powers of town meetings. Now, anyone accused of murdering a British colonial official could be tried in Britain, rather than in the colonies. Finally, a fourth law strengthened the 1765 Quartering Act.

Parliament also passed the Quebec Act, which set up a government for the territory taken from France in 1763. The Quebec Act claimed land between the Ohio and the Missouri rivers as part of Canada. Quebec's new boundaries took away the western lands claimed by several colonies and blocked colonists from moving west.

**Main Idea**
The British reaction to the Boston Tea Party outraged colonists and led to the First Continental Congress.

**History** *Interactive*

**Discover the Events
That Led to
the Revolution**
**Visit:** PHSchool.com
**Web Code:** mvl-2054

**Roots of the Revolution**

Relations between Great Britain and the colonies changed after the French and Indian War. Years of colonial protest against laws passed by Parliament gradually led to open revolt. **Critical Thinking: Explain Problems** *Why did colonists view these laws as attacks on their rights as British citizens?*

French and
Indian War
(1754–1763)

The Stamp Act
(1765)

The Boston Tea Party (1773)

The Intolerable Acts (1774)

**Outbreak
of the
Revolution**

**Vocabulary** *Builder*
react (ree AKT) *v.* to act in return

**Draw Logical
Conclusions**
What conclusion can you make about how the Congress felt about independence at this time?

Americans in all the colonies <u>reacted</u> by trying to help the people of Boston. Food and other supplies poured into Boston from throughout the colonies. Meanwhile, the Committee of Correspondence organized a meeting to discuss what to do next.

That meeting, known as the First Continental Congress, took place in Philadelphia in September and October 1774. Twelve of the 13 colonies sent delegates. Only Georgia did not send representatives. Among the delegates were John Adams and Samuel Adams from Massachusetts, John Jay of New York, and George Washington and Patrick Henry from Virginia.

The Congress demanded the repeal, or official end, of the Intolerable Acts and declared that the colonies had a right to tax and govern themselves. It also called for the training of militias to stand up to British troops if necessary. The Congress also called for a new boycott of British goods. It then voted to meet again in May 1775 if its demands were not met.

☑**Checkpoint** **What did the First Continental Congress accomplish?**

**Main Idea**
The British attempt to seize Patriot arms led to the first open battle of the American Revolution.

## The Shot Heard Round the World

The British government had no intention of meeting the demands of the First Continental Congress. It chose, instead, to use force to restore its authority. Meanwhile, the colonists began to arm and form new militia units called minutemen—citizen soldiers who could be ready to fight at a minute's notice.

In April, General Thomas Gage, the new governor of Massachusetts, learned the minutemen were storing arms in Concord, about 20 miles from Boston. On April 18, 1775, he sent 700 troops to seize the arms and capture some important colonial leaders. As the troops set out, a signal sent by the Patriots appeared in the steeple of Boston's Old North Church. Two men, Paul Revere and William Dawes, then rode through the night to warn the minutemen.

Five miles from Concord in the town of Lexington, about 77 minutemen were waiting when the British arrived. The British commander ordered the minutemen to go home. They refused. Suddenly, a shot rang out. Nobody knows who fired it, but it turned out to be the first shot of the American Revolution—"the shot heard round the world." The British then opened fire, killing eight Americans.

A larger battle took place in nearby Concord. This time, 400 minutemen fought the British, killing three of them. As the British retreated toward Boston, about 4,000 Americans fired at them from behind trees and fences. By the time the British reached Boston, almost 300 of them had been killed or wounded.

Statue of a minuteman

✓**Checkpoint**   **What led to the conflict at Lexington and Concord?**

⭐ **Looking Back and Ahead**   News of the battles at Lexington and Concord traveled fast through the colonies. Many colonists saw their hopes of reaching an agreement with Britain fade. For many, the battles were proof that only war would decide the future of the 13 colonies.

---

## Section 3 | Check Your Progress

**Progress Monitoring** ⓞnline
**For:** Self-test with instant help
**Visit:** PHSchool.com
**Web Code:** mva-2053

### Comprehension and Critical Thinking

**1. (a) Recall** Why did Britain pass the Tea Act?
**(b) Identify Alternatives** What other ways, besides the Boston Tea Party, might colonists have protested the Tea Act?

**2. (a) Summarize** What were the Intolerable Acts?
**(b) Apply Information** How did the Intolerable Acts affect colonial unity?

**3. (a) Describe** How did the American Revolution begin?
**(b) Draw Conclusions** Why do you think the first shot fired at Lexington was called "the shot heard round the world"?

### 🔄 Reading Skill
**4. Draw Logical Conclusions** Based on the battles of Lexington and Concord, what can you conclude about the colonists' advantage in fighting?

### Vocabulary *Builder*
Fill in the blanks with the correct key terms.
**5.** The _____ were colonists who could prepare to fight in a very short time.
**6.** Because the East India Company had a _____ on selling British tea in the colonies, other countries could not sell their tea there.

**7.** The First Continental Congress provided for the training of _____ that could fight the British troops.

### Writing
**8.** One of the decisions of the First Continental Congress was to boycott British goods. In a paragraph, identify the problem that Congress was trying to solve by boycotting British goods. Did the boycott solve the problem? Explain.

# A Spirit of Protest

From the Stamp Act to the Boston Tea Party to the outbreak of fighting at Lexington and Concord, a spirit of protest steadily grew in the colonies. This defiant mood expressed itself in many ways.

## Boycotting British Goods

Women took a leading role in refusing to buy British goods. In October 1774, a group of women in Edenton, North Carolina, signed a pledge. They promised "not to conform to the Pernicious Custom of Drinking Tea." Above, the women of Edenton pour away tea.

## A Warning of Danger

Benjamin Franklin was the first to use a serpent as a symbol of the colonies. (See Section 1.) By 1775, the serpent had become a rattlesnake, which stood for the idea that the colonists would ▼ fight back against tyranny.

DONT TREAD ON ME

## The Pen as a Weapon

Mercy Otis Warren of Boston wrote plays that made fun of the British. The plays were not acted in theaters but were circulated privately. In *The Blockheads*, Warren shows how the Patriots made fools of the ▼ British troops after Lexington and Concord. One British soldier says:

Mercy Otis Warren

> ❝Ha, ha, ha,—yankee doodle forever. . . . We were sent here to ransack the country and hang up a parcel of leading fellows for the crows to pick, and awe all others into *peace* and *submission*—instead of this, in our first attempt, we were drove thro' the country, like a pack of *jackasses*.❞
>
> —Mercy Otis Warren, *The Blockheads*

## Violent Protests

The spirit of protest sometimes took a violent turn. The British cartoon below shows a tax official in Boston being tarred and feathered by members of the Sons of Liberty. Hot tar was poured over the body of the victim, who was then covered with chicken feathers. Tarring and feathering was not fatal, but it was painful and humiliating. In the background, colonists pour tea into Boston Harbor.

The first Liberty Tree was an elm in Boston, where dummies representing tax collectors were hanged. Patriots in many colonies raised Liberty Trees or Liberty Poles as symbols of protest.

In addition to being tarred and feathered, the unfortunate tax collector has tea poured down his throat.

### Analyze LIFE AT THE TIME

Choose a person pictured on these pages. As that person, write a letter to a friend describing how you feel about the new mood of protest in the colonies.

# The War Begins

## Objectives

1. Identify the issues facing the Second Continental Congress.
2. Describe the differences between Patriots and Loyalists.
3. Identify the Olive Branch Petition, and explain why it failed.
4. Explain the significance of the Battle at Bunker Hill.

## Prepare to Read

### Reading Skill

**Identify Supporting Evidence** Readers often draw conclusions without even realizing that they are doing so. However, like inferences, conclusions should be supported and challenged and the evidence identified. This ensures that your conclusions are logical and reliable. Remember, you may need to use evidence from prior reading to reach your conclusions.

### Vocabulary *Builder*

**High-Use Words**

**crisis**, p. 156
**restore**, p. 158

**Key Terms**

blockade, p. 161
mercenary, p. 161

### Main Idea
The Second Continental Congress was divided, at first, about what course to take in the dispute with Britain.

### Vocabulary *Builder*
**crisis** (KRĪ sihs) *n.* time of great danger or trouble

⭐ **Background Knowledge** Lexington and Concord were the first battles of the American Revolution. As war loomed, many colonists expected the British to give in quickly and meet the colonists' demands. Instead, a long struggle for independence lay ahead.

## The Second Continental Congress

Even after the battles of Lexington and Concord, most colonists still did not favor independence. At the same time, many of them were ready to use force, if necessary, to defend their rights against the British.

As the <u>crisis</u> with Britain deepened, the Second Continental Congress came together in Philadelphia in May 1775. The delegates included Thomas Jefferson, a young lawyer from Virginia; Boston merchant John Hancock; and Benjamin Franklin of Philadelphia.

The Congress, at first, was divided about what to do. A group of delegates from New England wanted to declare independence. A more moderate group from the Middle Colonies favored less drastic action. However, nearly all delegates felt they needed to prepare for war. The first step was to form an army.

The Congress chose George Washington as the commander of the newly formed Continental army. He had military experience and was well respected.

The Congress also took steps to pay for its army by printing paper money. The Second Continental Congress was starting to act like a government.

**Patriots Against Loyalists** By 1775, a split was developing in the American colonies. Colonists who favored independence and were willing to fight for it took the name Patriots. Those who remained loyal to Britain and the king called themselves Loyalists. Most colonists were Patriots. However, as many as one third of the colonists may have had Loyalist sympathies.

The Loyalists came from every colony and all sections of the population. Everywhere, however, they were a minority. During 1774 and 1775, the Patriots took control of local governments.

The Loyalists included some people from the wealthiest families in the colonies. Many leading merchants and large landowners were Loyalists. They feared a rebellion would lead to a change in government and that they would lose their property. Government officials who owed their jobs and place in society to the British Crown often were Loyalists.

At the same time, many enslaved African Americans sided with the British, hoping to win their freedom. So did most Native Americans, who feared they would lose their lands if the colonists won independence.

During the Revolution, thousands of Loyalists fought on the British side. During and after the Revolutionary War, about 100,000 Loyalists left the country forever. Many settled in Canada.

**Identify Supporting Evidence**
Give evidence to support the conclusion that Loyalists strongly supported social order.

## Lord Dunmore's Declaration

Lord Dunmore sent this declaration to the rebel Patriots in Virginia:

❝[So] that the peace and good order of this colony may be again restored . . . I do, [by] the authority to me given by His Majesty, determine to execute martial law. . . . I do require every person capable of bearing arms to resort to His Majesty's standard, or be looked upon as traitors to His Majesty's . . . government, and [subject to] the penalty . . . such as [loss] of life or lands. . . . ❞

—from Proclamation of Lord Dunmore, November 1775

Boys laughing at a Loyalist

### Reading Primary Sources
#### Skills Activity

In 1775, Patriots had taken over Virginia. In desperation, Lord Dunmore, the Loyalist governor, issued a declaration against the rebel Patriots.

**(a)** Apply Information According to Dunmore, why are the Patriots a danger to the colony?

**(b)** Make Predictions Do you think Dunmore's declaration will be obeyed? Explain.

**Petitioning the King** Even months after Lexington and Concord, many delegates at the Second Continental Congress hoped that peace could be <u>restored</u> between Britain and its American colonies. Two resolutions passed in July showed the uncertainty of Congress. The first resolution was called the Olive Branch Petition and was sent to King George. The petition stated that the colonists were loyal to the king. It asked George to stop the fighting so all disputes between the colonists and Britain could be solved peacefully. The petition got its name from the olive branch, a symbol of peace since ancient times.

The next day, the Congress passed a tougher statement called the Declaration of the Causes and Necessities of Taking Up Arms. Written in part by Thomas Jefferson, the document stated that the colonists were ready "to die freemen rather than to live as slaves."

The effort to make peace failed. King George did not bother to answer the Olive Branch Petition. Instead, he declared the colonies were "in open . . . rebellion." Parliament, meanwhile, voted to send 20,000 soldiers to the colonies to end the revolt.

**An Important American Victory** On May 10, 1775, the same day the Second Continental Congress began meeting, an important battle took place in northern New York. A daring band of colonists made a surprise attack on Fort Ticonderoga (ti kahn duh ROH guh).

The fort stood at the southern end of Lake Champlain and protected the water route to Canada. Leading the force was Ethan Allen, a blacksmith. Most of his followers came from the nearby Green Mountains of today's Vermont. Because of that, they were known as the Green Mountain Boys.

Allen's force of 83 men reached the fort by crossing the lake at night and surprising the British in the early morning. Only 42 British troops guarded the fort, and they surrendered almost immediately.

Fort Ticonderoga was important for two reasons. It controlled the main route between Canada and the Hudson River valley. It also held valuable weapons, especially cannons. The Americans needed the cannons to match the powerful British weapons. When the Green Mountain Boys took the fort, they seized several dozen cannons. Later, those cannons were moved to Boston, where George Washington used them to drive the British from the city.

Ethan Allen demanding the surrender of Fort Ticonderoga

☑**Checkpoint** **How did the divided loyalties of the colonists affect the Second Continental Congress?**

**Main Idea**
The battles at Bunker Hill and Ticonderoga proved Americans could fight and stand up to professional British soldiers.

# Early Battles

By June 1775, the British had 6,500 troops in Boston. The Americans had about 10,000 surrounding the city. About 1,600 of these troops occupied Breed's Hill overlooking the city. From this position, they could fire on British ships in Boston harbor. Nearby was Bunker Hill, also controlled by the Americans.

# Delivering the Cannons

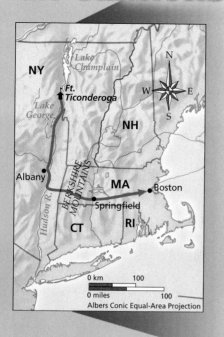

## From Fort Ticonderoga to Boston

The difficulty of dragging cannons from Fort Ticonderoga to Boston is evident in this painting of the event. **Critical Thinking: *Apply Information*** *What does this effort indicate about the Continental army's military forces?*

**Battle of Bunker Hill** The Americans surrounding Boston were farmers and workers, not trained soldiers. Nobody knew if they would stand and fight against tough British troops.

British General William Howe decided to attack straight up the hill. The American commander, Israel Putnam, knew his soldiers did not have much ammunition. The Americans waited until the British were only about 150 feet away. When they opened fire, hundreds of British soldiers fell dead and wounded.

The first British attack failed. So did the second. The third attack succeeded, only because the Americans ran out of ammunition and had to retreat. The British won the battle but at a terrible cost. More than 1000 were killed or wounded. American losses were about 400 killed or wounded. The Americans had proved they could fight and stand up to professional British soldiers.

The Battle of Bunker Hill did not solve Britain's problem in Boston. The city still was surrounded by American forces. In July 1775, George Washington arrived and took charge of the army.

Washington knew he had to build a regular army. Washington also needed powerful weapons to drive the British from Boston. He had the British cannons, which had been seized at Fort Ticonderoga, dragged on sleds across mountains and forests to Boston. That difficult 300-mile journey took three months.

In March, Washington placed the cannons on high ground overlooking Boston. This made it impossible for the British to defend the city. On March 17, 1776, they withdrew from Boston by sea and never returned.

# The Battle of Bunker Hill

On June 16, 1775, the colonists occupied Bunker Hill and Breed's Hill, two high points near Charles Town, which was across the harbor from Boston. The battle that took place there the following morning fueled the colonists' determination to fight. After this battle, it is said that "a frenzy of revenge" gripped the colonists. **Critical Thinking: Understand Sequence** *Based on the information on this page and on your reading, describe the sequence of events before, during, and after the battle.*

**Building the Fort**
The night before battle, as shown in this engraving, the colonists built a fort on Breed's Hill. The colonists hoped to take advantage of the hill when using cannons to attack the British warships in the harbor. ▼

◄ **The Attack**
This painting shows the attack on Bunker Hill and the burning of Charles Town.

◄ **The Battle Begins**
On the morning of June 17, British soldiers took position around the base of Breed's Hill. As shown in this painting, the British soldiers, wearing red coats, marched straight up the hill through tall grass and over fences.

Although the Americans won in Boston, Washington knew that the war was far from over. Britain still held most of the advantages. They had the most powerful navy in the world. They used it to transport troops and supplies and to blockade American ports. A blockade is the shutting off of a port by ships to keep people or supplies from moving in or out. The British also strengthened their army by hiring mercenaries—soldiers who serve another country for money.

**Invading Canada** While Washington was training one army outside Boston, two other American armies were moving north into Canada. One, led by Richard Montgomery, left from Fort Ticonderoga. The other, led by Benedict Arnold, moved north through Maine.

Arnold had a terrible journey through the Maine woods in winter. His troops were forced to boil candles, bark, and shoe leather for food. In late December 1775, the Americans attacked Quebec during a severe snowstorm. The attack was turned back. Montgomery was killed, and Arnold was wounded. The Americans stayed outside Quebec until May 1776, when the British landed new forces in Canada. Weakened by disease and hunger, the Americans withdrew, leaving Canada to the British.

☑**Checkpoint** **What did the Battle of Bunker Hill show about the American and British forces?**

⭐ **Looking Back and Ahead** After Bunker Hill, King George III was confident that he could soon restore order in the colonies. Meantime, colonists wondered what chance they had of defeating a well-armed, powerful nation such as Britain.

Section 4 | **Check Your Progress**

**Progress Monitoring** ●nline
**For:** Self-test with instant help
**Visit:** PHSchool.com
**Web Code:** mva-2054

**Comprehension and Critical Thinking**

1. **(a) Recall** What were the major achievements of the Second Continental Congress?
**(b) Apply Information** How did the Second Continental Congress influence the conflict between the colonists and Britain?

2. **(a) Recall** What did the Patriots want?
**(b) Apply Information** Why do you think Loyalists were described as "having their heads in England . . . but their bodies in America"?

**Reading Skill**

3. **Identify Supporting Evidence** Give evidence to support the conclusion that the war's momentum shifted after the Battle of Bunker Hill.

**Vocabulary Builder**

Read each sentence below. If the sentence is true, write YES. If the sentence is not true, write NO and explain why.

4. Countries set up blockades to help strengthen trade relations.

5. Most mercenaries are hired to fight for their own countries.

**Writing**

6. In a few sentences, describe how a Loyalist might have reacted to the Olive Branch Petition and to the Declaration of the Causes and Necessities of Taking Up Arms as possible solutions to the feud between Britain and the colonies. Then, write a brief response reflecting how a Patriot might have reacted to these documents as a solution to the feud.

You can increase your understanding of history by asking questions about what you see and read. Formulating, or asking, questions helps you become a more effective learner. The better your questions, the more you will learn.

**Primary Source**

Patrick Henry presented his views in this excerpt from a speech to the convention that gathered after the Virginia Assembly was suspended.

"Sir, we have done everything to avert the storm which is now coming on. We have petitioned; we have remonstrated; we have supplicated; we have prostrated ourselves before the throne. Our petitions have been slighted; our remonstrances have produced additional violence and insult; our supplications have been disregarded. . . .

*There is no longer any room for hope.* If we wish to be free; if we mean to preserve inviolate those inestimable privileges for which we have been so long contending; . . . we must fight! I repeat it, sir, we must fight! An appeal to arms and to the God of hosts is all that is left us!

—I know not what course others may take; but as for me,—give me liberty, or give me death!"

—Patrick Henry, March 23, 1775

## Learn the Skill

*Use these steps to formulate questions.*

1 **Examine the material.** Ask basic questions to summarize what you are reading. Formulate questions that begin with *who, what, when, where,* and *how much.*

2 **Think of analytical questions.** These are questions that reflect a thoughtful approach to the information. They might begin with *how* or *why.*

3 **Ask questions that evaluate.** These call for judgments and opinions based on evidence.

4 **Formulate hypothetical questions.** Hypothetical questions involve the word *if.* They suggest possible outcomes: *if this happens, would such and such occur?*

## Practice the Skill

*Answer the following questions about the primary source.*

1 **Examine the material.** What is Patrick Henry's view of the American Revolution?

2 **Think of analytical questions.** (a) How would you describe the tone or feeling? (b) Formulate an analytical question.

3 **Ask questions that evaluate.** (a) Why is this primary source persuasive? Explain. (b) Formulate a question to evaluate the source.

4 **Formulate hypothetical questions.** If the British had won the Revolution, what do you think would have happened to Patrick Henry and those who supported his views?

## Apply the Skill

*See the Review and Assessment at the end of this chapter.*

## Chapter Summary

### Section 1
### Trouble on the Frontier

- British settlers moved into lands claimed by the French in the Ohio River valley.
- After early British defeats at Fort Duquesne, Fort Niagara, and Lake George, France was defeated.
- Under the 1763 Treaty of Paris, Britain and Spain took control of all of France's North American possessions.

### Section 2
### The Colonists Resist Tighter Control

- To avoid conflict with Native Americans, Britain issued the Proclamation of 1763.
- After the end of the war, Britain strengthened its control over the American colonies by imposing a series of new taxes.
- Colonists protested Britain's actions by boycotting British goods.

### Section 3
### From Protest to Rebellion

- After Parliament passed the Tea Act, American colonists dumped cases of British tea into Boston Harbor.
- The Intolerable Acts further tightened Britain's control over the American colonies.
- The first major conflict between American colonists and British soldiers took place at Lexington and Concord on April 18, 1775.

### Section 4
### The War Begins

- The Second Continental Congress met in Philadelphia in May 1775 to deal with the deepening crisis with Great Britain.
- The British surrendered Fort Ticonderoga to a small American force led by Ethan Allen.
- When the Olive Branch Petition failed, the Continental Congress approved a more militant statement of purpose.
- Although the Patriots lost the Battle of Bunker Hill, George Washington finally drove the British from Boston.

## Key Concepts

These notes will help you prepare for questions about key concepts.

**From Protest to Revolution: Major Events**

**1763:** Britain wins French and Indian War

**1764–1766:** Britain tightens control of American colonies through a series of unpopular acts: Sugar Act; Quartering Act; Stamp Act; Townshend Acts

**1770:** Boston Massacre increases tensions between colonists and British

**1773:** Tea Act results in Boston Tea Party

**1774:** Intolerable Acts punish colonists for Boston Tea Party

**April 1775:** First battles of Revolution at Lexington and Concord

**May 1775:** Britain rejects Second Continental Congress's effort to make peace

**June 1775:** British win Battle of Bunker Hill but suffer heavy losses

**March 1776:** Americans drive British from Boston

## Vocabulary *Builder*

### Key Terms

Answer the following questions in complete sentences that show your understanding of the key terms.

1. Why did the British want to form an alliance with the Iroquois during the French and Indian War?

2. How did the role of the militia change after the battles of Lexington and Concord?

3. What did Britain hope to achieve by a blockade of American ports?

4. How did the English king react to the colonists' petition about the Sugar and Stamp Acts?

## Comprehension and Critical Thinking

5. **(a) Identify** What were three results of the French and Indian War?
   **(b) Make Predictions** What would have happened if the French had won the French and Indian War?

6. **(a) Recall** What was Pontiac's War?
   **(b) Draw Conclusions** What happened to the relationship between Native Americans and colonists after the French and Indian War? Explain your answer.

7. **(a) Recall** What did the First Continental Congress do?
   **(b) Recall** What did the Second Continental Congress do?
   **(c) Compare and Contrast** Compare and contrast the achievements of the First and Second Continental Congress.

8. **(a) Recall** What were the terms of the Olive Branch Petition?
   **(b) Identify** What was the Declaration of the Causes and Necessities of Taking Up Arms?
   **(c) Apply Information** Given the terms of each document, why might British leaders have felt the colonists were sending mixed messages about independence?

9. **(a) Describe** How did colonists react to the Battle of Bunker Hill?
   **(b) Make Predictions** How do you think this reaction would help colonial forces during the war?

## ⟳ History Reading Skill

10. **Make Inferences and Draw Conclusions** Draw a conclusion about George Washington as a military leader. Use evidence from throughout this chapter to support your conclusion.

## Writing

11. **Write two paragraphs on the following topic:** How did the French and Indian War affect the relationship between the 13 colonies and Britain?
   **Your paragraphs should:**
   • include a thesis statement that expresses your main idea;
   • develop that main idea with facts, examples, and other information;
   • conclude by describing the lasting impact of what happened.

12. **Write a Narrative:**
   Since 1766, you have been a colonial merchant living in Boston. Write a letter to a friend explaining why you feel it is important to serve on the correspondence committee in your town.

## Skills for Life

### Formulate Questions

Use the quotation below to answer the questions.

> "As to government matters, it is not in the power of Britain to do this continent justice; the business of it will soon be too weighty and intricate to be managed with any tolerable degree of convenience, by a power so distant from us, and so very ignorant of us; for if they cannot conquer us, they cannot govern us. . . .
> . . . Freedom have been hunted round the globe. . . . O receive the fugitive, and prepare in time an asylum for mankind."
>
> —Thomas Paine, *Common Sense*, January 1776

13. How does Thomas Paine feel about the American Revolution?

14. **(a)** Why does Thomas Paine compare "freedom" to a "fugitive"?
   **(b)** How would this comparison affect his readers?

## Test Yourself

**1. How did the Battle at Bunker Hill affect the colonists?**

A They needed to train their militia.

B They were proud of having stood their ground against the British soldiers.

C They were proud of their victory.

D They decided to call for a new commanding general.

**Refer to the quotation below to answer Question 2.**

> "Drive from the Ohio River any European foreigners, and do it in a way that will make them lose all taste for trying to return."

**2. The result of this policy by the French government**

A ended relations between France and Spain.

B increased tensions between England and Native Americans.

C increased tensions between France and England.

D pushed French colonists farther west.

**Refer to the map below to answer Question 3.**

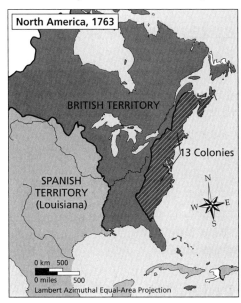

North America, 1763

BRITISH TERRITORY

13 Colonies

SPANISH TERRITORY (Louisiana)

N
W E
S

0 km 500
0 miles 500
Lambert Azimuthal Equal-Area Projection

**3. How did the boundaries after 1763 affect the British?**

A British colonists settled in Canada.

B Britain could not expand farther north.

C Britain could not expand farther west.

D Britain offered to buy Louisiana from Spain.

## Document-Based Questions

**Task:** Look at Documents 1 and 2, and answer their accompanying questions. Then, use the documents and your knowledge of history to complete this writing assignment:

> Use the evidence in the documents to write a two-paragraph essay explaining the causes and degree of colonial anger.

**Document 1:** Angered by the Stamp Act, in October 1765, representatives from nine colonies met in the Stamp Act Congress. Challenging Britain's right to tax the colonists, they issued a Declaration of Rights, excerpted below. *According to the delegates, why did Britain not have the right to tax the colonies?*

> "The members of this congress . . . make the following declarations. . . .
>
>   That His Majesty's . . . . subjects in these colonies are entitled to all the . . . rights and privileges of his natural born subjects [in] Great Britain.
>
>   That the people of these colonies are not . . . represented in the House of Commons in Great Britain. . . .
>
>   That the only representatives of the people of these colonies are persons chosen . . . by themselves; and that no taxes ever have been or can be constitutionally imposed on them but by their respective legislatures. . . ."

**Document 2:** Look at the 1774 engraving of the tarring and feathering of a British tax collector in the Life at the Time feature in this chapter. *The fury of the colonists surprised the British. Why do you think this was so?*

# Chapter Preview

The American Revolution began as a protest against unfair colonial rule. But after the colonists issued the Declaration of Independence, the war turned into a struggle to create a new nation.

## ☑ What You Will Learn

The Declaration of Independence proclaimed that the colonies were separating from Britain.

The American army faced many difficulties in the early years of the war.

The impact of the war was felt by all Americans in every part of the nation.

After a final victory, the Americans at last achieved independence from British rule.

**U.S. Events**

**1776**
Continental Congress issues Declaration of Independence.

**1777**
American victory at Saratoga marks turning point in war.

**1779**
American ship *Bonhomme Richard* defeats British ship in naval battle.

1776

1778

1780

**World Events**

**1778** France recognizes the United States.

**1779** Spain enters war against Britain.

By signing the Declaration of Independence, the Continental Congress proclaimed that the colonies were free of British rule.

**1781**
British troops surrender to Americans at Battle of Yorktown.

**1783**
Britain recognizes American independence in Treaty of Paris.

1780

1782

1784

**1780** Indians in Peru stage unsuccessful revolution.

**1783** Spain regains Florida.

**History Reading Skill** Analyze Word Parts

## What was the end of the American Revolution like?

In this chapter, you will learn how to analyze word parts to determine meaning. Read the following journal entry by an American army surgeon in the American Revolution. The side notes show you how to analyze word parts to determine meaning.

Dr. James Thacher served as a surgeon in the Continental Army. He wrote this journal entry to describe the official surrender of British General Cornwallis in 1781.

**Primary Source**

October 19, 1781

This is to us a most glorious day; but to the English, one of bitter chagrin and <u>disappointment.</u> . . .

> The prefix *dis-* means "not." To *disappoint* comes originally from *not* keeping an appointment.

At about twelve o'clock, the combined army was arranged and drawn up in two lines extending more than a mile in length. The Americans were drawn up in a line on the right side of the road, and the French occupied the left. . . .

The Americans were not all in <u>uniform,</u> nor was their dress so neat. Yet they exhibited an erect, soldierly air, and every [face] beamed with satisfaction and joy. The [crowd] of <u>spectators</u> from the country was . . . probably equal to the military, but universal silence and order prevailed.

> *Uni-* means "one." *Form* means "shape." Thus, *uniforms* all have one shape.

> The word root *spec* means "see." *Spectators* are people who watch.

—James Thacher, *Military Journal During the American Revolution*

## Analyze Word Parts

- Use the meanings of familiar prefixes to help you construct meanings for unfamiliar words.
- Combine the meanings of prefixes with those of word roots to build meanings for new words.
- Find word roots that you know, then use them to determine the meanings of unfamiliar words.

## Document-Based Questions

1. Who wrote this selection? What was his relationship to the event being described?
2. Identify four groups of people who were present at the event.
3. Why was this event important to the people who were there?
4. Why do you think the crowd greeted the event with "universal silence"?

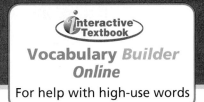
# Vocabulary *Builder*

## Previewing High-Use Academic Words

| High-Use Word | Definition | Sample History Sentence |
|---|---|---|
| **prospect** (PRAHS pehkt) (Section 1, p. 170) | *n.* possibility; expectation | The <u>prospect</u> of wealth attracted many settlers to the colonies. |
| **logic** (LAH jihk) (Section 1, p. 171) | *n.* reason; careful thought | Thinkers of the Enlightenment believed in using <u>logic</u> to support their opinions. |
| **vital** (vī tuhl) (Section 2, p. 183) | *adj.* necessary; of great importance | Shipbuilding played a <u>vital</u> role in the New England economy. |
| **transform** (trans FORM) (Section 2, p. 183) | *v.* to change from one thing or condition to another | The battles of Lexington and Concord <u>transformed</u> the colonial struggle from a protest to a revolution. |
| **confine** (kuhn FĪN) (Section 3, p. 188) | *v.* to keep within certain limits | Captives on slave ships were <u>confined</u> in small, crowded spaces. |
| **resource** (REE sors) (Section 3, p. 188) | *n.* supply of something to meet a particular need | For New England shipbuilders, wood was a valuable <u>resource</u>. |
| **efficient** (ee FISH ehnt) (Section 4, p. 191) | *adj.* acting effectively, without wasted cost or effort | The printing press provided an <u>efficient</u> way to make books. |
| **option** (AHP shuhn) (Section 4, p. 192) | *n.* choice; possible course of action | A poor person who wanted to go to the colonies had the <u>option</u> of becoming an indentured servant. |

## Previewing Key Terms and People

# A Nation Declares Independence

## Objectives

1. Find out how Thomas Paine stirred support for independence.
2. Understand the meaning and structure of the Declaration of Independence.
3. Learn how Congress finally agreed to separate from England.

## Prepare to Read

### Reading Skill

**Analyze Word Roots** Many English words have common word roots or parts. For example, the root *mot* means "move." That root appears in the words *motion, motor, promote,* and *demote*. Those words have different meanings, but all share some connection to movement. Learn to recognize familiar word roots and trace their origins.

### Vocabulary *Builder*

**High-Use Words**

**prospect,** p. 170
**logic,** p. 171

**Key Terms and People**

Thomas Paine, p. 170
Richard Henry Lee, p. 171
resolution, p. 171
preamble, p. 172
grievance, p. 172

---

⭐ **Background Knowledge** In the last chapter, you saw why many Americans became angry with British rule. In this section, you will learn how Patriots moved from protesting injustice to seeking independence.

## A Call for Independence

**Main Idea**
Thomas Paine's *Common Sense* helped increase support for independence in the colonies.

When the year 1776 began, few colonists could have predicted what lay ahead. Most colonists still hoped for a peaceful end to the quarrel with Britain.

**Colonists Divided** Both Patriots and Loyalists were in a minority at the start of 1776. Many colonists were in the middle, with no strong feelings about the dispute with Britain.

Even within the Continental Congress, support for independence was limited to about one third of the delegates. Patriots such as John Adams found it hard to win others to the cause of independence. Adams complained that Loyalists used the <u>prospect</u> of independence as a way to frighten people into giving up the struggle.

**Vocabulary** *Builder*
**prospect** (PRAHS pehkt) *n.*
possibility; expectation

**Common Sense** In January 1776, a 50-page pamphlet titled *Common Sense* was published in Philadelphia. The pamphlet stimulated broad support for independence.

The author, Thomas Paine, called King George III a "royal brute." Paine ridiculed the very idea of rule by kings. Americans, he said, would be far better off if they governed themselves. (See Reading Primary Sources on the next page.)

Paine's strong <u>logic</u> and powerful words inspired people in all the colonies. Some 500,000 copies of the pamphlet were sold between January and July of 1776. George Washington wrote, "*Common Sense* is working a powerful change in the minds of men."

**Vocabulary *Builder***
<u>logic</u> (LAH jihk) *n.* reason; careful thought

**Virginia's Resolution** Paine's pamphlet increased support for independence within the Continental Congress. In May 1776, Virginia authorized its delegates to support independence. Soon after, Richard Henry Lee introduced a resolution, or formal statement of opinion, to Congress. The Virginia resolution proclaimed that "these United Colonies are, and of right ought to be, free and independent States."

Before voting on Lee's resolution, Congress appointed a committee to draw up a statement stating the reasons for separation from Britain. Thomas Jefferson, a 33-year-old delegate from Virginia, was given the task of composing the declaration. Highly educated but shy, Jefferson spoke little in Congress. However, he was known for his graceful writing style.

In the heat of the Philadelphia summer, Jefferson struggled to find the words that would convince Americans and the world of the rightness of independence. The result was masterful. John Adams and Benjamin Franklin, who were also on the committee, suggested only minor changes.

☑**Checkpoint**   **What proposal did Richard Henry Lee make to Congress?**

## *Common Sense*

"I challenge the warmest advocate for reconciliation, to show a single advantage that this continent can reap, by being connected with Great Britain. I repeat the challenge, not a single advantage is derived. Our corn will fetch its price in any market in Europe, and our imported goods must be paid for, buy them where we will. . . . Whenever a war breaks out between England and any foreign power, the trade of America goes to ruin, because of her connection with Britain. . . . Every thing that is right or natural pleads for separation. The blood of the slain, the weeping voice of nature cries, 'TIS TIME TO PART.'"

—Thomas Paine, *Common Sense*

Thomas Paine

### Reading Primary Sources
#### Skills Activity

In *Common Sense*, Thomas Paine gives political, military, and moral arguments for breaking away from Britain. In the excerpt above, Paine discusses some economic reasons.

**(a) Identify Costs** Why does Paine think that association with Britain hurts American trade?

**(b) Make Inferences** What do you think Paine means by "the blood of the slain"?

Main Idea
The Declaration of
Independence is based on the
idea of natural rights.

**Analyze Word Roots**
Determine the meaning of
the word *respect*. The root
*spec* means "see." Also read how
the word is used in context.

# The Declaration of Independence

The Declaration of Independence is a brilliant piece of writing. Building on the ideas of the Enlightenment, it uses step-by-step logic to explain why the colonists wanted to break away from British rule. (See the Declaration of Independence following this section.)

The Declaration begins with a preamble, or introduction. It says that "a decent respect to the opinions of mankind" requires that Americans explain why they are breaking away from Britain.

**Natural Rights** The Declaration is divided into three main sections. The first section states some general ideas about society and government. "We hold these truths to be self-evident," or obvious to all. First among these truths is that "all men are created equal." Jefferson goes on to state that everyone is "endowed by their Creator with certain unalienable rights." This statement is based on John Locke's ideas about natural rights. (See Chapter 4.)

Like Locke, Jefferson goes on to state that governments are created in order to protect people's rights. And, like Locke, he concludes that, if a government violates those rights, the people have a right to abolish their government and create another.

**List of Grievances** Jefferson's next task was to prove that the British government had, in fact, violated the rights of the colonists. So the next section details a long list of specific grievances, or formal complaints, against King George III of England.

Many grievances accuse the king of ignoring rights that English citizens had enjoyed since the time of the Magna Carta. For example, the Magna Carta had established trial by jury as a basic right. The Declaration thus condemns the king "for depriving us, in many cases, of trial by jury." The Declaration also charges the king with "imposing taxes on us without our consent"—another violation of traditional English rights.

Time after time, says the Declaration, colonists have appealed to the king. But King George has ignored the petitions they sent. He must, therefore, be considered "unfit to be the ruler of a free people."

**Dissolving the Bonds** After stating the basic principle that the people have a right to abolish an unjust government and showing that the king has violated the rights of the colonists, the Declaration reaches a logical conclusion. It asserts that the colonies are "free and independent states . . . and that all political connection between them and the state of Great Britain is, and ought to be totally dissolved."

The document ends with a solemn pledge: "With a firm reliance on the protection of Divine Providence, we mutually pledge to each other our Lives, our Fortunes, and our sacred Honor."

The serious tone shows that, to the Patriots, declaring independence was a serious and deeply felt step.

King George III

✓Checkpoint **What does the Declaration of Independence say about people's rights?**

# Impact of the Declaration

**Main Idea**
The Declaration of Independence changed the nature of the American Revolution.

When Congress met to debate Lee's resolution, it still was not certain that they would declare independence. But on July 4, 1776, Congress approved the Declaration of Independence. Since then, Americans have celebrated July 4th as Independence Day.

The actual signing of the Declaration took place on August 2. According to tradition, as he stepped up to sign the document, Benjamin Franklin commented, "We must all hang together, or most assuredly we shall all hang separately." Indeed, for the delegates who signed, the personal risk was great. If captured by the British, they could be hanged.

The Declaration of Independence changed the nature of the Revolution. No longer were the Patriots fighting for fairer treatment from Britain. Now, they were fighting to create a new nation. There was no turning back.

Since then, the Declaration of Independence has become one of the world's enduring documents. The statement that "all men are created equal" still inspires Americans and people in other nations. In 1776, these words applied primarily to white, male property owners. Over the years, Americans worked to expand the notion of equality and natural rights.

☑**Checkpoint** **How did the Declaration change the nature of the American Revolution?**

⭐ **Looking Back and Ahead** Declaring independence from Britain was only a first step. For the Declaration to have real meaning, the Americans would have to win their liberties on the battlefield. In the next section, you will read about the progress of the war for independence.

Thomas Jefferson

## Section 1 | Check Your Progress

**Progress Monitoring** ⏼nline
**For:** Self-test with instant help
**Visit:** PHSchool.com
**Web Code:** mva-2061

### Comprehension and Critical Thinking

1. **(a) Recall** What was the main idea of Thomas Paine's *Common Sense*?
   **(b) Draw Conclusions** Why do you think *Common Sense* had such an impact on colonists?

2. **(a) Identify** What are the major parts of the Declaration of Independence?
   **(b) Apply Information** Why is the list of grievances against the king an important part of the Declaration?

### 🔁 Reading Skill

3. **Analyze Word Roots** Use the word root *spir*, meaning "breathe," to determine the meaning of the word *inspire* in this sentence: The statement that "all men are created equal" still *inspires* Americans and people in other nations.

### Vocabulary *Builder*

Complete each sentence so that the second part further explains the first part and clearly shows your understanding of the key term.

4. The Declaration of Independence began with a preamble, or _____.
5. Congress took a step toward independence when Lee introduced Virginia's resolution, or _____.
6. The Declaration includes a list of grievances, or _____.

### Writing

7. List two challenges you think Thomas Jefferson faced in writing the Declaration of Independence. Do you think he met these challenges? Explain.

# The Declaration of Independence

By signing the Declaration of Independence, members of the Continental Congress sent a clear message to Britain that the American colonies were free and independent states. Starting with its preamble, the document spells out all the reasons the people of the United States have the right to break away from Britain. **Critical Thinking:** *Detect Points of View How would a Loyalist react to the Declaration of Independence?*

**Explore More Video**
To learn more about the roots of the Declaration of Independence, view the video.

**Preamble**
The document first lists the reasons for writing the Declaration.

**Protection of Natural Rights**
If a government fails to protect people's natural rights, the people have a right to reject it and create another.

**Grievances Against the King**
King George has violated colonists' rights and ignored their petitions.

**Declaring Independence**
Therefore, the colonies declare their independence from Great Britain.

## The Unanimous Declaration of the Thirteen United States of America

When in the Course of human events, it becomes necessary for one people to dissolve the political bands which have connected them with another, and to assume among the powers of the earth, the separate and equal station to which the Laws of Nature and of Nature's God entitle them, a decent respect to the opinions of mankind requires that they should declare the causes which impel them to the separation.

We hold these truths to be self-evident, that all men are created equal, that they are endowed by their Creator with certain unalienable Rights, that among these are Life, Liberty and the pursuit of Happiness. That to secure these rights, Governments are instituted among Men, deriving their just powers from the consent of the governed. That whenever any Form of Government becomes destructive of these ends, it is the Right of the People to alter or to abolish it, and to institute new Government, laying its foundation on such principles and organizing its powers in such form, as to them shall seem most likely to effect their Safety and Happiness. Prudence, indeed, will dictate that Governments long established should not be changed for light and transient causes; and

The Declaration of Independence has four parts: the Preamble, the Declaration of Natural Rights, the List of Grievances, and the Resolution of Independence. The Preamble states why the Declaration was written. The document will explain to the world the reasons why the colonists feel **impelled**, or forced, to separate from Great Britain.

People set up governments to protect their basic rights. These rights are **unalienable**; they cannot be taken away. The purpose of government is to protect these natural rights. When a government does not protect the rights of the people, the people must change the government or create a new one. The colonists feel that the king's repeated **usurpations**, or unjust uses of power, are a form of **despotism**, or tyranny, that has denied them their basic rights.

accordingly all experience hath shown that mankind are more disposed to suffer, while evils are sufferable, than to right themselves by abolishing the forms to which they are accustomed. But when a long train of abuses and usurpations, pursuing invariably the same Object evinces a design to reduce them under absolute Despotism, it is their right, it is their duty, to throw off such Government, and to provide new Guards for their future security. Such has been the patient sufferance of these Colonies; and such is now the necessity which constrains them to alter their former Systems of Government. The history of the present King of Great Britain is a history of repeated injuries and usurpations, all having in direct object the establishment of an absolute Tyranny over these States. To prove this, let Facts be submitted to a candid world.

He has refused his Assent to Laws, the most wholesome and necessary for the public good.

He has forbidden his Governors to pass Laws of immediate and pressing importance, unless suspended in their operation till his Assent should be obtained; and when so suspended, he has utterly neglected to attend to them.

He has refused to pass other Laws for the accommodation of large districts of people, unless those people would relinquish the right of Representation in the Legislature, a right inestimable to them and formidable to tyrants only.

He has called together legislative bodies at places unusual, uncomfortable, and distant from the depository of their public Records, for the sole purpose of fatiguing them into compliance with his measures.

He has dissolved Representative Houses repeatedly, for opposing with manly firmness his invasions on the rights of the people.

He has refused for a long time, after such dissolutions, to cause others to be elected; whereby the Legislative powers, incapable of Annihilation, have returned to the People at large for their exercise; the State remaining in the mean time exposed to all the dangers of invasion from without, and convulsions within.

He has endeavoured to prevent the population of these States; for that purpose obstructing the Laws for Naturalization of Foreigners; refusing to pass others to encourage their migrations hither, and raising the conditions of new Appropriations of Lands.

He has obstructed the Administration of Justice by refusing his Assent to Laws for establishing Judiciary powers.

He has made Judges dependent on his Will alone, for the tenure of their offices, and the amount and payment of their salaries.

He has erected a multitude of New Offices, and sent hither swarms of Officers to harass our people, and eat out their substance.

He has kept among us, in times of peace, Standing Armies without the Consent of our legislatures.

The List of Grievances details the colonists' complaints against the British government, and King George III in particular. The colonists have no say in determining the laws that govern them and they feel King George's actions show little or no concern for the well being of the people.

The colonists refuse to **relinquish**, or give up, the right to representation, which they feel is **inestimable**, or priceless.

The king has refused to allow new legislators to be elected. As a result, the colonies have not been able to protect themselves against foreign enemies and **convulsions**, or riots, within the colonies.

The king has tried to stop foreigners from coming to the colonies by refusing to pass naturalization laws. Laws for naturalization of foreigners are laws that set up the process for foreigners to become legal citizens.

The king alone has decided a judge's **tenure**, or term. This grievance later would result in Article 3, Section 1, of the Constitution, which states that federal judges hold office for life.

He has affected to render the Military independent of and superior to the Civil power.

He has combined with others to subject us to a jurisdiction foreign to our constitution, and unacknowledged by our laws; giving his Assent to their Acts of pretended Legislation:

For quartering large bodies of armed troops among us:

> Forced by the king, the colonists have been **quartering**, or lodging, troops in their homes. This grievance found its way into the Constitution in the Third Amendment.

For protecting them, by a mock Trial, from punishment for any Murders which they should commit on the Inhabitants of these States:

For cutting off our Trade with all parts of the world:

For imposing Taxes on us without our Consent:

For depriving us in many cases, of the benefit of Trial by Jury:

For transporting us beyond Seas to be tried for pretended offences:

For abolishing the free System of English Laws in a neighbouring Province, establishing therein an Arbitrary government, and enlarging its Boundaries so as to render it at once an example and fit instrument for introducing the same absolute rule into these Colonies:

> The king has taken away the rights of the people in a nearby province (Canada). The colonists feared he could do the same to the colonies if he so wished.

For taking away our Charters, abolishing our most valuable Laws, and altering fundamentally the Forms of our Governments:

For suspending our own Legislatures, and declaring themselves invested with power to legislate for us in all cases whatsoever.

He has abdicated Government here, by declaring us out of his Protection and waging War against us.

He has plundered our seas, ravaged our Coasts, burnt our towns, and destroyed the lives of our people.

He is at this time transporting large Armies of foreign Mercenaries to complete the works of death, desolation, and tyranny, already begun with circumstances of Cruelty and perfidy scarcely paralleled in the most barbarous ages, and totally unworthy the Head of a civilized nation.

> The king has hired foreign **mercenaries**, or soldiers, to bring death and destruction to the colonists. The head of a civilized country should never act with the cruelty and **perfidy**, or dishonesty, that the king has.

He has constrained our fellow Citizens taken Captive on the high Seas to bear Arms against their Country, to become the executioners of their friends and Brethren, or to fall themselves by their Hands.

He has excited domestic insurrections amongst us, and has endeavoured to bring on the inhabitants of our frontiers, the merciless Indian Savages whose known rule of warfare, is an undistinguished destruction of all ages, sexes and conditions.

In every stage of these Oppressions We have Petitioned for Redress in the most humble terms: Our repeated Petitions have been answered only by repeated injury. A Prince, whose character is thus marked by every act which may define a Tyrant, is unfit to be the ruler of a free People.

> The colonists have tried repeatedly to petition the king to **redress,** or correct, these wrongs. Each time, they have been ignored by the king or punished by new laws. Because of the way he treats his subjects, the king is not fit to rule a free people.

The colonists have appealed to the British people. They have asked their fellow British subjects to support them. However, like the king, the British people have ignored the colonists' requests.

The Resolution of Independence boldly asserts that the colonies are now "free and independent states." The colonists have proven the **rectitude**, or justness, of their cause. The Declaration concludes by stating that these new states have the power to wage war, establish alliances, and trade with other countries.

Nor have We been wanting in attentions to our British brethren. We have warned them from time to time of attempts by their legislature to extend an unwarrantable jurisdiction over us. We have reminded them of the circumstances of our emigration and settlement here. We have appealed to their native justice and magnanimity, and we have conjured them by the ties of our common kindred, to disavow these usurpations, which would inevitably interrupt our connections and correspondence. They too have been deaf to the voice of justice and of consanguinity. We must, therefore, acquiesce in the necessity, which denounces our Separation, and hold them, as we hold the rest of mankind, Enemies in War, in Peace Friends.

We, therefore, the Representatives of the United States of America, in General Congress, Assembled, appealing to the Supreme Judge of the world for the rectitude of our intentions, do, in the Name, and by Authority of the good People of these Colonies, solemnly publish and declare, That these United Colonies are, and of Right ought to be Free and Independent States; that they are Absolved from all Allegiance to the British Crown, and that all political connection between them and the State of Great Britain, is and ought to be totally dissolved; and that as Free and Independent States, they have full Power to levy War, conclude Peace, contract Alliances, establish Commerce, and to do all other Acts and Things which Independent States may of right do. And for the support of this Declaration, with a firm reliance on the protection of Divine Providence, we mutually pledge to each other our Lives, our Fortunes and our sacred Honor.

John Hancock, *President*
Charles Thomson, *Secretary*

*Georgia*
Button Gwinnett
Lyman Hall
George Walton

*North Carolina*
William Hooper
Joseph Hewes
John Penn

*South Carolina*
Edward Rutledge
Thomas Heyward, Jr.
Thomas Lynch, Jr.
Arthur Middleton

*Maryland*
Samuel Chase
William Paca
Thomas Stone
Charles Carroll

*Virginia*
George Wythe
Richard Henry Lee
Thomas Jefferson
Benjamin Harrison
Thomas Nelson, Jr.
Francis Lightfoot Lee
Carter Braxton

*Pennsylvania*
Robert Morris
Benjamin Rush
Benjamin Franklin
John Morton
George Clymer
James Smith
George Taylor
James Wilson
George Ross

*Delaware*
Caesar Rodney
George Read
Thomas McKean

*New York*
William Floyd
Philip Livingston
Francis Lewis
Lewis Morris

*New Jersey*
Richard Stockton
John Witherspoon
Francis Hopkinson
John Hart
Abraham Clark

*New Hampshire*
Josiah Bartlett
William Whipple
Matthew Thornton

*Massachusetts*
Samuel Adams
John Adams
Robert Treat Paine
Elbridge Gerry

*Rhode Island*
Stephen Hopkins
William Ellery

*Connecticut*
Samuel Huntington
William Williams
Oliver Wolcott
Roger Sherman

## Objectives

1. Discover the results of fighting in the Middle States.
2. Understand why the Battle of Saratoga was a turning point in the American Revolution.
3. Learn how foreign nations and volunteers helped the Americans.

## Prepare to Read

### ⊙ Reading Skill

**Apply the Meanings of Prefixes** Prefixes—word parts added to the beginning of words or word roots—can dramatically affect a word's meaning. Applying the meanings of common prefixes will help you define unfamiliar words. Piece together a likely meaning. Check how the word is used within the content of the surrounding text. If necessary, use a dictionary.

### Vocabulary *Builder*

**High-Use Words**

<u>vital</u>, p. 183

<u>transform</u>, p. 183

**Key Terms and People**

Nathan Hale, p. 180

mercenary, p. 181

alliance, p. 183

Marquis de Lafayette, p. 183

cavalry, p. 183

Friedrich von Steuben, p. 183

☆ **Background Knowledge** In the last section, you saw how the 13 colonies proclaimed their independence. This section describes how American fortunes shifted back and forth on the battlefield in 1776 and 1777.

## Retreat From New York

In mid-1776, the heavy fighting shifted from New England to the Middle States. There, the Continental army suffered through the worst days of the war.

**Attack and Retreat** In June 1776, just as the Continental Congress was considering independence, a large British fleet arrived off New York. Sir William Howe, the British commander, gathered his forces on Staten Island, at the southern edge of New York harbor.

Washington expected Howe's attack. He already had led his forces south from Boston to Brooklyn on Long Island. However, his army was no match for the British. Howe had about 34,000 well-trained troops and 10,000 sailors, as well as ships to ferry them ashore. Washington had fewer than 20,000 poorly trained troops and no navy.

That summer saw a long series of battles and American retreats. In the Battle of Long Island, in August 1776, the British drove Washington's troops out of Brooklyn. The following month, Washington had to abandon New York City. The British pursued the Americans north to White Plains, then west and south across New Jersey.

**Main Idea**
Washington and the Continental army suffered severe setbacks in New York.

British fleet off Long Island

179

**Nathan Hale** During the fight for New York, Nathan Hale became an American legend. Hale was a Connecticut officer, and he volunteered for dangerous spy duty. His mission was to collect information about British battle plans on Long Island.

Caught behind British lines, Hale was tried and condemned to death. He was hanged the next morning. Later, it was reported that his last words had been, "I only regret that I have but one life to lose for my country."

☑ **Checkpoint**  **What was the result of the Battle of Long Island?**

**Main Idea**
The surprise victory at Trenton raised American spirits.

## Surprises for the British

Under relentless British pursuit, the Continental army kept retreating. In December, it crossed the Delaware River into Pennsylvania. The British now threatened Philadelphia. Patriot spirits were low. Many soldiers deserted. Others seemed ready to go home as soon as their terms of service ended.

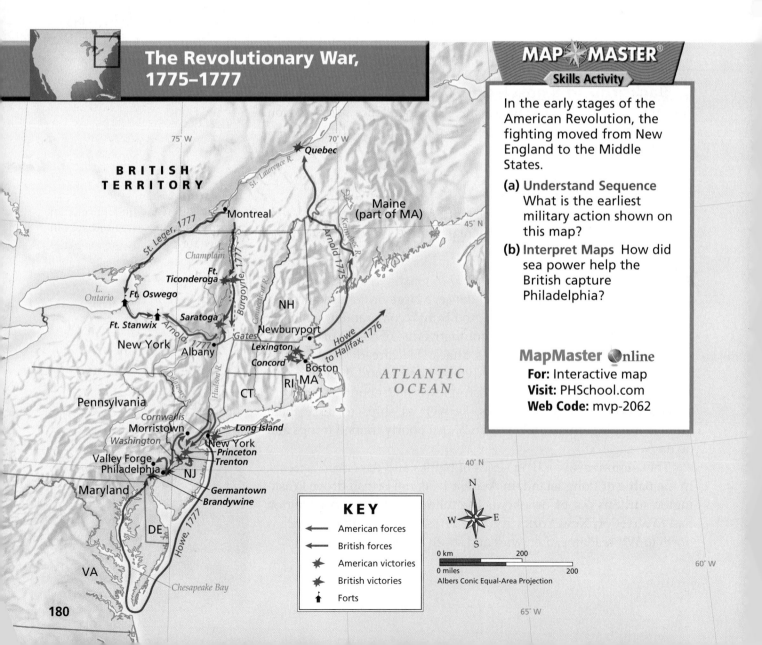

**The Revolutionary War, 1775–1777**

**MAP MASTER**
**Skills Activity**

In the early stages of the American Revolution, the fighting moved from New England to the Middle States.

**(a) Understand Sequence** What is the earliest military action shown on this map?

**(b) Interpret Maps** How did sea power help the British capture Philadelphia?

**MapMaster ⦿nline**
**For:** Interactive map
**Visit:** PHSchool.com
**Web Code:** mvp-2062

KEY
← American forces
← British forces
★ American victories
✶ British victories
⬆ Forts

0 km   200
0 miles   200
Albers Conic Equal-Area Projection

Thomas Paine had retreated with the army through New Jersey. To raise morale, he wrote another pamphlet, *The Crisis*. Paine urged Americans to support the army, despite hard times. He wrote:

> **❝**These are the times that try men's souls. The summer soldier and the sunshine patriot will, in this crisis, shrink from the service of his country; but he that stands it now deserves the love and thanks of man and woman.**❞**
>
> —Thomas Paine, *The Crisis*

Washington had *The Crisis* read aloud to his troops. At the same time, he made plans for a bold attack.

**Crossing the Delaware** On Christmas night, 1776, Washington led 2,400 men across the river in small boats. Soldiers huddled in the boats as the spray from the river froze on their faces. So poorly supplied were the troops that some had no shoes. Once across the river, the soldiers marched in the swirling snow. To keep their feet from freezing, the soldiers bound them in rags.

On the far bank, the men trudged several miles with Washington urging them on. Early on December 26, they attacked Trenton from two sides, achieving complete surprise.

**An American Victory** The attack brought a ringing American victory. The soldiers in Trenton were Hessians (men from Hesse, a small German state). They were among thousands of German mercenaries who were fighting for the British. Mercenaries are soldiers who are paid to fight for a country other than their own. Washington's army captured almost a thousand Hessian mercenaries.

Pursued by the British, Washington used a clever trick to escape. His soldiers made camp near Trenton and lit campfires. After dark, most of the men packed up and quietly withdrew. The British did not discover the trick until daylight, when the main body of soldiers attacked and heavily damaged a British force near Princeton.

☑ **Checkpoint** How did Washington attack Trenton?

# Saratoga: A Turning Point

British general John Burgoyne came up with a plan he hoped would quickly end the rebellion. His goal was to cut New England off from the rest of the states.

**Washington at Trenton**
During Washington's surprise attack on Trenton, the commander of the Hessian mercenaries was seriously wounded. In this picture, Washington orders his men to help the dying Hessian officer to his bed. **Critical Thinking: Apply Information** *Why was Washington able to win the battle at Trenton?*

**Main Idea**
The Battle of Saratoga ended Britain's hopes of a quick victory.

**The British Plan** Burgoyne's plan called for British forces to drive toward Albany, New York, from three directions. From Canada, an army of 8,000 would move south to capture the forts on Lake Champlain, Lake George, and the upper Hudson River. From the west, a smaller British force would drive through the Mohawk Valley toward Albany. And from the south, General Howe would lead a large army up the Hudson River from New York City.

Burgoyne's plan ran into trouble almost immediately. George III ordered Howe to move south from New York in a misguided attempt to attack Philadelphia. Not until November were Howe's forces ready to march north again. At the same time, American forces cut off the British troops coming through the Mohawk Valley.

**An American Victory** Burgoyne led the main British force from Canada in June. After recapturing Fort Ticonderoga, they slowly pushed south, dragging a large train of baggage carts through the woods. Supplies were running short.

Americans were rushing to block the British. By September, the American commander in New York, General Horatio Gates, had 6,000 men ready to fight. At the village of Saratoga, New York, the Americans surrounded the British. After suffering heavy casualties, Burgoyne surrendered on October 17, 1777.

**Apply the Meanings of Prefixes**

The prefix *mis-* means "badly" or "wrongly." What does the word *misguided* mean?

**History** *Interactive*

**Explore a Soldier's Life**

**Visit:** PHSchool.com
**Web Code:** mvl-2062

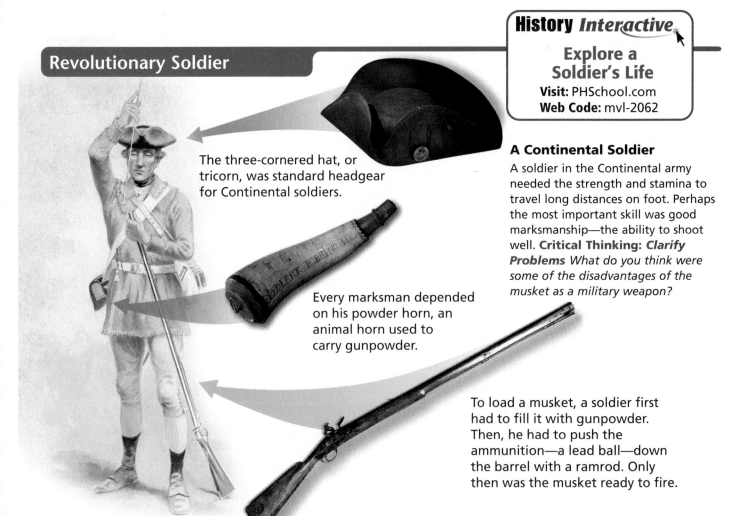

**Revolutionary Soldier**

The three-cornered hat, or tricorn, was standard headgear for Continental soldiers.

Every marksman depended on his powder horn, an animal horn used to carry gunpowder.

**A Continental Soldier**

A soldier in the Continental army needed the strength and stamina to travel long distances on foot. Perhaps the most important skill was good marksmanship—the ability to shoot well. **Critical Thinking:** *Clarify Problems What do you think were some of the disadvantages of the musket as a military weapon?*

To load a musket, a soldier first had to fill it with gunpowder. Then, he had to push the ammunition—a lead ball—down the barrel with a ramrod. Only then was the musket ready to fire.

**Results of the Battle** The Battle of Saratoga marked a major turning point in the war. The American victory ended the British threat to New England and destroyed British hopes of an easy victory. It also lifted Patriot spirits at a time when Washington's army was suffering defeats. Perhaps most important, the Battle of Saratoga helped convince Europeans that the Americans had a sound chance of winning.

☑**Checkpoint** **List two results of the Battle of Saratoga.**

## Help From Overseas

Soon after Saratoga, France agreed to openly support American independence. In February 1778, France officially formed an alliance with the United States. An alliance is a formal agreement between two powers to work together toward a common goal.

**The French Alliance** France was eager to weaken Britain. Even before Saratoga, the French had secretly supplied money and arms to the Americans. But the French did not want to take an open stand until it seemed the Americans might win. The Battle of Saratoga convinced the French government to help the struggling young nation. In February 1778, France became the first nation to sign a treaty with the United States.

France and its allies in the Netherlands and Spain also went to war with Britain. By carrying the fight to Europe and the Caribbean, the allies forced Britain to wage war on many fronts. This helped the American cause, because the British could spare fewer troops to fight in North America.

**European Volunteers** A number of Europeans volunteered to serve with the American forces. They were inspired by the American struggle for liberty.

A French noble, the Marquis de Lafayette (lah fay YET), became a high-ranking officer in Washington's army. He and Washington became close friends. When Lafayette was wounded in battle, Washington told a surgeon, "Treat him as though he were my son."

Volunteers from Poland also made <u>vital</u> contributions to the Patriot war effort. Thaddeus Kosciusko (kawsh CHUSH koh) was an engineer who took charge of building fortifications at West Point. Casimir Pulaski led and trained cavalry, or units of troops on horseback.

**Baron von Steuben** A German baron, Friedrich von Steuben (STOO buhn), helped train the Continental army. Steuben had served in the Prussian army, which was considered the best in Europe.

Before Steuben arrived in early 1778, American troops were often poorly trained and undisciplined. Steuben taught the soldiers how to march, how to improve their aim, and how to attack with bayonets. His methods helped to <u>transform</u> raw recruits into soldiers and shaped the Continental army into a more effective force.

☑**Checkpoint** **How did France aid the Patriot cause?**

**Main Idea**
Both foreign nations and individuals from Europe gave valuable help to the Patriot cause.

Medals commemorating the American-French alliance

**Vocabulary *Builder***
<u>vital</u> (VĪ tuhl) *adj.* necessary; of great importance

**Vocabulary *Builder***
<u>transform</u> (trans FORM) *v.* to change from one thing or condition to another

# Valley Forge

Washington's Continental army suffered through the cruel winter of 1777–1778 in a hastily built camp at Valley Forge in Pennsylvania. Meanwhile, some 22 miles away, British officers in Philadelphia danced the winter away in a merry round of parties and balls.

The 11,000 Continental soldiers were not sufficiently fed, clothed, or housed. Many lacked socks, shoes, and even trousers. Throughout the winter, they shivered in drafty huts. At any one time, about one soldier in four was sick with chills, fever, or worse.

Because food was so scarce, the soldiers mainly ate thin soup and dry bread patties. One private later recalled that he went without food for two days. He was so hungry he would have grabbed food away from anyone, even his best friend. Finally, he found half a pumpkin. He cooked it "upon a rock, the skin side up, by making a fire on it."

When Americans learned about conditions at Valley Forge, they sent help. Women collected food, medicine, warm clothes, and ammunition. Some women, including George Washington's wife, Martha, went to Valley Forge to tend the sick and wounded.

Despite its woes, the Continental army used that winter to gather its strength for the battles that lay ahead. Steuben's drills sharpened the soldiers' skills and discipline.

✓**Checkpoint  Why was the winter at Valley Forge so difficult?**

☆ **Looking Back and Ahead** By the spring of 1778, the army at Valley Forge was ready to resume the fight. "The army grows stronger every day," wrote one New Jersey soldier. While soldiers drilled, Washington and his staff planned new campaigns against the British.

Washington at Valley Forge

---

Section 2 | **Check Your Progress**

**Progress Monitoring** ⓞnline
**For:** Self-test with instant help
**Visit:** PHSchool.com
**Web Code:** mva-2062

## Comprehension and Critical Thinking

**1. (a) Recall** What happened at Trenton in December 1776?
**(b) Draw Inferences** What did Washington's actions at the Battle of Trenton show about his character and leadership?

**2. (a) List** What were three important results of the American victory at Saratoga?
**(b) Make Predictions** What do you think would have happened if the Americans had lost the battle?

## Reading Skill

**3. Apply the Meanings of Prefixes** The prefix *trans-* means "change." The word root *form* means "shape" or "structure." Use this information to explain the meaning of *transform* in this sentence: His methods helped to *transform* raw recruits into soldiers.

## Vocabulary *Builder*

Read each sentence below. If the sentence is true, write YES and explain why. If the sentence is not true, write NO and explain why not.

**4.** German mercenaries helped the British because they believed the king should rule the Americans.
**5.** After making an alliance with the Americans, France contributed money and arms to the Patriots.
**6.** The cavalry soldiers fired at the British soldiers from the ground before running away.

## Writing

**7.** In order to gather enough soldiers to fight the battle in America, the British had to hire German mercenaries. List one strong argument for and one strong argument against this solution.

# Valley Forge
## by Maxwell Anderson

**Prepare to Read**

## Introduction

Maxwell Anderson's play *Valley Forge* depicts the hardships faced by Washington's army in the winter of 1778. One problem the army faced was men trying to go home. Here, Washington hears the complaints of a soldier named Teague.

##  Reading Skill

**Analyze Dramatic Conflict** An important element in any drama is conflict, when two characters want different things. As you read this scene, try to identify the source of the conflict between Washington and Teague.

## Vocabulary *Builder*

As you read this literature selection, look for the following underlined words:

**commissary** (KAH muh sehr ee) *n.* food supplies

**munitions** (myoo NIH shuhns) *n.* weapons and ammunition

---

TEAGUE: I'm going hungry here and my woman's going hungry at home. You let me go home for the winter, and you won't have to feed me, and that relieves the <u>commissary</u>. I rustle some wild meat for the younguns and the old woman, and they don't starve and I don't starve. More'n that, everybody knows there's two or three thousand men gone home already for that same reason, and if they was here now they'd be chewing the bark off the second-growth birch like so many cottontails. I don't hold it against you and I don't hold it against anybody because I don't know who in thunder to hold it against, but there's nothing to eat here. . . .

WASHINGTON: Well, Master Teague, if they catch you they'll give you seventy-five lashes, and that's a good deal to take and live. On the other hand, you're quite right from your own angle, and if I were you I'd feel as you do. If you go home, and we all go home this winter, you won't need to bother about coming back in the spring. There'll be not fighting to come back to. General Howe will march out of Philadelphia and take over these states of ours. If he knew now how many have deserted, how many are sick, how many unfit for duty on account of the lack of food and clothes and <u>munitions</u>, he'd come back in force and wring our necks one by one, and the neck of our sickly little revolution along with us.

> From *America On Stage: Ten Great Plays of American History,*
> ed. Stanley Richards. Doubleday & Co., 1976.

**Analyze Dramatic Conflict**

What does Teague want? What does Washington want? How are their wishes in conflict?

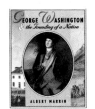

If you liked this excerpt and want to learn more about George Washington, you might want to read *George Washington and the Founding of a Nation* by Albert Marrin. Dutton Books, 2001.

## *Analyze* LITERATURE

Do you think that Washington should permit Teague to go home without punishment? Write a paragraph explaining the reasons for your opinion.

# The War Widens

## Objectives

1. Discover the role that African Americans played in the American Revolution.

2. Find out how the war affected women and other civilians.

3. Learn about the progress of the fighting on the western frontier and at sea.

## Prepare to Read

### Reading Skill

**Analyze Word Roots** Word roots can do more than help you define unfamiliar words. They can help you expand your vocabulary. As you read Section 3, use word roots to determine meanings. Then, list other words you know that come from the same word roots. Think about how they share meanings with the text words—and how the meanings differ. Notice the shades of meaning that can derive from a single word root.

### Vocabulary *Builder*

**High-Use Words**
**confine**, p. 188
**resource**, p. 188

**Key Terms and People**
enlist, p. 187
civilian, p. 187
continental, p. 188
George Rogers Clark, p. 189
Bernardo de Gálvez, p. 189
John Paul Jones, p. 190
privateer, p. 190

⭐ **Background Knowledge** You have learned about the early stages of the American Revolution. In this section, you will read how the war affected Americans in all parts of the country.

## African Americans in the War

**Main Idea**
The promise of freedom led many African Americans to serve in the American Revolution.

African Americans fought on both sides of the American Revolution. For them, the war meant both danger and opportunity.

**Free and Slave** From the beginning, free African Americans took part in the war. At least nine served as minutemen at Lexington and Concord. Peter Salem fought at Bunker Hill and Saratoga.

Enslaved people served as well. After fleeing his master in Rhode Island, Jehu Grant served in the American army for nine months. He later recalled:

> **❝**When I saw liberty poles and the people all engaged for the support of freedom, I could not but like and be pleased with such thing. . . . The songs of liberty . . . thrilled through my heart.**❞**
>
> —Jehu Grant, letter, December 1, 1836

### Analyze Word Roots

The word root *port* means "to carry." The prefix *sub-* means "under," and *sub-* becomes *sup-* when used before the letter *p*. Use these word parts to explain the meaning of *support*. List three other words that build on the root *port*.

The British offered freedom to enslaved people who deserted and joined the British. Many thousands did so. They served mainly in support roles as cooks, blacksmiths, and teamsters. However, some people who had formerly been enslaved fought for the British.

On the American side, Washington at first refused to accept African American soldiers. But the British offer of freedom to enslaved people made Washington change his policy. By the end of the war, some 7,000 African Americans had served on the American side, including 2,000 in the navy. African Americans also served in northern militias and state armies. Most southern states, however, refused to accept African American soldiers. Slave owners feared armed slave revolts.

**Freedom Beckons**  During the Revolution, a number of northern states took steps to end slavery. For example, a Pennsylvania law of 1780 provided for a gradual end to slavery. It allowed slaveholders to keep their existing slaves but barred them from getting more.

 **Checkpoint**  **Why did some enslaved African Americans choose to fight for the British?**

## The War at Home

Many men **enlisted,** or signed up for duty, in the military. After a set term, usually one year, they were free to leave. Thus, Washington had to struggle constantly to keep the ranks of his army filled.

**Civilians,** or people not in the military, also faced hardships. They were often subject to food shortages and military attack.

**Main Idea**
The war brought hardships and new responsibilities to women and others.

1951 American soldiers in Korea

### African American Soldiers

**1777**  Reversing his earlier policy, Washington permits free African Americans to enlist in the Continental army.

**1863**  During the last half of the Civil War, African Americans were allowed to join the Union army. Black and white soldiers served in separate units.

**1948**  President Harry Truman ended racial separation in the military. Two years later, black and white troops served side by side in the Korean War.

### Link to Today  **Online**

**The Military Today**  In today's all-volunteer military, African Americans make up 21 percent of all military personnel.

**For:** U.S. military in the news
**Visit:** PHSchool.com
**Web Code:** mvc-2063

**A Woman in Battle**
When her husband was wounded at the Battle of Monmouth, Mary Ludwig Hays dropped her water bucket and took up his cannon. Her heroic actions made her a legendary American hero, known as Molly Pitcher. **Critical Thinking:** *Evaluate Information* Why do you think Molly Pitcher has become a popular subject for American artists? What image of women does she represent?

**Vocabulary** *Builder*
<u>confine</u> (kuhn FĪN) *v.* to keep within certain limits

**Vocabulary** *Builder*
<u>resource</u> (REE sors) *n.* supply of something to meet a particular need

**Women** As men went to war, women took over many of their duties. On farms, women planted crops and cared for livestock. In towns, women often ran their husbands' businesses.

Some women accompanied their husbands to military camps. In battles, they cared for the wounded. One woman, Deborah Sampson, joined the army, disguised as a man. Wounded in battle, Sampson tended her own wounds in order to keep her secret.

The added responsibilities of wartime gave many women a new confidence. At a time when women's roles were largely <u>confined</u>, the war opened up new opportunities for many women.

**Financial Burdens** Paying for the war was a difficult task. Congress had limited <u>resources</u>. With no power to tax, Congress had to plead with the states for money. However, the states had little money themselves.

To pay and supply troops, Congress printed continentals, or paper money. But the more money Congress printed, the less the money was worth. By the end of the war, paper money had lost almost all its value. Something worthless was said to be "not worth a continental."

☑**Checkpoint** **What roles did women play in the Revolution?**

**Main Idea**
Fighting on the western frontier brought Native Americans into the war.

# Fighting in the West

Throughout most of the American Revolution, attention was mainly focused on the 13 states along the Atlantic coast. However, skirmishes and battles occurred on the western frontier as well.

**Native Americans Take Sides** Americans tried to keep the Native Americans neutral. They offered payments to groups willing to remain at peace. They brought leaders to Philadelphia to impress them with parades of Continental troops.

Still, most Native American groups sided with Britain. They feared that an American victory would mean more settlers moving west or south onto Native American lands.

**Defending the Frontier** Seeking to defend against attacks on the frontier, Virginia sent George Rogers Clark and a militia force to strike British forts beyond the Appalachian Mountains in 1778. Clark's forces easily captured two Mississippi River outposts, Kaskaskia and Cahokia.

Early in 1779, Clark and his men trudged across 200 miles, at times splashing through icy floodwaters up to their chests. Their midwinter attack on the fort at Vincennes caught the British by surprise. The British and their Native American allies surrendered.

Clark's victories allowed settlers to remain on the frontier. This strengthened the American claim on the Ohio Valley area.

**Help From the Spanish** The Americans got unofficial help from Spain. At the time, Spain governed Louisiana, the land west of the Mississippi stretching as far north as Canada. The Spanish were eager to get back Florida, which they had lost to Britain at the end of the French and Indian War.

Even before Spain declared war against Britain in 1779, Louisiana governor Bernardo de Gálvez began helping the Americans. He secretly provided money and munitions to George Rogers Clark and other Americans. He also gave American ships safe refuge in New Orleans harbor. From 1779 to 1781, Gálvez played a key role in Spanish attacks that captured British forts on the Mississippi River and the Gulf of Mexico.

In 1781, the Americans sought financial help from the Spanish colony of Cuba. A group of wealthy women, the "Havana's Ladies," were especially generous. They sent some 7 million dollars to the Americans along with a letter saying, "So the American mothers' sons are not born as slaves." Without the contribution of these women, Washington's army might have run short of needed funds at a critical point in the war. A commander in the Continental army later wrote with gratitude of "the generous gesture and solidarity of the Cuban ladies and how they had donated money and jewelry."

✔**Checkpoint** What was the result of the fighting in the West?

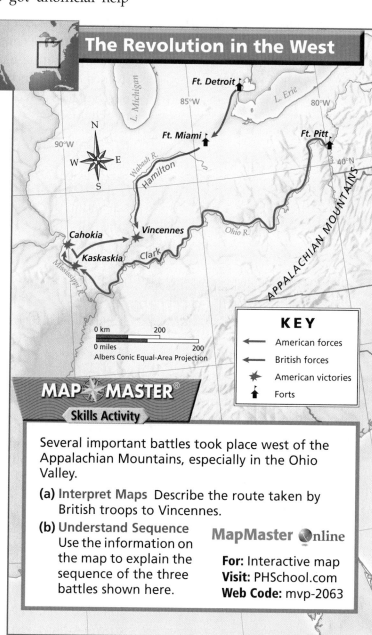

**The Revolution in the West**

**KEY**
← American forces
← British forces
✳ American victories
⬆ Forts

0 km 200
0 miles 200
Albers Conic Equal-Area Projection

**MAP ✳ MASTER®**
**Skills Activity**

Several important battles took place west of the Appalachian Mountains, especially in the Ohio Valley.

**(a) Interpret Maps** Describe the route taken by British troops to Vincennes.

**(b) Understand Sequence** Use the information on the map to explain the sequence of the three battles shown here.

**MapMaster** ⬤**nline**

**For:** Interactive map
**Visit:** PHSchool.com
**Web Code:** mvp-2063

## The War at Sea

Congress had voted to create a Continental navy as early as 1775. But American shipyards were able to build only a few warships. With only a small navy to go against the powerful British fleet, the Americans became skilled at making hit-and-run attacks on British shipping. Still, Britain dominated the seas. The British fleet blocked most ships from entering or leaving American ports.

The most famous naval battle took place off the coast of England in 1779. The American ship *Bonhomme Richard* (bon ohm ree CHARD), under the command of John Paul Jones, fought side by side with the larger British warship *Serapis.* Cannon and musket fire ripped the sails of both ships to shreds and blasted holes in their wooden sides. Though his ship was in tatters, Jones refused to give up. "I have not yet begun to fight," he vowed. Finally, with dozens of sailors dead on each side, the captain of the *Serapis* surrendered.

The navy had help from some 800 privateers that harassed British shipping. **Privateers** were armed civilian ships that had their government's permission to attack enemy ships and keep their goods. Operating like pirate ships, privateers seized cargoes of rum from the West Indies, wool from England, and furs from Canada. Such attacks forced Britain to spend valuable resources protecting merchant ships.

John Paul Jones

☑**Checkpoint**  How did privateers help the American war effort?

⭐ **Looking Back and Ahead**  Despite important battles at sea and in the west, the main war effort was concentrated in the colonies. In the next section, you will read about the final phase of the war.

---

**Section 3 | Check Your Progress**

Progress Monitoring Online
For: Self-test with instant help
Visit: PHSchool.com
Web Code: mva-2063

### Comprehension and Critical Thinking

**1. (a) Recall**  How did Washington's policy toward African American soldiers change? What was the reason for this change?
**(b) Identify Benefits**  How did African Americans expect to benefit from serving in the military?

**2. (a) Describe**  What challenges did the American navy face?
**(b) Draw Conclusions**  Why do you think John Paul Jones is considered a great American hero?

### Reading Skill

**3. Analyze Word Roots**  The root *fid* means "faith." The prefix *con-* means "with." Use these word parts to determine the meaning of *confidence* in this sentence: The added responsibilities of wartime gave many women a new *confidence.*

### Vocabulary *Builder*

**4.** Draw a table with four rows and three columns. In the first column, list the key terms from this section: enlist, civilian, continental, privateer. In the next column, write the definition of each word. In the last column, make a small illustration that shows the meaning of the word.

### Writing

**5.** Identify the problems facing the Continental Congress during the war. Then, brainstorm one or two possible solutions.

# Winning Independence

## Objectives

1. Find out how the Americans won the final battle of the Revolution.

2. Learn the terms of the peace treaty with England.

3. Explore the reasons that the Americans were victorious.

4. Examine the effects of the American Revolution.

## Prepare to Read

 **Reading Skill**

**Apply the Meanings of the Prefix *re-*** Prefixes sometimes have more than one meaning. For example, the prefix *re-* can mean "again" or "anew," but it can also mean "back" or "backward." You must think about the surrounding words and context in which the word is used before deciding which meaning of the prefix to apply.

### Vocabulary *Builder*

**High-Use Words**

efficient, p. 191

option, p. 192

**Key Terms and People**

Charles Cornwallis, p. 191

guerrilla, p. 191

Francis Marion, p. 191

Nathanael Greene, p. 192

traitor, p. 192

⭐ **Background Knowledge** In the last section, you read about battles at sea and in the West. In this section, you will see how fighting shifted to the South the final stages of Revolution.

## Fighting Moves South

The British shifted their attention to the South late in 1778. Their aim was to capture some key cities, win over the local population, and then march north, acquiring one state after another.

**British Advance** At first, the plan seemed to work. British soldiers moved north from Florida to Georgia. In December 1778, the British took the city of Savannah. Within a month, they controlled most of Georgia.

Moving on to South Carolina, the British captured the main port, Charles Town, and then the rest of the state. The British commander, Lord Charles Cornwallis, then carried the war into North Carolina. It looked as if the British might be unstoppable.

To slow the British advance, Americans used guerrilla tactics. Guerrillas are fighters who work in small bands to make hit-and-run attacks. In South Carolina, Francis Marion led his men silently through the swamps. They attacked without warning, then escaped. Marion's guerrilla attacks were so efficient that he won the nickname the Swamp Fox. Other bands of guerrillas were also active.

Elsewhere in the South, Loyalist bands roamed the backcountry. They plundered and burned Patriot farms, killing men, women, and children. "If a stop cannot be put to these massacres," wrote one Continental general, "the country will be depopulated in a few months more."

**Main Idea**
After fighting shifted to the South, the war ended with an American victory at Yorktown.

**Vocabulary *Builder***
**efficient** (ee FISH ehnt) *adj.* acting effectively, without wasted cost or effort

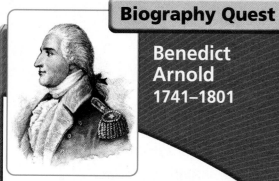 
**Vocabulary** *Builder*
<u>option</u> (AHP shuhn) *n.* choice; possible course of action

**Brighter Days** Patriot fortunes began to improve in October 1780. Some 900 frontier fighters defeated a larger force of British troops and Loyalists atop Kings Mountain in South Carolina.

In December 1780, General Nathanael Greene took over command of the Continental army in the South. Greene split his small army in two. He led 1,200 men into eastern South Carolina, leaving General Daniel Morgan with 800 men in the west.

In January 1781, Morgan won a clear victory at the Battle of Cowpens. He put a small militia force in front, telling the men to fire three shots and then retreat. The British rushed forward, only to be met by charging cavalry and a line of skilled riflemen.

**American Traitor** Still, the British seemed to have the upper hand in the South. In addition to Cornwallis's forces, the British had troops under the command of an American traitor, Benedict Arnold. A **traitor** is a person who turns against one side in a conflict to help the other side.

Early in the war, Arnold had fought bravely for the Patriots. But Arnold felt Congress undervalued him. He plotted to turn West Point, a key fort on the Hudson River in New York, over to the British. When the plot was discovered in September 1780, Arnold escaped. He and his Loyalist soldiers then staged a series of destructive raids in Virginia.

**Final Battle** Weakened by battles like Cowpens, Cornwallis headed to Virginia. That gave Greene an excellent opportunity. Over a five-month period, Patriot forces swept through the Deep South. By late summer, only Charles Town and Savannah remained in British hands.

Cornwallis then made a fateful mistake. He moved his main army to the Yorktown peninsula, a tongue of Virginia land poking into Chesapeake Bay. There, he thought, the British fleet could reinforce his position. But at the end of August, the French fleet arrived off Yorktown and chased off British ships.

At the same time, Washington rushed toward Virginia with American and French troops. Cornwallis found himself in a trap. American and French soldiers barred escape by land, while the French fleet blocked escape by sea. After three weeks, Cornwallis had no <u>option</u> but to surrender.

On October 19, 1781, the Americans and French lined up in two facing columns. The British marched glumly between the two columns and tossed their weapons into a large pile on the ground. The victory at Yorktown was the last major battle of the war.

✔**Checkpoint** **How were Cornwallis and his troops trapped at Yorktown?**

# Making Peace With Britain

The news from Yorktown caused shockwaves in Britain. Although the king wanted to keep fighting, Parliament voted in favor of peace.

Peace talks began in Paris in 1782. The American delegation included Benjamin Franklin and John Adams. Britain was eager for peace, so the Americans got most of what they wanted.

**Treaty of Paris** The talks led to an agreement, the Treaty of Paris. Britain recognized the independence of the United States. The boundaries of the new nation were set at the Atlantic on the east, Canada on the north, the Mississippi River on the west, and Florida on the south. Florida itself was returned to Spain.

For its part, the United States agreed to "earnestly recommend" that the states restore rights and property taken from Loyalists during the war. However, most states ignored this pledge.

On April 15, 1783, Congress approved the treaty. The war was officially over. It had been almost exactly eight years since the "shot heard round the world" started the fighting at Lexington.

**Main Idea**

In the Treaty of Paris, Britain recognized American independence.

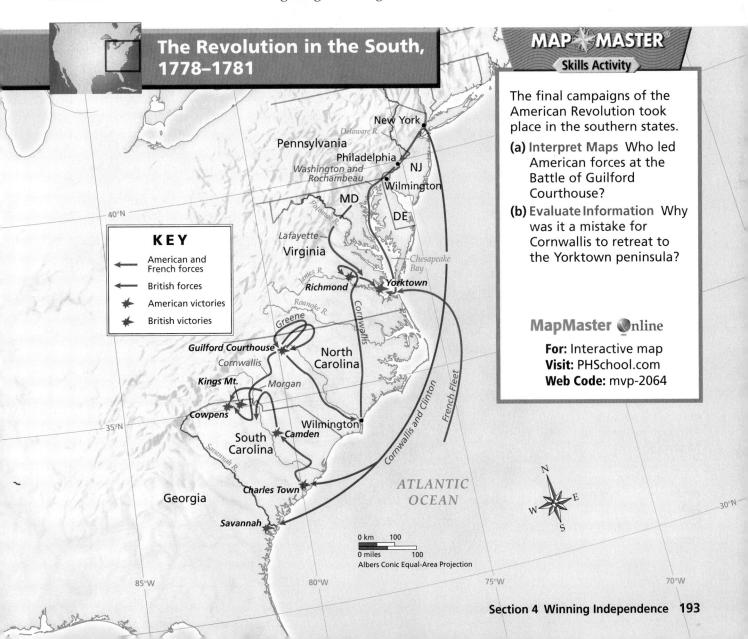

## The Revolution in the South, 1778–1781

**KEY**

← American and French forces

← British forces

✦ American victories

✦ British victories

### MAP MASTER®
#### Skills Activity

The final campaigns of the American Revolution took place in the southern states.

**(a) Interpret Maps** Who led American forces at the Battle of Guilford Courthouse?

**(b) Evaluate Information** Why was it a mistake for Cornwallis to retreat to the Yorktown peninsula?

**MapMaster Online**

**For:** Interactive map
**Visit:** PHSchool.com
**Web Code:** mvp-2064

# Why Did the Americans Win?

Many factors contributed to the American victory. They fell into four main groups: geographic advantages, help from abroad, patriotic spirit, and skilled leadership.
**Critical Thinking:** *Evaluate Information* What do you think was the most important reason for the American victory?

## Geography

Americans, such as Francis Marion (pictured below), were on their home ground. They knew the forests, hills, and swamps. But British forces were far from their home country. They had to depend on longer supply lines, stretching across the Atlantic Ocean. ▼

## Patriotic Spirit ▲

A key asset of the Americans was patriotism. Americans were fighting to create a new nation. Many soldiers stayed in the army for years, at great financial and personal sacrifice. Leaders such as Jefferson and Adams risked their lives and fortunes to champion independence.

## Skilled Leadership ▶

Despite great odds, George Washington (left) never gave up. Although he sometimes faced sharp criticism in Congress, his courage and knowledge won him broad support in the army. By the end of the war, he was the new nation's most admired hero.

## ◀ Help From Abroad

The Americans might never have won without French military help. Men such as Lafayette (right) provided needed leadership and support. Money from such countries as Spain and the Netherlands was also crucial.

**Washington's Farewell** On December 4, 1783, Washington and his ranking officers were reunited for one last meal together at Fraunces Tavern in New York City. In parting, each man, in turn, embraced Washington. One officer wrote, "Such a scene of sorrow and weeping I had never before witnessed."

Washington wished to retire to his plantation. Soon, though, he would again be called to the aid of the nation he had helped create.

☑ **Checkpoint** What was the Treaty of Paris?

# Impact of the Revolution

The immediate effect of the American Revolution was to create a new nation of 13 independent states, linked by ties of custom and history. The long-term effects are still being felt today. The Declaration of Independence cemented ideas like equality and liberty in the American mind. Over time, those concepts have gained broader meanings.

The impact of American independence reached beyond the borders of the infant nation. In 1789, revolution shook France. Leaders of the French Revolution, including Lafayette, looked to the American example. They issued the Declaration of the Rights of Man and the Citizen, modeled in part on the Declaration of Independence. The American Revolution also inspired later independence movements in Latin America.

☑ **Checkpoint** How did the American Revolution affect France?

⭐ **Looking Back and Ahead** The United States emerged from the American Revolution as a proud nation—but also weak and deeply in debt. In the next chapter, you will read how the new nation met the challenge of forming a democratic government.

**Main Idea**
The American Revolution affected people both in the United States and around the world.

**Apply the Meaning of the Prefix re-**
The word root *belli* means "war." Apply a meaning of *re-* to determine the meaning of *rebelled.* Identify the prefix meaning that you applied.

---

**Section 4 | Check Your Progress**

**Progress Monitoring** Online
**For:** Self-test with instant help
**Visit:** PHSchool.com
**Web Code:** mva-2064

**Comprehension and Critical Thinking**

**1. (a) Recall** What military strategy defeated Cornwallis at Yorktown?
**(b) Apply Information** What was one important factor that contributed to the American victory at Yorktown?

**2. (a) Describe** What were the provisions of the Treaty of Paris?
**(b) Identify Benefits** Why was setting the nation's western border important economically to the new country?

🔄 **Reading Skill**

**3. Apply the Meanings of the Prefix re-** Read the text under the heading "Making Peace With Britain," and find at least two words that use the prefix *re-*. Apply the meanings of the prefix to define those words.

**Vocabulary *Builder***

Answer the following questions in complete sentences that show your understanding of the key terms.
**4.** What advantages did guerrillas have against larger forces?

**5.** Why did Americans consider Benedict Arnold to be a traitor?

**Writing**

**6.** Once the Treaty of Paris was signed, the Americans had to address a new set of problems. Prepare a thesis statement for an essay about the challenges facing the new nation.

By comparing maps from different time periods, you can see how historical changes affected an area. The two maps below show North America before and after the Revolutionary War.

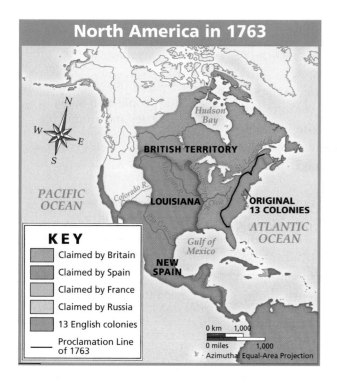

**North America in 1763**

PACIFIC OCEAN

Hudson Bay

BRITISH TERRITORY

LOUISIANA

ORIGINAL 13 COLONIES

ATLANTIC OCEAN

Gulf of Mexico

NEW SPAIN

**KEY**
- Claimed by Britain
- Claimed by Spain
- Claimed by France
- Claimed by Russia
- 13 English colonies
- Proclamation Line of 1763

0 km 1,000
0 miles 1,000
Azimuthal Equal-Area Projection

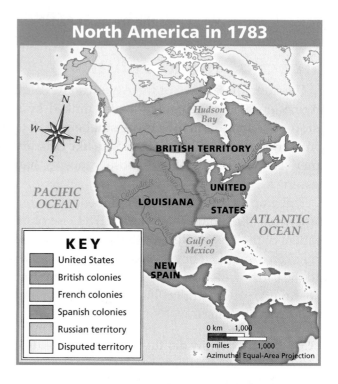

**North America in 1783**

PACIFIC OCEAN

Hudson Bay

BRITISH TERRITORY

UNITED STATES

LOUISIANA

ATLANTIC OCEAN

Gulf of Mexico

NEW SPAIN

**KEY**
- United States
- British colonies
- French colonies
- Spanish colonies
- Russian territory
- Disputed territory

0 km 1,000
0 miles 1,000
Azimuthal Equal-Area Projection

## Learn the Skill

*Use these steps to compare maps.*

1. **Check the subject and area shown on each map.** What do the map titles and labels tell you? Is the same geographical area shown on each map?

2. **Study the map key.** Determine what symbols are used to present specific information that you can compare.

3. **Compare the maps.** Use the data on the maps to make comparisons and note changes over time.

4. **Interpret the maps.** Think over what you already know about this period from other sources. Draw conclusions or make predictions based on your own knowledge and the information on the maps.

## Practice the Skill

*Answer the following questions about the two maps on this page.*

1. **Check the subject and area shown on each map.** (a) What area is shown on both maps? (b) What is the date of each map?

2. **Study the map key.** (a) What do the colors on the 1763 map key represent? (b) What color was added to the map key on the 1783 map?

3. **Compare the maps.** (a) What was the major difference between North America in 1763 and in 1783? (b) How was North America the same in 1763 and in 1783?

4. **Interpret the maps.** How did the 1783 Treaty of Paris affect the distribution of land in North America?

## Apply the Skill

*See the Review and Assessment at the end of this chapter.*

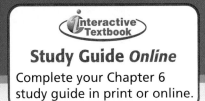

## Chapter Summary

### Section 1
### A Nation Declares Independence

- Thomas Paine's pamphlet *Common Sense* convinced more Americans to support independence from Britain.
- The Declaration of Independence used Enlightenment ideas and careful logic to show why Americans wanted to be free of British rule.

### Section 2
### A Critical Time

- As fighting moved from New England to the Middle States, American troops faced many setbacks.
- The Battle of Saratoga was a turning point in the war.
- As a result of the American victory at Saratoga, France decided to aid the American cause.

### Section 3
### The War Widens

- African Americans fought on both sides of the Revolution, often in the hope of gaining freedom.
- As men went to war, women took on added responsibilities.
- Important battles took place on the western frontier and at sea.

### Section 4
### Winning Independence

- In the final stages of the war, fighting shifted to the South, ending in the British surrender at Yorktown.
- In the Treaty of Paris, Britain recognized American independence.
- The American Revolution and the Declaration of Independence have inspired people in other nations who sought freedom.

## Key Concepts

These notes will help you prepare for questions about key concepts.

### Major Ideas of the Declaration of Independence

- All men are created equal.
- All people are born with rights that cannot be taken away.
- People form governments to protect people's rights.
- If people are dissatisfied with their government, they have the right to form another.
- The king has violated the rights of the colonists.
- Therefore, the colonies declare their independence.

### Some Key Figures of the American Revolution

- **Thomas Paine:** Wrote *Common Sense* and *The Crisis*
- **John Adams:** Led fight for independence in Congress
- **Richard Henry Lee:** Introduced resolution in Congress calling for independence
- **Thomas Jefferson:** Wrote Declaration of Independence
- **George Washington:** Commanded Continental army
- **Nathan Hale:** Executed by British in New York for spying
- **Marquis de Lafayette:** French volunteer; helped Washington
- **Friedrich von Steuben:** Trained American troops
- **George Rogers Clark:** Won victories in West
- **Bernardo de Gálvez:** Spanish governor; supported Americans
- **John Paul Jones:** Won major naval victory
- **Francis Marion:** Led guerrilla attacks on British troops
- **Nathanael Greene:** Commanded troops in South
- **Benedict Arnold:** American general; turned traitor
- **Lord Charles Cornwallis:** British general; surrendered at Yorktown

## Vocabulary *Builder*

### Key Terms

Complete each of the following sentences so that the second part explains the first part and shows your understanding of the key term.

1. Congress decided to pay the soldiers and buy their food and equipment by printing continentals _____.

2. The Declaration of Independence declared that people have unalienable rights _____.

3. One of the reasons that America won the war was because of its French and Spanish alliances _____.

4. During the Revolution, the small American navy had help from privateers _____.

5. A Polish volunteer led the American cavalry _____.

## Comprehension and Critical Thinking

6. **(a) Recall** Why was the publication of *Common Sense* so important?
   **(b) Describe** What was the political importance of the Declaration of Independence?
   **(c) Draw Conclusions** How do you think that *Common Sense* influenced people's reaction to the Declaration of Independence?

7. **(a) Review** How did the course of the war change from June to the end of December 1776?
   **(b) Analyze Cause and Effect** What effect do you think this change had on the Patriots?

8. **(a) Summarize** How did France help America during the Revolution?
   **(b) Make Predictions** What do you think might have happened if France had not come to the aid of America during the Revolution?

9. **(a) Summarize** What financial problems faced Congress during the Revolution?
   **(b) Identify Alternatives** What are some ways the new American government might avoid these same financial problems in the future?

10. **(a) Recall** How did the victories of the militia led by George Clark in the West benefit the frontier settlers?
    **(b) Identify Benefits** What were the economic benefits of these victories for the new nation?

## History Reading Skill

11. **Analyze Word Parts** Choose a word that contains any of the word parts discussed in this chapter. Use the word part to define the word. Then, write a sentence that contains the word and clarifies its meaning.

## Writing

12. **Write two paragraphs discussing the problem of winning support from other nations for the Patriot cause. Your paragraph should:**
    - include a thesis statement that expresses your main idea;
    - develop the main idea with facts, examples, and other information;
    - conclude by describing the lasting impact of what happened.

13. **Write a Dialogue:**
    It is May 1775. Your family is seriously divided over which course to take. Choose one of the following roles: a parent concerned about the safety of the children, a Loyalist supporter, a Patriot supporter. Write one page of conversation about the situation.

## Skills for Life

### Compare Maps

Use the maps in Sections 3 and 4 to answer the following questions.

14. **(a)** What areas are shown on both maps?
    **(b)** What is the date of each map?

15. What information is provided in the map key for "The Revolution in the West" that is not included in the map key for "The Revolution in the South"?

16. Based on the information in the maps, how would you compare the success of the British troops in the South and the West?

# Test Yourself

1. **Which statement best describes the effects of the American Revolution on women?**

   A The political rights of women were reduced.

   B Women had to take on many new responsibilities.

   C Many women were forced to serve in the army.

   D The Declaration of Independence granted equal rights to women.

2. **One effect of the Treaty of Paris was that Britain**

   A gave up all its colonies in North America.

   B surrendered to the Patriots.

   C recognized American independence.

   D formed an alliance with the United States.

**Refer to the map below to answer Question 3.**

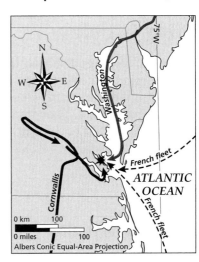

3. **What battle is shown on the map?**

   A Battle of Saratoga

   B Battle of Cowpens

   C Battle of Yorktown

   D Battle of Trenton

# Document-Based Questions

**Task:** Look at Documents 1 and 2, and answer their accompanying questions. Then, use the documents and your knowledge of history to complete this writing assignment:

> Write an essay comparing the ways in which these two documents proclaim people's basic rights. How do they reflect the Enlightenment ideas of John Locke?

**Document 1:** This excerpt describes the basic principles behind the Declaration of Independence. *According to the Declaration, what basic rights do people have?*

> "We hold these truths to be self-evident, that all men are created equal, that they are endowed by their Creator with certain unalienable Rights, that among these are Life, Liberty, and the pursuit of Happiness. That to secure these rights, Governments are instituted among Men, deriving their just powers from the consent of the governed."
>
> —Declaration of Independence

**Document 2:** In 1789, on the eve of the French Revolution, the French Assembly issued the Declaration of the Rights of Man and the Citizen. As you can see from the excerpt below, this document was modeled in part on the American Declaration of Independence. *According to the Declaration of the Rights of Man and the Citizen, what is the aim of government?*

> "The representatives of the French people . . . have determined to set forth in a solemn declaration the natural, unalienable, and sacred rights of man.
>
> 1. Men are born and remain free and equal in rights. . . .
>
> 2. The aim of all political association is the preservation of the natural and imprescriptable rights of man. These rights are liberty, property, security, and resistance to oppression."
>
> —Declaration of the Rights of Man and the Citizen

## Chapter Preview

In 1776, the 13 colonies declared their independence from Britain. In the American Revolution, they fought a long, hard battle for freedom. Now they faced another challenge. They had to find a new form of government to replace British rule.

The Constitution

U.S.
Events

World
Events

**1777**
Congress adopts
Articles of
Confederation.

**1781**
Articles of
Confederation
approved by last
of 13 states.

1776 · 1780 · 1784

**1778** France and United
States sign treaty of alliance.

**Discovery SCHOOL**

**Quick View Video**
View the chapter video for a quick preview of the main ideas.

Proud of their new nation, American artisans wove this rug featuring important patriotic symbols.

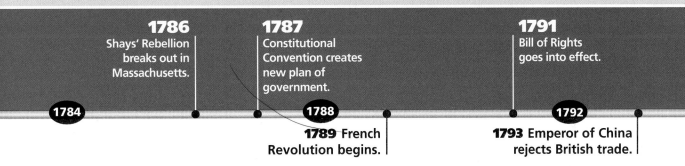

**1786**
Shays' Rebellion breaks out in Massachusetts.

**1787**
Constitutional Convention creates new plan of government.

**1791**
Bill of Rights goes into effect.

1784

**1789** French Revolution begins.

1788

**1793** Emperor of China rejects British trade.

1792

**History Reading Skill** Analyze Propositions and Support

## What arguments had been used to support the American Revolution?

In this chapter, you will learn how to analyze propositions—arguments—and the evidence used to support them.

**Primary Source**

A leader in the American Revolution, Patrick Henry, argued on the eve of that conflict that England was readying itself for war despite colonial efforts to resolve the problems through diplomacy.

Ask yourselves . . . [about] . . . these warlike preparations which cover our waters and darken our land. Are fleets and armies necessary to a work of love and reconciliation? Have we shown ourselves so unwilling to be reconciled, that force must be called in to win back our love? Let us not deceive ourselves, sir. These are implements of war and subjugation; the last arguments to which kings resort. I ask gentlemen, sir, what means this martial array, if its purpose be not to be to force us into submission? Can gentlemen assign any other possible motives for it? Has Great Britain any enemy, in this quarter of the world, to call for all this accumulation of navies and armies? No, sir, she has none. They are meant for us; they can be meant for no other. . . .

. . . Beside, sir, we have no election [choice]. If we were base enough to desire it, it is now too late to retire from the contest. There is no retreat but in submission and slavery! Our chains are forged! . . . The war is inevitable—and let it come! I repeat it, sir, let it come!

— Patrick Henry, speech to the Second Virginia Convention, March 23, 1775

> These questions support Henry's argument.

> Henry sees that England is massing troops in the colonies and proposes that England is preparing to fight its colonies.

> Here, Henry states the problem that war is unavoidable and proposes that the colonies must prepare for it.

> These are the supporting reasons for Henry's views.

## Analyze Propositions and Support

- Ask yourself what problems Patrick Henry identifies and what he proposes in response to those problems.
- Evaluate Henry's propositions and support. Does he support his propositions convincingly? Do you agree with them?

## Document-Based Questions

1. When was this speech given?
2. What events were taking place in Massachusetts around this time?
3. What action do you think Henry wants the Virginia Convention to take?

# Vocabulary *Builder*

## Previewing High-Use Academic Words

| High-Use Word | Definition | Sample History Sentence |
|---|---|---|
| **minimize** (MIHN ah mīz) (Section 1, p. 204) | *v.* to reduce to the lowest possible amount | To <u>minimize</u> the chances of rebellion, England sent troops to the colonies. |
| **devise** (dee vīz) (Section 1, p. 206) | *v.* to think up an idea for something and figure out how it will work | Athens was the first city-state to <u>devise</u> a system of direct democracy. |
| **contrast** (KAHN trast) (Section 2, p. 214) | *n.* difference | In <u>contrast</u> with previous European explorers, Columbus sailed westward across the Atlantic Ocean. |
| **emotion** (ee MOH shuhn) (Section 2, p. 214) | *n.* strong feeling about something or someone | The people of Massachusetts reacted with <u>emotion</u> when they heard of the Boston Massacre. |
| **flexible** (FLEHKS ah bahl) (Section 3, p. 221) | *adj.* able to change | The Puritans of Massachusetts found it difficult to be <u>flexible</u> on religious matters. |
| **amendment** (ah MEHND mehnt) (Section 3, p. 221) | *n.* addition or alteration to a document | The Twenty-sixth <u>Amendment</u> allows citizens who are 18 years old to vote in state and national elections. |

James Wilson

## Previewing Key Terms and People

constitution, p. 204
executive, p. 205
economic depression, p. 208
Daniel Shays, p. 209
James Madison, p. 213
judicial branch, p. 213
Roger Sherman, p. 214

James Wilson, p. 214
compromise, p. 214
Gouverneur Morris, p. 217

ratify, p. 218
Alexander Hamilton, p. 218
John Jay, p. 218
George Mason, p. 219

Roger Sherman

# Governing a New Nation

## Objectives

1. Discuss the ideas that guided the new state governments.

2. Describe the government under the Articles of Confederation.

3. Explain the Ordinances of 1785 and 1787 and their importance to westward expansion.

4. Identify the problems created by a weak central government.

## Prepare to Read

### 🔁 Reading Skill

**Identify Propositions** The study of history often takes you inside important debates and arguments over ideas and actions. People argue—or propose—their ideas and then give reasons to support those ideas. Identifying those propositions will help you to understand the beliefs and experiences of people in an earlier time. One way to identify propositions is to ask yourself what problems people had and how they proposed solving those problems.

### Vocabulary *Builder*

**High-Use Words**

minimize, p. 204

devise, p. 206

**Key Terms and People**

constitution, p. 204

executive, p. 205

economic depression, p. 208

Daniel Shays, p. 209

⭐ **Background Knowledge** You have read about the causes of the American Revolution. Leaders of the new nation remembered what they had hated about British rule. They had seen how the king and Parliament in faraway England had exerted power over elected colonial legislatures. Americans sought instead to create a republic in which the states had more power than the central government.

**Main Idea**
The first state constitutions were designed to support the principles fought for in the American Revolution.

## Government by the States

As the Continental Congress began moving toward independence in 1776, leaders in the individual states began creating governments. Eleven of the 13 states wrote new constitutions to support their governments. A constitution is a document stating the rules under which a government will operate. The other two states—Rhode Island and Connecticut—kept using their colonial charters. However, they removed all references to the British king.

**Writing State Constitutions** In writing state constitutions, Americans were well aware of the problems that had led to the Revolution. Colonists had been unhappy with governors appointed by the British Crown. Thus, the new constitutions <u>minimized</u> the powers of state governors. Instead, they gave most of the power to state legislatures elected by the people.

**Vocabulary *Builder***
<u>minimize</u> (MIHN ah mīz) *v.* to reduce to the lowest possible amount

The governor served as the state's executive. In a government, the **executive** is the person who runs the government and sees that the laws are carried out. Governors appointed key state officials, but usually the legislature had to approve the appointments.

The new constitutions allowed more people to vote than in colonial times. Nonetheless, all but a few states barred African Americans (including those who were free) from voting. New Jersey allowed some women to vote until 1807, but women could not vote in any other state. In order to vote, white males had to be 21 or older. In most states, they also had to own a certain amount of property.

**Protecting Rights** The Declaration of Independence listed ways that Britain had violated the rights of colonists. To prevent such abuses, states sought to protect individual rights. Virginia was the first state to include a bill of rights in its constitution. Virginia's list included freedom of the press and the right to trial by jury, and it also barred "cruel and unusual punishments." The final clause guaranteed freedom of religion:

> **❝**That religion, or the duty which we owe to our Creator, and the manner of discharging it, can be directed only by reason and conviction, not by force or violence; and therefore all men are equally entitled to the free exercise of religion, according to the dictates of conscience.**❞**
>
> —Virginia Bill of Rights, 1776

Many other states followed Virginia's lead. For example, the New York state constitution also included a bill of rights that guaranteed freedom of religion:

> **❝**This convention doth further, in the name and by the authority of the good people of this State, ordain, determine, and declare, that the free exercise and enjoyment of religious profession and worship, without discrimination or preference, shall forever hereafter be allowed, within this State, to all mankind.**❞**
>
> —New York Constitution of 1777

Massachusetts also included freedom of religion in its bill of rights. However, Massachusetts did retain its official church. Massachusetts's bill of rights declared that people have the freedom to worship as they please, so long as they did not disturb the public peace or interfere with other people's freedom of worship.

**✓Checkpoint** **Why did many state constitutions limit the power of state governors?**

**Protecting Rights**

Virginia included a bill of rights in its constitution. The Virginia bill of rights became a model for other states and, later, for the national Constitution. **Critical Thinking: Link Past and Present** *Which protections in the Virginia bill of rights are enjoyed by all Americans today?*

**Virginia Bill of Rights**

- Freedom of Religion
- Freedom of the Press
- Trial by Jury
- Limits on Searches
- Limits on Arrests
- No Cruel and Unusual Punishment

# The Articles of Confederation

While the states were writing their constitutions, the Continental Congress created a plan for the nation as a whole. It was called the Articles of Confederation. Congress adopted the Articles in 1777.

**Form of Government** Instead of having three branches of government like those of most states, the government under the Articles had just one branch—a one-house legislature, called Congress. There was no executive and no system of national courts.

Within Congress, all states would be equal and each had a single vote. Moreover, for the most important matters, nine states had to agree before a law could go into effect.

**Limited Government** The framers of the Articles of Confederation kept in mind their complaints against Britain. Parliament had passed laws the colonists considered unfair. The new states did not want to risk giving too much power to a central government far from the people. Thus, the Articles provided for a limited central government.

Under the Articles, most power remained in the hands of the states. Congress could not regulate trade or collect taxes. Instead, it had to ask the states for the money it needed.

Congress did have some powers under the Articles. It could deal with foreign nations and with Native Americans outside the 13 states. It could make laws, declare war, coin or borrow money, and run a postal service. However, the national government had no power to enforce the laws that it made. For that, it depended on the states.

**Identify Propositions**
What issues concerned the framers when they were drafting the Articles of Confederation? What did they propose in response?

**✔Checkpoint** How did the Articles of Confederation ensure the power of the states?

# Settling the Western Lands

The Articles had to be approved by all 13 states. But some states would not give their approval until other states dropped their claims to vast areas of land west of the Appalachian Mountains. It took years to get all the states to give up their claims to western lands. In 1781, Virginia was the final state to agree. Only then did Maryland approve the Articles of Confederation, the final state to do so.

The western lands that the states had given up were turned over to the national government. They proved to be very valuable. Land was in great demand. It could be sold off, piece by piece, to private companies seeking to develop western settlements.

**Main Idea**
The ordinances of 1785 and 1787 created a way for national lands to be sold to the public.

**Vocabulary** *Builder*
**devise** (dee vīz) *v.* to think up an idea for something and figure out how it will work

**Land Ordinance of 1785** Congress had to <u>devise</u> a system for land sales and settlement. Under the Land Ordinance of 1785, surveyors were to divide public lands into townships, 6 miles on each side. This would result in a grid of squares. Within each township there would also be a grid, 1 mile on each side. These 36 sections would be sold for no less than $1 an acre.

Within each township, one section was set aside to support schools. This reflected the belief of the nation's leaders that democracy depended on education. Thomas Jefferson later wrote:

&#9830;&#9830;If a nation expects to be ignorant and free, in a state of civilization, it expects what never was and never will be.&#9830;&#9830;

—Thomas Jefferson, letter to Charles Yancey, 1816

**Northwest Ordinance of 1787** Investors were eager to buy land in the Northwest Territory, north of the Ohio River. They pressed Congress to determine how this area would be governed. In response, Congress passed the Northwest Ordinance of 1787. It guaranteed basic rights for settlers and banned slavery there.

The Northwest Ordinance set a three-step process for admitting new states. When a territory was just starting to be settled, Congress would appoint a governor, a secretary, and three judges. Once the territory had 5,000 free adult male settlers, it could elect a legislature. When the free population reached 60,000, the territory could ask to become a state. In time, five states—Ohio, Indiana, Illinois, Michigan, and Wisconsin—were carved out of the Northwest Territory. (For more on the settling of the Northwest Territory, see the Geography and History feature.)

**✓Checkpoint** How did the two ordinances turn national land into private holdings?

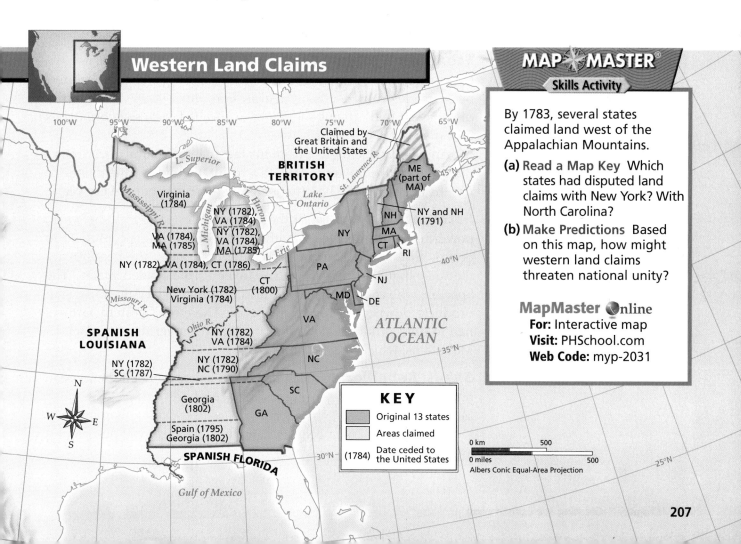

## Western Land Claims

**MAP MASTER**
**Skills Activity**

By 1783, several states claimed land west of the Appalachian Mountains.

(a) **Read a Map Key** Which states had disputed land claims with New York? With North Carolina?

(b) **Make Predictions** Based on this map, how might western land claims threaten national unity?

**MapMaster Online**
**For:** Interactive map
**Visit:** PHSchool.com
**Web Code:** myp-2031

**KEY**
- Original 13 states
- Areas claimed
- (1784) Date ceded to the United States

0 km    500
0 miles    500
Albers Conic Equal-Area Projection

207

**Shays' Rebellion**

Abigail Adams called the leaders of Shays' Rebellion "ignorant, restless desperadoes without conscience or principles." However, many felt that the Massachusetts farmers had good reason for their anger. Here, farmers attack the Massachusetts statehouse. **Critical Thinking: *Analyze Cause and Effect*** *What was the main cause of Shays' Rebellion?*

**Main Idea**

The Articles of Confederation denied the central government the power to deal effectively with several key issues facing the nation.

# Growing Problems

Under the Articles of Confederation, the United States had many successes. It waged a successful war for independence, negotiated a peace treaty with Britain, and set up rules for settling new territories. But the United States faced growing problems during the 1780s. Many Americans concluded that the Articles did not give the government enough power to solve these problems.

**Economic Problems** Under the Articles, each state set its own trade policy. Each state tried to help its own farmers and manufacturers by setting taxes on goods brought in from other states. This practice discouraged trade among the states. In addition, each state printed its own money, making trade between states harder.

Another problem grew from the fact that the central government did not have the power to tax. As a result, there was little money to run the government. The situation grew more desperate every year.

**Foreign Affairs** Because the United States seemed to be weak, powerful nations viewed it with scorn. British troops continued to occupy forts in the Northwest Territory, although the peace treaty required that the forts be turned over to the United States. The Spanish, who controlled New Orleans, refused to let Americans ship products down the Mississippi River. Therefore, western farmers had to send products along the rugged trails over the Appalachian Mountains, which was far more costly.

**Shays' Rebellion** In the mid-1780s, a severe economic depression hit the United States. An **economic depression** is a period when business activity slows, prices and wages drop, and unemployment rises. As the depression deepened, there was widespread despair and anger.

The depression hit farmers in Massachusetts especially hard. As crop prices declined, many were unable to pay their taxes. The state government then began seizing some farms and selling them in order to get the back taxes. Angry farmers demanded that the legislature stop the farm sales. They also demanded that the state issue more paper money to make it easier to get loans. Still, the legislators took no action.

In August 1786, a former Revolutionary War captain named Daniel Shays led an uprising of about 1,000 Massachusetts farmers. When the farmers tried to seize arms from a state warehouse, the state called out the militia. Shays and other leaders were arrested.

Although Shays' Rebellion fizzled, it had frightened some leading Americans. They believed that a stronger central government would protect against popular unrest. In response, Congress asked the states to send delegates to a convention in Philadelphia in 1787. Their task was to revise the Articles of Confederation.

✓Checkpoint **What did Shays' Rebellion demonstrate about the strength of the national government under the Articles of Confederation?**

⭐ **Looking Back and Ahead** After 10 years of independence, some leading Americans had come to the conclusion that the Articles of Confederation needed improvement. The Philadelphia convention was called to revise the Articles. But were the Articles of Confederation worth saving? Or was an entirely new framework required? This decision would be one of the first issues that the delegates at the Philadelphia convention would confront.

Section 1 | **Check Your Progress**

**Progress Monitoring** Online
**For:** Self-test with instant help
**Visit:** PHSchool.com
**Web Code:** mya-2031

## Comprehension and Critical Thinking

**1. (a) Recall** Why did the Continental Congress make the federal government weak when it drew up the Articles of Confederation?
**(b) Explain Problems** Why did foreign powers treat the U.S. government under the Articles of Confederation with scorn?

**2. (a) Recall** Why was a section of public land set aside to support public schools under the Land Ordinance of 1785?
**(b) Analyze Cause and Effect** How does education contribute to a successful democracy?

## Reading Skill

**3. Identify Propositions** Reread the text following the heading "Land Ordinance of 1785." What belief did the nation's leaders have about education? What did they propose to further this belief?

## Vocabulary *Builder*

Fill in the blanks with the correct key terms.
**4.** After the break with Britain, each of the states wrote a new _____, a framework for the state government.

**5.** The _____ is the person in a government responsible for carrying out the laws.
**6.** In the 1780s, when business slowed and unemployment rose, the nation entered a period of _____.

## Writing

**7.** Identify two problems caused by the creation of a weak national government under the Articles of Confederation. Write a sentence about each problem, explaining why it was important that it be solved.

# Settling the Northwest Territory

By the end of the American Revolution, the United States had acquired a vast territory west of the Appalachian Mountains. Congress passed two land ordinances, one in 1785 and another in 1787. The ordinances served as a framework for moving settlers into—and forming states out of—this Northwest Territory. The states of Ohio, Indiana, Illinois, Michigan, Wisconsin, and part of Minnesota were eventually carved out of the expanse.

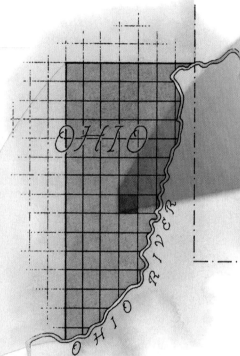

NORTHWEST TERRITORY WITH PRESENT-DAY STATE BOUNDARIES

## ▲ A New Organization

The Land Ordinance of 1785 established a system for settling the Northwest Territory. Surveyors laid out a grid of lines spaced 6 miles apart. These lines marked off townships. Each township was divided into 36 sections, and these 1-mile square sections could be divided into smaller units for sale to farmers.

1 mile

1 mile

Half Section
320 Acres

Quarter
Section
160 Acres

| 6 | 5 | 4 | 3 | 2 | 1 |
| 7 | 8 | 9 | 10 | 11 | 12 |
| 18 | 17 | 16* | 15 | 14 | 13 |
| 19 | 20 | 21 | 22 | 23 | 24 |
| 30 | 29 | 28 | 27 | 26 | 25 |
| 31 | 32 | 33 | 34 | 35 | 36 |

6 miles

6 miles

\* Income reserved to support schools

*Understand Effects:*
## Slavery and the Northwest Ordinance

Congress banned slavery in the Northwest Territory in 1787. Eventually, five free states were formed from the territory. Decades later, the balance between free states and slave states would lead to a national crisis.

### ▼ An Enduring Landscape

The grid established more than 200 years ago remains the basis for land division across the Midwest. Many roads and property lines still follow the straight lines and right angles the original surveyors laid out.

### ▲ Support for Education

The 1785 ordinance set aside one section in every township to support public schools. Lands were often reserved for school buildings like the one shown here.

*Analyze* **GEOGRAPHY AND HISTORY**

Write a pamphlet recruiting settlers to live in the Northwest Territory.

# The Constitutional Convention

## Objectives

1. Describe the proceedings of the Constitutional Convention.

2. Identify the specifics of the Virginia Plan.

3. Explain how the Great Compromise satisfied both large and small states.

4. Describe the disputes over slavery and the compromises that were reached.

5. Discuss the drafting of the new Constitution.

## Prepare to Read

### Reading Skill

**Identify Support for Propositions** As you read about the propositions that people from history made to solve their problems and advance their ideas, look for supporting evidence. How did people try to convince those around them to support these propositions? What reasons did they give to explain their views? Identifying supporting evidence helps you understand and respond to propositions.

### Vocabulary *Builder*

**High-Use Words**

contrast, p. 214

emotion, p. 214

**Key Terms and People**

James Madison, p. 213

judicial branch, p. 213

Roger Sherman, p. 214

James Wilson, p. 214

compromise, p. 214

Gouverneur Morris, p. 217

---

⭐ **Background Knowledge** In Section 1, you learned that many Americans worried about the weaknesses of the Articles of Confederation. These weaknesses prompted the states to call a meeting in Philadelphia to revise the Articles. In this section, you will learn how the Constitutional Convention instead led to the creation of an entirely new framework of government.

**Main Idea**
The original aim of the Constitutional Convention was to revise the Articles of Confederation.

## The Constitutional Convention Begins

An air of mystery hung over Philadelphia in the summer of 1787. Every day, the nation's great leaders passed in and out of the state-house. One Philadelphia resident, Susannah Dillwyn, wrote to her father, "There is now sitting in this city a grand convention, who are to form some new system of government or mend the old one."

**Aims of the Convention** In fact, members of the convention did not have the authority to "form some new system of government." Congress had called the meeting "for the sole and express purpose of revising the Articles of Confederation." However, many delegates argued that revising the Articles would not be enough.

Early on, the delegates voted to keep their debates secret. Despite the heat, windows remained tightly shut. Guards kept out members of the public. The delegates would be free to speak their minds—even if their discussions took the convention far beyond its original aims.

**The Delegates** In all, 55 delegates from 12 states took part in the convention. Only Rhode Island did not send any representatives.

Some delegates, such as George Washington and Ben Franklin, had been respected leaders of the Revolution. Washington was quickly voted president of the convention. Most delegates, however, were younger. Alexander Hamilton of New York was only 32. Another influential delegate was 36-year-old James Madison of Virginia. Madison took careful notes on the meetings. Published after his death, Madison's notes became a rich source of historical information.

☑ **Checkpoint** Why did delegates to the Constitutional Convention keep their debates secret?

## The Virginia Plan

On the third day of the convention, Edmund Randolph of Virginia proposed a plan for a new, strong central government. James Madison was the principal author of this Virginia Plan. For the next month, debate focused on this proposal.

**Three Branches of Government** The Virginia Plan called for the central government to have three separate branches. Congress would continue to be the legislative branch. But two additional branches would be created. The executive branch would carry out the laws. The judicial branch would consist of a system of courts to interpret the law.

Many delegates believed that a strong executive was necessary to correct the weaknesses of the Articles of Confederation. But should the executive be one person or a group of people?

**Main Idea**
The Virginia Plan set forth an entirely new framework for the national government.

**Birthplace of the United States**
In 1787, delegates met in this room in Philadelphia's statehouse to debate a new plan of government. Today, the building is known as Independence Hall, in honor of another important event that took place there, the signing of the Declaration of Independence. **Critical Thinking:** *Draw Conclusions* *Why do you think many Americans today visit Independence Hall and other historic places?*

James Wilson

Randolph proposed that Congress appoint three people to serve jointly as chief executive. One person alone, he said, would never be able to win the people's confidence. Others objected. A single executive, they said, could act more quickly when urgent action was required. Eventually, the delegates voted to have one person, called the President, serve as executive.

**A Two-House Legislature** The Virginia Plan called for a change in the composition of Congress. Rather than a single legislative body, it would consist of two parts—a lower house and an upper house.

Delegates argued long and hard about methods of choosing members of the two houses. Some wanted state legislatures to elect both houses. Roger Sherman of Connecticut said the people "should have as little to do" with the selection process as possible because they can be misled.

On the other hand, James Wilson of Pennsylvania warned against shutting the people out of the process. According to Wilson, election of the legislature by the people was "not only the cornerstone, but the foundation of the fabric."

☑**Checkpoint** How was the national government organized under the Virginia Plan?

## The Great Compromise

**Main Idea**
After fierce debate, delegates agreed on a plan that satisfied both large and small states.

One part of the Virginia Plan nearly tore the convention apart. The plan called for representation based on population. The more people a state had, the more seats it would have in each house. Naturally, this idea drew support from big states like Virginia, Pennsylvania, and Massachusetts.

**New Jersey Plan** The smaller states strongly opposed this idea. They wanted each state to have the same number of votes in Congress, as was the case under the Articles of Confederation.

On June 15, William Paterson of New Jersey introduced a modified plan on behalf of the small states. This New Jersey Plan stood in sharp <u>contrast</u> to the Virginia Plan. It called for a single house of Congress, with equal representation for each state. The plan also expanded the powers of Congress to raise money and regulate commerce.

**Vocabulary** *Builder*
<u>contrast</u> (KAHN trast) *n.* difference

In the summer heat, delegates argued day after day over the great issues at stake. <u>Emotions</u> ran so high that some feared the convention would fail and the Union would break apart.

**Vocabulary** *Builder*
<u>emotion</u> (ee MOH shuhn) *n.* strong feeling about something or someone

**Terms of the Compromise** Finally, Roger Sherman of Connecticut worked out a compromise that he hoped would satisfy both the large and small states. A compromise is an agreement in which each side gives up part of what it wants. On July 16, 1787, delegates narrowly voted to accept Sherman's proposals, which came to be known as the Great Compromise.

The key to Sherman's plan was a two-house Congress. To please the large states, the lower house, called the House of Representatives, was to be based on population. Bigger states would thus have more votes. Representatives would be chosen by a vote of the people to serve two-year terms. To please the small states, each state would have two seats in the upper house, or Senate. State legislatures would choose senators, who would serve six-year terms.

The Great Compromise was a vital step in creating a new Constitution. Now, small-state delegates were willing to support a strong central government.

✓Checkpoint **What was the main difference between the Virginia Plan and the New Jersey Plan?**

**Identify Support for Propositions**
Roger Sherman proposed a two-house Congress, hoping to satisfy both small and large states. What support did he give to show how this solution would meet the needs of all states?

## Debates Over Slavery

Other issues also divided the delegates—none more so than the question of slavery. The issue touched off bitter debates between northerners and southerners.

**Main Idea**
Disputes among the delegates over slavery indicated just how deeply divided the North and the South were.

**Three-Fifths Compromise** Southern delegates said that enslaved people should be counted in calculating how many representatives a state should have in Congress. Northern delegates said that because enslaved people could not vote, they should not be counted toward a state's representation.

Finally, Congress agreed to a plan called the Three-Fifths Compromise. Each enslaved person would be counted as three fifths of a free person. Thus, 500 enslaved people would count as 300 free people. The Three-Fifths Compromise was a gain for the South, which got more seats in the House. Northern delegates reluctantly agreed in order to keep the South in the Union.

The Three-Fifths Compromise was a blow to African Americans. It helped preserve slavery in the new Constitution by making a distinction between "free persons" and "all other persons." The compromise was finally overturned when slavery was banned in 1865.

**Slave Trade** Some northern delegates wanted to ban the buying and selling of people anywhere in the country. Southern delegates protested that a ban would ruin the South's economy.

Once again, a compromise was reached. Ships would be allowed to bring enslaved people into the country for a period of 20 years. After 1808, Congress could bar the importation of enslaved people. But the slave trade *within* the United States was not affected.

✓Checkpoint **What was the Three-Fifths Compromise?**

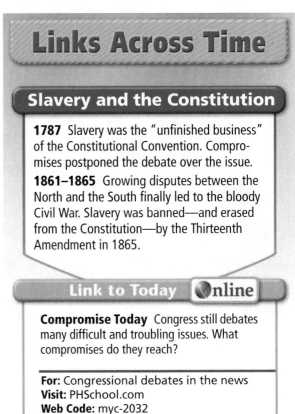

## Links Across Time

### Slavery and the Constitution

**1787** Slavery was the "unfinished business" of the Constitutional Convention. Compromises postponed the debate over the issue.

**1861–1865** Growing disputes between the North and the South finally led to the bloody Civil War. Slavery was banned—and erased from the Constitution—by the Thirteenth Amendment in 1865.

### Link to Today  Online

**Compromise Today** Congress still debates many difficult and troubling issues. What compromises do they reach?

**For:** Congressional debates in the news
**Visit:** PHSchool.com
**Web Code:** myc-2032

# Signing the CONSTITUTION

In his *Signing of the Constitution*, painter Howard Chandler Christy captured the moment on September 17, 1787, when delegates signed the historic document that has guided our government for more than 200 years.

**1** **Roger Sherman** helped draft the Great Compromise that determined how states would be represented in Congress. After months of bitter debate, the compromise satisfied both large and small states.

**2** **George Washington** was voted president of the meeting. His firm leadership held the convention together when it seemed close to breaking up.

**3** **Benjamin Franklin,** though frail and ailing, was one of the convention's most respected delegates. At the end, he wrote a masterful speech supporting the Constitution.

**4** **James Madison** wrote much of the Constitution and led the fight to get it approved by the states. He is often called the Father of the Constitution.

▶ **The Constitution**

**Critical Thinking:** *Interpret Paintings*
*How does the artist draw attention to certain Framers?*

# A New Constitution

**Main Idea**
The Constitution of the United States derives its authority from "We the People of the United States."

After many more weeks of debate, the delegates agreed on all the terms. A so-called Committee of Style was appointed to draw up the final wording of the new Constitution. Gouverneur Morris, a gifted writer, was largely responsible for writing the Preamble, or introduction.

The Preamble highlights a major difference between the Constitution and the Articles of Confederation. The Articles were a pact between separate states. By contrast, the Constitution opens with the words, "We the People of the United States, in order to form a more perfect union, . . . do ordain and establish this Constitution for the United States of America." The Constitution thus claims to take its authority from the people rather than from the states.

The aging Ben Franklin gave some final advice on the day of the signing. Because he was so ill, Franklin remained seated and another delegate read Franklin's speech. Like many other delegates, Franklin had some doubts about parts of the Constitution. Still, he said, "I agree to this Constitution with all its faults," and he urged others to do the same. At last, the delegates stepped forward to place their signatures on the document.

☑Checkpoint  **What is the significance of the Constitution's first phrase: "We the People of the United States"?**

⭐ **Looking Back and Ahead** Once the Constitution had been signed, secrecy ended. Public debates began. These debates would stretch over 10 months. And, as the Constitution's supporters soon learned, the battle for approval would be hard-fought and bitter.

---

## Section 2 | Check Your Progress

**Progress Monitoring** Online
**For:** Self-test with instant help
**Visit:** PHSchool.com
**Web Code:** mya-2032

### Comprehension and Critical Thinking

**1. (a) Summarize** Summarize the arguments for and against having a single executive.
**(b) Explain Problems** What problems do you think might arise during a crisis if the executive power in the U.S. government was held by three people?

**2. (a) Describe** How was representation in Congress to be based, according to the terms of the Great Compromise?
**(b) Apply Information** Why did the small states decide to support a strong central government after the compromise?

### Reading Skill

**3. Identify Support for Propositions** Reread the text following the heading "Slave Trade." What reason did southerners give to support their position against ending the slave trade?

### Vocabulary *Builder*

Fill in the blanks with the correct key terms.
**4.** The Virginia Plan called for a _____, or system of courts to interpret the law.

**5.** Under a _____ between northern and southern states, Congress could bar slaves from being imported after 1808.

### Writing

**6.** Choose one of the problems that the delegates at the Constitutional Convention had to solve. List several possible solutions for that problem, and then write a few sentences explaining the solution that the convention eventually chose. What were the advantages and disadvantages of this solution?

# Debating the Constitution

## Objectives

1. Compare the positions of the Federalists and the Antifederalists.

2. Discuss the debate over ratification.

3. Describe the Bill of Rights and how it protects the people.

## Prepare to Read

 **Reading Skill**

**Evaluate Support for Propositions** When a person argues a proposition using reasons and support, listeners or readers must evaluate that support—that is, whether the evidence given really supports the proposition. As you read, ask yourself if the propositions are well supported and whether or not they convince you.

**Vocabulary** *Builder*

**High-Use Words**
flexible, p. 221
amendment, p. 221

**Key Terms and People**
ratify, p. 218
Alexander Hamilton, p. 218
John Jay, p. 218
George Mason, p. 219

⭐ **Background Knowledge** As you have read, the original purpose of the 1787 convention had been to revise the Articles of Confederation. Instead, the delegates produced an entirely new frame of government. How would the states greet the new Constitution?

**Main Idea**
Supporters and opponents of the new Constitution argued over the need for a strong central government.

## Federalists Versus Antifederalists

The convention had set a process for states to ratify, or approve, the Constitution. Each state was to hold a convention. The Constitution would go into effect once it was ratified by nine states.

**The Federalist Position** Supporters of the new Constitution called themselves Federalists because they favored a strong federal, or national, government. James Madison, Alexander Hamilton, and John Jay published the *Federalist Papers,* a series of 85 newspaper essays in support of the Constitution.

At the heart of the Federalist position was the need for a stronger central government. For the Union to last, they argued, the national government had to have powers denied to it under the Articles of Confederation, including the power to enforce laws. Hamilton wrote:

**Evaluate Support for Propositions**
How does Hamilton support the proposition that the national government needed more powers?

❝Government implies the power of making laws. It is essential to the idea of a law, that it be attended with . . . a penalty or punishment for disobedience. If there be no penalty . . . the resolutions or commands which pretend to be laws will, in fact, amount to nothing more than advice.❞

—Alexander Hamilton, *The Federalist* No. 15

**The Antifederalist Position** Opponents of ratification were called Antifederalists. Leading Antifederalists, such as George Mason and Patrick Henry of Virginia, agreed that the Articles of Confederation were not strong enough. However, they felt the Constitutional Convention had gone too far.

Antifederalists were not all united in their reasons for opposing the Constitution. Some of their most frequent arguments included:

- **Weakening the States** Antifederalists argued that the Constitution dangerously weakened the state governments. They feared that a too-strong central government, like that of England, would wipe out state power and individual freedom. "There never was a government over a very extensive country without destroying the liberties of the people," warned Mason.

- **No Bill of Rights** Some Antifederalists pointed out that the proposed Constitution offered no protections for basic freedoms. Unlike the constitutions of many states, it had no bill of rights.

- **President or King?** Another objection was that the Constitution provided for a President who could be reelected again and again. Said Henry, "Your President may easily become a king."

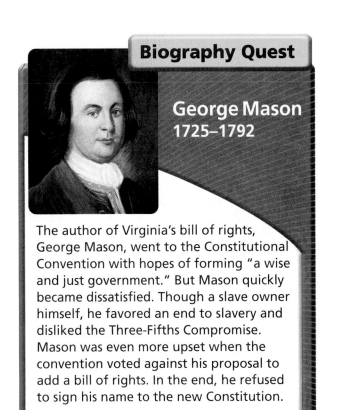 
✓ **Checkpoint** Why did Antifederalists believe that the Constitutional Convention had gone too far?

## The Ratification Debate

The debate between Federalists and Antifederalists heated up as states held their ratification conventions. Without the approval of nine states, the Constitution would not go into effect.

Delaware acted first. Its convention unanimously approved the Constitution on December 7, 1787. Pennsylvania, New Jersey, Georgia, and Connecticut quickly followed.

Antifederalists hoped to win in Massachusetts. Opposition to the Constitution was strong in the rural areas from which Shays' Rebellion had drawn its strength. Only a major campaign by Constitution supporters won ratification by the state.

All eyes moved to Virginia. By then, Maryland and South Carolina had ratified, which made a total of eight state ratifications. Only one more was needed. But if large and powerful Virginia rejected the pact, New York and other remaining states might do so, too.

**Main Idea**
After intense debates, each of the 13 states ratified the Constitution.

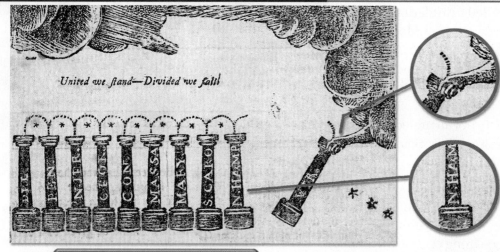

United we stand—Divided we fall!

A hand reaches from the heavens to put Virginia in place.

New Hampshire was the ninth state to ratify, allowing the Constitution to go into effect.

## Reading Political Cartoons
### Skills Activity

The cartoon above appeared in an American newspaper in 1788—at a time when the states were debating whether or not to ratify the Constitution.

**(a) Identify Main Ideas** What do the pillars represent? Which pillar is first? What pillars are missing?

**(b) Detect Points of View** Do you think the cartoonist favored the Federalists or the Antifederalists?

Patrick Henry led the attack on the Constitution in Virginia. "There will be no checks, no real balances, in this government," he said. James Madison supported the Constitution and warned of the possible breakup of the Union. In the end, the Federalist view narrowly won out. Virginia's convention approved the Constitution by a vote of 89 to 79.

Meanwhile, in June 1788—while Virginia was still debating—New Hampshire became the ninth state to ratify. The Constitution could now go into effect. In time, New York and North Carolina followed. Finally, in May 1790, Rhode Island became the last of the original 13 states to ratify the Constitution.

On July 4, 1788, Philadelphia celebrated the ratification of the Constitution. A huge parade snaked along Market Street, led by soldiers who had served in the Revolution. Benjamin Rush, a Philadelphia doctor and strong supporter of the Constitution, wrote to a friend, "Tis done. We have become a nation."

✓ **Checkpoint** Why was the vote in Virginia so important?

**Main Idea**
The Bill of Rights aims to protect Americans against unfair use of government powers.

## The Bill of Rights

Once the ninth state had ratified the Constitution, Congress took steps to prepare for a new government. George Washington was elected the first President, with John Adams as Vice President.

During the debate on the Constitution, many of the states had insisted that a bill of rights be added. This became one of the first tasks of the new Congress that met in March 1789.

The Framers had provided a way to amend the Constitution. They wanted to make the Constitution <u>flexible</u> enough to change. But they did not want changes made lightly. So, they made the process fairly difficult. (You will read more about the amendment process in the Citizenship Handbook.)

In 1789, the first Congress passed a series of <u>amendments</u>. By December 1791, three fourths of the states had ratified 10 amendments. These amendments are known as the Bill of Rights. The Bill of Rights aims to protect people against abuses by the federal government. Many of them came out of the colonists' struggle with Britain.

The First Amendment guarantees freedom of religion, speech, and the press. The Second Amendment deals with the right to bear arms. The Third Amendment bars Congress from forcing citizens to keep troops in their homes, as Britain had done.

The Fourth Amendment protects citizens from unreasonable searches of their homes or seizure of their property. Amendments Five through Eight protect citizens who are accused of crimes and are brought to trial. The last two amendments limit the powers of the federal government to those that are granted in the Constitution.

**Vocabulary** *Builder*
<u>flexible</u> (FLEHKS ah bahl) *adj.* able to change

<u>amendment</u> (ah MEHND mehnt) *n.* addition or alteration to a document

✓**Checkpoint**  **Why did Congress move quickly to pass the Bill of Rights?**

⭐ **Looking Back and Ahead** The delegates to the Constitutional Convention are often called the Framers because they framed, or shaped, our form of government. The Constitution they wrote established a republic that has thrived for more than 200 years. On the following pages, you will read the actual text of the Constitution and study its meaning in more detail.

## Section 3 | Check Your Progress

**Progress Monitoring** Online
**For:** Self-test with instant help
**Visit:** PHSchool.com
**Web Code:** mya-2033

### Comprehension and Critical Thinking

**1. (a) Summarize** In complete sentences, list three arguments of the Antifederalists against the Constitution.
**(b) Draw Conclusions** Why might the Antifederalists think the Constitution would reduce the power of the states?

**2. (a) Recall** Compare the attitudes of Patrick Henry and James Madison toward ratification.
**(b) Apply Information** How did the passage of the Bill of Rights help deal with Patrick Henry's concerns?

### Reading Skill

**3. Evaluate Support for Propositions** Patrick Henry led the attack on the Constitution. "There will be no checks, no real balances, in this government," he said. Evaluate his supporting argument. Do you think it is an effective argument?

### Vocabulary *Builder*

Answer the following question in a complete sentence that shows your understanding of the key term.
**4.** Why was it important that Virginia ratify the Constitution?

### Writing

**5.** Write a paragraph discussing the Bill of Rights as the solution to a problem faced by the early U.S. government after the Constitution was ratified. Complete the following topic sentence, and then write four more sentences developing this idea with specific information. **Topic sentence:** In 1789, the first Congress passed 10 amendments to the Constitution, known as the Bill of Rights, in order to protect _____.

Major historical events have both causes and effects. Sometimes causes and effects are short term. They take place shortly before or after the major event. Causes and effects can also be long term. They build up over a period of time.

## CAUSES

- King George III had limited colonists' liberty.
- America had fought a revolution to protect freedoms.
- Antifederalists wanted a specific list of rights that protected citizens' basic liberties.
- Some states refused to ratify the Constitution unless a bill of rights was added later.

## BILL OF RIGHTS ADDED TO CONSTITUTION IN 1791

## EFFECTS

- First 10 amendments identify and guarantee basic rights and freedoms.
- The federal government cannot take away rights spelled out in the Bill of Rights.

## Learn the Skill

*Use these steps to analyze cause-and-effect relationships.*

1. **Read labels.** The labels on the chart tell which event is the focus of study and which statements are the causes and which are the effects.

2. **Identify causes.** Causal statements give reasons why an event occurred. Major events have both long- and short-term causes.

3. **Identify effects.** Effect statements tell what happened because of the events. Major events have both long- and short-term effects.

4. **Analyze cause-and-effect relationships.** Think about why certain causes led to the event and why the event in turn had the results it did.

## Practice the Skill

*Answer the following questions about cause and effect based on the chart above.*

1. **Read labels.** To what event do the causes lead?

2. **Identify causes.** (a) What was one cause of the Bill of Rights? (b) Was this a long- or short-term cause? Explain.

3. **Identify effects.** (a) What was one effect of the Bill of Rights? (b) Was this a long- or short-term effect? Explain.

4. **Analyze cause-and-effect relationships.** How did colonial history lead to a concern about protecting citizens' rights?

## Apply the Skill

*See the Review and Assessment at the end of this chapter.*

**Interactive Textbook**

**Study Guide** *Online*
Complete your Chapter 7
study guide in print or online.

## Chapter Summary

### Section 1
### Governing a New Nation

- Many states added a bill of rights to their constitutions to protect individual freedoms.
- The Northwest Ordinance established a three-stage process for transforming a territory into a state.
- An increasing number of Americans came to believe that a stronger federal government was needed to deal with the country's pressing problems.

### Section 2
### The Constitutional Convention

- The Virginia Plan, calling for a strong central government with three branches, formed the basis of the U.S. Constitution.
- The Great Compromise set up a Congress with two houses, which pleased both the large and small states.

- As part of the compromise that won support for the Constitution, northern and southern delegates agreed that each enslaved person would count as three fifths of a free person.

### Section 3
### Debating the Constitution

- Federalists believed that three competing branches of government would keep any one part of the federal government from becoming too strong.
- Antifederalists were concerned that a strong federal government threatened states' rights and individual freedoms.
- A bill of rights was added to the Constitution to protect the people against abuses by the federal government.

## Key Concepts

These notes will help you prepare for questions about key concepts.

| Weaknesses of the National Government Under the Articles | Reforms of the National Government by the Constitutional Convention | Federalists Versus Antifederalists |
|---|---|---|
| • No power to tax or regulate trade<br>• Seen as weak by foreign powers<br>• Only one branch of government, the Congress<br>• Congress had few powers<br>• No means of enforcing its laws<br>• Unable to put down internal disturbances | • Set up three branches of government<br>• Congress to consist of two houses<br>• Established a single executive<br>• Expanded powers to raise money and regulate trade<br>• Compromise over issues related to slavery<br>• Constitution based on "we the people," not "we the states" | **Federalists**<br>• Need a stronger national government<br><br>**Antifederalists**<br>• Constitutional Convention had no authority to write a new constitution<br>• Constitution threatens to weaken powers of the states<br>• No bill of rights to protect individual freedoms<br>• President may become too powerful |

## Vocabulary *Builder*

### Key Terms

Answer the questions in complete sentences that show your understanding of the key terms.

1. How did the economic depression of the mid-1780s impact farmers?

2. What is the role of the judicial branch in government?

3. What process did the Constitutional Convention set forth for states to ratify the Constitution?

## Comprehension and Critical Thinking

4. **(a) Recall** Which powers did the Congress not have under the Articles of Confederation?
   **(b) Apply Information** How did not having these powers make the national government weak?

5. **(a) Recall** List the three stages a territory had to go through to become a state under the Northwest Ordinance of 1787.
   **(b) Draw Conclusions** How did this process help a territory prepare for statehood?

6. **(a) Describe** What were the causes of Shays' Rebellion of 1786?
   **(b) Detect Points of View** Thomas Jefferson called Shays' Rebellion "a medicine necessary for the sound health of government." What do you think he meant?

7. **(a) Contrast** How did the New Jersey Plan differ from the Virginia Plan?
   **(b) Link Past and Present** Which key part of the New Jersey Plan is not part of our Constitution today? Why not?

8. **(a) Recall** Describe one contribution made by each of the following to the writing and ratification of the Constitution: George Washington; James Madison; Roger Sherman; Gouverneur Morris.
   **(b) Evaluate Information** Whose contribution do you think was most important? Give reasons for your answer.

9. **(a) Summarize** Which freedoms and rights are protected in the Bill of Rights?
   **(b) Draw Conclusions** The Bill of Rights limited the powers of the federal government to those granted in the Constitution. Why do you think these limits were included?

## History Reading Skill

10. **Analyze Propositions and Support** Reread the text under the heading "The Great Compromise." What did the Virginia Plan propose about representation in Congress? How did delegates from smaller states respond? What support did they give for their different responses? Evaluate that support.

## Writing

11. **Write two paragraphs on the following topic:** Explain how the Constitution addressed weaknesses in the Articles of Confederation.
    **Your paragraphs should:**
    • include a thesis statement that expresses your main idea;
    • develop that main idea with facts, examples, and other information;
    • conclude by describing the lasting impact of what happened.

12. **Write a Narrative:**
    You are a delegate who has just arrived in Philadelphia in May 1787. Write a letter home explaining your feelings about the upcoming convention.

## Skills for Life

### Analyze Cause and Effect

Use the information below to answer the questions that follow.

> **Cause:** In 1774, the British Parliament passes an act that forces American colonists to house British troops in their homes.
>
> **Event:** Bill of Rights, Third Amendment
>
> "No soldier shall, in time of peace, be quartered in any house without the consent of the owner; nor in time of war, but in a manner to be prescribed by law."

13. What right does the Third Amendment protect?

14. **(a)** What was one cause of the Third Amendment?
    **(b)** Was this cause long term or short term? Explain.

15. How did the colonists' experiences under British rule influence their decision to change the Constitution?

# Test Yourself

1. **The Great Compromise settled a dispute between**

   A the North and the South.

   B Britain and the new United States.

   C the large states and the small states.

   D the President and Congress.

2. **Antifederalists opposed the Constitution because it**

   A did not give the President enough power.

   B weakened the state governments.

   C contained a bill of rights.

   D could not be amended.

**Study the political cartoon below to answer Question 3. Consider how it is similar to and different from the cartoon in Section 3.**

3. **What event is the creator of this political cartoon celebrating?**

   A the approval of the Constitution

   B the abolition of the slave trade

   C the failure of Shays' Rebellion

   D the passage of the Northwest Ordinance

# Document-Based Questions

**Task:** Look at Documents 1 and 2, and answer their accompanying questions. Then, use the documents and your knowledge of history to complete this writing assignment:

> Write an essay explaining why the writers of the Constitution felt it was necessary to create a new plan of government.

**Document 1:** This excerpt from the Articles of Confederation defines the limitations on the powers of the national Congress. *According to this excerpt, what is Congress not allowed to do without the consent of the states?*

"The United States in Congress assembled shall never engage in a war . . . nor coin money, nor regulate the value thereof, nor [spend] the sums and expenses necessary for the defense and welfare of the United States . . . nor borrow money on the credit of the United States . . . nor agree upon the number of vessels of war, to be built or purchased, or the number of land or sea forces to be raised, nor appoint a commander in chief of the army or navy, unless nine States [agree] to the same. . . ."

**Document 2:** This excerpt from the Constitution defines some of the powers granted to Congress. *Why do you think the Framers of the Constitution gave Congress the power to set standards for weights and measures, rather than leaving it up to each state?*

"The Congress shall have power:

1. To lay and collect taxes . . . to pay the debts and provide for the common defense and general welfare of the United States. . . .

2. To borrow money on the credit of the United States. . . .

3. To coin money, regulate the value thereof, and of foreign coin, and for the standard of weights and measures. . . .

4. To declare war. . . .

5. To raise and support armies. . . .

6. To provide and maintain a navy."

# The United States Constitution: An Outline

## Original Constitution

### Preamble

| Article I | Legislative Branch |
|---|---|
| Section 1 | A Two-House Legislature |
| Section 2 | House of Representatives |
| Section 3 | Senate |
| Section 4 | Elections and Meetings |
| Section 5 | Legislative Proceedings |
| Section 6 | Compensation, Immunities, and Disabilities of Members |
| Section 7 | Law-Making Process |
| Section 8 | Powers of Congress |
| Section 9 | Powers Denied to Congress |
| Section 10 | Powers Denied to the States |

| Article II | Executive Branch |
|---|---|
| Section 1 | President and Vice President |
| Section 2 | Powers of the President |
| Section 3 | Duties of the President |
| Section 4 | Impeachment |

| Article III | Judicial Branch |
|---|---|
| Section 1 | Courts, Terms of Office |
| Section 2 | Jurisdiction |
| Section 3 | Treason |

| Article IV | Relations Among the States |
|---|---|
| Section 1 | Full Faith and Credit |
| Section 2 | Privileges and Immunities of Citizens |
| Section 3 | New States and Territories |
| Section 4 | Protection Afforded to States by the Nation |

| Article V | Provisions for Amendment |
|---|---|

**Explore More Video**
To learn more about the first 10 amendments to the Constitution, view the video.

# The Constitution of the United States

**A Note on the Text of the Constitution**

*The complete text of the Constitution, including amendments, appears on the pages that follow. Spelling, capitalization, and punctuation have been modernized, and headings have been added.* Portions of the Constitution altered by later amendments or that no longer apply are printed in blue. *Commentary appears in the outside column of each page.*

> **The Preamble** The Preamble describes the purpose of the government as set up by the Constitution. Americans expect their government to defend justice and liberty and provide peace and safety from foreign enemies.

## Preamble

We the people of the United States, in order to form a more perfect union, establish justice, insure domestic tranquillity, provide for the common defense, promote the general welfare, and secure the blessings of liberty to ourselves and our posterity, do ordain and establish this Constitution for the United States of America.

## Article I ★ Legislative Branch

### Section 1. A Two-House Legislature

> **Section 1** The Constitution gives Congress the power to make laws. Congress is divided into the Senate and the House of Representatives.

All legislative powers herein granted shall be vested in a Congress of the United States, which shall consist of a Senate and House of Representatives.

## Section 2. House of Representatives

**1. Election of Members** The House of Representatives shall be composed of members chosen every second year by the people of the several states, and the electors in each state shall have the qualifications requisite for electors of the most numerous branch of the state legislature.

**2. Qualifications** No person shall be a representative who shall not have attained to the age of twenty-five years, and been seven years a citizen of the United States, and who shall not, when elected, be an inhabitant of that state in which he shall be chosen.

**3. Apportionment** Representatives and direct taxes shall be apportioned among the several states which may be included within this Union, according to their respective numbers, which shall be determined by adding to the whole number of free persons, including those bound to service for a term of years and excluding Indians not taxed, three fifths of all other persons. The actual enumeration shall be made within three years after the first meeting of the Congress of the United States, and within every subsequent term of ten years, in such manner as they shall by law direct. The number of representatives shall not exceed one for every thirty thousand, but each state shall have at least one representative; and until such enumeration shall be made, the state of New Hampshire shall be entitled to choose three, Massachusetts eight, Rhode Island and Providence Plantations one, Connecticut five, New York six, New Jersey four, Pennsylvania eight, Delaware one, Maryland six, Virginia ten, North Carolina five, South Carolina five, and Georgia three.

**4. Filling Vacancies** When vacancies happen in the representation from any state, the executive authority thereof shall issue writs of election to fill such vacancies.

**5. Officers; Impeachment** The House of Representatives shall choose their Speaker and other officers; and shall have the sole power of impeachment.

## Section 3. Senate

**1. Composition; Term** The Senate of the United States shall be composed of two senators from each state chosen by the legislature thereof, for six years, and each senator shall have one vote.

**2. Classification; Filling Vacancies** Immediately after they shall be assembled in consequence of the first election, they shall be divided as equally as may be into three classes. The seats of the senators of the first class shall be vacated at the expiration of the second year, of the second class at the expiration of the fourth year, and of the third class at the expiration of the sixth year, so that one third may be chosen every second year; and if vacancies happen by resignation, or otherwise, during the recess of the legislature of any State, the executive thereof may make temporary appointments until the next meeting of the legislature, which shall then fill such vacancies.

**Clause 1** Electors refers to voters. Members of the House of Representatives are elected every two years. Any citizen allowed to vote for members of the larger house of the state legislature can also vote for members of the House.

**Clause 3** The number of representatives each state elects is based on its population. An enumeration, or census, must be taken every 10 years to determine population. Today, the number of representatives in the House is fixed at 435. Clause 3 contains the Three-Fifths Compromise worked out at the Constitutional Convention. Persons bound to service meant indentured servants. All other persons meant slaves. All free people in a state were counted. However, only three fifths of the slaves were included in the population count. This three-fifths clause became meaningless when slaves were freed by the Thirteenth Amendment.

**Clause 4** Executive authority means the governor of a state. If a member of the House leaves office before his or her term ends, the governor must call a special election to fill the seat.

**Clause 5** The House elects a Speaker. Only the House has the power to impeach, or accuse, a federal official of wrongdoing.

**Clause 2** Every two years, one third of the senators run for reelection. The Seventeenth Amendment changed the way of filling vacancies, or empty seats. Today, the governor of a state must choose a senator to fill a vacancy that occurs between elections.

**3. Qualifications** No person shall be a senator who shall not have attained to the age of thirty years, and been nine years a citizen of the United States, and who shall not, when elected, be an inhabitant of that state for which he shall be chosen.

**4. President of the Senate** The Vice President of the United States shall be president of the Senate, but shall have no vote, unless they be equally divided.

**5. Other Officers** The Senate shall choose their other officers, and also a president pro tempore, in the absence of the Vice President, or when he shall exercise the office of the President of the United States.

**6. Impeachment Trials** The Senate shall have the sole power to try all impeachments. When sitting for that purpose, they shall be on oath or affirmation. When the President of the United States is tried, the Chief Justice shall preside; and no person shall be convicted without the concurrence of two thirds of the members present.

**7. Penalty on Conviction** Judgment in cases of impeachment shall not extend further than to removal from office, and disqualification to hold and enjoy any office of honor, trust or profit under the United States: but the party convicted shall nevertheless be liable and subject to indictment, trial, judgment, and punishment, according to law.

## Section 4. Elections and Meetings

**1. Election of Congress** The times, places, and manner of holding elections for senators and representatives, shall be prescribed in each state by the legislature thereof; but the Congress may at any time by law make or alter such regulations, except as to the places of choosing senators.

**2. Sessions** The Congress shall assemble at least once in every year, and such meeting shall be on the first Monday in December, unless they shall by law appoint a different day.

## Section 5. Legislative Proceedings

**1. Organization** Each house shall be the judge of the elections, returns, and qualifications of its own members, and a majority of each shall constitute a quorum to do business; but a smaller number may adjourn from day to day, and may be authorized to compel the attendance of absent members, in such manner, and under such penalties, as each house may provide.

**2. Rules** Each house may determine the rules of its proceedings, punish its members for disorderly behavior, and with the concurrence of two thirds, expel a member.

**3. Record** Each house shall keep a journal of its proceedings, and from time to time publish the same, excepting such parts as may in their judgment require secrecy; and the yeas and nays of the members of either house on any question shall, at the desire of one fifth of those present, be entered on the journal.

**Clause 5** Pro tempore means temporary. The Senate chooses one of its members to serve as president pro tempore when the Vice President is absent.

**Clause 6** The Senate acts as a jury if the House impeaches a federal official. The Chief Justice of the Supreme Court presides if the President is on trial. Two thirds of all senators present must vote for conviction, or finding the accused guilty. No President has ever been convicted. The House impeached President Andrew Johnson in 1868, but the Senate acquitted him of the charges. In 1998–99, President Bill Clinton became the second President to be impeached and acquitted.

**Clause 1** Each state legislature can decide when and how congressional elections take place, but Congress can overrule these decisions. In 1842, Congress required each state to set up congressional districts with one representative elected from each district. In 1872, Congress decided that congressional elections must be held in every state on the same date in even-numbered years.

**Clause 1** Each house decides whether a member has the qualifications for office set by the Constitution. A quorum is the smallest number of members who must be present for business to be conducted. Each house can set its own rules about absent members.

Portions of the Constitution altered by later amendments or that no longer apply are printed in blue.

**4. Adjournment** Neither house, during the session of Congress, shall, without the consent of the other, adjourn for more than three days, nor to any other place than that in which the two houses shall be sitting.

## Section 6. Compensation, Immunities, and Disabilities of Members

**1. Salaries; Immunities** The senators and representatives shall receive a compensation for their services, to be ascertained by law, and paid out of the Treasury of the United States. They shall in all cases, except treason, felony, and breach of the peace, be privileged from arrest during their attendance at the session of their respective houses, and in going to and returning from the same; and for any speech or debate in either house, they shall not be questioned in any other place.

**2. Restrictions on Other Employment** No senator or representative shall, during the time for which he was elected, be appointed to any civil office under the authority of the United States, which shall have been created, or the emoluments whereof shall have been increased during such time; and no person holding any office under the United States shall be a member of either house during his continuance in office.

## Section 7. Law-Making Process

**1. Revenue Bills** All bills for raising revenue shall originate in the House of Representatives; but the Senate may propose or concur with amendments as on other bills.

**2. How a Bill Becomes Law; the Veto** Every bill which shall have passed the House of Representatives and the Senate shall, before it become a law, be presented to the President of the United States; if he approve, he shall sign it, but if not, he shall return it, with his objections, to that house in which it shall have originated, who shall enter the objections at large on their journal, and proceed to reconsider it. If after such reconsideration two thirds of that house shall agree to pass the bill, it shall be sent, together with the objections, to the other house, by which it shall likewise be reconsidered, and if approved by two thirds of that house, it shall become a law. But in all such cases the votes of both houses shall be determined by yeas and nays, and the names of the persons voting for and against the bill shall be entered on the journal of each house respectively. If any bill shall not be returned by the President within ten days (Sundays excepted) after it shall have been presented to him, the same shall be a law, in like manner as if he had signed it, unless the Congress by their adjournment prevent its return, in which case it shall not be a law.

**3. Resolutions Passed by Congress** Every order, resolution, or vote to which the concurrence of the Senate and House of Representatives may be necessary (except on a question of adjournment) shall be presented to the President of the United States; and before the same shall take effect, shall be approved by him, or being disapproved by him, shall be repassed by two thirds of the Senate and House of Representatives, according to the rules and limitations prescribed in the case of a bill.

**Clause 4** Neither house can adjourn, or stop meeting, for more than three days unless the other house approves. Both houses must meet in the same city.

**Clause 1** Congress decides the salary for its members. While Congress is in session, a member is free from arrest in civil cases and cannot be sued for anything he or she says on the floor of Congress. This allows for freedom of debate. However, a member can be arrested for a criminal offense.

**Clause 2** Emolument means salary. A member of Congress cannot hold another federal office during his or her term. A former member of Congress cannot hold an office created while he or she was in Congress. An official in another branch of government cannot serve at the same time in Congress.

**Clause 1** Revenue is money raised by the government through taxes. Tax bills must be introduced in the House. The Senate, however, can make changes in tax bills.

**Clause 2** A bill, or proposed law, that is passed by a majority of the House and Senate is sent to the President. If the President signs the bill, it becomes law.

A bill can also become law without the President's signature. The President can refuse to act on a bill. If Congress is in session at the time, the bill becomes law 10 days after the President receives it.

The President can veto, or reject, a bill by sending it back to the house where it was introduced. If the President refuses to act on a bill and Congress adjourns within 10 days, then the bill dies. This way of killing a bill without taking action is called the pocket veto.

Congress can override the President's veto if each house of Congress passes the bill again by a two-thirds vote.

Congress's power is expressed directly in the Constitution. Numbered from 1 to 18, these powers are also known as enumerated powers.

**Clause 1** Duties are tariffs. Imposts are taxes in general. Excises are taxes on the production or sale of certain goods.

**Clause 3** Only Congress has the power to regulate foreign and interstate commerce. This allows a "common market" with a unified set of laws governing trade. This clause has also been interpreted as giving the federal government authority over Native American nations.

**Clause 4** Naturalization is the process whereby a foreigner becomes a citizen. Bankruptcy is the condition in which a person or business cannot pay its debts.

**Clause 5** Congressional power to coin money and set its value is one of the keys to creating a stable economy.

**Clause 6** Counterfeiting is the making of imitation money. Securities are bonds. Congress can make laws to punish counterfeiters.

**Clause 11** Only Congress can declare war. Declarations of war are granted at the request of the President. Letters of marque and reprisal were documents issued by a government allowing merchant ships to arm themselves and attack ships of an enemy nation. They are no longer issued.

**Clauses 15, 16** The militia is a body of citizen soldiers. Each state has its own militia, today called the National Guard. Normally, the militia is under the command of a state's governor. However, it can be placed under the command of the President.

Portions of the Constitution altered by later amendments or that no longer apply are printed in blue.

## Section 8. Powers of Congress

### The Congress shall have power

**1.** To lay and collect taxes, duties, imposts, and excises, to pay the debts and provide for the common defense and general welfare of the United States; but all duties, imposts and excises shall be uniform throughout the United States;

**2.** To borrow money on the credit of the United States;

**3.** To regulate commerce with foreign nations, and among the several states, and with the Indian tribes;

**4.** To establish an uniform rule of naturalization, and uniform laws on the subject of bankruptcies throughout the United States;

**5.** To coin money, regulate the value thereof, and of foreign coin, and fix the standard of weights and measures;

**6.** To provide for the punishment of counterfeiting the securities and current coin of the United States;

**7.** To establish post offices and post roads;

**8.** To promote the progress of science and useful arts by securing for limited times to authors and inventors the exclusive right to their respective writings and discoveries;

**9.** To constitute tribunals inferior to the Supreme Court;

**10.** To define and punish piracies and felonies committed on the high seas and offenses against the law of nations;

**11.** To declare war, grant letters of marque and reprisal, and make rules concerning captures on land and water;

**12.** To raise and support armies, but no appropriation of money to that use shall be for a longer term than two years;

**13.** To provide and maintain a navy;

**14.** To make rules for the government and regulation of the land and naval forces;

**15.** To provide for calling forth the militia to execute the laws of the Union, suppress insurrections, and repel invasions;

**16.** To provide for organizing, arming, and disciplining the militia, and for governing such part of them as may be employed in the service of the United States, reserving to the states, respectively, the appointment of the officers, and the authority of training the militia according to the discipline prescribed by Congress;

**17.** To exercise exclusive legislation in all cases whatsoever, over such district (not exceeding ten miles square) as may, by cession of particular states, and the acceptance of Congress, become the seat of the government of the United States, and to exercise like authority over all places purchased by the consent of the legislature of the state in which the same shall be, for the erection of forts, magazines, arsenals, dock-yards, and other needful buildings; —and

**18.** To make all laws which shall be necessary and proper for carrying into execution the foregoing powers, and all other powers vested by this Constitution in the government of the United States, or in any department or officer thereof.

## Section 9. Powers Denied to Congress

**1. The Slave Trade** The migration or importation of such persons as any of the states now existing shall think proper to admit, shall not be prohibited by the Congress prior to the year one thousand eight hundred and eight, but a tax or duty may be imposed on such importation, not exceeding ten dollars for each person.

**2. Writ of Habeas Corpus** The privilege of the writ of habeas corpus shall not be suspended, unless when in cases of rebellion or invasion the public safety may require it.

**3. Bills of Attainder; Ex Post Facto Laws** No bill of attainder or ex post facto law shall be passed.

**4. Apportionment of Direct Taxes** No capitation, or other direct, tax shall be laid, unless in proportion to the census or enumeration herein before directed to be taken.

**5. Taxes on Exports** No tax or duty shall be laid on articles exported from any state.

**6. Special Preference for Trade** No preference shall be given by any regulation of commerce or revenue to the ports of one state over those of another; nor shall vessels bound to, or from, one state, be obliged to enter, clear, or pay duties in another.

**7. Spending** No money shall be drawn from the Treasury, but in consequence of appropriations made by law; and a regular statement and account of the receipts and expenditures of all public money shall be published from time to time.

**8. Titles of Nobility** No title of nobility shall be granted by the United States; and no person holding any office of profit or trust under them, shall, without the consent of the Congress, accept of any present, emolument, office, or title, of any kind whatever, from any king, prince or foreign state.

## Section 10. Powers Denied to the States

**1. Unconditional Prohibitions** No state shall enter into any treaty, alliance, or confederation; grant letters of marque and reprisal; coin money; emit bills of credit; make any thing but gold and silver coin a tender in payment of debts; pass any bill of attainder, ex post facto law, or law impairing the obligation of contracts, or grant any title of nobility.

**2. Powers Conditionally Denied** No state shall, without the consent of the Congress, lay any imposts or duties on imports or exports, except what may be absolutely necessary for executing its inspection laws; and the net produce of all duties and imposts, laid by any state on imports or exports, shall be for the use of the Treasury of the United States; and all such laws shall be subject to the revision and control of the Congress.

**Clause 18** Clause 18 gives Congress the power to make laws as needed to carry out the first 17 clauses. It is sometimes called the elastic clause because it lets Congress stretch the meaning of its power.

**Clause 1** "Such persons" means slaves. In 1808, as soon as Congress was permitted to abolish the slave trade, it did so.

**Clause 2** A writ of habeas corpus is a court order requiring government officials to bring a prisoner to court and explain why he or she is being held. A writ of habeas corpus protects people from unlawful imprisonment. The government cannot suspend this right except in times of rebellion or invasion.

**Clause 3** A bill of attainder is a law declaring that a person is guilty of a particular crime. An ex post facto law punishes an act which was not illegal when it was committed. Congress cannot pass a bill of attainder or ex post facto laws.

**Clause 7** The federal government cannot spend money unless Congress appropriates it, or passes a law allowing it. The government must publish a statement showing how it spends public funds.

**Clause 1** The writers of the Constitution did not want the states to act like separate nations, so they prohibited states from making treaties or coining money. Some powers denied to the federal government are also denied to the states.

**Clauses 2, 3** Powers listed here are forbidden to the states, but Congress can pass laws that give these powers to the states. **Clause 2** forbids states from taxing imports and exports without the consent of Congress. States may charge inspection fees on goods entering the states. Any profits go to the United States Treasury.

**Clause 3** forbids states from keeping an army or navy without the consent of Congress. States cannot make treaties or declare war unless an enemy invades or is about to invade.

**Clauses 2, 3** Some writers of the Constitution were afraid to allow the people to elect the President directly. Therefore, the Constitutional Convention set up the electoral college. Clause 2 directs each state to choose electors, or delegates to the electoral college, to vote for President. A state's electoral vote is equal to the combined number of senators and representatives. Each state may decide how to choose its electors. Members of Congress and federal officeholders may not serve as electors. This much of the original electoral college system is still in effect.

**Clause 3** Clause 3 called upon each elector to vote for two candidates. The candidate who received a majority of the electoral votes would become President. The runner-up would become Vice President. If no candidate won a majority, the House would choose the President. The Senate would choose the Vice President.

The election of 1800 showed a problem with the original electoral college system. Thomas Jefferson was the Republican candidate for President, and Aaron Burr was the Republican candidate for Vice President. In the electoral college, the vote ended in a tie. The election was finally decided in the House, where Jefferson was chosen President. The Twelfth Amendment changed the electoral college system so that this could not happen again.

Portions of the Constitution altered by later amendments or that no longer apply are printed in blue.

**3. Other Denied Powers** No state shall, without the consent of Congress, lay any duty of tonnage, keep troops, or ships of war in time of peace, enter into any agreement or compact with another state, or with a foreign power, or engage in war, unless actually invaded, or in such imminent danger as will not admit of delay.

## Article II ★ Executive Branch

### Section 1. President and Vice President

**1. Chief Executive; Term** The executive power shall be vested in a President of the United States of America. He shall hold his office during the term of four years, and, together with the Vice President, chosen for the same term, be elected as follows:

**2. Electoral College** Each state shall appoint, in such manner as the legislature thereof may direct, a number of electors, equal to the whole number of senators and representatives to which the state may be entitled in the Congress: but no senator or representative, or person holding an office of trust or profit under the United States, shall be appointed an elector.

**3. Former Electoral Method** The electors shall meet in their respective states, and vote by ballot for two persons, of whom one at least shall not be an inhabitant of the same state with themselves. And they shall make a list of all the persons voted for, and of the number of votes for each; which list they shall sign and certify, and transmit sealed to the seat of the government of the United States, directed to the president of the Senate. The president of the Senate shall, in the presence of the Senate and House of Representatives, open all the certificates, and the votes shall then be counted. The person having the greatest number of votes shall be the President, if such number be a majority of the whole number of Electors appointed; and if there be more than one who have such majority, and have an equal number of votes, then the House of Representatives shall immediately choose by ballot one of them for President; and if no person have a majority, then from the five highest on the list the said House shall in like manner choose the President. But in choosing the President, the votes shall be taken by states, the representation from each state having one vote; a quorum for this purpose shall consist of a member or members from two thirds of the states, and a majority of all the states shall be necessary to a choice. In every case, after the choice of the President, the person having the greatest number of votes of the electors shall be the Vice President. But if there should remain two or more who have equal votes, the Senate shall choose from them by ballot the Vice President.

**4. Time of Elections** The Congress may determine the time of choosing the electors, and the day on which they shall give their votes; which day shall be the same throughout the United States.

**5. Qualifications for President** No person except a natural-born citizen, or a citizen of the United States at the time of the adoption of this Constitution, shall be eligible to the office of President; neither shall any person be eligible to that office who shall not have attained to the age of thirty-five years, and been fourteen years a resident within the United States.

**6. Presidential Succession** In case of the removal of the President from office, or of his death, resignation, or inability to discharge the powers and duties of the said office, the same shall devolve on the Vice President, and the Congress may by law provide for the case of removal, death, resignation or inability, both of the President and Vice President, declaring what officer shall then act as President, and such officer shall act accordingly, until the disability be removed, or a President shall be elected.

**7. Salary** The President shall, at stated times, receive for his services, a compensation, which shall neither be increased nor diminished during the period for which he shall have been elected, and he shall not receive within that period any other emolument from the United States, or any of them.

**8. Oath of Office** Before he enter on the execution of his office, he shall take the following oath or affirmation:—"I do solemnly swear (or affirm) that I will faithfully execute the office of the President of the United States, and will to the best of my ability, preserve, protect, and defend the Constitution of the United States."

## Section 2. Powers of the President

**1. Military Powers** The President shall be commander in chief of the army and navy of the United States, and of the militia of the several states, when called into the actual service of the United States; he may require the opinion, in writing, of the principal officer in each of the executive departments, upon any subject relating to the duties of their respective offices, and he shall have power to grant reprieves and pardons for offenses against the United States, except in cases of impeachment.

**2. Treaties; Appointments** He shall have power, by and with the advice and consent of the Senate, to make treaties, provided two thirds of the senators present concur; and he shall nominate, and by and with the advice and consent of the Senate, shall appoint ambassadors, other public ministers and consuls, judges of the Supreme Court, and all other officers of the United States, whose appointments are not herein otherwise provided for, and which shall be established by law: but the Congress may by law vest the appointment of such inferior officers, as they think proper, in the President alone, in the courts of law, or in the heads of departments.

**3. Temporary Appointments** The President shall have power to fill up all vacancies that may happen during the recess of the Senate, by granting commissions which shall expire at the end of their next session.

**Clause 6** The powers of the President pass to the Vice President if the President leaves office or cannot discharge his or her duties. The Twenty-fifth Amendment replaced this clause.

**Clause 7** The President is paid a salary. It cannot be raised or lowered during his or her term of office. The President is not allowed to hold any other federal or state position while in office.

**Clause 1** The President is the head of the armed forces and the state militias when they are called into national service. So the military is under civilian, or nonmilitary, control. The President can get advice from the heads of executive departments. In most cases, the President has the power to grant reprieves and pardons. A reprieve suspends punishment ordered by law. A pardon prevents prosecution for a crime or overrides the judgment of a court.

**Clause 2** The President has the power to make treaties with other nations. Under the system of checks and balances, all treaties must be approved by two thirds of the Senate.

The President has the power to appoint ambassadors to foreign countries and to appoint other high officials. The Senate must confirm, or approve, these appointments.

## Section 3. Duties of the President

He shall from time to time give to the Congress information of the state of the Union, and recommend to their consideration such measures as he shall judge necessary and expedient; he may, on extraordinary occasions, convene both houses, or either of them, and in case of disagreement between them, with respect to the time of adjournment, he may adjourn them to such time as he shall think proper; he shall receive ambassadors and other public ministers; he shall take care that the laws be faithfully executed, and shall commission all the officers of the United States.

## Section 4. Impeachment

**Section 4**
Civil officers include federal judges and members of the Cabinet. High crimes are major crimes. Misdemeanors are lesser crimes. The President, Vice President, and others can be forced out of office if impeached and found guilty of certain crimes.

The President, Vice President and all civil officers of the United States, shall be removed from office on impeachment for, and conviction of, treason, bribery, or other high crimes and misdemeanors.

# Article III ★ Judicial Branch

## Section 1. Courts, Terms of Office

The judicial power of the United States shall be vested in one Supreme Court, and in such inferior courts as the Congress may from time to time ordain and establish. The judges, both of the Supreme and inferior courts, shall hold their offices during good behavior, and shall, at stated times, receive for their services, a compensation, which shall not be diminished during their continuance in office.

## Section 2. Jurisdiction

**Clause 1** Jurisdiction refers to the right of a court to hear a case. Federal courts have jurisdiction over cases that involve the Constitution, federal laws, treaties, foreign ambassadors and diplomats, naval and maritime laws, disagreements between states or between citizens from different states, and disputes between a state or citizen and a foreign state or citizen.

**1. Scope of Judicial Power** The judicial power shall extend to all cases, in law and equity, arising under this Constitution, the laws of the United States, and treaties made, or which shall be made, under their authority;—to all cases affecting ambassadors, other public ministers and consuls;—to all cases of admiralty and maritime jurisdiction;—to controversies to which the United States shall be a party;—to controversies between two or more states; between a state and citizens of another state; —between citizens of different states;—between citizens of the same state claiming lands under grants of different states, and between a state, or the citizens thereof, and foreign states, citizens, or subjects.

**Clause 2** Original jurisdiction means the power of a court to hear a case where it first arises. The Supreme Court has original jurisdiction over only a few cases, such as those involving foreign diplomats. More often, the Supreme Court acts as an appellate court. An appellate court does not decide guilt. It decides whether the lower court trial was properly conducted and reviews the lower court's decision.

**2. Supreme Court** In all cases affecting ambassadors, other public ministers and consuls, and those in which a state shall be a party, the Supreme Court shall have original jurisdiction. In all the other cases before mentioned, the Supreme Court shall have appellate jurisdiction, both as to law and fact, with such exceptions, and under such regulations as the Congress shall make.

Portions of the Constitution altered by later amendments or that no longer apply are printed in blue.

**3. Trial by Jury** The trial of all crimes, except in cases of impeachment, shall be by jury; and such trial shall be held in the state where the said crimes shall have been committed; but when not committed within any state, the trial shall be at such place or places as the Congress may by law have directed.

## Section 3. Treason

**1. Definition** Treason against the United States shall consist only in levying war against them, or in adhering to their enemies, giving them aid and comfort. No person shall be convicted of treason unless on the testimony of two witnesses to the same overt act, or on confession in open court.

> **Clause 1** Treason is clearly defined. An <u>overt act</u> is an actual action.

**2. Punishment** The Congress shall have power to declare the punishment of treason, but no attainder of treason shall work corruption of blood or forfeiture except during the life of the person attained.

> **Clause 2** Congress has the power to set the punishment for the traitors. Congress may not punish the children of convicted traitors by taking away their civil rights or property.

## Article IV ★ Relations Among the States

### Section 1. Full Faith and Credit

Full faith and credit shall be given in each state to the public acts, records, and judicial proceedings of every other state. And the Congress may by general laws prescribe the manner in which such acts, records, and proceedings shall be proved, and the effect thereof.

> Each state must recognize the official acts and records of any other state. For example, each state must recognize marriage certificates issued by another state. Congress can pass laws to ensure this.

### Section 2. Privileges and Immunities of Citizens

**1. Privileges** The citizens of each state shall be entitled to all privileges and immunities of citizens in the several states.

**2. Extradition** A person charged in any state with treason, felony, or other crime, who shall flee from justice, and be found in another state, shall on demand of the executive authority of the state from which he fled, be delivered up, to be removed to the state having jurisdiction of the crime.

> **Clause 2** <u>Extradition</u> means the act of returning a suspected criminal or escaped prisoner to a state where he or she is wanted. State governors must return a suspect to another state. However, the Supreme Court has ruled that a governor cannot be forced to do so if he or she feels that justice will not be done.

**3. Fugitive Slaves** No person held to service or labor in one state, under the laws thereof, escaping into another, shall in consequence of any law or regulation therein, be discharged from such service or labor, but shall be delivered up on claim of the party to whom such service or labor may be due.

> **Clause 3** "Persons held to service or labor" refers to slaves or indentured servants. This clause required states to return runaway slaves to their owners. The Thirteenth Amendment replaces this clause.

### Section 3. New States and Territories

**1. New States** New states may be admitted by the Congress into this Union; but no new states shall be formed or erected within the jurisdiction of any other state; nor any state be formed by the junction of two or more states, or parts of states, without the consent of the legislatures of the states concerned as well as of the Congress.

> **Clause 1** Congress has the power to admit new states to the Union. Existing states cannot be split up or joined together to form new states unless both Congress and the state legislatures approve. New states are equal to all other states.

**2. Federal Lands** The Congress shall have power to dispose of and make all needful rules and regulations respecting the territory or other property belonging to the United States; and nothing in this Constitution shall be so construed as to prejudice any claims of the United States, or of any particular state.

## Section 4. Protection Afforded to States by the Nation

The United States shall guarantee to every state in this Union a republican form of government, and shall protect each of them against invasion; and on application of the legislature, or of the executive (when the legislature cannot be convened) against domestic violence.

## Article V ★ Provisions for Amendment

The Congress, whenever two thirds of both houses shall deem it necessary, shall propose amendments to this Constitution, or, on the application of the legislatures of two thirds of the several states, shall call a convention for proposing amendments, which, in either case, shall be valid to all intents and purposes, as part of this Constitution, when ratified by the legislatures of three fourths of the several states, or by conventions in three fourths thereof, as the one or the other mode of ratification may be proposed by the Congress; provided that no amendment which may be made prior to the year one thousand eight hundred and eight shall in any manner affect the first and fourth clauses in the ninth section of the first Article; and that no state, without its consent, shall be deprived of its equal suffrage in the Senate.

## Article VI ★ National Debts, Supremacy of National Law, Oath

### Section 1. Validity of Debts

All debts contracted and engagements entered into, before the adoption of this Constitution, shall be as valid against the United States under this Constitution, as under the Confederation.

### Section 2. Supremacy of National Law

This Constitution, and the laws of the United States which shall be made in pursuance thereof, and all treaties made, or which shall be made, under the authority of the United States, shall be the supreme law of the land; and the judges in every state shall be bound thereby, anything in the constitution or laws of any state to the contrary notwithstanding.

---

**Section 4** In a <u>republic</u>, voters choose representatives to govern them. The federal government must protect the states from foreign invasion and from domestic, or internal, disorder if asked to do so by a state.

The Constitution can be <u>amended</u>, or changed, if necessary. An amendment can be proposed by (1) a two-thirds vote of both houses of Congress or (2) a national convention called by Congress at the request of two thirds of the state legislatures. (This second method has never been used.) An amendment must be <u>ratified</u>, or approved, by (1) three fourths of the state legislatures or (2) special conventions in three fourths of the states. Congress decides which method will be used.

Congress has proposed each of the 27 amendments to the Constitution by a vote of two-thirds in both houses. The only amendment ratified by constitutional conventions of the states was the Twenty-first Amendment. State legislatures have ratified all other amendments.

**Section 2** The "supremacy clause" in this section establishes the Constitution, federal laws, and treaties that the Senate has ratified as the <u>supreme</u>, or highest, law of the land. Thus, they outweigh state laws. A state judge must overturn a state law that conflicts with the Constitution or with a federal law.

Portions of the Constitution altered by later amendments or that no longer apply are printed in blue.

## Section 3. Oaths of Office

The senators and representatives before mentioned, and the members of the several state legislatures, and all executive and judicial officers, both of the United States and of the several states, shall be bound by oath or affirmation, to support this Constitution; but no religious test shall ever be required as a qualification to any office or public trust under the United States.

## Article VII ★ Ratification of Constitution

The ratification of the conventions of nine states shall be sufficient for the establishment of this Constitution between the states so ratifying the same.

Done in convention by the unanimous consent of the states present the seventeenth day of September, in the year of our Lord one thousand seven hundred and eighty-seven, and of the independence of the United States of America the twelfth. In Witness whereof, we have hereunto subscribed our names.

> **Article VII** During 1787 and 1788, states held special conventions. By October 1788, the required nine states had ratified the United States Constitution.

Attest: William Jackson, SECRETARY
George Washington, PRESIDENT and deputy from Virginia

*New Hampshire*
  John Langdon
  Nicholas Gilman

*Massachusetts*
  Nathaniel Gorham
  Rufus King

*Connecticut*
  William Samuel Johnson
  Roger Sherman

*New York*
  Alexander Hamilton

*New Jersey*
  William Livingston
  David Brearley
  William Paterson
  Jonathan Dayton

*Pennsylvania*
  Benjamin Franklin
  Thomas Mifflin
  Robert Morris
  George Clymer
  Thomas Fitzsimons
  Jared Ingersoll
  James Wilson
  Gouverneur Morris

*Delaware*
  George Read
  Gunning Bedford, Jr.
  John Dickinson
  Richard Bassett
  Jacob Broom

*Maryland*
  James McHenry
  Dan of St. Thomas Jennifer
  Daniel Carroll

*Virginia*
  John Blair
  James Madison, Jr.

*North Carolina*
  William Blount
  Richard Dobbs Spaight
  Hugh Williamson

*South Carolina*
  John Rutledge
  Charles Cotesworth Pinckney
  Charles Pinckney
  Pierce Butler

*Georgia*
  William Few
  Abraham Baldwin

**The Amendments** Amendments are changes. The Constitution has been amended 27 times since it was ratified in 1788. The first 10 amendments are referred to as the Bill of Rights. These amendments give rights to the people and states, thus putting limits on the power of government.

**First Amendment** The First Amendment protects five basic rights: freedom of religion, speech, the press, assembly, and petition. Congress cannot set up an established, or official, church or religion for the nation. It cannot forbid the practice of religion, nor can it force the practice of religion.

Congress may not abridge, or limit, the freedom to speak and write freely. The government may not censor, or review, books and newspapers before they are printed. This amendment also protects the right to assemble, or hold public meetings. Petition means ask. Redress means to correct. Grievances are wrongs. The people have the right to ask the government for wrongs to be corrected.

**Second Amendment** Americans debate the exact meaning of the Second Amendment. Some believe that it guarantees the right of individuals to own firearms. Others argue that it guarantees the right of each state to maintain a militia. Gun control, or the passage of laws to regulate the ownership and use of firearms, is one of the most controversial issues today.

**Third Amendment** In colonial times, the British could quarter, or house, soldiers in private homes without permission of the owners. The Third Amendment prevents such abuses.

Portions of the Constitution altered by later amendments or that no longer apply are printed in blue.

# Amendments

## First Amendment ★

### (1791) Freedom of Religion, Speech, Press, Assembly, and Petition

Congress shall make no law respecting an establishment of religion, or prohibiting the free exercise thereof; or abridging the freedom of speech, or of the press; or the right of the people peaceably to assemble, and to petition the government for a redress of grievances.

## Second Amendment ★

### (1791) Bearing Arms

A well-regulated militia being necessary to the security of a free state, the right of the people to keep and bear arms shall not be infringed.

## Third Amendment ★

### (1791) Quartering of Troops

No soldier shall, in time of peace, be quartered in any house, without the consent of the owner; nor in time of war, but in a manner to be prescribed by law.

## Fourth Amendment ★

### (1791) Searches and Seizures

The right of the people to be secure in their persons, houses, papers, and effects, against unreasonable searches and seizures, shall not be violated, and no warrants shall issue, but upon probable cause, supported by oath or affirmation, and particularly describing the place to be searched, and the persons or things to be seized.

## Fifth Amendment ★

### (1791) Criminal Proceedings; Due Process; Eminent Domain

No person shall be held to answer for a capital, or otherwise infamous, crime, unless on a presentment or indictment of a grand jury, except in cases arising in the land or naval forces, or in the militia, when in actual service in time of war or public danger; nor shall any person be subject for the same offense to be twice put in jeopardy of life and limb; nor shall be compelled, in any criminal case, to be a witness against himself; nor be deprived of life, liberty, or property, without due process of law; nor shall private property be taken for public use, without just compensation.

## Sixth Amendment ★

### (1791) Criminal Proceedings

In all criminal prosecutions, the accused shall enjoy the right to a speedy and public trial, by an impartial jury of the state and district wherein the crime shall have been committed, which district shall have been previously ascertained by law, and to be informed of the nature and cause of the accusation; to be confronted with the witnesses against him; to have compulsory process for obtaining witnesses in his favor, and to have the assistance of counsel for his defense.

**Fourth Amendment** This amendment protects Americans from unreasonable searches and seizures. Search and seizure are permitted only if a judge has issued a warrant, or written court order. A warrant is issued only if there is probable cause. This means an officer must show that it is probable, or likely, that the search will produce evidence of a crime.

**Fifth Amendment** This amendment protects the rights of the accused. Capital crimes are those that can be punished with death. Infamous crimes are those that can be punished with prison or loss of rights. The federal government must obtain an indictment, or formal accusation, from a grand jury to prosecute anyone for such crimes. A grand jury is a panel of between 12 and 23 citizens who decide if the government has enough evidence to justify a trial.

Double jeopardy is forbidden by this amendment. This means that a person cannot be tried twice for the same crime. However, if a court sets aside a conviction because of a legal error, the accused can be tried again. A person on trial cannot be forced to testify, or give evidence, against himself or herself. A person accused of a crime is entitled to due process of law, or a fair hearing or trial.

Finally, the government cannot seize private property for public use without paying the owner a fair price for it.

**Sixth Amendment** In criminal cases, the jury must be impartial, or not favor either side. The accused is guaranteed the right to a trial by jury. The trial must be speedy. If the government purposely postpones the trial so that it becomes hard for the person to get a fair hearing, the charge may be dismissed. The accused must be told the charges and be allowed to question all witnesses. Witnesses who can help the accused can be ordered to appear in court. The accused must be allowed a lawyer.

**Seventh Amendment** <u>Common law</u> refers to rules of law established by judges in past cases. This amendment guarantees the right to a jury trial in lawsuits where the sum of money at stake is more than $20. An appeals court can set aside a verdict only if legal errors made the trial unfair.

**Eighth Amendment** <u>Bail</u> is money that the accused leaves with the court as a pledge to appear for trial. If the accused does not appear, the court keeps the money. This amendment prevents the court from imposing bail or fines that are <u>excessive</u>, or too high. The amendment also forbids cruel and unusual punishments, such as physical torture.

**Ninth Amendment** The rights of the people are not limited to those listed in the Bill of Rights. In the Ninth Amendment, the government is prevented from claiming these are the only rights people have.

**Tenth Amendment** Powers not given to the federal government belong to the states. Powers reserved to the states are not listed in the Constitution.

**Eleventh Amendment** A private citizen from one state cannot sue the government of another state in federal court. However, a citizen can sue a state government in a state court.

Portions of the Constitution altered by later amendments or that no longer apply are printed in blue.

## Seventh Amendment ★

### (1791) Civil Trials

In suits at common law, where the value in controversy shall exceed twenty dollars, the right of trial by jury shall be preserved, and no fact tried by a jury shall be otherwise re-examined in any court of the United States, than according to the rules of the common law.

## Eighth Amendment ★

### (1791) Punishment for Crimes

Excessive bail shall not be required, nor excessive fines imposed, nor cruel and unusual punishments inflicted.

## Ninth Amendment ★

### (1791) Unenumerated Rights

The enumeration in the Constitution, of certain rights, shall not be construed to deny or disparage others retained by the people.

## Tenth Amendment ★

### (1791) Powers Reserved to the States

The powers not delegated to the United States by the Constitution, nor prohibited by it to the states, are reserved to the states respectively, or to the people.

## Eleventh Amendment ★

### (1795) Suits Against States

The judicial power of the United States shall not be construed to extend to any suit in law or equity, commenced or prosecuted against one of the United States by citizens of another state, or by citizens or subjects of any foreign state.

## Twelfth Amendment ★

### (1804) Election of President and Vice President

The electors shall meet in their respective states, and vote by ballot for President and Vice President, one of whom, at least, shall not be an inhabitant of the same state with themselves; they shall name in their ballots the person voted for as President, and in distinct ballots the person voted for as Vice President, and they shall make distinct lists of all persons voted for as President, and of all persons voted for as Vice President, and of the number of votes for each, which lists they shall sign and certify, and transmit sealed to the seat of the government of the United States, directed to the president of the Senate; the president of the Senate shall, in the presence of the Senate and the House of Representatives, open all the certificates and the votes shall then be counted;—the person having the greatest number of votes for President shall be the President, if such number be a majority of the whole number of electors appointed; and if no person have such a majority, then from the persons having the highest numbers not exceeding three on the list of those voted for as President, the House of Representatives shall choose immediately, by ballot, the President.

But in choosing the President, the votes shall be taken by states, the representation from each state having one vote; a quorum for this purpose shall consist of a member or members from two thirds of the states, and a majority of all states shall be necessary to a choice. And if the House of Representatives shall not choose a President whenever the right of choice shall devolve upon them, before the fourth day of March next following, then the Vice President, shall act as President, as in the case of death or other constitutional disability of the President—The person having the greatest number of votes as Vice President, shall be the Vice President, if such a number be a majority of the whole number of electors appointed, and if no person have a majority, then from the two highest numbers on the list, the Senate shall choose the Vice President; a quorum for the purpose shall consist of two thirds of the whole number of senators, and a majority of the whole number shall be necessary to a choice. But no person constitutionally ineligible to the office of President shall be eligible to that of Vice President of the United States.

## Thirteenth Amendment ★

### (1865) Slavery and Involuntary Servitude

**Section 1. Outlawing Slavery** Neither slavery nor involuntary servitude, except as a punishment for crime whereof the party shall have been duly convicted, shall exist within the United States, or any place subject to their jurisdiction.

**Section 2. Enforcement** Congress shall have power to enforce this article by appropriate legislation.

**Twelfth Amendment** This amendment changed the way the electoral college voted as outlined in Article II, Clause 3.

This amendment provides that each elector choose one candidate for President and one candidate for Vice President. If no candidate for President receives a majority of electoral votes, the House of Representatives chooses the President. If no candidate for Vice President receives a majority, the Senate elects the Vice President. The Vice President must be a person who is eligible to be President.

This system is still in use today. However, it is possible for a candidate to win the popular vote and lose in the electoral college. This happened in 1888 and in 2000.

**Thirteenth Amendment** The Emancipation Proclamation (1863) freed slaves only in areas controlled by the Confederacy. This amendment freed all slaves. It also forbids involuntary servitude, or labor done against one's will. However, it does not prevent prison wardens from making prisoners work. Congress can pass laws to carry out this amendment.

# Fourteenth Amendment ★

## (1868) Rights of Citizens

**Section 1. Citizenship** All persons born or naturalized in the United States, and subject to the jurisdiction thereof, are citizens of the United States and of the state wherein they reside. No state shall make or enforce any law which shall abridge the privileges or immunities of citizens of the United States; nor shall any state deprive any person of life, liberty, or property, without due process of law; nor deny to any person within its jurisdiction the equal protection of the laws.

**Section 2. Apportionment of Representatives** Representatives shall be apportioned among the several states according to their respective numbers, counting the whole number of persons in each state, excluding Indians not taxed. But when the right to vote at any election for the choice of electors for President and Vice President of the United States, representatives in Congress, the executive and judicial officers of a state, or the members of the legislature thereof, is denied to any of the male inhabitants of such state, being twenty-one years of age, and citizens of the United States, or in any way abridged, except for participation in rebellion, or other crime, the basis of representation therein shall be reduced in the proportion which the number of such male citizens shall bear to the whole number of male citizens twenty-one years of age in such state.

**Section 3. Former Confederate Officials** No person shall be a senator or representative in Congress, or elector of President and Vice President, or hold any office, civil or military, under the United States, or under any state, who having previously taken an oath, as a member of Congress, or as an officer of the United States, or as a member of any state legislature, or as an executive or judicial officer of any state, to support the Constitution of the United States, shall have engaged in insurrection or rebellion against the same, or given aid or comfort to the enemies thereof. But Congress may, by a vote of two thirds of each house, remove such disability.

**Section 4. Public Debt** The validity of the public debt of the United States, authorized by law, including debts incurred for payment of pensions and bounties for services in suppressing insurrection or rebellion, shall not be questioned. But neither the United States nor any state shall assume or pay any debt or obligation incurred in aid of insurrection or rebellion against the United States, or any claim for the loss of emancipation of any slave; but all such debts, obligations and claims shall be held illegal and void.

**Section 5. Enforcement** The Congress shall have power to enforce, by appropriate legislation, the provisions of this article.

# Fifteenth Amendment ★

## (1870) Right to Vote—Race, Color, Servitude

**Section 1. Extending the Right to Vote** The right of citizens of the United States to vote shall not be denied or abridged by the United States or by any state on account of race, color, or previous condition of servitude.

**Section 2. Enforcement** The Congress shall have power to enforce this article by appropriate legislation.

# Sixteenth Amendment ★

## (1913) Income Tax

The Congress shall have power to lay and collect taxes on incomes, from whatever source derived, without apportionment among the several states, and without regard to any census or enumeration.

# Seventeenth Amendment ★

## (1913) Popular Election of Senators

**Section 1. Method of Election** The Senate of the United States shall be composed of two senators from each state, elected by the people thereof, for six years; and each senator shall have one vote. The electors in each state shall have the qualifications requisite for electors of the most numerous branch of the state legislatures.

**Section 2. Vacancies** When vacancies happen in the representation of any state in the Senate, the executive authority of such state shall issue writs of election to fill such vacancies: provided, that the legislature of any state may empower the executive thereof to make temporary appointments until the people fill the vacancies by election as the legislature may direct.

**Section 3. Those Elected Under Previous Procedure** This amendment shall not be so construed as to affect the election or term of any senator chosen before it becomes valid as part of the Constitution.

**Fifteenth Amendment, Section 1**
Previous condition of servitude refers to slavery. This amendment gave African Americans, both former slaves and free African Americans, the right to vote. In the late 1800s, southern states used grandfather clauses, literacy tests, and poll taxes to keep African Americans from voting.

**Fifteenth Amendment, Section 2**
Congress can pass laws to carry out this amendment. The Twenty-fourth Amendment barred the use of poll taxes in national elections. The Voting Rights Act of 1965 gave federal officials the power to register voters where there was voting discrimination.

**Sixteenth Amendment** Congress has the power to collect taxes on people's income. An income tax can be collected without regard to a state's population. This amendment changed Article 1, Section 9, Clause 4.

**Seventeenth Amendment, Section 1**
This amendment replaced Article 1, Section 2, Clause 1. Before it was adopted, state legislatures chose senators. This amendment provides that senators are directly elected by the people of each state.

## Eighteenth Amendment ★

### (1919) Prohibition of Alcoholic Beverages

**Section 1. Ban on Alcohol** After one year from the ratification of this article, the manufacture, sale, or transportation of intoxicating liquors within, the importation thereof into, or the exportation thereof from the United States and all territory subject to the jurisdiction thereof for beverage purposes is hereby prohibited.

**Section 2. Enforcement** The Congress and the several states shall have concurrent power to enforce this article by appropriate legislation.

**Section 3. Method of Ratification** This article shall be inoperative unless it shall have been ratified as an amendment to the Constitution by the legislatures of the several states, as provided in the Constitution, within seven years from the date of the submission hereof to the states by Congress.

## Nineteenth Amendment ★

### (1920) Women's Suffrage

**Section 1. The Right to Vote** The right of citizens of the United States to vote shall not be denied or abridged by the United States or by any state on account of sex.

**Section 2. Enforcement** Congress shall have power to enforce this article by appropriate legislation.

## Twentieth Amendment ★

### (1933) Presidential Terms; Sessions of Congress; Death or Disqualification of President-Elect

**Section 1. Beginning of Terms** The terms of the President and Vice President shall end at noon on the $20^{th}$ day of January, and the terms of senators and representatives at noon on the $3^{rd}$ day of January, of the years in which such terms would have ended if this article had not been ratified; and the terms of their successors shall then begin.

**Section 2. Congressional Sessions** The Congress shall assemble at least once in every year, and such meeting shall begin at noon on the $3^{rd}$ day of January, unless they shall by law appoint a different day.

**Section 3. Presidential Succession** If, at the time fixed for the beginning of the term of the President, the President-elect shall have died, the Vice President-elect shall become President. If a President shall not have been chosen before the time fixed for the beginning of his term, or if the President-elect shall have failed to qualify, the Vice President-elect shall act as President until a President shall have qualified; and the Congress may by law provide for the case wherein neither a President-elect nor a Vice President-elect shall have qualified, declaring who shall then act as President, or the manner in which one who is to act shall be selected, and such person shall act accordingly until a President or Vice President shall have qualified.

**Section 4. Elections Decided by Congress** The Congress may by law provide for the case of the death of any persons from whom the House of Representatives may choose a President whenever the right of choice shall have devolved upon them, and for the case of the death of any of the persons from whom the Senate may choose a Vice President whenever the right of choice shall have devolved upon them.

**Section 5. Date of Implementation** Sections 1 and 2 shall take effect on the 15th day of October following the ratification of this article.

**Section 6. Ratification Period** This article shall be inoperative unless it shall have been ratified as an amendment to the Constitution by the legislatures of three fourths of the several states within seven years from the date of its submission.

## Twenty-first Amendment ★

### (1933) Repeal of Prohibition

**Section 1. Repeal** The eighteenth article of amendment to the Constitution of the United States is hereby repealed.

**Section 2. State Laws** The transportation or importation into any state, territory, or possession of the United States for delivery or use therein of intoxicating liquors, in violation of the laws thereof, is hereby prohibited.

**Section 3. Ratification Period** This article shall be inoperative unless it shall have been ratified as an amendment to the Constitution by conventions in the several states, as provided in the Constitution, within seven years from the date of the submission hereof to the states by the Congress.

**Twentieth Amendment, Section 3.** If the President-elect dies before taking office, the Vice President-elect becomes President. If no President has been chosen by January 20 or if the elected candidate fails to qualify for office, the Vice President-elect acts as President, but only until a qualified President is chosen.

Finally, Congress has the power to choose a person to act as President if neither the President-elect nor the Vice President-elect is qualified to take office.

**Twenty-first Amendment, Section 1** The Eighteenth Amendment is repealed, making it legal to make and sell alcoholic beverages. Prohibition ended December 5, 1933.

## Twenty-second Amendment ★

### (1951) Presidential Tenure

**Section 1. Two-Term Limit** No person shall be elected to the office of the President more than twice, and no person who has held the office of President, or acted as President, for more than two years of a term to which some other person was elected President shall be elected to the office of President more than once. But this article shall not apply to any person holding the office of President when this article was proposed by the Congress, and shall not prevent any person who may be holding the office of President, or acting as President, during the term within which this article becomes operative from holding the office of President or acting as President during the remainder of such term.

**Section 2. Ratification Period** This article shall be inoperative unless it shall have been ratified as an amendment to the Constitution by the legislatures of three fourths of the several states within seven years from the date of its submission to the state by the Congress.

## Twenty-third Amendment ★

### (1961) Presidential Electors for the District of Columbia

**Section 1. Determining the Number of Electors** The district constituting the seat of government of the United States shall appoint in such manner as the Congress may direct:

A number of electors of President and Vice President equal to the whole number of senators and representatives in Congress to which the district would be entitled if it were a state, but in no event more than the least populous state; they shall be in addition to those appointed by the states, but they shall be considered, for the purposes of the election of President and Vice President, to be electors appointed by a state; and they shall meet in the district and perform such duties as provided by the twelfth article of amendment.

**Section 2. Enforcement** The Congress shall have power to enforce this article by appropriate legislation.

## Twenty-fourth Amendment ★

### (1964) Right to Vote in Federal Elections—Tax Payment

**Section 1. Poll Tax Banned** The right of citizens of the United States to vote in any primary or other election for President or Vice President, for electors for President or Vice President, or for senator or representative in Congress, shall not be denied or abridged by the United States or any state by reason of failure to pay any poll tax or other tax.

**Section 2. Enforcement** The Congress shall have the power to enforce this article by appropriate legislation.

---

**Twenty-second Amendment, Section 1**
This amendment provides that no President may serve more than two terms. A President who has already served more than half of someone else's term can serve only one more full term. Before Franklin Roosevelt became President, no President served more than two terms in office. Roosevelt broke with this custom and was elected to four terms. The amendment, however, did not apply to Harry Truman, who became President after Franklin Roosevelt's death in 1945.

**Twenty-third Amendment, Section 1**
This amendment gives the residents of Washington, D.C., the right to vote in presidential elections. Until this amendment was adopted, people living in Washington, D.C., could not vote for President because the Constitution had made no provision for choosing electors from the nation's capital. Washington, D.C., now has three electoral votes.

**Twenty-fourth Amendment, Section 1**
A poll tax is a tax on voters. This amendment bans poll taxes in national elections. Some states used poll taxes to keep African Americans from voting. In 1966, the Supreme Court struck down poll taxes in state elections, also.

Portions of the Constitution altered by later amendments or that no longer apply are printed in blue.

## Twenty-fifth Amendment ★

### (1967) Presidential Succession, Vice Presidential Vacancy, Presidential Inability

**Section 1. President's Death or Resignation** In case of the removal of the President from office or of his death or resignation, the Vice President shall become President.

**Section 2. Vacancies in Vice Presidency** Whenever there is a vacancy in the office of the Vice President, the President shall nominate a Vice President who shall take office upon confirmation by a majority vote of both houses of Congress.

**Section 3. Disability of the President** Whenever the President transmits to the President pro tempore of the Senate and the Speaker of the House of Representatives his written declaration that he is unable to discharge the powers and duties of his office, and until he transmits to them a written declaration to the contrary, such powers and duties shall be discharged by the Vice President as acting President.

**Section 4. Vice President as Acting President** Whenever the Vice President and a majority of either the principal officers of the executive departments or of such other body as Congress may by law provide, transmit to the President pro tempore of the Senate and the Speaker of the House of Representatives their written declaration that the President is unable to discharge the powers and duties of his office, the Vice President shall immediately assume the powers and duties of the office as acting President.

Thereafter, when the President transmits to the President pro tempore of the Senate and the Speaker of the House of Representatives his written declaration that no inability exists, he shall resume the powers and duties of his office unless the Vice President and a majority of either the principal officers of the executive department or of such other body as Congress may by law provide, transmit within four days to the President pro tempore of the Senate and the Speaker of the House of Representatives their written declaration that the President is unable to discharge the powers and duties of his office. Thereupon Congress shall decide the issue, assembling within forty-eight hours for that purpose if not in session. If the Congress, within twenty-one days after receipt of the latter written declaration, or, if Congress is not in session, within twenty-one days after Congress is required to assemble, determines by two-thirds vote of both Houses that the President is unable to discharge the powers and duties of his office, the Vice President shall continue to discharge the same as acting President; otherwise, the President shall resume the powers and duties of his office.

**Twenty-fifth Amendment, Section 1**
If the President dies or resigns, the Vice President becomes President. This section clarifies Article 2, Section 1, Clause 6.

**Twenty-fifth Amendment, Section 3**
If the President declares in writing that he or she is unable to perform the duties of office, the Vice President serves as acting President until the President recovers.

**Twenty-fifth Amendment, Section 4**
Two Presidents, Woodrow Wilson and Dwight Eisenhower, fell gravely ill while in office. The Constitution contained no provision for this kind of emergency. Section 3 provided that the President can inform Congress he or she is too sick to perform the duties of office. However, if the President is unconscious or refuses to admit to a disabling illness, Section 4 provides that the Vice President and Cabinet may declare the President disabled. The Vice President becomes the acting President until the President can return to the duties of office. In case of a disagreement between the President and the Vice President and Cabinet over the President's ability to perform the duties of office, Congress must decide the issue. A two-thirds vote of both houses is needed to find the President is disabled or unable to fulfill the duties of office.

## Twenty-sixth Amendment ★

### (1971) Right to Vote—Age

**Twenty-sixth Amendment, Section 1**
In 1970, Congress passed a law allowing 18-year-olds to vote. However, the Supreme Court decided that Congress could not set a minimum age for state elections.

**Section 1. Lowering the Voting Age** The right of citizens of the United States, who are eighteen years of age or older, to vote shall not be denied or abridged by the United States or by any state on account of age.

**Section 2. Enforcement** The Congress shall have the power to enforce this article by appropriate legislation.

## Twenty-seventh Amendment ★

### (1992) Congressional Pay

**Twenty-seventh Amendment**
If members of Congress vote themselves a pay increase, it cannot go into effect until after the next congressional election. This amendment was proposed in 1789. In 1992, Michigan became the thirty-eighth state to ratify it.

No law, varying the compensation for the services of the senators and representatives, shall take effect until an election of representatives shall have intervened.

Independence Hall room where the Constitution was signed

Portions of the Constitution altered by later amendments or that no longer apply are printed in blue.

# CITIZENSHIP HANDBOOK

## Table of Contents

## Key Terms

amend, p. 264

appeal, p. 262

bill, p. 259

censorship, p. 267

checks and balances, p. 257

citizen, p. 270

dictatorship, p. 252

dissent, p. 267

federalism, p. 257

habeas corpus, p. 252

interest group, p. 271

jurisdiction, p. 262

libel, p. 267

limited government, p. 256

naturalization, p. 270

override, p. 259

popular sovereignty, p. 256

private property, p. 252

ratify, p. 264

repeal, p. 255

republic, p. 252

separation of powers, p. 253

unconstitutional, p. 263

veto, p. 259

# Ideas Behind the Constitution

The delegates to the Constitutional Convention who gathered in Philadelphia were greatly influenced by past experiments with democracy and natural rights. As they debated the new document for American government, the Founders considered a variety of past political ideas.

## Ancient Rome

Earlier in this textbook, you read about the ancient Roman Republic. The Framers of the United States Constitution looked to Rome as a model. Like the early Romans, they sought to create a lasting **republic,** or a government in which citizens rule themselves through elected representatives. American leaders also admired what they saw as the independent thinking and public service of Roman citizens. Romans, Americans said, had been willing to serve in public office out of devotion to the republic.

However, Americans also took the fate of Rome as a warning. The Roman Republic eventually collapsed and became a **dictatorship,** a government in which one person or a small group holds complete authority. American leaders believed that the Roman Republic faltered when citizens began to value luxury and comfort more than freedom and public service. The Framers of the Constitution wanted to avoid Rome's fate. They hoped to build a system in which informed, independent citizens played an active role in their own government.

## Two Historic Documents

You also learned earlier about the following two important documents in British history: the Magna Carta, which British nobles forced King John to sign in 1215; and the Bill of Rights, which William and Mary issued in 1689 after the Glorious Revolution. These two documents created an English tradition of liberty, which the colonists brought to America.

The following principles found in the these two documents became part of the American system of government:

- Citizens have rights which the government must protect.
- Even the head of the government must obey the law.
- Taxes cannot be raised without the consent of the people.
- Elections should be held frequently.
- People accused of crimes have the right to trial by jury and the right of **habeas corpus,** meaning no person may be held in prison without being charged with a specific crime.
- People have the right to **private property,** or property owned by an individual.

King John signing the Magna Carta

## Teachings of the Enlightenment

Many of the Framers were influenced by the works of European Enlightenment thinkers. In his book *Two Treatises on Government*, the English writer John Locke declared that every individual has natural rights to life, liberty, and property. Locke said government is an agreement between the ruler and the ruled. Further, he argued, if a ruler violates the people's natural rights, the people have a right to rebel.

The French thinker Baron de Montesquieu (MOHN tehs kyoo) suggested a concept known as **separation of powers**—the idea that powers of government must be clearly defined and divided into legislative, executive, and judicial branches. This concept was designed to keep one person or group from gaining too much power.

John Locke

## Representative Traditions and the Declaration of Independence

Americans enjoyed a long tradition of representative government. The Virginia colonists set up the House of Burgesses, and the Pilgrims drafted the Mayflower Compact in 1620. The compact was the first document of self-government in North America.

Each of the 13 colonies had a written charter that identified the powers and limits of government granted by the British Crown. In addition to these traditions, the Framers of the Constitution drew on the grievances Thomas Jefferson had listed against George III in the Declaration of Independence. In writing the Constitution, they sought to prevent similar abuses in the new American government.

Baron de Montesquieu

**Declaring Independence**
Delegates sign the Declaration of Independence.

### Assessment

1. Identify two principles of American government that came from the Magna Carta or the English Bill of Rights.

2. How did Montesquieu's ideas affect the crafting of the Constitution?

# Structure of the Constitution

The principles of the Constitution have guided the United States for more than 200 years. The Constitution is divided into three main parts: the Preamble, or opening statement; the Articles; and the Amendments. The Preamble begins with the words, "We the people of the United States." These words show that the authority of the government comes from its citizens. The Preamble then goes on to outline six basic goals for the new government. They are shown on the chart below.

## Goals of the Preamble

| Goals | What It Means to Us |
|---|---|
| ■ To form a more perfect union | All states should work together as a unified nation. |
| ■ To establish justice | Everyone should be treated equally and fairly under the law. |
| ■ To ensure domestic tranquillity | The government has the responsibility to ensure peace and order at home. |
| ■ To provide for the common defense | The government has the responsibility to protect its citizens against foreign attack. |
| ■ To promote the general welfare | The government has the responsibility to promote the well-being of all its citizens. |
| ■ To secure the blessings of liberty | The government should value and protect the rights of its citizens. |

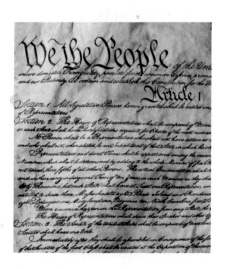

The Constitution

## Articles

The main body of the Constitution is divided into seven sections called articles. Together, they establish the framework for American government. The first three articles describe the three branches of the national government: legislative, executive, and judicial. Article 1 establishes the powers and limits on Congress. Articles 2 and 3 do the same for the President and the courts.

Article 4 deals with relations between states. It requires states to honor one another's laws and also sets out a system for admitting new states. Article 5 provides a process to amend the Constitution. Article 6 states that the Constitution is the "supreme law of the land." States cannot make laws that violate the Constitution and federal laws prevail in all disputes. The final article, Article 7, sets up a procedure for the states to ratify the Constitution.

## Amendments

The Amendments are formal changes that have been made to the Constitution. Some of these changes added new ideas to the document. Others repealed, or canceled, other parts of the Constitution.

In more than 200 years, only 27 changes have been made to the Constitution. The first 10 amendments, known as the Bill of Rights, were added in 1791. You will read more about the Bill of Rights later in this handbook.

Some later amendments had an immediate and powerful impact on American society. A few of them are illustrated below.

The Thirteenth Amendment ended slavery throughout the United States. ▼

The Eighteenth Amendment prohibited, or banned, the manufacture and sale of alcoholic beverages. This amendment was later repealed by the Twenty-first Amendment.

▲ The Nineteenth Amendment guaranteed women the right to vote.

▲ The Twenty-sixth Amendment lowered the minimum voting age from 21 to 18.

### Assessment

1. What are the three main parts of the Constitution?

2. What does the goal "to provide for the common defense" mean? How might this be done?

# Principles of the Constitution

The Constitution rests on seven basic principles. They are popular sovereignty, limited government, separation of powers, federalism, checks and balances, republicanism, and individual rights.

- **Popular Sovereignty** The Framers of the Constitution lived at a time when monarchs claimed that their power came from God. The Preamble, which begins "We the people," reflects a revolutionary new idea: a government gets its authority from the people. This principle, known as popular sovereignty, asserts that the people are the primary source of the government's authority.

- **Limited Government** The colonists believed that the British king had ruled them harshly. To avoid a repeat of this rule in their new government, the Framers made limited government a principle of the Constitution. In a limited government, the government has only the powers that the Constitution gives it. Equally important, every citizen of the United States—including the President—must obey the law.

- **Separation of Powers** To further limit the power of the government, the Framers provided for separation of powers. The Constitution divides the government into three branches, and each branch has its own duties. The chart below outlines the duties of each branch of government.

## Separation of Powers

| Legislative Branch (Congress)  | Executive Branch (President)  | Judicial Branch (Supreme Court and Other Federal Courts)  |
|---|---|---|
| **Passes Laws** | **Carries Out Laws** | **Interprets Laws** |
| ■ Can override President's veto<br>■ Approves treaties<br>■ Can impeach and remove President and other high officials<br>■ Prints and coins money<br>■ Raises and supports armed forces<br>■ Can declare war<br>■ Regulates foreign and interstate trade | ■ Proposes laws<br>■ Can veto laws<br>■ Negotiates foreign treaties<br>■ Serves as commander in chief of armed forces<br>■ Appoints federal judges, ambassadors, and other high officials<br>■ Can grant pardons to federal offenders | ■ Can declare laws unconstitutional<br>■ Can declare executive actions unconstitutional |

## Checks and Balances

**Legislative Branch**
(Congress makes laws)

**Checks on the Executive Branch**
- Can override President's veto
- Confirms executive appointments
- Ratifies treaties
- Can declare war
- Appropriates money
- Can impeach and remove President

**Checks on the Judicial Branch**
- Creates lower federal courts
- Can impeach and remove judges
- Can propose amendments to overrule judicial decisions
- Approves appointments of federal judges

**Executive Branch**
(President carries out laws)

**Checks on the Legislative Branch**
- Can propose laws
- Can veto laws
- Can call special sessions of Congress
- Makes appointments
- Negotiates foreign treaties

**Checks on the Judicial Branch**
- Appoints federal judges
- Can grant pardons to federal offenders

**Judicial Branch**
(Supreme Court interprets laws)

**Check on the Executive Branch**
- Can declare executive actions unconstitutional

**Check on the Legislative Branch**
- Can declare acts of Congress unconstitutional

---

- **Checks and Balances** A system of checks and balances safeguards against abuse of power. Each branch of government has the power to check, or limit, the actions of the other two. This arrangement guarantees that no branch of government will become too powerful. The chart above describes the specific checks each branch has on the other two. The next six pages of this handbook will detail how each branch of government works.

- **Federalism** The Constitution also establishes the principle of federalism, or division of power between the federal government and the states. The Constitution grants specific powers to the federal government and other powers to the states. Powers that are not clearly given to the federal government belong to the states.

- **Republicanism** The Constitution provides for a republican form of government. Instead of direct participation in government, citizens elect representatives to carry out their will.

- **Individual Rights** The Constitution protects individual rights, such as freedom of speech, freedom of religion, and the right to trial by jury. You will learn more about the rights protected by the Constitution later in this handbook.

### Assessment

1. How does the Constitution reflect the principle of separation of powers?

2. How can the judicial branch check the powers of the executive and legislative branches?

The first and longest article of the Constitution deals with the legislative, or lawmaking, branch. Article 1 sets up the Congress to make the nation's laws. Congress is made up of two bodies: the House of Representatives and the Senate.

## The Senate

The Senate is based on equal representation, with two senators for each state. Senators are elected to six-year terms. The Vice President of the United States is the president of the Senate. The Vice President presides over the Senate—casting a vote when there is a tie—but cannot take part in Senate debates.

## The House of Representatives

The larger of the two bodies is the House of Representatives, which currently has 435 members. Representation in the House is based on population, with larger states having more representatives than smaller states. Every state has at least one representative. Representatives are elected by the people of their district for two-year terms. The leader of the House is called the Speaker. The Speaker, who is chosen by the representatives, regulates debates and controls the agenda.

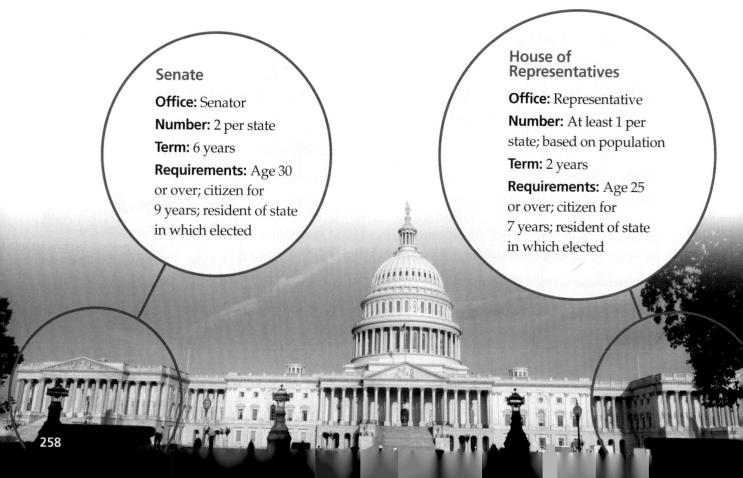

**Senate**

**Office:** Senator
**Number:** 2 per state
**Term:** 6 years
**Requirements:** Age 30 or over; citizen for 9 years; resident of state in which elected

**House of Representatives**

**Office:** Representative
**Number:** At least 1 per state; based on population
**Term:** 2 years
**Requirements:** Age 25 or over; citizen for 7 years; resident of state in which elected

## How a Bill Becomes a Law

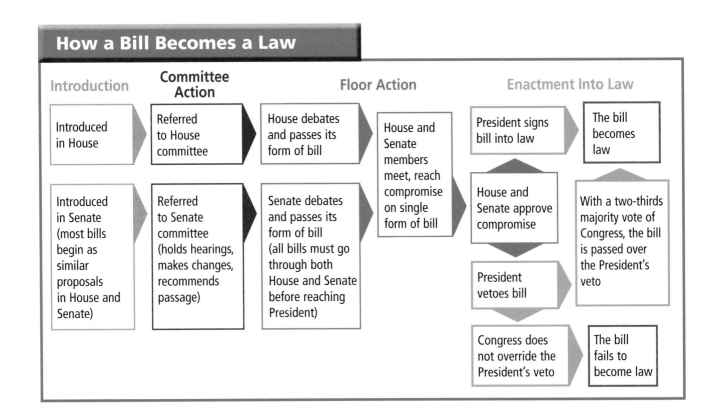

**Introduction** | **Committee Action** | **Floor Action** | **Enactment Into Law**

Introduced in House → Referred to House committee → House debates and passes its form of bill →

Introduced in Senate (most bills begin as similar proposals in House and Senate) → Referred to Senate committee (holds hearings, makes changes, recommends passage) → Senate debates and passes its form of bill (all bills must go through both House and Senate before reaching President) →

House and Senate members meet, reach compromise on single form of bill →

President signs bill into law → The bill becomes law

House and Senate approve compromise →

President vetoes bill →

With a two-thirds majority vote of Congress, the bill is passed over the President's veto

Congress does not override the President's veto → The bill fails to become law

## Powers of Congress

The most important power of Congress is the power to make the nation's laws. A **bill**, or proposal for a new law, may be introduced either in the House or the Senate. After debate and changes, the bill is voted on. If both houses vote to approve the bill, it then goes to the President to be signed. If the President signs the bill, it becomes a law. The President, however, has the power to **veto**, or reject, the bill. Congress may vote to **override**, or pass a law despite a presidential veto. A two-thirds vote is needed to override. (See flowchart above.)

Other powers of Congress are listed in Article 1, Section 8. These include the power to collect taxes, to coin money, to establish post offices, to fix standard weights and measures, and to declare war.

## Congressional Committees

Much of the work in Congress is done through committees. Each committee deals with a specific topic. For example, if someone in Congress introduces a bill to improve the nation's railroad service, the bill would first go to the Transportation Committee for study. Other standing committees deal with such areas as defense, education, taxation, foreign affairs, agriculture, or science.

### Assessment

1. What are the major differences between membership in the Senate and membership in the House?

2. How can Congress pass a bill over a presidential veto?

# PART 5

# How the Federal Government Works: The Executive Branch

Article 2 of the Constitution sets up an executive branch to carry out the laws and run the affairs of the national government. The President is the head of the executive branch. Other members include the Vice President, the Cabinet, and people in the many departments and agencies that help run the government.

## Powers of the President

The Framers of the Constitution intended Congress to be the most powerful branch of government. Therefore, although the Constitution is very specific about the powers of the legislature, it offers few details about the powers of the President. (See the graphic organizer below.)

Beginning with George Washington, Presidents have often taken those actions they thought were necessary to carry out their job. Thus, they shaped the presidency to meet the nation's changing needs.

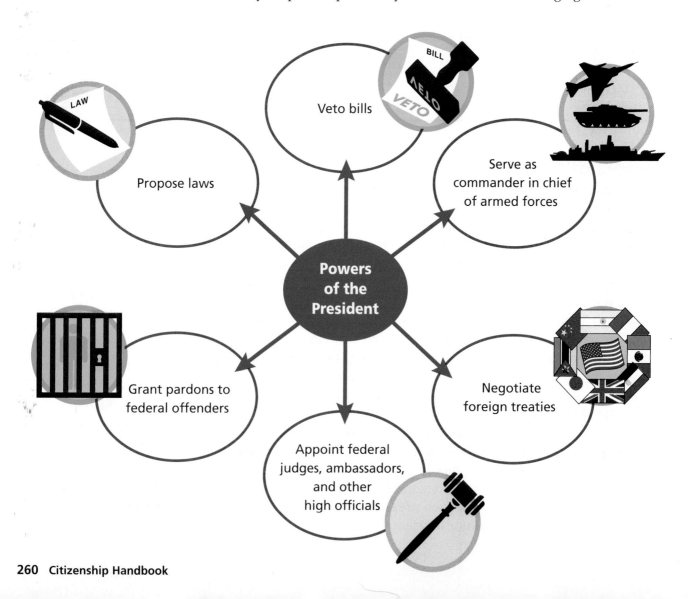

Veto bills

Propose laws

Serve as commander in chief of armed forces

**Powers of the President**

Grant pardons to federal offenders

Negotiate foreign treaties

Appoint federal judges, ambassadors, and other high officials

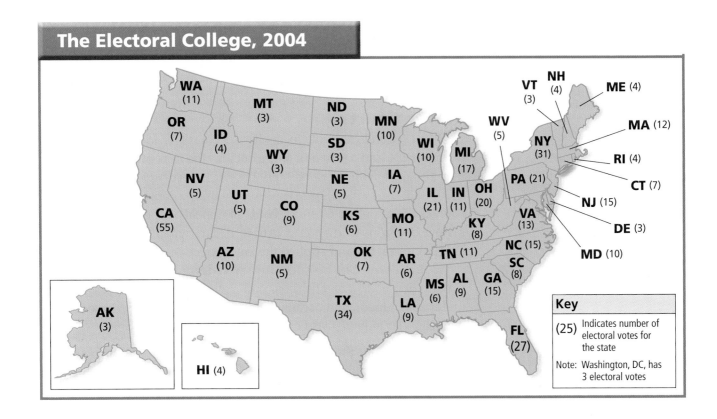

**The Electoral College, 2004**

WA (11)
OR (7)
ID (4)
MT (3)
ND (3)
MN (10)
WI (10)
MI (17)
NY (31)
VT (3)
NH (4)
ME (4)
MA (12)
RI (4)
CT (7)
WV (5)
NV (5)
UT (5)
WY (3)
SD (3)
NE (5)
IA (7)
IL (21)
IN (11)
OH (20)
PA (21)
NJ (15)
DE (3)
CA (55)
CO (9)
KS (6)
MO (11)
KY (8)
VA (13)
MD (10)
AZ (10)
NM (5)
OK (7)
AR (6)
TN (11)
NC (15)
SC (8)
AK (3)
TX (34)
LA (9)
MS (6)
AL (9)
GA (15)
HI (4)
FL (27)

**Key**

(25) Indicates number of electoral votes for the state

Note: Washington, DC, has 3 electoral votes

## Electing the President

The President is elected for a four-year term. As a result of the Twenty-second Amendment, adopted in 1951, no President may be elected to more than two complete terms.

The Framers set up a complex system for electing the President, known as the electoral college. When Americans vote for President, they do not vote directly for the candidate of their choice. Rather, they vote for a group of "electors" who are pledged to the candidate. The number of a state's electors depends on the number of its senators and representatives. (See the map above.)

A few weeks after Election Day, these electors meet in each state to cast their votes for President. In most states, the candidate with the majority of the popular vote receives all that state's electoral votes. The candidate who receives a majority of the electoral votes nationwide becomes President. Although electors are not required by federal law to vote for their pledged candidate, only a few have broken their pledges and voted for other candidates in past elections.

# How the Federal Government Works: The Judicial Branch

The Constitution establishes a Supreme Court and authorizes Congress to establish any other courts that are needed. Under the Judiciary Act of 1789, Congress set up the system of federal courts that is still in place today.

## Lower Courts

Most federal cases begin in district courts. Evidence is presented during trials, and a jury or a judge decides the facts of the case. A party that disagrees with the decision of the judge or jury may appeal it, that is, ask that the decision be reviewed by a higher court. The next level of court is the appellate court, or court of appeal. Appellate court judges review decisions of district courts to decide whether the lower court judges interpreted and applied the law correctly.

Court cases can be filed under federal or state jurisdiction. Jurisdiction is the power to hear and decide cases. Most cases are tried under state jurisdiction because they involve state laws. A case may be placed under federal jurisdiction if any of the following apply:

- The United States is either suing another party or being sued by another party.

- The case is based on the Constitution or on a federal law.

- The case involves disputes between different states.

## Federal Court System

**State Route** → **United States Supreme Court** ← **Federal Route**

**State Supreme Court**
- Highest state court
- Hears appeals of appellate court cases

**Appellate Court**
- Hears appeals of trial court cases

**Trial Court**
- Handles civil and criminal cases

**United States Supreme Court**
- Nation's highest court
- Reviews the decisions of lower courts
- Decides cases involving U.S. Constitution and federal laws

**Court of Appeal**
- Hears appeals of cases originating in U.S. district courts
- Can review decisions by federal administrative agencies

**District Court**
- Federal trial court
- Handles civil and criminal cases

**The Supreme Court**

The nine members of the Supreme Court pose for their annual portrait in 2004. Chief Justice William Rehnquist is seated, center. To his left is Associate Justice Sandra Day O'Connor, the first woman ever appointed to the Supreme Court.

## The Supreme Court

At the top of the American judicial system is the Supreme Court. (See the chart on the facing page.) The Court is made up of a chief justice and eight associate justices. The President appoints the justices, but Congress must approve the appointments. Justices serve until they resign, retire, or die. However, like other federal officials, Supreme Court justices may be impeached and removed from office.

The main job of the Supreme Court is to serve as the nation's final court of appeal. It hears the cases that have been tried and appealed in lower federal and state courts. The Court hears and decides fewer than 100 cases each year.

Decisions rest on a majority vote of at least five justices. One justice then writes a majority opinion, a document that explains the constitutional reasons for the decision. A justice who voted against the majority may submit a dissenting opinion, explaining his or her reasons for disagreeing with the majority opinion.

There is no court of appeal beyond the Supreme Court. However, if another case dealing with the same issues comes up, the Supreme Court may sometimes reverse its own past decisions.

## Judicial Review

The most important power of the Supreme Court is the power to decide what the Constitution means. At the beginning of the 1800s, the Court asserted the right to declare whether acts of the President or laws passed by Congress are **unconstitutional,** that is, not allowed under the Constitution. The landmark 1803 case of *Marbury* v. *Madison* established this power of judicial review for the Supreme Court.

## Assessment

1. How does a case reach the United States Supreme Court?

2. What is judicial review?

# Amending the Constitution

Although the Framers were pleased with the government they had established through the Constitution, some were dissatisfied with the final document. For one thing, while establishing the powers of the state and federal governments, the document said nothing about the rights of the American people. In 1791, the new nation would do something about this omission when it added the Bill of Rights, the first 10 amendments to the Constitution.

This addition was possible because the founders had written a Constitution that allowed for change. The Constitution was flexible enough to be changed but not so flexible that it could be *easily* changed. Article 5 laid out the method for amending, or changing, the Constitution. The flowchart below shows the amendment process.

## The Amendment Process

The Constitution can be changed in one of four ways. There are two different procedures for proposing amendments to the Constitution. There are also two different procedures for ratifying, or approving, amendments to the Constitution, the second step in the process.

**Proposing an Amendment** Congress can propose an amendment if both the House and Senate vote for a change to the Constitution. Each of the Constitution's 27 amendments has been proposed in this way.

The second way to propose an amendment begins at the state level. Currently, the legislatures of 34 states must call for a national convention. It is then up to the national convention to formally propose an amendment.

**Ratifying an Amendment** An amendment can be ratified through the action of state legislatures. Currently, the yes vote of 38 states is needed. Twenty-six of the 27 amendments to the Constitution have been ratified in this way.

An amendment can also be ratified through the action of state conventions rather than through state legislatures. Conventions, are special meetings that are called to address a specific issue. Only the Twenty-first Amendment was added through the process of state conventions.

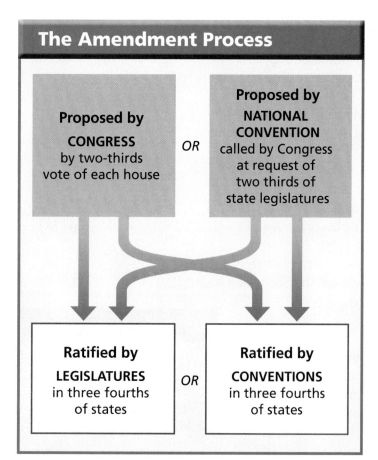

**The Amendment Process**

**Proposed by CONGRESS** by two-thirds vote of each house

OR

**Proposed by NATIONAL CONVENTION** called by Congress at request of two thirds of state legislatures

**Ratified by LEGISLATURES** in three fourths of states

OR

**Ratified by CONVENTIONS** in three fourths of states

**The Sixth Amendment**
The right to trial by jury in a criminal case is guaranteed by the Sixth Amendment. It also ensures that a person accused of a crime has the right to be represented by a lawyer and to hear the testimony given by witnesses in the trial.

## The Bill of Rights

The Preamble of the Constitution begins with the words, "We the People of the United States." However, the seven articles of the original document deal mostly with issues involving the structure and powers of the branches of government, not with the rights of individuals. The Bill of Rights, the name given to the first 10 amendments to the Constitution, addresses the freedoms guaranteed to citizens.

- *First Amendment:* freedom of religion, speech, and the press; right of petition and assembly (See the following page.)
- *Second Amendment:* right to bear arms
- *Third Amendment:* government cannot force people to quarter troops in their homes
- *Fourth Amendment:* protects against unreasonable search and seizure
- *Fifth Amendment:* rights of people accused of crimes
- *Sixth Amendment:* right to trial by jury in criminal cases
- *Seventh Amendment:* right to trial by jury in civil cases
- *Eighth Amendment:* forbids excessive bail and cruel or unusual punishment
- *Ninth Amendment:* people's rights are not limited to those listed in the Constitution
- *Tenth Amendment:* states or people have all powers not denied or given to federal government by the Constitution

### Assessment

1. Which one of the four different two-step processes has most often been used to add amendments to the Constitution?

2. Why do you think the Founders added the Ninth Amendment to the Bill of Rights?

# The First Amendment

The colonial past was very much on the minds of American leaders when they set out to write the Bill of Rights in the early 1790s. It is not surprising, therefore, that the colonial experience inspired the very first amendment to the Constitution.

## First Amendment

Congress shall make no law respecting an establishment of religion, or prohibiting the free exercise thereof; or abridging the freedom of speech, or of the press; or the right of the people peaceably to assemble, and to petition the government for a redress of grievances.

**Freedom of Religion**
This painting by Norman Rockwell illustrates the principle of freedom of religion.

**Freedom of Religion** As you have learned, Pilgrims, Puritans, Quakers, and Catholics had come to North America because they wanted to practice their religion freely. Yet, colonial religious leaders such as Thomas Hooker, Roger Williams, and Anne Hutchinson were later driven from Massachusetts after clashing with community leaders over religious questions. The Founders wanted to avoid such church-versus-state disputes. Thus, the First Amendment affirms freedom of religion as a basic right. Americans are free to follow any religion or no religion, as they choose.

This part of the First Amendment was inspired by the Virginia Statute on Religious Freedom, written by Thomas Jefferson. Jefferson later spoke of a "wall of separation between Church and State." However, not everyone agrees on the nature of that separation. Some people believe that the First Amendment means that religion should play no role in government. Others argue that the Amendment merely says that Congress cannot establish an official, state-supported church or make any laws that interfere with freedom of worship.

NORMAN ROCKWELL

**Freedom of the Press**
American reporters do their jobs without fear of government interference.

**Peaceful Assembly**
These striking workers are exercising their right of peaceful assembly.

**Freedom of Speech and Freedom of the Press** Dictators understand that their power depends on silencing dissent, or disagreement. They will often shut down newspapers and jail people who criticize the government. By contrast, the First Amendment protects the right of Americans to speak without fear of punishment.

The First Amendment also protects the press from government censorship. Censorship is the power to review, change, or prevent the publication of news. Freedom of the press also means that journalists cannot be arrested for criticizing the government or public officials. (As you have read, this principle was established in the colonies by the case of John Peter Zenger.)

The Framers knew that a free flow of ideas is vital to a democratic government. Still, freedom of the press is not unlimited. The press has a responsibility to present the news fairly and accurately. Individuals may sue journalists for libel, or the publication of false and malicious information that damages a person's reputation.

**Peaceful Assembly and Petition** As you have read, King George III and Parliament ignored the colonists' petition protesting the Stamp Act. Such experiences had a powerful effect on the leaders who wrote the Bill of Rights. The First Amendment thus guarantees the right of Americans to assemble in peaceful protest. It also protects their right to petition the government for a change in policy.

## Assessment

1. What does the First Amendment say about freedom of religion?

2. Identify two rights of a free press.

# State and Local Governments

As you have learned, under the principle of federalism, the Constitution assigns some powers to the government in Washington, D.C., and other powers to the states. You have already read about the role of the federal government in our nation's life. Now you will learn about the role played by state and local governments.

## State Governments

In general, the federal government deals with national issues. The states concern themselves with needs within each state.

State governments resemble the federal government in many ways. Each state has a constitution of its own, for example, and each state constitution can be amended. In addition, every state is divided into three branches of government. Each state has a legislature, a governor who serves as the chief executive, and a judiciary. But there are some differences between the state and federal governments. Nebraska, for instance, is the only state in the Union with a one-house legislature.

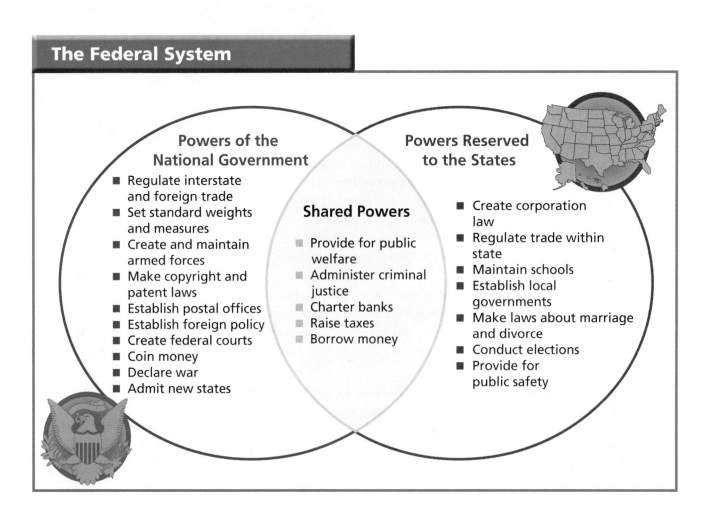

## The Federal System

**Powers of the National Government**
- Regulate interstate and foreign trade
- Set standard weights and measures
- Create and maintain armed forces
- Make copyright and patent laws
- Establish postal offices
- Establish foreign policy
- Create federal courts
- Coin money
- Declare war
- Admit new states

**Shared Powers**
- Provide for public welfare
- Administer criminal justice
- Charter banks
- Raise taxes
- Borrow money

**Powers Reserved to the States**
- Create corporation law
- Regulate trade within state
- Maintain schools
- Establish local governments
- Make laws about marriage and divorce
- Conduct elections
- Provide for public safety

## State Services

Enforcing the law, protecting property, regulating business, building and maintaining highways, and operating state parks are just a few of the many tasks the state oversees. In addition, states supervise public education by setting standards and by funding school programs.

## Local Governments

As we have seen, the Constitution carefully identifies the powers of state and federal governments. However, it says nothing about local government. Local governments administer smaller units, such as counties, cities, and towns.

Local governments have budgets just like the federal government and state government. Most of the money in their budgets is spent on education. Cities, towns, or school districts hire teachers and staff, buy books and supplies, and maintain school buildings. But local governments do not have sole control over the school system. They are required by law to meet the state's education standards.

Local government generally plays a more direct role in our lives than federal or state government does. For example, local governments hire people who interact with us on a regular basis, such as firefighters, police officers, and garbage collectors. In addition, local governments maintain local roads and hospitals, provide sewers and water, run libraries, oversee parks and recreational facilities, and conduct safety inspections of buildings.

## Assessment

1. Name two powers the federal goverment and state governments share. Name two powers that are reserved to the states.

2. What permits local governments to function even though they are not mentioned in the Constitution? Explain your answer.

What is a citizen? A **citizen** is someone who is entitled to all the rights and privileges of a particular nation. Not everyone who lives in a certain nation is a citizen of that nation. On the other hand, some citizens live outside the nation to which they belong.

## Becoming an American Citizen

To become a citizen of the United States, you must fulfill one of the following three requirements:

- You were born in the United States or have at least one parent who is a citizen of the United States.
- You were naturalized. **Naturalization** is the official legal process of becoming a citizen.
- You were 18 years old or younger when your parents were naturalized.

Each year, millions of people born in other countries and living in the United States become naturalized. To become a naturalized citizen, a person must live legally in the United States for at least five years. The person then applies for citizenship. He or she must take a citizenship examination and undergo a series of interviews. Finally, the applicant takes the citizenship oath before a judge, swearing to "support and defend the Constitution and laws of the United States."

A naturalized citizen enjoys every right of a natural-born citizen except one. Only natural-born citizens may serve as President or Vice President.

**Naturalization**
New citizens of the United States proudly take the citizenship oath.

## Rights of Citizens

As you have seen, the Bill of Rights guarantees certain rights to citizens. You have the right to worship as you please, the right to express your opinion, and the right to consult a lawyer if you are arrested. But the Ninth Amendment states that citizens' rights are not limited to those listed in the Constitution. Over the years, federal and state laws have identified other rights. For example, the Constitution does not mention education. But today, laws in every state guarantee that children have the right to an education.

## Responsibilities of Citizens

In addition to rights, citizens have responsibilities. Some actions are required of every citizen. For example, all citizens *must*

- obey federal, state, and local laws;
- pay their fair share of taxes;
- serve on juries if called;
- defend the nation if called.

Citizens have other responsibilities that are not required by law. Good citizens *should*

- vote in federal, state, and local elections;
- stay informed on important issues;
- serve the community;
- help to create a just society.

Some citizens participate in the political process through interest groups. An **interest group** is an organization that represents the concerns of a particular group. The American Association of Retired Persons, the National Rifle Association, and the Sierra Club are examples of interest groups that try to influence lawmakers and raise public awareness of certain issues.

Young people, too, can get involved in the political process. For example, in one California community, poor children could not afford to pay for public transportation to school every day. Some students organized to solve this problem. Using their First Amendment rights, they collected signatures on petitions and held public rallies. As a result, the local transportation board took up the issue. Like thousands of other Americans, these students used their rights as citizens to voice their views and help their communities.

**Registering to Vote**
Before a U.S. citizen can vote, he or she must register.

## Assessment

1. How does a person become an American citizen?

2. Identify three ways that Americans can participate in the political process.

# Writing Workshop

## Problem-Solution Essay

### ▶ Introduction

In a problem-solution essay, you analyze a problem and propose a method for solving it. The problem you choose to analyze should be one that offers some challenges but is still possible to resolve. A problem-solution essay should have the following characteristics:

- a problem that needs to be solved

- a thesis statement that identifies the problem and points toward the solution

- identification of several possible solutions

- specific facts, details, examples, and reasons indicating why one solution is best

- an analytical tone

**Assignment** On the following pages, you will learn how to write a problem-solution essay. You will get step-by-step instructions. Each step will include an example from a sample essay discussing the Articles of Confederation.

Read the instructions and the examples. Then, follow each step to plan and write a 500–700 word essay.

> **Analyze a problem faced by the writers of the Constitution and discuss the solution that the Constitutional Convention chose.**

For a review of the steps in the writing process see the **Historian's Toolkit,** *Write Like a Historian.*

> **Sample notes about a problem arising from the Articles of Confederation**
>
> - The Articles did not include a central executive because the states didn't want to give up power to central authority.
>
> - Congress had to manage everything.
>
> - Nine states had to vote for any action to take place.
>
> - Foreign governments saw the new nation as weak and ignored its demands.
>
> - Americans also defied the national government (Shays' Rebellion).
>
> - It was difficult for Congress to act quickly or make changes in policy.

### ▶ Prewriting

**Define the problem to be solved.** In order to write a problem-solution essay, you need to start with a clear vision of the problem itself.

Once you have broken your problem down and looked at it from different angles, sit back and look at the big picture. Think about your ultimate goal in solving the problem.

> **Sample goal:**
> The problems with the Articles needed to be solved so that the new nation could survive and adapt to change.

**Brainstorm to identify several solutions.** Look for as many solutions as you can, even if they solve only part of the problem. List each solution and evaluate it. One good technique is to ask questions. Create a chart like this one to help you evaluate your various solutions.

**Write a thesis statement.** Write a thesis statement briefly identifying the problem. Your thesis statement may also indicate possible solutions, but you may also save that information for later in your essay.

**Gather supporting information.** Look for facts, details, and reasons to support your solutions to the problem.

> **Sample thesis statement:**
> The Articles of Confederation left the new nation too weak because they allowed for no central authority besides Congress. The Articles needed to be changed in some way—or something new had to replace them.

| Problem | Possible Solution | Evaluation |
|---|---|---|
| The Articles of Confederation left the nation weak because there was no central authority. | Leave the Articles as is, persuade other countries and Americans to respect the new nation | Not practical—what would make more established governments and local rebels accept a weak authority? |
| | Leave the basic Articles in place but have Congress elect a new executive each year, rotating from state to state | Possible, but amendments needed to be agreed on by all the states. Also, how does the central authority work with the Congress, which was used to running everything? |
| | Get rid of the Articles, create an entirely new plan | Possible, but it would be a huge task to start all over again. |

## ▶ Drafting

**Decide how to organize your writing.** The simplest way to organize a problem-solution essay is to begin by identifying the problem in the first paragraph, leading up to your thesis statement. Present the solution that you think works best, explaining why it is the most promising one.

**Support your thesis with examples and details.** Use your lists of supporting information to back up your ideas about the best solution to the problem.

**Use an analytical tone.** As you write your draft, remember that you are appealing to people's ability to reason, not to their emotions. Describe the problem and the various possible solutions objectively.

**Write a strong conclusion.** In your final paragraph, restate your ideas about the problem and its solution.

# Writing Workshop *continued*

## ▶ Model Essay

Read the following model of a problem-solution essay. Notice how it includes the characteristics you have learned about.

### The Articles of Confederation: Problems and Solutions

In November 1777, the Continental Congress approved the first American constitution: the Articles of Confederation. Soon after the Articles were ratified by the states in 1781, problems arose. One of the most serious of these problems was that the Articles of Confederation left the new nation too weak. It allowed for no central authority besides Congress.

> The thesis statement identifies the problem.

The Articles of Confederation created a loose alliance of 13 independent states. No state wanted to give up its power to a strong central government. Even Congress had little power. For example, Congress could pass a law, but nine states had to approve the law before it went into effect. Congress had no power to tax the states, so the nation could not pay its war debts.

> This paragraph describes the problem in greater detail.

Recognizing that many problems existed with the Articles of Confederation, the Continental Congress met again in 1787. There were a number of solutions they could have considered. First, Congress could change the Articles so that Congress would elect a new central authority each year. Second, Congress could give itself more power. These solutions might solve some of the nation's problems, but not all. Finally, Congress could get rid of the Articles and create an entirely new plan of government. The delegates saw this as the best solution, but one that would take a great deal of work.

> Each paragraph describes possible solutions and discusses their pros and cons.

> The analytical tone presents the information fairly, using straightforward language.

Most of the delegates to what became known as the Constitutional Convention recognized that the Articles of Confederation had serious weaknesses. Their decision to formulate a new plan of government was a bold one. Nevertheless, it proved to be the best solution. The delegates created a new and lasting form of government for the United States.

> The conclusion restates the thesis. It shows the importance of solving the problem and explaining why the solution was a good one.

## ▶ Revising

After completing your draft, read it again carefully to find ways to make your writing better. Here are some questions to ask yourself.

### Revise to strengthen your thesis and support
- Do the introduction and thesis statement identify the problem?
- Do the body paragraphs explain the problem thoroughly? Do they examine several solutions and describe the most effective solution clearly?
- Is your proposal supported by convincing reasons, facts, and examples?

### Revise to meet written English-language conventions
- Are all sentences complete, with a subject and a verb?
- Are all the words spelled correctly? Use a spell-checker or a dictionary to make sure.
- Are all proper nouns capitalized, including names of people and places?
- Did you use proper punctuation? Check punctuation within sentences as well as at the ends of sentences.

## ▶ Rubric for Self-Assessment

*Evaluate your problem-solution essay using the following rating scale:*

|  | Score 4 | Score 3 | Score 2 | Score 1 |
|---|---|---|---|---|
| **Organization** | Supports the thesis with a series of paragraphs exploring a problem and its various solutions, ending with a discussion of the one proposed by the writer | Uses a reasonably clear organization, but occasionally wanders from the topic | Chooses an organization not suited to the topic (for example, presents the solution without having explained the problem) | Shows lack of organizational strategy |
| **Presentation** | Explores the problem and solutions thoroughly with facts, details, and reasons; links all information to the goal of solving the problem | Explores the problem and solutions adequately with several facts, details, or examples; links most information to the goal of solving the problem | Does not explore the problem and solutions adequately; does not link supporting information to the goal of solving the problem | Does not provide any facts, details, or examples to explore the problem and solutions |
| **Use of Language** | Varies sentence structure and vocabulary successfully; includes none or very few mechanical errors | Uses some variety in sentence structure and vocabulary; includes few mechanical errors | Uses the same types of sentences without varying them; repeats words; includes many mechanical errors | Writes incomplete sentences; uses language poorly; sounds confused; includes many mechanical errors |

# Unit 3

## Think Like a Historian

As you read this unit, think about this question: *What problems might a new nation face?*

**George Washington** After leading U.S. troops to victory against the British, Washington led the new nation as its first President. His actions set precedents that future Presidents would follow.

# 1789

**Andrew Jackson** A veteran of the War of 1812 and wars against Native Americans, Jackson was the first President from the West.

# 1828

# The New Republic

**Exploring the Louisiana Territory**
President Thomas Jefferson acquired the Louisiana Territory and sent an expedition to explore lands west of the Mississippi River.

## 1803

**War of 1812** In June 1812, the United States declared war on Great Britain. One reason for war was Britain's refusal to stop seizing U.S. Navy vessels and sailors.

## 1812

**Trail of Tears** Forced to move west to Indian Territory under harsh conditions, thousands of Native Americans lost their lives on what became known as the Trail of Tears.

## 1838

## Chapter Preview

The Constitution had created a framework of government. Now the young nation faced many decisions about how to make the plan work. Meanwhile, challenges arose inside the nation's borders and on the high seas.

### ☑ What You Will Learn

George Washington oversaw the creation of new federal departments and asked Alexander Hamilton to tackle the nation's debt problem.

Two political parties began to take shape—the Federalists and the Republicans.

Under Washington, the United States dealt with challenges from Native Americans in the Northwest Territory and from the British navy at sea.

Political divisions grew bitter during the presidency of John Adams, as he struggled to keep peace with France.

**U.S. Events**

**1789**
George Washington becomes first President of the United States.

**1790**
Alexander Hamilton announces economic plan.

**1794**
Whiskey Rebellion is crushed.

1789

1792

1795

**World Events**

**1789** French Revolution begins.

**1793** France and Britain go to war. "Reign of Terror" occurs in France.

Washington had to leave his comfortable estate at Mount Vernon, Virginia (below), and move to New York to assume the presidency of the United States.

**1795**
Senate approves Jay Treaty with Britain.

**1798**
"XYZ Affair" becomes public. Congress passes Alien and Sedition acts.

**1800**
France agrees to stop seizing American ships.

1795

1798

1801

**1799** Napoleon Bonaparte gains political power in France.

## History Reading Skill  Analyze Comparisons

### What questions did America's founders have about their new government?

In this chapter, you will learn how to analyze comparisons made through similes, metaphors, and analogies. Read the following speech given by Benjamin Franklin. The side notes point out the comparisons.

**Primary Source**

Benjamin Franklin was one of the many state representatives who gathered in Philadelphia in 1787 to create the Constitution. Here, Franklin gives his views about the completed Constitution.

. . . It . . . astonishes me, Sir, to find this system approaching so near to perfection as it does; and I think it will astonish our enemies, who are waiting with confidence to hear, that our councils are confounded like those of the builders of Babel, and that our States are on the point of separation, only to meet hereafter for the purpose of cutting one another's throats. Thus I consent, Sir, to this Constitution, because I expect no better, and because I am not sure that it is not the best. The opinions I have had of its errors I sacrifice to the public good. I have never whispered a syllable of them abroad. Within these walls they were born, and here they shall die. . . .

—Benjamin Franklin, Closing Speech to the Constitutional Convention, September 17, 1787

The word *like* signals a simile comparing the representatives to the builders of the Tower of Babel.

Franklin draws an analogy between his giving up his views to help the overall good and ancient peoples who made sacrifices to please their gods.

Here, Franklin uses a metaphor, discussing his criticisms as if they were living things.

### Analyze Comparisons

- Find similes—comparisons of different things linked by the words *like* or *as.*
- Find metaphors—implied comparisons that do not have the words *like* or *as* but suggest that one thing is like another.
- Draw analogies—find ideas in the text that are connected in some way.

### Document-Based Questions

1. Who was Franklin addressing?
2. What was his purpose for giving this speech?
3. Would the reference to "our enemies" help to achieve this purpose? Why or why not?

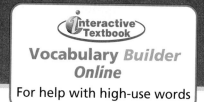

# Vocabulary *Builder*

## Previewing High-Use Academic Words

| High-Use Word | Definition | Sample History Sentence |
|---|---|---|
| **invest** (ihn VEHST) (Section 1, p. 284) | ***v.*** to purchase something with the hope that its value will grow | Wealthy Americans <u>invested</u> in land, believing that they could sell it later for a profit. |
| **impose** (ihm POHZ) (Section 1, p. 285) | ***v.*** to place a burden on something or someone | Manufacturers wanted the government to <u>impose</u> a high tax on imports. |
| **hostile** (HAHS tihl) (Section 2, p. 291) | ***adj.*** unfriendly; adverse or opposed | Native Americans were often <u>hostile</u> to colonial settlements established on Native American lands. |
| **fundamental** (fuhn duh MEHN tahl) (Section 2, p. 293) | ***adj.*** basic; most important; forming the foundation of an idea or action; essential | The most <u>fundamental</u> principle of democracy is that the people rule. |
| **cease** (sees) (Section 3, p. 296) | ***v.*** to cause to come to an end; to stop | After hours of battle, the soldiers on both sides <u>ceased</u> their firing. |
| **emphasize** (EHM fah sīz) (Section 3, p. 297) | ***v.*** to stress; to give more importance to | The Declaration of Independence <u>emphasizes</u> equality and the natural rights of humankind. |
| **react** (ree AKT) (Section 4, p. 298) | ***v.*** to act in response to another action; to respond | Delegates to the Constitutional Convention <u>reacted</u> cautiously to Roger Sherman's Great Compromise. |
| **provoke** (prah VOHK) (Section 4, p. 301) | ***v.*** to cause to anger; to excite; to cause an action | When France seized U.S. ships, it must have known that its actions would <u>provoke</u> great anger among the American people. |

## Previewing Key Terms and People

inauguration, p. 283
precedent, p. 283
bond, p. 284
speculator, p. 284
unconstitutional, p. 285
tariff, p. 286
faction, p. 290

James Madison, p. 290
Thomas Jefferson, p. 290
Alexander Hamilton, p. 290
John Adams, p. 293
Anthony Wayne, p. 295
neutral, p. 295
impressment, p. 296

John Jay, p. 296
alien, p. 300
sedition, p. 300
nullify, p. 301
states' rights, p. 301

# Washington Takes Office

## Objectives

1. Discuss how the new government was organized during Washington's presidency.

2. Explain why the new nation faced an economic crisis.

3. Identify the three parts of Hamilton's financial plan.

4. Describe how Washington responded to the Whiskey Rebellion.

## Prepare to Read

###  Reading Skill

**Identify Similes** Similes use the signal words *like* or *as* to connect two items being compared. The comparison helps the reader to imagine the description more fully. For example, "the gunfire echoed like thunder" creates a mental image of the sound of a battle. Look for similes as you read this section.

### Vocabulary *Builder*

**High-Use Words**

**invest**, p. 284
**impose**, p. 285

**Key Terms**

inauguration, p. 283
precedent, p. 283
bond, p. 284
speculator, p. 284
unconstitutional, p. 285
tariff, p. 286

⭐ **Background Knowledge** In 1789, the United States was one fourth of its size today. All 13 states were in the East. The nation's western border followed the Mississippi River. The enormous Northwest Territory lay between that river and the Appalachian Mountains. In the North, the Great Lakes formed much of the border separating the United States from British-controlled Canada. In the South, the United States bordered on Spanish-controlled Florida and Louisiana.

The American people had a new Constitution. They now had a new Congress and their first President. In this section, you will learn how the nation's leaders made this brand-new government work.

## The First President

**Main Idea**
Congress and the President chose people to run the institutions created by the Constitution.

In April of 1789, George Washington traveled from Virginia to the nation's capital, New York City, to begin his term as the first President of the United States. Washington's journey along bumpy roads took eight days. Large crowds lined the streets. As one newspaper reported, Americans greatly admired the tall, stately war hero:

❝Many persons in the crowd were heard to say they should now die contented—nothing being wanted to complete their happiness . . . but the sight of the savior of his country.❞
—*Gazette of the United States*, April 1789

Washington's inauguration—a ceremony in which the President takes the oath of office—was held on April 30, 1789. Despite all he had achieved, Washington was anxious. The country was divided on many issues. Washington understood how much the new nation depended on him. His actions would set a precedent—an example to be followed by others in the future.

**The Executive Branch** The Constitution of the United States provided only a general outline for organizing the government. When the President took office, the entire federal government was made up of little more than 75 post offices, a few clerks, and a tiny army of 672 soldiers.

The first job of the President and the Congress, therefore, was to put a working government in place. First, Congress passed laws to set up three departments for the executive branch: Treasury, State, and War. Each department was to be headed by a secretary nominated by the President. The President would also appoint an attorney general to advise him on legal matters.

Washington appointed four well-known men to take the new posts. He chose Alexander Hamilton to be secretary of the treasury. Hamilton was considered one of the country's outstanding leaders and an expert on economic affairs. Thomas Jefferson, the author of the Declaration of Independence, became secretary of state. His task was to manage relations with foreign countries. Henry Knox, a former general, was Washington's choice for secretary of war. Edmund Randolph, who had played an important role at the Constitutional Convention, became attorney general.

Washington soon began meeting regularly with these leaders as a group. Over time, this group became known as the Cabinet.

**Explore More Video**
To learn more about George Washington's presidency, view the video.

**Washington's Inauguration**
George Washington took the oath of office on a balcony of Federal Hall in New York City as well-wishers watched from the street below. **Critical Thinking:** *Link Past and Present* *Who attended Washington's oath-taking? How would a modern-day President's inauguration be different?*

**Establishing the Judiciary** The Constitution also called for a judiciary, or court system. The Judiciary Act of 1789 provided for a Supreme Court of 6 justices. Under the Supreme Court were 3 circuit courts and 13 district courts. The main job of the federal courts was to hear appeals from the state courts. Washington appointed John Jay of New York as the first Chief Justice of the Supreme Court.

✓**Checkpoint** **What were the new executive departments?**

## The Nation's First Economic Crisis

The American Revolution had left the nation deeply in debt. The federal government owed $52 million. That debt was mainly in the form of bonds. A **bond** is a certificate issued by a government for an amount of money that the government promises to pay back with interest. Both Americans and foreigners had <u>invested</u> in bonds to help the war effort. Would the government pay back this debt?

The issue was complicated because most people who had originally bought the bonds had sold them for less than they were worth. The buyers were **speculators**—people who invest in a risky venture in the hope of making a large profit. It seemed unfair to many Americans that speculators would make a profit after the original bondholders had lost money. Also in dispute was whether or not the federal government should pay back state debts.

The government was operating on a shoestring. It did not even have the money for George Washington's move to New York. Washington had to borrow $3,000 to pay his moving expenses.

✓**Checkpoint** **Why was there such a large public debt?**

**Main Idea**
The federal government owed millions of dollars but lacked money with which to pay its debts.

**Vocabulary** *Builder*
**invest** (ihn VEHST) *v.* to purchase something with the hope that its value will grow

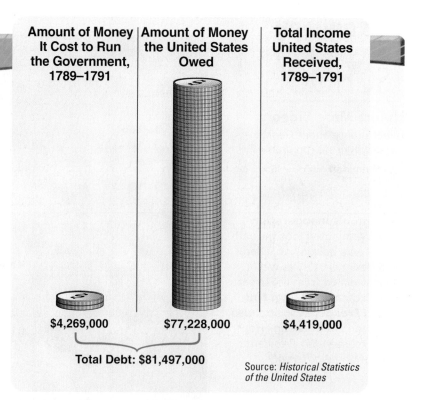

**Links to Economics**

### The Debt Problem

The U.S. government was collecting enough in taxes to pay its expenses, but hardly enough to pay back the debt. Hamilton's financial plan sought to find new sources of income to repay the debt. **Critical Thinking: Identifying Economic Costs** *Without the amount of money owed, how much would the government have had left over after paying its costs?*

| Amount of Money It Cost to Run the Government, 1789–1791 | Amount of Money the United States Owed | Total Income United States Received, 1789–1791 |
| --- | --- | --- |
| $4,269,000 | $77,228,000 | $4,419,000 |

**Total Debt: $81,497,000**

Source: *Historical Statistics of the United States*

# Hamilton's Financial Plan

The person responsible for developing a plan to solve the country's financial crisis was Alexander Hamilton, the secretary of the treasury.

Hamilton's program had three parts: (1) The U.S. government would fully assume, or agree to pay, all federal *and* state debts. (2) The U.S. government would charter a national bank for depositing government funds. (3) The government would impose a high tax on goods imported into the country.

**Paying the Debt** Hamilton knew that paying the debt would be a huge burden on the U.S. government. However, he wanted to prove to people here and abroad that the United States would honor its debts in full. Then, people would be willing to invest again in the future.

Many southerners opposed the plan to repay state debts. Several southern states had paid off their wartime debts on their own. Southerners thought other states should do the same.

Congress debated the plan for six months in 1790. Then, an agreement was reached. Southerners would support Hamilton's plan to have the federal government repay the wartime debt. In return, the government would build its new capital city in the South. The capital would rise along the banks of the Potomac River, between Virginia and Maryland.

**A National Bank** The second part of Hamilton's plan called for the creation of a privately owned bank of the United States. It would provide a safe place to deposit government funds. The bank would be able to issue paper money that would serve as a national currency.

The debate over the bank of the United States went beyond the bank itself and focused on the powers the government had under the Constitution. Opponents of the bank, such as Thomas Jefferson, insisted that the law establishing the bank was unconstitutional—contrary to what is permitted by the Constitution.

Jefferson argued that nowhere in the Constitution was there a provision allowing Congress to set up a national bank. Jefferson's view, that the Constitution permits only what it specifically says, is called a "strict" interpretation of the Constitution. Hamilton argued for a "loose" interpretation. He pointed out that Article 1, Section 8 of the Constitution gave Congress the power to make all laws "necessary and proper" for fulfilling its duties. This suggested that there were things not directly permitted by the Constitution that Congress could do.

## Biography Quest

### Alexander Hamilton
### 1755–1804

If not for Aaron Burr, Alexander Hamilton might have made even greater contributions to the nation. In 1804, Burr ran for governor of New York. Hamilton opposed Burr and criticized his character. After losing the election, Burr challenged Hamilton to a duel. Hamilton was against dueling because his son had been killed in a duel. He purposely missed his shot at Burr. However, Burr took careful aim and killed Hamilton.

**Biography Quest** ⬤nline

**Why did Hamilton defend Loyalists in court after the American Revolution?**

**For:** The answer to the question about Hamilton
**Visit:** PHSchool.com
**Web Code:** myd-3041

# The Whiskey Rebellion

Farmers thought that having to pay a tax on the whiskey they produced from their corn was too heavy a burden. The tax was part of Alexander Hamilton's plan to pay the nation's war debt. **Critical Thinking: *Detect Points of View*** *Why did the farmers resist the tax? Why did George Washington think it was important to put down the Whiskey Rebellion?*

**"We Won't Pay the Tax"** ▲
Angry Pennsylvania farmers and militia members tar and feather a would-be tax collector (second from left). Farmers thought it was unfair to tax their "liquid corn," or whiskey.

**No Tolerance for Rebellion** ▶
George Washington reviews U.S. troops as they start off to Pennsylvania to put down the rebellion. He said the farmers' actions threatened both "the just authority of government" and "the rights of individuals."

In 1791, Congress did pass a law establishing the bank, and the President signed it. However, to this day Americans disagree about whether the Constitution should be interpreted strictly or loosely.

**A High Tariff** The final part of Hamilton's plan called for a high tariff—a tax on imported goods. It would raise money for the federal government. It would also protect U.S. manufacturers from foreign competition.

The tariff was the only part of Hamilton's plan that Congress did not pass, and that was because southerners opposed it. They argued that a high tariff would help the North, where most industries were located, while making southerners pay more for the goods they bought.

☑**Checkpoint** How did Congress respond to Hamilton's plan?

# The Whiskey Rebellion

In 1791, Congress imposed a tax on all whiskey made and sold in the United States. Hamilton hoped this tax would raise funds for the Treasury. Instead, it led to a revolt that tested the strength of the new government.

Many backcountry farmers made extra money by turning the corn they grew into whiskey. Therefore, they bitterly resented the new whiskey tax. Farmers compared it to the hated taxes that Britain had imposed on the colonies before the Revolution. Many farmers organized protests and refused to pay the tax.

In 1794, officials in western Pennsylvania tried to collect the tax. Farmers rebelled, burning down the home of a tax collector. Soon, a large, angry mob was marching through Pittsburgh like a gathering storm. The violent protest became known as the Whiskey Rebellion.

Washington responded quickly to this challenge to federal authority. He sent the militia to Pennsylvania. When the rebels heard that 13,000 troops were marching against them, they quickly scattered. Washington later pardoned the leaders of the rebellion.

The Whiskey Rebellion tested the will of the new government. Washington's forceful response showed Americans that armed rebellion was not acceptable in a republic.

✓**Checkpoint** **What was the cause of the Whiskey Rebellion?**

⭐ **Looking Back and Ahead** George Washington set a firm course for the federal government, while Alexander Hamilton began to attack the debt problem. In the next section, you will read how the nation's first political parties developed.

**Main Idea**

When Pennsylvania farmers rebelled against a federal tax on whiskey, President Washington responded with armed force.

**Identify Similes**
Find the simile in this paragraph. What two things are being compared?

---

Section 1 | **Check Your Progress**

**Progress Monitoring** Online
**For:** Self-test with instant help
**Visit:** PHSchool.com
**Web Code:** mya-3041

## Comprehension and Critical Thinking

1. **(a) Describe** How did Washington's inauguration reflect the nation's deep respect for him?
**(b) Organize Information** Create a chart showing the top posts in the executive branch and judiciary at this time. Define each position and name the first person to occupy each post.

2. **(a) Recall** What was the nation's first economic crisis? How was it further complicated?
**(b) Explain Problems** What was Hamilton's plan to solve the crisis? Why was it controversial?

## Reading Skill

3. **Identify Similes** Identify the simile in this sentence: The new President was as tough as nails. What two things does it compare?

## Vocabulary *Builder*

4. Write two definitions for each key term: inauguration, precedent, bond, speculator, unconstitutional, tariff. First, write a formal definition for your teacher. Second, write a definition in everyday English for a classmate.

## Writing

5. A newspaper account of George Washington's inauguration referred to him as "the savior of his country." That was a reference to Washington's service as commander in chief during the Revolutionary War. If you were to begin reading an essay about the life of George Washington, list five questions you would like it to answer.

# The Arts of Early America

After winning independence, Americans began to develop their own styles in the arts. Often, they deliberately turned away from the model of their former British rulers.

## Architecture

American architects of the Federal Period (1790–1830) turned away from the influence of England. They looked instead to two ancient civilizations, Greece and Rome. Domes and pillars were common. Buildings were designed to create a sense of harmony and balance. This picture shows the White House as it looked in 1807.

**History** *Interactive*

**Explore Art and Music of the 1800s**
**Visit:** PHSchool.com
**Web Code:** myp-3047

Arches were common in Roman architecture.

Pillars were modeled on Greek style.

Equal numbers of doors and windows on each side gave a sense of balance.

▲ The White House, 1807

## Folk Art

Folk art is art created by ordinary people rather than trained artists. Common types of American folk art included hand-stitched samplers, weather vanes, ships' figureheads, and tavern signs. Much of the folk art of this time included patriotic images that revealed pride in the new nation. This Pennsylvania Dutch watercolor shows George Washington and his wife, Martha.

Pennsylvania Dutch watercolor

## Music

Many early American popular songs—including "Yankee Doodle"(below, right)—were adapted from old English melodies. In 1796, Americans put a new set of words to "Yankee Doodle" (below, left) to show pride in their democracy.

### THE RIGHT OF FREE ELECTIONS

Should enemies beset us round,

Of foreign, fierce complexions;

Undaunted we will stand our ground,

Upheld by free elections.

We'll never from our duty swerve,

Let who will make objections;

But while we live, unchanged preserve

The freedom of elections.

### YANKEE DOODLE

There was Captain Washington
Upon a slapping stallion
A-giving orders to his men
I guess there was a million.
Yankee Doodle, keep it up
Yankee Doodle dandy
Mind the music and the step
And with the girls be handy.

Early American flute ▲

### Analyze LIFE AT THE TIME

Choose one of the examples of art, architecture, or music shown on these pages. Write a paragraph explaining how it shows a sense of pride in being an American.

# The Birth of Political Parties

## Objectives

1. Explain how early political parties emerged.
2. Compare the political views of the Republicans and the Federalists.
3. Discuss the result of the election of 1796.

## Prepare to Read

### 🕐 Reading Skill

**Infer Meanings of Similes**
Similes compare things that may seem unrelated. The comparison helps you to see things in a new way. When you read a simile, think about how the items being compared are similar. Try to determine what point the writer is making.

### Vocabulary *Builder*

**High-Use Words**
<u>hostile</u>, p. 291
<u>fundamental</u>, p. 293

**Key Terms and People**
faction, p. 290
James Madison, p. 290
Thomas Jefferson, p. 290
Alexander Hamilton, p. 290
John Adams, p. 293

**Main Idea**
Against the expectations of the Framers of the Constitution, two political parties soon came into being.

⭐ **Background Knowledge** The arguments over Hamilton's financial plan reflected serious disagreements among the new nation's leaders. In this section, you will learn how those differences led to the formation of political parties in the United States.

## Political Parties Emerge

The Framers of the Constitution did not expect political parties to develop in the United States. Rather, they thought that government leaders would rise above personal or local interests. The leaders, they believed, would work together for the sake of the country.

In those days, people spoke of *factions* rather than *political parties*. A **faction** was an organized political group, and the word was not complimentary. James Madison considered factions to be selfish groups, unconcerned with the well-being of the whole nation. Madison argued in the *Federalist Papers* that an effective national government would prevent the growth of factions. As he put it,

> ❝Among the numerous advantages promised by a well-constructed Union, none deserves to be more accurately developed than its tendency to break and control the violence of faction.❞
>
> —James Madison, *The Federalist* No. 10, 1787

Thomas Jefferson and Alexander Hamilton, who were rarely in agreement, both disliked factions. Hamilton warned that the "spirit of faction" might work like a spark to bring mob rule and chaos.

### 🕐 Infer Meanings of Simile

To what is "the spirit of faction" compared in the final sentence of this paragraph? What does the comparison mean?

No one was more <u>hostile</u> to factions than George Washington. The President watched unhappily as Jefferson and Hamilton, the leading members of his Cabinet, grew apart. Washington tried to reduce the quarreling. In a letter to Henry Lee, he predicted that factions would destroy the "best fabric of human government and happiness."

Despite Washington's efforts, by the early 1790s two political parties were beginning to form. One group supported Thomas Jefferson and his close ally, James Madison. The other supported Alexander Hamilton and his ideas.

✓**Checkpoint**  **Why did many of the nation's leaders dislike political parties?**

**Vocabulary** *Builder*
<u>hostile</u> (HAHS tihl) *adj.* unfriendly; adverse or opposed

# Republicans Against Federalists

The two parties that took shape during the first half of the 1790s eventually got the names Republicans and Federalists.

The Republicans took their name from political clubs called Democratic-Republican Societies that had been organized in various parts of the country. They argued that the federal government was growing too strong under President Washington. They wanted to keep most power at the state or local level. They feared that a strong central government would act like a monarchy.

**Main Idea**
The Republicans and the Federalists disagreed on how powerful the federal government should be.

## Republicans Versus Federalists

### Republicans

1. Were led by Thomas Jefferson
2. Believed people should have political power
3. Favored strong state government
4. Emphasized agriculture
5. Favored strict interpretation of Constitution
6. Were pro-French
7. Opposed national bank
8. Opposed protective tariff

### Federalists

1. Were led by Alexander Hamilton
2. Believed wealthy and educated should lead
3. Favored strong central government
4. Emphasized manufacturing, shipping, and trade
5. Favored loose interpretation of Constitution
6. Were pro-British
7. Favored national bank
8. Favored protective tariff

**Reading Charts**
**Skills Activity**

The nation's first political parties were the Federalists and the Republicans. They took opposing stands on many political issues.

**(a) Read a Chart** How did the parties differ on federal power?

**(b) Apply Information** Why did the party that favored strong state governments insist on a strict interpretation of the Constitution?

# Links Across Time

## Political Parties Then and Now

**1790s** Political differences between Thomas Jefferson and Alexander Hamilton led to the development of America's first political parties.

**1850s** By the 1850s, the parties we know today had taken shape. Today's Democratic Party actually traces its roots to Jefferson's Republican Party. The modern Republican Party, which was born during the 1850s over the issue of slavery, has no connection to Jefferson's Republicans.

## Link to Today  nline

**Political Parties Today** The two major parties play a leading role in the American political system. How do the parties stand on today's political issues?

---

**For:** Political parties in the news
**Visit:** PHSchool.com
**Web Code:** myc-3042

The donkey is the modern-day symbol associated with the Democratic Party.

The symbol for today's Republican Party is an elephant.

This early Republican Party drew its main strength from southern planters and northern farmers and artisans. Key leaders were James Madison and Thomas Jefferson. Unhappy with the federal government's policies, Jefferson resigned as secretary of state in 1793.

The Federalists took their name from the people who had supported the adoption of the Constitution after 1787. A prominent leader was Alexander Hamilton. As in the debates over the Constitution, Federalists said the United States needed a strong federal government to hold the country together and deal with its problems.

Federalists drew support mainly from merchants, other property owners, and ordinary workers whose jobs depended on manufacturing and trade. They were especially strong in the North.

**Organizing and Arguing** At the time that both parties were organizing, the Federalists had an advantage. President Washington usually supported Hamilton and his policies. One Hamilton supporter running for office proudly said, "I am a FEDERALIST, the friend of order, of government, and of the present administration."

A newspaper editor who supported the Republicans saw the situation very differently. In 1792, he printed a series of questions in the *National Gazette* implying that the Federalists wanted to betray the Constitution and bring back a king. "Are not some amongst us . . . advocates for monarchy and aristocracy?" he asked. "Are not the principles of all such [people] hostile to the principles of the constitution?"

**A Series of Battles** In 1790, Washington sent a small force to end the Native American attacks on settlers. Warriors led by Little Turtle of the Miami Nation and Blue Jacket of the Shawnees defeated the soldiers. The next year, Washington sent a larger force. This time, Little Turtle won an even bigger victory. More than 900 soldiers were killed or wounded. It was the worst defeat the army would ever suffer in a battle with Native Americans.

Washington then turned to a Revolutionary War hero, General Anthony Wayne, to lead the forces against the Native Americans. Native Americans gathered for battle at a place where fallen trees covered the ground. They thought the trees would cause trouble for Wayne and his soldiers. But in August 1794, Wayne won a major victory at the Battle of Fallen Timbers.

That battle broke the Native American hold on the Northwest. In the 1795 Treaty of Greenville, leaders of the defeated Native American nations gave up most of their lands from the Ohio River in the south to Lake Erie in the north. Today, that is most of the state of Ohio.

☑ **Checkpoint** How were the conflicting claims of settlers and Native Americans resolved?

## Treaty of Greenville

In the Treaty of Greenville, Native Americans gave up, or ceded, territory to the United States. The cessions (lands ceded) are shown in color.

**(a) Read a Map** How many areas were ceded?

**(b) Analyze Cause and Effect** What event shown on the map led to the cessions?

**MapMaster Online**

**For:** Interactive map
**Visit:** PHSchool.com
**Web Code:** myp-3043

# The French Revolution

The French Revolution began in 1789. Most Americans at first supported the French revolutionaries. In their eyes, France was following the lead of the United States in fighting monarchy.

Soon, though, the French Revolution became controversial in the United States. One reason was that it became more violent. This process peaked in mid-1793 with a period called the Reign of Terror. The French revolutionaries executed about 17,000 people, including the king and queen. The Federalists denounced the violence. But Jefferson and his supporters argued that in a fight by oppressed people to win freedom, some injustices were to be expected.

Secondly, by early 1793, France and Britain were at war. In that war, said President Washington, the United States would remain neutral—not favoring either side in a dispute.

The United States wanted to trade with both sides. However, each European country feared such trade would benefit the other. Both countries began stopping American ships and seizing their cargoes.

**Main Idea**

Americans at first welcomed the French Revolution, but they divided over how to respond.

## American Reaction to the Reign of Terror

In this excerpt, a British observer describes the reactions of some Americans to the execution of Louis XVI.

❝Never was the memory of any man so cruelly insulted as that of this mild and humane monarch [Louis XVI]. He was guillotined in effigy [using a dummy to represent a real person], in the capital of the Union [Philadelphia], twenty or thirty times every day, during one whole winter and part of the summer. Men, women, and children flocked to the tragical exhibition, and not a single paragraph appeared in the papers to shame them from it.❞

—William Cobbett, *History of the American Jacobins*
(Philadelphia, 1796)

In this illustration, an executioner displays the severed head of Louis XVI.

### Reading Primary Sources
#### Skills Activity

During the Reign of Terror, revolutionaries used the guillotine to behead the French king Louis XVI in January 1793. Queen Marie Antoinette was executed in October 1793.

**(a) Detect Points of View** How did the author view Louis XVI's execution?

**(b) Draw Conclusions** How do you think Philadelphians who attended the "tragical exhibition" felt about the king's execution? Explain.

The British made matters worse by the **impressment** of sailors on American ships, which meant seizing the sailors and forcing them to serve in the British navy. Some of the sailors were British sailors who had fled the British navy, but many were Americans.

As tensions rose, Hamilton urged the President to stay friendly with Britain. He argued that American prosperity depended on trade with Britain. The British purchased 75 percent of American exports and supplied 90 percent of American imports.

Washington agreed and tried to repair relations with Britain. He sent John Jay to London to try to solve the most serious problems.

Jay returned with a treaty in 1795. In it, the United States agreed to pay debts long owed to British merchants. In return, Britain agreed to pay for the ships it had seized. It also agreed to withdraw its troops from the Northwest Territory and stop aiding Native Americans there. However, the British refused to recognize a U.S. right to trade with France. They also refused to <u>cease</u> impressment of U.S. sailors.

The Jay Treaty angered Republicans. They claimed the United States had given away too much and gotten too little. Federalists, in contrast, liked the treaty because it kept peace with Britain. Since Federalists controlled the Senate, the Jay Treaty won approval by a narrow margin.

**Vocabulary** *Builder*
<u>cease</u> (sees) *v.* to cause to come to an end; to stop

✓**Checkpoint** How did Americans react to the Jay Treaty?

# Washington Retires From Public Life

In 1796, Washington published a letter to fellow Americans that had lasting influence. Washington's Farewell Address made two major points. First, the President warned against political divisions at home. He feared that violent divisions might tear the nation apart.

Washington's second piece of advice concerned foreign policy. In a famous passage, Washington emphasized his belief that the United States must not get entangled in the affairs of Europe. He said:

> **"**Europe has a set of primary interests which to us have none or a very remote relation. . . . Why . . . entangle our peace and prosperity in the toils [traps] of European ambition? . . . It is our true policy to steer clear of permanent alliances with any portion of the foreign world.**"**
>
> —George Washington, Farewell Address, 1796

As he left office, Washington could take pride in his accomplishments: (1) The United States now had a functioning federal government. (2) The economy was improving. (3) Washington had avoided war. (4) The British had been forced to leave their forts in the Northwest Territory, an area that was now safe for settlement.

Still, political divisions were growing and challenges remained.

☑ **Checkpoint** What were Washington's chief accomplishments?

⭐ **Looking Back and Ahead** As President, George Washington created conditions for a strong federal government. In the next section, you will read how his successor sought to deal with divisions at home and challenges abroad.

**Main Idea**
Washington's Farewell Address has had lasting influence.

**Vocabulary** *Builder*
emphasize (EHM fah sīz) *v.* to stress; to give more importance to

---

**Section 3** | **Check Your Progress**

**Progress Monitoring** 🌐nline
**For:** Self-test with instant help
**Visit:** PHSchool.com
**Web Code:** mya-3043

## Comprehension and Critical Thinking

**1. (a) Describe** How did Washington deal with Britain's policy of impressment?
**(b) Compare and Contrast** How did Washington's policy on matters at home differ from his foreign policy?

**2. (a) Recall** What were the two main arguments Washington made in his Farewell Address?
**(b) Distinguish Facts From Opinions** Support the following opinion with facts from the chapter: George Washington was a great first President.

## Reading Skill

**3. Infer Meanings of Metaphors** Identify and explain the metaphor in this sentence: In the heated political atmosphere, this warning had little impact.

## Vocabulary *Builder*

Read each sentence that follows. If the sentence is true, write YES. If the sentence is not true, write NO and explain why.
**4.** As a neutral nation, the United States should trade only with Britain and not France.

**5.** The Jay Treaty did not end the impressment of American sailors by the British navy.

## Writing

**6.** Based on what you have read about George Washington in this section, write a description of the personality traits he showed as President of the United States. Include at least two specific examples of actions that he took as President.

# The Presidency of John Adams

## Objectives

1. Discuss the reasons for tension between the United States and France.

2. Describe the main provisions of the Alien and Sedition acts.

3. Explain how controversy arose over states' rights.

## Prepare to Read

### 🔊 Reading Skill

**Identify Analogies** In an analogy, two pairs of items are connected with the same sort of comparison. For example, both pairs might compare synonyms, or words with similar meanings. You must understand the comparison between the first pair in order to complete the comparison between the second pair. Some common types of analogies are cause-effect, antonyms, and synonyms.

### Vocabulary *Builder*

**High-Use Words**

**react**, p. 298

**provoke**, p. 301

**Key Terms**

alien, p. 300

sedition, p. 300

nullify, p. 301

states' rights, p. 301

### ⭐ Background Knowledge

As you have read, John Adams was elected to succeed George Washington as President. Like Washington, he struggled to reduce the country's divisions and to steer a neutral course in foreign policy.

## Main Idea

Despite many Americans' desire for war against France, John Adams managed to resolve differences peacefully.

## Vocabulary *Builder*

**react** (ree AKT) *v.* to act in response to another action; to respond

## Troubles With France

Adams immediately faced a crisis over relations with France. The French were angered by U.S. neutrality in the war between France and Britain. France had hoped for U.S. support. Had not French assistance been the key to success in the American Revolution? Why didn't Americans show their gratitude by helping the French now?

The Jay Treaty only increased tensions with France. As the French saw it, the treaty put the United States on Britain's side. France <u>reacted</u> late in 1796 by snubbing a U.S. diplomat. Moreover, the French continued to attack American merchant ships.

**The XYZ Affair** In 1797, Adams sent a new three-person mission to France. Agents of the French government demanded that the United States pay a bribe of $250,000. The agents also wanted the United States to lend France several million dollars.

The Americans said they would pay "not a sixpence [a coin worth six pennies]." Later, that statement led to the slogan, "Millions for defense, but not one sixpence for tribute [a forced payment]."

The bribe attempt was a sensation when it became public. Because the names of the French agents were kept secret, they were called X, Y, and Z. The incident became known as the XYZ Affair.

**War Fever** The XYZ Affair caused an outbreak of war fever in the United States. Many Federalists demanded that Adams ask Congress to declare war on France.

With war fever rising, Adams asked Congress to increase the size of the army and rebuild the navy. It did both, thus enhancing the power of the central government. Adams also convinced Congress to create a separate department of the navy. Between 1798 and 1800, the United States fought an undeclared naval war with France.

Nonetheless, the President and many other Americans opposed a full-scale war. To avoid war, Adams sent a new mission to France. Napoleon Bonaparte, France's dictator, was busy dealing with war in Europe. In 1800, he agreed to stop seizing American ships.

President Adams had avoided war. But the agreement angered leaders of his own Federalist Party, especially the pro-British Hamilton. This disapproval weakened Adams politically.

Still, Adams was satisfied. He told a friend that he wanted his tombstone to read: "Here lies John Adams, who took upon himself the responsibility of peace with France in the year 1800."

☑**Checkpoint**  **How did Adams settle differences with France?**

## The Alien and Sedition Acts

The war fever deepened the split between Federalists and Republicans. Federalists' fear of revolutionary France spilled over into a mistrust of immigrants. Federalists suspected them of bringing in dangerous ideas and feared that they would back the Republicans.

**Identify Analogies**
The phrase *war fever* is an analogy. Think about what having a fever does to a person's body. How is that similar to what the desire for war might do to the country?

**Main Idea**
During the troubles with France, Federalists in Congress passed drastic laws to limit immigration and restrict free speech.

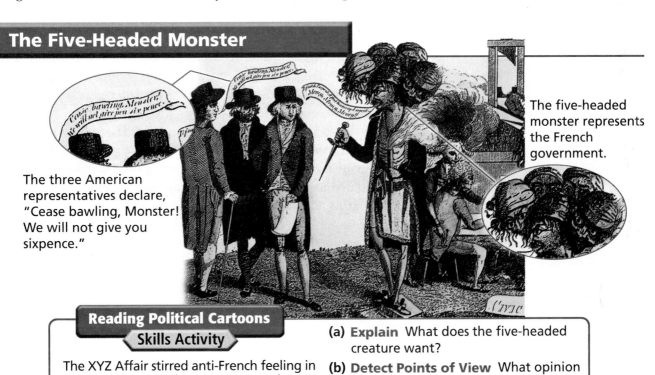

**The Five-Headed Monster**

The three American representatives declare, "Cease bawling, Monster! We will not give you sixpence."

The five-headed monster represents the French government.

**Reading Political Cartoons**
**Skills Activity**

The XYZ Affair stirred anti-French feeling in the United States. This 1798 cartoon shows a five-headed creature demanding a bribe from the three American representatives (at left).

(a) **Explain** What does the five-headed creature want?

(b) **Detect Points of View** What opinion do you think the cartoonist has of the French government? What evidence supports your view?

### New Life for a Debate

Passage of the Alien and Sedition acts renewed the debate over federal versus state power. Jefferson and Madison wrote the Kentucky and Virginia resolutions in defense of states' rights. **Critical Thinking:** *Detect Points of View According to defenders of states' rights in 1798, what could states do if they disliked a federal law?*

| Arguments for States' Rights | Arguments for Federal Power |
| --- | --- |
| ■ The federal government derives its power from rights given to it by the states. <br><br> ■ Because the states created the United States, individual states have the power to nullify a federal law. | ■ The federal government derives its power from rights given to it by the American people. <br> ■ States have no power to nullify federal laws. <br> ■ States cannot revoke federal powers set forth in the Constitution. |

#### Trouble on the Horizon

Within 25 years of the Alien and Sedition acts, people in New England and South Carolina would threaten to leave the Union because they either disagreed with American foreign policy or opposed laws passed by Congress.

Federalist leaders decided that to restore order at home they must destroy their political opponents. Congress passed a group of laws in 1798 aimed at immigrants. Another 1798 law targeted Republicans.

The laws directed at immigrants were the Alien Act. An alien is an outsider or someone from another country. The Alien Act increased the length of time from 5 to 14 years that a person had to live in the United States to become a citizen. The President gained the power to deport or imprison any alien he considered dangerous.

The law targeting Republicans was the Sedition Act. Sedition is activity designed to overthrow a government. The Sedition Act probably was the harshest law limiting free speech ever passed in the United States. It made it a crime for anyone to write or say anything insulting or anything false about the President, Congress, or the government in general. During 1798 and 1799, ten people were convicted under the act. Most were Republican editors and printers.

☑**Checkpoint**   **What did the Alien and Sedition acts do?**

**Main Idea**
Critics of the Alien and Sedition acts argued that states could refuse to obey certain federal laws.

## States' Rights

The Republicans denounced the Alien and Sedition acts. They charged that the Sedition Act violated the Constitution, especially the First Amendment, which guarantees freedom of speech.

However, the Republicans faced a problem opposing the law. At the time, it was not clearly established that the Supreme Court had the power to strike down a law as unconstitutional. Because of this, the Republicans expressed their opposition through the state legislatures.

Republicans James Madison and Thomas Jefferson, both Virginians, led the campaign. Madison wrote a resolution attacking the Alien and Sedition acts. It was passed by the Virginia legislature. Jefferson wrote a similar resolution that was passed by the Kentucky legislature. Together, the Virginia and Kentucky resolutions stated that the Alien and Sedition acts were unconstitutional. They declared that states had the right to declare laws passed by Congress to be unconstitutional.

No other states supported Virginia and Kentucky, so the two resolutions had little immediate impact. As for the Alien and Sedition acts, they were not in force for long. The law that gave the President the power to imprison or deport dangerous aliens expired after two years. The Sedition Act expired in 1801. The waiting period for immigrants to become citizens was restored to five years in 1802.

However, over the long term the Virginia and Kentucky resolutions were far more important than the laws that provoked them. The resolutions claimed that states could nullify—deprive of legal force—a law passed by Congress. The resolutions also boosted the idea of states' rights. This is the idea that the union binding "these United States" is an agreement between the states and that they therefore can overrule federal law. In decades to come, a number of states would refuse to obey certain federal laws. States' rights would become the rallying cry for southern defenders of slavery.

James Madison

**Vocabulary Builder**
**provoke** (prah VOHK) *v.* to cause to anger; to excite; to cause an action

✔**Checkpoint** Why did the issue of states' rights arise at this time?

⭐ **Looking Back and Ahead** You have read how the United States got up and running under its first two Presidents. The next chapter deals with the next two Presidents, Thomas Jefferson and James Madison, and the challenges they faced.

---

Section 4 | **Check Your Progress**

**Progress Monitoring Online**
**For:** Self-test with instant help
**Visit:** PHSchool.com
**Web Code:** mya-3044

## Comprehension and Critical Thinking

**1. (a) Recall** What problem did President Adams face abroad?
**(b) Explain Problems** How did Adams resolve this problem?

**2. (a) Summarize** Why did the Federalist Congress pass the Alien and Sedition acts?
**(b) Analyze Cause and Effect** Explain the following statement: State reaction to the Alien and Sedition acts caused further tension between the political parties.

## Reading Skill

**3. Identify Analogies** Explain the analogy in this sentence: As the call for war heated up, John Adams tried to be the nation's firefighter.

## Vocabulary Builder

Answer the following questions in complete sentences that show your understanding of the key terms.
**4.** Why did Federalists mistrust aliens?
**5.** Why did newspaper editors accused of sedition tend to be Republicans?

**6.** Why did Republicans want to nullify the Alien and Sedition acts?
**7.** How can states' rights be used to oppose federal laws?

## Writing

**8.** Use Internet or library resources to research the life of John Adams. List the principal events in his life. Then, describe the personality traits he displayed as President of the United States. Write a thesis statement that could be used to introduce a biographical essay about Adams.

It is important to be able to tell the difference between facts and opinions when you read historical stories and narratives. A fact is something that can be proved to be true or can be observed. An opinion is a statement that reflects a person's feelings, judgments, or beliefs about a subject.

---

This diary entry, which is historical fiction, was written by a merchant living in colonial Philadelphia in the 1790s.

February 28

After dinner tonight I finished reading today's edition of the *Gazette of the United States.* The publisher of the newspaper is John Fenno. In my opinion, he is right to favor the Federalist leader, Alexander Hamilton. Of course, I am a merchant and I agree with Hamilton's support of trade and manufacturing. To me it is a more worthwhile policy than Mr. Jefferson's support of the farmers.

I believe that I have Hamilton alone to thank for the National Bank. This Bank, established by Congress in 1791, has the power to make loans to businesses, such as my dry goods store. Of course, the federal Bank is opposed by that friend of the states, Thomas Jefferson, who isn't thinking of our country's future. I only hope that Mr. Hamilton's party wins the next election.

—Isaac Smith

---

## Learn the Skill
*Use these steps to identify facts and opinions.*

❶ **Decide which statements are facts.** Facts are statements that are based on direct evidence and can be proved to be true. Facts tell what really happened. You can look up a statement in a research source to prove it is a fact.

❷ **Decide which statements are opinions.** An opinion is a personal interpretation of an event, an idea, or a person. Words such as "I think," "I believe," or "I feel" are often used in a statement of opinion. Look for these words when you read.

❸ **Recognize how writers or speakers mix facts and opinions.** Sometimes writers use facts to support their personal opinion. Or, writers use facts and opinions to persuade the reader to support their point of view.

## Practice the Skill
*Answer the following questions about the journal entry on this page.*

❶ **Decide which statements are facts.** (a) Find two facts in this journal entry. (b) How can you prove that each statement is a fact?

❷ **Decide which statements are opinions.** (a) Find two statements of opinion in this journal entry. (b) How can you tell that each is an opinion?

❸ **Recognize how writers or speakers mix facts and opinions.** (a) Find an example of a statement that mixes fact and opinion. What is the fact? What is the opinion? (b) Why do you think the writer mixed fact and opinion in this selection?

## Apply the Skill
*See the Review and Assessment at the end of this chapter.*

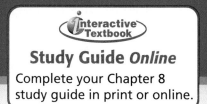

**Study Guide** *Online*
Complete your Chapter 8 study guide in print or online.

## Chapter Summary

### Section 1
### Launching a New Nation

- George Washington was inaugurated as the first President in April of 1789.
- Washington and Congress organized the executive and judiciary branches.
- Alexander Hamilton developed a financial plan to repay the country's large war debt.
- Federal forces put down the Whiskey Rebellion in 1794.

### Section 2
### The Birth of Political Parties

- Deepening differences between factions led to the first political parties.
- Republicans wanted a limited national government, while Federalists favored a strong federal government.
- John Adams, a Federalist, won the presidency in 1796. Thomas Jefferson, a Republican, won the vice presidency.

### Section 3
### Troubles at Home and Abroad

- Washington responded forcefully to conflict in the Northwest Territory between settlers and Native Americans.
- The United States remained neutral when France and Britain went to war.
- In his Farewell Address, George Washington warned the nation against disunity and against becoming involved in foreign wars.

### Section 4
### The Presidency of John Adams

- John Adams was elected President of the United States in 1796.
- The United States and France avoided full-scale war under Adams but fought an undeclared naval war.
- The Federalist-sponsored Alien and Sedition acts provoked a strong reaction by Republicans in favor of states' rights.

## Key Concepts

These notes will help you prepare for questions about key concepts.

| | George Washington's Presidency | John Adams's Presidency |
|---|---|---|
| **Key Events at Home** | First Cabinet forms | Tension continues between political parties |
| | National bank opens | Alien Act passes |
| | Rise of political parties | Sedition Act passes |
| | Whiskey Rebellion occurs | Issues over states' rights develop |
| | Battle of Fallen Timbers occurs | Adams's political party does not support him for second term |
| | Washington retires | |
| **Key Events Abroad** | Britain and France ignore U.S. policy of neutrality | XYZ Affair occurs |
| | Britain signs the Jay Treaty | Navy is enlarged for undeclared war with France |

## Vocabulary *Builder*

### Key Terms

Fill in the blanks with the correct key terms.

1. Many of the customs that Washington started set a _____ for how other Presidents were to act in the future.

2. Jefferson said the national bank was _____ because it was not written in the Constitution that Congress had authority to establish one.

3. Neither France nor Britain agreed that the United States could be a _____ nation and trade with both sides during their war.

4. The _____ Act violated the First Amendment of the Constitution.

## Comprehension and Critical Thinking

5. **(a) Recall** What was the purpose of George Washington's Cabinet?
   **(b) Link Past and Present** Why do you think current Presidents have more advisers than the number required in Washington's day?

6. **(a) Describe** What were two internal problems and their resolutions during Washington's second term as President?
   **(b) Explain Problems** What does the picture below indicate about Washington's view of the Whiskey Rebellion?

7. **(a) Recall** In Washington's Farewell Address, he talked about neutrality toward European nations. Why did Washington believe that the United States needed to be neutral in the war between France and Britain?
   **(b) Draw Conclusions** In Washington's Farewell Address, he also talked about national unity. Why was building unity an important goal for Washington?

8. **(a) Recall** Why were the Alien and Sedition acts unpopular with many people?
   **(b) Apply Information** Would you defend or oppose the government's right to silence people who criticize it? Explain.

## History Reading Skill

9. **Analyze Comparisons** George Washington is often referred to as the Father of Our Country. What is the meaning of this metaphor? Do you think this is a valid comparison? Explain.

## Writing

10. **Write a paragraph about either George Washington or John Adams.**
    Include major events and describe your subject's personality.
    **Your paragraph should:**
    - begin with a thesis statement;
    - expand on that main idea with facts, examples, and other information;
    - conclude by stating what you think was your subject's most important contribution to the new nation.

11. **Write a Narrative:**
    Study the pictures, map, and text in Section 1 about the Whiskey Rebellion. Write a two-paragraph narrative describing the rebellion. Write from the point of view of either a farmer or a soldier.

## Skills for Life

### Distinguish Facts From Opinions

Use the fictional journal entry below to answer the questions that follow.

> "I am grateful that at least our Vice President, Thomas Jefferson, is a Republican. I believe that his policies are the only hope for farmers, such as myself and my neighbors. In my opinion, our political leaders don't have to be rich or well-educated. The people can lead as well as follow. Of course, the Federalist Mr. Hamilton, with his fine clothes, favors the wealthy merchants."

12. **(a)** Identify one fact in the journal entry.
    **(b)** How can you prove the statement is a fact?

13. **(a)** What is an example of an opinion?
    **(b)** How can you tell the statement is an opinion?

14. Find a statement that mixes fact and opinion. What is the fact? What is the opinion?

# Test Yourself

1. **Which of the following led to tension between France and the United States during Adams's presidency?**

   A Treaty of Greenville

   B Jay Treaty

   C Treaty of Paris

   D Declaration of Independence

**Refer to the quotation below to answer Question 2.**

> "It is in my judgment necessary under the circumstances of the case to take measures for calling forth the militia in order to . . . cause the laws to be duly executed."

2. **What event is the subject of the quotation?**

   A French Revolution

   B XYZ Affair

   C Battle of Fallen Timbers

   D Whiskey Rebellion

**Refer to the chart below to answer Question 3.**

| The First Political Parties | |
|---|---|
| **Federalists** | **Republicans** |
| Favored strong central government | Favored state government |
| Emphasized manufacturing, shipping, and trade | Emphasized agriculture |
| Supported loose interpretation of the Constitution | Supported strict interpretation of the Constitution |
| Favored national bank | Opposed national bank |

3. **Which statement describes a fundamental difference between the two parties?**

   A Federalists believed in a strong central government, and Republicans did not.

   B Federalists believed in a strict interpretation of the Constitution, and Republicans did not.

   C Republicans believed in a strong central government, and Federalists did not.

   D Republicans believed in a loose interpretation of the Constitution, and Federalists did not.

# Document-Based Questions

**Task:** Look at Documents 1 and 2, and answer their accompanying questions. Then, use the documents and your knowledge of history to complete this writing assignment:

   Write a newspaper editorial supporting or attacking President Adams's decision to avoid war with France.

**Document 1:** In 1797, France began seizing American ships. Enraged Americans called for war, but President John Adams urged a policy of peace. *What action does Adams say he will take toward France?*

> "It is my sincere desire . . . to preserve peace and friendship with all nations; and believing that neither the honor nor the interest of the United States absolutely forbid the repetition of advances for securing these desirable objects with France, I shall institute a fresh attempt at negotiation, and shall not fail to promote and accelerate an accommodation on terms compatible with the rights, duties, interests, and honor of the nation."

**Document 2:** After the XYZ Affair, newspapers published cartoons such as the one shown below. It depicts the United States as a young woman surrounded by members of the French government. *What is the cartoonist's view of the XYZ Affair?*

PROPERTY PROTECTED. à la Françoise.

## Chapter Preview

By 1800, the Federalists faced many problems. The Alien and Sedition acts had angered many Americans. The party itself was divided. The election of 1800 would mark the end of the Federalist era. A new party took charge of the government, and a period of growth and national pride began.

**U.S. Events**

**1803** United States purchases Louisiana from France.

**1804** Lewis and Clark set out to explore Louisiana.

**1809** Embargo Act bans foreign trade.

1800

1805

1810

**World Events**

**1804** Napoleon becomes emperor of France.

**1810** Mexico declares independence from Spain.

The USS *Philadelphia* burns in Tripoli harbor, 1804. Although Americans wanted no involvement in foreign conflict, they were still drawn into a brief war with North African pirates.

**1811**
Americans defeat Native Americans at Tippecanoe.

**1812**
United States declares war on Britain.

**1815**
Battle of New Orleans is fought.

1810

1815

1820

**1815** Napoleon suffers final defeat at Battle of Waterloo.

**1819** Simón Bolívar seizes Bogotá from the Spanish.

**History Reading Skill** Relate Events in Time

## What did Americans discover as they explored new lands to the west?

In this chapter, you will learn how to relate events in time and understand their sequence. Read this account of an important exploration of the American West in the early 1800s. The side notes show you how to relate events in time and identify their sequence.

> **Primary Source**
>
> In 1804, President Jefferson sent Meriwether Lewis and William Clark to explore the Louisiana Territory. Lewis and Clark kept journals documenting their travels. The first paragraph below is a letter introducing part of those journals. The second paragraph is an excerpt from the journals.
>
> "They left the Pacific Ocean 23d March, 1806, where they arrived in November, 1805;—and where some Americans had been just before. . . . They have kept an ample journal of their tour, which will be published, and must afford much intelligence."
>
> "Here we remained during the day, the wind having risen at twelve so high that we could not proceed. It continued to blow violently all night, with occasional sprinklings of rain from sunset till midnight. On both sides of the river the country is rough and broken, the low grounds becoming narrower; the tops of the hills on the north exhibits some scattered pine and cedar, on the south, the pine has not yet commenced. . . ."
>
> —Journals of the Lewis and Clark expedition

*The dates clarify the sequence.*

*Words such as before, after, next, and soon show sequence.*

*Time descriptions tell readers what happened when.*

*This verb shows sequence by describing a process.*

## Relate Events in Time

- Sequence signal words tell you when events happen in time.
- Use sequence verbs to understand the order of events in time.
- Look for dates or times to relate events to one another in time.
- Notice when two or more events occur at the same time.

## Document-Based Questions

1. Why did Lewis and Clark keep a journal?
2. What kinds of information did they record? List five specific details in the journal excerpt.
3. Do you think their journals were a good source of information about the American West? Explain.

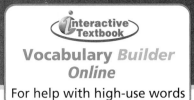

# Vocabulary *Builder*

## Previewing High-Use Academic Words

| High-Use Word | Definition | Sample History Sentence |
|---|---|---|
| **prospect** (PRAHS pehkt) (Section 1, p. 310) | *n.* expectation; likely outcome | Slaveholders in the southern colonies feared the <u>prospect</u> of a rebellion by enslaved people. |
| **cease** (sees) (Section 1, p. 313) | *v.* to stop; to come to an end | With Cornwallis's surrender at Yorktown, all Revolutionary War fighting <u>ceased</u>. |
| **crisis** (KRĪ sihs) (Section 2, p. 314) | *n.* turning point or deciding event in history | The Whiskey Rebellion created a <u>crisis</u> for George Washington's presidency. |
| **alter** (AWL ter) (Section 2, p. 315) | *v.* to change in some way; to make different | Cornwallis's decision to camp on the Yorktown peninsula <u>altered</u> the course of the American Revolution. |
| **decline** (dee KLĪN) (Section 3, p. 324) | *v.* to gradually lose strength or power | The strength of the Continental army <u>declined</u> after Valley Forge. |
| **restore** (ree STOR) (Section 3, p. 326) | *v.* to bring back to a former condition | The Loyalists hoped to <u>restore</u> British power to the colonies. |
| **reinforce** (ree ihn FORS) (Section 4, p. 328) | *v.* to strengthen with additional troops | At Yorktown, American forces were <u>reinforced</u> by the French navy. |
| **critic** (KRIHT ihk) (Section 4, p. 331) | *n.* someone who makes judgments on the value of actions | The Antifederalists were <u>critics</u> of the U.S. Constitution. |

Tecumseh

## Previewing Key Terms and People

Thomas Jefferson

**The Era of Thomas Jefferson 309**

# Jefferson Takes Office

## Objectives

1. Describe the outcome of the election of 1800.

2. Explain Jefferson's policies as President.

3. Discuss the importance of *Marbury* v. *Madison.*

**Main Idea**
After a bitter election campaign, Thomas Jefferson used his inaugural address to try to bring opposing sides together.

**Vocabulary** *Builder*
**prospect** (PRAHS pehkt) *n.*
expectation; likely outcome

**Understand Sequence of Events**
What words in this paragraph are clues to sequence?

## Prepare to Read

### 🎯 Reading Skill

**Understand Sequence of Events** A historian must master the sequence of events that make up a historical episode. To understand the sequence, determine what happened first, next, or last. Look for clues such as dates and sequence signal words. Compare when events occurred. This will help you identify connections between events.

### Vocabulary *Builder*

**High-Use Words**
prospect, p. 310
cease, p. 313

### Key Terms and People

Thomas Jefferson, p. 310
Aaron Burr, p. 310
laissez faire, p. 311
John Marshall, p. 313
judicial review, p. 313

⭐ **Background Knowledge** In the previous chapter, you learned how the Federalists controlled the national government until the election of 1800. As a result of this election, the new Republican administration of Thomas Jefferson reversed Federalist policies. This led to what Jefferson called the "Revolution of 1800."

## Republicans Take Charge

Margaret Smith attended the inauguration of Thomas Jefferson as President of the United States in March 1801. After the inauguration, she wrote a letter explaining how proud she was of the United States. In other countries, the transfer of power usually involved "confusion . . . and bloodshed." However, "in our happy country" that transfer was peaceful and orderly.

**A Bitter Campaign** The presidential election of 1800 was viciously contested. The Federalists raised the prospect of civil war if Jefferson were elected. Republicans accused John Adams of wanting to create a monarchy.

By receiving 73 electoral votes, Jefferson defeated Adams. According to the Constitution, the person who received the next highest total of electoral votes would be Vice President. However, Aaron Burr, Jefferson's running mate, also received 73 votes. It was up to the House of Representatives to decide who would be President. For six days, the House was deadlocked. On the 36th vote, Jefferson won the election.

To avoid this situation in the future, the Twelfth Amendment to the Constitution changed how electors voted. Beginning in 1804, electors would vote separately for President and Vice President.

**Jefferson's Inauguration** Thomas Jefferson was the first President to be inaugurated in Washington, D.C., the country's new capital. Jefferson believed the government should have simple customs. To make the point, he walked to his inauguration instead of riding in a fancy carriage. He also ended the custom of people bowing to the President. Instead, they just shook his hand.

Jefferson used his inaugural address to bring a divided country together. He told the American people:

> **❝**Let us, then, fellow-citizens, unite with one heart and one mind. . . . Every difference of opinion is not a difference of principle. . . . We are all Republicans; we are all Federalists.**❞**
> —Thomas Jefferson, First Inaugural Address, March 4, 1801

☑ **Checkpoint** **Why did the election of 1800 have to be decided in the House of Representatives?**

## Jefferson Charts a New Course

Jefferson thought of his election as the "Revolution of 1800." Jefferson's first goal as President was to limit the federal government's power over states and citizens. The new President thought that under Washington and Adams the federal government had become too involved in economic affairs. He believed in the idea known as laissez faire (LEHS ay fehr), from the French term for "let alone." **Laissez faire** means that the government should not interfere in the economy.

**New Republican Policies** Jefferson put his laissez faire ideas into practice when he reduced the number of people in government. He fired all tax collectors and cut the number of U.S. diplomats.

**Main Idea**
As President, Thomas Jefferson's main goal was to limit the federal government's power over states and citizens.

**Thomas Jefferson's Home**
Thomas Jefferson designed his home, Monticello. In the design, he included elements of Greek architecture, such as columns, and Roman architecture, such as domes. **Critical Thinking:** *Link Past and Present What elements of Greek and Roman culture are still important to us today?*

## Goals and Policies of Thomas Jefferson

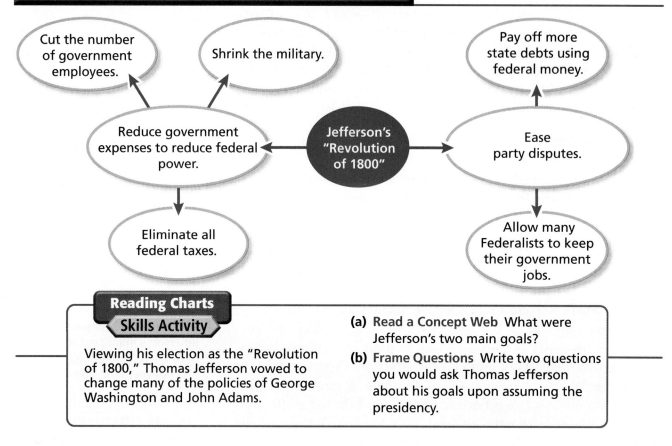

Cut the number of government employees.

Shrink the military.

Pay off more state debts using federal money.

Reduce government expenses to reduce federal power.

Jefferson's "Revolution of 1800"

Ease party disputes.

Eliminate all federal taxes.

Allow many Federalists to keep their government jobs.

**Reading Charts**

**Skills Activity**

Viewing his election as the "Revolution of 1800," Thomas Jefferson vowed to change many of the policies of George Washington and John Adams.

**(a) Read a Concept Web** What were Jefferson's two main goals?

**(b) Frame Questions** Write two questions you would ask Thomas Jefferson about his goals upon assuming the presidency.

Larger cuts came from shrinking the military. Jefferson cut the army's budget in half, reducing the army's size from 4,000 to about 2,500 soldiers. At the same time, Jefferson eliminated all federal taxes inside the country. Now, most tax revenue came from the tariff on imported goods.

The Sedition Act was another of Jefferson's targets. As you have read, a number of people had been convicted and fined under the act. Jefferson ordered those fines refunded. Those imprisoned under the Sedition Act were released.

**Federalist Policies Remain** Jefferson could not reverse all Federalist policies. He believed that the United States had to keep repaying its national debt. He also did not fire most of the Federalist officeholders. He said they could keep their jobs if they did them well and were loyal citizens.

☑Checkpoint **What action did Jefferson take as President to help those convicted under the Sedition Act?**

**Main Idea**

The Supreme Court ruling in *Marbury* v. *Madison* established the principle of judicial review.

## The Supreme Court and Judicial Review

One Federalist who did not keep his job was Judge William Marbury. Adams had appointed Marbury and several other judges in the last hours before he left office. The Republicans argued that these appointments were aimed at maintaining Federalist power.

When Jefferson took office, he ordered James Madison, his secretary of state, to <u>cease</u> work on the appointments. Marbury then sued Madison, citing the Judiciary Act of 1789. This act gave the Supreme Court the power to review cases brought against a federal official.

The outcome of the case forever changed the relationship of the three branches of government. In his ruling, Chief Justice John Marshall spoke for a unanimous Court. He ruled that the Judiciary Act of 1789 was unconstitutional. Marshall stated that the Court's powers came from the Constitution, not from Congress. Therefore, Congress did not have the right to give power to the Supreme Court in the Judiciary Act. Only the Constitution could do that.

The Court's actual decision—that it could not help Marbury gain his commission—was not highly significant. However, the ruling did set an important precedent. Marshall used the case of *Marbury* v. *Madison* to establish the principle of judicial review—the authority of the Supreme Court to strike down unconstitutional laws. Today, judicial review remains one of the most important powers of the Supreme Court.

✓**Checkpoint** What is judicial review?

⭐ **Looking Back and Ahead** Thomas Jefferson had long argued that the federal government's powers were limited to what was set down in the Constitution. The Constitution did not specifically give the government the power to buy land from a foreign country. In the next section, you will read of Jefferson's dilemma when France offered to sell the United States the huge territory known as Louisiana.

**Progress Monitoring** Online
For: Self-test with instant help
Visit: PHSchool.com
Web Code: mya-3051

**Comprehension and Critical Thinking**

1. **(a) Recall** How did Jefferson's inauguration demonstrate the changes he planned for the U.S. government?
   **(b) Apply Information** How did Jefferson's policies change the American government?

2. **(a) Identify** What was Chief Justice Marshall's decision in the case of *Marbury* v. *Madison*?
   **(b) Make Predictions** How did the outcome of *Marbury* v. *Madison* affect the relationship of the three branches of government?

**Reading Skill**

3. **Understand Sequence of Events** Read the first paragraph under the heading "Jefferson Charts a New Course." What was Jefferson's *first* priority as President?

**Vocabulary** *Builder*

Read each sentence below. If the sentence is true, write YES. If the sentence is not true, write NO and explain why.

4. Jefferson believed in laissez faire, the idea that the federal government should not interfere in economic affairs.

5. John Marshall cited judicial review as the reason why only the Senate had the right to decide whether acts of Congress are constitutional.

**Writing**

6. Based on what you have read in this section about Jefferson's early days in office, write a thesis statement about Jefferson's influence on American government. Then, list the kinds of supporting information that would back up your thesis statement.

Vocabulary *Builder*
<u>cease</u> (sees) *v.* to stop; to come to an end

# The Louisiana Purchase

## Objectives

1. Explain the importance of New Orleans and the crisis over its port.

2. Describe how the United States gained the Louisiana Purchase.

3. Discuss Lewis and Clark's expedition.

## Prepare to Read

### Reading Skill

**Distinguish Events in Sequence** As you read, it will help you to identify events that occur at about the same time in different locations. Ask yourself if these events share a common cause. Was there any advantage for people to make these events happen at the same time? Would faster communication have changed the sequence at all?

### Vocabulary *Builder*

**High-Use Words**

crisis, p. 314
alter, p. 315

**Key Terms and People**

expedition, p. 317
Meriwether Lewis, p. 317
William Clark, p. 317
continental divide, p. 318
Zebulon Pike, p. 319

**Background Knowledge** In the previous section, you learned how Jefferson focused on reducing the size of the federal government upon becoming President. But Jefferson had a lifelong interest in the American West. In this section, you will learn how he expanded the country's borders far to the west.

## The Nation Looks West

**Main Idea**
U.S. leaders worried that France or Spain might close the port of New Orleans to the goods of western farmers.

The tide of westward settlement speeded up in the years after the United States won independence. By 1800, more than one million settlers lived between the Appalachian Mountains and the Mississippi River.

Most western settlers were farmers. Because there were few roads in the West, they relied on the Mississippi River to ship their crops to the port at New Orleans. From there, the goods were loaded on ships and carried to markets in the East.

Spain, which controlled the Mississippi and New Orleans, had several times threatened to close the port to American ships. To prevent this from happening again, in 1795 the United States negotiated a treaty with Spain. The Pinckney Treaty guaranteed the Americans' right to ship their goods down the Mississippi to New Orleans. There, they could be stored until they were transferred to oceangoing ships for the journey east.

For a time, Americans shipped their goods through New Orleans peacefully. Then, in 1801, a crisis developed. Jefferson discovered that Spain had secretly given New Orleans and the rest of its Louisiana Territory to France.

**Vocabulary** *Builder*
crisis (KRĪ sihs) *n.* turning point or deciding event in history

Jefferson was alarmed by this development. The French ruler, Napoleon Bonaparte, had already set out to conquer Europe. Jefferson feared that he now intended to make France the first power in America as well. If Napoleon controlled Louisiana, the westward expansion of the United States would be blocked.

☑**Checkpoint**  **What important right did the United States gain with the Pinckney Treaty of 1795?**

# Buying Louisiana

Even before the transfer of Louisiana to France took place, America's position in Louisiana was threatened. In 1802, the Spanish governor of Louisiana withdrew the right of Americans to ship their goods through New Orleans. Westerners exploded in anger. They demanded that Jefferson go to war to win back their rights.

The situation was explosive. What would happen, Jefferson worried, when the French took over New Orleans?

**A Surprise Offer**  The President decided the best approach was to try to buy the city of New Orleans from the French. He sent his friend James Monroe to France to make a deal. Monroe had the help of Robert Livingston, the American minister in Paris. Jefferson instructed the two men to buy New Orleans and a territory to the east called West Florida.

In Paris, the Americans discovered an <u>altered</u> situation. A revolution led by Toussaint L'Ouverture (too SAN loo vehr TYOOR) had driven the French from their Caribbean colony of Haiti. Without Haiti as a base, the French would have trouble defending Louisiana in the event of a war. At the same time, tensions between France and Britain were again on the rise. War was looming and Napoleon needed money to support the war effort. France offered to sell the United States not only New Orleans but the *entire* Louisiana Territory.

It would take months to get Jefferson's advice. So Livingston and Monroe agreed to buy the whole Louisiana Territory for $15 million—about 4 cents an acre. This included an enormous area stretching from the Gulf of Mexico to Canada and from the Mississippi River to the Rocky Mountains.

**Main Idea**
The Louisiana Purchase gave the United States a vast area with untold wealth.

**Vocabulary** *Builder*
<u>alter</u> (AWL ter) *v.* to change in some way; to make different

**Haitian Independence**
Toussaint L'Ouverture (right) helped lead the Haitian struggle to expel the French.
**Critical Thinking:** *Analyze Cause and Effect  Why would France have trouble defending Louisiana if it did not control Haiti?*

# Exploring the Louisiana Purchase

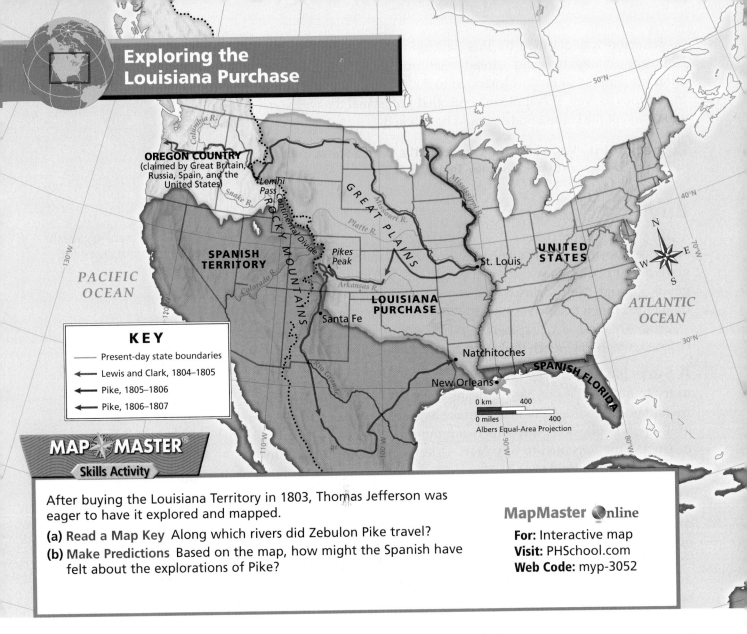

## KEY

— Present-day state boundaries
← Lewis and Clark, 1804–1805
← Pike, 1805–1806
← Pike, 1806–1807

**MAP MASTER**
**Skills Activity**

After buying the Louisiana Territory in 1803, Thomas Jefferson was eager to have it explored and mapped.

**(a) Read a Map Key** Along which rivers did Zebulon Pike travel?

**(b) Make Predictions** Based on the map, how might the Spanish have felt about the explorations of Pike?

**MapMaster Online**

**For:** Interactive map
**Visit:** PHSchool.com
**Web Code:** myp-3052

---

The Louisiana Purchase proved an amazing bargain for the United States. Its area almost doubled the size of the country. Although largely unexplored, the region clearly had millions of acres of fertile farmland and other natural resources. Ownership of Louisiana gave the United States control of the Mississippi River. As Livingston put it, "From this day, the United States take their place among the powers of the first rank."

**Jefferson's Dilemma** Jefferson was delighted with the deal. At the same time, he had a serious problem. The Constitution nowhere states that the President has the power to buy land from a foreign country. Adding the huge Louisiana Territory would dramatically change the character of the nation.

In the end, Jefferson decided that he did have authority to buy Louisiana. The Constitution, he reasoned, allowed the President to make treaties. The Senate approved the treaty and Congress quickly voted to pay for the land.

✓**Checkpoint** Why did President Jefferson hesitate to approve the purchase of the Louisiana Territory?

## Lewis and Clark Explore the West

In January 1803, even before the United States had bought Louisiana, Jefferson convinced Congress to spend $2,500 on a western expedition (eks puh DISH uhn). An **expedition** is a long and carefully organized journey.

Jefferson chose army captain Meriwether Lewis to lead the exploration. Lewis chose William Clark, also an army officer, as his coleader. The men were ordered to report back on the geography, plants, animals, and other natural features of the region.

The expedition also had other goals. Jefferson wanted Lewis and Clark to make contact with Native Americans who lived in the Louisiana Territory. The President also wanted Lewis and Clark to find out if a waterway existed between the Mississippi River and the Pacific Ocean.

**Into the Unknown** In the spring of 1804, Lewis and Clark left St. Louis and headed up the Missouri River. Their three boats carried tons of supplies and about 40 men. Most were Americans, although there were several French Canadians. The expedition also included an enslaved African American named York.

In mid-July, the party reached the mouth of the Platte River, a powerful tributary that flows into the Missouri. In early August, they met Native Americans for the first time. Three weeks later, the expedition reached the eastern edge of the Great Plains.

**Main Idea**
Lewis and Clark brought back valuable information on the area's people, plants, and animals.

## Links Across Time

1969 American astronauts Buzz Aldrin (shown here) and Neil Armstrong landed on the moon.

### Exploration

**1804–1806** Lewis and Clark explored the lands of the Louisiana Purchase. Their journals, maps, and drawings inspired the rapid settlement of the West.

**1960s** American explorers ventured into the "new frontier" of outer space. On July 20, 1969, the United States became the first nation to land a man on the moon. People around the world watched the landing on television.

### Link to Today

**Exploration Today** The United States has sent additional missions to the moon and beyond. What kinds of exploration are going on today?

**For:** Recent activities of the U.S. space program
**Visit:** PHSchool.com
**Web Code:** mvc-3052

**Explore More Video**
To learn more about Lewis and Clark's expedition, view the video.

**Lewis and Clark: A Hard Journey** At times during their travel up the Missouri River, members of the Lewis and Clark party had to carry their boats around rapids and falls. Here, Sacagawea, Clark, Lewis, and York examine the Great Falls in present-day Montana. **Critical Thinking: Apply Information** *What other hazards did Lewis and Clark face on their river voyages?*

In late October 1804, the expedition reached the territory of the Mandan people, in what is now North Dakota. Lewis and Clark decided to camp there for the winter. They were joined in camp by a French Canadian trader and his wife, a Native American named Sacagawea (sahk uh juh WEE uh). She was a Shoshone (shoh SHOH nee) who would travel with them and serve as translator.

**Crossing the Rockies** In April 1805, the party set out again. By summer they were in what is now Montana. They began to climb the Rockies. By August, they had reached the Continental Divide. A continental divide is the place on a continent that separates river systems flowing in opposite directions. The view to the west was beautiful but also deeply disappointing. Lewis had hoped to see a wide river that would take the group to the Pacific. Instead, all he saw were "immense ranges of mountains still to the west."

The next day, Lewis met a group of Shoshone warriors. When Sacagawea arrived to interpret, she was astonished to see that the Shoshone chief was her brother. She jumped up and threw her arms around him. Thanks to Sacagawea, the Shoshones agreed to sell the expedition horses that were needed to cross the mountains.

**At the Pacific** On the west side of the Rockies, Lewis and Clark reached the Columbia River. Here, they stopped to build canoes for the downriver voyage. At one point, they had to cross a 55-mile stretch of rapids and rough water. Finally, through a dense early November fog, they saw the Pacific Ocean.

The travelers spent the wet and gloomy winter of 1805–1806 near the point where the Columbia River flows into the Pacific. They began the return journey in March 1806. It took the party half a year to return to St. Louis. Their return, however, brought the American people a new awareness of a rich and beautiful part of the continent.

**Pike's Expedition** At the same time that Lewis and Clark were trekking back home, other Americans also hoped to learn more about the West. From 1805 to 1807, Zebulon Pike explored the southern part of the Louisiana Territory.

Pike led an expedition due west to the Rocky Mountains. There, he tried to climb a mountain that rose out of the Colorado plains. He made it about two thirds of the way to the top. Standing in snow up to his waist, he was forced to turn back. Today, this mountain is known as Pikes Peak.

Pike's return route took him into Spanish New Mexico. Early in 1807, Spanish troops arrested the members of the party as spies. The Spanish feared Pike was gathering information so that the Americans could take over the region. After several months of captivity, the men were released and escorted back to the United States. As the Spanish had feared, Pike's reports about the Spanish borderlands created great American interest in the region.

**Distinguish Events in Sequence**
What do the words "at the same time" tell you about the sequence of events? What was happening at the same time?

☑**Checkpoint** **What goals did President Jefferson set for Lewis and Clark's expedition?**

⭐ **Looking Back and Ahead** Lewis and Clark and Pike gave the United States detailed knowledge of the West. However, Americans had little time to digest this information. They soon found themselves caught up again in Europe's conflicts.

---

### Section 2 | Check Your Progress

**Progress Monitoring** ⬤nline
**For:** Self-test with instant help
**Visit:** PHSchool.com
**Web Code:** mya-3052

**Comprehension and Critical Thinking**

**1. (a) Recall** Why was New Orleans important to the United States?
**(b) Identify Benefits** What was the significance of the Louisiana Purchase?

**2. (a) Identify** Who was Sacagawea, and how was she important to the success of the Lewis and Clark expedition?
**(b) Compare and Contrast** How was Pike's expedition similar to that of Lewis and Clark's? How was it different?

**Reading Skill**

**3. Distinguish Events in Sequence** Describe how the sequence of Lewis and Clark's expedition related to that of Zebulon Pike.

**Vocabulary *Builder***

**4.** Draw a table with two rows and two columns. In the first column, list the key terms from this section: expedition, continental divide. In the next column, write the definition of each word.

**Writing**

**5.** Use this section and the following items to write a thesis statement about the life of Meriwether Lewis. **Items:** Born in 1774; Virginian; family friend of Jefferson; in 1792 asked by Jefferson to lead exploration of the Northwest; with Clark led expedition through Louisiana Territory; was appointed governor of Louisiana Territory in 1808; died mysteriously in 1809.

# Exploring the Louisiana Purchase

An atmosphere of eager anticipation filled the air as Meriwether Lewis and William Clark and their men set out to explore the vast lands that lay west of the Mississippi River. Use the map below to follow Lewis and Clark on their journey to the Pacific Ocean.

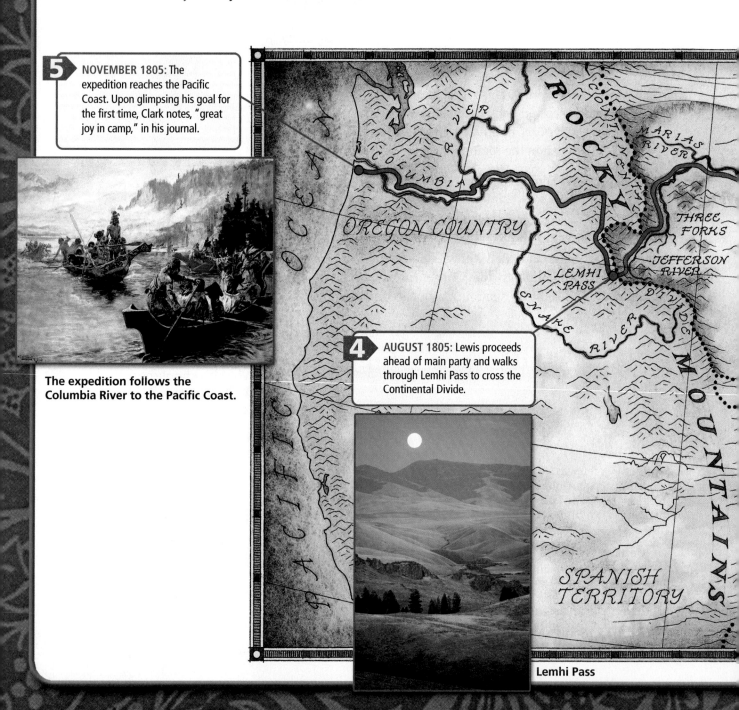

**5** NOVEMBER 1805: The expedition reaches the Pacific Coast. Upon glimpsing his goal for the first time, Clark notes, "great joy in camp," in his journal.

**The expedition follows the Columbia River to the Pacific Coast.**

**4** AUGUST 1805: Lewis proceeds ahead of main party and walks through Lemhi Pass to cross the Continental Divide.

Lemhi Pass

**William Clark**

**Clark's compass**

## Legacy of the Expedition

The explorers returned to St. Louis in 1806. Though the expedition was a success, it failed to excite the majority of Americans. Over time, however, the journey of Lewis and Clark contributed to a national feeling that Americans had a Manifest Destiny, a duty to expand west across the continent.

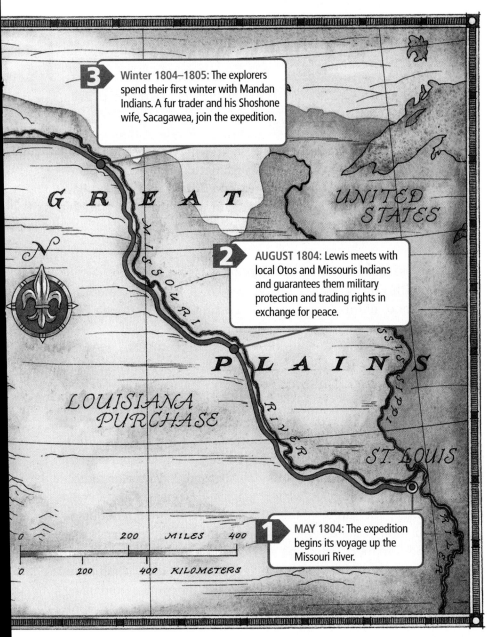

**3** Winter 1804–1805: The explorers spend their first winter with Mandan Indians. A fur trader and his Shoshone wife, Sacagawea, join the expedition.

GREAT

UNITED STATES

**2** AUGUST 1804: Lewis meets with local Otos and Missouris Indians and guarantees them military protection and trading rights in exchange for peace.

PLAINS

LOUISIANA PURCHASE

MISSOURI RIVER

MISSISSIPPI

ST. LOUIS

| 0 | 200 | MILES | 400 |
| 0 | 200 | 400 | KILOMETERS |

**1** MAY 1804: The expedition begins its voyage up the Missouri River.

RIVER

**Meriwether Lewis**

▲ A page from Lewis's journal

### Analyze GEOGRAPHY AND HISTORY

Write a journal entry that expresses Lewis and Clark's excitement about crossing the Continental Divide. How did the explorers know they were closer to their goal?

# A Time of Conflict

## Objectives

1. Discuss how the United States defeated the Barbary pirates.
2. Explain how war in Europe hurt American trade.
3. Discuss the causes and effects of the Embargo Act.
4. Identify the events leading up to the Battle of Tippecanoe.

## Prepare to Read

###  Reading Skill

**Explain How Events Are Related in Time** Many events that occur in sequence have cause-and-effect relationships. Explaining how events are related in time will help you find these cause-and-effect links. As you read this section, look for events that have this relationship.

### Vocabulary *Builder*

**High-Use Words**

decline, p. 324

restore, p. 326

**Key Terms and People**

tribute, p. 322

Stephen Decatur, p. 322

embargo, p. 324

smuggle, p. 324

Tecumseh, p. 326

William Henry Harrison, p. 326

⭐ **Background Knowledge** In the previous chapter, you learned how the United States under Washington and Adams became entangled in the dispute between France and Britain. That dispute did not go away. As you will learn, it rose again with added fury during the administration of Thomas Jefferson.

**Main Idea**
Threats to American shipping led the United States to capture Tripoli, stronghold of the Barbary pirates.

## Defeating the Barbary States

Trade with Europe was critical to the U.S. economy. Americans sold crops and natural resources to customers in Europe. They purchased manufactured goods made in Europe.

After the American Revolution, pirates began attacking American ships in the Mediterranean Sea. The pirates came from four small countries on the North African coast—Morocco, Algiers, Tunisia, and Tripoli. Together, these countries were known as the Barbary States.

**Explain How Events Are Related in Time**
Explain why the United States stopped paying tribute to the Barbary States.

Barbary pirates raided European and American ships, taking property and enslaving sailors and holding them for ransom. European governments stopped such raids by paying the Barbary States tribute—money paid by one country to another in return for protection. In exchange, their rulers agreed to leave European ships alone.

For a time, the United States also paid tribute. But Jefferson stopped this practice and sent warships to the Mediterranean Sea to protect American merchant ships. At first, these military patrols went badly. The warship *Philadelphia* ran aground near the Tripoli coast and its 300-man crew was imprisoned. To keep the pirates from using the ship, 60 American sailors led by Stephen Decatur raided Tripoli harbor and burned the *Philadelphia* down to the waterline.

The next year, a small force of American marines marched 600 miles across the Sahara and captured Tripoli. A line in the U.S. Marine Corps anthem—"To the shores of Tripoli"—recalls that victory. It inspired a wave of confidence in the ability of the United States to deal forcefully with foreign powers that threatened American security and prosperity.

☑**Checkpoint** **How did European nations protect themselves against raids by the Barbary pirates?**

## American Neutrality Is Challenged

A more serious threat to American overseas trade came from two much more powerful countries, Britain and France. By 1803, the two nations once again were at war. The United States remained neutral.

Because it was neutral, the United States continued trading with both Britain and France. The war in Europe had created opportunities for Americans to sell their products there.

Meanwhile, Britain and France looked for ways to weaken each other. One method was to cut off the other country's foreign trade. British warships started seizing American ships trading with France. French warships did the same to American ships trading with Britain. Between 1803 and 1807, France seized 500 American ships and Britain seized more than 1,000.

Britain badly needed sailors for its war against France. So it turned again to impressment. As a result, thousands of American sailors were forced to serve in the British navy.

**Main Idea**
Britain and France interfered with American shipping, increasing tensions between the United States and the two European nations.

**Impressment**
A nineteenth-century woodprint shows unfortunate American sailors being impressed by British gangs. Conditions on board British warships were harsh.
**Critical Thinking: *Draw Conclusions*** *What impact do you think impressment had on the performance of the British navy?*

## Carving Up the World

George III

Napoleon

**Reading Political Cartoons**

**Skills Activity**

Britain's King George III and French leader Napoleon Bonaparte are shown dividing the world in this American cartoon. Their rivalry drew the United States into a conflict it did not want to enter.

**(a) Identify Main Ideas** What portion of the globe is Napoleon taking? What portion is King George taking?

**(b) Detect Points of View** What do you think the cartoonist's opinion is of the two European leaders?

Beginning in 1805, Britain and France increased their efforts to attack trade with their foes. No matter what American merchant ships did, they risked being seized by either Britain or France.

☑**Checkpoint**   **What was impressment, and why did it anger Americans?**

**Main Idea**
The Embargo Act hurt the United States far more than it hurt Britain or France.

## Jefferson Responds With an Embargo

The President looked for peaceful methods to force Britain and France to respect American neutrality. He decided to use an embargo—a government order that forbids foreign trade. In 1807, Congress passed the Embargo Act. It imposed a total embargo on American ships sailing to any foreign port. Jefferson predicted that both countries would soon cease attacking American ships.

Things did not turn out as Jefferson expected. Indeed, the big loser proved to be the United States. In just one year, American exports fell from $109 million to $25 million. Prices of American crops declined, hurting farmers and planters. Tens of thousands of Americans lost their jobs.

**Vocabulary Builder**
decline (dee KLĪN) v. to gradually lose strength or power

Many Americans were outraged by the embargo. Anger was greatest in New England, where merchants depended heavily on foreign trade. Thousands of Americans turned to smuggling—the act of illegally importing or exporting goods—in order to evade the embargo.

Congress finally repealed the Embargo Act in 1809, just before Jefferson left office. Then, Congress passed a less severe law that reopened foreign trade with every country except Britain and France. The law stated that the United States would reopen trade with those countries when they started respecting America's trading rights as a neutral nation.

☑**Checkpoint** **Why did President Jefferson place an embargo on foreign goods in 1807?**

## Tecumseh and the Prophet

In the years after the Battle of Fallen Timbers, tens of thousands of settlers moved westward. Ohio became a state in 1803. Americans continued to push into new areas. They settled in the territory of Indiana and other lands farther west.

The tide of settlement had a grave impact on Native Americans. Diseases such as measles, smallpox, and influenza killed thousands of Native Americans who had never been exposed to such diseases before. Settlers took over large parts of the Native American hunting grounds. Deer and other animals the Native Americans depended on were driven away as farmers cleared the forests for planting. The Native American population decreased, and the power of their traditional leaders declined.

**Main Idea**
Native Americans led by Tecumseh resisted white settlement but suffered a severe setback at the Battle of Tippecanoe.

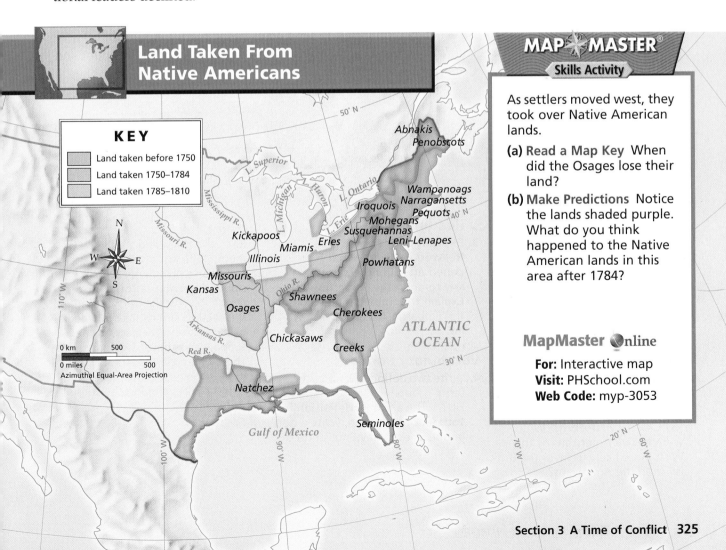

**Land Taken From Native Americans**

**KEY**
- Land taken before 1750
- Land taken 1750–1784
- Land taken 1785–1810

Abnakis
Penobscots
Wampanoags
Narragansetts
Iroquois    Pequots
Mohegans
Susquehannas
Eries    Leni–Lenapes
Miamis
Illinois
Powhatans
Kickapoos
Missouris
Kansas
Osages    Shawnees
Ohio R.
Cherokees
Chickasaws    ATLANTIC OCEAN
Creeks
Natchez
Seminoles
Gulf of Mexico

L. Superior
L. Michigan
L. Huron
L. Ontario
L. Erie
Mississippi R.
Missouri R.
Arkansas R.
Red R.

0 km 500
0 miles 500
Azimuthal Equal-Area Projection

**MAP MASTER®**
**Skills Activity**

As settlers moved west, they took over Native American lands.

**(a) Read a Map Key** When did the Osages lose their land?

**(b) Make Predictions** Notice the lands shaded purple. What do you think happened to the Native American lands in this area after 1784?

**MapMaster Online**

**For:** Interactive map
**Visit:** PHSchool.com
**Web Code:** myp-3053

**New Leaders Take Charge** The Shawnee people were hard hit by these developments. After 1805, two Shawnee brothers—Tenskwatawa (tehn SKWAH tuh wuh) and Tecumseh (tih KUHM suh)—began urging Native American resistance. Tecumseh and Tenskwatawa, who was also known as the Prophet, called on Native Americans to preserve traditional ways.

Tecumseh organized the western tribes into a league to <u>restore</u> Indian lands. He traveled widely spreading his message.

**Harrison's Victory** American officials were deeply concerned by Tecumseh's activities. William Henry Harrison, governor of the Indiana Territory, decided to take action. While Tecumseh was traveling in search of allies, Harrison marched a thousand soldiers against Shawnee villages on the Tippecanoe River. In the Battle of Tippecanoe, Harrison defeated the Native Americans.

The Battle of Tippecanoe marked the high point of Native American opposition to settlement. Even though the alliance declined in power after the battle, Tecumseh and his warriors continued their struggle during the next several years.

✓**Checkpoint** What actions did Tecumseh and the Prophet urge on their followers?

☆ **Looking Back and Ahead** Tensions remained high in the West even after Harrison's victory. Many Americans blamed the British, who continued to send arms to the Native Americans. There were widespread calls for war with Britain. Could the President and Congress resist them?

---

**Section 3** | **Check Your Progress**

**Progress Monitoring** Online
**For:** Self-test with instant help
**Visit:** PHSchool.com
**Web Code:** mya-3053

## Comprehension and Critical Thinking

1. **(a) Identify** Who were the Barbary pirates?
   **(b) Identify Costs** What was the United States risking when it refused to pay tribute to the Barbary pirates? Why do you think Jefferson believed it was worth the risk?

2. **(a) Describe** How did settlement in the West affect the Native Americans who lived there?
   **(b) Clarify Problems** Why were Native Americans of the West more likely to favor the British than the Americans?

## Reading Skill

3. **Explain How Events Are Related in Time** What happened after Congress passed a law to undo the Embargo Act? Explain the connection between the Embargo Act and the new law.

## Vocabulary *Builder*

4. Write two definitions for each key term: tribute, embargo, smuggle. First, write a formal definition for your teacher. Second, write a definition in everyday English for a classmate.

## Writing

5. Read the following thesis statement: "The last years of Thomas Jefferson's presidency were clouded by international problems." Review the information in this section and choose four facts or details from the section that support this thesis statement. Then, based on the supporting items you chose, write several sentences developing the thesis statement.

# The War of 1812

## Objectives

1. Explain why the United States declared war on Britain.

2. Describe what happened in the early days of the war.

3. Discuss the American invasion of Canada and the fighting in the South.

4. Identify the events leading to the end of the War of 1812.

## Prepare to Read

### Reading Skill

**Explain How Events Are Related in Time** Events can be related in time in many ways. One event may directly cause another or events may unfold over time. As you read this section, try to relate the many events to one another in time. Use the skills you practiced in Sections 1–3 as tools. Also, use sequence verbs as a tool. These verbs describe how events progress over time.

### Vocabulary *Builder*

**High-Use Words**

reinforce, p. 328

critic, p. 331

**Key Terms and People**

nationalism, p. 327

war hawk, p. 327

blockade, p. 328

Oliver Hazard Perry, p. 329

Andrew Jackson, p. 330

secede, p. 331

⭐ **Background Knowledge** In previous sections, you have learned how the first three U.S. Presidents worked hard to avoid war with Britain and France. In this section, you will learn why, despite these efforts, the United States finally went to war.

## The Move Toward War

Tension with Britain was high when James Madison took office in 1809. Americans were angry at Britain for arming Native Americans in the Northwest. Americans also resented the continued impressment of American sailors by the British.

To most Americans, the country's honor was at stake. They felt a new sense of American nationalism—pride in one's country. In 1810, two strong nationalists, Henry Clay of Kentucky and John C. Calhoun of South Carolina, became leaders in the House of Representatives.

Clay, Calhoun, and their supporters were called war hawks—those who were eager for war with Britain. Opposition to war was strongest in New England. Many New Englanders believed war with Britain would harm American trade.

Relations with Britain worsened steadily in the early months of 1812. In the spring, the British told the United States they would continue impressing sailors. Meanwhile, Native Americans in the Northwest began new attacks on frontier settlements. In June, Congress declared war on Britain.

✓**Checkpoint** In what regions of the United States was the support for war with Britain the strongest?

**Main Idea**

Led by the war hawks, Congress declared war on Britain in June 1812.

Andrew Jackson, a young war hawk

## Early Days of the War

The war did not come at a good time for the British, who were still at war in Europe. However, Britain was not willing to meet American demands to avoid war. Providing Native Americans with support was one way of protecting Canada against an American invasion.

When the war began, Americans were confident that they would win. It soon became apparent that the United States was not prepared for war. Jefferson's spending cuts had weakened American military strength. The navy had only 16 warships ready for action. The army also was small, with fewer than 7,000 men.

In the first days of the war, the British set up a blockade of the American coast. A **blockade** is the action of shutting a port or road to prevent people or supplies from coming into an area or leaving it. By 1814, the British navy had 135 warships blockading American ports. After reinforcing their troops, the British were able to close off all American ports by war's end.

A major sea battle was fought at the beginning of the war. In August 1812, the USS *Constitution* defeated the British warship *Guerrière* (gai ree AIR) in a fierce battle. According to tradition, American sailors nicknamed the *Constitution* "Old Ironsides" because British artillery fire bounced off the ship's thick wooden hull. To the Americans, it seemed as if the *Constitution* were made of iron.

✔**Checkpoint**  **Why was the United States unprepared for war?**

# "Old Ironsides"

**History** *Interactive*
**Explore
Old Ironsides**
**Visit:** PHSchool.com
**Web Code:** myp-3054

In the most famous sea battle of the War of 1812, the USS *Constitution* engaged the British frigate *Guerrière* in the North Atlantic Ocean.

For nearly an hour, the two ships closed in on each other. Then, the *Constitution* fired a barrage that tore off both of the *Guerrière* masts. Meanwhile, British cannonballs bounced harmlessly off the reinforced hull of the *Constitution*. **Critical Thinking:** *Identify Benefits How were ships like the* Constitution *helpful to the American naval effort?*

A cutaway of the ▶
*Constitution*'s hull.

The ship's hull, which was more than two feet thick at the waterline, was made up of three layers of extremely tough and durable oak wood.

USS *Constitution*

*Guerrière*

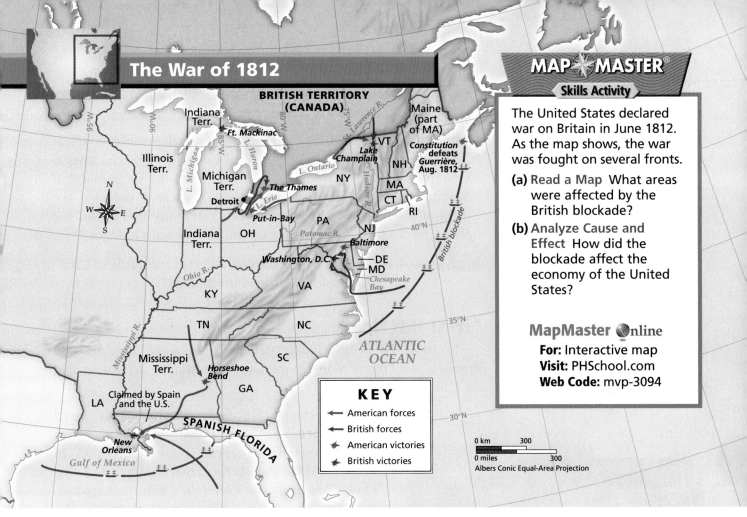

## The War of 1812

BRITISH TERRITORY (CANADA)

Indiana Terr.
Ft. Mackinac
Illinois Terr.
Michigan Terr.
L. Michigan
L. Huron
The Thames
Detroit
L. Erie
Put-in-Bay
Indiana Terr.
OH
Ohio R.
KY
TN
Mississippi Terr.
Horseshoe Bend
LA
Claimed by Spain and the U.S.
New Orleans
Gulf of Mexico
SPANISH FLORIDA
MS
GA
SC
NC
VA
Potomac R.
Washington, D.C.
Baltimore
Chesapeake Bay
DE
MD
NJ
PA
NY
Hudson R.
CT
RI
MA
NH
VT
Lake Champlain
L. Ontario
St. Lawrence R.
Maine (part of MA)
Constitution defeats Guerrière, Aug. 1812
ATLANTIC OCEAN
British blockade
40°N
35°N
30°N
95°W
90°W
85°W
80°W
75°W

### KEY
← American forces
← British forces
✴ American victories
✴ British victories

0 km 300
0 miles 300
Albers Conic Equal-Area Projection

**MAP MASTER**
**Skills Activity**

The United States declared war on Britain in June 1812. As the map shows, the war was fought on several fronts.

**(a) Read a Map** What areas were affected by the British blockade?

**(b) Analyze Cause and Effect** How did the blockade affect the economy of the United States?

**MapMaster Online**
**For:** Interactive map
**Visit:** PHSchool.com
**Web Code:** mvp-3094

## The War in the West and South

In the West, the Americans and British fought for control of the Great Lakes and the Mississippi River. Both sides had Native American allies.

**Invasion of Canada** Even before the war began, war hawks were demanding an invasion of Canada. They expected Canadians to welcome the chance to throw off British rule.

In July 1812, American troops under General William Hull invaded Canada from Detroit. Hull was unsure of himself. Fearing he did not have enough soldiers, he soon retreated.

The British commander, General Isaac Brock, took advantage of Hull's confusion. His army of British soldiers and Native American warriors quickly surrounded Hull's army and forced it to surrender. The British captured more than 2,000 American soldiers. It was a serious defeat for the United States.

American forces had better luck on Lake Erie. Both sides were aware of the importance of controlling the lake. A key three-hour battle took place at Put-In-Bay, in the western part of the lake, in 1813.

During the battle, the American flagship was badly damaged. The American commander, Oliver Hazard Perry, switched to another ship and continued the fight until it was won. Perry announced his victory with a dramatic message: "We have met the enemy and they are ours." With Americans in control of the lake, the British were forced to leave Detroit and retreat back into Canada.

**Main Idea**
Native Americans suffered severe setbacks during fighting in the West and South during 1814.

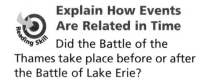
**Explain How Events Are Related in Time**
Did the Battle of the Thames take place before or after the Battle of Lake Erie?

As the British and their Native American allies retreated, the Americans under General William Henry Harrison pursued them. They followed the British into Canada, defeating them in the Battle of the Thames. Tecumseh was among those killed in the battle.

**Conflict in the South** Native Americans also suffered defeat in the South. In the summer of 1813, Creek warriors attacked several southern American settlements. Andrew Jackson took command of American forces in Georgia. In March 1814, Jackson defeated the Creeks at the Battle of Horseshoe Bend. The treaty that ended the fighting forced the Creeks to give up millions of acres of land.

☑**Checkpoint** **What is the connection between the Battle of Lake Erie and the Battle of the Thames?**

**Main Idea**
Although the War of 1812 had no clear victor, Americans gained new confidence after its end.

# Final Battles

In 1814, the British finally defeated Napoleon. This allowed Britain to send many more troops across the Atlantic to fight against the United States.

**The British Attack Washington and Baltimore** The new British strategy was to attack the nation's capital, Washington, D.C. In August 1814, a British force marched into the city. Dolley Madison, the President's wife, gathered up the President's important papers and fled the White House. The British set fire to several government buildings, including the White House. Americans were shocked to learn that their army could not defend Washington.

The British now moved on to Baltimore. Their first objective was Fort McHenry, which defended the city's harbor. British warships bombarded the fort throughout the night of September 13, 1814. Francis Scott Key, a young American, watched the attack. At dawn, Key saw the American flag still flying over the fort. The Americans had beaten off the attack.

On the back of an old envelope, Key wrote a poem that he called "The Star-Spangled Banner." It told the story of his night's watch. The poem became popular and was set to music. In 1931, Congress made it the national anthem of the United States.

**The War Ends** By 1814, Britain had tired of war. Peace talks began in Ghent (gehnt), Belgium. On Christmas Eve 1814, the two sides signed the Treaty of Ghent, which ended the war. The treaty returned things to the way they had been before the war.

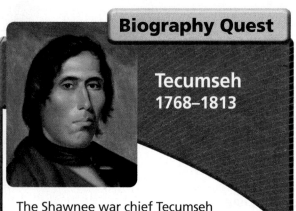

## Biography Quest

### Tecumseh
### 1768–1813

The Shawnee war chief Tecumseh challenged the tide of white settlement. Tecumseh visited Native Americans from the Great Lakes to Florida, urging them to unite. He was away recruiting when General Harrison defeated the Shawnee at Tippecanoe. After the battle, Tecumseh allied his forces with the British, hoping that a British victory would mean the return of Native American lands. His death at the Battle of the Thames dealt a blow to Native American resistance.

**Biography Quest** ⬤**nline**

**Why did Tecumseh issue an angry challenge to his allies, the British?**

**For:** The answer to the question about Tecumseh
**Visit:** PHSchool.com
**Web Code:** myd-3054

# Building the National Economy

After 1815, many Americans believed the federal government should take action to increase economic prosperity in all regions of the country. Even the Republicans began to see merit in certain federal programs. This was a change, because in previous years Republicans had been known for stressing states' rights. Support for federal measures to promote economic prosperity came from many regions.

These beliefs were expressed by a number of bright young members of Congress from different regions. Outstanding among those who favored federal action were Henry Clay of Kentucky, John C. Calhoun of South Carolina, and Daniel Webster of Massachusetts.

- Clay spoke for people in the West who thought the country needed better roads and canals to transport goods from one region to another.

- Calhoun spoke for the interests of the South. While first a defender of national unity, he later put more emphasis on the idea of states' rights.

- Webster became a spokesperson for the Northeast. At first, he opposed high tariffs, but he later came to support them as a way of protecting industry.

**Main Idea**
Congress and the President encouraged U.S. manufacturing with high tariffs and a second Bank of the United States.

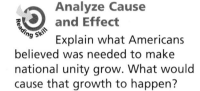

**Analyze Cause and Effect**
Explain what Americans believed was needed to make national unity grow. What would cause that growth to happen?

Henry Clay

Daniel Webster

NORTH

WEST

SOUTH

John C. Calhoun

# New Leaders Speak for Their Regions

During the Era of Good Feelings, three young members of Congress became spokespersons for their regions.

**Daniel Webster - Massachusetts**
*He supported tariffs because they allowed New England's factories to compete against European manufacturers.*

**John C. Calhoun - South Carolina**
*He opposed tariffs because they raised the price of goods that southerners bought.*

**Henry Clay - Kentucky**
*He supported the construction of roads and canals because they would enable the three regions of the country to trade with one another.*

**Critical Thinking:** *Apply Information Which of the three leaders would you expect to be the strongest supporter of slavery? Explain.*

341

## Links to Economics

### How Tariffs Work

By increasing the cost of imported goods, tariffs helped U.S. manufacturers to compete with foreign manufacturers. But the higher prices hurt consumers. **Critical Thinking:** *Identify Economic Costs* Why was the cost of cloth higher in the United States than in Britain?

**History** *Interactive*

**Find Out How Tariffs Work**

**Visit:** PHSchool.com
**Web Code:** myp-3061

|  | United States | Great Britain |
|---|---|---|
| Cost of cloth | $6.00 | $5.00 |
| Cost to manufacture final product | $0.85 | $0.50 |
| Shipping costs | $0.20 | $0.25 |
| Tariff | — | $1.50 |
| Total | **$7.05** | **$7.25** |

**The Second Bank of the United States** As you have read, Congress passed a law in 1791 creating the first Bank of the United States. In 1811, the Bank ceased to exist. Its charter—a legal document giving certain rights to a person or company—had run out. Without the Bank, the economy suffered. State banks made too many loans and issued too much money. This caused an increase in spending and led to rising prices.

To cure these problems, Congress established the second Bank of the United States in 1816. Like the first Bank, the new Bank was privately owned and had a charter to operate for twenty years. It lent money to individuals and controlled the money supply. This gave a boost to American businesses.

**The Tariff of 1816** Another problem the nation faced after the War of 1812 was foreign competition. Most British goods had been kept out of the United States by the Embargo Act and the War of 1812. This helped American industry grow rapidly. New American factories made textiles, smelted iron, and produced many other products.

After the War of 1812, British manufacturers looked to sell their goods in the United States. They could still produce goods more cheaply than the Americans because they had well-established factories and more customers. This gave the British an opportunity to drive their American competitors out of business by dumping their goods in the United States. Dumping is selling goods in another country below market prices.

British dumping caused dozens of New England businesses to fail. As their investments collapsed, angry factory owners turned to Congress for help. They demanded protective tariffs to raise the price of foreign goods.

Congress responded with the Tariff of 1816, which put a tax on foreign textiles, iron, leather goods, paper, and other products. In 1818 and 1824, Congress passed even higher tariffs.

These tariffs were popular in the North, where most factories were located. However, the tariffs were deeply resented in the South, where they forced southerners to pay more for their goods. John C. Calhoun became a bitter foe of tariffs. He argued that they made northern manufacturers rich at the expense of the South.

### Clay's American System

As the debate over tariffs raged, Henry Clay came up with a plan that he believed would help the economy of each section of the country. He called his plan the American System. It proposed high tariffs and a federal program of public works.

Clay believed that high tariffs helped all regions of the country, not just the North. According to Clay, the wealth produced by tariffs would enable northerners to buy farm products from the West and the South. The tariff also would provide revenue for the federal government. The government could then use the money to build up the infrastructure—roads, bridges, and canals—in the South and West.

Clay's American System never fully became government policy. Presidents Madison and Monroe both refused to support some of Clay's projects. Also, southerners continued to oppose protective tariffs. They were not convinced by Clay's argument that high tariffs would aid the South in the long run.

✔**Checkpoint** **According to Henry Clay, how would his American System benefit the economy?**

**British Leather Boots**
The U.S. tariff on imports such as leather goods helped New England manufacturers to compete.

**Vocabulary** *Builder*
**infrastructure** (IHN frah struhk chahr) *n.* basic public works, like bridges and roads, needed for a society to function

# Three Important Supreme Court Rulings

The Supreme Court also promoted national economic growth and the power of the federal government during this era. Led by Chief Justice John Marshall, a Federalist sympathizer, the Court issued a series of important rulings between 1819 and 1824.

In *McCulloch* v. *Maryland* (1819), the Court protected the second Bank of the United States. The case grew out of an attempt by the state of Maryland to put a tax on the branch of the Bank operating in that state. The Bank refused to pay the tax.

The Court's 1819 decision, written by Marshall, strengthened the power of the federal government. It ruled that states had no power to interfere with federal institutions. A tax, said the Court, was a dangerous interference because "the power to tax involves the power to destroy." Moreover, according to Marshall, a state cannot pass any law that violates a federal law. This reasoning would be used in future years to expand the power of the federal government.

**Main Idea**
A number of Supreme Court rulings strengthened the federal government and supported economic growth.

**Interstate Commerce**

No individual state could grant a monopoly to a steamboat company to use a river that divides two states, the Supreme Court ruled in *Gibbons* v. *Ogden.*

Two other decisions helped shape American life. In *Dartmouth College* v. *Woodward* (1819), the Court ruled that the charter of Dartmouth College in New Hampshire was a private contract. A contract is an agreement between two or more parties that can be enforced by law. Since the Constitution protected private contracts, New Hampshire could not change Dartmouth's charter. In protecting private contracts, the Court was protecting private businesses. In doing that, it helped promote capitalism—the economic system in which privately owned businesses compete in a free market.

In *Gibbons* v. *Ogden* (1824), the Court again supported federal power. It ruled that New York State could not give a steamboat company a monopoly to carry passengers on the Hudson River. The Court pointed out that travel on the Hudson River included stops in New Jersey as well as New York. Therefore, it was interstate commerce—trade between two or more states. Under the Constitution, only Congress can regulate interstate commerce. Again, the Court had strengthened the federal government at the expense of the states.

**✓Checkpoint** How did the Supreme Court ruling in *Dartmouth College* v. *Woodward* support economic growth?

⭐ **Looking Back and Ahead** Americans turned their attention to economic growth after the War of 1812. But while Americans were debating Henry Clay's American System, events in Latin America were drawing the concern of American leaders.

---

**Section 1** | **Check Your Progress**

**Progress Monitoring** ⬤nline
**For:** Self-test with instant help
**Visit:** PHSchool.com
**Web Code:** mya-3061

**Comprehension and Critical Thinking**

1. **(a) Recall** Which groups supported and which opposed tariffs?
**(b) Draw Conclusions** Do you think the American System offered a good solution to regional differences? Explain.

2. **(a) Recall** What did *McCulloch* v. *Maryland* decide?
**(b) Compare** What did the Supreme Court decisions in *McCulloch* v. *Maryland* and *Gibbons* v. *Ogden* have in common?

**Reading Skill**

3. **Analyze Cause and Effect** Reread the text following the headings "The Tariff of 1816" and "Clay's American System." What did Clay believe would result from high tariffs?

**Vocabulary** *Builder*

Fill in the blanks with the correct key terms.

4. To set up the Bank of the United States, the government granted it a _____.

5. Private businesses compete in the American economic system called _____.

**Writing**

6. Decide which is the best closing sentence for an essay on James Monroe. Explain your choice.
**Sentences:**

(a) James Monroe, the fifth President of the United States, won two landslide victories.

(b) Clearly, James Monroe deserved to have his presidency called the Era of Good Feelings.

(c) James Monroe is, without a doubt, one of the greatest men ever elected President.

# Dealing With Other Nations

## Objectives

1. Explain why Spain ceded Florida to the United States.

2. Describe how Spanish territories in the Americas gained independence.

3. Explain why the Monroe Doctrine was issued.

4. Discuss how Canada became self-governing.

## Prepare to Read

### ◉ Reading Skill

**Identify Multiple Effects** As you read about historical events, note that some events have multiple, or more than one, effects. Several effects may happen at the same time or one effect may lead to the next. As you read this section, look for multiple effects of each event.

### Vocabulary *Builder*

**High-Use Words**

**province**, p. 346
**domestic**, p. 348

**Key Terms and People**

cede, p. 345
Miguel Hidalgo, p. 346
Simón Bolívar, p. 346
James Monroe, p. 347
John Quincy Adams, p. 347
self-government, p. 348

⭐ **Background Knowledge** In the previous section, you learned how the United States dealt with problems at home after 1815. In this section, you will learn why the United States took a firm position in challenging European influence in the Americas.

## Relations With Spain

At the time of the War of 1812, the United States and Haiti were the only parts of the Americas not under European control. Spain controlled more territory in the Americas than any other European country. However, Spain's power had steadily weakened over several hundred years.

Spain's control was especially weak in Florida. Spain could not stop enslaved African Americans who escaped from plantations in Georgia and Alabama from crossing into Florida. Once in Florida, many of the escapees joined the Seminole Nation. The Seminoles often crossed into the United States to raid American settlements.

In 1817, the U.S. government sent Andrew Jackson to recapture those who had escaped slavery. Jackson attacked and destroyed Seminole villages. He then went far beyond his orders. He seized two important Spanish towns and forced the governor to flee Florida.

Jackson's attack on Florida showed that the United States could take over Florida whenever it wanted. Since Spain could not protect Florida, it decided to give up the territory. In the Adams-Onís Treaty of 1819, Spain ceded, or gave up, Florida to the United States.

☑**Checkpoint** What effect did Andrew Jackson's attack on Florida have on the government of Spain?

**Main Idea**
Spain's inability to defend Florida led it to turn the colony over to the United States.

◉ **Identify Multiple Effects**
Spain's control was especially weak in Florida. What were all the effects of this situation?

# Spanish Colonies Win Independence

By 1810, opposition to Spanish rule ran strong in Spain's American colonies. The American and French revolutions had inspired Latin Americans to want to control their own affairs. Revolutionary movements were growing in almost all of the Spanish colonies. Spain seemed unable to control the pressure for change in Latin America.

**Mexico Breaks Away** Mexico's struggle for independence began in 1810. In that year, Father Miguel Hidalgo (ee DAHL goh) organized an army of Native Americans that freed several Mexican <u>provinces</u>. However, in 1811, Hidalgo was captured and executed by troops loyal to Spain.

Another revolution broke out in Mexico in 1820. This time, Spain was unable to end the fighting. In 1821, Spain agreed to Mexico's independence.

At first, Mexico was ruled by an emperor. Then, in 1823, the monarchy was overthrown. A new constitution, patterned after the United States Constitution, made Mexico a federal republic of nineteen states and four territories.

**Independence for South and Central America** South America, too, was affected by revolutionary change. Here, the best-known leader of the struggle for independence from Spain was Simón Bolívar (see MOHN boh LEE vahr).

**New Nations of Latin America**

**MAP MASTER®**
**Skills Activity**

Wars of independence led to the creation of many new countries in Latin America in the first half of the 1800s.

**(a) Read a Map** What parts of Latin America remained colonies of European nations?

**(b) Apply Information** Use the world map in the Atlas in this textbook to identify how the border between the United States and Mexico has changed.

**MapMaster** Online

**For:** Interactive map
**Visit:** PHSchool.com
**Web Code:** myp-3062

KEY
New nations
European colonies

0 km    2,000
0 miles    2,000
Azimuthal Equal-Area Projection

Bolívar is often called the Liberator for his role in leading independence movements in the northern part of South America. In August 1819, he led an army on a daring march from Venezuela over the ice-capped Andes Mountains and into Colombia. There, he defeated the Spanish and became president of the independent Republic of Great Colombia. It included today's nations of Venezuela, Colombia, Ecuador, and Panama.

Farther north, the people of Central America declared their independence from Spain in 1821. Two years later, they formed the United Provinces of Central America. It included today's nations of Nicaragua, Costa Rica, El Salvador, Honduras, and Guatemala.

In 1822, Brazil announced its independence from Portugal. Soon after, the United States recognized the independence of Mexico and six other former colonies in Central and South America. By 1825, most parts of Latin America had thrown off European rule.

✓Checkpoint **Why was Miguel Hidalgo important to the history of Mexico?**

## Links Across Time

### Beyond the Monroe Doctrine

**1823** The Monroe Doctrine warned European nations not to interfere in Latin America.

**1900s** U.S. Presidents cited the Monroe Doctrine to justify armed actions in Latin America. The actions often angered Latin Americans.

**1930s** President Franklin D. Roosevelt launched a Good Neighbor Policy. It stressed cooperation and trade to promote U.S. interests in the hemisphere.

### Link to Today  nline

**Connection to Today** What is the state of our relations with the countries of Latin America today?

**For:** U.S. relations with Latin America today
**Visit:** PHSchool.com
**Web Code:** myc-3062

## The Monroe Doctrine

The future of these new countries was soon clouded. Several European powers, including France and Russia, indicated that they might help Spain regain its colonies.

This worried President James Monroe and Secretary of State John Quincy Adams. It also worried the British. Both nations wanted to protect trade with Latin America. In 1823, Britain suggested that the two countries issue a joint statement. The statement would announce their determination to protect the freedom of the new nations of Latin America.

Adams told President Monroe he thought the United States should take action alone. He believed a joint statement would make the United States look like Britain's junior partner. Monroe agreed.

In a message to Congress in December 1823, the President stated what is known as the Monroe Doctrine. The United States would not allow European nations to create American colonies or interfere with the free nations of Latin America. The United States would consider any attempt to do so "dangerous to our peace and safety."

At the time, the United States was not strong enough to block European action. Only the British navy could do that. As U.S. power grew, however, the Monroe Doctrine boosted the influence of the United States in the region.

✓Checkpoint **What was Adams's advice to Monroe?**

**Main Idea**
In the Monroe Doctrine, the United States warned European nations against reestablishing colonies in Latin America.

# Relations With Canada

Canada remained a British colony after the American Revolution. In 1791, the country was divided into two parts. Upper Canada was mainly English, and Lower Canada was mainly French. In 1837, there were rebellions against British rule in both parts of Canada.

Although the British put down the rebellions, they learned a lesson. They could no longer deny rights to Canadians. Britain would have to give Canadians more powers of self-government—the right of people to rule themselves independently. The Act of Union of 1841 was a major step in that direction. It merged Canada's two parts into a single unit governed by a Canadian legislature. Britain, however, still had ultimate control.

Canada and the United States had their own disagreements. Tensions were particularly high when the United States unsuccessfully tried to invade Canada during the War of 1812.

The situation slowly improved after the war. Between 1818 and 1846, the United States and Britain settled several border disputes regarding Canada. Eventually, the United States and Canada established excellent relations. Their relations remain strong to this day.

☑**Checkpoint** Why did Britain grant some self-government to Canada?

☆ **Looking Back and Ahead** The Monroe Doctrine convinced Americans that their southern borders were safe from European expansion. Treaties with Britain lessened the tensions along the northern border with Canada. With a new sense of confidence, Americans prepared to make great strides on the domestic front. The 1820s and 1830s would see an upsurge in the democratic spirit.

**Vocabulary** *Builder*
domestic (doh MEHS tihk) *adj.*
relating to one's country; internal

---

Section 2 | **Check Your Progress**

**Progress Monitoring** ⊕nline
**For:** Self-test with instant help
**Visit:** PHSchool.com
**Web Code:** mya-3062

## Comprehension and Critical Thinking

**1. (a) Summarize** What was the Monroe Doctrine?
**(b) Clarify Problems** Would the United States have looked weak if it had jointly issued a warning with Britain? Explain.

**2. (a) List** Name six of today's Latin American countries that were independent by 1825.
**(b) Identify Economic Benefits** How did Great Britain and the United States benefit from the independence of Spain's American colonies?

## ⟳ Reading Skill
**3. Identify Multiple Effects** European powers, such as France and Russia, considered helping Spain regain its South and Central American colonies. What were the effects of this situation? Reread the text under the heading "The Monroe Doctrine."

## Vocabulary *Builder*
Answer the following questions in complete sentences that show your understanding of the key terms.
**4.** What did Spain cede to the United States in the Adams-Onís Treaty?

**5.** How did Canadians benefit when Britain granted them more self-government?

## Writing
**6.** Revise the following sentences to make them flow better. **Sentences:** The Monroe Doctrine stated that the United States would not allow Spain to take back its former colonies. The doctrine helped the new Latin American states remain free. The doctrine supported the cause of democracy in the Western Hemisphere.

## Objectives

1. Discuss the conflict between Andrew Jackson and John Quincy Adams over the election of 1824.

2. Explain how the right to vote expanded in the United States.

3. Describe Andrew Jackson's victory in the election of 1828.

## Prepare to Read

### Reading Skill

**Identify Short-Term Effects**
Some events have effects that take place shortly after the event. Other events create changes that last only a short time. Both of these types of effects are short-term effects. As you read Section 3, look for examples of the short-term effects of events.

### Vocabulary *Builder*

**High-Use Words**
participate, p. 349
react, p. 350

**Key Terms and People**
Andrew Jackson, p. 349
suffrage, p. 351
caucus, p. 352
nominating convention, p. 352
spoils system, p. 354

⭐ **Background Knowledge** Earlier, you read how one party dominated the political scene during the Era of Good Feelings. In this section, you will learn how important changes in American political life during the 1820s and 1830s led to an era of vigorous competition in political life.

## Adams and Jackson in Conflict

Andrew Jackson served two terms as President, from 1829 to 1837. His presidency marked the opening of a new and more democratic era in American political life. So great was his influence that the twenty-year period after he became President is often called the Age of Jackson.

Andrew Jackson was a wealthy man by the time he became President. However, he began life with very little. Born in a log cabin on the border of North and South Carolina, he was an orphan by the age of 14. Jackson was ambitious, brave, and tough. He survived smallpox as a child and severe gunshot wounds as an adult.

During a difficult march with his troops in 1812, one soldier described him as "tough as hickory." Hickory trees are extremely strong, and their wood is very hard. The description fit Jackson so well that it stuck as a nickname. Jackson became known as Old Hickory.

Jackson stood for the idea that ordinary people should <u>participate</u> in American political life. As a general and later as President, Andrew Jackson was deeply loved by millions of ordinary Americans. They loved him for his humble beginnings and his firm leadership.

**Main Idea**
Andrew Jackson was deeply loved by millions of Americans. John Quincy Adams never won the trust of the American people.

**Vocabulary** *Builder*
**participate** (pahr TIHS ah payt) *v.* to take part in; to share in an activity

**The Election of 1824** Jackson first ran for President in 1824. His opponents were John Quincy Adams, Henry Clay, and William H. Crawford of Georgia. Jackson received the most electoral votes, but not a majority. According to the Constitution, the House of Representatives would have to decide the election.

The choice was between Jackson and Adams, the two who had received the most votes. As Speaker of the House, Clay had great influence. He told his supporters to vote for Adams. The House then elected Adams on the first ballot.

Jackson <u>reacted</u> with fury. He had won the most popular votes and the most electoral votes, but still had lost the election. When Adams appointed Clay secretary of state, Jackson's supporters claimed the two men had made a "corrupt bargain."

**The Presidency of John Quincy Adams** Adams was burdened by the charges of a secret deal. He accomplished little, even though he had ambitious plans for the nation. He supported Clay's American System and wanted the federal government to play a larger role in supporting the American economy.

Adams proposed a national program to build roads and canals and a high tariff to protect industry. He also planned to set up a national university and an observatory for astronomers in Washington, D.C. However, he lacked the political skill to push his programs through Congress. Adams never won the trust of the American people. As a result, he served only one term.

**Vocabulary** *Builder*
<u>react</u> (ree AKT) *v.* to act in response to another action

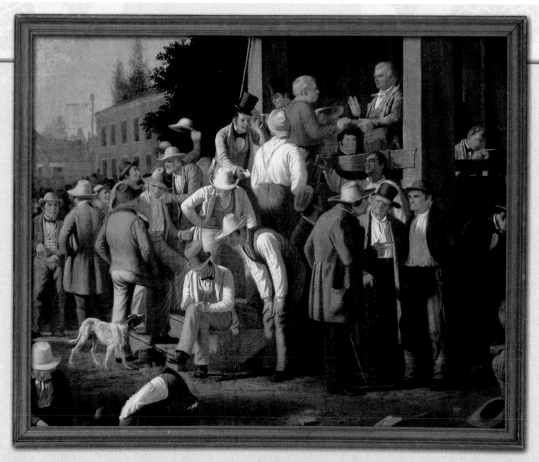

▲ *The County Election*, George Caleb Bingham

Despite his failures, Adams was an eloquent supporter of what he saw as America's special place in the world. He stated his ideas in a Fourth of July speech in 1821. He said the United States had no designs on the territory of other nations:

> "Wherever the standard of freedom and independence has been or shall be unfurled, there will her [America's] heart, . . . and her prayers be. But she goes not abroad in search of monsters to destroy. She is the well-wisher to the freedom and independence of all."
>
> —John Quincy Adams, Fourth of July 1821 Address

☑**Checkpoint** Why did Jackson's supporters claim there had been a "corrupt bargain" in the election of 1824?

## A New Era in Politics

The election of 1824 disappointed Andrew Jackson and his followers. Still, that election began a new era in American politics.

Back in the 1790s, states had begun extending suffrage—the right to vote. Many states dropped the requirement that men had to own property to be able to vote. Voting requirements varied slightly from state to state. However, almost all adult white males now could vote and hold office.

**Main Idea**
A growing spirit of democracy resulted in more white American males gaining the right to vote.

# *Democracy in Action*

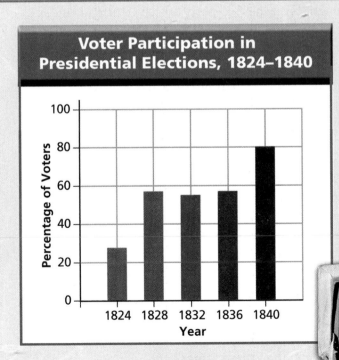

**Voter Participation in Presidential Elections, 1824–1840**

The Age of Jackson saw the first stirrings of democracy in action in the United States. More men could and did vote, and many more people joined political parties and participated in election campaigns.

It would be many years until women and African Americans also gained the right to vote. However, the kinds of political contests that are familiar to Americans today had their beginnings in the presidential elections of the 1820s and 1830s. **Critical Thinking:** *Draw Conclusions Why would people become more actively involved in political campaigns as the right to vote was extended to new groups?*

◄ Portrait of Andrew Jackson shown inside a souvenir box from an early presidential campaign.

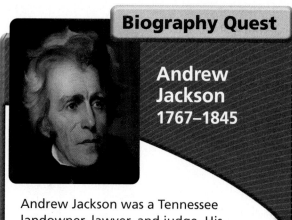

### Andrew Jackson
### 1767–1845

Andrew Jackson was a Tennessee landowner, lawyer, and judge. His military campaigns against the British in the War of 1812 and against Native Americans in Florida made him a war hero. Political opponents called him a country hick. But supporters admired him as a self-made man who spoke out for ordinary people. His election as President was a sign that the United States was becoming a more democratic nation.

**Biography Quest**

**How did Jackson gain a reputation as a supporter of ordinary people?**

**For:** The answer to the question about Jackson

**Visit:** PHSchool.com

**Web Code:** myd-3063

States also were changing how they chose presidential electors. Previously, state legislatures chose them. Now, that right went to the voters. In 1824, voters chose the presidential electors in 18 out of 24 states.

Of course, suffrage was still restricted in the United States. Women could not participate in government. Nor could enslaved African Americans, male or female. In most states, even free African Americans could not vote.

### Democracy in the Age of Jackson

Extending the right to vote was part of a larger spread of democratic ideas. Supporters of Andrew Jackson believed that ordinary people should vote in elections, hold public office, and do anything else they had the ability to do. Jackson's supporters strongly opposed special privileges for those of high social status.

Wealthy observers were sometimes dismayed by this spirit of equality. One visitor complained, "the rich and the poor, the educated and the ignorant, the polite and the vulgar, all . . . feed at the same table."

Jackson and his supporters did not trust government. They believed it often favored the rich and powerful. The Jacksonians also were suspicious of banks, which they believed favored the rich.

**New Political Parties** The Age of Jackson brought back the two-party system that had briefly ended during the Era of Good Feelings. During the 1824 election, the Republican Party split. Supporters of Adams called themselves National Republicans. Jackson's supporters used the name Democrats.

In 1831, the National Republicans nominated Henry Clay to run against Jackson. Jackson won easily, with strength in all parts of the country. However, by 1836, the anti-Jackson forces had formed a new party, the Whigs. From then until 1852, the Democrats and the Whigs were the country's two major political parties.

The new parties adopted a new way of choosing their presidential candidates. Previously, a party's members of Congress held a caucus—a meeting of members of a political party. These caucuses involved only a small group of people. Beginning in 1831, political parties started holding national nominating conventions—large meetings of party delegates to choose candidates for office. National conventions opened the nominating process to many more people and made it more democratic.

### Identify Short-Term Effects

What was the immediate effect of using nominating conventions to choose presidential candidates?

☑ Checkpoint    **Which groups did not benefit from increased suffrage in the United States?**

# Jackson Becomes President

Three times as many people voted in the election of 1828 as had voted in 1824. Most of these new voters supported Jackson, who easily defeated Adams.

The election revealed growing sectional and class divisions among American voters. Jackson did best in the West and the South, where planters and small farmers supported him. He also did well among small business people, artisans, and workers in cities and towns nationwide. Adams was most popular in his home region of New England.

**Jackson's Inauguration** Jackson's supporters called the election a victory for the "common man." His inauguration in March 1829 showed what they meant. Thousands of ordinary working people jammed into Washington for the event. After the inauguration at the Capitol, Jackson rode a horse to the White House. A journalist described the scene:

> **❝**As far as the eye could reach, the sidewalks of the Avenue were covered with people on foot . . . with . . . carriages and persons on horseback. . . . For a full half hour, I stood waiting for the stream to run by; but like a never failing fountain people continued pouring forth.**❞**
>
> —Amos Kendall in the *Argus of Western America*, March 29, 1829

**Main Idea**
Andrew Jackson's victory in 1828 was a result of widespread support among farmers, workers, and artisans.

**Jackson's Inauguration**
Joyful crowds welcomed Andrew Jackson to the White House upon his inauguration in 1829. The artist who created this picture made sly fun of the celebrants. **Critical Thinking: Apply Information** *Why were some people upset by what happened at Jackson's inauguration?*

Twenty thousand people crowded in and around the White House for a reception in Jackson's honor. They did not all behave well. Some broke furniture, spilled drinks, trampled rugs, and broke several thousand dollars worth of glassware and dishes. Officials finally lured the unruly crowd outside by moving the punch bowl onto the White House lawn.

Jackson's opponents were shocked. One member of the Supreme Court complained about the "reign of King Mob." A Jackson supporter saw things more positively: "It was the People's day, and the People's President, and the People would rule."

**The Spoils of Victory** Jackson began his term by replacing some government officials with his supporters. Previous Presidents had done the same thing. In fact, during his two terms Jackson replaced only about 20 percent of federal officeholders.

The difference was that Jackson openly defended what he was doing. He claimed putting new people into government jobs furthered democracy. One of his supporters put it more selfishly when he compared the process to a conquering army after a war, saying "to the victors belong the spoils [loot]." People quickly applied the term **spoils system** to the practice of rewarding government jobs to loyal supporters of the party that wins an election.

☑**Checkpoint** How did Andrew Jackson justify the spoils system?

⭐ **Looking Back and Ahead** As President, Andrew Jackson supported the right of ordinary people to participate in government. Jackson's belief in equality, however, left out many, including Native Americans. In the next section, you will read how government policies denied basic rights to Native Americans.

---

Section 3 | **Check Your Progress**

**Progress Monitoring** ●nline
**For:** Self-test with instant help
**Visit:** PHSchool.com
**Web Code:** mya-3063

**Comprehension and Critical Thinking**

**1. (a) Recall** What was the "corrupt bargain"?
**(b) Evaluate Information** Who benefited from accusations of a "corrupt bargain"?

**2. (a) Recall** How did the United States become more democratic between the 1790s and the 1830s?
**(b) Draw Conclusions** How did these democratic changes contribute to Jackson's election in 1828?

**Reading Skill**

**3. Identify Short-Term Effects** What was the immediate effect when Henry Clay told his supporters to vote for Adams?

**Vocabulary Builder**

Read each sentence below. If the sentence is true, write YES. If the sentence is not true, write NO and explain why.

**4.** By 1828, suffrage had been extended to white women and African Americans.

**5.** In 1824, a nominating convention chose John Quincy Adams to run for President.

**6.** Tens of thousands of ordinary citizens showed up for the caucus celebrating Jackson's victory.

**Writing**

**7.** Using vivid, specific words will make your writing livelier and more accurate. Rewrite these sentences using more specific, colorful words. **Sentences:** Many people liked Andrew Jackson, and he was very popular. People liked Jackson better than John Quincy Adams. They felt Jackson was a man of the people and Adams was not a man of the people.

# Indian Removal

## Prepare to Read

### 🔁 Reading Skill

**Identify Long-Term Effects** Many historical events have long-term effects—lasting effects that build up over time. As you read Section 4, look for events that have long-term effects. Think about why these causes have had such a lasting effect.

### Vocabulary *Builder*

**High-Use Words**
voluntary, p. 357
quote, p. 357

**Key Person**
Sequoyah, p. 355

⭐ **Background Knowledge** As a general, Andrew Jackson won great popularity for his victories over Native Americans in Georgia and Florida. As President, Jackson worked to remove Native Americans from their homelands in the Southeast.

## Native Americans of the Southeast

When Andrew Jackson became President, more than 100,000 Native Americans still lived east of the Mississippi River. Many of these Native Americans were farmers or lived in towns.

The Choctaw, Chickasaw, Cherokee, and Creek nations lived in parts of Mississippi, Alabama, northern Georgia, western North Carolina, and southern Tennessee. The Seminoles, who lived in Florida, had an unusual origin. They were a combination of Creeks who had moved into Florida in the late 1700s, Florida Native Americans, and escaped African American slaves.

The Cherokees had adopted some white customs. Aside from farming, they ran successful businesses, such as grain and lumber mills. The Cherokees had their own schools, and some could speak and read English. Many had converted to Christianity.

The Cherokees even had a written alphabet for their language. It had been created by a learned leader named Sequoyah (sih KWOY uh). In 1827, the Cherokees established a government based on a written constitution. They claimed status as a separate nation. The next year, they started a newspaper in both English and Cherokee.

✅**Checkpoint** What were some of the customs and ways of life of the Cherokees?

**Main Idea**
The Native Americans of the Southeast followed a variety of customs.

Seminole woman

# Indian Removal

WISCONSIN TERRITORY

Sauk

Fox

ME
VT
NH
NY
MA
CT
RI

MI

PA
NJ
MD
DE

IL
IN
OH

MO

Ohio R.

VA

KY

NC

INDIAN TERRITORY

Ft. Smith
Ft. Gibson
Ft. Coffee
Memphis

TN

SC

AR

Red R.

GA

LA

AL

Vicksburg
MS

FLORIDA TERRITORY

New Orleans

Gulf of Mexico

ATLANTIC OCEAN

40° N

70° W

30° N

0 km    200
0 miles    200
Azimuthal Equal-Area Projection

100° W

90° W

80° W

20° N

### KEY

Ceded to Native Americans
Ceded by Native Americans
Common removal route
Cherokee removal route (Trail of Tears)
Chickasaw removal route
Choctaw removal route
Creek removal route
Seminole removal route
Forts

## MAP★MASTER®

### Skills Activity

In the 1830s, some 100,000 Native Americans of the Southeast were driven from their homes and forced to walk to a new home across the Mississippi River.

**(a) Read a Map** Which five Southeast nations were affected by the movement?

**(b) Apply Information** Use the scale of miles and the map above to answer the following question: About how far did the Seminoles have to travel to get from Florida Territory to New Orleans?

**MapMaster ⦿nline**

**For:** Interactive map
**Visit:** PHSchool.com
**Web Code:** myp-3064

# Conflict Over Land

To government leaders, the presence of Native Americans in the Southeast stood in the way of westward expansion of the United States. Furthermore, the Native Americans lived on fertile land. White farmers wanted that land for growing cotton.

**Forced Movement** Policies to move Native Americans from their lands dated from the presidency of Thomas Jefferson. Jefferson hoped the movement would be <u>voluntary</u>. He believed that moving west was the only way the Native Americans could preserve their cultures.

After the War of 1812, the federal government signed treaties with several Native American groups of the Old Northwest. Under those treaties, the groups gave up their lands and moved west of the Mississippi River.

However, the Native Americans of the Southeast would not move. In 1825, President James Monroe suggested a plan to move all Native Americans living east of the Mississippi to land west of the river. However, nothing came of the plan. Yet, year by year, the pressure on the Native Americans of the Southeast grew. By the 1820s, many white southerners were demanding that Native Americans be removed by force.

In 1825 and 1827, the state of Georgia passed a law forcing the Creeks to give up most of their land. In 1828, Georgia tried to get the Cherokees to do the same. The state said the Cherokees were not a separate nation and they had to move off their land.

**Support for Native Americans** Georgia's actions were challenged in two suits that reached the Supreme Court. The decision in the first suit went against the Cherokees. In *Cherokee Nation* v. *Georgia* (1831), the Court refused to stop Georgia from enforcing its law. But in *Worcester* v. *Georgia* (1832), the Court declared that Georgia's laws "can have no force" within Cherokee territory.

Chief Justice John Marshall wrote the Court's majority opinion in *Worcester* v. *Georgia*. He <u>quoted</u> treaties that the United States had signed, guaranteeing certain territory to Native Americans. Under the Constitution, treaties are the supreme law of the land. Therefore, Marshall said, Georgia had no say over Cherokee territory.

Like the state of Georgia, President Jackson wanted to remove the Native Americans from their land. He was furious when he heard of the ruling in *Worcester* v. *Georgia*. "John Marshall has made his decision," he is reported to have said. "Now let him enforce it!"

Jackson was already putting into effect a federal law called the Indian Removal Act of 1830. The law gave him authority to offer Native American nations land west of the Mississippi in exchange for their lands in the East. It also provided money so the law could be carried out.

✓ **Checkpoint**   **According to Marshall, why was Georgia barred from applying its laws to Cherokee territory?**

**Main Idea**
Andrew Jackson objected to a Supreme Court ruling in favor of Native Americans.

**Vocabulary** *Builder*
**voluntary** (VAHL ahn tair ee) *adj.* done willingly, of one's own free will

**Vocabulary** *Builder*
**quote** (kwoht) *v.* to repeat the exact words spoken or written

**A Tragic Journey** This painting, *Shadow of the Owl*, by Cherokee artist John Guthrie portrays the Trail of Tears. More than 4,000 Cherokees died along the trail. The tombstone of one of them is shown below. **Critical Thinking: *Interpret Art*** *What do you think the owl in the main picture represents?*

**Main Idea**
Native Americans were moved to the West under harsh and dangerous conditions.

# On the Trail of Tears

Believing they had no choice, most Native American leaders signed new treaties giving up their lands. They agreed to move to what was called the Indian Territory. Today most of that area is in the state of Oklahoma.

**Removal of the Choctaws** The Choctaws signed the first treaty in 1830. The Treaty of Dancing Rabbit Creek stated that

> **❝**the United States under a grant . . . shall cause to be conveyed to the Choctaw Nation a tract of country west of the Mississippi river . . .**❞**
> —Article II, Treaty of Dancing Rabbit Creek, 1830

Closely guarded by American soldiers, the Choctaws moved west between 1831 and 1833.

The federal government did not provide enough tents, food, blankets, shoes, winter clothes, or other supplies. Heavy rain and snow caused enormous suffering. An army lieutenant wrote that one group "walked for 24 hours barefoot through the snow and ice" before reaching shelter.

**Cherokee Removal** The Cherokees held out a few years longer. They were still on their land in 1837 when Jackson left office.

Finally, in 1838, President Martin Van Buren forced the Cherokees to move. In the winter of 1838–39, they went to Indian Territory, guarded by 7,000 soldiers. The route is called the Trail of Tears. A soldier's description helps explain why:

> **"**On the morning of November 17th, we encountered a terrific sleet and snow storm with freezing temperatures, and from that day until we reached the end of the fateful journey on March the 26th, 1839, the sufferings of the Cherokee were awful. The trail of the exiles was a trail of death.**"**
>
> —Memoirs of Private John G. Burnett, December 1890

The Cherokees were forced to march hundreds of miles. They had little food or shelter. Many did not survive. Of 15,000 Cherokees who began the trip, 4,000 died along the way.

One group refused to move. The Seminoles fought three wars against removal. However, in the 1840s most Seminoles were forced to move. In their new homes in the Indian Territory, Native Americans struggled to rebuild their lives under very difficult conditions.

☑**Checkpoint** **What mistakes in planning did the government make before removing Native Americans?**

⭐ **Looking Back and Ahead** Andrew Jackson was determined to be a strong President. He defied the Supreme Court by enforcing the Indian Removal Act. In Section 5, you will learn about his stands against the nation's bankers and his dramatic actions to save the Union.

**Identify Long-Term Effects**

President Jackson sent federal agents to finalize treaties for Native American removal. Summarize the long-term effects of this policy. Explain how the policy affected the Native Americans in the region.

---

Section 4 | **Check Your Progress**

**Progress Monitoring** ⬤nline
**For:** Self-test with instant help
**Visit:** PHSchool.com
**Web Code:** mya-3064

**Comprehension and Critical Thinking**

**1. (a) Recall** How did the Supreme Court rule in the case of *Worcester* v. *Georgia*?
**(b) Detect Bias** Why do you suppose President Jackson objected to the Court's decision?

**2. (a) Compare and Contrast** Describe the removal of the Choctaws and the Cherokees.
**(b) Identify Economic Benefits** Why would the Cherokees be particularly opposed to removal from their land?

**Reading Skill**

**3. Identify Long-Term Effects** A long-term effect is an effect that lasts over a long period of time. White farmers wanted the lands belonging to Native Americans of the Southeast. Write three sentences summarizing the long-term effects of this desire for land.

**Writing**

**4.** A paragraph should focus on a single topic. Rewrite the following paragraph to get rid of any sentences that stray from the topic. **Paragraph:** By the 1830s, Native Americans had fought several legal battles over land. Many Native Americans wore traditional clothing. The states tried to make the Native Americans move. However, the Supreme Court decided that states could not force them from their homes.

# Sequoyah and the Cherokee Alphabet by Robert Cwiklik

## Prepare to Read

### Introduction

The leader Sequoyah became convinced that the Cherokee needed a system to write in their own language. The following selection is from a biography of Sequoyah. In this excerpt, Sequoyah becomes interested in the "talking leaves" of an English book.

###  Reading Skill

**Analyze Motivation** A character's motives are the reason for his or her actions. As you read this excerpt, look for clues that tell why Sequoyah wanted the book.

### Vocabulary *Builder*

As you read this literature selection, look for the following underlined words:

**leaves** (leevz) *n.* pages or sheets

**wampum belt** (WAHM pum) *n.* belt woven with images made with beads or shells, used to record historic events

**pelts** (pehltz) *n.* animal skins

**bristled** (BRIHS ahld) *v.* became angry

###  Background

The images on the wampum belt were a record of events in Cherokee history. Details like names of people and places were passed down from one medicine man to the next. The medicine men would tell the history of the tribe based on the images on the belt.

Sequoyah picked up the book to examine it. He saw that it was made of thin <u>leaves</u> of paper. Instead of the pictures on a <u>wampum belt</u>, there were marks of some kind on the paper, like the footprints of a crow. And the marks were in neat rows like the rows of corn planted in a garden. When the reader looked at those rows, the leaves of the book "talked" to him. The reader then told his friends what the leaves said. Sequoyah found these talking leaves fascinating.

Sequoyah mentally compared the markings on the talking leaves to the designs on a wampum belt. The colorful belt was much prettier, but the book was filled with many thin leaves, each covered with markings. It must surely "remember" more than the wampum belt. Wu The had told Sequoyah that books made the white people's medicine powerful. She had said that just one of their books of talking leaves could remember more than all the medicine men of Taskigi together. And the white men had many, many such books. This is why Wu The wanted Sequoyah to learn English—so he could learn the secret of the talking leaves, the secret of the white people's powerful medicine.

Sequoyah was so curious about the talking leaves that he bought the book from the hunter for two good deer <u>pelts</u>. The men laughed, thinking they had again cheated an Indian. Sequoyah knew his pelts were worth more in silver than this book. Still he wished to have it. He wanted to ponder the secret of its talking leaves.

Agi Li and Rabbit Eyes kidded Sequoyah as the three hiked home after the rain stopped, "You gave good pelts for a book you cannot even understand," they said, laughing.

Later the boys fell to talking about the talking leaves. "Surely," Rabbit Eyes said, "it was a magic power of the white man to be able to put his speeches into books."

"Surely," Agi Li said, "one must learn the white man's language to gain the power of the talking leaves."

Sequoyah <u>bristled</u> at this. "Bah," he said. "These are mere scratchings, mere crow's prints. It is not magic. I could invent them for the Cherokee language, and we, too, could have our own talking leaves."

The other boys laughed at this. "How can you do such a thing?" asked Agi Li, chuckling.

Sequoyah picked up a flat stone and scratched out a picture of a deer on it with the blade of his knife. "There," he said, showing them the stone. "That means 'deer,' see?" Then Sequoyah drew an arrow through the deer. "And that means 'to hunt a deer,'" he said.

His friends laughed again. "At this rate, you will be scratching on stones until you are an old man, Sequoyah, to make pictures of every word there is in our language. It is impossible. The talking leaves belong to the white man. They are not meant for us."

Sequoyah stood his ground. "You are wrong," he said. "You think the white man has special medicine. That is why you wear his clothes," Sequoyah said, pointing to their trousers and shirts. "Well, our medicine can be just as strong, if we wish it."

From *Sequoyah and the Cherokee Alphabet,* by Robert Cwiklik.
© 1989 Silver Burdett Press.

**Analyze Motivation**
At the beginning of the excerpt, Sequoyah's curiosity motivates him to buy the book. What is his motivation for wanting to write his language?

☑ **Checkpoint**   **Why did Wu The want Sequoyah to learn English?**

If you liked this story about Sequoyah, you might want to read more about the Cherokees in *The Cherokee Dragon: A Novel of the Real People* by Robert J. Conley. St. Martin's Press. 2000.

Sequoyah and his Cherokee alphabet

*Analyze* **LITERATURE**
Sequoyah went on to create an alphabet for the Cherokees. Imagine that you are Sequoyah. Write a paragraph explaining to the Cherokees why they should learn to write.

## Objectives

1. Describe the disagreement over the Bank of the United States.

2. Discuss the differing viewpoints on the balance of federal and state powers.

3. Explain why South Carolina threatened to secede from the Union.

4. Describe the economic crisis that began in 1837.

## Prepare to Read

### ⦿ Reading Skill

**Identify Multiple Causes** Just as events can have multiple effects, so too can they have multiple causes. Major events in history often have many causes. As you read Section 5, look for events that have multiple causes.

### Vocabulary *Builder*

**High-Use Words**

**enrich**, p. 362
**resolve**, p. 364

**Key Terms and People**

nullification, p. 364
Martin Van Buren, p. 366
William Henry Harrison, p. 367

---

### Main Idea
Andrew Jackson opposed the Bank of the United States, saying he believed it gave too much power to the wealthy.

⭐ **Background Knowledge** As you learned in Section 3, Andrew Jackson believed that common people needed support against powerful forces of wealth. This belief led Jackson to take a strong stand against the Bank of the United States.

## The Bank War

Between 1816 and the early 1830s, the second Bank of the United States earned strong support from business people. They liked the fact that the Bank made loans to businesses. Moreover, the Bank was a safe place for the federal government to keep its money. The paper money it issued formed a stable currency. Its careful policies helped create confidence in banks all over the country.

On the other hand, many Americans disliked the Bank. They opposed the way the Bank restricted loans made by state banks. Fearing that state banks were making too many loans, Bank directors often limited the amount of money banks could lend. This angered farmers and merchants who wanted to borrow money to buy land. Many southerners and westerners blamed the Bank for the economic crisis that broke out in 1819. In that crisis, many people lost their farms.

**Vocabulary *Builder***
**enrich** (ehn RIHCH) *v.* to make wealthy

The Bank's most powerful enemy was Andrew Jackson, who called the Bank "the Monster." According to Jackson, the Bank allowed a small group of the wealthy people to enrich themselves at the expense of ordinary people. Jackson believed that the wealthy stood for unfair privilege. Jackson especially disliked Nicholas Biddle, the Bank's president. Biddle, who came from a wealthy Philadelphia family, was skilled at doing favors for powerful politicians.

Biddle got Congress to renew the Bank's charter in 1832, although the charter still had four years to go. The news reached Jackson when he was sick in bed. The President vowed, "The Bank . . . is trying to kill me, but I will kill it!"

Jackson immediately vetoed the bill. The fight over the Bank became a major issue in the 1832 presidential election. Henry Clay, who ran against Jackson, strongly supported the Bank. But most voters stood solidly behind Jackson's veto of the Bank bill. Jackson won reelection by a huge margin.

Jackson's victory over the Bank helped to increase the powers of the presidency. It showed that a determined President could stir up the voters and face down powerful opponents in Congress.

The second Bank ceased to exist when its charter ran out in 1836. Unfortunately for Jackson's successor, an economic crisis struck a few months after Jackson left office. Without a Bank of the United States, it was harder for the new President to end the crisis.

☑**Checkpoint** **What were the arguments for and against the second Bank of the United States?**

## The Question of States' Rights

Since the founding of the United States, Americans had debated what should be the balance between the powers of the states and the powers of the federal government.

**Main Idea**
The balance of federal and state powers had been an issue since the early days of the Union.

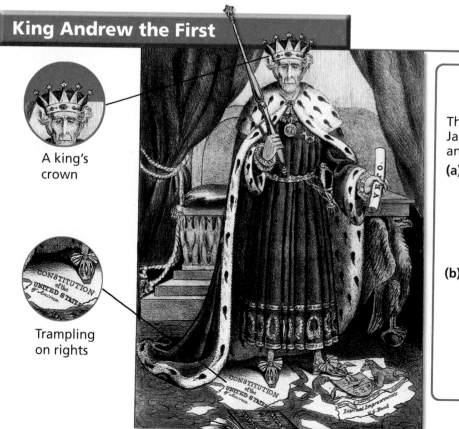

**King Andrew the First**

A king's crown

Trampling on rights

CONSTITUTION of the UNITED STATES of America

**Reading Political Cartoons**

**Skills Activity**

The national press ridiculed Jackson for his quick temper and steely will.

**(a) Detect Points of View** Name two negative images in the cartoon. Why do you think Jackson is shown stepping on the bank document?

**(b) Distinguish Relevant Information** Would this cartoon have the same impact in Britain if, instead of Jackson, it showed a British leader? Explain your answer.

The Constitutional Convention of 1787 had created a government based on federalism, the division of power between the national government and the states. The Constitution gave the federal government many significant powers. At the same time, the Tenth Amendment set limits on federal power. It states that any powers not specifically given to the federal government are "reserved to the States respectively, or to the people."

Over the years, the issue of balancing federal and state power had come up repeatedly. The Alien and Sedition acts had raised the issue. So had the Virginia and Kentucky resolutions and the Hartford convention. The issue could never be fully <u>resolved</u>. During Andrew Jackson's presidency, arguments over federal power and states' rights caused a serious crisis.

**Vocabulary** *Builder*
<u>resolve</u> (ree SAHLV) *v.* to decide; to solve

☑**Checkpoint** **How does the Tenth Amendment limit federal powers?**

**Main Idea**
Andrew Jackson forcefully opposed South Carolina's threat to leave the Union.

## The Nullification Crisis

The crisis erupted when Congress passed a law in 1828 raising the tariff on iron, textiles, and other products. The tariff helped manufacturers in the North and some parts of the West. But it made southerners pay more for manufactured goods. It seemed to southerners that the federal government was forcing them to obey an unfair law.

Vice President John C. Calhoun of South Carolina argued that the states had the right of **nullification,** an action by a state that cancels a federal law to which the state objects. If accepted, Calhoun's ideas would seriously weaken the federal government.

**Arguments for Nullification** To many southerners, the tariff issue was part of a much larger problem. If the federal government could enforce what they considered an unjust law, could it also use its power to end slavery?

John C. Calhoun had based his theory of nullification on his view of how the Union was formed. He said the Union grew from an agreement between the various states. After the Union was formed, each state kept certain powers. One of them was the power to nullify federal laws the people of the state considered unfair.

## Milestones in the States' Rights Debate

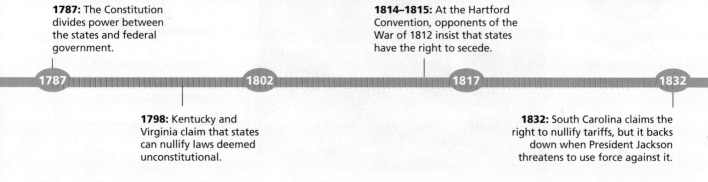

**1787:** The Constitution divides power between the states and federal government.

**1814–1815:** At the Hartford Convention, opponents of the War of 1812 insist that states have the right to secede.

1787    1802    1817    1832

**1798:** Kentucky and Virginia claim that states can nullify laws deemed unconstitutional.

**1832:** South Carolina claims the right to nullify tariffs, but it backs down when President Jackson threatens to use force against it.

## Links to Government

### Federal Power Versus States' Rights

President Andrew Jackson and Vice President John C. Calhoun took opposing views on states' rights and nullification. They had once been friends. However, by 1830, the two men were fierce enemies. **Critical Thinking: *Detect Points of View*** *How may Andrew Jackson's views about nullification have been affected by his responsibility as President of the United States?*

"The Union—next to our liberty, the most dear"

"Our Federal Union—It must be preserved"

John C. Calhoun

Andrew Jackson

**Arguments Against Nullification** The clearest argument against nullification came from Massachusetts Senator Daniel Webster. He argued that the United States had not been formed by the states, but by the entire American people. In a dramatic speech on the floor of the Senate in January 1830, Webster defended his belief, saying "We are all agents of the same supreme power, the people."

A few months later, President Jackson dramatically defended the Union. At a banquet, Jackson stared directly at Vice President Calhoun and said, "Our Federal Union—It must be preserved." Ominously, Calhoun responded: "The Union—next to our liberty, the most dear." The challenge was clear. To Calhoun, states' rights was more important than saving the Union.

**South Carolina Threatens to Secede** In 1832, Congress passed another tariff law. Although it lowered some tariffs, it passed high tariffs on iron and textiles. South Carolina then called a state convention, which voted to nullify the tariffs. The tariffs of 1828 and 1832, it said, did not apply to South Carolina. The state also warned the federal government not to use force to impose the tariffs. If it did, South Carolina would secede from the Union.

A furious Jackson responded strongly. In December 1832, he put federal troops in South Carolina on alert. Then he issued a "Proclamation to the People of South Carolina." It said that the Union could not be dissolved. It also warned that "disunion by armed force is treason." With tensions running high, Calhoun resigned as Vice President.

Early in 1833, Jackson asked Congress to allow the federal government to collect its tariff in South Carolina by force if necessary. At the same time, he supported a compromise bill that would lower the tariffs. In March 1833, Congress passed both laws.

Unable to win support for its position from other states, South Carolina then repealed its tariff nullification. Many Americans breathed a sigh of relief. The crisis had been settled peacefully.

**The Election of 1840**
Both the Whigs and the Democrats tried new methods in the presidential election of 1840. They broadened their appeal, hoping to win the vote of the "common man."
**Critical Thinking:** *Link Past and Present* How are presidential campaigns today similar to the 1840 campaign? How are they different?

Jackson had successfully defended federal power, while states' rights supporters had suffered a setback. However, the issue of states' rights would not go away. Americans would continue to debate the balance between states' rights and federal powers until the Civil War broke out in 1861.

✓**Checkpoint**   What was the position of Vice President John C. Calhoun on nullification?

## The End of the Jackson Era

**Main Idea**
Jackson's successor, Martin Van Buren, faced an economic crisis known as the Panic of 1837.

A weary Andrew Jackson retired from office after two terms. Martin Van Buren was Andrew Jackson's choice to succeed him. Van Buren, the son of a New York tavern owner, had played a central role in organizing Jackson's first election victory in 1828. He had been secretary of state during Jackson's first term and Vice President during his second term. He had long been a close political adviser to Jackson.

In the election of 1836, the Whigs ran three candidates, each from a different region of the country. Their goal was to prevent any candidate from receiving a majority of electoral votes. This would throw the election into the House of Representatives. However, the strategy did not work. Van Buren received a majority of both the electoral and the popular vote.

**The Panic of 1837** Van Buren took office at a time when the American economy was beginning a severe slump. Because Britain was experiencing an economic slowdown, British manufacturers were buying less cotton. This caused cotton prices to fall sharply. American banks could not collect on the loans they had made to cotton growers. As a result, hundreds of banks went bankrupt.

The result was an economic collapse in the United States called the Panic of 1837. The economic hard times that followed lasted six years. The hardships of those years ruined Van Buren's presidency.

**The Election of 1840** Van Buren ran for reelection in 1840 against the Whig candidate, William Henry Harrison. This time the Whigs ran a skillful campaign. They used parades, barbecues, and other forms of entertainment to reach ordinary voters. They portrayed Harrison as a "man of the people" who would feel right at home in a simple log cabin. Helped by his "log cabin" campaign, Harrison easily defeated Van Buren. The Whigs were in power and the Age of Jackson was over.

☑ **Checkpoint** What was the main cause of the Panic of 1837?

☆ **Looking Back and Ahead** Throughout the administrations of John Quincy Adams, Andrew Jackson, and Martin Van Buren, Americans continued to push westward. By the 1830s, Americans had settled most of the land east of the Mississippi River. By the 1840s, they were crossing the Mississippi in large numbers. You will read about this movement in the next unit.

**Identify Multiple Causes**

In 1837, the United States experienced an economic collapse. What were two causes of this collapse?

---

Section 5 | **Check Your Progress**

**Progress Monitoring** ⬤nline
**For:** Self-test with instant help
**Visit:** PHSchool.com
**Web Code:** mya-3065

**Comprehension and Critical Thinking**

1. **(a) Recall** Why did states' rights become an issue in the 1820s?
**(b) Distinguish Relevant Information** Agree or disagree with the following statement and provide relevant facts to support your position: "The issue of states' rights had plagued the nation from the time of the Constitutional Convention."

2. **(a) Summarize** What were John C. Calhoun's and Daniel Webster's positions on nullification?
**(b) Detect Points of View** What did John C. Calhoun mean when he said, "The Union—next to our liberty, the most dear"?

**↻ Reading Skill**

3. **Identify Multiple Causes** After the nullification crisis, South Carolina repealed its nullification of the federal tariffs. What were two causes of the state's action?

**Vocabulary Builder**

4. Write two definitions for the key term nullification. First, write a formal definition for your teacher. Second, write a definition in everyday English for a classmate.

**Writing**

5. Correct the errors in grammar, spelling, and punctuation in the following passage. **Passage:** The Nullification Crises represent a conflict between the South and the federal government. president Jackson at a banquet said that the Union must be preserved. John Calhoun answered "The Union—next to our liberty, the most dearest."

Bias is slanted writing that communicates a certain point of view about an idea or event. The writer either leaves out information or purposely changes the facts in order to create a certain impression. Bias is different from objective writing, which presents the facts in a balanced way.

> The following excerpt, from Andrew Jackson's seventh annual message to Congress, focuses on his Indian removal policy.
>
> **Primary Source**
>
> ". . . The plan of removing the [native] people to . . . country west of the Mississippi River approaches its [conclusion]. . . . All preceding experiments for the improvement of the Indians have failed. It seems now to be an established fact that they can not live in contact with a civilized community and prosper. . . .
>
> The plan for their removal . . . is founded upon the knowledge we have gained of their character and habits, and has been dictated by a spirit of [generosity]. A territory exceeding in extent that [given up] has been granted to each tribe. Of its climate, fertility, and capacity to support an Indian population the representations are highly favorable. . . .
>
> . . . A country west of Missouri and Arkansas has been assigned to them, into which the white settlements are not to be pushed. . . . A barrier has thus been raised for their protection . . . guarding the Indians as far as possible from those evils which have brought them to their present condition."
>
> —Andrew Jackson, December 7, 1835

## Learn the Skill

*Use these steps to identify bias.*

**1** **Identify the source.** Knowing the speaker or writer and the audience helps you understand why the point of view might be biased.

**2** **Find the main idea.** Summarize the main point in the primary source.

**3** **Compare the primary source with objective writing.** Look for differences between the biased writing and an objective account of the same subject. Does the biased writer leave out information or alter facts? Does the biased writer use broad generalizations that support a particular point of view? Does the biased writer use emotionally charged words?

**4** **Draw conclusions.** What does the writer or speaker hope to accomplish?

## Practice the Skill

*Answer the following questions about the primary source on this page.*

**1** **Identify the source.** (a) Who is the author? (b) Why might the author's position be biased?

**2** **Find the main idea.** What is the main point of the speech?

**3** **Compare the primary source with objective writing.** Read the information about the government's Indian removal policy in Section 4. (a) What is one way that this account differs from the account in Section 4? (b) What is an example of a broad generalization that creates a biased view? (c) What information about the real reason for Indian removal is not included?

**4** **Draw conclusions.** What message does the author want to present to the audience?

### Apply the Skill

*See the Review and Assessment at the end of this chapter.*

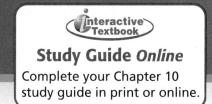

**Study Guide** *Online*
Complete your Chapter 10
study guide in print or online.

## Chapter Summary

### Section 1
### Building a National Identity

- James Monroe's time as President was called the Era of Good Feelings.
- Tariffs protected northern factories but forced the South to pay more for goods.
- Key Supreme Court decisions strengthened the power of the federal government.

### Section 2
### Dealing With Other Nations

- The United States acquired Florida in 1819.
- Spanish territories in the Americas revolted and gained their independence.
- Britain granted Canadians more rights.

### Section 3
### The Age of Jackson

- John Quincy Adams served only one term.
- Democratic reforms allowed more white men to vote.

### Section 4
### Indian Removal

- The government forced Native Americans to move west of the Mississippi River.
- Thousands of Native Americans died resisting removal or along the journey west.

### Section 5
### States' Rights and the Economy

- Jackson vetoed a bill to renew the charter of the second Bank.
- South Carolina said that states had the right to nullify federal laws.
- Jackson insisted that states could not nullify federal laws.
- Eventually, South Carolina backed down on nullification.

## Key Concepts

These notes will help you prepare for questions about key concepts.

### Democratic Reforms in the Age of Jackson

- States dropped property requirements for voting.
- Presidential electors were chosen by voters instead of state legislators.
- Candidates for office were chosen by nominating conventions instead of caucuses.

### Key Supreme Court Rulings and Their Impact

*McCulloch v. Maryland*
- The Court ruled that a state law could not go against a federal law.
- The decision strengthened federal power.

*Dartmouth College v. Woodward*
- The Court said the charter of Dartmouth College was a private contract, which New Hampshire could not change.
- The protection of contracts helped promote capitalism.

*Gibbons v. Ogden*
- The Court ruled that only the federal government had the power to regulate interstate commerce.
- The decision further strengthened federal powers.

## Vocabulary *Builder*

### Key Terms

Answer the following questions in complete sentences that show your understanding of the key terms.

1. How would British dumping hurt American business?

2. What are the advantages of suffrage?

3. Which group of people might hold a caucus?

4. Who did John C. Calhoun believe had the right of nullification?

## Comprehension and Critical Thinking

5. **(a) List** How did Henry Clay believe the United States would benefit from his American System?
   **(b) Analyze Cause and Effect** Which regions of the country were likely to benefit most from the plan? Why?

6. **(a) Explain** Why did President Monroe issue the Monroe Doctrine?
   **(b) Apply Information** How might the Monroe Doctrine aid Latin American nations?
   **(c) Draw Conclusions** How do you think Latin American leaders felt about the Monroe Doctrine?

7. **(a) Describe** Why did Andrew Jackson lose the presidential election in 1824?
   **(b) Analyze Cause and Effect** What changes occurred between 1824 and 1828 that resulted in Jackson winning the 1828 election?

8. **(a) Identify** What was the Trail of Tears?
   **(b) Link Past and Present** Why does the state of Oklahoma today have a large Native American population?

9. **(a) Describe** How did the spoils system work?
   **(b) Draw Conclusions** How would it affect a political party?
   **(c) Detect Points of View** Why did Jackson say the spoils system furthered democracy?

10. **(a) Identify** What was the Panic of 1837?
    **(b) Draw Inferences** How might the panic have contributed to the election of William Henry Harrison in 1840?

## History Reading Skill

11. **Analyze Cause and Effect** Reread the text in Section 1 under the heading "Three Important Supreme Court Rulings." What was the cause of the Supreme Court's decision in *McCulloch* v. *Maryland*? What were the results of the decision? Which results were short-term? Which were long-term?

## Writing

12. **Revise the following paragraph to correct the errors in grammar, spelling, and punctuation:**
    In 1832, congress pass a new law, which lowered some tariffs but continued the high tarriffs on iron and textiles. Generally the South opposed tarifs. South Caroline actually voted to oppose the tariff legislation. Because President Jackson regard this act as a challenge to his authority. He issued a "Proclamation to the People of South Carolina." Which said that leaving the Union would be an act of treeson.

13. **Write a Narrative:**
    Imagine you are a Cherokee in 1838–1839. Write a narrative describing your journey to the Indian Territory.

## Skills for Life

### Identify Bias

Use the excerpt below to answer the questions.

"More than eight millions of the stock of this bank are held by foreigners. By this act the American Republic proposes virtually to make them a present of some millions of dollars. . . . If we must have a bank with private stockholders, every consideration of sound policy and every impulse of American feeling admonishes that it should be *purely American*. . . ."

—Andrew Jackson, "Bank Veto Message,"
July 10, 1832

14. **(a)** Who is the author? **(b)** Why would the author's position be biased?

15. What is the main point of the message?

16. Give an example of emotionally charged words used to support the writer's point of view.

17. What message does the writer want to convey to the audience?

## Test Yourself

1. **What was the principal reason Andrew Jackson opposed the second Bank of the United States?**

   **A** Its policies hurt revenue Jackson expected to get from tariffs.

   **B** The second Bank refused to loan money to state banks.

   **C** Jackson believed it gave power to a small group of wealthy people.

   **D** The second Bank backed John C. Calhoun on the issue of nullification.

2. **Which issue was Andrew Jackson referring to when he said, "John Marshall has made his decision. Now let him enforce it"?**

   **A** a case about the importance of private contracts

   **B** a state attempt to apply its laws to Cherokee territory

   **C** interstate commerce

   **D** the dumping of goods by Britain in the United States

**Refer to the map below to answer Question 3.**

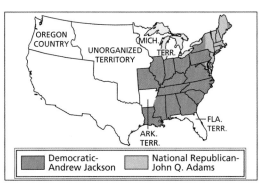

Legend: Democratic-Andrew Jackson | National Republican-John Q. Adams

3. **Based on the map above, what was the major reason Jackson won the election of 1828?**

   **A** Jackson won only the states with large electoral vote totals.

   **B** New states that joined the Union between 1824 and 1828 voted for Jackson.

   **C** Many states that had voted for Adams in 1824 switched to Jackson.

   **D** Jackson swept the electoral votes of states in the South and West.

## Document-Based Questions

**Task:** Look at Documents 1 and 2, and answer their accompanying questions. Then, use the documents and your knowledge of history to complete this writing assignment:

Write a short essay describing how changing political practices reflected new views of democracy that began to take hold during the Age of Jackson.

**Document 1:** William Henry Harrison's 1840 presidential campaign was filled with advertising, slogans, organized rallies, and campaign songs like this one. *What image of Harrison was this song trying to create?*

"Come swell the throng and join the song,
Make the circle wider
Join the round for Harrison, Log Cabin and Hard Cider.
With Harrison our country's won,
No treachery can divide her.
Thy will be done
With Harrison, Log Cabin and Hard Cider."

**Document 2:** This campaign poster combines images of a humble log cabin with slogans about Harrison's exploits as a general. *What image of Harrison does this poster create? How does this image compare to Andrew Jackson's image?*

# Writing Workshop

## Narrative Essay
## Biographical Essay

### ▶ Introduction

In a biographical essay, you write about the life and personality of a person who actually lived. A biographical essay should have the following characteristics:

- a real-life subject

- a thesis statement that states a specific idea about that person's life and achievements

- an account of one or more major events in the subject's life

- a description of the subject's key character traits

**Assignment** On the following pages, you will learn how to write a biographical essay. You will get step-by-step instructions. Each step will include an example from a sample essay discussing the life of George Washington.

Read the instructions and the examples. Then, follow each step to plan and write a 500–700 word essay.

> **Discuss one of the historical people from Unit 3. Review his or her most important contribution to the nation, giving reasons for your choice.**

For a review of the steps in the writing process, see the **Historian's Toolkit**, *Write Like a Historian.*

### ▶ Prewriting

**Choose your subject.** Choose a person whose life seems especially appealing to you. Once you have decided on a subject, make notes about what you already know about his or her life and personality.

### Sample notes about George Washington

- "father of his country"

- "first in war, first in peace, first in the hearts of his countrymen"

- Washington's father was a wealthy Virginia planter.

- Washington fought in the French and Indian War.

- led disorganized, poorly funded Continental army in the Revolution against better-trained, better-funded professional British soldiers

- struggled with Continental Congress for money

- encountered many tough situations as President and knew each decision would have impact on the future

- the nation faced financial problems: debt crisis, Hamilton's plan

- faced other crises: Whiskey Rebellion, conflict in Northwest Territory, European wars

**Gather information.** Once you have reviewed what you know, think about what areas of this person's life you would like to focus on. Then, write down some questions to help you direct your research.

**Draw conclusions.** Based on your research, make some decisions about your subject's personality. What did he or she value most? Is there a connection between your subject's character traits and his or her role in history?

**Write a thesis statement.** You have learned more about your subject and reflected on his or her life and personality. You are ready to write a thesis statement.

> Sample questions about George Washington:
>
> - What was Washington's family background like? What about his education?
>
> - What qualities made him a good general? Were they the same things that made him a good President?
>
> - How did his soldiers feel about him? How did other leaders feel about him?
>
> - How effective was he as a President?
>
> - What was Washington like as a person?
>
> - What were his personality strengths and weaknesses? What did he do best? What did he not do as well?

> **Sample thesis statement:**
> George Washington was not a very imaginative man, but he had a practical, steady mind—a quality that was necessary to give stability to our new nation.

## ▶ Drafting

**Decide how to organize your writing.** The simplest way to organize a biographical essay is to cover the main events of the subject's life chronologically.

Another type of organization focuses on a few important events in the person's life, building up to the one that you think is most important.

**Write an introduction.** The first paragraph of your essay introduces your subject. The introduction leads up to the thesis statement, which expresses the idea you will develop in your essay.

**Support your thesis with examples and details.** Use the information you have gathered to support and develop your idea about your subject.

**Use an informative, lively tone.** As you write your draft, enliven your writing with vivid language and colorful details that appeal to the senses.

**Write a strong conclusion.** In your final paragraph, restate your view of the person about whom you are writing. Tell the reader what this individual has contributed to the country.

# Writing Workshop *continued*

## ▶ Model Essay

Read the following model of a biographical essay about George Washington. Notice how it includes the characteristics you have learned about.

### George Washington: A Quiet American Hero

When George Washington was a boy, he liked to make up his own sayings. "Lean not on anyone" was one of them. As he grew older, a strong sense of self-reliance and responsibility—to his family, his soldiers, and his country —shaped Washington's character. It gave him a quiet strength that helped him direct the course of our nation.

Washington grew up on his family's Virginia plantation. As a young man, he decided to learn a trade as a land surveyor. George Washington was only sixteen years old when he set out on his first surveying expedition. Sleeping outdoors and hunting for his food made the teenager more mature. This maturity and sense of responsibility were the perfect qualities for a military leader.

Seven years later, Washington was already a colonel commanding Virginia's colonial troops. At six feet two inches tall, he was a forceful leader who inspired his men to defend the colony's 350-mile western frontier.

In 1775, Washington's leadership was called upon one more time. The Second Continental Congress named him commander in chief of the army. From 1775 to 1783 his strength helped his soldiers overcome many problems. Washington's troops didn't have enough supplies, and many soldiers deserted. The men suffered horribly during the bitterly cold winter at Valley Forge.

After Washington's death, Thomas Jefferson said about the leader, "His integrity was most pure, his justice the most inflexible I have ever known." Without this quiet American hero, with his strong sense of responsibility, our nation's early history would have been very different.

**The opening paragraph is an introduction to the subject. It can include an anecdote.**

**The thesis statement introduces the idea that will be developed in the essay.**

**Is this essay organized chronologically; by focusing on a few events; or by contrasting the public's opinion with the real man?**

**Each paragraph includes examples and details to develop ideas about the subject.**

**The conclusion restates the thesis statement in a new way.**

# Vocabulary *Builder*

## Previewing High-Use Academic Words

| High-Use Word | Definition | Sample History Sentence |
|---|---|---|
| **invest** (ihn VEHST) (Section 1, p. 383) | *v.* to supply money for a project in order to make a profit | Shipowners <u>invested</u> in voyages to distant lands. |
| **efficient** (ee FISH ehnt) (Section 1, p. 386) | *adj.* acting effectively, without wasted cost or effort | New inventions often led to more <u>efficient</u> ways of doing business. |
| **reign** (rayn) (Section 2, p. 393) | *n.* period of dominance or rule | The American Revolution took place during the <u>reign</u> of King George III. |
| **inferior** (ihn FIR ee uhr) (Section 2, p. 395) | *adj.* less worthy; less valuable; of lower rank | Old factories are <u>inferior</u> to newer, more modern ones. |
| **devote** (dee VOHT) (Section 3, p. 397) | *v.* to commit; to apply (time and energy, for example) | To become a judge, one must <u>devote</u> many years to the study of law. |
| **revolt** (ree VOHLT) (Section 3, p. 400) | *n.* uprising; rebellion | Slaveholders feared times when enslaved African Americans would rise up in <u>revolt</u> and fight for freedom. |
| **pursue** (per SYOO) (Section 4, p. 402) | *v.* to chase after; to try to capture | Latin American leaders vowed to <u>pursue</u> liberty in their fight for freedom from European control. |
| **isolated** (ī sah lay tehd) (Section 4, p. 403) | *adj.* set apart | Lord Cornwallis was trapped on the <u>isolated</u> Yorktown peninsula. |

## Previewing Key Terms and People

Nat Turner

Industrial Revolution, p. 382
factory system, p. 383
capitalist, p. 383
Francis Cabot Lowell, p. 384
mass production, p. 386
interchangeable parts, p. 386
urbanization, p. 390

telegraph, p. 391
Samuel F.B. Morse, p. 391
famine, p. 394
nativist, p. 394
discrimination, p. 395
cotton gin, p. 396
slave code, p. 399

spiritual, p. 400
Nat Turner, p. 400
Daniel Boone, p. 401
turnpike, p. 402
corduroy road, p. 403
canal, p. 403
Henry Clay, p. 404

# The Industrial Revolution

## Objectives

1. Explain the changes that the Industrial Revolution brought to American life.

2. Discuss the importance of Samuel Slater's cotton mill.

3. Describe the growth of industry in the United States after 1812.

4. Identify important developments in factories and the problems that factory life produced.

**Main Idea**
The Industrial Revolution introduced great changes in the way Americans lived.

## Prepare to Read

### Reading Skill

**Identify Central Issues From the Past** To effectively study history, you can identify important— or central—issues and then seek to make generalizations from them. To make a generalization, identify main points or ideas in a text. Then, devise a general principle or broad statement that applies to all of them and to other situations.

### Vocabulary *Builder*

**High-Use Words**

**invest**, p. 383
**efficient**, p. 386

**Key Terms and People**

Industrial Revolution, p. 382
factory system, p. 383
capitalist, p. 383
Francis Cabot Lowell, p. 384
mass production, p. 386
interchangeable parts, p. 386

⭐ **Background Knowledge** In the early 1700s, most people worked as farmers. Men worked in the fields to produce food for their families. Women helped in the fields and made simple goods, like candles and soap, at home. In this section, you will see how new inventions began to change the way people lived and worked.

## A Revolution in Technology

In the 1700s, a great change began that we now call the Industrial Revolution. Gradually, machines took the place of many hand tools. Much of the power once provided by people and horses began to be replaced, first by flowing water and then by steam engines.

The Industrial Revolution began in Britain, in the textile, or cloth-making, industry. For centuries, workers had spun thread in their homes on spinning wheels. The thread was then woven into cloth on hand looms. Making thread was time-consuming. It took one person, spinning one strand at a time, almost two weeks to produce a pound of cotton thread.

**Machines and Factories** In the 1760s, the spinning jenny speeded up the thread-making process. The jenny allowed a person to spin many strands at once. However, thread still had to be made by hand.

Then, in 1764, Richard Arkwright invented the water frame, a spinning machine powered by running water rather than human energy. Other inventions speeded up the weaving process. To house the large machines, manufacturers built textile mills on the banks of rivers.

The new mills created a new way of working, known as the factory system. The factory system brings workers and machinery together in one place. Instead of spinning at home, textile workers had to go to the factories and begin and end work at specific hours. Workers now had to keep up with the machines instead of working at their own pace.

British mill owners soon recognized the potential of the new water frames and the factory system. However, the system required huge amounts of money to be <u>invested</u> in buildings and machines. Thus, the mill owners turned to capitalists, people who invest capital, or money, in a business to earn a profit. Factories proved to be a good investment for the capitalists and mill owners. By 1784, British workers were producing 24 times as much thread as they had in 1765.

**Steam Power** Building factories on riverbanks had some disadvantages. In a dry season, the machines had no power. Also, most factories were far from cities, and labor was hard to find in rural areas.

In 1790, Arkwright built the first steam-powered textile plant. The steam engine was a reliable source of power. Factories no longer had to be built on riverbanks. They could be built in cities, where young women and children provided cheap labor.

Britain tried to guard the secrets of its industrial success. It forbade anyone to take information about textile machinery out of Britain. Skilled workers were forbidden to leave the country.

☑**Checkpoint** How did the Industrial Revolution change the way work was performed?

Vocabulary *Builder*
<u>invest</u> (ihn VEHST) *v.* to supply money for a project in order to make a profit

**A Steam Engine**

**❶ Cylinder** Steam from boiling water rises into the cylinder.

**❸ Flywheel** The other end of the beam goes down, moving gears to turn the flywheel.

**❷ Piston rod** Pressure from the rising steam pushes the piston rod up and raises one end of the beam.

**History** *Interactive*
**Steam Engine in Action**
**Visit:** PHSchool.com
**Web Code:** myp-4071

**Steam Engine**
Steam engines use the energy created by boiling water to push rods and wheels. **Critical Thinking:** *Identify Economic Benefits What advantage would the steam engine have given to a manufacturer over competitors who depended on water power to operate their machinery?*

**Main Idea**
Britain tried but failed to prevent the spread of the new industrial methods.

# The American Industrial Revolution

In 1789, a young apprentice in one of Arkwright's factories decided to immigrate to the United States. Samuel Slater knew that his knowledge of Arkwright's machines could be worth a fortune. He studied hard and memorized the plans of Arkwright's machines. Then, he boarded a ship for New York.

In the United States, Slater joined forces with a wealthy merchant, Moses Brown. Brown had rented a textile mill in Pawtucket, Rhode Island. Relying entirely on his memory, Slater constructed a spinning machine based on Arkwright's. Slater's factory began producing cotton thread at a rate never before seen in the United States.

 **Checkpoint** **Why did Samuel Slater have to build his machines from memory?**

**Main Idea**
The factory system changed the way Americans worked and encouraged the growth of U.S. industry.

## American Industry Grows

The success of Slater's mill marked the beginning of American industrialization. Industrialization began in the Northeast. The region was home to a class of merchants who had capital to build factories and to buy raw materials.

Still, U.S. industry did not grow significantly until the War of 1812. As the British navy blockaded U.S. ports, Americans had to depend on their own industries to supply goods.

**The Lowell Mills** Francis Cabot Lowell found a way. Before the war, he had visited England and seen the latest weaving machines. When he returned to the United States, Lowell and an associate built an improved version of the English machines.

With several other capitalists, Lowell opened a mill in Waltham, Massachusetts. The mill was organized in a new way. Instead of obtaining thread from separate spinning mills, Lowell's factory brought together spinning and weaving in one building.

After Lowell died in 1817, his partners expanded the business. Wanting better lives for their workers, the partners built a new town, with boardinghouses, a library, and a hospital. They named their mill town Lowell after their late partner.

**Lowell Girls** The new factories were staffed with young women from nearby farms. "Lowell girls" lived in boardinghouses under strict supervision. After work, they might attend lectures or visit libraries. As a result, many women gained an education they probably would not have received on their family farms. The British novelist Charles Dickens was amazed when he saw Lowell:

> **"** Firstly, there is a . . . piano in a great many of the boardinghouses. Secondly, nearly all these young ladies subscribe to circulating libraries. Thirdly, they have [created] a periodical called 'The Lowell Offering.' . . . **"**
>
> —Charles Dickens, *American Notes,* 1842

**Identify Central Issues From the Past**

Reading Skill  What generalization can you make about the link between war, trade, and inventiveness?

✅**Checkpoint**  **How was the Lowell factory system different from the European factory system?**

# Links Across Time

2000s Office workers and researchers use computers for much of what they do.

## Technology and Work

**1820s** The Industrial Revolution opened the way for new developments in technology, which changed the way people worked.

**1981–2000s** Since the invention of the personal computer, changes in technology have affected not only *how* people work but also *where* they work. With speedy laptops and hand-held devices, workers are able to work successfully at home or at the office.

## Link to Today  nline

**Technology's Impact**  Technology continues to advance. How are technological innovations changing people's lives today?

**For:** Technology in the workplace
**Visit:** PHSchool.com
**Web Code:** myc-4071

**Factory Workers**
This picture shows young girls at work in a textile factory about 1834.
**Critical Thinking:** *Draw Conclusions* *What were some disadvantages for children who worked in early American factories?*

**Main Idea**
American inventors developed new ways for factories to produce large amounts of goods quickly.

**Vocabulary** *Builder*
**efficient** (ee FISH ehnt) *adj.* acting effectively, without wasted cost or effort

# The Revolution Takes Hold

The Lowell system was an example of a unique American outlook. Without a long tradition of doing things a certain way, Americans experimented with new methods. One of the most important developments was **mass production**, or the rapid manufacture of large numbers of identical objects.

Before the 1800s, skilled craftsworkers manufactured clocks, guns, and other mechanical products. Each part of the gun or clock was handcrafted. When a part broke, a craftsworker had to create a unique piece to fit the product. In the 1790s, American inventor Eli Whitney devised a system of **interchangeable parts**, identical pieces that could be assembled quickly by unskilled workers.

Interchangeable parts soon came to be used in the manufacture of other products. Manufacturing became more <u>efficient</u>. The price of many goods dropped. As people bought more goods, U.S. industry expanded to satisfy their needs.

**Factory Life** As you have read, the Lowell mills treated factory workers in a new and kinder way. However, this was not the general rule. Samuel Slater employed children in his textile mill, as had been done for decades in British factories. As time went on, working conditions for children and adults became harsher.

**Child Labor** Children routinely worked on family farms in the 1800s. Their labor was often needed to help feed their families. Working on a home farm was different from working in a factory, however. American textile mills, coal mines, and steel foundries employed children as young as 7 or 8. These children had no opportunities for education. They often worked in unsafe conditions. By 1880, more than a million children between the ages of 10 and 15 worked for pay.

**Factory Conditions** Working conditions were appalling. Factories were poorly lighted. There was little fresh air. Machines were designed to perform a task, not to protect the worker. As a result, many workers were injured on the job. A worker who lost a hand or a foot received no help. He or she needed to depend on family for support. Business owners provided no payments for disabled workers, as they do by law today.

To keep machines running as long as possible, workdays lasted 12 or 14 hours. By 1844, workers were demanding shorter days. "Eight hours for work, eight hours for sleep, and eight hours for God and the brethren" was an early slogan. Conditions gradually improved, but the 8-hour workday was far in the future.

☑**Checkpoint** **How did Eli Whitney's system of interchangeable parts speed up the manufacturing process?**

☆ **Looking Back and Ahead** Although the new factories were hard on workers, industrialization led to vastly increased production and lower prices. In the next section, you will read how the growth of northern industry helped to widen the gap between the North and the South.

---

**Section 1 | Check Your Progress**

**Progress Monitoring** ⬤nline
**For:** Self-test with instant help
**Visit:** PHSchool.com
**Web Code:** mya-4071

## Comprehension and Critical Thinking

**1. (a) Describe** How did the War of 1812 affect U.S. industry?
**(b) Draw Conclusions** Why did advances in industry occur mainly in the North?

**2. (a) Recall** What are interchangeable parts?
**(b) Draw Conclusions** How did the system of interchangeable parts affect employment in the United States?

## Reading Skill

**3. Identify Central Issues From the Past** Based on this section, what generalization can you make about the impact of inventiveness during the early Industrial Revolution?

## Vocabulary *Builder*

**4.** Write two definitions for each key term: factory system, capitalist, interchangeable parts. First, write a formal definition for your teacher. Second, write a definition in everyday English for a classmate.

## Writing

**5.** Rewrite the following lists of causes and effects, so that causes are correctly paired up with their effects.

**Causes:** Francis Lowell; Arkwright's textile plant; Samuel Slater's emigration; Eli Whitney

**Effects:** efficiency in mass production; libraries for factory workers; factories built in cities; increased American production of cotton thread

# Mill Workers
### by Lucy Larcom

## Introduction

Lucy Larcom was born in Massachusetts in 1824. After her father died when she was 11, Lucy went to work in the Lowell textile mills. Years later, she wrote about her experiences. The following selection is an excerpt from her memoirs.

## Reading Skill

**Analyze Setting** In literature, a character's actions and attitudes often are affected by his or her surroundings. In the memoir below, we learn how the physical conditions in a textile mill affect Lucy Larcom's outlook on work. As you read, pay attention to her descriptions of the mill.

## Vocabulary *Builder*

As you read this literature selection, look for the following underlined words:

**bobbin** (BAHB ihn) *n.* spool for thread or yarn, used in spinning, weaving, or in a sewing machine

**board** (bord) *n.* meals provided regularly for pay

**drudge** (druhj) *n.* person who does hard, menial, or tedious work

 **Background**

Women and girls who worked in northern mills were educated. Some mills published collections of workers' essays and poetry.

I went to my first day's work in the mill with a light heart. The novelty of it made it seem easy, and it really was not hard just to change the <u>bobbins</u> on the spinning-frames every three-quarters of an hour or so, with half a dozen other little girls who were doing the same thing. When I came back at night, the family began to pity me for my long, tiresome day's work, but I laughed and said, "Why, it is nothing but fun. It is just like play."

And for a while it was only a new amusement. . . . We were not occupied more than half the time. The intervals were spent frolicking around the spinning-frames, teasing and talking to the older girls, or entertaining ourselves with games and stories in the corner, or exploring, with the overseer's permission, the mysteries of the carding-room, the dressing-room, and the weaving-room.

I never cared much for machinery. The buzzing and hissing of pulleys and rollers and spindles and flyers around me often grew tiresome. I could not see into their complications, or feel interested in them. But in a room below us we were sometimes allowed to peer in through a sort of blind door at the great waterwheel that carried the works of the whole mill. It was so huge that we could only watch a few of its spokes at a time, and part of its dripping rim, moving with a slow, measured strength through the darkness that shut it in. It impressed me with something of the awe which comes to us in thinking of the great Power which keeps the mechanism of the universe in motion. . . .

When I took my next three months at the grammar school, everything there was changed, and I too was changed. . . . It was a great delight to me to study, and at the end of the three months the master told me that I was prepared for the high school.

Lowell girls weaving in a Massachusetts textile mill in the 1850s

But alas! I could not go. The little money I could earn—one dollar a week, besides the price of my <u>board</u>—was needed in the family, and I must return to the mill. . . .

At this time I had learned to do a spinner's work, and I obtained permission to tend some frames that stood directly in front of the windows, with only them and the wall behind me, extending half the length of the mill. . . .

The last window in the row behind me was filled with flourishing houseplants—fragrant-leaved geraniums, the overseer's pets. . . . T[he] perfume and freshness tempted me there often. . . . On the whole, it was far from being a disagreeable place to stay in. The girls were bright looking and neat, and everything was kept clean and shining. The effect of the whole was rather attractive to strangers. . . .

Still, we did not call ourselves ladies. We did not forget that we were working girls, wearing coarse aprons suitable to our work, and that there was some danger to our becoming <u>drudges</u>. I know that sometimes the confinement of the mill became very wearisome to me. In the sweet June weather I would lean far out of the window, and try not to hear the unceasing clash of the sound inside. Looking away to the hills, my whole stifled being would cry out, "Oh that I had wings!"

From *A New England Girlhood*, by Lucy Larcom.
Peter Smith, 1973. First published in 1887 by Macmillan.

✓ **Checkpoint** **Why did Larcom return to the mill after finishing three months at grammar school?**

## *Analyze* LITERATURE

Lucy Larcom's words describe a mill in New England during the 1800s. Consider the sights and sounds around her, and how working in the mill made her feel. Write a paragraph in which you describe what it is like to work in a mill.

 **Background**
The wages paid for millwork offered new opportunities to many women and girls, but workers lived apart from their families and often felt lonely.

 **Analyze Setting**
Lucy's attitude toward the mill changes somewhat over the course of this excerpt. How does setting contribute to this change?

If you liked this passage from *A New England Girlhood*, you might want to read more first-person accounts in *Ordinary Americans: U.S. History Through the Eyes of Everyday People*, edited by Linda R. Monk. Close Up Foundation. 2003.

# The North Transformed

## Objectives

1. Explain why American cities grew in the 1800s.

2. List the new inventions and advances in agriculture and manufacturing.

3. Describe the improvements in transportation during the early 1800s.

4. Discuss the wave of immigration to the United States in the 1840s and 1850s.

5. Describe the problems African Americans faced in the North.

## Prepare to Read

 **Reading Skill**

**Explain Central Issues From the Past** As you read about the events of the past, you'll discover that people struggled with issues, much as they do today. Explain those issues to yourself—try to identify what people's concerns were, how they felt about issues, what the issues were about. This will make issues more real and understandable for you.

### Vocabulary *Builder*

**High-Use Words**

<u>reign</u>, p. 393
<u>inferior</u>, p. 395

**Key Terms and People**

urbanization, p. 390
telegraph, p. 391
Samuel F.B. Morse, p. 391
famine, p. 394
nativist, p. 394
discrimination, p. 395

**Main Idea**
As cities in the United States grew, Americans faced a variety of urban problems.

⭐ **Background Knowledge** You have read that from colonial times, the North and the South developed as distinct regions. At first these differences were small. But during the Industrial Revolution, the differences between the North and South widened dramatically.

## Northern Cities

American cities had long been the centers of commerce and culture. By today's standards, these early cities were small. New York, the largest, had a population of slightly more than 33,000 in 1790. Compared to the major cities of Europe, or even the ancient Aztec capital of Tenochtitl´n, New York was hardly more than a town.

**Growth of Cities** In the 1800s, however, U.S. cities grew larger. The Industrial Revolution spurred urbanization, or the growth of cities due to movement of people from rural areas to cities. As capitalists built more factories, agricultural workers were attracted to the new types of work available in the cities.

As cities along the eastern coast became crowded, newly arrived immigrants headed west. Pittsburgh, Pennsylvania, had about 23,000 people in 1840. Ten years later, the city had more than doubled in population. Farther west, the Kentucky city of Louisville was also growing. German and Irish immigrants increased the city's population to more than 43,000 by 1850, making Louisville larger than Washington, D.C.

**Urban Problems** Growing cities faced many problems. Filthy streets, the absence of good sewage systems, and a lack of clean drinking water encouraged the spread of disease.

> "One finds in the streets [of New York] dead cats and dogs, which make the air very bad; dust and ashes are thrown out into the streets, which are swept perhaps once every [two weeks]."
>
> —Baron Axel Klinckowstrom of Sweden

Citywide fires were another common problem. Most structures were made of wood. Volunteer firefighters were often poorly trained and equipped. Insurance companies paid firefighters for saving an insured building. Racing to fire scenes to earn the insurance money, rival fire companies sometimes ended up fighting one another instead of the fire.

☑**Checkpoint** **What problems did cities face in the early 1800s?**

# The Growth of Northern Industry

New inventions revolutionized communications. The most important was the telegraph, a device that used electrical signals to send messages quickly over long distances.

**The Telegraph** Samuel F.B. Morse's invention worked by sending electrical signals over a wire. A code devised by Morse used shorter and longer bursts of electricity. In his system, known as the Morse code, each letter of the alphabet is represented by its own mix of short signals ("dots") and long signals ("dashes").

**Explain Central Issues From the Past**
Explain the link between industrialization and urban problems.

**Main Idea**
New inventions and other advances in agriculture and manufacturing boosted industrial growth.

**Growing Cities**
American cities became bustling centers of enterprise during the 1800s. This is a view along Broadway in New York City.
**Critical Thinking: Explain Problems** What problems did the rapid growth of cities pose for city dwellers?

391

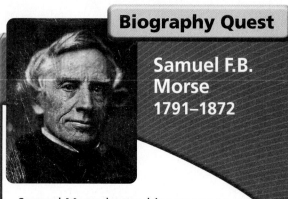

### Samuel F.B. Morse
### 1791–1872

Samuel Morse began his career as a painter. By 1835, however, he was working on the invention that would make him famous. For years, he struggled to find funding. In 1843, he convinced Congress to back his efforts.

The following year, he arranged to link the nation's capital and the city of Baltimore with telegraph lines. The historic first message was sent from the Capitol building in Washington, D.C.

**Biography Quest**

**What chance event led Morse to attempt to develop the telegraph?**

**For:** The answer to the question about Morse

**Visit:** PHSchool.com

**Web Code:** myd-4072

In 1844, Morse tested his system. He wired a message from Washington, D.C., to his assistant in Baltimore: "What hath God wrought?" A few minutes later, a response came back from Baltimore.

The telegraph soon became part of American life. Thousands of miles of wires were strung across the nation. Factories in the East could communicate with their markets in the West in a matter of hours rather than weeks.

**Advances in Agriculture** The mechanical reaper, invented by Cyrus McCormick, made it easier for farmers to settle the prairies of the Midwest. The reaper cut stalks of wheat many times faster than a human worker could. This enabled farmers to cultivate more land and harvest their crops with fewer workers.

Improvements in threshers also speeded up the harvesting of grain. Threshers separate the grains of wheat from their stalks. The wheat grains are then ground into flour. Eventually, the mechanical reaper and the thresher were put together into one machine called a combine.

These advances in agriculture also affected industry. Farm laborers who had been replaced by machines went to cities to work in shops and factories. Cities like Cincinnati grew as both agricultural and industrial centers.

**Advances in Manufacturing** Other inventions revolutionized the way goods were made. In 1846, Elias Howe patented a machine that could sew seams in fabric. A few years later, Isaac Singer improved on Howe's design. The sewing machine made it much more efficient to produce clothing in quantity. As clothes became less expensive, people of modest means began to dress almost as well as wealthier Americans.

By 1860, factories in New England and the Middle Atlantic states were producing most of the nation's manufactured goods. That year, Americans had over $1 billion invested in businesses. Of that total, more than 90 percent was invested in businesses in the North.

✓**Checkpoint** **What new inventions helped northern industry to grow?**

**Main Idea**
Advances in transportation made it easier for businesses to obtain raw materials and get goods to market.

## A Transportation Revolution

Improvements in transportation spurred the growth of American industry. As transportation became faster and easier, factories could make use of raw materials from farther away. Improved transportation also allowed factory owners to ship their goods to distant markets.

**Steamboats and Clipper Ships** In 1807, Robert Fulton, an American inventor, used a steam engine to power a boat. Fulton's *Clermont* was the first practical steamboat. It was 133 feet long and had wooden side paddles that pulled it through the water.

Although side-paddle steamboats were ideal for traveling on rivers, they were not suited to ocean travel. In 1850, a new type of American-built ship appeared, the clipper ship. Long and slender, with tall masts, the clipper ships were magnificent, swift vessels. The Yankee clippers, as they were called, were the world's fastest ships. Their <u>reign</u> was brief, however. By the 1850s, Great Britain was producing oceangoing steamships. These ironclad steamships were faster and could carry more cargo.

**Vocabulary** *Builder*
<u>reign</u> (rayn) *n.* period of dominance or rule

**Railroads** Of all forms of transportation, railroads did the most to tie together raw materials, manufacturers, and markets. Steamboats had to follow the paths of rivers, which sometimes froze in winter. Railroads, however, could be built almost anywhere.

America's first railroad, the Baltimore and Ohio, was begun in 1828. As with most European railroads, its cars were drawn along the track by horses. Then, in 1830, Peter Cooper built the first American-made steam locomotive. By 1840, about 3,000 miles of railway track had been built in the United States.

☑Checkpoint **Why were railroads a better means of transportation than steamboats?**

# A New Wave of Immigrants

The American population grew rapidly in the 1840s. Millions of immigrants entered the United States, mostly from western Europe. Some came because they had heard of opportunities to buy cheap land. Others believed their skills would serve them well in the United States. Still others had little choice, because they could not survive at home.

**Main Idea**
Hunger and political unrest in Europe increased immigration to the United States in the 1840s.

**Fulton's Steamboat**
Robert Fulton's steamboat, the *Clermont,* carried passengers between New York and Albany on the Hudson River. **Critical Thinking:** *Interpret Pictures Why would the* Clermont *not be suitable for ocean travel?*

# Irish Immigration, 1845–1853

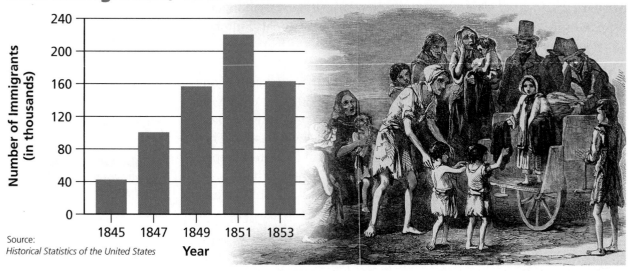

**Number of Immigrants (in thousands)**

240
200
160
120
80
40
0

1845  1847  1849  1851  1853

**Year**

Source:
*Historical Statistics of the United States*

## Fleeing the Famine

A famine in the 1840s drove many Irish to the United States. They contributed to a sharp rise in immigration. **Critical Thinking: Draw Inferences** *Why do you suppose the peak did not come immediately after the famine started in 1845?*

**The Great Hunger** Ireland had long been under British rule. While the best farmland was owned by British landlords, the potato was the staple, or basic, food for most of the population. Then, in 1845, a fungus destroyed the potato crop, leading to famine, or widespread starvation. The years that followed are often called the Great Hunger. More than a million people starved to death. About a million more left Ireland.

Most of the Irish immigrants who came to the United States during this period had been farm laborers at home. The men found work doing the lowliest jobs in construction or laying railroad track in the East and Midwest. Young Irish women were often employed as household workers.

**German Newcomers** Germans came to America during this period as well. Many had taken part in revolutions against harsh rulers. When the revolutions failed, the Germans fled to the United States.

Unlike the Irish, German immigrants came from many different levels of society. After arriving in the United States, most Germans moved west. Many settled in the Ohio Valley and the Great Lakes region.

**Reaction Against Immigrants** Some Americans worried about the growing foreign population. These were nativists, or people who wanted to preserve the country for white, American-born Protestants. Nativists especially opposed Irish immigration because most of the Irish were Roman Catholics.

One group of nativists in New York formed a secret group. When asked about their secret order, members replied, "I know nothing." In time, the Know-Nothings became a political party. In 1856, the Know-Nothing candidate for President won 21 percent of the vote. Soon after, the party split over the issue of slavery and dissolved.

☑ **Checkpoint** Why did Irish and German immigration to the United States increase in the 1840s?

# African Americans in the North

Even more than immigrants, African Americans in the North faced discrimination. Discrimination is the denial of equal rights or equal treatment to certain groups of people.

Slavery had largely ended in the North by the early 1800s. Free African Americans there were joined by new arrivals from the South. Freedom, however, did not grant equal treatment. African Americans were often denied the right to vote. They were not allowed to work in factories or in skilled trades. Even when they sought the least desirable jobs, they were at a disadvantage. Many employers preferred to hire white immigrants rather than African Americans.

Prejudice against African Americans led to the racial segregation of schools and public facilities. Turned away by white congregations, African Americans formed their own churches. For example, people who had been freed from slavery started the African Methodist Episcopal Church in Philadelphia in 1816.

White newspapers often portrayed African Americans as underlined. African Americans responded by starting their own publications. The first newspaper owned and run by African Americans was *Freedom's Journal,* which was established in 1827 in New York. Its editor, John B. Russwurm, had been one of the first African Americans to graduate from an American college.

☑Checkpoint **What obstacles did African Americans face in the North?**

☆ **Looking Back and Ahead** Northern cities grew with the arrival of immigrants from abroad and African Americans from rural areas. Meanwhile, as you will read in the next section, the South depended more and more on cotton and slavery.

**Main Idea**
Although slavery ended in the North, free African Americans struggled to overcome discrimination and prejudice.

**Vocabulary** *Builder*
**inferior** (ihn FIR ee uhr) *adj.* less worthy; less valuable; of lower rank

---

## Section 2 | Check Your Progress

**Progress Monitoring** ⓝnline
**For:** Self-test with instant help
**Visit:** PHSchool.com
**Web Code:** mya-4072

**Comprehension and Critical Thinking**

1. **(a) Recall** What factors led to the growth of cities?
**(b) Evaluate Information** How did the rapid growth of cities affect urban living conditions?

2. **(a) Recall** How did the telegraph improve communication?
**(b) Identify Economic Benefits** How might improved communication help the growing economy?

**Reading Skill**

3. **Explain Central Issues From the Past** Reread the text following the heading "Advances in Agriculture." Explain how changes in agriculture affected workers in the nineteenth century.

**Vocabulary** *Builder*

Read each sentence below. If the sentence is true, write YES. If the sentence is not true, write NO and explain why.

4. Urbanization is the movement of people from urban areas to farms.

5. More than a million people died in a famine during "the Great Hunger" that started in Ireland in 1845.

6. Even though many African Americans living in the North were legally free, they still suffered from discrimination.

**Writing**

7. Based on what you have read in this section, list as many causes as you can for the growth of industry in the North. Put stars next to the causes that you think are most important.

## Objectives

1. Explain the significance of cotton and the cotton gin to the South.

2. Describe what life was like for free and enslaved African Americans in the South.

## Prepare to Read

### Reading Skill

**Explain Problems From the Past** Why did problems occur in the past? Try to answer this question as you read. It will help you connect events and understand people's beliefs and actions. Put yourself in the shoes of the people about whom you read. What problems would you have with these same issues? Explain these problems to clarify them.

### Vocabulary *Builder*

**High-Use Words**

**devote**, p. 397

**revolt**, p. 400

### Key Terms and People

cotton gin, p. 396

slave code, p. 399

spiritual, p. 400

Nat Turner, p. 400

⭐ **Background Knowledge** As you have read, Eli Whitney's system of interchangeable parts revolutionized industry. Another of Whitney's inventions had an equally powerful impact on the rural South.

## The Cotton Kingdom

**Main Idea**
As cotton production expanded in the South to supply the northern textile industry, planters increased their use of slave labor.

As the North became more urban and industrialized, the South remained largely rural. Two events changed life in the South. First, a boom in textiles caused by the Industrial Revolution created a huge demand for cotton. Second, a new invention allowed the South to satisfy that demand.

**The Cotton Gin** In 1793, Eli Whitney devised a simple machine that speeded the processing of cotton. His cotton gin used a spiked cylinder to remove seeds from cotton fibers.

Before the introduction of the cotton gin, the seeds had to be picked out of the cotton fibers by hand. This was a slow process. Working by hand, a laborer could clean only a pound of cotton a day.

The cotton gin was revolutionary technology. A worker could process fifty times more cotton fiber with the gin than by hand. Cotton growing became far more profitable.

**Slave Labor** To grow more cotton, planters used more slave labor. In 1790, there were about 698,000 enslaved African Americans in the United States. By 1860, the census recorded nearly 4 million. During that time, the price of a slave increased ten or twenty times.

Cotton became the greatest source of wealth for the United States. It enriched planters in the South, as well as bankers and shipowners in the North. Cotton production rose at an astonishing rate. Planters grew one and a half millon pounds of cotton in 1790. In 1820, they grew ten times as much.

Southern states were not all alike. States like Alabama and Mississippi, which depended on cotton, had large populations of enslaved people. Other states, such as Kentucky, <u>devoted</u> less attention to cotton. Fewer enslaved people lived there.

In the southern "Cotton Kingdom," society was dominated by owners of large plantations. This small but wealthy class lived in luxury and sent their children to the finest schools. But more than half of all southern farmers did not have slaves. They grew corn and raised hogs and chickens.

**Defending Slavery** Most southern whites accepted the system of slavery. Many feared that any weakening of controls over African Americans might encourage violent uprisings. By the 1830s, some people in the North were urging that slavery be banned. (You will read about the movement to end slavery in the next chapter.) In response, southern whites hardened their support for slavery.

Supporters of slavery said it was more humane than the free labor system of the North. Unlike northern factory workers, they argued, enslaved African Americans did not worry about unemployment.

**Vocabulary** *Builder*
<u>devote</u> (dee VOHT) *v.* to commit; to apply (time and energy, for example)

**Explain Problems From the Past**
Explain the disagreements between supporters and critics of slavery.

# Cotton Production and Slavery

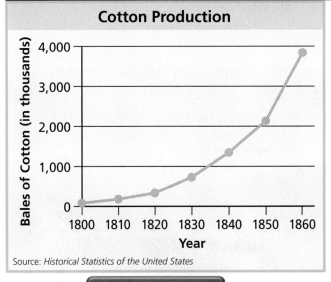

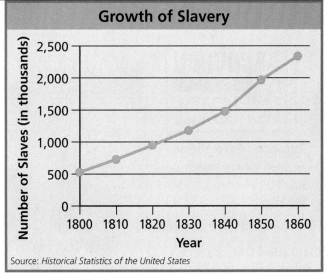

**Reading Charts**
**Skills Activity**

The rise in cotton production in the South was paralleled by a rise in the number of enslaved African Americans.

(a) **Read Graphs** How much did cotton production increase between 1800 and 1850? In what 10-year period did slavery grow the fastest?

(b) **Make Predictions** If cotton production had decreased, would the number of slaves have declined? Explain your reasoning.

Critics of slavery, however, challenged this reasoning. They argued that northern workers were free to quit a job and take another if conditions became too harsh. Also, the critics said, people held in slavery often suffered physical or other abuse from white owners. There was no satisfactory substitute for freedom.

☑ **Checkpoint**  How widespread was slave ownership?

## African Americans in the South

**Main Idea**
Whether free or enslaved, African Americans in the South were subject to harsh rules and unequal treatment.

Not all of the 4 million African Americans in the South were enslaved. About 253,000 (or 6 percent) were free. Many had purchased their freedom. A few did well, especially in cities like New Orleans. But most did not share in the prosperity around them.

**Restrictions on Free African Americans** Laws denied basic rights even to African Americans who were free. By law, they were excluded from all but the most menial jobs. Their children were denied the right to attend public schools. African Americans could not vote, serve on juries, or testify against white defendants in court.

Free African Americans were discouraged from traveling. In a petition, some described the conditions they faced:

> ❝[When] we have occasion to . . . Travel . . . [b]y Steem boat or Stage, we have been exceedingly anoyd And put to very considerable inconvenience and eaven compeled to Leave the boat and thereby entirely defeated from accomplishing our just and lawful business because we have not [had] a certificate from some White person.❞
> —petition to Delaware legislature, 1850s

**Explore More Video**
To learn more about southern plantations, view the video.

**Plantation Life** Life on a southern plantation showed vast contrasts. The families of large plantation owners enjoyed many luxuries. Families bound to slavery experienced hard work and many cruelties. **Critical Thinking: Compare and Contrast** How do these pictures support the view that plantation owners and enslaved African Americans lived very

▼ **A Family on the Patio** A wealthy southern family relaxes on their patio as they survey their estate.

◀ **Keeping Cool** Refreshing breezes from fans like this kept wealthy women cool.

The freedom of African Americans in the South was never secure. Slave catchers prowled the streets looking for escapees. They often kidnapped free African Americans and sold them into slavery.

In spite of all the restrictions placed upon them, many free African Americans made valuable contributions to southern life. Norbert Rillieux revolutionized the sugar industry. His method of refining sugar made the process faster, safer, and less costly. Another African American inventor, Henry Blair, developed a seed-planting device that reduced the time a farmer spent sowing a crop.

**Life Under Slavery** For all the problems faced by free African Americans, those who were enslaved faced much greater trials. They had no rights at all. Laws known as **slave codes** controlled every aspect of their lives. As a Kentucky court ruled in 1828, ". . . a slave by our code is not treated as a person but as a . . . thing. . . ."

Many enslaved African Americans became skilled workers. Their skills kept the plantations operating efficiently. Others worked in the owners' homes as housekeepers, butlers, or nannies and became trusted house servants.

The vast majority did heavy farm labor. Most slaveholders stopped short of working a laborer to death. Some came close, however. On the large plantations, white overseers administered punishment—often a whipping—for many offenses.

Enslaved African Americans had only one real protection against mistreatment: Owners looked on them as valuable property that they needed to keep healthy and productive.

Families of enslaved African Americans were often broken apart when slave owners sold one or more of their family members. Many children had only the slightest memory of their parents.

◄ **A Family in the Fields**
Children worked in the fields with their enslaved parents. This Georgia family was picking cotton.

◄ **Bonds of Slavery**
Shackles such as these were used to restrain slaves who tried to escape or who otherwise displeased a master.

Nat Turner captured

**Vocabulary** *Builder*
revolt (ree VOHLT) *n.* uprising; rebellion

After 1808, it was illegal to import enslaved Africans to the United States. As a result, African Americans had little direct contact with Africa. Nevertheless, African customs, music, and dance survived in their daily lives from one generation to another.

Many African Americans found a message of hope in the Bible. African Americans composed **spirituals,** religious folk songs that blended biblical themes with the realities of slavery.

**Resistance to Slavery** Many African Americans did what they could to resist the slaveholders. Some worked slowly or pretended not to understand what they were told to do. Others deliberately broke farm equipment. The most daring fled north to freedom.

Sometimes, resistance became rebellion. Nat Turner led the most famous slave revolt in 1831. Turner said he had a vision that told him to kill whites. He and others killed about 60 whites. In reprisal, many innocent African Americans were executed.

☑**Checkpoint** **How did enslaved African Americans adapt to slavery and resist it?**

⭐ **Looking Back and Ahead** The more cotton they grew, the more southern planters depended on the labor of enslaved African Americans. At the same time, African Americans in the South struggled to endure or resist slavery. In the next section, you will read how the settling of western areas caused new tensions between North and South.

---

Section 3 | **Check Your Progress**

**Progress Monitoring** ⏾nline
**For:** Self-test with instant help
**Visit:** PHSchool.com
**Web Code:** mya-4073

**Comprehension and Critical Thinking**

1. **(a) Summarize** How were northern textile mills and southern cotton plantations linked? What key invention deepened this connection?
**(b) Understand Sequence** Place the following events in the order in which they happened: population of cotton-producing states triples; Whitney invents the cotton gin; Nat Turner leads slave revolt; the need for slaves increases; northern textile factories have need for cotton; support for slavery hardens among southern whites.

2. **(a) Describe** What might a typical workday be like for an enslaved African American on a southern cotton plantation?
**(b) Draw Conclusions** Why do you think enslaved people rebelled, even though the risk was so great and the likelihood of success so small?

**⏵ Reading Skill**
3. **Explain Problems From the Past** Connect the problems facing southern planters and southern African Americans.

**Vocabulary** *Builder*
Answer the following questions in complete sentences that show your understanding of the key terms.

4. How does the cotton gin work?
5. How did slave codes control every aspect of the lives of enslaved African Americans?
6. What would be a common theme of an African American spiritual?

**Writing**
7. Based on what you have read in this section, list as many effects as you can that resulted from the invention of the cotton gin by Eli Whitney. List the effects in the order in which they happened. If one effect led to another effect, draw an arrow between those two developments.

# The Challenges of Growth

## Objectives

1. Identify the problems Americans moving westward faced.
2. Describe the impact of the building of the Erie Canal.
3. Discuss the debate over slavery and the Missouri Compromise.

## Prepare to Read

### Reading Skill

**Place Events in a Matrix of Time and Place** Each event in history takes place in the context of a specific time and place. As you read this textbook or other history textbooks, try to remember additional events from the same time or place. Then, look for possible connections among the events discussed in the different parts of a chapter or unit.

### Vocabulary *Builder*

**High-Use Words**

<u>pursue</u>, p. 402

<u>isolated</u>, p. 403

**Key Terms and People**

Daniel Boone, p. 401

turnpike, p. 402

corduroy road, p. 403

canal, p. 403

Henry Clay, p. 404

---

⭐ **Background Knowledge** You have learned that there was a boom in cotton production after the invention of the cotton gin. Settlers moved west from southern states to find new land for cotton. Farther north, a different stream of settlers headed west, seeking land for other crops.

## Moving West

During colonial times, Americans looked on the backcountry between the Atlantic Coast and the Appalachian Mountains as the western frontier. By the 1750s, the Scotch-Irish and the Germans of Pennsylvania had begun to settle the backcountry.

The most famous early pioneer was Daniel Boone. In 1775, Boone and a party of 30 men cleared a new route to the West—the Wilderness Road. It crossed the Appalachian Mountains through the Cumberland Gap into Kentucky. The Wilderness Road became the main route across the Appalachians. In time, pioneers created many other routes for westward travel. (See the map on the next page.)

**A Growing Population** By the early 1800s, the flow of immigrants to the West had become a flood. As western populations grew, many areas applied to become states. From 1792 to 1819, eight states joined the Union: Kentucky (1792), Tennessee (1796), Ohio (1803), Louisiana (1812), Indiana (1816), Mississippi (1817), Illinois (1818), and Alabama (1819).

**Main Idea**

During the early 1800s, a flood of settlers pushed the frontier ever farther to the west.

**Place Events in a Matrix of Time and Place**

Name two important events from the early nineteenth century that contributed to America's growth as a nation. Consider the topics covered in this chapter and in previous chapters.

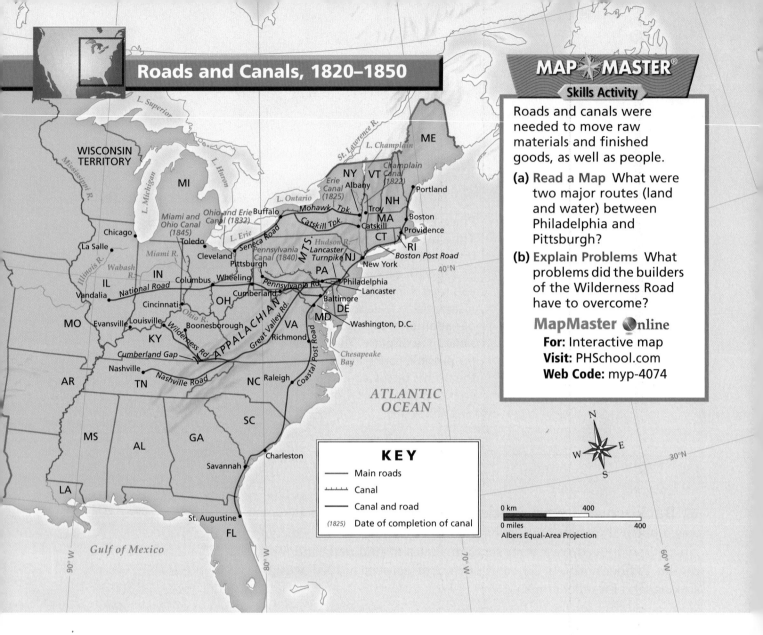

## Roads and Canals, 1820–1850

**MAP MASTER®**

**Skills Activity**

Roads and canals were needed to move raw materials and finished goods, as well as people.

**(a) Read a Map** What were two major routes (land and water) between Philadelphia and Pittsburgh?

**(b) Explain Problems** What problems did the builders of the Wilderness Road have to overcome?

**MapMaster Online**
**For:** Interactive map
**Visit:** PHSchool.com
**Web Code:** myp-4074

**KEY**
— Main roads
+++ Canal
— Canal and road
(1825) Date of completion of canal

**Vocabulary** *Builder*
**pursue** (per SYOO) *v.* to chase after; to try to capture

Traveling west was not easy. Many early roads began as paths for deer or bison. Indians used these well-worn paths to <u>pursue</u> game. Then, white settlers began to drive their wagons over these paths. Not surprisingly, the roads were terrible. They were unpaved, dotted with tree stumps, and easily washed out by rain.

✓**Checkpoint** How did American settlers heading west reach their new homes?

**Main Idea**
Both private investors and the government helped to extend the network of American roads.

## Roads and Turnpikes

Clearly the nation needed better roads. Farmers and merchants had to have a way to move their goods to market quickly and cheaply. Some capitalists decided to provide that way.

Private companies began to build turnpikes, or toll roads. At certain points, a bar on a hinge swung out across the road. The bar resembled a spear, or pike. Travelers would have to stop and pay a toll in order to pass.

In 1795, a private company in Pennsylvania built a turnpike between Lancaster and Philadelphia. The Lancaster Turnpike was the first long-distance stone road in the United States. The road provided cheap, reliable transportation to <u>isolated</u> agricultural areas.

In marshy areas, wagons traveled on **corduroy roads,** roads made of sawed-off logs, laid side by side. This meant a bumpy ride as wagons bounced over each log. Corduroy roads were a hazard to horses, because they could break their legs if they slipped through the logs.

The National Road was the first federally funded road. Begun in 1811 in Cumberland, Maryland, it stretched to Wheeling, in western Virginia, by 1818 and reached Vandalia, Illinois, in 1850. The road crossed hundreds of miles of varying terrain. Bridges carried it over many rivers and streams.

☑**Checkpoint** **What was the National Road?**

**Vocabulary** *Builder*
<u>isolated</u> (ī sah lay tehd) *adj.* set apart

# Canals

Slow road travel isolated western farmers from eastern markets. The fastest, cheapest way to ship goods was by water. However, the major rivers ran north and south. The solution was to build canals from east to west. A **canal** is a channel that is dug across land and filled with water. Canals allow boats to reach more places.

In 1816, New York Governor DeWitt Clinton proposed a canal from the Hudson River to Lake Erie. Critics scoffed at the idea. Still, work began on "Clinton's Ditch" in 1817.

Building the canal was a challenge for canal engineers—and for workers, who were mostly Irish immigrants. The land in upstate New York is not level. Locks had to be built to raise or lower boats in the canal. Locks are chambers just big enough to hold a boat. When a boat enters a lock, gates close at both ends of the chamber. If the boat is to be raised, water flows into the lock. If the boat must be lowered, water drains out.

At Lockport, five double locks raised the canal 50 feet. One canal traveler wrote:

> **"**As one passes along this deep cavern and sees . . . the rough perpendicular walls pierced in every part with drill-holes used for blasting the rock, he is astonished at the perseverance, labor, and expense which it cost.**"**
>
> —from the *Diary of Jonathan Pearson,* 1833

Within two years of its opening in 1825, the canal had paid for itself. Produce from the Midwest came across Lake Erie, passed through the Erie Canal, and was carried down the Hudson River to New York City. Because of its location at the end of the canal, New York soon became the richest city in the nation.

**Main Idea**
The Erie Canal was one of many canals built to fill gaps in the nation's system of transportation.

**Crazy Over Canals**
American popular culture celebrated the new canals with songs, stories, and even jokes.

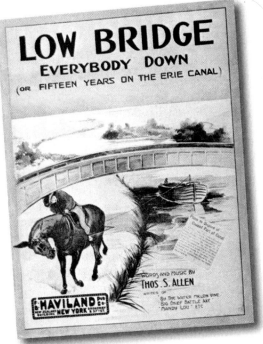

The success of the Erie Canal sparked a surge of canal building. In 1829, a canal was built through Delaware. Canals were soon underway in Virginia, Pennsylvania, Ohio, Indiana, and Illinois.

✓**Checkpoint** **How did the building of the Erie Canal help farmers in the interior of the country?**

## The Extension of Slavery

**Main Idea**
As new states applied to enter the Union, a renewed debate over slavery added to tensions between the North and the South.

Westward expansion strengthened the nation. It also caused problems. The most serious problem was the extension of slavery.

**Slave and Free States** In 1819, the nation consisted of 11 "slave states," which permitted slavery, and 11 "free states," which prohibited slavery. However, Missouri had been seeking admission as a slave state since 1817.

Northerners had reacted strongly. Adding another slave state would upset the balance in the Senate, where each state had two votes. Adding two more senators from a slave state would make the South more powerful than the North.

In 1819, Representative James Tallmadge of New York proposed that Missouri be admitted as a slave state. However, once it was admitted, no more slaves could be brought into the state.

The bill passed the House of Representatives, but it failed in the Senate. Southern senators feared that slavery itself—and thus the South's economic well-being—was being threatened.

**The Missouri Compromise** In the next session of Congress, Maine applied for admission to the Union. Unlike Missouri, Maine prohibited slavery. The admission of both a free state and a slave state would maintain the balance in the Senate.

In 1820, Senator Henry Clay persuaded Congress to adopt the Missouri Compromise. It permitted Maine to be admitted to the Union as a free state and Missouri to be admitted as a slave state. In addition, the compromise provided that the Louisiana Territory north of the southern border of Missouri would be free of slavery. The compromise had one other important feature. It gave southern slave owners a clear right to pursue escaped fugitives into "free" regions and return them to slavery.

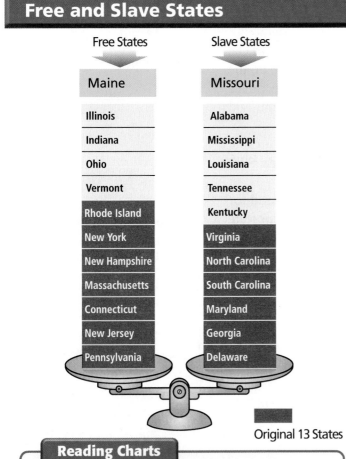

## Free and Slave States

| Free States | Slave States |
| --- | --- |
| Maine | Missouri |
| Illinois | Alabama |
| Indiana | Mississippi |
| Ohio | Louisiana |
| Vermont | Tennessee |
| Rhode Island | Kentucky |
| New York | Virginia |
| New Hampshire | North Carolina |
| Massachusetts | South Carolina |
| Connecticut | Maryland |
| New Jersey | Georgia |
| Pennsylvania | Delaware |

Original 13 States

### Reading Charts
#### Skills Activity

The addition of Missouri to the Union threatened to upset the balance between free states and slave states.

**(a) Read a Chart** Which of the following was a free state: Kentucky, Tennessee, or Ohio?

**(b) Explain Problems** Why did northern states wish to have Missouri and Maine enter the Union at the same time?

**A Continuing Problem** The Missouri Compromise revealed how much sectional rivalries divided the states of the Union. The compromise seemed to balance the interests of the North and the South. However, white southerners were not happy that Congress had given itself the power to make laws regarding slavery. Many northerners, in turn, were angry that Congress had allowed slavery to expand into another state.

Thomas Jefferson was alarmed by the fierce debate over the Missouri Compromise. The former President, much older now, saw that the issues raised by the compromise could tear the nation apart. He wrote to a friend:

> **❝** This momentous question, like a firebell in the night, awakened and filled me with terror. I considered it at once as the knell of the Union. . . . [W]e have the wolf by the ears, and we can neither hold him, nor safely let him go. **❞**
> —Thomas Jefferson, letter of April 22, 1820

As Jefferson observed, the bitterness of feelings about slavery posed a serious threat to national unity. In time, the issue of slavery would indeed split the nation in two.

**☑ Checkpoint** **Why was Jefferson alarmed at the bitterness of the debate over the extension of slavery?**

**⭐ Looking Back and Ahead** In this chapter, you learned about increasing differences between North and South. In the next chapter, you will read about the movement to end slavery and other efforts to bring social change.

---

**Section 4 | Check Your Progress**

**Progress Monitoring ◐nline**
**For:** Self-test with instant help
**Visit:** PHSchool.com
**Web Code:** mya-4074

**Comprehension and Critical Thinking**

1. **(a) Recall** How did building better roads and canals transform the United States?
**(b) Identify Economic Benefits** How did improved transportation lead to economic growth?

2. **(a) List** What were the main points of the Missouri Compromise?
**(b) Make Predictions** Why would the issues addressed by the Missouri Compromise continue to tear the nation apart?

**⟳ Reading Skill**

3. **Place Events in a Matrix of Time and Place** What event in the early nineteenth century led to the creation of the Missouri Territory and later to the state of Missouri? Describe this event.

**Vocabulary *Builder***

4. Draw a table with three rows and three columns. In the first column, list the key terms from this section: turnpike, corduroy road, canal. In the next column, write the definition of each term. In the last column, make a small illustration that shows the meaning of the term.

**Writing**

5. Based on what you have read in this section, write a thesis statement about the most important change caused by the development of new routes to the West.

When you are doing research on the Internet, it is important to evaluate the Web sites to determine if the information is valid and objective. The page below is from a Web site about Samuel F.B. Morse.

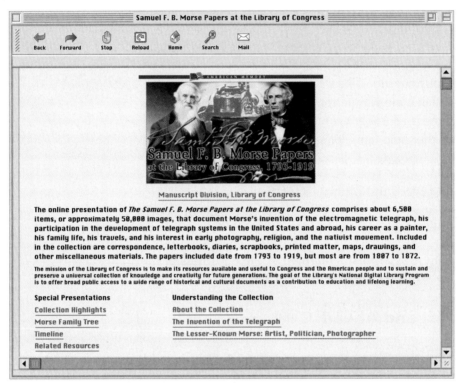

Source: The Library of Congress

## Learn the Skill

*Use these steps to learn how to evaluate Internet sources.*

**1** **Determine the Web site's purpose.** Does the Web site provide information? Is it trying to sell something or to promote a particular point of view?

**2** **Examine the information.** Does the site include visuals? Does it include first-person accounts and other primary source materials?

**3** **Compare the information to what you already know.** Does the information agree with what you have read in a textbook or in another reliable print source? What other information is provided?

**4** **Evaluate the source.** Is the source an established organization? Can you tell who provided the information?

## Practice the Skill

*Use the information above to answer the following questions.*

**1** **Determine the Web site's purpose.** What is the purpose of this Web site?

**2** **Examine the information.** (a) What kinds of information can you find on this page? (b) What other features does it include?

**3** **Compare the information to what you already know.** What additional information does this Web site give that supplements the information in this chapter?

**4** **Evaluate the source.** (a) Who is the provider for this site? (b) If you were writing a paper about Samuel F.B. Morse, do you think you could use the information on this Web site? Why or why not?

## Apply the Skill

*See the Review and Assessment at the end of this chapter.*

## Chapter Summary

### Section 1
### The Industrial Revolution

- By the end of the 1700s, advances in technology allowed goods to be produced cheaply and quickly by machines.
- In the United States, the Industrial Revolution centered in the Northeast, which had an ample supply of labor and raw materials.
- Factory conditions became increasingly dangerous, and laborers fought for better working conditions.

### Section 2
### The North Transformed

- Cities grew rapidly during the 1800s, and crowding, disease, and fast-spreading fires were common problems.
- Northern industries grew due to advances in technology.

### Section 3
### The Plantation South

- Eli Whitney's cotton gin made possible a huge increase in cotton production.
- As cotton production grew, the number and value of enslaved African Americans increased dramatically.
- In the face of cruel conditions, many enslaved African Americans resisted slavery.

### Section 4
### The Challenges of Growth

- By the early 1800s, a flood of settlers westward helped many territories qualify for statehood.
- Better roads and canals further increased the rate of western settlement.
- Tension arose over slavery in the territories, but the Missouri Compromise settled the issue temporarily.

## Key Concepts

These notes will help you prepare for questions about key concepts.

### Key Inventions and Innovations

**Manufacturing**
- Spinning jenny
- Steam engine
- Factory system
- Interchangeable parts and mass production
- Sewing machine

**Agriculture**
- Mechanical reaper
- Thresher
- Combine
- Cotton gin

### Transportation and Communication

**Improvements**
- Roads are improved.
- Canals link waterways.
- Clipper ships speed traffic over oceans.
- Steamships ply rivers.
- Use of railroads is increased.
- The telegraph speeds communication.

**Effects of Improvements**
- Goods get to market faster and cheaper.
- People migrate to the West.

### Impact of Immigration

**Population Movement**
- Irish immigrate to the United States due to famine.
- German immigration is sparked by revolutions against harsh rulers.
- Free African Americans in the South move north and west.

**Effects of Immigration**
- Large numbers of people fill factory jobs.
- Nativists become politically active in reaction to European immigration.

## Vocabulary *Builder*

### Key Terms
Fill in the blanks with the correct key terms.

1. The _____ was the change in the way people made goods beginning in the late 1700s.

2. People who wanted to keep immigrants out of the country were called _____.

3. African Americans sang _____ to keep hope during their difficult lives.

4. Travelers had to pay tolls on _____ in order to pass.

## Comprehension and Critical Thinking

5. **(a) Describe** Who were the Lowell girls?
   **(b) Apply Information** How do you think the Lowell system affected production?

6. **(a) Identify** What contribution did Eli Whitney make to manufacturing?
   **(b) Identify Economic Benefits** How did this contribution benefit consumers?

7. **(a) Summarize** How did the physical limitations of steamboats differ from those of railroads?
   **(b) Draw Conclusions** Why were both means of transportation important to the growth of industry?

8. **(a) Summarize** How did the cotton gin benefit southern planters? How did it benefit northern textile manufacturers?
   **(b) Analyze Cause and Effect** How did the cotton gin change life for enslaved people?

9. **(a) Contrast** What arguments did some southerners use to defend slavery? What were some points raised by northern critics of slavery to challenge those arguments?
   **(b) Apply Information** What were some tactics that enslaved African Americans employed in order to endure or resist slavery?

10. **(a) Describe** What were some of the difficulties Americans faced as they traveled west?
    **(b) Analyze Cause and Effect** How did improved transportation affect western settlement? How did it affect industry?
    **(c) Draw Conclusions** How were immigrants important to the transportation revolution?

11. **(a) Recall** How was slavery an issue in the debate over Missouri's statehood?
    **(b) Detect Points of View** Why did northerners believe that it would be damaging to the North if the South became more powerful in the Senate?

## History Reading Skill

12. **Identify and Explain Central Issues** Write a paragraph that explains the issues central to the Missouri Compromise. Orient the issues in the context of the times and places in which they occurred.

## Writing

13. Write a paragraph explaining *either* the causes *or* the effects of one of the following developments:
    - Industrialization of the North
    - The cotton empire of the South

    **Your paragraph should:**
    - begin with a sentence that expresses your main idea;
    - indicate whether you will focus on the subject's causes or its effects;
    - expand on your main idea with facts, examples, and other information.

14. **Write a Narrative:**
    Choose one of the inventions developed during the first half of the nineteenth century. Write a narrative that describes how people were affected by the invention.

## Skills for Life
### Evaluate Internet Sources
Visit this Web site: www.eriecanalmuseum.org. Then, use the information to answer the following questions.

15. What seems to be the purpose of this Web site?

16. **(a)** What kinds of information can you find on this page? **(b)** What other features and links does it include?

17. What additional information does this Web site give to supplement the information in your textbook?

18. **(a)** Who is the provider for this site? **(b)** If you were writing a paper about the Erie Canal, do you think you could use the information on this Web site? Why or why not?

# Test Yourself

1. **Which of the following inventions did the most to advance the connection between goods, raw materials, and markets?**

   A interchangeable parts

   B steamboats

   C telegraphs

   D railroads

2. **In the mid-1800s, many immigrants came to the United States from Ireland to escape**

   A revolutions.

   B famine.

   C political unrest.

   D religious persecution.

**Refer to the quotation below to answer Question 3.**

> "This momentous question, like a firebell in the night, awakened and filled me with terror. I considered it at once as the knell of the Union. . . ."

3. **To which issue does this quotation refer?**

   A transportation

   B slavery

   C immigration

   D mass production

# Document-Based Questions

**Task:** Look at Documents 1 and 2, and answer their accompanying questions. Then, use the documents and your knowledge of history to complete this writing assignment:

> Write an essay describing what life was like for enslaved African Americans in the South. Use information from the graph to explain why slaveholders felt restrictive measures were necessary.

**Document 1:** This graph gives information about the population of some slave-holding states in 1840. *Use the graph to make a generalization about the South's slave population.*

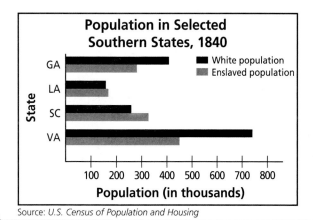

**Population in Selected Southern States, 1840**

- White population
- Enslaved population

State: GA, LA, SC, VA

Population (in thousands): 100 200 300 400 500 600 700 800

Source: *U.S. Census of Population and Housing*

**Document 2:** The excerpt below is from a 1930s interview with Fountain Hughes, born a slave in 1848 near Charlottesville, Virginia. *How does Fountain Hughes describe what it meant to be a slave?*

> "Well, I belonged to B., when I was a slave. My mother belonged to B. But we was all slave children. . . .
>
> Now I couldn' go from here across the street . . . [with]out I have a note, or something from my master. . . . Whoever he sent me to, they'd give me another pass an' I'd bring that back so as to show how long I'd been gone. . . . An' when I come back, why I carry it to my master an' give that to him, that'd be all right. But I couldn' jus' walk away like the people does now. . . .
>
> We belonged to people. They'd sell us like they sell horses an' cows an' hogs an' all like that. Have a auction bench, an' they'd put you on, up on the bench an' bid on you jus' same as you bidding on cattle."

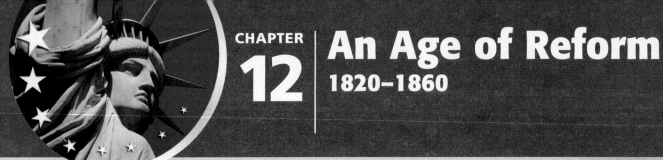
## Chapter Preview

As the country grew, efforts to bring social reforms increased. In the mid-1800s, Americans worked for change in many areas. Meanwhile, American culture flowered as artists and writers began to develop uniquely American styles.

**1826**
Charles Finney begins holding religious revival meetings.

**1831**
William Lloyd Garrison founds antislavery newspaper.

**1837**
Horace Mann begins campaign to improve public schools.

**U.S. Events**

1820

1830

1840

**World Events**

**1822** Colony of Liberia is founded in West Africa.

**1833** Slavery is banned in all British colonies.

410

In this painting, the women riding in the sleigh were campaigning to win the right to vote.

**Discovery SCHOOL**

**Quick View Video**
View the chapter video for a quick preview of the main ideas.

**1848**
Women's rights convention is held in Seneca Falls, New York.

**1850s**
American writers publish *The Scarlet Letter, Moby-Dick, Walden,* and *Leaves of Grass.*

1840

**1845** Britain passes law to reform mental hospitals.

1850

**1860** Charles Dickens publishes *Great Expectations.*

1860

**History Reading Skill** **Draw Conclusions From Sources**

## For which rights were nineteenth-century women fighting?

In this chapter, you will learn how to use details to draw conclusions from sources. Read the following selection by women's rights advocate Elizabeth Cady Stanton. The side notes show you how to draw conclusions from sources.

The Declaration of Sentiments was issued in 1848 during a women's rights convention in Seneca Falls, New York.

**Primary Source**

...We hold these truths to be self-evident: that all men and women are created equal; that they are endowed by their Creator with certain inalienable rights; ... that to secure these rights governments are instituted, deriving their just powers from the consent of the governed. Whenever any form of government becomes destructive of these ends, it is the right of those who suffer from it to refuse allegiance to it, and to insist upon the institution of a new government. ....

The history of mankind is a history of repeated injuries and usurpations [unlawful seizure of power] on the part of man toward woman, having in direct object the establishment of an absolute tyranny over her. ....

He has never permitted her to exercise her inalienable right to the elective franchise [right to vote]. ....

He has taken from her all right in property, even to the wages she earns. ....

He has denied her the facilities [means] for obtaining a thorough education, all colleges being closed against her.

—Elizabeth Cady Stanton, Declaration of Sentiments

> This detail shows that Stanton believes action is necessary to win rights for women.

> Women did not get the same type of education as men.

> This detail points out that women could not vote.

## Draw a Conclusion

- Stanton provides details of injustices women have faced.
- You can conclude that Stanton believes women have been denied rights and that they must fight for these rights.

## Document-Based Questions

1. Compare this excerpt to the opening of the Declaration of Independence. Identify two similarities in language.
2. Why do you think Stanton deliberately repeated language from the Declaration of Independence?

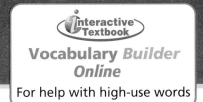
# Vocabulary *Builder*

## Previewing High-Use Academic Words

| High-Use Word | Definition | Sample History Sentence |
|---|---|---|
| **impulse** (IHM puhls) (Section 1, p. 415) | *n.* sudden push or driving force | Reformers had an <u>impulse</u> to try to improve society. |
| **convert** (kahn VERT) (Section 1, p. 415) | *v.* to change from one political party, religion, or way of life to another | The preacher's goal was to <u>convert</u> his listeners from a life of sin to a life of good works. |
| **eliminate** (ee LIHM ih nayt) (Section 2, p. 422) | *v.* to get rid of | Some people worked to <u>eliminate</u> the problem of alcohol abuse. |
| **via** (VEE ah) (Section 2, p. 424) | *prep.* by way of | Settlers went west <u>via</u> the Great Wagon Road. |
| **exclude** (ehks KLYOOD) (Section 3, p. 428) | *v.* to keep out or expel; to reject | Most colleges at that time <u>excluded</u> women and African Americans. |
| **emotion** (ee MOH shuhn) (Section 4, p. 432) | *n.* strong feeling such as sadness, anger, or love | His speech about the evils of slavery stirred the <u>emotions</u> of the audience. |
| **reproduce** (ree prah DYOOS) (Section 4, p. 435) | *v.* to make a copy | In her paintings, she tried to <u>reproduce</u> the beauty of the natural world. |

## Previewing Key Terms and People

# Improving Society

## Objectives

1. Discuss what led many Americans to try to improve society in the 1800s.

2. Identify the social problems that reformers tried to solve.

3. Summarize the improvements in public education in the 1800s.

## Prepare to Read

### 🔄 Reading Skill

**Assess Evidence for a Conclusion** In reading history, you will encounter many descriptive details that help you draw conclusions about historical events. Evaluate the details carefully with questions such as these: Are they accurate and from reliable sources? Do the sources have firsthand knowledge of the situations? What conclusions do the details point to?

### Vocabulary *Builder*

**High-Use Words**

<u>impulse</u>, p. 415

<u>convert</u>, p. 415

**Key Terms and People**

social reform, p. 414

predestination, p. 415

Charles Finney, p. 415

revival, p. 415

temperance movement, p. 416

prohibition, p. 416

Dorothea Dix, p. 417

public school, p. 417

Horace Mann, p. 418

⭐ **Background Knowledge** As you have read, the presidency of Andrew Jackson was a time of expanding democracy in the United States. This democratic spirit was one factor that helped spark efforts to improve American society. In this section, you will read about some of these efforts.

## The Reforming Spirit

**Main Idea**
Political and religious ideas inspired Americans to seek ways to improve society.

In the 1830s, many Americans became interested in social reform, or organized attempts to improve conditions of life. The effort to create a better society had both political and religious roots.

**Jacksonian Democracy** The expansion of democracy in the Age of Jackson encouraged reform. Most states dropped property requirements for voting. As a result, more white American men were able to vote than ever before. Political parties also developed a more open way of choosing candidates for President.

In the spirit of Jacksonian democracy, some people worked to make the political system even fairer. A number of reformers believed that all men should vote and be able to hold office. Others supported greater legal rights for women. Increasingly, reformers also spoke out strongly against slavery. They argued that no society that allowed one human being to own another could call itself democratic.

**The Second Great Awakening** Religious feelings and ideas also sparked the reforming <u>impulse</u>. Beginning in the early 1800s, a new generation of ministers challenged some traditional views. This movement became known as the Second Great Awakening.

Changing religious ideas sparked the Second Great Awakening. In colonial days, many American Protestants believed in **predestination**, the idea that God decided the fate of a person's soul even before birth. But leaders of the Second Great Awakening preached that people's own actions determined their salvation. This "doctrine of free will" blended easily with political ideas about democracy and independence.

The most important of this new generation of preachers was **Charles Finney**. Finney held the first of many religious revivals in 1826. A **revival** is a huge outdoor religious meeting. Before long, Finney and other preachers were conducting revivals across the nation. A single revival might go on for several days or even a week. Ministers of different faiths preached day and night, trying to <u>convert</u> sinners and urging people to reform their lives.

Finney believed that the emotion of a revival could touch even the most hopeless sinner. "All sorts of abandoned characters are awakened and converted," he wrote. "The worst part of human society is softened and reclaimed, and made to appear as a lovely specimen of the beauty of holiness."

**Vocabulary** *Builder*
<u>impulse</u> (IHM puhls) *n.* sudden push or driving force

**Vocabulary** *Builder*
<u>convert</u> (kahn VERT) *v.* to change from one political party, religion, or way of life to another

Drinking alcohol is a step toward Hell.

Education is a step toward self-improvement.

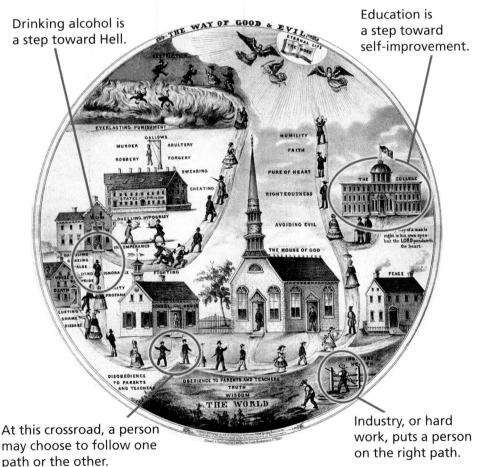

**The Way to Salvation**

This symbolic painting, *The Way of Good and Evil,* shows two paths a person can take. One path leads to Hell and the other leads to Heaven. **Critical Thinking: Apply Information** *How does this painting reflect the doctrine of free will that was part of the Second Great Awakening?*

At this crossroad, a person may choose to follow one path or the other.

Industry, or hard work, puts a person on the right path.

Preaching at a revival meeting

Thus, the religious revivals of the Second Great Awakening encouraged reform. People came to believe that, if they had the power to improve themselves, they could improve society as well.

**Utopian Communities** The desire to create a more perfect society spurred some reformers to found utopian communities. (*Utopia* was a book about a fictional ideal society.) Utopian reformers hoped their communities would become models for others to follow.

Robert Owen founded a utopian community in Indiana in 1825. He called this colony New Harmony. New Harmony was based on common ownership of property. Residents were to raise their own food and manufacture their own goods. However, New Harmony turned out to be anything but harmonious. Members argued among themselves about goals and actions. The colony dissolved after about two years. Indeed, most utopian communities did not last very long.

☑**Checkpoint** **What was the goal of the Second Great Awakening?**

**Main Idea**
Reformers worked to solve a variety of social problems, including alcohol abuse and poor treatment of prisoners and persons with mental illnesses.

## Social Reformers at Work

Utopian reformers tried to create perfect, separate communities. However, most reform-minded Americans chose to work within the existing society. The reforming impulse took many forms.

**The Temperance Movement** Many reformers supported the temperance movement, an organized effort to end alcohol abuse and the problems created by it. Alcohol was widely used in the United States. Whiskey was cheaper than milk or beer. Often, it was safer to drink than water, which was frequently contaminated. As a result, alcohol abuse reached epidemic proportions.

Many women were drawn to the temperance movement. They pointed out how many women and children suffered at the hands of husbands and fathers who drank too much. Such organizations as the American Temperance Society published pamphlets denouncing "strong drink."

Most reformers favored temperance, or moderation in drinking. But others called for prohibition, a total ban on the sale and consumption of alcohol. During the 1850s, supporters of prohibition got nine states to pass laws banning the sale of alcohol. The movement was interrupted by the Civil War but reemerged later.

**Prison Reform** Other reformers sought to improve the nation's prison system. Prisons had traditionally been harsh places, designed to make people want to stay out of them. Poorly heated buildings, inadequate food, and cramped conditions were typical. Many people in prison were not criminals at all but were people who owed money they could not pay back. Because debtors could seldom earn money while in jail, they often remained locked up for years.

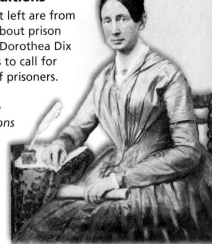

**Reforming Prison Conditions**
The two drawings shown at left are from an 1858 magazine article about prison conditions. Such sights led Dorothea Dix (right) and other reformers to call for more humane treatment of prisoners. **Critical Thinking:** *Frame Questions Based on these drawings, write two questions that you would ask Dorothea Dix to answer.*

Chains and cages used on prisoners

Dorothea Dix

Social reformers began investigating conditions in jails. Dorothea Dix, a Massachusetts schoolteacher, was one of those who took up the cause of prison reform. Over the years, she worked to convince state legislatures to build new, more sanitary, and more humane prisons. In addition, debtors were no longer sent to jail.

**Reforms for the Mentally Ill** Dix was outraged to find that prisons were also used to house individuals with mental illnesses. After a careful investigation, she reported to the Massachusetts legislature on the horrifying conditions she had witnessed: "A woman in a cage . . . [One man] losing the use of his limbs from want of exercise . . . One man and one woman chained."

Dix's shocking report helped persuade the Massachusetts legislature to fund a new mental hospital. She then continued her efforts in other states. She urged city and state governments around the country to create separate institutions, called asylums, for those with mental illnesses. The new asylums provided treatment, rather than punishment.

☑ **Checkpoint**  How did Dorothea Dix contribute to social reform?

# Education Reform

Education was another area of concern to reformers. The first American schools were set up for religious purposes. The Puritans of Massachusetts believed that all people needed to be able to read and understand the Bible. In 1642, they passed a law requiring all large towns to hire teachers and build schools. In this way, Massachusetts set up the first public schools, or free schools supported by taxes.

**Need for Better Education** By the early 1800s, Massachusetts was still the only state to require public schools. In other states, children from wealthy families were educated privately, whereas poor children generally received no education outside the home. Under these circumstances, many Americans could not read or write.

**Main Idea**
Gradually, states took steps to improve education and make it available to more people.

# Links Across Time

## Public Education

**1852** Massachusetts became the first state to pass a law that required all children to attend school up to a certain age. This was known as compulsory education.

**1918** By this date, compulsory education laws had been passed in every state in the Union. As a result, for the first time, every state required children to attend school at least up to the tenth grade.

## Link to Today   Online

**Education Today** Today, billions of dollars in federal, state, and local taxes go to support public education. But not everybody agrees on the best way to spend that money and to educate American children.

**For:** Education in the news
**Visit:** PHSchool.com
**Web Code:** myc-4081

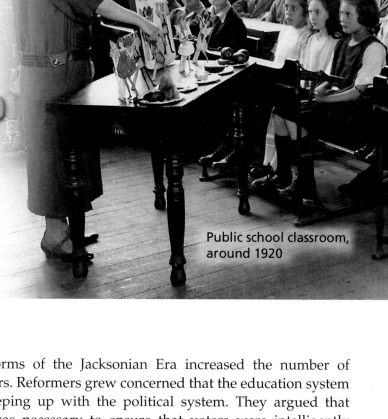

Public school classroom, around 1920

The reforms of the Jacksonian Era increased the number of eligible voters. Reformers grew concerned that the education system was not keeping up with the political system. They argued that education was necessary to ensure that voters were intelligently informed. With immigration on the rise, reformers also pointed out that better schools would help immigrants assimilate, or become part of, American culture.

**Mann and Public Education** Horace Mann of Massachusetts took the lead in education reform. To Mann, public financing of education was essential for democracy to work. He said:

> **❝** If we do not prepare children to become good citizens; if we do not develop their capacities, if we do not enrich their minds with knowledge . . . then our republic must go down to destruction as others have gone before it. **❞**
>
> —Horace Mann, quoted in *A Century of Childhood* (Heininger)

After becoming head of the state board of education in 1837, Mann convinced Massachusetts to improve its public school system. It created colleges to train teachers, raised the salaries of teachers, and lengthened the school year. (To learn more about public education in the 1800s, see the Life at the Time feature.)

### Assess Evidence for a Conclusion

**Reading Skill**

Read the quotation by Horace Mann. Assess the credibility of this source in supporting the following conclusion: Mann believed that strong character, moral behavior, and wide knowledge were equally important qualities. List three examples from the quotation that support this conclusion.

Other states soon followed Massachusetts's example. By the 1850s, public schools had gained much acceptance in the Northeast. Southern and western states lagged behind, however. They would not create their own public school systems until many decades later.

**Education for African Americans** The improvements in public education did little for African Americans. Southern states prohibited teaching enslaved persons to read. In the North, free black children were seldom admitted to the same schools as white children.

Reformers who tried to improve educational opportunities for African Americans often met with resistance. Prudence Crandall, a Quaker teacher, opened a school for African American girls in Connecticut. Hostile neighbors attacked and destroyed the school.

Still, some opportunities did open up. In major northern cities, free African American educators opened their own schools. In 1855, Massachusetts became the first state to admit African American students to public schools. Some African Americans attended private colleges such as Harvard and Oberlin. In 1854, Pennsylvania chartered Ashmun Institute (later called Lincoln University), the nation's first college for African American men.

**✓ Checkpoint** How did public education improve in the mid-1800s?

**☆ Looking Back and Ahead** Inspired by political or religious ideals, reformers tackled many social problems. But one issue towered above all others in the minds of reformers. In the next section, you will read about the growing efforts to end slavery.

---

**Section 1 | Check Your Progress**

**Progress Monitoring** Online
**For:** Self-test with instant help
**Visit:** PHSchool.com
**Web Code:** mya-4081

**Comprehension and Critical Thinking**

1. **(a) Identify** What were the ideas of predestination and the doctrine of free will?
   **(b) Draw Conclusions** How might the doctrine of free will promote democracy?

2. **(a) Recall** Which reforms did Horace Mann convince the state of Massachusetts to make?
   **(b) Detect Points of View** According to Mann, why is it important for a democracy to have educated citizens?

**⊙ Reading Skill**

3. **Assess Evidence for a Conclusion** Assess the quotation that follows by Dorothea Dix. Is the evidence reliable? Does it support the conclusion that the mentally ill were poorly treated?
   **Quotation:** "[T]wo females . . . lie in wooden bunks filled with straw; always shut up. . . . The use of cages [is] all but universal."

**Vocabulary *Builder***

Answer the following questions in complete sentences that show your understanding of the key terms.

4. What did the temperance movement seek?

5. What was the goal of social reform in the 1830s?

6. What is a religious revival?

**Writing**

7. A topic sentence sets the focus for a single paragraph. A thesis statement expresses a broader idea to be developed in an entire essay. Write three topic sentences for paragraphs that would support and develop the following thesis statement: A powerful reforming spirit swept through this country in the 1830s.

# Going to School

Following the lead of Massachusetts, other states in the North began to fund public schools. Not all children were able to attend school, and most of those who did only got as far as the eighth grade. What were these early American classrooms like?

## The Classroom

Schools in the early 1800s were not like the large public buildings we know today. In rural areas especially, many children went to one-room schoolhouses, where children of all ages were taught together. Students wrote on chalk slates and were expected to recite their lessons when called upon by the teacher.

**History** *Interactive*
**Explore an Early American Classroom**
**Visit:** PHSchool.com
**Web Code:** myp-4081

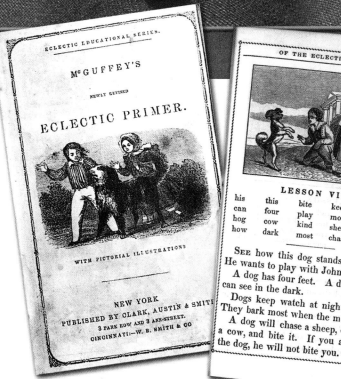

## A Popular Textbook ▲

In elementary schools, the most popular text-books were *McGuffey's Eclectic Readers* (Primer through Sixth). First published in 1836, the Readers offered moral lessons along with the "three Rs"– reading, 'riting, and 'rithmetic. The lesson shown above was used to teach children how to read and how to treat pets.

## Rewards and Punishments ▶

Discipline was strict in early classrooms. Students who failed to learn their lessons might have to sit in a corner wearing a "dunce cap" (right). But there were also rewards. Students might get certificates for learning their lesson well, for good behavior, or just for coming to school on time (below).

▼

### Analyze LIFE AT THE TIME

Look at the pages from *McGuffey's Eclectic Primer* shown at the top of this page. Then, write a lesson for the Primer about the importance of going to school. Use simple language that can be understood by elementary school students.

# The Fight Against Slavery

## Objectives

1. Describe efforts in the North to end slavery.
2. Discuss the contributions of William Lloyd Garrison, Frederick Douglass, and other abolitionists.
3. Describe the purpose and risks of the Underground Railroad.
4. Explain why many people in the North and South defended slavery.

### Prepare to Read

#### Reading Skill

**Form an Opinion Based on Evidence** You can use details and evidence in primary and secondary sources to help you form opinions about history. Remember that primary sources come from people who saw or experienced events, whereas secondary sources (such as this textbook) build on many sources to recount historical information.

### Vocabulary *Builder*

**High-Use Words**

eliminate, p. 422

via, p. 424

**Key Terms and People**

abolitionist, p. 423

William Lloyd Garrison, p. 423

Frederick Douglass, p. 424

Harriet Tubman, p. 424

⭐ **Background Knowledge** As early as colonial times, some Americans had opposed slavery. Most Quakers, in particular, condemned slavery on religious and moral grounds. In this section, you will see how the reforming impulse of the 1800s spurred a vigorous new effort to end slavery.

**Main Idea**
Soon after the American Revolution, northern states began to do away with slavery.

**Vocabulary *Builder***
eliminate (ee LIHM ih nayt) *v.* to get rid of

## Roots of the Antislavery Movement

A number of prominent leaders of the early republic, such as Alexander Hamilton and Benjamin Franklin, opposed slavery. They believed that slavery violated the most basic principle of the Declaration of Independence, "that all men are created equal."

**Slavery Ends in the North** In 1780, Pennsylvania became the first state to pass a law that gradually eliminated slavery. By 1804, every northern state had ended or pledged to end slavery. Congress also outlawed slavery in the Northwest Territory. As a result, when Ohio entered the Union in 1803, it became the first state to ban slavery in its state constitution.

**The Colonization Movement** The American Colonization Society, established in 1817, was an early antislavery organization. This society proposed that slaves be freed gradually and transported to Liberia, a colony founded in 1822 on the west coast of Africa.

The colonization movement did not work. Most enslaved people had grown up in the United States and did not desire to leave. By 1830 only about 1,400 African Americans had migrated to Liberia.

✓**Checkpoint** How did slavery end in the North?

# Growing Opposition to Slavery

The Second Great Awakening inspired further opposition to slavery. Many people were influenced by the preaching of Charles Finney, who condemned slavery. By the mid-1800s, a small but growing number of people were **abolitionists**, reformers who wanted to abolish, or end, slavery. Rejecting gradual emancipation, abolitionists called for a complete and immediate end to slavery.

**Garrison** One of the most forceful voices for abolition was William Lloyd Garrison. A Quaker, he strongly opposed the use of violence to end slavery. Still, Garrison was more radical than many others, because he favored full political rights for all African Americans.

In 1831, Garrison launched an abolitionist newspaper, the *Liberator.* It became the nation's leading antislavery publication for 34 years, ending only when slavery itself ended.

Garrison cofounded the New England Anti-Slavery Society, which later became the American Anti-Slavery Society. Leaders of this group included Theodore Weld, a minister who had been a pupil of Charles Finney. Weld brought the zeal of a religious revival to antislavery rallies. Other members included Sarah and Angelina Grimke, daughters of a South Carolina slaveholder.

**African American Abolitionists** Prominent African Americans in the North took a leading role in the abolitionist movement. In 1829, David Walker published his *Appeal: to the Coloured Citizens of the World.* This strongly worded pamphlet urged enslaved people to rebel, if necessary, to gain their freedom.

**Main Idea**

A growing number of people in the North began to call for an end to slavery.

## The Liberator

"Let Southern oppressors tremble—let all the enemies of the persecuted blacks tremble. . . . On this subject, I do not wish to think, or to speak, or write, with moderation. No! No! Tell a man whose house is on fire to give a moderate alarm . . . but urge me not to use moderation in a cause like the present. I am in earnest—I will not equivocate—I will not excuse—I will not retreat a single inch—AND I WILL BE HEARD."

—William Lloyd Garrison, *Liberator,* January 1831

William Lloyd Garrison

### Reading Primary Sources
#### Skills Activity

In the above excerpt from the first issue of the *Liberator,* William Lloyd Garrison vows to take a firm stand against slavery.

(a) **Detect Points of View** What is Garrison's attitude toward slaveholders?

(b) **Draw Conclusions** What does Garrison mean when he writes, "Tell a man whose house is on fire to give a moderate alarm"?

Perhaps the most powerful speaker for abolitionism was Frederick Douglass. Born into slavery, Douglass had broken the law by learning to read. He later escaped to freedom in the North. Garrison and other abolitionists encouraged Douglass to describe his experiences at antislavery rallies. Douglass told one crowd:

> **❝** I appear this evening as a thief and a robber. I stole this head, these limbs, this body from my master, and ran off with them. **❞**
>
> —Frederick Douglass, speech, 1842

By appearing in public, Douglass risked being sent back into slavery. Yet, he continued to speak before larger and larger audiences. He also published his own antislavery newspaper, the *North Star.*

**A Former President Takes a Stand** Abolitionists won the support of a few powerful people. Former President John Quincy Adams, now a member of Congress, read antislavery petitions from the floor of the House of Representatives. In 1839, Adams proposed a constitutional amendment that would ban slavery in any new state joining the Union. However, the amendment was not passed.

Two years later, Adams made a dramatic stand against slavery. Captive Africans aboard the slave ship *Amistad* had rebelled, killing the captain and ordering the crew to sail back to Africa. Instead, the crew sailed the ship to America. The 73-year-old Adams spoke to the Supreme Court for nine hours and helped the captives regain their freedom.

✔**Checkpoint** **What role did Frederick Douglass play in the abolitionist movement?**

## The Underground Railroad

Some courageous abolitionists dedicated themselves to helping people escape from slavery. They established a system known as the Underground Railroad. Despite its name, it was neither underground nor a railroad. It was a network of people—black and white, northerners and southerners—who secretly helped slaves reach freedom.

Working for the Underground Railroad was illegal and dangerous. "Conductors" led fugitive slaves from one "station" to the next. Stations were usually the homes of abolitionists, but might be churches or caves. Supporters helped by donating clothing, food, and money to pay for passage on trains and boats. Many people risked their lives to help runaway slaves. Levi Coffin, an Indiana Quaker, assisted more than 3,000 fugitives.

Harriet Tubman, who had herself escaped from slavery, escorted more than 300 people to freedom via the Underground Railroad. Tubman was nicknamed the Black Moses after the biblical leader who led the Israelites out of slavery in Egypt. She proudly told Frederick Douglass that, in 19 trips to the South, she "never lost a single passenger." Slave owners promised a $40,000 reward for her capture.

**Form an Opinion Based on Evidence**

*Reading Skill*

What is your opinion of Frederick Douglass's speech? Do you think it was an effective statement against slavery? Use evidence to support your opinion.

Antislavery medallion

**Main Idea**
Some abolitionists secretly worked to help African Americans escape from slavery.

**Vocabulary** *Builder*
**via** (VEE ah) *prep.* by way of

# THE Underground Railroad

As many as 50,000 African Americans escaped from slavery in the South to freedom in the North or in Canada via the Underground Railroad.
**Critical Thinking:** *Identify Costs and Benefits*
*What were the risks of helping fugitive slaves escape? Why do you think conductors on the Underground Railroad chose to take those risks?*

**Explore More Video**
To learn more about how African Americans escaped slavery, view the video.

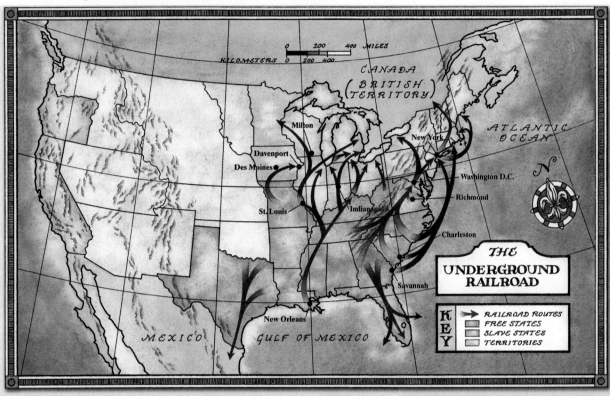

THE UNDERGROUND RAILROAD

KEY
RAILROAD ROUTES
FREE STATES
SLAVE STATES
TERRITORIES

▼ This modern quilt honors Harriet Tubman, the most famous conductor on the Underground Railroad.

HARRIET TUBMAN 1820-1913

The homes of some conductors ▶ had secret rooms to hide runaway slaves. In this room, the bed would be moved to hide the doorway.

▶
This song contained directions for escaping slaves. The "drinking gourd" is the Big Dipper.

*"The riverbank makes a very good road.*
*The dead trees will show you the way.*
*Left foot, peg foot, traveling on,*
*If you follow the drinking gourd."*

Each year, hundreds of slaves moved along the Underground Railroad to freedom in the North or in Canada. In total, perhaps as many as 50,000 gained their freedom in this way.

☑**Checkpoint** How did the Underground Railroad work?

**Main Idea**

Many people in both the North and the South defended slavery.

## Opposing Abolition

Abolitionists faced powerful obstacles in the North as well as in the South. Many northerners profited from the existence of slavery. Northern textile mill owners and merchants relied on the cotton produced by southern slave labor. Northern workers feared that freed slaves might come north and take their jobs.

Such fears sometimes prompted violence against abolitionists. Mobs attacked antislavery meetings. In 1835, William Lloyd Garrison was dragged through the streets of Boston with a rope around his neck.

As you have read, southerners had long defended slavery as a positive force. Now, as support for abolition grew louder, they went on the offensive. The state of Georgia offered a $5,000 reward for the arrest and conviction for libel of William Lloyd Garrison. Southerners in Congress won passage of a "gag rule" that blocked discussion of antislavery petitions. John Quincy Adams unsuccessfully fought for repeal of the gag rule.

☑**Checkpoint** Why did some northerners oppose abolition?

⭐ **Looking Back and Ahead** By the 1840s, the North and the South were increasingly divided by the issue of slavery. Abolitionists succeeded in making converts in the North. Slavery was spreading along with the cotton boom in the South.

---

### Section 2 | Check Your Progress

**Progress Monitoring** ⏳nline
**For:** Self-test with instant help
**Visit:** PHSchool.com
**Web Code:** mya-4082

**Comprehension and Critical Thinking**

1. **(a) List** What solutions did the American Colonization Society propose to end slavery?
**(b) Explain Problems** Why did most African Americans reject the society's goals?

2. **(a) Identify** Which groups in the North were opposed to abolition? Why?
**(b) Identify Alternatives** How might the concerns of these groups have been calmed?

**Reading Skill**

3. **Form an Opinion Based on Evidence** Henry Brown mailed himself to freedom in a crate. What do you think was important to him? Use evidence quoted from his own narrative to form your opinion: "I was . . . placed on my head. . . . In this dreadful position, I remained the space of an hour and a half . . . my eyes were almost swollen out of their sockets, and the veins on my temples seemed ready to burst. I made no noise, however, determining to obtain *'victory or death.'*"

**Vocabulary *Builder***

4. Write two definitions for the key term abolitionist. First, write a formal definition for your teacher. Second, write a definition in everyday English for a classmate.

**Writing**

5. Choose three details from Section 2 that support the topic sentence that follows. Then, write a paragraph developing the topic based on these details.
**Topic sentence:** Abolitionists used a variety of tactics to oppose slavery.

# A Call for Women's Rights

## Objectives

1. Explain how the women's suffrage movement began.

2. Describe the goals of the Seneca Falls Convention in 1848.

3. Identify the new opportunities that women gained in the mid-1800s.

## Prepare to Read

### 🎯 Reading Skill

**State the Meaning of Evidence** One way to draw conclusions from source material is to make a statement about the meaning of the evidence. This statement will be a conclusion drawn from the details of the evidence. Your statement should use your own words, fit with all the details, and make sense to you.

### Vocabulary *Builder*

**High-Use Word**

exclude, p. 428

### Key Terms and People

Sojourner Truth, p. 427

Lucretia Mott, p. 427

Elizabeth Cady Stanton, p. 428

women's suffrage, p. 428

women's rights movement, p. 429

Susan B. Anthony, p. 429

⭐ **Background Knowledge** You have read how abolitionists fought to rid the country of slavery. In this section, you will see how abolitionism helped spark another reform movement, which was dedicated to rights for women.

## The Struggle Begins

In 1820, the rights of American women were limited. They could not vote, serve on juries, attend college, or enter such professions as medicine or law. Married women could not own property or keep their own wages. Most Americans—both men and women—believed that a woman's place was in the private world of the home.

Women who were active in abolition or other social reform movements believed that they had important contributions to make to American society. They began to demand rights as equal citizens. Among these women was Sojourner Truth. Born into slavery in New York State, she was illiterate, but her words inspired the crowds that heard her. Truth became a powerful voice on behalf of both enslaved African Americans and women.

Lucretia Mott, a Quaker, had spent years working in the anti-slavery movement. Quakers allowed women to take public roles that other religions prohibited. Mott thus had organizing skills and public speaking experience that most women of her day did not.

**✓Checkpoint** Why did some reformers turn to the issue of women's rights?

**Main Idea**
Women who were involved in abolition and other reform movements began to speak out about the status of women.

Sojourner Truth

# Seneca Falls Convention

In 1840, Mott traveled to London to attend an international anti-slavery convention. There, she met another abolitionist, Elizabeth Cady Stanton. Stanton was honeymooning in London with her husband, a delegate to the conference. But when Mott and Stanton tried to attend a meeting, they were told that women were not permitted to take an active role in the proceedings.

Mott and Stanton were infuriated at being <u>excluded</u>. Sitting outside the convention hall, they agreed on the need for a convention to advance women's rights. They followed through on that idea in the summer of 1848. Their convention met in Seneca Falls, New York, "to discuss the social, civil, and religious rights of women." The Seneca Falls Convention attracted over 300 men and women.

**Declaration of Sentiments** Stanton wrote a Declaration of Sentiments, modeled on the Declaration of Independence. It began, "We hold these truths to be self-evident: that all men and women are created equal. . . ." The declaration then listed injustices women suffered, including being shut out from educational opportunities and good jobs. The Declaration of Sentiments demanded full equality for women in every area of life.

Like the colonial Patriots, Stanton opposed "taxation without representation." In a speech just before the convention, she declared:

> ❝[W]e are assembled to protest against a form of government existing without the consent of the governed—to declare our right to be free as man is free, to be represented in the government which we are taxed to support.❞
>
> —Elizabeth Cady Stanton, speech, July 19, 1848

**Call for Suffrage** Stanton's argument was the beginning of the long battle for women's suffrage, or the right of women to vote. However, not all of the delegates agreed when Stanton included a call for women's suffrage in the Declaration of Sentiments. Some, such as Frederick Douglass, strongly supported it. Others, including Lucretia Mott, feared that the call for women's suffrage would be so controversial that it would harm their other causes. Still, the convention narrowly voted to support the demand for women's suffrage.

☑Checkpoint   What was the purpose of the Declaration of Sentiments?

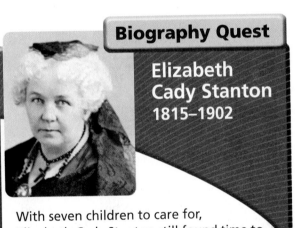

## Biography Quest

### Elizabeth Cady Stanton
### 1815–1902

With seven children to care for, Elizabeth Cady Stanton still found time to try to change the world. She began her long political partnership with Susan B. Anthony in 1851. For much of the next 50 years, the two women pooled their talents to try to win women the right to vote. "[I am] a fine writer," Stanton noted. "Miss Anthony is a thorough manager." Sadly, Stanton died 18 years before women finally won the vote.

**Biography Quest**

**Why was Stanton's wedding ceremony unusual for its day?**

**For:** The answer to the question about Stanton

**Visit:** PHSchool.com

**Web Code:** myd-4083

# New Opportunities for Women

The Seneca Falls Convention launched the women's rights movement in the United States. The **women's rights movement** was an organized effort to improve the political, legal, and economic status of women in American society.

**Political Victories** In the years after the Seneca Falls Convention, Susan B. Anthony became a close ally of Stanton. The two made a dynamic team. As an unmarried woman, Anthony was free to travel and devote herself to reform work. Stanton, the mother of a growing family, more often wrote speeches from her home. Together, they founded the National Woman Suffrage Association in 1869.

The fight for women's suffrage made little progress at first. Yet the women's rights movement won some victories. In 1860, Stanton and Anthony convinced New York to pass a law protecting women's property rights. Many other states followed. Some states revised their laws to allow married women to keep their wages.

**Education for Women** The women's rights movement focused much attention on education. American schools emphasized education for boys, who would grow up to be voters, citizens, and professionals. Girls seldom studied advanced subjects like math and science.

Even before the Seneca Falls Convention, reformers worked to give girls a chance for a better education. In 1821, Emma Willard started an academy in Troy, New York, that soon became the model for girls' schools everywhere. The Troy Female Seminary attracted the daughters of lawyers and doctors. The first year, 90 students enrolled. By 1831, the seminary had more than 300 students. Many female reformers of this era attended Willard's school.

Mary Lyon began an even bolder experiment when she opened Mount Holyoke Female Seminary in Massachusetts, in 1837. Lyon did not call her school a college. However, Mount Holyoke was, in fact, the first college for women in the United States. The school showed that women could indeed learn subjects like Latin, geometry, and chemistry.

**Main Idea**
In the mid-1800s, women gained new opportunities for education and careers.

## Cause and Effect

**CAUSES**
- Women could not vote, serve on juries, own property, or divorce abusive husbands.
- Many abolitionists believed that women also deserved equal rights.
- Women were denied equal educational opportunities.
- Seneca Falls Convention launched the women's rights movement.

**THE WOMEN'S RIGHTS MOVEMENT**

**EFFECTS**
- Suffragist movement demanded that women get the right to vote.
- States passed laws that protected women's property rights.
- Private schools for women opened, and some colleges accepted women as students.
- Women entered careers once closed to them.

### Reading Charts
#### Skills Activity

The Seneca Falls Convention marked the start of an organized women's rights movement in the United States.

**(a) Read a Chart** Identify two effects of the women's rights movement.

**(b) Analyze Cause and Effect** Why is the abolition movement shown as a cause of the women's rights movement?

State the Meaning of Evidence

Make a general statement that is supported by the evidence in these three paragraphs.

Maria Mitchell (left) at her telescope

**New Careers** Gradually, American society came to accept that girls could be educated and that women could be teachers. More and more schools began hiring women teachers who had been trained at one of the new academies or colleges for women. Some women began trying to enter other professions as well.

Margaret Fuller made a career as a journalist, scholar, and literary critic. She spoke in public for pay at a time when it was illegal for women to do so. In 1845, Fuller published an influential book, *Women in the Nineteenth Century.* "We would have every . . . barrier thrown down. We would have every path laid open to Woman as freely as to Man," she wrote.

Other women excelled in science. Elizabeth Blackwell was admitted to Geneva Medical College in New York. Blackwell graduated first in her class in January 1849, becoming the first woman to graduate from an American medical school. The astronomer Maria Mitchell was the first professor hired at Vassar College. She was also the first woman elected to the American Academy of Arts and Sciences in 1848. A crater on the moon was later named in her honor.

**✓Checkpoint** Give two examples of advances in education for women.

☆ **Looking Back and Ahead** The delegates at the Seneca Falls Convention hesitated to demand women's suffrage. As it turned out, getting the vote was a long struggle. Not until 1920 did a constitutional amendment guarantee women's right to vote. You will read more about the women's suffrage movement in a later chapter.

---

Section 3 | **Check Your Progress**

**Progress Monitoring ⊙nline**
For: Self-test with instant help
Visit: PHSchool.com
Web Code: mya-4083

## Comprehension and Critical Thinking

**1. (a) Summarize** What were the goals of the women's rights movement?

**(b) Compare and Contrast** How were the goals of the women's rights movement similar to and different from those of the abolitionist movement?

**2. (a) Recall** Why was it considered more important for boys to get a good education than girls in the early 1800s?

**(b) Explain Problems** How did the lack of equal educational opportunities hurt women?

## Reading Skill

**3. State the Meaning of Evidence** Make a statement about public views regarding women in politics, and then support it with the evidence in this paragraph: "Hers is the domestic altar; there she ministers and commands . . .; let her not seek madly to descend from this eminence to mix with the strife and ambition of the cares of government; the field of politics is not her appropriate arena."

## Vocabulary *Builder*

Read each sentence below. If the sentence is true, write YES and explain why. If the sentence is not true, write NO and explain why not.

**4.** Supporters of women's suffrage opposed the right to vote.

**5.** The Seneca Falls Convention marked the start of the women's rights movement.

## Writing

**6.** Imagine that you are a reporter in 1848 writing an article about the Seneca Falls Convention. Write a few sentences explaining why the convention met. Then, predict what might be the long-term effects of the convention.

## Objectives

1. Identify the common themes in American literature and art in the mid-1800s.

2. Describe the flowering of American literature in the mid-1800s.

3. Discuss the development of unique American styles in art and music.

## Prepare to Read

### Reading Skill

**Draw Logical Conclusions** As you review the details and evidence in text, make sure that the conclusions you draw are logical. In other words, they should make sense with all the details and with what you know about the events and about the world. Use your own experience to test, for example, whether particular attitudes make sense in a given situation. Do they fit the historical context?

### Vocabulary *Builder*

**High-Use Words**

emotion, p. 432

reproduce, p. 435

**Key Terms and People**

transcendentalism, p. 432

Ralph Waldo Emerson, p. 432

individualism, p. 432

Henry David Thoreau, p. 432

civil disobedience, p. 433

Herman Melville, p. 433

Nathaniel Hawthorne, p. 433

Louisa May Alcott, p. 434

⭐ **Background Knowledge** The reformers that you have read about in this chapter all shared a sense of optimism. They believed that individuals could reform themselves and that society could be improved. In this section, you will see how this same optimistic spirit inspired a new generation of American writers.

## An American Culture Develops

Before 1800, American writers and artists modeled their work on European styles. Poets used complex, formal language and filled their poems with references to Greek and Roman myths. Most artists trained in Europe and learned European approaches to painting.

**American Themes** By the mid-1800s, American writers and artists had begun to develop styles that reflected American optimism and energy. Their work explored subjects that were uniquely American. Two early writers, Washington Irving and James Fenimore Cooper, reflected this interest in American themes.

Irving drew upon the Dutch history of New York in his stories "The Legend of Sleepy Hollow" and "Rip Van Winkle." Rip Van Winkle was a lazy farmer who slept through the American Revolution.

Cooper created the popular character Natty Bumppo, a frontiersman who kept moving westward. Uncomfortable with life in cities and towns, Bumppo criticized the destruction of nature. Cooper's novels about Bumppo, such as *The Deerslayer* and *The Last of the Mohicans,* helped American literature gain popularity in Europe.

**Main Idea**

In the 1800s, American writers explored uniquely American themes and developed new ideas about people and nature.

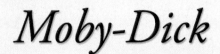

**Vocabulary** *Builder*
<u>emotion</u> (ee MOH shuhn) *n.* strong feeling such as sadness, anger, or love

### Transcendentalism

By the early 1800s, a new artistic movement took shape in Europe, called Romanticism. Unlike thinkers of the Enlightenment, who emphasized reason, Romantics placed greater value on nature, <u>emotions</u>, and imagination.

A small but influential group of writers and thinkers in New England developed an American form of Romanticism, called transcendentalism (trahnz ehn DEHNT uhl ihzm). Transcendentalism was a movement that sought to explore the relationship between humans and nature through emotions rather than through reason. It got its name because its goal was to transcend, or go beyond, human reason.

Transcendentalists believed in a close link between humans and nature. They urged people to live simply and to seek beauty, goodness, and truth within their own souls.

### Emerson and Thoreau

Ralph Waldo Emerson was the leading transcendentalist. In his popular speeches and essays, Emerson asked Americans to question the value of material goods. Civilization might provide wealth, he said, but nature reflected higher values that came from God. Emerson also stressed individualism, the unique importance of each individual. "Trust thyself," he taught. He challenged people to use their "inner light" to guide their lives and improve society.

Henry David Thoreau (thuh ROW) took up Emerson's challenge. He spent two years living in the woods at Walden Pond, meditating on nature. In his 1854 book *Walden*, Thoreau urged people to live

## *Moby-Dick*

Herman Melville's novel *Moby-Dick* tells the story of a sea captain's mad pursuit of a white whale. The novel is still widely read and has been filmed several times. **Critical Thinking:** *Apply Information* *You have read that Melville was interested in extreme, dark emotions. How does the excerpt on the facing page reflect that interest?*

**Herman Melville**

CHAPTER CXXXIV    THE CHASE—SECOND DAY

AT day-break, the three mast-heads were punctually manned afresh.

"D'ye see him?" cried Ahab, after allowing a little space for the light to spread.

"See nothing, Sir."

← 794 →

simply. "Most of the luxuries, and many of the so-called comforts of life, are not only not indispensable, but positive hindrances to the elevation of mankind," he wrote.

Like Emerson, Thoreau believed that individuals must judge right and wrong for themselves. He encouraged civil disobedience, the idea that people should peacefully disobey unjust laws if their consciences demand it. Thoreau spent a night in jail for refusing to pay a tax that he felt supported slavery. Thoreau's ideas about civil disobedience and nonviolent protest influenced later leaders like Martin Luther King, Jr.

☑**Checkpoint** **What was the goal of transcendentalism?**

## Flowering of American Literature

Irving and Cooper set a high standard for American writers. Two later novelists, Herman Melville and Nathaniel Hawthorne, began to change the tone of American literature.

**Melville and Hawthorne** Both Hawthorne and Melville were fascinated by psychology and extreme emotions. Melville's novel *Moby-Dick* (1851) told the story of a sea captain who is obsessed with pursuing a white whale. In the end, Captain Ahab's mad pursuit destroys himself, his ship, and his crew. *Moby-Dick* was largely ignored when it was first published. Today, however, it is considered one of the greatest American novels.

**Draw Logical Conclusions**
Reading Skill
Draw a logical conclusion about Thoreau's values from the information and quotation in this paragraph.

**Main Idea**
American fiction and poetry reached new heights in the 1840s and 1850s.

▼ Captain Ahab tells his crew that he lost his leg because of the white whale Moby Dick.

❝ 'Aye, my hearties all round; it was Moby Dick that dismasted me; Moby Dick that brought me to this dead stump I stand on now. Aye aye,' he shouted with a terrific, loud, animal sob, like that of a heart-stricken moose; 'Aye, aye! it was that accursed white whale that razeed me; made a poor pegging lubber for me for ever and a day!' Then, tossing both arms, with measure-less imprecations he shouted out, 'Aye, aye! and I'll chase him round Good Hope, and round the Horn, and round the Norway Maelstrom, and round perdition's flames before I give him up. And this is what ye have shipped for, men! To chase that white whale on both sides of land, and over all sides of the earth. . . .' ❞

▲ Captain Ahab in a movie version of *Moby-Dick*.

### The Hudson River School

This landscape painting by Thomas Cole shows Americans building a home in the middle of the wilderness. Like other paintings of the Hudson River school, it reflects a sense of the beauty and power of nature. **Critical Thinking:** *Evaluate Information* What is the relationship between people and nature in this painting?

Hawthorne was descended from the Puritans of Massachusetts. He often used historical themes to explore the dark side of the mind. In his 1850 novel *The Scarlet Letter,* a young minister is destroyed by secret guilt. The novel paints a grim picture of Puritan life.

**Alcott** Louisa May Alcott presented a gentler view of New England life. In 1868, Alcott published *Little Women*, a novel based on her own experiences growing up with three sisters. The main character, Jo March, was one of the first young American heroines to be presented as a believable, imperfect person rather than as a shining ideal.

**Poets of Democracy** Poets helped create a new national voice. Henry Wadsworth Longfellow based poems on American history, such as "Paul Revere's Ride." His long poem *The Song of Hiawatha* was one of the first works to honor Native Americans.

Walt Whitman published *Leaves of Grass* in 1855. This book of poems shocked many readers because it rejected formal rules. But today, Whitman is seen as the poet who best expresses the democratic American spirit. His poetry celebrated common people:

> **"**[T]he policeman travels his beat—the gate-keeper marks who pass; . . .
>
> The clean-hair'd Yankee girl works with her sewing-machine, or in the factory or mill.**"**
>
> —Walt Whitman, "Song of Myself"

Some poets used their pens to support social reform. John Greenleaf Whittier, a Massachusetts Quaker, and Frances Watkins Harper, an African American woman from Maryland, wrote poems that described and condemned the evils of slavery.

☑**Checkpoint** **How did writers explore the American past?**

# Art and Music

After 1820, artists also began to create a unique American style. Turning away from European themes, they focused on the landscapes around them or on the daily lives of common Americans.

**Painting America** A group of artists painted scenes of the Hudson River valley. This group became known as the Hudson River school. Thomas Cole and the other painters of this school reflected the values of Romanticism. They sought to stir emotions by reproducing the beauty and power of nature.

Other American painters were inspired by everyday life. George Caleb Bingham created a timeless picture of life on the great rivers. George Catlin captured the ways and dignity of Native Americans.

**Popular Songs** Most early American songs, such as "Yankee Doodle," had roots in English, Irish, or Scottish tunes. Over time, a wide variety of new American songs emerged. Many were work songs, chanted by men as they sailed on whaling ships, laid railroad tracks, or hauled barges along canals. The spiritual was a special type of song developed by enslaved African Americans.

The most popular American songwriter of the 1800s was Stephen Foster. Many of his tunes, such as "Camptown Races" and "Old Folks at Home," are still familiar today.

☑ **Checkpoint**  Identify two themes of American painting.

☆ **Looking Back and Ahead**  American culture of the 1800s had an influence that is still felt today. People still read *Moby-Dick* and *Little Women*. Concepts like individualism and civil disobedience continue to affect people's ideas and actions.

**Main Idea**
American painters and songwriters also used their skills to explore American life.

**Vocabulary** *Builder*
**reproduce** (ree prah DYOOS) *v.* to make a copy of

---

**Section 4** | **Check Your Progress**

**Progress Monitoring** ⬤nline
**For:** Self-test with instant help
**Visit:** PHSchool.com
**Web Code:** mya-4084

## Comprehension and Critical Thinking

**1. (a) Recall** Before 1800, what models influenced American writers and painters?
**(b) Draw Conclusions** How did later works like *The Scarlet Letter* and the paintings of the Hudson River school reflect a change in American art and literature?

**2. (a) Recall** What did Henry David Thoreau mean by "civil disobedience"?
**(b) Link Past and Present** How did Thoreau's ideas influence Martin Luther King, Jr.?

## Reading Skill

**3. Draw Logical Conclusions** In a novel by James Fenimore Cooper, Natty Bumppo watches as settlers shoot hundreds of pigeons. Based on the following quotation, what conclusion can you draw about Natty's feelings for nature? Explain why your conclusion is logical. **Quotation:** "It's much better to kill only such as you want, without wasting your powder and lead, than to be firing into God's creatures in this wicked manner. . . . Wasn't the woods made for the beasts and birds to harbor in?"

## Vocabulary *Builder*

**4.** Write two definitions for the key term transcendentalism. First, write a formal definition for your teacher. Second, write a definition in everyday English for a classmate.

## Writing

**5.** What is the relationship between artists and society? Using examples from this section, write a paragraph explaining how writers, painters, and musicians reflect the society in which they lived and how they help to influence it.

A summary briefly retells the main ideas of a selection, using different words. It also includes the most important details about the main ideas. Summaries should not include personal opinions about the selection. Read the primary source below, then read summaries A–C.

**Primary Source**

> In 1852, Frederick Douglass, African American abolitionist, was invited to speak at a July 4th gathering in Rochester, New York.

> Fellow citizens, pardon me, allow me to ask, why am I called upon to speak here today? What have I, or those I represent, to do with your national independence? Are the great principles of political freedom and of natural justice, embodied in that Declaration of Independence, extended to us? . . . This Fourth of July is yours, not mine. You may rejoice. I must mourn. . . . Do you mean, citizens, to mock me by asking me to speak today? . . . My subject then, fellow citizens, is American slavery. I shall see this day and its popular characteristics from the slave's point of view.
>
> —Frederick Douglass,
> Independence Day speech,
> Rochester, 1852

**Summary A:** Douglass believes that all Americans should celebrate the Fourth of July. The freedoms established in the Declaration of Independence are meant for all.

**Summary B:** Douglass does not feel he is able to speak. He is a poor man who does not enjoy the wealth and good fortune shared by many members of the audience.

**Summary C:** Douglass reminds his audience that African Americans did not enjoy the freedoms and independence guaranteed in the Declaration of Independence.

## Learn the Skill

*Use these steps to determine which summary accurately captures the main idea of the speech.*

1. **Identify the subject of the selection.** What is the selection about?

2. **Find the main idea of the selection.** Determine the writer or speaker's most important point about the subject.

3. **Find important details.** What details provide key information about the main idea?

4. **Evaluate the summary.** Does it accurately restate the main idea of the original in different words? Does it include important details? Does it communicate the basic meaning of the original text?

## Practice the Skill

*Answer the following questions about the summaries on this page.*

1. **Identify the subject of the selection.** What is the selection about?

2. **Find the main idea of the selection.** What main point does Frederick Douglass make?

3. **Find important details.** What is one detail that provides information about the main idea?

4. **Evaluate the summary.** Which is the best summary of Douglass's speech? Give three reasons for your answer.

## Apply the Skill

*See the Review and Assessment at the end of this chapter.*

CHAPTER 12 | **Quick Study Guide**

*interactive Textbook*

**Study Guide** *Online*
Complete your Chapter 12 study guide in print or online.

## Chapter Summary

### Section 1
### Improving Society

- Jacksonian democracy encouraged reform by focusing on ideals of liberty and equality.
- In the Second Great Awakening, ministers preached that people had free will and could reform their own lives.
- Reformers tackled a variety of causes, including temperance, prison reform, improved conditions for those with mental illnesses, and public education.

### Section 2
### The Fight Against Slavery

- Abolitionists such as William Lloyd Garrison and Frederick Douglass called for an end to slavery.
- Conductors on the Underground Railroad helped people escape from slavery to freedom.
- Abolitionists faced strong opposition in both the North and the South.

### Section 3
### A Call for Women's Rights

- People active in social reform began to demand equal rights for women.
- The Declaration of Sentiments at the Seneca Falls Convention called for women's equality in many areas of public life.
- The women's rights movement focused much of its attention on gaining better education for women.

### Section 4
### American Literature and Arts

- American writers and artists began to explore American themes in their work.
- Transcendentalists emphasized emotions, nature, and individualism.
- Melville and Hawthorne explored dark areas of psychology, while Whitman wrote poems celebrating democracy.

## Key Concepts

These notes will help you prepare for questions about key concepts.

| Major Movements of the Early 1800s | |
|---|---|
| **MOVEMENT** | **GOAL** |
| Second Great Awakening | Individuals reform their lives through use of free will |
| Utopian communities | Perfect humankind by building perfect communities |
| Temperance movement | End abuses related to alcohol use |
| Prison and mental hospital reform | Improve conditions in prisons and build separate asylums |
| Public education | Public financing of education to strengthen democracy |
| Abolition | End slavery |
| Underground Railroad | Help slaves escape to freedom |
| Women's rights | Improve condition of women in society |
| Transcendentalism | Individuals seek divine within themselves |

## Vocabulary *Builder*

### Key Terms

Complete each of the following sentences so that the second part further explains the first part and clearly shows your understanding of the key term.

1. The doctrine of free will was almost the exact opposite of predestination, the belief that _____.

2. People in the United States who wanted to end slavery were called abolitionists because they wanted to _____.

3. Women who wanted to _____ supported women's suffrage.

## Comprehension and Critical Thinking

4. (a) **Describe** Describe two problems Dorothea Dix uncovered.
(b) **Apply Information** What did she do to correct them?
(c) **Link Past and Present** How do you think Dix's work benefits people today?

5. (a) **List** Give two reasons why Americans opposed slavery.
(b) **Compare and Contrast** Compare how northern abolitionists and southern slave-holders viewed slavery.

6. (a) **Recall** Which rights were denied women in the early 1800s?
(b) **Draw Conclusions** What rights did women gain as a result of the victories won in the struggle for equal rights in the 1800s?

## History Reading Skill

7. **Draw Conclusions From Sources** Based on the following quotation, what conclusion can you draw about the writer's view regarding education? Explain how you reached this conclusion.

"Those who have been blessed with a good common-school education rise to a higher and higher point in the kinds of labor performed and also in the rate of wages paid, while the ignorant sink like dregs and are always found at the bottom."

—Annual Reports of the Secretary of the Board of Education of Massachusetts, 1839–1844

## Writing

8. **Read the following poem by Frances Watkins Harper. Then, write a paragraph explaining how this poem is related to the spirit of change that swept the United States in the mid-1800s:**

"I ask no monument, proud and high,
To arrest the gaze of passers-by;
All that my yearning spirit craves,
Is bury me not in a land of slaves."

—Frances Watkins Harper,
"Bury Me in a Free Land"

9. **Write a Narrative:**
You are a student in the 1850s. Your parents have taken you to a public meeting about temperance, abolition, or women's rights. Write a letter to a friend describing what you saw and heard at the meeting and how it made you feel. Use information from this chapter to create your description.

## Skills for Life

**Evaluate Summaries**
Review Section 3, "A Call for Women's Rights." Then, look at the three summaries below and answer the questions that follow.

**Summary A:** The Seneca Falls Convention was a failure. American women failed to make any political or economic gains.

**Summary B:** The Seneca Falls Convention did not change American society overnight. Still, the convention marked the start of a long struggle for women's rights that eventually succeeded.

**Summary C:** The Seneca Falls Convention was a great success. Before long, many states gave women property rights and passed laws giving women suffrage.

10. What is the main idea of the section?

11. Which is the best summary of the section? Give three reasons for your answer.

# Test Yourself

1. **The idea that God decides the fate of each person is called**

   A prohibition.

   B transcendentalism.

   C romanticism.

   D predestination.

2. **Frederick Douglass and William Lloyd Garrison were**

   A founders of the American Colonization Society.

   B leaders of the antislavery movement.

   C conductors on the Underground Railroad.

   D delegates to the Seneca Falls Convention.

**Refer to the quotation below to answer Question 3.**

> "Most of the luxuries, and many of the so-called comforts of life, are not only not indispensable, but positive hindrances to the elevation of mankind."

3. **The quotation above describes the core ideas of which American author?**

   A Herman Melville

   B Louisa May Alcott

   C Henry David Thoreau

   D James Fenimore Cooper

# Document-Based Questions

**Task:** Look at Documents 1 and 2, and answer their accompanying questions. Then, use the documents and your knowledge of history to complete this writing assignment:

> Write a short essay about the Second Great Awakening. Include details about the emotional and moral impact of the movement.

**Document 1:** Charles Grandison Finney, a leading figure of the Second Great Awakening, conducted spellbinding revival meetings in many eastern cities. This excerpt is from Finney's Revival Lectures. *According to Finney, what role do revivals play in religion?*

> "Almost all the religion in the world has been produced by revivals. God has found it necessary to take advantage of the excitability there is in mankind, to produce powerful excitements among them, before he can lead them to obey. Men are so spiritually sluggish, there are so many things to lead their minds off from religion, and to oppose the influence of the Gospel, that it is necessary to raise an excitement among them, till the tide rises so high as to sweep away the opposing obstacles. They must be so excited that they will break over these counteracting influences, before they will obey God."

**Document 2:** Millions of American flocked to revival meetings, sometimes camping at the sites for several days. *Why were so many Americans attracted to the revival movement?*

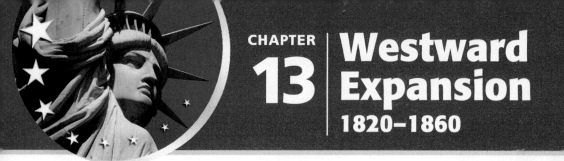

CHAPTER
# 13 Westward Expansion
## 1820–1860

## Chapter Preview

The Louisiana Purchase in 1803 had almost doubled the size of the nation. In the years that followed, Americans continued to push westward. New territories, settled by a diverse mix of people, were added to the nation. By 1853, the United States would stretch from coast to coast.

**U.S. Events**

**1821**
William Becknell opens Santa Fe Trail.

**1830**
Joseph Smith founds Mormon Church.

**1836**
Texas declares independence from Mexico.

1820

1830

1840

**World Events**

**1821** Mexico wins independence from Spain.

**1833** Santa Anna becomes president of Mexico.

**Discovery**
**SCHOOL**

**Quick View Video**
View the chapter video for a quick preview of the main ideas.

In this painting, settlers traveling to the West by wagon train pause on their long journey.

**1846**
Mexican-American War begins.

**1849**
California gold rush begins.

**1853**
United States buys land from Mexico in Gadsden Purchase.

1840

1850

1860

**1851** Australian gold rush begins.

**1858** British government takes control of India.

**History Reading Skill** **Frame Research Questions**

## What questions could you ask to learn more about the California gold rush?

In this chapter, you will learn how to frame, or ask, questions that can be answered through research. Read the following letter from Louise Amelia Clappe about her experiences as a gold miner in California in 1851. The side notes show you how to frame research questions.

**Primary Source**

> Nothing of importance has happened since I last wrote you, except that I have become a miner. I can truly say that I am sorry I "learned the trade," for I wet my feet, tore my dress, spoilt a pair of new gloves, nearly froze my fingers, got an awful headache, took cold, and lost a valuable pin in this, my labor of love.
>
> I myself thought . . . that one had but to stroll gracefully along romantic streamlets . . . and to stop now and then to . . . carelessly rinse out a small panful of yellow sand in order to fill one's work bag with the . . . precious mineral. Since I have been here, I have discovered my mistake. . . .
>
> . . . To be sure, there are now and then "lucky strikes." Once a person took $256 out of a single basinful of soil. But such luck is as rare as the winning of a $100,000 prize in a lottery. We are acquainted with many here whose gains have never amounted to much more than wages:—that is, from $6 to $8 a day.
>
> —Louise Amelia Clappe,
> letter of November 25, 1851

**Build on a unique event:** What happened to the few "lucky strikers"? How did their experience encourage the thousands of gold miners who came to the American West?

**Build on the details:** What problems did 19th century customs about women's dress present for miners?

**Build on her beliefs:** Why did miners believe that getting gold would be so easy? How did propaganda play a role in this mistaken belief?

### Frame Research Questions

- Ask questions that explain details. These often require you to combine information from the text with information you have from other readings.
- Ask questions that explain attitudes. These often require you to make an inference from the text (figure out information that is not directly stated).
- Ask questions that explore individual situations and how they demonstrate beliefs, values, or other larger ideas.
- Use these question types to frame research questions that go beyond the text. Focus on larger issues, such as cause-effect or comparison of historical situations with present situations.

### Document-Based Questions

1. When was this letter written?
2. What was the purpose of the letter?
3. How does Clappe's experience compare with that of immigrants to America today?

# Vocabulary *Builder*

## Previewing High-Use Academic Words

| High-Use Word | Definition | Sample History Sentence |
|---|---|---|
| **manual** (MAN yoo ahl) (Section 1, p. 444) | *adj.* done by using one's hands | Mining for gold required people to do a lot of <u>manual</u> labor. |
| **distinct** (dihs TIHNKT) (Section 1, p. 446) | *adj.* clear or definite; different in its quality | The Southwest had a <u>distinct</u> culture different from that of other parts of the country. |
| **isolated** (ī sah lay tehd) (Section 2, p. 449) | *adj.* set apart; separated | People living in remote parts of the West often led <u>isolated</u> lives. |
| **hostile** (HAHS tihl) (Section 2, p. 450) | *adj.* unfriendly; intending to do harm | Native Americans and new settlers from the East were sometimes <u>hostile</u> to one another. |
| **levy** (LEHV ee) (Section 3, p. 454) | *v.* to force to be paid | To protect local manufacturers, Congress <u>levied</u> a tax on imports. |
| **provoke** (prah VOHK) (Section 3, p. 457) | *v.* to cause to anger; to excite; to cause an action | Laws that forced Native Americans off their land <u>provoked</u> an angry response. |
| **efficient** (ee FISH ehnt) (Section 4, p. 463) | *adj.* done in a way that increases production with the least amount of waste | The cotton gin provided a more <u>efficient</u> way of processing cotton. |
| **prospect** (PRAHS pehkt) (Section 4, p. 464) | *n.* promise; something looked forward to | The <u>prospect</u> of owning good farmland attracted many settlers to the West. |

## Previewing Key Terms and People

frontier, p. 444
land grant, p. 446
ranchero, p. 446
expansion, p. 447
William Becknell, p. 448
John Jacob Astor, p. 448
mountain man, p. 449
rendezvous, p. 449

Marcus and Narcissa Whitman, p. 450
Stephen Austin, p. 454
dictatorship, p. 455
siege, p. 455
Sam Houston, p. 455
annex, p. 456
James K. Polk, p. 456

cede, p. 457
John C. Frémont, p. 457
Joseph Smith, p. 462
polygamy, p. 462
Brigham Young, p. 463
forty-niner, p. 464
water rights, p. 464
vigilante, p. 465

## Objectives

1. Identify the destinations of settlers heading west in the early 1800s.

2. Describe the unique culture of the Southwest.

3. Explain the meaning of Manifest Destiny.

## Prepare to Read

### 🔊 Reading Skill

**Ask Analytical Questions**
Reading about historical events will often lead you to ask questions. When these questions are analytical—or require you to solve puzzles in the text to answer them—they can yield interesting research. Think about the *why* and *how* of history to help you ask questions about the text and then to frame possible research questions.

### Vocabulary *Builder*

**High-Use Words**

manual, p. 444
distinct, p. 446

**Key Terms**

frontier, p. 444
land grant, p. 446
ranchero, p. 446
expansion, p. 447

⭐ **Background Knowledge** Since colonial times, settlers had been moving westward from the Atlantic coast toward the Appalachian Mountains. In this section, you will see how settlers in the early 1800s began to look even farther west.

**Main Idea**
By the early 1800s, Americans thought of the area beyond the Great Plains as the western frontier.

## What Was "The West"?

As the nation grew, Americans' idea of "the West" changed. Early Americans thought of the area between the Appalachians and the Mississippi River as the western frontier. A frontier is the land that forms the farthest extent of a nation's settled regions. By the 1820s, however, much of the land in this area had been settled. As the population soared, Americans began to look beyond the Mississippi River.

**The Great Plains** Stretching for seemingly endless miles to the west, the Great Plains lie between the Mississippi River and the Rocky Mountains. The Plains were easy to reach from eastern and southern states. However, settlers in the early 1800s were not attracted to this vast region. Farmers did not consider the land suitable for agriculture. The Plains were covered by grass that was anchored to the ground by deep root systems. Breaking up the dense sod would be hard manual labor.

**Vocabulary *Builder***
manual (MAN yoo ahl) *adj.* done by using one's hands

For many settlers in the early 1800s, the Great Plains were simply a route to the Far West. Some were attracted to the area known as Oregon Country in the Northwest. Others were interested in the Mexican lands of the Southwest.

**The Northwest** In the Northwest, settlers were attracted to the fertile land stretching from beyond the Rocky Mountains to the Pacific Ocean. This region is now occupied by the states of Oregon and Washington as well as by most of British Columbia in Canada. In the early 1800s, the United States, Great Britain, Russia, and Spain all claimed this land as their own.

**The Southwest** The Mexican settlements in the Southwest were another major destination for settlers heading west. This area, known as the Spanish Borderlands, was part of New Spain. Together with Mexico, these lands had been claimed for Spain in the 1500s.

The lands of the Southwest included present-day California, Utah, Nevada, Arizona, New Mexico, Texas, and about half of Colorado. Ruled first by Spain, then by Mexico, these lands had a culture and history very different from that of the eastern United States.

✓**Checkpoint** What did "the West" mean to Americans in the 1800s?

**Ask Analytical Questions**
*Reading Skill* What do you think were the land and climate features that attracted people to the Northwest? Suggest a possible research question to build on this topic.

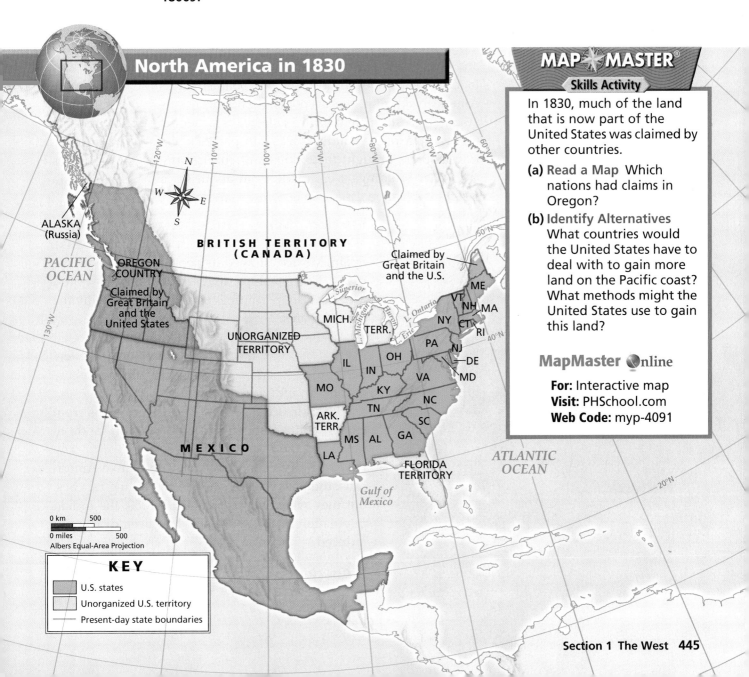

**North America in 1830**

**MAP★MASTER®**

**Skills Activity**

In 1830, much of the land that is now part of the United States was claimed by other countries.

**(a) Read a Map** Which nations had claims in Oregon?

**(b) Identify Alternatives** What countries would the United States have to deal with to gain more land on the Pacific coast? What methods might the United States use to gain this land?

**MapMaster ●nline**

**For:** Interactive map
**Visit:** PHSchool.com
**Web Code:** myp-4091

**KEY**
- U.S. states
- Unorganized U.S. territory
- Present-day state boundaries

0 km 500
0 miles 500
Albers Equal-Area Projection

**Mission in the Southwest**
Old Spanish missions, like this one in California, still dot the Southwest. Native Americans were forced to live and work on the mission grounds, where Spanish priests taught them about Christianity. **Critical Thinking: Apply Information** *How were missions like these an example of cultural blending?*

# Mexican Settlements

Like England and France, Spain followed a policy of mercantilism toward its colonies. It was illegal for settlers in New Spain to trade with other countries. Raw materials were sent to Spain. Manufactured goods were shipped to the Spanish colonies for sale.

Over the years, many Spanish settlers, or peninsulares, had children. These American-born children were called creoles. Spanish settlers, Native Americans, and Africans also intermarried. The result was another group, the mestizos. By the 1800s, this combination of ethnic groups had created a <u>distinct</u> Southwestern culture.

**Native Americans** Spanish missionaries, such as Junípero Serro (ho NEE peh roh SEHR rah) in California, were determined to convert Native Americans to Catholicism. Many Indians in the borderlands were forced to live and work at missions. There, they herded sheep and cattle and raised crops. They also learned about the Catholic religion. In the end, the mission system took a terrible toll on Native Americans. Thousands died from overwork or disease.

Spanish settlers and Native Americans exchanged language, foods, and customs. The Spanish brought their language, religion, and laws to the region. The Indians introduced the Spanish to such foods as beans, squash, and potatoes. Spanish settlers adopted Native American clothing, such as ponchos and moccasins.

Southwestern architecture reflected this blending of cultures. The general style of the buildings was European. However, Native American laborers brought their skills and cultural traditions. Churches and other buildings were made from adobe, or sun-dried brick, a traditional Native American building material.

**Mexico Wins Independence** In 1821, Mexico won its independence from Spain. Unlike Spain, Mexico allowed its people to trade with the many foreign ships that landed on its shores. Mexico also permitted overland trade with the United States.

Under Spanish rule, land grants, or government gifts of land, had been given only to a few peninsulares. Mexico, however, made many grants to individual rancheros, or owners of ranches. Mexico also removed the missions from church control and distributed mission lands to rancheros and a few American settlers.

Much of this land belonged to Native Americans. Indians often responded by raiding ranches, but they were soon crushed. By 1850, the Indian population in the Southwest had been drastically reduced.

☑**Checkpoint** **What groups shaped the culture of the Southwest?**

# Manifest Destiny

From the beginning, Americans had been interested in westward expansion, or extending the nation beyond its existing borders. Thomas Jefferson was one of many who believed that the nation must increase in size to make room for its growing population. As you have read, under Jefferson, the Louisiana Purchase doubled the territory of the nation.

By the 1840s, many Americans strongly favored westward expansion. Newspaper editor John L. O'Sullivan wrote in 1845:

> " The American claim is by the right of our manifest [obvious] destiny to overspread and possess the whole of the continent which Providence has given us for the development of the great experiment of liberty and . . . self-government entrusted to us. "
>
> —John L. O'Sullivan, *United States Magazine and Democratic Review*

The phrase Manifest Destiny quickly became popular. It described the belief that the United States was destined, or meant, to extend from the Atlantic to the Pacific—"from sea to shining sea."

☑ **Checkpoint**  What did Americans mean by Manifest Destiny?

☆ **Looking Back and Ahead**  The drive to achieve Manifest Destiny would become one of the most powerful forces shaping American history. In the next sections, you will see how Americans pursued the goal of Manifest Destiny.

**Main Idea**
Many Americans believed that the United States should extend to the Pacific Ocean.

---

Section 1 | **Check Your Progress**

**Progress Monitoring** ●nline
**For:** Self-test with instant help
**Visit:** PHSchool.com
**Web Code:** mya-4091

## Comprehension and Critical Thinking

**1. (a) Recall** Why did American farmers prefer to settle in the Northwest rather than the Great Plains?
**(b) Evaluate Information** How did the geography of the Great Plains affect U.S. settlement of that region in the early 1800s?

**2. (a) Explain** What is Manifest Destiny?
**(b) Detect Points of View** How do you think the Mexican government felt about the idea of Manifest Destiny?

## ◉ Reading Skill

**3. Ask Analytical Questions**
Suggest a possible research question related to this topic: The effect of Native American labor on slavery in Mexican settlements.

### Vocabulary *Builder*

Fill in the blanks with the correct key terms.
**4.** Each time Americans settled farther west, the _____ moved.
**5.** Under Spanish rule, only peninsulares received _____, but under Mexican rule, rancheros received them as well.

## Writing

**6.** Decide which is the best closing sentence for an essay discussing why Americans were drawn to the lands west of the Mississippi River. Explain your choice.
**Sentences:**

(a) So for many Americans, the West was a promise—of wealth, adventure, and freedom.

(b) The fertile lands of the Northwest drew many people who wanted to own farms.

(c) Therefore, the southwestern lands ruled by Mexico had developed a culture very different from that of easterners.

## Objectives

1. Explain how traders and fur trappers helped open the West.

2. List the reasons pioneers traveled along the Oregon Trail and describe the hardships they faced.

3. Discuss the issues for women, Native Americans, and new settlers in the West.

## Prepare to Read

### 🕦 Reading Skill

**Ask Inferential Questions** You can also ask inferential questions to explore a text and generate research ideas. Inferential questions require you to read between the lines. In other words, you have to use clues in the text and your own knowledge to make reasonable guesses about history. You can then conduct research to confirm or disprove your guesses.

### Vocabulary *Builder*

**High-Use Words**

<u>isolated</u>, p. 449

<u>hostile</u>, p. 450

### Key Terms and People

William Becknell, p. 448

John Jacob Astor, p. 448

mountain man, p. 449

rendezvous, p. 449

Marcus and Narcissa Whitman, p. 450

---

☆ **Background Knowledge** As you know, the earliest Europeans who came to the Americas included merchants and Christian missionaries. As Americans moved westward in the 1800s, traders and missionaries continued to play an important role.

## Traders Lead the Way

**Main Idea**
Merchants and fur traders blazed important trails to both Oregon and the Southwest.

The first Americans to move into the Far West were traders. They were looking for new markets in which to sell their goods. In the process, they blazed important trails for the people who followed.

**The Santa Fe Trail** As you have read, when Mexico won independence, it began to allow overland trade with the United States. In 1821, Captain William Becknell led a wagon train filled with merchandise from Independence, Missouri, to Santa Fe, New Mexico. The route stretched for about 800 miles.

Becknell crossed treacherous rivers with bottoms of quicksand. He and the traders traveling with him barely survived the desert. Then, he had to find a way through nearly impassable mountains. In spite of these obstacles, Becknell's group reached Santa Fe with their wagons. Other Americans followed Becknell's route. It became known as the Santa Fe Trail. The Santa Fe Trail soon became a busy international trading route.

**The Oregon Fur Trade** Farther north, fur traders were making huge fortunes. John Jacob Astor, a German immigrant, sent the first American fur-trading expedition to Oregon. Astor established the American Fur Company in 1808 at Fort Astor, now Astoria, Oregon.

Astor's expedition consisted of two groups. The first group sailed around South America and up the Pacific coast. The second group traveled across the continent, using information that had been recorded by Lewis and Clark. On the way, they found the South Pass through the Rocky Mountains. This important route helped to open the Northwest for the missionaries and settlers who followed.

**Mountain Men** The fur trade made Astor the richest man in the country. The trappers who supplied him with furs were also eager to become rich. These mountain men, or fur trappers of the Northwest, would become legendary.

For most of the year, trappers led <u>isolated</u>, dangerous lives. They endured bitter cold, intense heat, and attacks from wild animals. Jedediah Smith was once scalped by a grizzly bear. He persuaded a companion to sew his scalp back onto his head and to piece together his severed ear. Several weeks later, Smith returned to his work.

Once a year, trappers would bring their furs to a rendezvous (RAHN day voo), a meeting where the trappers would trade furs for supplies. Here, the mountain men would celebrate their time together—singing, laughing, and competing in contests. Then, they got down to serious bargaining. Beaver fur was in great demand in the East, so trappers were able to command high prices for their furs.

By the 1830s, the supply of beavers was nearly exhausted. Most trappers moved back east to become farmers, merchants, or even bankers. Others stayed as guides for the wagon trains that brought thousands of settlers west in the 1840s. One mountain man, an African American named James Beckwourth, discovered a pass through the Sierras that later became a major route to California.

☑**Checkpoint** **Why did the mountain men travel to Oregon?**

**Vocabulary** *Builder*
<u>isolated</u> (ī sah lay tehd) *adj.* set apart; separated

## Links to Economics

### The Oregon Fur Trade

What do the beaver (1), the mountain man (2), and the man in the fancy cloak (3) have in common? They were all part of the same economic process, called supply and demand. Fashions in the East created a demand for beaver fur, used in hats and fur-lined cloaks. Mountain men supplied the furs to meet the demand. **Critical Thinking:** *Draw Conclusions What other people were needed to complete the link between the mountain man and the man wearing the fur cloak?*

## The Oregon Trail

The first white easterners to build permanent homes in Oregon were missionaries. In the 1830s, they began to travel west for the purpose of bringing their religious beliefs to the Indians.

**Missionaries** One couple, Marcus and Narcissa Whitman, set up a mission in Oregon to serve the Cayuse Indians. The Whitmans had trouble from the start. The Cayuses mistrusted them, partly because the Whitmans made little effort to understand Cayuse ways.

As more settlers arrived and took over Indian lands, the Cayuses grew increasingly hostile. Then, in 1847, an epidemic of measles killed many Cayuse adults and nearly all their children. Blaming the Whitmans, the Indians killed them along with 12 other settlers.

Still, missionaries like the Whitmans greatly spurred settlement of the West. Their glowing reports of Oregon led more easterners to make the journey west. Farmers sought the free and fertile land, the mild climate, and the plentiful rainfall of the river valleys. Settlers from all over the country were in the grip of "Oregon Fever."

**On the Oregon Trail** Most settlers followed the Oregon Trail, a route that stretched more than 2,000 miles from Missouri to Oregon. They set out in spring and had to be in Oregon within five months. Travelers caught by winter in the Rockies risked a slow death. The trip itself was hazardous. Disease and accidents killed about one traveler out of every ten on the Oregon Trail.

# On the Oregon Trail

To many easterners, Oregon held out the promise of fertile, available farmland and greater freedom. But first, they had to pack their belongings and set off on the long, difficult Oregon Trail. **Critical Thinking:** *Identify Costs and Benefits Do you think the benefits of moving to Oregon outweighed the risks? Why or why not?*

▲ Covered wagons were designed to carry cargo, not passengers.

*"Monday June 13. This has been a long hard day's travel. Came 30 miles through sand and dust. . . . Tomorrow we will come to the first poison water. There will be no more good water for about 25 miles."*

— diary of Mrs. Amelia Stewart Knight, 1853

Pioneers on the Oregon Trail banded together for mutual protection. Most traveled in long trains of covered wagons drawn by teams of horses or oxen. The wagons carried food and possessions, while the people walked. They traveled for up to 15 hours each day. At night, wagons were drawn up in a circle to keep the cattle from wandering.

As the miles went by, the horses and oxen tired more easily. People began to discard personal items to lighten their wagons. The trail was scattered with "leeverites," short for "leave 'er right here." There was so much debris that passersby would gather up wagon-loads of flour, bacon—even cast-iron stoves!

Dust got into everything. Some people wore masks to keep it out of their faces and lungs. Clean, safe water was hard to find. Francis Parkman, a famous historian, observed the following incident:

> **❝**I saw a tall slouching fellow . . . contemplating the contents of his tin cup, which he had just filled with water. 'Look here, you,' said he; 'it's chock full of animals!' The cup . . . exhibited in fact an extraordinary variety and profusion of animal life.**❞**
>
> —Francis Parkman, *The Oregon Trail*

Despite such hardships, more than 50,000 people reached Oregon between 1840 and 1860.

☑**Checkpoint** **Why did settlers travel by wagon train?**

**Ask Inferential Questions**

Reading Skill

Why do you think so many Americans were willing to face the hardships of westward settlement? Suggest a possible research topic to answer this question.

◄ Coffee grinder

Trunk carefully packed with dishware ►

◄ Butter churn

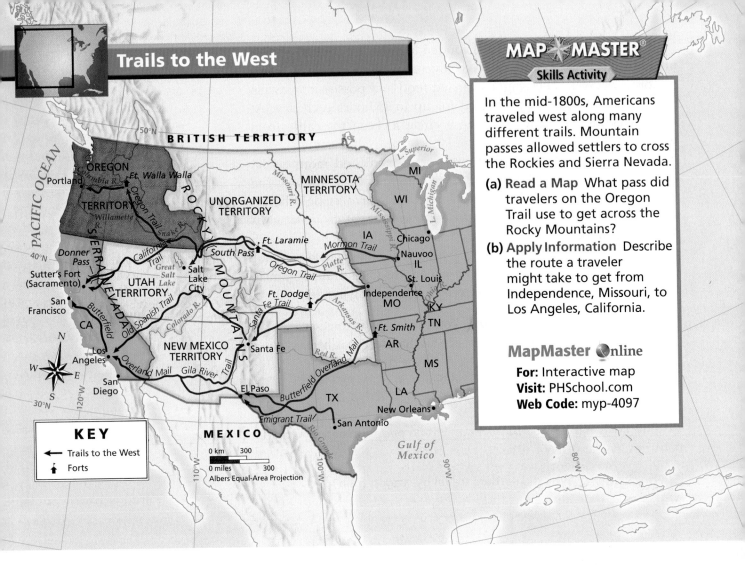

## Trails to the West

### MAP MASTER
#### Skills Activity

In the mid-1800s, Americans traveled west along many different trails. Mountain passes allowed settlers to cross the Rockies and Sierra Nevada.

**(a) Read a Map** What pass did travelers on the Oregon Trail use to get across the Rocky Mountains?

**(b) Apply Information** Describe the route a traveler might take to get from Independence, Missouri, to Los Angeles, California.

**MapMaster Online**

**For:** Interactive map
**Visit:** PHSchool.com
**Web Code:** myp-4097

**KEY**
← Trails to the West
↑ Forts

0 km 300
0 miles 300
Albers Equal-Area Projection

---

**Main Idea**

Women enjoyed new status in the West, but settlers faced conflicts with Native Americans already living on the land.

# Life in the West

Pioneer life was filled with hardships. Settlers arrived with few possessions. Working only with hand tools, they had to clear the land, plant crops, and build shelters. Disease, accidents, and natural disasters like storms and floods were an ever-present threat.

A. H. Garrison was 15 years old when his family went west in 1846. He later recalled the hardships of their first winter in Oregon.

> "On Christmas day, it began to snow, and it continued until the ground was covered to a depth of twenty inches. . . . At the beginning of the storm, father had thirteen head of oxen, and twelve head of cows, and one fine American mare. There was no feed to be had, and the grass was so covered that the cattle could get nothing to eat. . . . When spring came, we had four oxen and three cows left."
>
> —*Reminiscences of A. H. Garrison*

Some settlers gave up and returned to the East. Others, like John Bidwell of California, met the challenges and went on to live extraordinary lives. Bidwell and his wife Annie each became civic leaders. Annie Bidwell later fought for the right of women to vote.

**Women in the West** Women in the West worked alongside men to make a success of their family farms. The fact that their labor was necessary for a family's survival raised the status of western women.

Meanwhile, as you have read, women in the East had begun to campaign for greater political and legal rights. Chief among these was the right to vote. On a national level, women's struggle for the vote would take many years. But the West was quicker to reward the hard work of its women. In 1869, the Wyoming Territory became the first area of the United States to grant women the vote.

**Native Americans and Settlers** Native Americans in Oregon lived in an uneasy peace with the white settlers. Indians in the southern part of Oregon usually got along with whites. In northern Oregon, however, Native Americans were angered by the presence of strangers on their lands.

The discovery of gold in northern Oregon in the 1850s brought large numbers of white and Chinese miners into the area. War broke out there in 1855. The miners killed several dozen Native American men. Three months later, miners massacred an equal number of Indian women, children, and old men.

The Indians fought back, killing white and Chinese alike. The brief war ended when the U.S. government intervened. The Native Americans were forced to accept peace treaties.

Woman harvesting hay on a western farm

✓**Checkpoint** **Why did women enjoy greater equality in the West than in the East?**

☆ **Looking Back and Ahead** The Oregon and Santa Fe trails created close links between east and west. In the next section, you will see how western lands became part of the United States.

---

## Section 2 | Check Your Progress

**Progress Monitoring** Online
**For:** Self-test with instant help
**Visit:** PHSchool.com
**Web Code:** mya-4092

**Comprehension and Critical Thinking**

1. **(a) Recall** Why did Americans go to Oregon in the early 1800s?
   **(b) Analyze Cause and Effect** What factors might have discouraged Americans from traveling to Oregon?

2. **(a) Explain** Why did conflict arise between Native Americans and settlers in Oregon?
   **(b) Make Predictions** Do you think such conflicts would be likely to continue later in the 1800s? Explain.

**Reading Skill**

3. **Ask Inferential Questions** Reread the text following the heading "The Oregon Fur Trade." What qualities were needed to be successful as a fur trapper in Oregon? Suggest a possible research question to take this topic further.

**Vocabulary Builder**

Read each sentence below. If the sentence is true, write YES and explain why. If the sentence is not true, write NO and explain why not.

4. **Mountain men** made their living by farming the Great Plains.

5. A trapper would often trade his furs for supplies at a rendezvous.

**Writing**

6. For each of these transitions (connecting words), write a sentence that expresses a cause-effect relationship about the topic in parentheses. **Transitions:**
   **(a)** *because* (Astor and the Oregon Trail)
   **(b)** *as a result* (the decline in the fur trade)
   **(c)** *therefore* (hardships on the Oregon Trail)

# Conflict With Mexico

## Objectives

1. Explain how Texas became independent from Mexico.

2. Discuss the issues involved in annexing Texas and Oregon.

3. Summarize the main events in the Mexican-American War.

4. Explain how the United States achieved Manifest Destiny.

## Prepare to Read

### Reading Skill

**Ask Questions to Synthesize Information** As you read history, recall what you already know about the topic. Consider as well what you know about related topics or experiences—even from modern times. Pull these many pieces of information together to ask and answer questions about the text. Then, use your questions to build research topics.

### Vocabulary *Builder*

**High-Use Words**

**levy**, p. 454

**provoke**, p. 457

### Key Terms and People

Stephen Austin, p. 454

dictatorship, p. 455

siege, p. 455

Sam Houston, p. 455

annex, p. 456

James K. Polk, p. 456

cede, p. 457

John C. Frémont, p. 457

⭐ **Background Knowledge** Mexico became independent in 1821. That year, American traders began to travel to the Southwest along the Santa Fe Trail. In this section, you will see how increasing tensions between the United States and Mexico led to war.

## Texas Wins Independence

**Main Idea**
Conflicts with the Mexican government led American settlers in Texas to declare independence.

In 1820, the Spanish governor of Texas gave Moses Austin a land grant to establish a small colony in Texas. After Moses died, his son, Stephen Austin, led a group of some 300 Americans into Texas.

Soon after, Mexico won independence from Spain. The Mexican government agreed to honor Austin's claim to the land. In return, Austin and his colonists agreed to become Mexican citizens and to worship in the Roman Catholic Church.

**Growing Conflict** Thousands of Americans flooded into Texas. They soon came into conflict with the Mexican government. The new settlers were Protestant, not Catholic. Also, many of the settlers were slaveholders from the American South who wanted to grow cotton in Texas. However, Mexico had abolished slavery.

For a while, Mexico tolerated these violations of its laws. Then, in 1830, Mexico banned further American settlement. Still, Americans kept arriving in Texas. Tensions increased as Mexico tried to enforce its laws banning slavery and requiring settlers to worship in the Catholic Church. Mexico also began to levy heavy taxes on American imports.

**Vocabulary *Builder***
**levy** (LEHV ee) *v.* to force to be paid

**Declaring Independence** American settlers wanted more representation in the Mexican legislature. Some Tejanos (teh HAH nos), Texans of Mexican descent, also hoped for a democratic government that gave less power to the central government.

These hopes were dashed in 1833 when General Antonio López de Santa Anna became president of Mexico. Santa Anna wanted a strong central government, with himself at the head. Soon after, Santa Anna overturned Mexico's democratic constitution and started a **dictatorship**, or one-person rule.

Austin urged Texans to revolt against the Mexican government. In 1836, Texans declared independence from Mexico and created the Republic of Texas.

**Texans at War** Santa Anna responded with force. His troops laid siege to the Alamo, a mission in San Antonio where about 185 Anglo-Americans and Tejanos were gathered. A **siege** is an attack in which one force surrounds a city or fort. The defenders of the Alamo held out for 12 days under heavy cannon fire. At last, Mexican forces overran the Alamo. All of the defenders were killed in battle or executed afterward. Inspired by the bravery of the Alamo defenders, many American volunteers joined the Texan army.

The following April, the commander of the Texan forces, **Sam Houston,** led a small army in a surprise attack against Santa Anna's army at San Jacinto. Texans shouted "Remember the Alamo!" Within 18 minutes, the Texans had captured Santa Anna. They forced him to sign a treaty recognizing Texan independence.

**Discovery SCHOOL**

**Explore More Video**
To learn more about the Texas War for Independence, view the video.

**Siege at the Alamo** For 12 days, a small group of Texans held off Mexican troops at the Alamo. This print from the 1800s is not an eyewitness portrayal, but it gives an idea of the odds against the defenders of the Alamo. **Critical Thinking: *Detect Points of View*** *Based on this print (right), why do you think many Americans admired the defenders of the Alamo?*

The Alamo today

## Ask Questions to Synthesize Information

Why was it important whether a new state was a slave state or a free state? Suggest a possible research topic building on this question.

**Main Idea**

Americans elected a new President in 1844 who promised to expand the territory of the United States.

**Republic of Texas** Sam Houston became president of the new Republic of Texas. He hoped that the United States would annex, or add on, Texas. But public opinion in the United States was divided. Southerners supported annexation of Texas as a slave state. Northerners opposed this, but still hoped for western expansion.

Presidents Andrew Jackson and Martin Van Buren refused to support annexation. Both feared that adding a slave state might spark a huge political fight that could split the Union.

☑**Checkpoint** Why did Texans want independence from Mexico?

## Annexing Texas and Oregon

A decade after Texas won its independence, the annexation of Texas remained an unsettled question. It became a major issue in the presidential election of 1844.

**Election of 1844** President John Tyler favored the annexation of Texas. But Tyler was not nominated for a second term. In 1844, the Whigs nominated Henry Clay instead.

Clay hoped to avoid the issue of annexation. But the Democratic candidate, James K. Polk, called for the annexation of both Texas and Oregon. At the time, Oregon was jointly held by Britain and the United States. Polk demanded that the British withdraw from all territory south of latitude 54°40'N. Polk, the candidate of expansion, won the election.

**Annexation** Shortly before Polk took office, Tyler asked Congress to annex Texas. Congress voted for admission of Texas as a state in 1845, three days before Tyler left office. A convention of Texan delegates quickly met and voted for annexation.

In keeping with his campaign promise, President Polk negotiated a treaty with Britain to divide Oregon. The United States got the lands south of latitude 49°N. Eventually, this territory became the states of Washington, Oregon, and part of Idaho.

**Tensions With Mexico** The annexation of Texas increased tensions with Mexico. Mexico had never formally recognized Texan independence. The treaty that Santa Anna had been forced to sign at San Jacinto set the southern boundary of Texas at the Rio Grande. The Mexican government claimed that the southern boundary of Texas was the Nueces River, farther to the north.

### The Texas War for Independence

**KEY**

← Texan forces  ← Mexican forces

✴ Texan victories  ✴ Mexican victories

UNITED STATES

AR

Disputed Area

LA

MEXICO

REPUBLIC OF TEXAS

The Alamo

San Antonio

San Jacinto

Gonzales

Goliad

Nueces R.

Gulf of California

Gulf of Mexico

0 km 300
0 miles 300
Albers Equal-Area Projection

## MAP✴MASTER

**Skills Activity**

After a brief but bloody war, the Republic of Texas won its independence from Mexico.

**(a) Read a Map Key** Who won the battle at Goliad?

**(b) Make Predictions**
Based on this map, why might there be future conflict between Texas and Mexico?

**MapMaster Online**

**For:** Interactive map
**Visit:** PHSchool.com
**Web Code:** myp-4094

In fact, Texas had never controlled the area between the two rivers. But setting the Rio Grande as the border between Texas and Mexico would have given Texas much more land. President Polk put pressure on Mexico to accept this claim. Still, Mexico refused.

☑Checkpoint **How did the annexation of Texas increase tensions with Mexico?**

## The Mexican-American War

Polk knew that the Mexican government needed cash. He offered money to settle the claim for the Rio Grande border. He also offered to purchase California and the rest of New Mexico. Outraged Mexicans refused the offer. They did not want to cede, or give up, more land to the United States.

Polk then changed his tactics. Hoping to <u>provoke</u> a Mexican attack on U.S. troops, he sent General Zachary Taylor south to the disputed land south of the Nueces. The Mexicans saw this as an act of war. After Mexican troops ambushed an American patrol on the disputed land, Polk asked Congress for a declaration of war. He claimed that Mexico had forced this war by shedding "American blood upon American soil."

**Opposition to War** Overall, the war with Mexico was very popular among Americans. Support for the war was strongest among southerners and westerners, who were willing to take up arms to gain more land.

Many northerners, however, argued that Polk had provoked the war. They scornfully referred to it as "Mr. Polk's war" and claimed that he was trying to extend slavery. Abraham Lincoln, a member of the House of Representatives from Illinois, pointed out that the land under dispute was not "American soil." He held that General Taylor's troops had invaded Mexico, not the other way around.

**Rebellion in California** Polk ordered troops under the command of Stephen Kearny to invade and capture Santa Fe, New Mexico. From there, Kearny was to lead his troops into California.

Even before Kearny's troops reached California, settlers near San Francisco had begun their own revolt against Mexico. Taking up arms, they raised a grizzly bear flag and declared California an independent republic. A bold young explorer, John C. Frémont, soon took command of the Bear Flag Rebellion. He moved to join forces with U.S. troops under the command of Kearny.

**Main Idea**
Expansionists favored war with Mexico, but some Americans disapproved.

**Vocabulary** *Builder*
<u>provoke</u> (prah VOHK) *v.* to cause to anger; to excite; to cause an action

## Biography Quest

### John C. Frémont
### 1813–1890

John C. Frémont changed Americans' view of the West. Frémont led several expeditions to explore the area. During one expedition, he helped to map out the Oregon Trail. For this, he became known as the Great Pathfinder.

It was Frémont's salesmanship that did the most to advance the cause of Manifest Destiny. His published accounts of his journeys excited people's interest in the vast, untapped riches of the Great Plains.

**Biography Quest**

**How did Frémont become involved in the California rebellion?**

**For:** The answer to the question about Frémont
**Visit:** PHSchool.com
**Web Code:** myd-4093

# Growth of the United States to 1853

BRITISH TERRITORY

(Ceded by Britain, 1818)

**OREGON COUNTRY** (Agreement with Britain, 1846)

L. Superior

L. Michigan

L. Huron

L. Ontario

L. Erie

**LOUISIANA PURCHASE** (Purchased from France, 1803)

**THE UNITED STATES, 1783**

ORIGINAL 13 STATES

ATLANTIC OCEAN

**MEXICAN CESSION** (Treaty of Guadalupe-Hidalgo, 1848)

PACIFIC OCEAN

0 km 500
0 miles 500
Albers Equal-Area Projection

**TEXAS ANNEXATION** (Annexed by Congress, 1845)

**GADSDEN PURCHASE** (Purchased from Mexico, 1853)

**FLORIDA** (Ceded by Spain, 1819)

(Annexed, 1810)

(Annexed, 1812)

Gulf of Mexico

MEXICO

**KEY**

— Present-day state boundaries

**MAP MASTER®**

**Skills Activity**

By 1848, the United States stretched from the Atlantic Ocean to the Pacific Ocean.

**(a) Read a Map** What areas on the map did the United States own in 1853 that it did not own in 1830?

**(b) Apply Information** Look at a map of the present-day United States. When and how did your state become part of the United States?

**MapMaster Online**

**For:** Interactive map
**Visit:** PHSchool.com
**Web Code:** myp-4093

Mexico had very little military presence in California. Frémont's forces quickly captured Monterey and San Francisco. Meanwhile, General Kearny's troops captured Santa Fe and San Diego. There they united with naval units to occupy more of California. By early 1847, all of southern California was also under American control.

**Invasion of Mexico** Moving south from the Rio Grande, General Zachary Taylor captured the Mexican city of Monterrey. Santa Anna attacked Taylor at the Battle of Buena Vista. Though greatly outnumbered, Taylor's forces were better armed. Santa Anna retreated.

An American army under General Winfield Scott captured Veracruz, an important Mexican port. Scott then marched from Veracruz to Mexico City. Scott's army forced the Mexican army into the capital. Still, Santa Anna would not surrender.

Scott's campaign ended at Chapultepec, a stone palace above Mexico City. Like the Texans at the Alamo, the Mexicans fought bravely to defend Chapultepec. Most of them were killed. In Mexico, these young men are still honored for their bravery and patriotism.

After Mexico's defeat at Chapultepec, Santa Anna left Mexico City. The Mexican capital was now in American hands. The United States had won the war. (To learn more about the key battles in the Mexican-American War, see the Geography and History feature.)

☑ Checkpoint  **How did Polk's actions lead to war with Mexico?**

## Achieving Manifest Destiny

Polk sent a representative, Nicholas Trist, to help General Scott negotiate a treaty with the Mexican government. Despite many difficulties, Trist negotiated the Treaty of Guadalupe-Hidalgo, which was signed in 1848. It formally ended the Mexican-American War.

Under the treaty, Mexico recognized the annexation of Texas and ceded a vast territory to the United States. This territory, known as the Mexican Cession, included present-day California, Nevada, and Utah, as well as parts of Wyoming, Colorado, Arizona, and New Mexico. In return, the United States paid $18 million to Mexico.

In the Gadsden Purchase of 1853, the United States paid Mexico $10 million for a narrow strip of present-day Arizona and New Mexico. Manifest Destiny had been achieved.

☑ Checkpoint  **What was the Mexican Cession?**

⭐ **Looking Back and Ahead**  By 1853, the United States owned all the territory that would make up the first 48 states. Not until Alaska and Hawaii joined the Union in 1959 would any states outside this area be added.

**Main Idea**
As a result of the Mexican-American War, the United States gained a huge new territory.

---

Section 3 | **Check Your Progress**

**Progress Monitoring** ⓦnline
**For:** Self-test with instant help
**Visit:** PHSchool.com
**Web Code:** mya-4093

**Comprehension and Critical Thinking**

**1. (a) Recall** Why did the Republic of Texas hope the United States would annex Texas?
**(b) Analyze Cause and Effect** How would the addition of Texas as a slave state affect the Union? Explain.

**2. (a) Recall** What did the United States gain as a result of the Mexican-American War?
**(b) Draw Conclusions** How do you think the Mexican-American War affected the relationship between Mexico and the United States?

**🔄 Reading Skill**

**3. Ask Questions to Synthesize Information** Reread the text following the heading "Invasion of Mexico." Why might Santa Anna have been unwilling to surrender? Suggest a possible research topic to explore this question.

**Vocabulary** *Builder*

Complete each of the following sentences so that the second part clearly shows your understanding of the key term.

**4.** Many U.S. senators wanted to annex Texas, _____.

**5.** In Mexico, Santa Anna established a dictatorship, _____.

**6.** The Mexicans laid siege to the Alamo, _____.

**Writing**

**7.** Rewrite the following paragraph to eliminate sentence errors and improve sentence variety. **Paragraph:** Conflict between Mexicans and Anglo-Americans. There was a difference in religion. Mexicans were Catholics. Many Anglo-Americans Protestants. Mexico had outlawed slavery. but many Anglo-Americans owned slaves. This also created problems. Mexico began to tax American imports. Hostilities finally broke out. When Santa Anna attacked the Alamo.

# The Mexican-American War

By 1846, the United States and Mexico stood on the brink of war. Mexicans were furious at the American annexation of Texas the year before. Americans felt that Mexico stood in the way of Manifest Destiny. After a border dispute erupted in hostilities, U.S. troops attacked Mexico on two fronts in order to achieve quick victory.

**History** *Interactive*

**Learn More About the Mexican-American War**

**Visit:** PHSchool.com
**Web Code:** myp-4095

► U.S. soldier at the Battle of Buena Vista

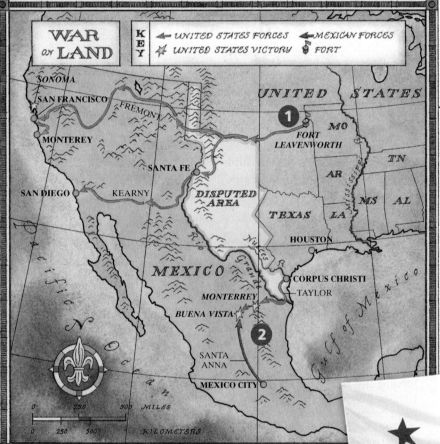

► Rebel American settlers declared California a new nation—the Bear Flag Republic.

## War on Land

American forces invaded Mexico in two directions. John C. Frémont and Stephen Kearny moved west from Fort Leavenworth ❶ to take control of California. They were aided by a revolt of American settlers near San Francisco. Zachary Taylor marched south across the Rio Grande and defeated a large Mexican force at Buena Vista ❷.

CALIFORNIA REPUBLIC

## War at Sea

The U.S. Navy blockaded Mexico's east and west coasts. American sailors helped secure California ❸ while another fleet in the Gulf of Mexico supported the assault at Veracruz ❹. Winfield Scott won a last battle against Mexican soldiers at the Battle of Chapultepec.

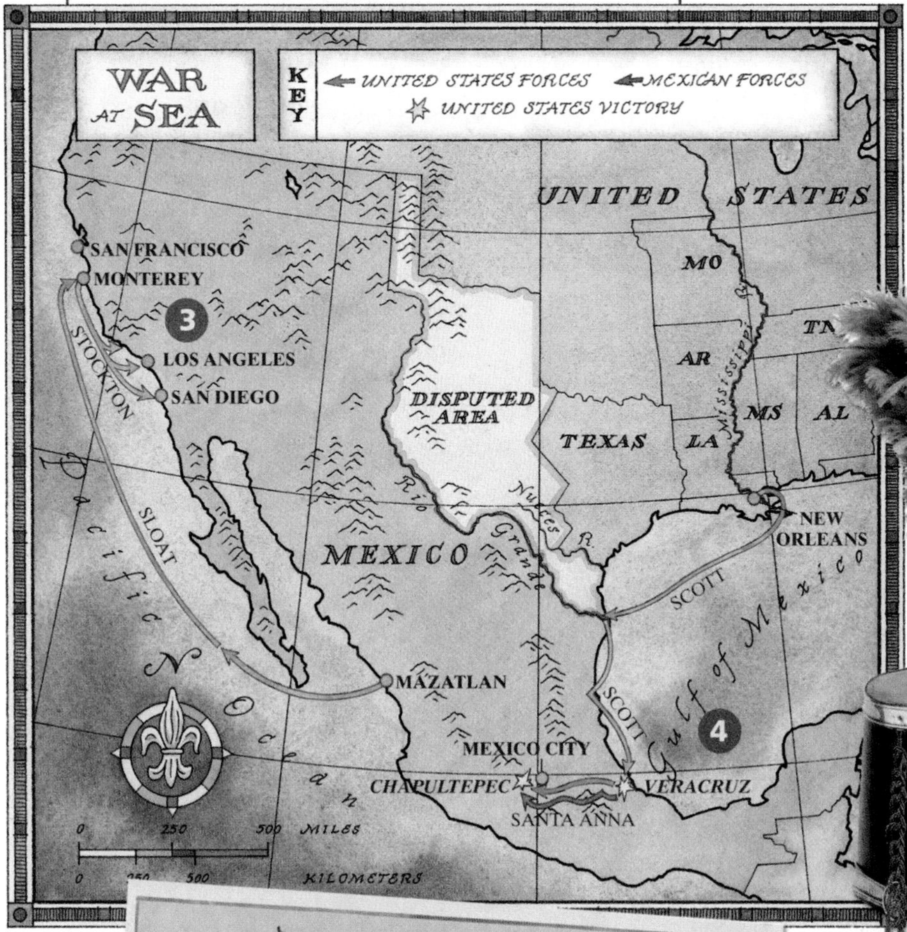

## The War's Final Days

By the time of General Scott's victory outside Mexico City, U.S. forces had surrounded the Mexican capital. The northern territories of California and New Mexico were under Frémont's and Kearny's control, and Taylor had moved south to press for attack. With the loss of Mexico City, the Mexican government moved to make peace.

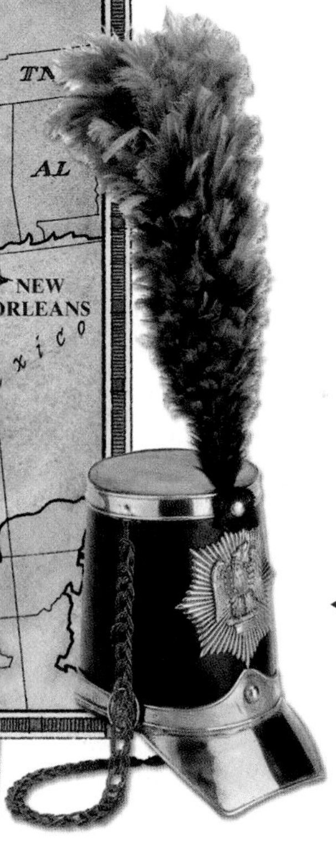

### WAR AT SEA

**KEY**
- ◀━ UNITED STATES FORCES
- ◀━ MEXICAN FORCES
- ✦ UNITED STATES VICTORY

UNITED STATES

SAN FRANCISCO
MONTEREY

❸

LOS ANGELES

SAN DIEGO

STOCKTON

SLOAT

Pacific Ocean

MEXICO

MAZATLAN

MEXICO CITY

CHAPULTEPEC

SANTA ANNA

VERACRUZ

DISPUTED AREA

TEXAS

Rio Grande R.

Nueces R.

MO

TX

AR

MS   AL

LA

NEW ORLEANS

SCOTT

SCOTT

❹

Gulf of Mexico

0    250    500 MILES
0    250    500 KILOMETERS

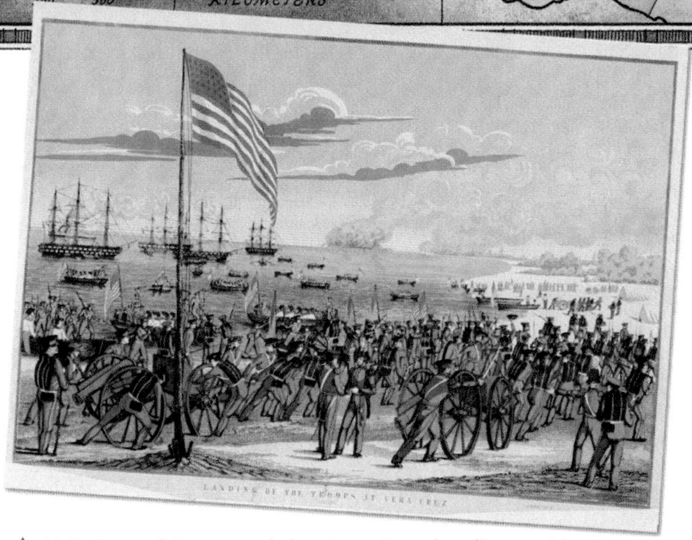

◀ The shako cap—topped with a tall plume of feathers—was part of the American uniform during the war.

▲ U.S. Navy ships guard the American landing at Veracruz.

### Analyze GEOGRAPHY AND HISTORY

Select a key battle from the Mexican-American War, and write a journal entry about it from a U.S. soldier's point of view.

# A Rush to the West

## Objectives

1. Explain why the Mormons settled in Utah and the issues that divided Mormons and the federal government.

2. Discuss the effects of the 1849 California gold rush.

3. Describe how California's population had changed by 1850.

## Prepare to Read

### Reading Skill

**Ask Questions That Go Beyond the Text** Research questions should build on the information you learn in your textbook. Use the many strategies you practiced in Sections 1–3 to build questions that link the text topic to larger issues. For example, you might look at how history fits with modern situations or why the people of history made the decisions they made. Check yourself to be sure that your questions cannot be answered with *yes* or *no*.

### Vocabulary *Builder*

**High-Use Words**
efficient, p. 463
prospect, p. 464

**Key Terms and People**
Joseph Smith, p. 462
polygamy, p. 462
Brigham Young, p. 463
forty-niner, p. 464
water rights, p. 464
vigilante, p. 465

⭐ **Background Knowledge** You have seen that, as a result of the war with Mexico, the United States gained the lands known as the Mexican Cession. In this section, you will see why large numbers of Americans began to settle in this vast region.

## Mormons Settle Utah

**Main Idea**
The Mormons journeyed westward seeking a safe place to practice their religion.

Even before the end of the war, a group of Americans had begun moving into the part of the Mexican Cession that is today Utah. These were the Mormons, members of the Church of Jesus Christ of Latter-day Saints. The church was founded in 1830 by Joseph Smith, a New York farmer. Smith said that heavenly visions had revealed to him the text of a holy book called the *Book of Mormon.*

**Seeking Refuge** The Mormon Church grew quickly, but some of its teachings often placed its followers in conflict with their neighbors. For example, Mormons at first believed that property should be held in common. Smith also favored polygamy, the practice of having more than one wife at a time.

Hostile communities forced the Mormons to move from New York to Ohio and then to Missouri. By 1844, the Mormons had settled in Nauvoo, Illinois. There, Joseph Smith was murdered by an angry mob.

**Brigham Young,** the new Mormon leader, realized that Nauvoo was no longer safe. He had heard about a great valley in the Utah desert, which at the time was still owned by Mexico. In 1847, he led a party of Mormons on a long, hazardous journey to the valley of the Great Salt Lake. Over the next few years, some 15,000 Mormon men, women, and children made the trek to Utah.

Although Utah was a safe refuge, the land was not hospitable. Farming was difficult in the dry desert. Then, in the summer of 1849, enormous swarms of crickets nearly destroyed the Mormons' first harvest. But a flock of seagulls flew in from the Pacific and devoured the crickets. The Mormons then set out to make the desert bloom. Under strict church supervision, they enclosed and distributed farmland and set up an <u>efficient</u> system of irrigation.

### Conflict With the Government

In 1848, as a result of the Mexican Cession, Utah became part of the United States. Congress then created the Utah Territory. Mormon leaders immediately came into conflict with officials appointed to govern the territory.

Three issues divided the Mormons and the federal government. First, the Mormon Church controlled the election process in the Utah Territory. Non-Mormons had no say. Second, the church supported businesses that were owned by Mormons. "Outsiders" had difficulty doing business. The third issue was polygamy, which was illegal in the rest of the country.

These issues were not resolved for more than 40 years. In time, Congress passed a law that took control of elections away from the Mormon Church. Church leaders agreed to ban polygamy and to stop favoring Mormon-owned businesses. Finally, in 1896, Utah became a state.

☑ **Checkpoint** **Why did the Mormons leave Illinois?**

**Vocabulary** *Builder*
<u>efficient</u> (ee FISH ehnt) *adj.* done in a way that increases production with the least amount of waste

**Mormons Come to Utah**
Brigham Young (below) led the first wave of Mormons to migrate to Utah. In later years, settlers continued to arrive. Some, like those shown in the painting, were so poor they had to haul their belongings along the Mormon Trail by hand. **Critical Thinking:** *Identify Benefits  Identify two benefits these Mormons might look forward to from settling in Utah.*

# The California Gold Rush

When California was ceded to the United States in 1848, about 10,000 Californios, or Mexican Californians, were living in the territory. A handful of wealthy families owned most of the land. They lived an elegant, aristocratic life. Their ranches were worked by poorer Californios or by Native Americans.

After the Mexican Cession, easterners began to migrate to California. The wealthy Californios looked down on the newcomers from the East, and the newcomers felt contempt for the Californios. The two groups rarely mixed or intermarried.

**Gold Is Discovered** An event in January 1848 would bring a flood of other settlers to California. James Marshall was building a sawmill on John Sutter's land near Sacramento. One morning, he found a small gold nugget in a ditch. Sutter tried to keep his discovery a secret. But the news spread like wildfire throughout the country and abroad. By 1849, the California gold rush had begun.

The prospect of finding gold attracted about 80,000 fortune seekers. The nickname **"forty-niners"** was given to these people who came to California in search of gold. In just two years, the population of California zoomed from 14,000 to 100,000.

Sutter's Mill was just the beginning. Prospectors, or gold seekers, searched throughout the Sacramento Valley for gold. They dug into the land using picks and shovels. They also looked in streams. This process, called placer mining, did not take much labor, money, or skill. Miners washed dirt from a stream in a pan, leaving grains of gold in the bottom. Finding gold was called "hitting pay dirt."

Gold above ground was quickly found. But there was more gold in underground deposits, or lodes. Gold in lodes was difficult and expensive to mine. It required heavy and expensive machinery. As a result, large companies took over the mining of underground lodes.

**Water Rights** In the gold fields, disputes over water rights were common. **Water rights** are the legal rights to use the water in a river, stream, or other body. California has an abundance of land, but much of it is desert. Settlers needed water for irrigation and mining.

California had kept older Mexican laws regarding water rights. Landowners had the right to use the water that flowed through their land. At the same time, it was illegal to cut off water to one's neighbors. In most gold rush territories, though, the law was ignored. The first people to reach a stream used as much water as they wanted—sometimes even the whole stream! Disputes over water rights often erupted into violence.

**Life in Mining Towns** Mining towns were not very permanent places. Most sprang up overnight and emptied just as quickly when miners heard news of a gold strike in another place.

Mining towns attracted both miners and people hoping to make money from miners. Miners were often willing to pay high prices for food and supplies. They also needed entertainment. A typical mining town was made up of a row of businesses with a saloon at its center.

**Vocabulary** *Builder*
**prospect** (PRAHS pehkt) *n.* promise; something looked forward to

**Panning for Gold**

Forty-niners, like the man in this picture, spent many back-breaking hours sifting through sand at the edge of the river. If they were lucky, their reward was a glimmer of gold in their pan. **Critical Thinking: Apply Information** *Based on your reading, what method of gold mining did this prospector use?*

California was not yet a state, so federal law did not apply within the mining towns. To impose some order, miners banded together and created their own rules. Punishment for crimes was often quick and brutal. Vigilantes, or self-appointed law enforcers, punished people for crimes, though they had no legal right to do so.

**Role of Women** Gold rushes were not like other migrations in American history. Most migrations included men and women, young and old. Most forty-niners, however, were young men. By 1850, the ratio of men to women in California was twelve to one!

Still, some women did come to California in search of fortune, work, or adventure. Unlike other areas of the country, California offered women profitable work. Some women mined, but many more stayed in town. They worked in or ran boardinghouses, hotels, restaurants, laundries, and stores.

**Drifting and Settling** Few forty-niners struck it rich. After the gold rush ended, many people continued to search for gold throughout the West. There were gold or silver strikes in British Columbia, Idaho, Montana, Colorado, Arizona, and Nevada. Other miners gave up the drifting life and settled in the West for good.

 **Checkpoint** Why were water rights an important issue?

# Links Across Time

## Water Rights in the West

**1849** During the gold rush, California law generally gave water rights to the first person to make use of a body of water.

**1905** Los Angeles, still a small city, won rights to the Owens River, 200 miles away. Engineers later built aqueducts and dams to carry the water to the city. This water helped Los Angeles grow rapidly. But ranchers and farmers in the Owens Valley protested the loss of their water rights.

## Link to Today  Online

**Connection to Today** Water rights remain an issue in many areas of the nation today. Farms and communities still compete to win access to clean, available water.

**For:** Water rights in the news
**Visit:** PHSchool.com
**Web Code:** myc-4094

**1913** Workers opened the gates of the newly completed Los Angeles aqueduct.

**San Francisco During the Gold Rush**

This painting shows San Francisco in the 1850s. "Where there was a vacant piece of ground one day," wrote one witness, "the next saw it covered with half a dozen tents or shanties." **Critical Thinking: Distinguish Relevant Information** *What information in this picture supports the conclusion that San Francisco had a diverse population?*

**Main Idea**

The gold rush permanently altered the makeup of California's population.

# California's Changing Population

Many gold rush towns were temporary, but some grew and prospered. San Francisco had only 200 inhabitants in 1848. During the gold rush, immigrants who sailed to California passed through San Francisco's harbor. Its merchants provided miners with goods and services. Many newcomers remained in the city. Others returned to settle there after working in the mines. By 1870, San Francisco had a population of more than 100,000.

**An Unusual Mix of People** The gold rush brought enormous ethnic diversity to California. People came from Europe, Asia, Australia, and South America. By 1860, the population of California was almost 40 percent foreign-born.

European immigrants often enjoyed more freedom in California than in Europe. They also faced less prejudice than in the East. In some ways, mining societies were more democratic, as men in the gold fields had to rely on one another. One immigrant wrote home:

> **"**We live a free life, and the best thing . . . is that no human being here sets himself up as your lord and master. It is true that we do not have many of the luxuries of life, but I do not miss them.**"**
>
> —quoted in *Land of Their Choice* (Blegen)

**Chinese Immigrants** China's economy was in trouble in the 1840s. After news reached China of a "mountain of gold," about 45,000 Chinese men went to California. Most hoped to return home to China with enough money to take care of their families.

Chinese laborers faced prejudice. They generally were not given higher-paying jobs in the mines. Instead, they were hired to do menial labor. Some cooked or did laundry. Despite many difficulties, the Chinese worked hard. They helped build railroads and worked on farms. Their labor also helped cities like San Francisco to prosper.

**African Americans** Several thousand free African Americans lived in California by 1850. They had their own churches and newspapers. Many ran their own businesses. However, they did not have equal rights. They could not vote or serve on juries.

Slavery did not take root in California. Some southerners did bring their slaves with them during the gold rush. However, the other miners objected. They believed that anyone who profited from mining should participate in the hard labor of finding gold.

**Native Americans** For Native Americans, the gold rush brought even more tragedy. Miners swarmed onto Indian lands to search for gold. Vigilante gangs killed Indians and stole their land. About 100,000 Indians, nearly two thirds of the Native American population of California, died during the gold rush.

**Impact on Californios** By 1850, only 15 percent of Californians were Mexican. The old ruling families did not have a strong say in the new territorial government. When a constitutional convention was held, only 8 of the 48 delegates were Californios.

Californio politicians could not stop the passage of laws that discriminated against their people. The legislature levied a high tax on ranches and required rancheros to prove that they owned their land. This was often difficult, because most had received their land grants from Spain or Mexico. By the time many Californios could prove ownership, they had had to sell their land to pay legal bills.

☑ **Checkpoint**  What effects did the gold rush have on Californios?

⭐ **Looking Back and Ahead**  California had enough people by 1850 to apply for admission to the Union as a free state. As you will read in the next chapter, California's request for statehood would cause a national crisis.

**Ask Questions That Go Beyond the Text**
Ask a question that explores beyond the text and requires research to answer. You might focus on the ways that the lives of Mexicans in California changed after the gold rush.

---

Section 4 | **Check Your Progress**

**Progress Monitoring** ⬤nline
**For:** Self-test with instant help
**Visit:** PHSchool.com
**Web Code:** mya-4094

**Comprehension and Critical Thinking**

1. **(a) Recall** Why did the Mormons decide to move to Utah?
**(b) Identify Alternatives** What other options might the Mormons have considered?

2. **(a) List** Which groups migrated to California after 1848?
**(b) Make Inferences** Which groups benefited most from the discovery of gold? Which groups suffered most? Explain.

**Reading Skill**

3. **Ask Questions That Go Beyond the Text** Recall what you just read about California during the gold rush. Ask a question that goes beyond the text and requires research to answer.

**Vocabulary** *Builder*

4. Write two definitions of the term water rights. First, write a formal definition for your teacher. Second, write a definition in everyday English for a classmate.

**Writing**

5. Write a short paragraph explaining what happened as a result of the California gold rush in 1849. Then, exchange paragraphs with another student. Check your partner's work for errors. Work together to take the best elements from each paragraph and to create a new version.

Historical evidence comes from many sources. Evaluating the validity of written sources is important in putting together a picture of the past.

The following journal entries, written by Elizabeth Wood, describe portions of her two-and-a-half-month journey from Fort Laramie, Wyoming, to eastern Oregon in 1851.

**Primary Source**

"July 25. Since last date we camped at the ford where emigrants cross from the south to the north side of the Platte. . . . We stopped near the Red Buttes, where the hills are of a red color, nearly square and have the appearance of houses with flat roofs. . . . We also passed Independence Rock and the Devil's Gate, which is high enough to make one's head swim, and the posts reach an altitude of some 4 or 500 feet."

"Monday, September 15th. . . . Mount St. Elias is in the distance, and is covered with snow, so you can imagine somewhat the beauty and grandeur of the scene. We are now among the tribe of Wallawalla Indians."

—Journal of a Trip to Oregon,
Elizabeth Wood

## Learn the Skill
*Use these steps to evaluate written sources.*

1 **Identify the source.** Knowing who the writer is helps you to evaluate that person's account of events.

2 **Note the context.** When was the account written? In what form did it appear? What was the purpose of the account?

3 **Analyze the point of view.** What is the writer trying to say? How does the writer feel about the subject?

4 **Evaluate the validity of the material.** How true is this account? Why do you think so?

## Practice the Skill
*Answer the following questions to evaluate the source on this page.*

1 **Identify the source.** Who wrote these journal entries?

2 **Note the context.** (a) When were these entries written? (b) What was their purpose?

3 **Analyze the point of view.** (a) How does the writer feel about the journey? (b) What words or phrases express the writer's feelings?

4 **Evaluate the validity of the material.** Do you think this journal entry accurately describes the journey west? Why or why not?

## Apply the Skill
*See the Review and Assessment at the end of this chapter.*

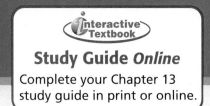

## Chapter Summary

### Section 1
### The West

- By the 1820s, land-hungry Americans often had to look west of the Mississippi River for territory to settle.
- Some Americans moved to the Mexican-controlled lands of the Southwest.
- Manifest Destiny was the idea that the United States had the right to "spread and possess the whole of the continent."

### Section 2
### Trails to the West

- Traders and trappers helped open the West for settlement.
- Free land and the mild climate attracted settlers from all parts of the United States to Oregon.

### Section 3
### Conflict With Mexico

- American settlers in Texas rebelled against Mexico and created the independent Republic of Texas.
- American forces defeated Mexican troops in what became known as the Mexican-American War.
- The United States gained vast new territories as a result of the Treaty of Guadalupe-Hidalgo.

### Section 4
### A Rush to the West

- The Mormons moved west to Utah for religious freedom.
- Gold fever brought thousands of immigrants to California.

## Key Concepts

These notes will help you prepare for questions about key concepts.

### U.S. Territorial Acquisitions in the West

**Oregon**
- Also claimed by Britain
- Region divided by agreement with Britain, 1846

**Texas**
- Won independence from Mexico in 1836; became independent republic
- Annexed by Congress, 1845

**Mexican Cession**
- Acquired from Mexico after Mexican-American War, 1848
- Included California, Utah, most of Southwest

**Gadsden Purchase**
- Purchased from Mexico, 1853
- Small portion of southern Arizona and New Mexico

### Key Groups That Settled the American West

- Traders—first Americans to move to the West
- Trappers—made their living in the fur trade
- Missionaries—came west to convert Native Americans
- Farmers—attracted to the West by land
- Mormons—moved west for religious freedom
- Forty-niners—flocked to California to hunt for gold

## Vocabulary *Builder*

### Key Terms

Answer the following questions in complete sentences that show your understanding of the key terms.

1. Why did settlers in California argue over water rights?

2. What did rancheros own?

3. How did wealthy families benefit from land grants?

4. To what did General Santa Anna lay siege in San Antonio during the war for Texas independence?

## Comprehension and Critical Thinking

5. **(a) Identify** Who were the peninsulares, the creoles, and the mestizos?
   **(b) Draw Inferences** Which of these groups were most likely to support Mexican independence from Spain? Why?

6. **(a) Recall** What was Manifest Destiny?
   **(b) Identify Economic Benefits** What economic benefits could the United States get from following the ideals of Manifest Destiny?

7. **(a) Describe** Describe the life of a mountain man like the one pictured at right.
   **(b) Draw Inferences** How did these men contribute to the goal of Manifest Destiny?

Mountain man

8. **(a) Explain** What did President James Polk do to bring about Manifest Destiny?
   **(b) Draw Conclusions** How did Great Britain threaten Manifest Destiny?

9. **(a) Recall** Why did the Mormons immigrate to Utah?
   **(b) Compare** What other groups in earlier American history came to North America for similar reasons?

10. **(a) Identify** Who were the forty-niners?
    **(b) Analyze Cause and Effect** How did the forty-niners contribute to California becoming a state?

## 🎧 History Reading Skill

11. **Frame Research Questions** Frame a research question about any aspect of this chapter. Start by reviewing headings and choosing one that interests you. Remember to frame questions that go beyond the text and require research to answer.

## Writing

12. **Write two paragraphs discussing the results of the Mexican-American War.** Then, exchange papers with another student.
    **As you look at your partner's paragraphs, you should:**
    • correct every error you can find;
    • look for places to add transitions to make the sentences flow better and to connect the two paragraphs;
    • find opportunities to mix short and long sentences.

13. **Write a Narrative:**
    You are an easterner in the 1840s trying to decide whether to go to Oregon, Utah, or California. Write a diary entry in which you weigh the possible costs and benefits of such a trip and reach a final decision.

## Skills for Life

### Evaluate Written Sources

Use the diary entry below to answer the questions.

> "Tuesday May 20th. Travelled 20 miles and camped . . . saw several antelope, and an animal called prairie dogs, which resemble a puppy. There are acres of them . . . they plough the ground up and form little knolls all over the ground. . . ."
>
> —Journal of Travels to Oregon, Amelia Hadley, 1851

14. Who wrote this journal entry?

15. When was it written?

16. How does the writer feel about the journey?

17. Do you think this journal entry accurately describes prairie wildlife? Why or why not?

# Test Yourself

1. **Which of the following most directly led to achieving Manifest Destiny?**

   **A** Women vote in the West.

   **B** Mormons settle Utah.

   **C** Santa Anna establishes dictatorship in Mexico.

   **D** President Polk negotiates a treaty with Great Britain to divide Oregon.

   **Refer to the quotation below to answer Question 2.**

   > "I am determined to sustain myself as long as possible and die like a soldier, who never forgets what is due to his honor and that of his country. Victory or Death!"

2. **The person who made this statement was mostly likely**

   **A** at the Alamo.

   **B** at a rendezvous.

   **C** at John Sutter's sawmill.

   **D** on the Oregon Trail.

**Refer to the map below to answer Question 3.**

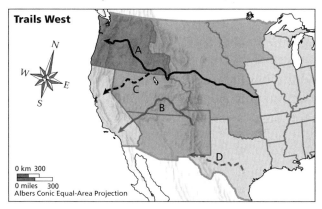

**Trails West**

0 km 300
0 miles 300
Albers Conic Equal-Area Projection

3. **Which of the trails marked on the map led the forty-niners to their final destination?**

   **A** trail A

   **B** trail B

   **C** trail C

   **D** trail D

## Document-Based Questions

**Task:** Look at Documents 1 and 2, and answer their accompanying questions. Then, use the documents and your knowledge of history to complete this writing assignment:

   List the reasons for and against the Mexican-American War. Then, write a short essay analyzing the arguments of each side. Draw a conclusion about the validity of each argument.

**Document 1:** In 1846, President Polk asked Congress to declare war against Mexico. *What does Polk accuse Mexico of doing?*

> "The grievous wrongs perpetrated by Mexico upon our citizens throughout a long period of years remains unredressed. . . . We have tried every effort of reconciliation. . . . But now . . . Mexico has passed the boundary of the United States, has invaded our territory and shed American blood upon the American soil. . . .
>
> . . . I involve the prompt action of Congress to recognize the existence of the war, and to place at the disposition of the Executive the means of prosecuting the war with vigor, and thus hastening the restoration of peace."

**Document 2:** Abraham Lincoln, then a member of Congress, spoke out against the Mexican-American War. *How does Lincoln challenge Polk's reasons for war with Mexico?*

> "I carefully examined the President's messages. . . . The result of this examination was to make the impression that . . . he falls far short of proving his justification [for the war]. . . . The President . . . declares that the soil was ours on which hostilities were commenced by Mexico. . . .
>
> Let [the President] remember he sits where Washington sat, and so remembering, let him answer as Washington would answer. . . . And if, so answering, he can show that the soil was ours, where the first blood of the war was shed, . . . then I am with him. . . . But if he can not do this . . . then I shall be fully convinced . . . that he is deeply conscious of being in the wrong."

# Writing Workshop

## Expository Essay
## Multiple Causes or Effects

### ▶ Introduction

In a cause-effect essay, you either explain what caused an event to happen or describe the effects of an event. Most important events in history have several causes and several effects. An essay analyzing multiple causes or effects should have the following characteristics:

- an event or development that has several causes or effects

- a thesis statement that makes a point about these causes or effects

- supporting information that shows how the causes or effects are related to the development (and often to each other)

**Assignment**   On the following pages, you will learn how to write an essay analyzing multiple causes or effects. You will get step-by-step instructions. Each step will include an example from a sample essay discussing the gold rush.

Read the instructions and the examples. Then, follow each step to plan and write a 500–700 word essay.

> **Write an essay analyzing either the causes or the effects of the antislavery movement.**

For a review of the steps in the writing process, see the **Historian's Toolkit, *Write Like a Historian.***

### ▶ Prewriting

**Define your subject and brainstorm about its causes and effects.** Begin by thinking about the central historical event or development about which you are going to write. Brainstorm about causes or effects using the following guidelines:

| | |
|---|---|
| **If you can choose whether to write about *causes* or *effects*** | Decide which seems more interesting or complex. If a development has only one principal cause, it would make more sense to write about its effects. |
| **If you are asked to focus on the *causes* of a historical event** | Try to go back as far as you can to find the earliest factors leading to the event. List the various causes in chronological order. See if any of the causes have caused one another, and draw arrows showing these connections. |
| **If you are asked to focus on the *effects* of a historical event** | See if any effects can still be felt today. If some of the effects are connected, with one result leading to another, draw arrows between them. Be specific: What seems to be a single effect may turn out to be several different effects. |

**Decide on the major causes or effects to analyze.** Now you need to decide which causes or effects you will actually write about. You can choose from several different approaches.

- Analyze causes or effects that are related to one another in a chain, each one leading to the next.
- Examine in depth two or three most important causes or effects of the historical development.
- Discuss the kinds of causes or effects involved. For example, you could look at the economic, social, and cultural causes or effects.

**Write a thesis statement.** Once you have chosen the causes or effects you will discuss, you are ready to write a thesis statement expressing an idea about these causes or effects.

> **Sample thesis statement:** The California gold rush of 1849 had a number of social, political, economic, and cultural effects on the history of California.

## ▶ Drafting

**Decide how to organize your writing.** Essays analyzing causes and effects may be organized chronologically, by order of importance, or according to types of causes or effects.

- **Chronological organization** You could organize a cause-effect essay chronologically, moving from earlier events to later ones.

- **Order of importance** You could also organize your causes or effects by order of importance, saving the most important one for last.

- **Types** You might organize your analysis according to types of causes or effects. For example, in discussing the gold rush, you might look first at the population changes that occurred as thousands of settlers moved to California. Then you could discuss the economic changes and, finally, the cultural changes.

**Write an introduction.** The first paragraph of your essay introduces your subject to the reader. Lead up to your thesis statement in which you announce your main idea about these causes or effects.

**Support your thesis with examples and details.** You should devote one or two paragraphs to each of the major causes or effects. Be sure to include relevant facts and details.

**Write a strong conclusion.** In your final paragraph, show the reader how you have supported your thesis.

# Writing Workshop continued

## ▶ Model Essay

Read the following model of an essay discussing the effects of the gold rush. Notice how it includes the characteristics you have learned about.

**The first paragraph is an introduction to the subject of the essay.**

**Is this essay organized using chronology, order of importance, or types?**

### Effects of the California Gold Rush

Tens of thousands of people from around the world caught gold fever in 1848. They came to California with big dreams of becoming rich overnight. The gold rush, as this movement was called, had social, political, and cultural effects on California.

Because so many people moved there, the population of the territory soared. By 1852, it totaled more than 250,000. San Francisco changed from a small town to a busy city almost overnight.

But the huge population growth also caused serious social problems. Miners disregarded laws. There was an increase in murders and robbery in many mining camps. Criminals were often hanged without a legal trial.

Californians knew this lawlessness could not continue. They drafted a state constitution in 1849 and asked for admission to the Union. After much debate, in 1850 California was admitted as a free state. This political change was an important result of the gold rush.

The gold rush also affected the culture of California. Many thousands of people from countries in Europe, Australia, and South America moved there. Beginning in 1849, thousands of Chinese began to immigrate to California to work. They joined the many Mexican Americans and African Americans who were arriving.

The gold rush changed life in California forever. This historic event pushed the economy forward and transformed a territory into a state. It also created a society that became a rich mix of people and cultures, which is still seen today.

**The thesis statement identifies the main idea about the effects of the gold rush.**

**Each paragraph includes facts and details about the effect being discussed.**

**The conclusion restates the main ideas about the effects of the gold rush and relates it to later events.**

# ▶ Revising

After completing your draft, read it again carefully to find ways to make your writing better. Here are some questions to ask yourself.

## Revise to strengthen your thesis and support
- Do the introduction and thesis statement establish a clear relationship between your topic and its causes or effects?
- Do the body paragraphs develop the connection with logical facts, examples, and reasons?

## Revise to use helpful transitions and clear language
- Does the essay include transitions showing cause or effect and connecting words or phrases such as *because, as a result, therefore*?
- Are the causes or effects clearly described, and their connections clear?

## Revise to meet written English-language conversions
- Are all sentences complete, with a subject and a verb?
- Are all the words spelled correctly?
- Are all proper nouns capitalized, including names of people and places?
- Did you use proper punctuation?

# ▶ Rubric for Self-Assessment

*Evaluate your cause-effect essay using the following rating scale:*

|  | Score 4 | Score 3 | Score 2 | Score 1 |
|---|---|---|---|---|
| **Organization** | Supports the thesis with logically ordered paragraphs linking a historical development to earlier events (its causes) or later ones (its effects) | Uses a reasonably clear organization, but occasionally fails to follow it or includes less relevant information (for example, events that are not really causes or effects of the subject) | Chooses an organization not suited to the topic (for example, presents causes or effects without showing how they are linked to the subject) | Shows lack of organizational strategy |
| **Presentation** | Clearly shows how the causes led to the development or how the effects grew from it; uses facts, examples, and reasons to support the thesis | Discusses the causes or effects of the development adequately but could go into greater depth; links most supporting information to the thesis | Does not discuss the causes or effects of the historical development adequately or in any detail; does not link supporting information to the thesis | Does not provide any facts, reasons, or examples about the causes or effects of the historical development being analyzed |
| **Use of Language** | Varies sentence structure and vocabulary successfully; includes no or very few mechanical errors | Uses some variety in sentence structure and vocabulary; includes few mechanical errors | Uses the same types of sentences without varying them; repeats words; includes many mechanical errors | Writes incomplete sentences; uses language poorly; includes many mechanical errors |

**Underground Railroad** By the middle of the 1830s, opposition to slavery was rising among reformers. Abolitionists aided enslaved people who sought to escape via the Underground Railroad to the North or to Canada.

## 1830s

**Lincoln's Gettysburg Address** Lincoln's firm leadership inspired the Union side. In the Gettysburg Address, he vowed that "these dead shall not have died in vain . . . and that government of the people, by the people, for the people, shall not perish from the earth."

## 1863

# Civil War and Reunion

**Decision at Gettysburg** All attempts at compromise having failed, the United States endured a bloody four-year civil war. After the Battle of Gettysburg, the war turned in favor of the Union army.

## 1863

**A New Voice in Government** Before the Civil War, African Americans had no voice in southern government. During Reconstruction, they became a powerful voting force in southern elections. African Americans were elected to public office as sheriffs, mayors, state legislators, and members of Congress.

## 1868

# 14 | The Nation Divided
## 1846–1861

## Chapter Preview

The conflict over the issue of slavery continued to divide the country. A series of events in the 1850s caused the crisis to deepen. Eventually the conflict erupted into war between North and South.

☑ **What You Will Learn**

With the addition of new western land, debate over the spread of slavery increased.

After all efforts at compromise failed, violent fighting broke out in the Kansas Territory.

As tensions increased, a new antislavery political party emerged.

Abraham Lincoln's election led seven southern states to leave the Union.

**U.S. Events**

**1850**
Fugitive Slave Act requires citizens to help catch runaway slaves.

**1852**
Harriet Beecher Stowe publishes *Uncle Tom's Cabin*.

**1854**
Kansas-Nebraska Act leads to violence.

1850

1853

1856

**World Events**

**1853** Commodore Matthew Perry arrives in Japan to open trade.

In Eastman Johnson's painting, *A Ride for Liberty—The Fugitive Slaves,* a mother holding a small child looks back for possible pursuers.

**1857**
Supreme Court declares Missouri Compromise unconstitutional.

**1860**
Abraham Lincoln is elected President.

**1861**
Civil War begins with bombardment of Fort Sumter.

1856

1859

1862

**1857** Soldiers in India revolt against the British.

**1861** Russian tsar frees serfs.

## History Reading Skill  Analyze Cause and Effect

### What causes brought the Union to the brink of war in the 1850s?

In this chapter, you will learn how to analyze cause-and-effect relationships. Read the following speech by Senator John C. Calhoun in which he explains why he thinks the nation is so divided. The side notes show you how to analyze causes and effects.

**Primary Source**

In 1850, South Carolina Senator Calhoun wrote this speech in defense of slavery and gave his view of the reasons for the current division in the nation.

It is a great mistake to suppose that disunion can be effected by a single blow. The cords which bound these states together in one common union are far too numerous and powerful for that. Disunion must be the work of time. It is only through a long process that the cords can be snapped, until the whole fabric falls asunder. Already the agitation of the slavery question has snapped some of the most important and has greatly weakened all the others.

If the agitation goes on, the same force, acting with increased intensity, will finally snap every cord. Then nothing will be left to hold the states together except force.

So, the question again recurs—how can the Union be saved? To this I answer, there is but one way by which it can be—and that is by adopting such measures as will satisfy the states belonging to the southern section so that they can remain in the Union consistently with their honor and their safety.

—Senator John C. Calhoun, speech to the Senate, 1850

> Phrases such as "the work of" and "through a long process" highlight the cause-and-effect link.

> Two effects: The agitation of slavery has weakened some ties and destroyed others.

> Here is another example of cause and effect.

> Two causes: Southern states must be able to feel both safe and honorable in order to save the Union.

### Analyze Cause and Effect

- Look for verbs and phrases that suggest how one event led to another: *lead to, snapped, saved, weakened.*
- Consider whether a cause has more than one effect and whether an effect has more than one cause.
- Confirm that one event actually results from another, rather than just occurring after it.

### Document-Based Questions

1. Who gave this speech?
2. What issue does he say is dividing the Union?
3. How does he say the Union can be saved?

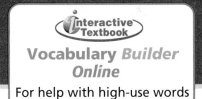

# Vocabulary *Builder*

## Previewing High-Use Academic Words

| High-Use Word | Definition | Sample History Sentence |
|---|---|---|
| **vital** (VĪ tahl) (Section 1, p. 482) | *adj.* necessary for life; of great importance | The buffalo was <u>vital</u> to the way of life of the Plains Indians. |
| **crisis** (KRĪ sihs) (Section 1, p. 484) | *n.* turning point or deciding event in history | During the winter at Valley Forge, General Washington faced a <u>crisis</u> in keeping his force together. |
| **deprive** (dee PRĪV) (Section 2, p. 487) | *v.* to keep from happening; to take away by force or intent | During the administration of Andrew Jackson, many Native Americans were <u>deprived</u> of their homelands. |
| **impose** (ihm POHZ) (Section 2, p. 490) | *v.* to place a burden on someone or something | After the Boston Tea Party, the British <u>imposed</u> a harsh rule on Massachusetts. |
| **embrace** (ehm BRAYS) (Section 3, p. 496) | *v.* to hold tight; to readily accept | With the battles of Lexington and Concord, many Americans <u>embraced</u> the idea of independence from Britain. |
| **clarify** (KLAIR ih fī) (Section 3, p. 497) | *v.* to make the meaning of something clear | The Virginia and Tennessee resolutions <u>clarified</u> the reasons for opposing the Alien and Sedition acts. |
| **accommodation** (ak kom moh DAY shuhn) (Section 4, p. 501) | *n.* adjustment; adaptation | With the Treaty of Ghent, Britain and the United States reached an <u>accommodation</u> to end the War of 1812. |
| **isolate** (Ī sah layt) (Section 4, p. 503) | *v.* to set apart; to separate | With the French fleet in place, Cornwallis was <u>isolated</u> on the Yorktown peninsula. |

## Previewing Key Terms and People

Dred Scott

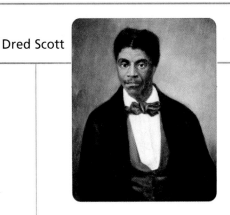

popular sovereignty, p. 483
secede, p. 484
fugitive, p. 484
Henry Clay, p. 484
John C. Calhoun, p. 485
Daniel Webster, p. 485
Harriet Beecher Stowe, p. 488

propaganda, p. 488
Stephen Douglas, p. 489
John Brown, p. 491
Dred Scott, p. 495
Roger B. Taney, p. 495
Abraham Lincoln, p. 495
civil war, p. 503

# Growing Tensions Over Slavery

## Objectives

1. Explain why conflict arose over the issue of slavery in the territories after the Mexican-American War.

2. Identify the goal of the Free-Soil Party.

3. Describe the compromise Henry Clay proposed to settle the issues that divided the North and the South.

## Prepare to Read

### Reading Skill

**Analyze Causes** Causes are the reasons that events happen. As the United States struggled over the issue of slavery, events such as new laws or important speeches had dramatic effects on the struggle. Understanding how these events made such an impact will help you make sense of this turbulent time in American history.

### Vocabulary *Builder*

**High-Use Words**

vital, p. 482
crisis, p. 484

**Key Terms and People**

popular sovereignty, p. 483
secede, p. 484
fugitive, p. 484
Henry Clay, p. 484
John C. Calhoun, p. 485
Daniel Webster, p. 485

---

**Main Idea**
The vast territory acquired as a result of the Mexican-American War reignited the controversy over slavery.

**Vocabulary *Builder***
vital (vī tahl) *adj.* necessary for life; of great importance

⭐ **Background Knowledge** The Missouri Compromise of 1820 seemed to have quieted the differences between North and South. Then, the American victory in the Mexican-American War added new territory to the United States. In this section, you will learn how this development recharged the slavery issue.

## Slavery and the Mexican-American War

Between 1820 and 1848, four new slaveholding states and four new free states were admitted to the Union. This maintained the balance between free and slaveholding states, with 15 of each. However, territory gained by the Mexican-American War threatened to destroy the balance.

**The Wilmot Proviso** The Missouri Compromise did not apply to the huge territory gained from Mexico in 1848. Would this territory be organized as states that allowed slavery? The issue was vital to northerners who wanted to stop slavery from spreading.

Fearing that the South would gain too much power, in 1846 Representative David Wilmot of Pennsylvania proposed that Congress ban slavery in all territory that might become part of the United States as a result of the Mexican-American War.

This proposal was called the Wilmot Proviso. The provision was passed in the House of Representatives, but it failed in the Senate.

Although the Wilmot Proviso never became law, it aroused great concern in the South. Many supporters of slavery viewed it as an attack on slavery by the North.

**An Antislavery Party** The controversy over the Wilmot Proviso also led to the rise of a new political party. Neither the Democrats nor the Whigs took a firm stand on slavery. Each hoped to win support in both North and South in the election of 1848.

The Democratic candidate for President in 1848, Senator Lewis Cass of Michigan, proposed a solution that he hoped would appeal to everyone. Cass suggested letting the people in each new territory or state decide for themselves whether to allow slavery. This process, called **popular sovereignty**, meant that people in the territory or state would vote directly on issues, rather than having their elected representatives decide.

Many Whigs and Democrats wanted to take a stronger stand against the spread of slavery. In August 1848, antislavery Whigs and Democrats joined forces to form a new party, which they called the Free-Soil Party. It called for the territory gained in the Mexican-American War to be "free soil," a place where slavery was banned.

The party chose former Democratic President Martin Van Buren as its candidate. Van Buren did poorly in the election. However, he won enough votes from the Democrats to keep Cass from winning. General Zachary Taylor, a Whig and a hero of the Mexican-American War, was elected instead.

☑**Checkpoint** Why was the Free-Soil Party founded?

## The Election of 1848

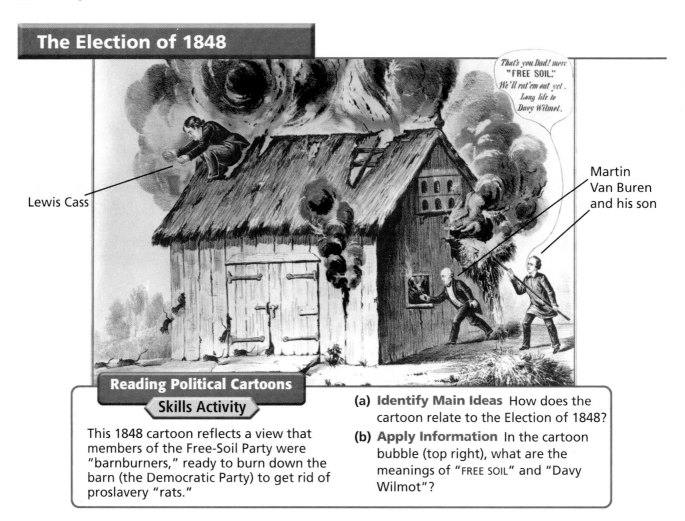

*That's you Dad! more "FREE SOIL." We'll rat 'em out yet. Long life to Davy Wilmot.*

Lewis Cass

Martin Van Buren and his son

**Reading Political Cartoons**

**Skills Activity**

This 1848 cartoon reflects a view that members of the Free-Soil Party were "barnburners," ready to burn down the barn (the Democratic Party) to get rid of proslavery "rats."

**(a) Identify Main Ideas** How does the cartoon relate to the Election of 1848?

**(b) Apply Information** In the cartoon bubble (top right), what are the meanings of "FREE SOIL" and "Davy Wilmot"?

## Calhoun Versus Webster

"[If] something is not done to arrest it, the South will be forced to choose between abolition and secession. . . . If you are unwilling we should part in peace, tell us so; and we shall know what to do when you reduce the question to submission or resistance."

—John C. Calhoun, March 4, 1850

John C. Calhoun

"I wish to speak today, not as a Massachusetts man, nor as a Northern man, but as an American. . . . I speak today for the preservation of the Union. . . . I speak today . . . for the restoration to the country of that quiet and that harmony which make the blessings of this Union so rich, and so dear to us all."

—Daniel Webster, March 7, 1850

Daniel Webster

### Reading Primary Sources

**Skills Activity**

During the Senate debate on Clay's Compromise of 1850, John C. Calhoun and Daniel Webster wrote dramatic speeches evaluating the compromise.

**(a) Detect Points of View** For what region does Daniel Webster claim to be speaking?

**(b) Apply Information** Calhoun says "[If] something is not done to arrest it, the South will be forced to choose between abolition and secession." To what does "it" refer?

---

**Main Idea**

The compromise proposed by Henry Clay produced one of the greatest debates in American history.

**Analyze Causes**

What event did both southerners and northerners worry would destroy the balance of power between them?

**Vocabulary Builder**

**crisis** (KRĪ sihs) *n.* turning point or deciding event in history

## A Bitter Debate

After the discovery of gold in California, thousands of people rushed west. California soon had enough people to become a state. Both sides realized that California's admission to the Union as a free state would upset the balance between free and slave states in the Senate.

Northerners argued that California should be a free state because most of the territory lay north of the Missouri Compromise line. But southerners feared that if free states gained a majority in the Senate, the South would not be able to block antislavery attacks like the Wilmot Proviso. Southern leaders began to threaten to secede, or withdraw, from the nation if California was admitted to the Union as a free state.

There were other issues dividing the North and South. Northerners wanted the slave trade abolished in Washington, D.C. Southerners wanted northerners to catch people who had escaped from slavery. Southerners called for a law that would force the return of fugitives, or runaway enslaved people.

For months it looked as if there was no solution. Then, in January 1850, Senator Henry Clay of Kentucky stepped forward with a plan to calm the crisis. Clay had won the nickname the Great Compromiser for working out the Missouri Compromise. Now, Clay made another series of proposals that he hoped would forever resolve the issues that bitterly divided northerners and southerners.

The Senate's discussion of Clay's proposals produced one of the greatest debates in American political history. South Carolina Senator John C. Calhoun was against compromise. Calhoun was gravely ill and just four weeks from death. He was too weak to give his speech, but he struggled to sit upright while his final speech was read to the Senate.

The admission of California as a free state, Calhoun wrote, would expose the South to continued attacks on slavery. There were only two ways to preserve the South's way of life. One was a constitutional amendment to protect states' rights. The other was secession.

Three days later, Massachusetts Senator Daniel Webster rose to support Clay's proposals and called for an end to the bitter sectionalism that was dividing the nation. Webster argued for Clay's compromise in order to preserve the Union.

Which view would prevail? The very existence of the United States depended on the answer.

✓ **Checkpoint**  **How did California's proposed admission to the Union affect the debate between the North and the South over slavery?**

⭐ **Looking Back and Ahead**  With the territories acquired by the Mexican-American War, the nation could no longer overlook the slavery issue. Statehood for each of these territories would upset the balance between free states and slaveholding states. For a short while, it seemed to many that Henry Clay's proposed compromise gave concessions to both sides. But, as you will read in the next section, the compromise soon fell apart. When it did, the nation once again plunged down the road to all-out war between the regions.

## Section 1 | Check Your Progress

**Progress Monitoring** Online
**For:** Self-test with instant help
**Visit:** PHSchool.com
**Web Code:** mya-5101

### Comprehension and Critical Thinking

**1. (a) Recall** What was the Wilmot Proviso?
**(b) Analyze Cause and Effect** Did the Wilmot Proviso successfully address the nation's divisions over slavery? What effect *did* it have on the nation?

**2. (a) List** What were the main issues that led to Henry Clay's proposed compromise?
**(b) Detect Points of View** Write a sentence describing how you would feel about the need to compromise if you were a member of Congress from the North.

### Reading Skill
**3. Analyze Causes** What did southerners want Congress to do about enslaved people who had fled to the North?

### Vocabulary *Builder*
Complete these sentences so they clearly show your understanding of the key terms.
**4.** The status of new western territories would be decided by popular sovereignty, which is _____.

**5.** If southern states seceded from the Union, then _____.

**6.** Many northerners would not report fugitives, who were _____.

### Writing
**7.** Consider the broad topic "Conflicts Between Slave States and Free States Before the Civil War." Divide it into four or five narrower topics. Each of these narrower topics should be covered in a research paper of a few pages.

# Compromises Fail

## Objectives

1. Summarize the main points of the Compromise of 1850.

2. Describe the impact of the novel *Uncle Tom's Cabin*.

3. Explain how the Kansas-Nebraska Act reopened the issue of slavery in the territories.

4. Describe the effect of the Kansas-Nebraska Act.

## Prepare to Read

### ⟳ Reading Skill

**Analyze Effects** The important events of the 1850s had far-reaching effects around the nation. As you read Section 2, try to identify and understand these effects. Remember that two events do not necessarily have a cause-and-effect link just because they occur in sequence. Use signal words such as *result* to help you identify effects.

### Vocabulary *Builder*

**High-Use Words**

deprive, p. 487

impose, p. 490

### Key Terms and People

Harriet Beecher Stowe, p. 488

propaganda, p. 488

Stephen Douglas, p. 489

John Brown, p. 491

⭐ **Background Knowledge** In the previous section, you learned how many Americans hoped that Henry Clay's proposed compromise would quiet the controversy over slavery. Their hopes were soon dashed. In this section, you will learn how new disputes about slavery destroyed the compromise and led to new crises.

## The Compromise of 1850

**Main Idea**
The key part of the Compromise of 1850 related to the Fugitive Slave Act.

In September 1850, Congress finally passed five bills based on Clay's proposals. This series of laws became known as the Compromise of 1850. President Zachary Taylor had opposed the Compromise. However, Taylor died in 1850. The new President, Millard Fillmore, supported the Compromise and signed it into law.

**To Please the North** The Compromise of 1850 was designed to end the crisis by giving both supporters and opponents of slavery part of what they wanted. To please the North, California was admitted to the Union as a free state. In addition, the Compromise banned the slave trade in the nation's capital. (However, Congress declared that it had no power to regulate the slave trade between slave states.)

**To Please the South** Under the terms of the Compromise, popular sovereignty would be used to decide the question of slavery in the rest of the Mexican Cession. People in the states created from that territory would vote whether to be a free state or a slave state when they requested admission to the Union. Also, in return for agreeing to outlaw the slave trade in Washington, D.C., southerners got a tough new fugitive slave law.

The Fugitive Slave Act of 1850 allowed special government officials to arrest any person accused of being a runaway slave. Suspects had no right to a trial to prove that they had been falsely accused. All that was required to <u>deprive</u> them of their freedom was for a slaveholder or any white witness to swear that the suspect was the slaveholder's property. In addition, the law required northern citizens to help capture accused runaways if authorities requested assistance.

**Outrage in the North** The Fugitive Slave Act became the most controversial part of the Compromise of 1850. Many northerners swore that they would resist the hated new law.

Northerners were outraged to see people accused of being fugitive slaves deprived of their freedom. An Indiana man was torn from his wife and children and given to an owner who claimed the man had escaped 19 years earlier. A wealthy African American tailor was carried back to South Carolina after living in New York for years. His friends quickly raised enough money to buy his freedom. But most who were shipped south remained there. Thousands of northern African Americans fled to the safety of Canada, including many who had never been enslaved.

In city after city, residents banded together to resist the Fugitive Slave Law. When two white Georgians arrived in Boston to seize fugitives, Bostonians threatened the slave catchers with harm if they did not leave the city right away. Another group rescued an accused runaway and sent him to safety in Canada. When the mob leaders were arrested, local juries refused to convict them.

John C. Calhoun had hoped that the Fugitive Slave Law would force northerners to admit that slaveholders had rights to their property. Instead, every time the law was enforced, it convinced more northerners that slavery was evil.

✔Checkpoint **How did the Compromise of 1850 deal with the admission of California to the Union?**

Vocabulary *Builder*
<u>deprive</u> (dee PRĪV) *v.* to keep from happening; to take away by force or intent

**Returned to Slavery**
Guarded by federal troops, fugitives Anthony Burns and Thomas Sims are captured in Boston and returned to enslavement in South Carolina. Below is a poster distributed by a southern slaveholder. **Critical Thinking:** *Draw Conclusions* *What details show the attitude of Bostonians to the return of Burns and Sims?*

RAN AWAY!

FROM THE SUBSCRIBER. My Mulatto Boy, GEORGE. Said George is 5 feet 8 inches in height, brown curly hair, dark coat. I will give $400 for him alive, and the same sum for satisfactory proof that he has been killed. WM. HARRIS.
*Vide ANTHONY & ELLIS MAMMOTH "UNCLE TOM'S CABIN."*

# Uncle Tom's Cabin

One northerner deeply affected by the Fugitive Slave Act was Harriet Beecher Stowe. The daughter of an abolitionist minister, Stowe met many people who had escaped from slavery. She decided to write "something that will make this whole nation feel what an accursed thing slavery is."

In 1852, Stowe published *Uncle Tom's Cabin,* a novel about kindly Uncle Tom, an enslaved man who is abused by the cruel Simon Legree. In this passage, Tom dies after a severe beating:

> **"**Tom opened his eyes, and looked upon his master. . . . 'There an't no more ye can do! I forgive ye with all my soul!' and he fainted entirely away.
>
> 'I b'lieve, my soul, he's done for, finally,' said Legree, stepping forward, to look at him. 'Yes, he is! Well, his mouth's shut up, at last,—that's one comfort!'**"**
>
> —Harriet Beecher Stowe, *Uncle Tom's Cabin,* Chapter 38

Stowe's book was a bestseller in the North. It shocked thousands of people who previously had been unconcerned about slavery. As a result, readers began to view slavery as more than just a political conflict. It was a human, moral problem facing every American.

Many white southerners were outraged by Stowe's book. They criticized it as **propaganda,** false or misleading information that is spread to further a cause. They claimed the novel did not give a fair or accurate picture of the lives of enslaved African Americans.

☑**Checkpoint** **What impact did *Uncle Tom's Cabin* have?**

**Analyze Effects**
What was one effect of Harriet Beecher Stowe's horror over slavery? What word in this paragraph highlights the cause-effect link?

**Explore More Video**
To learn more about Harriet Beecher Stowe's book, view the video.

*Uncle Tom's Cabin* The novel *Uncle Tom's Cabin* had an impact that lasted long after slavery ended. An original illustration from the book and a scene on a decorative plate are shown here.
**Critical Thinking: *Identify Costs*** *You are a northerner during the 1850s. A fugitive comes to your door seeking help. Will you help her? List the costs and benefits of helping the person.*

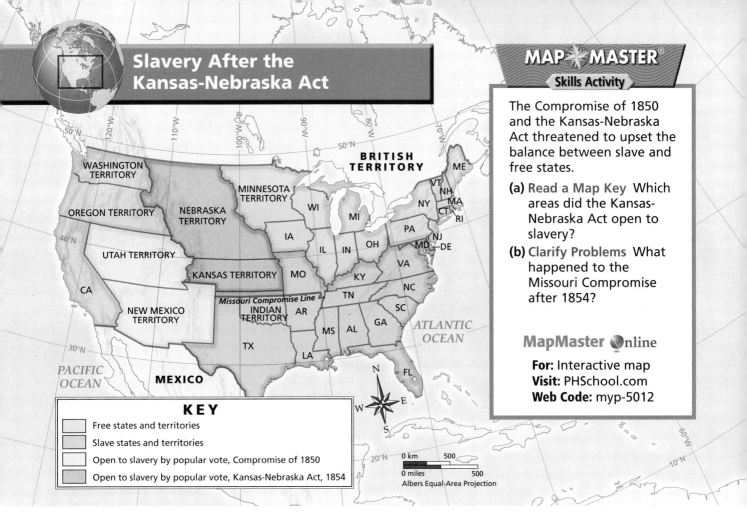

## Slavery After the Kansas-Nebraska Act

WASHINGTON TERRITORY

OREGON TERRITORY

UTAH TERRITORY

CA

NEW MEXICO TERRITORY

NEBRASKA TERRITORY

MINNESOTA TERRITORY

KANSAS TERRITORY

MO

Missouri Compromise Line

INDIAN TERRITORY

AR

TX

LA

MS AL GA

WI

IA

IL IN OH

MI

KY

TN

NC

SC

FL

BRITISH TERRITORY

ME

VT NH

NY MA

CT RI

PA

NJ

MD DE

VA

ATLANTIC OCEAN

PACIFIC OCEAN

MEXICO

### KEY

- Free states and territories
- Slave states and territories
- Open to slavery by popular vote, Compromise of 1850
- Open to slavery by popular vote, Kansas-Nebraska Act, 1854

0 km 500
0 miles 500
Albers Equal-Area Projection

### MAP MASTER®
**Skills Activity**

The Compromise of 1850 and the Kansas-Nebraska Act threatened to upset the balance between slave and free states.

**(a) Read a Map Key** Which areas did the Kansas-Nebraska Act open to slavery?

**(b) Clarify Problems** What happened to the Missouri Compromise after 1854?

**MapMaster Online**

**For:** Interactive map
**Visit:** PHSchool.com
**Web Code:** myp-5012

## The Kansas-Nebraska Act

The nation moved closer to war after Congress passed the Kansas-Nebraska Act in 1854. The act was pushed through by Senator Stephen Douglas. Douglas was eager to develop the lands west of his home state of Illinois. He wanted to see a railroad built from Illinois through the Nebraska Territory to the Pacific Coast.

In 1853, Douglas suggested forming two new territories—the Kansas Territory and the Nebraska Territory. Southerners at once objected. Both territories lay in an area closed to slavery by the Missouri Compromise. This meant that the states eventually created from these territories would enter the Union as free states.

To win southern support, Douglas proposed that slavery in the new territories be decided by popular sovereignty. Thus, in effect, the Kansas-Nebraska Act undid the Missouri Compromise.

As Douglas hoped, southerners supported the Kansas-Nebraska Act. They were sure that slave owners from Missouri would move across the border into Kansas. In time, they hoped that Kansas would enter the union as a slave state.

Northerners, however, were outraged by the Kansas-Nebraska Act. They believed that Douglas had betrayed them by reopening the issue of slavery in the territories. "The more I look at it the more enraged I become," said one northern senator of Douglas's bill. "It needs but little to make me an out-and-out abolitionist."

**Main Idea**

The Kansas-Nebraska Act allowed settlers in the territories to decide whether their territory would allow slavery.

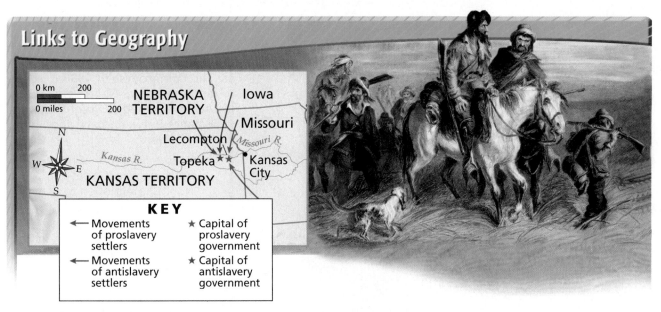

## Links to Geography

NEBRASKA TERRITORY

Iowa

Missouri

Lecompton

Topeka

Kansas City

KANSAS TERRITORY

0 km 200
0 miles 200

Kansas R.

Missouri R.

**KEY**

← Movements of proslavery settlers

★ Capital of proslavery government

← Movements of antislavery settlers

★ Capital of antislavery government

***Bleeding Kansas***

The migration of proslavery and antislavery settlers into Kansas led to the outbreak of violence known as Bleeding Kansas. **Critical Thinking:** *Interpret Maps Why did some proslavery settlers take a more southerly route than did antislavery settlers?*

After months of debate, southern support enabled the Kansas-Nebraska Act to pass in both houses of Congress. President Franklin Pierce, a Democrat elected in 1852, then signed the bill into law. Douglas predicted that, as a result of the Kansas-Nebraska Act, the slavery question would be "forever banished from the halls of Congress." But events would soon prove how wrong he was.

☑**Checkpoint**   How did Stephen Douglas's plan undo the Missouri Compromise?

**Main Idea**

Kansas suffered widespread violence as proslavery and antislavery settlers battled for control.

## Bleeding Kansas

The Kansas-Nebraska Act left it to the white citizens of the territory to decide whether Kansas would be free or slave territory. Both proslavery and antislavery settlers flooded into Kansas within weeks after Douglas's bill became law. Each side was determined to hold the majority in the territory when it came time for the vote.

Thousands of Missourians entered Kansas in March 1855 to illegally vote in the election to select a territorial legislature. Although Kansas had only 3,000 voters, nearly 8,000 votes were cast on election day! Of 39 legislators elected, all but 3 supported slavery. The antislavery settlers refused to accept these results and held a second election.

**Vocabulary** *Builder*
**impose** (ihm POHZ) *v.* to place a burden on someone or something

**Growing Violence** Kansas now had two governments, each claiming the right to <u>impose</u> their government on the territory. Not surprisingly, violence soon broke out. In April, a proslavery sheriff was shot when he tried to arrest some antislavery settlers in the town of Lawrence. The next month, he returned with 800 men and attacked the town.

Three days later, John Brown, an antislavery settler from Connecticut, led seven men to a proslavery settlement near Pottawatomie (paht uh wah TOH mee) Creek. There, they murdered five proslavery men and boys.

These incidents set off widespread fighting in Kansas. Bands of proslavery and antislavery fighters roamed the countryside, terrorizing those who did not support their views. The violence was so bad that it earned Kansas the name Bleeding Kansas.

**Bloodshed in the Senate** Even before Brown's raid at Pottawatomie Creek, the violence in Kansas spilled over into the United States Senate. Charles Sumner of Massachusetts was the leading abolitionist senator. In a fiery speech, Sumner denounced the proslavery legislature in Kansas. He then attacked his southern foes, singling out Andrew Butler, an elderly senator from South Carolina.

Butler was not present the day Sumner made his speech. A few days later, however, Butler's nephew, Congressman Preston Brooks, marched into the Senate chamber. Using a heavy cane, Brooks beat Sumner until he fell to the floor, bloody and unconscious. Sumner never completely recovered from his injuries.

Many southerners felt that Sumner got what he deserved. Hundreds of people sent canes to Brooks to show their support. To northerners, however, Brooks's violent act was just more evidence that slavery was brutal and inhuman.

☑**Checkpoint** **What was the outcome of the election to select a legislature in the Kansas Territory?**

⭐ **Looking Back and Ahead** By 1856, all attempts at compromise had failed. The bitterness between the North and the South was about to alter the political landscape of the United States.

**Analyze Effects** Describe the effect of the Kansas-Nebraska Act on Kansas.

---

**Section 2 | Check Your Progress**

**Progress Monitoring** Online
For: Self-test with instant help
Visit: PHSchool.com
Web Code: mya-5102

**Comprehension and Critical Thinking**
1. **(a) Recall** What parts of the Compromise of 1850 were included to please the North?
**(b) Draw Conclusions** Why do you think northerners were still not satisfied?

2. **(a) Recall** What was the Kansas-Nebraska Act?
**(b) Evaluate Information** How did the Kansas-Nebraska Act contribute to tension between the North and the South?

**Reading Skill**
3. **Analyze Effects** What was one effect of Harriet Beecher Stowe's book *Uncle Tom's Cabin*?

**Vocabulary** *Builder*
Complete the following sentence so that the second part further explains the first part and clearly shows your understanding of the key term.
4. Many white southerners considered *Uncle Tom's Cabin* propaganda; _____ an unfair picture of slavery.

**Writing**
5. Imagine that you are researching the effects of Harriet Beecher Stowe's book *Uncle Tom's Cabin*. Write down five questions that would help you focus your research on this topic. The questions should point you to areas where you need to find more information about the influence of Stowe's book.

# Uncle Tom's Cabin

## by Harriet Beecher Stowe

## Prepare to Read

### Introduction

Harriet Beecher Stowe rocked the nation in 1851 when she published *Uncle Tom's Cabin.* The novel won many converts to the antislavery cause. The excerpt below is from the opening chapter. Shelby, a Kentucky slave owner, must sell some of his enslaved servants to Mr. Haley, a slave trader. Haley is especially interested in buying a young woman named Eliza.

### Reading Skill

**Judging Characters** In a work of fiction, characters may say things that the author thinks are wrong. We have to read carefully in order to understand how the author wants us to judge the characters. In the selection below, look for clues as to what Stowe really thinks of Mr. Haley, the slave trader.

### Vocabulary *Builder*

As you read this literature selection, look for the following underlined words:

**calculation** (kal kyoo LAY shuhn) *n.* ability to figure out exactly what something is worth

**humane** (hyoo MAYN) *adj.* kind; considerate; merciful

**candid** (KAN dihd) *adj.* frank; honest

**virtuous** (VIR choo uhs) *adj.* highly moral

### ⭐ Background

Much of *Uncle Tom's Cabin* is written in dialect that reproduces how different types of characters speak. For example, to show the way Haley speaks, Stowe uses "ha'nt" for "haven't," "this yer" for "this here," "uns" for "ones," and "onpleasant" for "unpleasant."

"Come, how will you trade about the gal?—what shall I say for her—what'll you take?"

"Mr. Haley, she is not to be sold," said Shelby. "My wife would not part with her for her weight in gold."

"Ay, ay! women always say such things, cause they ha'nt no sort of <u>calculation</u>. Just show 'em how many watches, feathers, and trinkets, one's weight in gold would buy, and that alters the case, I reckon."

"I tell you, Haley, this must not be spoken of; I say no, and I mean no," said Shelby, decidedly.

"Well, you'll let me have the boy, though," said the trader; "you must own I've come down pretty handsomely for him."

"What on earth can you want with the child?" said Shelby.

"Why, I've got a friend that's going into this yer branch of the business—wants to buy up handsome boys to raise for the market. Fancy articles entirely—sell for waiters, and so on, to rich 'uns, that can pay for handsome 'uns. It sets off one of yer great places—a real handsome boy to open door, wait, and tend. They fetch a good sum; and this little devil is such a comical, musical concern, he's just the article!"

"I would rather not sell him," said Mr. Shelby, thoughtfully; "the fact is, sir, I'm a <u>humane</u> man, and I hate to take the boy from his mother, sir."

"O, you do?—La! yes—something of that ar natur. I understand, perfectly. It is mighty onpleasant getting on with women, sometimes, I al'ays hates these yer screechin', screamin' times. They are *mighty* onpleasant; but, as I manages business, I generally avoids

Slave auction

'em, sir. Now, what if you get the girl off for a day, or a week, or so; then the thing's done quietly,—all over before she comes home. Your wife might get her some ear-rings, or a new gown, or some such truck, to make up with her."

"I'm afraid not."

"Lor bless ye, yes! These critters ain't like white folks, you know; they gets over things, only manage right. Now, they say," said Haley, assuming a <u>candid</u> and confidential air, "that this kind o' trade is hardening to the feelings; but I never found it so. Fact is, I never could do things up the way some fellers manage the business. I've seen 'em as would pull a woman's child out of her arms, and set him up to sell, and she screechin' like mad all the time;—very bad policy—damages the article—makes 'em quite unfit for service sometimes. I knew a real handsome gal once, in Orleans, as was entirely ruined by this sort o' handling. The fellow that was trading for her didn't want her baby; and she was one of your real high sort, when her blood was up. I tell you, she squeezed up her child in her arms, and talked, and went on real awful. It kinder makes my blood run cold to think on 't; and when they carried off the child, and locked her up, she jest went ravin' mad, and died in a week. Clear waste, sir, of a thousand dollars, just for want of management,—there's where 't is. It's always best to do the humane thing, sir; that's been my experience." And the trader leaned back in his chair, and folded his arm, with an air of <u>virtuous</u> decision, apparently considering himself a second Wilberforce.

From *Uncle Tom's Cabin*, by Harriet Beecher Stowe

**Judging Characters**
Stowe has Haley refer to enslaved Africans as "critters," showing he does not think of them as human beings. Yet, he also claims that slave-trading has not hardened his feelings. What does this indicate about Stowe's view of Haley?

★ **Background**
William Wilberforce was a famous English clergyman who campaigned to end slavery.

If you liked this selection, you might want to read more about the antislavery movement in *Escape From Slavery: Five Journeys to Freedom* by Doreen Rappaport, illustrated by Charles Lilly. Harper Collins Publishers. 1991.

## *Analyze* LITERATURE

Imagine that you are a northerner in 1851 reading *Uncle Tom's Cabin* for the first time. Write a letter to a friend explaining how this excerpt made you feel about the slave trade.

## Objectives

1. Explain why the Republican Party came into being in the 1850s.

2. Summarize the issues involved in the Dred Scott decision.

3. Identify Abraham Lincoln's and Stephen Douglas's views on slavery.

4. Describe the differing reactions in the North and the South to John Brown's raid.

## Prepare to Read

### Reading Skill

**Analyze Causes and Effects**
Historians often disagree over exactly what caused the Civil War. As you read Section 3, watch carefully for cause-and-effect links. Analyzing these links will help you answer this difficult question for yourself. Remember that sometimes the link is not directly stated. Identify an event, then ask yourself: What caused this event to happen? What were the effects of this event?

### Vocabulary *Builder*

**High-Use Words**

embrace, p. 496

clarify, p. 497

**Key People**

Dred Scott, p. 495

Roger B. Taney, p. 495

Abraham Lincoln, p. 495

---

**Main Idea**
The goal of the new Republican Party was to stop the spread of slavery into the western territories.

**Analyze Causes and Effects**
How did growing northern concern about the growth of slavery affect the 1856 presidential election?

☆ **Background Knowledge** You have learned that bitterness between northerners and southerners over slavery weakened the nation's two major political parties. In this section, you will learn about a new party that rapidly came to dominate northern politics.

## A New Antislavery Party

As the Whig Party split apart in 1854, many northern Whigs joined a new political party. It was called the Republican Party, and its main goal was to stop the spread of slavery into the western territories. The Republicans' antislavery stand also attracted northern Democrats and Free-Soil Party members.

The Republicans quickly became a powerful force in politics. The congressional elections of 1854 were held only months after the party was founded. Of the 245 candidates elected to the U.S. House of Representatives, 105 were Republicans. Republican victories in state races also cost the Democrats control of all but two northern state legislatures.

Two years later, in 1856, the Republican Party ran its first candidate for President. It chose John C. Frémont, the army officer who had helped California win independence during the Mexican-American War. The Republicans waged a strong antislavery campaign. Although the Democrat James Buchanan was elected, Frémont won in 11 of the nation's 16 free states.

☑ **Checkpoint** What was the result of the election of 1856?

# The Dred Scott Decision

In March 1857—only three days after Buchanan took office—the U.S. Supreme Court delivered a shattering blow to antislavery forces. It decided the case of *Dred Scott* v. *Sandford*.

Dred Scott was an enslaved person who had once been owned by a U.S. Army doctor. The doctor, and Scott, lived for a time in Illinois and in the Wisconsin Territory. Slavery was illegal in both places. After leaving the army, the doctor settled with Scott in Missouri.

With the help of antislavery lawyers, Scott sued for his freedom. He argued that he was free because he had lived where slavery was illegal. In time, the case reached the Supreme Court. Neither northerners nor southerners were prepared for what the Court decided.

**The Court Decides** Chief Justice Roger B. Taney wrote the decision for the Court. Scott was not a free man, he said, for two reasons. First, according to Taney, Scott had no right to sue in federal court because African Americans were not citizens. Second, Taney said, merely living in free territory did not make an enslaved person free. Slaves were property, Taney declared, and property rights were protected by the U.S. Constitution.

But the ruling went even further. Taney wrote that Congress did not have the power to prohibit slavery in any territory. Thus, the Missouri Compromise was unconstitutional.

**Reaction** Supporters of slavery rejoiced at the Dred Scott decision. The decision meant that slavery was legal in all territories—just as white southern leaders had been demanding all along.

Northerners, however, were stunned. African American leaders such as Frederick Douglass condemned the ruling. Still, Douglass declared, "my hopes were never brighter than now." He believed that outrage against the decision would bring more whites to the abolitionist cause.

Indeed, white northerners were also shocked by the ruling. Many had hoped that slavery would eventually die out if it were restricted to the South. Now, however, slavery could spread throughout the West.

One northerner who spoke out against the Dred Scott decision was an Illinois lawyer named Abraham Lincoln. The idea that African Americans could not be citizens, he said, was based on a false view of American history. In a very short time, Lincoln would become a central figure in the fight against the spread of slavery.

☑**Checkpoint** **Why did Dred Scott claim he was no longer enslaved?**

**Main Idea**
The Dred Scott ruling meant that all American territories were open to slavery.

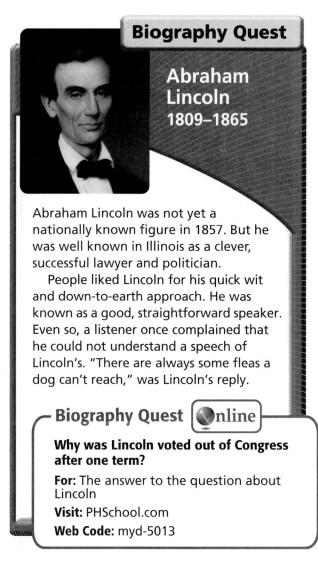

**Biography Quest**

**Abraham Lincoln**
**1809–1865**

Abraham Lincoln was not yet a nationally known figure in 1857. But he was well known in Illinois as a clever, successful lawyer and politician.

People liked Lincoln for his quick wit and down-to-earth approach. He was known as a good, straightforward speaker. Even so, a listener once complained that he could not understand a speech of Lincoln's. "There are always some fleas a dog can't reach," was Lincoln's reply.

**Biography Quest** ●**nline**

**Why was Lincoln voted out of Congress after one term?**

**For:** The answer to the question about Lincoln

**Visit:** PHSchool.com

**Web Code:** myd-5013

# Links Across Time

## Elections and the Media

**1858** Americans followed the Lincoln-Douglas debates as telegraph reports circulated around the country.

**1960** Americans were for the first time able to watch presidential candidates debate live on television. Richard Nixon and John F. Kennedy debated before an enormous television audience. Many experts believe that the debates played a major role in Kennedy's victory.

### Link to Today

**Elections and the Media Today** The digital revolution is again changing American political campaigns. What media do candidates use today?

**For:** Voting and the media
**Visit:** PHSchool.com
**Web Code:** myc-5103

**Main Idea**
Abraham Lincoln took a strong stand against slavery's expansion in the Lincoln-Douglas debates.

**Vocabulary** *Builder*
**embrace** (ehm BRAYS) *v.* to hold tight; to readily accept

## The Lincoln-Douglas Debates

Lincoln had had only a brief career in politics. After serving in the Illinois state legislature, he was elected to Congress as a Whig. There, he voted for the Wilmot Proviso. After a single term, he returned to Illinois to practice law.

Lincoln's opposition to the Kansas-Nebraska Act brought him back into politics, this time embracing the Republican cause. He had long been a rival of Illinois Senator Stephen Douglas, the author of the Kansas-Nebraska Act. Their rivalry was personal as well as political. Both men had courted Mary Todd, who married Lincoln.

**A House Divided** In 1858, Illinois Republicans chose Lincoln to run for the Senate against Douglas. Accepting the nomination, Lincoln made a stirring speech in favor of the Union:

> **"**A house divided against itself cannot stand. I do not believe this government can endure, permanently, half slave and half free. I do not expect the Union to be dissolved—I do not expect the house to fall—but I do expect it will cease to be divided. It will become all one thing or all the other.**"**
>
> —Abraham Lincoln, Springfield, Illinois, June 16, 1858

Lincoln did not state that he wanted to ban slavery. Still, many southerners became convinced that Lincoln was an abolitionist.

**Debating Slavery** Lincoln then challenged Douglas to a series of public debates. Thousands of people gathered to hear them speak. Newspapers throughout the nation reported what each man said.

Douglas strongly defended popular sovereignty. "Each state of this Union has a right to do as it pleases on the subject of slavery," he said. "In Illinois we have exercised that sovereign right by prohibiting slavery. . . . It is none of our business whether slavery exists in Missouri." Douglas also painted Lincoln as a dangerous abolitionist who wanted equality for African Americans.

Lincoln took a stand against the spread of slavery. He declared, "If slavery is not wrong, nothing is wrong." Lincoln predicted that slavery would die on its own. In the meantime, he said, it was the obligation of Americans to keep it out of the western territories.

In reply to Douglas, Lincoln stated: "I am not, nor ever have been in favor of bringing about in any way the social and political equality of the white and black races." But he did <u>clarify</u> this view. He insisted that "there is no reason in the world why the Negro is not entitled to all the rights enumerated in the Declaration of Independence, the right to life, liberty and the pursuit of happiness."

In the end, Douglas won the Senate election. However, the debates had made Lincoln known throughout the country. Two years later, the men would be rivals again—this time for the presidency.

**☑Checkpoint** **What position did Douglas take on slavery?**

**Vocabulary** *Builder*
**clarify** (KLAIR ih fī) *v.* to make the meaning of something clear

# John Brown's Raid

The nation's attention soon was captured by the actions of John Brown. Driven out of Kansas after the Pottawatomie Massacre, Brown had returned to New England. There he hatched a plot to raise an army and free people in the South who were enslaved.

In 1859, Brown and a small band of supporters attacked the town of Harpers Ferry in Virginia. His goal was to seize guns the U.S. Army had stored there. He thought that enslaved African Americans would support him. He would then give them weapons and lead them in a revolt.

Brown quickly gained control of the arms. But troops commanded by Colonel Robert E. Lee surrounded Brown's force before it could escape. Ten of Brown's followers were killed. Brown was wounded and captured.

**Main Idea**
Northern support of John Brown shocked and angered southern slaveholders.

**John Brown in Kansas**
John Steuart Curry began painting this 10-foot-high mural in 1937. It shows John Brown as a fiery abolitionist with a rifle in one hand and a Bible in the other. **Critical Thinking:** *Detect Points of View Based on this painting, do you think Curry admired John Brown?*

**Death of John Brown**

Thomas Hovenden painted this portrait of a saintly John Brown. On his way to his death, Brown stops to kiss a child. Hovenden did not personally witness the events he showed here. **Critical Thinking:** *Contrast Compare this painting to the one on the previous page. How do these two paintings try to stir different emotions?*

At his trial, Brown sat quietly as the court found him guilty of murder and treason. Before hearing his sentence, he gave a moving defense of his actions. The Bible, he said, instructed him to care for the poor and enslaved. "If it is deemed necessary that I should forfeit my life for the furtherance of the ends of justice . . . I say, let it be done." He showed no emotion as he was sentenced to death.

When the state of Virginia hanged Brown for treason on December 2, 1859, church bells across the North tolled to mourn the man who many considered a hero. But southerners were shocked. People in the North were praising a man who had tried to lead a slave revolt! More than ever, many southerners were convinced that the North was out to destroy their way of life.

✔**Checkpoint** **What was John Brown's goal in launching the raid on Harpers Ferry?**

⭐ **Looking Back and Ahead** The nation had suffered one dispute after another over the expansion of slavery since the end of the Mexican-American War in 1846. By the election of 1860, talk of the breakup of the United States was everywhere. In the next section, you will read how that breakup came about.

---

**Section 3 | Check Your Progress**

**Progress Monitoring** ⬤nline
**For:** Self-test with instant help
**Visit:** PHSchool.com
**Web Code:** mya-5103

**Comprehension and Critical Thinking**

1. **(a) Summarize** Which groups supported the newly formed Republican Party?
   **(b) Draw Conclusions** How did the outcomes of the elections of 1854 and 1856 affect the Republican Party?

2. **(a) Identify** On what grounds did Dred Scott sue for his freedom in court?
   **(b) Draw Conclusions** How did Taney's ruling further divide the North and the South?

3. **(a) Recall** What were the Lincoln-Douglas debates?
   **(b) Apply Information** Why do you think the Lincoln-Douglas debates received national attention?

**Reading Skill**

4. **Analyze Causes and Effects** Identify one cause and one effect of John Brown's raid. Why did Brown and his followers attack Harpers Ferry? What happened as a result?

**Writing**

5. Reread the paragraphs in this section that describe the Lincoln-Douglas debates. When you have finished, paraphrase the excerpt from Lincoln's Springfield speech. Remember, when you paraphrase, you restate something said by someone else, using only your own words.

# The Coming of the Civil War

## Objectives

1. Describe the results of the election of 1860.

2. Explain why southern states seceded from the Union.

3. Summarize the events that led to the outbreak of the Civil War.

## Prepare to Read

### ➲ Reading Skill

**Analyze Multiple Causes or Effects** Many events in history have more than one cause, as the Civil War certainly did. Other events lead to more than one effect, which is also certainly true of the Civil War. As you read about this turning point in American history, look for causes with multiple effects and effects with multiple causes.

### Vocabulary *Builder*

**High-Use Words**
<u>accommodation</u>, p. 501
<u>isolate</u>, p. 503

**Key Term**
civil war, p. 503

---

⭐ **Background Knowledge** John Brown's raid steadily increased tensions between North and South over slavery. In this section, you will learn how Abraham Lincoln's election as President created a crisis that shattered the nation and led to war.

## The Nation Divides

As the election of 1860 drew near, Americans everywhere felt a sense of crisis. The long and bitter debate over slavery had left the nation seriously divided.

**Election of 1860** The Republicans chose Abraham Lincoln as their presidential candidate. His criticisms of slavery during his debates with Douglas had made him popular in the North.

Southern Democrats wanted the party to support slavery in the territories. But northerners refused to do so. In the end, the party split in two. Northern Democrats chose Stephen Douglas as their candidate. Southern Democrats picked Vice President John Breckinridge of Kentucky.

Some southerners still hoped to heal the split between North and South. They formed the Constitutional Union Party and nominated John Bell of Tennessee. Bell promised to protect slavery *and* keep the nation together.

Stephen Douglas was sure that Lincoln would win the election. However, he believed that Democrats "must try to save the Union." He pleaded with southern voters to stay with the Union, no matter who was elected. However, when Douglas campaigned in the South, hostile southerners often pelted him with eggs and rotten fruit.

**Main Idea**
The election of 1860 led to the breakup of the Union.

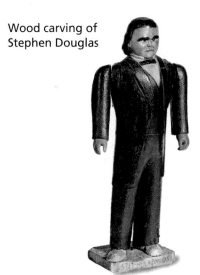

Wood carving of Stephen Douglas

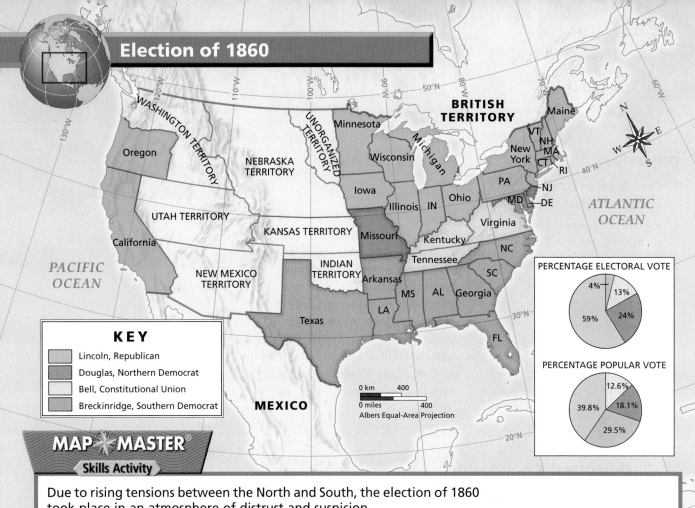

KEY

- Lincoln, Republican
- Douglas, Northern Democrat
- Bell, Constitutional Union
- Breckinridge, Southern Democrat

PERCENTAGE ELECTORAL VOTE

4% 13%
24%
59%

PERCENTAGE POPULAR VOTE

12.6%
18.1%
29.5%
39.8%

0 km 400
0 miles 400
Albers Equal-Area Projection

## MAP★MASTER®
### Skills Activity

Due to rising tensions between the North and South, the election of 1860 took place in an atmosphere of distrust and suspicion.

**(a) Read a Map Key** What do the four colors on the map stand for? Which party won nearly all the northern states? Which party won nearly all the southern states?

**(b) Draw Conclusions** How does the map show that sectionalism was important in the election?

**MapMaster ⬤nline**

**For:** Interactive map
**Visit:** PHSchool.com
**Web Code:** myp-5104

---

The election showed just how fragmented the nation had become. Lincoln won in every free state and Breckinridge in all the slave-holding states except four. Bell won Kentucky, Tennessee, and Virginia—all in the upper South. Douglas carried only Missouri. Although Lincoln got only 40 percent of the popular votes, he received enough electoral votes to win the election.

**Southern States Secede** Lincoln's election sent shock waves through the South. To many southerners, it seemed that the South no longer had a voice in the national government. They believed that the President and Congress were now set against their interests—especially slavery.

One Virginia newspaper expressed the feelings of many southerners. "A party founded on the single sentiment . . . of hatred of African slavery, is now the controlling power," it observed. "The honor, safety, and independence of the Southern people are to be found only in a Southern Confederacy."

South Carolina was the first southern state to secede from the Union. When news of Lincoln's election reached the state, the legislature called for a special convention. On December 20, 1860, the convention passed a declaration that "the union now subsisting between South Carolina and the other states, under the name of the 'United States of America' is hereby dissolved."

**The Confederate States of America** With hope of <u>accommodation</u> all but gone, six more states followed South Carolina out of the Union. However, not all southerners favored secession. Tennessee Senator Andrew Johnson and Texas Governor Sam Houston were among those who opposed it. Yet, the voices of the moderates were overwhelmed. "People are wild," said one opponent of secession. "You might as well attempt to control a tornado as attempt to stop them."

In early February, leaders from the seven seceding states met in Montgomery, Alabama, to form a new nation that they called the Confederate States of America. By the time Lincoln took office in March, they had written a constitution and named former Mississippi Senator Jefferson Davis as their president.

☑**Checkpoint** **Why did southern states secede from the Union?**

## The Civil War Begins

On March 4, 1861, Abraham Lincoln became President of a nation facing the greatest crisis in its history. In his inaugural address, he assured the seceded states that he meant them no harm. "I have no purpose, directly or indirectly, to interfere with the institution of slavery where it exists," he promised. But he also warned them about continuing on the course they had chosen:

> **"**In your hands, my dissatisfied fellow countrymen, and not in mine, is the momentous issue of . . . war. The government will not assail [attack] you. . . . We are not enemies, but friends. We must not be enemies. Though passion may have strained, it must not break our bonds of affection.**"**
>
> —Abraham Lincoln, Inaugural Address, March 4, 1861

Lincoln's assurance of friendship was rejected. The seceding states took over post offices, forts, and other federal property within their borders. The new President had to decide how to respond.

**Fort Sumter** Lincoln's most urgent problem was Fort Sumter, located on an island in the harbor of Charleston, South Carolina. The fort's commander would not surrender it. South Carolina authorities decided to starve the fort's 100 troops into surrender. They had been cut off from supplies since late December and could not hold out much longer.

**Main Idea**
President Lincoln's assurances of friendship in his inaugural address were rejected by the South.

Abraham Lincoln speaks at his first inauguration

501

# Attack on Fort Sumter

**History Interactive**
**Inside Fort Sumter**
Visit: PHSchool.com
Web Code: myp-5107

America's most tragic conflict began early on the morning of April 12, 1861, at Fort Sumter. The dark night was suddenly lit up by Confederate shells fired from the mainland. Within a few hours, the fort's wooden barracks had caught fire and portions of the fort had crumbled. At midday, a Confederate shell knocked over the fort's flagpole. The firing went on throughout the day and evening. By the next day, the Union garrison was exhausted and every wooden structure in the fort was ablaze. "The men lay . . . on the ground, with wet handkerchiefs over their mouths and eyes, gasping for breath."

**Critical Thinking:** *Analyze Cause and Effect What was the cause of the Confederate attack on Fort Sumter? What were the effects?*

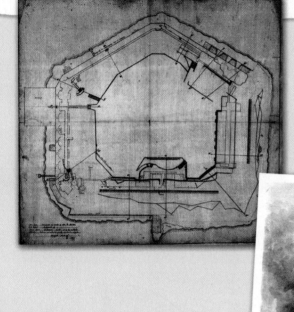

◀ **Blueprint of the Fort**

This overhead diagram of the fort shows its pentagonal, or five-sided, shape. The square-shaped area on the left side of the diagram shows a small wharf. Prior to the Confederate attack, Union ships used this dock to unload supplies to the fort.

▼ **American flag from Fort Sumter**

▲ **Confederate Troops Fire on the Fort**

Confederate artillery pounded Fort Sumter for 34 hours. Fires raged out of control and threatened to ignite the fort's magazine, where many barrels of gunpowder were stored. Facing shortages of food and ammunition, the Union commander surrendered. The bloodiest of all American wars had begun.

Lincoln did not want to give up the fort. But he feared that sending troops might cause other states to secede. Therefore, he announced that he would send food to the fort, but that the supply ships would carry no troops or guns.

Confederate leaders decided to capture the fort while it was isolated. On April 12, Confederate artillery opened fire on the fort. After 34 hours, with the fort on fire, the U.S. troops surrendered.

**Vocabulary** *Builder*
isolate (ī sah layt) *v.* to set apart; to separate

**Why War Came** The Confederate attack on Fort Sumter marked the beginning of a long civil war. A civil war is a war between opposing groups of citizens of the same country.

The Civil War probably attracts more public interest today than any other event in American history. Americans continue to debate why the war took place and whether it could have been avoided.

In 1850, southerners might have been satisfied if they had been left alone. But by 1861, many Americans in both the North and the South had come to accept the idea that war could not be avoided. At stake was the nation's future. Four years later, a weary Lincoln looked back to the beginning of the conflict. He noted:

> ❝Both parties [condemned] war, but one of them would *make* war rather than let the nation survive, and the other would *accept* war rather than let it perish, and the war came.❞
>
> —Abraham Lincoln, Second Inaugural Address, March 4, 1865

**Analyze Multiple Causes or Effects**
According to this section, what were two causes of the Civil War?

☑**Checkpoint** **Why was Lincoln reluctant to give up Fort Sumter?**

⭐ **Looking Back and Ahead** Confederate cannons had nearly destroyed Fort Sumter. To many, it seemed like a huge fireworks display. No one knew that the fireworks marked the beginning of a terrible war that would last four years.

Section 4 | **Check Your Progress**

**Progress Monitoring** ⬤nline
**For:** Self-test with instant help
**Visit:** PHSchool.com
**Web Code:** mya-5104

**Comprehension and Critical Thinking**

**1. (a) Recall** How did divisions among the Democrats help lead to the election of Republican Abraham Lincoln in 1860?
**(b) Explain Problems** What was the South's reaction to Lincoln's election? How did Lincoln try to reassure the South?

**2. (a) Identify** What event marked the start of war between the North and the South?

**(b) Evaluate Information** Explain what Abraham Lincoln meant by the following remark: "Both parties [condemned] war, but one of them would *make* war rather than let the nation survive. . . ."

🕹 **Reading Skill**
**3. Analyze Multiple Causes or Effects** What were three effects of Lincoln's warning to the South?

**Vocabulary** *Builder*
**4.** Write two definitions for the key term civil war. First, write a formal definition for your teacher. Second, write a definition in everyday English for a classmate.

**Writing**
**5.** Based on what you have read in this section, write a thesis statement for an essay explaining why the election of Abraham Lincoln caused the South to secede.

Not everything a writer includes in a selection is equally important. Some information is relevant because it is directly related to the subject of the text. Other information is less relevant because it does not directly relate to the subject. When you read, you must focus your attention on the main topic and the most relevant information. Read the fictional letter below to determine relevance.

The letter below is historical fiction. That means that it is based on history, but is not a primary source. In the letter, William, a farmer who had moved to Kansas Territory, writes to his brother Joseph in Vermont.

November 20, 1854
Dear Joseph,
　　I was pleased to receive your last letter. The success of your store is a great achievement. Our new farm continues to prosper and little Sarah has recovered from the fever that had sickened her for a month. Of course, the issue of the Kansas-Nebraska Act continues to trouble me. I do not agree with your support of Senator Stephen Douglas of Illinois; however, I enjoy reading his speeches. Those who oppose slavery, as I do, do not want that cruel system in place in a territory where it had been banned. Under the terms of the Kansas-Nebraska Act, it is up to the people to decide the issue peacefully by voting their hearts. Yet, settlers who are for and against slavery in the territory seem intent on using force, instead of the ballot box. The elections next year will settle the issue once and for all.

Your loving brother,
William

## Learn the Skill

*Use these steps to determine which information is relevant and which is irrelevant.*

1. **Identify the subject or topic.** What is the main topic of the selection?

2. **Identify your purpose for reading the selection.** Ask yourself: What am I trying to find out?

3. **Identify the information that is relevant to the topic.** What information is directly related to the subject? Why is it relevant?

4. **Identify the information that is irrelevant to the topic.** What information is not directly related to the subject? Why is it irrelevant?

## Practice the Skill

*Answer the following questions about the letter on the page.*

1. **Identify the subject or topic.** What is the main topic of the letter?

2. **Identify the purpose for reading the selection.** Why am I reading this letter?

3. **Identify the information that is relevant to the subject.** (a) What are two statements that are directly related to the topic of the letter? (b) Why is each statement relevant?

4. **Identify the information that is irrelevant to the topic.** (a) What are two statements that are not directly related to the subject? (b) Why is each statement irrelevant?

## Apply the Skill

*See the Review and Assessment at the end of this chapter.*

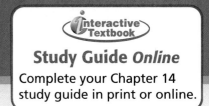

## Chapter Summary

### Section 1
### Growing Tensions Over Slavery

- The acquisition of new territories in the West reopened the issue of slavery.
- Lawmakers debated how to keep a balance of power between free and slave-holding states.

### Section 2
### Compromises Fail

- The Compromise of 1850 attempted to settle the slavery question, but northerners refused to accept the Fugitive Slave Act.
- *Uncle Tom's Cabin* increased northern hatred of slavery and antagonized southern slaveholders.
- Popular sovereignty established by the Kansas-Nebraska Act triggered bloody fighting in Kansas.

### Section 3
### The Crisis Deepens

- The Republican Party was formed to oppose the spread of slavery.
- In the Dred Scott decision, the Supreme Court ruled that Congress could not ban slavery in any territory.
- Abraham Lincoln became a central political figure when he and Stephen Douglas debated slavery.
- John Brown, an abolitionist, and his followers attacked the federal arsenal at Harpers Ferry, Virginia, to protest slavery.

### Section 4
### The Coming of the Civil War

- After Lincoln won the presidential election of 1860, some southern states seceded from the Union.
- The Civil War began when Confederate troops fired on Fort Sumter.

## Key Concepts

These notes will help you prepare for questions about key concepts.

### Main Provisions of the Compromise of 1850

- California was admitted to the Union as a free state.
- Popular sovereignty would decide the issue of slavery in the territories won in the Mexican-American War.
- The slave trade was banned in Washington, D.C.
- Congress passed a strong Fugitive Slave Act.

### Election of 1860

- Lincoln-Douglas debates attract attention to Lincoln.
- Republicans chose Lincoln as presidential candidate.
- Democratic Party splits.
- John Bell supports slavery and opposes secession.
- Lincoln wins every free state and is elected President.
- Southern states secede.

### Events That Led to Civil War

- Compromise of 1850
- Publication of *Uncle Tom's Cabin*
- Kansas-Nebraska Act
- John Brown's raid on Harpers Ferry
- Dred Scott decision
- Election of Abraham Lincoln as President
- Secession of southern states and formation of the Confederate States of America
- Confederate attack on Fort Sumter

## Vocabulary *Builder*

**Key Terms**

Fill in the blanks with the correct key terms.

1. Many southern states threatened to _____ from the Union if California was admitted as a free state.

2. Southerners claimed that *Uncle Tom's Cabin* was _____ because it did not give a fair picture of the lives of enslaved African Americans.

3. Slavery was the main issue that split the nation apart and led to a violent _____.

## Comprehension and Critical Thinking

4. **(a) Recall** Why did Senator Stephen Douglas introduce the Kansas-Nebraska Act?
   **(b) Understand Sequence** How did the events in Kansas demonstrate the unrest that would eventually take shape throughout the nation?

5. **(a) Summarize** What was the Supreme Court's verdict in the Dred Scott case?
   **(b) Detect Points of View** How do you think Harriet Beecher Stowe reacted to the verdict?

6. **(a) Identify** What was the main goal of the Republican Party in the election of 1854?
   **(b) Distinguish Relevant Information** How did Abraham Lincoln represent Republican principles during the Lincoln-Douglas debates?

7. **(a) Identify** What is the subject of the painting below?
   **(b) Draw Conclusions** Do you agree with the artist's view of this person? Why or why not?

8. **(a) Describe** What happened at Fort Sumter?
   **(b) Draw Conclusions** Do you think southerners were justified in seceding despite Lincoln's assurances? Explain.

## History Reading Skill

9. **Analyze Cause and Effect** Reread the text in Section 4 under the heading "The Nation Divides." How did the election of 1860 affect the unity of the United States?

## Writing

10. **Choose one of the following topics for a research report:**
   • the Kansas-Nebraska Act
   • the Dred Scott decision
   • the early career of Abraham Lincoln

   List five questions you would want to pursue if you were going to research that topic. Write a thesis statement for the topic and find supporting evidence for that thesis from the chapter.

11. **Write a Narrative:**
   Imagine you are from a northern farm family and have just heard of the attack on Fort Sumter. Write a narrative describing your hopes and fears about the future.

## Skills for Life

**Determine Relevance**

Use the fictional letter below to answer the questions that follow.

> October 18, 1856
>
> Dear Margaret,
>
> When the Republican Party was formed two years ago, we had no idea it would grow so quickly. I am so pleased with the party's choice of John Frémont as the Republican candidate for President. I know Mother would have agreed with me. I only hope you and I will be able to cast our votes in a presidential election soon.
>
> Your loving sister, Ellen

12. What is the letter about?

13. What is one statement directly related to the subject of the letter? Why is it relevant?

14. What is one statement that is irrelevant to the subject of the letter? Why is it irrelevant?

# Test Yourself

1. All of the following were causes of the Civil War EXCEPT

   A John Brown's raid on Harpers Ferry.

   B the Dred Scott decision.

   C the use of child labor in northern factories.

   D the publication of Stowe's *Uncle Tom's Cabin*.

**Refer to the quotation below to answer Question 2.**

> "A house divided against itself cannot stand. . . .
> I do not expect the Union to be dissolved—I do
> not expect the house to fall—but I do expect it
> will cease to be divided. It will become all one
> thing or all the other."

2. What division does this quotation describe?

   A church and state

   B free states and slaveholding states

   C the House of Representatives and the Senate

   D Republicans and Democrats

**Refer to the pie chart below to answer Question 3.**

### Percentage of Popular Vote, 1860

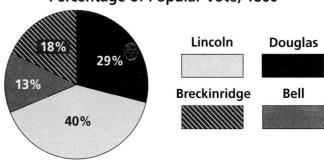

- 18%
- 29%
- 13%
- 40%

Lincoln   Douglas

Breckinridge   Bell

3. What conclusion can you draw from this pie chart?

   A Southerners voted for Douglas.

   B Lincoln won most of the popular vote.

   C Bell had little support in the North.

   D The two Democrats combined won more votes than Lincoln.

# Document-Based Questions

**Task:** Look at Documents 1 and 2, and answer their accompanying questions. Then, use the documents and your knowledge of history to complete this writing assignment:

> Write a two-paragraph essay comparing the goals of the Fugitive Slave Law with its actual effects.

**Document 1:** In this speech, Senator John Calhoun of South Carolina explained the need for the Fugitive Slave Law. *According to Calhoun, what would happen if Congress did not pass the law?*

> "How can the Union be saved? . . . There is but one
> way . . . , and that is by adopting such measures as will
> satisfy . . . the southern section that they can remain
> in the Union consistently with their honor and their
> safety. . . .
>     But can this be done? Yes, easily. . . . The North has
> only . . . to conced[e] to the South an equal right in
> [newly] acquired territory, and to caus[e] the stipula-
> tions relative to fugitive slaves to be faithfully ful-
> filled—to cease the agitation of the slave
> question. . . ."

**Document 2:** This poster reveals Bostonians' commitment to protect runaways or kidnapped African Americans. *Why were posters like this illegal?*

A MAN KIDNAPPED!

A PUBLIC MEETING AT

FANEUIL HALL!

WILL BE HELD

THIS FRIDAY EVEN'G,

May 26th, at 7 o'clock,

To secure justice for A MAN CLAIMED AS A SLAVE by a

VIRGINIA KIDNAPPER!

And NOW IMPRISONED IN BOSTON COURT HOUSE, in
defiance of the Laws of Massachusetts. Shall he be plunged into the Hell of
Virginia Slavery by a Massachusetts Judge of Probate !

BOSTON, May 26th, 1854.

# CHAPTER 15 | The Civil War
## 1861–1865

## Chapter Preview

In 1861, war broke out between North and South. For more than four years, Americans fought other Americans. The Civil War was a long, difficult struggle that caused much suffering for both sides.

**1861**
Eleven states secede from the Union.

**1862**
President Lincoln announces plan of emancipation.

**1863**
Union wins victory at Gettysburg.

**U.S. Events**

1861

1862

1863

**World Events**

**1861** Napoleon III sends French troops to invade Mexico.

**1862** Otto von Bismarck becomes prime minister of Prussia.

All is peaceful now at Cemetery Hill
in Gettysburg, Pennsylvania. But in
July 1863, a terrible, bloody battle
took place there that marked a
turning point in the Civil War.

**1864**
Grant invades the South
and lays siege to Petersburg.

**1865**
Lee surrenders at
Appomattox.

1863

1864

1865

**1864** French-backed
Maximilian of Austria
becomes emperor of Mexico.

**History Reading Skill** Understand Sequence

## What was a Civil War battle like?

In this chapter, you will learn how to relate events in time and understand sequence. Read the following report about a major Civil War battle. The side notes show you how to relate events in time and identify their sequence.

**Primary Source**

In 1862, George Washburn Smalley was a war journalist for a northern newspaper. Here, he describes the Battle of Antietam, a major battle during the early years of the Civil War.

Fierce and desperate battle between 200,000 men has raged since daylight. Finally, at four o'clock, [Union General] McClellan was to advance . . . [at] . . . any cost. . . . [General] Burnside was to carry the woods next in front of him to the right, which the Rebels still held. . . .

There is a halt. The Rebel left gives way and scatters over the field. The rest stand fast and fire. More infantry comes up. Burnside is outnumbered, flanked, compelled to yield the hill he took so bravely. His position is no longer one of attack. He defends himself with unfaltering firmness. . . .

The sun is already down. Not half an hour of daylight is left. None suspected how near was the peril of defeat. But the Rebels halted instead of pushing on. Before it was quite dark, the battle was over.

—*New York Daily Tribune*, September 20, 1862

> Signal words—*since daylight, at four-o'clock*—show the sequence.

> Here, events are described in order: (1) There is a halt. (2) The Rebel left gives way.

> After new infantry shows up, the course of the battle is changed. These events are related in time.

> The sequence of events—the Union is losing, but then the Rebels halt—causes the Union to unexpectedly win the battle.

## Understand Sequence

- Sequence signal words and dates tell you when events happened.
- Look for events described in time, or chronological, order.
- Ask yourself how events are connected: Are they happening at the same time? Did one event cause another that follows?

## Document-Based Questions

1. In which newspaper was this article published?
2. Describe the sequence of events in the battle.
3. Do you think this is a reliable account? Explain your answer.

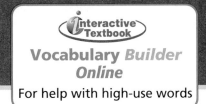
## Vocabulary *Builder*

### Previewing High-Use Academic Words

| High-Use Word | Definition | Sample History Sentence |
|---|---|---|
| **distinct** (dihs TIHNKT) (Section 1, p. 514) | *adj.* clear or definite; different in quality | Each Civil War general had his own distinct methods of fighting. |
| **resource** (REE sors) (Section 1, p. 514) | *n.* supply of something to meet a particular need | As the war dragged on, the South's war effort suffered from a lack of resources. |
| **superior** (sah PIR ee ahr) (Section 2, p. 519) | *adj.* of greater importance or value; above average | In some battles, a smaller force proved superior to a larger one. |
| **reinforce** (ree ihn FORS) (Section 2, p. 519) | *v.* to make stronger; to make more effective | Expecting an enemy attack, soldiers tried to reinforce their defenses. |
| **restore** (ree STOR) (Section 3, p. 524) | *v.* to bring back to a normal state; to put back; to reestablish | If a building was only damaged in the war, its owner might try to restore it by ordering repairs. |
| **sustain** (suh STAYN) (Section 3, p. 525) | *v.* to keep going; to endure; to supply with food; to support as just | Using horse carts to haul food and ammunition, the army was able to sustain its troops through a long campaign. |
| **levy** (LEHV ee) (Section 4, p. 531) | *v.* to impose by law | It is common for governments to levy a tax on imports. |
| **currency** (KER rehn see) (Section 4, p. 531) | *n.* money used to make purchases | The government prints paper currency that people can use for their purchases. |
| **encounter** (ehn KOWN ter) (Section 5, p. 534) | *v.* to meet in an unexpected way; to experience | Soldiers who entered enemy territory did not know what dangers they might encounter. |
| **exceed** (ehks SEED) (Section 5, p. 535) | *v.* to go beyond what is expected; to be greater than what was planned | The general had expected to win, but his victory exceeded his greatest hopes. |

### Previewing Key Terms and People

border state, p. 513
neutral, p. 513
martial law, p. 513
blockade, p. 515
ironclad, p. 518
George McClellan, p. 519

casualty, p. 520
Ulysses S. Grant, p. 520
emancipate, p. 524
Horace Greeley, p. 524
habeas corpus, p. 529
draft, p. 530

income tax, p. 531
inflation, p. 531
siege, p. 535
William Tecumseh Sherman, p. 536
total war, p. 536

# The Call to Arms

## Objectives

1. Identify the states that supported the Union, the states that seceded, and the states whose loyalties were divided.

2. Describe the advantages each side had in the war.

3. Compare the different strategies used by the North and the South.

4. Summarize the results of the First Battle of Bull Run.

5. Describe the conditions soldiers in camp faced.

## Prepare to Read

### Reading Skill

**Understand Sequence of Events** The Civil War began as a result of a complex sequence of events. As that war proceeded in its early days, events continued at a furious pace. To form a full understanding of this phase of the war, pause regularly to summarize the sequence of events. Use your own words to recount the important events in the correct order.

### Vocabulary *Builder*

**High-Use Words**
distinct, p. 514
resource, p. 514

**Key Terms**
border state, p. 513
neutral, p. 513
martial law, p. 513
blockade, p. 515

### Main Idea
As the war began and states chose sides, loyalties in the four border states were divided.

⭐ **Background Knowledge** In the previous chapter, you learned how tensions over slavery troubled the nation throughout the 1850s. Southern slaveholders became committed to protecting the system on which they depended. In this section, you will learn how this determination led to the Civil War.

## Taking Sides in the War

Two days after Fort Sumter's surrender, President Lincoln declared that a rebellion existed in the South. To put it down, he asked the nation's governors to raise 75,000 troops. Across the North, young men eagerly volunteered. Support was so widespread that the governors of Ohio, Indiana, and several other states begged to send more troops than the President had requested.

**More States Secede** Not all states were so enthusiastic, however. In Tennessee, the governor said that his state "will not furnish a single man" to fight against "our southern brothers." The governors of Kentucky and Missouri made similar replies to Lincoln's request. Maryland and Delaware did not respond at all.

The President's call for troops led more southern states to secede. On April 17, Virginia left the Union. In May, Arkansas, Tennessee, and North Carolina also joined the Confederacy. However, the western counties of Virginia, where there was little support for slavery, refused to secede. In 1863, these 50 counties were admitted to the Union as the state of West Virginia.

**The Border States** Loyalties remained divided in the border states—slave states that did not secede. Delaware had few enslaved people, and its support of the Union was strong. However, many people in Kentucky, Missouri, and Maryland favored the South. Kentucky and Missouri were important to controlling the Ohio and Mississippi rivers. And unless the Union could hold Maryland, Washington would be surrounded by the Confederacy.

At first, Kentucky declared itself neutral, or not favoring either side. Union generals wanted to occupy Kentucky, but Lincoln refused. He feared that such a move would push the state to secede. His strategy was wise. When Confederate forces invaded it in September 1861, Kentucky decided to support the North.

By contrast, the President acted forcefully to hold Missouri and Maryland. When Missouri's government sided with the South, Union supporters set up their own state government. Fighting broke out within the state. Finally, Lincoln sent troops, and the state stayed in the Union throughout the war.

In Maryland, southern sympathizers destroyed railroad and telegraph lines. So Lincoln placed eastern Maryland under martial law. This is a type of rule in which the military is in charge and citizens' rights are suspended. Maryland officials and others suspected of disloyalty were jailed without trials.

**Reading Skill**

**Understand Sequence of Events** Summarize the events as North and South geared up for full-scale conflict. Make sure to recount events in the correct sequence.

✔**Checkpoint** How did the border states line up in the war?

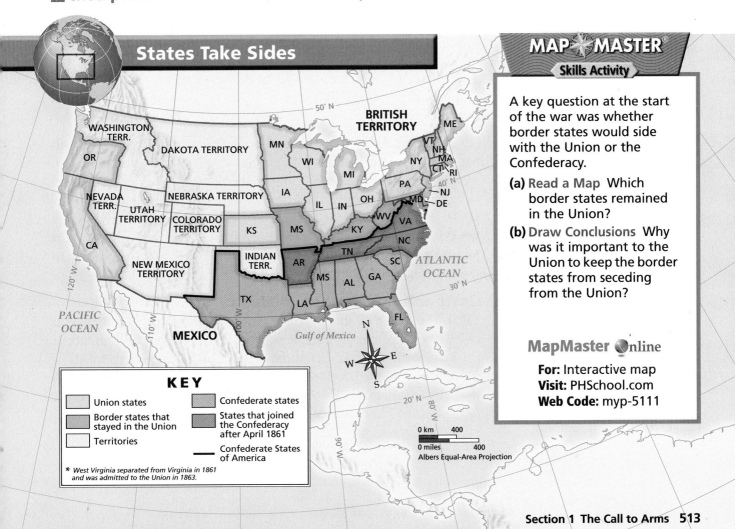

**States Take Sides**

**MAP MASTER®**

**Skills Activity**

A key question at the start of the war was whether border states would side with the Union or the Confederacy.

**(a) Read a Map** Which border states remained in the Union?

**(b) Draw Conclusions** Why was it important to the Union to keep the border states from seceding from the Union?

**MapMaster Online**

**For:** Interactive map
**Visit:** PHSchool.com
**Web Code:** myp-5111

**KEY**

- ☐ Union states
- ☐ Border states that stayed in the Union
- ☐ Territories
- ☐ Confederate states
- ☐ States that joined the Confederacy after April 1861
- — Confederate States of America

*\* West Virginia separated from Virginia in 1861 and was admitted to the Union in 1863.*

0 km 400
0 miles 400
Albers Equal-Area Projection

## Comparing Resources, 1861

Source: *The Times Atlas of World History*

**Reading Charts**
**Skills Activity**

The Union had an advantage over the Confederacy in a number of resources.

(a) **Read a Bar Graph** In which of the three comparisons is the Union's advantage the greatest?

(b) **Draw Conclusions** For each of these three resources, how would you expect the Union to benefit from its advantage?

(c) **Make Predictions** Based on the information in these graphs, which side would you expect to win the war? Explain.

**Main Idea**
Each side had its advantages and disadvantages, and each side was sure it would win.

**Vocabulary** *Builder*
__distinct__ (dihs TIHNKT) *adj.* clear or definite; different in quality

**Vocabulary** *Builder*
__resource__ (REE sors) *n.* supply of something to meet a particular need

# North Against South

As the armies prepared, people on both sides were confident. A Union soldier declared that he was "willing . . . to lay down all my joys in this life to help maintain this government." Southerners compared themselves to Americans of 1776. A New Orleans poet wrote of Confederates: "Yes, call them rebels! 'tis the name/Their patriot fathers bore."

**Southern Advantages** Although outnumbered, the South had some __distinct__ military advantages. To win, northern armies would have to invade and conquer the South. Confederates would be fighting on their own territory, with help from the local people.

In addition, most of the nation's experienced military officers were southerners. The Confederacy's three top generals—Albert Johnston, Joseph Johnston, and Robert E. Lee—all had resigned from the U.S. Army to fight for the South.

**Northern Advantages** In 1861, the United States had about 130,000 factories. Of those, 110,000 were in the North. The North had twice as much railroad track and almost twice as much farmland.

The North also had a population advantage. Some two thirds of the nation's people lived in states that remained in the Union, and in the South more than a third of the people were enslaved. With more __resources__, the North was able to field, feed, and equip larger armies.

✓**Checkpoint** What were each side's advantages?

## The Two Sides Plan Strategies

Union leaders hoped to win a quick victory. To isolate the Confederacy, Lincoln had the navy blockade southern seaports. A **blockade** is a military action to prevent traffic from coming into an area or leaving it. Lincoln hoped to cut off the South's supply of manufactured goods and block overseas sales of cotton.

An important part of northern strategy was to gain control of the Mississippi River, the South's major transportation link. This would split the South in two. The Union also planned to invade Virginia and seize Richmond, the Confederate capital. It was just 100 miles from Washington, D.C.

The South's strategy was simpler. The Confederates did not need to invade the North. They had only to defend their land until northerners got tired of fighting. The Confederates sought aid from Britain and other European nations. They hoped that Britain's need of cotton for its textile mills would force the British to support the South.

☑Checkpoint **How did strategies on the two sides differ?**

**Main Idea**
While the North wanted to isolate the South and invade it, the South hoped to get help from Europe.

## Americans Against Americans

On both sides, men rushed to be part of the fight. "I had never dreamed that New England . . . could be fired with so warlike a spirit," wrote Mary Ashton Livermore in Boston. In South Carolina, Mary Chesnut said that men rushed to enlist in the army for "fear the war will be over before they get a sight of the fun."

This war between Americans broke families apart, setting brother against brother, father against son. Kentucky Senator John Crittenden had two sons in the war fighting on different sides. Four brothers of Mary Lincoln, the President's wife, fought for the Confederacy.

**Main Idea**
The war often divided families as it drew most adult males on both sides into the military.

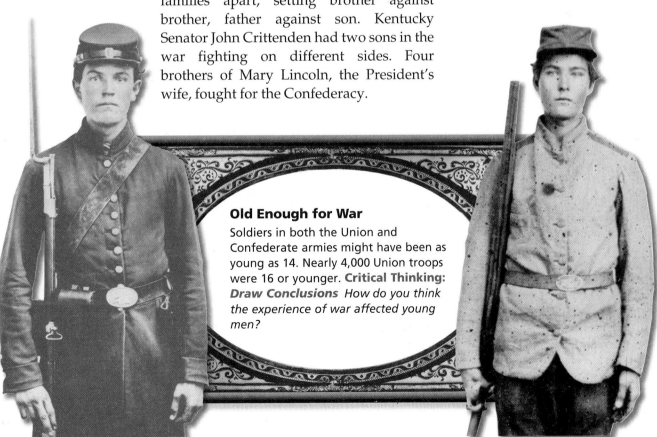

**Old Enough for War**
Soldiers in both the Union and Confederate armies might have been as young as 14. Nearly 4,000 Union troops were 16 or younger. **Critical Thinking: Draw Conclusions** *How do you think the experience of war affected young men?*

## Fleeing Bull Run

Before the First Battle of Bull Run, both sides expected an easy victory. But they were wrong. Here, Union soldiers have panicked and are fleeing the Bull Run battlefield. Bull Run was an early sign that the war would be long and costly. **Critical Thinking:** *Draw Conclusions What reasons did each side have to think it would win an early victory? Why were both sides' expectations unreasonable?*

**History** *Interactive*
**Explore the Lessons of a Battle**
Visit: PHSchool.com
Web Code: myp-5177

The soldiers came from many backgrounds. Nearly half of the North's troops were farmers. One fourth were immigrants.

Three fourths of the South's 1 million white males between ages 18 and 45 served in the army. Two thirds of the 3.5 million northern males of the same age fought for the Union. Some soldiers were as young as 14.

☑ **Checkpoint** Who were the soldiers in this war?

**Main Idea**
Expectations of a quick victory were dashed at Bull Run in July 1861.

## First Battle of Bull Run

Union General Irvin McDowell wanted time to turn his soldiers into an effective fighting force. But by July 1861, northern newspapers were demanding the capture of Richmond and a quick end to the war.

McDowell's 30,000 men left Washington and marched southwest into Virginia. About the same number of Confederates waited at Manassas, a railroad center about 25 miles away. Hundreds of people rode out from Washington to see the battle, expecting an easy Union victory.

The armies clashed along Bull Run, a river just north of Manassas, on July 21. At first, the Union army pushed forward. But a southern commander rallied his men to hold firm. "Look, there is Jackson with his Virginians, standing like a stone wall," he shouted. From then on, the general, Thomas Jackson, was known as "Stonewall" Jackson.

Slowly the battle turned in favor of the Confederates. The poorly trained Union troops began to panic. Soldiers and sightseers fled back to Washington. The Confederates were too exhausted to pursue them.

☑ **Checkpoint** What was the result of the First Battle of Bull Run?

# A Soldier's Life

Most soldiers spent three fourths of their time in camp, not fighting. Training took up to 10 hours a day. When not training, soldiers stood guard, wrote home, and gathered firewood. A meal might be simply a dry, cracker-like product called hardtack.

**Harsh Conditions** Camp conditions were often miserable, especially when wet weather created muddy roads and fields. The lack of clean water was a major health threat. Outbreaks of smallpox, typhoid fever, and other diseases swept through the ranks. It was not unusual for half the men in a regiment to be too sick to fight.

**Prisoners of War** Both sides built prison camps for captured soldiers. Overcrowded prison camps became deathtraps. Nearly 10 percent of soldiers who died in the war perished in prison camps.

The camps at Elmira, New York, and Andersonville, Georgia, were the worst. Elmira camp, built to hold 5,000 Confederate prisoners, held 10,000. The camp cut rations to bread and water, forcing prisoners to eat rats to survive. Thousands died. At Andersonville, nearly 35,000 Union soldiers lived in a fenced, open field intended to hold 10,000 men. As many as 100 prisoners died each day, usually from starvation or exposure.

✓**Checkpoint** What conditions did soldiers have to endure?

☆ **Looking Back and Ahead** The North's hopes for an early victory had been dashed. The war would be long and brutal. In the next section, you will read more about the early years of the war.

**Main Idea**
Rain, mud, disease, and crowded prison camps took a heavy toll on both sides.

Hardtack

---

Section 1 | **Check Your Progress**

**Progress Monitoring** ⏺nline
**For:** Self-test with instant help
**Visit:** PHSchool.com
**Web Code:** mya-5111

## Comprehension and Critical Thinking

**1. (a) Recall** How did President Lincoln respond to the surrender of Fort Sumter?
**(b) Apply Information** What caused three border states to remain in the Union?

**2. (a) List** What were three advantages held by the South? What were three advantages held by the North?
**(b) Analyze Cause and Effect** How did the First Battle of Bull Run shatter the belief that the Civil War would be a quick Union victory?

## 🔵 Reading Skill

**3. Understand Sequence of Events** Choose a state that wavered about supporting the North or the South. Summarize the sequence of events that led this state to a final decision.

## Vocabulary *Builder*

Complete each of the following sentences so that the second part explains the first and shows your understanding of the key term.
**4.** Union leaders planned a blockade; _____.
**5.** Lincoln placed Maryland under martial law; _____.

## Writing

**6.** Create an outline that covers the information presented in this section, copying the form below. A few entries have been filled in.

  **I.** Taking sides in the war (first important topic)
    **A.** More states secede (first issue for that topic)
      **1.** A number of border states refused to send troops to support the Union (first point)
      **2.** _____ (second point)
    **B.**
      **1.**
      **2.**
  **II.**

# Early Years of the War

## Objectives

1. Explain how new weapons made fighting the war more dangerous.

2. Describe the course of the war in the East in 1862.

3. Describe the early days of the war in the West and at sea.

## Prepare to Read

### ⟳ Reading Skill

**Distinguish Events in Sequence** As you read this section, it is important to keep events in sequence. Ask yourself: Which event happened first? Next? Last? You might number events to help you organize their sequence. This will help you to understand the unfolding drama of the Civil War.

### Vocabulary *Builder*

**High-Use Words**
**superior,** p. 519
**reinforce,** p. 519

**Key Terms and People**
ironclad, p. 518
George McClellan, p. 519
casualty, p. 520
Ulysses S. Grant, p. 520

## Main Idea

The use of new weapons forced commanders to rethink their tactics.

☆ **Background Knowledge** The Union's crushing defeat at Bull Run made northerners realize that a long and difficult struggle lay ahead. In this section, you will learn how the bloody early years of war caused many to worry that the North might not win.

## New Technology in the War

New weapons made the Civil War more deadly than any previous war. Traditionally, generals had relied on an all-out charge of troops to overwhelm the enemy. But new rifles and cannons were far more accurate and had a greater range than the old muskets and artillery. They could also be loaded much faster. As a result, the attacking army could be bombarded long before it arrived at the defenders' position.

Unfortunately, Civil War generals were slow to recognize the problem and change tactics. Thousands of soldiers on both sides were slaughtered by following orders to cross open fields against these deadly new weapons.

Both sides also made use of ironclads. These were warships covered with protective iron plates. Cannon fire bounced harmlessly off this armor. The most famous naval battle of the war occurred when two ironclads, the Union's *Monitor* and the Confederacy's *Merrimack,* fought to a draw in March 1862. The use of ironclads marked the end of thousands of years of wooden warships. The Confederates used ironclads against the Union's naval blockade. Ironclad Union gunboats played an important role in the North's efforts to gain control of the Mississippi River.

✓**Checkpoint** What new technologies were used in the Civil War?

## The War in the East

After the Union's defeat at Bull Run, Lincoln removed McDowell and put General George McClellan in command. The general was a good organizer, but he was very cautious. For seven months, he trained his army but did not attack. "If General McClellan does not want to use the army," a frustrated Lincoln complained, "I would like to borrow it for a time."

In March 1862, McClellan was finally ready. He moved some 100,000 soldiers by boat along Chesapeake Bay to a peninsula southeast of Richmond. As McClellan advanced toward the Confederate capital, he discovered that his force was far <u>superior</u> to the 15,000 enemy soldiers blocking the way. However, McClellan still did not have as many soldiers as he wanted because Lincoln had ordered 37,000 soldiers to stay behind to guard Washington, D.C. The general stopped his advance and asked for more troops.

McClellan waited nearly a month before moving again. This delay gave the Confederates time to <u>reinforce</u> their small army of defenders. On May 31, 1862, the Confederates stopped McClellan's advance near Richmond. In late June, McClellan had to retreat.

With Richmond no longer threatened, Lee decided to invade the North. He hoped that a victory on Union soil would help win support for the South in Europe and turn northern public opinion against the war. In early September, he slipped his army into western Maryland.

Now McClellan had a stroke of luck. A Union officer found a paper showing Lee's battle plan. McClellan thus learned that the Confederate army had divided into two parts.

**Main Idea**
Each side suffered setbacks in the East in 1862.

**Vocabulary** *Builder*
<u>superior</u> (sah PIR ee ahr) *adj.* of greater importance or value; above average

**Vocabulary** *Builder*
<u>reinforce</u> (ree ihn FORS) *v.* to make stronger; to make more effective

Inset shows the recovery of the *Monitor*'s turret, or gun chamber, in 2002.

**Explore More Video**
To learn more about this historic battle, view the video.

**Battle of Two Ironclads**
The Civil War introduced ironclad warships. Here, an artist shows the battle between the Confederacy's *Merrimack* (left) and the Union's *Monitor* (right) off Hampton Roads, Virginia, in 1862. **Critical Thinking:** *Draw Conclusions* *How would you expect an ironclad ship to fare in a battle against an older warship that lacked armor? Explain.*

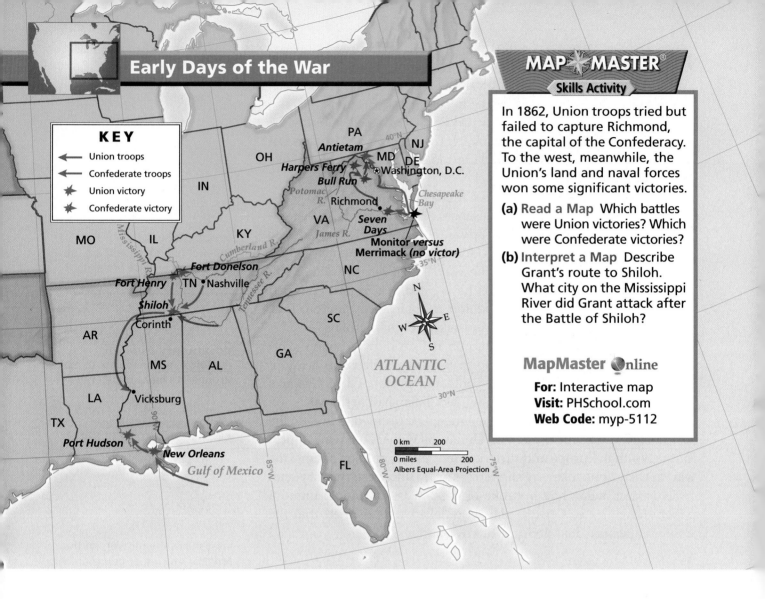

## Early Days of the War

**KEY**

⬅ Union troops
⬅ Confederate troops
✦ Union victory
✦ Confederate victory

**MapMaster Online**

**For:** Interactive map
**Visit:** PHSchool.com
**Web Code:** myp-5112

**MAP MASTER**
**Skills Activity**

In 1862, Union troops tried but failed to capture Richmond, the capital of the Confederacy. To the west, meanwhile, the Union's land and naval forces won some significant victories.

**(a) Read a Map** Which battles were Union victories? Which were Confederate victories?

**(b) Interpret a Map** Describe Grant's route to Shiloh. What city on the Mississippi River did Grant attack after the Battle of Shiloh?

---

McClellan's troops attacked the larger part of Lee's army at Antietam Creek, near Sharpsburg, Maryland, on September 17, 1862. This was the bloodiest day of the Civil War. The Union army attacked again and again. It suffered about 12,000 casualties—the military term for persons killed, wounded, or missing in action. Lee lost nearly 14,000 men—almost one third of his army. He was forced to pull his battered army back into Virginia. To Lincoln's dismay, McClellan did not press his advantage by pursuing Lee.

Neither side won a clear victory at the Battle of Antietam. But because Lee had ordered a retreat, the North claimed victory.

☑**Checkpoint** How did McClellan's caution hurt the Union?

## The War in the West

**Main Idea**
In the West, Union forces seized control of most of the Mississippi River in 1862.

As McClellan moved cautiously, Union armies in the West went on the attack. General Ulysses S. Grant led the most successful of these armies. McClellan and Grant were very different. McClellan wore carefully fitted uniforms. Grant, once a poor store clerk, wore rumpled clothes. McClellan was cautious. Grant took chances.

Union forces made major advances in western land and naval battles in 1862, seizing control of most of the Mississippi River. In February 1862, Grant moved his army south from Kentucky. First, he captured Fort Henry on the Tennessee River. Then, he captured Fort Donelson on the Cumberland River.

Two water routes into the western Confederacy were now wide open. Grant's army continued south along the Tennessee River toward Corinth, Mississippi, an important railroad center.

Before Grant could advance on Corinth, Confederate General Albert Sidney Johnston attacked. On April 6, 1862, he surprised Grant's troops at the Battle of Shiloh. (For more on this battle, see the Geography and History feature in this chapter.)

The Battle of Shiloh was costly yet important for both sides. The South suffered nearly 11,000 casualties and the North more than 13,000. However, the Union forced the Confederate army to withdraw from the railroad center. Union forces also gained control of western Tennessee and part of the Mississippi River.

Two weeks after the Battle of Shiloh, a Union fleet commanded by David Farragut entered the Mississippi River from the Gulf of Mexico. On April 26, Farragut captured New Orleans, Louisiana. By summer, nearly the entire river was in Union hands.

**Distinguish Events in Sequence** What was the sequence of battles in the West? When did these occur?

✓**Checkpoint** **What was the result of the Battle of Shiloh?**

☆ **Looking Back and Ahead** Northern and southern generals both tried to carry the war into enemy territory. At first, neither side gained a decisive advantage. In the next section, you will read how the Emancipation Proclamation changed the nature of the war.

## Section 2 | Check Your Progress

**Progress Monitoring** Online
**For:** Self-test with instant help
**Visit:** PHSchool.com
**Web Code:** mya-5112

### Comprehension and Critical Thinking

1. (a) **Describe** Explain what life was like for a Civil War soldier.
   (b) **Evaluate Information** How did harsh conditions and new technology result in a high number of casualties?

2. (a) **Summarize** Why was General McClellan considered to be an ineffective leader?
   (b) **Organize Information** Make a chart that shows the place, casualties, leaders, outcome, and importance of the battles at Shiloh and Antietam Creek.

### Reading Skill

3. **Distinguish Events in Sequence** During the Battle of Shiloh, which came first: Grant captured Fort Henry, Johnston attacked, Grant won a stunning victory? Identify the signal clues that you used.

### Vocabulary *Builder*

Read each sentence. If the sentence is true, write YES. If the sentence is not true, write NO and explain why.
4. Both the Union and the Confederacy suffered many casualties.
5. Ironclads were of little importance in the war at sea.

### Writing

6. Use library or Internet resources to find more information about one of the topics covered in this section. Suggestions for topics include the ironclad warships, the Battle of Shiloh, or the Battle of Antietam. Then, write a short introduction to a research paper that would present information about the topic.

# The Battle of Shiloh

In April 1862, the Confederacy seized an opportunity to attack Union forces in the West. Two Union armies were attempting to join each other in southwestern Tennessee. Confederate troops were camped close by in Corinth, Mississippi. The Confederates attacked near Pittsburgh Landing, Tennessee, on April 6, hoping to crush one Union force before the other could arrive.

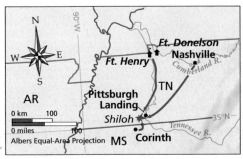

**KEY**

← Union troops

← Confederate troops

Confederate troops attacked Union forces at the Battle of Shiloh.

**1** **A Sunken Road**

The initial Confederate attack caught Union troops by surprise. They retreated a mile before establishing a defensive position along a sunken road. Troops crouched behind the road bank and fought off a dozen Confederate charges.

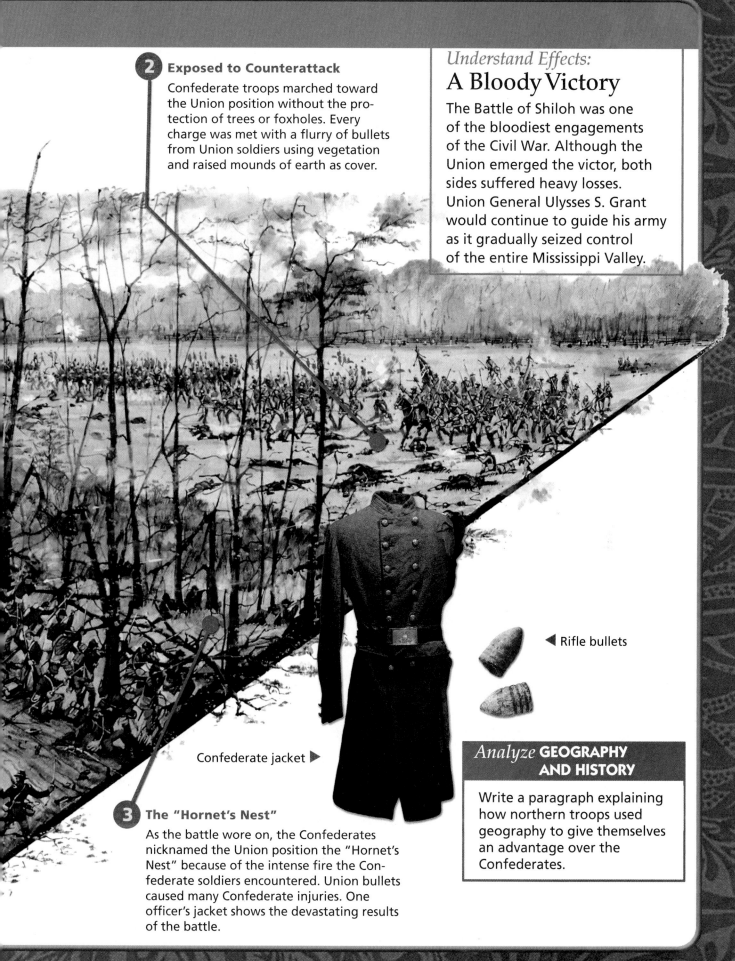

**2 Exposed to Counterattack**

Confederate troops marched toward the Union position without the protection of trees or foxholes. Every charge was met with a flurry of bullets from Union soldiers using vegetation and raised mounds of earth as cover.

*Understand Effects:*
## A Bloody Victory

The Battle of Shiloh was one of the bloodiest engagements of the Civil War. Although the Union emerged the victor, both sides suffered heavy losses. Union General Ulysses S. Grant would continue to guide his army as it gradually seized control of the entire Mississippi Valley.

◀ Rifle bullets

Confederate jacket ▶

**3 The "Hornet's Nest"**

As the battle wore on, the Confederates nicknamed the Union position the "Hornet's Nest" because of the intense fire the Confederate soldiers encountered. Union bullets caused many Confederate injuries. One officer's jacket shows the devastating results of the battle.

*Analyze* **GEOGRAPHY AND HISTORY**

Write a paragraph explaining how northern troops used geography to give themselves an advantage over the Confederates.

# The Emancipation Proclamation

## Objectives

1. Explain why Lincoln issued the Emancipation Proclamation.
2. Identify the effects of the proclamation.
3. Describe the contributions of African Americans to the Union.

## Prepare to Read

### 🎯 Reading Skill

**Explain How Events Are Related in Time** President Lincoln and others made many choices in fighting the war. They made these choices in the context of the events at the time. When reading about history, it is important to see how events in a period are related in time. Do events influence the attitudes and decisions of people going forward in time? Do they change people's actions and freedoms?

### Vocabulary *Builder*

**High-Use Words**

restore, p. 524

sustain, p. 525

**Key Terms and People**

emancipate, p. 524

Horace Greeley, p. 524

**Main Idea**

Lincoln was slow to decide on emancipation but finally embraced it as a necessary war measure.

**Vocabulary *Builder***

restore (ree STOR) *v.* to bring back to a normal state; to put back; to reestablish

⭐ **Background Knowledge** The first two years of war had not been good for the North. However, the North's victory at Antietam was a turning point. As you will now learn, that battle created the conditions that ended slavery and led to a Union victory.

## Emancipating the Enslaved

Many abolitionists rejoiced when the war began. They urged Lincoln to end slavery and thus punish the South for starting the war.

**Lincoln Changes His Mind** At first, the President resisted. He knew most northerners did not want to end slavery. "You ... overestimate the number in the country who hold such views," he told one abolitionist. He feared that any action to emancipate, or free, enslaved African Americans might make the border states secede.

Lincoln said his goal was to restore the Union, even if that meant letting slavery continue. He stated this very clearly in a letter to abolitionist newspaper publisher Horace Greeley.

> ❝If I could save the Union without freeing *any* slave, I would do it, and if I could save it by freeing *all* the slaves, I would do it. . . . What I do about slavery . . . I do because I believe it helps to save the Union.❞
>
> —Abraham Lincoln, letter to Horace Greeley, August 1862

Gradually, Lincoln began to change his mind. He realized how important slavery was to the South's war effort. He told his Cabinet that he intended to issue an Emancipation Proclamation. But Cabinet members advised him to wait until after a success on the battlefield.

**A Famous Proclamation** On September 22, 1862, a few days after Lee's retreat from Antietam, Lincoln met again with his Cabinet and issued a preliminary proclamation.

On January 1, 1863, Lincoln issued the final Emancipation Proclamation. This document had little immediate effect, however, because it freed enslaved people only in areas that were fighting the Union. Those were places where the Union had no power. The proclamation did not apply to parts of the South already under Union control. Nor did it free anyone in the border states.

The proclamation was both criticized and praised. Some abolitionists said it should be applied throughout the country. White southerners accused Lincoln of trying to cause a slave revolt. But many Union soldiers were enthusiastic. They welcomed anything that weakened the South. "This army will <u>sustain</u> the Emancipation Proclamation and enforce it with the bayonet," an Indiana soldier said.

**Effects of the Proclamation** Even though the proclamation freed few slaves at first, it had other important effects. Above all, it changed the Civil War into a struggle for freedom. This was no longer just a fight to save the nation. It was now also a fight to end slavery.

**Vocabulary** *Builder*
<u>sustain</u> (suh STAYN) *v.* to keep going; to endure; to supply with food; to support as just

## The Emancipation Proclamation

❝That on the first day of January, in the year of our Lord [1863], all persons held as slaves within any State or designated part of a State, the people whereof shall then be in rebellion against the United States, shall be then, thenceforward, and forever free. . . .❞

—Emancipation Proclamation, January 1, 1863

# FREEDOM TO SLAVES!

*Whereas,* the President of the United States did, on the first day of the present month, issue his *Proclamation* declaring "that *all persons held as Slaves* in certain designated States, and parts of States, are, and henceforward shall be *free,*" and that the Executive Government of the United States, including the Military and Naval authorities thereof, would recognize and maintain the freedom of said persons. *And Whereas,* the county of *Frederick* is included in the territory designated by the Proclamation of the President, in which the *Slaves should become free,* I therefore hereby notify the citizens of the city of Winchester, and of said County, of said Proclamation, and of my intention to maintain and enforce the same.

I expect all citizens to yield a ready compliance with the Proclamation of the Chief Executive, and I admonish all persons disposed to resist its peaceful enforcement, that upon manifesting such disposition by acts, they will be regarded as rebels in arms against the lawful authority of the Federal Government and dealt with accordingly.

All persons liberated by said Proclamation are admonished to abstain from all violence, and immediately betake themselves to useful occupations.

The officers of this command are admonished and ordered to act in accordance with said proclamation and to yield their ready co-operation in its enforcement.

Winchester Va
Jan. 5th, 1863.

**R. H. Milroy,**
Brig. Gen'l Commanding.

A Union general posted the announcement at right, declaring the freedom of enslaved African Americans in the part of Virginia occupied by his troops.

### Reading Primary Sources
### Skills Activity

President Lincoln's proclamation specified that it applied only to certain parts of the United States.

**(a) Understand Sequence** In what order were these two declarations issued?

**(b) Compare** In what way is the declaration on the right more specific than the one by President Lincoln?

**African American Soldiers**

These are guards of the 107th Colored Infantry at Fort Corcoran in Washington, D.C. **Critical Thinking: *Apply Information*** *How did conditions for African American soldiers differ from those for white soldiers?*

**Main Idea**

African Americans fought for the Union and made other contributions to the war effort.

**Explain How Events Are Related in Time**

Explain why these two events are related in time: African American soldiers fought for the Union; President Lincoln issued the Emancipation Proclamation.

Also, the Emancipation Proclamation dashed any hopes that Britain would recognize the South's independence. Britain would not help a government that was fighting to keep people enslaved.

In both North and South, Lincoln's proclamation united African Americans in support of the war. "We shout for joy that we live to record this righteous decree," wrote Frederick Douglass.

**✓Checkpoint** How did the proclamation affect the war?

## African Americans Help the Union

When the Civil War began, African American volunteers were not permitted to join the Union army. Northern African Americans appealed for the chance to help fight for the nation. However, not until after the Emancipation Proclamation were many allowed to serve.

**Volunteering for Service** The Emancipation Proclamation encouraged African Americans to enlist. Ultimately, 189,000 African Americans served in the Union army or navy. More than half were former slaves who had escaped or been freed by the fighting. All faced extra risks. If captured, they were not treated as prisoners of war. Most were returned to slavery and some were killed.

Black and white sailors served together on warships. In the army, however, African American soldiers served in all-black regiments under white officers. They earned less pay than white soldiers.

Despite these disadvantages, African American regiments fought with pride and courage. "They make better soldiers in every respect than any troops I have ever had under my command," a Union general said of an African American regiment from Kansas.

African American troops took part in about 40 major battles and hundreds of minor ones. The most famous was the attack on Fort Wagner in South Carolina by the 54th Massachusetts Infantry on July 18, 1863. The unit volunteered to lead the assault. As the soldiers charged, Confederate cannon fire rained down. Yet the 54th reached the top of the fort's walls before being turned back in fierce hand-to-hand fighting. The regiment suffered terrible losses. Nearly half of its soldiers were casualties.

Thousands of African Americans supported the Union in noncombat roles. Free northern and emancipated southern African Americans often worked for Union armies as cooks, wagon drivers, and hospital aides.

**Resisting Slavery** In the South, many enslaved African Americans did what they could to hurt the Confederate war effort. Some provided military and other kinds of information to Union armies. Enslaved people had always quietly resisted slavery by deliberately working slowly or damaging equipment. But with many slaveholders off fighting the war, large numbers of slaves refused to work.

✓**Checkpoint** How did African Americans help the Union cause?

⭐ **Looking Back and Ahead** The Emancipation Proclamation made the Civil War a fight to end slavery. After the war, the Thirteenth Amendment banned slavery throughout the nation. The next section tells how the war affected civilians on both sides.

---

## Section 3 | Check Your Progress

**Progress Monitoring** ⬤nline
**For:** Self-test with instant help
**Visit:** PHSchool.com
**Web Code:** mya-5113

### Comprehension and Critical Thinking

1. **(a) Identify** Why did Lincoln at first resist identifying slavery as an issue of the Civil War?
   **(b) Analyze Cause and Effect** What effect did the Emancipation Proclamation have on slavery?

2. **(a) Recall** In what ways did African Americans participate in the Civil War?
   **(b) Explain Problems** What were three problems faced by African American soldiers?

### Reading Skill

3. **Explain How Events Are Related in Time** Identify events that happened after the Emancipation Proclamation. Explain how these events are connected.

### Vocabulary *Builder*

4. Write two definitions for emancipate. First, write a formal definition for your teacher. Second, write a definition in everyday English for a classmate.

### Writing

5. Use library or Internet resources to find information about the African American 54th Massachusetts Infantry. Then, list the subtopics to be included in a research paper about the regiment. Write a paragraph about one of those subtopics. Identify some photographs and other nontext items that you would include in a research report on the 54th.

## Objectives

1. Explain how opposition to the war caused problems for both sides.
2. Identify the reasons that both sides passed draft laws.
3. Describe the economic hardships the war caused in the North and the South.
4. Describe the contributions of women to the war efforts.

## Prepare to Read

### Reading Skill

**Explain How Events Are Related in Time** As soldiers were fighting the Civil War on the battlefield, Americans in both the North and the South were facing other wartime challenges. You will have a better understanding of the Civil War Era if you can relate events on the battlefield to events in civilian life.

### Vocabulary *Builder*

**High-Use Words**

levy, p. 531
currency, p. 531

**Key Terms**

habeas corpus, p. 529
draft, p. 530
income tax, p. 531
inflation, p. 531

⭐ **Background Knowledge** The Emancipation Proclamation ended the South's hope for help from Britain and France. It also encouraged African Americans to fight for the Union. However, it also increased tensions in both the North and the South. In this section, you will learn about the changes and strains the Civil War caused in American life.

**Main Idea**
On both sides, pursuit of the war was hampered by disagreements among the people.

## Divisions Over the War

The Civil War not only divided the nation. It also caused divisions *within* the North and the South. Not all northerners supported a war to end slavery or even to restore the Union. Not all white southerners supported a war to defend slavery or secession.

**Division in the South** In the South, opposition to the war was strongest in Georgia and North Carolina. Barely half of Georgians supported secession. There were nearly 100 peace protests in North Carolina in 1863 alone. Yet only Virginia provided more troops to Confederate armies than did North Carolina. Generally, regions with large slaveholding plantations supported the war more strongly than poor backcountry regions, where there were fewer enslaved people.

Strong support for states' rights created other divisions. For example, South Carolina's governor objected to officers from other states leading South Carolina troops. And the governors of Georgia and North Carolina did not want the Confederate government to force men from their states to do military service.

**Division in the North** Northerners were also divided over the war. Many opposed the Emancipation Proclamation. Others believed that the South had a right to secede. Some northern Democrats blamed Lincoln and the Republicans for forcing the South into a war. Northern Democrats who opposed the war were called Copperheads, after the poisonous snake. Copperheads were strongest in Ohio, Indiana, and Illinois. They criticized the war and called for peace with the Confederacy.

**Dealing With Disruptions** Some people on both sides tried to disrupt the war effort. A common tactic was to encourage soldiers to desert. Some northerners helped Confederate prisoners of war to escape. In the South, peace groups tried to end the war by working against the Confederacy. They tried to prevent men from volunteering for military service and urged Confederate soldiers to desert.

To deal with such problems, both Lincoln and Confederate President Jefferson Davis suspended the right of habeas corpus in some places during the war. Habeas corpus is a constitutional protection against unlawful imprisonment. It empowers judges to order that imprisoned persons be brought into court to determine if they are being legally held. In the North, more than 13,000 people were arrested and jailed without trials.

**Explain How Events Are Related in Time** As the Civil War progressed on the battlefield, what was happening at home? Include information about both North and South in your answer.

☑**Checkpoint** How did the Civil War divide both North and South?

## Copperheads

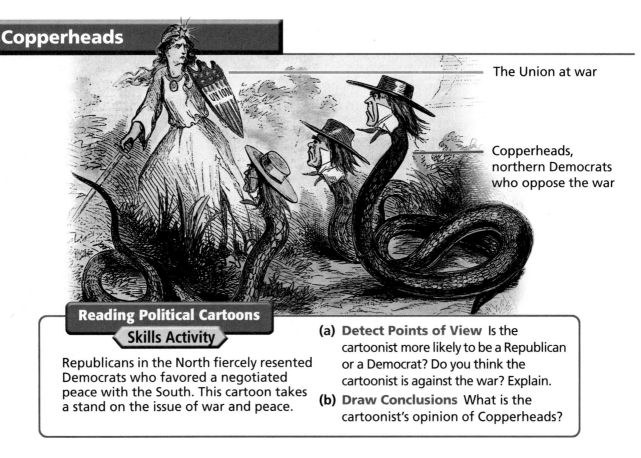

The Union at war

Copperheads, northern Democrats who oppose the war

**Reading Political Cartoons**
**Skills Activity**

Republicans in the North fiercely resented Democrats who favored a negotiated peace with the South. This cartoon takes a stand on the issue of war and peace.

(a) **Detect Points of View** Is the cartoonist more likely to be a Republican or a Democrat? Do you think the cartoonist is against the war? Explain.

(b) **Draw Conclusions** What is the cartoonist's opinion of Copperheads?

**Join or Be Drafted**

Volunteers rushed to enlist at first, but antiwar feeling soon grew. During the New York draft riots of 1863, a mob set fire to a home for African American orphans.
**Critical Thinking: *Detect Points of View*** *What motivated the people who rioted against the draft?*

**Main Idea**

Both sides found it necessary to draft men into military service.

## The Draft Laws

Desertion was a problem for both sides. Between 300,000 and 550,000 Union and Confederate soldiers left their units and went home. About half returned after their crops were planted or harvested. However, at times, from one third to one half of an army's soldiers were away from their units without permission.

To meet the need for troops, each side established a draft, a system of required military service. The South, with its smaller population, was first to act. In April 1862, the Confederacy passed a law requiring white men between ages 18 and 35 to serve in the military for three years. Later, the age range expanded to cover men from 17 to 50. The North adopted a similar draft law in 1863, for men ages 20 to 45.

Exceptions existed, however. Wealthy people had many ways of escaping fighting. In the South, a man who held at least 20 enslaved people did not have to serve. Both sides allowed draftees to hire substitutes to serve in their place. Northerners could avoid the draft by paying the government $300. For many workers, however, this was about a year's pay.

People on both sides complained that the draft made the war "a poor man's fight." Anger against the draft led to violent riots in the North in July 1863. The worst took place in New York City. Mobs of factory workers and laborers rioted for several days, destroying property and attacking African Americans and wealthy white men.

☑**Checkpoint** **Why was the Civil War sometimes called a poor man's fight?**

# The War and Economic Strains

Northern industries boomed as they turned out goods the Union needed in the war. Plenty of jobs were available. But the draft drained away workers so there was a constant shortage.

To pay the costs of fighting the war, Congress <u>levied</u> the first income tax in American history in August 1861. An income tax is a tax on the money people receive. The Union also printed $400 million of paper money to help pay its expenses. This was the first federal paper money, or <u>currency</u>. Putting this additional money into circulation led to inflation, or a general rise in prices. In the North, the prices of goods increased an average of 80 percent during the war.

The South was less able than the North to sustain a war. The Union blockade prevented the South from raising money by selling cotton overseas. Shortages made goods more expensive. This led to much greater inflation than in the North. A pair of shoes that had cost $18 dollars in 1862 cost up to $800 in the South in 1864. The price of a pound of beef soared from 12 cents in 1862 to $8 in 1865.

Southern food production fell as invading Union armies destroyed farmland and crops. Shortages of food led to riots in some southern cities. In Richmond, more than 1,000 women looted shops for food, cloth, and shoes in 1863. A woman in North Carolina complained:

> **"**A crowd of we poor women went to Greensboro yesterday for something to eat as we do not have a mouthful of bread nor meat. . . . I have 6 little children and my husband in the army and what am I to do?**"**
>
> —farm woman in North Carolina, April 1863

Enslaved people also suffered from wartime shortages. What little they did have was often seized by Confederate soldiers.

☑ **Checkpoint**  **What strains did the war put on people?**

# Women in the Civil War

Women in both the North and the South contributed to the war in many ways. At least 400 women disguised themselves as men and joined the Union or Confederate armies. Others became spies behind enemy lines. Many women took over businesses, farms, and plantations while their fathers, brothers, and husbands served on the battlefields.

In both North and South, women ran farms and plantations. Some southern women worked in the fields to help meet the needs of the Confederacy. They continued to work despite fighting that destroyed their crops and killed their livestock.

Women also ran many northern farms. "I saw more women driving teams [of horses] on the road and saw more at work in the fields than men," a traveler in Iowa reported in 1862.

**Main Idea**
The war strained the finances of governments and individuals.

**Vocabulary** *Builder*
<u>levy</u> (LEHV ee) *v.* to impose by law

**Vocabulary** *Builder*
<u>currency</u> (KER rehn see) *n.* money used to make purchases

**Main Idea**
The war opened many new opportunities for women, who contributed greatly to the war effort.

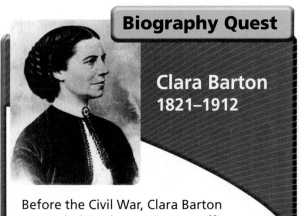

## Biography Quest

### Clara Barton
### 1821–1912

Before the Civil War, Clara Barton was a clerk in the U.S. Patent Office. When hostilities began, she became a nurse. Her work under dangerous conditions earned her the nickname Angel of the Battlefield from her Union and Confederate patients.

After the war, Barton worked for a time with the International Red Cross. Returning to the United States, Barton helped set up an American branch of the Red Cross.

### Biography Quest ⬤nline

**How did Barton become involved in a European war?**

**For:** The answer to the question about Barton

**Visit:** PHSchool.com

**Web Code:** myd-5114

Women on both sides did factory work. Some performed dangerous jobs, such as making ammunition. Others took government jobs. For example, the Confederate government employed dozens of women to sign and number Confederate currency.

The war created many new opportunities for women. Some women became teachers. About 10,000 northern women became nurses. Men had dominated these professions before the war.

Barriers to women especially fell in the field of nursing. Elizabeth Blackwell, America's first female physician, trained nurses for the Union army. Social reformer Dorothea Dix became the head of Union army nurses. Harriet Tubman, who continued to lead enslaved people to freedom during the war, also served as a Union nurse. Clara Barton cared for wounded soldiers on the battlefield. Although nursing was not considered a "proper" job for respectable southern women, some volunteered anyway.

✓**Checkpoint** **How did the war affect women?**

⭐ **Looking Back and Ahead** Both sides suffered political and economic hardships during the war. Draft laws affected every family, while new jobs opened up for women. In the next section, you will read how the war finally ended in the defeat of the Confederacy.

---

### Section 4 | Check Your Progress

**Progress Monitoring ⬤nline**
**For:** Self-test with instant help
**Visit:** PHSchool.com
**Web Code:** mya-5114

### Comprehension and Critical Thinking

**1. (a) Identify** What were two reasons some northerners opposed the war? What were two reasons some southerners opposed the war?
**(b) Explain Problems** Why did the military draft lead some people to describe the war as a poor man's fight?

**2. (a) Describe** Explain the changing role for women during the Civil War.
**(b) Identify Costs** What effects did the Civil War have on the economies of the North and of the South?

### 🎯 Reading Skill

**3. Explain How Events Are Related in Time** What was happening to the American economy as the Civil War raged on?

### Vocabulary *Builder*

**4.** Draw a table with four rows and three columns. In the first column, list the key terms from this section: habeas corpus, draft, income tax, inflation. In the next column, write the definition of each term. In the last column, make a small illustration that shows the meaning of the term.

### Writing

**5.** Reread the text under the heading "Women in the Civil War." Then, write a short paragraph about the role that women played in the Civil War. Include material directly quoted from this section. Be sure to copy the quotation exactly, to punctuate it correctly, and to identify the source.

## Objectives

1. Describe the significance of the battles at Vicksburg and Gettysburg.

2. Explain how Union generals used a new type of war to defeat the Confederacy.

3. Explain how the war ended.

## Prepare to Read

### Reading Skill

**Relate Events in a Sequence**
Events in sequence are often connected by a cause-and-effect link. One event causes an event that occurs next. This event in turn can cause another to occur. As you read Section 5, look for sequential events, and then determine if they have a cause-and-effect relationship. Remember, however, that not all events in sequence have this link.

### Vocabulary *Builder*

**High-Use Words**

encounter, p. 534

exceed, p. 535

**Key Terms and People**

siege, p. 535

William Tecumseh Sherman, p. 536

total war, p. 536

---

⭐ **Background Knowledge** By 1865, four years of Civil War had produced hundreds of thousands of deaths. In this section, you will learn how the Civil War finally came to an end.

## The Tide Turns

After the Union victory at the 1862 Battle of Antietam, the war again began to go badly for the North. As before, the problem was poor leadership. When McClellan failed to pursue Lee's beaten army, Lincoln replaced him with General Ambrose Burnside.

**Confederate Victories** Burnside knew McClellan had been fired for being too cautious. So Burnside decided on a bold stroke. In December 1862, he marched his army of 120,000 men directly toward Richmond. Lee massed 75,000 men at Fredericksburg, Virginia, to block their path. Using traditional tactics, Burnside ordered charge after charge. The Union suffered nearly 13,000 casualties in the Battle of Fredericksburg and the Confederates nearly 5,000.

Lincoln next turned to General Joseph Hooker, nicknamed "Fighting Joe." "May God have mercy on General Lee, for I will have none," Hooker boasted as he marched the Union army toward Richmond. In May 1863, Hooker's army was smashed at the Battle of Chancellorsville by a force that was half its size. But the victory was a costly one for the South. During the battle, Stonewall Jackson was shot and wounded. A few days later, Jackson died.

**Main Idea**
After suffering some defeats, Union forces gained the upper hand by winning major battles at Gettysburg and Vicksburg.

Union General Joseph Hooker

## The Battle of Gettysburg

These Confederate victories made Lee bolder. He was convinced that a major victory on Union soil would force northerners to end the war. In June 1863, Lee's troops crossed Maryland and marched into Pennsylvania. The Union army, which was now commanded by General George Meade, pursued them.

On July 1, some Confederate soldiers approached the quiet town of Gettysburg. They were looking for shoes, which were in short supply in the South because of the Union blockade. Instead of shoes, the Confederates <u>encountered</u> part of Meade's army. Shots were exchanged. More troops joined the fight on both sides. By evening, the southerners had pushed the Union forces back through Gettysburg.

The next day, more than 85,000 Union soldiers faced some 75,000 Confederates. The center of the Union army was on a hill called Cemetery Ridge. The center of the Confederate position was nearly a mile away, on Seminary Ridge. The fighting raged into the next day as Confederate troops attacked each end of the Union line.

On the afternoon of July 3, Lee ordered an all-out attack on the center of the Union line. General George E. Pickett led about 15,000 Confederates across nearly a mile of open field toward Cemetery Ridge. As they advanced, Union artillery shells and rifle fire rained down on them. Only a few hundred men reached the Union lines, and they were quickly driven back. About 7,500 Confederates were killed or wounded in what is known as Pickett's Charge.

**Vocabulary** *Builder*
<u>encounter</u> (ehn KOWN ter) *v.* to meet in an unexpected way; to experience

## Final Battles of the Civil War

**KEY**
← Union troops
← Confederate troops
★ Union victory
✦ Confederate victory
⚓ Union naval blockade

**MAP MASTER**
**Skills Activity**

Union victories at Gettysburg and Vicksburg in July 1863 marked a turning point. This map shows the battles in the final years of the Civil War.

**(a) Read a Map** Which battles were fought in Confederate territory? In Union territory?

**(b) Draw Inferences** What can this map tell you about the damage suffered by North and South between 1863 and 1865?

**MapMaster** ●**nline**

**For:** Interactive map
**Visit:** PHSchool.com
**Web Code:** myp-5113

In all, the Confederacy suffered more than 28,000 casualties during the three-day Battle of Gettysburg. Union losses <u>exceeded</u> 23,000. For a second time, Lee had lost nearly a third of his troops. "It's all my fault," he said as he rode among his surviving soldiers. "It is I who have lost this fight."

**Vocabulary *Builder***
**exceed** (ehks SEED) *v.* to go beyond what is expected; to be greater than what was planned

**The Fall of Vicksburg** On July 4, 1863, as Lee's shattered army began its retreat from Gettysburg, the South suffered another major blow far to the south and west. Vicksburg surrendered to General Grant. It had been one of the last cities on the Mississippi River to remain in Confederate hands. Unable to take Vicksburg by force, Grant had begun a siege of the city in May 1863. A **siege** is an attempt to capture a place by surrounding it with military forces and cutting it off until the people inside surrender.

Day after day, Union guns bombarded Vicksburg. Residents took shelter in cellars and in caves they dug in hillsides. They ate mules and rats to keep from starving. After six weeks, the 30,000 Confederate troops at Vicksburg finally gave up. A few days later, the last Confederate stronghold on the Mississippi River, Port Hudson, Louisiana, also gave up. The entire river was now under Union control.

These events, coupled with Lee's defeat at Gettysburg, make July 1863 the major turning point of the Civil War. Now the Union had the upper hand.

**The Gettysburg Address** In November 1863, about 15,000 people gathered on the battlefield at Gettysburg to honor the soldiers who had died there. In what is now known as the Gettysburg Address, Lincoln looked ahead to a final Union victory. He said:

> **❝**We here highly resolve that these dead shall not have died in vain—that this nation, under God, shall have a new birth of freedom—and that government of the people, by the people, for the people, shall not perish from the earth.**❞**
> —Abraham Lincoln, Gettysburg Address, November 19, 1863

Union General Ulysses S. Grant

☑**Checkpoint** **Identify two events that marked turning points in the Civil War.**

## Closing In on the Confederacy

In Ulysses S. Grant, President Lincoln found the kind of commander he had long sought. In 1864, the President gave him command of all Union forces. Grant decided that he must attack Richmond, no matter how large the Union losses.

**Grant versus Lee** Grant's huge army hammered at the Confederates in a series of battles in northern Virginia in the spring of 1864. Grant was unable to break through Lee's troops. But Grant did not retreat. Instead, he continued the attack.

**Main Idea**
With Grant in command, Union forces carried the war to the heart of the Confederacy.

## Cause and Effect

### CAUSES

- Issue of slavery in the territories divides the North and South.
- Abolitionists want slavery to end.
- Southern states secede after Lincoln's election.

### THE CIVIL WAR

### EFFECTS

- Lincoln issues the Emancipation Proclamation.
- Total war destroys the South's economy.
- Hundreds of thousands of Americans killed.

### Reading Charts
### Skills Activity

The Civil War had multiple causes—and multiple effects.

**(a) Analyze Cause and Effect** Why did the North fear the extension of slavery to the West?

**(b) Draw Conclusions** Which effects were felt mainly in the South? Which effects were felt mainly in the North?

**Relate Events in a Sequence**
What happened first, the Union's victory in Atlanta or President Lincoln's reelection? Explain how these events are related in sequence.

**Main Idea**
Lee surrendered to Grant at Appomattox, putting an end to the long and bloody war.

After seven weeks of fighting, Grant had lost about 55,000 men; the Confederates had lost 35,000. Grant realized that his army could count on a steady stream of men and supplies. Lee, on the other hand, was running out of both.

The two armies clashed at Petersburg, an important railroad center south of Richmond. There, in June 1864, Grant began a siege, the tactic he had used at Vicksburg.

While Grant besieged Lee, another Union army under General William Tecumseh Sherman advanced toward Atlanta. Like Grant, Sherman was a tough soldier. He believed in total war—all-out attacks aimed at destroying an enemy's army, its resources, and its people's will to fight. Sherman later said:

> ❝We are not only fighting hostile armies, but a hostile people, and must make young and old, rich and poor, feel the hard hand of war.❞
>
> —William T. Sherman,
> *Memoirs*, 1886

**March to the Sea** The Confederates could not stop Sherman's advance. The Union army marched into Atlanta on September 2, 1864. Atlanta's capture gave President Lincoln's reelection campaign a boost. In the months before the capture of Atlanta, many northerners had grown tired of the war. Support for Lincoln had been lagging. But after Atlanta's fall, Lincoln won a huge election victory over General George McClellan, the Democrats' candidate.

In November, Sherman ordered Atlanta burned. He then marched east toward the Atlantic Ocean. Along the way, Union troops set fire to buildings, seized crops and livestock, and pulled up railroad tracks. They left a path of destruction up to 60 miles wide. In February 1865, the army headed north across the Carolinas.

✓**Checkpoint** How did Sherman show "the hard hand of war"?

## Peace at Last

In March 1865, Grant's army still waited outside Petersburg. For months, Grant had been extending his battle lines east and west of Petersburg. Lee knew it was only a matter of time before Grant would capture the city.

Lincoln, too, saw that the end of the war was near. In his Second Inaugural Address in March 1865, he asked Americans to forgive and forget. "With malice toward none; with charity for all; . . . let us strive together . . . to bind up the nation's wounds," said Lincoln.

**Surrender at Appomattox** On April 2, Grant's troops finally broke through Confederate lines. By evening, Richmond was in Union hands. Lee's army retreated to the town of Appomattox Court House. There, on April 9, 1865, his escape cut off, Lee surrendered.

Grant offered Lee generous surrender terms. The Confederates had only to give up their weapons and leave in peace. As Lee rode off, some Union troops started to celebrate the surrender. But Grant silenced them. "The war is over," he said. "The rebels are our countrymen again."

**The War's Terrible Toll** The Civil War was the bloodiest conflict the United States has ever fought. About 260,000 Confederate soldiers gave their lives in the war. The number of Union dead exceeded 360,000, including 37,000 African Americans. Nearly a half million men were wounded. Many returned home disfigured for life.

The war had two key results: It reunited the nation and put an end to slavery. However, a century would pass before African Americans would begin to experience the full meaning of freedom.

✓**Checkpoint** **Why did Lee finally decide to surrender?**

⭐ **Looking Back and Ahead** With Lee's surrender, the long and bitter war came to an end. In the next chapter, you will read how U.S. leaders tried to patch the Union together again.

## Section 5 | Check Your Progress

**Progress Monitoring** Online
**For:** Self-test with instant help
**Visit:** PHSchool.com
**Web Code:** mya-5115

### Comprehension and Critical Thinking

**1. (a) Identify** Why are the battles at Gettysburg and Vicksburg considered a turning point?
**(b) Understand Sequence** How did the advantages of the North at the start of the war continue to be advantages?

**2. (a) Classify** President Lincoln called for "charity for all." How would you classify his words to the country?
**(b) Distinguish Facts From Opinions** Write three facts and three opinions Grant might have stated about the Civil War.

### Reading Skill

**3. Relate Events in a Sequence** What events led to the turning point of the Civil War in July 1863? How did those events change the war?

### Vocabulary *Builder*

Complete each of the following sentences so that the second part further explains the first part and clearly shows your understanding of the key term.

**4.** Grant placed Vicksburg under a siege; _____.
**5.** Sherman pursued a total war; _____.

### Writing

**6.** This section says that the Civil War took more than 620,000 American lives. Research and record the number of American deaths in World War I, World War II, Korea, and Vietnam. Compare the total number of American lives lost in these wars to the number lost in the Civil War. Then, write a paragraph to make a point about your findings. Also, credit the sources of published information you used.

A primary source is information about people or events presented by someone who lived through what is being described. Speeches are primary sources that can give important information about historical figures and events.

**Primary Source**

President Lincoln gave this speech at the dedication of the battlefield cemetery at Gettysburg.

"Fourscore and seven years ago our fathers brought forth on this continent a new nation, conceived in Liberty, and dedicated to the proposition that all men are created equal.

Now we are engaged in a great civil war, testing whether that nation, or any nation so conceived and so dedicated, can long endure. We are met on a great battlefield of that war. We have come to dedicate a portion of that field as a final resting place for those who here gave their lives that the nation might live. It is altogether fitting and proper that we should do this.

But in a larger sense, we cannot dedicate, we cannot consecrate, we cannot hallow, this ground. The brave men, living and dead, who struggled here have consecrated it, far above our poor power to add or detract. The world will little note, nor long remember, what we say here, but it can never forget what they did here. It is for us the living, rather, to be dedicated here to the unfinished work which they who fought here have thus far so nobly advanced. It is rather for us to be here dedicated to the great task remaining before us—that from these honored dead we take increased devotion to that cause for which they gave the last full measure of devotion—that we here highly resolve that these dead shall not have died in vain—that this nation, under God, shall have a new birth of freedom—and that government of the people, by the people, for the people, shall not perish from the earth."

—Abraham Lincoln, November 19, 1863

## Learn the Skill

*Use these steps to analyze a speech.*

① **Identify the source.** Find out who gave the speech, when it was given, and why it was given.

② **Identify the main idea.** Read carefully to discover what the main idea of the speech is. What do you think the speaker wanted to tell his or her audience?

③ **Identify the point of view.** Often a speechmaker wants to persuade listeners to share his or her feelings. Read carefully to determine the point of view of the speechmaker. Look for language that expresses strong feelings.

## Practice the Skill

*Answer the questions about the speech above.*

① **Identify the source.** (a) Who wrote the speech? (b) When was the speech given? (c) Why was it given?

② **Identify the main idea.** What is the most important idea in the speech?

③ **Identify the point of view.** (a) What is the speaker's opinion of the Civil War? (b) What words or phrases express his feelings? (c) Why do you think he feels this way?

## Apply the Skill

*See the Review and Assessment at the end of this chapter.*

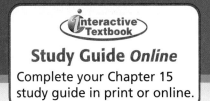

**Study Guide Online**
Complete your Chapter 15 study guide in print or online.

## Chapter Summary

### Section 1
### The Call to Arms

- The Civil War was a war of Americans against Americans.
- Both the North and the South used their advantages in planning military strategy.

### Section 2
### Early Years of the War

- Civil War soldiers lived under harsh and dangerous conditions.
- Battles at Antietam Creek and Shiloh were important victories for the North.

### Section 3
### The Emancipation Proclamation

- The Emancipation Proclamation freed enslaved people in areas of rebellion.
- The Emancipation Proclamation changed the Civil War into a fight to end slavery.
- Approximately 189,000 African Americans served in the Union army and navy.

### Section 4
### The Civil War and American Life

- The Civil War caused divisions in both the North and the South.
- Draft laws that seemed to favor the wealthy led to protests and riots.
- The Civil War caused economic hardships and also led to changes in women's roles.

### Section 5
### Decisive Battles

- Major Confederate losses at Gettysburg and Vicksburg marked a turning point.
- Lee surrendered to Grant on April 9, 1865, at Appomattox Court House.
- Some 620,000 soldiers died in the Civil War.

## Key Concepts

These notes will help you prepare for questions about key concepts.

| Causes of the Civil War | Effects of the Emancipation Proclamation | Major Civil War Events, 1861–1865 |
|---|---|---|
| • Spread of slavery in western territories divides North and South. <br>• Abolitionists want to end all slavery. <br>• South fears it will lose power in the federal government. <br>• Southern states secede after Lincoln's election. <br>• Confederates bomb Fort Sumter. | (Issued by President Abraham Lincoln on January 1, 1863) <br>• Freed enslaved people in areas that were in rebellion <br>• Turned war into a fight to end slavery <br>• Ended South's hopes for recognition of independence by Britain <br>• Encouraged African Americans to join Union army | • First Bull Run, July 1861 <br>• Shiloh, April 1862 <br>• Antietam Creek, September 1862 <br>• Fredericksburg, December 1862 <br>• Vicksburg, May–July 1863 <br>• Gettysburg, July 1863 <br>• Surrender of Confederate army, April 9, 1865, Appomattox Court House |

## Vocabulary *Builder*

### Key Terms

Answer the following questions in complete sentences that show your understanding of the key terms.

1. Which army, the Union or the Confederate, sustained more casualties?

2. Why did Kentucky cease being neutral?

3. What was both Lincoln's and Davis's purpose in suspending habeas corpus?

4. How did Grant's siege of Vicksburg lead to the surrender of Confederate troops?

## Comprehension and Critical Thinking

5. **(a) Recall** Why was it critical to keep Maryland in the Union?
   **(b) Analyze Cause and Effect** What was the effect of Lincoln's declaring martial law in Maryland?

6. **(a) Identify** Why did President Lincoln issue the Emancipation Proclamation?
   **(b) Explain Problems** What were two limitations of the Emancipation Proclamation?

7. **(a) Describe** What roles did women play in the Civil War?
   **(b) Identify Economic Benefits** In what way did the hardships of the Civil War provide new opportunities for women?
   **(c) Link Past and Present** Make a list of three opportunities that are open to women today that once were limited to men.

8. **(a) Classify** Create a chart of the battles fought at these places: Bull Run, Antietam Creek, Shiloh, Fredericksburg, Vicksburg, Gettysburg, Petersburg. Classify each battle as either a Union victory or a Confederate victory.
   **(b) Detect Bias** Reread the excerpt from Lincoln's Gettysburg Address found in Section 5. Do you think the address gave more comfort to northerners or to southerners? Why?

9. **(a) Summarize** Write three sentences that explain how the Civil War ended.
   **(b) Make Predictions** Do you think the surrender of the Confederate army at Appomattox Court House brought an end to the conflict between the northern and southern states? Explain.

## History Reading Skill

10. **Understand Sequence** In a paragraph, summarize the events in the Civil War on the battlefield and on the home front. Use signal words to clarify the sequence. Where appropriate, show cause-effect links between events in sequence.

## Writing

11. **Write on the following topic:**
    Find more information about a Civil War general. Write four paragraphs about him, using the guidelines below.
    - The first paragraph should introduce the general and present a thesis.
    - The second and third paragraphs should support this thesis by giving some background about the general's life, actions, and character.
    - The fourth paragraph should draw a conclusion about the general.

12. **Write a Narrative:**
    Choose one of the following roles: soldier, civilian, or nurse. Write two paragraphs of descriptive narrative telling about your experience in the Civil War.

## Skills for Life

### Analyze a Speech
Use the quotation below to answer the questions.

> ". . . the people of the Confederate States, in their conventions, determined that the wrongs which they had suffered and the evils with which they were menaced required that they should revoke the delegation of powers to the Federal Government which they had ratified in their several conventions. They consequently passed ordinances [laws] resuming all their rights as sovereign and independent States. . . ."
>
> —Jefferson Davis, April 29, 1861

13. **(a)** Who is the writer?
    **(b)** When was this written?

14. What is the main idea?

15. **(a)** What words or phrases show the writer's feelings?
    **(b)** Why do you think he feels this way?

## Test Yourself

**Refer to the quotation below to answer Question 1.**

"I now hold in contemplation of universal law and of the Constitution [that] the Union of these States is perpetual. . . . It follows from these views that no State upon its own mere motion can lawfully get out of the Union. . . ."

—Abraham Lincoln, March 4, 1861

1. **This quotation shows that Lincoln wanted to**
   A allow southern states to secede.
   B amend the Constitution.
   C abolish slavery.
   D preserve the Union.

2. **Which of the following granted freedom to all African Americans in areas of rebellion against the Union in 1863?**
   A Gettysburg Address
   B Thirteenth Amendment
   C Emancipation Proclamation
   D surrender at Appomattox Court House

3. **Which of the following was the North's most important advantage in the Civil War?**
   A Britain and other European nations sent economic aid.
   B The nation's most experienced military leaders were northerners.
   C The North had a larger population and more resources than the South.
   D Northerners were united in their support for the war.

## Document-Based Questions

**Task:** Look at Documents 1 and 2, and answer their accompanying questions. Then, use the documents and your knowledge of history to complete this writing assignment:

Write an essay describing the disagreement between the Copperheads and northern supporters of the Civil War. Include specific details about each side's position.

**Document 1:** Clement L. Vallandigham, an Ohio congressman, gave this speech in New York City in March 1863. *What does Vallandigham propose? How does that represent the Copperhead position?*

"When I see that the experiment of blood has failed, . . . I am not one of those who proclaim . . . that we shall have separation and disunion. I am for going back to the instrumentality through which this Union was first made, and by which alone it can be restored.

I am for peace, because it is the first step toward conciliation and compromise. You cannot move until you have first taken that indispensable preliminary—a cessation of hostilities. . . .

Let men of intelligence judge: let history attest it hereafter. My theory . . . then, is this—stop this war."

**Document 2:** Copperheads were probably the most outspoken critics of the war in the North. *What opinion of Copperheads does this cartoon present?*

## Chapter Preview

The Civil War was the bloodiest war fought on U.S. territory. The war ended slavery and reunited the North and the South. After the war, the nation faced the task of rebuilding the South—a region ruined by war.

Northerners who moved south after the Civil War were called carpetbaggers. A carpetbag was a carpet rolled up or stitched together to hold belongings.

**U.S. Events**

**1863**
President Lincoln proposes mild Reconstruction plan.

**1865**
Lincoln is assassinated five days after war ends.

**1867**
Radical Reconstruction begins.

1860      1865      1870

**World Events**

**1867** Dominion of Canada is formed.

**Quick View Video**
View the chapter video for a quick preview of the main ideas.

Students and teachers pose outside the Freedmen's Bureau school in Beaufort, South Carolina.

## 1870
15th Amendment is ratified by the states.

## 1877
Rutherford B. Hayes becomes President after disputed election.

## 1896
Supreme Court upholds separate facilities for blacks and whites.

**1870**

**1875**

**1900**

**1870** Italy becomes unified nation.

**1873** Slave markets are abolished in Zanzibar, in Africa.

**1876** Porfirio Díaz becomes leader of Mexico.

**History Reading Skill** **Analyze and Evaluate Proposals**

## How did the Civil War affect plantation owners?

Thomas Dabney's plantation lay in ruins after the Civil War. In the excerpt below, his daughter describes the way Dabney dealt with his personal crisis.

**Primary Source**

Thomas Dabney was a southern plantation owner. At the close of the Civil War, his property was in ruins and the plantation economic system had ended. His daughter, Susan Dabney Smedes, describes the proposals he made to face those challenges and the methods he used to carry out his proposals.

> He informed [former slaves] . . . that they were now free. His advice was that they should continue to work the crop as they had been doing. At the end of the year they should receive such pay for their labor as he thought just. . . .
>
> He owned nothing that could be turned into money without great sacrifice but five bales of cotton. There were yet two sons and two daughters to be educated. He decided to get a tutor for them and to receive several other pupils in his house in order to make up the salary.
>
> His chivalrous nature had always revolted from the sight of a woman doing hard work. He determined to spare his daughters all such labor as he could perform. General Sherman had said that he would like to bring every southern woman to the washtub. "He shall never bring my daughter to the washtub," Thomas Dabney said. "I will do the washing myself." And he did it for two years.
>
> — Susan Dabney Smedes, *Memorials of a Southern Planter*

**Thomas Dabney proposes to his former slaves that they keep working.**

**Here, he gives a reason to support his proposal: They will get paid at the end of the year.**

**Dabney proposes a way to get an education for his children.**

**Here, Dabney proposes how he will treat the women of his family.**

**He shows how he will carry out his proposal.**

## Analyze and Evaluate Proposals

- Ask yourself what goals Thomas Dabney has and how he proposes to meet those goals.
- You can identify Thomas Dabney's proposals in the decisions he makes. Support follows in the reasons for those decisions or the methods of carrying them forward.
- Evaluate Dabney's proposals. Do you think his proposals will help him meet his goals?

## Document-Based Questions

1. Who is the author of this source?
2. What is the relationship of the author to Thomas Dabney?
3. How might the opinion of Dabney's former slaves compare with the author's opinion of Dabney?

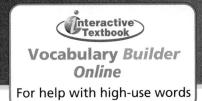

# Vocabulary *Builder*

## Previewing High-Use Academic Words

| High-Use Word | Definition | Sample History Sentence |
|---|---|---|
| **voluntary** (VAHL ahn tair ee) (Section 1, p. 547) | **adj.** not forced; done of one's own free will | The state of Virginia's ceding of western land to the U.S. government was <u>voluntary</u>. |
| **resolve** (ree SAHLV) (Section 1, p. 548) | **v.** to decide; to solve | The colonists <u>resolved</u> to fight the British. |
| **critic** (KRIHT ihk) (Section 2, p. 553) | **n.** someone who makes judgments on the value of objects or actions | The war hawks were <u>critics</u> of Madison's lenient policy toward the British. |
| **impose** (ihm POHZ) (Section 2, p. 555) | **v.** to place a burden on something or someone | The Tariff of 1816 <u>imposed</u> a high tax on certain goods imported into the country. |
| **factor** (FAK tor) (Section 3, p. 558) | **n.** condition or quality that causes something else to happen | Distance was the most important <u>factor</u> in the colonies developing cultures different from the British. |
| **inferior** (ihn FIR ee uhr) (Section 3, p. 561) | **adj.** of lower rank or status, or of poorer quality | At first, American manufactures were <u>inferior</u> in quality to British goods. |

## Previewing Key Terms and People

Hiram Revels

Abraham Lincoln

Andrew Johnson

# Rebuilding the Nation

## Objectives

1. Describe the postwar challenges that faced the nation.

2. Compare and contrast President Lincoln's plan for Reconstruction with the plan proposed by Congress.

3. Identify the goals of the Freedmen's Bureau.

4. Describe the immediate impact of Lincoln's assassination.

## Prepare to Read

### Reading Skill

**Identify Proposals** In turbulent times, such as after the Civil War, people may have many different ideas about how to move forward. They identify goals to achieve and propose solutions to problems. For example, each proposal made by a government leader was intended to achieve a specific goal. As you read Section 1, identify these proposals and goals.

### Vocabulary *Builder*

**High-Use Words**
voluntary, p. 547
resolve, p. 548

**Key Terms and People**
Abraham Lincoln, p. 546
amnesty, p. 547
freedman, p. 548
John Wilkes Booth, p. 549

**Main Idea**
President Lincoln and Congress did not agree about how to bring the Union back together.

⭐ **Background Knowledge** After four years of bitter war, the Union finally had won the Civil War. Even though the fighting had ended, the nation remained divided. In this section, you will read of early plans for rebuilding national unity after the war.

## Preparing for Reunion

As the Civil War ended, enormous problems faced the nation, especially the South. Vast stretches of the South lay in ruins. What provisions would be made for people who had been freed from slavery? Homeless refugees—both African American and white—needed food, shelter, and work. (For more on conditions in the South after the Civil War, see the Life at the Time feature at the end of this section.)

Somehow, though, Americans had to master their hard feelings and bring the North and the South together again. This process, known as Reconstruction, would occupy the nation for years to come.

**Lincoln's Ten Percent Plan** Abraham Lincoln wanted to make it easy for the southern states to rejoin the Union. His goal was to bind up the wounds of war as quickly as possible.

In December 1863, Lincoln introduced what was called the Ten Percent Plan. As soon as ten percent of a state's voters swore an oath of loyalty to the United States, the voters could organize a new state government. That government would have to declare an end to slavery. Then, the state could send members to Congress and take part in the national government again.

Lincoln's plan included amnesty for former Confederates who took the loyalty oath. An amnesty is a group pardon. The offer of amnesty did not apply to Confederate government leaders and top military officers.

**The Wade-Davis Bill** Six months later, Congress passed a much stricter plan for Reconstruction called the Wade-Davis Bill. Under that bill, 50 percent of voters would have to sign a loyalty oath before a state could return to the Union. Moreover, anyone who had <u>voluntarily</u> fought for the Confederacy would be barred from voting for delegates to a convention to write a new state constitution. The bill did not give them a right to vote. Lincoln would not sign the Wade-Davis Bill, so it never became law.

Lincoln and his fellow Republicans hoped to see a strong Republican Party in the new South. Lincoln thought that his "soft," or lenient, Reconstruction policy would win support from influential southerners. Supporters of a strict policy toward the South, known as Radical Republicans, disagreed. They argued that only a strict plan would keep the people who had led the South into secession from regaining power and weakening the control of the Radical Republicans.

**☑Checkpoint** **How did Lincoln's plan for Reconstruction differ from that of the Radical Republicans in Congress?**

**Identify Proposals**
What did Lincoln propose in his Ten Percent Plan?

**Vocabulary *Builder***
**voluntary** (VAHL ahn tair ee) *adj.* not forced; done of one's own free will

**Destruction in the South**
Parts of Richmond, capital of the Confederacy, lay in ruins at war's end. **Critical Thinking:** *Interpret Photographs* What do you think would be the most urgent need of the people of Richmond?

# The Freedmen's Bureau

It was urgent to deal with the needs of freedmen, enslaved people who had been freed by the war, as well as other war refugees. Congress created the Freedmen's Bureau in March 1865. The bureau's first duty was to provide emergency relief to people displaced by the war.

**Education** The Freedmen's Bureau set up schools to teach freedmen to read and write. So great was the hunger for education that many African American communities started schools on their own. To pay a teacher, people pooled their pennies and dollars.

Many teachers were northern white women, but a large number were northern African American women. Edmonia Highgate, the daughter of freed slaves, taught at a Freedmen's Bureau school in Louisiana. "The majority of my pupils come from plantations, three, four and even eight miles distant," she wrote. "So anxious are they to learn that they walk these distances so early in the morning."

Most southern states had lacked systems of public education before the war. Now, public schools began to educate both blacks and whites. The Freedmen's Bureau helped to start schools at which African Americans could extend their education. These schools gave rise to such present-day institutions as Fisk University in Tennessee and Hampton University in Virginia.

**Defending Freedmen** The Freedmen's Bureau helped freedmen find jobs and <u>resolved</u> disputes between whites and blacks. Some people tried to cheat the freedmen. The Freedmen's Bureau set up its own courts to deal with such disputes.

✔**Checkpoint** What was the Freedmen's Bureau?

**Vocabulary** *Builder*
<u>resolve</u> (ree SAHLV) *v.* to decide; to solve

**Explore More Video**
To learn more about Lincoln's life and presidency, view the video.

**Assassinated!**
Lincoln's assassination set off an intense hunt for the killer, John Wilkes Booth. **Critical Thinking: Make Predictions** *What effect do you think the assassination of Lincoln would have on the nation?*

# Lincoln Is Murdered

As the war drew to a close, President Lincoln hoped for a peaceful Reconstruction. But Lincoln had no chance to put his plans into practice. He was shot dead on April 14, 1865, five days after Lee's surrender.

A Confederate sympathizer, John Wilkes Booth, slipped up behind Lincoln while he and his wife were attending a play at the Ford's Theatre in Washington. Booth fired a single pistol shot into the President's head. Lincoln died a few hours later.

Booth was shot dead two weeks later after pursuers trapped him in a barn and set it on fire. Eight people were convicted and four were hanged for their parts in the plot to kill Lincoln.

News of Lincoln's death shocked the nation. A special funeral train carried Lincoln's body back to Illinois for burial. In town after town, vast crowds paid their last respects.

Lincoln's successor was Vice President Andrew Johnson of Tennessee. Johnson was a southern Democrat who had remained loyal to the Union. Because Johnson had expressed bitterness toward the Confederates, many expected him to take a strict approach to Reconstruction.

☑ **Checkpoint** **Why did many people expect Johnson to take a hard line on Reconstruction?**

☆ **Looking Back and Ahead** Many people feared the effect of Lincoln's assassination on the process of Reconstruction. In the next section, you will learn how Reconstruction was affected by tensions between Lincoln's successor and members of Congress.

**Main Idea**
Abraham Lincoln's assassination ended the chance of a lenient Reconstruction.

## Section 1 | Check Your Progress

**Progress Monitoring** Online
**For:** Self-test with instant help
**Visit:** PHSchool.com
**Web Code:** mya-5121

### Comprehension and Critical Thinking

**1. (a) Recall** How did the Civil War affect the North? How did the war affect the South?
**(b) Contrast** Why did the South have greater difficulty than the North in recovering from the Civil War?

**2. (a) Recall** How did Lincoln's plan for Reconstruction differ from the Wade-Davis Bill?
**(b) Explain Problems** What problems do you see for reuniting the nation in each plan?

### Reading Skill

**3. Identify Proposals** Reread the paragraphs under the heading "The Freedmen's Bureau." What did the bureau propose to do to help the freedmen?

### Vocabulary *Builder*

Answer the following questions in complete sentences that show your understanding of the key terms.
**4.** What did former Confederates have to do to get amnesty under Lincoln's plan to rebuild the Union?
**5.** Who were the freedmen?

### Writing

**6.** Choose the best sentence to end a research paper about Abraham Lincoln. Explain your choice.
**Sentences:**

**(a)** Abraham Lincoln was humbly born on February 12, 1809, but he went on to be one of our greatest Presidents.

**(b)** Because Abraham Lincoln did not win a majority of the votes cast, his presidency turned out to be the nation's most turbulent period.

**(c)** His trials as President changed Lincoln into the steady leader who saved the Union in its darkest hour.

# The South After the Civil War

The Civil War had a devastating impact on the South. All southerners—rich and poor, black and white—faced a long struggle to rebuild their lives and their land.

Confederate flag

Destroyed plantation

## ▲ Physical Destruction

Most of the fighting during the Civil War took place in the South. Cities and plantations lay in charred ruins. Two thirds of the railroads were destroyed.

## ► Wounded Soldiers

A quarter of a million Confederate soldiers died in the war. Thousands more were disabled by their wounds.

Returning Confederate veteran

Freedmen's school

Teaching people to read

## ▲ Freedmen

For nearly 4 million freedmen, the end of the Civil War was a time of both hope and fear. They were no longer enslaved. But most had no land, no jobs, and no education. The first task was to teach them to read.

## ◄ Financial Ruin

The economy of the South was ruined. Confederate money was suddenly worthless. Many banks closed, and people lost their life's savings.

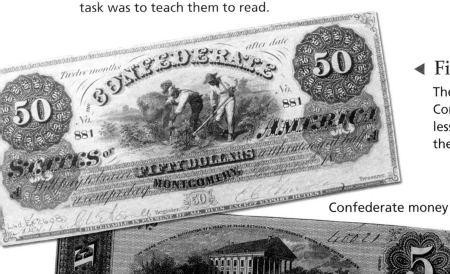

Confederate money

### Analyze LIFE AT THE TIME

Take one of the following roles: a wounded veteran; a planter whose plantation has been destroyed; a freedman. Write a paragraph explaining how you feel about the end of the war and the possibilities for the future.

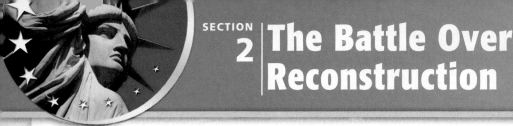

## Objectives

1. Explain why conflicts developed over plans for Reconstruction.

2. Describe the changes in the South brought about by Radical Reconstruction.

3. Explain how Congress tried to remove President Johnson from office.

4. Describe how the Ku Klux Klan and other secret societies tried to prevent African Americans from exercising their rights.

## Prepare to Read

### ⟳ Reading Skill

**Analyze Proposals** Proposals must be carried out in order to be effective. The proposal must include details on how to put the proposal into action. As you read Section 2, look at the suggested ideas for carrying out proposals.

### Vocabulary *Builder*

**High-Use Words**

critic, p. 553

impose, p. 555

### Key Terms and People

Andrew Johnson, p. 552

black codes, p. 553

Hiram Revels, p. 555

Blanche Bruce, p. 555

scalawag, p. 555

carpetbagger, p. 555

impeachment, p. 556

☆ **Background Knowledge** You have read that Radical Republicans in Congress wanted a strict Reconstruction. In this section, you will learn how President Johnson's Reconstruction plans set the stage for a bitter battle between Johnson and Congress.

## A Growing Conflict

Like President Lincoln, Andrew Johnson proposed a relatively lenient plan of Reconstruction. He followed Lincoln's example in putting his plan into effect himself, without consulting legislators.

**Main Idea**
Andrew Johnson's lenient Reconstruction plan was rejected by Congress.

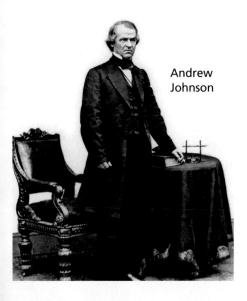

Andrew Johnson

**The Thirteenth Amendment** In January 1865, Congress approved a constitutional amendment to abolish slavery throughout the nation. The Thirteenth Amendment banned both slavery and forced labor. The amendment gave Congress the power to make laws to enforce its terms.

**Johnson's Plan** Like Lincoln, Johnson issued a broad amnesty to most former Confederates. Johnson allowed southern states to organize new governments and elect representatives to Congress. Each state, though, was required to abolish slavery and ratify the Thirteenth Amendment. By late fall, most of the states had met Johnson's requirements. When Congress met in December 1865, the representatives and senators elected by white southerners included many former Confederate leaders.

Congress quickly rejected Johnson's approach. First, it refused to seat the southern senators and representatives. Next, the two houses appointed a committee to form a new plan for the South.

In a series of public hearings, the committee heard testimony about black codes—new laws used by southern states to control African Americans. Critics claimed that the codes replaced the system of slavery with near-slavery. In Mississippi, for example, African Americans could not vote or serve on juries. If unable to pay a fine as ordered by a court, they might be hired out by the sheriff to any white person who paid the fine.

Anger at these developments led Congress to adopt an increasingly hard line. The hardest line was taken by the Radical Republicans. The Radicals had two key goals. One was to prevent former Confederates from regaining control over southern politics. The other was to protect the freedmen and guarantee them a right to vote.

**Vocabulary** *Builder*
critic (KRIHT ihk) *n.* someone who makes judgments on the value of objects or actions

✔**Checkpoint** How did Congress respond to Johnson's plan for Reconstruction?

## The Fourteenth Amendment

The struggle over Reconstruction led to direct clashes between the President and Congress during 1866. At issue were two laws and a constitutional amendment.

Voicing alarm at the treatment of African Americans in the South, Congress passed the Civil Rights Act of 1866. It granted citizenship rights to African Americans and guaranteed the civil rights of all people except Native Americans.

President Johnson vetoed the bill and another one extending the life of the Freedmen's Bureau. Congress voted to overturn both vetoes. Under the Constitution, a vetoed bill becomes law if it wins the votes of two thirds of each house. Both bills received enough votes to become law.

**Main Idea**
Alarmed by violence against African Americans in the South, Congress approved the Fourteenth Amendment.

## Opposing Plans for Reconstruction

I want a quick reunion.

| President Andrew Johnson (1865) | Radical Republicans (1867) |
|---|---|
| • Majority of white men must swear oath of loyalty<br>• Must ratify 13th Amendment<br>• Former Confederate officials may vote and hold office | • Must disband state government<br>• Must write new constitution<br>• Must ratify 13th and 14th Amendments<br>• Must allow African American men to vote |

President Andrew Johnson

We want real change.

Congressman Thaddeus Stevens

### Reading Charts
#### Skills Activity

President Andrew Johnson and Republican members of Congress, led by Thaddeus Stevens, disagreed about the process of Reconstruction.

(a) **Read a Chart** Which plan required states to write new constitutions?

(b) **Detect Points of View** Why did Radical Republicans think Johnson's plan was not strict enough?

---

**Analyze Proposals**

Congress proposed the Fourteenth Amendment to give freedmen a way to defend their rights. How would the amendment put that goal into action?

Congress also drew up the Fourteenth Amendment to the Constitution, seeking to make sure that the Supreme Court did not strike down the Civil Rights Act. Republicans remembered the Court's Dred Scott decision. In that ruling, the Court declared that no one descended from an enslaved person could be a United States citizen.

The amendment failed at first to win the approval of three fourths of the states. It finally was approved in 1868, after Radicals took control of Reconstruction.

The Fourteenth Amendment says that all people born or naturalized in the United States are citizens. The amendment also declares that states may not pass laws that take away a citizen's rights. Nor can a state "deprive any person of life, liberty, or property, without due process of law; nor deny to any person . . . the equal protection of the laws."

Another provision declares that any state that denies the vote to any male citizen over the age of 21 will have its representation in Congress reduced. That provision was not enforced until the 1970s.

The Fourteenth Amendment became a powerful tool for enforcing civil rights. However, almost a century passed before it was used for that purpose.

✓**Checkpoint** How did the Fourteenth Amendment seek to protect the freedmen?

## Radical Reconstruction

**Main Idea**
During Radical Reconstruction, African Americans played an active part in the political life of the South.

Tempers rose as the elections of 1866 approached. White rioters and police attacked and killed many African Americans in two southern cities, Memphis and New Orleans. Outrage at this violence led Congress to push a stricter form of Reconstruction.

**Radicals in Charge** By early 1867, the Radical Republicans had won enough support from moderates to begin a "hard" Reconstruction. This period is known as Radical Reconstruction.

The Reconstruction Act of 1867 removed the governments of all southern states that had refused to ratify the Fourteenth Amendment. It then <u>imposed</u> military rule on these states, dividing them into five military districts. Before returning to the Union, each state had to write a new constitution and ratify the Fourteenth Amendment. Each state also had to let African Americans vote.

Under military rule, the South took on a new look. Soldiers helped register southern blacks to vote. In five states, African American voters outnumbered white voters. In the election of 1868, Republicans won all southern states. The states wrote new constitutions and, in June 1868, Congress seated representatives from seven "reconstructed" states.

**Time of Hope and Advancement** For the first time, African Americans in the South played an active role in politics. Prominent among them were free-born African Americans—carpenters, barbers, preachers—and former Union soldiers.

African Americans were elected as sheriffs, mayors, judges, and legislators. Sixteen African Americans served in the U.S. House of Representatives between 1872 and 1901. Two others, Hiram Revels and Blanche Bruce, served in the Senate.

Historians once took a critical view of Radical Reconstruction, focusing on the widespread corruption and excessive spending during this period. More recently, however, historians have written about important accomplishments of Reconstruction. They noted that during Reconstruction, southern states opened public schools for the first time. Legislators spread taxes more evenly and made fairer voting rules. They gave property rights to women. In addition, states rebuilt bridges, roads, and buildings destroyed by the war.

Radical Reconstruction brought other sweeping changes to the South. Old leaders lost much of their power. The Republican Party built a strong following based on three key groups. One group, called scalawags by their opponents, were southern whites who had opposed secession. Freedmen voters made up a second group.

The third group were carpetbaggers, a name given by southerners to northern whites who went south to start businesses or pursue political office. Critics claimed that these northerners were in such a rush to head south that they just tossed their clothes into cheap satchels called carpetbags.

**Vocabulary Builder**
**impose** (ihm POHZ) *v.* to place a burden on something or someone

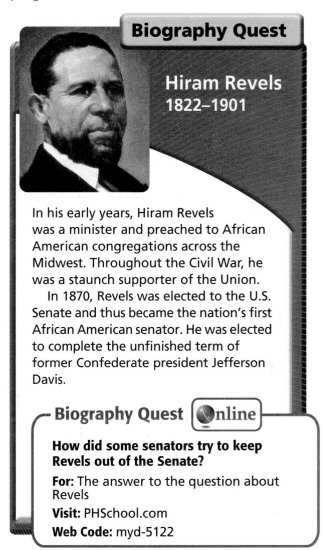

**Biography Quest**

**Hiram Revels**
**1822–1901**

In his early years, Hiram Revels was a minister and preached to African American congregations across the Midwest. Throughout the Civil War, he was a staunch supporter of the Union.

In 1870, Revels was elected to the U.S. Senate and thus became the nation's first African American senator. He was elected to complete the unfinished term of former Confederate president Jefferson Davis.

**Biography Quest** **Online**

**How did some senators try to keep Revels out of the Senate?**

**For:** The answer to the question about Revels

**Visit:** PHSchool.com

**Web Code:** myd-5122

## The Impact of Violence

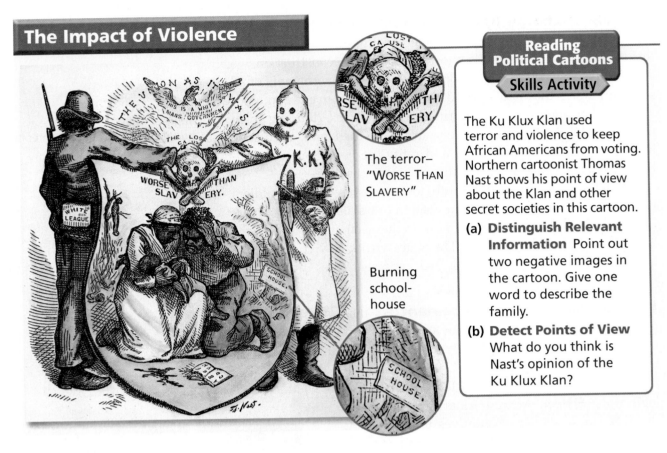

The terror—"WORSE THAN SLAVERY"

Burning school-house

**Reading Political Cartoons**

**Skills Activity**

The Ku Klux Klan used terror and violence to keep African Americans from voting. Northern cartoonist Thomas Nast shows his point of view about the Klan and other secret societies in this cartoon.

**(a) Distinguish Relevant Information** Point out two negative images in the cartoon. Give one word to describe the family.

**(b) Detect Points of View** What do you think is Nast's opinion of the Ku Klux Klan?

**Targeting President Johnson** Meanwhile, the Radicals mounted a major challenge against President Johnson. The Radicals tried to remove Johnson from office by impeachment. Impeachment is the bringing of formal charges against a public official. The Constitution says the House may impeach a President for "treason, bribery, or other high crimes and misdemeanors." After impeachment, there is a trial in the Senate. If convicted, the President is removed from office.

Johnson escaped removal—but barely. The House voted to impeach him in February 1868. The Senate trial took place from March to May. In the end, the votes went 35 for and 19 against Johnson. This was one vote short of the required two-thirds majority.

**The Election of 1868** General Ulysses S. Grant, a war hero, won the presidential election for the Republicans in the fall of 1868. With southern states back in the Union under military rule, some 500,000 African Americans voted, mainly for Republicans. Grant won the electoral votes of 26 of the 34 states.

Grant was a moderate who had support from many northern business leaders. With his election, the Radicals began losing their grip on the Republican Party.

**Fifteenth Amendment** Over opposition from Democrats, Congress approved the Fifteenth Amendment in 1869. It barred all states from denying African American males the right to vote "on account of race, color, or previous condition of servitude."

Some African Americans said the amendment was too weak. It did not prevent states from requiring voters to own property or pay a voting tax. The amendment took effect in 1870, after three fourths of the states gave their approval.

**The Ku Klux Klan** Angry at being shut out of power, some whites resorted to violence. They created secret societies to terrorize African Americans and their white allies.

The best-known secret society was the Ku Klux Klan. Its members donned white robes with hoods that hid their faces. Klansmen rode by night to the homes of African American voters, shouting threats and burning wooden crosses. If threats failed, the Klan would whip, torture, shoot, or hang African Americans and white Republicans. Klan violence took hundreds of lives during the election of 1868.

The terror went on even after Congress responded with new laws. The Ku Klux Klan Acts of 1870 and 1871 barred the use of force against voters. Although the original Klan dissolved, new groups took its place. In the face of the terrorism, voting by African Americans declined. The stage was set for the end of Reconstruction.

✓Checkpoint **What were the key elements of Radical Reconstruction?**

⭐ **Looking Back and Ahead** Although Reconstruction guaranteed rights to more Americans, huge challenges remained. In the next section, you will learn more about the process of rebuilding the South. You will also learn that as time went on, Americans became less interested in Reconstruction. This set the scene for a return of power to former Confederates.

**Terror and Violence**
To spread terror, Ku Klux Klan members wore hoods like the one above when they attacked their victims. They also left miniature coffins as warnings. **Critical Thinking: *Draw Conclusions*** *Why do you think the hoods helped spread terror?*

---

Section 2 | **Check Your Progress**

**Progress Monitoring** 🔍nline
**For:** Self-test with instant help
**Visit:** PHSchool.com
**Web Code:** mya-5122

**Comprehension and Critical Thinking**

1. **(a) Recall** Which amendment guaranteed African Americans the right to vote: the Thirteenth, Fourteenth, or Fifteenth?
   **(b) Apply Information** How did each of these three amendments help to expand democracy?

2. **(a) Recall** What was the Ku Klux Klan?
   **(b) Evaluate Information** Why do you think the Klan was not formed before the Civil War?

**Reading Skill**

3. **Analyze Proposals** In 1867, the Radical Republicans in Congress proposed the Reconstruction Act. What actions did this proposal involve?

**Vocabulary *Builder***
Complete each of the following sentences so that the second part clearly shows your understanding of the key term.

4. Radical Republicans in the House of Representatives tried to remove the President by impeachment, which is _____.

5. Former Confederates wanted to control the lives of freedmen through black codes, which were _____.

**Writing**

6. Rewrite the following passage to correct the grammar, spelling, and punctuation errors that you find. **Passage:** President Johnson wanting to show mercy to the defeated confederacy. Many of the republicans in Congress, however, opposed him. Because they wanted to protect the freedman. This conflict led congress to held impeachment hearings.

## Objectives

1. Explain why support for Reconstruction declined.
2. Describe how African Americans in the South lost many newly gained rights.
3. Describe the sharecropping system and how it trapped many in a cycle of poverty.
4. Identify the signs that the South began to develop a stronger economy by the 1880s.

## Prepare to Read

### Reading Skill

**Evaluate Proposals** When you read a proposal, ask yourself: Is the proposal likely to work as a way of advancing its goal?

### Vocabulary *Builder*

**High-Use Words**

**factor**, p. 558

**inferior**, p. 561

**Key Terms and People**

poll tax, p. 560

literacy test, p. 560

grandfather clause, p. 560

segregation, p. 560

Homer Plessy, p. 561

sharecropper, p. 561

---

**Background Knowledge** You have read how Reconstruction brought both positive change and turmoil to the South. In this section, you will learn how Reconstruction's end led to new hardships for African Americans in the South.

## Reconstruction's Conclusion

**Main Idea**
A deal between President Hayes and southern Democrats led to the end of Reconstruction.

Support for Radical Republicans declined as Americans began to forget the Civil War and focus on bettering their own lives. Scandals within President Grant's administration played an important role. Grant made poor appointments to public offices, often appointing personal friends. Many of the appointees proved to be corrupt. Although Grant himself had no part in the corruption that took place, his reputation suffered. Grant won reelection in 1872, but many northerners lost faith in the Republicans and their policies.

**Self-rule for the South** Meanwhile, many people in both North and South were calling for the withdrawal of federal troops and full amnesty for former Confederates. Starting with Virginia in 1869, opponents of Republicans began to take back the South, state by state. Slowly, they chipped away at the rights of African Americans.

**Vocabulary *Builder***
factor (FAK tor) *n.* condition or quality that causes something else to happen

In some states, campaigns of terror by secret societies were a major factor in restoring their power. By 1874, Republicans had lost control of all but three southern states. By 1877, Democrats controlled those, too.

**The Election of 1876** The end of Reconstruction was a direct result of the presidential election of 1876. Because of disputes over election returns, the choice of the President was decided by

Congress. There, a deal between the Republicans and Democrats settled the election—and sealed the fate of Reconstruction.

The candidates in 1876 were Rutherford B. Hayes of Ohio for the Republicans and Samuel J. Tilden of New York for the Democrats. The Republicans said they would continue Reconstruction, and the Democrats said they would end it.

Tilden won the popular vote by 250,000 votes. However, 20 electoral votes were in dispute. Without them, Tilden fell one vote short of the 185 needed to win in the electoral college.

To resolve the issue, Congress appointed a special commission of 15 members. Most of them were Republicans. The commission gave all 20 electoral votes to Hayes. Rather than fight the decision in Congress, Democrats agreed to accept it. Hayes had privately told them that he would end Reconstruction. Once in office, Hayes removed all federal troops from the South.

**Evaluate Proposals**
What proposal did Hayes make to the Democrats in order to end their opposition? How did this proposal meet the goals of both the Democrats and Republicans?

☑ **Checkpoint**  **What factors contributed to the end of Reconstruction?**

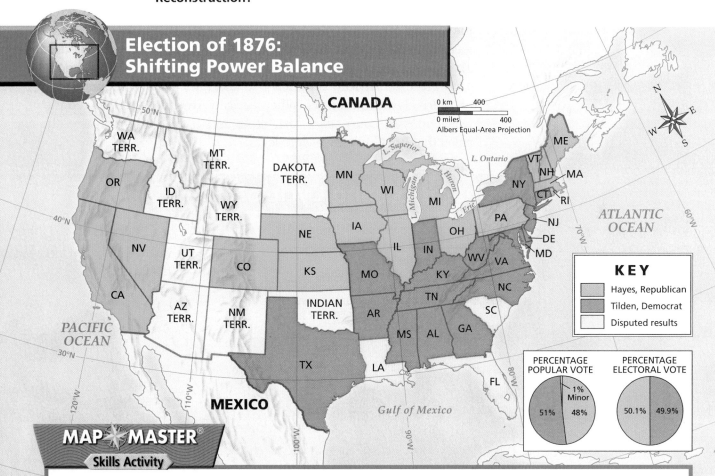

## Election of 1876: Shifting Power Balance

0 km  400
0 miles  400
Albers Equal-Area Projection

**KEY**

| | Hayes, Republican |
| | Tilden, Democrat |
| | Disputed results |

PERCENTAGE POPULAR VOTE — 51%  48%  1% Minor

PERCENTAGE ELECTORAL VOTE — 50.1%  49.9%

**MAP✷MASTER®**
**Skills Activity**

Although Samuel Tilden won the popular vote, Rutherford B. Hayes was declared the winner in the election.

**(a)** Read a Map Key  In which region did Tilden have the most support?

**(b)** Draw Conclusions  Based on this map, do you think the Civil War ended sectionalism? Explain.

**MapMaster ●nline**

**For:** Interactive map
**Visit:** PHSchool.com
**Web Code:** myp-5123

# African Americans Lose Rights

With the end of Reconstruction, African Americans began to lose their remaining political and civil rights in the South. Southern whites used a variety of techniques to stop African Americans from voting. They passed laws that applied to whites and African Americans but were enforced mainly against African Americans.

One such law imposed a **poll tax**—a personal tax to be paid before voting. This kept a few poor whites and many poor freedmen from voting. Another law required voters to pass a **literacy test,** or a test to see if a person can read and write. In this case, voters were required to read a section of the Constitution and explain it.

However, a grandfather clause allowed illiterate white males to vote. The **grandfather clause** was a provision that allowed a voter to avoid a literacy test if his father or grandfather had been eligible to vote on January 1, 1867. Because no African American in the South could vote before 1868, nearly all were denied the right to vote.

Southern states created a network of laws requiring **segregation,** or enforced separation of races. These so-called Jim Crow laws barred the mixing of races in almost every aspect of life. Blacks and whites were born in separate hospitals and buried in separate cemeteries. The laws decreed separate playgrounds, restaurants, and schools. They required African Americans to take back seats or separate cars on railroads and streetcars. When African Americans challenged the restrictions in court, they lost. State and local courts consistently ruled that Jim Crow laws were legal.

## Sharecropping Cycle of Poverty

**Planting the crop**
Landowners give the sharecropper land, seed, and tools in exchange for a share in the crop. Sharecroppers buy goods and supplies from the landowner on credit.

1

In 1896, the U.S. Supreme Court upheld segregation laws. Homer Plessy had been arrested for sitting in a coach marked "for whites only." In the case of *Plessy* v. *Ferguson,* the Court ruled in favor of a Louisiana law requiring segregated railroad cars. The Court said a law could require "separate" facilities, so long as they were "equal."

This "separate but equal" rule was in effect until the 1950s. In fact, facilities for African Americans were rarely equal. For example, public schools for African Americans were almost always <u>inferior</u> to schools for whites.

☑Checkpoint **What methods did southern states use to deprive African Americans of their rights?**

## A Cycle of Poverty

At emancipation, many freedmen owned little more than the clothes they wore. Poverty forced many African Americans, as well as poor whites, to become sharecroppers. A **sharecropper** is a laborer who works the land for the farmer who owns it, in exchange for a share of the value of the crop.

The landlord supplied living quarters, tools, seed, and food on credit. At harvest time, the landlord sold the crop and tallied up how much went to the sharecroppers. Often, especially in years of low crop prices or bad harvests, the sharecroppers' share was not enough to cover what they owed the landlord for rent and supplies. As a result, most sharecroppers became locked into a cycle of debt.

**Vocabulary** *Builder*
<u>inferior</u> (ihn FIR ee uhr) *adj.* of lower rank or status, or of poorer quality

**Main Idea**
Freedmen farmers were forced into a cycle of poverty nearly impossible to escape.

**History** *Interactive*
**Explore the Sharecropping Cycle**
**Visit:** PHSchool.com
**Web Code:** myp-5127

Farming land they did not own, sharecroppers were locked in a cycle of debt, as shown by the illustration. **Critical Thinking: Draw Conclusions** *Why was it hard for sharecroppers to escape the debt cycle?*

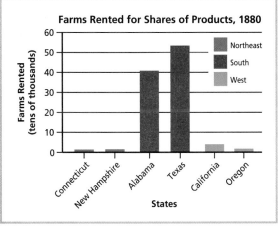

**2** **Harvesting the crop and settling accounts** The sharecropper gives the landowner his crop. Landowner sells it and gives the tenant his share, minus the amount owed at the company store.

**3** **Cycle of debt** After a year of hard work, the sharecroppers often owed more than they had earned and had no choice but to offer the landlord a greater percentage of next year's crop.

**Farms Rented for Shares of Products, 1880**

Farms Rented (tens of thousands)

Legend: Northeast, South, West

| States | Connecticut | New Hampshire | Alabama | Texas | California | Oregon |
|--------|-------------|---------------|---------|-------|------------|--------|

*Source: Inter-university Consortium for Political and Social Research*

# Links Across Time

**1963** Dr. Martin Luther King, Jr., speaks to Americans in Washington, D.C.

## Fighting for Civil Rights

**1896** In *Plessy* v. *Ferguson*, the Supreme Court upheld segregation laws in the South. These restrictions continued for more than 50 years.

**1950s–1960s** Some Americans launched a campaign to bring equal rights to African Americans. This civil rights movement used marches, petitions, and other public actions to end discrimination in education, use of public facilities, and voting.

## Link to Today  Online

**Civil Rights Today** Did the civil rights movement win equal rights for all Americans? Not everyone agrees. Go online to find out more about recent developments in civil rights.

**For:** Civil rights in the news
**Visit:** PHSchool.com
**Web Code:** myc-5123

---

Opportunities dwindled for African Americans in southern towns and cities, too. African American artisans who had been able to find skilled jobs during Reconstruction increasingly found such jobs closed to them. Those with some education could become schoolteachers, lawyers, or preachers in the African American community. But most urban African Americans had to take whatever menial job they could find.

✓**Checkpoint** **How did many freedmen and whites become locked in a cycle of poverty?**

## Industrial Growth

**Main Idea**
By the 1880s, the South had begun to develop its own resources and industries.

It would be a long process, but during Reconstruction the South's economy began to recover. By the 1880s, new industries appeared. Southerners hailed a "New South," based on industrial growth.

The first element of the South's economy to begin recovery was agriculture. Cotton production, which had lagged during the war, quickly revived. By 1875, it was setting new records. Planters put more land into tobacco production, and output grew.

Southern investors started or expanded industries to turn raw materials into finished products. The textile industry came to play an important role in the southern economy.

The South had natural resources in abundance, but it had done little to develop them in the past. Atlanta newspaper editor Henry Grady described the funeral of a man from Georgia as follows:

❝They buried him in the heart of a pine forest, and yet the pine coffin was imported from Cincinnati. They buried him within touch of an iron mine, and yet the nails in his coffin and the iron in the shovel that dug his grave were imported from Pittsburgh.❞

—Henry Grady to the Bay State Club of Boston, 1889

The South began to develop its own resources. New mills and factories grew up to use the South's iron, timber, and oil. Lumber mills and furniture factories processed yellow pine and hardwoods from southern forests.

Southern leaders took great pride in the region's progress. They spoke of a "New South" that was no longer dependent on "King Cotton." An industrial age was underway, although the North was still far more industrialized.

Factory in the "New South"

☑Checkpoint  **What was the "New South" that was emerging by 1900?**

⭐ **Looking Back and Ahead** When Reconstruction ended in 1877, its record showed many successes and some failures. Most importantly, all African Americans were finally citizens. Laws passed during Reconstruction, such as the Fourteenth Amendment, became the basis of the civil rights movement that took place almost 100 years later.

---

Section 3 | **Check Your Progress**

**Progress Monitoring** ⬤nline

**For:** Self-test with instant help
**Visit:** PHSchool.com
**Web Code:** mya-5123

**Comprehension and Critical Thinking**

1. **(a) Identify** Who were sharecroppers? How did they differ from landowners?
   **(b) Draw Conclusions** Why did so many sharecroppers live in poverty?

2. **(a) Recall** What is segregation?
   **(b) Analyze Cause and Effect** How did *Plessy* v. *Ferguson* make the fight against segregation more difficult?

**Reading Skill**

3. **Evaluate Proposals** In *Plessy* v. *Ferguson*, the Supreme Court proposed the idea of "separate but equal" facilities. Do you think this idea meets the goal of ensuring equal rights?

**Vocabulary Builder**

Complete each of the following sentences so that the second part clearly shows your understanding of the key term.

4. African Americans and whites had to pay a poll tax before _____.

5. Because of laws in the South requiring segregation, African Americans and whites _____.

**Writing**

6. Rewrite the following passage to correct the errors. **Passage:** The 1876 presidential election decided by a special commission. Samuel J. Tilden a democrat won the Popular vote over republican Rutherford B. Hayes. However, their were 20 disputed electorial votes. A special commission made an agreement with the democrats.

Thematic maps focus on special topics, such as food products, physical features, or political boundaries. Information presented in a visual way is easier to understand and absorb. One type of thematic map shows the migration or movement of people within a particular area.

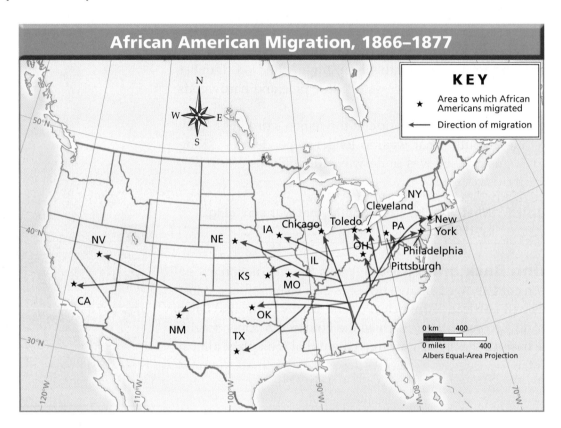

### African American Migration, 1866–1877

**KEY**

★ Area to which African Americans migrated

← Direction of migration

## Learn the Skill

*Use these steps to learn how to trace migrations on maps.*

1. **Identify the subject of the map.** Read the title of the map. Look for dates that identify the time period.

2. **Look at the map key.** The map key explains special symbols and colors used on the map.

3. **Determine direction.** To trace the route of a migration, use the direction arrows on the compass rose to identify north, south, east, and west. Then, identify the direction or directions of the route.

4. **Make a generalization.** Use the information on the map to make a general statement about the historic migration.

## Practice the Skill

*Answer the following questions about the map on this page.*

1. **Identify the subject of the map.** What is the title of the map?

2. **Look at the map key.** What does the star symbol show?

3. **Determine direction.** In which direction did African Americans travel to migrate to New York?

4. **Make a generalization.** In general, to which areas of the country did African Americans migrate during Reconstruction?

## Apply the Skill

*See the Review and Assessment at the end of this chapter.*

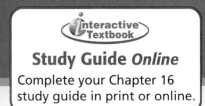

**Study Guide *Online***
Complete your Chapter 16
study guide in print or online.

## Chapter Summary

### Section 1
### Rebuilding the Nation

- The South faced major economic and social challenges at the end of the Civil War.
- Reconstruction plans and programs like the Freedmen's Bureau were designed to rebuild the South.
- The death of Abraham Lincoln threatened lenient plans for Reconstruction.

### Section 2
### The Battle Over Reconstruction

- President Andrew Johnson and the Radical Republicans clashed over Reconstruction plans.
- Conflict over Reconstruction led to Andrew Johnson's impeachment.
- During Reconstruction, African American males gained the right to vote. Republicans came to power in each southern state.

### Section 3
### The End of Reconstruction

- With the end of Reconstruction, African Americans in the South lost many rights they had gained after the Civil War.
- Many African Americans and poor whites were forced to become sharecroppers.
- The South's agriculture revived, and its industries expanded.

## Key Concepts

These notes will help you prepare for questions about key concepts.

### Freedmen Rights and Restrictions

**Rights**
- Were granted freedom from slavery
- Were given citizenship and the right to vote
- Could no longer be legally discriminated against

**Restrictions**
- Black codes
- Voting limited by laws and violence
- Legal segregation

### The Civil War Amendments

**Amendment 13**
- Abolished slavery

**Amendment 14**
- Defined citizenship to include African Americans
- Guaranteed equal protection under the law

**Amendment 15**
- Guaranteed voting rights

### Successes and Failures of Reconstruction

**Successes**
- The Union was restored, and the South began rebuilding.
- African Americans gained the right to vote.
- African Americans gained legal rights to equal treatment.

**Failures**
- Southern governments kept African Americans from voting.
- Federal troops were unable to stop the violence against African Americans.

## Vocabulary *Builder*

### Key Terms

Fill in the blanks with the correct key terms.

1. _____ were people who had been enslaved before emancipation.

2. Northerners who moved south after the Civil War were sometimes called _____.

3. Southern states gave _____, which required voters to read and explain part of the Constitution.

4. A _____ farmed land in return for a portion of the value of the crop.

## Comprehension and Critical Thinking

5. **(a) Recall** How did the Wade-Davis Bill differ from Lincoln's plan for reuniting the country?
   **(b) Make Predictions** How do you think southerners would have reacted to Reconstruction if Lincoln's plan had been followed?

6. **(a) Recall** How did Johnson and the Radicals come into conflict?
   **(b) Analyze Cause and Effect** How effective do you think Johnson was after the failure of the impeachment process?

7. **(a) Recall** What right is guaranteed by the Fifteenth Amendment?
   **(b) Interpret Art** How does the painting *His First Vote* (below) reflect how the Fifteenth Amendment affected African Americans?

8. **(a) Recall** How did the Freedman's Bureau help African Americans after the Civil War?
   **(b) Make Predictions** Which of the actions of the Freedmen's Bureau has probably had the longest lasting impact on African Americans? How?

9. **(a) Recall** What were the terms of the compromise that gave Rutherford B. Hayes the presidency in 1876?
   **(b) Draw Conclusions** How were African Americans in the South affected by this compromise?

## History Reading Skill

10. **Analyze and Evaluate Proposals** Review what you have read about the conflict between Johnson and Radical Republicans. What did each side propose? Which proposal makes the most sense to you? Explain.

## Writing

11. **Write an essay on the following topic:**
   Explain how events and developments during Reconstruction highlighted differences between North and South, even as the two tried to reunite.

   **Your essay should:**
   • state a thesis or purpose for writing;
   • explain the subject you are writing about;
   • offer evidence, examples, or details to support your explanation;
   • conclude with a short summary of your main points.

12. **Write a Narrative:**
   Imagine you are Hiram Revels. Write a narrative describing your first days in the Senate.

## Skills for Life

### Analyze a Migration Map

Use the map in the Skills for Life feature to answer the questions that follow.

13. What time period is covered in this map?

14. What does the arrow symbol show?

15. In which direction did African Americans travel to migrate to Oklahoma and New Mexico?

16. Based on the information in the map, what decision did many African Americans make during Reconstruction?

# Test Yourself

**Refer to the quotation below to answer Question 1.**

> "A system of oppression so rank that nothing could make it seem small except the fact that [African Americans] had already been ground under it for a century and a half."

**1. Which system does this quotation refer to?**

- **A** amnesty
- **B** Reconstruction
- **C** sharecropping
- **D** segregation

**2. How did African Americans benefit from the passage of the Fourteenth Amendment?**

- **A** Their right to vote was protected.
- **B** They became citizens.
- **C** They were given land.
- **D** They no longer had to pass literacy tests.

**3. A chief goal of the Freedmen's Bureau was to promote**

- **A** abolition.
- **B** industrial growth.
- **C** education.
- **D** segregation.

# Document-Based Questions

**Task:** Look at Documents 1 and 2, and answer their accompanying questions. Then, use the documents and your knowledge of history to complete the following writing assignment:

> Write a two-paragraph essay about the goals and methods of the Ku Klux Klan. Using specific details, draw a conclusion about whether Document 1 or Document 2 gives a more accurate description of the Klan.

**Document 1:** The "Organization and Principles" of the Ku Klux Klan, stated below, was written in 1868. It describes the goals of the Klan. *What does the Klan say is its attitude toward violence?*

> "This is an institution of chivalry, humanity, mercy, and patriotism; embodying in its genius and its principles all that is chivalric in conduct, noble in sentiment, generous in manhood, and patriotic in purpose; its peculiar objects being:
>
> First, to protect the weak, the innocent, and the defenseless from the [insults], wrongs, and outrages of the lawless, the violent, and the brutal; to relieve the injured and oppressed. . . .
>
> *Questions to be asked each [Klan] candidate:*
>
> - Are you in favor of a white man's government in this country? . . ."

**Document 2:** This political cartoon was published in a northern magazine in 1874. *Describe what has happened to the African American family.*

# Writing Workshop

## Research Paper

### ▶ Introduction

In a research paper, you gather information about a subject from several different sources. Then, you tie this information together with a single unifying idea and present it to your readers. A research paper should have the following characteristics:

- an interesting topic about which you need to find outside information

- information about that topic drawn from several different sources

- a thesis statement expressing an idea about the topic, based on the research

- information that identifies the sources used

**Assignment** On the following pages, you will learn how to plan, collect information for, and write a research paper. You will get step-by-step instructions. Each step will include an example from research about the Battle of Gettysburg.

Read the instructions and the examples. Then, follow each step to plan a research paper.

> **Write a research paper about a Civil War battle of your choice.**

For a review of the steps in the writing process, see the **Historian's Toolkit,** *Write Like a Historian.*

### ▶ Planning Your Research

**Find a research subject.** Start by listing subjects that interest you. Think about which of these subjects are likely to have information that you can readily find. Then, write a few questions you would like to answer about each subject.

**Narrow your topic.** One of the most important steps in writing a research paper is narrowing your topic to something you can cover in the space you have. If you have access to the Internet, you can use it to help you narrow your topic.

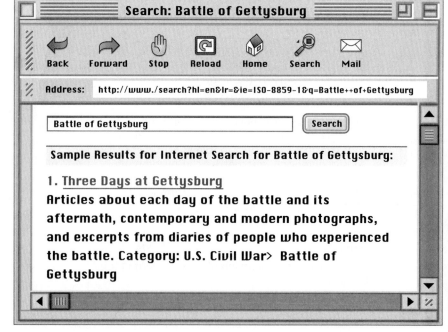

# ▶ Doing Your Research

**Find your sources.** A research paper involves consulting outside sources as you seek information you do not already have. Look for more recent sources to avoid relying on information that is out of date. Using library and Internet resources, keep researching until you have five good sources of information about your narrowed topic.

**Take notes from your sources.** As you read a source, write down and define key terms. Summarize longer passages and paraphrase important ideas, restating them in your own words. When you come across quotations you want to use, copy them exactly and identify their sources. Using someone else's words as if they were your own is called plagiarism, which is dishonest and can result in severe penalties.

**Keep track of your sources.** You need to identify each source that you use, whether the source is an encyclopedia, a book, a newspaper, a magazine, a television program, or an Internet site. In your final paper, you will create a bibliography that identifies all the sources you used.

# ▶ Writing Your Research Paper

**Create a working thesis.** After you review your notes, write a sentence that states the main idea of your paper.

**Plan your organization.** Depending on your topic, you can use various methods to organize your research paper. If you are discussing two items, one approach would be to compare and contrast them. If you are focusing on a complex event or a process, you could use a chronological organization.

> **Sample working thesis:**
> The Battle of Gettysburg consisted of a series of mistakes on the part of both North and South. Perhaps the greatest and most horrendous mistake of them all was Pickett's Charge.

**Create an outline.** Creating an outline can help you when you have a great deal of material to present. Decide the order that you think best suits your information and your thesis. Here is a portion of an outline for a research paper about Pickett's Charge at the Battle of Gettysburg.

> **Part of sample outline**
>
> I. Before Pickett's Charge
>   A. Status of Battle of Gettysburg on the morning of July 3
>   B. Lee's need to have decisive attack
>   C. Preparing Pickett's, Armistead's and Trimble's divisions
>     1. Pickett's was fullest division
>     2. Armistead and Trimble had lost many more men

# Writing Workshop *continued*

**Write your introduction.** Write an introductory paragraph that grips your audience's attention. Set up your research topic, indicating what aspects of the topic you will cover. Lead up to your thesis statement.

**Support your thesis with examples and details.** Now write the body of your paper, presenting the best information that you found in your research. Writing a topic sentence for each paragraph will help you stay on target as you write. Keep the relationships between your ideas clear with transitions.

**Write a strong conclusion.** In your final paragraph, review the ground you have covered. Find a lively or powerful way to say what you found most interesting, moving, or surprising in what you learned.

## ▶ Giving Credit to Your Sources

You must identify the sources you use to support your ideas. Whenever you present statistics, little-known facts, direct quotations, or paraphrases of others' views, you need to give credit to the source of the information—both within your paper and in a bibliography listing the sources you used at the end of the paper.

**Include citations within the paper.** You have a few options for identifying sources within your paper. You can identify the source in parentheses. You can use a number corresponding to a footnote at the bottom of the page or an endnote at the end of the paper.

**List your sources in a bibliography.** At the end of your paper, you need to list the sources that you used. List them in alphabetical order by author, using accepted formats.

## ▶ Revising Your Research Paper

After completing your draft, read it again carefully, looking for ways to make your writing better. Here are questions to ask yourself.

---

### Sample introduction

By the morning of July 3, 1863, the Battle of Gettysburg was two days old, and both armies were exhausted. The South had penetrated Northern defenses as far as Cemetery Ridge. The Union and Confederate armies were spread out over a large battlefield of rolling hills, and the ground in some places did not allow much visibility. Both sides had already made a number of mistakes in the two previous days of battle—mistaking the strength of the enemy and misrepresenting each other's positions. Perhaps the greatest, and most heroic, mistake of all was the one that was about to happen: the charge by General George Pickett, who led 15,000 Confederate soldiers with bayonets against the Union position on Cemetery Ridge.

### Sample conclusion

Pickett's Charge is remembered as one of the most noble and tragic moments in military history. The Confederate soldiers fought bravely, but were no match for the Union weapons. Robert E. Lee had miscalculated, and his army paid the price. They staggered away from Gettysburg and never reached as far into the North again. The Civil War went on for almost two more years, but the tide had turned against the South. It turned on the heroic but mistaken charge by George Pickett and his men.

## Revise to heighten interest and clarify research

- Does the first paragraph capture the reader's attention?
- Have you presented your information in the most compelling order?
- Are the relationships between ideas clear? Can you add any transitions to make them clearer?

## Revise to meet written English-language conventions

- Are all sentences complete, with a subject and a verb?
- Are all the words spelled correctly?
- Are all proper nouns capitalized, including names of people and places?
- Did you use proper punctuation?

## Revise to meet research-paper conventions

- Have you properly identified all of your sources?
- Are all quotations clearly marked, with credit given to the original writer or speaker?
- Is the bibliography complete and correctly formatted?

## ▶ Rubric for Self-Assessment

*Evaluate your research paper using the following rating scale:*

|  | Score 4 | Score 3 | Score 2 | Score 1 |
|---|---|---|---|---|
| **Topic** | Appropriate for a research paper, since it requires outside research; well focused and suits the scope of the paper | Appropriate for a research paper, requiring outside research; reasonably focused but may be a little too broad or too narrow | Barely appropriate for a research paper; not well focused, since it is too broad or too narrow | Not appropriate for a research paper; not focused at all |
| **Organization** | Uses order of importance correctly and makes the relationships between the items and the reasons for their relative importance clear | Uses order of importance and makes most of the reasons for their relative importance clear | Organization not suited to the topic | Shows lack of organizational strategy |
| **Presentation** | Develops ideas with relevant facts, details, or examples; links all information to the issue being analyzed | Develops most ideas with facts, details, or examples; links most information to the issue being analyzed | Does not give most ideas in depth; does not link some information to the issue being analyzed | Does not provide facts, details, or examples to support ideas |
| **Use of Language** | Varies sentence structure and vocabulary successfully; includes no or very few mechanical errors | Uses some variety in sentence structure and vocabulary; includes few mechanical errors | Uses the same types of sentences without varying them; does not vary vocabulary; includes many mechanical errors | Writes incomplete sentences; uses language poorly; sounds confused; includes many mechanical errors |

**Plains Farm Family** Out on the Great Plains, settlers faced enormous challenges, including lack of schools and medical care. Families built their homes from sod, tightknit bricks of dirt and roots. Above all, Plains families had to face the terrible isolation of the western prairies.

## 1880s

### Think Like a Historian

As you read this unit, think about this question: *How did the industrialization of the United States change the economy, society, and politics of the nation?*

**Bull Moose** Denied the Republican nomination for President in 1912, Theodore Roosevelt campaigned vigorously under the banner of the Bull Moose Party. Democrat Woodrow Wilson won the election.

## 1912

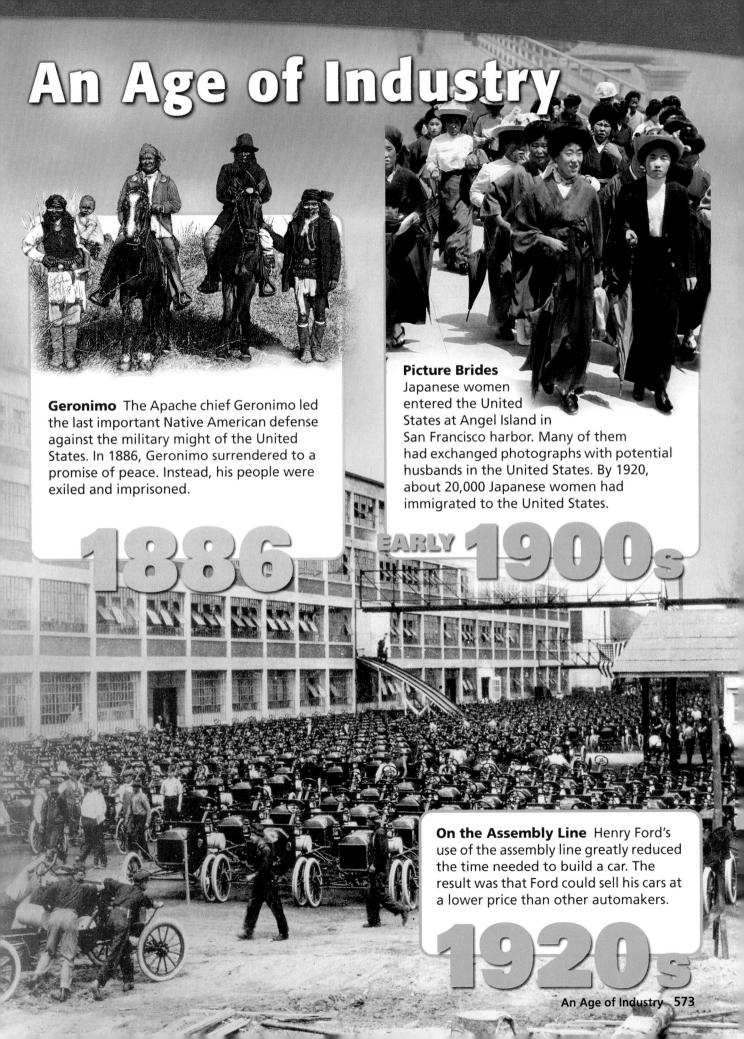

# An Age of Industry

**Geronimo** The Apache chief Geronimo led the last important Native American defense against the military might of the United States. In 1886, Geronimo surrendered to a promise of peace. Instead, his people were exiled and imprisoned.

**1886**

**Picture Brides** Japanese women entered the United States at Angel Island in San Francisco harbor. Many of them had exchanged photographs with potential husbands in the United States. By 1920, about 20,000 Japanese women had immigrated to the United States.

**EARLY 1900s**

**On the Assembly Line** Henry Ford's use of the assembly line greatly reduced the time needed to build a car. The result was that Ford could sell his cars at a lower price than other automakers.

**1920s**

## Chapter Preview

After the Civil War, Americans moved west in greater numbers. Miners, ranchers, and farmers settled on the Great Plains, changing the region forever. Meanwhile, Native Americans on the western lands struggled to keep their homelands.

| | ✓ **What You Will Learn** |
|---|---|
| **Section 1**<br>**Mining and Railroads**<br>Pages 578–581 | Miners and railroad builders helped bring new settlers to the West and link it to the rest of the nation. |
| **Section 2**<br>**Native Americans Struggle to Survive**<br>Pages 584–589 | As settlers poured into the West, Native Americans struggled to maintain their way of life. |
| **Section 3**<br>**The Cattle Kingdom**<br>Pages 590–594 | An extensive cattle industry developed in the West to provide meat for the nation. |
| **Section 4**<br>**Farming in the West**<br>Pages 595–599 | Many western settlers took up farming and adapted their lives to meet many new challenges. |

**U.S. Events**

**1862**
Congress passes Homestead Act.

**1869**
Transcontinental railroad is completed.

1860  1868  1876

**World Events**

**1864** Taiping Rebellion in China ends.

**1869** Suez Canal opens.

**Quick View Video**
View the chapter video
for a quick preview of the
main ideas.

Cowhands drove cattle long distances
along dusty trails to reach railroad
towns where the cattle could be
shipped east.

**1876**
Sioux defeat Custer's
army at Little Big Horn.

**1887**
Dawes Act breaks up
Native American
tribal lands.

**1889**
Oklahoma
opens to
homesteaders.

**1892**
Populist Party
organizes at
national level.

1876

1884

1892

**1885** Indian National
Congress forms to
seek self-rule for India.

**1888** Brazil
bans slavery.

**History Reading Skill** Use Context Clues to Verify Meaning

**What was life like for Sioux families in the late 1800s?**

In this chapter, you will practice using context clues to define unfamiliar words. Read the following account by Chief Standing Bear in which he describes the tasks and daily activities of a typical Lakota Sioux family. The side notes suggest ways to use context clues to define unfamiliar words.

**Primary Source**

The Lakota Sioux were a large Plains Indian culture. They lived in tepees and hunted buffalo as their way of life. The buffalo provided many items for the Sioux, from clothing to shelter to tools.

*Split for thread* describes the use of the unfamiliar word sinew.

**Unfamiliar word**

Sinew was split for thread, coarse strands for heavy work and medium fine or very fine strands for decorative work, then folded into little bundles and placed in a sewing kit. . . .

When the men came home from the hunt there were skins to be cleaned and tanned. . . . From rawhide were made **Unfamiliar word** moccasin soles, bags and trunks for holding ceremonial garments, headdresses, and other articles to be kept in neatness and order. . . .

Here, examples give you information about the meaning of the unfamiliar word rawhide.

Grandmother, next to mother, was the most important person in the home. . . . As a storyteller, she was a delight. . . . Her sense of humor was keen, . . . she laughed as readily **Unfamiliar word** as we. . . .

This phrase defines the unfamiliar word keen as it applies to sense of humor.

— Chief Standing Bear, *Cry of the Thunderbird: The American Indian's Own Story*

**Use Context Clues to Verify Meaning**

- Restatements use different language to restate a word's meaning. Definitions tell you what a word means. Examples help you piece together a word's meaning by showing how the word is used.
- Also, look for comparison or contrast clues, in which unfamiliar words are described as similar to or different from familiar terms.

**Document-Based Questions**

1. Who wrote this account?
2. What were some of the daily activities of a Lakota Sioux family?
3. How do you think the roles of men and women in the family differed?

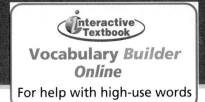

Vocabulary Builder Online
For help with high-use words

# Vocabulary *Builder*

## Previewing High-Use Academic Words

| High-Use Word | Definition | Sample History Sentence |
|---|---|---|
| **immigrate** (IHM mah grayt) (Section 1, p. 581) | **v.** to move to a foreign region or country | Thousands of Chinese immigrated to the United States to work on western railroads. |
| **manual** (MAN yoo ahl) (Section 1, p. 581) | **adj.** involving work done by hand | The miners were exhausted after ten hours of manual labor. |
| **transform** (trans FORM) (Section 2, p. 584) | **v.** to change in appearance or form; to change the condition of something | The arrival of horses in Spanish times transformed the lives of Native Americans. |
| **violate** (VĪ ah layt) (Section 2, p. 589) | **v.** to break a rule or law; to disrespect; to disturb | Time after time, the government violated treaties it had made with Native Americans. |
| **persist** (per SIHST) (Section 3, p. 591) | **v.** to endure; to continue in the face of difficulty | Farmers on the frontier persisted despite the hardships they faced. |
| **myth** (mihth) (Section 3, p. 593) | **n.** story or legend; imaginary object; invented story | In discussing the "Wild West," it is difficult to separate fact from myth. |
| **reside** (ree ZĪD) (Section 4, p. 595) | **v.** to live (in or at); to dwell for a while; to exist (in) | The rancher resided in a large house with a view of distant mountains. |
| **surplus** (SER pluhs) (Section 4, p. 598) | **n.** excess; quantity that is left over | The company's expenses were very high that year; there was no surplus to invest in research. |

## Previewing Key Terms and People

Sitting Bull

vigilante, p. 580
subsidy, p. 580
transcontinental railroad, p. 581
travois, p. 584
tepee, p. 584
reservation, p. 586
Sitting Bull, p. 586

open range, p. 590
cattle drive, p. 590
vaquero, p. 592
cow town, p. 592
cattle kingdom, p. 593
homesteader, p. 595
sod, p. 596

sodbuster, p. 596
sooner, p. 598
grange, p. 598
farm cooperative, p. 598
inflation, p. 599
William Jennings Bryan, p. 599

**The West Transformed  577**

# Mining and Railroads

## Objectives

1. Explain how the discovery of gold and silver affected the West.

2. Describe life in the western mining towns.

3. Summarize how railroads spread and helped the West to develop.

## Prepare to Read

 **Reading Skill**

**Use Definition Clues** As you read about history, you will come across unfamiliar words. In this textbook, definitions for many unfamiliar words are included in the text that surrounds the word. When you read a word that you do not know, look at nearby sentences. The unfamiliar word may be repeated and defined.

## Vocabulary *Builder*

**High-Use Words**

immigrate, p. 581

manual, p. 581

**Key Terms**

vigilante, p. 580

subsidy, p. 580

transcontinental railroad, p. 581

⭐ **Background Knowledge** With the Civil War over, the nation turned its attention to its western frontier. This stretched from the Mississippi River to the Pacific Ocean. The frontier had prairies, mountains, and forests. Even though Americans thought of it as unsettled, it was the home of Mexican settlers and Native Americans.

Moving west, settlers first crossed the Great Plains. Most of the Plains receives little rainfall and has few trees. Thinking that crops could not grow there, settlers called the area the Great American Desert. In this section, you will learn how railroad builders and miners made the West a vital part of the nation's economy.

**Main Idea**
Settlement of the West often came in a rush, but many boomtowns soon died out.

## Boom and Bust

In many parts of the West, settlement came in a rush. This was especially true in areas where prospectors found gold or silver. New mining towns sprang up in a flash—but many did not last long.

The gold rush of 1849 in California excited the nation. Before long, miners spread from California to the Sierra Nevada and the Rocky Mountains and to the Black Hills of the Dakota Territory.

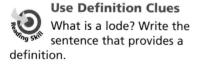

**Use Definition Clues**
What is a lode? Write the sentence that provides a definition.

**The Comstock Lode** Just before the Civil War, prospectors began searching for gold in the Sierra Nevada. In 1859, two Irish prospectors found the gold they were looking for. However, a third man, Henry Comstock, said the claim was on his land. The find became known as the Comstock Lode. A lode is a rich vein of ore.

At the Comstock Lode, a blue-tinted sand stuck to all the equipment and made the gold hard to dig out. The blue mud turned out to be loaded with silver. In fact, the silver was far more valuable than the gold. This was one of the richest silver mines in the world.

In the next 20 years, the Comstock Lode produced $300 million worth of silver and made Nevada a center of mining. A tent city near the mines grew into the boomtown of Virginia City, Nevada.

**The Boom Spreads** After the Civil War, prospectors fanned out over the West. They found valuable ores in Montana, Idaho, and Colorado. They made a gold strike in South Dakota's Black Hills. In the 1890s, a gold find drew people from all over the world to Alaska.

Although each strike caused great excitement, few prospectors got rich. The ore was deep underground and expensive to extract. Comstock gave up and sold his mining rights for $11,000 and two mules. Many other prospectors sold their claims to large mining companies. By the 1880s, western mining had become a big business.

**Boomtown Life** Tent cities like Virginia City often arose around the diggings. Soon hotels, stores, and other wood-frame buildings appeared. Mining camps quickly grew into boomtowns.

Where prospectors went, others followed. Merchants brought mule teams hauling tools, food, and clothing. Nothing was cheap in the boomtown stores. Sometimes, miners paid high prices for bottles of pure drinking water. They did not want to drink from streams that might be polluted with chemicals, like arsenic, used in mining.

Women who joined the mining boom could make a good living. Some opened restaurants. Others washed clothes or took in boarders. One woman just baked pies. In a year, she became quite wealthy.

Nearly half the miners were foreign-born. The streets of the mining towns rang with Irish accents as well as Italian, German, Spanish, Chinese, and other languages. The foreign miners often faced hostility. For example, laws restricted Chinese miners to claims abandoned by others. Mobs often drove the Chinese from towns.

**Discovery SCHOOL**

**Explore More Video**
To learn more about boomtowns and ghost towns, view the video.

**From Boomtown to Ghost Town** In the 1870s, Virginia City, Nevada, had close to 30,000 inhabitants. When the Comstock Lode ran out, Virginia City became a ghost town. Today, it is a thriving tourist attraction. **Critical Thinking: *Identify Economic Alternatives*** *Why did Virginia City become a ghost town? How did it later restore its economy?*

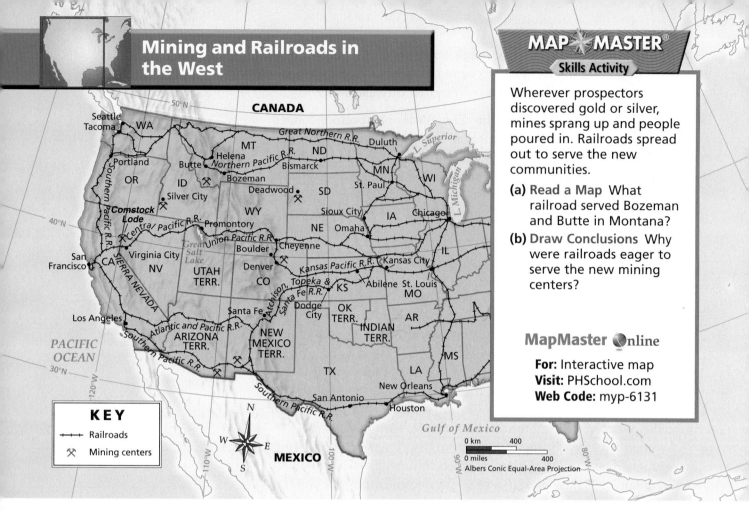

## Mining and Railroads in the West

**MAP MASTER®**

**Skills Activity**

Wherever prospectors discovered gold or silver, mines sprang up and people poured in. Railroads spread out to serve the new communities.

**(a) Read a Map** What railroad served Bozeman and Butte in Montana?

**(b) Draw Conclusions** Why were railroads eager to serve the new mining centers?

**MapMaster ◉nline**

**For:** Interactive map
**Visit:** PHSchool.com
**Web Code:** myp-6131

**KEY**
- ┼─┼─┼ Railroads
- ⚒ Mining centers

---

**Frontier Justice** Mining towns sprouted so fast that law and order were hard to find. Miners formed groups of vigilantes, or self-appointed law keepers. Such groups hunted down bandits and imposed their own rough brands of justice.

As boomtowns grew, local residents began to seek more lasting forms of government. Sheriffs, marshals, and judges replaced vigilantes. Colorado, Dakota, and Nevada organized into territories in 1861, followed by Arizona and Idaho in 1863 and Montana in 1864.

In some mining towns, all the ore was soon extracted. Mines shut down and miners moved away. With few customers, businesses failed and merchants left. Boomtowns became ghost towns.

✓**Checkpoint** **Why did boomtowns use vigilante justice?**

**Main Idea**
Backed by federal aid, railroad companies had laid tracks from coast to coast by 1869.

## The Railroad Boom

Railroads raced to lay track to the mines and boomtowns. They received generous help from the federal government.

**Aid to Railroads** Before 1860, railroad lines ended at the Mississippi River. Then, the federal government began to offer subsidies. Subsidies are grants of land or money. For every mile of track, the government gave the railroad 10 square miles of land next to the track. Railroads got more than 180 million acres, an area the size of Texas. They also received federal loans.

**Spanning the Continent** Many westerners dreamed of a transcontinental railroad, a railroad line that spanned the continent. In 1862, Leland Stanford and his partners won the right to build a line eastward from Sacramento. Their railroad was the Central Pacific. Another railroad, the Union Pacific, would build west from Omaha. When the lines met, tracks would stretch from coast to coast.

The railroads hired thousands of workers—native-born whites, Mexican Americans, and African Americans. Workers also <u>immigrated</u> to the United States from Mexico and Ireland. The Central Pacific brought 10,000 Chinese to the United States.

The work was hazardous; the pay low. Cutting through the Sierra Nevada, Chinese <u>manual</u> laborers were lashed by snow and winds. Avalanches buried weeks of work in moments and killed workers by the score. Daily progress sometimes came in inches. (For more on the building of the railroad, see the Geography and History feature.)

At last, on May 10, 1869, the two lines met at Promontory, Utah. Stanford drove the final spike into the last rail with a silver mallet.

**Effects of the Railroads** New towns sprang up in the West. People and supplies poured in. Gold and silver poured out.

Rapid population growth brought political changes. Nevada became a state in 1864; Colorado in 1876; North Dakota, South Dakota, Montana, and Washington in 1889; Idaho and Wyoming in 1890.

✔**Checkpoint** How did the railroads change the West?

☆ **Looking Back and Ahead** Gold and silver discoveries brought boomtowns to the West. Then came railroads and more settlers. In the next section, you will read how these developments affected the Native Americans who lived in the West.

**Vocabulary** *Builder*
**immigrate** (IHM mah grayt) *v.* to move to a foreign region or country

**Vocabulary** *Builder*
**manual** (MAN yoo ahl) *adj.* involving work done by hand

---

Section 1 | **Check Your Progress**

**Progress Monitoring** ⏾nline
**For:** Self-test with instant help
**Visit:** PHSchool.com
**Web Code:** mya-6131

**Comprehension and Critical Thinking**

1. **(a) Recall** In 1850, what region of the United States was considered the western frontier?
**(b) Detect Points of View** Explain how each of the following groups viewed the western frontier: Americans, Spanish settlers, Native Americans.

2. **(a) Identify** Why did the government believe it was important to extend railroad lines west?
**(b) Identify Economic Benefits** What incentives did the government offer to railroad builders to extend railroad lines westward?

**🎯 Reading Skill**

3. **Use Definition Clues** Define the term subsidies in the following context, and describe the clue you used: Congress offered generous subsidies to railroads. Subsidies are grants of land or money.

**Vocabulary** *Builder*

Read each sentence. If the sentence is true, write YES. If the sentence is not true, write NO and explain why.

4. Vigilante groups in the West were replaced by homesteaders.

5. The transcontinental railroad connected the East with the West.

**Writing**

6. Persuasive writing always centers on an opinion—an idea about which there can be disagreement. Tell whether each of the following statements expresses an opinion or states a fact. **Statements:**

   **(a)** A valuable gold strike was made in South Dakota's Black Hills.

   **(b)** The unjust treatment of foreign miners was shameful.

   **(c)** Creating a coast-to-coast railway was the most important factor in U.S. economic history.

   **(d)** Some mining camps quickly grew into boomtowns.

# Transcontinental Railroad

During the Civil War, Congress passed a bill that provided for the construction of a transcontinental railroad. The new law assigned two companies to build the railroad: the Central Pacific Railroad and the Union Pacific Railroad.

### ▼ Two Railroads

The Central Pacific headed east from Sacramento. The Union Pacific headed west from Omaha.

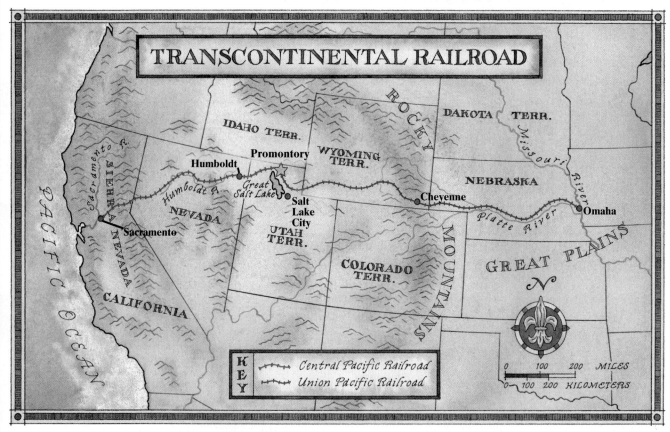

TRANSCONTINENTAL RAILROAD

**KEY**
Central Pacific Railroad
Union Pacific Railroad

### Physical Obstacles ▶

Foul weather and rugged landscapes hampered construction efforts on both lines. The Central Pacific took almost five years to cross the Sierra Nevada.

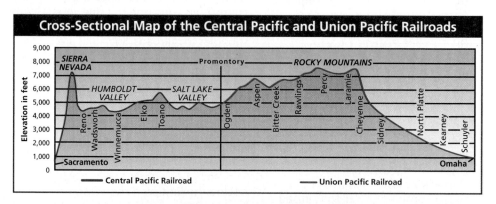

**Cross-Sectional Map of the Central Pacific and Union Pacific Railroads**

Central Pacific Railroad
Union Pacific Railroad

**▲ Blasting Through Mountains**

The Central Pacific recruited large numbers of Chinese workers to build the railroad. The workers would climb down steep cliffs in the Sierra Nevada and stuff explosives into the rocks to blast tunnels.

## Understand Effects:
# Moving West

The completion of the transcontinental railroad paved the way for increased settlement of the West. Additional railroads were built in the decades after 1869, and populations of western territories surged. Native Americans were increasingly hemmed in by steady tides of new settlers.

**History Interactive**
**Travel the Transcontinental Railroad**
Visit: PHSchool.com
Web Code: myp-6137

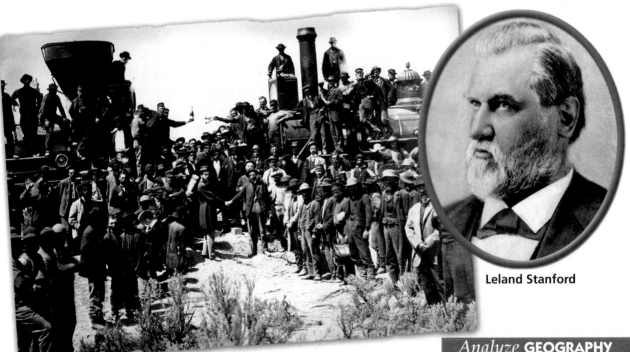

**Leland Stanford**

**▲ A Golden Spike**

With the engines No. 119 and Jupiter pulled nose to nose at Promontory, Utah, the railroads were joined by a golden spike on May 10, 1869. Leland Stanford, a railroad executive and later governor of California, supervised construction of the Central Pacific.

## Analyze GEOGRAPHY AND HISTORY

Write a paragraph describing how geography affected the construction of the transcontinental railroad. Think about the physical obstacles each railroad company faced along the way.

## Objectives

1. Describe the importance of the buffalo to Native Americans of the Plains.

2. Explain how Native Americans and settlers came into conflict.

3. Summarize the struggles of Native American groups to maintain their traditional ways of life.

4. Explain why Congress passed the Dawes Act in 1887.

### Prepare to Read

#### 🔄 Reading Skill

**Use Restatement Clues** Like a definition clue, a restatement clue tells you what an unfamiliar word means. It restates in simple language what the word means. Restatement clues often follow the unfamiliar word, linked by a comma and the word *or*. This textbook often uses restatement clues to define key terms and highlights them in blue.

#### Vocabulary *Builder*

**High-Use Words**

**transform**, p. 584

**violate**, p. 589

**Key Terms and People**

travois, p. 584

tepee, p. 584

reservation, p. 586

Sitting Bull, p. 586

---

**Main Idea**
Native Americans of the Plains relied on the buffalo to meet many basic needs.

**Vocabulary *Builder***
**transform** (trans FORM) *v.* to change in appearance or form; to change the condition of something

⭐ **Background Knowledge** Mining and railroading brought people to the West and turned it into a booming region. But Native Americans struggled to survive there.

## People of the Plains

At the end of the Civil War, some 360,000 Native Americans lived in the West, mainly on the Great Plains. Many, like the Arikaras and the Lakotas, had been there for centuries.

**Life in Transition** People of the Plains lived by gathering wild foods, hunting, and fishing. Some raised crops. Early Native Americans hunted buffalo and other game on foot. The arrival of the Europeans  transformed their lives. Plains nations tamed herds of wild horses, descended from tough breeds brought by the Spanish. They also traded with the French and British for guns.

With guns, Native Americans could kill more game. On horseback, they could travel faster and farther. Some groups became wanderers, carrying belongings on travois (truh VOIZ), or small sleds. They lived in tepees, cone-shaped tents made of buffalo skins.

Many Plains nations followed the buffalo herds. In winter, they trailed the herds into protected valleys and forests. In summer, when grass on the Plains grew tall, hunters tracked the buffalo as they gathered to graze.

People found many uses for the buffalo. Its meat was a protein-rich food. Horns and bones could be made into tools, and tendons could be made into thread. Buffalo hunting thus played a key role in people's survival.

**Division of Labors** In many Plains nations, women managed village life. They cared for children and prepared food. They carved tools and made clothing and tepees. Sometimes they went to war. In 1876, a Crow woman named The Other Magpie rode against the Sioux for killing her brother. In some groups, a wise woman ruled.

Men were hunters and warriors. Often, they also led religious life. One important ritual was the Sun Dance. The four-day ceremony brought together thousands of Native Americans from many nations. Men would make pledges to the Great Spirit, or ruler of the universe.

☑**Checkpoint** Why was the buffalo important to many groups?

## Broken Treaties

U.S. treaties promised to safeguard Native American lands. As miners and railroad crews pushed west, they broke those treaties.

**Fort Laramie Treaty** In 1851, ten thousand people from many Plains nations gathered near Fort Laramie in Wyoming for a "big talk" with U.S. officials. The officials wanted the nations to stop following the buffalo. If they would settle permanently, the government promised to protect their lands "as long as the grass shall grow."

No sooner had some Native American leaders signed the Fort Laramie Treaty than settlers moved onto their lands. In 1859, a gold strike at Pikes Peak in Colorado sent miners swarming to the region.

**Main Idea**
Treaties to protect Native American lands were quickly broken, and wars broke out.

**Uses of the Buffalo**
The buffalo was central to the life of Native Americans living on the Great Plains. It furnished not only food but also many other necessities of life. **Critical Thinking: *Draw Conclusions*** *Why did the nations of the Plains depend so heavily on the buffalo? How did they cope when the buffalo herds began to disappear?*

**Covering Tepees** Buffalo hides were used to cover the tepees in which the people of the Plains lived.

**Keeping Warm** The hairy hides of the buffalo provided clothing and warm coverings, such as this Cheyenne robe. Buffalo tendons made a strong thread for sewing garments together.

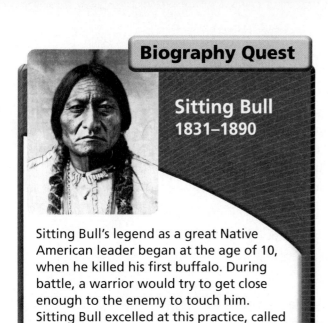 
**Main Idea**
Warfare continued even as some Native American nations tried to adapt to life on reservations.

**Sand Creek Massacre** In the early 1860s, new treaties forced Native Americans to give up land around Pikes Peak. Many warriors resisted. They attacked supply trains and homes.

In response, Colonel John Chivington and 700 volunteers attacked a band of Cheyennes at Sand Creek in eastern Colorado in 1864. These Cheyennes were friendly and under army protection. They raised a white flag to signal peace, but Chivington ordered his men to attack. In the end, more than 100 men, women, and children died.

**Buffalo Soldiers** The Sand Creek Massacre helped to ignite an era of war. Among the soldiers most feared on the Plains were African American veterans of the Civil War. The Native Americans called them Buffalo Soldiers. The Buffalo Soldiers fought on the Plains for 20 years. They also captured bandits from Texas to the Dakotas.

**End of the Buffalo** The giant herds of buffalo, so central to Native American life, began to shrink in the 1870s. Railroads had hunters kill the animals to feed their crews. Others also slaughtered buffalo because buffalo robes drew high prices in eastern cities. One hunter might kill 2,000 buffalo in a month.

✓**Checkpoint** Why did the buffalo begin to disappear?

## Last Stand for Custer and the Sioux

New treaties in the late 1860s sought to end the wars on the Plains. Federal officials urged Plains nations to settle down and farm.

**Reservations** The southern Plains nations—the Kiowas, Comanches, and Arapahos—moved to reservations in Oklahoma. A reservation is land set aside for Native Americans to live on. Life there was a disaster. Poor soil in Oklahoma made farming difficult.

Many Sioux and Cheyennes gathered on land set aside for them in the Black Hills of the Dakotas. An 1874 gold strike brought a flood of miners. Sitting Bull and Crazy Horse led attacks to keep whites out.

**Little Bighorn** In June of 1876, under orders to force the Native Americans onto a reservation, Colonel George Armstrong Custer entered the Little Bighorn Valley in Montana Territory. Although outnumbered, he attacked a large band of Sioux and Cheyennes.

Custer and all his men died at the Battle of Little Bighorn. But the victory of Sitting Bull and Crazy Horse was fleeting. One Sioux recalled, "A winter or so later, more soldiers came to round us up on reservations. There were too many of them to fight now."

✓**Checkpoint** Why did Custer attack at Little Bighorn?

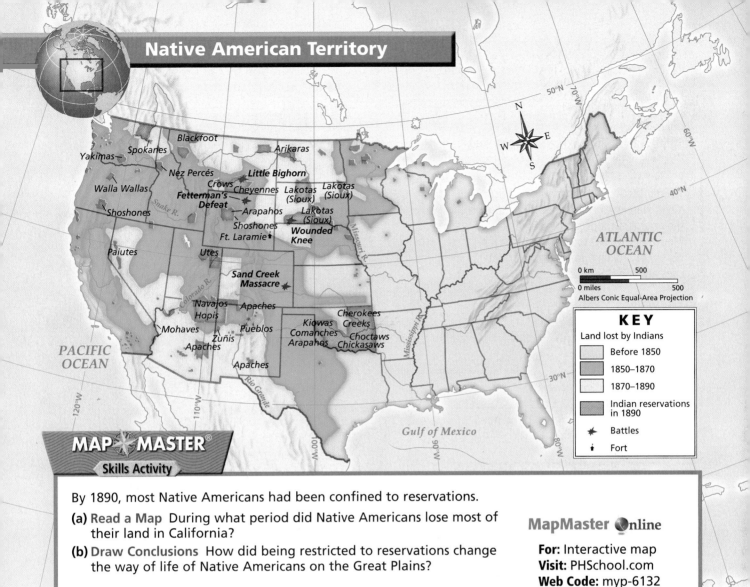

## Native American Territory

**MAP MASTER**

Skills Activity

By 1890, most Native Americans had been confined to reservations.

**(a) Read a Map** During what period did Native Americans lose most of their land in California?

**(b) Draw Conclusions** How did being restricted to reservations change the way of life of Native Americans on the Great Plains?

**MapMaster Online**

**For:** Interactive map
**Visit:** PHSchool.com
**Web Code:** myp-6132

**KEY**

Land lost by Indians

- Before 1850
- 1850–1870
- 1870–1890
- Indian reservations in 1890

★ Battles
⚓ Fort

Albers Conic Equal-Area Projection

## Other Efforts at Resistance

Other Native American nations in the West also came under pressure. Among them were the Nez Percés to the north and the Navajos and Apaches to the south.

**The Nez Percés** The Nez Percés lived where Idaho, Oregon, and Washington now meet. They bred horses and cattle in the Snake River valley. Under pressure, many agreed to go to a reservation.

Rather than see his nation humiliated, Chief Joseph fled toward Canada with a large band of Nez Percés in 1877. The U.S. Army pursued them. In 75 days, the Nez Percés traveled 1,300 miles.

The army caught the Nez Percés near Canada's border. As Chief Joseph surrendered, he said, "I shall fight no more forever."

**The Navajos** Navajos raised sheep, horses, and cattle in the Southwest. Bands of Navajos also raided settlers' farms for livestock. To stop raids, white settlers called in the army. After a series of wars, the Navajos were defeated in 1864 in Arizona. Soldiers took them on what the Navajos called a "Long Walk" to a spot near the Pecos River. There, they suffered years of disease and hunger.

**Main Idea**

Efforts by Native Americans to preserve their traditional way of life did not succeed.

# Links Across Time

**1968** Native Americans demonstrate in the nation's capital against a bill under consideration by Congress.

## Civil Rights for Native Americans

**1890** Some 200 Sioux were killed by soldiers at Wounded Knee. This incident brought the period of the Indian Wars to a violent close.

**1960s** Inspired in part by the civil rights movement, Native Americans organized to demand their rights. Groups such as the American Indian Movement sought to remind Americans of the history of broken treaties between Native Americans and the U.S. government.

### Link to Today

**Native American Rights Today** Many Native American rights groups now focus their attention on the Supreme Court. What legal issues affect Native Americans in modern society?

**For:** Native American rights in the news
**Visit:** PHSchool.com
**Web Code:** myc-6132

---

**The Apaches** Fierce resistance came from Apaches like Geronimo, who refused to go to a reservation. From Mexico, Geronimo and his men attacked settlers in Arizona and New Mexico for 10 years. After his capture in 1886, he was sent to a reservation in Oklahoma.

**Use Restatement Clues**
What is a trance? Use a restatement clue in your answer.

**The Ghost Dance** Some Native Americans dreamed of returning to old ways. In the late 1880s, Native Americans across the Plains began performing a unique, swaying dance. Dancers fell into a trance, or dreamlike state. They believed they were talking to ghosts of their ancestors, so the dance was called the Ghost Dance. Dancers believed their ancestors and the buffalo would return and white people would leave the Plains. Soldiers guarding reservations saw the dance as the beginning of an uprising. In December 1890, Native American police went to a Sioux village to stop the dances. In a struggle to arrest Sitting Bull, police killed him.

Fearful of further violence, a band of Sioux tried to flee to safety. Army troops surrounded them at Wounded Knee Creek in South Dakota. As the Sioux were giving up their guns, a shot rang out. The troops opened fire with machine guns and rifles. Nearly 200 Sioux men, women, and children were killed. Some 30 soldiers died.

The Battle of Wounded Knee marked the end of the era of Indian Wars. "A people's dream died there," said one chief.

✓**Checkpoint** **What was the purpose of the Ghost Dance?**

# The Failure of Reform

Reformers criticized the government for its harsh treatment of Native American nations. Criticism grew as more groups were forced onto reservations in the late 1800s.

**Calls for Reform** Susette La Flesche knew all about the calamity befalling Native Americans. Her father was an Omaha chief. In lectures and articles, she told of the destruction of native culture.

In 1881, inspired by La Flesche, the poet Helen Hunt Jackson wrote *A Century of Dishonor*. The book recorded the many treaties <u>violated</u> by the government at Native American expense. Alice Fletcher also promoted native rights. She became an agent for the U.S. Bureau of Indian Affairs, which dealt with Native Americans.

**The Dawes Act** Hoping to improve Native American life, Congress passed the Dawes Act in 1887. It tried to end Native Americans' wandering and turn them into farmers. Native American males each received 160 acres to farm. The act set up schools to make Native American children more like other Americans.

The Dawes Act failed. Few Native Americans took to farming. Many sold their land cheaply to dishonest whites. Federal agents replaced native leaders, and Native Americans had to give up traditional ways like the buffalo hunt. As a result, they remained poor. Many grew dependent on the government for food and supplies.

✓**Checkpoint** What was the purpose of the Dawes Act?

⭐ **Looking Back and Ahead** As settlers poured into the West, buffalo grew scarce. Native Americans were moved onto reservations and forced to change their way of life. In the next section, you will read how some of the settlers made a living in the West.

**Main Idea**
The Dawes Act encouraged Native Americans to become farmers, but it failed.

**Vocabulary *Builder***
**violate** (vī ah layt) *v.* to break a rule or law; to disrespect; to disturb

---

**Section 2 | Check Your Progress**

**Progress Monitoring** ⬤nline
**For:** Self-test with instant help
**Visit:** PHSchool.com
**Web Code:** mya-6132

## Comprehension and Critical Thinking

**1. (a) Describe** How did guns and horses change the lives of Plains Native Americans?
**(b) Analyze Cause and Effect** What were the short- and long-term effects of hunting buffalo on Native American life?

**2. (a) Identify** Who was Chief Joseph?
**(b) Detect Points of View** In 1879, Chief Joseph appeared before Congress. He said, "Treat all men alike. Give them all the same law. Give them all an even chance to live and grow. All men were made by the same Great Spirit Chief." What was Chief Joseph trying to tell Congress? How do you think members of Congress responded to his words?

### Reading Skill

**3. Use Restatement Clues** Use a restatement clue to define the term tepees in the following sentence: They lived in cone-shaped tepees, portable tents made of buffalo skins.

### Vocabulary *Builder*

**4.** Write two definitions for each key term: travois, reservation. First, write a formal definition for your teacher. Second, write a definition in everyday English for a classmate.

### Writing

**5.** Find three pieces of evidence in this section that support or refute the following opinion: In the nineteenth century, the U.S. government treated Native Americans in an unfair way.

# The Cattle Kingdom

## Objectives

1. Explain how the cattle industry began.

2. Describe the life of a cowhand on the trail.

3. Discuss the myth of the Wild West.

4. Identify reasons for the end of the cattle boom.

## Prepare to Read

### Reading Skill

**Use Example Clues** Writers may offer clues to a word's meaning by giving examples. Consider this sentence: "Canines such as poodles and spaniels make good companions." The examples show that *canines* means "dogs." A writer may describe an example in depth or tell what something does to help you visualize the unfamiliar word. Look for the phrases *such as* and *for example.*

### Vocabulary *Builder*

**High-Use Words**

persist, p. 591

myth, p. 593

**Key Terms**

open range, p. 590

cattle drive, p. 590

vaquero, p. 592

cow town, p. 592

cattle kingdom, p. 593

⭐ **Background Knowledge** You have read how Native Americans were forced onto reservations. Now, you will learn how ranchers created a cattle industry that supplied beef to the nation.

## The Rise of the Cattle Industry

### Main Idea
The coming of railroads gave western ranchers a way to get cattle to distant markets.

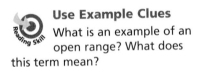

**Use Example Clues**
What is an example of an open range? What does this term mean?

For years, wild cattle wandered the open range, or unfenced land, of Texas. Called longhorns for their broad horns, they needed almost no care. They survived on prairie grass and watering holes.

**Means and Markets** The herds of cattle had grown from strays lost by Spanish ranchers. As American settlers moved in, they set up new ranches. But they did not bother to round up the stray herds because they had no means of getting the cattle to distant markets.

As railroads swept across the Plains in the 1860s, Texans at last saw a way to reach those markets. Protein-rich beef was in demand to feed city dwellers in the East and miners and soldiers in the West.

**The Long Drives** Ranchers began rounding up the cattle in the 1860s. They hired cowhands—skilled riders who know how to herd cattle—to move the cattle to rail lines in Kansas, Missouri, and Wyoming. Some rail lines were as far away as 1,000 miles.

Spring was an ideal time to begin a cattle drive—the herding and moving of cattle over long distances. Grass grew tall, and rivers flowed full from spring rains. The work was so demanding that cowhands brought a number of horses so that each day a fresh one would be available.

The long drives lasted two to three months. They followed well-worn trails. To the east lay the famous Chisholm Trail from San Antonio, Texas, to Abilene, Kansas. To the west, the Goodnight-Loving Trail led to rail towns in Wyoming. In just one year, as many as 600,000 cattle might be moved north.

☑**Checkpoint**   **Why did cattle drives cover long distances?**

## Life on the Trail

Life on the trail was hard and dangerous. The long cattle drives tested the nerve and skill of every cowhand.

**A Risky Ride**   Andy Adams had driven many herds north. Never before had he seen cattle going blind with thirst. All he could do was "let them pass." When the crazed cattle finally sniffed out water and drank, their sight returned.

Cowhands such as Andy Adams kept the herds together as the cattle moved along the trails. The cowhands developed nerves of steel, staying calm even in times of extreme stress. Trip after trip, they <u>persisted</u> in performing their exciting but dangerous job.

Herding cattle was certainly risky. A lightning bolt could send a herd stampeding in all directions. Swift river currents sometimes carried the longhorns away, and cowhands would have to struggle to get the panicked animals back on solid ground. Cowhands also fought grass fires, pulled the cattle from swamps, and chased off thieves.

**Main Idea**
Cowhands, working long hours for low pay, learned skills developed earlier by Spanish and Mexican vaqueros.

**Vocabulary** *Builder*
**persist** (per SIHST) *v.* to endure; to continue in the face of difficulty

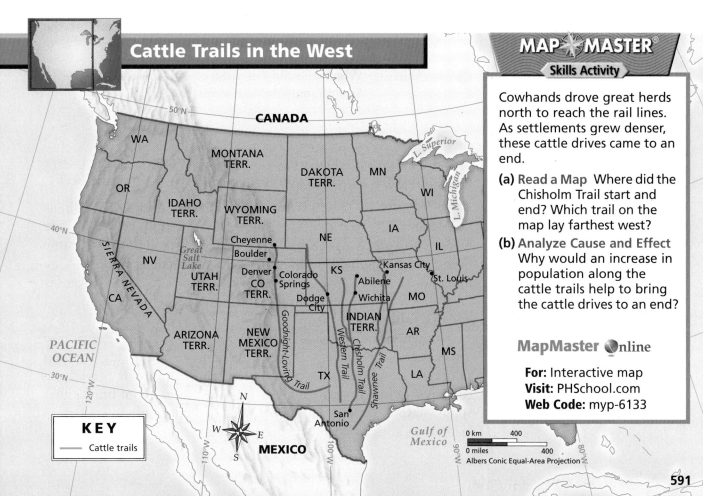

**Cattle Trails in the West**

**MAP MASTER®**
**Skills Activity**

Cowhands drove great herds north to reach the rail lines. As settlements grew denser, these cattle drives came to an end.

**(a) Read a Map** Where did the Chisholm Trail start and end? Which trail on the map lay farthest west?

**(b) Analyze Cause and Effect** Why would an increase in population along the cattle trails help to bring the cattle drives to an end?

**MapMaster** ⬤**nline**

**For:** Interactive map
**Visit:** PHSchool.com
**Web Code:** myp-6133

**KEY**
— Cattle trails

591

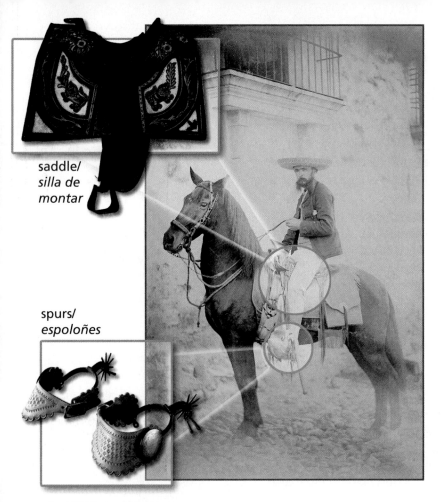

saddle/
*silla de
montar*

spurs/
*espoloñes*

**Outfitting a Vaquero**
Cowhands borrowed much from early Spanish and Mexican vaqueros. The labels provide the English and Spanish names of the gear shown. **Critical Thinking:** *Frame Questions* *What question would you want to ask a vaquero about the objects pictured here?*

**Main Idea**
The West gained an exaggerated reputation for lawlessness and violence.

On the hot, dusty trails, cowhands could spend 18 hours a day in the saddle. Yet, for all their efforts, they earned wages of less than $1 a day. Like mining, cattle ranching relied on a workforce of low-paid laborers.

**Spanish Roots** The cowhands driving herds north owed much to Spanish and Mexican vaqueros (vah KAYR os). **Vaquero** (from *vaca*, meaning "cow") is the Spanish word for cowhand, or cowboy. Vaqueros tended cattle on ranches in Mexico, California, and the Southwest.

When Americans started to herd cattle, they learned from vaqueros how to ride, rope, and brand. Cowboys wore Mexican spurs and leather chaps that kept their legs safe from thorny shrubs. The broad-brimmed cowboy hat came from the Mexican *sombrero*, or "hat that provides shade." Cowboys used a leather lariat, or lasso (from the Spanish word *lazo*), to catch cattle and horses.

Approximately one third of all western cowhands were Mexican. Many others were African American and white veterans of the Civil War.

☑**Checkpoint**  **What skills did American cowboys learn from Spanish and Mexican vaqueros?**

## The Wild West
Cattle drives ended at towns along railroad lines. These towns—often unruly places—helped to create the fantasy of the Wild West.

**Cow Towns** In 1867, Joseph McCoy hit on an idea. The Illinois businessman figured that after months on the trail, cowboys were ready for a bath, a good meal, a soft bed, and some fun. Also, cattle needed to be penned as they awaited shipment east. So McCoy founded Abilene, Kansas, where the Chisholm Trail met the Kansas Pacific Railroad. Abilene was the first **cow town,** or settlement at the end of a cattle trail.

With money to be made from cowboys and their herds, rival cow towns such as Wichita and Dodge City, Kansas, soon sprang up along rail lines. Dance halls, saloons, hotels, and restaurants served the cowboys. Drinking and gambling often led to barroom brawls that spilled onto the streets. Gunfights were rare but common enough to lead towns such as Wichita to ban carrying pistols.

**The Myth of the West** Rough-and-tumble life in cow towns helped to spread the <u>myth</u> of the West as a place of violence, adventure, and endless opportunity. Easterners called it the Wild West.

No one did more to promote this fantasy than William "Buffalo Bill" Cody. A former buffalo hunter, Cody created a traveling Wild West show in 1883. Gun-slinging cowboys and Native Americans performed daring feats of sharp shooting and horseback riding. They staged performances depicting frontier events, including Custer's Last Stand. Annie Oakley broke the stereotype of the dainty woman with shooting as precise as any man's.

The myth of the Wild West had some basis in fact. But, as you have read, the West was also being transformed. Native Americans were being forced onto reservations. Mining and ranching were big businesses. Independent miners were becoming wage earners, like cowboys. Even wild cow towns were being quieted down by settlers and ministers who wanted peaceful communities for their families and their faiths.

☑ **Checkpoint** **How true was the myth of the Wild West?**

**Vocabulary** *Builder*
<u>myth</u> (mihth) *n.* story or legend; imaginary object; invented story

# Boom and Bust in the Cattle Kingdom

The cattle boom lasted from the 1860s to the 1880s. The region dominated by the cattle industry and its ranches, trails, and cow towns came to be called the **cattle kingdom.** Ranchers made large profits as herds and markets grew. But then the cattle industry collapsed.

**The Cattle Boom** At the height of the cattle boom, ranchers could buy a young calf for $5 and sell a mature steer for $60. Even after the expense of a cattle drive, profits were extremely high.

**Main Idea**
Overstocking and a spell of bad weather eventually put an end to the cattle boom.

## Links to Art

### *Cold Morning on the Range, 1904*

**by Frederic Remington**

Frederic Remington was a Yale-educated easterner who became a famous painter and sculptor of western scenes. His work highlighted such themes as self-reliance and mastery over nature. In *Cold Morning on the Range* (seen here), he portrays a rider in the process of taming a wild horse. **Critical Thinking:** *Evaluate Information* How do you think Remington's work added to the myth of the Wild West?

Profits rose still higher with the introduction of new breeds of cattle. These breeds caught fewer diseases and had more meat than longhorns. As a result, backers from the East and Europe invested millions in huge cattle companies. The ranches of one company alone covered almost 800 square miles in three states.

**The Boom Ends** By the mid-1880s, more than 7 million cattle roamed the open range. That was more than the land could feed. Then, beginning in 1886 and 1887, a cycle of scorching summers and frigid winters killed millions of cattle. Meanwhile, an economic depression threw many city dwellers out of work. Demand for beef dropped.

To make things worse, sheep began competing with cattle for prairie grasses across the Plains. Farmers fenced in the open range to keep cattle away from crops. Without free grazing for their herds, ranchers had to buy expensive feed.

Giant cattle ranches slowly gave way to smaller spreads that grew their own feed. As railroads expanded, their lines moved closer to the ranches. Large roundups and long cattle drives vanished. The cattle boom was over.

☑**Checkpoint** **What factors ended the cattle boom?**

☆ **Looking Back and Ahead** As railroads pushed across the West, the cattle industry boomed. Cowhands moved herds north on long drives to meet trains that took the cattle east. The cattle boom lasted into the 1880s. In the next section, you will read how farming changed the West.

**Texas Longhorn**
The horns of longhorn cattle can be six feet wide or more. The cattle use them for both attack and defense.

---

**Section 3** | **Check Your Progress**

**Progress Monitoring** Online
**For:** Self-test with instant help
**Visit:** PHSchool.com
**Web Code:** mya-6133

**Comprehension and Critical Thinking**

1. **(a) Describe** What dangers did cowhands face on cattle drives?
   **(b) Draw Conclusions** Why do you think cowhands took these risks?

2. **(a) Recall** How did the expansion of railroads help to create a cattle boom?
   **(b) Identify Economic Benefits** How did the cattle boom lead to economic prosperity for many new towns in the West?

**Reading Skill**

3. **Use Example Clues** Reread the text following the subheading "Cow Towns." How do example and description help you understand the term cow town? What is a cow town?

**Vocabulary Builder**

Complete each of the following sentences so that the second part further explains the first and clearly shows your understanding of the key term.

4. Cattle drives brought thousands of cattle to rail lines; _____.

5. Vaqueros tended cattle herds; _____.

6. The cattle kingdom supplied meat to a growing nation; _____.

**Writing**

7. Based on what you have read in this section about the Wild West myth, write an opinion about the effects of this myth on American life. Back up your opinion with reasons and examples from the section and from your own knowledge.

# Farming in the West

## Objectives

1. Identify what attracted farmers to settle on the Great Plains.
2. Describe how people adapted to life on the Plains.
3. Summarize the result of the Oklahoma Land Rush.
4. Explain how economic issues led farmers to organize to seek reform.

## Prepare to Read

### Reading Skill

**Use Comparison or Contrast Clues** Comparison and contrast can also help you define unfamiliar words. Comparison clues show how an unfamiliar word is similar to a familiar word, phrase, or example. Look for signal words such as *similar to* or *like* to highlight these clues. Contrast clues show how an unfamiliar word is different from a familiar word, phrase, or example. Look for signal words such as *unlike* or *instead* to highlight these clues.

### Vocabulary *Builder*

**High-Use Words**
reside, p. 595
surplus, p. 598

**Key Terms and People**
homesteader, p. 595
sod, p. 596
sodbuster, p. 596
sooner, p. 598
grange, p. 598
farm cooperative, p. 598
inflation, p. 599
William Jennings Bryan, p. 599

⭐ **Background Knowledge** While ranchers and cowhands were building a cattle kingdom, hundreds of thousands of farmers were flooding onto the Great Plains.

## Homesteading

By 1900, half a million farmers had settled on the Great Plains. Many were attracted by an offer of free land.

**Homestead Act** During the Civil War, Congress passed the Homestead Act of 1862. It offered a 160-acre plot to anyone who resided on the land for five years. Congress wanted to give the poor a chance to own farms. Thousands became homesteaders—settlers who acquired free land from the government—on the Great Plains.

But few had the money to move west and start a farm. Also, land companies took over large areas illegally. And on the dry Plains, 160 acres was too small to grow enough grain to profit. Only one homesteader in three lasted the required five years.

**Railroads Promote Farming** In fact, railroads promoted more farming than did the Homestead Act. More farms meant more shipping for western railroads. So the railroads gave away some of the 180 million acres they got from the government. They recruited thousands of people from the eastern United States, Ireland, Germany, and Scandinavia to settle on the Great Plains.

☑**Checkpoint** How did the Homestead Act help people gain land?

**Main Idea**
Would-be settlers could get a homestead from the government or land from railroad companies.

**Vocabulary *Builder***
reside (ree ZĪD) *v.* to live (in or at); to dwell for a while; to exist (in)

## A Hard Life on the Plains

Life on the Great Plains was not easy. Water was scarce, and crops were hard to grow. Farmers struggled to make ends meet.

**Busting Sod** The first farmers on the eastern Plains staked out sites near water and trees. Later arrivals continued on to the treeless prairie. The farther west one went, the drier the climate became.

The soil of the Plains was fertile. It was covered with a thick sod, or a surface layer of earth in which the roots of grasses tangle with soil. With little rain, sod baked into a hardened mass. Early settlers, lacking wood, cut sod into bricks to build walls. Two rows of sod bricks made walls that kept homes cool in summer and warm in winter.

**New Farming Methods** Farmers broke through the tough sod with plows. The sod often cracked plows made of wood or iron. In 1877, John Deere of Illinois invented a sodbusting plow made of steel. Steel plows were stronger and lighter than other plows.

Plains farmers, or sodbusters as they were known, used machines called drills to plant crops. The drills buried seeds deep in the ground where there was moisture. Farmers used reapers to harvest crops and threshers to beat off the hard coverings of the grains.

Water often lay hundreds of feet below ground. Farmers used windmills to pump the water out. To keep cattle from trampling crops, farmers put up fences. Lacking wood, they used barbed wire. Joseph Glidden, an Illinois farmer, invented this twisted metal wire in 1874.

# Sodbusters

Thickly matted grass roots held the fertile Plains soil in a tight grip. Even with a four-horse plow, sodbusting (breaking up the sod) was backbreaking work. Worse, once exposed by plowing, the fertile soil might be blown away by winds. **Critical Thinking: *Clarify Problems*** *What problems did settlers face on the Plains? How did they overcome their problems?*

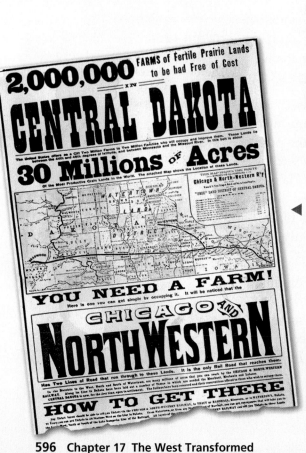

◀ **Railroads Lure Settlers**
Railroads, eager for customers, offered free land to lure settlers to the Great Plains. People came from eastern cities and from many countries in Europe.

**Sod ▶**
Deep, thick roots allowed grasses to thrive in areas of the Great Plains that received limited amounts of moisture.

**Farm Families** Whole families worked on the farms. Men labored from dawn to dusk. Children tended animals and helped with other chores. Life was also hard for women. Besides keeping house, they helped plant and harvest. They educated children. They nursed the sick. They sewed clothing, preserved food, and made such basics as candles and soap.

**Exodusters** Thousands of African Americans, many of them former slaves, streamed onto the Plains. By the early 1880s, perhaps 70,000 African Americans had settled in Kansas. These settlers were known as Exodusters because they believed they were like the Jews fleeing slavery in Egypt, a biblical story told in the book of Exodus.

Some Exodusters took up farming. Others moved to towns. Men often worked as hired hands and women as laundresses.

**The Spanish Southwest** In the Southwest along the border with Mexico, arriving settlers found Spanish-speaking farmers and sheepherders. Many had been there since before the Mexican-American War, when the United States had acquired this territory.

The coming of the railroads brought more immigrants from Mexico. Many helped build the new lines. Some of the older Hispanic residents were large landowners, known as *ricos* (REE kos). They fought to keep their lands, deeded under Spanish or Mexican law.

☑ **Checkpoint** Who were the sodbusters and the Exodusters?

**Reading Skill**

**Use Comparison or Contrast Clues** What comparison clue is included in this paragraph to help you define the term *Exodusters*? What are Exodusters?

◄ **A Sod House**
Settlers cut sod into bricks that they used to construct sturdy sod houses like the one at left.

◄ **Care With Resources**
Like the Native Americans, early farm families had few resources to spare. The woman in this picture gathers dried buffalo manure to use as a fuel for heating or cooking, or to use as a fertilizer for crops.

597

# A Last Rush for Land

By the 1880s, few areas on the Plains remained free to settlers. The federal government agreed to open Oklahoma to homesteaders.

**Boomers and Sooners** In April 1889, nearly 100,000 people gathered at a line near present-day Oklahoma City. These were the "boomers." They had come to claim some of the 2 million acres of free homesteads in what was once Indian Territory.

At noon, a volley of gunfire signaled the start of the Oklahoma Land Rush. A few people, known as **sooners,** had already sneaked onto the land. They jumped from hiding and grabbed the best land. Other rushes followed until all 2 million acres had been claimed.

**The Frontier Closes** In 1890, the national census reported that the United States no longer had land available for homesteading. In the West, "there can hardly be said to be a frontier line," the report stated.

☑**Checkpoint** **Where was the last land rush in the West?**

**Main Idea**
Facing an economic crisis, farmers formed groups like the National Grange and the Populist Party.

**Vocabulary** *Builder*
<u>surplus</u> (SER pluhs) *n.* excess; quantity that is left over

# Farmers Organize

Wheat and grain from Plains farms fed the growing cities of America and Europe. A few big farmers prospered. But small farmers faced an economic crisis and quickly organized to end it.

**Crisis on the Farm** The more grain that farmers hauled to market, the lower grain prices fell. Farmers were producing a <u>surplus</u> of crops. One Kansas farmer complained that "we are poorer by many dollars than we were years ago."

Small farmers were hit the hardest by low grain prices. Many had borrowed money for land and machinery. As prices fell, Plains farmers could not repay their loans and lost their land. In the South, tenants and sharecroppers fell deeper into debt as cotton prices fell.

**Cooperatives and Political Parties** Many farmers lived in poverty and isolation. Some communities began to form granges, groups of farmers who met for lectures, sewing bees, and other events. In 1867, local granges joined to form the National Grange.

What began as a social and educational movement evolved into an economic protest. In the 1870s and 1880s, Grangers demanded the same low rates from railroads and warehouses that were given to big farmers. They elected state officials who passed laws limiting rates.

A group called the Farmers' Alliance organized in the late 1870s to help farmers. It set up **farm cooperatives**—groups of farmers who pool their money to make large purchases of tools, seed, and other supplies at a discount. In the South, both whites and blacks joined the Alliance.

In 1892, unhappy farmers joined with members of labor unions to form the Populist Party. This was a political party that pushed for social reforms. It demanded public ownership of railroads and warehouses to control rates, a tax on income to replace property taxes, an eight-hour workday, and other reforms.

Populists wanted to use silver in addition to gold as a basis for the money supply. With more money circulating, Populists hoped to see inflation, or a general rise in prices. They believed rising grain prices would help farmers pay off their debts. In that way, the farmers could avoid foreclosure—the taking of property to settle a debt. Summing up Populist demands, Kansas activist Mary Elizabeth Lease said:

> ❝We want money, land, and transportation. We . . . want the power to make loans direct from the government. We want the accursed foreclosure system wiped out. . . .❞
>
> —Mary Elizabeth Lease, 1890 speech

**The Election of 1896** In the presidential election of 1896, Populists supported Democrat William Jennings Bryan, known as the "Great Commoner." Bryan won the votes of farmers from the South and West for supporting the use of silver to raise prices.

Bankers and business owners claimed rising prices would ruin the economy. They backed Republican William McKinley and his gold-alone standard. McKinley won. Republicans took both the White House and Congress for the first time in decades. The Populists faded. Although the major parties absorbed many of their ideas, most Americans saw no link between farm problems and their own.

These presidential campaign buttons show the two major candidates in 1896. William McKinley (right) won for the Republicans. William Jennings Bryan (left) had the backing of Democrats and Populists but lost.

☑**Checkpoint** What did the Populists demand?

⭐ **Looking Back and Ahead** Farmers found it hard to make a living, so they organized to demand reforms. In the next chapter, you will read about the rise of big business and labor.

---

**Section 4 | Check Your Progress**

**Progress Monitoring** Online
**For:** Self-test with instant help
**Visit:** PHSchool.com
**Web Code:** mya-6134

**Comprehension and Critical Thinking**

1. **(a) Recall** What was a homesteader?
   **(b) Explain Problems** What were three problems associated with the Homestead Act?

2. **(a) Recall** What is a surplus?
   **(b) Clarify Problems** How did a surplus of grain contribute to low grain prices? How did the National Grange, the Farmers' Alliance, and the Populist Party try to address the economic crisis caused by low prices?

**Reading Skill**

3. **Use Comparison or Contrast Clues** Define the term inflation in the following sentence: Like the wind under a child's runaway balloon, inflation pushed prices higher and higher.

**Vocabulary Builder**

Answer the following questions in complete sentences that show your understanding of the key terms.

4. How did tough sod make living on the Great Plains difficult?
5. Why were Great Plains farmers called sodbusters?
6. Who were the sooners?

7. How did forming a farm cooperative help farmers?
8. How did Populists think inflation would help them economically?

**Writing**

9. Imagine that you will be writing an editorial meant to influence readers of your school newspaper about coed sports teams. Write a few sentences creating an audience profile describing these readers. Think about who they are: How old are they? What types of interests do they have? What sports interest them the most?

As you learned in the Skills for Life in the previous chapter, thematic maps focus on topics such as agricultural products, migrations, or physical regions. The map below is a climate map. Climate refers to the average weather of a place over a period of time. The visual information included on a climate map can help you understand the economy of a region.

**Climates of the United States**

| | KEY | |
|---|---|---|
| | Marine | Abundant rainfall; warm summers and cool winters |
| | Mediterranean | Hot summers and cool winters |
| | Highland | Varies, depending on elevation |
| | Steppe | Limited rainfall; hot summers and cold winters |
| | Desert | Hot summers and mild-to-cold winters; hot days and cold nights |
| | Humid continental | Mild summers and cold winters |
| | Humid subtropical | Hot summers and cool winters |
| | Tropical | Hot all year |
| | Tundra | Cold summers and very cold winters |
| | Subarctic | Cool summers and very cold winters |

## Learn the Skill
*Use these steps to interpret climate maps.*

**1** **Use the map key to read the map.** The map key explains special symbols and colors used on the map.

**2** **Look for patterns on the map.** Study the information on the map to notice trends or patterns.

**3** **Make inferences.** Make generalizations. Use the information on the map to make a general statement about the climate.

## Practice the Skill
*Answer the following questions about the map on this page.*

**1** **Use the map key to read the map.** What does the key on this map tell you? What do the colors tell you? What other information is on this key?

**2** **Look for patterns on the map.** How does the climate change as you move across the Great Plains states from east to west?

**3** **Make inferences.** How do you think the climate of the Great Plains affects farming?

## Apply the Skill
*See the Review and Assessment at the end of this chapter.*

**Study Guide Online**
Complete your Chapter 17 study guide in print or online.

## Chapter Summary

### Section 1
### Mining and Railroads

- Gold and silver strikes in the West attracted many newcomers.
- Some mining towns became ghost towns after the metals were mined out.
- Immigrants came to the West from many countries to help build railroads.
- In 1869, a transcontinental railroad linked the East with the West.

### Section 2
### Native Americans Struggle to Survive

- Native Americans lost their lands, despite treaties aimed at protecting them.
- Native American nations were forced onto reservations.
- Native Americans fought for their way of life.
- The 1887 Dawes Act tried to promote new ways of living among Native Americans.

### Section 3
### The Cattle Kingdom

- Railroads provided a way for cattle ranchers to get their herds to distant markets.
- Unruly cattle towns helped to give rise to the myth of the Wild West.
- Economic depression, bad weather, and the fencing of crops brought the cattle boom to an end in the late 1800s.

### Section 4
### Farming in the West

- Free land for homesteaders helped to populate the Great Plains.
- Plains settlers faced a hard and isolated life.
- Disgruntled farmers and workers organized to demand reforms from government.
- The Populist Party shook up American politics in the 1890s.

## Key Concepts

These notes will help you prepare for questions about key concepts.

### The Western Frontier Disappears

**Causes**
- Gold and silver are discovered.
- A transcontinental railroad is built.
- The Homestead Act is passed.

**Effects**
- Mining towns rise and fall.
- More settlers, including immigrants, move west.
- Native American nations lose their lands.
- Wars break out between Native Americans and the U.S. Army.

### Native Americans: A Chronology

- **1851** The Fort Laramie Treaty is signed.
- **1859** Miners discover gold at Pikes Peak, Colorado.
- **1864** The Sand Creek Massacre occurs in eastern Colorado.
- **1874** Gold is found in the Black Hills.
- **1876** Sioux and Cheyennes defeat Custer's forces at the Battle of Little Bighorn.
- **1887** Congress passes the Dawes Act.
- **1890** Nearly 200 Sioux die in the Battle of Wounded Knee.

### Facts About Cowhands and Farmers

**Cowhands**
- Spanish and Mexican vaqueros passed on many skills.
- About one third of all western cowhands were Mexican.
- Cowhands worked long hours for low pay.

**Farmers**
- Farmers overcame great difficulties to survive on the Plains.
- Crop surpluses kept prices low.
- Farmers joined together to demand reforms.

## Vocabulary *Builder*

### Key Terms

Complete each of the following sentences so that the second part further explains the first part and clearly shows your understanding of the key term.

1. Plains Indians used *travois* in their travels; _____.

2. Farmers thought *inflation* would benefit farm prices; _____.

3. *Vaqueros* were important in cattle ranching; _____.

4. Railroads benefited from generous government *subsidies*; _____.

## Comprehension and Critical Thinking

5. **(a) Describe** What difficulties did immigrants face in mining towns?
   **(b) Evaluate Information** How did immigrants help to develop the West?

6. **(a) List** What types of changes did the transcontinental railroad bring to the West?
   **(b) Draw Inferences** What were the effects of the building of railroads on Native Americans?

7. **(a) List** Describe three ways in which Native Americans made use of buffalo.
   **(b) Recall** Why did the buffalo begin to disappear from the Great Plains in the 1870s?
   **(c) Draw Conclusions** How did the disappearance of the buffalo change the lives of Native Americans?

8. **(a) Summarize** How did the U.S. government and settlers treat Native Americans?
   **(b) Detect Points of View** What do you think the Native American chief meant when he said after the Battle of Wounded Knee, "A people's dream died there"?

9. **(a) Recall** Who was Buffalo Bill Cody?
   **(b) Apply Information** Why do you think Americans characterize the West as "wild"?

10. **(a) Describe** What was life like for individuals who settled on the Great Plains?
    **(b) Draw Conclusions** Why do you think families risked moving west?

## History Reading Skill

11. **Use Context Clues** Choose four key terms or other unfamiliar words from this chapter. Write sentences that define these words. Include at least one of each clue type: example, comparison or contrast, definition, or restatement.

## Writing

12. **Choose one of the following issues discussed in this chapter:**
    - the rise and fall of the cattle kingdom;
    - the settlement of the West and disappearance of the frontier;
    - relations between Native Americans and the U.S. government.

    State an opinion about the issue, and list several facts and reasons from the chapter to support your opinion.

13. **Write a Narrative:**
    Write one or two diary entries from the point of view of a family member who is moving west in the 1870s. Describe why your family is moving west and how you feel about it. Tell what you expect to see in the West and the type of life you think you will have.

## Skills for Life

### Interpret a Climate Map

Use the map below to answer the questions.

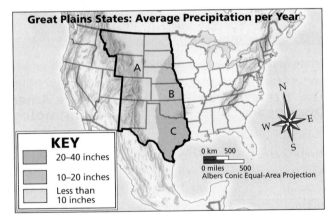

Great Plains States: Average Precipitation per Year

KEY
- 20–40 inches
- 10–20 inches
- Less than 10 inches

14. Study the key. What does the green color mean?

15. As you move east to west across the Great Plains states, how does the amount of precipitation change?

16. How do you think the amount of rain in the Great Plains states affects farming there?

# Test Yourself

1. **Which of the following turned Virginia City, Nevada, into a boomtown?**

   **A** transcontinental railroad

   **B** Comstock Lode

   **C** Fort Laramie Treaty

   **D** Oklahoma Land Rush

**Refer to the quotation below to answer Question 2.**

> "Let me be a free man, free to travel, free to stop, free to work, . . . free to choose my own teachers, free to follow the religion of my fathers, free to think and talk and act for myself. . . ."
>
> —Chief Joseph of the Nez Percés, 1879

2. **Chief Joseph referred to which event?**

   **A** Reconstruction

   **B** Homestead Act

   **C** National Grange

   **D** Dawes Act

**Refer to the photograph below to answer Question 3.**

3. **The photograph best reflects which of the following?**

   **A** gold rush of 1849

   **B** Fort Laramie Treaty

   **C** Populist movement

   **D** Homestead Act

# Document-Based Questions

**Task:** Look at Documents 1 and 2, and answer their accompanying questions. Then, use the documents and your knowledge of history to complete this writing assignment:

> Write an essay about the economic crisis facing farmers in the 1890s.

**Document 1:** Mary Elizabeth Lease gave this speech in 1890. *What hardship does Lease say farmers are suffering? What does she say is the cause?*

> "After all our years of toil . . . and hardships upon the Western frontier, monopoly is taking our homes from us by an infamous system of mortgage foreclosure. . . . How did it happen? The government, at the bid of Wall Street, repudiated its contracts with the people. . . . As Senator Stewart [of Nevada] puts it, 'For twenty years the market value of the dollar has gone up and the market value of labor has gone down, till today the American laborer . . . asks which is the worst—the black slavery that has gone or the white slavery that has come?'"

**Document 2:** The more farmers harvested, the less they earned. *How does this graph help to explain the farmers' problem?*

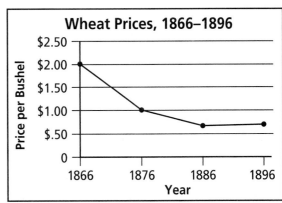

**Wheat Prices, 1866–1896**

Source: *Historical Statistics of the United States*

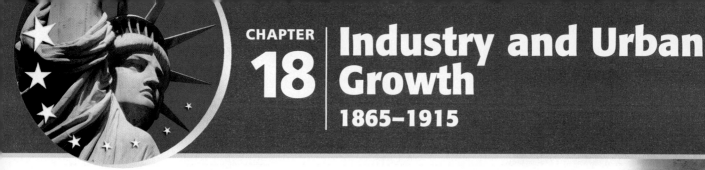

## Chapter Preview

After the Civil War, the United States continued to change in many ways. Cities grew, industry boomed, and vast numbers of immigrants came to the United States. With these changes came new challenges.

**1869**
Workers organize Knights of Labor.

**1882**
John D. Rockefeller forms Standard Oil.

**1889**
Jane Addams founds Hull House to help city poor.

**U.S. Events**

1860

1875

1890

**World Events**

**1878** Salvation Army is formed in London.

**1889** German engineers build first gas-powered automobile.

**Quick View Video**
View the chapter video for a quick preview of the main ideas.

Steel bridges like the Brooklyn Bridge in New York, shown here, helped change the face of American cities.

**1892**
Ellis Island opens as entry station for immigrants.

**1903**
Wright Brothers make first airplane flight.

**1913**
Henry Ford sets up assembly line to mass-produce automobiles.

1890

1905

1920

**1901** First wireless radio message is sent across Atlantic.

**History Reading Skill** Use Word Origins

## How have immigrants changed America?

Many new words in English evolved from the languages of immigrants, as well as from the long-ago influences of Latin and Greek. In this chapter, you will practice using word origins to determine word meanings and to understand how other languages have affected the English language. Read the following account. The side notes suggest ways to use word origins.

**Primary Source**

Many immigrants came to America in the 1900s. One was Mary Antin, who came to Boston as a young girl. Here, she describes the adjustments her family made to their new home.

> The word *banana* comes to English from Spanish or Portuguese but probably was first used in West Africa.

"Our initiation into American ways began with the first step on the new soil. My father corrected us even on the way from the pier. . . . [W]e paid the strictest attention to my father's instructions.

The first meal was an object lesson of much variety. . . . [My father] tried to introduce us to a . . . slippery kind of fruit which he called <u>banana</u>. . . . After the meal he had better luck with a curious piece of furniture on runners . . . called rocking chair. . . . [W]e found . . . ways of getting into the American <u>machine</u> of perpetual <u>motion</u>. . . . We laughed over . . . [its] novelty. . . .

[Next] we had to visit the stores and be dressed . . . in American clothing. . . . With our <u>immigrant</u> clothing we shed also our impossible Hebrew names."

—Mary Antin, *The Promised Land*

> The words *motion* and *immigrant* both come from the Latin roots *mot* and *migr*, meaning "move."

> The word *machine* builds on the Greek root *mech*, meaning "machine."

## Use Word Origins

- Words may be built on Greek or Latin roots. Get to know those roots to help you recognize related English words.
- Some words come into English more or less the same as in their original language.
- Use context to adapt a root's meaning to modern usage.

## Document-Based Questions

1. What new food did Mary's father want the family to try?
2. What did they think of the rocking chair?
3. What did Mary mean when she said: "With our immigrant clothing we shed also our impossible Hebrew names"?

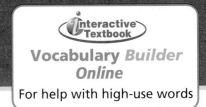

# Vocabulary *Builder*

## Previewing High-Use Academic Words

| High-Use Word | Definition | Sample History Sentence |
|---|---|---|
| **factor** (FAK tor) (Section 1, p. 608) | *n.* condition or quality that causes something else to happen | Technology was one <u>factor</u> that led to the Industrial Revolution. |
| **alter** (AWL ter) (Section 1, p. 613) | *v.* to change; to make different | Bridges and tall buildings <u>altered</u> the look of American cities. |
| **eliminate** (ee LIHM ih nayt) (Section 2, p. 615) | *v.* to get rid of | For many Americans, the automobile <u>eliminated</u> the need for horses. |
| **justify** (JUHS tih fī) (Section 2, p. 616) | *v.* to give good reason for an action | Industrialists said that competition <u>justified</u> tough ways of doing business. |
| **accelerate** (ak SEL er ayt) (Section 3, p. 621) | *v.* to increase in speed | Immigration <u>accelerated</u> population growth in the United States. |
| **clinic** (KLIHN ihk) (Section 3, p. 622) | *n.* place where people receive medical treatment, often for free or for a small fee | Poor families went to free <u>clinics</u> because they could not afford medical care. |
| **isolate** (ī sah layt) (Section 4, p. 627) | *v.* to set apart; to separate | Many farmers felt <u>isolated</u> after moving to large, crowded cities. |
| **exclude** (ehks KLYOOD) (Section 4, p. 629) | *v.* to keep out, expel, or reject | All-white schools in the South <u>excluded</u> African American students. |
| **minimum** (MIHN ah muhm) (Section 5, p. 632) | *adj.* smallest amount possible or allowed | The law did not set a <u>minimum</u> wage for factory workers. |
| **circuit** (SIR kuht) (Section 5, p. 633) | *n.* route repeatedly traveled | Preachers followed a regular <u>circuit</u> as they traveled from state to state. |

## Previewing Key Terms and People

patent, p. 610
Thomas Edison, p. 610
Alexander Graham Bell, p. 611
Henry Ford, p. 612
assembly line, p. 613
Wilbur and Orville Wright, p. 613
entrepreneur, p. 614
corporation, p. 614
monopoly, p. 615

Andrew Carnegie, p. 615
John D. Rockefeller, p. 615
trust, p. 615
free enterprise, p. 616
Samuel Gompers, p. 618
collective bargaining, p. 618
urbanization, p. 620
tenement, p. 622
Jane Addams, p. 622

settlement house, p. 622
steerage, p. 626
assimilation, p. 627
anarchist, p. 629
compulsory education, p. 632
realist, p. 634
Mark Twain, p. 634
Joseph Pulitzer, p. 635
yellow journalism, p. 635

# A New Industrial Revolution

## Objectives

1. List reasons industry grew rapidly after the Civil War.

2. Identify inventions and inventors that changed the way Americans lived.

3. Describe the advances that revolutionized transportation.

## Prepare to Read

### 🔄 Reading Skill

**Use Greek Word Origins**
English words may be built on several Greek roots, and each of these may be adapted to modern usage. Thus, once you know the roots of a word, you may need to experiment with different ways to shape an up-to-date word. Use the modern context as your final clue to a word's modern English meaning.

### Vocabulary *Builder*

**High-Use Words**

factor, p. 608

alter, p. 613

### Key Terms and People

patent, p. 610

Thomas Edison, p. 610

Alexander Graham Bell, p. 611

Henry Ford, p. 612

assembly line, p. 613

Wilbur and Orville Wright, p. 613

---

⭐ **Background Knowledge** You have seen how the Industrial Revolution of the early 1800s changed the way Americans lived and worked. In this section, you will learn how a new Industrial Revolution changed life after the Civil War.

## Why Industry Boomed

As the nation expanded westward, conditions were ripe for industrial growth. Vast deposits of coal, iron, lead, and copper now lay within reach of the miner's pickax. The towering forests of the Pacific Northwest furnished lumber for building.

Government policy favored industrial growth. Congress gave generous land grants and other subsidies to railroads and other businesses. The government also kept high tariffs on imports. Tariffs helped American industry by making foreign goods more expensive.

**Steel and Oil** Technology was another <u>factor</u> that spurred industrial growth. In the 1850s, inventors developed the Bessemer process, a method to make stronger steel at a low cost. Steel quickly replaced iron as the basic building material of cities and industry.

Pittsburgh became the nation's steel-making capital. Nearby coal mines and good transportation helped Pittsburgh steel mills thrive. Other steel mills sprang up across the Midwest.

**Main Idea**
Abundant resources, new technology, government aid to business, and a railroad boom all contributed to industrial growth.

**Vocabulary *Builder***
factor (FAK tor) *n.* condition or quality that causes something else to happen

Workers near Titusville, Pennsylvania, tapped a new source of energy in 1859. As they drilled into the ground, a stream of dark liquid gushed upward. It was the nation's first oil strike. The oil industry soon devised methods to refine crude oil into lubricants for machines—and, later, into gasoline to power engines and automobiles. Oil was so valuable it became known as "black gold."

**A Railroad Boom** Railroads fueled industrial growth. Trains carried people and goods to the West and raw materials to eastern factories. Companies improved service by adding sleeping and dining cars and laying down thousands of miles of new tracks.

As more lines were built, railroads sought ways to limit competition and keep prices high. Some big lines consolidated, or combined. They bought up smaller lines or forced them out of business. The Pennsylvania Railroad, for example, consolidated 73 smaller companies. Railroads also gave secret rebates, or discounts, to their best customers. In some places, rival rail lines made agreements to fix rates at a high level.

Such practices helped giant railroads control grain traffic in the West and South. However, high rates angered small farmers, who relied on the railroads to get their goods to market. As a result, many farmers joined the Granger and Populist movements.

☑**Checkpoint** **How did the government support business?**

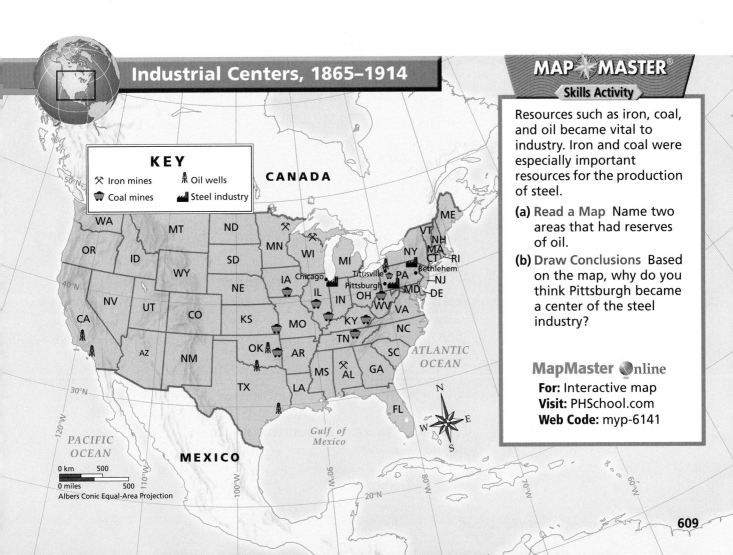

## Industrial Centers, 1865–1914

**KEY**
⚒ Iron mines     🛢 Oil wells
⛏ Coal mines     ⚒ Steel industry

**MAP MASTER**
*Skills Activity*

Resources such as iron, coal, and oil became vital to industry. Iron and coal were especially important resources for the production of steel.

**(a) Read a Map** Name two areas that had reserves of oil.

**(b) Draw Conclusions** Based on the map, why do you think Pittsburgh became a center of the steel industry?

**MapMaster ●nline**
**For:** Interactive map
**Visit:** PHSchool.com
**Web Code:** myp-6141

**609**

# America: Land of Inventors

Thomas Edison once said, "Genius is one percent inspiration and ninety-nine percent perspiration." This combination of imagination and hard work enabled Americans to produce a flood of new inventions in the late 1800s. **Critical Thinking:** *Evaluate Information Which of the inventions shown here do you think did the most to change daily life? Explain your answer.*

**Thomas Edison**
Electric light bulb, 1879

*Extra daylight for work and leisure!*

**Alexander Graham Bell**
Telephone, 1876

*Instant communication over the miles!*

**Main Idea**
Thomas Edison and other inventors created hundreds of devices that made life easier.

## Inventors and Inventions

In the late 1800s, enterprising Americans created an astonishing flood of new inventions. In fact, the government issued more patents in 1897 alone than in the ten years before the Civil War! A **patent** is a document giving someone the sole right to make and sell an invention.

Around the world, the United States became known as a land of invention. Almost every day, it seemed, American inventions made business and life easier.

**Edison's Invention Factory** In 1876, Thomas Edison set up a research laboratory in Menlo Park, New Jersey. At this "invention factory," Edison and other scientists produced the light bulb, the phonograph, the motion picture camera, and hundreds of other useful devices.

Still, such inventions would be worthless without a reliable source of energy. In 1882, Edison opened the nation's first electrical power plant in New York City. Other power plants soon sprang up all over the country. They supplied the electricity that lit up homes, powered city streetcars, and enabled factories to replace steam engines with safer electric engines. The modern age of electricity had begun.

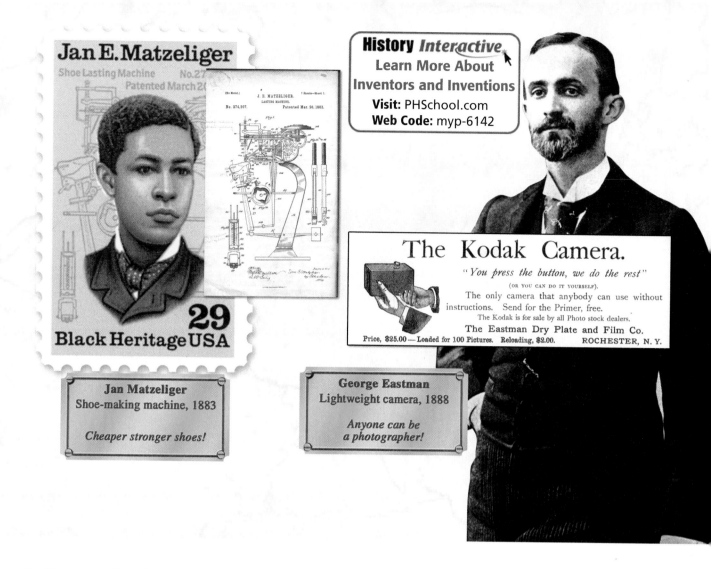

Jan E. Matzeliger
Shoe Lasting Machine   No.27
Patented March 2(

**29**
**Black Heritage USA**

**The Kodak Camera.**
*"You press the button, we do the rest"*
(OR YOU CAN DO IT YOURSELF).
The only camera that anybody can use without
instructions.   Send for the Primer, free.
The Kodak is for sale by all Photo stock dealers.
**The Eastman Dry Plate and Film Co.**
Price, $25.00 — Loaded for 100 Pictures.   Reloading, $2.00.   ROCHESTER, N. Y.

**Jan Matzeliger**
Shoe-making machine, 1883

*Cheaper stronger shoes!*

**George Eastman**
Lightweight camera, 1888

*Anyone can be
a photographer!*

## A Communications Revolution

Improved communication was vital to growing American businesses. The telegraph, in use since 1844, helped people stay in touch with one another. But Americans still had to wait weeks for news from Europe to arrive by boat. In 1866, Cyrus Field had an underwater telegraph cable laid across the Atlantic Ocean that sped communications from Europe.

The telegraph used a code of dots and dashes. Alexander Graham Bell wanted to build a device that would carry the human voice. Bell worked for years inventing this device, which he called the telephone. Finally, in 1876, he sent the first telephone message to his assistant in another room: "Mr. Watson, come here. I want you."

Bell's patent for the telephone was the most valuable patent ever issued. By 1885, more than 300,000 phones had been sold, most of them to businesses. Instead of going to a telegraph office, people could buy, sell, and get information about prices or supplies simply by picking up the telephone. In time, Bell organized over 100 local companies into the giant American Telephone and Telegraph Company.

## Devices for Home and Office

Some inventions made office work faster and cheaper. In 1868, Christopher Sholes invented a letter-writing device called the "Type-Writer." Soon, female typists in offices were churning out letters at 60 words per minute.

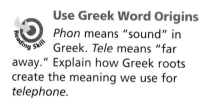

**Use Greek Word Origins**
*Phon* means "sound" in Greek. *Tele* means "far away." Explain how Greek roots create the meaning we use for *telephone*.

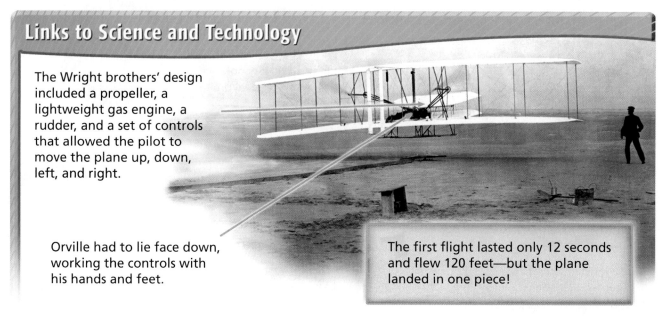

The Wright brothers' design included a propeller, a lightweight gas engine, a rudder, and a set of controls that allowed the pilot to move the plane up, down, left, and right.

Orville had to lie face down, working the controls with his hands and feet.

The first flight lasted only 12 seconds and flew 120 feet—but the plane landed in one piece!

## Human Flight

Until the Wright brothers invented the airplane, people had flown only by wind power, in balloons and gliders. The airplane was revolutionary because it powered itself. In addition, the pilot controlled the movement of the plane. This photograph shows the Wright brothers' first flight on December 17, 1903. **Critical Thinking: *Contrast*** *Identify two ways that the Wright brothers' airplane differed from modern airplanes.*

Some inventions, such as the camera, affected individuals more than businesses. George Eastman introduced a lightweight camera in 1888. It replaced hundreds of pounds of chemicals and equipment. Because Eastman's camera sold at a low price, ordinary people could record their lives on film.

African Americans contributed to the flood of inventions. Jan Matzeliger revolutionized the shoe industry with a machine that sewed the tops to the soles. Granville Woods devised a way to send telegraph messages between moving trains.

☑**Checkpoint**   **Why was Edison's power plant important?**

**Main Idea**
The automobile and the airplane launched an age of fast transportation.

## A Transportation Revolution

Technology also revolutionized transportation. For thousands of years, people had traveled by foot or by horse. Railroads went faster and farther but only where tracks ran.

Then, in the late 1800s, European engineers developed the automobile. Suddenly, people were able to travel almost anywhere and at any time. The development of the automobile ushered in an era of freer and faster transportation.

**Henry Ford** Only 8,000 Americans owned automobiles in 1900. Then, Henry Ford, an American manufacturer, made the automobile available to millions. Ford perfected a system to mass-produce cars and make them available at a lower price.

To speed construction and lower costs, Ford introduced the assembly line in 1913. The **assembly line** is a manufacturing method in which a product is put together as it moves along a belt. As each car frame moved along the belt, one set of workers hooked up the engine, another attached the wheels, and so on. The assembly line sliced production time in half. Lower costs allowed Ford to charge lower prices. By 1917, more than 4.5 million Americans owned cars.

Cars changed the nation's landscape. A web of roads spread across the country. Cities began sprawling into the countryside.

**The Wright Brothers** Another transportation revolution took place in 1903. Wilbur and Orville Wright tested a gas-powered airplane at Kitty Hawk, North Carolina. On its first flight, the plane stayed in the air for 12 seconds and flew 120 feet. Orville made four flights that day. His longest flight lasted 59 seconds.

Surprisingly, the first flights did not attract much interest. No one could see any practical use for a flying machine. The military uses of the airplane did not become clear until World War I (1914–1918). By the 1920s, the airplane had begun to <u>alter</u> the world by making travel quicker and trade easier.

**Vocabulary** *Builder*
<u>alter</u> (AWL ter) *v.* to change; to make different

☑ **Checkpoint** **Why did the cost of automobiles decrease?**

⭐ **Looking Back and Ahead** Resources and technology set the stage for growth. In the next section, you will see how business leaders built on this foundation to create giant industries.

---

**Section 1** | **Check Your Progress**

**Progress Monitoring** 🌐nline
**For:** Self-test with instant help
**Visit:** PHSchool.com
**Web Code:** mya-6141

**Comprehension and Critical Thinking**

**1. (a) Identify** What factors were in place at the end of the Civil War that helped create a surge in industrial growth?
**(b) Analyze Cause and Effect** What effect did the discovery of new energy sources have on the Industrial Revolution?

**2. (a) List** What inventions revolutionized American life in the late 1800s?
**(b) Make Predictions** What impact did Ford's assembly line have on changing American lifestyles?

🔊 **Reading Skill**

**3. Use Greek Word Origins** The Greek root *graph* means "writing," and the Greek root *phon* means "sound." The name of what Edison invention combines these roots?

**Vocabulary** *Builder*

Answer the following questions in complete sentences that show your understanding of the key terms.
**4.** How does a patent protect inventors?
**5.** How did the assembly line revolutionize factories?

**Writing**

**6.** Which of the following statements are logical, and which are not logical? Explain why.
**Statements:**
**(a)** Abundant natural resources aid economic growth because they provide energy and raw materials for manufacturing.
**(b)** Secret rebates are unfair because they encourage business but not the arts.
**(c)** Secret rebates are unfair because they were given to some customers but not to others.
**(d)** Inventions aid industrial growth because they show Americans' special ingenuity.

# Big Business and Organized Labor

## Objectives

1. Describe how new business methods helped American industry grow.

2. Identify the leaders of "big business" and the practices they used.

3. Summarize how working conditions changed as industry grew.

4. Describe workers' efforts to organize during the late 1800s.

## Prepare to Read

### ⟳ Reading Skill

**Use Latin Word Origins**
English words may also combine several Latin roots or words to build one word. Knowledge of the several roots can help you make a general guess of the English word's meaning. Context offers confirming information. As you read Section 2, look for words built on Latin word origins. Notice how this ancient language continues to influence English today.

### Vocabulary *Builder*

**High-Use Words**
eliminate, p. 615
justify, p. 616

**Key Terms and People**
entrepreneur, p. 614
corporation, p. 614
monopoly, p. 615
Andrew Carnegie, p. 615
John D. Rockefeller, p. 615
trust, p. 615
free enterprise, p. 616
Samuel Gompers, p. 618
collective bargaining, p. 618

⭐ **Background Knowledge** You have learned about the new Industrial Revolution that took place after the Civil War. In this section, you will see how this industrial boom had a very different impact on business owners and on workers.

**Main Idea**
Business leaders developed new ways to raise money needed for expansion.

## New Ways of Doing Business

Business expansion was led by bold entrepreneurs (ahn treh preh NYOORZ). An **entrepreneur** is someone who sets up new businesses to make a profit. To raise capital, or money, entrepreneurs adopted new ways of organizing business.

**The Corporation** Many businesses became corporations, or businesses owned by many investors. Corporations raise large amounts of capital by selling stock, or shares. Stockholders receive a share of the profits and pick directors to run the company.

Corporations limited the risk of investors. Owners of other types of businesses could lose their savings, homes, and other property if the business failed. Stockholders risked only the amount of money they had invested.

**Banking** Banks lent huge amounts of capital to corporations. These loans helped American industry grow faster than ever before. They also made huge profits for the bankers.

One banker, J. Pierpont Morgan, made himself the most powerful force in the American economy. Morgan gained control of key industries, such as railroads and steel. In hard times, Morgan and his friends bought stock in troubled corporations. They then ran the companies in ways that <u>eliminated</u> competition and increased profits.

☑ **Checkpoint**  **How did corporations raise capital?**

**Vocabulary** *Builder*
**eliminate** (ee LIHM ih nayt) *v.* to get rid of

## Growth of Big Business

As in Jefferson's time, the government took a laissez-faire approach to business in the late 1800s. Congress rarely made laws to regulate business practices. This atmosphere of freedom encouraged the growth of what came to be known as "big business." Entrepreneurs formed giant corporations and monopolies. A **monopoly** is a company that controls most or all business in a particular industry.

**Main Idea**
By the late 1800s, many major industries were dominated by a few giant companies.

**Carnegie** One of the giants of big business was Andrew Carnegie. A poor Scottish immigrant, he worked his way up in the railroad business. He then entered the growing steel industry. Slowly, Carnegie gained control of every step in making steel. His companies owned iron mines, steel mills, railroads, and shipping lines. In 1892, Carnegie combined his businesses into the giant Carnegie Steel Company. It soon produced more steel than all the mills of England.

As a business leader, Carnegie could be ruthless. Still, he believed that the rich had a duty to improve society. He called his philosophy the Gospel of Wealth. Carnegie donated hundreds of millions of dollars to build libraries and support other charities. "I started life as a poor man," he said, "and I wish to end it that way." Carnegie set up a foundation that continued to fund worthy causes after his death. Many business leaders followed his example.

**Rockefeller** Another business giant, John D. Rockefeller, also came from humble beginnings. Rockefeller was the son of a peddler in New York. At age 23, he invested in an oil refinery. He used the profits to buy other oil companies. Rockefeller was a brilliant entrepreneur. He also did not hesitate to crush competitors, slashing prices to drive rivals out of business.

In 1882, Rockefeller ended competition in the oil industry by forming the Standard Oil Trust. A **trust** is a group of corporations run by a single board of directors. Other industries followed his lead. By 1900, trusts dominated many of the nation's key industries, from meatpacking to sugar refining to the manufacture of copper wire.

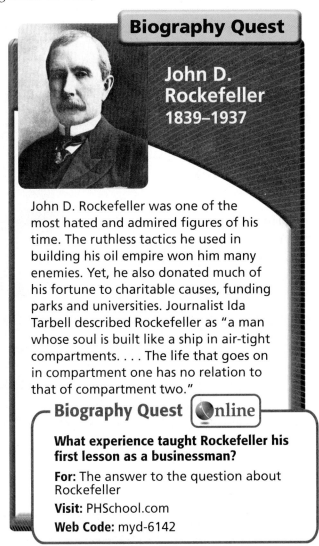

**Biography Quest**

### John D. Rockefeller
**1839–1937**

John D. Rockefeller was one of the most hated and admired figures of his time. The ruthless tactics he used in building his oil empire won him many enemies. Yet, he also donated much of his fortune to charitable causes, funding parks and universities. Journalist Ida Tarbell described Rockefeller as "a man whose soul is built like a ship in air-tight compartments. . . . The life that goes on in compartment one has no relation to that of compartment two."

**Biography Quest** 🌐**nline**

**What experience taught Rockefeller his first lesson as a businessman?**

**For:** The answer to the question about Rockefeller
**Visit:** PHSchool.com
**Web Code:** myd-6142

**Debate Over Trusts** Was big business good or bad for the nation? Americans at the time hotly debated that issue. Today, many historians believe that both views are partly true.

Critics saw trusts as a threat to **free enterprise,** the system in which privately owned businesses compete freely. They saw leaders like Carnegie and Rockefeller as "robber barons" who unfairly eliminated competition. Critics also pointed out that business leaders used their wealth to influence politicians.

Others saw big business leaders as bold "captains of industry" who built up the economy and created jobs. They argued that limiting costly competition allowed companies to lower prices for their products. As a result, American consumers were able to afford more goods and services.

**Social Darwinism** A new philosophy called Social Darwinism also supported the trend toward trusts. Scientist Charles Darwin had said that, in nature, forms of animal and plant life survived if they could adapt to change better than others. Social Darwinism applied this idea of "survival of the fittest" to human affairs.

Big business leaders used Social Darwinism to <u>justify</u> efforts to limit competition. Businesses that drove out their competitors, they said, were "fittest" and deserved to survive. As you will see, Social Darwinism was also used to justify harsh working conditions.

 **Use Latin Word Origins**
The Latin word *ducere* can mean "to draw out." Combine this with *pro-*, meaning "forth." Connect these word origins to the modern usage of the word *products.*

**Vocabulary *Builder***
<u>justify</u> (JUHS tih fī) *v.* to give good reason for an action

✓**Checkpoint** **How did Rockefeller control the oil industry?**

## Trusts and Monopolies: Good or Bad?

A newspaper editor, quoted below, defends the right of businesses to cooperate in forming trusts and monopolies.

❝The right to cooperate is as unquestionable as the right to compete. . . . The trust denies competition only by producing and selling more cheaply than those outside the trust can produce and sell.❞

—Benjamin R. Tucker, Chicago Conference on Trusts

This cartoon presents a different view of giant business monopolies.

**Reading Primary Sources**
**Skills Activity**

By 1900, the question of trusts and monopolies had become one of the most hotly debated issues in the United States.

**(a)** **Interpret Primary Sources** According to Tucker, how does the public benefit from trusts?

**(b)** **Detect Points of View** How does the view of monopoly expressed in the cartoon differ from Tucker's view?

# Changes in the Workplace

Before the Civil War, most factories were small. A boss knew every worker in the shop. As giant industries grew, however, the close relationships between owners and workers ended.

American industry attracted millions of new workers. Most were immigrants or native-born whites. Others were African Americans who left southern farms for northern factories.

**Women and Children** In some industries, the majority of workers were women. They outnumbered men in the textile mills of New England, the tobacco factories of the South, and the garment sweatshops of New York. A sweatshop is a manufacturing workshop where workers toil long hours under poor conditions for low pay.

Children also worked in industry, often in hazardous jobs. In bottle factories, eight-year-old boys ran with white-hot bottles to cooling racks. Children toiled in textile mills, tobacco factories, coal mines, and garment sweatshops. Most child laborers could not go to school. Therefore, they had little chance of improving their lives.

**Dangerous Conditions** Factory work could be dangerous. Breathing in fibers or dust all day, textile workers and miners came down with lung diseases. Steelworkers risked burns and death from vats of molten metal. Employers were not required to pay compensation for injuries suffered on the job. Social Darwinists claimed that such harsh conditions were necessary to cut costs, increase production, and ensure survival of the business.

An accident at a New York sweatshop tragically called attention to the dangers many workers faced. On March 25, 1911, fire broke out in the Triangle Shirtwaist Factory. Within minutes, the upper stories were ablaze. Hundreds of workers raced for the exits only to find them locked. The company had locked the doors to keep workers at their jobs. Panicked workers piled up against the exits.

Firetrucks rushed to the scene, but their ladders were too short to reach the fire. One after another, workers trying to escape the flames leaped to their deaths. Nearly 150 people, most of them young women, died in the Triangle Fire. As a result, New York and other states approved safety laws to help protect factory workers.

☑**Checkpoint** **What dangers did factory workers face?**

# Workers Organize

Since the early days of the Industrial Revolution, factory workers had made attempts to organize. Most early efforts to form unions failed, however. Companies hired private security guards to attack strikers or union organizers. In addition, laws made it illegal for workers to go on strike. Still, workers continued their attempts to form unions, often in secret. Labor unions sought safer working conditions, higher wages, and shorter hours.

**Main Idea**
As industry grew, working conditions often got worse.

Child coal miners

**Main Idea**
Despite many obstacles, organized labor began to grow in the late 1800s.

## A Violent Strike

Strikes often turned violent. This 1877 picture shows a confrontation between Maryland state militia and workers during a railroad strike. At least 10 strikers were killed. **Critical Thinking: *Evaluate Information*** *How does this picture suggest that there was violence on both sides?*

**Knights of Labor** In 1869, a group of Philadelphia clothing workers formed a union called the Knights of Labor. At first, the union was small and secret. Then, in 1879, the Knights elected Terence Powderly as president. Powderly rejected the use of strikes as a tool. Instead, he tried to win support by holding public rallies.

Under Powderly, the Knights of Labor admitted women, African Americans, immigrants, and unskilled workers. No earlier labor union had included all workers. For a time, the Knights became the biggest union in the country.

Union successes were undercut by a series of violent labor disputes. One of the worst episodes occurred in Chicago. On May 4, 1886, striking workers rallied in Haymarket Square. Suddenly, a bomb exploded and killed seven policemen. Police sprayed the crowd with bullets. As a result of such violence, public opinion turned against unions. The Knights of Labor, some of whom were at Haymarket Square, lost much of their influence.

**Rise of the AFL** In 1886, the year of the Haymarket Riot, Samuel Gompers formed a new union in Columbus, Ohio. It was called the American Federation of Labor, or AFL. The AFL soon replaced the Knights of Labor as the leading union in the country.

Unlike the Knights, the AFL admitted skilled workers only. Gompers argued that skilled workers could create a powerful union because their skills made it costly and difficult to train replacements. He also believed that the most effective way to win improvements was through collective bargaining. In collective bargaining, unions negotiate with management for workers as a group. Gompers believed in using strikes, but only if all else failed.

This practical approach worked well. By 1904, the AFL had grown to more than a million members. But because it barred African Americans, immigrants, and unskilled workers, the AFL still included only a tiny fraction of American workers.

**Women in the Labor Movement** Women played leading roles in building unions. Mary Harris Jones tirelessly traveled the country, campaigning for unions and giving support to striking miners. She called attention to the hard lives of children in textile mills. Because of her work with children, people began calling her Mother Jones.

**Bitter Strikes** In 1893, the nation was hit by a severe enconomic depression. Many business owners cut production, fired workers, and slashed wages. A wave of violent strikes swept the country. One of the worst occurred near Chicago. George Pullman, a manufacturer of railroad cars, cut his workers' pay by 25 percent. Still, he refused to lower rents on company-owned housing.

Angry workers struck the Pullman plant. Railroad workers walked off their jobs in support. By July, rail lines were shut down from coast to coast. President Grover Cleveland then sent federal troops to Chicago to end the strike. They were joined by deputies paid by the railroads. Marshals fired on the crowds, killing two protesters.

In such violent labor disputes, the public generally sided with the owners. Most Americans saw striking unions as radical and violent. By 1900, only about 3 percent of American workers belonged to a union.

✓**Checkpoint** **What methods did the AFL use?**

⭐ **Looking Back and Ahead** Big business grew at a rapid pace. Organized labor also grew but faced many obstacles. In the next chapter, you will learn how these trends began to shift.

Mother Jones

---

Section 2 | **Check Your Progress**

**Progress Monitoring** ⏺nline
**For:** Self-test with instant help
**Visit:** PHSchool.com
**Web Code:** mya-6142

**Comprehension and Critical Thinking**

1. (a) **Recall** What big business tactic did Rockefeller use to eliminate competition?
   (b) **Compare and Contrast** How were trusts viewed as both a threat and an advantage to the free enterprise system?

2. (a) **List** How did changes in the factory system affect workers in the late 1800s?
   (b) **Draw Conclusions** Why was there an effort to organize workers into labor unions?

**Reading Skill**

3. **Use Latin Word Origins** Connect the roots *ad-*, meaning "out," and *optare*, meaning "choose or wish," to the modern English word *adopted* as it is used in the following sentence: To raise capital, Americans adopted new ways of organizing business.

**Vocabulary Builder**

4. Draw a table with six rows and two columns. In the first column, list these terms: entrepreneur, corporation, monopoly, trust, free enterprise, collective bargaining. In the next column, write the definition of each word.

**Writing**

5. Which of the following statements seems the most emotional in its appeal? Which seems the most persuasive? Why?
   **Statements:**
   (a) One cause of the Pullman strike was George Pullman's failure to lower rents on company-owned housing.
   (b) One cause of the Pullman strike was George Pullman's unfair treatment of workers.
   (c) One cause of the Pullman strike was a conflict between George Pullman and his workers over wages and rent.

# Cities Grow and Change

## Objectives

1. Explain why cities grew in the late 1800s.

2. Describe the problems city dwellers faced and the efforts to improve city life.

3. Identify the attractions and leisure activities cities offered.

## Prepare to Read

###  Reading Skill

**Use Latin Word Origins** Latin roots can be paired with different prefixes or suffixes to create related words. For example, the root *port* means "carry." Paired with the prefix *sub-,* meaning "beneath," it is the root of the English word *support,* meaning "carry from beneath." Paired with the prefix *im-,* meaning "in or toward," it is the root of the English word *import,* meaning "carry into." As you read, look for examples of words that share a Latin root.

### Vocabulary *Builder*

**High-Use Words**

<u>accelerate</u>, p. 621

<u>clinic</u>, p. 622

**Key Terms and People**

urbanization, p. 620

tenement, p. 622

Jane Addams, p. 622

settlement house, p. 622

---

**Main Idea**
Industrialization, migration, and technology all contributed to the growth of American cities.

**Use Latin Word Origins**
Use the Latin root *tract,* meaning "pull or drag," to define the word *attracting.* Then, name at least one other related word that shows the influence of this root.

☆ **Background Knowledge** You have seen how American industry boomed in the late 1800s. In this section, you will learn how the industrial age reshaped American cities.

## Rapid Growth of Cities

"We cannot all live in cities," wrote journalist Horace Greeley, "yet nearly all seem determined to do so." Greeley was describing the growth of American cities in the late 1800s.

**Urbanization** The rate of urbanization was astonishing. Urbanization is the rapid growth of city populations. In 1860, only one American in five was a city dweller. By 1890, one in three lived in a city. For the first time, the United States had cities the sizes of London and Paris.

The reason for this rapid urbanization was simple. Cities attracted industry, and industry attracted people. Farmers, immigrants, and African Americans from the South all migrated to cities in search of jobs and excitement.

Many fast-growing cities were located near waterways. New York and San Francisco had excellent ocean harbors. Chicago rose on the shores of Lake Michigan. Cities near waterways drew industry because they provided easy transport for goods.

**Growing Out and Up** New technology helped cities grow. Elevated trains carried passengers over crowded streets. In 1887, the first electric streetcar system opened in Richmond, Virginia. Ten years later, the nation's first electric subway trains began running beneath the streets of Boston.

Public transportation gave rise to suburbs, living areas on the outskirts of a city. People no longer had to live in cities to work in cities. Steel bridges also <u>accelerated</u> suburban growth. The Brooklyn Bridge, completed in 1883, linked the city center in Manhattan to outlying Brooklyn. As a result, New York City was able to spread out to house its growing population.

Cities began to expand upward as well as outward. In 1885, architects in Chicago constructed the first 10-story building. People called it a "skyscraper" because its top seemed to touch the sky. By 1900, steel-framed skyscrapers up to 30 stories high towered over cities. Electric elevators whisked office workers to the upper floors.

As cities grew outward from their old downtown sections, living patterns changed. Many cities took on a similar shape. Poor families crowded into the oldest sections at the city's center. Middle-class people lived farther out in row houses or new apartment buildings. The rich built fine homes on the outskirts of the city.

☑Checkpoint **How did technology change city life?**

## Problems of Urban Life

Rapid urbanization brought many problems. Fire was a constant threat in tightly packed neighborhoods. In 1871, fire engulfed Chicago. Winds blew flames across the city faster than a person could run. The Chicago Fire leveled 3 square miles of downtown, killed 300 people, and left 18,000 homeless.

**Main Idea**
As cities grew, they faced a variety of problems, especially in the poorest neighborhoods.

**Discovery SCHOOL**

**Explore More Video**
To learn more about the changes in city life, view the video.

**A Changing City** Cities underwent great changes in the late 1800s. The photograph shows a Chicago street in 1900. **Critical Thinking:** *Link Past and Present* Describe two ways a picture of this street today might look different.

Elevated railroad

12-story skyscraper

BOSTON STORE

Rapidly growing population

Electric streetcar

**A Tenement Family**
This photograph shows a family in their New York tenement apartment. **Critical Thinking: Clarify Problems** *Based on this photograph and your reading, identify one problem this family might face daily.*

**Vocabulary *Builder***
<u>clinic</u> (KLIHN ihk) *n.* place where people receive medical treatment, often for free or for a small fee

**Tenement Life** In downtown slums, the poor lived in bleak conditions. People crowded into tenements, buildings divided into many tiny apartments. Many apartments had no windows, heat, or indoor plumbing. Often, 10 people might live in a single room. Several families shared a single bathroom.

Slum streets were littered with garbage. Outbreaks of cholera and other diseases were common. Babies ran the greatest risk. In one Chicago slum, half of all babies died before the age of one.

**Improving City Life** In the 1880s, cities began to improve urban life. They installed streetlights and set up fire, sanitation, and police departments. Public health officials waged war on disease.

Religious groups served the poor. Mother Cabrini, a Catholic nun, set up hospitals and <u>clinics</u> for people who could not afford a doctor. The Salvation Army, founded by a Methodist minister, gave food, clothing, and shelter to the homeless.

**Settlement Houses** Reformers like Jane Addams worked hard for poor city dwellers. Addams came from a well-to-do family, but she felt strong sympathy for the poor. In 1889, she opened Hull House, a settlement house in the slums of Chicago. A settlement house is a center offering help to the urban poor. Soon, reformers—most of them women—had started settlement houses in other major cities.

At settlement houses, volunteers taught English to immigrants, sponsored music and sports for young people, and provided nurseries for children of working mothers. Addams and other settlement house leaders also pressured state legislatures to outlaw child labor.

✔**Checkpoint** **What problems did tenement dwellers face?**

# The Excitement of City Life

Despite hardships, cities offered attractions that were not available in the country. Newcomers were awed by electric lights that turned night into day, elevated railroads rumbling overhead, and tall buildings that seemed to pierce the clouds.

**Department Stores** Downtown shopping areas attracted hordes of people. People came to buy the goods pouring in from American factories. To meet the needs of shoppers, merchants developed a new type of store, the department store.

Earlier, people had bought shirts in one store, boots in another, and lamps in a third. A department store offered all of these goods in separate sections of the same store. Shoppers could wander from floor to floor, bathed in light from crystal chandeliers. Elegant window displays advertised the goods for sale.

**Leisure Activities** Long hours on the job made people value their free time. This strict division between work and play led to a new interest in leisure. To meet this need, cities provided a wealth of entertainment. Almost every museum, orchestra, art gallery, and theater was located in a city. Circuses drew audiences with elephants, lions, acrobats, and clowns.

In the 1850s, Frederick Law Olmsted planned Central Park in New York. Other cities followed suit. Parks, zoos, and gardens allowed urban dwellers to enjoy green grass and open air.

**Main Idea**
Cities lured newcomers with a wide variety of attractions and leisure activities.

## Cause and Effect

### CAUSES
- Growth of industries in cities attracted workers.
- African Americans from the South and immigrants sought a better life.
- Many cities near waterways attracted industries.
- Technological advances led cities to construct subways, trolleys, streetlights, bridges, and skyscrapers.
- Many leisure activities that cities provided drew people to urban areas.

### URBANIZATION

### EFFECTS
- Urban transportation systems enabled people to live in one part of the city and work in another.
- Flood of people into cities led to teeming neighborhoods that became slums.
- Improvements in transportation gave rise to suburbs.

### Reading Charts
#### Skills Activity

The movement of large numbers of people to cities was one of the biggest social changes of the late 1800s.

**(a) Interpret Charts** How did technology encourage the growth of cities?

**(b) Analyze Cause and Effect** Why was the growth of industry a cause of urbanization?

**Sports** Americans had always enjoyed outdoor games. Not until after the Civil War, however, did professional sports teams begin to spring up in cities. The most popular sport by far was baseball. A guidebook of the time noted:

> "Base ball first taught us Americans the value of physical exercise as an important aid . . . in cultivating the mind up to its highest point. It is to the introduction of base ball as a national pastime, in fact, that the growth of athletic sports in general in popularity is largely due."
>
> —*Spalding's Official Base Ball Guide,* 1889

The first professional team, the Cincinnati Red Stockings, appeared in 1869. Only seven years later, teams from eight cities formed the National League of Professional Baseball Clubs. A game might draw as many as 5,000 fans, loudly rooting for their city's home team. African American players, banned from the majors in the 1880s, formed their own professional baseball league.

In 1891, James Naismith nailed two peach baskets to the walls of a gym in Springfield, Massachusetts. He handed players a soccer ball and challenged them to throw the ball in the basket. The new game, called basketball, became a favorite winter sport. Football was also popular. At the time, the sport was brutal and dangerous. Players wore no helmets. In one season, 44 college players died of injuries.

Early baseball glove and baseball card

✓**Checkpoint** What leisure activities did city dwellers enjoy?

☆ **Looking Back and Ahead** You have already learned that immigration contributed to the growth of cities. In the next section, you will take a closer look at immigrant life.

---

**Section 3** | **Check Your Progress**

**Progress Monitoring** Online
**For:** Self-test with instant help
**Visit:** PHSchool.com
**Web Code:** mya-6143

**Comprehension and Critical Thinking**

**1. (a) Describe** Why did cities grow rapidly after the Civil War?
**(b) Apply Information** What role did technology play in urbanization? Give at least two examples.

**2. (a) Identify** What type of housing did poor city dwellers live in?
**(b) Identify Benefits** Why do you think many people wanted to live in cities in spite of harsh conditions?

**Reading Skill**

**3. Use Latin Word Origins** The Latin root *urb* means "city." How does this influence the meaning of the term suburb? What other word in Section 3 shows the influence of the root *urb*?

**Vocabulary** *Builder*

Read each sentence below. If the sentence is true, write YES. If the sentence is not true, write NO and explain why.

**4.** Urbanization was the result of people moving to western farms.

**5.** Tenements were apartments used by the wealthy.

**6.** Settlement houses provided needed services for city dwellers.

**Writing**

**7.** "Life in a city is more rewarding than life outside a city." List two or three arguments in favor of this opinion and two or three arguments opposing this opinion.

# 4 The New Immigrants

## Objectives

1. Identify the reasons immigration to the United States increased in the late 1800s.

2. Describe the difficulties immigrants faced adjusting to their new lives.

3. Discuss how immigrants assimilated and contributed to American life.

4. Describe efforts to limit immigration.

## Prepare to Read

 **Reading Skill**

**Use Other Word Origins** The English language reflects interactions with cultures from around the world. Some words have been adopted in their original form. Others have changed in spelling or pronunciation but still show the influence of the original language.

## Vocabulary *Builder*

**High-Use Words**

<u>isolate</u>, p. 627

<u>exclude</u>, p. 629

**Key Terms**

steerage, p. 626

assimilation, p. 627

anarchist, p. 629

⭐ **Background Knowledge** The industrial age changed the face of cities with new buildings and bridges. It also changed the population. In this section, you will learn about the millions of people immigrating to the United States during this time.

## A Fresh Start

Between 1865 and 1915, some 25 million immigrants entered the United States—more than the population of the entire country in 1850! They were part of a worldwide surge of migration.

**Reasons for Migration** There were many reasons for this vast migration. In European nations such as Italy, the amount of farmland was shrinking as populations swelled. Machines were replacing farmhands, forcing more people from the land. They looked to the United States as a "land of opportunity" where they could build a better life.

Other immigrants sought religious freedom. In the 1880s, Jews in Russia became targets of government-sponsored pogroms (POH grohmz), or violent attacks against Jews. Armenian Christians faced similar persecution in Turkey.

Finally, political unrest drove many from their native lands. In 1910, a revolution in Mexico pushed tens of thousands of refugees across the Rio Grande.

Jobs pulled immigrants to the United States. Steamship companies and railroads, which profited from immigration, sent agents to Asia and Europe to advertise cheap land and plentiful jobs. The promise of freedom also drew people from lands without traditions of democracy and liberty.

**Main Idea**

In the late 1800s, a new wave of immigrants came to the United States for economic and political reasons.

Poor Italian villager

## Immigration, 1865–1915

### Immigration to the United States, 1865–1915

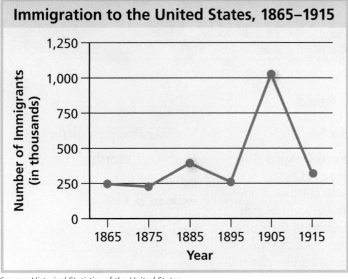

Source: *Historical Statistics of the United States*

### Sources of Emigration, 1865–1915

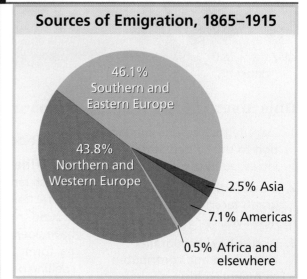

46.1% Southern and Eastern Europe

43.8% Northern and Western Europe

2.5% Asia

7.1% Americas

0.5% Africa and elsewhere

Source: *Historical Statistics of the United States*

### Reading Charts
#### Skills Activity

The line graph at left shows how immigration increased in the decades after the Civil War. The pie chart on the right shows where these "new immigrants" in the United States came from.

**(a) Read a Graph** Approximately how many immigrants entered the United States in 1875? In 1905?

**(b) Draw Inferences** Based on your reading, how would the pie chart have looked different in the 1830s?

**The New Immigrants** In the early 1800s, most immigrants were Protestants from northern and western Europe. Many spoke English and had experience in democracy.

By contrast, most of the "new immigrants" who began to arrive in the late 1800s came from nations of southern and eastern Europe, such as Italy, Poland, Russia, and Greece. Most were Catholic or Jewish. A smaller number came from Asia and the Pacific. Few understood English or had experience living in a democracy or in a city.

☑**Checkpoint** Why did many people leave their homelands?

**Main Idea**
Immigrants faced many challenges to settle in the United States.

## Starting a New Life

The decision to emigrate was difficult. It meant leaving home, family, and friends and starting a strange life. (For more on the immigrants' experiences, see the Life at the Time feature in this chapter.)

**Coming to America** The passage by boat was miserable. Immigrants were crammed below decks in steerage, large compartments that usually held cattle. The tight, airless berths were breeding grounds for disease. Rough seas sickened the travelers.

Most people coming from Europe landed in New York. After 1892, they went to the receiving center on Ellis Island. Asian immigrants entered through Angel Island in San Francisco Bay.

New arrivals faced a rigorous physical examination at the receiving centers. Did they limp? Were their eyes free of disease? Those judged to be disabled or seriously ill might be sent home.

**Immigrant Neighborhoods** Once admitted to the United States, about two thirds of immigrants settled in cities, near other people from the same country. Ethnic neighborhoods helped people feel less <u>isolated</u> in their new homes.

In immigrant neighborhoods, sidewalks rang with the sounds of Italian, Chinese, Yiddish, and other languages. Newcomers celebrated familiar holidays and cooked foods from the old country, such as kielbasa (Polish sausage) and goulash (Hungarian stew). Italians joined social groups such as the Sons of Italy. Greeks read newspapers in Greek. Small storefronts were turned into Jewish synagogues or Buddhist temples.

**Vocabulary** *Builder*
**isolate** (ī sah layt) *v.* to set apart; to separate

☑**Checkpoint**   **What hardships did immigrants face?**

# Becoming American

Immigrant neighborhoods were springboards to a new life. Organizations called immigrant aid societies helped new arrivals with clothing, housing, and language classes.

**Main Idea**
For many immigrants, the goal was to become part of American life and culture.

**Assimilation** Newcomers often felt caught between the old world and new. Most clung to traditional modes of worship, family life, and community relations. At the same time, they worked hard to assimilate. Assimilation is the process of becoming part of another culture.

Children of immigrants assimilated more rapidly than their parents. Surrounded by English-speakers in school and on the street, they learned the language quickly. They played baseball and dressed like native-born Americans. Immigrant parents felt both pride and pain as they saw their children change.

**Becoming American**
Citizenship classes, like the one shown here, were an important step toward assimilation. **Critical Thinking:** *Draw Inferences What subjects do you think students like these might study in citizenship classes?*

This man is labeled *Russian Anarchist.*

This man is labeled *Italian Brigand.* A brigand is a bandit.

### A Nativist View of Immigration

In this 1891 cartoon, the man in the suit tells Uncle Sam that he can get rid of anarchy, crime, and other ills by restricting immigration. **Critical Thinking: *Detect Bias*** *What details create a negative picture of immigrants?*

Still, the fondest dream of many immigrants was to educate their children so that the next generation could be better off. One Russian Jewish immigrant called education "the essence of American opportunity, the treasure that no thief could touch . . . surer, safer than bread or shelter."

**Contributions of Immigrants** The labor of immigrants was essential to the new American economy. Desperate for money, newcomers took whatever jobs they could find. Immigrants worked in steel mills, meatpacking plants, mines, and garment sweatshops. They helped build subways, skyscrapers, and bridges. Chinese, Irish, and Mexican workers laid down hundreds of miles of railroad track in the West.

Through hard work and saving, many immigrants slowly advanced economically. Often, they began by opening small businesses, such as stores or barbershops, to serve their communities. In time, their customers expanded beyond the neighborhood. Outsiders might bring their clothing to Chinese laundries or buy foods they had never tasted before. In this way, ethnic foods such as spaghetti, chow mein, and bagels became part of American life.

Individual immigrants made major contributions. Andrew Carnegie and Alexander Graham Bell were born in Scotland. Samuel Goldwyn and Louis Mayer, Jewish immigrants from Eastern Europe, established the motion picture industry in California. Italian-born Arturo Toscanini became a famous orchestra conductor. Belgian immigrant Leo Baekeland invented the first plastic.

☑**Checkpoint** **How did immigrants assimilate?**

**Use Other Word Origins**
Identify the words in this paragraph that came into English from the Yiddish word *beygl,* meaning "ring or bracelet," and the Italian word *spago,* meaning "string or cord."

# A New Wave of Nativism

As in the 1840s, increased immigration led to a wave of nativism. Nativists sought to preserve the United States for native-born American citizens.

Nativists argued that the new immigrants would not assimilate because their languages, religions, and customs were too different. They also charged that immigrants took jobs away from Americans. Nativists associated immigrants with violence, crime, and anarchy. An **anarchist** is a person who opposes all forms of government.

On the West Coast, nativist feelings against Chinese immigrants ran high. Mobs drove Chinese from mining camps and cities and sometimes killed them. In 1882, Congress passed a law to <u>exclude</u> Chinese laborers from the United States. The Chinese Exclusion Act was the first law limiting immigration based on race. It was finally repealed in 1943.

In 1917, Congress passed a law that denied entry to immigrants who could not read their own languages. Since education at the time was usually restricted to the wealthy, this law barred most of the world's poor people from immigrating to the United States.

☑**Checkpoint**  **Why did nativists oppose immigration?**

☆ **Looking Back and Ahead**  Although immigration slowed after 1917, it never stopped. In the 1960s, Congress finally eased restrictions on immigration.

**Main Idea**
Many Americans distrusted immigrants and called for limits on immigration.

**Vocabulary Builder**
**exclude** (ehks KLYOOD) *v.* to keep out, expel, or reject

---

Section 4 | **Check Your Progress**

**Progress Monitoring ⊕nline**
**For:** Self-test with instant help
**Visit:** PHSchool.com
**Web Code:** mya-6144

## Comprehension and Critical Thinking

**1. (a) List** Why did people immigrate to the United States in the late 1800s?
**(b) Frame Questions** What five questions could you ask one of those immigrants?

**2. (a) Describe** How did immigrants try to assimilate?
**(b) Detect Bias** How did nativists feel about the ability of immigrants to assimilate?

## ⊙ Reading Skill

**3. Use Other Word Origins** The text lists *kielbasa* and *goulash*, food items introduced to America by immigrants. The Polish and Hungarian words are used because these foods have no English-word counterparts. On your own or with a partner, name foods from other cultures. Do we use the original name or an English word?

## Vocabulary *Builder*

Complete each of the following sentences so that the second part explains the first part and shows your understanding of the term.
**4.** Many immigrants traveled across the ocean in steerage; _____.
**5.** Immigrants blended into American life through a process called assimilation; _____.

## Writing

**6.** Imagine that you are writing an editorial in which you object to a bill that excludes immigrants who could not read their own languages. Which of the following arguments is most persuasive? Why? **Arguments:**

**(a)** Many native-born American citizens do not know how to read, so the bill uses an unfair standard for immigrants.

**(b)** Immigrants come to this country for a better life, which includes getting an education.

**(c)** The bill is being used as a trick to restrict all immigration.

# An Immigrant's Journey

From all over the world, immigrants poured into the United States. Wherever they came from, these newcomers shared many of the same hopes, fears, and challenges.

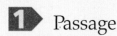 **Passage**

Immigrants faced a long, difficult ocean crossing crowded into ship holds that were designed to carry cargo or cattle.

*"Day after day the weather was bad and the sea stormy. The hatch was tightly closed and there was no circulation of air, so we were all tortured by the bad odor."*

—Japanese immigrant
describes the voyage

**European immigrants arrive in New York**

**2 Arrival**

New York's Ellis Island was the point of entry for many European immigrants. Asians were detained on Angel Island outside San Francisco.

*"Immigration officials slammed a tag on you with your name, address, country of origin, etc. . . . Then they pushed you and they'd point, because they didn't know whether you spoke English or not."*

—Irish immigrant
describes arrival at Ellis Island

## 3 ▶ Ethnic Neighborhoods

Crowded into ethnic neighborhoods, immigrants preserved familiar ways as they adjusted to their new culture.

A street in a Jewish neighborhood in New York

*"When we first arrived we still wore our wooden shoes. . . . We conquered the English language beautifully. My father spoke well. But in the home we spoke Frisian."*

**–Dutch immigrant describes life in America**

## 4 ▶ Citizenship

For many immigrants, becoming a citizen was the proudest moment of their lives.

A new citizen is sworn in

*"I am the youngest of America's children, and into my hands is given all her priceless heritage. . . . Mine is the whole majestic past, and mine is the shining future."*

**–Russian immigrant expresses pride in becoming U.S. citizen**

### *Analyze* LIFE AT THE TIME

Suppose that you are an immigrant in 1900. For each stage of the journey from passage to citizenship, write a sentence describing your hopes or your fears.

## Objectives

1. Explain how public education changed after 1870.

2. Identify new American writers and the topics they wrote about.

3. Describe the growth of the American newspaper industry.

## Prepare to Read

### 🔁 Reading Skill

**Use Popular Word Origins**
Some words and phrases do not come from formal languages. Instead, they arise from popular use. For example, in the previous section, you saw that *basketball* got its name because it was originally played using peach baskets. The term *basketball* remained even when people stopped using real baskets to play with. Other words and phrases also have origins in popular usage that have since gone out of date.

### Vocabulary *Builder*

**High-Use Words**
**minimum**, p. 632
**circuit**, p. 633

**Key Terms and People**
compulsory education, p. 632
realist, p. 634
Mark Twain, p. 634
Joseph Pulitzer, p. 635
yellow journalism, p. 635

⭐ **Background Knowledge** You have learned how northern states established tax-supported public schools in the mid-1800s. In this section, you will learn how the expansion of public education was linked to other changes in American culture.

## Educating Americans

**Main Idea**
States took steps to expand education, including requiring children to attend school.

Before 1870, fewer than half of American children went to school. Many attended one-room schoolhouses, with all age levels and only one teacher. As industry grew, people realized that the nation needed an educated workforce. As a result, states improved public schools at all levels.

**Vocabulary *Builder***
**minimum** (MIHN ah muhm) *adj.*
smallest amount possible or allowed

**Education Expands** In 1852, Massachusetts passed the first compulsory education law. Compulsory education is the requirement that children attend school up to a certain age. Other states in the North, Midwest, and West followed. Most states required a minimum tenth-grade education.

In the South, which had no tradition of public schools, the Freedmen's Bureau built grade schools for both white and black students. Southern states were more reluctant to pass compulsory education laws than states in the North or West. Still, by 1918, every state required children to attend school.

After the Civil War, many cities and towns built public high schools. By 1900, there were 6,000 high schools in the country. Still, not until 1950 did the majority of Americans of high school age graduate.

Higher education also expanded. New private colleges for both women and men opened. Many states built universities that offered free or low-cost education.

**The School Day** For elementary school students, the typical school day lasted from 8:00 A.M. to 4:00 P.M. Pupils learned the "three Rs": reading, 'riting, and 'rithmetic.

The most widely used textbooks were *McGuffey's Eclectic Readers.* Students memorized and recited lessons that had titles like "Waste Not, Want Not." Such poems and stories taught not only reading but also moral values and the Christian religion.

**Education for Adults** Older Americans also got more opportunity to widen their knowledge. Wealthy individuals such as Andrew Carnegie gave money to towns and cities to build public libraries. Libraries offered more than books and magazines. Speakers often gave talks on important topics of the day.

In 1874, a Methodist minister opened a summer school for Bible teachers along Lake Chautauqua (shuh TAWK wuh) in New York. The next year, the camp was opened to the public. Mostly middle-class men and women gathered at Chautauqua to hear lectures on a wide variety of subjects. The Chautauqua Society later began sending out traveling companies on a wide <u>circuit</u>. In time, Chautauquas reached as many as 5 million people in 10,000 towns each year.

**Vocabulary *Builder***
**circuit** (SIR kuht) *n.* route repeatedly traveled

✓**Checkpoint**   **How did states expand public education?**

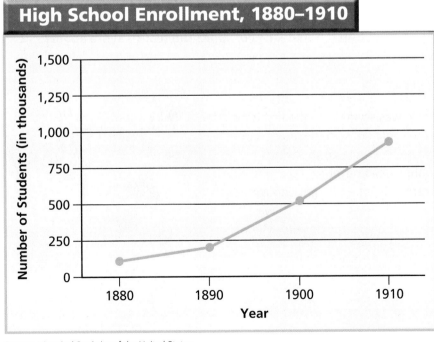

**High School Enrollment, 1880–1910**

Source: *Historical Statistics of the United States*

**Reading Charts**
**Skills Activity**

The late 1800s saw a dramatic rise in public high school enrollment.

**(a) Read a Chart** How many Americans attended public high schools in 1880? In 1910?

**(b) Distinguish Relevant Information** Which of the following might help you understand the reasons for the trend shown on the graph: a mathematics textbook from 1890; a list showing when states passed compulsory education laws; a population graph? Explain.

# New American Writers

As learning became available to more people, Americans began to read more books and magazines. Many bestsellers were dime novels, low-priced paperbacks that often told thrilling tales of the "Wild West." One popular writer, Horatio Alger, wrote "rags-to-riches" stories about poor boys who became successful through hard work, courage, and honesty.

**Realism** Other American writers were realists, writers who try to show life as it is. They often emphasized the harsh side. Some, such as Stephen Crane, had been newspaper reporters. Crane depicted the hardships of slum life in his novel *Maggie: A Girl of the Streets.*

California-born Jack London wrote of miners and sailors who risked their lives in backbreaking jobs. Kate Chopin shocked readers with *The Awakening,* a novel about an unhappily married woman. The poems of Paul Laurence Dunbar described the joys and sorrows of black life. He was the first African American to earn a living as a writer.

**Mark Twain** The most popular author of the time was Mark Twain, the pen name of Samuel Clemens. Twain made his stories realistic by capturing the speech patterns of southerners who lived and worked along the Mississippi River.

Twain set his novel *Huckleberry Finn* in the days before the Civil War. Huck, an uneducated boy, and Jim, an escaped slave, raft down the Mississippi River together. Though brought up to believe slavery is right, Huck comes to respect Jim and decides to help him win his freedom.

Some parents complained that Huck was a crude character who would have a bad effect on children. But today, many critics consider *Huckleberry Finn* to be one of the greatest American novels.

✓**Checkpoint**   What kinds of topics did realists write about?

**Use Popular Word Origins**
Based on context clues, what do you think the phrase *pen name* means? What do you think was the origin of this term?

**Huckleberry Finn**
In this passage from Mark Twain's *Huckleberry Finn*, shown below, Huck recounts a conversation with his friend Jim, an escaped slave. **Critical Thinking:** *Evaluate Information* How does the language in this passage give a sense of realism?

Mark Twain

"He was saying how the first thing he would do when he got to a free State he would go to saving up money and never spend a single cent, and when he got enough he would buy his wife, which was owned on a farm close to where Miss Watson lived; and then they would both work to buy the two children, and if their master wouldn't sell them, they'd get an Ab'litionist to go and steal them."

Cover of an early edition of *Huckleberry Finn*

# A Newspaper Boom

The number of American newspapers grew dramatically in the late 1800s. By 1900, half the newspapers in the world were printed in the United States.

**Causes** The spread of education was one reason for the growth of the newspaper industry. As more Americans could read, they bought more newspapers and magazines.

The newspaper boom was also linked to urbanization. In towns and villages, neighbors could share news face to face. In cities, people needed newspapers to stay informed.

**A New Kind of Newspaper** A Hungarian immigrant, Joseph Pulitzer, created the first modern, mass-circulation newspaper. In 1883, Pulitzer bought the *New York World*. He immediately cut the price so that more people could afford it.

Pulitzer added crowd-pleasing features to his newspaper, including color comics. The Yellow Kid, a tough but sweet slum boy, became the first popular American comic strip character.

The *New York World* became known for sensational headlines that screamed of crime and scandal. Readership skyrocketed, and other papers followed his lead. Because of the Yellow Kid, critics coined the term yellow journalism to describe the sensational reporting style of the *New York World* and other papers.

☑️**Checkpoint**  Why did the newspaper industry grow?

⭐ **Looking Back and Ahead** In this section, you saw how education increased the popularity and influence of newspapers. In the next chapter, you will see how newspapers and magazines contributed to a growing reform movement.

**Main Idea**

Education contributed to a rapid growth in American newspapers.

The Yellow Kid

---

Section 5 | **Check Your Progress**

**Progress Monitoring** 🌐nline
**For:** Self-test with instant help
**Visit:** PHSchool.com
**Web Code:** mya-6145

## Comprehension and Critical Thinking

1. **(a) Describe** What were schools like before 1870?
   **(b) Draw Inferences** Why do you think compulsory education laws were important for the industrialized North?

2. **(a) Identify** What were the goals of realists?
   **(b) Apply Information** How did Mark Twain's use of language make his stories more realistic?

## 🔵 Reading Skill

3. **Use Popular Word Origins** The phrase "yellow journalism" is still used to describe one type of reporting. How has the meaning separated from its origin?

## Vocabulary *Builder*

Read each sentence below. If the sentence is true, write YES and explain why. If the sentence is not true, write NO and explain why not.

4. Yellow journalism used sensational headlines to attract readers.

5. Mark Twain was not a realist because he wrote about people.

6. Compulsory education allowed parents to choose whether or not to send children to school.

## Writing

7. Do you think memorizing and reciting lessons from books like *McGuffey's Readers* is a useful way for children to learn? Write a paragraph explaining your opinion. Give at least two reasons.

Economic and social factors often affect political decisions. A cost-benefit analysis is one tool that helps people make these decisions. A cost-benefit analysis compares the costs and benefits, or rewards, that would result if a certain choice were made.

This is an excerpt from the 1902 book *The Battle With the Slum* by Jacob Riis. He was a journalist, photographer, and reformer who focused attention on the conditions in the slums of New York City.

**Primary Source**

"The East Side, that had been orderly, became a hotbed of child crime. . . . Yesterday, Mayor Low's reform government voted $6 million for new schools. . . . In the most crowded neighborhood in all the world, where the superintendent lately pleaded in vain for three new schools, half a dozen have been built, the finest in this or any other land—great, light, and airy structures, with playgrounds on the roof; and all over the city the like are going up.

The briefest of our laws . . . says that never one shall be built without its playground. And not for the child's use only. The band shall play there yet and neighbor meet neighbor in such social contact as the slum has never known to its undoing . . . Clergymen applaud the opening of the school buildings on Sunday for concerts, lectures, and neighborhood meetings. Common sense is having its day. The streets are cleaned."

—Jacob Riis, *The Battle With the Slum*

## Learn the Skill
*Use these steps to conduct a cost-benefit analysis.*

1. **Identify the issue.** What is the economic, social, or political issue being considered? Look for the main idea and important details.

2. **List the costs and benefits.** Make a two-column chart. List the benefits in the first column and the costs in the second column.

3. **Compare the costs and the benefits.** Are the benefits greater than the costs? Are the costs greater than the benefits?

4. **Make the best decision.** Based on the costs and benefits in the chart, choose the option that makes the best sense. Be able to give reasons for your choice.

## Practice the Skill
*Answer the following questions about the primary source on this page.*

1. **Identify the issue.** (a) What issue is discussed? (b) What are two details relating to the issue?

2. **List the costs and benefits.** Make a chart listing the costs and benefits.

3. **Compare the costs and the benefits.** Are the benefits greater than the costs? Explain.

4. **Make the best decision.** Based on the information in your chart, what decision would you make about the issue? Explain your answer.

## Apply the Skill
*See the Review and Assessment at the end of this chapter.*

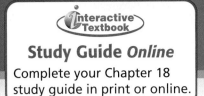

**Interactive Textbook**

**Study Guide** *Online*
Complete your Chapter 18 study guide in print or online.

## Chapter Summary

### Section 1
### A New Industrial Revolution

- The discovery of valuable resources fed a major growth in industry.
- Inventions such as the electric light, the telephone, and the automobile changed life.

### Section 2
### Big Business and Organized Labor

- Industrial growth gave rise to new forms of business, such as corporations and trusts.
- Harsh working conditions led to the formation of labor unions.

### Section 3
### Cities Grow and Change

- People migrated to cities to find jobs.
- Rapid urbanization created such problems as poor housing and sanitation.

### Section 4
### The New Immigrants

- Twenty-five million immigrants entered the United States between 1865 and 1915.
- The work of immigrants contributed to the growth of the American economy.
- A new wave of nativists sought to limit immigration.

### Section 5
### Education and Culture

- Education expanded in response to the needs of industry.
- As more people learned to read, popular books and newspapers boomed.

Immigrant family

## Key Concepts

These notes will help you to prepare for questions about the key concepts.

### The Growth of Big Business

**Causes**
- A growing network of railroads allows access to natural resources.
- U.S. government gives land grants and other subsidies to businesses.
- New inventions and the assembly line lower costs and raise profit.
- Banks loan corporations large amounts of money.
- Stockholders invest money in large corporations.

**Effects**
- Heads of corporations and bankers gain money and influence.
- Some business leaders use their wealth to set up charities.
- Corporations form trusts that get control of key industries and crush the competition.
- Facing hazardous conditions in large factories, workers begin to organize and demand better working conditions.

### Facts About Immigration in the Late 1800s

**Reasons for Coming to America**
- Hope of gaining land or work
- Escape from religious persecution
- Desire to benefit from public education system

**Hardships Faced**
- Traveling in steerage
- Getting examined at the port of entry
- Learning a new language and a new culture
- Facing the prejudice of "nativists"

## Vocabulary *Builder*

### Key Terms

Answer the questions in complete sentences that show your understanding of the key terms.

1. Why did inventors apply for patents?

2. How did forming corporations help entrepreneurs raise capital?

3. Why did Samuel Gompers favor collective bargaining?

4. Why was assimilation a goal of many immigrants?

5. What services did settlement houses provide?

## Comprehension and Critical Thinking

6. (a) **Describe** What government policies helped to spark industrial growth?
   (b) **Clarify Problems** How did the policies of the federal government create problems for small businesses?

7. (a) **Identify** Identify two devices invented by Thomas Edison.
   (b) **Draw Conclusions** Some people think Edison's creation of a research laboratory was more important than any of his inventions. Give one reason for this opinion.

8. (a) **Recall** What happened at Haymarket Square on May 4, 1886?
   (b) **Analyze Cause and Effect** How did the events at Haymarket Square and the Pullman plant affect public opinion toward unions?

9. (a) **Summarize** What did Horace Greeley mean when he said, "We cannot all live in cities, yet nearly all seem determined to do so"?
   (b) **Identify Costs and Benefits** How did the new Industrial Revolution affect the way of life in cities?

10. (a) **Describe** What jobs did immigrants hold after arriving in the United States?
    (b) **Identify Economic Benefits** Why do you think immigrants were willing to work long hours in dangerous conditions for little pay?

11. (a) **Describe** What was a typical school day like for a child in the 1880s?
    (b) **Draw Conclusions** What impact did the Industrial Revolution have on education in America?

## ⊙ History Reading Skill

12. **Use Word Origins** Choose an English word from this chapter, and trace its language influences. Use a print or online dictionary. Most entries will show the languages a word has passed through, in order from most recent to most distant. List the languages your chosen word has moved through.

## Writing

13. **Write a Persuasive Paragraph:**
    Choose one headline from the list below and write a persuasive paragraph that gives your opinion on the issue. Remember to support your opinion with facts, examples, and reasons.
    • Captains of Industry: Heroes or Tyrants?
    • Immigration: A Benefit or a Danger?
    • The New Industrial Revolution: A Better Life or a Less Human One?

14. **Write a Narrative:**
    Imagine that you are a settlement house worker in a large city in the late 1800s. Write a letter to a friend describing why you have chosen to live among the poor.

## Skills for Life

### Conduct a Cost-Benefit Analysis

The document below describes piecework, a system in which garment workers are paid a certain amount for each piece of clothing they make. Use the document to answer the questions.

> "The differential rate system of piecework consists briefly in offering two different rates for the same job; a high price per piece, in case the work is finished in the shortest possible time and in perfect condition, and a low price, if it takes a longer time to do the job or if there are any imperfections in the work. . . . The advantages of this [system] are: First, that the manufactures are produced cheaper under it, while at the same time the workmen earn higher wages."
>
> —Frederick Taylor, "A Piece-Rate System," 1895

15. (a) What is the cost of the system discussed in the text? (b) What is one benefit of the system?

16. Do you think the benefits are greater than the costs? Explain.

# Test Yourself

1. **Which of the following most benefited big business?**

   **A** creation of the Knights of Labor

   **B** passage of the Chinese Exclusion Act

   **C** laissez-faire government policies

   **D** yellow journalism

**Refer to the quotation below to answer Question 2.**

> "Give me your tired, your poor,
> Your huddled masses yearning to breathe free,
> The wretched refuse of your teeming shore,
> Send these, the homeless, tempest-tossed to me,
> I lift my lamp beside the golden door!"
>
> —poem by Emma Lazarus, inscribed
> on the Statue of Liberty pedestal

2. **To whom does the poem refer?**

   **A** inventors

   **B** nativists

   **C** realists

   **D** immigrants

**Refer to the graph below to answer Question 3.**

## U.S. Rural and Urban Population, 1870–1920

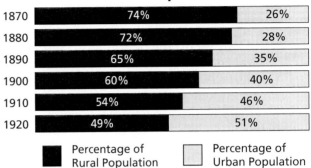

| Year | Percentage of Rural Population | Percentage of Urban Population |
|------|------|------|
| 1870 | 74% | 26% |
| 1880 | 72% | 28% |
| 1890 | 65% | 35% |
| 1900 | 60% | 40% |
| 1910 | 54% | 46% |
| 1920 | 49% | 51% |

Sources: *Historical Statistics of the United States* and *Statistical Abstract of the United States*

3. **In what year was the urban population larger than the rural population?**

   **A** 1870

   **B** 1890

   **C** 1910

   **D** 1920

# Document-Based Questions

**Task:** Look at Documents 1 and 2, and answer their accompanying questions. Then, use the documents and your knowledge of history to complete this writing assignment:

Write an essay analyzing the reasons for the success of the AFL.

**Document 1:** In a speech in 1898, Samuel Gompers described the need for trade unions. *State three purposes of trade unions cited by Gompers.*

> "The trade unions . . . were born of the necessity of workers to protect and defend themselves from encroachment, injustice and wrong. . . . To protect the workers in their inalienable rights to a higher and better life; to protect them, not only as equals before the law, but also in their health, their homes, their firesides, their liberties as men, as workers, and as citizens; to overcome and conquer prejudices and antagonism; to secure to them the right to life; the right to be full sharers in the abundance which is the result of their brain and brawn. . . . The attainment of these is the glorious mission of the trade unions."

**Document 2:** Unions enjoyed enormous growth in the late 1800s and early 1900s. *What was the increase in union membership between 1897 and 1915?*

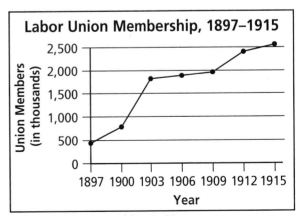

Labor Union Membership, 1897–1915

Source: *Historical Statistics of the United States*

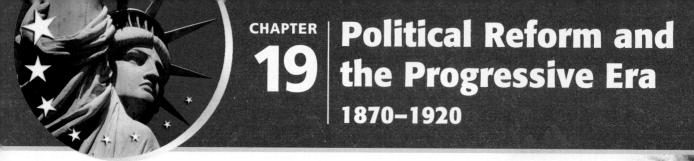

## Chapter Preview

In the late 1800s, the nation faced serious problems. Political corruption was common, and many Americans continued to face inequality. A period of reform known as the Progressive Era took shape as reformers worked to improve government and society.

☑ **What You Will Learn**

Reformers known as Progressives tried to end government corruption and limit the influence of big business.

Presidents Theodore Roosevelt, William Howard Taft, and Woodrow Wilson backed Progressive reforms.

After decades of effort, women finally won the right to vote.

African Americans, Mexican Americans, Asian Americans, and religious minorities all faced challenges.

**U.S. Events**

**1865**

**1874** Opponents of alcohol use form Woman's Christian Temperance Union.

**1880**

**1883** Civil service begins system of tests for government jobs.

**1890** Sherman Antitrust Act is passed.

**1895**

**World Events**

**1800s** Pogroms against Russian Jews increase.

**1893** New Zealand is first nation to give women the vote.

Photographs like this one by Jacob Riis called public attention to the problems of city slums.

**1901**
Theodore Roosevelt becomes President.

**1909**
Reformers found NAACP to promote rights of African Americans.

**1920**
19th Amendment guarantees women right to vote.

1895

1910

1925

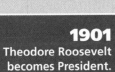

**1905** Japanese navy wins victory in war with Russia.

**1910** Revolution breaks out in Mexico.

**History Reading Skill** Identify and Explain Central Issues

## What central problems and issues did America face in the late nineteenth century?

In this chapter, you will practice identifying and explaining central issues. You will also practice placing events in the context of the time and place in which they occurred. Read the following essay by Walt Whitman, in which he identifies the problems he sees in late nineteenth-century America. The side notes suggest ways to analyze central issues and orient them in time and place.

> **Primary Source**

> Here, Whitman outlines some specific problems that he believes industrialization is causing, for example, business and government corruption.

**To find a problem, identify the main idea: People no longer hold honest beliefs.**

> I say we had best look our times and lands searchingly in the face, like a physician diagnosing some deep disease. . . . Genuine belief seems to have left us. The underlying principles of the States are not honestly believed in nor is humanity itself believed in. What penetrating eye does not see through the mask?
>
> We live in an atmosphere of hypocrisy throughout. . . . The depravity of the businesses classes of our country is not less than has been supposed, but infinitely greater. The official services of America, national, state, and municipal, . . . are deep in corruption, bribery, and falsehood.
>
> I say that our New World democracy, however great a success in uplifting the masses and in developing products, is, so far, an almost complete failure in its social, religious, moral, [and] literary . . . results. It is as if we were somehow being endowed with more and more body, and left with little or no soul.
>
> —Walt Whitman, *Democratic Vistas in Complete Prose*

**Orient events in the larger context: Whitman refers here to business and government corruption that was common in the late 1800s.**

**Reword text to explain problems: Whitman believes that Americans are sacrificing morality for material gain.**

## Identify and Explain Central Issues

- Look for important issues and problems of a historical period. What concerned people of the time?
- Restate problems to understand and explain them.
- Place the problems and issues in the context of other historical events you know about, such as westward expansion.

## Document-Based Questions

1. What problems does Whitman see in business and government?
2. What is his opinion of democracy?
3. What do you think Whitman means by "the underlying principles of the States"?

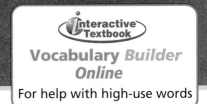

## Vocabulary *Builder*

### Previewing High-Use Academic Words

| High-Use Word | Definition | Sample History Sentence |
|---|---|---|
| **enrich** (ehn RIHCH) (Section 1, p. 644) | *v.* to make wealthy; to increase in quality or wealth | Industrial expansion after the Civil War <u>enriched</u> business leaders. |
| **exert** (ehks ZERT) (Section 1, p. 645) | *v.* to use; to put into action | Temperance leaders tried to <u>exert</u> pressure on lawmakers to ban alcohol. |
| **efficient** (ee FISH ehnt) (Section 2, p. 650) | *adj.* done in a way that minimizes waste and gets better results | During the Industrial Revolution, new machines and new sources of power made manufacturing more <u>efficient</u>. |
| **rigid** (RIH jihd) (Section 2, p. 653) | *adj.* strict; not easily bent or changed | When it came to women's rights, Susan B. Anthony was <u>rigid</u> and refused to compromise. |
| **devise** (dee VĪZ) (Section 3, p. 657) | *v.* to carefully think out; to invent | John D. Rockefeller <u>devised</u> a way to gain a monopoly on the oil business. |
| **commit** (kah MIHT) (Section 3, p. 658) | *v.* to make a pledge or promise | Some women <u>committed</u> themselves to ending child labor. |
| **submit** (sahb MIHT) (Section 4, p. 661) | *v.* to yield; to give up power or control | The reformer argued that people should not <u>submit</u> to injustice. |
| **crisis** (KRĪ sihs) (Section 4, p. 664) | *n.* turning point; situation involving great risk | The Civil War was the greatest <u>crisis</u> in American history. |

Woodrow Wilson

### Previewing Key Terms and People

## Objectives

1. Identify the problems in American politics during the Gilded Age.

2. Describe the political reforms the Progressives supported.

3. Explain how journalists contributed to reform efforts.

### Prepare to Read

 **Reading Skill**

**Place Events in a Matrix of Time and Place** As you read this textbook, notice that chapters often cover overlapping time periods. History is complex and involves many continuing issues. To gain a better understanding of a period, place events from one chapter in the context of other events from the same time period. Think back to other chapters and to your own knowledge for these connections.

### Vocabulary *Builder*

**High-Use Words**

enrich, p. 644
exert, p. 645

**Key Terms**

civil service, p. 645
primary, p. 646
recall, p. 647
initiative, p. 647
referendum, p. 647
graduated income tax, p. 647
muckraker, p. 648

---

**Main Idea**
Many Americans sought to fight corruption by ending the spoils system and controlling big business.

**Vocabulary *Builder***
enrich (ehn RIHCH) *v.* to make wealthy; to increase in quality or wealth

⭐ **Background Knowledge** As you have read, by the late 1800s giant corporations controlled much of American business. In this section, you will learn why many Americans began to demand that the government control the power of these huge trusts and monopolies.

## Reform in the Gilded Age

The period after the Civil War came to be known as the Gilded Age. *Gilded* means "coated with a thin layer of gold paint." It suggests falseness beneath surface glitter. Some Americans worried that the glitter of American society was hiding serious problems. The Gilded Age lasted from the 1870s through the 1890s.

Two concerns shaped politics during the Gilded Age. Many Americans feared that industrialists and other wealthy men were <u>enriching</u> themselves at the expense of the public. The other worry was corruption, or dishonesty in government. Bribery and voter fraud appeared to be widespread.

**Taming the Spoils System** Critics said a key source of corruption was the spoils system, the practice of rewarding political supporters with government jobs. The spoils system had grown since the Age of Jackson. Whenever a new President took office, job seekers swarmed to Washington, demanding rewards for their political support.

In 1881, James Garfield became President. He was soon swamped with people seeking jobs. Four months later, Garfield was shot by a disappointed office seeker. He died two months later. The assassination sparked new efforts to end the spoils system.

Vice President Chester A. Arthur succeeded Garfield. Arthur, a New York politician, owed his own rise to the spoils system. Yet, he worked with Congress to reform how people got government jobs.

In 1883, Arthur signed the Pendleton Act. It created the Civil Service Commission. The **civil service** is a system that includes most government jobs, except elected positions, the judiciary, and the military. The aim of the Civil Service Commission was to fill jobs on the basis of merit. Jobs went to those with the highest scores on civil service examinations. At first, the Commission controlled only a few jobs. Over time, however, the civil service grew to include more jobs.

**Controlling Big Business** In the late 1800s, big business <u>exerted</u> a strong influence over politics. Railroad owners and industrialists bribed members of Congress in order to secure their votes. Outraged by such actions, many Americans demanded that something be done to limit the power of railroads and monopolies.

Under the Constitution, the federal government has the power to regulate interstate commerce, or trade that crosses state lines. In 1887, President Grover Cleveland signed the Interstate Commerce Act. It forbade practices such as rebates. It also set up the Interstate Commerce Commission to oversee railroads.

**Vocabulary Builder**
**exert** (ehks ZERT) *v.* to use; to put into action

## The Problem of Corruption

The Capitol building is where Congress meets.

This hand is coming out of a window labeled "Trusts."

### Reading Political Cartoons
#### Skills Activity

In many cities, illegal businesses often paid "protection" to police in order to avoid arrest. This 1894 cartoon compares this practice to corruption in the federal government.

**(a) Interpret Cartoons** Who is the man on the right? What is he getting from the man in the window?

**(b) Draw Inferences** What do you think the giver expects in return?

Thomas Nast cartoon of Boss Tweed

President Benjamin Harrison signed the Sherman Antitrust Act in 1890. It prohibited businesses from trying to limit or destroy competition. The law sounded tough but proved difficult to enforce. Judges sympathetic to business ruled in favor of trusts. Instead of regulating trusts, the Sherman Act was used to limit the power of labor unions. The courts said strikes blocked free trade and thus threatened competition.

**Corruption in the Cities** Corruption was a particularly serious problem in city governments. As cities grew, they needed to expand services such as sewers, garbage collection, and roads. Often, politicians accepted money to award these jobs to friends. As a result, corruption became a way of life.

In many cities, powerful politicians called bosses controlled work done locally and demanded payoffs from businesses. City bosses were popular with the poor, especially immigrants. The bosses handed out turkeys at Thanksgiving and extra coal in winter. Often, they provided jobs. In return, the poor voted for the boss or his chosen candidate.

William Tweed, commonly known as Boss Tweed, carried corruption to new extremes. During the 1860s and 1870s, he cheated New York City out of more than $100 million. Journalists exposed Tweed's crimes. Cartoonist Thomas Nast pictured Tweed as a greedy giant and as a vulture feeding on the city. Faced with prison, Tweed fled to Spain. There, local police arrested him when they recognized him from Nast's cartoons. Still, when Tweed died in jail in 1878, thousands of poor New Yorkers mourned for him.

☑**Checkpoint** How did the civil service system limit corruption?

**Main Idea**
Political reformers called Progressives worked to give more power to voters and expose social problems.

## Progressives and Political Reform

Opposition to corruption led to the rise of the Progressive movement. The Progressives were a diverse group of reformers united by a belief in the public interest, or the good of all the people. The public interest, they said, must not be sacrificed to the greed of a few huge trusts and city bosses.

**The Wisconsin Idea** Wisconsin was one of the first states to adopt Progressive reforms. Wisconsin governor Robert La Follette, known as Battling Bob, introduced various Progressive reforms that became known as the Wisconsin Idea.

La Follette opposed political bosses. He appointed commissions of experts to solve problems. For example, his railroad commission recommended lowering railroad rates. As rates decreased, rail traffic increased, which helped both railroad owners and customers.

Since the Age of Jackson, party leaders had picked candidates for local and state offices. In 1903, Wisconsin was the first state to adopt a primary run by state government officials. A **primary** is an election in which voters, rather than party leaders, choose their party's candidate. By 1917, all but four states had followed Wisconsin's lead.

## Progressive Political Reforms

| Before | | After |
|--------|--------|--------|
| Party leaders pick candidates for state and local offices | **PRIMARY** → | Voters select their party candidates |
| Only members of state legislature can introduce bills | **INDIRECT INITIATIVE** → | Voters can propose bills to the legislature |
| Only legislators pass laws | **REFERENDUM** → | Voters can vote on bills directly |
| Only courts or legislature can remove corrupt officials | **RECALL** → | Voters can remove elected officials from office |

**More Power to Voters** Some states instituted reforms to put more power in the hands of voters. One such reform was the recall, a process by which people may vote to remove an elected official from office. The recall made it easier to get rid of corrupt officials.

Other reforms gave voters a direct say in the lawmaking process. The initiative is a process that allows voters to put a bill before a state legislature. In order to propose an initiative, voters must collect a certain number of signatures on a petition. The referendum is a way for people to vote directly on a proposed new law.

**Two Constitutional Amendments** Many Progressive reformers backed a graduated income tax, a method of taxation that taxes people at different rates depending on income. The wealthy pay taxes at a higher rate than the poor or the middle class. When the Supreme Court ruled that a federal income tax was unconstitutional, Progressives called for a constitutional amendment. The Sixteenth Amendment, which gave Congress the power to pass an income tax, was ratified in 1913.

Since 1789, United States senators had been elected by state legislatures. Powerful interest groups often bribed lawmakers to vote for certain candidates. Progressives wanted to end this abuse by having people vote for senators directly. The Seventeenth Amendment, ratified in 1913, required the direct election of senators.

**Place Events in a Matrix of Time and Place**
In the 1890s, the Populists had also supported an income tax. How did the roots of Populism differ from the roots of Progressivism?

✓**Checkpoint** What reforms put more power in the hands of voters?

# The Muckrakers

The press played an important role in exposing corruption and other problems. President Theodore Roosevelt compared reporters who uncovered problems to men who raked up dirt, or muck, in stables. Muckraker became a term for a crusading journalist.

Some muckrakers targeted big business. Ida Tarbell's work led to demands for more controls on trusts. She accused oil baron John D. Rockefeller of unfair business methods. Tarbell wrote:

> **"**Every great campaign against rival interests which the Standard Oil Company has carried on has been inaugurated . . . to build up and sustain a monopoly in the oil industry.**"**
>
> —Ida M. Tarbell, *History of the Standard Oil Company*

Others described how corruption in city government led to inadequate fire, police, and sanitation services. Jacob Riis (REES), a photographer and writer, provided shocking images of slum life.

In 1906, Upton Sinclair's novel *The Jungle* told grisly details about the meatpacking industry. Sinclair described how packers used meat from sick animals and how rats often got ground up in the meat.

**✓Checkpoint** **How did muckrakers stir public opinion?**

★ **Looking Back and Ahead** The Progressive movement began at local and state levels. In the next section, you will see how three Presidents brought Progressive ideas into the White House.

---

## Section 1 | Check Your Progress

**Progress Monitoring** Online
**For:** Self-test with instant help
**Visit:** PHSchool.com
**Web Code:** mya-6151

### Comprehension and Critical Thinking

1. **(a) Recall** How was the spoils system reformed during the Gilded Age?
   **(b) Analyze Cause and Effect** What abuses do you think were occurring under the spoils system that made reform necessary?

2. **(a) Identify** Who were some of the principal muckrakers during the Progressive Era, and what did each try to do?
   **(b) Link Past and Present** What impact do you think their efforts had on life in the United States today?

### Reading Skill

3. **Place Events in a Matrix of Time and Place** Ida Tarbell wrote muckraking articles about the Standard Oil Company. Why did she think this was necessary? How had Standard Oil's business practices changed American industry? Think back to the previous chapter to answer these questions.

### Vocabulary *Builder*

Answer the following questions in complete sentences that show your understanding of the key terms.
4. Which jobs are civil service positions?

5. What happens in a primary election?
6. What did muckrakers try to do?
7. What happens in a successful referendum?
8. How are tax rates structured under the graduated income tax?

### Writing

9. Write a statement supporting the work of the muckrakers. Then, write a statement opposing their work. For each statement, write one question to ask the muckrakers about their methods and their goals.

# The Progressive Presidents

## Objectives

1. Describe how Theodore Roosevelt tried to limit the power of business.

2. Summarize the main points of Roosevelt's Square Deal.

3. Identify the reforms promoted by Presidents Taft and Wilson.

## Prepare to Read

### Reading Skill

**Explain Issues From the Past** Every era in history has its issues—the ideas or problems that people think about, argue about, and put their energies into. As you read about history, explain these issues to yourself as a way of understanding what mattered to people of that time. Use headings and main ideas to help you identify and explain the issues.

## Vocabulary *Builder*

### High-Use Words

efficient, p. 650

rigid, p. 653

### Key Terms and People

Theodore Roosevelt, p. 649

trustbuster, p. 650

conservation, p. 651

national park, p. 651

William Howard Taft, p. 652

Woodrow Wilson, p. 652

⭐ **Background Knowledge** Although Progressives made many gains at the state and local levels, they had little success at the national level. William McKinley, who was elected President in 1896 and 1900, had the strong support of bankers and business leaders. Then, a shocking assassination thrust a Progressive into the presidency.

## The First Progressive President

On September 6, 1901, an unemployed anarchist stood nervously in line at the world's fair in Buffalo, New York. He was waiting to shake the hand of President William McKinley. When McKinley extended his hand, the assassin fired two shots into the President. McKinley died eight days later.

Vice President Theodore Roosevelt then became President. At age 42, he was the youngest President to take office. He was also a strong supporter of Progressive goals.

**Teddy Roosevelt** Teddy Roosevelt—or TR, as he was called—came from a wealthy New York family. As a child, he suffered from asthma and often was sick. To build his strength, he lifted weights, ran, and boxed. For a time, he worked on a cattle ranch.

TR wanted to serve the public. At the age of 23, he was elected to the New York state legislature. Later, he served on the Civil Service Commission. He then headed New York City's police department and served as assistant secretary of the navy.

**Main Idea**

Theodore Roosevelt was the first President to support limits on the power of business.

Campaign tray showing Teddy Roosevelt as a soldier

In 1898, the United States went to war against Spain. (You will read about this in the next chapter.) Roosevelt led a unit of troops in some daring exploits that received widespread publicity. He returned home to a hero's welcome and was elected governor of New York. Two years later, Roosevelt was elected Vice President under McKinley.

**TR and Big Business** As President, Roosevelt won a reputation as a trustbuster, a person working to destroy monopolies and trusts. He was not against big business, he said. Indeed, he liked big business. But he saw a difference between "good trusts" and "bad trusts." Good trusts, he said, were efficient and fair and should be left alone. Bad ones took advantage of workers and cheated the public by eliminating competition. The government, he said, must either control bad trusts or break them up.

Roosevelt resolved to do just that. In 1902, he had the government bring a lawsuit against the Northern Securities Company. Northern Securities was a trust that had been formed to control competition among railroads. TR argued that the company used unfair business practices.

In 1904, the Supreme Court ruled that Northern Securities had violated the Sherman Antitrust Act. It ordered the trust to be broken up. The decision was a victory for Progressives. For the first time, the Sherman Antitrust Act had been used to break up trusts, not unions.

Roosevelt later launched suits against other trusts, including Standard Oil and the American Tobacco Company. In time, the courts broke up both trusts because they attempted to limit free trade.

**A Boost for Organized Labor** Roosevelt also clashed with mine owners. In 1902, Pennsylvania coal miners went on strike for better pay and a shorter workday. Mine owners refused to negotiate with the miners' union.

As winter approached, schools and hospitals ran out of coal. Furious at the owners, Roosevelt threatened to send in troops to run the mines. Finally, the mine owners sat down with the union and reached an agreement. Roosevelt was the first President to side with strikers.

✓**Checkpoint** What was Theodore Roosevelt's attitude toward big business?

## The Square Deal

Roosevelt ran for President in his own right in 1904. During the campaign, he promised Americans a Square Deal. By this, he meant that everyone from farmers and consumers to workers and owners should have the same opportunity to succeed. That promise helped Roosevelt win a huge victory.

**Vocabulary** *Builder*
efficient (ee FISH ehnt) *adj.* done in a way that minimizes waste and gets better results

**Main Idea**
Roosevelt's program of Progressive reform included measures to conserve natural resources and protect consumers.

**Discovery SCHOOL™**

**Explore More Video**
To learn more about protecting wilderness areas, view the video.

**Conserving Natural Resources** Roosevelt took action to protect the nation's wilderness areas. To fuel the nation's surging industrial growth, lumber companies were cutting down entire forests. Miners were removing iron and coal at a frantic pace, leaving gaping holes in the earth.

Roosevelt loved the outdoors and worried about the destruction of the wilderness. He pressed for conservation, or the protection of natural resources. Roosevelt was not against using resources, but he believed they had to be used wisely, with an eye toward the future. For example, he urged lumber companies to plant new trees in the forests they were clearing. Roosevelt declared:

> **❝** I recognize the right and duty of this generation to develop and use the natural resources of our land; but I do not recognize the right to waste them, or to rob, by wasteful use, the generations that come after us. **❞**
>
> —Theodore Roosevelt, "The New Nationalism"

Under Roosevelt, the U.S. Forest Service was formed in 1905 to conserve the nation's woodlands. Roosevelt also had thousands of acres of land set aside for national parks. A national park is a natural area protected and managed by the federal government.

**Roosevelt and Conservation**
In 1903, President Roosevelt (left) went camping in California's Yosemite Valley with conservationist John Muir (right). The trip strengthened Roosevelt's commitment to conservation. Today, you can still enjoy the wilderness areas of Yosemite National Park. **Critical Thinking: Link Past and Present** What do the two pictures above suggest about the long-term effects of Roosevelt's conservation policies?

**Explain Issues From the Past**
*Reading Skill* Explain Roosevelt's reasons for supporting conservation and how they affected his approach to big business.

**Protecting Consumers** Roosevelt also supported reforms to protect consumers. Upton Sinclair's novel *The Jungle* had shocked Roosevelt. The President made public a report exposing unhealthy conditions in meatpacking plants. The public outcry forced Congress to pass a law in 1906 allowing closer inspections of meatpacking houses.

Muckrakers had also exposed drug companies for making false claims about medicines and adding harmful chemicals to canned foods. In response, Congress passed the Pure Food and Drug Act, which required food and drug makers to list all the ingredients on packages.

☑**Checkpoint** **Why did Roosevelt support conservation?**

## Taft and Wilson

Roosevelt did not want to run for reelection in 1908. Instead, he backed William Howard Taft, his secretary of war. Taft won easily.

**Troubles for Taft** Taft's approach to the presidency was far different from Roosevelt's. Unlike the energetic Roosevelt, Taft was quiet and cautious. Roosevelt loved power, Taft was wary of it.

Nevertheless, Taft supported many Progressive causes. He broke up even more trusts than TR. He favored the graduated income tax, approved new safety rules for mines, and signed laws giving government workers the eight-hour workday. He also oversaw the creation of a federal office to make regulations controlling child labor.

Despite such actions, Taft lost Progressive support. In 1909, he signed a bill that raised most tariffs. Progressives opposed the new law, arguing that tariffs raised prices for consumers. Also, Taft modified some conservation policies. Progressives accused the President of blocking conservation efforts.

**Election of 1912** By 1912, Roosevelt had broken with Taft. He decided to run against Taft for the Republican nomination. Roosevelt had massive popular support, but Taft controlled the Republican Party leadership. At its convention, the Republican Party nominated Taft.

Roosevelt and his supporters stormed out of the convention. They set up a new party, called the Progressive Party, and chose Roosevelt as their candidate. He accepted, saying "I feel as strong as a bull moose." Roosevelt's Progressive Party became known as the Bull Moose Party.

Democrats chose Woodrow Wilson, also a Progressive, as their candidate. Wilson had served as president of Princeton University and as governor of New Jersey. Wilson was known as a brilliant

**Three-Way Race**

TR, the "bull moose" candidate, made the presidential election of 1912 a three-way race. **Critical Thinking: *Draw Inferences*** *Why does the cartoonist show the "moose" nipping at the elephant?*

scholar and a cautious reformer. Though honest and idealistic, he was often criticized for being <u>rigid</u> and unwilling to compromise with others.

Together, Taft and Roosevelt won more votes than Wilson. However, they split the Republican vote, and so Wilson won the 1912 presidential election.

**Wilson and the New Freedom** Wilson hoped to restore free competition among American corporations. He called his program to achieve this goal the New Freedom. To ensure fair competition, Wilson persuaded Congress to create the Federal Trade Commission (FTC) in 1914. The FTC had the power to investigate companies and order them to stop using unfair practices to destroy competitors.

Wilson signed the Clayton Antitrust Act in 1914. The new law banned some business practices that limited competition. In addition, it stopped antitrust laws from being used against unions.

To regulate banking, Congress passed the Federal Reserve Act in 1913. The act set up a system of federal banks and gave the government the power to raise or lower interest rates and control the money supply.

☑**Checkpoint** **How did a split among Republicans enable Woodrow Wilson to become President?**

⭐ **Looking Back and Ahead** Despite Wilson's successes, the Progressive movement slowed after 1914. By then, Progressives had achieved many of their goals. Also, in 1914, war broke out in Europe. Americans worried that the war might soon affect them. You will read about World War I in the next unit.

**Vocabulary** *Builder*
**rigid** (RIH jihd) *adj.* strict; not easily bent or changed

Woodrow Wilson

Section 2 | **Check Your Progress**

**Progress Monitoring** ⬤nline
**For:** Self-test with instant help
**Visit:** PHSchool.com
**Web Code:** mya-6152

## Comprehension and Critical Thinking

**1. (a) Recall** Why did Theodore Roosevelt want to break up Northern Securities and Standard Oil?
**(b) Identify Benefits** Which groups of people might have benefited from Roosevelt's actions as a trustbuster?

**2. (a) Recall** Why did the Republican Party split during the 1912 presidential election campaign?
**(b) Draw Conclusions** What impact might a powerful third party such as the Bull Moose Party have on a presidential election?

## 🎯 Reading Skill

**3. Explain Issues From the Past** Reread the text following the subheading "A Boost for Organized Labor." Explain the central issues that moved Roosevelt. How did he interact with big business over these issues?

## Vocabulary *Builder*

Read each sentence below. If the sentence is true, write YES. If the sentence is not true, write NO and explain why.
**4.** Theodore Roosevelt was called a trustbuster because he lost the trust of the people.

**5.** Roosevelt was a strong supporter of conservation, which is the protection of natural resources.

## Writing

**6.** Write the opening paragraph to an editorial evaluating TR's presidency. Complete the following topic sentence, and introduce each point that follows with a transition word: Theodore Roosevelt's Square Deal created a number of reforms that were *(express your opinion here).* For example, he _____. In addition, he _____. Most important *(OR worst of all)*, he _____.

# The Jungle
## by Upton Sinclair

## Prepare to Read

### Introduction

The main characters in *The Jungle* are a family of immigrants who have recently immigrated to Chicago from Eastern Europe. Several of them find jobs at a meatpacking plant. In this excerpt, Elzbieta, one family member, learns the gruesome details of the sausage-making process.

###  Reading Skill

**Analyze Symbolism** Symbolism is the use of concrete images or objects to represent abstract ideas. Upton Sinclair wrote *The Jungle* in order to make a statement about the excesses of unrestricted free enterprise. As you read this passage, consider what the practices Sinclair describes might represent.

### Vocabulary *Builder*

As you read this literature selection, look for the following underlined words:

**scheme** (skeem) *n.* dishonest plan

**hopper** (HAH per) *n.* a bin in which material is temporarily stored

**nuisance** (NOO sehns) *n.* annoyance

**enforce** (ehn FORS) *v.* bring about by force

### ⭐ Background

This passage describes, among other things, the working conditions for laborers. Though Sinclair wrote *The Jungle* in order to speak out against working conditions for laborers, the public's reaction was not what Sinclair intended. The public outcry over this book's description of meat-packaging practices helped lead to the passage of the Pure Food and Drug Act of 1906.

The packers were always originating such <u>schemes</u>—they had what they called "boneless hams," which were all the odds and ends of pork stuffed into casings; and "California hams," which were the shoulders, with big knuckle joints, and nearly all the meat cut out; and fancy "skinned hams," which were made of the oldest hogs, whose skins were so heavy and coarse that no one would buy them—that is, until they had been cooked and chopped fine and labeled "head cheese"!

It was only when the whole ham was spoiled that it came into the department of Elzbieta. Cut up by the two-thousand-revolutions-a-minute flyers, and mixed with half a ton of other meat, no odor that ever was in a ham could make any difference. There was never the least attention paid to what was cut up for sausage; there would come all the way back from Europe old sausage that had been rejected, and that was mouldy and white—it would be dosed with borax and glycerine, and dumped into the <u>hoppers</u>, and made over again for home consumption. There would be meat that had tumbled out onto the floor, in the dirt and sawdust, where the workers had tramped and spit uncounted billions of consumption germs. There would be meat stored in great piles in rooms, and the water from leaky roofs would drip over it, and thousands of rats would race about on it. It was too dark in those storage places to see well, but a man could run his hands over these piles of meat and sweep off handfuls of the dried dung of rats. These rats were <u>nuisances</u>, and the packers would put out poisoned bread for them, they would die, and then rats, bread, and meat would go into the hoppers together. This is no fairy story and no joke: the meat would be shoveled into carts, and the man who did the shoveling would not trouble to lift out a rat even when he saw one—there were things that went into the sausage in comparison with which a poisoned rat was a tidbit. There was no place for the men to wash their hands before they ate their dinner, and so they made a practice of washing them in the water that was to be ladled into the sausage. There were the butt-ends of smoked meat, and the scraps of corned beef, and all the odds and ends of the waste of the plants, that would be dumped into old barrels in the cellar and left there. Under the system of rigid economy which the packers <u>enforced</u>, there were some jobs that it only paid to do once in a long time, and among these was the cleaning out of the waste barrels. Every spring they did it; and in the barrels would be dirt and rust and old nails and stale water— and cartload after cartload of it would be taken up and dumped into the hoppers with fresh meat, and sent out to the public's breakfast. Some of it they would make into "smoked" sausage—but as the smoking took time, and was therefore expensive, they would call upon the chemistry department, and preserve it with borax and color it with gelatine to make it brown. All of their sausage came out of the same bowl, but when they came to wrap it they would stamp some of it "special," and for this they would charge two cents more a pound.

From *The Jungle*, by Upton Sinclair. © 1981. Bantam.

**☑Checkpoint** **What was wrong with the way the packers cleaned out the waste barrels?**

**Analyze Symbolism**
Reading Skill

Upton Sinclair wrote at a time when few laws controlled how people worked and what they produced. Sinclair blamed the capitalist system for these abuses, rather than the lack of laws. Knowing Sinclair's motivation for writing this book, what abstract idea might the "special" and "fancy" packaging of the meat represent?

### Analyze LITERATURE

After reading this passage, what images are the most striking? Are the images powerful? Now imagine that you are a member of the general public reading this passage. Write a short letter to your local newspaper expressing your reaction to this passage.

If you liked this passage from *The Jungle*, you might enjoy reading more about the labor movement in America in *Ashes of Roses* by Mary Jane Auch. Henry Holt and Company, 2002.

# The Rights of Women

## Objectives

1. Describe how women won the right to vote.
2. Identify the new opportunities that women gained during the Progressive Era.
3. Explain how the temperance movement gained strength during the early 1900s.

## Prepare to Read

### ⟳ Reading Skill

**Identify Central Issues From the Past** What changes did people of the past work to achieve? As you read Section 3, try to identify the central issues at the core of women's efforts for change. In your own words, answer the questions: What was this struggle about? What change did these people seek?

### Vocabulary *Builder*

**High-Use Words**

**devise**, p. 657
**commit**, p. 658

**Key Terms and People**

Carrie Chapman Catt, p. 657
suffragist, p. 657
Alice Paul, p. 658
Frances Willard, p. 659
prohibition, p. 659

☆ **Background Knowledge** The Progressives' desire for reform touched many parts of society. However, Progressives were not particularly interested in women's rights. In this section, you will learn how American women finally won the right to vote.

## Women Win the Vote

**Main Idea**
After more than 70 years of effort, American women won the right to vote in all elections.

The Seneca Falls Convention of 1848 marked the start of an organized women's rights movement in the United States. After the Civil War, Elizabeth Cady Stanton and Susan B. Anthony formed the National Woman Suffrage Association. This group pushed for a constitutional amendment to give women the right to vote.

Anthony spoke all over the country for the cause. In 1872, she was arrested for trying to vote. At her trial, she told the judge:

> **“**My natural rights, my civil rights, my political rights, my judicial rights, are all alike ignored. Robbed of the fundamental privilege of citizenship, I am degraded from the status of a citizen to that of a subject.**”**
> —*Proceedings of the Trial of Susan B. Anthony*

**Women Vote in the West** In most states, leading politicians opposed women's suffrage. Still, in the late 1800s, women won voting rights in four western states: Wyoming, Utah, Colorado, and Idaho. Pioneer women had worked alongside men to build farms and cities. By giving women the vote at least in local or state elections, these states recognized the women's contributions.

When Wyoming applied for statehood in 1890, many members of Congress wanted it to bar women from voting. Wyoming lawmakers stood firm. "We may stay out of the Union for 100 years, but we will come in with our women." Wyoming was admitted.

**Growing Support** In the early 1900s, support for women's suffrage grew. More than 5 million women worked outside the home. Although women were paid less than men, wages gave them some power. Many demanded a say in making the laws.

After Stanton and Anthony died, a new generation of leaders took up the cause. Carrie Chapman Catt <u>devised</u> a detailed strategy to win suffrage, state by state. Across the nation, suffragists, or people who worked for women's right to vote, followed her plan. Their efforts brought steady gains. One by one, states in the West and Midwest gave women the right to vote.

**The Nineteenth Amendment** Still, in some of these states, women could not vote in federal elections. More women joined the call for a federal amendment to allow them to vote in all elections.

**Vocabulary** *Builder*
**devise** (dee vīz) *v.* to carefully think out; to invent

**Identify Central Issues From the Past**
Identify the central issue, or goal, for suffragists.

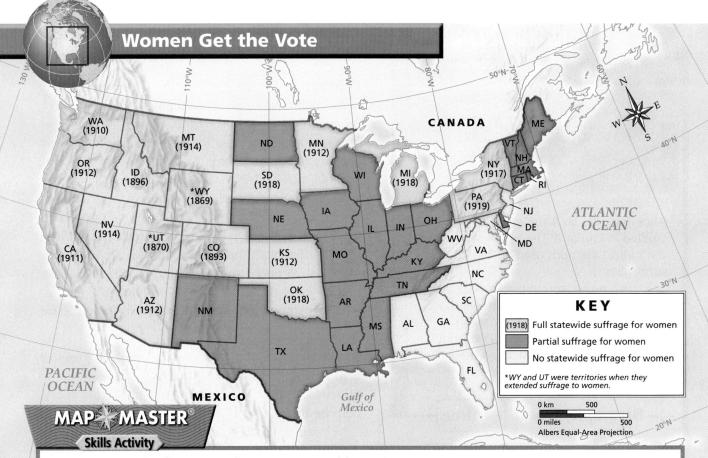

**Women Get the Vote**

WA (1910)
MT (1914)
OR (1912)
ID (1896)
*WY (1869)
NV (1914)
*UT (1870)
CA (1911)
CO (1893)
AZ (1912)
NM
ND
SD (1918)
NE
KS (1912)
OK (1918)
TX
MN (1912)
IA
MO
AR
LA
WI
IL
IN
OH
KY
TN
MS
AL
GA
MI (1918)
WV
VA
NC
SC
FL
NY (1917)
PA (1919)
NJ
DE
MD
ME
VT
NH
MA
CT
RI

CANADA
ATLANTIC OCEAN
PACIFIC OCEAN
MEXICO
Gulf of Mexico

**KEY**
(1918) Full statewide suffrage for women
Partial suffrage for women
No statewide suffrage for women
*WY and UT were territories when they extended suffrage to women.

0 km 500
0 miles 500
Albers Equal-Area Projection

**MAP MASTER®**
**Skills Activity**

Wyoming was the first state where women could vote in state elections. By 1919, some states (shown in yellow) still did not allow women to vote.

**(a) Read a Map** In what year did women win suffrage in Colorado? In California?

**(b) Apply Information** How would this map change after passage of the Nineteenth Amendment?

**MapMaster Online**
**For:** Interactive map
**Visit:** PHSchool.com
**Web Code:** myp-6153

As the struggle dragged on, suffragists such as Alice Paul took more forceful steps. Paul met with President Woodrow Wilson in 1913. Paul told Wilson that suffragists had <u>committed</u> themselves to achieving such an amendment. Wilson pledged his support.

By 1919, the tide had turned. Congress passed the Nineteenth Amendment guaranteeing women the right to vote. By August 1920, three fourths of the states had ratified the amendment. The Nineteenth Amendment doubled the number of eligible voters.

☑ **Checkpoint** **Why did suffragists want a constitutional amendment?**

## New Opportunities for Women

Besides working for the vote, women struggled to gain access to jobs and education. Most states refused to grant women licenses to practice law or medicine.

**Higher Education** Despite obstacles, a few women managed to get the higher education needed to enter a profession. In 1877, Boston University granted the first Ph.D., or doctoral degree, to a woman. Slowly, more women earned advanced degrees. By 1900, the nation had 1,000 women lawyers and 7,000 women doctors.

**Women's Clubs** During the late 1800s, many middle-class women joined women's clubs. At first, most clubwomen read books and sought other ways to advance their knowledge. In time, many became reformers. They raised money for libraries, schools, and parks. They pressed for laws to protect women and children, to ensure pure food and drugs, and to win the vote.

Faced with racial barriers, African American women formed their own clubs, such as the National Association of Colored Women. They battled to end segregation and violence against African Americans. They also joined the battle for suffrage.

**Women Reformers** During the Progressive Era, many women committed themselves to reform. Some entered the field of social work, helping the poor in cities.

Florence Kelley investigated conditions in sweatshops. In time, she was made the chief factory inspector for Illinois. Kelley's main concern was child labor. She organized a boycott of goods produced in factories that employed young children.

☑ **Checkpoint** **What gains did women make in education?**

**Biography Quest**

**Alice Paul**
**1885–1977**

Alice Paul was an American who studied in England. There, she saw the radical methods used by English suffragists.

Returning to the United States, Paul formed a new suffrage group, which merged into the National Woman's Party in 1917. Paul called on President Wilson many times and worked tirelessly for the Nineteenth Amendment.

**Biography Quest**  **Online**

**How did Paul become involved in the struggle for a voting rights amendment?**

**For:** The answer to the question about Paul
**Visit:** PHSchool.com
**Web Code:** myd-6153

# The Crusade Against Alcohol

You have read that reformers began a temperance movement, or campaign against alcohol abuse, in the 1820s. Women took a leading role in the temperance movement. In the late 1800s, the movement gained new strength.

In 1874, a group of women organized the Woman's Christian Temperance Union, or WCTU. Frances Willard became its president in 1879. Willard spoke tirelessly about the evils of alcohol. She called for state laws to ban the sale of liquor. She also worked to close saloons. In time, Willard joined the suffrage movement, bringing many WCTU members along with her.

Carry Nation was a more radical temperance crusader. After her husband died from heavy drinking, Nation often stormed into saloons. Swinging a hatchet, she smashed beer kegs and liquor bottles. Nation won publicity, but her actions embarrassed the WCTU.

After years of effort, temperance leaders persuaded Congress to pass the Eighteenth Amendment in 1917. The amendment enforced prohibition, a ban on the sale and consumption of alcohol. The amendment was ratified in 1919.

✓**Checkpoint** How did supporters of temperance seek to influence public policy?

⭐ **Looking Back and Ahead** For many women, the Nineteenth Amendment was a final victory. Others saw it as just one step on the road to full equality. Today, Americans still debate issues involving the roles of women in society, government, the family, and the workplace.

**Main Idea**
Temperance supporters won passage of a constitutional amendment banning alcohol.

Cartoon of a temperance supporter

---

**Progress Monitoring** ⓠnline

**For:** Self-test with instant help
**Visit:** PHSchool.com
**Web Code:** mya-6153

## Comprehension and Critical Thinking

1. **(a) Recall** What did the Nineteenth Amendment to the Constitution do?
   **(b) Link Past and Present** How has its passage helped women?

2. **(a) Recall** What did the Eighteenth Amendment to the Constitution do?
   **(b) Make Predictions** What would be the results of the Eighteenth Amendment? Explain your reasoning.

## 🔁 Reading Skill

3. **Identify Central Issues From the Past** Reread the text under the heading "New Opportunities for Women." Identify the central issues for the women mentioned in those paragraphs.

## Vocabulary *Builder*

Read each sentence below. If the sentence is true, write YES. If the sentence is not true, write NO and explain why.

4. Suffragists were people who worked to ban alcohol.

5. During prohibition, the sale and use of tobacco in the United States were outlawed.

## Writing

6. Imagine that you are working with a group of people in 1912 promoting women's suffrage. Create four slogans for banners and leaflets supporting the right of women to vote. Then, write a short persuasive paragraph supporting and developing one of those slogans.

# Struggles for Justice

## Objectives

1. Describe the efforts of African American leaders to fight discrimination.

2. Describe the life of Mexican Americans and the challenges they faced.

3. Explain why some Americans called for limits on Japanese immigration.

4. Discuss the problems facing religious minorities.

## Prepare to Read

### Reading Skill

**Identify Central Problems From the Past** Understanding the problems of the past helps you understand the reactions of people from that time. As you read, identify problems and restate them in your own words. Think about how people of that time responded and how people today might respond to similar problems.

### Vocabulary *Builder*

**High-Use Words**

submit, p. 661

crisis, p. 664

**Key Terms and People**

Booker T. Washington, p. 660

W.E.B. Du Bois, p. 661

lynching, p. 661

parochial school, p. 665

anti-Semitism, p. 665

⭐ **Background Knowledge** After Reconstruction, African Americans in the South lost many rights. Jim Crow laws led to segregation in public places. In this section, you will see how African Americans and other groups opposed discrimination.

## African Americans

**Main Idea**
African American leaders took different approaches to the problems of segregation and discrimination.

African Americans faced discrimination in the North as well as in the South. Landlords often refused to rent homes in white areas to African Americans. Across the nation, they were restricted to the worst housing and the poorest jobs.

**Booker T. Washington** During this time, educator Booker T. Washington emerged as the most prominent African American. Born into slavery, Washington taught himself to read. Later, he worked in coal mines, attending school whenever he could. In 1881, Washington helped found the Tuskegee Institute in Alabama. The school offered training in industrial and agricultural skills.

Washington advised African Americans to learn trades and seek to move up gradually in society. Eventually, they would have money and the power to demand equality. Washington declared:

> **❝**No race can prosper till it learns that there is as much dignity in tilling a field as in writing a poem. It is at the bottom of life we must begin, and not at the top. Nor should we permit our grievances to overshadow our opportunities.**❞**
>
> —Booker T. Washington, speech to Atlanta Exposition

Washington's practical approach won the support of business leaders such as Andrew Carnegie and John D. Rockefeller. They helped him build trade schools for African Americans. At the same time, Presidents sought his advice on racial issues.

**W.E.B. Du Bois** W.E.B. Du Bois (doo BOYS) had a different view. A brilliant scholar, Du Bois was the first African American to receive a Ph.D. from Harvard University. He agreed with Booker T. Washington on the need for "thrift, patience and industrial training." However, Du Bois criticized Washington for being willing to accept segregation:

> "So far as Mr. Washington apologizes for injustice, North or South, does not rightly value the privilege and duty of voting . . . and opposes the higher training and ambition of our brighter minds,—so far as he, the South, or the Nation, does this,—we must unceasingly and firmly oppose them."
> —W.E.B. Du Bois, *The Souls of Black Folk*

Du Bois urged blacks to fight discrimination rather than patiently <u>submit</u> to it. In 1909, he joined Jane Addams and other reformers in forming the National Association for the Advancement of Colored People, or NAACP. Blacks and whites in the NAACP worked for equal rights for African Americans.

**Campaign Against Lynching** In the 1890s, more than 1,000 African Americans in the South and elsewhere were victims of lynching, or murder by a mob. The epidemic of violence worsened after the depression of 1893. Often, jobless whites took out their anger on blacks.

**Vocabulary** *Builder*
<u>submit</u> (sahb MIHT) *v.* to yield; to give up power or control

**Identify Central Problems From the Past**
*Reading Skill*
Identify the central problems facing African Americans in the late 1800s. How did people of the time respond to those problems?

**History** *Interactive*
**Booker T. Washington and W.E.B. Du Bois**
**Visit:** PHSchool.com
**Web Code:** myp-6152

## Two African American Leaders

**Two African American Leaders**
Booker T. Washington (left) was the most prominent African American leader of his day. He urged African Americans to work patiently to move up in society. W.E.B. Du Bois (right) admired Washington but criticized many of his ideas. Rather than patiently accepting discrimination, Du Bois urged African Americans to fight it actively.
**Critical Thinking:** *Contrast How did Washington's and Du Bois's ideas about how to fight segregation differ?*

Booker T. Washington

W.E.B. Du Bois

## Ida B. Wells Fights Against Lynching

"The real purpose of these savage demonstrations is to teach the Negro that in the South he has no rights that the law will enforce. Samuel Hose [a lynching victim] was burned to teach the Negroes that no matter what a white man does to them, they must not resist. . . . The daily press offered reward for [Hose's] capture and . . . incited the people to burn him as soon as caught."

—Ida B. Wells, "Lynch Law in Georgia," 1899

Antilynching protesters

### Reading Primary Sources
#### Skills Activity

In 1895, journalist Ida B. Wells published an analysis that exposed the truth about the lynching of African Americans.

(a) **Interpret a Primary Source** According to Wells, why do lynchings occur?

(b) **Compare** Ida Wells is often classified as a muckraker. How was her work similar to the work of Jacob Riis?

The murders outraged Ida B. Wells, an African American journalist. In her newspaper, *Free Speech,* Wells urged African Americans to protest the lynchings. She called for a boycott of segregated streetcars and white-owned stores. Wells spoke out despite threats to her life.

**Setbacks and Successes** Few white Progressives gave much thought to the problems faced by African Americans. President Wilson ordered the segregation of workers in the federal civil service. "Segregation is not humiliating, but a benefit," he told protesters who came to talk to him.

Despite obstacles, some African Americans succeeded. Scientist George Washington Carver discovered hundreds of new uses for peanuts and other crops grown in the South. Sarah Walker created a line of hair care products for African American women. She became the first American woman to earn more than $1 million.

Black-owned insurance companies, banks, and other businesses served the needs of African Americans. Black colleges trained young people for the professions. Churches like the African Methodist Episcopal Church became the training ground for generations of African American leaders.

✓ **Checkpoint**  On what grounds did W.E.B. Du Bois disagree with Booker T. Washington?

# Mexican Americans

By 1900, about half a million Mexican Americans lived in the United States. Like African Americans, Mexican Americans often faced legal segregation. In 1910, the town of San Angelo, Texas, built new schools for its Anglo children. Mexican children were forced to go to separate, inferior schools. When Mexican children tried to attend one of the new schools, officials barred their way.

**Increased Immigration** In 1910, revolution and famine swept Mexico. Thousands of Mexicans fled into the United States. They came from all levels of Mexican society. Many were poor farmers, but some came from middle-class and upper-class families.

At first, 90 percent of Mexican immigrants settled in the Southwest. In time, the migration spread to other parts of the country. People who could not find work in the Southwest began moving to the Midwest and the Rocky Mountain region.

**Daily Life** Mexican immigrants often worked as field hands, built roads, or dug irrigation ditches. Some lived near the railroads they helped build. Still others worked in city factories under harsh conditions. They were paid less than Anglo workers and were denied skilled jobs.

Like other immigrants, Mexican Americans sought to preserve their language and culture. They created barrios, or ethnic Mexican American neighborhoods. Los Angeles was home to the nation's largest barrio. Its population almost tripled between 1910 and 1920.

Within the barrio, Mexican immigrants and Mexican Americans took many steps to help each other. Some formed mutualistas, or mutual aid groups. These groups worked like other immigrant aid societies. Members of mutualistas pooled money to pay for insurance and legal advice. They also collected money for the sick and needy.

✓**Checkpoint** Why did emigration from Mexico rise after 1910?

**Mexican Americans Helping One Another**

Like other groups, Mexican Americans formed mutual aid groups. Members of a mutualista in Arizona are shown marching in a parade (bottom left). Below is the symbol of the Cruz Azul Mexicana, or Mexican Blue Cross, which aided poor families.
**Critical Thinking: *Draw Conclusions*** *Why were mutual aid groups like these important to Mexican American communities?*

**Japanese Brides Arrive in the United States**

The Gentlemen's Agreement between President Roosevelt and Japan allowed Japanese wives to join their husbands who were already in the United States. Here, a group of Japanese women arrive at San Francisco. **Critical Thinking:** *Clarify Problems* What problem was Roosevelt trying to solve by allowing Japanese women to enter the United States?

**Main Idea**

As large numbers of immigrants arrived from Japan, some Americans called for limits on Japanese immigration.

**Vocabulary** *Builder*
**crisis** (KRĪ sihs) *n.* turning point; situation involving great risk

# Asian Americans

As you learned in the previous chapter, the Chinese Exclusion Act of 1882 kept Chinese from settling in the United States. Employers on the West Coast and in Hawaii began hiring workers from other Asian countries, mainly the Philippines and Japan.

**Japanese Immigrants** More than 100,000 Japanese entered the United States in the early 1900s. Most went first to Hawaii to work on sugar plantations. When the United States annexed Hawaii in 1898, many Japanese decided to seek a better life on the mainland.

Many of the newcomers were farmers. They settled on dry, barren land that Americans thought was useless. Through hard work, the Japanese made their farms profitable. Soon, they were producing a large percentage of southern California's fruits and vegetables.

**A Gentlemen's Agreement** Prejudice against Asians was high. In 1906, San Francisco forced all Asian students, including Japanese children, to attend separate schools. When Japan protested the insult, the issue threatened to cause an international crisis.

Unions and other groups put pressure on President Theodore Roosevelt to limit immigration from Japan. Because Roosevelt did not want to antagonize a growing naval power, he tried to soothe Japanese feelings. He condemned the segregated schools and proposed that if San Francisco ended segregation, he would restrict Japanese immigration.

In 1907, Roosevelt reached a "Gentlemen's Agreement" with Japan. Japan would stop any more workers from going to the United States. The United States, in exchange, would allow Japanese women to join their husbands who were already in the country.

Anti-Japanese feeling remained high. In 1913, California banned Asians who were not American citizens from owning land.

✓**Checkpoint**   **What was the Gentlemen's Agreement?**

# Religious Minorities

Religious minorities also faced prejudice. As you have read, the immigration boom included large numbers of Roman Catholics and Jews. Nativist groups, such as the Anti-Catholic American Protective Association, worked to restrict immigration. Even Jews and Catholics who were not immigrants faced discrimination in jobs and housing.

Anti-Catholic feeling was common in schools. Some teachers lectured against the Pope, and textbooks contained references to "deceitful Catholics." In response, American Catholics set up their own parochial schools, or schools sponsored by a church.

The most notorious case of anti-Semitism, or prejudice against Jews, in the United States took place in Georgia in 1913. Leo Frank, a Jewish man, was falsely accused of murdering a young girl. Newspapers inflamed public feeling against "the Jew." Despite a lack of evidence, he was sentenced to death. When the governor of Georgia reduced the sentence, a mob took Frank from prison and lynched him.

In response to the lynching and other cases of anti-Semitism, American Jews founded the Anti-Defamation League. (Defamation is the spreading of false, hateful information.) The League worked to promote understanding and fight prejudice against Jews.

**☑Checkpoint**  **What problems did Jews and Catholics face?**

⭐ **Looking Back and Ahead** Groups such as the NAACP and the Anti-Defamation League were formed to fight discrimination. Today, many Americans continue to work against prejudice.

**Main Idea**
Immigration also led to increased prejudice against Jews and Roman Catholics.

---

## Section 4 | Check Your Progress

**Progress Monitoring Online**
**For:** Self-test with instant help
**Visit:** PHSchool.com
**Web Code:** mya-6154

### Comprehension and Critical Thinking

**1. (a) Contrast** How did Booker T. Washington and W.E.B. Du Bois propose to improve life for African Americans?
**(b) Draw Conclusions** Whose ideas do you think would be more likely to help African Americans in the long run? Explain your reasons.

**2. (a) Identify** What was the Gentlemen's Agreement?
**(b) Analyze Cause and Effect** How did the Gentlemen's Agreement affect Japanese immigration?

### Reading Skill

**3. Identify Central Problems From the Past** What central problems faced Asian Americans in the late 1800s? How did Japan respond to these problems? Can you connect their problems to the attitudes toward immigrants today?

### Vocabulary *Builder*

**4.** Write two definitions for the key terms lynching and anti-Semitism. First, write a formal definition for your teacher. Second, write a definition in everyday English for a classmate.

### Writing

**5.** Imagine that you are an editorial writer who attended a debate between Booker T. Washington and W.E.B. Du Bois about the best tactics for fighting discrimination. Write a topic sentence that states the central idea of each man's argument. Then, write a paragraph endorsing one of these points of view and explaining your position.

Photographs are one type of primary source. By capturing a moment in time, they can provide important details about a historical period or event. The photographs below were taken by Jacob Riis.

Baxter Street, New York
(From *Battle With the Slums*, 1902.)

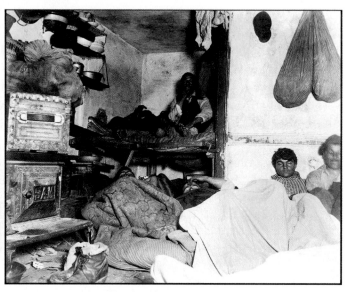

Lodgers in a New York tenement
(From *How the Other Half Lives*, 1890.)

## Learn the Skill

*Use these steps to analyze photographs.*

**1** **Find out information about the photograph.** Read the caption to identify the time and place.

**2** **Identify the subject.** Look carefully at the photograph. What does it show? If there are people in the photograph, what are they doing?

**3** **Decide what the photograph tells about history.** Study the photograph to find out what it illustrates about the past. Try to determine the photographer's point of view or opinion about the scene.

**4** **Decide if the photograph is a reliable source of information.** The photographer may have shot the photograph for a special reason or left out certain details in the scene. You should ask questions to determine the reliability of the photograph.

## Practice the Skill

*Answer the following questions about the photographs on this page.*

**1** **Find out information about the photograph.** (a) Where was the left photograph taken? (b) When was it published?

**2** **Identify the subject.** (a) Who are the people in the right photograph? (b) What are they doing?

**3** **Decide what the photograph tells about history.** (a) What do these photographs show about life in New York City slums at the time? (b) How do you think the photographer felt about these scenes? Explain.

**4** **Decide if the photograph is a reliable source.** Do you think these photographs give a reliable idea of how poor people lived in New York City? Explain.

## Apply the Skill

*See the Review and Assessment at the end of this chapter.*

**interactive Textbook**

**Study Guide** *Online*
Complete your Chapter 19 study guide in print or online.

## Chapter Summary

### Section 1
### The Gilded Age and Progressive Reform

- Corrupt political bosses sometimes gained power over cities during the Gilded Age.
- Progressives supported reforms that gave more power to the voters.
- Muckrakers exposed political, social, and business corruption.

### Section 2
### The Progressive Presidents

- Theodore Roosevelt tried to break up business trusts that hurt competition.
- Roosevelt's Square Deal called for conservation and consumer protection.
- Roosevelt and Progressive Republicans established the Bull Moose Party.
- Woodrow Wilson continued Progressive reforms in his New Freedom program.

### Section 3
### The Rights of Women

- The Nineteenth Amendment guaranteed women the right to vote.
- The Eighteenth Amendment banned the sale and consumption of alcoholic beverages.

### Section 4
### Struggles for Justice

- Booker T. Washington said African Americans should work patiently to move up in society, whereas W.E.B. Du Bois said blacks should actively fight discrimination.
- Mexican immigrants worked in low-paying jobs in the fields and factories and lived in ethnic neighborhoods called barrios.
- Asians faced discrimination, especially on the West Coast.
- Roman Catholics and Jews also faced different forms of discrimination.

## Key Concepts

These notes will help you prepare for questions about key concepts.

### Progressive Era Amendments

- **Sixteenth**—Congress gains power to pass an income tax
- **Seventeenth**—provides for direct election of senators
- **Eighteenth**—bans sale and consumption of alcohol nationally (later repealed)
- **Nineteenth**—gives women the right to vote in all elections

| Major Reform Legislation During the Gilded Age | | |
|---|---|---|
| **Date** | **Legislation** | **Major Purpose** |
| 1883 | Pendleton Act | Fill government jobs on basis of merit |
| 1887 | Interstate Commerce Act | Regulate railroads, stop pools and rebates |
| 1890 | Sherman Antitrust Act | Prohibit attempts to destroy competition |

| Major Reform Legislation During the Progressive Era | | |
|---|---|---|
| 1906 | Pure Food and Drug Act | Protect consumers from unsafe food and drugs; stop false advertising |
| 1914 | Federal Trade Commission | Investigate attempts to destroy competition |
| 1914 | Clayton Antitrust Act | Ban practices limiting free enterprise; stop use of antitrust laws against unions |

## Vocabulary *Builder*

**Key Terms**

Answer the following questions in complete sentences that show your understanding of the key terms.

1. Why would Upton Sinclair be considered a muckraker?

2. Why would William Howard Taft be considered a trustbuster?

3. Why would Alice Paul and Carrie Chapman Catt be considered suffragists?

4. What happened to the more than 1,000 African Americans who were lynched in the South during the 1890s?

## Comprehension and Critical Thinking

5. **(a) List** Which legislation did Congress pass to curb big business, and what were the goals of the legislation?
**(b) Make Predictions** How effective do you think the legislation was?

6. **(a) Describe** Which four reforms were instituted during the Progressive Era to give voters more power?
**(b) Apply Information** How would voters in your state use each of these reforms to get what they want done?

7. **(a) Recall** What did Theodore Roosevelt do to protect the nation's natural areas?
**(b) Draw Conclusions** How have Americans benefited from Roosevelt's actions?

8. **(a) Recall** How did the role of President change during the administration of Theodore Roosevelt?
**(b) Evaluate Information** Suggest one reason for the change.

9. **(a) Recall** What was the principal goal of the women's rights movement after the Civil War?
**(b) Draw Inferences** Why was that an important goal?

10. **(a) Summarize** What kind of discrimination did African Americans, Mexican Americans, and Asian Americans face during this period?
**(b) Link Past and Present** How do these groups still face similar discrimination today? Which types of discrimination are no longer legal?

## History Reading Skill

11. **Identify and Explain Central Issues** Explain the issues central to corruption in city government, placing them in the context of the nation's growth in the late 1800s. Give an example of a problem that resulted from this corruption. How did people respond to that corruption?

## Writing

12. **Write a two-paragraph persuasive composition:**
Choose one particular present-day problem that you feel needs to be corrected. (You do not need to provide a solution.) Express your opinion about this problem, explaining why it needs to be addressed. Include several facts and reasons supporting your opinion. Then, end with a strong statement meant to persuade your readers to take action against the problem.

13. **Write a Narrative:**
Imagine you are a Japanese immigrant in California around 1910. Write a narrative describing your experiences since arriving in the state.

## Skills for Life

**Analyze Photographs**

Use the photograph below by Jacob Riis to answer the questions that follow.

Seventh Avenue night school, New York
(From *Children of the Poor*, 1892.)

14. **(a)** Who are the people in the photograph?
**(b)** What are they doing?

15. How do you think the photographer feels about the situation in the photograph? Explain.

16. In general, does the photograph give a reliable idea of how poor people lived in New York City? Explain.

# Test Yourself

1. **The principal reason Theodore Roosevelt wanted to break up certain trusts was that he believed they**

   A were unfair to entrepreneurs.

   B hurt workers and the public.

   C made a few Americans rich and kept the majority poor.

   D threatened to slow the growth of foreign trade.

2. **Unlike Booker T. Washington, W.E.B. Du Bois believed that African Americans should**

   A work to achieve equal rights gradually.

   B accept racial segregation laws.

   C actively resist discrimination.

   D focus on gaining industrial and agricultural skills.

Refer to the quotation below to answer Question 3.

> "I recognize the right and duty of this generation to develop and use the natural resources of our land; but I do not recognize the right to waste them, or to rob, by wasteful use, the generations that come after us."

3. **The person who made the above statement would best be described as a**

   A muckraker.

   B suffragist.

   C prohibitionist.

   D conservationist.

# Document-Based Questions

**Task:** Look at Documents 1 and 2, and answer their accompanying questions. Then, use the documents and your knowledge of history to complete this writing assignment:

> Write a short essay about the muckrakers of the late 1800s and early 1900s. Be sure to identify the different muckrakers and to describe their goals and accomplishments. Include information about how they got their name.

**Document 1:** The excerpt below is from journalist Ida Tarbell's *History of the Standard Oil Company. What does Tarbell say is the goal of a trust?*

> "Standard Oil Trust is the most perfectly developed trust in existence; that is, it satisfies most nearly the trust ideal of entire control of the commodity in which it deals. Its vast profits have led its officers into various allied interests, such as railroads, shipping, gas, copper, iron, steel, as well as into banks and trust companies. . . . It has led in the struggle against legislation directed against combinations. Its power in state and Federal government, in the press, in the college, in the pulpit, is generally recognized."

**Document 2:** In *How the Other Half Lives,* Jacob Riis called attention to the misery of tenement living. *What aspect of tenement living is Riis describing in this excerpt?*

> "It is said that nowhere in the world are so many people crowded together on a square mile as here. . . . In this house . . . there were fifty-eight babies and thirty-eight children that were over five years of age. In Essex Street, two small rooms in a six-story tenement were made to hold a "family" of father and mother, twelve children, and six boarders. These are samples of the packing of the population that has run up the record here to the rate of three hundred and thirty thousand per square mile.
>
> The densest crowding of Old London . . . never got beyond a hundred and seventy-five thousand. Even the alley is crowded out. Through dark hallways and filthy cellars, crowded, as is every foot of the street, with dirty children, the settlements in the rear are reached."

# Writing Workshop

## Persuasive Editorial

### ▶ Introduction

In a persuasive editorial, you express an opinion about an issue of public interest. You support that opinion with facts, reasons, and examples, and communicate your viewpoint to a particular audience. A persuasive editorial should have the following characteristics:

- a topic that involves a matter of opinion
- an issue of public (rather than personal) interest
- a thesis statement that clearly expresses an opinion about that issue
- specific facts, details, examples, and reasons that support the opinion
- reasonable tone and persuasive language

**Assignment** On the following pages, you will learn how to write a persuasive editorial. You will get step-by-step instructions. Each step will include an example from a sample editorial expressing an opinion about suffrage for women.

Read the instructions and the examples. Then, follow each step to plan and write a 500–700 word persuasive editorial.

> **Write about the settlement of the West and the disappearance of the frontier.**

### ▶ Prewriting

**Find a persuasive topic.** A persuasive editorial presents an opinion about an issue of public interest. Opinions deal with matters of interpretation—with questions that can be viewed in more than one way.

**Define your audience.** When you plan to write a persuasive editorial, you need to know your audience. Ask the following questions to create an audience profile:

- What issues is my audience most concerned about?
- Where do they live?
- How much do they know about this issue? How are they likely to feel about it?

> For a review of the steps in the writing process, see the **Historian's Toolkit, *Write Like a Historian.***

> **Sample thesis statement:**
> A constitutional amendment giving women the right to vote should be passed.

> **Sample supporting fact:**
> More than 5 million women are in the workforce.
>
> **Sample supporting reason:**
> It is only fair that women in the workforce, as well as homemakers, have a say in the laws that govern them.

**Create a working thesis.** Your thesis should express an informed opinion based on a knowledge of the facts and reflect logical thinking.

**Brainstorm for supporting information.** You need to find facts, details, examples, and reasons that support your opinion.

**Think about opposing arguments.** Your editorial will be especially persuasive if you pay attention to opposing arguments—opinions that are different from the one you are expressing. It is a good idea to mention such arguments and then answer them in support of your own opinion.

## ▶ Drafting

**Decide how to organize your writing.** Persuasive editorials may be organized in a number of different ways. Three effective methods of organization are order of importance, process of elimination, and contrast.

- **Order of importance** List three or four major reasons for supporting your opinion, and then support and develop each of these reasons, going from the least significant reason to the most important one.
- **Process of elimination** Lead the reader step by step through several possible interpretations. Show why each interpretation is not valid or does not fit the facts as well as your approach does.
- **Contrast** If you are focusing on just two alternative viewpoints, you could contrast them, hoping to persuade your audience that one is more valid than the other.

**Introduce your thesis.** Draft an introductory paragraph that sets up the issue you will be writing about. State your opinion on the matter and the main reasons that support your opinion.

**Support your thesis with examples and details.** Use your notes to write paragraphs supporting your opinion with facts and reasons. The more specific and concrete your supporting details are, the more convincing your essay will be.

**Use a persuasive tone.** As you write your draft, keep in mind that you are addressing an audience that does not necessarily agree with you. Present your ideas tactfully. Acknowledge but do not insult opposing opinions.

**Write a strong conclusion.** In your final paragraph, restate your opinion as forcefully as you can.

# Writing Workshop *continued*

## ▶ Model Essay

Read the following model of a persuasive essay. Notice how it includes the characteristics you have learned about.

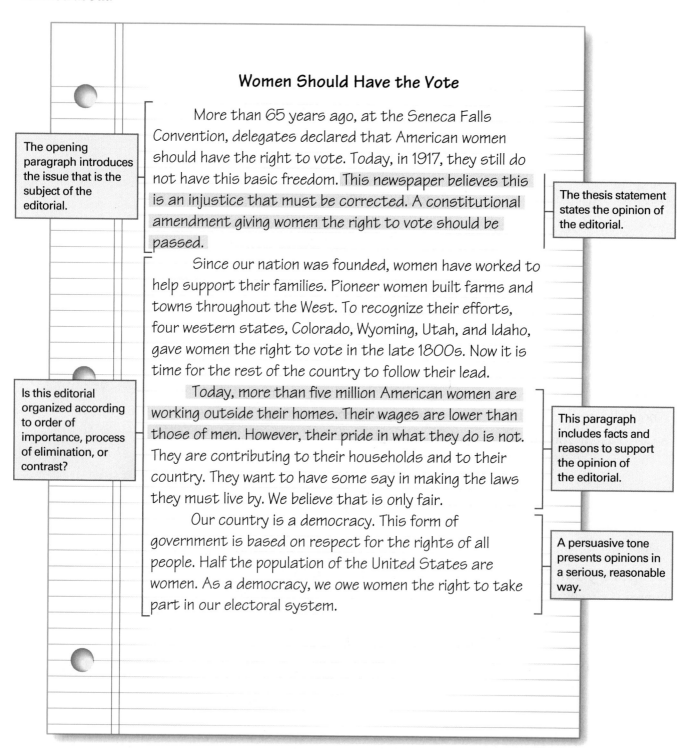

**The opening paragraph introduces the issue that is the subject of the editorial.**

**Is this editorial organized according to order of importance, process of elimination, or contrast?**

### Women Should Have the Vote

More than 65 years ago, at the Seneca Falls Convention, delegates declared that American women should have the right to vote. Today, in 1917, they still do not have this basic freedom. This newspaper believes this is an injustice that must be corrected. A constitutional amendment giving women the right to vote should be passed.

Since our nation was founded, women have worked to help support their families. Pioneer women built farms and towns throughout the West. To recognize their efforts, four western states, Colorado, Wyoming, Utah, and Idaho, gave women the right to vote in the late 1800s. Now it is time for the rest of the country to follow their lead.

Today, more than five million American women are working outside their homes. Their wages are lower than those of men. However, their pride in what they do is not. They are contributing to their households and to their country. They want to have some say in making the laws they must live by. We believe that is only fair.

Our country is a democracy. This form of government is based on respect for the rights of all people. Half the population of the United States are women. As a democracy, we owe women the right to take part in our electoral system.

**The thesis statement states the opinion of the editorial.**

**This paragraph includes facts and reasons to support the opinion of the editorial.**

**A persuasive tone presents opinions in a serious, reasonable way.**

# ▶ Revising

After completing your draft, read it again carefully to find ways to make your writing better. Here are some questions to ask yourself.

## Revise to strengthen your thesis and support
- Does the thesis state your opinion clearly and strongly?
- Does each paragraph offer valid reasons and solid facts that support that opinion?

## Revise to be more convincing
- Is the tone of the editorial reasonable but persuasive?
- Are the opposing arguments dealt with effectively and respectfully?
- Does the editorial make the reader feel that the issue is important?

## Revise to meet written English-language conventions
- Are all sentences complete, with a subject and a verb?
- Are all the words spelled correctly?
- Are all proper nouns capitalized, including names of people and places?
- Did you use proper punctuation?

# ▶ Rubric for Self-Assessment

*Evaluate your persuasive editorial using the following rating scale:*

|  | Score 4 | Score 3 | Score 2 | Score 1 |
|---|---|---|---|---|
| **Organization** | Supports the thesis with a series of paragraphs guided by a reason stated in a topic sentence | Uses order of importance or some other effective way of organizing the composition; uses a reasonably clear organization to present the supporting information | Chooses an organization not suited to the topic | Shows lack of organizational strategy |
| **Presentation** | Supports the opinion effectively with relevant facts, details, or examples; links all information to the opinion being supported | Supports the opinion adequately with several facts, details, or examples; links most information to the opinion being supported | Does not support the opinion adequately; does not link supporting information to the opinion | Does not provide facts, details, or examples to support the opinion |
| **Use of Language** | Uses persuasive language and reasonable tone; varies sentence structure and vocabulary successfully; includes no or very few mechanical errors | Is often persuasive and usually reasonable; uses some variety in sentence structure and vocabulary; includes few mechanical errors | Is not respectful of opposing views; repeats sentence style; does not vary vocabulary; includes many mechanical errors | Does not have a persuasive tone; is not respectful of opposing views; includes incomplete sentences; uses language poorly; includes many mechanical errors |

# Unit 7

**Americans Look Overseas** By 1900, the United States Navy had enlarged and modernized its naval fleet. The nation showed growing interest in overseas trade and in playing a larger role in world affairs.

## 1900

## 1917

**United States Enters World War I** America joined with France and the other Allies to push back Germany and Austria-Hungary in the First World War. President Wilson hoped this would be the war to make the world "safe for democracy."

# A New Role in the World

**Panama Canal** The United States began building a canal across a narrow strip of land in Central America. The new canal made it possible for oceangoing ships to sail more quickly between the west and east coasts of the United States.

## 1904

**The Roaring Twenties** Radios, cars, and motion pictures brought enormous changes to popular culture. New forms of advertising helped popularize products and styles.

## 1920s

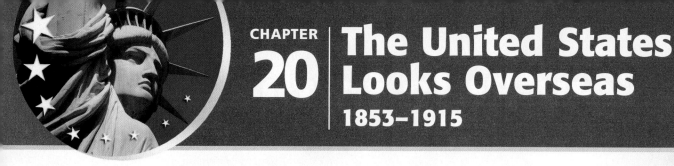

# Chapter Preview

By the late 1800s, the United States was taking a larger role in world affairs. The nation acquired new territories in the Pacific and strengthened its trade ties with Asia. In addition, the Spanish-American War led to increased involvement in Latin America.

✓ **What You Will Learn**

During the last half of the 1800s, the United States acquired territories and built up trade in the Asia-Pacific region.

A quick U.S. victory in the Spanish-American War of 1898 gave the United States an overseas empire.

The United States expanded the Monroe Doctrine and became more involved in Latin America.

**U.S. Events**

**1854** United States signs trade treaty with Japan.

**1893** American planters stage revolt in Hawaii.

**1898** United States wins Spanish-American War.

1850

1890

1900

**World Events**

**1858** France begins conquest of Indochina.

**1880s** European powers carve up Africa.

**1900** Boxer Rebellion breaks out in China.

President Theodore Roosevelt followed a "big stick" policy as he sought to block European nations from interfering when Latin American nations could not pay their debts.

**Discovery SCHOOL**

**Quick View Video**
View the chapter video for a quick preview of the main ideas.

**1904**
United States begins to build Panama Canal.

**1914**
United States Navy occupies port of Veracruz, Mexico.

1900

1910

1920

**1910** Japan annexes Korea.

**1914** World War I begins in Europe.

**History Reading Skill** **Frame Research Questions**

### What questions could you ask to learn more about the Panama Canal?

In this chapter, you will practice framing, or asking, questions that can be answered through research. Read the following account of the history of the Panama Canal. The side notes show you how to frame research questions.

**Primary Source**

In 1914, the United States completed the Panama Canal after overcoming many challenges. The waterway across Central America's narrowest point connected the Pacific and Atlantic oceans.

For at least 400 years people dreamed about digging a canal across the Isthmus of Panama. . . .

The first dreamer was King Charles V of Spain. In 1534 his soldiers had to struggle across the Isthmus on a bumpy stone road . . . with the stolen riches of Bolivia and Peru piled on the backs of mules and horses. . . .

By 1855, despite many deaths from malaria and yellow fever, an American company succeeded in completing a railroad across the Isthmus to transport [gold] prospectors and their families. . . .

In 1882 the French began digging a great trench . . . across the Isthmus. It had been the dream of Ferdinand de Lesseps, but his canal company ultimately collapsed because of disease, corruption, and mismanagement.

—Nancy Winslow Parker, *Locks, Crocs, & Skeeters: The Story of the Panama Canal*

**Ask questions to extend the text:** How did the Spanish interact with local populations?

**Ask questions to solve puzzles:** Why build this railroad? How did the risks balance with the likely rewards?

**Ask questions to connect across time periods:** How did Americans overcome the challenges that defeated Lesseps?

### Frame Research Questions

- Ask questions that are narrow enough to realistically answer. For example, questions should focus on a specific time period.
- Ask questions about *who* and *what* to find out important details. Then, ask *why* and *how* to go even further.
- Ask questions that require you to extend into related topics of interest to you.

### Document-Based Questions

1. According to the excerpt, who was the first European to think about building a canal across the Isthmus of Panama?
2. How would a canal have benefited the Spanish?
3. What challenge faced both the railroad builders and the canal builders?

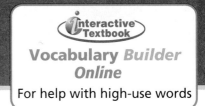
# Vocabulary *Builder*

## Previewing High-Use Academic Words

| High-Use Word | Definition | Sample History Sentence |
|---|---|---|
| **critic** (KRIHT ihk) (Section 1, p. 681) | *n.* someone who makes judgments about objects or actions | Critics are often quick to find fault with a president's actions. |
| **exclude** (ehks KLYOOD) (Section 1, p. 684) | *v.* to keep out or expel; to reject or not be considered | The United States objected to the attempts by some nations to exclude U.S. merchants from trade in China. |
| **revolt** (ree VOHLT) (Section 2, p. 688) | *n.* uprising; rebellion | Spain struggled to put down revolts in Cuba and the Philippines. |
| **prospect** (PRAHS pehkt) (Section 2, p. 690) | *n.* expectation; likely outcome | American businesses wanted to invest in China, lured by the prospect of great profits. |
| **hostile** (HAHS tihl) (Section 3, p. 694) | *adj.* unfriendly; intending to do harm; like an enemy | U.S. forces had little trouble defeating hostile forces in Puerto Rico. |
| **invest** (ihn VEHST) (Section 3, p. 696) | *v.* to supply money for a project in order to make a profit | If you invest in a stock today, you are hoping that its value will grow so that you can sell it at a profit later. |

## Previewing Key Terms and People

Liliuokalani

Matthew C. Perry, p. 680
isolationism, p. 681
imperialism, p. 681
Frederick Jackson Turner, p. 682
Liliuokalani, p. 683
sphere of influence, p. 684
reconcentration, p. 688
José Martí, p. 688
William Randolph Hearst, p. 689
Emilio Aguinaldo, p. 690

protectorate, p. 692
isthmus, p. 693
William C. Gorgas, p. 694
corollary, p. 696

dollar diplomacy, p. 696
Francisco Villa, p. 697

José Martí

# Eyes on the Pacific

## Objectives

1. Describe early attempts by the United States to expand in the Pacific.

2. List the reasons many Americans came to favor expansion.

3. Explain how the United States gained the territories of Samoa and Hawaii.

4. Describe how the United States protected its trading rights in China.

## Prepare to Read

### 🔊 Reading Skill

**Ask Extension Questions** In discussing one central event, history books will often mention a related event. You may find yourself interested in the related event. Why did it happen? What made it important? How did it affect those involved? Framing questions in specific language will help you research to find the answers.

### Vocabulary *Builder*

**High-Use Words**

critic, p. 681
exclude, p. 684

### Key Terms and People

Matthew C. Perry, p. 680
isolationism, p. 681
imperialism, p. 681
Frederick Jackson Turner, p. 682
Liliuokalani, p. 683
sphere of influence, p. 684

⭐ **Background Knowledge** You have seen how the United States extended its borders under the banner of Manifest Destiny. In this chapter, you will learn how the United States began to seek new opportunities overseas.

### Main Idea
The United States opened trade with Japan and purchased Alaska from Russia.

Japanese statuette of Commodore Perry

## The United States Looks Overseas

In the mid-1800s, the United States was ready to take on new challenges. It found new trading partners and acquired more land.

**Opening Japan to Trade** U.S. merchants longed to engage Japan in a profitable trade. However, for 250 years, Japan had blocked outside trade and barred foreigners from entering or leaving the country.

In 1853, a squadron of heavily armed U.S. warships, commanded by Commodore Matthew C. Perry, sailed into Tokyo Bay. Perry presented the Japanese with a letter from the President calling for Japan to grant trading rights to Americans. The Japanese were awed by Perry's powerful ships and menacing guns. When Perry returned in 1854, they signed a treaty opening Japan for trade.

Perry's visit had another important effect. Faced with the technology and power of the United States, the Japanese recognized their own weakness. They set out to transform their feudal society into an industrial nation that could compete in the modern world.

**Purchasing Alaska** In 1867, Alaska was a Russian colony. Russia told U.S. Secretary of State William Seward that it wanted to sell Alaska. Seward strongly favored U.S. expansion. He saw Alaska as a stepping stone for trade with Asia and the Pacific.

Alaska is twice the size of Texas. The United States purchased the territory for $7.2 million, about 2 cents an acre. The purchase increased the area of the United States by almost one fifth.

Many Americans opposed the purchase. Some saw Alaska as a frozen wasteland—"Seward's Folly" or "Seward's Icebox." But the critics changed their tune when valuable discoveries of gold led to the Klondike and Alaska gold rushes of 1897–1898. Alaska, it turned out, was rich in an amazing array of resources.

**Vocabulary** *Builder*
critic (KRIHT ihk) *n.* someone who makes judgments about objects or actions

✔**Checkpoint**  **How did the United States get Japan to open trade?**

## The Expansionist Mood

Until the late 1800s, Americans heeded George Washington's advice to "steer clear of permanent alliances." The nation generally pursued a policy of isolationism—that is, avoiding involvement in other countries' affairs. Americans stood aside as the nations of Europe undertook a policy of imperialism—building empires by imposing political and economic control over peoples around the world.

In the late 1800s, however, a new spirit of expansion gripped the nation. Americans began to consider a new sort of Manifest Destiny that would extend overseas. Supporters of expansion offered a variety of arguments for increased involvement in world affairs. These included promoting economic growth and spreading American values. A new view of history also encouraged expansionism.

**Main Idea**
In the late nineteenth century, the United States began to turn away from isolationism in a bid to acquire overseas territories.

### Seward's Folly

Russia offers Alaska.

Will "Billy" Seward trade?

**Reading Political Cartoons**

**Skills Activity**

The cartoonist shows a Russian stranger offering to trade "bears, seals, icebergs," and more.

**(a) Recognize Points of View** What is the cartoonist's opinion about the purchase of Alaska? What symbols does the cartoonist use to make the point?

**(b) Apply Information** What did people learn about Alaska after 1898? How would you change the cartoon, based on that information?

## Cause and Effect

### CAUSES

- Western frontier closes.
- European nations acquire overseas colonies and compete for resources and markets.
- U.S. industry needs to acquire raw materials and to find new markets in which to sell its products.
- Some in the United States want to spread American culture and values to other parts of the world.

### U.S. OVERSEAS EXPANSION

### EFFECTS

- U.S. Navy grows in size and power.
- United States gains control of territories in the Caribbean and the Pacific.
- The United States issues Open Door Policy, which allows all nations to trade with China.
- U.S. builds Panama Canal.
- United States sends troops to Latin American nations to protect its interests.

### Reading a Chart
#### Skills Activity

American expansionists wanted an overseas empire. By 1900, they had achieved their goal.

**(a)** **Read a Chart** Which causes listed on the chart relate to benefits for the U.S. economy?

**(b)** **Apply Information** How was a strong navy related to the expansionists' goals?

**The Turner Thesis** In 1893, historian Frederick Jackson Turner put forth the thesis, or idea, that the western frontier had defined American history. Westward movement, he said, had built individualism and democratic values. Turner concluded:

> "And now, four centuries from the discovery of America, at the end of a hundred years of life under the Constitution, the frontier has gone, and with its going has closed the first period of American history."
>
> —Frederick Jackson Turner, *The Significance of the Frontier in American History*

Today, few historians accept Turner's thesis. But the idea of a closing frontier influenced expansionists such as Theodore Roosevelt. Overseas expansion, they said, was the new frontier that would help the nation renew its vitality and strength.

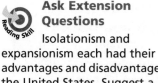

**Ask Extension Questions**

Isolationism and expansionism each had their advantages and disadvantages for the United States. Suggest a possible research question that builds on this topic.

**Promoting Economic Growth** The United States had a powerful industrial economy. It produced far more than Americans would buy. U.S. leaders watched nervously as European powers seized land in Africa and Asia. If the United States did not act soon, it might be shut out of global markets and denied raw materials.

A top supporter of expansion was Alfred T. Mahan, naval captain and author. Mahan said that future U.S. prosperity depended on building up trade. The key to strong trade, he argued, was a powerful navy that would control the world's sea lanes and thus protect U.S. access to foreign markets.

**Spreading American Values** In the late 1800s, many Americans believed that Americans of the "Anglo-Saxon race" were superior to "lesser races" in other nations. Therefore, the argument went, Americans had a divine duty to spread Christian values and western civilization around the world.

✓**Checkpoint** What arguments did expansionists make?

## Gaining Footholds in the Pacific

Supporters of expansion expressed interest in various Pacific islands. They saw them as essential for expanding U.S. influence and trade.

**Rivalry for Samoa** U.S. steamship companies and missionaries fanned interest in Samoa, a chain of islands in the South Pacific. The steamship companies and the U.S. Navy wanted to set up coaling stations, where ships could stock up on coal.

Britain and Germany also wanted Samoa. Armed conflict loomed in 1889, as Britain, Germany, and the United States all sent warships to Samoa. But fighting was averted when a typhoon struck, disabling or destroying most of the warships. Ten years later, in 1899, the United States and Germany divided the islands of Samoa between them. The people of Samoa, however, had no say in the matter.

**Interest in Hawaii** Expansionists also eyed Hawaii, a group of islands in the North Pacific. The islands have great natural beauty, sunshine, beaches, and rolling surf. But beauty was secondary. Located between Asia and the United States, Hawaii could serve as a "military and commercial outpost in the Pacific."

The first people to settle Hawaii arrived by canoe from other islands in the Pacific around the 600s. They lived undisturbed until 1778, when Captain James Cook, an English explorer, arrived.

In 1820, the first American missionaries came, hoping to convert Hawaiians to Christianity. Later, other Americans acquired land and set up huge sugar plantations.

As the sugar industry in Hawaii grew, so did the power of American planters. In 1887, planters forced the Hawaiian king, Kalakaua, to accept a new constitution that gave them great influence.

When Kalakaua died in 1891, his sister Liliuokalani (lih lee oo oh kah LAH nee) succeeded him. The new queen was a strong advocate of Hawaiian independence. She refused to recognize the 1887 constitution. She wanted to restore the power of the monarchy and reduce foreign influence in Hawaii.

**Main Idea**
The United States gained Pacific footholds in Samoa and Hawaii.

## Biography Quest

### Liliuokalani
1838–1917

Queen Liliuokalani championed several women's causes during her long life. She supported the establishment of a college that would train young Hawaiian women to be scholars. Other efforts led to the 1890 founding of a maternity home to help mothers and to provide care for newborns. She also championed the idea of a women's bank for Hawaii.

**Biography Quest** ●**nline**

**In what other field is Liliuokalani remembered for her contributions?**

**For:** The answer to the question about Liliuokalani

**Visit:** PHSchool.com

**Web Code:** myd-6162

**Boxer Rebellion**

U.S. troops joined soldiers from other powers in crushing the Boxer Rebellion of 1900 in China. **Critical Thinking:** *Detect Points of View This painting shows the event from the foreigner's point of view. Describe how a Chinese artist's painting would have differed.*

**Annexing Hawaii** In 1893, American planters organized an uprising. Without consulting the U.S. government, they persuaded a U.S. official to land 50 U.S. Marines to help overthrow the queen and set up a pro-American government. But President Grover Cleveland rejected a proposal to annex Hawaii. He argued that the revolt had been illegal and was not supported by the people of the islands.

Cleveland's successor, William McKinley, however, favored annexation and supported a treaty to achieve it. On July 7, 1898, Congress voted to make Hawaii a territory of the United States.

☑ **Checkpoint** **How did the United States acquire Hawaii?**

## Carving Up China

**Main Idea**
After other powers grabbed spheres of influence in China, the United States campaigned for equal trading rights there.

In the late 1800s, China had just emerged from an unsuccessful war. Taking advantage of China's weakness, European powers and Japan forced the Chinese empire to grant them land and trading rights. They set about dividing China into spheres of influence, or areas where another nation has economic and political control.

**Open Door Policy** At first, Americans were not part of this activity. But as the other powers carved up China, U.S. leaders feared that Americans would be <u>excluded</u> from the China trade.

**Vocabulary** *Builder*
<u>exclude</u> (ehks KLYOOD) *v.* to keep out or expel; to reject or not be considered

In 1899, U.S. Secretary of State John Hay issued a message to the other powers. He called on them to keep an "open door" in China. By this, he meant that he wanted them to guarantee the rights of all nations to trade with China on an equal basis. The various nations responded cautiously, most saying neither yes nor no. But Hay declared publicly that the Open Door Policy had been accepted.

**Boxer Rebellion** Many Chinese resented foreign influences in their country. They organized a secret society to combat the foreigners. The society called itself the Righteous and Harmonious Fists. Europeans called this society and its members Boxers, because they performed ceremonial exercises that resembled shadowboxing.

In the spring of 1900, the Boxers began a rebellion to expel the foreigners. Backed by China's government, they attacked and killed westerners and Chinese Christians. Mobs burned churches and the homes of foreigners. Hundreds of foreigners and some 2,000 Chinese sought safety in a walled section of Beijing, the Chinese capital.

Eventually, the outside powers, including the United States, sent in 18,000 troops armed with modern weapons. The troops freed the trapped foreigners, crushed the rebellion, looted the capital, and killed thousands of Chinese.

**The Open Door Again** Secretary Hay feared that the other powers would use the Boxer Rebellion as an excuse to seize more Chinese territory. To prevent this, he issued a second Open Door note. In it, he repeated the principle of open trade and made an even stronger statement about American intentions to preserve trade. He also said that China should remain one country and not be broken up into separate pieces.

☑ **Checkpoint**   **What was the goal of the U.S. Open Door Policy?**

⭐ **Looking Back and Ahead** Under the urging of expansionists, the government promoted U.S. trade and began to acquire territories overseas. In the next section, you will read of how the Spanish-American War gave the United States an empire.

---

Section 1 | **Check Your Progress**

**Progress Monitoring** Online
**For:** Self-test with instant help
**Visit:** PHSchool.com
**Web Code:** mya-6161

## Comprehension and Critical Thinking

**1. (a) Recall** What benefit did Seward see in acquiring Alaska?
**(b) Detect Points of View** Why did people call the purchase of Alaskan lands "Seward's Folly"?

**2. (a) Summarize** In what three ways did U.S. supporters of expansion justify increased involvement in world affairs?
**(b) Identify Economic Benefits** How did the division of Samoa and the annexation of the Hawaiian Islands benefit the United States?

## Reading Skill

**3. Ask Extension Questions** American acquisition of territory in the Pacific region was controversial. Suggest a possible research question building on this topic.

## Vocabulary Builder

Complete each of the following sentences so that the second part further explains the first part.
**4.** During much of the 1800s, the nation followed a policy of isolationism; _____.
**5.** Competing European nations followed policies of imperialism; _____.

**6.** China was divided into spheres of influence; _____.

## Writing

**7.** The paragraph that follows contains some vague, incorrect, or illogical arguments. Revise the paragraph to strengthen the passage. **Paragraph:** The United States could no longer be isolated by the rest of the world. The nation had to look overseas to promote economic growth because we were out of raw materials at home. The United States also needed to protect overseas trade, because trade is always useful.

# Economic Interests in the Pacific

After the Civil War, the United States became a world leader in industry and agriculture. American leaders believed that expansion was essential in order to compete with European factories. They favored expansion across the Pacific to gain resources, open new markets, and encourage trade.

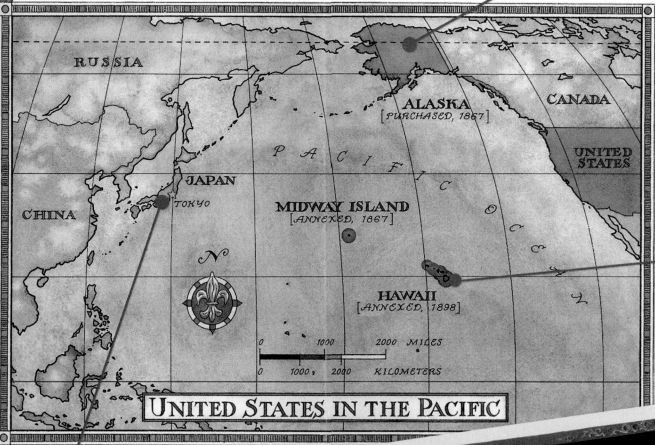

**UNITED STATES IN THE PACIFIC**

RUSSIA

ALASKA
[PURCHASED, 1867]

CANADA

UNITED STATES

PACIFIC

JAPAN

TOKYO

CHINA

MIDWAY ISLAND
[ANNEXED, 1867]

OCEAN

N

HAWAII
[ANNEXED, 1898]

0      1000      2000  MILES

0    1000    2000   KILOMETERS

**1  A New Market in Asia**
Seeking to pressure Japan into opening its ports to trade, Commodore Matthew C. Perry led a fleet of warships that entered Tokyo Bay in 1853. Japan realized it could not compete with American naval power. It decided to open trade relations with the United States.

### 2 "Seward's Folly"

Critics called Alaska "Seward's Folly" because they thought it was an icy wasteland. However, a gold rush in the 1890s proved the critics wrong. These miners pose for a photograph next to their Alaskan claim.

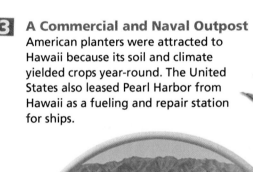

## America Expands Its Influence

By the start of the Spanish-American War in 1898, the United States had expanded its influence across the entire Pacific Ocean. It acquired valuable raw materials from its new territories and increased its influence on global trade.

**Secretary of State William Seward**

### 3 A Commercial and Naval Outpost

American planters were attracted to Hawaii because its soil and climate yielded crops year-round. The United States also leased Pearl Harbor from Hawaii as a fueling and repair station for ships.

### Analyze GEOGRAPHY AND HISTORY

What were American goals in the Pacific and Asia? Write a paragraph describing how Hawaii's climate and location made it vital to reaching those goals.

# The Spanish-American War

## Objectives

1. Describe how Americans reacted to the revolt in Cuba.

2. Identify the reasons the United States declared war on Spain.

3. Explain how the Spanish-American War led to the creation of an American overseas empire.

## Prepare to Read

### 🎯 Reading Skill

**Ask Analytical Questions**
Reading about history may sometimes leave you puzzled. Ask questions that focus on these puzzles, then research to find answers. Start by looking at what doesn't make sense to you, such as why people acted in a particular way. Use the question starters *who, what, when, why,* and *how* to begin. Then, think about how events changed over time and what caused the changes.

### Vocabulary *Builder*

**High-Use Words**

<u>revolt</u>, p. 688

<u>prospect</u>, p. 690

**Key Terms and People**

reconcentration, p. 688

José Martí, p. 688

William Randolph Hearst, p. 689

Emilio Aguinaldo, p. 690

protectorate, p. 692

⭐ **Background Knowledge** In the previous section, you read how the United States took its first steps on the world stage in the late 1800s. In this section, you will learn how it fought a war that transformed it into a major world power.

## War Clouds Loom

**Main Idea**
Americans sympathized with rebels who sought to gain Cuba's independence.

Cuba, 90 miles off the coast of Florida, had been under Spanish rule since Columbus came in 1492. Over the centuries, Cubans grew increasingly discontented with Spain's harsh rule. In 1868, the Cubans began an uprising that was finally put down 10 years later.

**Rebellion in Cuba** Cubans rose up again in 1895. To suppress this new <u>revolt</u>, the Spanish began a policy of reconcentration. Reconcentration is the forced movement of large numbers of people into detention camps for military or political reasons. In the Spanish camps, food was scarce and sanitation poor. As a result, an estimated 200,000 Cubans died.

**Vocabulary *Builder***
**revolt** (ree VOHLT) *n.* uprising; rebellion

Cuban exiles in the United States, led by José Martí, urged the United States to help the rebels. Martí, Cuba's greatest poet, had long dreamed of an independent Cuba. However, he was killed in a skirmish in Cuba before he could see his dream come true.

**Americans React** Many Americans were sympathetic to the Cuban rebels. They called on the U.S. government to intervene to oust the Spanish. Other Americans wanted to intervene for economic reasons, to safeguard American investments in Cuba. At the time,

🎯 **Ask Analytical Questions**
Revolts in Cuba interested many Americans. Suggest a possible research question on this topic.

Americans had about $50 million invested in Cuban sugar and rice plantations, railroads, and iron mines.

President Cleveland ignored the calls for intervention. He remarked that "there seems to be an epidemic of insanity in the country." When William McKinley became President in 1897, he also tried to maintain neutrality. Still, the clamor for war continued.

Some of the loudest cries came from the New York press. As you have read, Joseph Pulitzer of the *New York World* had developed a style of reporting that became known as yellow journalism. Pulitzer's rival, William Randolph Hearst of the *New York Journal*, tried to outdo Pulitzer in the use of sensational stories and headlines.

The two publishers focused much of their attention on Cuba. "FEEDING PRISONERS TO THE SHARKS," read one headline in the *Journal*. The *World* called Cuba a land of "blood on the roadsides, blood in the fields, blood on the doorsteps, blood, blood, blood." This daily barrage of horror stories fed American outrage against Spain.

**"Remember the *Maine*"** Early in 1898, fighting broke out in Havana, Cuba's capital. President McKinley ordered the battleship *Maine* to Havana harbor to protect American lives and property.

On February 15, at 9:40 P.M., a great explosion sank the *Maine* and killed 260 men. To this day, no one knows what caused the explosion. However, the press and the public blamed Spain. With cries of "Remember the *Maine*," Americans demanded revenge.

☑**Checkpoint** Why was the *Maine* in Havana harbor?

**Explore More Video**
To learn more about the sinking of the *Maine*, view the video.

**The Yellow Press Reports on the *Maine*** Sensational coverage of the explosion of the battleship *Maine* by New York's yellow press helped feed the fever for war.
**Critical Thinking:**
***Distinguish Facts From Opinions*** From these examples and from what you have read, state two facts and two opinions that appeared in coverage of the *Maine*.

**Vocabulary** *Builder*
prospect (PRAHS pehkt) *n.*
expectation; likely outcome

# The United States Goes to War

War fever swept the United States. At first, President McKinley favored a peaceful settlement between Spain and the rebels. He feared that war would disrupt the U.S. economy. In the end, though, McKinley gave in to the public pressure. On April 11, 1898, he asked Congress to declare war on Spain. Nine days later, Congress did so.

**Surprise in the Philippines** The first great battle of the war was not fought in Cuba. It took place halfway around the world.

Assistant Secretary of the Navy Theodore Roosevelt was eager to expand U.S. naval power. After the *Maine* blew up, Roosevelt saw the prospect of war growing. Roosevelt telegraphed Commodore George Dewey, head of the Pacific fleet. He ordered Dewey to move his ships so as to strike the Philippines when war broke out. On May 1, Dewey, with a small fleet of American warships, sank the entire Spanish squadron at Manila Bay, in the Philippines. The Americans did not lose a single ship or life.

**Fall of Manila** Like the Cubans, many Filipinos were in rebellion against the Spanish. Dewey enlisted Emilio Aguinaldo, a rebel leader, to help him seize Manila from the Spanish. Soon, the United States found itself in control of the Philippine Islands. Aguinaldo was a major help to the Americans. But the Americans overlooked the fact that Aguinaldo was fighting for Philippine independence. Soon he would be fighting against the Americans.

**War in the Caribbean** The war's focus next shifted to Cuba. The main fighting took place around Santiago and at sea. American ground forces arrived in Santiago in late June. They were poorly trained and poorly equipped—but eager to fight.

One of the best known units was the Rough Riders, led by Theodore Roosevelt. Roosevelt had given up his navy post to join the war. On July 1, Roosevelt helped lead his men in a successful charge up San Juan Hill that became the most celebrated event of the war.

Americans—both black and white—fought in the Santiago campaign. First Lieutenant John J. Pershing wrote:

> **❝**White regiments, black regiments . . . fought shoulder to shoulder, unmindful of race or color . . . and mindful only of their common duty as Americans.**❞**
> —First Lieutenant John J. Pershing, speech, November 27, 1898

Meanwhile, U.S. ships had trapped the Spanish fleet in Santiago harbor. When the fleet tried to escape, U.S. ships destroyed it. The 24,000 Spanish soldiers at Santiago surrendered two weeks later.

After the Spanish surrendered Cuba, American troops invaded Puerto Rico, another Spanish possession in the Caribbean. They quickly brought the island under U.S. control.

Theodore Roosevelt, Rough Rider

☑**Checkpoint** What lands did Spain lose in the Caribbean?

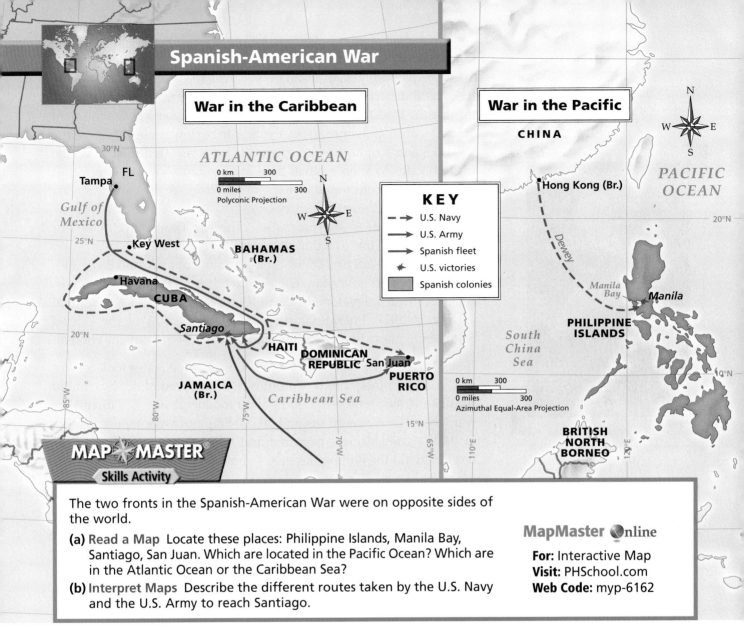

# Spanish-American War

## War in the Caribbean

## War in the Pacific

**KEY**

- – – → U.S. Navy
- ——→ U.S. Army
- ——→ Spanish fleet
- ✶ U.S. victories
- ▨ Spanish colonies

**MAP MASTER®**
**Skills Activity**

The two fronts in the Spanish-American War were on opposite sides of the world.

**(a) Read a Map** Locate these places: Philippine Islands, Manila Bay, Santiago, San Juan. Which are located in the Pacific Ocean? Which are in the Atlantic Ocean or the Caribbean Sea?

**(b) Interpret Maps** Describe the different routes taken by the U.S. Navy and the U.S. Army to reach Santiago.

**MapMaster ●nline**

**For:** Interactive Map
**Visit:** PHSchool.com
**Web Code:** myp-6162

## An American Empire

In December 1898, Spain and the United States signed a peace treaty. Spain accepted Cuban independence. It granted Puerto Rico, the Philippines, and the Pacific islands of Guam and Wake to the United States. In return, the United States paid Spain $20 million.

**Debating the Treaty** The treaty triggered an angry debate in the United States. Many Americans said taking colonies violated the principle of the Declaration of Independence—that all people had a right to self-government. Besides, they said, acquiring colonies brought the risk of future wars.

Expansionists, by contrast, welcomed the treaty. It gave the United States important bases, they said, and provided new business opportunities. Also, they argued, the United States had a duty to spread the ideas of democratic government to other parts of the world.

In a close vote, the Senate ratified the treaty on February 6, 1899. The United States now had an overseas empire.

**Main Idea**

Over opposition from some Americans, the United States took on an overseas empire.

**Governing Cuba and Puerto Rico** The United States replaced Spain as the leading Caribbean power. As a result, Cuba did not gain the true independence it sought. In 1902, Congress forced Cuba to include the Platt Amendment in its new constitution. The amendment limited Cuba's power to make treaties or borrow money. It gave the United States a right to intervene in Cuban affairs. It also allowed the United States to keep a naval base at Guantánamo Bay. In effect, it made Cuba a protectorate of the United States. A protectorate is an independent country whose policies are controlled by an outside power. Wrote one Cuban journalist, "The Americans have made our country free. As free as a dog on a leash."

The Foraker Act of 1900 set up a government in Puerto Rico, with a U.S.-appointed governor. The act gave Puerto Ricans limited self-rule. Americans developed Puerto Rico's economy and educational system. In 1917, Puerto Ricans were made citizens of the United States. Still, many Puerto Ricans wanted to be free of outside control.

**Revolt in the Philippines** When the United States took control of the Philippines, many Filipinos felt betrayed. Led by Emilio Aguinaldo, they renewed their fight for independence. In a three-year war, about 4,000 Americans and 20,000 Filipinos were killed. Finally, in 1901, Aguinaldo was captured and fighting came to an end. Not until 1946 did the Philippines gain independence.

Emilio Aguinaldo

✓**Checkpoint** How did the treatment of Cuba, Puerto Rico, and the Philippines differ?

⭐ **Looking Back and Ahead** The Spanish-American War gave the United States an overseas empire. Next, you will read how the United States extended its influence in Latin America.

---

**Section 2 | Check Your Progress**

**Progress Monitoring** 🌐nline
**For:** Self-test with instant help
**Visit:** PHSchool.com
**Web Code:** mya-6162

**Comprehension and Critical Thinking**

1. **(a) Identify** What role did the press play in rallying American support for a war in Cuba?
**(b) Draw Inferences** What motivated the United States to enter into a war with Spain?

2. **(a) List** What were the terms of the peace treaty between the United States and Spain?
**(b) Analyze Cause and Effect** How had the United States replaced Spain as a colonial power in the world?

**Reading Skill**

3. **Ask Analytical Questions** Reread the text following the subheading "Debating the Treaty." What were the arguments in the debate? Suggest a possible research question on this topic.

**Vocabulary** *Builder*

Answer the following questions in complete sentences that show your understanding of the key terms.

4. How did reconcentration suppress the people of Cuba?

5. Why did a Cuban describe protectorate status as like being a "dog on a leash"?

**Writing**

6. Write a persuasive paragraph either for or against the Spanish-American War. Exchange papers with a classmate who took the opposite view. Next, write comments opposing the other person's arguments. Finally, take back your own paper and rewrite it to respond to your classmate's notes.

# The United States and Latin America

## Objectives

1. Explain why and how the United States built the Panama Canal.

2. Discuss how Presidents expanded the Monroe Doctrine to intervene in the affairs of Caribbean nations.

3. Describe how relations between the United States and Mexico became strained under President Wilson.

## Prepare to Read

### 🎯 Reading Skill

**Focus Research Topics** Research topics must be specific. Frame questions to a particular time and place. Avoid questions that would require yes or no answers. Connect questions to the context of your history reading. Work toward asking questions that can be answered with evidence from available and reliable research sources.

### Vocabulary *Builder*

**High-Use Words**

<u>hostile</u>, p. 694

<u>invest</u>, p. 696

**Key Terms and People**

isthmus, p. 693

William C. Gorgas, p. 694

corollary, p. 696

dollar diplomacy, p. 696

Francisco Villa, p. 697

⭐ **Background Knowledge** By 1902, the United States was a world power, with colonies overseas and a strong economy. In this section, you will learn how it used its power in Latin America.

## Linking the Oceans

During the Spanish-American War, the U.S. Navy sent the battleship *Oregon* from San Francisco to Cuba. The trip—14,000 miles around the tip of South America—took more than two months.

Clearly, a shorter route was needed. A canal across Central America would link the Atlantic and Pacific oceans. President Theodore Roosevelt was determined to build that canal. Not only would it improve global shipping, but it would also make it easier for the U.S. Navy to defend the nation's new overseas empire.

**Choosing a Site** At 50 miles wide, the Isthmus of Panama was the ideal location for a canal. An isthmus is a narrow strip of land joining two larger areas of land. In 1902, Panama was a province of Colombia. Roosevelt offered Colombia $10 million in cash and $250,000 yearly in rent to allow the United States to build a canal through Panama.

Many Colombians opposed the deal because it would give the United States permanent control over a 6-mile-wide stretch of Colombian territory. Other Colombians claimed that the rights were worth far more than the United States had offered. Colombia's government held out for more money. However, Roosevelt was impatient. He did not want to lose time in bargaining.

**Main Idea**

In order to build a canal between the oceans, Teddy Roosevelt helped Panama to break away from Colombia.

Route of the USS *Oregon*

**Revolt in Panama** Roosevelt knew that many Panamanians disliked Colombian rule. Secretly, he let them know that the United States would help if they claimed independence. The Panamanians, of course, would then reap the rewards of a canal.

A revolt took place on November 3, 1903. U.S. gunboats waited in the harbor to provide support for the rebels. U.S. Marines landed in Colón to prevent <u>hostile</u> Colombian troops from reaching Panama City. Many Americans were alarmed by Roosevelt's role in the revolt, criticizing his "gunboat diplomacy."

The United States immediately recognized the independent Republic of Panama. Three days later, a Frenchman acting for Panama signed a treaty giving the United States permanent use and control of a 10-mile-wide zone across the Isthmus of Panama. The United States agreed to pay $10 million plus $250,000 a year in rent.

☑**Checkpoint**   **How did the United States help rebels in Panama?**

**Main Idea**
Despite many obstacles, construction was completed and ships began traveling through the Panama Canal in 1914.

## The Panama Canal

In 1904, the U.S. government began to build a canal across Panama. President Roosevelt urged the engineers to "Make the dirt fly!"

**Fighting Disease** The first great obstacle to building the canal was not an engineering problem. It was disease. Malaria and yellow fever were widespread in Panama. Real work on the canal could not begin until those diseases were controlled.

William C. Gorgas, an American expert on tropical diseases, took up the problem. Most people at the time believed that the damp night air caused yellow fever and malaria. A major breakthrough came when a Cuban doctor, Carlos Juan Finlay, discovered that yellow fever was transmitted by a certain kind of mosquito. An English doctor, Ronald Ross, found that a different kind of mosquito carried malaria.

At Gorgas's direction, workers cleared brush and drained swamps where mosquitoes lived. The huge effort paid off. By 1906, Gorgas had nearly wiped out yellow fever and reduced malaria in Panama.

**Focus Research Topics**
Suggest a more focused research question that builds on the following topic: How do science and economics work together?

**The "Big Ditch"** Construction of the canal involved three major tasks. Workers had to cut through a mountain, dam a river, and erect the canal's giant locks. By raising or lowering the water level, the locks would allow ships to cross Panama's Cordillera Mountains.

The most challenging job was digging the Gaillard Cut, a 9-mile ditch through the mountains. Thousands of men worked day after day under the tropical sun or in drenching rainstorms. Mudslides were a constant problem. To many workers, it seemed that the digging would never end. One later recalled, "I load cement, I unload cement. I carry lumber until my shoulders peel."

While engineers and supervisors came from the United States, most of the laborers were West Indians of African descent. Some 20,000 were from Barbados. More than 6,000 workers lost their lives during the construction of the canal.

# THE Panama Canal

**History Interactive**
**Tour the Panama Canal**
Visit: PHSchool.com
Web Code: myp-6163

The building of the Panama Canal was one of the greatest engineering feats of all time. Construction of the canal began in 1904 and was finished in 1914. When it was completed, the Atlantic and Pacific oceans were linked.
**Critical Thinking: *Synthesize Information*** *What were the costs and benefits of building the canal?*

## Panama Canal

**KEY**
Canal Zone
Locks
Canal

Caribbean Sea

Colón

80°W

PANAMA

Gatún Lake

PANAMA

Gaillard Cut

Panama City

9°N

0 km 10
0 miles 10
Conformal Conic Projection

Balboa

PACIFIC OCEAN

▲ Ships passing through the canal from the Pacific to the Caribbean are actually traveling northwest.

**Locks Under Construction ▲**
Because of the uneven elevation in the Canal Zone, the canal planners designed a system of locks to raise and lower the water level. This photograph shows construction of a lock in 1913. The huge gates open and close to let water in and out.

**Locks in ▶ Use Today**
Locks were built in pairs, allowing ships to pass in both directions at the same time.

## FAST FACTS

**Length:** 50 miles

**Cost to build:** $375 million

**Time to build:** 10 years

**Amount of earth removed during construction:** more than 230 million cubic yards

Source: Panama Canal Authority

Despite unexpected delays, work on the canal was finished six months ahead of schedule. The Panama Canal opened on August 15, 1914. After years of work, the Atlantic and the Pacific were joined.

☑ **Checkpoint**   **What problems did canal builders overcome?**

# Wielding a "Big Stick" in Latin America

**Main Idea**
Under Presidents Roosevelt and Taft, the United States often sent soldiers into Latin American nations.

Theodore Roosevelt was fond of quoting an old West African proverb: "Speak softly and carry a big stick; you will go far." He wanted the world to know that if diplomacy failed, the United States would not hesitate to use military force to protect its interests.

**Roosevelt Corollary**  Roosevelt applied his "big stick" policy in Latin America. He asserted the claim of the United States to be the leader in the Western Hemisphere. He especially wanted to prevent European nations from becoming too powerful in the region.

In 1904, European nations considered using military force to collect overdue debts from the Dominican Republic. To prevent any such action, Roosevelt announced a new policy. It came to be known as the Roosevelt Corollary to the Monroe Doctrine. A corollary is a logical extension of a doctrine or proposition.

Roosevelt argued that when the neighbors of the United States got into disputes with foreign nations, the United States had the right to "exercise . . . an international police power" to restore order.

Roosevelt sent marines to the Dominican Republic and took over the country's finances. Later Presidents often cited the Roosevelt Corollary when intervening in Latin America.

**Dollar Diplomacy**  William Howard Taft, who followed Roosevelt as President, had a different approach. Taft favored dollar diplomacy, a policy based on the idea that economic ties were the best way to expand American influence. Taft urged U.S. bankers and businesses to <u>invest</u> heavily in Asia and Latin America.

**Vocabulary Builder**
<u>invest</u> (ihn VEHST) v. to supply money for a project in order to make a profit

Dollar diplomacy led to as many military interventions as Roosevelt's "big stick." When a revolution broke out in Nicaragua, the United States sent in marines to protect U.S. investments. Later, American troops also occupied Haiti and Honduras. Many Latin Americans bitterly resented interference in their affairs.

☑ **Checkpoint**   **How did Roosevelt build on the Monroe Doctrine?**

**The U.S. and Latin America**
Fearing European intervention in Latin America, U.S. foreign policy asserted U.S. power in the Western Hemisphere. **Critical Thinking: *Identify Effects*** *Use information in the text to provide one effect of each policy listed in the chart.*

| U.S. Policy in Latin America, 1823–1909 | | |
|---|---|---|
| **Monroe Doctrine** (1823) Monroe asserts that the United States will not permit European nations to interfere with the free nations of Latin America. | **Roosevelt Corollary** (1904) Theodore Roosevelt reinforces the Monroe Doctrine by claiming the right to use force to prevent intervention in Latin America. | **Dollar Diplomacy** (1909) Taft's policy aims to protect U.S. economic investments in Latin America and in other regions. |

# Relations With Mexico

Woodrow Wilson, who became President in 1913, had his own ideas about foreign relations. He stated that U.S. foreign policy should aim to support and nurture democracy throughout the world.

Wilson's policy got its first test in relations with Mexico. In 1911, Mexicans had overthrown longtime dictator Porfírio Díaz. Mexico was plunged into a violent revolution that went on until 1917. Wilson at first followed a policy that he called "watchful waiting." He said he hoped Mexico would develop a democratic government.

In 1914, a minor incident led Wilson to intervene in Mexico. U.S. sailors who went ashore in Tampico were briefly arrested. Although they were released promptly with an apology, Wilson sent the navy to occupy the port of Veracruz. More than 100 Mexicans died. The incident brought Mexico and the United States close to war. Tempers cooled after South American nations arranged for peace talks.

Wilson was drawn into Mexican affairs again by the actions of Francisco Villa, a Mexican rebel general nicknamed Pancho. In 1916, Villa's rebels crossed into New Mexico. They raided and burned the town of Columbus, killing 18 Americans.

Mexico's president reluctantly let the United States pursue Villa into Mexico. On Wilson's orders, General John J. Pershing led several thousand soldiers across the border. After 11 months, Wilson ordered Pershing to withdraw without capturing Villa.

✓Checkpoint   **What was Wilson's policy toward Mexico?**

⭐ **Looking Back and Ahead**  World events provided the backdrop for the withdrawal of troops from Mexico. In 1917, war was raging in Europe and parts of Africa, Asia, and the Pacific. In the next chapter, you will learn about that world war and the U.S. role in it.

Pancho Villa

---

Section 3 | **Check Your Progress**

**Progress Monitoring** ⬤nline
**For:** Self-test with instant help
**Visit:** PHSchool.com
**Web Code:** mya-6163

## Comprehension and Critical Thinking

**1. (a) Recall** Why was the building of a canal important to the United States?
**(b) Understand Sequence** What events led to the eventual building of the Panama Canal?

**2. (a) Describe** According to President Wilson, what was the goal of U.S. foreign policy?
**(b) Compare and Contrast** How did the foreign policies of Presidents Roosevelt and Taft differ?

## ↻ Reading Skill

**3. Focus Research Topics** Reread the text following the subheading "Roosevelt Corollary." Suggest a more focused research question based on the following: How did Latin Americans respond to U.S. actions under the Roosevelt Corollary?

## Vocabulary *Builder*

Read the sentence below. If it is true, write YES. If it is not true, write NO and explain why.
**4.** Engineers built the canal through an isthmus river bed.

## Writing

**5.** Choose one of the following statements about U.S. support of the Panamanian rebels in 1903. Revise the statement to make its language more restrained and persuasive. **Statements:**

**(a)** The greedy Colombian government stood in the way of progress, but Roosevelt found a way around it.

**(b)** When Colombia stood up to Roosevelt, he acted like a bully and took what he wanted anyhow.

History is the story of change. Changes can result from a combination of causes, including war, natural or human disasters, economic needs, or new political ideas. Over time, new patterns of historical events develop. Identifying them will help you understand historical change.

**United States Involvement in the Caribbean**

UNITED STATES

Gulf of Mexico

**KEY**
United States and possessions
Areas of United States activity

BAHAMAS

ATLANTIC OCEAN

MEXICO

**CUBA**
(Occupied, 1898)

**PUERTO RICO**
(Won from Spain, 1898)

**HAITI**
(Occupied, 1915)

**DOMINICAN REPUBLIC**
(Marines sent, 1916)

**BRITISH HONDURAS**

**JAMAICA**

**GUATEMALA**

**HONDURAS**
(Marines sent, 1911)

Caribbean Sea

**EL SALVADOR**

**NICARAGUA**
(Marines sent, 1912)

**Canal Zone**
(Granted to U.S., 1903)

**COSTA RICA**

PACIFIC OCEAN

**PANAMA**
(Supported revolutionary government, 1903)

0 km 500
0 miles 500
Azimuthal Equal-Area Projection

## Learn the Skill

*Use these steps to recognize new historical patterns.*

**1** **Identify the main idea.** Look at the title of the map or chart to determine the subject.

**2** **Evaluate information.** How is the information presented? Look for dates of specific events. What important facts do you find out about the events? Framing questions can help you better evaluate the information.

**3** **Look for a historical pattern.** Make generalizations about the events. Add information from other sources to determine and extend the historical pattern.

**4** **Draw conclusions.** Use the information to draw conclusions about the historical pattern.

## Practice the Skill

*Answer the following questions about the map on this page.*

**1** **Identify the main idea.** What is the subject of the map?

**2** **Evaluate information.** (a) What happened in 1903? (b) What happened as a result?

**3** **Look for a historical pattern.** (a) What do the events on this map show about the change in U.S. foreign policy during this period? (b) What information about the Panama Canal can you add to this map from Section 3?

**4** **Draw conclusions.** How did the events on this map affect U.S. power in the Caribbean?

## Apply the Skill

*See the Review and Assessment at the end of the chapter.*

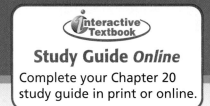

## Chapter Summary

### Section 1
### Eyes on the Pacific

- The United States purchased Alaska and acquired Pacific territories.
- The United States recognized the Pacific islands as important military outposts.
- The Open Door Policy was meant to give the United States equal trading opportunities with other nations in China.

### Section 2
### The Spanish-American War

- The United States went to war against Spain over Cuba and the Philippines.
- Naval and land battles in the Philippines and in Cuba and Puerto Rico resulted in victory for the United States.
- The United States took control of lands from which it had evicted Spain.

### Section 3
### The United States and Latin America

- The United States built the Panama Canal to improve global shipping and to strengthen American defense.
- Disease and tough terrain made building the Panama Canal very difficult.
- Foreign policy in the early 1900s aimed to build U.S. influence in Latin America.

Teddy Roosevelt

## Key Concepts

These notes will help you prepare for questions about key concepts.

### U.S. Influence in Asia

**Japan**
- U.S. Navy warships under Matthew C. Perry sail into Tokyo Bay in 1853.
- Japan opens its ports in 1854.
- Japan begins to modernize.

**China**
- European powers carve China into spheres of influence.
- U.S. Open Door Policy claims the right of all nations to trade with China.
- Western powers crush Chinese rebels in the Boxer Rebellion.

### U.S. Territorial Gains

**Territory Acquired or Controlled by the United States in the Pacific**
- Alaska: purchased in 1867
- Hawaii: annexed in 1898
- Samoa: a portion annexed in 1899

**Territory Gained in Spanish-American War**
- Puerto Rico
- Cuba
- Philippines
- Guam

### United States in Latin America

- United States backs Panamanians and builds the Panama Canal.
- President Theodore Roosevelt issues the Roosevelt Corollary to the Monroe Doctrine.
- President William Howard Taft promotes dollar diplomacy.
- United States sends troops to many Latin American nations.
- President Woodrow Wilson has U.S. Navy seize Mexican port.
- U.S. General Pershing pursues Pancho Villa into Mexico.

## Vocabulary *Builder*

### Key Terms

Answer the questions in complete sentences that show your understanding of the key terms.

1. How did imperialism conflict with isolationism in U.S. foreign policy?

2. Why did foreign nations want to establish spheres of influence in China?

3. Why was Theodore Roosevelt's foreign policy seen as a corollary to the Monroe Doctrine?

4. What was the goal of Taft's dollar diplomacy?

5. Why was an isthmus a good place to build a canal?

## Comprehension and Critical Thinking

6. **(a) Recall** Why was Secretary of State Seward interested in buying Alaska?
   **(b) Detect Points of View** How does the cartoon below reflect what many Americans thought of the purchase at first?
   **(c) Identify Economic Benefits** How did buying Alaska provide economic benefits?

7. **(a) Identify** In which regions of the world did European powers gain control by 1900?
   **(b) Evaluate Information** What impact did the expansion policies of European countries have on the foreign policy of the United States?

8. **(a) Recall** What event was the immediate cause of the Spanish-American War?
   **(b) Draw Conclusions** Do you think this event by itself was enough to start the war? Why or why not?

9. **(a) Explain** How did the United States gain an overseas empire?
   **(b) Detect Points of View** Why do you think some critics felt that having an empire was against American ideals?

10. **(a) Summarize** How did Roosevelt apply his "big stick" policy to Latin America?
    **(b) Compare** How was Taft's dollar diplomacy like the Roosevelt Corollary?

## History Reading Skill

11. **Frame Research Questions** Review the sections in this chapter, and frame one research question for each section. Remember to frame questions that go beyond the text and require research to answer.

## Writing

12. **Write two persuasive paragraphs about one of the following issues:**
    - American expansionism in the Pacific
    - U.S. relations with Latin America
    - The Spanish-American War

    **Your paragraphs should:**
    - Include a thesis statement expressing your opinion.
    - Use facts, reasons, and examples from the chapter.

    When you are finished, exchange papers with another student. Correct errors. Try to make the language more persuasive.

13. **Write a Narrative:**
    Imagine you are a Cuban nationalist visiting the United States with José Martí. Write a paragraph describing how you sought U.S. help for Cuba.

## Skills for Life

### Recognize New Historical Patterns

Create a list of key events related to the Spanish-American War, based on information in the chapter. Use your list and the map in Section 2 to answer the questions.

14. What is the subject of the map?

15. **(a)** What key event took place on February 15, 1898?
    **(b)** What happened as a result of this event?

16. Based on the events on your list, what historical pattern can you identify?

17. Why did this pattern emerge at this time?

## Test Yourself

1. **The chief goal of the Open Door Policy was to**

   A divide China into spheres of influence.

   B open Japan for trade.

   C put down the Boxer Rebellion.

   D protect U.S. trading rights in China.

2. **In the late 1800s, expansionists argued that the United States**

   A should avoid involvement with other nations.

   B needed new markets for its products.

   C should reject the Turner thesis.

   D should accept the Roosevelt Corollary.

**Refer to the cartoon below to answer Question 3.**

THE BIG STICK IN THE CARIBBEAN SEA

3. **What is the subject of this cartoon?**

   A yellow journalism

   B the Spanish-American War

   C the Roosevelt Corollary

   D the war in the Philippines

## Document-Based Questions

**Task:** Look at Documents 1 and 2, and answer their accompanying questions. Then, use the documents and your knowledge of history to complete this writing assignment:

> Write a short essay comparing the viewpoints of supporters and opponents of overseas expansion. Evaluate the validity of the arguments on each side.

**Document 1:** In January 1899, Senator Orville H. Platt explained why he supported annexing the Philippines. *What arguments does Platt give?*

"I believe the same force was behind . . . our ships in Manila Bay that was behind the landing of Pilgrims on Plymouth Rock. . . . [We] have been chosen to carry forward this great work of uplifting humanity . . . . From the time of the landing on Plymouth Rock in the spirit of the Declaration of Independence, in the spirit of the Constitution, believing that all men are equal and endowed by their Creator with inalienable rights, believing that governments derive their just powers from the consent of the governed, we have spread that civilization . . . until it stood at the Pacific Ocean looking ever westward."

**Document 2:** Senator George F. Hoar responded to Platt's argument in favor of annexing the Philippines. *Why does Senator Hoar oppose annexing the Philippines?*

"You have no right at the cannon's mouth to impose on an unwilling people your Declaration of Independence and your Constitution and your notions of freedom and notions of what is good. . . . Now the people of the Philippine Islands are clearly a nation— a people three and one-third times as numerous as our fathers were when they set up this nation. . . . The people there have got a government, with courts and judges . . . and it is proposed to turn your guns on them and say, 'We think that our notion of government is better than the notion you have got yourselves.'"

## Chapter Preview

In 1914, a massive war broke out in Europe. Although the United States at first remained neutral, the nation eventually got involved. The conflict, which we now call World War I, had important effects both at home and in the world.

**U.S. Events**

**1912**
Woodrow Wilson is elected President.

**1914**
Wilson declares U.S. neutrality in war in Europe.

**1915**
128 Americans die when the *Lusitania* is sunk.

1912    1914    1916

**World Events**

**1914** World War I begins in Europe.

In this picture, American soldiers fight from trenches in the French countryside in July 1918.

**Discovery SCHOOL**

**Quick View Video**
View the chapter video for a quick preview of the main ideas.

**1917**
United States declares war on Germany.

**1918**
Armistice ends World War I.

**1919**
U.S. Senate rejects Treaty of Versailles.

1916

1918

1920

**1917** Revolution in Russia overthrows the tsar.

**1918** Treaty of Versailles punishes Germany.

### ⊙ History Reading Skill  Identify and Connect Main Ideas

## How did Americans react to war in Europe?

In this chapter, you will practice identifying and connecting main ideas. Read the following historical document. The side notes show you how to identify and connect main ideas.

> In 1914, war broke out in Europe. At this point, President Woodrow Wilson urged Americans not to take sides.
>
> **Primary Source**
>
> The effect of the war upon the United States will depend upon what American citizens say and do. Every man who really loves America will act and speak in the true spirit of neutrality, which is the spirit of impartiality and fairness and friendliness to all concerned. . . .
>
> The people of the United States are drawn from many nations, and chiefly from the nations now at war. It is natural and inevitable that there should be the utmost variety of sympathy and desire among them. . . . Some will wish one nation, others another, to succeed in the momentous struggle. . . . The people of the United States, whose love of their country and whose loyalty to its government should unite them as Americans all, bound in honor and affection to think first of her and her interests, may be divided in camps of hostile opinion . . . .
>
> Such divisions amongst us would be fatal to our peace of mind and might seriously stand in the way of the proper performance of our duty as the one great nation at peace.
>
> —Woodrow Wilson,
> August 19, 1914

**Here is the main idea of the excerpt.** You can connect it to other main ideas in the excerpt.

**Connect this information** with what you have learned in other chapters about immigration in the early 1900s.

**Connect this main idea to the main idea in the first paragraph.** Wilson reminds Americans to remain neutral because of the danger of causing disunity within the nation.

**Connect main ideas to current events:** Does the United States still try to act as a peacemaker between warring nations?

## Identify and Connect Main Ideas

- Ask yourself how the main idea in one piece of text relates to that in another piece. Connections might include cause and effect, comparison and contrast, explanations and examples, and so on.
- Connect main ideas from this chapter to those from other chapters. Ask yourself how different times in history influenced others.
- Connect main ideas to current events.

## Document-Based Questions

1. What policy does Wilson think the United States should follow in the war?
2. Why does he fear the war in Europe may cause conflict among Americans?
3. What role does Wilson think the United States should play in foreign wars?

# Vocabulary *Builder*

## Previewing High-Use Academic Words

| High-Use Word | Definition | Sample History Sentence |
|---|---|---|
| **provoke** (prah VOHK) (Section 1, p. 706) | *v.* to cause; to stir to action | The sinking of the *Maine* provoked the United States to declare war on Spain. |
| **liable** (LĪ ah bahl) (Section 1, p. 710) | *adj.* likely to cause or have an effect | In the 1850s, many Americans warned that the slavery issue was liable to split the Union in two. |
| **accelerate** (ak SEL er ayt) (Section 2, p. 713) | *v.* to increase in speed; to move faster | The rate of immigration began to accelerate in the late 1800s. |
| **collide** (koh LĪD) (Section 2, p. 715) | *v.* to clash; to come together with great force | The North and South collided over the issue of slavery. |
| **sustain** (suh STAYN) (Section 3, p. 718) | *v.* to nourish or strengthen; to keep going | During the American Revolution, support from overseas helped to sustain the American army. |
| **dictate** (DIHK tayt) (Section 3, p. 721) | *v.* to direct or order a specific action | During Reconstruction, Radical Republicans dictated policy in the South. |
| **eliminate** (ee LIHM ih nayt) (Section 4, p. 723) | *v.* to remove; to get rid of | The Thirteenth Amendment eliminated slavery in the United States. |
| **clause** (klawz) (Section 4, p. 724) | *n.* part of a law, treaty, or other written agreement | Different clauses of the Constitution describe the three branches of government. |

## Previewing Key Terms and People

militarism, p. 706
nationalism, p. 706
stalemate, p. 707
trench warfare, p. 707
propaganda, p. 709
mobilize, p. 712
Jeannette Rankin, p. 713
illiterate, p. 713
Herbert Hoover, p. 714
Eugene V. Debs, p. 715
convoy, p. 718

John J. Pershing, p. 718
Vladimir Lenin, p. 719
communism, p. 719
armistice, p. 721

self-determination, p. 723
reparations, p. 724
Henry Cabot Lodge, p. 725
deport, p. 727

John J. Pershing

Jeannette Rankin

## Objectives

1. Discover the factors that led to the outbreak of war in Europe.

2. Find out why World War I was deadlier than any earlier conflict.

3. Learn how the United States moved from neutrality to involvement in the war.

## Prepare to Read

### Reading Skill

**Identify Main Ideas and Support** In this textbook, a main idea is stated in the margin next to each main heading. Also look for supporting ideas within the text paragraphs that begin with subheadings. As you read, use the headings to guide you in identifying main ideas and supporting ideas.

### Vocabulary *Builder*

**High-Use Words**

provoke, p. 706
liable, p. 710

**Key Terms**

militarism, p. 706
nationalism, p. 706
stalemate, p. 707
trench warfare, p. 707
propaganda, p. 709

⭐ **Background Knowledge** In the last chapter, you traced the growing American role in world affairs. Here, you will see how the United States became involved in a huge world war.

**Main Idea**
Imperialism, nationalism, and a complex alliance system helped spark war in Europe.

# Origins of World War I

In 1914, tensions in Europe erupted into the largest war the world had yet seen. There were many different causes for the conflict that later became known as World War I.

**Imperialism** European nations competed for trade and territory in Africa, Asia, and the Pacific. France and England looked on distrustfully as Germany expanded its overseas holdings.

Imperialism fed a rise in militarism, or the glorification of the military. For self-protection and for national glory, nations built up their armed forces. Military leaders gained great influence in European governments.

**Vocabulary *Builder***
provoke (prah VOHK) *v.* to cause; to stir to action

**Nationalism** A surge of nationalism, or pride in one's nation or ethnic group, boosted tensions. In the Balkan region of southeastern Europe, different national groups sought to break free from Austria-Hungary. Russia encouraged Serbians and other Balkan nationalists to do so. Many people compared the Balkans to a "powder keg," or barrel of gunpowder. A single spark could easily provoke a major war.

**Alliance System** As tensions mounted, European nations formed alliance systems. Germany formed an alliance with Austria-Hungary. France, Britain, and Russia pledged to come to one another's aid if attacked. The alliance system meant that any conflict between two powers would quickly involve others.

**War Begins** The spark that set off the war came on June 28, 1914, in the Bosnian city of Sarajevo. A Serbian nationalist assassinated Archduke Franz Ferdinand, heir to the Austro-Hungarian throne. Austria-Hungary accused the government of Serbia of supporting terrorism. On July 29, Austria-Hungary declared war on Serbia.

The alliance system drew one country after another into war. (See the chart below.) In time, more than 20 countries became involved in the fighting. Britain, France, and Russia led the Allies. Opposing them were the Central powers, including Germany, Austria-Hungary, and the Ottoman Empire.

✓**Checkpoint** **How did nationalism contribute to war?**

## The Deadliest War

Both sides hoped for a quick victory. By early September, German forces had advanced to within 30 miles of Paris. At the First Battle of the Marne, however, French and British troops halted the German advance. This area became known as the Western Front. Fighting quickly settled into a long stalemate, or deadlock, in which neither side could score a clear victory. The stalemate dragged on for more than three grueling years.

Along the Western Front, trench warfare fed the stalemate. In trench warfare, soldiers fire on one another from opposing lines of dugout trenches. Between the lines was an unoccupied territory known as "no man's land." After days of shelling, officers would order troops to charge into no man's land and attack the enemy trenches. There, they were mowed down by enemy fire. As death tolls mounted, the two sides fought back and forth over the same patches of land.

**Main Idea**
Advanced technology contributed to a long, deadly stalemate in Europe.

**The Road to World War I**
During the summer of 1914, one European power after another was drawn into the conflict that became known as World War I.
**Critical Thinking: *Apply Information*** *How does the information on the map help explain the sequence of events listed here?*

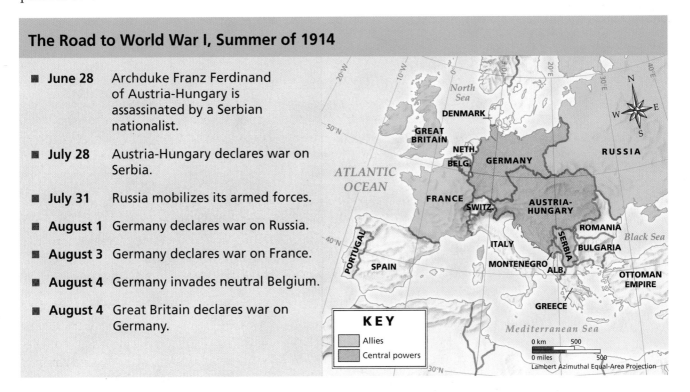

## The Road to World War I, Summer of 1914

- **June 28** Archduke Franz Ferdinand of Austria-Hungary is assassinated by a Serbian nationalist.

- **July 28** Austria-Hungary declares war on Serbia.

- **July 31** Russia mobilizes its armed forces.

- **August 1** Germany declares war on Russia.

- **August 3** Germany declares war on France.

- **August 4** Germany invades neutral Belgium.

- **August 4** Great Britain declares war on Germany.

**KEY**
- Allies
- Central powers

Lambert Azimuthal Equal-Area Projection

Technological advances made the war more lethal. Airplanes, invented a few years before, were used for scouting and support of ground forces. Armored tanks appeared on the battlefield. More than any other weapons, rapid-fire machine guns and heavy artillery raised the death toll.

But the most feared new weapon was poison gas. It was first used by Germany, then by the Allies. Various gases caused choking, blinding, or severe skin blisters. Even some soldiers who survived gas attacks suffered lung problems for years afterward. In 1925, after the war, a group of 140 nations agreed to ban the use of chemical weapons in war.

☑**Checkpoint** How did technology make the war more deadly?

**Main Idea**
At first, the United States tried to stay out of the war in Europe.

## American Neutrality

Horrified by the bloodshed, President Woodrow Wilson sought to keep the United States out of the war. Soon after the fighting began, he issued a proclamation of "strict and impartial neutrality."

**Ethnic Loyalties** Still, many Americans had strong ties to one side or the other. German Americans generally supported the Central powers. Many Irish Americans also favored the Central powers, out of hatred for England's long domination of Ireland.

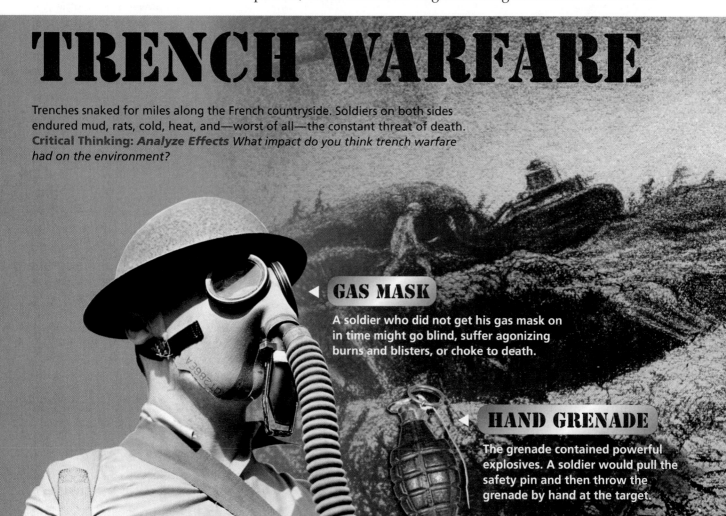

# TRENCH WARFARE

Trenches snaked for miles along the French countryside. Soldiers on both sides endured mud, rats, cold, heat, and—worst of all—the constant threat of death.
**Critical Thinking: *Analyze Effects*** *What impact do you think trench warfare had on the environment?*

### GAS MASK
A soldier who did not get his gas mask on in time might go blind, suffer agonizing burns and blisters, or choke to death.

### HAND GRENADE
The grenade contained powerful explosives. A soldier would pull the safety pin and then throw the grenade by hand at the target.

Other Americans favored the Allies. Britain and the United States shared a common language and history. Americans of Slavic or Italian descent also generally supported the Allied side.

Britain used propaganda to win American support. Propaganda is the spread of information designed to win support for a cause. British propaganda often focused on Germany's brutal treatment of the Belgians at the start of the war. Many of the most horrifying tales were exaggerated or completely made up.

**Supplying the Allies** Legally, American firms were free to sell to both sides. Still, most American trade was with the Allies. In addition, American banks made large loans to the Allies.

Contributing to this imbalance was a British naval blockade of Germany. British ships stopped supplies from reaching German ports. The British intercepted not only weapons, but also food and cotton. Although Wilson objected, he reached an agreement with Britain. For instance, he required Britain to buy more American cotton to make up for lost sales to Germany.

**The *Lusitania*** Germany's navy had too few surface vessels to enforce a blockade of Britain and France. But the Germans had a large supply of U-boats, or submarines. In February 1915, Germany announced it would use its U-boats to blockade Britain.

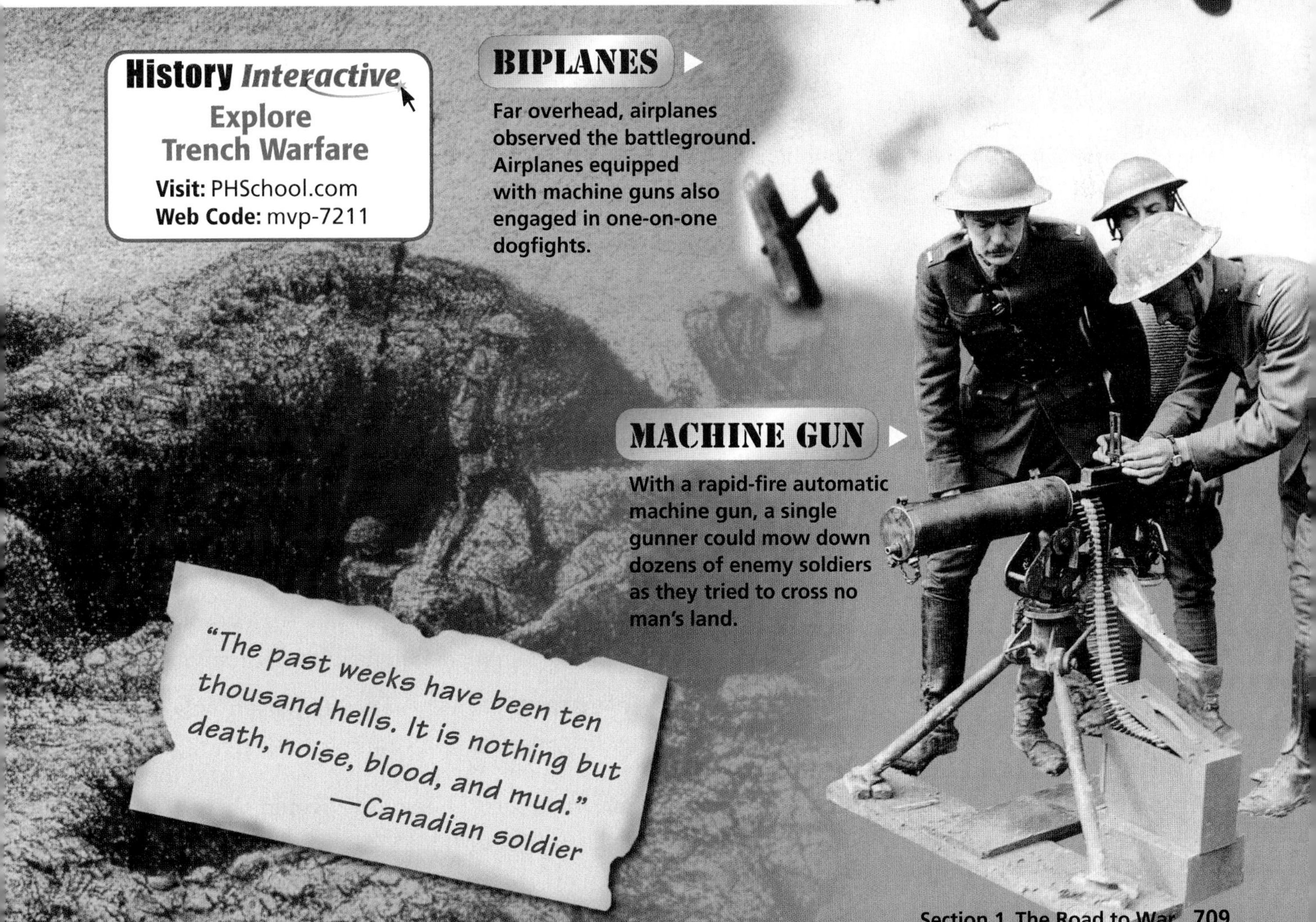

**History** *Interactive*

**Explore Trench Warfare**

**Visit:** PHSchool.com
**Web Code:** mvp-7211

**BIPLANES** ▶

Far overhead, airplanes observed the battleground. Airplanes equipped with machine guns also engaged in one-on-one dogfights.

**MACHINE GUN** ▶

With a rapid-fire automatic machine gun, a single gunner could mow down dozens of enemy soldiers as they tried to cross no man's land.

"The past weeks have been ten thousand hells. It is nothing but death, noise, blood, and mud."
—Canadian soldier

**Explore More Video**
To learn more about the American entry into World War I, view the video.

**Sinking of the Lusitania** On May 7, 1915, German U-boats torpedoed the British liner *Lusitania*. One passenger wrote the note shown here, sealed it in a bottle, and tossed it into the sea. **Critical Thinking: Analyze Cause and Effect** What impact did the sinking of the *Lusitania* have?

**Vocabulary Builder**
**liable** (LĪ ah bahl) *adj.* likely to cause or have an effect

**Main Idea**
German submarine attacks were a major factor that led the United States to enter the war on the Allied side.

On May 7, 1915, a U-boat sank a British passenger liner, the *Lusitania,* off the coast of Ireland. Nearly 1,200 people died, 128 of them Americans. Wilson made angry protests to Germany. The Germans responded that the ship was carrying a load of ammunition to England. This argument mattered little to an outraged American public. Fearing that further attacks were <u>liable</u> to provoke the United States to declare war, Germany said its U-boats would no longer target passenger liners and neutral merchant ships.

☑**Checkpoint**   How did the war in Europe divide Americans?

## Entering the War

Wilson was reelected in November 1916 on the slogan "He kept us out of war." He then called on the warring powers to accept "peace without victory." Such a peace, he said, should be based on the principles of democracy, freedom of the seas, and the avoidance of "entangling alliances." But Wilson's attempt to make peace failed.

Germany resumed unrestricted submarine warfare in February 1917. Germany hoped that cutting off American supplies to the British would break the stalemate on the Western Front. In response, Wilson cut off diplomatic relations with Germany.

**Zimmermann Telegram** On February 24, Wilson was shown a telegram that the British had intercepted. Germany's foreign minister, Arthur Zimmermann, proposed that Mexico join the war on Germany's side. In return, Germany would help Mexico "reconquer" New Mexico, Texas, and Arizona.

The Zimmermann Telegram was released to the press on March 1. American anger exploded. Anger soon turned to thoughts of war after U-boats sank three American merchant ships.

**Russian Revolution** A revolution in Russia removed the final obstacle to America's entry. Russia was one of the three main Allies. Its ruler, Tsar Nicholas II, was an absolute monarch who had long resisted calls for democratic reforms. In March 1917, military defeats and food shortages led to an uprising. The tsar was overthrown. A new government vowed to keep Russia in the war.

The fall of the tsar made it easier for the United States to enter the war. By joining with the Allied powers, the United States would not be siding with a tyrant. Instead, Wilson reasoned, it would be joining with other democracies to fight tyranny.

**Declaring War** On April 2, Wilson asked Congress to declare war against the Central powers. His goal, he declared, was to fight

> **❝** . . . for the rights of nations great and small and the privilege of men everywhere to choose their way of life and of obedience. The world must be made safe for democracy. **❞**
>
> —Woodrow Wilson, war message, April 2, 1917

President Wilson asks Congress to declare war on Germany.

Congress overwhelmingly gave its approval. After nearly three years on the sidelines, the United States was at war.

☑**Checkpoint** How did submarine warfare help lead the United States into World War I?

⭐ **Looking Back and Ahead** Following its traditional policy of isolationism, the United States tried to stay out of World War I. Now that it had joined the war, American life would be greatly changed.

---

## Section 1 | Check Your Progress

**Progress Monitoring** ⏻nline
**For:** Self-test with instant help
**Visit:** PHSchool.com
**Web Code:** mva-7211

### Comprehension and Critical Thinking

**1. (a) List** Identify three factors that led to the outbreak of World War I.
**(b) Identify Alternatives** What alternatives did European nations face when their Allies entered the war?

**2. (a) Recall** How did Wilson try to maintain neutrality?
**(b) Draw Conclusions** Do you think the United States could have avoided entering the war? Why or why not?

### ↻ Reading Skill

**3. Identify Main Ideas and Support** Reread the text under the heading "American Neutrality." Identify the main idea of this portion of text. Then, list supporting ideas.

### Vocabulary *Builder*

Complete each of the following sentences so that the second part further explains the first part and clearly shows your understanding of the key term.

**4.** Serbs and other ethnic groups favored nationalism, or _____.
**5.** The British tried to gain support by using propaganda, or _____.
**6.** Technology contributed to a long stalemate, or _____.
**7.** War fever was partly the result of militarism, or _____.

### Writing

**8.** Based on what you have read in this section, write a thesis statement for an essay contrasting trench warfare with present-day warfare.

# Supporting the War Effort

## Objectives

1. Find out how the United States quickly prepared for entry into World War I.

2. Learn what measures the government took to control the wartime economy.

3. Discover how the need to build support for the war sometimes clashed with civil liberties.

## Prepare to Read

### Reading Skill

**Connect Main Ideas** All the ideas in a section relate to one another. Look for several types of connections. For example, these connections may be cause and effect, parts of a category, or comparison-contrast. In addition, some ideas simply provide more information about a larger idea.

### Vocabulary *Builder*

**High-Use Words**

accelerate, p. 713

collide, p. 715

**Key Terms and People**

mobilize, p. 712

Jeannette Rankin, p. 713

illiterate, p. 713

Herbert Hoover, p. 714

Eugene V. Debs, p. 715

☆ **Background Knowledge** As you have learned, President Wilson had been unable to maintain American neutrality. Now that the nation had declared war on Germany, it faced enormous challenges.

## Building the Military

### Main Idea
After entering World War I, the United States quickly had to increase its military force.

The United States entered the war with a large navy. However, it had only the world's sixteenth largest army, numbering just 125,000 men. In order to contribute to an Allied victory, the nation would have to mobilize quickly. To **mobilize** is to prepare for war.

**Selective Service** Immediately after the United States declared war, eager young men began volunteering for military service. Still, volunteers alone would not be enough to expand the army quickly. Wilson called upon Congress to establish a draft.

After a month of debate, Congress passed the Selective Service Act. The law required all young men between the ages of 21 and 30 to register for the military draft. By war's end, almost four million Americans had served in uniform.

**Women in the Military** Women were not subject to the draft. Still, American women had a long history of volunteerism, especially during the Progressive Era. More than 30,000 women volunteered for service. Two thirds of these women served in the U.S. Army and U.S. Navy Nurse Corps. The rest performed clerical work, such as filing papers or sending and receiving telegraph messages, as members of the U.S. Navy and U.S. Marine Corps. They became the first women in American history to hold official military rank.

Women of the U.S. Navy drilling

Still, leading American women were divided over the war. Some opposed war under all circumstances. Jane Addams cofounded the Women's Peace Party in 1915 and continued to speak out for peace even after the United States entered the war. Representative Jeannette Rankin of Montana, the first woman elected to Congress, voted against Wilson's war resolution. "As a woman I can't go to war," Rankin said, "and I refuse to send anyone else."

Others, such as suffragist Carrie Chapman Catt, urged women to support the war effort. Catt hoped that women's wartime service would <u>accelerate</u> their drive to win the vote. In fact, this proved to be the case. As you have read, Congress passed the Nineteenth Amendment in 1919, shortly after the end of World War I.

**Vocabulary Builder**
<u>accelerate</u> (ak SEL er ayt) v. to increase in speed; to move faster

**A Diverse Force** The military reflected the increasingly diverse makeup of the nation. About one in every five recruits had been born in foreign lands such as the Philippines, Mexico, or Italy. Many others were children of immigrants.

Native Americans were not American citizens at the time. Therefore, they were not subject to the draft. Still, a large number of Native Americans volunteered for service.

**African Americans Serve** Some 380,000 African Americans also served during the war. Their opportunities were restricted by official segregation and widespread racism. Still, civil rights leader W.E.B. Du Bois encouraged African Americans to support the war effort. "Let us, while the war lasts, forget our special grievances and close ranks . . . with our fellow citizens," Du Bois urged.

Still, African Americans faced discrimination in the military. They were placed in all-black units, of which only 10 percent were sent to combat. Most African American troops were confined to such noncombat duties as unloading ships, working in kitchens, or constructing barracks.

Some African American units fought under French command. Several members of a unit known as the Harlem Hell Fighters received France's highest medal for bravery, the *Croix de Guerre,* or cross of war.

**The Military as Educator** One in four draftees and recruits were illiterate, or unable to read and write. They could not read newspapers or even write letters home to their families. In addition, some young men from poor rural areas were not used to eating daily meals, taking regular baths, or using indoor plumbing.

For these young men, the military served as a great educator. The army taught millions not only how to fight, but how to read. Recruits learned about nutrition, personal hygiene, and patriotism.

✔**Checkpoint** How did the United States build its military force?

**An African American Soldier**

As in earlier wars, African American soldiers served in separate units. This bugler served in France with the 15th New York Infantry. **Critical Thinking: *Evaluate Information*** *What image of this soldier does this painting create?*

# Managing the War Effort

Entry into the war forced a reshaping of the nation's economy. Both agriculture and industry mobilized for war.

**Managing Food Supplies** President Wilson chose Herbert Hoover to head a new Food Administration. Early in the war, Hoover had directed relief efforts in Belgium. His new job was to assure adequate food supplies for both civilians and troops.

Hoover urged Americans to conserve valuable food resources. To save on food, Americans observed "wheatless Mondays" and "meatless Tuesdays." Many grew their own vegetables in "victory gardens." The President's wife had one on the White House lawn.

**Producing for War** The war greatly increased demands on American industries. For example, the government placed orders for two million rifles and 130 million pairs of socks. To oversee the shift to war production, Wilson set up a new agency, the War Industries Board (WIB).

At first, the WIB had limited power. During an unusually cold winter in 1917 to 1918, there were shortages of fuel and crippling congestion at ports and on railroads. Wilson strengthened the war board and gave it a new head, Bernard Baruch. The board told industries what to produce, how much to charge, and how to use scarce resources. For example, to make sure there was enough tin for military use, the WIB forbade toy makers to use tin for toys.

**Finding Workers** War brought a labor shortage, as millions of men joined the military. Also, there was a steep drop in immigration, to a tenth of its prewar rate. To meet war demands, American industry needed workers.

To fill the jobs, business owners turned to two main sources. Women took on roles previously denied them, for example, as factory workers or elevator operators. And more than half a million African Americans left the rural South to work in factories of the Midwest and Northeast. They were drawn by the opportunity to earn money and to escape segregation.

✓**Checkpoint** What was the role of the War Industries Board?

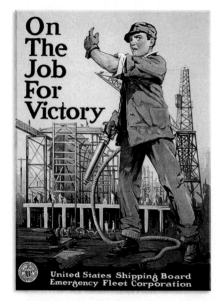

Propaganda posters such as this one encouraged industrial workers to increase production for the war effort.

# Shaping Public Opinion

The government worked to whip up support for the war. At the same time, it took measures to stifle antiwar sentiments.

**Calling on Patriotism** An effective propaganda tool was the Committee on Public Information, appointed by the President. The committee recruited 75,000 "Four-Minute Men" to deliver brief patriotic speeches at places like movie theaters and ball parks. It also enlisted artists to produce pro-war cartoons and posters. One famous poster had Uncle Sam pointing a finger and sternly saying, "Uncle Sam wants YOU!"

The government issued Liberty Bonds to help finance the war. Movie stars toured the nation, urging Americans to buy bonds.

**Suppressing Dissent** The government took stern measures to suppress criticism of the war. Under the Espionage Act of 1917 and the Sedition Act of 1918, authorities closed newspapers and jailed individuals for expressing antiwar views.

Among those jailed was labor leader Eugene V. Debs, a five-time presidential candidate of the Socialist Party. Debs was jailed in 1918 for giving a speech in which he urged workers not to support the war effort. "It is extremely dangerous to exercise the constitutional right of free speech in a country fighting to make democracy safe in the world," Debs commented.

At times, war fever collided with personal freedoms. Private organizations sprang up that encouraged people to spy on their neighbors. The largest of these, the 200,000-strong American Protective League, opened people's mail, tapped phones, and pried into medical records.

**Anti-German Hysteria** German Americans suffered, too. In towns across the country, citizens shunned, harassed, and even assaulted German Americans who might once have been their friends. Some German Americans were tarred and feathered. Many schools stopped teaching the German language.

Anti-German feeling even affected the language. People referred to sauerkraut as "liberty cabbage." German measles became "liberty measles."

**✓ Checkpoint** How did the government build public support for the war effort?

⭐ **Looking Back and Ahead** The war effort deeply affected life at home. In the next section, you will see how America's entry into the war helped to turn the tide in favor of the Allies.

**Vocabulary Builder**
collide (koh LĪD) v. to clash; to come together with great force

**Connect Main Ideas**
Connect the main ideas following the subheading "Calling on Patriotism" to those following the subheading "Suppressing Dissent."

---

## Section 2 | Check Your Progress

**Progress Monitoring** Online
**For:** Self-test with instant help
**Visit:** PHSchool.com
**Web Code:** mva-7212

**Comprehension and Critical Thinking**

1. **(a) Recall** What steps did the United States take to mobilize for the war?
**(b) Identify Alternatives** Some Americans opposed the Selective Service Act. Do you think the government had other alternatives? Explain.

2. **(a) Recall** How did the government suppress dissent during World War I?

**(b) Support a Point of View** Do you think the government is justified in suppressing civil liberties during wartime? Give reasons for your opinion.

🎯 **Reading Skill**

3. **Connect Main Ideas** How are the main ideas of the text under the heading "Managing the War Effort" connected to the main ideas of the text under the heading "Shaping Public Opinion"?

**Vocabulary Builder**

4. Write two definitions of the key term mobilize—one a formal definition for a teacher, the other an informal definition for a younger child.

**Writing**

5. List supporting information to include in a short essay discussing how the war effort at times conflicted with personal freedom.

# On the Home Front

During World War I, all Americans were encouraged to do their part for the war effort. However, some Americans faced the added burden of hatred and mistrust.

## Food Will Win the War!

Americans planted "victory gardens" to grow vegetables so that there would be an adequate supply of food. Even children were expected to do their part. ▼

JOIN THE
UNITED-
STATES
SCHOOL
GARDEN
ARMY

ENLIST NOW

Write to The United States School Garden Army.
Bureau of Education, Department of Interior. Washington, D.C.

## ◄ Mistrust of German Americans

German Americans faced wartime restrictions and even violence. Here, police in New York fingerprint a German immigrant woman. The passage below describes an attack on a German community in Iowa.

"People acted like savages. They came in mobs from towns all around. . . . One mob got the minister and made him march through town carrying a flag. Then, they made him stand on a coffin which was a rough box and kiss the flag. . . . Then, he was ordered out of town."

### Buy a Victory Bond! ▶

To raise money for the war effort, the government issued Victory Bonds and Savings Stamps. Here, Charlie Chaplin—the most popular movie comedian of his day—addresses a huge crowd at a War Bond rally.

AMERICAN RED CROSS

OUR BOYS NEED SOX KNIT YOUR BIT

KEEP HIM FREE

BUY WAR SAVINGS STAMPS
ISSUED BY THE UNITED STATES TREASURY DEPT.

W.S.S.
WAR SAVINGS STAMPS
ISSUED BY THE UNITED STATES GOVERNMENT

### ◀ Support the Troops!

Volunteer organizations such as the Red Cross worked to keep soldiers healthy and comfortable. You did not have to be somebody's mother to knit a pair of warm socks!

*Analyze* **LIFE AT THE TIME**

Choose one of the posters shown on these pages. Restate the message of the poster in your own words and explain how the picture on that poster supports the message.

# 3 | Americans at War

## Objectives

1. Understand the setbacks that the Allies faced in 1917 and 1918.

2. Discover how American forces contributed to the Allied victory.

3. Explain the agreement that ended the fighting.

## Prepare to Read

 **Reading Skill**

**Connect Main Ideas to Earlier Ideas** Each chapter in this textbook focuses on a different time period or aspect of American history. As you read the chapters, think about how the events of one time period connect to events of other periods. Finding the connections will increase your understanding of history.

**Vocabulary** *Builder*

**High-Use Words**

sustain, p. 718

dictate, p. 721

**Key Terms and People**

convoy, p. 718

John J. Pershing, p. 718

Vladimir Lenin, p. 719

communism, p. 719

armistice, p. 721

⭐ **Background Knowledge** As you have read, Congress declared war in April 1917. However, more than a year passed before American troops made a significant contribution to the war.

## Main Idea
After the United States declared war, it took time before American troops were ready for combat.

## Joining the Fight

While the United States prepared its army, the Allies in Europe were growing increasingly desperate. From February through April 1917, German submarines sank 844 Allied vessels. Britain's top naval official predicted that Germany would win the war unless the flow of supplies from America increased.

**Protecting Allied Shipping** In order to maintain the flow of products needed to sustain the war effort, Allied naval leaders developed a convoy system. A convoy is a large group of merchant vessels sailing together. Light, fast Allied destroyers accompanied the convoys. The first convoys reached Britain in May. Soon, Allied ship losses fell to a fraction of what they had been.

## Vocabulary *Builder*
sustain (suh STAYN) *v.* to nourish or strengthen; to keep going

**American Expeditionary Force** Meanwhile, American forces were preparing to go overseas. The U.S. Army chose John J. Pershing to command the American Expeditionary Force, as American troops in Europe were known. A dashing and dedicated general, Pershing had led the pursuit of Pancho Villa in Mexico.

Pershing insisted that American soldiers fight in separate units under American command. Only rarely were they integrated with British or French units. This was in keeping with Wilson's orders. To influence the postwar settlement, Wilson believed, the United States had to make a victorious showing, on its own, in battle.

**Connect Main Ideas to Earlier Events/Ideas**

Recall that Pershing spoke admiringly of American soldiers from many backgrounds fighting together in the Spanish-American War. Connect that main idea to Pershing's actions in World War I.

718 Chapter 21 World War I

The first American troops reached Europe in June 1917. The unit was not ready for combat. Its purpose was to prop up sagging French morale. This First Division symbolized America's commitment to the fight and its intention to send more troops. As the newly arrived Americans paraded through Paris, crowds cheered and threw flowers.

**✓Checkpoint** How did the convoy system help the Allies?

## Setbacks and Advances

During 1917, as the Allies waited for more American troops to arrive, their situation grew increasingly desperate. On the Western Front, a three-month British offensive bogged down in the mud in Belgium. To the south, Austria-Hungary and Germany scored a major victory over the Italians at Caporetto.

**Russia Makes Peace** In Russia, the new government that had replaced the tsar struggled to keep up the war effort. But the Russian army was exhausted. Two million soldiers deserted the front lines. By July, German troops were driving deep into Russia.

Under the leadership of Vladimir Lenin, a radical faction known as the Bolsheviks seized the government on November 7, 1917. Lenin intended to set Russia on the road to communism. Communism is an economic and political system based on the idea that social classes and the right to private property should be eliminated. Lenin embraced the ideas of the German thinker Karl Marx, who had predicted that workers around the world would unite to overthrow the ruling class.

Lenin's first order of business was to pull Russia out of the war. In March 1918, Russia and Germany signed a peace agreement, called the Treaty of Brest-Litovsk. It transferred some 30 percent of Russia's territory to Germany.

The peace in the east was a huge setback to the Allies. It allowed the German army to shift 40 divisions to the Western Front. The stage was now set for a crucial showdown. Could Germany knock out the Allies before the bulk of American forces reached Europe?

**Germany Attacks** On March 21, 1918, the German army unleashed a series of daring attacks. The goal of this "peace offensive," as Germany called it, was to defeat the Allies quickly and bring peace on German terms.

**Main Idea**
The arrival of American troops eventually helped turn the war in favor of the Allies.

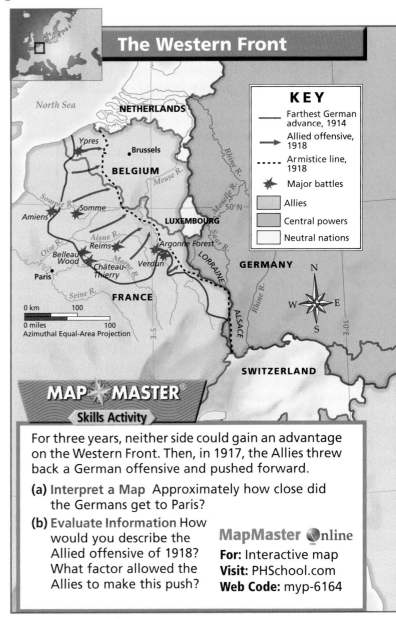

**The Western Front**

**KEY**
— Farthest German advance, 1914
→ Allied offensive, 1918
···· Armistice line, 1918
★ Major battles
▨ Allies
▨ Central powers
▢ Neutral nations

**MAP✦MASTER®**

**Skills Activity**

For three years, neither side could gain an advantage on the Western Front. Then, in 1917, the Allies threw back a German offensive and pushed forward.

**(a) Interpret a Map** Approximately how close did the Germans get to Paris?

**(b) Evaluate Information** How would you describe the Allied offensive of 1918? What factor allowed the Allies to make this push?

**MapMaster ◉nline**
**For:** Interactive map
**Visit:** PHSchool.com
**Web Code:** myp-6164

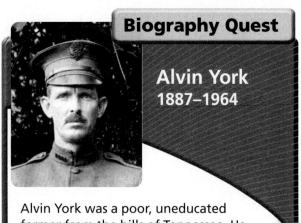

## Alvin York
### 1887–1964

Alvin York was a poor, uneducated farmer from the hills of Tennessee. He was also a man of deep religious beliefs. "I didn't want to go and fight and kill," he later wrote. "But I had to answer the call of my country."

Sergeant York became the most decorated American soldier of World War I. During one battle, he captured 132 Germans and 35 machine guns almost single-handedly.

**Biography Quest** nline

**After the war, how did York use his fame to help children?**

**For:** The answer to the question about York

**Visit:** PHSchool.com

**Web Code:** mvd-7213

Pershing traveled to the French army's head-quarters to pledge that American troops would now fight under French command. "Infantry, artillery, aviation, all that we have are yours," he declared. "Use them as you wish." The vow, made public, raised French spirits. But two months passed before the Americans could make a significant contribution to the Allied cause.

The advancing Germans broke through Allied lines in Belgium and France. By the beginning of June, Germany had reached the town of Château-Thierry (shah TOE tyeh REE), on the Marne River, less than 50 miles from Paris. As many as a million Parisians fled in panic before the approaching enemy. By this time, however, American troops had arrived to reinforce the Allies.

**Turning the Tide** American and French troops counterattacked near Château-Thierry. The French commander assigned American units to evict German troops from a narrow, heavily forested area called Belleau (BEH loh) Wood. The Germans had fortified the forest with barbed wire, artillery, and machine guns.

During three weeks of intense, often hand-to-hand combat, U.S. Marines suffered heavy casualties. But, in their first major battle of the war, they succeeded in driving the Germans out.

Germany had lost some 800,000 men since the start of 1918. Yet, the offensive continued. In mid-July, the Germans attempted a new drive toward Paris. The drive gained a bit of ground and then stalled. With more than a quarter million Americans participating, the Allies counterattacked. The Germans had to pull back. Costs to both sides were high in this Second Battle of the Marne.

**Battle of the Argonne Forest** Weakened by influenza and deprived of supplies by the Allied blockade that had tightened since America's entry into the war, Germany's army was losing the will to fight. Now, it was the Allies' turn to take the offensive.

In September 1918, Allied forces pushed forward along a line that stretched from the North Sea to Verdun. The Americans were toward the right. More than one million American soldiers advanced on heavily fortified German positions between the Meuse River and the Argonne Forest in northeastern France.

At first, the Americans advanced slowly. But as November began, German defenses finally crumbled under the unrelenting assault. Farther north, French and British forces advanced as well.

✓**Checkpoint** **What role did American troops play at Belleau Wood?**

## The Armistice

By early autumn, Germany's military and political leaders realized that their cause was lost. Their army had no reserves, whereas the arrival of Americans had assured the Allies of a fresh supply of soldiers. The German leaders decided to seek an armistice. An **armistice** is a halt in fighting that allows peace talks to begin.

Germany knew that France and Britain wanted to impose a harsh settlement. But President Wilson had recently proposed a "Fourteen Points" peace plan, founded on principles for international cooperation. (See Section 4.) On October 6, the head of the German government sent Wilson a note requesting an armistice based on the Fourteen Points. But Wilson ultimately had little say.

**A Harsh Armistice** France and Britain <u>dictated</u> the terms of the armistice. They required Germany to pull back its troops on the Western Front. Germany also had to cancel the Treaty of Brest-Litovsk and hand over its entire fleet of U-boats.

Meanwhile, the other Central powers—Bulgaria, Austria-Hungary, and the Ottoman Empire—had asked for an armistice, too. None of them was in any position to resist Allied demands.

Wilson's major impact during this period was his insistence that the Kaiser, the absolute monarch of Germany, must step down. On November 9, Kaiser Wilhelm II fled to Holland. There, he soon gave up the throne. Germany became a republic.

**Main Idea**
After more than four years of fighting, the war finally ended in November 1918.

**Vocabulary** *Builder*
**dictate** (DIHK tayt) *v.* to direct or order a specific action

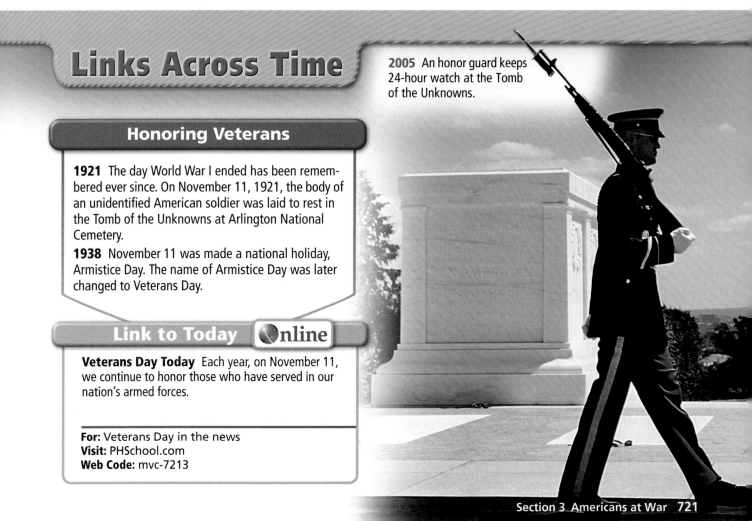

# Links Across Time

2005 An honor guard keeps 24-hour watch at the Tomb of the Unknowns.

### Honoring Veterans

**1921** The day World War I ended has been remembered ever since. On November 11, 1921, the body of an unidentified American soldier was laid to rest in the Tomb of the Unknowns at Arlington National Cemetery.

**1938** November 11 was made a national holiday, Armistice Day. The name of Armistice Day was later changed to Veterans Day.

### Link to Today  ⊙nline

**Veterans Day Today** Each year, on November 11, we continue to honor those who have served in our nation's armed forces.

**For:** Veterans Day in the news
**Visit:** PHSchool.com
**Web Code:** mvc-7213

A wounded soldier returns home

**War's Deadly Toll** The armistice took effect at 11 A.M. on November 11—the eleventh day of the eleventh month of 1918. The war had finally ended. At the front, soldiers could hardly believe it was true. One American soldier later recalled:

> **❝**After the long months of intense strain, of keying themselves up to the daily mortal danger, of thinking always in terms of war and the enemy, the abrupt release from it all was physical and psychological agony. Some suffered a total nervous collapse.**❞**
>
> —Thomas Gowenlock, *Soldiers of Darkness*

World War I was the most destructive war history had yet seen. It cost the lives of approximately 10 million military personnel—more than had died in all the wars fought in Europe during the previous 100 years combined.

In Europe, a generation of young men had lost their lives. France suffered approximately 1.3 million military deaths; Britain, 900,000; Germany, 1.6 million; and Russia, 1.7 million. American combat deaths numbered 50,000 in less than a year of fighting. Millions of other soldiers were blinded, lost limbs, suffered permanent lung damage from poison gas, or experienced psychological problems.

No one knows how many civilians died of disease, starvation, or other war-related causes. Some historians believe that as many civilians died as did soldiers. Much of northern France lay in ruins. Millions of children were left orphaned or homeless.

**✓Checkpoint** How did the war end?

⭐ **Looking Back and Ahead** The war had ended in an overwhelming Allied victory. In Section 4, you will read about the next great challenge: creating the peace.

---

Section 3 | **Check Your Progress**

**Progress Monitoring** ⏺nline
**For:** Self-test with instant help
**Visit:** PHSchool.com
**Web Code:** mva-7213

**Comprehension and Critical Thinking**

1. **(a) Identify** Identify two ways the Americans contributed to the Allied victory.
   **(b) Make Predictions** How do you think the war might have ended if the United States had not entered? Explain.

2. **(a) Recall** What were the terms of the armistice that ended the war?

**(b) Draw Conclusions** Why do you think Germany agreed to these terms?

🔁 **Reading Skill**

3. **Connect Main Ideas to Earlier Events** Connect America's role in World War I with its role in the Spanish-American War. What was the United States fighting for in each case?

**Vocabulary** *Builder*

4. Write a sentence using each of the key terms from this section: convoy, communism, armistice. Include a definition of the key term in each sentence.

**Writing**

5. Create an outline for an essay tracing the progress of Allied forces during World War I. List the information in the order you would present it in the essay.

# Shaping the Peace

## Objectives

1. Examine Woodrow Wilson's plan for a lasting and just peace.

2. Understand how the Treaty of Versailles punished Germany.

3. Explain why many Americans opposed membership in the League of Nations.

## Prepare to Read

### Reading Skill

**Connect Main Ideas to Current Events** Events and ideas from history often connect to events and issues of importance today. Finding these connections will bring history to life for you, as well as increase your understanding of current events. Look for these connections as you read this section.

### Vocabulary *Builder*

**High-Use Words**

eliminate, p. 723

clause, p. 724

**Key Terms and People**

self-determination, p. 723

reparations, p. 724

Henry Cabot Lodge, p. 725

deport, p. 727

⭐ **Background Knowledge** With the end of the war, the struggle began to determine the shape of peace. Wilson's ideas for the postwar world found opponents both abroad and at home.

## The Fourteen Points

Even before the war ended, President Wilson had presented his peace plan, known as the Fourteen Points, to Congress. He framed his plan in idealistic terms, saying he hoped to prevent future wars.

The first five points dealt with the factors that had led to the war. Wilson wanted to <u>eliminate</u> secret international agreements. He called for freedom of the seas, free trade among nations, and a sharp reduction in the world's military forces. He also favored settlement of colonial claims, balancing the interests of native populations and colonizing powers.

Points 6 through 13 dealt with specific territorial issues arising from the war. One of these issues involved self-rule for national minority groups in Austria-Hungary and the Ottoman Empire. Later, Wilson turned this point into a call for self-determination. Self-determination is the right of a group to decide its own form of government. Wilson knew that one of the causes of World War I was the struggle of Bosnians, Serbs, and other peoples to rule themselves.

For Wilson, Point 14 was the most important. It called for setting up an international organization, or association of nations, to guarantee world peace. Underlying his plan, Wilson said, was "the principle of justice to all peoples and nationalities . . . whether they be strong or weak."

**Main Idea**

Woodrow Wilson proposed a peace plan that he hoped would prevent future wars.

**Vocabulary *Builder***

eliminate (ee LIHM ih nayt) *v.* to remove; to get rid of

✅**Checkpoint** **What was the goal of the Fourteen Points?**

# Peace Conference in Paris

The victorious powers organized a peace conference in Paris. Although American Presidents had seldom gone abroad, Wilson decided that he himself would lead the American delegation.

The Fourteen Points had thrilled Europe's war-weary population. Two million people turned out to cheer Wilson when he arrived in Paris in January 1919. One newspaper likened him to Moses.

**The Big Four** At the conference, major decisions were made by the "Big Four." They were Wilson and the prime ministers of the three top European Allies: Georges Clemenceau of France, David Lloyd George of Britain, and Vittorio Orlando of Italy.

The other Allies did not share Wilson's idealistic goal of "peace without victory." They were determined to punish Germany and to ensure that Germany would not threaten its neighbors again. Also, during the war, several Allies had signed secret treaties for dividing up the territories and colonies of the Central powers.

**The Treaty of Versailles** After difficult negotiations, the Allies came to an agreement. The Treaty of Versailles (ver sī) dealt severely with Germany. Various clauses took away territory on Germany's borders and stripped Germany of colonies. The treaty forced Germany to accept full responsibility for the war and to pay the Allies huge reparations, or payments to cover war damages. It also placed limits on the size and nature of Germany's military.

**Vocabulary** *Builder*
clause (klawz) *n.* part of a law, treaty, or other written agreement

Lloyd George, Clemenceau, and Wilson (left to right) at the peace talks

Wilson disagreed with these harsh demands. However, he had agreed in order to win his cherished peacekeeping organization. The Treaty of Versailles also called for the creation of an international organization to be called the League of Nations. It would provide a place for countries to meet, settle disputes peacefully, and punish any nation that broke the peace.

On June 28, 1919, German delegates reluctantly signed the treaty. However, German anger at the Treaty of Versailles would later set the stage for another world war.

**Other Treaties** Negotiators arranged separate treaties with the other Central powers. The treaties applied the principle of self-determination to the peoples of Eastern Europe.

Some changes had already taken place. Austria-Hungary had collapsed. From its ruins arose the separate states of Austria, Hungary, and Czechoslovakia. In addition, the Serbs of Serbia had joined with other Balkan peoples to form Yugoslavia. Poland had declared independence. The peace treaties recognized all these changes, making adjustments to the new borders.

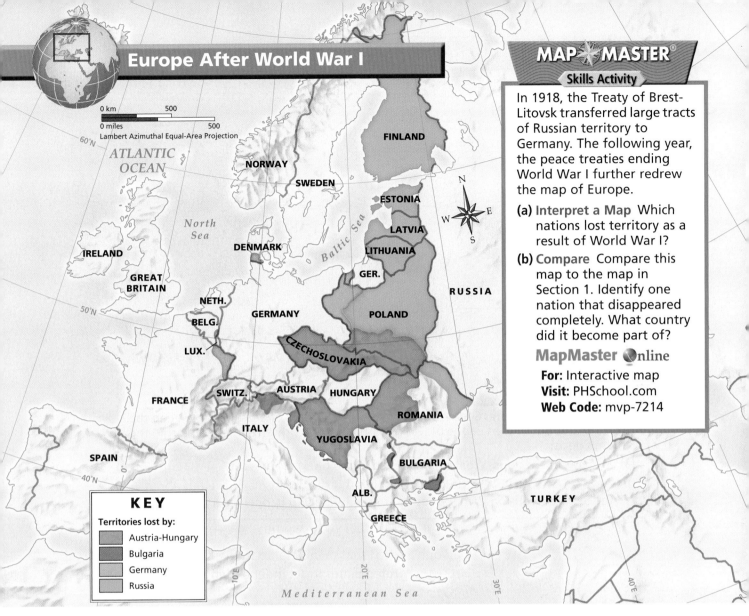

## Europe After World War I

0 km 500
0 miles 500
Lambert Azimuthal Equal-Area Projection

ATLANTIC OCEAN

60°N

50°N

40°N

North Sea

Baltic Sea

Mediterranean Sea

FINLAND

NORWAY

SWEDEN

ESTONIA

LATVIA

LITHUANIA

DENMARK

IRELAND

GREAT BRITAIN

NETH.

GER.

GERMANY

POLAND

RUSSIA

BELG.

LUX.

CZECHOSLOVAKIA

SWITZ.

AUSTRIA

HUNGARY

FRANCE

ITALY

YUGOSLAVIA

ROMANIA

BULGARIA

SPAIN

ALB.

GREECE

TURKEY

**KEY**

Territories lost by:

Austria-Hungary

Bulgaria

Germany

Russia

**MAP MASTER®**
Skills Activity

In 1918, the Treaty of Brest-Litovsk transferred large tracts of Russian territory to Germany. The following year, the peace treaties ending World War I further redrew the map of Europe.

**(a) Interpret a Map** Which nations lost territory as a result of World War I?

**(b) Compare** Compare this map to the map in Section 1. Identify one nation that disappeared completely. What country did it become part of?

**MapMaster ⬤nline**

**For:** Interactive map
**Visit:** PHSchool.com
**Web Code:** mvp-7214

However, the peacemakers at Paris did not apply the principle of self-determination to non-Europeans. Britain and France divided Germany's African colonies, as well as the Middle Eastern lands of the Ottoman Empire. The Ottoman Empire itself was disbanded, replaced by the new republic of Turkey. Many people living in Europe's African and Asian colonies felt betrayed by the peace settlements.

**✔Checkpoint** How did the Treaty of Versailles punish Germany?

## Battle Over the League

Returning to the United States, Wilson urged the Senate to ratify the Treaty of Versailles. Wilson forcefully backed the treaty's most controversial element, the League of Nations. The United States, he declared, must accept its "destiny" to lead the world on a new path.

**Lodge Opposes** Many Senators opposed the treaty. Leading the opposition was Henry Cabot Lodge, a powerful Republican from Massachusetts. Lodge's chief objection was to the proposal that the United States join the League of Nations.

**Main Idea**
Wilson's plan for a League of Nations met sharp opposition in the Senate.

U.S. participation is key to building the League of Nations.

The keystone is not in place.

In 1919, the United States Senate voted to reject the Treaty of Versailles and keep the United States out of the League of Nations. This cartoon presents one reaction to the Senate's decision.

(a) **Interpret Cartoons** What does the gap in the bridge represent?

(b) **Detect Points of View** How do you think this cartoonist may have felt about the Senate's decision? What does he convey is likely to happen as a result?

Lodge argued that membership in the League would restrict the right of the United States to act independently in its own interest:

> **"**The United States is the world's best hope, but if you [chain] her in the interests and quarrels of other nations, if you tangle her in the intrigues of Europe, you will destroy her power for good and endanger her very existence.**"**
>
> —Henry Cabot Lodge, speech, August 1919

Lodge asked for major changes that would reduce the United States ties to the League. But Wilson refused to compromise.

**Wilson's Last Battle** In early September, Wilson set out on a nationwide tour to stir public support for his position. Traveling 8,000 miles by train in three weeks, he gave 40 speeches.

On October 2, Wilson suffered a massive stroke that paralyzed his left side. His wife and his physician kept secret the severity of his illness. From his White House sickbed, Wilson continued to reject all compromise on the treaty.

In November 1919, the Senate voted to reject the treaty. The absence of the United States crippled the League's ability to stem the crises that shook the world in the 1930s.

**Connect Main Ideas to Current Events**

Connect the role of the United States in the League of Nations with the role of the United States in world affairs today.

☑**Checkpoint** **Why did Lodge oppose the League of Nations?**

# Postwar Troubles

The United States did not easily adjust to the return of peace. The postwar years brought a variety of troubles.

**Influenza Epidemic** Toward the end of the war, troop movements contributed to a worldwide influenza epidemic. In the United States alone, the disease took more than 500,000 lives in 1918 and 1919. Worldwide, the epidemic killed more people than had died in four years of war.

**Labor Unrest** During the war, unions and businesses had cooperated to meet production goals. But peacetime brought high unemployment, as soldiers came home to seek jobs. With prices rising, unions' demands for higher wages met stiff resistance from management. In 1919, four million laborers—20 percent of the American industrial work force—went on strike.

**Red Scare** Many Americans feared that Communists, or "Reds," were behind the labor unrest. After all, in Russia, Lenin had called for a worldwide workers' revolution. From 1919 into 1920 a "Red Scare," or fear of Communist revolution, gripped the nation.

Attorney General A. Mitchell Palmer ordered immigrants suspected of radical views to be rounded up and deported, or returned to their home countries. These Palmer Raids reached their height on January 2, 1920, when authorities arrested more than 4,000 people in 33 cities. But public opinion soon turned against Palmer. In time, the panic cooled.

This policeman is wearing a mask to avoid catching influenza.

✓**Checkpoint** **What problems affected the postwar United States?**

⭐ **Looking Back and Ahead** After World War I, many Americans longed for a return to peace and prosperity. In the next chapter, you will see how these goals were met in the 1920s.

---

## Section 4 | Check Your Progress

**Progress Monitoring** Online
**For:** Self-test with instant help
**Visit:** PHSchool.com
**Web Code:** mva-7214

### Comprehension and Critical Thinking

1. **(a) Describe** What were Woodrow Wilson's goals for peace?
   **(b) Evaluate Information** How well did the Treaty of Versailles meet Wilson's goals?

2. **(a) Recall** Why did Wilson refuse to compromise with critics of the League of Nations?
   **(b) Support a Point of View** Do you think Wilson was right? Why or why not?

### 🔄 Reading Skill

3. **Connect Main Ideas to Current Events** Reread the text under the heading "Battle Over the League." Connect Wilson's actions to those of current political leaders when seeking support for their policies.

### Vocabulary *Builder*

Answer the following questions in complete sentences that show your understanding of the key terms.

4. What was the principle behind the idea of self-determination?
5. What happened to immigrants who were deported?
6. What did the reparations clause require Germany to do?

### Writing

7. Write the opening paragraph to an essay taking a stand about whether or not Congress should have ratified the Treaty of Versailles. End the paragraph with a thesis statement expressing your main idea.

People use propaganda to shape public opinion and encourage popular support for or against something, including an idea, political group, or government. During World War I, newspapers and governments on both sides used propaganda to win public support for the war effort. Study the American World War I poster below.

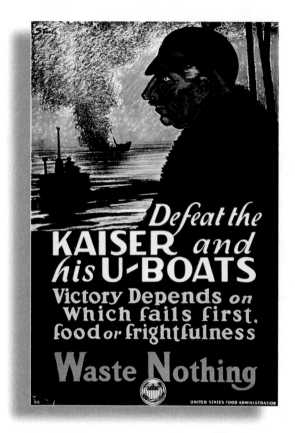

## Learn the Skill

*Use these steps to recognize propaganda.*

**1** **Identify the point of view.** Study the words and visuals to find the main idea. Identify the person or organization responsible for the propaganda and when it was created.

**2** **Identify the propaganda technique.** Propaganda can shape public opinion in several ways, such as by (1) using exaggeration, including strong words and images; (2) using symbols and/or offensive names to show the other side in a negative way; and (3) including only some of the facts about the subject or event.

**3** **Draw conclusions.** Evaluate the visuals and text. Decide whether or not the propaganda was effective and influenced public opinion.

## Practice the Skill

*Answer the following questions about the poster.*

**1** **Identify the point of view.** (a) Who created the poster? (b) When was it created? (c) What is the point of view expressed in the poster?

**2** **Identify the propaganda technique.** What technique or techniques are used in the poster?

**3** **Draw conclusions.** How do you think the poster affected public opinion in the United States?

## Apply the Skill

*See the Review and Assessment at the end of this chapter.*

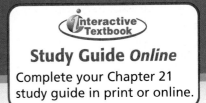

**Interactive Textbook**

**Study Guide** *Online*
Complete your Chapter 21 study guide in print or online.

## Chapter Summary

### Section 1
### The Road to War

- The massive war that broke out in Europe in 1914 quickly settled into a long, bloody stalemate.
- At first, President Wilson was determined to maintain American neutrality.
- German submarine warfare and the Zimmermann Telegram contributed to Wilson's decision to declare war on Germany in 1917.

### Section 2
### Supporting the War Effort

- The United States moved quickly to build up its armed forces.
- To support the war effort, the government took steps to control the economy, build public support for the war, and suppress dissent.

### Section 3
### Americans at War

- American troops were finally ready for combat in 1918.
- With fresh American troops and supplies, the Allies were able to resist a German advance and push on to victory.
- An armistice ended the war in November 1918.

### Section 4
### Shaping the Peace

- Wilson's Fourteen Points were an effort to create a just peace and prevent future wars.
- The Treaty of Versailles imposed harsh conditions on Germany.
- Opposition to the League of Nations led the Senate to reject the treaty.

## Key Concepts

These notes will help you prepare for questions about key concepts.

### Causes of World War I

- **Imperialism:** European nations competed for trade and territory.
- **Militarism:** Nations glorified the military and military leaders.
- **Nationalism:** Ethnic groups in the Balkans and elsewhere sought to create their own nations.
- **Alliance System:** Defensive alliances meant many nations would be drawn into conflict.
- **Immediate Cause:** Archduke Franz Ferdinand was assassinated by Serbian nationalists.

### Technology of World War I

New technology contributed to the stalemate and made World War I more deadly than any previous war.
- Trench warfare
- Machine guns
- Airplanes
- Tanks
- Poison gas
- Submarines

### The Fourteen Points

Wilson's peace plan included these principles:
- End of secret agreements
- Freedom of the seas
- Free trade
- Arms reduction
- Settlement of colonial claims
- Self-determination
- League of Nations

## Vocabulary *Builder*

### Key Terms

Fill in the blanks with the correct key terms from this chapter.

1. The Treaty of Versailles punished Germany by making it pay _____.

2. In _____, armies fired at each other across a barren patch called no man's land.

3. The principle of _____ meant that nations could choose their own form of government.

4. The use of _____ helped stir support for the war effort.

5. _____ led nations to place great pride and trust in their armies and navies.

## Comprehension and Critical Thinking

6. **(a) Describe** Describe the events that led the United States to declare war on Germany.
   **(b) Contrast** Review what you learned about the Spanish-American War. How were the reasons for declaring war on Spain similar to the reasons for declaring war on Germany? How were they different?

7. **(a) Recall** How did American women support the war effort?
   **(b) Analyze Cause and Effect** How did the role of women during the war affect their political status?

8. **(a) Recall** What problems did German Americans face during World War I?
   **(b) Identify Bias** How is the use of an expression such as "liberty cabbage" for "sauerkraut" an example of bias?
   **(c) Apply Information** Suggest one way that people can avoid such bias during wartime.

9. **(a) Explain** Why did Wilson want American forces to fight separately from French and British armies?
   **(b) Evaluate Information** Did Wilson's plan succeed?

10. **(a) Recall** How did Wilson and Lodge disagree over the League of Nations?
    **(b) Detect Points of View** Recall what you learned about George Washington's Farewell Address. Do you think Washington's viewpoint was closer to that of Wilson or to that of Lodge?

## History Reading Skill

11. **Identify and Connect Main Ideas** Identify a main idea from each of the four sections in this chapter. Explain how these ideas connect to one another. If possible, find a connection to an earlier event or to a current event.

## Writing

12. **Write two paragraphs about one of the following issues involving World War I:**
    - Describe what happened on the "home front" during the war.
    - Evaluate the effectiveness of President Wilson as a leader.
    - Take a stand about America's entry into World War I.

    **Your paragraph should:**
    - begin with a sentence stating your main idea about your subject;
    - include facts, reasons, and examples from the chapter to develop your ideas.

13. **Write a Letter:**
    Imagine that you are an American soldier in France during World War I. Write a letter home describing your experiences.

## Skills for Life

**Recognize Propaganda**
Use the poster below to answer the questions.

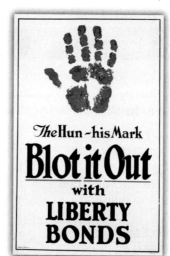

14. **(a)** Who do you think created this poster?
    **(b)** What did the creator of the poster want people to do?

15. What propaganda techniques are used?

16. Do you think the poster was an effective form of propaganda? Why or why not?

# Test Yourself

1. **During World War I, African American soldiers**

   A were banned from joining the army.

   B refused to support the war effort.

   C served in combat with white soldiers.

   D served in segregated units.

**Refer to this excerpt from the Treaty of Versailles to answer Question 2.**

> "Germany accepts the responsibility of Germany and her allies for causing all the loss and damage to which the Allied and Associated Governments and their nationals have been subjected."

2. **Which of the Big Four would have been most likely to oppose the above clause?**

   A Wilson

   B Lloyd George

   C Clemenceau

   D Orlando

**Refer to the graph below to answer Question 3.**

Source: R.E. Dupay and T.N. Dupay, *The Encyclopedia of Military History*

3. **Which Allied power shown on the graph had the most casualties?**

   A Russia

   B Germany

   C France

   D United States

# Document-Based Questions

**Task:** Look at Documents 1 and 2, and answer their accompanying questions. Then, use the documents and your knowledge of history to complete the following writing assignment:

> Write a short essay discussing whether or not the government has the right to limit freedom of speech during war time.

**Document 1:** The Espionage Act of 1917 was passed after Congress declared war with Germany. *What is the punishment for someone who violates this portion of the Espionage Act?*

> "SEC. 3 Whoever, when the United States is at war, shall willfully make or convey false reports or false statements with intent to interfere with the operation or success of the military or naval forces of the United States or to promote the success of its enemies . . . or shall willfully obstruct the recruiting or enlistment service of the United States, to the injury of the service or of the United States, shall be punished by a fine of not more than $10,000 or imprisonment for not more than twenty years, or both."

**Document 2:** Rose Pastor Stokes was a socialist and outspoken critic of the war. In 1918, she was convicted under the Espionage Act and sentenced to 10 years in federal prison for writing to the editor of the *Kansas City Star* the following letter. *Why did Stokes write to the* Kansas City Star?

> "To the Star:
> . . . A headline in the evening's issue of the Star reads: 'Mrs. Stokes for Government and Against War at the Same Time.' I am <u>not</u> for the government. In the interview that follows I am quoted as having said 'I believe the government of the United States should have the unqualified support of every citizen in its war aims.' I made no such statement, and I believe no such thing. No government which is <u>for</u> the profiteers can also be <u>for</u> the people, while the government is for the profiteers.
>
> Rose Pastor Stokes"

CHAPTER 22

# The Roaring Twenties

## 1919–1929

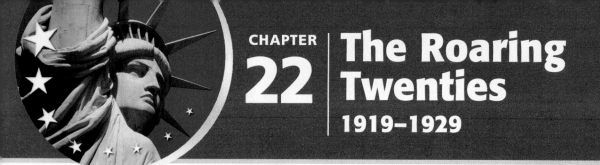

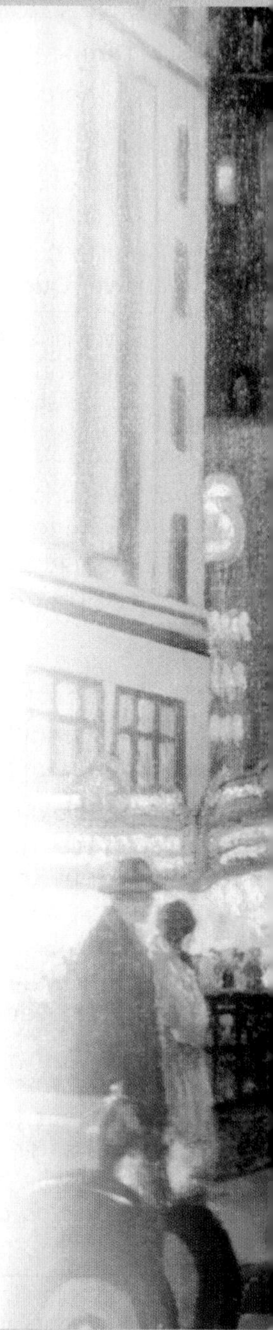

## Chapter Preview

The decade after World War I marked dramatic changes for the nation. With Republicans in command, the nation returned to prewar isolationism, while policies supporting big business cleared the way for the growth of industries. Cultural changes affected the lifestyles and values of Americans. However, these changes also sparked conflicts and tensions.



**U.S. Events**

**1918** World War I ends.

**1920** 19th Amendment extends right to vote to women.

1916 — 1918 — 1920 — 1922

**World Events**

**1917** Bolshevik Revolution gives Communists control of Russia.

**1922** The Soviet Union is formed. Mussolini comes to power in Italy.

The 1920s were years of prosperity for many, as reflected in this scene of Times Square in New York City.

**1924**
Teapot Dome and other government scandals become public.

**1925**
John Scopes is convicted of teaching the theory of evolution.

**1927**
*The Jazz Singer* introduces sound to movies. Lindbergh flies alone across the Atlantic.

1922

**1924**

**1926**

1928

**1923** An economic crisis shakes Germany.

**1927** U.S. Marines are sent to Nicaragua.

**1928** Kellogg-Briand Pact outlaws war.

733

**History Reading Skill  Clarify Understanding**

## What financial risks were Americans willing to take during the 1920s?

In this chapter, you will practice clarifying your understanding of a reading by paraphrasing and summarizing. Read the following discussion of real estate speculation in the 1920s. The side notes show you how to clarify your understanding.

> Economist John Kenneth Galbraith looked back at the 1920s to try to understand people's behavior with money. Here, he discusses their desire to get rich quickly and easily.
>
> **Primary Source**
>
> [Americans] were also displaying a . . . desire to get rich quickly with a minimum of physical effort. The first [evidence] of this . . . was in Florida. . . .
>
> The Florida [real estate] boom contained all of the elements of a classic speculative bubble. Florida had a better winter climate than New York, Chicago, or Minneapolis. Higher incomes and better transportation were making it increasingly accessible to the frostbound North. . . .
>
> [Based on that] fact, men and women had proceeded to build a world of speculative make-believe. This is a world inhabited not by people who have to be persuaded to believe but by people who want an excuse to believe. In this case of Florida, they wanted to believe that the whole peninsula would soon be populated by the . . . sun worshipers. . . . So great would be the crush that . . . [even] common scrubland would have value.
>
> —John Kenneth Galbraith, *The Great Crash*

**Restate in your own words:** Americans wanted to get rich quickly and easily.

**Use essential details to flesh out your summary:** Florida had a better winter climate and better transportation.

**Clarify the main idea:** Like other speculative, or uncertain, deals, the Florida real estate boom built on some truths.

**Clarify and summarize the paragraph:** Investors wanted to believe in the Florida real estate schemes. They convinced themselves that so many people would want to go to Florida that even worthless land would become valuable.

## Clarify Understanding

- Paraphrase text by restating it in your own words.
- Summarize the main ideas by choosing an important idea from each paragraph.
- List only the most important details in the summary.
- Summarize larger portions of text by including several ideas with important details.

## Document-Based Questions

1. Who is the author of this source?
2. Why would an investor in the Florida real estate "bubble" probably have lost money?
3. Why do you think people invested in deals that seemed "to good to be true"?

# Vocabulary *Builder*

## Previewing High-Use Academic Words

| High-Use Word | Definition | Sample History Sentence |
|---|---|---|
| **domestic** (doh MEHS tihk) (Section 1, p. 736) | *adj.* having to do with a country's internal affairs | The President plays a key role in both <u>domestic</u> and foreign affairs. |
| **impose** (ihm POHZ) (Section 1, p. 738) | *v.* to place a burden on something or someone | Congress holds the power to <u>impose</u> taxes on goods, services, and income. |
| **restrict** (ree STRIHKT) (Section 2, p. 742) | *v.* to confine; to keep within a certain boundary or limit; to place limitations on something or somebody | Racial discrimination has <u>restricted</u> the opportunities of African Americans. |
| **isolate** (ī sah layt) (Section 2, p. 743) | *v.* to set apart; to separate | The great distances between homesteads <u>isolated</u> frontier families from their neighbors. |
| **critic** (KRIHT ihk) (Section 3, p. 749) | *n.* someone who makes judgments on the value of objects or actions | Many American writers have been <u>critics</u> of middle-class values. |
| **analyze** (AN ah līz) (Section 3, p. 750) | *v.* to critically examine an idea or object by separating it into parts | Nathaniel Hawthorne wrote novels that <u>analyzed</u> people's actions and decisions. |
| **accumulate** (uh KYOOM yoo layt) (Section 4, p. 753) | *v.* to slowly collect; to increase in amount over time | As losses mounted, investors <u>accumulated</u> many debts. |
| **participate** (pahr TIHS ah payt) (Section 4, p. 754) | *v.* to take part in; to share in an activity | Native Americans, African Americans, and women could not <u>participate</u> in the voting process. |

## Previewing Key Terms and People

Warren Harding, p. 737
Calvin Coolidge, p. 737
disarmament, p. 738
communism, p. 738
anarchist, p. 739

prohibition, p. 741
bootlegger, p. 741
speakeasy, p. 741
Charles Lindbergh, p. 747
jazz, p. 747

Sinclair Lewis, p. 749
Langston Hughes, p. 750
installment buying, p. 752
bull market, p. 753
buying on margin, p. 753

# Adjusting to Peacetime

## Objectives

1. Explain how economic factors led to the election of Republican Warren Harding.

2. Compare and contrast the administrations of Harding and Calvin Coolidge.

3. Describe the U.S. policy of isolationism.

4. Explain how the threat of communism abroad raised concerns in the United States.

## Prepare to Read

### ⏺ Reading Skill

**Paraphrase Text for Understanding** One way to clarify text is to paraphrase. Paraphrasing is simply restating the text in your own words. If you can restate text in your own words, you will be more likely to understand it. As you read Section 1, pause at an indicated side note, read the side note and corresponding text, then paraphrase the idea in your own words.

### Vocabulary *Builder*

**High-Use Words**

domestic, p. 736

impose, p. 738

**Key Terms and People**

Warren Harding, p. 737

Calvin Coolidge, p. 737

disarmament, p. 738

communism, p. 738

anarchist, p. 739

☆ **Background Knowledge** During World War I, the United States emerged as a world power. Yet, at the end of the war, Americans rejected any major role in world affairs and instead turned to dealing with problems at home.

### Main Idea
After World War I, voters rejected the Democrats and elected Republicans to the presidency.

### Vocabulary *Builder*
domestic (doh MEHS tihk) *adj.* having to do with a country's internal affairs

## Return to Normalcy

President Woodrow Wilson might have expected to return from the Paris Peace Conference as a popular hero. Instead, he and his party were rejected by the voters at the next election. By 1920, the mishandling of the peace treaty at Versailles and a failing economy combined to make Wilson and the Democrats very unpopular.

The end of the Great War was followed by an economic recession. During the war, the domestic economy had expanded rapidly to produce all the extra goods needed by the military. With war's end, munitions factories shut down and workers lost their jobs. Soldiers returning from the war found it difficult to find work.

Labor unions had made a no-strike pledge as a patriotic gesture in wartime. But labor disputes led to many strikes after the war. In 1919, four million workers—one fifth of the labor force—took part in strikes. Accounts of strike-related violence filled the newspapers.

Many Americans feared other types of violence as well. Some feared that Communists would overthrow the government, as they had recently done in Russia. Racial violence also frightened some. Many Americans hoped that a change of leadership would restore peace and prosperity.

**The Harding Administration** In 1920, the Republican nominee for President, Warren Harding of Ohio, promised a return to "normalcy." It was what the public wanted. He won by a landslide.

Harding was a firm supporter of business. He filled his administration with like-minded men. For secretary of the treasury, he chose Andrew Mellon, a banker and industrialist. Mellon was one of the nation's richest men. He got Congress to lower taxes on businesses and the wealthy. He also helped slash the federal budget.

Some of Harding's other appointees were personal friends. Some saw their government jobs as opportunities to make personal fortunes, legally or illegally. Harding's presidency was marred by several major scandals involving these men. In one case, Charles Forbes, the head of the Veterans Bureau, was convicted of taking bribes totaling about $200 million.

The biggest scandal centered on Teapot Dome, Wyoming, a government-owned oil reserve. The secretary of the Department of the Interior, Albert B. Fall, secretly leased the land and its reserves to an oil man. Fall received a bribe of $400,000. After the scandal broke, Fall was tried and convicted. He was the first Cabinet member ever sent to prison.

Harding himself was never linked to any of the crimes and did not live to see the worst of the scandals unfold. In 1923, he suffered a heart attack and died, leaving his Vice President, Calvin Coolidge, to deal with the Teapot Dome and other scandals.

## The Harding Scandals

Billboards show the "sale" of government institutions.

### Reading Political Cartoons
#### Skills Activity

What part of the federal government was *not* for sale, cartoonists asked, as the Harding administration's many scandals came to light.

**(a) Apply Information** What symbols of the nation's government are used?

**(b) Detect Points of View** Does the cartoonist seem to think the scandals are a serious problem? Explain.

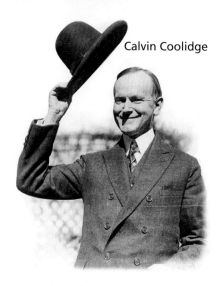

Calvin Coolidge

**The Coolidge Administration** Coolidge was very different from Harding. He was a soft-spoken, serious New Englander who was known for his honesty and integrity. By cooperating with the investigations into the Harding White House, Coolidge helped to restore the public's trust in government. When Coolidge ran for President in 1924, he won by a large margin.

Coolidge's prospects were helped by the prosperity of the mid-1920s. The postwar recession was over, and the economy had rebounded. The 1920s had begun to "roar," and the voters wanted to keep the Republicans in power.

✓**Checkpoint**  **Why did voters reject Wilson's Democrats?**

# Foreign Policy

World War I had made the United States an international power. Still, most Americans did not want their nation to play a leading role in world affairs. As you have read, this sentiment is known as isolationism.

Isolationism did not mean cutting off contact with the rest of the world. Throughout the 1920s, the United States participated in international conferences intended to promote world peace and to encourage disarmament. **Disarmament** means the reduction or limitation of military armaments. The United States joined the Washington Naval Arms Conference of 1921. The conference resulted in a treaty limiting the navies of the United States, Britain, France, Italy, and Japan. In 1928, the United States joined France in sponsoring the Kellogg-Briand Pact. The pact condemned military aggression and outlawed war. However, it <u>imposed</u> no punishment on a country that acted aggressively, so it was ineffective at preventing war.

President Coolidge believed that the government had a right to intervene in foreign matters that affected American business. In 1926, a revolution broke out in Nicaragua. Coolidge sent in troops to protect American business interests there. Defending his actions to send troops to Nicaragua, Coolidge stated:

> ❝It has always been . . . the policy of the United States . . . to take steps that may be necessary for the . . . protection of the lives, the property, and the interests of [U.S.] citizens. In this respect, I propose to follow the path of my predecessors. ❞
> —Calvin Coolidge, message before Congress, January 10, 1927

The following year, Mexico announced plans to take over all foreign-owned oil lands, including those owned by U.S. companies. Although many Americans wanted to send troops, Coolidge managed to resolve this dispute by diplomacy.

In the Bolshevik Revolution of 1917, Communists had taken power in Russia. They created the Soviet Union, the world's first Communist state. **Communism** is an economic and political system in which the state owns the means of production and a single party rules. In the Soviet Union, the Communist Party crushed all opposition.

**Main Idea**
Isolationist sentiment kept the United States from taking a leading role in world affairs.

**Vocabulary** *Builder*
**impose** (ihm POHZ) *v.* to place a burden on something or someone

**Paraphrase Text for Understanding**
Reading Skill
Paraphrase this paragraph. Be sure to use your own words to restate the main ideas and details.

In an effort to weaken the Soviet government, the United States refused to grant it diplomatic recognition. In 1918, President Wilson sent troops to aid the opponents of communism. Yet, when a devastating famine hit Russia in 1921, the United States sent aid. That aid may have saved 10 million people from starvation.

**✓Checkpoint** How did President Coolidge solve disputes in Latin America?

## The Red Scare

Alarm about communism affected not only American foreign policy but also events at home. The postwar strikes that rocked the United States made some Americans afraid that a revolution was beginning.

The fears reached a fever pitch in the spring and summer of 1919, when a series of bombings occurred. The bombings were the work of anarchists, people who oppose all organized government. Many anarchists were foreign-born, and the bombings led to an outcry against all foreigners. During this Red Scare, thousands of anarchists and Communists, or "Reds," were hunted down and arrested. Many were deported, or expelled from the country.

**Sacco and Vanzetti** In May 1920, at the height of the Red Scare, two Italian immigrants, Nicola Sacco and Bartolomeo Vanzetti, were arrested. They were charged with robbing and murdering two payroll employees in Massachusetts.

At the trial, little evidence was presented that Sacco and Vanzetti, were guilty of the charges. Rather, the prosecution focused on the fact that both defendants were foreigners and anarchists. Sacco and Vanzetti were convicted in 1921 and executed in 1927.

**Main Idea**
Labor unrest and anarchist bombings caused a Red Scare, during which the government expelled many foreigners.

### Links to Art

#### *Sacco and Vanzetti*
**by Ben Shahn**

The artist Ben Shahn viewed the execution of Sacco and Vanzetti as an outrage against justice. This portrait of the two men is one in a series of 23 paintings by Shahn about their trial, conviction, and execution. **Critical Thinking: Apply Information** *Why did the Sacco-Vanzetti case stir such strong feelings among Americans of the 1920s?*

The case was controversial at the time and remains so today. Were innocent people put to death because of public hysteria? Or did two murderers receive the punishment they deserved?

**Limiting Immigration** Fears about radicals led to new limits on immigration into the United States. There were other reasons, as well. Many Americans had long worried that the mainstream culture of the United States was being overwhelmed by immigrants from southern and eastern Europe. In addition, American workers were often concerned that newcomers would compete for their jobs.

An emergency immigration law was passed by Congress in 1921. It limited the number of people admitted from eastern and southern Europe. In 1924 and 1929, Congress imposed even more restrictions on immigrants. In addition, the United States completely prohibited immigration from Asia.

The new immigration limits, however, did not apply to people from the Americas. In the 1920s, nearly 500,000 people migrated from Mexico and 950,000 from Canada. Most Mexicans migrated to the Southwest, where their labors played a vital role in the growth of farmlands, railroads, and mines. Canadians, mainly from Quebec, took jobs in factories in New York and New England.

Mexican workers pick cotton

☑**Checkpoint**  What caused the Red Scare after World War I?

⭐ **Looking Back and Ahead**  After World War I, Americans elected Republicans, who promised a return to "normalcy" and prosperity. Next we will see how, during the 1920s, the nation experienced an era of social and economic change.

---

Section 1 | **Check Your Progress**

**Progress Monitoring** ⬤nline
**For:** Self-test with instant help
**Visit:** PHSchool.com
**Web Code:** mva-7221

**Comprehension and Critical Thinking**

1. **(a) Recall** How had World War I been good for the economy?
   **(b) Analyze Cause and Effect** Why might a country face economic problems even after a victorious war?

2. **(a) Recall** Why was secretary of the Interior Albert B. Fall sent to prison?
   **(b) Draw Conclusions** Why do most historians consider Warren Harding to have been a poor President?

**Reading Skill**

3. **Paraphrase Text for Understanding** Reread the first paragraph under the heading "The Red Scare." Paraphrase the text, using your own words.

**Vocabulary *Builder***

Answer the following questions in complete sentences that show your understanding of the key terms:
4. What is the goal of supporters of disarmament?
5. Who owns the means of production under communism?
6. What are anarchists against?

**Writing**

7. Based on what you have read in this section, write a thesis statement and one supporting paragraph for an essay about the mood in the country the first few years after World War I.

## Objectives

1. Identify the causes and effects of the Eighteenth Amendment.

2. Explain how the Nineteenth Amendment changed the role of women in society.

3. Describe how the automobile, radio, and movies changed American culture.

4. Explain why tension and unrest lay beneath the surface during the 1920s.

## Prepare to Read

### 🎯 Reading Skill

**Summarize Main Ideas** In an earlier chapter, you practiced identifying main ideas. You can build on that skill here, by summarizing main ideas. Clarify your understanding of the text by stating the main ideas. You will find that you must understand the main ideas in order to weave them together into a summary.

### Vocabulary *Builder*

**High-Use Words**

restrict, p. 742

isolate, p. 743

**Key Terms**

prohibition, p. 741

bootlegger, p. 741

speakeasy, p. 741

⭐ **Background Knowledge** The political changes of the 1920s were accompanied by far-reaching social and economic changes. The goals of some nineteenth-century reform movements were achieved in the early twentieth century. In this section, you will learn how a changing economy affected American society.

## Prohibition

During the 1800s, many reformers had worked to reduce alcohol use in the United States. Eventually, supporters of temperance began supporting prohibition, a total ban on alcoholic drinks. During World War I, support for prohibition grew. Many Americans saw it as a way to conserve grains during the war. In part, due to this reasoning, the states ratified the Eighteenth Amendment in 1919. It prohibited making, selling, or transporting alcohol and began a specific time of federal enforcement known as Prohibition.

**The Experiment Fails** Saloons shut down, and arrests for drunkenness declined. There was a drop in the amount of alcohol that people consumed, especially working people for whom the high price of illegal liquor was an obstacle.

However, the law proved impossible to enforce. It was easy to smuggle liquor across the border from Canada and the Caribbean. Liquor smugglers, called bootleggers, made huge profits importing illegal alcohol. Every large town had its speakeasies, or illegal taverns that served liquor.

**Main Idea**
In 1919, the Eighteenth Amendment bans the use and sale of alcohol.

Poster in support of prohibition

**Dumping Whiskey**

Prohibition was intended to solve such social problems as drunkenness and family violence. Yet, the amendment was repealed in 1933. **Critical Thinking:** *Identify Costs* What were the unintended consequences of the Prohibition Amendment that led to its repeal?

**The Growth of Organized Crime** The money to be made through bootlegging encouraged the growth of organized crime. A series of gang wars broke out in some parts of the country.

By the end of the decade, it was clear that Prohibition had failed. Many people called for the repeal of the Eighteenth Amendment. In February 1933, Congress approved the Twenty-first Amendment, repealing Prohibition. Before the year was out, the states had ratified the amendment and Prohibition was over. The federal government returned the control of alcoholic beverages to the states.

✓**Checkpoint**   **Why did many people want to end Prohibition?**

## Changing Lives of Women

**Main Idea**

Women, now able to vote, sought more freedom in the 1920s.

**Vocabulary** *Builder*

restrict (ree STRIHKT) *v.* to confine; to keep within a certain boundary or limit; to place limitations on something or somebody

Due to the Nineteenth Amendment, American women voted in their first presidential election in 1920. They also joined political parties and were elected to offices previously closed to them. In 1924, the first women governors were elected: Nellie Tayloe Ross in Wyoming and Miriam "Ma" Ferguson in Texas.

Other areas of life remained more <u>restricted</u>. Many universities and professional schools, such as medical schools, still barred women from admission. In some states, women still could not serve on juries or keep their own earnings if they were married. But more women were holding jobs.

**A New Attitude** Many younger women during the 1920s did not seem interested in women's rights. Called "flappers," these young women shocked the older generation. Even though their numbers were small, the flappers became the symbol of women in the 1920s.

✓**Checkpoint**   **How did flappers represent the spirit of the 1920s?**

# A New Mass Culture

The automobile also became a symbol of the 1920s—especially the Model T Ford. Henry Ford introduced the assembly line which reduced the time in making cars from about 12 hours to about 1½ hours. Middle-class families could now afford to buy a car since prices dropped.

**Impact of the Automobile** The automobile changed American life in many ways. In a restless age, it became the symbol of individual freedom and independence. The automobile also created new businesses. Gas stations, roadside restaurants, and cabins sprang up along newly built highways.

Cars affected society in other ways. Cars and new roads made it easier for many families to move to the suburbs. Cars made people in rural areas less <u>isolated</u>. Furthermore, they encouraged tourism.

**The Radio** Another important part of the new culture was the radio. Introduced in the 1920s, commercial radio was an instant success. Almost any family could afford to buy a radio.

The radio became a leading supplier of entertainment. Families listened together at night after dinner. Radio put Americans in the stands at baseball games and on the floor of political conventions. It turned band leaders, singers, and comedians into household names.

The first commercial radio station, KDKA, began broadcasting in Pittsburgh in 1920. By 1926, there were more than 700 radio stations and a national radio network, NBC. People all over the country could hear the same songs and thrill to the same radio dramas.

**Main Idea**
The automobile, the radio, and the movies brought sweeping changes to American life.

**Vocabulary** *Builder*
<u>isolate</u> (ī sah layt) *v.* to set apart; to separate

**Summarize Main Ideas**
Summarize the main ideas under the heading "A New Mass Culture."

## Portrait of a Flapper

"She is frankly, heavily made up . . . pallor mortis, poisonously scarlet lips, richly ringed eyes. . . . And there are, finally, her clothes. . . . Her dress . . . is cut low where it might be high, and vice versa. The skirt comes just an inch below her knees, overlapping by a faint fraction her rolled and twisted stockings. The idea is that when she walks in a bit of a breeze, you shall now and then observe the knee. . . . [The flapper's] haircut is also abbreviated. She wears of course the very newest thing in bobs. . . ."

—Bruce Bliven, "Flapper Jane," *The New Republic,* Sept. 9, 1925

### Reading Primary Sources
#### Skills Activity

Some younger Americans shocked their elders by acting with a new freedom during the 1920s. In the quotation above, a magazine writer describes a 19-year-old flapper. **Critical Thinking:** *Evaluate Information* How did changes in American society help to create the flapper generation?

**The Movies** Movies were another new form of entertainment. They provided an escape from everyday life. Millions of Americans went to the movies at least once a week. The movie industry grew up in Hollywood, where mild weather allowed for filming year-round.

The first films were silent. A pianist or small musical group in each theater provided an accompaniment. In 1927, the first major "talkie," *The Jazz Singer,* created a sensation.

Americans especially loved action films. Comedies were also popular, and actors, such as Charlie Chaplin, became celebrities. Animated movies began in the 1920s, and the Walt Disney company was founded in 1923.

Out of the love of films grew a fascination with movie stars. Fan magazines and gossip columns contributed to the worship of celebrities.

☑**Checkpoint** **What new forms of entertainment became popular in the 1920s?**

**Main Idea**
The rapid changes of the 1920s also brought social tensions and racial unrest.

**Magic of the Silver Screen**
Charles Chaplin was among many Hollywood stars who became household names during the 1920s. **Critical Thinking:** *Draw Conclusions How did new forms of mass culture like radio and movies help to bring Americans together?*

This is the great picture upon which the famous comedian has worked a whole year.

6 reels of Joy.

*Charles Chaplin*
IN
"THE KID"

Written and directed by Charles Chaplin
A First National ● Attraction

## Social Conflict

Not everyone shared in the new postwar social values. Some were offended by what they saw. They feared that rapid social and economic changes would destroy a treasured way of life.

**The Scopes Trial** Some of those conflicts were at the heart of the Scopes trial of 1925. John Scopes was a high school biology teacher in Dayton, Tennessee. He was accused of violating Tennessee law by teaching the theory of evolution to his students.

Evolution is the scientific theory devised by Charles Darwin in the nineteenth century. Darwin claimed that all life evolved, or developed, from simpler forms over a long period of time.

Some religious leaders rejected evolution, saying it denied the word of the Bible. A number of states, including Tennessee, passed laws that banned the teaching of Darwin's theory. Scopes wanted to challenge the law, so he announced that he taught evolution.

The trial became a national sensation. The prosecutor was William Jennings Bryan, who had run for President three times. The defense attorney was Clarence Darrow, a famous Chicago criminal defense lawyer. The trial seemed to pit modern, urban Americans against traditional, rural Americans.

In the end, Scopes was convicted and lost his job. Laws against teaching evolution remained but were rarely enforced.

**Racial Conflict** African Americans returned from service in World War I with new hope for equality at home. They tried to get better paying jobs and to move to better neighborhoods.

The 1920s saw large numbers of African Americans move north in what was called the Great Migration. Leaving the South, they headed for cities such as Chicago, Detroit, and New York. They crowded into the few neighborhoods that allowed black residents.

Racial tensions mounted, and race riots broke out in several cities. Some of the worst violence occurred in Chicago, where 13 days of rioting in 1919 left 38 people dead and some 500 injured.

Under these conditions, the Jamaican immigrant Marcus Garvey gained a wide following. Arriving in America in 1916, Garvey, a spellbinding speaker, created the Universal Negro Improvement Association (UNIA). "Up, you mighty race," Garvey told his followers, "you can accomplish what you will." The UNIA sponsored activities to promote black pride and black unity. It also encouraged African Americans to move permanently to Africa.

The social tensions of the 1920s were also expressed in the growth of the Ku Klux Klan. The whites-only Klan scorned not just blacks but also immigrants, Catholics, and Jews. The organization's power spread from the South to the Midwest and the West. In Oregon and Indiana, Klan-backed candidates were elected as governors.

However, several public scandals at the end of the 1920s cost the Klan much of its support. The general economic prosperity also contributed to the organization's decline.

✓**Checkpoint**  **What was one cause of the Great Migration?**

⭐ **Looking Back and Ahead** The economic and social pressures unleashed by World War I greatly changed U.S. society. The changes helped bring a burst of creative energy in the arts.

Marcus Garvey

---

Section 2 | **Check Your Progress**

**Progress Monitoring** Online
**For:** Self-test with instant help
**Visit:** PHSchool.com
**Web Code:** mva-7222

**Comprehension and Critical Thinking**

1. **(a) List** How did automobiles change the lives of Americans?
   **(b) Draw Conclusions** How did the production of the automobile change life in small towns?

2. **(a) Recall** What did Marcus Garvey encourage?
   **(b) Link Past to Present** Which of Garvey's ideas have African Americans embraced and which have they rejected?

**Reading Skill**

3. **Summarize Main Ideas** Reread the text following the subheading "The Movies." Summarize its main ideas.

**Vocabulary Builder**

Complete the following sentence so that the second part further explains the first part and clearly shows your understanding of the key term.

4. Supporters of the temperance movement favored prohibition, _____.

**Writing**

5. Which sentence is a better conclusion for a short essay about Prohibition? (a) "The Nineteenth Amendment outlawed the sale of alcohol." (b) "Given its unexpected effects, it is no surprise that Prohibition was repealed."

# The Jazz Age

## Objectives

1. Describe the new fads and heroes that emerged during the 1920s and how they affected American culture.

2. Identify the origins, importance, and spread of a new musical style—jazz.

3. Explain how new literature styles described American society in a new, more critical way.

## Prepare to Read

### ⊙ Reading Skill

**Summarize Main Ideas and Essential Details** A summary includes more than just main ideas. It must also include essential details. Still, a summary should not repeat everything in the text, but it should include those details necessary for understanding the main ideas. To find these details, ask yourself if the main idea would make sense without a detail. If not, then include the detail.

### Vocabulary *Builder*

**High-Use Words**

critic, p. 749

analyze, p. 750

**Key Terms and People**

Charles Lindbergh, p. 747

jazz, p. 747

Sinclair Lewis, p. 749

Langston Hughes, p. 750

---

⭐ **Background Knowledge** In the previous section, you learned how social changes and conflicts shaped American society during the 1920s. This section will examine the arts and culture produced by a society undergoing great changes.

**Main Idea**

Optimistic Americans in the 1920s eagerly embraced new fads and hailed new heroes.

Women playing mah-jongg

## Fads and Heroes

The energy and enthusiasm of the 1920s reflected the optimism felt by many Americans of the time. One hit song put it this way: "Ev'ry morning, ev'ry evening, ain't we got fun?"

As the economy soared and the culture roared, young people expressed their joy for life in dancing. Dance fads became popular quickly and then disappeared. The Charleston swept the nation, followed by the Lindy Hop, the Black Bottom, and then the Breakaway.

Other fads also became part of popular culture in the 1920s. Flagpole sitting was all the rage. Young people competed to see who could sit the longest atop a flagpole. Some did it for hours, others for days. Another fad that tested young people's endurance was the dance marathon. Couples danced for hundreds of hours until only one last bleary-eyed pair remained shuffling wearily about the dance floor.

The Chinese game of mah-jongg became extremely popular. Women went to mah-jongg clubs wearing Chinese-style silk gowns. College students formed their own mah-jongg clubs. Guests brought mah-jongg sets to dinner parties and set up their ivory and bamboo tiles on playing tables. In 1923, mah-jongg sets outsold radios.

**Heroes of the New Age** The growing popularity of sports entertainment produced a new kind of celebrity: the sports hero. Baseball great Babe Ruth became one such celebrity. His record of hitting 60 home runs in one season lasted for more than 30 years.

Other celebrities of the decade included swimmer Johnny Weissmuller, football player Red Grange, golf champion Bobby Jones, tennis stars Bill Tilden and Helen Wills, and boxer Jack Dempsey.

The mass media helped to make these celebrities style setters, too. When Babe Ruth began wearing a camel's-hair coat, so did millions of other Americans.

Charles Lindbergh, nicknamed Lucky Lindy, was the most beloved hero of the era. The handsome young airplane pilot gained his fame by being the first to fly nonstop across the Atlantic in 1927. He became an instant hero. New York City gave him the biggest ticker tape parade ever. Lindbergh seemed to symbolize American energy and optimism.

☑ **Checkpoint** What sports events became popular during the 1920s?

## An American Sound

During the 1920s, a new musical sound achieved wide popularity. Jazz was created by black musicians in the nightclubs and dance halls of New Orleans. New Orleans was a major port city, where people and cultures from around the world came together. Jazz combined rhythms from West Africa and the Caribbean, work chants and spirituals from the rural South, and harmonies from Europe into an original new style of music.

Jazz quickly spread to other American cities, following along with the Great Migration. African American musicians also found eager audiences for their music in St. Louis, New York, Chicago, Kansas City, and Detroit. Among the most famous of the new jazz artists were trumpet player and singer Louis Armstrong, singer Bessie Smith, and band leader Duke Ellington. All had roots in the South.

Armstrong, who was known as Satchmo, learned to play the trumpet while growing up in a New Orleans orphanage. Like other jazz players, he developed the ability to take a simple melody and recombine the notes and rhythms in new ways to produce a cascade of rich and exciting sounds. Because of jazz's emphasis on improvisation and experimentation, listeners heard many different versions of the basic tune.

**Main Idea**
Jazz originated among African American musicians and became the dominant music form of the 1920s.

**Summarize Main Ideas and Essential Details** List three essential details from the text under the heading "An American Sound" that could be used in a summary. Use your own words.

# THE JAZZ AGE

**Discovery SCHOOL™**

**Explore More Video**
To learn more about the culture of the Jazz Age, view the video.

Jazz spread from the dance halls of New Orleans to Chicago, Harlem, and beyond. Its rollicking beat was soon being heard all over the world. **Critical Thinking: *Apply Information*** *How did the Jazz Age open up new opportunities for African Americans?*

**Jazz Greats** The leading jazz performers were African Americans, such as Louis Armstrong, Duke Ellington, and Bessie Smith. Many became "goodwill ambassadors" abroad, performing in many countries.

Bessie ▶
Smith

The song sheet for ▶
"Tin Roof Blues"

◀ Louis
Armstrong

Duke
Ellington
▼

TIN ROOF BLUES

MUSIC BY NEW ORLEANS RHYTHM KINGS · LEON ROPPOLO · PA...
TIN ROOF CAFE
DANC...
WORDS BY WALTER MELROSE

Duke Ellington
and his band

Radio helped to spread jazz beyond the African American community. During the 1920s, white audiences, white band leaders such as Paul Whiteman, and white composers such as George Gershwin embraced jazz. Jazz became one of the most important American contributions to world culture. It was so popular that the decade of the 1920s became known as the Jazz Age.

However, jazz did not set everyone's feet to tapping. The rhythms of the new music were jarring to many older Americans. And jazz alarmed people who thought it encouraged an overemphasis on frivolity and pleasure and undermined the morals of America's young people.

☑ **Checkpoint** **Why was jazz considered an American art form?**

## Literature of the 1920s

American literature flourished during the 1920s. Writers both reflected the exuberance of the era and criticized its excesses. Many writers seemed disillusioned by the postwar generation. They complained that Americans had turned from international idealism to greedy selfishness. Some of these writers found American society so intolerable that they became "expatriates," people who leave their own country to live abroad.

**Social Critics** F. Scott Fitzgerald's 1925 novel *The Great Gatsby* captured the luxurious society of the wealthy. Fitzgerald was a <u>critic</u> of what he saw as the emptiness of rich people's lives. He seemed both fascinated and disgusted by the people he described.

Fitzgerald's friend Ernest Hemingway was another important writer of the decade. A one-time newspaper reporter, Hemingway was noted for his short, direct sentences using everyday language. Living among American expatriates in France, Hemingway wrote *The Sun Also Rises* (1926) about a group of young Americans who drifted around Spain after the war. Another Hemingway novel, *A Farewell to Arms* (1929), powerfully captured the growing antiwar sentiments of his generation.

Sinclair Lewis reacted against what he saw as the hypocrisies of middle-class culture. In *Babbitt* (1922), Lewis used a fictional real estate agent named George F. Babbitt to criticize American society.

> **❝** Babbitt was virtuous. He advocated, though he did not practice, the prohibition of alcohol; he praised, though he did not obey, the laws against motor-speeding; he paid his debts; he contributed to the church, the Red Cross, and the Y.M.C.A.; he followed the custom of his clan and cheated only as it was sanctified by precedent. . . . **❞**
> —Sinclair Lewis, *Babbitt*

Based on this character's moral faults, "babbitry" became a common term for mediocrity combined with an unthinking conformity to middle-class standards and prejudices.

**Main Idea**
Writers of the Harlem Renaissance cast a critical eye on American society.

**Vocabulary *Builder***
**critic** (KRIHT ihk) *n.* someone who makes judgments on the value of objects or actions

F. Scott Fitzgerald's *The Great Gatsby* calls attention to the excesses of the Roaring Twenties.

Zora Neale Hurston

**Vocabulary** *Builder*
**analyze** (AN ah līz) *v.* to critically examine an idea or object by separating it into parts

**The Harlem Renaissance** During the 1920s, a vibrant African American culture grew in Harlem, a part of New York City that attracted thousands of migrants from the South. Writers, musicians, and poets reacted against the prejudice they faced while expressing the hopes of black Americans. Jazz clubs and the music scene were one part of the Harlem Renaissance. Perhaps even more important were the writers.

Poet Langston Hughes won praise not only for the beauty of his poems but also for his moving expressions of racial pride. He wanted his poems to sound like jazz music. He said, "I tried to write poems like the songs they sang on Seventh Street. . . . [These songs] had the pulse beat of the people who keep on going."

James Weldon Johnson was another Harlem Renaissance figure who combined poetry and politics. Johnson wrote editorials for the *New York Age,* one of the most important black-owned newspapers in the country. He also worked as an organizer for the NAACP.

Zora Neale Hurston moved to New York to study anthropology at Barnard College. She, too, became swept up in the cultural excitement of the Harlem Renaissance. Hurston spent much time recording folk songs and folk tales to both preserve and analyze them. She also became an accomplished writer and is most remembered today for her novel *Their Eyes Were Watching God.*

☑**Checkpoint** **What was the Harlem Renaissance?**

☆ **Looking Back and Ahead** While Americans benefited from the general prosperity of the 1920s, it was easy to overlook a number of disturbing economic trends. In the next section, you will learn why a frenzied stock market boom concealed signs of an economy that was facing serious problems.

Section 3 | **Check Your Progress**

**Progress Monitoring** ⏺nline
**For:** Self-test with instant help
**Visit:** PHSchool.com
**Web Code:** mva-7223

**Comprehension and Critical Thinking**

1. **(a) Identify** Who was Charles Lindbergh?
   **(b) Draw Inferences** How did Lindbergh symbolize the American hero of the 1920s?

2. **(a) List** Who were the leading writers of the 1920s and what were their major works?
   **(b) Explain Problems** Which problems were the writers addressing in their works?

🔁 **Reading Skill**

3. **Summarize Main Ideas and Essential Details** Reread the text following the subheading "The Harlem Renaissance." List three essential details, in your own words, for a summary.

**Vocabulary** *Builder*

Read the sentence that follows. If the sentence is true, write YES. If the sentence is not true, write NO and explain why.

4. Jazz began in New Orleans when musicians of French heritage combined sounds from Europe with Native American music.

**Writing**

5. Proofread and correct the following sentences: The Jazz age is similer to currant life in America in a many ways. Four example, the people of both periods warshiped sports heros and other selebrities. Both ages was known for there populous fads. I think I druther live today than in the past.

# I, Too
## by Langston Hughes

### Introduction

Langston Hughes is considered one of the greatest of all African American poets. His short poem "I, Too" expresses two major themes of the Harlem Renaissance. The first is pride in being African American. The second is protest against injustice.

### Reading Skill

**Analyze Poetic Voices** Poets often write in voices other than their own. Sometimes, a poet may take on the voice of a character totally unlike himself or herself. At other times, the "I" of a poem may be symbolic of a group or idea. As you read this poem, look for clues as to who the "I" is supposed to be.

### Vocabulary *Builder*

As you read this literature selection, look for the following underlined word:

**ashamed** (uh SHAYMD) *adj.* feeling sorry and guilty about a wrong action

---

I, too, sing America.

I am the darker brother.
They send me to eat in the kitchen
When company comes,
But I laugh,
And eat well,
And grow strong.

Tomorrow,
I'll be at the table
When company comes.
Nobody'll dare
Say to me,
"Eat in the kitchen,"
Then.

Besides,
They'll see how beautiful I am
And be <u>ashamed</u>—

I, too, am America.

**Langston Hughes**

### Analyze Poetic Voices

The speaker of the poem says, "I am the darker brother." Who do you think the "I" represents? Who are "they" who send the speaker to "eat in the kitchen"? Only by identifying the "I" and "they" can you understand what the poem is saying.

### *Analyze* **LITERATURE**

Make a two-column chart. In the first column, list the ways in which this poem expresses a sense of injustice. In the second column, list ways in which this poem expresses a sense of optimism and patriotism.

If you want to learn more about the Harlem Renaissance, you might want to read *Harlem Stomp!: A Cultural History of the Harlem Renaissance,* by Laban Carrick Hill. Little, Brown & Co., 2004.

# The Economy of the 1920s

## Objectives

1. Describe the causes and effects of the industrial boom that occurred in the 1920s.

2. Explain how rising stock prices encouraged many to borrow money to invest in the stock market.

3. Identify groups that did not profit from the prosperity of the 1920s.

4. Describe the election of 1928 and Herbert Hoover's victory.

## Prepare to Read

### Reading Skill

**Summarize a Passage** Combine the skills you practiced in Sections 1 through 3 as you read Section 4. Pause after each major portion of text. Summarize the main ideas that fall under the major heading. Remember to paraphrase in your own words and to include all the important ideas.

### Vocabulary *Builder*

**High-Use Words**

<u>accumulate</u>, p. 753
<u>participate</u>, p. 754

**Key Terms**

installment buying, p. 752
bull market, p. 753
buying on margin, p. 753

⭐ **Background Knowledge** The social and economic changes of the 1920s were accompanied by a prolonged period of prosperity. This section will describe the economic boom while explaining some key problems that were hidden beneath the prosperity.

## Industrial Growth

**Main Idea**
After a brief postwar recession, industry revived and offered Americans a bounty of consumer goods.

The end of World War I was followed by a severe recession in agriculture and industry. For industry, that downturn did not last long. Industrial production recovered, and from 1922 to 1928 it climbed 70 percent. Many companies successfully switched from producing military goods to producing consumer goods. The market was filled with refrigerators, radios, and cars.

As more goods came to market, prices dropped. Meanwhile, rising incomes gave consumers more to spend. To encourage spending, businesses offered installment buying, or buying on credit. In 1925, Americans got 75 percent of their cars on the installment plan.

New forms of advertising surrounded customers with images of things they should consume. Chain stores and mail-order catalogs made it easier for people outside of major cities to buy these goods. A new consumer culture arose.

Middle-class women were especially affected by these changes. Many of the new electric appliances were designed to appeal to the American homemaker. Vacuum cleaners, toasters, washing machines, and refrigerators all lightened the household workload.

*Twice* the cleaning...
*twice* the leisure!

New product to make life easier

Government policies helped boost the economy. High tariffs on imports kept out goods that might compete with domestic products. Taxes on the wealthy were cut to encourage greater spending.

These measures did stimulate the economy. But they also helped Americans develop a recklessness about spending. In 1928, when Ford announced its new Model A, half a million people made a down payment on the car without even having seen it.

☑Checkpoint **What factors caused an increase in consumer spending?**

## A Booming Stock Market

With a strong economy, more people chose to invest in the stock market. Many people could now afford to purchase stocks, or shares of companies. With money pouring into stocks, stock values kept rising. A period of rising stock prices is called a **bull market.**

Stocks were so profitable that many people began buying on margin—borrowing money in order to buy stocks. The investor put down a portion of a stock's cost and paid the rest later with the profits earned from selling the stock. So long as the market continued to rise, the investor had no problem paying the loan back.

Many Americans grew wealthy buying and selling stocks. Newspapers were filled with stories of investors who <u>accumulated</u> fortunes. However, by 1928, some economists began to worry. High stock prices seemed to have little to do with the actual value of the company that issued them. A few experts warned that the stock market was overvalued. But investors mostly ignored the warnings.

**Main Idea**

Rising stock prices lured many Americans into buying stocks with borrowed money.

**Vocabulary** *Builder*

**accumulate** (uh KYOOM yoo layt) *v.* to slowly collect; to increase in amount over time

**History** *Interactive*
**Buying Stocks on Margin**
**Visit:** PHSchool.com
**Web Code:** mvl-7224

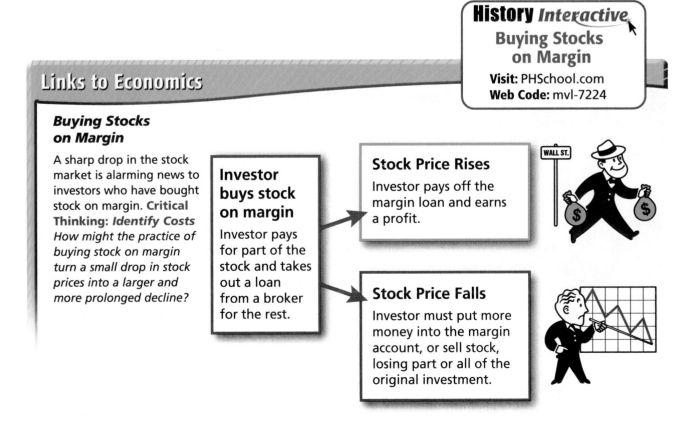

**Links to Economics**

**Buying Stocks on Margin**

A sharp drop in the stock market is alarming news to investors who have bought stock on margin. **Critical Thinking:** *Identify Costs How might the practice of buying stock on margin turn a small drop in stock prices into a larger and more prolonged decline?*

**Investor buys stock on margin**

Investor pays for part of the stock and takes out a loan from a broker for the rest.

**Stock Price Rises**

Investor pays off the margin loan and earns a profit.

**Stock Price Falls**

Investor must put more money into the margin account, or sell stock, losing part or all of the original investment.

**Summarize a Passage**
Use what you have learned in this chapter to summarize the text under the heading "A Booming Stock Market."

**Main Idea**
Many farmers and workers did not share in the era's prosperity.

**Vocabulary** *Builder*
**participate** (pahr TIHS ah payt) *v.* to take part in; to share in an activity

They preferred to listen to predictions like this one spoken by Irwin Fisher, a professor of economics in 1929: "The nation is marching along a permanently high plateau of prosperity." However, most people at the time were far from prosperous. The wealthiest Americans made up about 5 percent of the population. Most people just worked hard to make ends meet.

☑ **Checkpoint** **Why did rising stock prices encourage people to gamble on the stock market?**

## Signs of Trouble

There were other signs of potential trouble, too. In fact, for many Americans, the 1920s were years of poverty rather than prosperity.

**Farmers** Farmers were among the groups that did not <u>participate</u> in the good times. About one fifth of Americans made their living on the land and many of them lived in serious poverty.

There were several reasons for the agricultural depression. American farmers grew far more crops than the American public could consume. Before World War I, farmers had sold their surplus abroad. However, demand for American farm products declined after the war, because many nations were too poor to purchase them.

High debt was another reason for rural poverty. In the good years before the world war, farmers had taken out loans to buy new lands and equipment. After the war, though, sales went down. Many farmers were unable to pay off their debts.

**Workers** The 1920s were years of mixed results for American workers. On the one hand, wages were rising. Companies also began offering new benefits, such as pensions and paid vacations, in an attempt to keep their workers from joining unions.

On the other hand, unemployment was high. During the 1920s, it was about 5 percent of the workforce each year. Those who had jobs found that their jobs were changing. The assembly line system was squeezing out skilled labor. Each step had been reduced to its simplest methods. Unskilled workers could handle the work—and they received lower pay.

☑ **Checkpoint** **Why were farmers left out of the prosperity of the 1920s?**

**Farmers in Trouble**
Drought and erosion contributed to the troubles of farmers, who made up one fifth of the population. **Critical Thinking: Draw Conclusions** *Why might bad times for farmers also be bad for the American economy in general?*

# The Election of 1928

The Republicans had held the presidency throughout the 1920s, and they claimed responsibility for the decade's prosperity. For their candidate in the 1928 presidential election, they chose Secretary of Commerce Herbert Hoover. The Democrats nominated New York Governor Alfred E. Smith.

The campaign highlighted some of the continuing divisions in American society. Smith was the first Catholic ever to run for President, and religion became one of the issues. Immigrants, Catholics, and urban residents tended to support Smith. Rural residents and Protestants tended to support Hoover, a Quaker born in Iowa.

The economy was another major issue. Hoover pledged to continue the policies he credited for prosperity. He campaigned on the slogan "a chicken in every pot and a car in every garage." He said the nation was near to "the final triumph over poverty."

Although Alfred Smith won the largest cities, he lost every state but Massachusetts and six Deep South states. Hoover won with special strength in rural areas. Herbert Hoover entered the White House in 1929 with great expectations for a prosperous future.

☑ Checkpoint **Among what groups was Hoover strong?**

☆ **Looking Back and Ahead** A widespread prosperity and sweeping changes in society made the 1920s an exciting time. Within months of Hoover's election, however, a stock market crash plunged the nation into a great depression that spread misery across the land.

## Main Idea

Expectations of continued prosperity helped Herbert Hoover win the 1928 election for the Republicans.

Hoover campaign plugs

---

Section 4 | **Check Your Progress**

**Progress Monitoring ⬤nline**
**For:** Self-test with instant help
**Visit:** PHSchool.com
**Web Code:** mva-7224

## Comprehension and Critical Thinking

**1. (a) List** What were the reasons the economy, after a short slump, boomed following World War I?
**(b) Identify Economic Benefits** Explain how high tariffs and low taxes boosted the economy during the 1920s.

**2. (a) Recall** Which groups of Americans did not benefit from the prosperity of the 1920s?
**(b) Synthesize Information** Why might some farmers have felt government support was necessary at this time?

## ⟳ Reading Skill

**3. Summarize a Passage** Reread and then summarize the text under the heading "Signs of Trouble."

## Vocabulary *Builder*

Complete each of the following sentences so that the second part further explains the first part and clearly shows your understanding of the key term.
**4.** To purchase a car, a person can turn to installment buying, _____.
**5.** People make money during a bull market, _____.
**6.** In order to purchase even more stock in the 1920s, people began buying on margin, _____.

## Writing

**7.** Revise the following paragraph by putting the sentences in logical order: In the mid-1920s, however, reduced taxes and extended credit encouraged consumer spending. By 1929, the economy had grown to the point of being overheated. In the early 1920s the economy declined, partly as a result of World War I. The U.S. economy improved a great deal from the beginning to the end of the 1920s. The war had badly weakened European economies, and the overseas market for American goods shrank.

Facts and figures that measure how an economy is performing are called economic indicators. Examples include wages, income levels, price levels, and interest rates. Sometimes these economic indicators are shown on a graph.

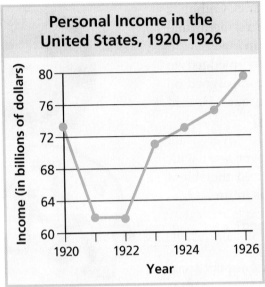

**Personal Income in the United States, 1920–1926**

Source: *Historical Statistics of the United States*

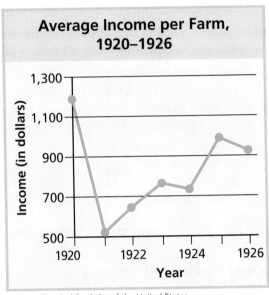

**Average Income per Farm, 1920–1926**

Source: *Historical Statistics of the United States*

## Learn the Skill

*Use these steps to interpret economic data on line graphs.*

**1** **Identify the topic.** Look for a title, a date, and a source. The title tells you what the subject is; the date tells what time period is covered; the source tells you where the information was found.

**2** **Read the labels.** Chart labels identify the given information and how it is measured. Both the horizontal axis and the vertical axis on a graph have labels organizing the information.

**3** **Practice interpreting the data.** Find information based on the economic data presented on the graph. The words "in billions" means you must add nine zeroes to the number shown. Sometimes you can compare and contrast information on the graph.

**4** **Draw Conclusions.** Use the information on the graph to draw conclusions about the topic. You can also use other information you might know about the subject of the graph.

## Practice the Skill

*Answer the following questions about the graphs on this page.*

**1** **Identify the topic.** (a) What is the subject of the first graph (left)? The second graph (right)? (b) What time periods do both graphs show? (c) What is the source for the graphs?

**2** **Read the labels.** (a) What do the numbers on the vertical axis of the first graph show? (b) Of the second graph?

**3** **Practice interpreting the data.** (a) What was the personal income of all U.S. citizens in 1920? In 1926? (b) What was the average net income per farm in 1920? In 1926? (c) How would you compare the income of farmers to the income of the general population?

**4** **Draw conclusions.** (a) What happened to the personal income of Americans in the 1920s? (b) How did the agricultural depression of the 1920s affect the farmer's income during this period?

## Apply the Skill

*See the Review and Assessment at the end of this chapter.*

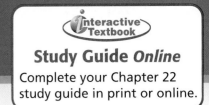

## Chapter Summary

### Section 1
### Adjusting to Peacetime

- A slumping economy and other missteps hurt the Democrats in the election of 1920.
- Scandals marred the Harding administration.
- Calvin Coolidge helped to restore the public trust in government.
- Isolationism and a fear of communism affected U.S. foreign and domestic policy.

### Section 2
### Changes in American Society

- The United States abandoned Prohibition.
- Flappers became the symbol of 1920s women.
- The automobile, radio, and the movies dramatically changed people's lives.
- Tough living conditions in northern cities led many African Americans to accept the black-pride message of Marcus Garvey.

### Section 3
### The Jazz Age

- Jazz gains a worldwide audience.
- Americans celebrated heroes, such as aviator Charles Lindbergh who flew nonstop across the Atlantic.
- Writers such as F. Scott Fitzgerald and Ernest Hemingway criticized the excesses of the period.
- The Harlem Renaissance celebrated African American culture.

### Section 4
### The Economy of the 1920s

- In a time of prosperity, rising stock prices attracted many new investors.
- Farmers and workers did not share in the overall prosperity.
- In 1928, voters elected another Republican President, Herbert Hoover.

## Key Concepts

These notes will help you prepare for questions about key concepts.

**Political and Social Controversy in the 1920s**
- Scandals during Harding's administration
- Isolationism
- Fear of communism and the Red Scare
- Great Migration
- Rebirth of the Ku Klux Klan
- Scopes Trial

**The Changing Economy**
- Support for big business
- Stock market boom
- Buying on credit
- New consumer goods
- Growth of the automobile industry

**The Changing Society**
- African Americans migrate to northern cities
- New roles for women

**A New Culture**
- Jazz
- Movies
- Radio
- Beginning of the Harlem Renaissance
- Rise of a new group of writers who question social values

## Vocabulary *Builder*

### Key Terms

Answer the following questions in complete sentences that show your understanding of the key terms.

1. Why would anarchists oppose the U.S. government?

2. How did communism abroad affect immigrants in the United States?

3. Why did many in the United States support prohibition?

4. How did bootleggers make a living during the 1920s?

5. When would an investor not want to purchase stocks by buying on margin?

## Comprehension and Critical Thinking

6. **(a) Compare** Compare the presidencies of William Harding and Calvin Coolidge.
   **(b) Make Predictions** Who would have made a stronger presidential candidate for the Republicans in the 1924 election, Harding or Coolidge? Why?

7. **(a) Describe** What is an isolationist foreign policy?
   **(b) Evaluate Information** In your opinion, describe whether the United States did or did not have an isolationist foreign policy during the 1920s.

8. **(a) Recall** What action did the U.S. government take against immigrants and foreigners in the 1920s?

**(b) Summarize** Why did the government take those actions against immigrants and foreigners?
**(c) Draw Conclusions** What point of view is represented by the artist who painted the picture of Sacco and Vanzetti shown on this page?

9. **(a) Identify** How did businesses make it easy for people to spend more money during the 1920s?
   **(b) Explain Problems** How did that "easy money" threaten the security of the economy?

## History Reading Skill

10. **Clarify Understanding** Choose one major portion of text from this chapter. Summarize that text, including its main ideas and essential details. Paraphrase to put the ideas into your own words.

## Writing

11. **Write two paragraphs about one of the following topics:**
    - The problems that might arise from an economy built on credit
    - The image of women during the 1920s

    **Your paragraphs should:**
    - include an introduction and a thesis statement;
    - use facts and examples to develop your ideas;
    - end with a sentence that draws a conclusion about your topic.

    When you are finished, exchange papers with another student. Correct errors. Make sure the ideas flow logically.

12. **Write a Magazine Ad:**
    You are a writer for a magazine. The year is 1920. Your assignment is to write the text for an ad for one of the new consumer products (such as a refrigerator or a mah-jongg set).

## Skills for Life

### Interpret Economic Data

Use the graphs on the Skills for Life, "Interpret Economic Data," page to answer the following questions.

13. What happened to personal income between the years 1921 and 1922?

14. Did the average income for farmers follow a similar trend during the years 1921–1922?

15. Which group of Americans had more changes in their incomes during the 1920s? Why do you think this happened?

# Test Yourself

1. **Which term best describes what "Teapot Dome" meant to the Harding administration?**

   **A** boon

   **B** success

   **C** scandal

   **D** annoyance

2. **How does jazz reflect the spirit of the 1920s?**

   **A** Most of the music had a tender, quiet quality.

   **B** The music was based on folk melodies.

   **C** The music was energetic and expressive.

   **D** The music encouraged musicians to play old ballads.

3. **How did magazines, radio, and movies help shape new values during the 1920s?**

   **A** by reminding consumers to save money

   **B** by encouraging consumers to move to the city

   **C** by popularizing the latest products for living the good life

   **D** by encouraging consumers to borrow money

# Document-Based Questions

**Task:** Look at Documents 1 and 2, and answer their accompanying questions. Then, use the documents and your knowledge of history to complete the following writing assignment:

Use the evidence given here to discuss immigration during the early twentieth century. In your essay, explain whether or not you think that people's views have changed since the early 1900s.

**Document 1:**
*What years showed the greatest increase in immigrants to the United States? The greatest decrease?*

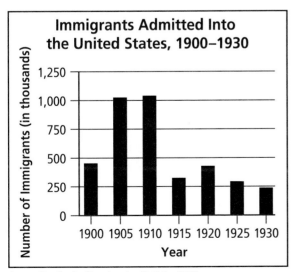

**Immigrants Admitted Into the United States, 1900–1930**

Source: *Yearbook of Immigration Statistics, 2003*

**Document 2:** In 1905, Commissioner General of Immigration Francis Sargent made the comments quoted below. In 1921 and again in 1924, Congress enacted laws that limited the number of immigrants allowed to enter from certain nations. These laws remained in effect until 1965. *What do you think Sargent meant by saying the nation would suffer from indigestion?*

"Put me down in the beginning as being fairly and unalterably opposed to what has been called the open door, for the time has come when every American citizen who is ambitious for the national future must regard with grave misgiving the mighty tide of immigration that, unless something is done, will soon poison or at least pollute the very fountainhead of American life and progress. Big as we are and blessed with an iron constitution, we cannot safely swallow such an endless-course dinner, so to say, without getting indigestion and perhaps national appendicitis."

—Francis Sargent, "Are We Facing an Immigration Peril?" *New York Times,* January 29, 1905

# Writing Workshop

## Writing for Assessment

### ▶ Introduction

In writing for assessment, you write an essay in response to a test question. To write a successful essay, you need to understand what is being asked in the question, answer the question clearly, and support your answer with examples or details. You also need to do all these things within a stated time limit. Essays written for assessment should have the following characteristics:

- a clearly worded thesis statement that answers the question
- strong supporting information that backs up the thesis statement
- a clear, logical organization
- a conclusion that sums up your views

**Assignment** On the following pages, you will learn how to write for assessment by responding in an essay to a test question. You will get step-by-step instructions. Each step will include an example from a sample test essay tracing U.S. involvement in World War I from 1914 to 1917.

Read the instructions and the examples. Then, follow each step to plan and write an essay of 300 to 400 words.

> **Write an essay comparing and contrasting the foreign policies of Presidents Theodore Roosevelt, Woodrow Wilson, and Calvin Coolidge.**

### ▶ Prewriting

**Budget your time.** Before you begin to write an essay, note how much time you have. If the essay question is part of a larger test, check to see what percentage of the test's grade the essay represents. In other words, if the essay counts for 20 percent of the total score, plan to spend 20 percent of your time to write the essay. If you have 30 minutes for your essay, spend about 5 minutes on prewriting (understanding the question, writing a thesis statement, and creating a rough outline); from 20 to 25 minutes on actually writing the essay; and from 2 to 5 minutes on reading over the essay and making revisions and corrections.

**Understand the essay-question prompt.** Begin by looking closely at the essay-question prompt and identifying the key words. The chart on the facing page shows examples of key words most often used in essay prompts.

> For a review of the steps in the writing process, see the **Historian's Toolkit, *Write Like a Historian.***

| Essay Question Prompts | |
|---|---|
| **Key Word** | **What It Means** |
| analyze | break the topic down into its parts; show causes and effects |
| compare | show how two or more things are similar |
| contrast | show how two or more things are different |
| defend | support an argument or position with facts, reasons, examples, and logic |
| define | state the meaning of a term; describe the basic nature of something |
| discuss | make observations about a subject in detail (similar to *examine* and *explain*) |
| evaluate | judge the significance, condition, or worth of something |
| summarize | give a condensed account or overview of an issue, event, or sequence of events |
| trace | describe a sequence of events; follow the development or progress of something |

When you read the essay question, underline or circle the key words, as well as the subject and time period you are to discuss and any special areas the prompt asks you to cover.

---

**Sample essay question:**

key word         subject             areas to cover
Trace the U.S. involvement in World War I, from neutrality to entrance

           time period
into the war, from 1914 to 1917.

---

**Write a thesis statement.** Based on your knowledge, write a sentence that clearly responds to the prompt. As in any other piece of writing, your thesis statement should present the main idea of your essay.

**Note your main points in a rough outline.** Create a quick outline that lists the main points you expect to cover in the order that you expect to follow. Be sure that your outline reflects the essay question prompt. For example, if the prompt asks you to "trace" something, you may want to use chronological order.

**Sample thesis statement:**
The United States had been neutral when war broke out in 1914, but entry to the war seemed inevitable by the spring of 1917 because a series of incidents had pushed the nation into the conflict.

## ▶ Drafting

**Write a short introductory paragraph.** In the first paragraph of your essay, introduce your subject and write your thesis statement.

**Support your thesis with examples and details.** Devote one body paragraph to each of the main points in your outline. Make sure you cover everything that the prompt requests. Include relevant, accurate information to develop each point you discuss.

**Write a strong conclusion.** In your final paragraph, sum up your support of your thesis statement.

# Writing Workshop *continued*

## ▶ Model Essay

Read the following model of an essay discussing the involvement of the United States in World War I from 1914 to 1917. Notice how it includes the characteristics you have learned about.

### The United States and the War in Europe, 1914–1917

> The thesis statement identifies the main idea about U.S. isolationism before WW I and hints at why the United States entered the war.

In the fall of 1914, Americans felt far removed from the European rush to war. By the spring of 1917, however, everything had changed. In less than three years, a string of events had pulled a reluctant United States into joining the battle in Europe.

Before the war, the United States had followed a policy of isolationism, keeping itself out of the complicated system of European alliances. President Wilson insisted on U.S. neutrality when the war started.

Despite its neutrality, the United States traded more with the Allies than with the Central powers. When Germany began to blockade Britain with U-boats, American ships were affected. In 1915, the sinking of the *Lusitania*, a British passenger ship with more than 100 Americans aboard, increased anti-German sentiment in the United States.

> Examples and details in these paragraphs support the thesis. Words highlighted in yellow show how chronology was used to trace the events.

In 1916, President Woodrow Wilson was reelected with the campaign slogan, "He kept us out of war." Wilson tried to convince the warring European countries to end the fighting. However, Wilson's efforts failed.

The tide in America turned toward war in early 1917 when the Zimmermann telegram came to light. Germany had secretly offered to help Mexico seize southwestern U.S. states if Mexico joined the Central powers. Americans were outraged.

> The conclusion reviews the content of the essay and restates the thesis.

So, it is not surprising that Congress voted overwhelmingly in favor of entering the war in April, 1917. The nation discovered that the ocean separating it from Europe could not guarantee protection from war.

# ▶ Revising

After completing your draft, read it again carefully to find ways to make your writing better. Here are some questions to ask yourself.

## Revise to strengthen your thesis
- Do the introduction and the thesis statement clearly respond to the prompt?
- Do the body paragraphs cover the issues set forth in the prompt and develop the thesis statement?
- Does the conclusion tie up the essay?

## Revise to use varied and clear vocabulary and helpful transitions
- Does the essay avoid repetition?
- Does the essay include transitions showing relationships appropriate to the key words in the prompt?

## Revise to meet written English-language conventions
- Are all sentences complete, with a subject and a verb?
- Are all the words spelled correctly?
- Are all proper nouns capitalized?
- Are all sentences punctuated properly?

# ▶ Rubric for Self-Assessment

*Evaluate your essay written for assessment using the following rating scale:*

|  | Score 4 | Score 3 | Score 2 | Score 1 |
|---|---|---|---|---|
| **Organization** | Supports the thesis with logically ordered paragraphs covering the areas specified in the prompt; paragraphs have an organizing principle that suits the prompt | Uses a reasonably clear organization but occasionally fails to follow it or includes less relevant information | Chooses an organization not suited to the topic (for example, uses chronological order for a comparison-and-contrast essay) | Shows lack of organizational strategy |
| **Presentation** | Clearly and accurately responds to the prompt and covers the areas specified in the prompt; uses facts, examples, and reasons intelligently to support the thesis; clearly links all supporting information to the thesis | Responds to the prompt accurately and covers the areas specified but does not go into greater depth; links most but not all supporting information to the thesis; could use more support | Responds to the prompt accurately but does not cover all the areas requested; includes some incorrect supporting information; does not link supporting information to the thesis | Does not respond accurately to the prompt; does not include a thesis; fails to provide any facts, reasons, or examples to support the thesis |
| **Use of Language** | Varies sentence structure and vocabulary successfully; includes almost no mechanical errors | Uses some variety in sentence structure and vocabulary; includes several mechanical errors | Uses the same types of sentences without varying them; repeats words; includes many mechanical errors | Writes incomplete sentences; uses language poorly; sounds confused; includes many mechanical errors |

# Unit 8

**Dust Bowl and Depression** Economic disaster coupled with drought in the prairies caused enormous hardships for Americans all over the country.

## 1930s

We Can Do It!

**United States Joins the Fighting in World War II** Americans contributed in many ways to the war effort during World War II. Thousands of soldiers fought in foreign lands, while many who stayed behind—including thousands of women—worked in war industries.

## 1941

# Depression and War

**President Roosevelt Launches the New Deal** President Franklin D. Roosevelt made frequent radio addresses to the American people. He explained his plans for improving the economy through numerous programs known as the New Deal.

## 1933

**Berlin Airlift** When East Germany closed off all access to the city of Berlin, the United States and other nations joined together to supply the city with food and other necessities.

## 1948

CHAPTER
# 23 | The Great Depression and the New Deal
## 1929–1941

## Chapter Preview

In 1929, the nation was hit with the most severe economic crisis in its history. During the Great Depression, millions of people lost their jobs, homes, and savings. A new President, Franklin Roosevelt, took sweeping measures that increased the size and power of the federal government.

**U.S. Events**

**1929**
Stock market crash marks the beginning of the Great Depression.

**1929**

**1933**
Franklin Roosevelt becomes President, launches the New Deal.

**1932**

**1935**
Congress passes Social Security Act.

**1935**

**World Events**

**1930** Depression spreads to Europe and Asia.

**1933** Adolf Hitler comes to power in Germany.

The Great Depression threw millions of Americans, such as this little girl, into poverty and homelessness.

**Quick View Video**
View the chapter video for a quick preview of the main ideas.

**1935**
John L. Lewis founds Comittee for Industrial Organization (CIO).

**1939**
John Steinbeck publishes *The Grapes of Wrath*.

**1941**
Great Depression ends as United States prepares for war.

1935

1938

1941

**1937** Japan invades China.

**1939** World War II begins in Europe.

## History Reading Skill  Analyze Cause and Effect

## What was life like during the Depression?

In this chapter, you will learn how to analyze cause-and-effect relationships. Read the following description of a young girl's life in the 1930s. The side notes show you how to analyze cause-and-effect relationships.

After the good times of the 1920s came the very bad times of the Great Depression. In this passage, a young girl describes the effect of the Depression on her family.

**Primary Source**

"It was a small mine under a big hill. . . . My father took me to work in the mine dressed up like a boy. . . . I wore shoes like the Boy Scouts, with a little knife in the side. . . . I liked going off to the mine in boys' clothes, with my hair cut short. It made me feel good to know I could help the family. . . . Before we went in, my father would set his pick upright and lay his leather cap over it. We knelt down on the dirt while he said a prayer in Slovak [their native language] to ask God to protect us underground. He'd do the same thing at the end of the day, to give thanks that we had come out safely. . . . We dug coal to buy flour, salt, sugar, and other essentials. . . . We'd trade coal. . . . for groceries. . . . My father could have gotten arrested for having a girl in the mine, but I never got caught."

Effect

Cause

Effect

Cause

Desired effect

Cause

—Elizabeth Zofchak, *Girls, A History of Growing Up Female in America*

## Analyze Cause and Effect
- Ask yourself: What caused this to happen?
- Make sentences that show cause-and-effect relationships: _____ *caused* _____ *to happen* or _____ *happened because of* _____.
- Remember that some causes have multiple effects and some effects have multiple causes.

## Document-Based Questions
1. What experience does the author describe?
2. How does she feel about this experience?
3. Do you think this experience was unusual for the time? Why or why not?

# Vocabulary *Builder*

## Previewing High-Use Academic Words

| High-Use Word | Definition | Sample History Sentence |
|---|---|---|
| **decline** (dee KLĪN) (Section 1, p. 770) | ***v.*** to lose strength or power over time | The Populist Party <u>declined</u> after the election of 1896. |
| **voluntary** (VAHL ahn tair ee) (Section 1, p. 775) | ***adj.*** not forced; done of one's own free will | Without a draft law, registration for the armed forces was completely <u>voluntary</u>. |
| **specify** (SPEHS ah fī) (Section 2, p. 777) | ***v.*** to name or describe in exact detail | In the Fourteen Points, Woodrow Wilson <u>specified</u> his goals for world peace. |
| **infrastructure** (IHN frah struhk chahr) (Section 2, p. 778) | ***n.*** underlying foundation on which a community or nation depends, such as its roads, bridges, etc. | Henry Clay's American system was designed to improve the nation's <u>infrastructure</u> by building roads and canals. |
| **domestic** (doh MEHS tihk) (Section 3, p. 782) | ***adj.*** having to do with the home or housework | The majority of American women spent most of their time on <u>domestic</u> duties. |
| **confer** (kahn FER) (Section 3, p. 783) | ***v.*** to exchange ideas with someone | The President <u>confers</u> with his Cabinet on important issues. |
| **minimum** (MIHN ah muhm) (Section 4, p. 791) | ***adj.*** smallest or least required or allowed | The <u>minimum</u> age for the President is 35 years. |
| **fundamental** (fuhn duh MEHN tahl) (Section 4, p. 793) | ***adj.*** basic; essential; most important | Freedom of speech is one of the <u>fundamental</u> rights guaranteed by the Constitution. |

John Steinbeck

## Previewing Key Terms and People

# Hoover and the Crash

## Objectives

1. Read about America's economic problems during the late 1920s.
2. Understand how the Great Depression started.
3. Find out how the Depression affected Americans.
4. Discover President Hoover's response to the Depression.

## Prepare to Read

### Reading Skill

**Analyze Causes** Analyzing causes will help you to understand the *why* and *how* of history. As you read the following section, try to answer the question: What caused the Great Depression to start? Remember that many causes can combine to yield one effect.

### Vocabulary *Builder*

**High-Use Words**

decline, p. 770

voluntary, p. 775

**Key Terms**

overproduction, p. 771

bankruptcy, p. 772

default, p. 772

bonus, p. 775

⭐ **Background Knowledge** As you have read in Chapter 22, the 1920s were a time of prosperity and a booming stock market. However, not everyone shared in the prosperity, and much of the boom was based on shaky practices such as buying on margin. In this section, you will see how the prosperity of the 1920s collapsed.

## A Collapsing Economy

In 1928, Herbert Hoover had predicted that the United States would soon achieve the "final triumph over poverty." In fact, the country was heading for the worst economic crisis in its history.

**Signs of Weakness** Several signs of economic weakness surfaced during the late 1920s. Older industries, such as coal mining, railroads, and clothing manufacture, were in decline. Agriculture was also experiencing a prolonged downturn.

Yet, as sections of the economy declined, stock prices continued to soar. As you have read, margin buying allowed people to purchase stocks by paying only a fraction of the cost at the outset and owing the balance. Margin buyers gambled that prices would be higher when they were ready to sell. The gamble seemed to pay off—for a while.

**The Stock Market Crashes** The prices for industrial stocks doubled between May 1928 and September 1929. But soon after, prices began a rapid slide. On Wednesday, October 23, six million shares of stock changed hands. Falling prices caused losses of $4 billion. Brokers who had lent people money to buy on margin now began to recall their loans. Investors who could not pay had to sell their stocks. This caused prices to drop even more.

### Main Idea

A series of economic weaknesses led to the collapse of the stock market in October 1929.

### Vocabulary *Builder*

decline (dee KLĪN) *v.* to lose strength or power over time

On October 29, 1929—known as Black Tuesday—the stock market crumbled completely. Panicked traders rushed to sell, but there were no buyers. Prices plummeted. Investors who thought they owned valuable shares of stock were left with worthless pieces of paper. Millionaires lost their fortunes overnight.

Over the next two weeks, stock prices continued to plunge. "Everybody wanted to tell his neighbor how much he had lost," observed a reporter for the *New York Times*. "Nobody wanted to listen. It was too repetitious a tale."

☑ **Checkpoint**  **What happened on Black Tuesday?**

## The Great Depression Begins

The stock market crash marked the start of a 12-year economic and social disaster known as the Great Depression. The crash, however, was less a cause than a symptom of a deepening crisis.

**Troubled Industries** One major cause of the Great Depression was **overproduction,** a situation in which the supply of manufactured goods exceeds the demand. Factories were producing more than people could afford to buy. With prices rising faster than salaries, many Americans cut back on their purchases.

At the same time, housing and automobile manufacture were in decline. These industries had supported American prosperity during the 1920s. By the end of the decade, though, most Americans who could afford houses and cars had already bought them. Between 1926 and 1929, spending on construction fell from $11 billion to $9 billion. In the first nine months of 1929, car sales dropped by more than one third.

**Main Idea**
Overproduction and bank failures contributed to a worsening economic crisis.

**The Stock Market Crash**
Screaming newspaper headlines announced the stock market crash of October 1929. Giant fortunes were lost overnight.
**Critical Thinking:** *Evaluate Information What is the young man in this picture trying to do? Do you think he will be successful? Explain.*

**Analyze Causes**
Identify two sentences on this page or the previous page that give causes of the Depression.

**Crisis in Banking** A nationwide banking crisis also contributed to the Depression. In the countryside, struggling farmers were finding it impossible to repay their bank loans. When their farms failed, many of the small banks that had loaned farmers money also went out of business.

City banks failed, too. Some of the largest banks had invested in the stock market or loaned huge amounts to speculators. After the crash, terrified depositors flocked into banks, demanding to withdraw their savings. More than 5,500 banks closed between 1930 and 1933. Many depositors were left penniless.

**The Downward Spiral** With people unable to buy what factories were producing, many workers lost their jobs. Thus, they had even less money with which to make purchases. In a vicious circle, declining sales led to more factory closings and layoffs. Many companies were forced into bankruptcy. Bankruptcy is financial failure caused by a company's inability to pay its debts. These bankruptcies, of course, caused even more layoffs.

The Great Depression soon spread worldwide. After World War I, many European nations owed America huge sums of money. A slowdown in international trade, however, caused these countries to default, or fail to repay their loans. European nations sank into their own economic depression.

☑ **Checkpoint**  **How did the Depression spread overseas?**

**Main Idea**
During the Great Depression, unemployment rose and millions of people faced poverty.

# The Human Cost

The Great Depression severely affected more people than any previous downturn. During earlier depressions, most Americans still lived on farms. They could feed their families in times of crisis. By 1930, however, far more Americans lived in cities and worked in factories or offices. When factories or businesses closed, the jobless had no money for food and no land on which to grow food.

**The Unemployed** Between 1929 and 1933, the unemployment rate skyrocketed from 3 percent to 25 percent. Nationwide, some 13 million people were unemployed. Some cities were harder hit than others. In Toledo, Ohio, four out of five workers had no work.

People lucky enough to have jobs saw their hours cut back and their salaries slashed. Coal miners who had earned $7 a day before the Depression now fought for the chance to work for a dollar.

**Growing Poverty** Grinding poverty crushed Americans' spirits. In cities, jobless people lined up at soup kitchens, waiting for meals. People tried to sell apples or pencils on the street or to pick up trash for food. Some men hopped freight trains in search of work.

On the outskirts of big cities, homeless people built communities of rundown shacks. They called these makeshift towns Hoovervilles, because they blamed the President for failing to solve the crisis. They slept under "Hoover blankets," or newspapers.

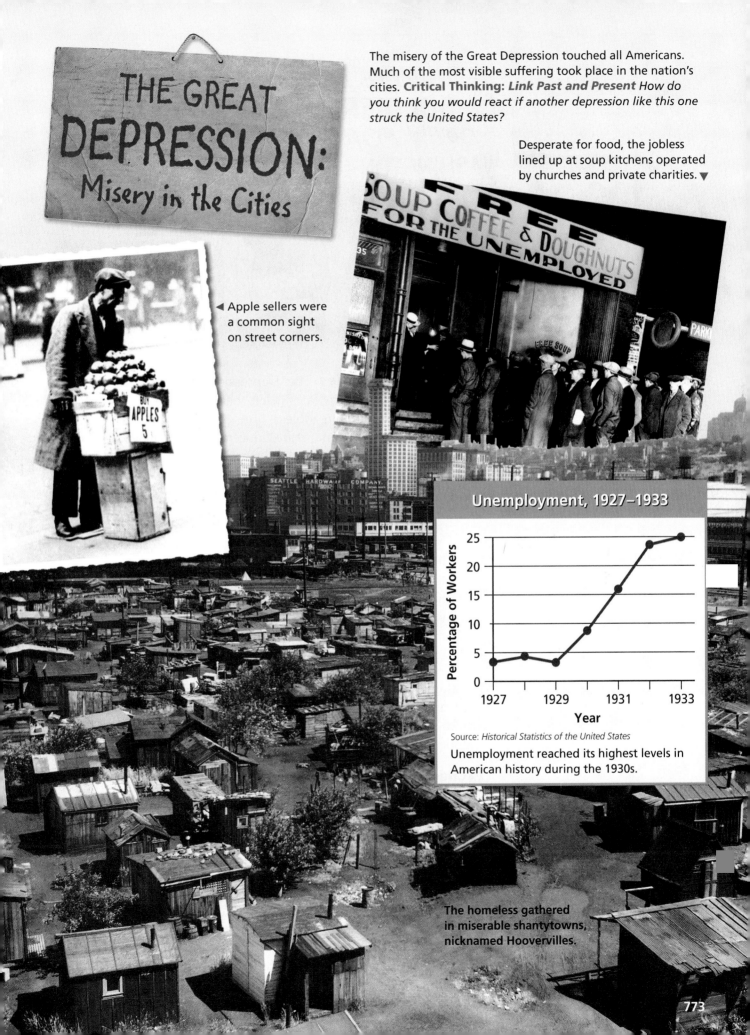

# THE GREAT DEPRESSION: Misery in the Cities

The misery of the Great Depression touched all Americans. Much of the most visible suffering took place in the nation's cities. **Critical Thinking:** *Link Past and Present How do you think you would react if another depression like this one struck the United States?*

Desperate for food, the jobless lined up at soup kitchens operated by churches and private charities. ▼

◄ Apple sellers were a common sight on street corners.

FREE SOUP COFFEE & DOUGHNUTS FOR THE UNEMPLOYED

## Unemployment, 1927–1933

Source: *Historical Statistics of the United States*

Unemployment reached its highest levels in American history during the 1930s.

The homeless gathered in miserable shantytowns, nicknamed Hoovervilles.

**The Bonus Army**

In 1932, these World War I veterans headed for Washington, D.C., to demand their bonus. **Critical Thinking: *Evaluate Information*** *What is the meaning of the poster on the right for the years 1918 and 1932?*

**Impact on Families** The Depression had a harsh effect on American families. Many fathers left their homes in search of work. Others, ashamed of being jobless, quit looking for work or deserted their families. With their futures uncertain, young people put off marriage plans. When couples did marry, they had fewer children.

For children, the Depression brought both hardship and a sense of uncertainty. One woman recalled that, after her father lost his job, her family had to move into a garage heated only by a coal stove:

> **❝**In the morning, we'd get out and get some snow and put it on the stove and melt it and wash around our faces. Never the neck or anything. Put on our two pairs of socks on each hand and two pairs of socks on our feet, and long underwear and lace it up with Goodwill shoes. Off we'd walk, three, four miles to school.**❞**
>
> —Dynamite Garland, quoted in *Hard Times* (Terkel)

Many children suffered lifelong health problems from a lack of food and dental care. Their education suffered as cash-strapped school boards cut the school year or closed schools. Almost one million rural children under the age of 13 did not attend school at all.

**✓Checkpoint** What were Hoovervilles?

## Hoover Responds

**Main Idea**
President Hoover's efforts to solve the Great Depression did not succeed.

As you saw, many Americans blamed President Hoover for the worsening crisis. Hoover's advisers considered the Depression a temporary setback. They recommended doing nothing.

**Government Aid** Hoover disagreed. After his brilliant career in mining and foreign aid administration, he believed in taking action. However, he thought business leaders and local governments should take the lead, rather than the federal government.

Hoover met with business executives and encouraged city and state governments to create public works projects to employ jobless people. He also urged private charities to set up soup kitchens.

Eventually, Hoover realized that <u>voluntary</u> action alone would not relieve the crisis. In 1932, he formed the Reconstruction Finance Corporation (RFC) to fund critical businesses, such as banks, insurance companies, and railroads. The RFC also gave money to local governments to fund public-works projects. Despite such measures, the economic situation continued to worsen.

**The Bonus Army** In June 1932, a protest began that would seal the President's fate. Eight years earlier, Congress had approved a bonus, or extra payment, of $1,000 for every veteran of World War I. This bonus was not to be paid until 1945. Made desperate by the Depression, some veterans demanded immediate payment.

When Hoover refused, an angry "Bonus Army" of at least 20,000 veterans marched to Washington, where they camped out. But Congress also rejected their plea. Most marchers left, but about 2,000 stubbornly remained in tents or abandoned buildings. To clear them out, government forces used tear gas, tanks, and machine guns. This lopsided attack killed at least one veteran, injured 100, and left the tent city a smoldering ruin. Many Americans were outraged by the image of government forces firing on unarmed veterans.

☑Checkpoint   **What was the goal of the Bonus Army?**

⭐ **Looking Back and Ahead**  The treatment of the Bonus Army further damaged Hoover's fading popularity. In the next section, you will see how voters turned to a dynamic new leader.

Vocabulary *Builder*
**voluntary** (VAHL ahn tair ee) *adj.* not forced; done of one's own free will

---

Section 1 | **Check Your Progress**

**Progress Monitoring** ⬤nline
**For:** Self-test with instant help
**Visit:** PHSchool.com
**Web Code:** mva-8231

## Comprehension and Critical Thinking

**1. (a) List** List the major troubles that industries faced in the Great Depression.
**(b) Analyze Cause and Effect** How did those troubles cost people their jobs?

**2. (a) Describe** What actions did President Hoover take to try to ease the economic crisis?
**(b) Detect Points of View** Why do you think Hoover wanted business leaders and local governments to take the lead?

## ↻ Reading Skill

**3. Analyze Causes** Reread the text following the subheading "The Downward Spiral." Identify the causes in this downward spiral.

## Vocabulary *Builder*

Answer the following questions in complete sentences that show your understanding of the key terms.
**4.** How can overproduction hurt the economy?
**5.** When would a company declare bankruptcy?
**6.** What happens when a company or individual defaults on a loan?

## Writing

**7.** Review this section, including photos and other visual elements. List three possible topics for a multimedia presentation that includes non-print media such as photographs, sound recordings, interviews, computer presentations, and film. Choose one of the three topics and write a sentence describing the topic and the kinds of materials you might use in your presentation.

## Objectives

1. Learn how Franklin Roosevelt won the 1932 presidential election.

2. Find out how the New Deal tried to promote economic recovery.

3. Understand what new laws regulated America's economic system.

4. Identify obstacles and criticisms faced by the New Deal.

## Prepare to Read

### Reading Skill

**Evaluate Causes and Effects**
When events have multiple effects, some may be positive and others negative. As you read the following section, look for events that have multiple effects or trigger cause-and-effect chains. Decide if you think the effects are positive or negative.

### Vocabulary *Builder*

**High-Use Words**
**specify**, p. 777
**infrastructure**, p. 778

**Key Terms and People**
Franklin D. Roosevelt, p. 776
fireside chat, p. 777
Huey Long, p. 781
Francis Townsend, p. 781
pension, p. 781
Charles Coughlin, p. 781

⭐ **Background Knowledge** In the last section, you learned how the Great Depression began. In this section, you will see how a new President tried to deal forcefully with the crisis.

**Main Idea**
In 1932, voters elected a new President, Franklin Roosevelt, who promised to take action against the Depression.

## Franklin D. Roosevelt

The Democrats nominated Franklin D. Roosevelt to run against Hoover in 1932. He became known to Americans as FDR.

**Background** FDR was a wealthy New Yorker and distant relative of Theodore Roosevelt. He had served as assistant secretary of the navy and was nominated for Vice President in 1920.

A year later, Roosevelt was stricken with polio, a deadly disease. For the rest of his life, he depended on steel leg braces to stand up. Determined to appear strong, Roosevelt never allowed photographers to take his picture in a wheelchair. In fact, most Americans never knew that Roosevelt's legs were paralyzed.

In 1928, he was elected governor of New York. Four years later, the Democrats tapped the popular governor to run for President.

**A Voice of Hope** During the campaign, Roosevelt pledged "a new deal for the American people." The term *New Deal* would later come to describe his entire political program. The election results were overwhelming. Roosevelt beat Hoover by a margin of 472 electoral votes to 59. Roosevelt received 57.4 percent of the popular vote.

Roosevelt bumper sticker

On March 4, 1933, supported on his son's arm, Roosevelt slowly shuffled a few steps to the platform. After taking the oath of office, the new President reassured Americans:

> "This great Nation will endure as it has endured, will revive and will prosper. So, first of all, let me assert my firm belief that the only thing we have to fear is fear itself—nameless, unreasoning, unjustified terror which paralyzes needed efforts to convert retreat into advance."
>
> —Franklin Roosevelt, First Inaugural Address, 1933

FDR did not <u>specify</u> what actions he would take. Still, the American people were encouraged by the new President's confidence.

**Vocabulary** *Builder*
**specify** (SPEHS ah fī) *v.* to name or describe in exact detail

**Bank Holiday** An optimistic FDR quickly went into action. The day after he took office, Roosevelt declared a bank holiday, a four-day closing of the nation's banks. Its goal was to halt the nationwide epidemic of bank failures. The bank holiday gave FDR time to propose an Emergency Banking Relief Act, which provided more careful government regulation of banks.

To restore Americans' confidence in their banks, Roosevelt delivered the first of many fireside chats, or radio talks. He told Americans, "It is safer to keep your money in a reopened bank than under the mattress." The next day, most of the nation's banks reopened. A relieved public began to redeposit its savings.

☑**Checkpoint** **What was the goal of FDR's bank holiday?**

# Relief for the Jobless

To decide what legislation to send to Congress, FDR conferred with a group of advisers. FDR's advisers were nicknamed the "brain trust" because several members had been college professors.

**Main Idea**
One goal of the New Deal was to provide jobs for the unemployed.

**History** *Interactive*
**Explore the Presidency of FDR**
**Visit:** PHSchool.com
**Web Code:** mvl-8231

## Fireside Chat

This coal miner (right) listens intently to a fireside chat by President Franklin Roosevelt (left). A friend of FDR said, "His face would smile and light up as though he were actually sitting on the front porch or in the parlor with them." **Critical Thinking:** *Link Past and Present How do Presidents communicate their ideas to the American people today?*

CCC badge (top) and WPA poster (bottom)

**Main Idea**
Other New Deal programs were aimed to help industry and tackle rural poverty.

During the whirlwind first hundred days of FDR's administration, Congress passed and the President signed a record 15 new bills. These New Deal measures had three goals: (1) relief for the jobless, (2) economic recovery, and (3) reforms to prevent future depressions.

**Unemployment Relief** Some measures helped the unemployed by providing financial assistance. The Federal Emergency Relief Administration, or FERA, granted funds to states so they could reopen shuttered relief agencies.

**Providing Jobs** Other programs employed jobless adults. The Civilian Conservation Corps (CCC) hired city dwellers to work in America's national parks, forests, wilderness areas, and countryside. Millions of young men planted trees, built reservoirs, constructed parks, and dug irrigation canals. In addition to providing jobs, the CCC conserved the nation's natural resources.

Another program, the Works Progress Administration (WPA), put people to work building or repairing public buildings, such as schools, post offices, and government offices. WPA workers paved 650,000 miles of roads, raised more than 75,000 bridges, and built more than 800 airports. The WPA also paid artists to paint murals in post offices and government buildings and hired writers to write stories, state guides, and histories.

☑**Checkpoint** **How did the CCC and WPA help the jobless?**

## Promoting Economic Recovery

In 1933, the President faced an enormous challenge. He needed to help two sectors of the economy recover: industry and agriculture.

**National Recovery Administration** As you saw, one of the causes of the Depression had been overproduction. Some competing businesses lured consumers by slashing prices. As a result, they had to lay off workers or cut wages.

A new federal agency, the National Recovery Administration (NRA) aimed to keep prices stable while boosting employment and buying power. Most of the country's major industries agreed to pay workers a minimum wage, to stop hiring children, and to keep wages and prices from falling too low.

The NRA succeeded in raising prices. However, critics charged that the agency's codes favored large businesses. More important, the NRA failed to improve the economy.

**Public Works Administration** Another agency, the Public Works Administration (PWA), was granted more than $3 billion to build large public-works projects. The PWA improved the nation's infrastructure and employed many people.

PWA projects included New York's Lincoln Tunnel, Florida's Key West Highway, and the Grand Coulee Dam in Washington. In fact, nearly every county in the nation could boast at least one PWA project. Even so, the Great Depression continued.

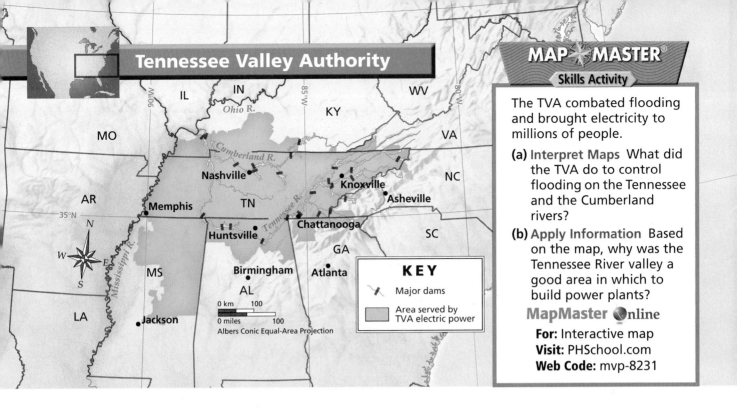

## Tennessee Valley Authority

**MAP MASTER®**
**Skills Activity**

The TVA combated flooding and brought electricity to millions of people.

**(a) Interpret Maps** What did the TVA do to control flooding on the Tennessee and the Cumberland rivers?

**(b) Apply Information** Based on the map, why was the Tennessee River valley a good area in which to build power plants?

**MapMaster ○nline**

**For:** Interactive map
**Visit:** PHSchool.com
**Web Code:** mvp-8231

**KEY**

⚒ Major dams

▨ Area served by TVA electric power

0 km    100
0 miles    100
Albers Conic Equal-Area Projection

**Tennessee Valley Authority** In 1933, Congress formed the Tennessee Valley Authority (TVA). This agency built giant dams along the Tennessee River. Planners believed that these dams would control flooding, provide cheap electricity, and increase jobs and prosperity in one of the country's poorest rural areas.

The TVA accomplished its major goals. By 1945, power from TVA plants lit thousands of farms that had never before enjoyed electricity. Still, the TVA failed to relieve the region's poverty. Conservatives criticized the TVA for driving some property owners off their land. They also argued that it was unfair for the government to compete with private power companies.

More recently, other critics have claimed that the TVA disrupted the natural environment and that some TVA projects led to increased air pollution. Still, in the 1930s, the popular TVA seemed to symbolize government planning at its best.

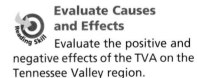

**Evaluate Causes and Effects**

Evaluate the positive and negative effects of the TVA on the Tennessee Valley region.

☑**Checkpoint**   **What was the goal of the NRA?**

## Reforming the Economic System

The third part of Roosevelt's plan—reforming the economic system—aimed to prevent future depressions. The Truth-in-Securities Act, for example, required corporations to inform the public fully about their stocks. This act corrected one of the conditions that had contributed to the stock market crash.

The Federal Deposit Insurance Corporation (FDIC), created in 1933, protected bank depositors. It guaranteed individual deposits up to $2,500. By raising public confidence in banks, the FDIC stemmed the tide of bank failures.

**Main Idea**
The third goal of the New Deal was to prevent another depression.

FDR beats a drum labeled "New Deal."

This man is Chief Justice Charles Evans Hughes.

**Reading Political Cartoons**

**Skills Activity**

Congress passed most New Deal legislation. However, the Supreme Court overturned some key measures. This cartoon is based on a famous painting about the American Revolution.

**(a) Interpret Cartoons** What do the three figures represent? What seems to be the attitude of FDR and Hughes toward each other?

**(b) Draw Conclusions** Summarize the main idea of this cartoon.

Other New Deal agencies set fairness and safety standards for various industries. The Federal Power Commission (FPC), for example, helped control the oil and gas industries. The New Deal also strengthened the power of the Food and Drug Administration to ensure product safety.

☑ **Checkpoint** How did the FDIC protect bank depositors?

**Main Idea**

New Deal programs were challenged by the Supreme Court and by a number of critics.

## Obstacles to the New Deal

Millions of Americans were enthusiastic about the New Deal. As a result, FDR won reelection in 1936 by a wide margin. Still, the New Deal faced a major challenge in the Supreme Court.

**Supreme Court** In 1935 and 1936, the Supreme Court declared several New Deal measures, including the NRA, to be unconstitutional. In response, Roosevelt proposed appointing up to six new Supreme Court justices. He claimed that he wanted to relieve the overworked judges. However, conservatives protested. They understood that FDR had designed this "court-packing plan" to gain a majority of justices.

Congress embarrassed the President by defeating his plan. Even so, FDR won a backdoor victory. When a conservative justice resigned in 1937, Roosevelt appointed a liberal in his place. FDR eventually named eight Supreme Court justices.

**New Deal Critics** Conservatives claimed that the New Deal went too far in regulating businesses and restricting individual freedom. On the other hand, some liberals thought it did not go far enough in helping the poor.

Three New Deal critics attracted widespread attention and some national support. Huey Long, a Democratic senator from Louisiana, argued that the government could end the Depression immediately. Long proposed to tax the wealthy and distribute their wealth to the poor. Long's radio speeches on behalf of what he called the Share Our Wealth plan won many enthusiastic followers.

A California doctor, Francis Townsend, called for a system of government pensions, or retirement payments. Under Townsend's plan, retired Americans over the age of 60 would receive $200 each month as long as they pledged to spend all the money. Congress never approved the Townsend plan, but it later helped set the stage for the government-supported pensions of the Social Security system. You will read about Social Security in Section 4.

Like Huey Long, Father Charles Coughlin used the radio to attract followers. A Catholic priest from Michigan, Coughlin came to distrust Roosevelt's policies on banking and money. Coughlin called on the government to take over the banks.

Supporters of Long, Townsend, and Coughlin eventually joined forces to back a third-party candidate in the 1936 election. However, they were not strong enough to combat FDR's popularity.

Huey Long addresses a rally in Louisiana.

✓**Checkpoint** **Why did FDR try to increase the size of the Supreme Court?**

⭐ **Looking Back and Ahead** In this section, you have read how Roosevelt tried to tackle the problems of the Great Depression. In the next section, you will see how the Depression affected American life.

## Section 2 | Check Your Progress

**Progress Monitoring** Online
**For:** Self-test with instant help
**Visit:** PHSchool.com
**Web Code:** mva-8232

**Comprehension and Critical Thinking**

**1. (a) Recall** What were the three goals of the New Deal?
**(b) Organize Information** Categorize five New Deal measures according to these three goals.

**2. (a) Recall** How did the Supreme Court threaten the New Deal?
**(b) Draw Inferences** How might Roosevelt's response have threatened separation of powers in the federal government?

**Reading Skill**
**3. Evaluate Causes and Effects** Reread the text under the heading "Relief for the Jobless." Evaluate the positive or negative effects of FDR's plan to help the poor and unemployed.

**Vocabulary *Builder***
Read each sentence below. If the sentence is true, write YES and explain why. If the sentence is not true, write NO and explain why.

**4.** Townsend's pension plan forced retired people to pay higher taxes.
**5.** In his fireside chats, FDR explained his programs directly to the American people.

**Writing**
**6.** List two topics for a multimedia presentation about Franklin Roosevelt's presidency.

# SECTION 3 | Life in the Great Depression

## Objectives

1. Discover how the Great Depression and the New Deal affected women, African Americans, Mexican Americans, and Native Americans.

2. Learn about the causes and effects of the Dust Bowl.

3. Understand how art, radio, and movies informed and entertained people during the Depression.

## Prepare to Read

### 🔊 Reading Skill

**Analyze Effects** Effects are the results of an action, event, or attitude. Often an action, event, or attitude will have several effects. Certainly, the events of the Great Depression had dramatic effects on American business, families, and culture. As you read this section, ask yourself: What happened to businesses and individuals because of these events? How did American culture change because of these events?

### Vocabulary *Builder*

**High-Use Words**

domestic, p. 782

confer, p. 783

### Key Terms and People

Eleanor Roosevelt, p. 783

civil rights, p. 784

Mary McLeod Bethune, p. 784

Marian Anderson, p. 784

migrant worker, p. 784

John Collier, p. 785

John Steinbeck, p. 786

---

⭐ **Background Knowledge** In Section 2, you saw how the New Deal attempted to relieve hard times. In this section, you will see how the Great Depression and New Deal affected everyday life.

## Women in the Depression

**Main Idea**
During the Depression, many women had to find ways to help support their families.

With so many men out of work, many Americans felt that women should stay at home. Yet, women often had to help support themselves or their families. By the end of the Great Depression, more women were working outside the home than at the start.

**Women in the Workplace** Women enjoyed two small advantages in the workplace. Female salesclerks and secretaries faced little competition from men. In addition, such jobs were less likely to disappear than the factory jobs many men held.

Still, most women with jobs struggled. For example, women who had trained to become schoolteachers or librarians suddenly found themselves competing for jobs with men who had lost other work. Female factory workers were more likely than men to lose their jobs or to have their wages cut. Many maids, seamstresses, and housekeepers also lost their jobs because fewer people could afford domestic help. African American women were especially hard hit because they held the majority of domestic jobs.

**Vocabulary** *Builder*
domestic (doh MEHS tihk) *adj.*
having to do with the home or housework

The Great Depression complicated life for most women, whether or not they worked outside the home. To save money, more women found themselves sewing clothes, canning fruits and vegetables, and baking bread instead of buying it.

**An Active First Lady** The most famous working woman in the country was FDR's wife, Eleanor Roosevelt. After polio had stricken her husband in 1921, Mrs. Roosevelt overcame her shyness to begin speaking and traveling on his behalf.

Eleanor Roosevelt helped transform the role of First Lady. The wives of earlier Presidents had hosted teas and stayed in the background. By contrast, the energetic Mrs. Roosevelt crisscrossed the country, serving as the President's "eyes and ears." Then, she conferred with FDR on what she had seen and what he should do. In 1933 alone, Eleanor Roosevelt logged 40,000 miles, including a trip down into a West Virginia coal mine. She also made frequent radio speeches and wrote a daily newspaper column.

Mrs. Roosevelt used her position to champion women's rights. She held press conferences limited to female reporters. She also urged FDR to appoint more women to government positions.

**Vocabulary Builder**
confer (kahn FER) *v.* to exchange ideas with someone

☑**Checkpoint** **What challenges did women face during the Great Depression?**

# African Americans in the Depression

African Americans had been hit hard by the Depression. They generally suffered more unemployment, homelessness, illness, and hunger than did whites.

**South and North** In the South, plunging cotton prices forced many African American sharecroppers off their land. Moving to southern cities, they found that many jobs traditionally done by blacks, such as cleaning streets, were now filled by jobless whites. By 1932, more than half the African Americans in the South were unemployed.

**Main Idea**
The New Deal offered some opportunities to African Americans, but many others faced even harder times.

Marian
Anderson
1897–1993

Marian Anderson began singing in a local Philadelphia church at the age of six. By 1934, she was singing for the kings of Sweden and Denmark.

Anderson is best remembered for her 1939 concert at the Lincoln Memorial. At first, she shied away from the attention. But she realized, "I had become, whether I liked it or not, a symbol, representing my people."

**Biography Quest**  **Online**

**What other barriers did Anderson break in her career?**

**For:** The answer to the question about Anderson
**Visit:** PHSchool.com
**Web Code:** mvd-8233

The migration of African Americans to the North, which had started after World War I, continued at an even faster pace. Even in northern cities, though, more black than white factory workers lost their jobs. African Americans were usually the last hired and the first fired. In New York, almost 50 percent of blacks were jobless.

**FDR's Mixed Record** The majority of African American voters had backed Roosevelt. Still, the President had a mixed record on civil rights. Civil rights are the rights guaranteed in the Constitution, especially voting and equal treatment under the law. For example, FDR failed to support a federal antilynching bill, which his wife strongly supported. The President feared that he might lose the support of southern senators for his New Deal programs.

Still, in part due to his wife's prodding, Roosevelt appointed at least 100 African Americans to government posts. Educator Mary McLeod Bethune, a friend of Eleanor Roosevelt's, became the top-ranking African American in the government.

Bethune was a member of FDR's "Black Cabinet," a group of high-ranking appointees who advised the President on African American issues. Other members of the Black Cabinet included William Hastie, who later became the first African American federal judge.

**A Symbolic Moment** In 1939, the Daughters of the American Revolution (DAR) refused to allow African American singer Marian Anderson to perform at their hall. Eleanor Roosevelt, a DAR member, resigned in protest. She then arranged for Anderson to sing on the steps of the Lincoln Memorial on Easter Sunday.

Anderson's performance drew a crowd of 75,000 listeners. The concert became a key symbol of the struggle for civil rights.

✓**Checkpoint** **What was the Black Cabinet?**

**Main Idea**
During the Great Depression, many Mexican Americans were expelled from the country, and new laws changed the lives of Native Americans.

## Other Americans in the Depression

All Americans were affected by the Depression. Yet, some faced special circumstances. Many Mexicans and Mexican Americans were not only forced out of work but also out of the country. Meanwhile, the New Deal meant a new government policy toward Native Americans.

**Mexican Immigrants Are Deported** Many Mexican immigrants lived in the Southwest as migrant workers, people who travel from farm to farm picking crops. During good times, farm owners had welcomed the Mexicans, who were willing to toil for low wages under harsh conditions. During the Depression, though, thousands of white migrant workers also flooded the area looking for work.

Many Americans wanted the government to force the Mexicans out of the country. Federal immigration officials rounded up hundreds of thousands of people and deported them to Mexico. Some of those deported were not immigrants but were citizens who had been born in the United States.

**The Indian New Deal** A law in 1924 had granted American citizenship to Native Americans. Still, when the Great Depression hit, most of the nation's 170,000 Indians lived in poverty on reservations administered by the government.

Under FDR, John Collier became Commissioner of Indian Affairs. Collier, a white man who had lived among the Pueblo Indians of New Mexico, embarked on an ambitious program that became known as the Indian New Deal. With funding from federal agencies, he hired Native Americans to build needed schools, hospitals, and irrigation systems. Collier also hoped to put reservations under Indian control, stop sales of Native American lands, and encourage Indian schools to teach Native American history and the arts.

Congress approved part of Collier's plan in the Indian Reorganization Act (IRA) of 1934. The IRA did restrict tribal land sales. Yet, it failed to bring self-government to the tribes or to promote education. Native Americans continued to be the poorest Americans.

☑**Checkpoint** **Why were many Mexican Americans expelled from the country during the Great Depression?**

**Native Americans and the New Deal**

In addition to the Indian Reorganization Act, Native Americans benefited from other New Deal programs. These farmers display the blue eagle, symbol of the National Recovery Act. **Critical Thinking: _Apply Information_** _What was the Indian New Deal?_

# The Dust Bowl

In the southwestern Plains, farmers already suffering the effects of the Great Depression faced another disaster. In 1930, very little rain fell. The resulting drought caused widespread crop failure and sent storms of dust swirling across the land. These gigantic dust storms lasted for five years, turning 100 million acres of rich farmland into a wasteland known as the Dust Bowl.

**Black Blizzards** Modern farming methods contributed to the Dust Bowl. Mechanical farming equipment, which had made farming easier, encouraged farmers to clear huge plots of land. They removed native grasses along with the sod formed by the grass roots. This sod layer, however, had held the dry Plains soil in place. When the rains failed, the rootless soil blew away like powder. (See the Geography and History feature following this section.)

Some dust storms arose so suddenly that people called them "black blizzards." Black blizzards made noon seem like midnight, buried fences, seeped into houses, and killed people and animals. "We went to school with headlights on and with dust masks on," recalled one man.

**Main Idea**
Drought and dust storms brought misery to farmers on the Plains.

## Links to Art

### Artists of the Depression

William Gropper created this painting, *Construction of the Dam*, for the Department of the Interior in 1937. The vibrant colors and dynamic poses reflect the strength of the men who labored on public works projects during the New Deal. **Critical Thinking: *Apply Information*** *Why was dam building a fitting subject for a painting during the era of the New Deal?*

**Analyze Effects**
Review and analyze the effects of the Great Depression and the Dust Bowl on farmers in the Great Plains.

**Okies Head West** By the thousands, ruined farm families abandoned their dusty homes to seek work elsewhere. In some of the worst-hit Dust Bowl counties, as many as one family in three left. Many headed west to the rich farmlands of California.

California residents scornfully called the migrants Okies because so many had come from Oklahoma. The migratory agricultural workers found conditions in California almost as miserable as the ones they had left. Unable to buy land, they competed with local workers to pick crops at starvation wages. The police eventually closed some roads entering the state. Still, the migrants kept coming.

☑**Checkpoint** **What were the causes of the Dust Bowl?**

**Main Idea**
Some artists and writers tried to give a realistic picture of hard times.

## Arts and Media of the Depression

In 1939, writer John Steinbeck captured the miseries of the Dust Bowl in *The Grapes of Wrath*. The novel told the story of the Joads, Okies who seek a better life in California. In one scene, Ma Joad describes how her family has been shattered by hard times:

❝They was the time when we was on the lan'. They was a boundary to us then. Ol' folks died off, and little fellas come, an' we was always one thing—we was the fambly—kinda whole and clear. An' now we ain't clear no more. Pa's lost his place. He ain't the head no more. We're cracking up, Tom. There ain't no fambly now.❞

—John Steinbeck, *The Grapes of Wrath*

Steinbeck's novel became the classic example of how American writers and artists tried to cope with the human toll of the Great Depression.

**Visual Arts** Photographers and painters used the Depression as a theme for their art. Under a New Deal program called the Farm Security Administration, photographer Dorothea Lange recorded the experiences of Dust Bowl migrants. Her classic photograph of a woman migrant farmworker remains the symbol of the Depression.

As you have read, the WPA hired artists to paint murals on public buildings. The realistic, colorful murals of artists such as Thomas Hart Benton paid tribute to the lives of ordinary working people.

**Movies and Radio** During the Depression, some movies dealt realistically with social problems. These included a 1940 movie version of *The Grapes of Wrath.* Gangster films, such as *The Public Enemy*, depicted the rise of organized crime in American cities.

Most movies of the era, however, were meant to help people forget their problems. Audiences laughed at the antics of Mickey Mouse and thrilled to the adventure fantasy *King Kong.* One of the most popular stars was Shirley Temple, a little girl who symbolized optimism in the face of trouble.

The radio was a vital part of everyday life. Families gathered in their living rooms to listen to FDR's fireside chats. For entertainment, people enjoyed popular bands and comedians. During the day, many listeners tuned in to continuing dramas sponsored by soap companies. Such serials are still known as soap operas.

Poster for the 1933 movie
*King Kong*

☑**Checkpoint** **How did movies and radio help Americans during the Great Depression?**

⭐ **Looking Back and Ahead** In this section, you saw how the Great Depression affected Americans of the time. In the next section, you will look at the lasting impact of the New Deal.

---

**Section 3 | Check Your Progress**

**Progress Monitoring** Online
**For:** Self-test with instant help
**Visit:** PHSchool.com
**Web Code:** mva-8233

**Comprehension and Critical Thinking**

**1. (a) Recall** How did Eleanor and Franklin Roosevelt differ in their position on a proposed antilynching bill?
**(b) Evaluate Information** Whose position do you agree with? Explain.

**2. (a) Describe** What caused the Dust Bowl in the 1930s?
**(b) Make Predictions** What do you think might finally end Dust Bowl conditions?

**Reading Skill**

**3. Analyze Effects** Reread the text under the heading "Other Americans in the Depression." Analyze the effects of the Depression on Mexican Americans.

**Vocabulary *Builder***

Answer the following questions in complete sentences that show your understanding of the key terms.
**4.** What is the goal of people who seek civil rights?
**5.** What did Mexican Americans and Okies do as migrant workers?

**Writing**

**6.** Choose one of the general topics from the list that follows. Narrow that topic down to a more specific subtopic that could be covered in a multimedia presentation of 5 minutes. List three elements for that presentation.
- popular media of the 1930s
- the Dust Bowl
- the Depression and women
- the Depression and African Americans
- family life in the 1930s

# The Dust Bowl

As the Depression tightened its grip on the country, a new enemy stalked farmers on the Plains. Drought came in the early 1930s. Farmers had to endure great dust storms, called black blizzards, that blotted out sunlight and swept away farmland. The Great Plains became a Dust Bowl, and thousands of Americans watched as the crops failed.

Windswept soil could bury farmhouses in drifts. ▶

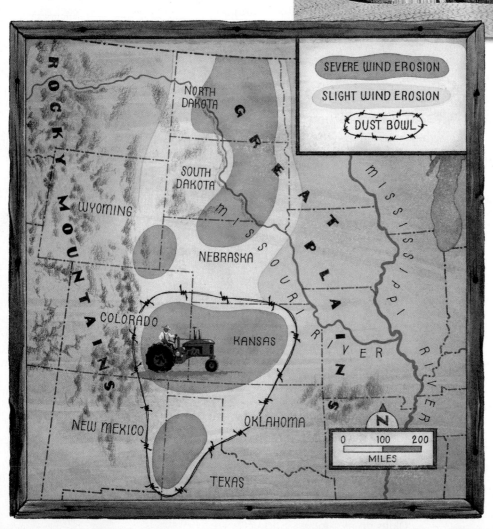

SEVERE WIND EROSION

SLIGHT WIND EROSION

DUST BOWL

ROCKY MOUNTAINS

NORTH DAKOTA

SOUTH DAKOTA

WYOMING

NEBRASKA

COLORADO

KANSAS

NEW MEXICO

OKLAHOMA

TEXAS

GREAT PLAINS

MISSISSIPPI RIVER

MISSOURI RIVER

N

0    100    200
MILES

◀ Dust Bowl, 1933–1940

The Dust Bowl spanned parts of six states in the southern plains. Wind erosion wore away soil beds in Nebraska and the Dakotas as well. Dirt from these areas swept east over the Mississippi River— far enough to darken the skies over New York and Washington!

**Explore More Video**
To learn more about
the Dust Bowl, view the
video.

*Understand Effects:*

# A Wave of Migrants

In the face of drought, wind, and low prices for their crops, thousands of Dust Bowl farmers lost their farms. Many headed west to California to look for work. Once they reached California, these displaced laborers often pushed African Americans, Mexican Americans, and Asian Americans out of their jobs.

The painting ▶ at right captures a Dust Bowl landscape after a pounding storm.

▲ Farmers and their families braced themselves against strong windstorms of swirling topsoil. After these storms passed, the sky and horizon often held the red tint of airborne prairie dirt for hours.

### Analyze **GEOGRAPHY AND HISTORY**

Drought and high winds created terrible dust storms on the Great Plains during the 1930s. Write a journal entry describing the effects of a dust storm on a farm family.

# Legacy of the New Deal

## Objectives

1. Discover how the New Deal reformed labor relations.

2. Find out how Social Security began.

3. Identify the main arguments for and against the New Deal.

## Prepare to Read

###  Reading Skill

**Evaluate Long-Term Effects**
Important historical events such as the Depression often have far-reaching effects. In fact, the Depression changed America permanently in some areas, such as its culture, political system, and economy. Read this section to identify these long-term effects. Think about how, if at all, they affect your life today.

### Vocabulary *Builder*

**High-Use Words**

<u>minimum</u>, p. 791
<u>fundamental</u>, p. 793

**Key Terms and People**

payroll tax, p. 790
Frances Perkins, p. 791
collective bargaining, p. 791
John L. Lewis, p. 791
sit-down strike, p. 791
deficit spending, p. 792

⭐ **Background Knowledge** You have seen how New Deal programs tried to combat the immediate effects of the Great Depression. Here, you will look at the lasting impact of the New Deal.

**Main Idea**
The Social Security Act provided aid to retired people and others in need.

## Social Security

"Those suffering hardship from no fault of their own have a right to call upon the government for aid," FDR argued. In 1935, he signed the Social Security Act. It gave the federal government a major and lasting role in providing support for the needy.

A key part of the Social Security Act was Old-Age Insurance. It guaranteed retired people a pension. To fund the pensions, the new law imposed a **payroll tax,** or a tax that removes money directly from workers' paychecks. Employers were required to make matching contributions. Business leaders opposed Old-Age Insurance, arguing that matching payments removed too much money from the economy.

The Social Security Act included Aid to Dependent Children (ADC) to help children whose fathers were dead, unemployed, or not living with the family. The ADC granted federal money to states to help mothers stay home to raise their young children. The Social Security Act also provided financial aid to the disabled and gave the states federal money to make temporary payments to the unemployed.

At first, the Social Security Act excluded some categories of labor. Employers of agricultural and domestic workers were not required to pay into the system. As a result, many African Americans, migrant workers, and poor rural whites did not benefit from Social Security.

Social Security poster

✓**Checkpoint** How did the Social Security Act pay for pensions for retired Americans?

# Lasting Labor Reforms

The committee that drafted the Social Security Act was chaired by FDR's secretary of labor, Frances Perkins. The first woman to serve in the Cabinet, Perkins backed major labor reforms. She said that "the ideal of government should be, through legislation and through cooperation between employers and workers, to make every job the best that the human mind can devise as to physical conditions, human relations, and wages."

**New Laws Favor Workers** In 1935, Congress passed the National Labor Relations Act. It became known as the Wagner Act, after the New York senator who sponsored it. The Wagner Act guaranteed workers' rights to organize into unions and prohibited unfair business practices, such as firing union members.

The Wagner Act also upheld collective bargaining, or the right of a union to negotiate wages and benefits for all of its members. A new National Labor Relations Board required employers to participate in collective bargaining with unions. Largely due to the Wagner Act, union membership tripled during the 1930s.

Workers gained additional benefits with the 1938 passage of the Fair Labor Standards Act. The new law set minimum wages at 25 cents per hour and maximum weekly work hours at 44. It also established time-and-a-half payment for overtime work and put an end to child labor in some businesses.

**A Powerful New Union** In 1935, John L. Lewis, head of the United Mine Workers, formed the Committee of Industrial Organization, later renamed the Congress of Industrial Organizations (CIO). The CIO was an umbrella organization consisting of many other unions. The CIO differed from the older American Federation of Labor (AFL).

The AFL organized member unions by their skills. However, Lewis thought that organizing unions differently would give workers more bargaining power. The CIO combined all the workers in a particular industry, skilled and non-skilled alike. This policy opened up union membership to more women and African Americans, many of whom worked in unskilled positions.

In 1936, the United Auto Workers—a member union of the CIO—launched a sit-down strike at the nation's largest auto factory. In a sit-down strike, workers stay in the factory but stop production. After six weeks, the strikers won their demands for higher wages and shorter hours. The Supreme Court later ruled sit-down strikes illegal.

✓Checkpoint **How did the Wagner Act protect workers?**

**Vocabulary** *Builder*
<u>minimum</u> (MIHN ah muhm) *adj.*
smallest or least required or allowed

**A Sit-Down Strike**
The sit-down strike was a new labor tactic in the 1930s. These auto workers are literally sitting down on the job—on unused car seats. **Critical Thinking: Evaluate Information** *Why do you think sit-down strikes were an effective means of protest?*

### CAUSES

- The gap between rich and poor Americans widens.
- Industries decline when people cannot afford new items.
- Margin buying leads to inflated stock prices.
- The stock market crashes in 1929.
- Banks fail because people cannot repay their loans.

### THE GREAT DEPRESSION

### EFFECTS

- Millions of people lose their jobs, farms, and property.
- The banking system nears collapse.
- Many businesses become bankrupt.
- FDR institutes New Deal legislation to promote economic recovery.
- The government's role in social welfare increases.

### Reading Charts
### Skills Activity

The economic collapse known as the Great Depression had multiple causes. Its effects reached every American.

**(a) Interpret Charts** Identify one economic cause of the Great Depression.

**(b) Analyze Cause and Effect** In what way are the effects of the Great Depression and the New Deal still felt today?

**Main Idea**

Critics of the New Deal argued that it made the government too powerful, whereas supporters claimed that it restored faith in government.

## Scorecard on the New Deal

The Social Security Act and other reforms permanently enlarged the role of the federal government. However, not everyone agreed that the government should take such an active approach to social problems. The debate over the New Deal continues to this day.

**Arguments Against the New Deal** Since the 1930s, critics have charged that the New Deal gave too much power to the federal government. They argue that government programs threaten both individual freedom and free enterprise. Herbert Hoover warned:

> "Either we shall have a society based upon ordered liberty and the initiative of the individual, or we shall have a planned society that means dictation, no matter what you call it or who does it. There is no halfway ground."
>
> —Herbert Hoover, speech, June 10, 1936

Such critics favor a return to the tradition of laissez faire, which stated that the government should interfere with the economy as little as possible.

Critics of the New Deal also worried about a massive increase in the nation's debt. To pay for his programs, FDR had resorted to a policy of deficit spending. **Deficit spending** is a situation in which the government spends more money than it receives in taxes.

**Evaluate Long-Term Effects**

Evaluate the long-term effects of the New Deal, as viewed by its critics.

Finally, critics pointed out that the New Deal failed to fulfill its most <u>fundamental</u> goal. FDR's programs did not end the Great Depression. Full economic recovery would not come until 1941, when the United States began producing goods in preparation for entering a new world war.

**Arguments for the New Deal** Supporters of the New Deal pointed out that FDR's active approach eased many problems. It employed millions of jobless people, ended the banking crisis, reformed the stock market, saved poor families from losing their homes, and improved working conditions. New Deal programs built dams and bridges, preserved 12 million acres of national parkland, brought electricity to rural America, and sponsored the creation of lasting works of art.

For many Americans, the New Deal restored their faith in government. They felt that their government would take care of them. Franklin and Eleanor Roosevelt received millions of letters from admirers. One writer said, "I have always felt like you and your wife and your children were as common as we were." In countless homes, FDR's picture held a place of honor.

✓**Checkpoint** **Summarize one argument against the New Deal.**

☆ **Looking Back and Ahead** Admirers of the New Deal said that people's faith in FDR helped American democracy survive the Great Depression. By contrast, several nations in Europe and Asia turned from democracy to dictatorship. In the next chapter, you will see how the rise of dictators led to World War II.

Eleanor and Franklin Roosevelt

**Vocabulary *Builder***
<u>fundamental</u> (fuhn duh MEHN tahl) *adj.* basic; essential; most important

---

**Section 4** | **Check Your Progress**

**Progress Monitoring** ⬤nline
**For:** Self-test with instant help
**Visit:** PHSchool.com
**Web Code:** mva-8234

## Comprehension and Critical Thinking

**1. (a) Identify** What were the main provisions of the Social Security Act?
**(b) Link Past and Present** Why is Social Security still important today?

**2. (a) Describe** How was the organization of the CIO different from that of the AFL?
**(b) Identify Benefits** How might the organization of the CIO have made it more effective in negotiating with companies on behalf of workers?

## ⟳ Reading Skill

**3. Evaluate Long-Term Effects** Reread "Arguments for the New Deal" on this page. Evaluate the long-term effects of the program, as viewed by its supporters.

## Vocabulary *Builder*

Complete each of the following sentences so that the second part further explains the first part and clearly shows your understanding of the key term.
**4.** Union and company representatives sit down together in collective bargaining, _____.
**5.** Many people fear a government might hurt the economy through deficit spending, _____.

**6.** Social Security was funded by a payroll tax, _____.

## Writing

**7.** Create a two-column checklist for a multimedia presentation on a topic from this section. Insert the topic at the top of the checklist. In the left column, list three of these media types: Music; Videos/DVDs; Art; Photographs; Computer Presentations; Interviews. In the right column, describe specific materials you would explore for each type. For example: Interviews (*left column*); Talk to grandmother about Social Security (*right column*).

Often, paintings and drawings include important evidence about daily life during a particular historical period. Studying works of art helps us draw conclusions about the society that created the art.

*Unemployment*, by Ben Shahn

## Learn the Skill

*Use these steps to analyze art.*

① **Identify the subject and artist.** The title or caption often identifies the subject and artist. Details in the painting may also tell you who or what is being shown.

② **Analyze the details in the work of art.** Look for the most important details to help you identify the focus of the painting.

③ **Draw conclusions based on the work of art.** Use information provided by the work of art and your own knowledge of the period or event. Does the art convey a particular mood or point of view? What can you conclude about the values and culture of the people who lived in that society?

## Practice the Skill

*Answer the following questions about the mural on this page.*

① **Identify the subject and artist.** (a) What is the title of the mural? (b) Who is the artist? (c) What is the subject matter?

② **Analyze the details in the work of art.** (a) Who are the people shown in this mural? (b) What are they doing? (c) What details in the mural attract your attention the most?

③ **Draw conclusions based on the work of art.** (a) What mood or feeling is created by this mural? (b) What does this mural show you about American society during this period? (c) What is the artist's point of view about the subject?

## Apply the Skill

*See the Review and Assessment at the end of this chapter.*

CHAPTER **23** | # Quick Study Guide

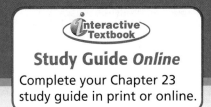

**Study Guide** *Online*
Complete your Chapter 23
study guide in print or online.

## Chapter Summary

### Section 1
### Hoover and the Crash

- The stock market crash in October 1929 marked the start of the Great Depression.
- Causes of the Depression included overproduction and a banking crisis.
- Unemployment led to widespread misery.
- President Hoover believed business and local government should lead the way out of the Depression.

### Section 2
### Roosevelt and the New Deal

- In 1933, President Roosevelt launched the New Deal, an ambitious program to bring relief to the jobless, spur economic recovery, and prevent future depressions.
- The Supreme Court overturned several major New Deal measures.
- Some critics felt that the New Deal did not do enough to improve conditions.

### Section 3
### Life in the Great Depression

- Women, African Americans, and Mexican Americans faced special challenges during the Depression.
- Droughts in the early 1930s turned much of the Plains region into a Dust Bowl.
- Painters, photographers, and writers in the 1930s depicted hard times in their works.

### Section 4
### Legacy of the New Deal

- The Social Security Act offered assistance to older Americans and others.
- Labor reforms and the founding of the CIO increased the power of unions.
- Critics of the New Deal feared it made the government too powerful, while supporters believed it strengthened faith in the democratic system.

## Key Concepts

These notes will help you prepare for questions about key concepts.

### Goals of the New Deal Programs

**Goal: Relieve joblessness**
- **Federal Relief Administration (FERA):** Fund states to reopen relief agencies
- **Civilian Conservation Corps (CCC):** Hire city dwellers to work in national parks and forests
- **Works Progress Administration (WPA):** Hire workers to repair public buildings, roads, and bridges and to build airports

**Goal: Promote economic recovery**
- **National Recovery Administration (NRA):** Keep prices stable and boost employment
- **Public Works Administration (PWA):** Build large public-works projects
- **Tennessee Valley Authority (TVA):** Build dams to control floods and provide electricity

**Goal: Reform the economic system**
- **Federal Deposit Insurance Corporation (FDIC):** Guarantee accounts up to $2,500

**Goal: Provide benefits for workers**
- **National Labor Relations Act (Wagner Act):** Guarantee workers' right to join a union; require employers to participate in collective bargaining
- **Fair Labor Standards Act (FLSA):** Set minimum wage and maximum number of work hours
- **Social Security Act:** Guarantee payments to retired persons and to unemployed

## Vocabulary *Builder*

### Key Terms

Read each sentence below. If the sentence is true, write YES and explain why. If the sentence is not true, write NO and explain why not.

1. The company declared bankruptcy to celebrate profits from selling stock.

2. European countries defaulted on loans, paying off their debts early.

3. His pension provided him with an income after he retired.

4. By spending more money that it took in, the government practiced deficit spending.

5. Migrant workers built permanent homes in the communities where they worked.

## Comprehension and Critical Thinking

6. (a) **Summarize** What were the causes of the stock market crash of 1929?
   (b) **Analyze Cause and Effect** How did the Crash contribute to increased unemployment?
   (c) **Apply Information** What measures did Roosevelt take to prevent another crash?

7. (a) **Recall** Why did Americans buy fewer and fewer cars and homes in the late 1920s?
   (b) **Analyze Cause and Effect** How did that trend contribute to the Great Depression?

8. (a) **Recall** How did Hoover propose to handle the economic crisis?
   (b) **Contrast** How did Roosevelt's approach differ from Hoover's?
   (c) **Evaluate Information** Why do you think more Americans responded favorably to Roosevelt's approach than to Hoover's?

9. (a) **Recall** How did the Great Depression affect women? African Americans? Mexican Americans?

(b) **Compare and Contrast** How were Depression experiences similar for all three groups? How were they different?

10. (a) **Describe** How did writers and artists tell the story of Americans during the Depression?
    (b) **Contrast** What approach did the movies take toward the Depression?
    (c) **Identify Benefits** Which approach do you think benefited Americans more? Explain.

11. (a) **List** How did Americans benefit from the Social Security Act of 1935?
    (b) **Analyze Cause and Effect** Why do you suppose legislators saw a need to pass the act?

## History Reading Skill

12. **Analyze Cause and Effect** Which effect of the Depression do you think was most devastating? Which effect do you think has caused the greatest change to today's world?

## Writing

13. Plan your research for a short multimedia presentation about one of the following topics:
    - Contrast Herbert Hoover and Franklin Roosevelt.
    - Show how the New Deal changed daily life.
    - Describe American arts and media in the 1930s.

    **Your plan should:**
    - narrow the issue into a topic that can be covered in a short multimedia presentation;
    - include a media checklist for that topic;
    - end with a few sentences describing the presentation you would like to create.

14. Write a Narrative:
    Write a short narrative describing an argument between two friends in the 1930s who have very different feelings about FDR and the New Deal.

## Skills for Life

### Analyzing Art

Use the painting in the Links to Art in Section 3 to answer the questions.

15. (a) What is the title of the painting? (b) Who is the artist? (c) When was the mural painted?

16. (a) What are the people doing? (b) What details attract your attention the most?

17. (a) What mood is created by this painting?
    (b) What does it illustrate about American government during this period?

# Test Yourself

1. **Which New Deal program met the goal of providing jobs for the unemployed?**

   **A** Civilian Conservation Corps

   **B** National Recovery Administration

   **C** Social Security Act

   **D** Federal Deposit Insurance Corporation

2. **Conservative critics argued that the New Deal**

   **A** did too little to help the poor.

   **B** made the federal government too powerful.

   **C** relied too much on private action.

   **D** was unfair to migrant workers.

3. **How did margin buying contribute to the stock market crash of October 1929?**

   **A** It made it harder to buy stocks.

   **B** It slowed down production of goods.

   **C** It encouraged risky investments.

   **D** It led to deficit spending.

**Refer to the graph below to answer Question 4.**

**Labor Union Membership, 1930–1940**

Union Members (in thousands)

Source: *Historical Statistics of the United States*

4. **Which of the following contributed most directly to the trend shown on this graph?**

   **A** the Wagner Act

   **B** the Social Security Act

   **C** the National Recovery Act

   **D** the bank holiday

# Document-Based Questions

**Task:** Look at Documents 1 and 2, and answer their accompanying questions. Then, use the documents and your knowledge of history to complete this writing assignment:

   Draw a conclusion about whether the New Deal succeeded in meeting Roosevelt's employment goals.

**Document 1:** In 1933, President Roosevelt asked Congress to take action to ease the crisis. *What three measures did Roosevelt propose?*

> **"**It is essential . . . that measures immediately be enacted aimed at unemployment relief. . . . The first is the enrollment of workers . . . by the Federal Government for . . . public employment. . . . The second is grants to States for relief work. The third extends to a broad public works labor-creating program. . . .
>
>    The first of these measures . . . can and should be immediately enacted. I propose to create a civilian conservation corps to be used in . . . forestry, prevention of soil erosion, . . . and similar projects. . . . I estimate that 250,000 men can be given temporary employment by early summer.**"**
>
> —Franklin Roosevelt, March 21, 1933

**Document 2:** The graph below shows the percentage of American workers who were unemployed between 1933 and 1941. *What trends in unemployment do you see in the graph?*

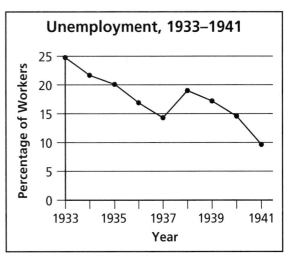

**Unemployment, 1933–1941**

Percentage of Workers

Source: *Historical Statistics of the United States*

## Chapter Preview

By the 1930s, powerful dictators had risen to power in a number of nations. Their aggressive attempts to conquer new lands led to the largest war the world has ever seen. After attempting to remain neutral, the United States became involved in the war and eventually emerged as a major world power.

☑ **What You Will Learn**

In the 1930s, dictators in Germany, Italy, and Japan tried to conquer neighboring nations, sparking a new world war.

The United States entered the war after Japanese airplanes bombed the American fleet at Pearl Harbor.

As the United States organized to win the war, women gained new opportunities, but Japanese Americans faced harsh restrictions.

The D-Day invasion of France was the first step to final victory in Europe, and the dropping of the atomic bomb brought the war in the Pacific to an end.

| | | |
|---|---|---|
| **1935** | **1939** | **1941** |
| Congress passes first Neutrality Act to keep nation out of foreign wars. | Roosevelt announces United States will remain neutral in war. | United States enters war after Japan attacks Pearl Harbor. |

**U.S. Events**

 1935

**World Events**

**1935** Italy invades Ethiopia.

1938

**1937** Japan invades China.

1941

**1939** Germany invades Poland; World War II begins.

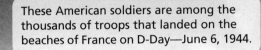

These American soldiers are among the
thousands of troops that landed on the
beaches of France on D-Day—June 6, 1944.

**1942**
U.S. Navy defeats
Japanese navy at
Battle of Midway.

**1944**
Allied troops
land in France
on D-Day.

**1945**
U.S. plane drops atomic
bomb on Hiroshima;
World War II ends.

1941

**1942** Britain defeats
German forces in
Egypt.

1944

1947

**1946** German leaders
convicted of war crimes.

**History Reading Skill** **Determine Meanings From Context**

## Why do countries start wars?

In this chapter, you will practice using context to determine word meanings. Read the following discussion of the ideas that motivated aggressor nations in World War II. The side notes show you how to use context to determine word meaning.

In the 1930s, several nations took aggressive action against their neighbors. Here, a scholar of the time discusses the reasons some gave to defend aggression.

**Primary Source** ▶ A distinguished Italian scholar . . . defended the right of the have-not nations to seek outlets for their population pressure and to control sources of raw materials. He frankly said: "Force is the only solution. The inferior races must be sacrificed for the benefit of the strong". . . .

These words, which still ring in my ears, sum up the philosophy of force preached by dictators and **apolog**ists of the aggressor nations which choose to call themselves "the have-nots," as if to have not would somehow justify their right to plunder the haves. . . .

Herein lies the fallacy of this philosophy of the have-nots. . . . It fails to appreciate the political importance of an international order which not merely protects the weak nations but also guarantees the power and prestige of the strong nations.

—Hu Shih, "To Have Not and Want to Have"

**Examples of** *apologists'* **actions and views**

**Unfamiliar word**

**Unfamiliar word; root in bold type is from the familiar word** *apology*

**Related familiar word** *fails* **introduces example of** *fallacy*

## Determine Meanings From Context

- Word clues, such as familiar base words, can suggest an unfamiliar word's meaning.
- Clues in the surrounding sentence or paragraph may include examples or descriptions of an unfamiliar word, as well as familiar related or contrasting words.
- Ask questions about unfamiliar words: What does that idea mean? How does it affect people or places?

## Document-Based Questions

1. According to the Italian scholar, why are some nations justified in attacking others?
2. Does Hu Shih agree with the Italian scholar? How can you tell?

# Vocabulary *Builder*

## Previewing High-Use Academic Words

| High-Use Word | Definition | Sample History Sentence |
|---|---|---|
| **superior** (soo PIR ee uhr) (Section 1, p. 803) | *adj.* of greater importance or value; of higher quality | Racism is the belief that one race is naturally superior to another. |
| **inferior** (ihn FIR ee uhr) (Section 1, p. 803) | *adj.* of lower rank or status; of poorer quality | In the early 1800s, British manufacturers tried to sell inferior goods to the United States. |
| **emphasize** (EHM fah sīz) (Section 2, p. 809) | *v.* to stress; to give particular importance to | The Declaration of Independence emphasizes the idea of natural rights. |
| **pendulum** (PEHN jah luhm) (Section 2, p. 811) | *n.* hanging weight that swings from side to side in a steady rhythm | In the early 1900s, the pendulum began to swing in favor of workers and unions. |
| **convert** (kuhn VERT) (Section 3, p. 816) | *v.* to change from one purpose to another | During the war, some factories converted from producing cars to making tanks. |
| **vague** (vayg) (Section 3, p. 819) | *adj.* uncertain; not precise or exact | The Bill of Rights requires that charges against an accused person must be precise rather than vague. |
| **dimension** (dih MEHN shuhn) (Section 4, p. 821) | *n.* size or extent; length, width, or height | In the late 1800s, American cities grew to greater dimensions than ever before. |
| **efficient** (ee FISH ehnt) (Section 4, p. 826) | *adj.* acting effectively, without wasted cost or effort | Edison's electric power plant provided industry with an efficient source of power. |

## Previewing Key Terms and People

Josef Stalin, p. 802
totalitarian state, p. 802
Benito Mussolini, p. 802
fascism, p. 803

Adolf Hitler, p. 803
aggression, p. 804
appeasement, p. 804
Winston Churchill, p. 807
total war, p. 811
Dwight D. Eisenhower, p. 812
Douglas MacArthur, p. 812
rationing, p. 817

intern, p. 818
A. Philip Randolph, p. 819
bracero, p. 820
Harry S Truman, p. 822
island hopping, p. 824
kamikaze, p. 824
genocide, p. 826
war crimes, p. 827

Dwight D. Eisenhower

# Aggression Leads to War

## Objectives

1. Learn why totalitarian dictators gained power after World War I.

2. Find out how Germany, Italy, and Japan embarked on a path of military conquest.

3. Discover how the United States tried to remain neutral in a new world conflict.

4. Understand how World War II began in Europe.

## Prepare to Read

### 🎯 Reading Skill

**Use Word Clues to Analyze Meaning** Start with word clues when you encounter an unfamiliar term such as *economic depression.* It is helpful to know that the familiar word *depress* means "weaken or make less active." Then, you might conclude that an economic depression is a period of weak or less active economy. Finally, learn about a word from its place in a sentence. A verb, for example, will describe an action.

### Vocabulary *Builder*

**High-Use Words**
<u>superior</u>, p. 803
<u>inferior</u>, p. 803

**Key Terms and People**
Josef Stalin, p. 802
totalitarian state, p. 802
Benito Mussolini, p. 802
fascism, p. 803
Adolf Hitler, p. 803
aggression, p. 804
appeasement, p. 804
Winston Churchill, p. 807

⭐ **Background Knowledge** As you have seen, the early decades of the twentieth century saw a series of major world crises. World War I and the Russian Revolution destroyed millions of lives and altered the political map of Europe. The Great Depression of the 1930s caused worldwide economic hardship. In this section, you will see how these conditions helped set the stage for a new world war.

**Main Idea**
Postwar problems led to the rise of dictators in several nations.

## The Rise of Dictators

In the 1920s and 1930s, people in several nations came to believe that democratic governments were too weak to solve their problems. They turned instead to dictators.

**Soviet Communism** By 1929, Josef Stalin was sole dictator of the Soviet Union. Stalin turned the Soviet Union into a totalitarian state. A totalitarian state is a nation in which a single party controls the government and every aspect of people's lives.

Stalin took brutal measures to control and modernize industry and agriculture. He ordered peasants to give crops, animals, and land to government-run farms. Millions of peasants who resisted were executed or sent to labor camps. In addition, an estimated four million Soviets, including many of Stalin's rivals in the Communist Party, were killed or imprisoned on false charges of disloyalty to the state.

**Fascism in Italy** After World War I, economic problems in Italy had led to unrest. Benito Mussolini promised to restore order through strong leadership. In October 1922, Mussolini and his

Josef Stalin

followers threatened to overthrow Italy's elected government. In response, the king appointed Mussolini prime minister.

Mussolini turned Italy into the world's first Fascist state. Fascism is a political system based on militarism, extreme nationalism, and blind loyalty to the state and its leader. Italy, he said, was a <u>superior</u> nation with a glorious destiny. He spoke of reviving the days when the Roman Empire dominated Europe. He also argued that a superior nation had a right and duty to conquer <u>inferior</u> nations.

Mussolini ended freedom of the press and banned all political parties except his own. Critics were jailed or murdered. In schools, children recited the motto "Mussolini is always right."

**Nazi Germany** Many Germans were angry over their defeat in World War I and the heavy reparation payments forced on them by the Allies. Among them was an extreme nationalist, Adolf Hitler. By 1921, Hitler had become leader of a small group known as the National Socialist, or Nazi, Party. Nazism was a form of fascism.

Racism lay at the core of Nazi beliefs. Hitler told Germans that they were a "master race," destined to rule over Slavs, Gypsies, and others they considered inferior. The cornerstone of Hitler's racial theories was anti-Semitism, or hatred of Jews. Hitler falsely claimed that Germany had not lost World War I but had been betrayed by Jews and other "traitors." This idea appealed to Germans eager to find a scapegoat, someone on whom to blame their problems.

The Great Depression increased Hitler's popularity. In 1933, he was named chancellor, or leader of the German parliament. Once in power, Hitler quickly created a totalitarian state. All other parties were outlawed. Hitler's secret police enforced strict loyalty.

Germany also passed anti-Semitic laws. Jews were banned from public schools and from professions such as medicine and law. Jewish communities were attacked. In 1938, troops began rounding up Jews and sending them to slave labor camps. But even worse was to come, as you will see.

**Two Fascist Dictators**
The Nazi propaganda poster (left) glorifies Adolf Hitler, dictator of Germany. At right, Italian dictator Benito Mussolini strikes a proud pose while standing atop a tank. **Critical Thinking: *Evaluate Information*** How does the propaganda poster create a heroic image of Hitler?

**Main Idea**
The rulers of Japan, Italy, and Germany sought to expand their territories and conquer other nations.

**Militarism in Japan** In Japan, too, the Great Depression undermined faith in democratic rule. Military leaders pressured the civilian government to take control of nearby countries. Militarists argued that their island nation needed more space, as well as raw materials for its booming industries.

By 1936, militarists were in complete control of the Japanese government. Like the Nazis in Germany, Japanese militarists preached racism. The Japanese, they said, were superior to other Asians as well as non-Asians.

☑**Checkpoint** How did the Great Depression aid Hitler?

## Military Aggression

Italy, Germany, and Japan each followed policies of ruthless aggression. **Aggression** is a warlike act by one country against another without cause.

**Japan Attacks China** In 1931, acting without the approval of Japan's elected government, the Japanese army seized Manchuria in northeastern China. The League of Nations, which had been founded to halt aggression, protested but took no action.

After 1937, Japan stepped up its aggression in China. Japanese armies treated the Chinese brutally. For six weeks, Japanese forces pillaged the Chinese city of Nanjing. In the assault, more than a quarter of a million civilians and prisoners of war were massacred.

**Italy Invades Ethiopia** In 1935, Mussolini's armies invaded the African country of Ethiopia. Though the Ethiopians fought bravely, their cavalry and outdated rifles were no match for Italy's modern tanks and airplanes.

Ethiopia's emperor, Haile Selassie (Hī lee suh LAS ee), appealed to the League of Nations for aid. However, the League responded weakly. Britain and France were weary of war and caught up in their own economic crises. Without help, Ethiopia fell to the invaders.

**German Aggression** Hitler vowed to create an empire that united all German-speaking people, including those outside Germany. In defiance of the Treaty of Versailles, he began to rebuild Germany's armed forces. He further defied the treaty by sending troops into the Rhineland region of western Germany in 1936. Two years later, German armies occupied Austria. As Hitler predicted, the European democracies did nothing to stop him.

Still, France and Britain protested when Hitler threatened to invade Czechoslovakia. In September 1938, European leaders met in the German city of Munich to ease the crisis. The leaders of France and Britain hoped to appease Hitler. **Appeasement** is a policy of giving in to aggression in order to avoid war.

In the Munich Pact, Britain and France agreed to let the German leader occupy the Sudetenland (soo DET ehn land), a portion of Czechoslovakia populated largely by people who spoke German. In return, Hitler promised he would seek no further territory.

Haile Selassie addressing the League of Nations

# Aggression in Europe to 1939

## KEY

Areas taken over by Germany by September 1939

Areas taken over by Italy by September 1939

Areas taken over by the Soviet Union by September 1939

0 km    400
0 miles    400
Azimuthal Equal-Area Projection

FINLAND
NORWAY
SWEDEN
ESTONIA
LATVIA
LITHUANIA
DENMARK
GER.
SOVIET UNION
IRELAND
GREAT BRITAIN
North Sea
Baltic Sea
NETH.
GERMANY
POLAND (Sept. 1939)
Rhineland (March 1936)
BELG.
CZECHOSLOVAKIA (March 1939)
LUX.
Saar Basin
Sudetenland (Sept. 1938)
ATLANTIC OCEAN
FRANCE
SWITZ.
AUSTRIA (March 1938)
HUNGARY
ROMANIA
YUGOSLAVIA
PORTUGAL
SPAIN
Corsica
ITALY
BULGARIA
Sardinia
ALBANIA (April 1939)
GREECE
TURKEY
Sicily
To Ethiopia (1935)
Dodecanese Is. (It.)
Mediterranean Sea
AFRICA

### MAP MASTER®
**Skills Activity**

In the late 1930s, aggressive acts by Italy and Germany threatened the peace of Europe and the world.

**(a) Interpret a Map** What was the earliest act of aggression shown on the map?

**(b) Apply Information** Based on the map and your reading, describe what happened to Czechoslovakia.

**MapMaster Online**

**For:** Interactive map
**Visit:** PHSchool.com
**Web Code:** mvp-8241

The British prime minister, Neville Chamberlain, returned from the Munich meeting announcing that he had won "peace for our time." But only a few months later, in March 1939, Hitler occupied the remainder of Czechoslovakia.

✓**Checkpoint** **How did the League of Nations respond to Italian and Japanese aggression?**

## American Neutrality

As you have seen, after World War I, the United States returned to a policy of isolationism. As aggression threatened to bring the world to war again, Americans were determined to avoid getting involved.

**Neutrality Act** In 1935, Congress passed the Neutrality Act. It was the first of several laws designed to keep the United States at peace. The Neutrality Act forbade the President from selling arms, making loans, or giving any other kind of assistance to any nation involved in war.

**Main Idea**

The United States sought to stay out of growing world conflict while strengthening ties to Latin America.

**Good Neighbor Policy** At the same time, the United States sought to strengthen ties to Latin America. In 1930, President Herbert Hoover rejected the Roosevelt Corollary to the Monroe Doctrine. The United States, he declared, no longer claimed the right to intervene in Latin American affairs.

Franklin Roosevelt went even further. Under what he called the Good Neighbor Policy, he withdrew American troops from Nicaragua and Haiti. He also cancelled the Platt Amendment, which had limited the independence of Cuba.

☑**Checkpoint** **What was the goal of the Neutrality Act?**

## War Begins in Europe

Meanwhile, in Europe, Poland loomed as Hitler's next target. France and Britain now realized that the policy of appeasement had failed. They promised to come to Poland's aid if Germany invaded Poland.

**Invasion of Poland** In late August 1939, the world was shocked to learn that Hitler and Stalin—two sworn and bitter enemies—had signed a nonaggression agreement. In the Nazi-Soviet Pact, the two dictators promised not to attack one another's countries. Secretly, they agreed to divide up Poland.

On September 1, 1939, Nazi troops invaded Poland. Sixteen days later, the Soviet Union seized eastern Poland. Stalin's forces also invaded Finland and later annexed Estonia, Lithuania, and Latvia.

Two days after Hitler's invasion of Poland, Britain and France declared war on Germany. World War II had begun.

In the early days of the war, Hitler's armies seemed unstoppable. In April 1940, they moved north, seizing Denmark and Norway. In May, they marched west to conquer the Netherlands, Luxembourg, and Belgium. They then moved into France.

**Fall of France** Britain sent troops to help France resist the assault. The British and French, however, were quickly overpowered. By May, the Germans had forced them to retreat to Dunkirk, a French port on the English Channel. In a bold action, the British sent every available ship and boat across the channel to rescue the trapped soldiers.

Unhindered, German armies entered France and marched on to Paris, the French capital. On June 22, 1940, barely six weeks later, Hitler gleefully accepted the surrender of France.

**Main Idea**

After invading Poland, German armies quickly conquered most of Europe.

**The Bombing of London**

For months, German planes bombed London and other British cities. Here, a group of London women sit outside the rubble of their homes. **Critical Thinking: Draw Conclusions** *Do you think the constant bombing attacks weakened or strengthened the British people? Explain.*

**Battle of Britain** Now, Britain stood alone against the Nazi war machine. Few thought the island nation stood a chance. Still, Winston Churchill, the British prime minister, expressed confidence:

> "We shall defend our island whatever the cost may be, we shall fight on the beaches . . . we shall fight in the fields and in the streets, we shall fight in the hills. We shall never surrender."
>
> —Winston Churchill, speech, June 4, 1940

Hitler ordered an air assault on Britain. Day after day, German planes attacked British cities. The raids took tens of thousands of lives, yet the British spirit never broke. By night, Londoners slept in subway stations. By day, they cleared the wreckage, buried the dead, and tried to carry on. Overhead, the British air force fought invading planes. The Battle of Britain continued through the summer and into the fall. By then, Hitler had abandoned all plans to invade Britain.

**Invasion of the Soviet Union** On June 22, 1941, Hitler broke his pact with Stalin. A huge German force crossed into the Soviet Union. The Soviet Union, which had remained out of the early days of the war, now joined Britain in fighting the Germans. Although Churchill and Stalin deeply mistrusted each other, they were now forced to work together to defeat their common enemy.

✓**Checkpoint**  What was the Nazi-Soviet Pact of 1939?

⭐ **Looking Back and Ahead**  Only 20 years after the end of World War I, the world was once again plunged into conflict. As you will see, World War II would be even more destructive.

---

## Section 1 | Check Your Progress

**Progress Monitoring** ⊕nline
**For:** Self-test with instant help
**Visit:** PHSchool.com
**Web Code:** mva-8241

### Comprehension and Critical Thinking

**1. (a) Describe** What kind of government did Hitler set up in Germany?
**(b) Compare** How was Nazi Germany similar to the Soviet Union under Stalin?

**2. (a) Recall** How did France and Britain respond to Nazi aggression?
**(b) Draw Conclusions** Do you think France and Britain could have prevented World War II if they had acted differently? Why or why not?

### Reading Skill

**3. Use Word Clues to Analyze Meaning** Explain how the root parts of the word *totalitarian* help you understand the meaning of the word.

### Vocabulary *Builder*

Answer the following questions in complete sentences that show your understanding of the key terms.
**4.** How does a totalitarian state such as Nazi Germany differ from a democratic nation such as the United States?
**5.** What are the main features of fascism?

**6.** How did Germany, Italy, and Japan practice aggression?
**7.** How was the Munich Pact an example of appeasement?

### Writing

**8.** Use library or Internet resources to find more information about one of the topics in this section. Suggestions for topics include Mussolini and fascism, the rise of Hitler, the invasion of Poland, Winston Churchill, and the Battle of Britain. Identify at least three sources of nonprint material on the topic. List the sources you find and describe their contents.

## Objectives

1. Understand how the United States prepared for war and strengthened its ties with the Allies.

2. Discover why the United States finally entered World War II.

3. Learn how, after many early setbacks, the Allies began to turn the tide of battle in North Africa and the Pacific.

## Prepare to Read

### ⊙ Reading Skill

**Use Sentence Clues to Analyze Meaning** After studying a word, look in the sentence for clues to its meaning. For example, you may find descriptions of what a verb does, examples of a noun, or details that explain an adjective.

### Vocabulary *Builder*

**High-Use Words**

emphasize, p. 809

pendulum, p. 811

### Key Terms and People

total war, p. 811

Dwight D. Eisenhower, p. 812

Douglas MacArthur, p. 812

⭐ **Background Knowledge** When the war began, most Americans hoped to remain neutral. In this section, you will learn how the United States finally entered the war.

**Main Idea**

Though the United States officially remained neutral, Roosevelt found ways to help Britain defend against the Nazis.

## Moving Toward War

In 1940, President Roosevelt sought reelection to a third term. His decision broke the precedent set by George Washington that Presidents serve only two terms. Roosevelt promised to maintain American neutrality. He told voters, "Your boys are not going to be sent into any foreign wars." FDR won reelection easily.

**Lend-Lease Act** Roosevelt sympathized with the Allies. Even before the campaign had begun, Winston Churchill had appealed to Roosevelt for military aid. Selling war supplies to Britain would violate the Neutrality Acts. Still, Roosevelt reached a compromise with Congress. The United States could sell supplies to Britain, but Britain would have to pay cash for all goods it received.

However, by the end of 1940, Britain's treasury was empty. Fearing that Britain would fall to the Nazis, Roosevelt persuaded Congress to pass a law he called Lend-Lease. It allowed the United States to lend or lease supplies to Britain and other nations fighting the Nazis. Isolationists objected that the law would draw the United States into war. Most Americans, however, favored the plan.

Lend-Lease convoys soon began moving across the Atlantic. Later, the Lend-Lease arrangement was extended to China and the Soviet Union. Under Lend-Lease, the United States became, in Roosevelt's words, "the great arsenal of democracy."

**Military Buildup** The United States took other steps to prepare for possible entry into the war. Congress approved greater spending

Franklin Roosevelt (left) and Winston Churchill (right)

for the army and navy. In September 1940, it passed a law that set up the first peacetime draft in American history.

Roosevelt took another unprecedented step in 1940. He ordered the Army Air Corps to organize an African American unit under the command of black officers. A flight training program was set up at Tuskegee Army Air Field in Alabama. The Tuskegee Airmen would later compile a superb combat record.

**Atlantic Charter** In August 1941, Roosevelt and Churchill issued the Atlantic Charter, outlining their goals for the postwar world. They agreed that their nations would seek no territorial gain from the war and <u>emphasized</u> the right of all people to choose their own government. They also called for a new international organization that might succeed where the League of Nations had failed.

**Vocabulary** *Builder*
**emphasize** (EHM fah sīz) *v.* to stress; to give particular importance to

☑**Checkpoint** **What was the Lend-Lease Act of 1941?**

## The United States Enters the War

Events in Asia, not Europe, finally drew the United States into war. In July 1941, Japan invaded the French colony of Indochina (present-day Vietnam, Laos, and Cambodia). In response, Roosevelt banned American exports of iron and steel scrap to Japan. He also restricted the sale of oil to Japan.

Facing a shortage of fuel for their navy, Japanese leaders decided on war. Plans for an attack on the United States were soon underway.

**Main Idea**
The Japanese attack on Pearl Harbor brought the United States into World War II.

### The Tuskegee Airmen

❝My own opinion was that blacks could best overcome racist attitudes through their achievements, even though those achievements had to take place within the hateful environment of segregation. . . . The coming war represented a golden opportunity. . . . We owned a fighter squadron—something that would have been unthinkable only a short time earlier. It was all ours. . . . Furthermore, we would be required to analyze our own problems and solve them with our own skills.❞

—Benjamin O. Davis, Jr., *Benjamin O. Davis, Jr., American*

Benjamin Davis at Tuskegee

**Reading Primary Sources**
**◄Skills Activity►**
Benjamin O. Davis, Jr., commanded the Tuskegee Airmen and later became the first African American general in the Air Force. Here, he describes his feelings about the formation of the flying program.

**(a)** **Detect Points of View** How does Davis feel about segregation?
**(b)** **Identify Benefits** How does Davis think African Americans might benefit from the United States entering World War II?

# ATTACK ON PEARL HARBOR

**History** *Interactive*

**Learn About Pearl Harbor**

**Visit:** PHSchool.com
**Web Code:** mvl-8242

President Roosevelt called December 7, 1941, "a day that will live in infamy." The attack on Pearl Harbor shocked Americans and propelled the United States into the most extensive war in history. **Critical Thinking:** *Link Past and Present* How was the reaction to Pearl Harbor similar to the reaction to terrorist attacks on the United States in our time?

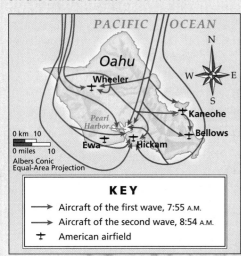

PACIFIC OCEAN

Oahu

Wheeler

Kaneohe

Pearl Harbor

Bellows

Ewa

Hickam

N W E S

0 km 10
0 miles 10
Albers Conic Equal-Area Projection

**KEY**

→ Aircraft of the first wave, 7:55 A.M.

→ Aircraft of the second wave, 8:54 A.M.

✝ American airfield

◄ At Pearl Harbor, the peace of a Sunday morning was shattered by Japanese bombers. Coming in two waves, the attack destroyed or seriously damaged much of the American fleet and killed thousands of Americans.

**EXTRA** NIGHT Pictorial

RACE RESULTS **Los Angeles Times** DAILY, FIVE CENTS

MONDAY MORNING, DECEMBER 8, 1941.

Vol. LXI Three Parts—28 Pages Page A

# IT'S WAR!

## Hostilities Declared by Japanese; 350 Reported Killed in Hawaii Raid

U.S. Battleships Hit; 7 Die in Honolulu

Air Bombs Rained on Pacific Bases

NEW YORK, Dec. 7. (A.P.)—Three hundred and fifty men were killed by a direct bomb hit on Hickam Field, an N.B.C. observer reported tonight from Honolulu.

LATE WAR BULLETINS

SHANGHAI, Dec. 8 (Monday.) (A.P.)—The Japanese have sunk the British gunboat Petrel as it lay off the International Settlement waterfront.

WASHINGTON, Dec. 7. (A.P.)—Th...

HONOLU...

"Remember Pearl Harbor" ▲ became the nation's battle cry. This poster was created the year after the attack.

◄ Newspaper headlines blared what everybody knew at once: The nation was now at war!

**Pearl Harbor** On December 7, 1941, Japanese bombers launched a surprise attack on American naval, air, and ground forces at Pearl Harbor, on the Hawaiian island of Oahu (oh AH hoo). The attack destroyed nearly half of the island's 400 military aircraft and damaged 8 battleships, two beyond repair. About 2,400 Americans were killed.

The assault on Pearl Harbor caught American military leaders by surprise. Though aware of the possibility of a Japanese attack, they did not expect the attack to come as far east as Hawaii.

The next day, a grave President Roosevelt addressed Congress.

> **"**Yesterday, December 7, 1941, a date which will live in infamy, the United States of America was suddenly and deliberately attacked by naval and air forces of the Empire of Japan.**"**
>
> —Franklin Roosevelt, speech, December 8, 1941

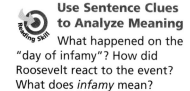
**Use Sentence Clues to Analyze Meaning** What happened on the "day of infamy"? How did Roosevelt react to the event? What does *infamy* mean?

Later that day, Congress declared war on Japan. Japan's allies, Germany and Italy, then declared war on the United States. Against their wishes, Americans were again involved in a world war.

**A Global Conflict** Even more than World War I, World War II was truly a global conflict. On one side were the Axis powers, an alliance made up of Germany, Italy, Japan, and six other nations. Opposing the Axis powers were the Allied powers. Before the war was over, the Allied powers would include Britain, France, the Soviet Union, the United States, China, and 45 other countries.

More than any war before it, World War II was a total war. Total war is conflict involving not just armies but entire nations. Countries on each side put all their resources into the war effort. Civilian populations often became targets of bombings.

☑**Checkpoint** Why did Japan attack United States forces?

# Europe and North Africa

In early 1942, the Allies faced a bleak situation on all fronts. Germany controlled most of Western Europe. Although Britain had not fallen, it was powerless to challenge the Nazi position on the continent. In Eastern Europe, the Nazis had advanced deep into Soviet territory. Soviet losses numbered in the millions. Still, in 1942, the <u>pendulum</u> began to swing in the Allies' favor.

**The Soviets Resist** Hitler had expected the Soviet Union to collapse swiftly in the face of his ferocious assault. But in December 1941, Soviet troops—assisted by the brutal Russian winter—halted the German advance just miles from Moscow.

The Germans mounted another offensive in mid-1942. A major battle took place in and around the Russian city of Stalingrad. Months of bitter fighting ended in a clear Soviet victory. From then on, the Soviets slowly drove the Germans back westward.

**Main Idea**
The German advance was slowed by Soviet resistance and by Allied victories in North Africa.

**Vocabulary** *Builder*
**pendulum** (PEHN jah luhm) *n.* hanging weight that swings from side to side in a steady rhythm

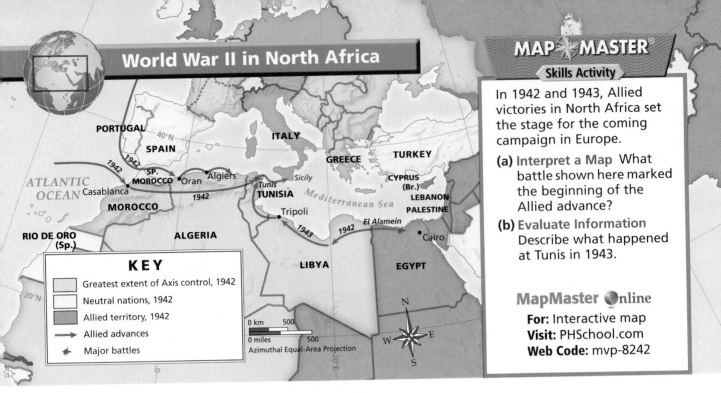

## World War II in North Africa

**MAP MASTER®**

**Skills Activity**

In 1942 and 1943, Allied victories in North Africa set the stage for the coming campaign in Europe.

**(a) Interpret a Map** What battle shown here marked the beginning of the Allied advance?

**(b) Evaluate Information** Describe what happened at Tunis in 1943.

**MapMaster Online**

**For:** Interactive map
**Visit:** PHSchool.com
**Web Code:** mvp-8242

**KEY**

- Greatest extent of Axis control, 1942
- Neutral nations, 1942
- Allied territory, 1942
- → Allied advances
- ⭑ Major battles

**The Tide Turns in North Africa** In North Africa, Erwin Rommel, Germany's most respected general, won a number of quick victories. Then, in October 1942, British troops defeated German forces at El Alamein (el AL uh mayn) in Egypt. Slowly, the British drove Rommel's tank corps westward into Tunisia.

Meanwhile, in November, the first American ground troops in combat landed in North Africa. Under the command of General Dwight D. Eisenhower, they occupied Morocco and Algeria. Hemmed in on both sides, Rommel's army surrendered in May 1943.

☑**Checkpoint** How did Allied fortunes change in North Africa?

## Japan Sweeps Through the Pacific

**Main Idea**
Japan's rapid advance across the Pacific was finally halted in two major naval battles.

In the days after Pearl Harbor, Japanese armies swiftly took control of Hong Kong, Malaya, Thailand, Burma, Guam, and Wake Island. To the south, they occupied the Dutch East Indies (present-day Indonesia) and the Solomon Islands and threatened Australia.

**The Philippines Fall** Hours after the attack on Pearl Harbor, Japanese aircraft bombed airfields in the Philippines, the island chain governed by the United States. The Japanese air force destroyed most of the planes that could defend the islands against their invasion.

Two weeks later, a Japanese invasion force landed on Luzon, the key Philippine island. There, General Douglas MacArthur commanded a Filipino–American force. As the enemy closed in on Manila, the capital city, MacArthur withdrew his forces onto the Bataan (bah TAHN) peninsula. He was then ordered by President Roosevelt to go to Australia and take command of all U.S. troops in the region. But as he left the Philippines, MacArthur vowed, "I shall return."

On Bataan and the nearby island of Corregidor, the trapped Americans and Filipinos waged a heroic defense. By early March, they were the only major forces in the Pacific that had not given way to the Japanese. The defenders of Bataan finally surrendered on April 9. Corregidor fell the following month.

**Bataan Death March** At Bataan, the Japanese captured nearly 70,000 soldiers. Already weak from hunger, the American and Filipino prisoners were then forced to walk 65 miles to a prison camp. Along the way, so many prisoners died of starvation, disease, or violence that their trek soon became known as the Bataan Death March.

**Coral Sea and Midway** The tide began to turn in the Pacific with two historic naval battles. In May 1942, at the Battle of the Coral Sea, American and Japanese navies waged a new form of warfare. For the first time, opposing ships did not see one another. Instead, planes taking off from the decks of huge aircraft carriers attacked enemy ships many miles away. Both sides suffered heavy losses, but the United States halted the Japanese drive to New Guinea.

A month later, the Japanese sought to take the island of Midway, home of a key American military base. But the Americans sank 4 Japanese aircraft carriers, destroyed 322 Japanese aircraft, and reduced Japan's supply of highly trained pilots. After the Battle of Midway, Japan's navy no longer ruled the Pacific.

**☑Checkpoint** What was the Bataan Death March?

⭐ **Looking Back and Ahead** The attack on Pearl Harbor brought American forces into the biggest war in history. In the next section, you will see how the war affected Americans at home.

Bataan Death March

## Section 2 | Check Your Progress

**Progress Monitoring** ⚓nline
**For:** Self-test with instant help
**Visit:** PHSchool.com
**Web Code:** mva-8242

**Comprehension and Critical Thinking**

1. **(a) Identify** Name two ways that President Roosevelt strengthened ties with Britain in the early years of the war.
   **(b) Detect Points of View** Why did some Americans view these actions as wrong?

2. **(a) Recall** Why did the situation look bad for the Allies in early 1942?
   **(b) Apply Information** Explain why each of the following places is considered a turning point in the war: Stalingrad, El Alamein, Midway.

**🔁 Reading Skill**

3. **Use Sentence Clues to Analyze Meaning** Use sentence clues to analyze the meaning of *ferocious* in the following sentence: Hitler had expected the Soviet Union to collapse swiftly in the face of his *ferocious* assault. According to that sentence, what did Hitler think would happen because his assault was ferocious? What does *ferocious* mean?

**Vocabulary** *Builder*

4. Write two definitions of the term total war—one a formal definition for a teacher, the other an informal definition for a younger child.

**Writing**

5. Use print or Internet resources to find more information about one of the battles or people discussed in this section. Identify at least three sources of nonprint material on the topic. List the sources you find and describe their contents.

# Dauntless: A Novel of Midway and Guadalcanal by Barrett Tillman

## Prepare to Read

### Introduction

Barrett Tillman is an expert on military aviation and best known for his nonfiction books. Though his 1992 novel *Dauntless* is a work of fiction, it is based on careful research about the war in the Pacific. The novel mixes real and fictional characters. In the excerpt below, Japanese and American fighter pilots prepare for the Battle of Midway in June 1942.

### Reading Skill

**Analyze Dramatic Irony** Often, when we read a novel or see a movie, we know something that the characters do not. This can lead to dramatic irony. Dramatic irony is the contrast between what a character thinks is true and what the audience knows is true. As you read this excerpt, look for two examples of dramatic irony.

### Vocabulary *Builder*

As you read this literature selection, look for the following underlined words:

**reconnaissance** (ree KAHN ah sihns) *n.* act of gathering advance information

**disposition** (dihs pah SIHSH ahn) *n.* arrangement; placement

**cryptanalysis** (krihpt ah NAHL uh sihs) *n.* science of breaking codes

**latitude** (LAH tih tyood) *n.* freedom from restrictions

**attrition** (uh TRIH shuhn) *n.* steady weakening or wearing away

---

*[Aboard a Japanese ship in the Pacific]*

"We are currently here," said Lieutenant Masatake Naito. The ship's air-operations officer pointed to a hash mark along the blue track, indicating a position 700 nautical miles off Japan. His audience, composed of the aircrews who would fly the reconnaissance planes, paid strict attention. After four days at sea, they were about to learn their mysterious destination. . . .

"At dawn four days from now, this force will launch powerful air attacks on the American base at Midway." He tapped the two specks indicating Sand and Eastern Islands, object of the multi-pronged assault. . . .

"We will take the enemy by surprise," Naito continued, "as we have evidence that their remaining fleet units are still in Pearl Harbor." He paused for emphasis, a confident look on his face. "The Americans will be unable to resist coming out to meet us. They must defend Midway or risk leaving Hawaii open to invasion. When they sail to defend Midway, our submarines and fleet units will destroy them in one decisive battle. . . .

"You division commanders—make certain everything is in order. Take nothing for granted." He stood with his hands on his hips, chin jutting forward. "I am counting on each of you. And so is the emperor!" Naito decided against a rousing series of "Banzai" cheers. He would save that emotional moment for later—at the inevitable victory celebration.

**Analyze Dramatic Irony**

In historical fiction, dramatic irony can occur because the audience knows how events really turned out. Why is the last line of this paragraph an example of dramatic irony?

*[Aboard the American aircraft carrier Yorktown]*

The ship's air-operations officer, Commander Murr Arnold, strode to the front of the room. . . . "Gentlemen," Arnold began, I wish to acquaint you with the <u>disposition</u> of our forces as we near Midway." His metallic voice cut through the crowded room, precise and clear. . . .

"Our course is designed to take us well north of the Hawaiian chain and arrive northeast of Midway day after tomorrow. If we remain undetected by the Japanese, we'll be in excellent position to launch surprise air strikes from their flank. We know they're coming, but apparently they don't know that we know."

Arnold then described the Japanese armada steaming toward Midway: the transport group, the main body and supporting force, but he emphasized the striking force of the four veteran carriers. As he did so, Burnett leaned into Rogers and whispered, "I tell you, Buck, that man of ours in Tokyo is worth every dime we pay him."

Rogers stifled a giggle but his mind registered one thought: *cryptanalysis.* . . .

"Admiral Nimitz has given us a great deal of <u>latitude</u> in the conduct of this engagement," Arnold continued. "We will be guided by the principle of calculated risk, employing maximum <u>attrition</u> tactics, but the actual conduct of the battle rests with us." He paused briefly, sweeping the room with his cobra gaze. "There's just one more thing, gentlemen. I have copied a message from Admiral Spruance to Task Force Sixteen, and I want to share it with you. He says, and I quote, 'The successful conclusion of the operations now commencing will be of great value to our country.'" Arnold looked up from the message firmly. "I cannot add anything to that."

From *Dauntless: A Novel of Midway and Guadalcanal* by Barrett Tillman. Bantam Books, 1992.

☑ **Checkpoint**    **What approach is used, by both the Japanese and the Americans, to prepare pilots for battle?**

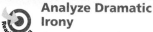

**Analyze Dramatic Irony**

Sometimes, the reader only recognizes that something is ironic when they read it for the second time, knowing the whole story. Read this paragraph, then reread the scene on the Japanese ship. Identify another example of dramatic irony.

**United States airplanes attack a Japanese aircraft carrier at the Battle of Midway.**

If you liked the excerpt from this novel and want to read more about the war in the Pacific, you might read *A Boy at War: A Novel of Pearl Harbor* by Harry Mazer. Simon and Schuster, 2001

*Analyze* **LITERATURE**

Imagine that you are one of the American pilots on board the *Yorktown* in the scene above. Write a letter home expressing your feelings about the coming battle.

## Objectives

1. Find out how the United States built its military and converted its economy to meet wartime needs.

2. Learn how American women contributed to the war effort.

3. Discover how World War II affected Japanese Americans and other groups of people at home.

## Prepare to Read

### 🔁 Reading Skill

**Use Context to Determine Meaning** By examining text around an unfamiliar word, you can often determine its meaning. For example, the unfamiliar word might be referred to or further described in the sentences before or after the sentence in which it is used.

### Vocabulary *Builder*

**High-Use Words**

<u>convert</u>, p. 816

<u>vague</u>, p. 819

**Key Terms and People**

rationing, p. 817

intern, p. 818

A. Philip Randolph, p. 819

bracero, p. 820

⭐ **Background Knowledge** As you have read, World War II totally involved all the people and resources of each nation. In this section, you will explore the American home front. You will also examine problems that certain groups of Americans faced.

**Main Idea**
The United States increased the size of its military and directed the economy toward the war effort.

## Organizing for War

The first challenge the United States faced was to build up its armed forces. Even before Pearl Harbor, Congress had enacted a draft law. Just days after the bombing of Pearl Harbor, Congress revised the law to require people to serve for the entire war.

**Building the Military** Eventually, more than 15 million volunteers and draftees would wear the American uniform during World War II. The number included Americans from every ethnic and religious group. In newly built military bases around the country, recruits trained to fight in the jungles of the Pacific, the deserts of North Africa, and the farmlands and towns of Europe.

Hundreds of thousands of American women were also in uniform during World War II. They served as nurses or in noncombat roles in special branches such as the Women's Army Corp (WACs). Women pilots ferried bombers from base to base, towed targets, and taught men to fly.

**Vocabulary *Builder***
<u>convert</u> (kuhn VERT) *v.* to change from one purpose to another

**A Wartime Economy** Industry quickly <u>converted</u> its output from consumer to military goods. The government established a War Production Board to supervise the changeover and set goals for production. As a result, military output nearly doubled.

The war quickly ended the Great Depression. Unemployment fell as millions of jobs opened up in factories. Minority workers found jobs where they had been rejected in the past.

**Supporting the War Effort** All Americans were expected to play a role in supplying Allied forces with food, clothing, and war equipment. As in World War I, Americans planted victory gardens to supplement food supplies and bought war bonds to help pay military costs.

To conserve needed resources, the government imposed rationing. Rationing is the act of setting limits on the amount of scarce goods people can buy. Americans were issued ration coupons to purchase coffee, sugar, meat, shoes, gasoline, tires, and many other goods.

War bond campaigns, rationing, and victory gardens did more than help pay for the war effort. They also gave citizens at home a sense that they were helping to win the war. Thus, they helped maintain public morale during the long struggle.

☑Checkpoint   **What was the War Production Board?**

# Women in Industry

With millions of men in uniform, defense industries needed a new source of labor. The government began a large-scale effort to recruit women for industry.

Millions of women took over jobs in factories and shipyards. Some welded, tended blast furnaces, and ran huge cranes. Others became bus drivers, police officers, and gas station attendants. A fictional character, "Rosie the Riveter," became a popular symbol of all women who worked for the war effort.

**Use Context to Determine Meaning**
*Reading Skill* To determine the meaning of the word *morale*, use paragraph clues and this question: How do people feel during difficult times?

**Main Idea**
During the war, American women took over many industrial jobs.

**Explore More Video**
To learn more about the role of women in World War II, view the video.

**Rosie the Riveter** This famous poster of Rosie the Riveter (right) assured American women that they were strong enough to handle the challenges of wartime factory work. At left, two real-life "Rosies" work together to build an aircraft. **Critical Thinking:** *Link Past and Present Why do you think this poster of Rosie the Riveter is still popular with many women today?*

Because women were needed in industry, they were able to gain better pay and working conditions. The government agreed that women and men should get the same pay for the same job. Some employers, however, found ways to avoid equal pay.

War work gave many American women a new sense of confidence and independence. "It gave me a good start in life," said welder Nova Lee Holbrook. "I decided that if I could learn to weld like a man, I could do anything it took to make a living."

✓**Checkpoint**  **What jobs did women do during the war?**

## Ordeal for Japanese Americans

**Main Idea**
Because of wartime fears, many Japanese Americans were forced to live in detention camps.

At the start of the war, about 300,000 people of Japanese origin lived in the United States. More than half resided in Hawaii. The rest lived mostly on the West Coast, especially in California.

After the attack on Pearl Harbor, many Americans feared that Japanese Americans would act as spies to help enemy submarines shell military bases or coastal cities. In truth, such suspicions were baseless. There was not a single documented case of disloyalty by a Japanese American.

**Internment** The intense anti-Japanese fears led President Roosevelt to issue Executive Order 9066 in February 1942. The order was used to intern, or temporarily imprison, some 110,000 Japanese Americans for the duration of the war.

**Japanese American Internment**

Two frightened boys line up for baggage inspection at an internment camp for Japanese Americans. One internee later recalled, "We didn't know where we were going, how long we'd be gone. We didn't know what to take." **Critical Thinking: *Apply Information*** *Why were these boys forced to leave their homes during World War II?*

Internees were allowed to bring with them only what they could carry. They had to sell the rest of their possessions quickly, at a fraction of their worth. The U.S. Army then transported them from the West Coast to small, remote internment camps enclosed by barbed wire. Armed soldiers looked down on them from guard towers.

In the 1944 case of *Korematsu* v. *United States*, the Supreme Court ruled that military necessity justified internment. Still, three of the nine justices dissented. One wrote:

❝We must accord great respect and consideration to the judgments of the military authorities who are on the scene and who have full knowledge of the military facts. . . . At the same time, however, it is essential that there be definite limits to military discretion. . . . Individuals must not be left impoverished of their constitutional rights on plea of military necessity that has neither substance nor support.❞

—Frank Murphy, dissenting opinion, *Korematsu* v. *United States*

As the war ended, the government released the internees. In 1948, it made a small payment to them for the property they had lost. However, a formal apology did not come until 1990. At that time, the government paid $20,000 to each surviving internee.

**Japanese Americans in Uniform** For Japanese Americans, being imprisoned on such <u>vague</u> charges was a humiliating experience. Still, about 17,000 Japanese Americans showed their loyalty by joining the armed services. All-Japanese units fought in North Africa, Italy, and France, winning thousands of military awards and medals. One group of Japanese American soldiers, the 442nd Nisei Regimental Combat Team, became the most highly decorated military unit in United States history.

**Vocabulary** *Builder*
<u>vague</u> (vayg) *adj.* uncertain; not precise or exact

☑**Checkpoint**   **Why were many Japanese Americans interned?**

## Tensions at Home

Japanese Americans were not the only group to face wartime restrictions. About 11,000 German Americans and several hundred Italian Americans were also held in government camps as "enemy aliens." Most of these were foreign-born residents who had not yet achieved citizenship. Other German Americans and Italian Americans faced curfews or travel restrictions.

**Main Idea**
Enemy aliens, African Americans, and Mexican Americans faced discrimination at home.

**African Americans** As in past wars, African Americans served in segregated units during World War II. Groups such as the NAACP and the National Association of Colored Graduate Nurses protested against the racial policy of the armed forces and the military nursing corps.

Discrimination was also widespread in industries doing business with the government. Some African American leaders pointed out that while the nation was fighting for democracy overseas, it still permitted injustice at home.

Union leader A. Philip Randolph, head of the Brotherhood of Sleeping Car Porters, threatened a mass protest unless Roosevelt moved to end discrimination in the armed forces. In response, the President ordered employers doing business with the government to support racial equality in hiring. To enforce the order, he set up the Fair Employment Practices Committee (FEPC) to investigate charges of discrimination.

The FEPC and the growing need for workers opened many jobs that previously had been closed to African Americans. By the end of 1944, about two million African Americans were working in war plants.

**Demanding Fair Employment**
This man is picketing at a dairy that hires only white people as drivers. **Critical Thinking:** *Analyze Information* *What is the main idea of the picket sign shown here?*

Young man in a "zoot suit"

However, as employment of African Americans increased, so did racial tension. Thousands of Americans—black people and white people—moved to cities to work in industry. Competition for scarce housing led to angry incidents and even violence. In 1943, race riots broke out in Detroit, New York, and other American cities.

**Mexican Americans** About half a million Mexican Americans served in the armed forces during World War II. At the same time, the Mexican American population was increasing. Because of the need for workers, the United States signed a treaty with Mexico in 1942. It allowed American companies to hire braceros, or Mexican laborers. As more Mexicans moved north to work on farms and railroads, they often faced prejudice and violent strife.

Young Mexican Americans in Los Angeles often dressed in showy "zoot suits." Their clothing and language set them apart. In June 1943, bands of sailors on shore leave attacked young Mexican Americans, beating them and clubbing them on the streets. The incident sparked several days of rioting.

Newspapers blamed the "Zoot Suit Riots" on the Mexican Americans. But in her newspaper column, Eleanor Roosevelt argued that the riots were the result of "longstanding discrimination against the Mexicans in the Southwest."

✔**Checkpoint** How did African Americans seek fairer treatment during the war?

⭐ **Looking Back and Ahead** Despite problems at home, Americans were united in their resolve to push on to victory in Europe and the Pacific. In the next section, you will see how that victory was won.

---

Section 3 | **Check Your Progress**

**Progress Monitoring** Online
**For:** Self-test with instant help
**Visit:** PHSchool.com
**Web Code:** mva-8243

**Comprehension and Critical Thinking**

1. **(a) Recall** What economic restrictions did Americans face during World War II?
   **(b) Identify Costs and Benefits** What were the costs of these restrictions? What were the benefits?

2. **(a) Recall** What happened to Japanese Americans on the West Coast during the war?
   **(b) Draw Conclusions** Do you think restricting people's civil liberties during wartime is ever justified? Why or why not?

**Reading Skill**

3. **Use Context to Determine Meaning** Reread the text following the subheading "Mexican Americans." Use different clues to determine the meaning of the word *strife*.

**Vocabulary Builder**

4. Draw a table with three rows and three columns. In the first column, list the following key terms: rationing, intern, bracero. In the next column, write the definition of each. In the last column, make a small illustration that shows the meaning.

**Writing**

5. A thesis statement expresses the main idea for a piece of writing. Based on what you have read in this section, write a thesis statement that could be developed using multimedia support on one of the following topics:
   • the internment of Japanese Americans
   • women's contribution to the war effort
   • rationing and other domestic war measures

Follow your thesis statement with a description of the kinds of multimedia materials you would use to support and develop it.

## Objectives

1. Learn how the Allies were finally able to defeat Germany.

2. Discover how a powerful new weapon brought the war in the Pacific to a close.

3. Explore the horrors of the Holocaust.

4. Understand the immediate aftereffects of World War II.

## Prepare to Read

### ⟳ Reading Skill

**Use Context to Determine Meaning** Here are additional clues to determine meaning. Draw on your own experience or knowledge. Look for contrast clues, in which a familiar word contrasts with the unfamiliar word. Search for synonym clues, in which a familiar word has a similar meaning.

### Vocabulary *Builder*

**High-Use Words**

dimension, p. 821

efficient, p. 826

**Key Terms and People**

Harry S Truman, p. 822

island hopping, p. 824

kamikaze, p. 824

genocide, p. 826

war crimes, p. 827

---

☆ **Background Knowledge** In Section 2, you saw how the Allies turned back Axis advances in the Pacific and in North Africa. In this section, you will follow World War II to its conclusion.

## Victory in Europe

In 1943, Russia was bearing the brunt of the Nazi assault. Stalin urged the Americans and British to open up a "second front" in Europe by invading France. However, Roosevelt and Churchill did not think their forces were ready for such a difficult task. Instead, they chose a more realistic goal—removing Italy from the war.

**Italy Surrenders** In July 1943, American and British troops crossed the Mediterranean from Tunisia. They swiftly took control of the Italian island of Sicily. By fall, they were fighting their way northward along the Italian Peninsula.

The king of Italy dismissed Mussolini from office. On September 8, 1943, the new government surrendered to the Allies. Even so, German troops in Italy continued to fight. The Allies would face a long struggle before they finally controlled Italy.

**D-Day** In 1944, Allied forces were ready to undertake the invasion of France. Under the command of General Eisenhower, the Allies carefully planned the landing. It would be an operation of massive dimensions, involving thousands of ships and aircraft.

On June 6, 1944—known as D-Day—more than 155,000 American, British, and Canadian troops crossed the English Channel. They landed on five beaches at Normandy, in western France. Troops at four of the beaches quickly overcame German opposition.

**Main Idea**
The invasion of Italy and the D-Day landing in France set the stage for the defeat of Germany.

**Vocabulary *Builder***
dimension (dih MEHN shuhn) *n.* size or extent; length, width, or height

On Omaha Beach, however, Americans met an especially fierce German defense. One American survivor of the assault later recalled being wounded by a shell as he tried to come ashore:

> **❝**The shrapnel hit my right shoulder and leg. The explosion and concussion seemed to push me into the ground and knocked the breath out of me. The force of the explosion blew my helmet off and cut the corner of my left eye. . . . The Germans were firing everything they could.**❞**
>
> —Roy Arnn, letter, November 10, 1990

By day's end, some 2,500 American soldiers lay dead on Omaha Beach. However, they had succeeded in their mission. Within a month, a million Allied troops had stormed ashore.

On August 25, 1944, the Allies entered Paris. After four years under Nazi rule, French men, women, and children greeted their liberators with joy.

**Battle of the Bulge** Allied forces pushed eastward. But on December 16, 1944, the Germans counterattacked in Belgium. Hitler poured his remaining reserves into the attack. Bad weather grounded Allied aircraft for the first week of the battle. This allowed German troops to create a "bulge" in the American lines.

The Germans came close to breaking through Allied lines. But, in the end, their attempt to fight off defeat proved futile. German troops were short of critical supplies, especially fuel. Also, though each side lost tens of thousands of men, the Allies had additional troops in reserve. Germany was running out of soldiers.

Fighting in Northern Europe's coldest winter in 40 years, Americans forces won the Battle of the Bulge. Germany now lay wide open from both east and west.

**Germany Invaded** In January 1945, a huge Soviet force entered Germany from the east. Soon, the Western Allies also entered in large numbers from the west. While the Allied armies advanced on the ground, their planes bombed German industries and cities.

On April 12, 1945, President Franklin D. Roosevelt died of a stroke. His death shattered Americans. Many could hardly remember anyone else as their leader. At a critical moment, Vice President Harry S Truman was suddenly thrust into the highest office in the country. Truman had little experience dealing with important policy issues. Would he be a decisive leader?

**Victory in Europe** Meanwhile, Germany was collapsing. On April 16, Soviet troops began an assault on Berlin. Hitler took shelter in a bunker built beneath the city's streets. There, with his Nazi empire in ruins, he committed suicide on April 30, 1945.

A week later, representatives of Germany's armed forces unconditionally surrendered at Eisenhower's headquarters in France. On May 8, the Allies celebrated V-E Day, Victory in Europe.

**✓Checkpoint** Why was D-Day important?

**Use Context to Determine Meaning**
Use clues in these paragraphs to determine the meaning of the word *futile*. Explain all the clues you used.

Anxious American soldiers wait to go into battle.

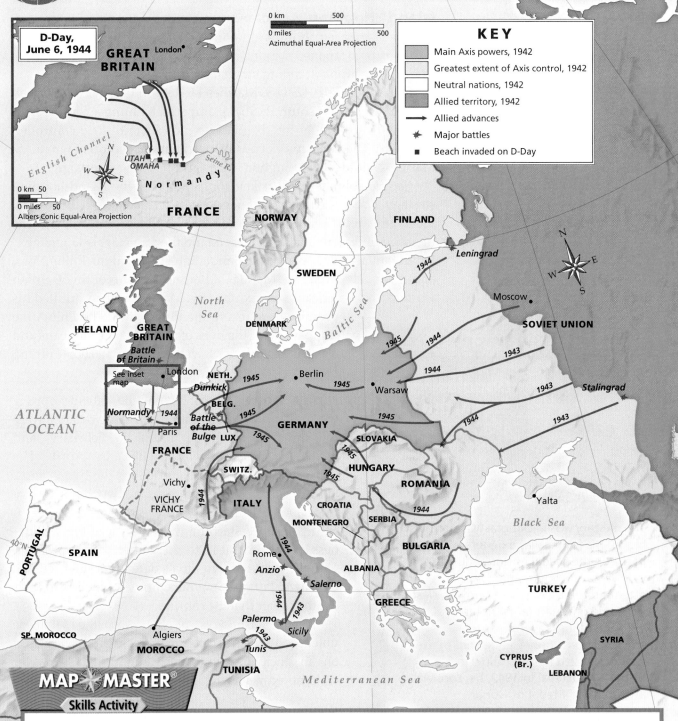

**D-Day, June 6, 1944**

GREAT BRITAIN
London

*English Channel*

UTAH
OMAHA

*Seine R.*

N o r m a n d y

FRANCE

0 km 50
0 miles 50
Albers Conic Equal-Area Projection

0 km 500
0 miles 500
Azimuthal Equal-Area Projection

**KEY**

Main Axis powers, 1942

Greatest extent of Axis control, 1942

Neutral nations, 1942

Allied territory, 1942

→ Allied advances

✶ Major battles

■ Beach invaded on D-Day

NORWAY

FINLAND

*Leningrad*

1944

Moscow

SOVIET UNION

SWEDEN

*North Sea*

DENMARK

*Baltic Sea*

1945

1944

1943

IRELAND

GREAT BRITAIN

*Battle of Britain*

See inset map

London

NETH.

*Dunkirk*

BELG.

Berlin

1945

1944

Warsaw

1943

*Stalingrad*

1945

1944

1943

1943

ATLANTIC OCEAN

*Normandy*

1944

Paris

*Battle of the Bulge*

LUX.

1945

1945

GERMANY

1945

SLOVAKIA

1945

HUNGARY

1945

ROMANIA

1944

*Yalta*

*Black Sea*

FRANCE

1944

SWITZ.

Vichy

VICHY FRANCE

ITALY

CROATIA

MONTENEGRO

SERBIA

BULGARIA

PORTUGAL

SPAIN

Rome

1944

*Anzio*

*Salerno*

1943

ALBANIA

TURKEY

1944

Palermo

1943

Sicily

GREECE

*Mediterranean Sea*

CYPRUS (Br.)

SYRIA

LEBANON

SP. MOROCCO

Algiers

MOROCCO

1943

Tunis

TUNISIA

# MAP✶MASTER®
### Skills Activity

After the massive Allied landing on D-Day, American and British troops pushed steadily eastward toward Germany. At the same time, Soviet troops were already advancing westward.

**(a) Interpret a Map** Describe the movement of Allied troops on D-Day. Where did they go next?

**(b) Evaluate Information** Why were there no troop movements or fighting in Spain?

**MapMaster ●nline**

**For:** Interactive map
**Visit:** PHSchool.com
**Web Code:** mvp-8244

# Victory in the Pacific

The Battle of Midway in 1942 had halted Japan's advance in the Pacific. After that, the Americans went on the offensive.

**Island Hopping** American commanders adopted a strategy known as island hopping, in which American forces would capture some Japanese-held islands and go around others. Each island taken was a stepping stone toward Japan.

On August 7, 1942, U.S. Marines landed on Guadalcanal (gwah dal cah NAL) in the south Pacific. Hampered by hunger and disease, the Americans fought for six grueling months until they controlled the island. The fierce combat on Guadalcanal was typical of what U.S. Marines would face throughout the island-hopping campaign.

Navajo soldiers made a key contribution to the island-hopping strategy. Using their own language, these code-talkers radioed vital messages from island to island. The Japanese intercepted the messages but were unable to understand the rare Navajo language.

In January 1945, army units landed on Luzon, in the Philippines, and then advanced on Manila. After nearly a month of urban warfare, the Americans secured the city. MacArthur had fulfilled his promise to return to the Philippines. The Philippine campaign cost the lives of over 14,000 Americans and 350,000 Japanese, as well as some 100,000 Filipino civilians.

**Japan Holds Firm** Meanwhile, island-hopping marines approached Japan. Their last two stops were Iwo Jima (EE woh JEE muh), in February, and Okinawa (oh kuh NAH wuh), in April. The Americans paid a terrible price for the two islands. Six thousand Americans died at Iwo Jima; twelve thousand at Okinawa.

Even more startling, however, was the willingness of the Japanese to die rather than surrender. Only 1 percent of Iwo Jima's defenders survived. On Okinawa, Japanese soldiers jumped off cliffs to their deaths rather than be captured.

In the last days of the war, the Japanese unleashed a deadly new form of combat. It was based on an ancient code which taught that surrender dishonored a warrior. In kamikaze (kah muh KAH zee) missions, suicide pilots crashed their planes into American ships. These events convinced American war planners that only a full-scale invasion of Japan's home islands would force a surrender.

After Hitler's defeat in Europe, the Allies were able to turn their full attention to the Pacific. By the spring of 1945, American bombers were pounding the Japanese home islands. American ships bombarded the coast and destroyed shipping.

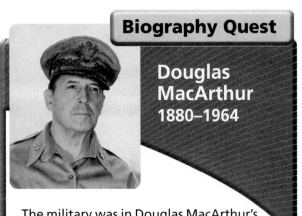

## Biography Quest

### Douglas MacArthur
### 1880–1964

The military was in Douglas MacArthur's blood. His father was a general who had won the Medal of Honor during the Civil War. As a young man, MacArthur attended the Military Academy at West Point. He graduated first in his class, with the highest average in years.

MacArthur's brave leadership in the Pacific allowed him to follow in his father's footsteps. In 1942, he, too, was awarded the Medal of Honor.

### Biography Quest

**How did MacArthur contribute to Japan after World War II ended?**

**For:** The answer to the question about MacArthur

**Visit:** PHSchool.com

**Web Code:** mvd-8244

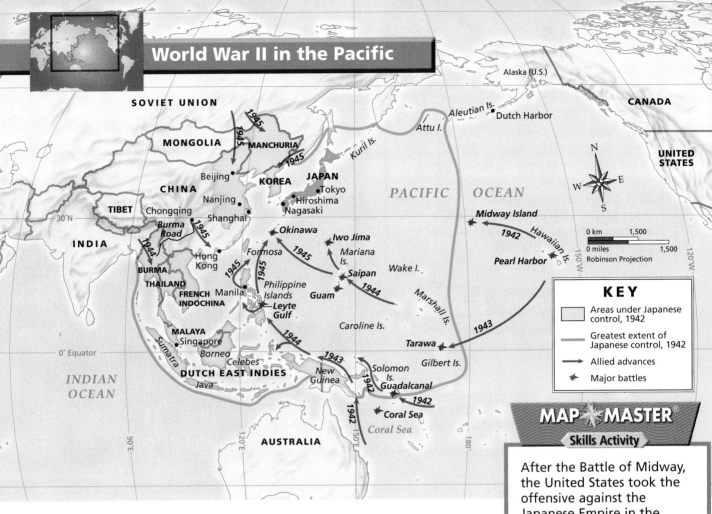

## World War II in the Pacific

**KEY**

| | Areas under Japanese control, 1942 |
| --- | --- |
| | Greatest extent of Japanese control, 1942 |
| → | Allied advances |
| ✹ | Major battles |

0 km 1,500
0 miles 1,500
Robinson Projection

**MAP MASTER®**

**Skills Activity**

After the Battle of Midway, the United States took the offensive against the Japanese Empire in the Pacific.

**(a) Interpret a Map** How close did the Allied island-hopping campaign get to Japan itself?

**(b) Understand Sequence** Describe the troop movements and sequence of battles that led to the recapture of the Philippines.

**MapMaster Online**

**For:** Interactive map
**Visit:** PHSchool.com
**Web Code:** mvp-8244

Millions of Japanese were short of food. Yet, Japanese leaders still talked of winning a glorious victory.

**The Atomic Bomb** President Truman made plans for invading Japan in the autumn. His military advisers warned him that the invasion might cost half a million American casualties. In July, however, Truman learned that a secret weapon—the atomic bomb—had been successfully tested in the New Mexico desert. The new weapon was so powerful that it could destroy an entire city.

On August 6, 1945, an American plane dropped an atomic bomb on the city of Hiroshima. The destruction was like nothing the world had ever seen. Within minutes, the blast and searing heat had killed more than 130,000 people. Still, the Japanese refused to surrender.

On August 9, a second atomic bomb was dropped on the city of Nagasaki. Some 35,000 people died instantly. Many more in both cities would die slower deaths from radiation poisoning.

At last, on August 14, 1945, the emperor of Japan announced that the nation would surrender. That day became known as V-J Day. On September 2, 1945, MacArthur formally accepted Japan's surrender aboard the battleship USS *Missouri,* anchored in Tokyo Bay. World War II was over at last.

✔**Checkpoint**  What was kamikaze warfare?

## Links Across Time

**1945** These survivors of a Nazi death camp can hardly believe they are free.

### The Holocaust and Genocide

**1945** Allied armies liberated the Nazi death camps, exposing the full horror of the Holocaust. People around the world asked how they could prevent such genocide from happening again.

**2004** Since 1945, genocides have occurred in such places as Cambodia, Bosnia, and Rwanda. In 2004, the U.S. secretary of state accused the Sudan government of starving or murdering up to 50,000 people in the Darfur region.

### Link to Today   Online

**Genocide in the Modern World** When attempts at genocide occur today, what actions do the United States and the world take to stop them?

**For:** The continuing legacy of the Holocaust
**Visit:** PHSchool.com
**Web Code:** mvc-8244

---

**Main Idea**
The world learned how the Nazis murdered 6 million Jews and millions of other people.

## The Holocaust

World War II was the bloodiest conflict in human history. It took the lives of up to 60 million people, including about 400,000 Americans. Some two thirds of those killed were civilians. Still, some of the worst horrors were not fully revealed until after Germany's defeat. Only then did the world learn the full extent of Nazi brutality.

**Victims of the Nazis** As you have read, Nazism was built on racism and extreme anti-Semitism. During the war, Hitler moved beyond restrictions on Jews to what he termed the "final solution to the Jewish problem"—the attempt to annihilate all Jews in Europe.

Some 6 million Jews were murdered under the Nazis. Entire families, from grandparents to infants, were wiped out. This mass slaughter is today known as the Holocaust. As a result of the Holocaust, a new word entered the English language: genocide. Genocide is the deliberate attempt to wipe out an entire nation or group of people.

Other groups also became victims of the Nazis. The Nazis murdered millions of Poles, Slavs, Gypsies, communists, and people with physical or mental disabilities.

**Vocabulary Builder**
**efficient** (ee FISH ehnt) *adj.* acting effectively, without wasted cost or effort

**Death Camps** The Nazis developed an <u>efficient</u> system of mass murder. They built six death camps in Poland. Millions of women, men, and children were transported to these camps in railway cattle cars. Hundreds at a time were killed in gas chambers. Others were subjected to torture or horrifying medical experiments.

As Allied soldiers liberated the death camps, they were shocked by the sight and smell of piles of corpses. The survivors were living skeletons. One American radio reporter told his listeners:

> **❝**In another part of the camp they showed me the children, hundreds of them. Some were only 6 years old. One rolled up his sleeves, showed me his number. It was tattooed on his arm. B-6030, it was. The others showed me their numbers. They will carry them till they die. . . . I could see their ribs through their thin shirts.**❞**
>
> —Edward R. Murrow, *PM*, April 16, 1945

Murrow concluded, "I reported what I saw and heard, but only part of it. For most of it, I have no words."

**War Crimes Trials** Shocked by the Holocaust and other Nazi actions, the Allies took an unprecedented step. For the first time in history, victors in a war prosecuted leaders of the losing side for war crimes. War crimes are wartime acts of cruelty and brutality that are judged to be beyond the accepted rules of war and human behavior.

In the German city of Nuremberg, Allied judges tried prominent Nazis for plunging the world into war and for the horrors of the death camps. In 1946, at the first Nuremberg Trials, 12 defendants were sentenced to death by hanging. Similar trials were held in Manila and Tokyo to try leaders of the Japanese war machine.

A veteran visits the National World War II Memorial.

✓**Checkpoint**　**Which people were killed in Nazi death camps?**

⭐ **Looking Back and Ahead**　After World War I, the United States returned to isolationism. But after World War II, Americans accepted a new role in the world. In the next chapter, you will see how the nation took the lead in a long global conflict—the Cold War.

---

**Section 4 | Check Your Progress**

**Progress Monitoring** ⬤nline
**For:** Self-test with instant help
**Visit:** PHSchool.com
**Web Code:** mva-8244

**Comprehension and Critical Thinking**

**1. (a) Identify** What was D-Day? What did it accomplish?
**(b) Draw Conclusions** What do you think might have happened if the D-Day landing had failed?

**2. (a) Recall** Why did the United States decide to drop the atomic bomb on Hiroshima?
**(b) Identify Alternatives** What other courses might the Americans have followed? Do you think the decision to drop the bomb was justified?

🔄 **Reading Skill**

**3. Use Context to Determine Meaning** Reread the paragraph with the subheading "Victims of the Nazis." Use different clues to determine the meaning of *annihilate*. Explain *all* the clues you used and where you found them.

**Vocabulary *Builder***

Fill in the blanks with the correct key terms from this chapter.

**4.** The leaders who planned the Nazi death camps were executed for _____.

**5.** Pilots who carried out _____ missions were certain to die.

**6.** The _____ campaign allowed Allied forces to inch slowly toward Japan.

**7.** The Nazi attempt to exterminate Jews was an example of _____.

**Writing**

**8.** Create an outline that would develop the following thesis statement for a multimedia report: "The D-Day landing was the single most decisive battle in World War II." Be sure to include ideas for media materials.

Sometimes the arguments in a primary source are weakened by faulty reasoning, that is, the author makes an error in thinking or argument. Common types of faulty reasoning include incorrectly stating cause-and-effect relationships or misinterpreting a situation, an event, or a character.

**Primary Source**

Read the excerpts below about the political consequences of the 1938 Munich Pact.

"I believe there is sincerity and goodwill on both sides. My main purpose has been to work for the pacification of Europe, for the removal of those suspicions and those [hatreds] which have so long poisoned the air. The path that leads to appeasement is long and bristles with obstacles. This question of Czechoslovakia is the latest and perhaps the most dangerous. Now that we have got past it I feel that it may be possible to make further progress along the road to sanity."

—Neville Chamberlain, address to the House of Commons, October 3, 1938

". . . Many people, no doubt, honestly believe that they are only giving away the interests of Czechoslovakia, whereas I fear we shall find that we have deeply compromised, and perhaps fatally endangered, the safety and even the independence of Great Britain and France. . . . I foresee and foretell that the policy of submission will carry with it restrictions upon the freedom of speech and debate in Parliament, on public platforms, and discussions in the Press."

—Winston Churchill, debate in the House of Commons, October 5, 1938

## Learn the Skill

*Use these steps to identify faulty reasoning.*

**1** **Identify the source.** If you know the identity of the speaker or writer, you can place his or her words in historical context.

**2** **Find main ideas.** What is the main point of the primary source? Does it support or oppose a particular position?

**3** **Compare the primary source with an objective presentation of facts.** What actually happened? Examining the historical events can help you identify mistakes in the writer's or speaker's thinking.

**4** **Identify errors in thinking or reasoning.** Frame questions to help you find examples of faulty reasoning. Does the source incorrectly state cause-and-effect relationships? Does the primary source misinterpret facts about a situation, an event, or a person?

## Practice the Skill

*Answer the following questions about the primary sources on this page.*

**1** **Identify the source.** When did Churchill deliver his speech?

**2** **Find main ideas.** (a) How does Chamberlain defend the Munich Pact? (b) What is the main idea of Churchill's speech?

**3** **Compare the primary source with an objective presentation of facts.** (a) How did Chamberlain view events in Czechoslovakia? (b) What actually happened there?

**4** **Identify errors in thinking or reasoning.** (a) How does Chamberlain incorrectly state cause-and-effect relationships surrounding the Munich Pact? (b) How does he misinterpret Hitler's character? (c) How does Churchill attack Chamberlain's reasoning?

### Apply the Skill

*See the Review and Assessment at the end of this chapter.*

## Chapter Summary

### Section 1
### Aggression Leads to War

- During the 1920s and 1930s, totalitarian dictators rose in several nations.
- Western democracies took little action to stop Italian, Japanese, and German aggression.
- To avoid involvement in world conflicts, the United States passed the Neutrality Act.
- Germany's invasion of Poland launched World War II.

### Section 2
### The United States at War

- Though officially neutral, the United States took steps to aid the Allies.
- The United States entered World War II after Japan bombed Pearl Harbor.
- By 1943, the Allies were beginning to turn back Axis advances in Europe, North Africa, and the Pacific.

### Section 3
### The War at Home

- As the economy switched to wartime production, the government rationed many valuable resources.
- During the war, women took over many jobs usually performed by men.
- On the West Coast, Japanese Americans were shipped to internment camps.

### Section 4
### Toward Victory

- With Allied troops closing in from the west and east, Germany surrendered in 1945.
- Japan is forced to surrender after two atomic bombs were dropped on Hiroshima and Nagasaki.
- After Germany surrendered, the Allies learned of the Nazi death camps where millions of people were murdered.

## Key Concepts

These notes will help you prepare for questions about key concepts.

### Steps to World War II

- **Rise of Dictatorships**
  Soviet Union (Stalin); Italy (Mussolini); Germany (Hitler); Japan (militarists)
- **Aggression**
  Japan occupies China; Italy invades Ethiopia; Germany moves across Eastern Europe
- **Appeasement**
  Democracies fail to take action against aggression
- **Nazi-Soviet Pact**
  Hitler and Stalin divide Poland
- **Hitler Invades Poland**
  France and Britain declare war on Germany

### Growing U.S. Involvement

**1935**
- Congress passes first Neutrality Act

**1940**
- U.S. sells supplies to Britain
- U.S. sets up first peacetime draft

**1941**
- Lend-Lease; U.S. supplies Allies
- Roosevelt and Churchill issue Atlantic Charter
- U.S. opposes Japanese aggression
- Japan bombs Pearl Harbor; U.S. enters war

### Turning Points of World War II

- **Battle of Britain, 1941:** Britain survives German bombing
- **Midway, 1942:** U.S. Navy turns back Japanese advance in Pacific
- **Stalingrad, 1942–1943:** Soviet Union resists Nazi attack
- **El Alamein, 1942:** British forces end Nazi advance in North Africa
- **Invasion of Italy, 1943:** Allied forces take Italy out of war
- **D-Day, 1942:** Allied troops begin drive toward Germany

## Vocabulary *Builder*

### Key Terms

1. Write one sentence giving the definition of each of these key terms: fascism; aggression; appeasement; total war; rationing; intern; genocide. Then, write a second sentence relating each of the key terms to World War II, its cause or its effects.

## Comprehension and Critical Thinking

2. (a) **Describe** Describe the features of a totalitarian state.
   (b) **Contrast** How does a totalitarian government differ from a democratic government, such as that of the United States?

3. (a) **Recall** How did Roosevelt try to improve relations with Latin American countries?
   (b) **Evaluate Information** Why do you think the United States was anxious to strengthen its ties to Latin America in the 1930s?

4. (a) **Recall** Why did the Japanese attack Pearl Harbor?
   (b) **Apply Information** After the attack, a Japanese admiral said, "I'm afraid we have awakened a sleeping tiger." What do you think he meant? Do you think he was correct?

5. (a) **Recall** How did American women contribute to the war effort?
   (b) **Analyze Cause and Effect** Why were African Americans able to make some gains during the war?
   (c) **Make Predictions** What impact do you think these wartime changes might have after the end of the war?

6. (a) **Explain** Why did Stalin want Britain and the United States to open a second front? How was this goal achieved?
   (b) **Evaluate Information** How did the opening of the second front hurt Germany?

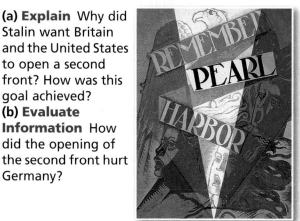

7. (a) **Describe** What was the Holocaust?
   (b) **Apply Information** Why were German actions during the Holocaust considered war crimes?
   (c) **Evaluate Information** Explain which of the following actions you would classify as war crimes: the Japanese attack on Nanjing; the German offensive at the Battle of the Bulge; the Bataan Death March.

## History Reading Skill

8. **Determine Meanings From Context** Find an unfamiliar word in this chapter. Use context clues to analyze its meaning. Explain the clues you used.

## Writing

9. **Write a thesis statement and create an outline for a multimedia presentation covering a topic in this chapter. You should**
   • focus on a topic that can be covered in a short multimedia presentation;
   • list the various parts of the presentation order in which they could be organized;
   • include ideas for the photographs, films, recordings, and other multimedia materials.

10. **Create an Interview:**
    Create a short radio interview, taking place just after V-J Day, between a journalist covering the war and an American sailor serving on a battleship in the Pacific.

## Skills for Life

**Identifying Faulty Reasoning**
Use the excerpt below to answer the questions.

> "Hitler . . . can be stopped and can be compelled to dig in. And that will be the beginning of the end of his downfall. . . . The facts of 1918 are proof that a mighty German Army and a tired German people can crumble rapidly and go to pieces when they are faced with successful resistance."
>
> —Franklin D. Roosevelt, October 27, 1941

11. When was this speech delivered?

12. (a) What prediction does Roosevelt make?
    (b) On what does he base this prediction?

13. (a) How long did the war against Germany actually last after this speech was made?
    (b) What may have been the flaw in Roosevelt's reasoning when he made his prediction?

# Test Yourself

1. The Supreme Court case of *Korematsu* v. *United States* dealt with the issue of
   A racial segregation in the military.
   B internment of Japanese Americans.
   C equal pay for women who worked in factories.
   D war crimes committed by the Japanese army.

2. **Which of the following was an example of appeasement?**
   A the Munich Pact
   B the Nazi-Soviet nonaggression agreement
   C the Atlantic Charter
   D the Lend-Lease Act

Refer to the table below to answer Question 3.

| Item | Amount per Person |
|------|-------------------|
| Sugar | 8–12 ounces per week |
| Meat | 28 ounces per week |
| Gasoline | 3 gallons per week |
| Shoes | 2 pairs per year |

Source: *Digital History*

3. **Which wartime economic policy is illustrated by the table above?**
   A conversion to wartime production
   B campaign to sell war bonds
   C rationing of consumer goods
   D hiring of braceros by American industry

# Document-Based Questions

**Task:** Look at Documents 1 and 2, and answer their accompanying questions. Then, use the documents and your knowledge of history to complete this writing assignment:

Use the evidence in the documents to write a newspaper editorial supporting or criticizing President Truman's decision to use the atomic bomb against Japan.

**Document 1:** In August 1945, the United States dropped two atomic bombs on Japan. The picture shows only a small part of the destruction caused by the bombs. *How was the atomic bomb different from conventional bombs?*

**Document 2:** In a public statement on August 9, 1945, President Truman gave his reasons for using the atomic bomb against Japan. *Why did Truman decide to use the bomb?*

"Having found the bomb we have used it. We have used it against those who attacked us without warning at Pearl Harbor, against those who have starved and beaten and executed American prisoners of war, against those who have abandoned all pretense of obeying international laws of warfare. We have used it in order to shorten the agony of war, in order to save the lives of thousands and thousands of young Americans.

We shall continue to use it until we completely destroy Japan's power to make war. Only a Japanese surrender will stop us."

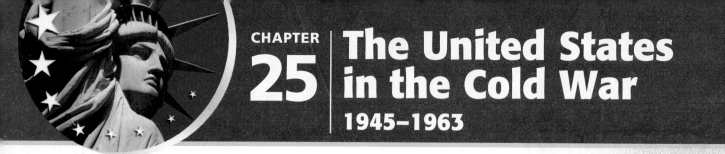
# Chapter Preview

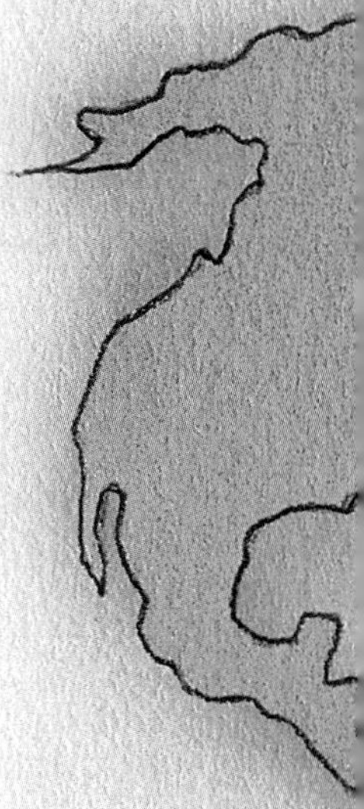

After World War II, the United States faced a new challenge—preventing the spread of communism. The conflict between the United States and the Soviet Union would dominate U.S. foreign policy for decades. At the same time, the United States entered a postwar prosperity as Americans began to rebuild their lives.

**U.S. Events**

**1947**
U.S. foreign policy changes with the Truman Doctrine and the Marshall Plan.

**1948**
United States joins Allies in Berlin Airlift.

1945

**World Events**

**1949** Soviets successfully test their first atomic bomb.

1950

**1950** Korean War begins.

1955

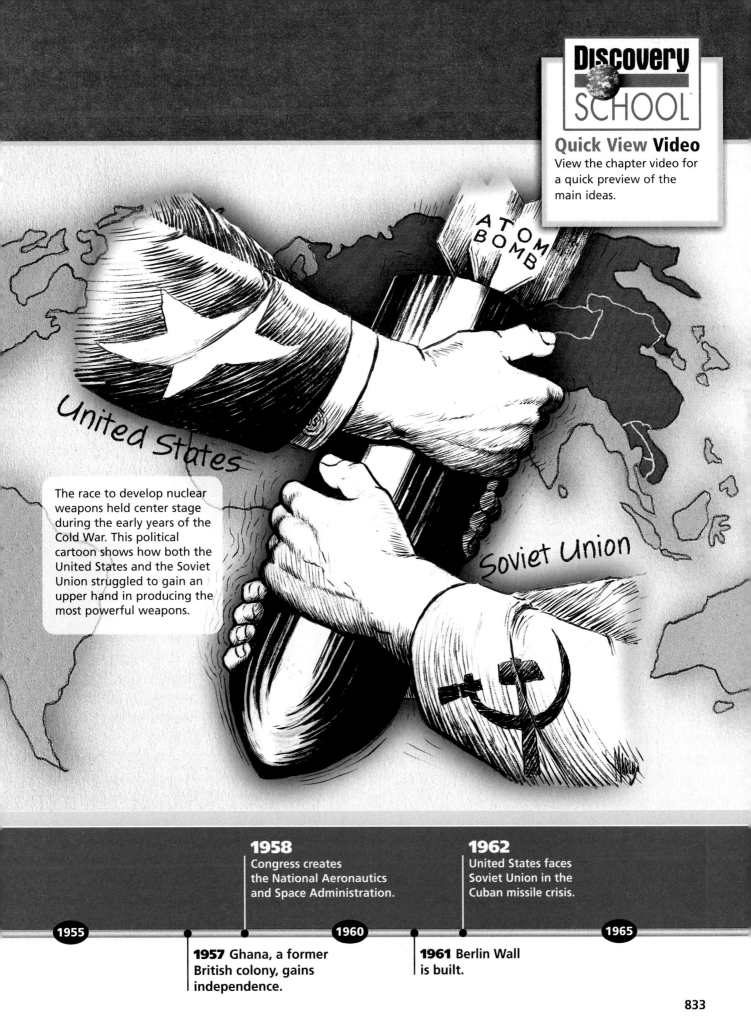

ATOM BOMB

United States

Soviet Union

The race to develop nuclear weapons held center stage during the early years of the Cold War. This political cartoon shows how both the United States and the Soviet Union struggled to gain an upper hand in producing the most powerful weapons.

**1958**
Congress creates the National Aeronautics and Space Administration.

**1962**
United States faces Soviet Union in the Cuban missile crisis.

1955

**1957** Ghana, a former British colony, gains independence.

1960

**1961** Berlin Wall is built.

1965

## 🎯 History Reading Skill  Analyze Cause and Effect

### How did the United States respond to civil war in China?

In this chapter, you will practice analyzing cause-and-effect relationships. Read the following account about U.S. efforts to end the civil war in China during the late 1940s. The side notes analyze the cause-and-effect relationships.

Chinese nationalists and communists had been fighting a civil war for many years by the 1940s. In 1945, President Truman sent General George Marshall to China in the hopes of ending the civil war.

> **Some causes must be inferred:** Truman clearly feels Chinese civil war is not in U.S. interests. This is the result.

> **Cause**

**Primary Source**

I . . . had sent General Marshall to China to try . . . to help put into effect the agreement between the nationalists and the communists to form a coalition government. He set up an executive headquarters, and the fighting stopped, temporarily. . . .

> **Short-term or immediate effect:** Fighting stopped.

. . . [F]ighting broke out again in 1946 and Chiang Kai-shek [nationalist leader] then decided . . . to occupy North China and Manchuria. General Marshall argued against it . . . , but he went ahead. They stayed there [in North China and Manchuria] until finally the whole thing disintegrated and they surrendered. . . .

> **Cause produces an effect, which then leads to conditions for the next cause and effect.**

At the beginning of 1947. . . both parties were unwilling to carry out their agreements. Chiang Kai-shek would not heed the advice of one of the greatest military strategists in history and lost to the communists.

> **Long-term effect:** China becomes a Communist country

> **Cause**

—Harry S Truman, *Memoirs by Harry S Truman: Years of Trial and Hope*

### Analyze Cause and Effect

- Causes produce effects, or events. Look for the related cause, or reason, as to why an event happened.
- Some causes have immediate, short-term effects, whereas others have long-term effects that last for years.
- An effect can create new conditions, leading to the next chain of events.

### Document-Based Questions

1. Which government did the United States support?
2. How did Marshall's presence affect the fighting?
3. How would the United States be affected by the outcome of the war?

# Vocabulary *Builder*

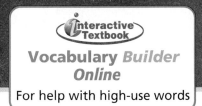
## Previewing High-Use Academic Words

| High-Use Word | Definition | Sample History Sentence |
|---|---|---|
| **sphere** (sfir) (Section 1, p. 837) | ***n.*** area of interest or influence | During the era of imperialism, many nations had <u>spheres</u> of influence in China. |
| **hostile** (HAHS tihl) (Section 1, p. 837) | ***adj.*** unfriendly; opposing | In the early 1940s, relations between the United States and Japan gradually became <u>hostile</u>. |
| **exceed** (ehks SEED) (Section 2, p. 842) | ***v.*** to go beyond | During World War II, the output of American war industries <u>exceeded</u> expectations. |
| **negative** (NEHG ah tihv) (Section 2, p. 846) | ***adj.*** in opposition to an idea; not positive | The Teapot Dome Scandal left a <u>negative</u> mark on Harding's administration. |
| **pursue** (per SYOO) (Section 3, p. 851) | ***v.*** to follow; to attempt to capture or achieve | The United Nations was formed to <u>pursue</u> the goal of world peace. |
| **resolve** (ree SAHLV) (Section 3, p. 853) | ***v.*** to settle or decide | Many people <u>resolved</u> never to let an event like the Holocaust happen again. |
| **revolt** (ree VOHLT) (Section 4, p. 858) | ***n.*** uprising; rebellion | The <u>revolt</u> between Britain and the Patriots led to a victory for the Patriots. |
| **encounter** (ehn KOWN ter) (Section 4, p. 859) | ***n.*** short, dangerous, or frightening meeting between people, groups, or things | At Stalingrad, the <u>encounter</u> between the German forces and the Russian people was brutal. |

## Previewing Key Terms and People

iron curtain, p. 837
satellite, p. 837
containment, p. 838
airlift, p. 838
veto, p. 840
closed shop, p. 843
productivity, p. 845

standard of living, p. 845
baby boom, p. 845
rock-and-roll, p. 846
Elvis Presley, p. 846
inner city, p. 847
stalemate, p. 851
demilitarized zone, p. 852

Joseph McCarthy, p. 854
censure, p. 854
superpower, p. 855
arms race, p. 855
stockpile, p. 856
John F. Kennedy, p. 857

# Roots of the Cold War

## Objectives

1. Explain how the friendships among the Allies broke down after the war.

2. Discover how the United States tried to limit the spread of communism.

3. Learn about three new international organizations.

4. Understand how the events of 1949 shook America's confidence.

## Prepare to Read

### 🔊 Reading Skill

**Analyze Underlying Causes** An event is the effect of a previous cause. However, some causes are not directly stated in the text. To identify these causes, you may need to collect information about how people's emotions affected their actions. For example, think of how the Cold War affected the attitude and actions of the nation.

### Vocabulary *Builder*

**High-Use Words**

**sphere**, p. 837
**hostile**, p. 837

**Key Terms**

iron curtain, p. 837
satellite, p. 837
containment, p. 838
airlift, p. 838
veto, p. 840

**Main Idea**
Conflict occurred when the United States and the Soviet Union disagreed over who would control Europe after World War II.

**☆ Background Knowledge** In an earlier chapter, you learned how the Allies defeated the Axis powers. In this section, you will learn how the wartime alliance broke down shortly after the war to be replaced by a struggle between Communist and non-Communist nations known as the Cold War.

## Growing Distrust

Differences arose among the wartime Allies even before the war had ended. In the final months of the war, Winston Churchill, Josef Stalin, and Franklin Roosevelt had met at Yalta, a resort in the Soviet Union. There, Stalin promised to hold free elections in the parts of Eastern Europe under his control. At the time, Soviet troops were occupying most of Eastern Europe. Instead, Stalin proceeded to establish Communist governments in these nations. He realized that free elections would result in non-Communist governments. Stalin wanted to construct a ring of friendly countries to protect the western borders of the Soviet Union. After the ring had been built, Stalin hoped to make the Soviet Union the world's dominant power.

Churchill expressed the fears of many in the West. Speaking at a college in Fulton, Missouri, he warned of the Soviet threat:

### 🔊 Analyze Underlying Causes

Why was the West worried about Soviet actions? Use the heading to help you infer the underlying cause.

> ❝[A]n iron curtain has descended across the continent. Behind that line lie all the capitals of the ancient states of Central and Eastern Europe . . . all these famous cities and populations around them lie in what I must call the Soviet sphere.❞
>
> —Winston Churchill, speech, Westminster College, March 5, 1946

**Vocabulary *Builder***
**sphere** (sfir) *n.* area of interest or influence

The term **iron curtain** is a way of referring to a barrier to understanding and information. Churchill's use of the term became a popular way of describing the conflict between the democratic nations of the West and the Soviet Union and the Communist-controlled nations of Eastern Europe.

By 1948, most of the nations of Eastern Europe had become satellites of the Soviet Union. A **satellite** is a country ruled by another nation. In addition, hostile Communist threats loomed in Southern and Western Europe. The wartime alliance among the Allies was no more.

☑Checkpoint **Why did nations of the West consider Stalin's actions a threat?**

## Containing Soviet Expansion

The Cold War began at a time when many Americans worried about the nation's leadership. Harry S Truman had become President after the sudden death of Franklin Roosevelt in April 1945. Truman was not well known; and, as Vice President, his leadership had not been tested. However, President Truman wasted little time in showing his leadership qualities. The first Cold War challenges he faced were in Greece, Iran, and Turkey. After the war, a Communist-led revolt broke out in Greece. Greek Communists threatened to take over the government. At the same time, the Soviet government began to threaten two nations on its southern border, Turkey and Iran.

**The Truman Doctrine and the Marshall Plan** In March 1947, President Truman made an urgent request to Congress to aid Greece and Turkey. He declared that the United States would oppose the spread of communism. He stated a principle that became known as the Truman Doctrine:

> ❝[I]t must be the policy of the United States to support free peoples who are resisting attempted subjugation by armed minorities or by outside pressures.❞
>
> —Harry S Truman, message to Congress, March 12, 1947

Truman's policy of blocking Communist expansion was known as containment. The goal of **containment** was to contain, or limit, Soviet expansion.

**Vocabulary** *Builder*
**hostile** (HAHS tihl) *adj.* unfriendly; opposing

**Main Idea**
The United States took steps to shape a foreign policy that would prevent or contain the spread of communism.

### Biography Quest

**Harry S Truman**
**1884–1972**

Harry S Truman became President upon the death of Franklin Roosevelt in 1945. During Truman's time in office, he acted decisively against the growing threat of communism in Eastern and Southern Europe. His policy of containment was adopted and expanded upon by the next presidential administrations. Truman did not run for a second term, but he remained active in politics.

**Biography Quest**

**Why did Truman dismiss MacArthur from his East Asian command in 1951?**

**For:** The answer to the question about Truman and MacArthur

**Visit:** PHSchool.com

**Web Code:** mvd-8251

Military aid alone could not contain communism. After World War II, much of Europe lay in ruins. Communists said the capitalist system was powerless to repair the damaged economies. Many desperate Europeans believed them. Communist parties gained strength in both Italy and France.

To meet this crisis, Secretary of State George Marshall proposed a plan in June 1947 that called for the United States to provide economic assistance to European nations. Between 1948 and 1951, the United States loaned 16 Western European countries more than $12 billion.

The Marshall Plan was a huge success. It helped countries such as France, West Germany, and Italy recover from the war. American dollars built new factories, schools, hospitals, railroads, and bridges.

**The Berlin Airlift** The focus of Cold War hostility now shifted to Germany. At the Yalta Conference, the Allies had agreed to divide Germany into four zones. American, British, French, and Soviet troops would each control one of the zones. Germany's capital city, Berlin, which lay inside Soviet-controlled territory, was also divided into four zones.

By 1948, the Western powers believed that it was time to reunite Germany. Stalin was bitterly opposed to this move. In June 1948, the Soviets set up a blockade around Berlin. They prevented delivery of food supplies to West Berlin's two million residents. Stalin gambled that the Western Allies would accept the Communist takeover of West Berlin. However, the Allies responded with a massive airlift—sending cargo planes to deliver tons of supplies to the people. For almost a year, Western planes delivered supplies to West Berlin.

The Soviets finally called off the blockade in May 1949. In October, France, Britain, and the United States combined their zones into one country, called the Federal Republic of Germany, or West Germany. The Soviet zone became the German Democratic Republic, or East Germany.

**Analyze Underlying Causes**

What was the stated cause of the Berlin blockade? What was the underlying, or overall, cause?

**Cold War Crisis** A divided Germany and Berlin remained a focus of Cold War tensions. Between 1949 and 1961, thousands of East Germans fled to West Berlin. From there, they went to West Germany. Suddenly, in August 1961, the East German government began building a wall between East and West Germany. For 28 years, the wall stood as a symbol of a divided Germany and a divided Europe.

✓**Checkpoint** How did Harry Truman respond to attempts by Greek Communists to seize control of Greece?

**Main Idea**
Nations joined the UN in the hopes of maintaining world peace and forming alliances with one another for further security.

# International Organizations

After World War II, the United States played a leading role in creating the United Nations (UN). This move signaled a turn away from isolationism.

# THE BERLIN AIRLIFT

**History** *Interactive*
**Learn More About the Berlin Airlift**
**Visit:** PHSchool.com
**Web Code:** mvl-8251

During the Berlin Airlift, British and U.S. forces made more than 200,000 flights to deliver goods to the people in West Berlin.
**Critical Thinking: *Draw Conclusions*** Why do you think Stalin chose not to prevent the airlift?

▲ Medal worn by Berlin Airlift workers

Residents of West Berlin watch an approaching cargo plane loaded with food and other goods. At one point, nearly 13,000 tons of goods arrived in West Berlin ▼ each day.

▲ A delivery of fresh milk

## Division of Berlin, 1949

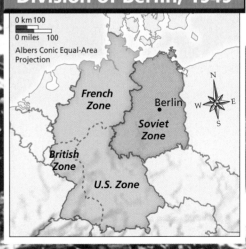

0 km 100
0 miles 100
Albers Conic Equal-Area Projection

French Zone

Berlin

Soviet Zone

British Zone

U.S. Zone

N W E S

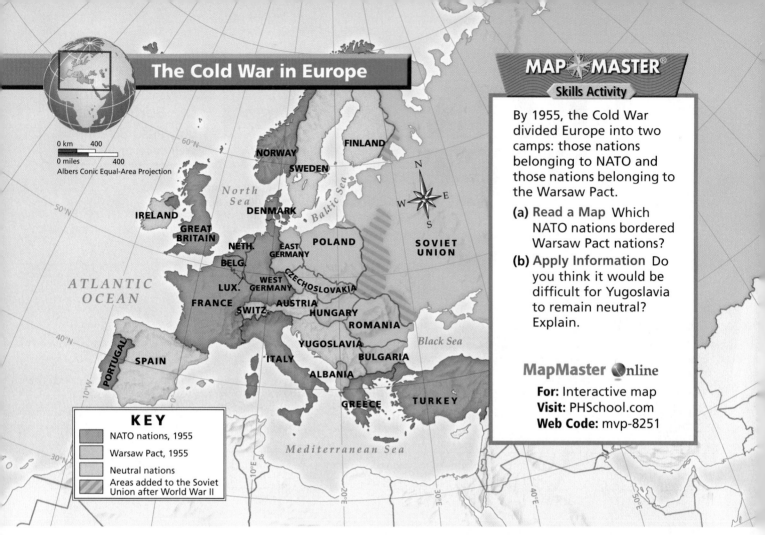

## The Cold War in Europe

0 km 400
0 miles 400
Albers Conic Equal-Area Projection

NORWAY
FINLAND
SWEDEN
North Sea
Baltic Sea
IRELAND
DENMARK
GREAT BRITAIN
NETH.
EAST GERMANY
POLAND
SOVIET UNION
BELG.
ATLANTIC OCEAN
LUX.
WEST GERMANY
CZECHOSLOVAKIA
FRANCE
SWITZ.
AUSTRIA
HUNGARY
ROMANIA
PORTUGAL
SPAIN
ITALY
YUGOSLAVIA
BULGARIA
Black Sea
ALBANIA
GREECE
TURKEY
Mediterranean Sea

**KEY**
- NATO nations, 1955
- Warsaw Pact, 1955
- Neutral nations
- Areas added to the Soviet Union after World War II

### MAP MASTER®
**Skills Activity**

By 1955, the Cold War divided Europe into two camps: those nations belonging to NATO and those nations belonging to the Warsaw Pact.

**(a) Read a Map** Which NATO nations bordered Warsaw Pact nations?

**(b) Apply Information** Do you think it would be difficult for Yugoslavia to remain neutral? Explain.

**MapMaster Online**

For: Interactive map
Visit: PHSchool.com
Web Code: mvp-8251

**The United Nations** The main goals of the UN were to maintain peace and settle international disputes. Under the UN Charter, member nations agreed to bring disputes before the UN.

At the core of the United Nations are the General Assembly and the Security Council. Every nation, large or small, has a single vote in the General Assembly. However, the General Assembly has no way to enforce its decisions. The Security Council has far more power. Its decisions are supposed to be followed by all UN nations. The Security Council has 15 members. Five of them are permanent members—the United States, Russia, China, Britain, and France. Each permanent member has the power to **veto,** or reject, any proposal before the Security Council. If only one permanent member votes no, the Security Council cannot act.

The UN's greatest successes have been in fighting hunger and disease and improving education. Through relief programs, the UN has provided tons of goods, clothing, and medicine to victims of disaster.

**NATO and the Warsaw Alliance** In April 1949, as Cold War tensions rose, the United States and other Western nations established the North Atlantic Treaty Organization (NATO), a formal military alliance to guard against a Soviet attack. Members of NATO agreed that an attack on one member would be considered an attack against the entire group.

In response, the Soviet Union and the satellite nations of Eastern Europe formed their own alliance, the Warsaw Pact, in 1955.

☑Checkpoint  **How does the Security Council help the UN meet its goals?**

## The Shocks of 1949

Until 1949, most Americans were confident that the United States was safe because it alone knew how to build the atomic bomb. However, in September 1949, the Soviet Union exploded its own atomic bomb. Now, the Cold War seemed much more deadly. Each nation had within its reach the power to destroy the other.

Shortly after, Americans received a second shock. Since the 1930s, China had been a battleground between the Chinese Nationalists and the Chinese Communists. In the final months of 1949, the Nationalist government collapsed. China fell under the control of the Communists.

Under their leader, Mao Zedong, the Chinese Communists established the People's Republic of China. The Chinese Nationalists fled to the island of Taiwan. The United States insisted that the Taiwan government was the legal government of China. It refused to recognize the People's Republic and kept the UN from admitting Communist China to China's seat on the Security Council.

☑Checkpoint  **How did events in the Soviet Union and China in 1949 affect the Cold War?**

⭐ **Looking Back and Ahead**  The United States faced a world in which the world's largest nation, the Soviet Union, and the world's most populous nation, China, were under Communist rule. While fears stemming from the Cold War haunted Americans, they still held hopes for a better life after 15 years of depression and war.

**Main Idea**
After 1949, the United States faced new challenges in the Cold War.

Dr. Leo Szilard, who participated in the development of the atomic bomb, reads about the Soviet Union's test bomb.

---

Section 1 | **Check Your Progress**

**Progress Monitoring** Online
**For:** Self-test with instant help
**Visit:** PHSchool.com
**Web Code:** mva-8251

**Comprehension and Critical Thinking**

**1. (a) Recall** What were Stalin's goals for the Soviet Union after World War II?
**(b) Apply Information** How did Stalin's goals affect the goals of U.S. foreign policy?

**2. (a) Recall** What is the purpose of the United Nations?
**(b) Evaluate Information** Does the organization of the UN make it possible for it to be successful? Explain.

**Reading Skill**

**3. Analyze Underlying Causes** Reread the text under the heading "International Organizations." Identify the underlying causes for the U.S. decision to join the UN and participate in NATO.

**Vocabulary Builder**

Answer the following questions in complete sentences that show your understanding of the key terms.
**4.** What was the goal of the American policy of containment of the Soviet Union after World War II?

**5.** What happens when one country becomes a satellite of another?

**Writing**

**6.** Organize the following elements for a multimedia presentation about the UN. Explain the reasons for your choices.

• Audiotape of opening ceremonies at the UN in 1945
• Current photograph of the UN
• Film clip of the Yalta Conference in 1945
• Audiotape of translators at a General Assembly session

# A Time of Prosperity

## Objectives

1. Identify the problems of the postwar economy.

2. Explain the effects of a changing society on the lives of Americans during the 1950s.

3. Contrast life in the suburbs with life in the cities.

## Prepare to Read

 **Reading Skill**

**Analyze Long-Term Effects**
Many events in history cause long-term effects. For example, World War II had lasting effects on the American economy and culture. Think about the difficulty of living through these times as you identify long-term effects in this section. Also, note how some of these effects may become the causes for the next effects.

## Vocabulary *Builder*

**High-Use Words**

<u>exceed</u>, p. 842
<u>negative</u>, p. 846

**Key Terms and People**

closed shop, p. 843
productivity, p. 845
standard of living, p. 845
baby boom, p. 845
rock-and-roll, p. 846
Elvis Presley, p. 846
inner city, p. 847

⭐ **Background Knowledge** In the previous section, you learned how the World War II Allies plunged into a "cold war" within a few years of the end of the war. Important economic, social, and political changes were also occurring at home during this time. In this section, you will learn about those changes.

## Adjusting to Peacetime

On the home front, Americans faced important economic challenges after the war. Defense industries had closed or had scaled back employment. Millions of soldiers would have to be absorbed into the postwar economy. The nation faced a serious problem—how to change back to a peacetime economy.

To help meet these needs, Congress had passed an act in 1944 that became known as the GI Bill of Rights. (GI, which stands for "government issue," was the name given to any member of the U.S. armed forces.) The bill gave veterans money to spend on business, homes, and schooling. The GI Bill helped more than two million former soldiers attend college to prepare for new careers.

**Inflation** During World War II, consumer goods had been in short supply. With the war's end, Americans were ready and eager to buy. Because demand far <u>exceeded</u> the supply of goods, the result was a

**Main Idea**
Returning soldiers and the problems of a postwar economy set new challenges for Americans.

**Analyze Long-Term Effects**
What was one long-term effect of millions of soldiers returning after the war? How do you think American civilians felt about those soldiers?

**Vocabulary *Builder***
<u>exceed</u> (ehks SEED) *v.* to go beyond

soaring inflation. As prices rose, workers demanded large pay increases. When employers refused, a wave of strikes swept the nation.

Although President Truman supported labor, he feared that wage increases would lead to even higher prices. In May 1946, he ended a United Mine Workers strike by taking over the mines. When railroad workers struck a month later, Truman threatened to order them back to work. That angered union members. When the President encouraged industries to raise salaries, inflation resulted. That made consumers angry.

During the 1946 elections, Republicans asked voters, "Had enough?" Voters seemed to agree. The election gave Republicans a majority in both the House and the Senate.

Armed with the power to cancel many New Deal programs, Congress passed the Taft-Hartley Act. The act let the government get a court order to delay a strike for 80 days if the strike threatened public safety. The act also forbade unions to contribute to political campaigns. Also, the act banned the closed shop. A closed shop is a workplace in which only union members can be hired. Truman vetoed the Taft-Hartley Act, but Congress passed the act over Truman's veto. Eventually, President Truman would try to extend the goal of the New Deal with his Fair Deal reforms.

## The Railroad Strike

Speaking before Congress in 1946, President Truman presented his proposal to end the railroad strike.

"I request . . . legislation [that] after the government has taken over an industry and . . . directed men to remain or return to work, the wage scale should be fixed . . . and . . . it shall be retroactive [effective from a particular date in the past]. This legislation must be . . . fair to capital and labor alike. . . . As part of this legislation, I request Congress to authorize the president to draft into the armed forces . . . all workers who are on strike against their government."

### Reading Primary Sources
#### Skills Activity

(a) **Apply Information** What role would the government have in Truman's plan?

(b) **Draw Conclusions** Do you think the workers would be pleased with the plan? Explain.

**A Truman Victory**

Harry Truman holds an early edition of the *Chicago Tribune* that mistakenly declares Dewey the winner of the 1948 election. **Critical Thinking: *Apply Information*** *What does this headline indicate about the election results?*

**The Election of 1948** In early 1948, President Truman's chances for reelection looked slim. Two out of three voters disapproved of the way he was leading the country. Even Truman's own Democrats were split. Angered by Truman's support of civil rights for African Americans, white southern Democrats nominated their own candidate, South Carolina Governor Strom Thurmond. Liberal Democrats, unhappy with Truman's policy of challenging Soviet expansion, formed the Progressive Party. They nominated former Vice President Henry Wallace to run for President.

Confident of victory, the Republicans nominated New York's governor, Thomas Dewey. Dewey did not campaign hard. Truman, on the other hand, campaigned tirelessly. He traveled more than 30,000 miles and made hundreds of speeches. Everywhere Truman went, he attacked what he called the "do-nothing" Republican Congress.

On election night, people still expected a Dewey victory. In fact, the *Chicago Tribune* printed its first edition with the headline "DEWEY DEFEATS TRUMAN."

The election was one of the biggest upsets in American history. Truman squeaked past Dewey to victory. The Democrats also regained control of both the House and the Senate.

President Truman saw his narrow victory as a chance to act on his Fair Deal program, which he had proposed during the campaign. Congress approved a few of the President's Fair Deal proposals. For example, lawmakers increased the minimum wage and provided funds for flood control and low-income housing. However, Congress refused to fund education and national health insurance. It also voted down Truman's proposals to reduce racial discrimination.

**Eisenhower's Middle Way** In 1952, Truman decided not to run again. In the election of 1952, the Democrats nominated Adlai Stevenson, governor of Illinois. The Republicans chose General Dwight D. Eisenhower, nicknamed Ike. A war hero, Eisenhower won a landslide victory.

In contrast to Roosevelt and Truman, Eisenhower believed that the federal government should play a smaller role in the economy. He called for cutting spending, though not for ending programs that helped people. In fact, he increased the number of people who could receive Social Security benefits.

Generally, Eisenhower followed a middle-of-the-road policy in his two terms as President. Running on a record of "peace, progress, and prosperity" won him another huge victory in 1956.

Perhaps Eisenhower's greatest achievement was the Interstate Highway Act of 1956. It provided funds for a vast system of freeways to link all parts of the United States. Increasingly, Americans used highways instead of railroads for traveling and for transporting goods.

☑**Checkpoint** **How did inflation affect the postwar economy?**

# A Changing Society

The Eisenhower years were prosperous ones for many Americans. Inflation slowed and employment soared. New technologies such as the use of computers helped increase American productivity. Increased productivity meant that workers were able to work more efficiently and produce more goods.

New jobs put money in consumers' pockets. Americans responded by spending money on homes, furniture, cars, and clothing. Delighted shoppers could also buy new products such as freezers, televisions, and air conditioners.

Throughout the 1950s, the American standard of living rose steadily. The standard of living is a measure of how comfortable life is for a person, group, or country. By the end of the decade, 6 out of 10 American families owned homes, and 3 out of 4 had cars. Americans manufactured and bought nearly 1 out of every 2 products produced anywhere in the entire world.

The United States was in the midst of change. After the dangers of war, Americans were looking for security. Many found it in their homes and families.

**Baby Boom** In the postwar years, Americans married earlier than their parents had. They also raised larger families. The increased birthrate became known as the **baby boom.** The baby boom increased demand for food, housing, and manufactured goods.

Meanwhile, people were living longer thanks to new medicines that became popular in the 1950s. For example, antibiotic medicines could now cure many serious infectious diseases. A new vaccine kept adults and children safe from the crippling disease of polio.

## Main Idea

The return of prosperity during the 1950s greatly improved the lives of many Americans—but not all.

**Analyze Long-Term Effects**
What caused the economic recovery of the prosperous 1950s? What long-term effects did the recovery cause?

## Increase in Car Ownership, 1948–1960

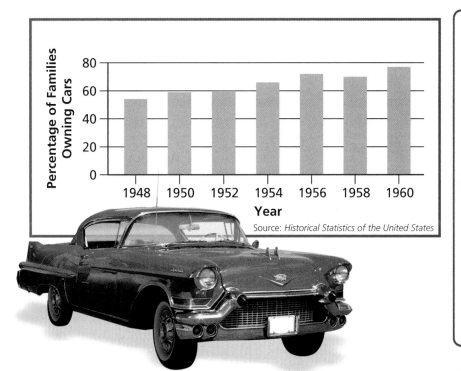

Source: *Historical Statistics of the United States*

### Reading Charts
#### Skills Activity

With the move to the suburbs, people depended more on automobiles. Manufacturers pushed to meet the demands.

(a) **Read a Bar Graph** During which years did automobile ownership remain about the same?

(b) **Identify Causes and Effects** Trace the change in car ownership between 1954 and 1960. List several events (political, social, and economic) that strongly affected the change in ownership at that time.

## A New Prosperity

In the decades following World War II, huge numbers of Americans moved to newly developed communities in the suburbs (shown at right). However, not everyone shared this good life. In the cities, many people were unemployed and living in poor housing (shown at left). **Critical Thinking: *Apply Information*** *Why do you think a book called* The Other America *was written about American life during this time?*

**Vocabulary *Builder***
<u>negative</u> (NEHG ah tihv) *adj.* in opposition to an idea; not positive

**Escaping the City** Americans bought automobiles as fast as auto plants could make them. Nowhere were these cars more appreciated than in the growing suburbs. During the 1950s, the number of Americans living in the suburbs grew by 50 percent.

Suburbs grew around cities throughout the United States. The growth was most pronounced in the West. As a result, states such as California, Arizona, and Texas gained both people and political power.

**Television** Of all the new products of the 1950s, the one that had the greatest impact on American life was television. In 1946, only 8,000 homes had a television set. By the mid-1950s, three out of four American homes had one. By the early 1960s, almost every house had one television set, and many homes had more than one.

Television brought news and entertainment into people's homes. Early programs included original dramas by top writers and situation comedies, or sitcoms, about the ideal middle-class family.

There were, however, some <u>negative</u> effects from television. During the 1950s, watching television became the most important activity of family life. In fact, by 1956, Americans were spending almost as much time watching television every week as they spent at work. The first frozen dinners, introduced in the 1950s, were designed for families who wanted to combine mealtime and television viewing.

**Rock-and-Roll** Television also helped to make popular a new kind of music, rock-and-roll. Rock-and-roll was a blend of black rhythm-and-blues and country music. By far the most popular singer of rock-and-roll was Elvis Presley. With hips shaking and knees bending,

Presley soon became a teen idol and national star. Adults, on the other hand, were shocked at his music and his dance moves. When he appeared on national television, the camera showed only his upper body.

**Signs of Trouble** Not everyone enjoyed this new prosperity. As jobs and people moved to the suburbs, cities lost important tax money. The inner cities, or centers of older cities, became home to poorer, less educated people. Cities could no longer raise enough tax money to repair old apartments, schools, and subways. City schools and other services declined. Crime rose. More and more, the people who stayed in the cities were those who could not afford to move.

Many social critics took note of this division between city and suburb. A small band of critics accused Americans of living in a closed society where differences were not tolerated. One critic, William H. White, wrote *The Organization Man* in 1956. It reported the ways Americans felt pressure to conform to group behavior. Others criticized what they saw as a growing emphasis on material possessions and spending.

**Analyze Long-Term Effects**
How did postwar prosperity create long-term changes in American life? Explain how effects became causes that led to more effects.

☑Checkpoint **How did the changes of the 1950s improve the lives of most Americans?**

⭐ **Looking Back and Ahead** As the United States was poised to enjoy a new burst of prosperity, a conflict was brewing in a faraway corner of the world, the Korean Peninsula. It would draw the United States into a very "hot" and bloody war, and set off a period of self-doubt among Americans.

---

## Section 2 | Check Your Progress

**Progress Monitoring** ⬤nline
**For:** Self-test with instant help
**Visit:** PHSchool.com
**Web Code:** mva-8252

### Comprehension and Critical Thinking

**1. (a) Recall** How did Truman attempt to end the strikes by mine workers and railroad workers?

**(b) Evaluate Information** Truman claimed to be a friend of labor. Based on his actions, do you think that was true? Explain.

**2. (a) Apply Information** What impact did television have on the American family in the 1950s?

**(b) Link Past and Present** How is television different today from television in the 1950s?

### Reading Skill

**3. Analyze Long-Term Effects** Reread the text following the subheading "Inflation." Explain that an increased demand for consumer goods led to effects that, in turn, caused other effects. Include the emotions that played a role in the process and identify any long-term effects.

### Vocabulary *Builder*

Answer the following questions in complete sentences that show your understanding of the key terms.

**4.** What would happen to a woman who wanted to work at a closed shop but refused to join a union?

**5.** What are inner cities? What happened to them in the 1950s?

**6.** What does a standard of living measure?

### Writing

**7.** Make a list of some materials you would use to prepare a multimedia presentation about American popular culture during the 1950s. (For suggestions, refer to the Life at the Time feature on the pages that follow). Write a few sentences introducing and explaining your choices.

# Growing Up in the 1950s

There were a lot of kids growing up in the 1950s. And they enjoyed themselves in ways that had never existed before. The changes that took place in American popular culture back then are still a part of our lives today.

## The Baby Boom

During the Great Depression and World War II, couples had fewer children. But after 1946, the birthrate soared.

**U.S. Births, 1944–1954**

Number of Births (in thousands) vs. Year

4,500
4,000
3,500
3,000
2,500

1944  1946  1948  1950  1952  1954

Source: *Historical Statistics of the United States*

The kids at this 1950s soda fountain were part of this ▼ postwar baby boom.

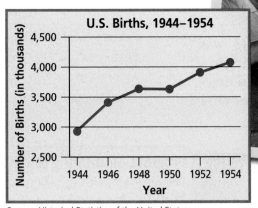

▶ The wild dancing of Elvis Presley outraged many parents. To a generation of teens, Elvis Presley was "The King."

## Rock and Roll

The baby boomers were the first generation to grow up with rock-and-roll. The pulsing new music blended elements of rhythm and blues, country and western, and pop music. Concerts by artists such as Chuck Berry and Little Richard brought white and black teenagers together, enjoying the same beat.

◀ Chuck Berry is often called the Father of Rock-and-Roll. He invented driving guitar riffs that are still being imitated by today's bands.

# Television

Television was invented in the 1920s. Not until the 1950s, however, did the TV set become a familiar feature in most homes. The baby boomers were the first generation to grow up watching "the tube."

◄ The most popular show of the 1950s was *I Love Lucy*, starring Lucille Ball and Desi Arnaz. The sitcom is still shown around the world.

The puppet Howdy Doody and his sidekick Buffalo Bob Smith starred in one of the best-loved children's programs of the day. ▼

◄ The Chantels were the first of the "girl groups" to win national popularity.

◄ Perhaps the most familiar rock-and-roll recording of the 1950s was "Rock Around the Clock" by Bill Haley and the Comets.

*Analyze* **LIFE AT THE TIME**

Prepare an interview with someone who grew up or went to school during the 1950s. Write 5–7 questions about television, music, or other topics of concern to teenagers.

# The Korean War Period

## Objectives

1. Explain how the situation in Korea became the Korean War, the first military conflict of the Cold War.

2. Describe how the Korean War ended.

3. Explain how the Cold War led to a Red Scare in the United States.

## Prepare to Read

### Reading Skill

**Analyze a Cause-and-Effect Chain** Consider how events can snowball out of control when a single cause has multiple effects that, in turn, lead to multiple causes. As the United States entered the Korean War period, this occurred often. Look for the multiple cause-and-effect chains in this section. To find them, read the text following each subheading, and then trace a chain. Watch for events having specific cause-and-effect relationships and not those just occurring in sequence.

### Vocabulary *Builder*

**High-Use Words**

<u>pursue</u>, p. 851

<u>resolve</u>, p. 853

**Key Terms and People**

stalemate, p. 851

demilitarized zone, p. 852

Joseph McCarthy, p. 854

censure, p. 854

⭐ **Background Knowledge** The United States had managed to contain communism in Europe and western Asia through a combination of bold action and economic aid. However, in the small Asian nation of Korea, the Cold War suddenly turned hot.

## Main Idea

Five years after the end of World War II, the United States and the United Nations defended South Korea against North Korea and China.

## Conflict in Korea

In 1910, Japan occupied the Korean Peninsula and ruled it harshly. After Japan's defeat in World War II, Korea was divided at the 38th parallel of latitude. The Soviet Union backed a Communist government in North Korea. The United States backed a non-Communist government in South Korea.

Tensions between North and South Korea continued to increase. Then, on June 25, 1950, North Korean troops suddenly invaded South Korea. Armed with Soviet tanks and artillery, the North Koreans shattered the South Korean army and pushed south. Within three days, the invasion had reached South Korea's capital, Seoul (sole). Korea, it appeared, would soon fall to the Communists.

President Truman quickly responded to the attack. At his urging, the UN Security Council voted to send a military force to Korea. Truman appointed World War II hero General Douglas MacArthur to lead the force. Although 16 nations sent troops to fight under the UN flag, 90 percent were American. The Soviet delegate was not present at the UN debate and so failed to veto the proposal.

The first UN forces to arrive at the front were badly outnumbered and poorly supplied. They fought bravely but were pushed back almost to the tip of the Korean Peninsula. As fresh troops and supplies arrived, however, the defensive line held.

Then, in September, General MacArthur launched a bold counter-attack. UN forces at Inchon, a port city near Seoul, were able to <u>pursue</u> the North Koreans back across the 38th parallel into North Korea. MacArthur's forces chased the North Koreans almost to the Yalu River, which separates North Korea from China.

China's government responded angrily. As UN soldiers neared the Yalu, masses of Chinese troops crossed the border. The UN forces were overwhelmed. Soon, the battle front was once again in South Korea. There, the war settled down into a stalemate, a situation in which neither side wins.

**Truman Versus MacArthur** General MacArthur believed that the United States could win in Korea only if it attacked China. MacArthur publicly called for the bombing of supply bases in China. President Truman was more cautious. He believed that an American attack on China might start a new world war. Truman warned MacArthur against making further public statements.

MacArthur disregarded these warnings. He publicly argued that he could not win the war because of politicians in Washington. Truman was furious and fired MacArthur.

**Peace Talks** Meanwhile, the stalemate in Korea continued. In July 1951, the opposing sides began peace talks. These talks would continue for two long years. All the while, the fighting and the killing continued.

**Vocabulary** *Builder*
<u>pursue</u> (per SYOO) *v.* to follow; to attempt to capture or achieve

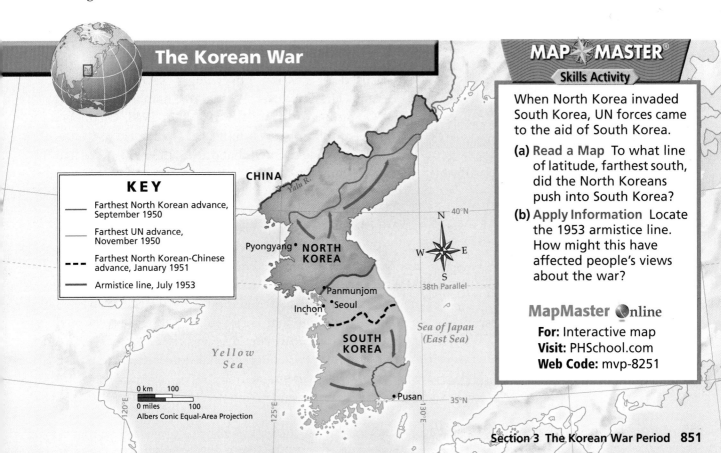

## The Korean War

**KEY**

— Farthest North Korean advance, September 1950

— Farthest UN advance, November 1950

- - - Farthest North Korean-Chinese advance, January 1951

— Armistice line, July 1953

CHINA

*Yalu R.*

Pyongyang • **NORTH KOREA**

40°N

Panmunjom
Inchon • • Seoul

38th Parallel

**SOUTH KOREA**

*Yellow Sea*

*Sea of Japan (East Sea)*

• Pusan

35°N

0 km 100
0 miles 100
Albers Conic Equal-Area Projection

**MAP MASTER®**

**Skills Activity**

When North Korea invaded South Korea, UN forces came to the aid of South Korea.

**(a) Read a Map** To what line of latitude, farthest south, did the North Koreans push into South Korea?

**(b) Apply Information** Locate the 1953 armistice line. How might this have affected people's views about the war?

**MapMaster ⬤nline**

**For:** Interactive map
**Visit:** PHSchool.com
**Web Code:** mvp-8251

A cease-fire finally ended the fighting in July 1953. The border between the warring sides stood almost exactly where it had been before the war. The two sides agreed to establish a demilitarized zone, an area which neither side controls. It still divides the two countries a half-century later.

The war's toll was horrendous. At least two million Koreans died in the fighting. Most of them were civilians. American losses totaled well over 30,000 dead and more than 100,000 wounded. Thousands of soldiers from other nations also were killed.

With the cease-fire, the fighting ended in Korea. However, tensions between North and South Korea continued well into the next century. Two heavily armed forces continued to face each other across the demilitarized zone.

☑Checkpoint  **How did the United States become involved in the Korean War?**

**Main Idea**
Events during the early years of the Cold War increased American fears of communism at home.

## Fears at Home

In Section 1 of this chapter, you learned how American confidence was shaken by the Communist victory in China and Soviet possession of the atomic bomb. The failure to win a decisive victory in the long stalemate in Korea further worried Americans.

**Communists in Government?** Americans had absorbed a number of blows during the Cold War. Soviet possession of atomic weapons, the fall of China to the Communists, and the stalemate in Korea all led to worries about the ability of the United States to defeat communism. Many Americans worried that Communist sympathizers and spies might be secretly working to overthrow the U.S. government.

Two cases seized public attention. In the first, Alger Hiss, a former State Department official, was accused of passing government secrets to Soviet agents. Hiss's accuser, Whittaker Chambers, had been a Communist during the 1930s. In 1948, Chambers appeared before a committee of the House of Representatives. He claimed that during the 1930s, Hiss had given him top-secret papers to pass to the Soviet Union.

Hiss strongly denied passing any secret papers to the Soviet Union and sued Chambers for making false accusations. Then, Chambers produced copies of the papers. They became known as the "pumpkin papers" because Chambers had hidden them on microfilm in a pumpkin in his garden. So many years had passed since the crime that Hiss could no longer be charged with spying. However, Hiss was convicted of perjury, or lying, to the congressional committee and spent several years in prison.

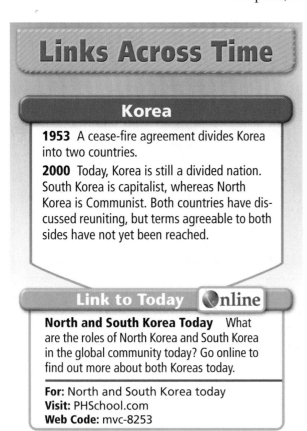

## Links Across Time

### Korea

**1953** A cease-fire agreement divides Korea into two countries.

**2000** Today, Korea is still a divided nation. South Korea is capitalist, whereas North Korea is Communist. Both countries have discussed reuniting, but terms agreeable to both sides have not yet been reached.

### Link to Today  Online

**North and South Korea Today**  What are the roles of North Korea and South Korea in the global community today? Go online to find out more about both Koreas today.

**For:** North and South Korea today
**Visit:** PHSchool.com
**Web Code:** mvc-8253

# The Hunt for Communists

"It's Okay—We're Hunting Communists"

The car is a symbol for the House Un-American Activities Committee.

Tire marks

**Reading Political Cartoons**

**Skills Activity**

In 1947, the House Un-American Activities Committee led an investigation to find Communists in the moviemaking industry.

**(a) Identify Main Ideas** What does the cartoon suggest about the way in which the investigation is being carried out?

**(b) Recognize Points of View** How does the cartoonist feel about the success of the investigation? Explain.

Fears about America's security rose even higher in 1950 when several Americans were arrested on charges of passing the secret of the atomic bomb to the Soviets. In the most famous trial of the times, a married couple, Julius and Ethel Rosenberg, were found guilty of supplying secret information to the Soviet Union. They were sentenced to death. A worldwide outcry arose, but the Rosenbergs were executed in 1953.

Today, more than half a century after the trials of Alger Hiss and Julius and Ethel Rosenberg, their roles are still debated. However, many questions of their involvement have been <u>resolved</u>. In the 1990s, the U.S. government released copies of secret Soviet messages that had been decoded after years of dedicated work. The messages appeared to show that both Alger Hiss and Julius Rosenberg had spied for the Soviets. Ethel Rosenberg apparently was aware of the spying and may even have assisted her husband.

**McCarthyism** A climate of fear contributed to the rise of Senator Joseph McCarthy of Wisconsin. McCarthy built his career by threatening to expose Communists. In a speech in Wheeling, West Virginia, in February 1950, McCarthy waved a paper in the air. He claimed it contained the names of 205 Communists who worked in the State Department. McCarthy later reduced this number to 81, then to 57.

**Vocabulary** *Builder*
<u>resolve</u> (ree SAHLV) *v.* to settle or decide

Senator Joseph McCarthy

McCarthy refused to show the list to anyone. He did not even need to do so because many Americans were eager to believe him. His dramatic charges gained him a large following.

During the next four years, McCarthy's charges became more sensational. He led Senate hearings in which he bullied witnesses and made exaggerated charges. Eventually, the term *McCarthyism* came to mean accusing someone of disloyalty without having any evidence.

Aware of McCarthy's power to destroy careers, few people were brave enough to oppose him and his scare tactics. McCarthy finally lost his following in 1954 when a television audience of millions saw him make false accusations against the United States Army. Many Americans came to realize that McCarthy could not support the charges. Unfortunately, many lives had been ruined by McCarthy's wild charges. Soon after, the U.S. Senate voted to censure, or condemn, him. McCarthy died three years later. By that time, the Communist scare was mostly finished.

✓**Checkpoint**  **What techniques did McCarthy use to accuse people of being Communists?**

⭐ **Looking Back and Ahead**  After McCarthy's fall, tensions between the United States and the Soviet Union continued. No one knew that the conflict between the two superpowers would drag on for almost 40 additional years.

---

**Section 3 | Check Your Progress**

**Progress Monitoring** Online
**For:** Self-test with instant help
**Visit:** PHSchool.com
**Web Code:** mva-8253

## Comprehension and Critical Thinking

**1. (a) Recall** How did the Korean War start?
**(b) Synthesize Information** How did the U.S. response to the Korean War reflect the goals of the Truman Doctrine?

**2. (a) Describe** What did Senator McCarthy do in the 1950s?
**(b) Analyze Cause and Effect** How did McCarthy's actions threaten democratic freedoms in the United States?

## 🔎 Reading Skill

**3. Analyze a Cause-and-Effect Chain** Reread the entire text under the heading "Fears at Home." Analyze the cause-and-effect chain from American worries about global communism to government investigations and spy trials.

## Vocabulary *Builder*

Read each sentence below. If the sentence is true, write YES. If the sentence is not true, write NO and explain why.
**4.** The Korean War ended in a stalemate; boundaries changed little and neither side won the war.

**5.** The United States censured Senator McCarthy by awarding him the Congressional Medal of honor for his work fighting communism.
**6.** The soldiers were preparing to occupy the demilitarized zone.

## Writing

**7.** You are preparing a multimedia presentation about McCarthyism. Write a few sentences to introduce your presentation. Then, write a brief introduction for a film clip of Senator McCarthy speaking. Finally, write a few sentences to conclude your presentation.

# Global Concerns in the Cold War

## Objectives

1. Explain how the Cold War turned into an arms race.

2. Describe how the Cold War divided the emerging countries in Asia and Africa.

3. Explain how communism gained influence in Latin America.

4. Explain why Cuba became a crisis spot during the Cold War.

## Prepare to Read

### 🎯 Reading Skill

**Evaluate Short- and Long-Term Effects** Some causes lead to both short- and long-term effects. For example, an event might cause an immediate reaction and also change a long-standing pattern in society. The Cold War had many immediate effects on the world. It also had long-term effects.

### Vocabulary *Builder*

**High-Use Words**

<u>revolt</u>, p. 858

<u>encounter</u>, p. 859

**Key Terms and People**

superpower, p. 855

arms race, p. 855

stockpile, p. 856

John F. Kennedy, p. 857

---

⭐ **Background Knowledge** The Korean War increased tensions between the United States and the Communist nations. In this section, you will discover how these Cold War tensions led the United States and the Soviet Union to engage in a dangerous competition to build up their supplies of nuclear arms.

## The Arms Race

After almost 30 years of totalitarian rule in the Soviet Union, Josef Stalin died in 1953. His death brought no letup in the Cold War tensions. A new Soviet leader, Nikita Khrushchev (KROO shawf), predicted that communism would destroy the Western democracies.

By the end of the 1950s, the United States and the Soviet Union had emerged as world superpowers. **Superpowers** are countries whose military, economic, and political strength are so great that they can influence events worldwide.

In the 1950s, the two nations began an expensive and dangerous arms race. An **arms race** is a contest in which nations compete to build more and more powerful weapons. In 1952, Americans exploded the first hydrogen bomb, or H-bomb. Soon the Soviets had their own H-bomb. China joined the race by exploding its own atomic bomb in 1964. Three years later, China exploded a hydrogen bomb. Britain and France also developed nuclear weapons.

**Main Idea**

As the Cold War continued, the Soviet Union and the United States competed in a race to build powerful weapons.

Models of missiles

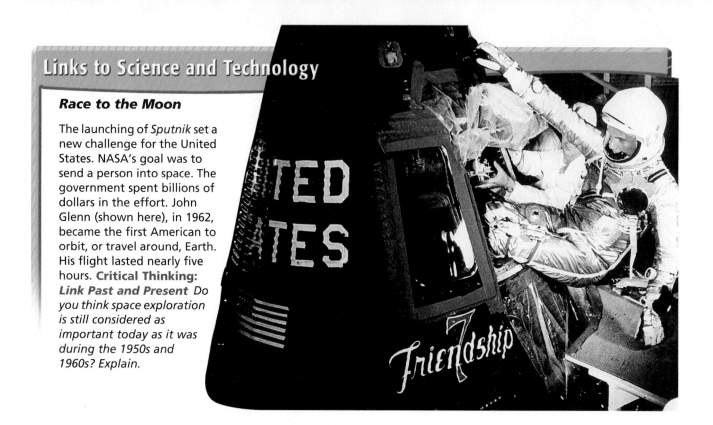

### Race to the Moon

The launching of *Sputnik* set a new challenge for the United States. NASA's goal was to send a person into space. The government spent billions of dollars in the effort. John Glenn (shown here), in 1962, became the first American to orbit, or travel around, Earth. His flight lasted nearly five hours. **Critical Thinking: Link Past and Present** *Do you think space exploration is still considered as important today as it was during the 1950s and 1960s? Explain.*

No country wanted to use nuclear weapons and risk a deadly counterattack. Instead, the nuclear nations stockpiled, or collected, their nuclear weapons. By the 1970s, the Soviet Union and the United States had enough weapons stockpiled to destroy each other many times over.

The superpowers also competed in space. In October 1957, the Soviet Union alarmed the West by launching the world's first human-made satellite. *Sputnik* weighed only 184 pounds, but the tiny satellite circling Earth at 18,000 miles an hour gave Americans a huge shock. If the Soviets could send satellites into space, they could also launch nuclear missiles at American cities.

The United States and the Soviets were now also in a race to develop the technology to control outer space. In response to *Sputnik*, Congress created the National Aeronautics and Space Administration (NASA) to launch its own space missions. Congress also passed the National Defense Education Act. Its goal was to produce more scientists and more teachers.

**Evaluate Short- and Long-Term Effects**
Evaluate the short- and long-term effects of the arms race.

☑**Checkpoint** How did the launch of *Sputnik* affect Americans?

**Main Idea**
Rivalry between the Soviet Union and the United States increased conflicts in other parts of the world.

## Emerging Nations

After World War II, many former colonies gained their independence. The United States and the Soviet Union soon were engaged in a competition to win allies among the new nations.

**The Peace Corps** The Soviet Union made a major effort to win support among the newly independent nations. To counter this appeal, President John F. Kennedy in 1961 proposed that Congress establish a Peace Corps. The new program sought to build friendships between Americans and the people of other nations. It also sought to encourage economic growth in developing countries.

Thousands of Americans, young and old, volunteered to serve in poor villages in Asia, Africa, and Latin America. They shared their skills and knowledge as teachers, doctors, nurses, carpenters, and farmers.

**Developments in Africa** The Soviet Union quickly extended aid to the new African nations of Ghana and Guinea. To counter Soviet influence, the United States expanded its own aid to other newly independent countries.

The Congo became a flash point for this competition between the United States and the Soviet Union to gain influence in a region. In 1960, the former Belgian Congo gained independence as the nation of Congo. Soon, opposing groups were fighting over control of the new country. The United States backed one side. The Soviet Union aided the other side. Each side supplied airplanes, trucks, and technical advisers to its Congo allies. The war became increasingly violent.

**The Philippines** With European nations weakened by World War II, many Asians saw an opportunity to seize the independence for which they had long hungered.

The first Asian country to win independence in the postwar period was the Philippine Islands. The United States had promised Filipinos independence in 1934. Twelve years later, in 1946, the United States lived up to its promise.

Unrest soon developed in the Philippines. Many Filipinos wanted reforms, especially land reforms. When the government moved too slowly toward making changes, fighting broke out. Some of the rebels were Communists. By 1954, the government had defeated the rebels. It also made some needed land reforms.

After Ferdinand Marcos became president in 1965, however, the government became less democratic. In the years that followed, many groups continued to push for greater reforms.

**Indochina** Indochina, which had been under French control, took a different path. After World War II, France struggled to maintain control. In one of the colonies, Vietnam, Ho Chi Minh (HOH CHEE MIHN) led the fight for independence from France. Because Ho was a Communist who had Soviet backing, the United States backed the French. In 1954, Ho's forces defeated the French and won control of the northern part of Vietnam. Fighting in Vietnam would last for almost 30 years. Before it ended, the fighting would draw the United States into a long and bitter war. You will read about the Vietnam War in another chapter.

☑**Checkpoint** How did the Peace Corps help the United States build friendships with other nations?

**Evaluate Short- and Long-Term Effects**
Evaluate the short- and long-term effects of growing independence among developing nations.

**A Volunteer**
This Peace Corps volunteer is reading to a child in Senegal. The Peace Corps logo is also shown.

**Explore More Video**
To learn more about the Cuban missile crisis, view the video.

**The Cuban Missile Crisis**
For 13 days in 1962, a standoff between President Kennedy and Soviet leader Nikita Khrushchev over missile bases inside Cuba drew the superpowers dangerously close to a nuclear war. **Critical Thinking:** *Analyze Cause and Effect How did the Cuban missile crisis affect the arms race?*

**Main Idea**
U.S. efforts to contain communism and prevent a nuclear attack increased after events in Latin America and Cuba.

**Vocabulary** *Builder*
<u>revolt</u> (ree VOHLT) *n.* uprising; rebellion

# Latin America and the Cold War

In the 1950s, the Cold War moved close to the United States, in Latin America. The nations of Latin America faced many critical problems, including widespread poverty and poor health care. The United States hoped that moderate Latin American governments would gradually improve these conditions.

Many Latin Americans, however, rejected gradual solutions. Instead, <u>revolts</u> brought anti-American groups to power. Many Americans worried about the threat to American security and American businesses in Latin America. As a result, the United States helped military dictators keep or gain power in several Latin American countries. This policy aroused hostile feelings in Latin America toward the United States.

**Fidel Castro Comes to Power** In January 1959, Fidel Castro, a Communist, led a successful revolution in Cuba. The Soviet Union promised Castro aid. Castro also began to encourage revolution in other parts of Latin America.

Castro's actions forced thousands of Cubans into exile. An exile is a person who is forced to leave his or her own country. Many came to live in the United States.

In April 1961, a group of Cuban exiles secretly trained by the U.S. Central Intelligence Agency landed at the Bay of Pigs on the southern coast of Cuba. The invasion failed. However, the invasion made Castro more popular in Cuba and embarrassed the United States.

**Cuban Missile Crisis** The next crisis was even more serious. In 1962, aerial photographs showed American leaders that the Soviets were building nuclear missile bases inside Cuba. The bases could be used to launch missiles against the United States.

Kennedy insisted that Soviet Premier Nikita Khrushchev remove the missiles. Kennedy called them "a threat to world peace." The President imposed a naval blockade on Cuba. He ordered the U.S. Navy to stop any Soviet ship from bringing missiles to Cuba.

For 13 days, the world held its breath, hoping that there would not be an <u>encounter</u> between the two superpowers. Soviet ships packed with more missiles steamed toward Cuba. American armed forces went on alert. Across the country, Americans wondered what would happen if the Soviet ships did not turn back.

At the last moment, the Soviet ships approaching the blockade turned back. Khrushchev agreed to withdraw the missiles. The United States pledged not to invade Cuba. U.S. Secretary of State Dean Rusk described the tense last hours of the crisis: "We were eyeball to eyeball, and I think the other fellow just blinked."

**Vocabulary** *Builder*
<u>encounter</u> (ehn KOWN ter) *n.* short, dangerous, or frightening meeting between people, groups, or things

✓**Checkpoint**  **Why were events in Cuba troubling to the American government?**

⭐ **Looking Back and Ahead** Dramatic changes occurred in United States foreign policy after World War II. Isolationism was no longer a valid response to world events. There were also critical changes on the home front, especially in the area of racial relations. You will learn about this historic era in the next chapter.

---

Section 4 | **Check Your Progress**

**Progress Monitoring** ⏻nline
**For:** Self-test with instant help
**Visit:** PHSchool.com
**Web Code:** mva-8254

**Comprehension and Critical Thinking**

**1. (a) Recall** Why did the United States become involved in the affairs of some Latin American countries?
**(b) Detect Points of View** How do you think the outcome of the Cuban missile crisis affected Kennedy's reputation in the United States? How do you think it affected Khrushchev's reputation in the Soviet Union?

**2. (a) Identify** What event in October 1957 shocked the United States?
**(b) Draw Conclusions** Why was the event seen as a grave threat?

**Reading Skill**
**3. Evaluate Short- and Long-Term Effects** Reread the text following the subheading "Developments in Africa and Asia." Evaluate the short- and long-term effects of civil war in the Congo.

**Vocabulary** *Builder*
Complete each of the following sentences so that the second part further explains the first part and clearly shows your understanding of the key term.
**4.** In the 1950s, the Soviet Union and the United States engaged in a dangerous arms race, _____.

**5.** After World War II, the United States and the Soviet Union emerged as the world's two superpowers, _____.

**Writing**
**6.** Add to the following list of items to be used in a multimedia presentation about the Cuban missile crisis: photograph of Soviet missiles in Cuba; photograph of Senator Kenneth Keating presenting aerial view of missile sites.

## Skills for Life

# Identify Alternatives

Throughout history, nations have made choices about their political futures. Making these choices often involves choosing between alternative, or different, solutions to a serious problem. By studying these alternatives, you can better understand how the actions of political leaders and governments affected history.

The excerpt below is from President Harry S Truman's speech to a joint session of Congress. In it, he discusses what has become known as the Truman Doctrine.

"... One aspect of the present situation which I . . . present to you . . . concerns Greece and Turkey. The United States has received from the Greek government an urgent appeal for financial and economic assistance. . . . The very existence of the Greek state is today threatened by the terrorist activities of several thousand armed men, led by Communists, who defy the government's authority at a number of points. . . .

Greece must have assistance if it is to become a self-supporting and self-respecting democracy. The United States must supply that assistance.

. . . I believe that it must be the policy of the United States to support free peoples who are resisting attempted subjugation by armed minorities or by outside pressures. . . . [O]ur help should be primarily through economic and financial aid, which is essential to economic stability and orderly political processes.

. . . I therefore ask the Congress to provide authority for assistance to Greece and Turkey in the amount of $400 million for the period ending June 30, 1948."

—Harry S Truman, March 12, 1947

## Learn the Skill

*Use these steps to identify alternatives.*

**1** **Identify the problem.** You must identify the problems before you identify the alternatives. What does the primary source address?

**2** **Identify the alternative solutions.** What choices are presented? Look for each main idea.

**3** **Evaluate the consequences of each alternative solution.** Alternative solutions will have certain results. Frame questions to help you identify these results, and draw conclusions about the best course of action.

## Practice the Skill

*Answer the following questions about the primary sources on this page.*

**1** **Identify the problem.** What political issue is the subject of Truman's speech to Congress?

**2** **Identify the alternative solutions.** What solution to the problem does Truman propose?

**3** **Evaluate the consequences of each alternative solution.** (a) What do you think may be the result of the solution proposed by Truman? (b) Do you think this is the best plan for dealing with postwar Greece? Explain.

## Apply the Skill

*See the Review and Assessment at the end of this chapter.*

**interactive Textbook**

**Study Guide** *Online*
Complete your Chapter 25 study guide in print or online.

## Chapter Summary

### Section 1
### Roots of the Cold War

- Truman established the policy of containment to limit Soviet expansion.
- The United Nations was established to maintain peace and to settle international disputes.
- The Soviet Union exploded its own atomic bomb in 1949, ending the U.S. monopoly on nuclear weapons.

### Section 2
### A Time of Prosperity

- The Republican Congress passed the Taft-Hartley Act over Truman's veto, limiting the power of unions.
- Truman and the Democrats won the 1948 election.
- The election of Eisenhower in 1952 marked a time of prosperity for most Americans.

### Section 3
### The Korean War Period

- In the early 1950s, American military forces prevented the Communists from taking over all of Korea.
- Senator Joseph McCarthy begins a career trying to expose Communists.

### Section 4
### Global Concerns in the Cold War

- The nuclear arms race between the United States and the Soviet Union begins.
- Fidel Castro took over Cuba and made it a Communist nation.
- Castro's attempt to make Cuba a Soviet military base in the Americas was checked by President Kennedy during the Cuban missile crisis.

## Key Concepts

These notes will help you prepare for questions about key concepts.

### Characteristics of Life in America in the 1950s

- Prosperity
- Baby boom
- Growth of suburbs
- Change of the inner city into a place of poverty
- Increasing importance of the automobile
- Television changes American life
- Birth of rock-and-roll
- Threat of communism and nuclear war

### United States Tries to Contain Communism

**Europe**
- Truman Doctrine and Marshall Plan—provided military and economic aid to countries threatened by Communist takeover
- Berlin Airlift—supplies sent to Berlin during Soviet blockade
- NATO—formed military alliance of United States and Western European countries against Soviet conquests

### Asia and Africa

- Korean War—sent American military forces to help South Korea
- Taiwan—protected Taiwan against Communist invasion
- Newly independent colonies—supported forces against pro-Communist movements

**Americas**
- Cuba—prevented Castro from making Cuba into a Soviet missile base
- Domestic spies—uncovered and tried Soviet agents working within the U.S. government

## Vocabulary *Builder*

### Key Terms and People

Answer the following questions in complete sentences.

1. How did the airlift in 1948 help people in Berlin?

2. What action did President John F. Kennedy take that brought about an end to the Cuban missile crisis?

3. In the 1950s, why were national television networks fearful of Elvis Presley's guest appearances?

4. What is a demilitarized zone, and what function does it serve?

## Comprehension and Critical Thinking

5. **(a) Recall** Why were Americans worried about Truman when he succeeded Roosevelt as President in 1945?
   **(b) Apply Information** Was Truman an effective leader for the United States in the postwar years? Why or why not?

6. **(a) List** Which major international organizations did the United States join in the postwar years to protect its interests?
   **(b) Identify Benefits** How would the United States benefit from being a member of those organizations?

7. **(a) Recall** Which domestic problems did Truman and Eisenhower face during their presidencies?
   **(b) Apply Information** What steps did each take to deal with the problems?
   **(c) Evaluate Information** Whose solutions have had a more lasting impact on the country? Explain your answer.

8. **(a) Describe** How did General MacArthur believe the United States could win the war in Korea?
   **(b) Make Predictions** Describe how history might have played out if MacArthur's proposal had been carried out.

9. **(a) Organize Information** Both the United States and the Soviet Union made gains in the Cold War that they probably considered important "successes." Create a chart of these events.

**(b) Evaluate Information** How effective do you believe the United States was in containing the spread of communism? Explain.

## History Reading Skill

10. **Analyze Cause and Effect** Write a paragraph summarizing the major cause-and-effect relationships of two events in this chapter.

## Writing

11. **Write an introduction, transitions, and conclusions for a multimedia presentation.**
   Review the activity you completed for Section 2 about popular culture during the 1950s. Use the Internet or library to find a few more multimedia sources on this topic. Choose the best order for the presentation.
   **Your writing should:**
   • include a thesis statement about popular culture in the 1950s;
   • include an introduction and transitions from one multimedia source to the other;
   • include an introduction and conclusion for the entire presentation.

12. **Write a Scene:**
   Write a short scene in which two children from today open a time capsule from 1952. Include their comments and what they find.

## Skills for Life

### Identify Alternatives

Use the newspaper excerpt below to answer the questions.

> "Moscow, Feb. 19—Western Europe was sternly warned today against the dangers of various economic and political attacks allegedly launched by the United States and Great Britain.
> . . . The countries of western Europe were advised to [keep] their economic independence and to [ignore] proposals for a United States of Europe. As an alternative, they were asked to consider the . . . friendship and postwar cooperation between the Soviet Union, Czechoslovakia, Poland, and Yugoslavia as 'models' of international agreements."

13. What is the political issue discussed?

14. What political alternative is suggested?

15. Based on what you have learned, is this the best alternative to the problem? Explain.

# Test Yourself

1. **Which activity took up the most family time in America by the late 1950s?**

   A attending football games

   B watching television

   C listening to rock-and-roll

   D driving around by automobile

2. **What did Winston Churchill mean when he said "an iron curtain has descended across the continent"?**

   A Europe has been divided into two hostile camps.

   B People can now travel anywhere on the continent by railroad.

   C Restricting Western journalists from going to Eastern Europe is breeding ignorance about that region of the world.

   D The whole of Europe has become dangerously oversupplied with weapons.

3. **How did the cases of Alger Hiss and the Rosenbergs contribute to the rise of Joseph McCarthy?**

   A The cases were an alert that laws were needed to protect foreigners.

   B The cases assured Americans that the spread of communism was not a threat.

   C The cases increased Americans' fears about the spread of communism.

   D The cases increased awareness that some investigations were unconstitutional.

## Document-Based Questions

**Task:** Look at Documents 1 and 2, and answer their accompanying questions. Then, use the documents and your knowledge of history to complete this writing assignment:

   Imagine that you live in East Berlin during the Cold War. Write a diary entry describing the building of the wall in 1961 and your reaction to President Kennedy's "Ich bin ein Berliner" speech two years later.

**Document 1:** The Berlin Wall, which sealed off Communist East Berlin from West Berlin, was a grim symbol of the Cold War. *Why did East Germany build the wall?*

**Document 2:** In June 1963, U.S. President John F. Kennedy delivered a speech at the Berlin Wall. Berliners loudly cheered his pledge of solidarity with the German people. *Why do you think the United States did not take direct action to remove the wall?*

"Freedom has many difficulties and democracy is not perfect. But we have never had to put a wall up to keep our people in. . . . I know of no town, no city, that has been besieged for 18 years that still lives with the vitality . . . and the determination of the city of West Berlin.

Freedom is indivisible, and when one man is enslaved, all are not free. . . . When all are free, then we can look forward to the day when this city will be joined as one and this country and this great Continent of Europe in a peaceful and hopeful globe.

All free men, wherever they may live, are citizens of Berlin.

And, therefore, as a free man, I take pride in the words 'Ich bin ein Berliner.'"

# Writing Workshop

## Multimedia Research Report

### ▶ Introduction

In a multimedia research report, you combine an oral research report with images and sounds from media, such as videotapes and DVDs, slides, sound CDs, audiotape recordings, live music, photographs, and fine art. A multimedia research report should have the following characteristics:

- an interesting topic for which you need to find outside information
- various media that add to or illustrate this information
- a thesis, or central idea, expressing an idea about the topic
- a clear, logical organization
- a conclusion that sums up what you learned

**Assignment** On the following pages, you will learn how to create and present a multimedia research report. You will get step-by-step instructions. Each step will include an example from a research report about President Franklin D. Roosevelt.

Read the instructions and the examples. Then, follow each step to plan and create a 10-minute multimedia research report:

> **Create a multimedia research report about *one year* during the period between 1930 and 1962.**

> For a review of the steps in the writing process, see the **Historian's Toolkit, *Write Like a Historian.***

### ▶ Prewriting

**Choose and narrow a topic.** You need to choose a topic for which media items are available. These could include documentary videos, live or recorded music, images of paintings and sculpture, news photographs, and voice recordings.

Think about the amount of time you have for your presentation, and narrow your topic so that you can cover it in that time.

**Create a media checklist.** Once you have a topic, list the various kinds of media that you could use to present information about it. In the left column, note each media category; and in the right column, describe more specifically the images and sounds you want to use.

| Media Checklist for a Report on Franklin D. Roosevelt | |
|---|---|
| ☑ Music and sound effects | "Happy Days Are Here Again"; other music from 1930s |
| ☑ Audio speech recordings | FDR's first inaugural address; fireside chat |
| ☑ Videos, film clips | Film clips from FDR's first inaugural; "Day of Infamy" speech after Pearl Harbor; FDR's funeral train with recorded spiritual, "Goin' Home" |
| ☑ Art and photographs | Still photos from FDR's early life; news photos of FDR and Mrs. Roosevelt, FDR and Churchill |
| ☑ Interviews | Interview Grandma about her memories |

**Research your topic.** You will find media materials in many places. Collections of libraries may include books of photographs, videotaped documentaries, music, and audio voice recordings. The Internet is also a good source, allowing you to locate items such as newspaper pages, videotapes, and recordings. In addition, consider recording interviews with people who have had firsthand experience of your topic—for example, older relatives and neighbors.

**Identify a thesis.** Consider the information and materials you have gathered, and write a thesis statement that expresses one main idea about this topic. You should plan to present your thesis statement early in your report. Consider using one or more of your materials to underscore your thesis statement—for example, a striking photograph or sound effect.

> **Sample thesis statement:**
> Franklin Delano Roosevelt's life combined great optimism with suffering, making him the right man for a time of this country's great need.

## ▶ Drafting

**Create an outline and organize your presentation.** Once you have gathered your information and materials, a detailed outline will help you determine what you would like to cover in your introduction and the various body paragraphs. It will also help you decide which materials to include and when to introduce them.

**Plan your delivery.** Draft a script that adds details to your outline. Indicate where you will be talking and where you will be including media.

Your script should include practical instructions to yourself in italics and brackets, such as *click to next slide, pause for sound effect,* or *speak over music.* You can also help yourself by suggesting the speaking volume, vocal inflections, and body language to use as you speak. However, keep your presentation from looking too "canned," or unnatural, by trying out various readings and gestures.

**List your sources in a bibliography.** Be sure to give credit to all your sources. Where feasible, work such citations into your presentation. In addition, include a typed bibliography, in alphabetical order, listing your sources and where you found them.

> **Sample outline for a multimedia presentation on Franklin D. Roosevelt**
>
> I. Introduction
>    A. Overview of Roosevelt's life (photo)
>    B. Thesis statement: the right man for a difficult time (recording of famous quotation: "The only thing we have to fear is fear itself" from FDR's first inaugural address)
>
> II. Body
>    A. Early years, marriage to Eleanor (period music from 1890s–1900s; photographs; excerpt from documentary)
>    B. Polio and aftermath (photographs about polio epidemics; photograph of Roosevelt recovering; excerpt from documentary)
>    C. Optimism battling handicap (music; photographs); winning presidency
>    D. Presidency: New Deal programs, fireside chats (interview with Grandma)
>
> III. Conclusion
>    A. Sum up research; restate thesis (final photograph)

# Writing Workshop continued

## ▶ Model Script

Read the following model of a multimedia presentation on President Franklin D. Roosevelt. Notice that it includes the characteristics you have learned.

### Model Script

The italic words in brackets tell when to show a slide or play audio or video. Directions like these will help you during your presentation.

[*cue slide:* Portrait of FDR from FDR Library] Franklin Delano Roosevelt became President at one of the darkest times in our history. [*cue audio:* "Happy Days Are Here Again"] The United States was fortunate that the man who took the oath of office on March 4, 1933, was an optimist, but he had also suffered. As a result, he had the qualities needed to rekindle Americans' belief in themselves and their country.

The thesis statement appears at the beginning of the presentation.

The script contains the words you will speak as you give your presentation.

Franklin Delano Roosevelt came from a privileged New York family. [*cue slides:* Series of pictures of Roosevelt as a boy, young man, marriage to Eleanor.] He was a distant cousin of Theodore Roosevelt and married TR's niece, Eleanor. He held a series of jobs in the government and had run for Vice President in 1920.

[*cue video:* Polio victims from the 1920s] FDR's privileged life came to an abrupt end when he was stricken with polio just before turning 40. Many people expected him to retire. However, Roosevelt was too active and optimistic a man to give up. [*cue slide:* Franklin and Eleanor after polio] He arranged for hydrotherapy treatments in Warm Springs, Georgia, where he established a clinic and where he swam to build his upper-body strength. [*cue video:* Roosevelt at Warm Springs] However, he never walked on his own again.

He won election as governor of New York in 1928. In 1929, the stock market crashed, and the country was plunged into the Great Depression. [*cue video:* Depression breadlines and audio "Brother, Can You Spare a Dime?"]

In 1932, the Democrats nominated Roosevelt to run for President. He won. His inaugural address told Americans that they had not been beaten by the Depression. [*cue audio:* Excerpt from inaugural address]

# ▶ Revising

After completing your script, read it again carefully to find ways to make your wording and presentation better. Here are some questions to ask yourself:

**Revise to clarify the sequence.**
- Is the thesis clearly stated?
- Does each section of the report develop the thesis, supporting it with facts, examples, and media?
- Does the conclusion tie up the presentation?

**Revise to add and vary the media.**
- Does the report balance the oral presentation and the various media?
- Does the report use a variety of different media?

**Practice and deliver your research report.**
- Have you practiced your script so that you can read it in a natural voice?
- Does all the equipment you are using work properly?

# ▶ Rubric for Self-Assessment

*Evaluate your multimedia research report using the following rating scale:*

|  | Score 4 | Score 3 | Score 2 | Score 1 |
|---|---|---|---|---|
| **Organization** | Includes an effectively ordered sequence of information | Includes a reasonably ordered sequence of information but includes some items that are less relevant | Includes several media items but not enough; some media items are not in logical order | Includes only one or two media items, in no logical order |
| **Presentation** | Smoothly combines media items with student's explanation and narration; uses facts, examples, and reasons intelligently to support the thesis; clearly links all supporting items to the thesis | Does not always combine media items with explanation and narration smoothly; links most but not all supporting information to the thesis; could use more support | Awkwardly combines media presentation with student's narration and explanation; does not link information clearly to the thesis | No effort to combine media items with student's narration and explanation; fails to provide facts, reasons, or examples to support the thesis |
| **Use of Language** | Varies sentence structure and vocabulary successfully | Uses some variety in sentence structure and vocabulary | Uses the same types of sentences without varying them; repeats words | Includes incomplete sentences; uses language poorly; sounds confused |

# Unit 9

## Think Like a Historian

**As you read this unit, think about this question:** ***How did the United States strive to strengthen democracy at home and to foster democracy abroad?***



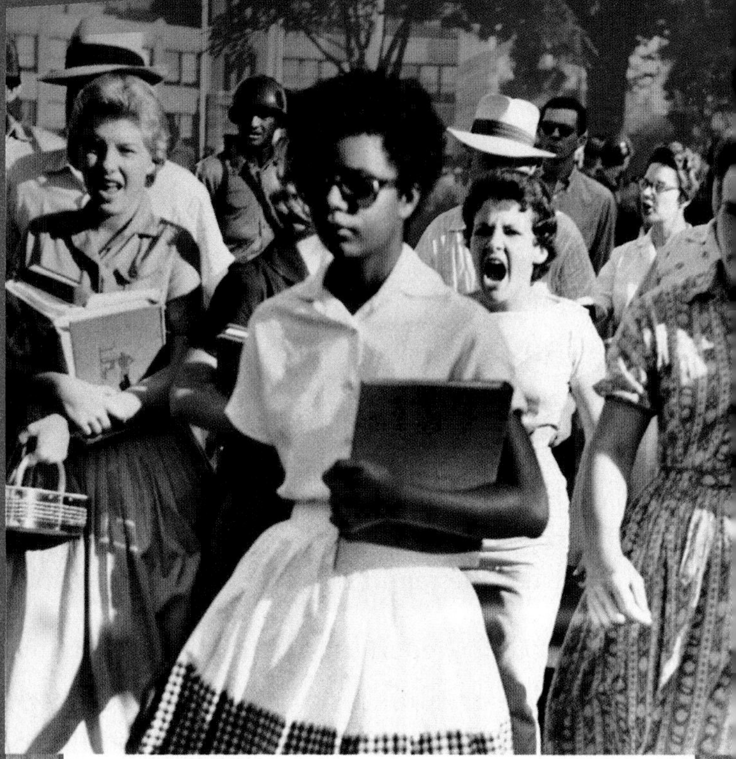

**Civil Rights Movement** African Americans struggled to gain the rights guaranteed them by the Constitution. Courageous individuals, such as Elizabeth Eckford, braved insults and violence to end segregation in public places and in other areas of American life.

**1950s**

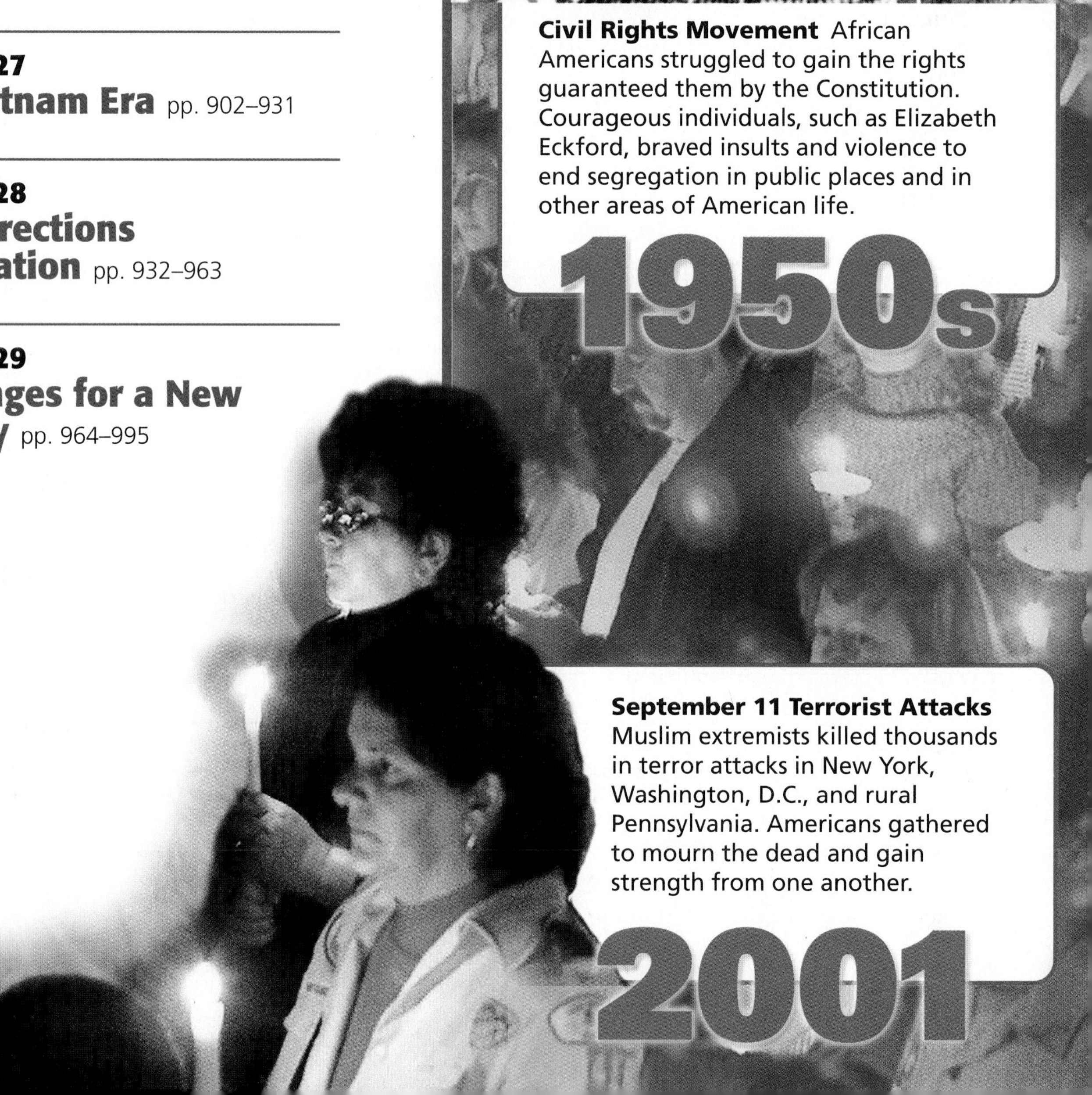

**September 11 Terrorist Attacks** Muslim extremists killed thousands in terror attacks in New York, Washington, D.C., and rural Pennsylvania. Americans gathered to mourn the dead and gain strength from one another.

**2001**

# Moving Toward the Future

**Vietnam War** The United States sent troops to Vietnam to help South Vietnam fight Communists there. By 1968, the number of American forces had reached more than 500,000. Meanwhile, at home, Americans debated whether the nation should be in the war.

## 1964

**The Cold War Ends** In 1989, the people in Berlin, Germany, knocked down the wall that had divided their city for nearly 30 years. Within a year, the Communist governments of the Soviet Union and numerous other countries had fallen.

## 1990

**America's Diverse Population** The U.S. population continues to grow more diverse, as immigrants come to America from all parts of the world. In recent years, Hispanics have become the largest minority.

## 21$^{ST}$ Century

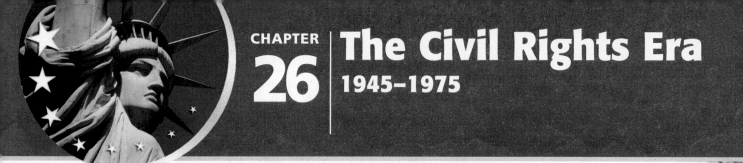

# CHAPTER 26 | The Civil Rights Era
## 1945–1975

## Chapter Preview

The long struggle of African Americans to win their full rights as citizens grew stronger after World War II. Under the leadership of such people as Martin Luther King, Jr., the civil rights movement changed American society. At the same time, other Americans also began to demand greater protections under the law.

**U.S. Events**

**1948** Truman ends segregation in the military.

**1954** Supreme Court strikes down school segregation in *Brown* v. *Board of Education.*

**1955** African Americans stage bus boycott in Montgomery, Alabama.

1940

**World Events**

**1947** India wins independence from British rule.

**1950** Korean War begins.

**1959** Fidel Castro comes to power in Cuba.

1950

1960

**Discovery SCHOOL**

**Quick View Video**
View the chapter video for a quick preview of the main ideas.

Dr. Martin Luther King, Jr., and his wife, Coretta, lead a peaceful march to protest racial segregation in 1965.

**1964**
Congress passes Civil Rights Act.

**1966**
National Organization for Women and the United Farm Workers are founded.

**1975**
Congress passes Education for the Handicapped Act.

1960

1970

1980

**1960** Nigeria, Somalia, and Congo win independence.

**1975** Helsinki Accords define basic human rights.

**History Reading Skill** Draw Inferences and Conclusions

## What was the South like during the civil rights era?

In this chapter, you will practice drawing inferences and conclusions. Read the following account of one African American woman's attempt to register to vote. The side notes highlight ways to draw inferences and conclusions.

In 1962, Mississippi still used literacy tests as a means of preventing African Americans from voting. Here, Fannie Lou Hamer describes what happened when she tried to register to vote.

**Primary Source**

You might infer that the goal of the election official was to stop Hamer from voting.

"He brought a big old book out there, and he gave me the sixteenth section of the Constitution of Mississippi, and that was dealing with de facto laws, and I didn't know nothin' about no de facto laws. . . . I could copy it like it was in the book, but after I got through copying it, he told me to give a reasonable interpretation and tell the meaning of that section that I had copied. Well, I flunked out. . . .

Evidence that supports the inference: The official asked Hamer to interpret a difficult and obscure part of the state constitution. Hamer could not interpret the passage.

You can conclude that the police want to harass the group yet have no real cause for doing so.

So then we started back to Ruleville . . . [O]n our way back . . . [the police] flagged the bus down . . . [and] told all of us to get off the bus. . . . They arrested Bob [an organizer] and told the bus driver he was under arrest. . . . The bus driver was fined $100 for driving a bus with too much yellow in it. Now ain't that ridiculous?"

Details that support the conclusion: The police stop the bus and arrest an organizer. They fine the driver for a ridiculous reason.

—Fannie Lou Hamer, in *My Soul Is Rested: Movement Days in the Deep South Remembered by Howell Raines*

## Draw Inferences and Conclusions

- An inference is an idea hinted at but not directly stated in the text. A conclusion is a larger or more definitive inference.
- Both inferences and conclusions must be supported by information in the text.
- Logic, previous knowledge, and personal experience can help you complete an inference or a conclusion.

## Document-Based Questions

1. What was Hamer's goal on the day she describes here?
2. Why does Hamer fail to achieve this goal?
3. Do you think Hamer has given up trying to achieve this goal? Explain.

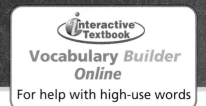

## Vocabulary *Builder*

### Previewing High-Use Academic Words

| High-Use Word | Definition | Sample History Sentence |
|---|---|---|
| **reinforce** (ree ihn FORS) (Section 1, p. 875) | *v.* to strengthen; to make more effective | Women's contributions during World War I <u>reinforced</u> their efforts to win the vote. |
| **persist** (pehr SIHST) (Section 1, p. 879) | *v.* to continue in the face of opposition or difficulty | Despite court rulings against them, labor leaders <u>persisted</u> in organizing unions. |
| **domestic** (doh MEHS tihk) (Section 2, p. 883) | *adj.* relating to matters within one's own country, rather than to foreign affairs | Creating jobs and reforming the economy were part of Franklin Roosevelt's <u>domestic</u> program. |
| **function** (FUHNK shuhn) (Section 2, p. 885) | *n.* purpose; proper use | The chief <u>function</u> of the legislative branch is to make laws. |
| **transform** (trahns FORM) (Section 3, p. 887) | *v.* to change the form, appearance, or nature of something | The machine gun and the airplane <u>transformed</u> the nature of modern warfare. |
| **restore** (ree STOR) (Section 3, p. 888) | *v.* to bring back to a normal state | After World War II, democratic rule was <u>restored</u> in West Germany. |
| **exert** (ehks ZERT) (Section 4, p. 897) | *v.* to put into action | American citizens <u>exert</u> their political rights by voting. |
| **modify** (MAH dih fi) (Section 4, p. 897) | *v.* to make changes to or in; to alter | The Wright Brothers <u>modified</u> their airplane design to make it capable of longer and longer flights. |

### Previewing Key Terms and People

## Objectives

1. Learn how the campaign for civil rights picked up pace after World War II.

2. Discover how the Supreme Court outlawed segregation in the nation's schools.

3. Find out why African Americans boycotted the buses in Montgomery, Alabama.

## Prepare to Read

###  Reading Skill

**Make Inferences** History textbooks may not directly state the views of people. Instead, the text may describe people's actions and leave the reader to figure out, or infer, the views and attitudes behind those actions. To make an inference, look at the actions people took and think about the attitudes that most likely produced those actions.

### Vocabulary *Builder*

**High-Use Words**

<u>reinforce</u>, p. 875

<u>persist</u>, p. 879

**Key Terms and People**

Thurgood Marshall, p. 875

integration, p. 875

Jackie Robinson, p. 876

Rosa Parks, p. 877

boycott, p. 877

Martin Luther King, Jr., p. 879

### Main Idea
The NAACP led the battle against laws that segregated African Americans.

⭐ **Background Knowledge** As you have read, African Americans in the South made important gains after the Civil War. But after Reconstruction ended, most of those gains were lost. In this section, you will see how the struggle for equal rights picked up strength after World War II.

## Separate but Unequal

Racial barriers existed in all parts of the country. However, they took different forms in the North and the South.

**In the North** Generally, there were no official segregation laws in the North. African Americans could vote and had legal access to jobs and colleges. Still, African Americans and whites rarely mixed. They tended to live in different communities. As a result, their children usually attended different schools.

African Americans in the North often faced prejudice in hiring and housing. Many qualified African Americans could not get high-paying jobs. Homeowners in white neighborhoods would often refuse to sell homes to African Americans. Other groups, such as Jews or immigrants, frequently faced similar forms of discrimination.

**In the South** In the South, segregation was a way of life supported by law. By the early 1900s, segregation was firmly in place in all southern states. The so-called Jim Crow laws enforced separation of races in schools and hospitals, on public transportation, and in theaters and restaurants. Even drinking fountains were for "whites only" or "colored only."

As you have learned, the 1896 Supreme Court ruling in *Plessy* v. *Ferguson* <u>reinforced</u> segregation. The Court ruled that segregation was legal as long as "separate-but-equal" facilities were provided. In fact, separate schools and other facilities for African Americans were rarely, if ever, equal to those for white southerners.

**The NAACP Leads the Fight** During the Progressive Era, reformers such as W.E.B. Du Bois and Jane Addams had founded the National Association for the Advancement of Colored People (NAACP). Its goals were to "eradicate . . . race prejudice" and to secure "complete equality before the law."

The NAACP challenged laws that prevented African Americans from exercising their full rights as citizens. It won its first major victory in 1915, when the Supreme Court declared grandfather clauses unconstitutional. As you learned, grandfather clauses had been used in the South to ensure that only whites voted. In the 1920s and 1930s, the NAACP won court victories in the areas of housing, employment, and education.

**Thurgood Marshall** In 1938, Thurgood Marshall became head of the NAACP's legal section. A brilliant lawyer, Marshall used his knowledge of the Constitution to attack the foundations of segregation. His legal strategy was largely based on the Fourteenth Amendment, which guarantees all citizens "equal protection of the laws."

It also forbids any state from making laws that interfere with the rights of U.S. citizens. Marshall argued that this meant that all rights in the federal Constitution applied to the states as well. Marshall's ultimate goal was integration, or an end to racial segregation. As you will see, his most important victory would come in 1954.

✓ **Checkpoint** Describe one accomplishment of the NAACP.

**Vocabulary** *Builder*
<u>reinforce</u> (ree ihn FORS) *v.* to strengthen; to make more effective

**Make Inferences**
Why do you think NAACP members went to court to fight against segregation? What do you think was their long-term goal?

**Segregation in the South**
Legal segregation was a way of life in southern states. The white man and black man at left were forbidden by law from drinking from the same water fountain. **Critical Thinking:** *Link Past and Present Would you see a road sign like the one shown here today? Why or why not?*

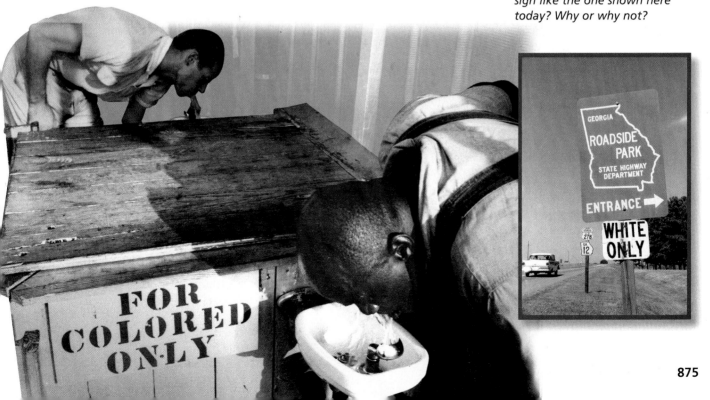

Postage stamp honoring Jackie Robinson

# Barriers Begin to Crumble

The campaign for equal rights gained speed after World War II. During the war, African Americans and other minorities had served with distinction in the armed forces. Returning home, they sought an end to discrimination in American society.

**Integrating Baseball** One of the first barriers to fall was in sports. Professional baseball had long been segregated into the all-white Major Leagues and the Negro League. Branch Rickey, general manager of the Brooklyn Dodgers, wanted to break the "color line" and tap into the vast pool of talent in the Negro League.

In 1947, Rickey signed an African American army veteran named Jackie Robinson. Robinson's first years in the majors were a test of endurance. While some teammates welcomed him, he was ignored by other players and jeered at by fans. Soon, however, his skill and daring on the field won him huge numbers of fans, both white and African American. At the end of his first season, Robinson was named Rookie of the Year. More important, he paved the way for other African American athletes to compete in professional sports.

**Integrating the Military** President Harry Truman was committed to civil rights. He proposed laws to make lynching a federal crime, to protect the rights of African American voters, and to ban discrimination in hiring. Because of southern opposition, though, not one of these laws was passed.

Still, as commander in chief, Truman did not need congressional approval to end segregation in the military. In 1948, he ordered the integration of all units of the armed forces. As a result, African American and white soldiers fought side by side in the Korean War.

☑**Checkpoint** **What actions did Truman take to further civil rights?**

# Desegregating the Schools

Spurred on by small victories, African Americans and their white supporters stepped up the struggle for equal rights. In 1954, the growing civil rights movement achieved a major triumph.

**Brown v. *Board of Education*** In 1951, Oliver Brown sued the board of education of Topeka, Kansas. Under Topeka's segregation laws, Brown's daughter Linda had to travel a great distance to a run-down school for African Americans. Brown wanted Linda to attend a school closer to her home, which also had better facilities. But the principal refused, saying that the school was for whites only.

The case of *Brown* v. *Board of Education of Topeka* reached the Supreme Court. Thurgood Marshall represented Brown. Marshall recognized that the moment had come to overthrow the doctrine of "separate but equal." He argued that segregation made equal education impossible. Segregation, he further stated, damaged African American youngsters by making them feel inferior.

The Court agreed. On May 17, 1954, the justices ruled that "in the field of public education, the doctrine of 'separate but equal' has no place." A year later, the Court ordered local school boards to desegregate "with all deliberate speed."

In a few places, schools were integrated smoothly. However, many white southerners were hostile to integration. The biggest battle over school integration took place in Little Rock, Arkansas.

**Trouble in Little Rock** The Little Rock school board approved a plan for gradual desegregation. According to the plan, nine African American students would attend the city's Central High School. But Arkansas governor Orval Faubus vowed, "No school district will be forced to mix the races as long as I am governor."

On September 4, 1957, Faubus called in the state's National Guard to keep the nine students out of Central High. An angry mob gathered outside the school. A few blocks away, eight of the students met so that they could walk together, protected by a band of black and white ministers. But Elizabeth Eckford did not get the message. Instead, she faced the mob alone. She recalled:

> **"**Somebody started yelling, 'Lynch her! Lynch her!' . . . I looked into the face of an old woman and it seemed a kind face, but when I looked at her again, she spat on me.**"**
>
> —Elizabeth Eckford, interview

After several weeks of turmoil, President Eisenhower stepped in. He sent in federal troops to enforce the Supreme Court's ruling. Under their protection, the students finally entered Central High.

✓**Checkpoint** **How did the Supreme Court rule in *Brown* v. *Board of Education*?**

## The Montgomery Bus Boycott

*Brown* v. *Board of Education of Topeka* was a milestone in the civil rights movement. Another milestone took place a year later.

**Rosa Parks** On December 1, 1955, Rosa Parks, an African American seamstress, boarded a bus in Montgomery, Alabama. Parks was secretary of the local chapter of the NAACP. In accordance with local segregation laws, she sat in the first row for "coloreds." As the bus filled up, the driver ordered her to give up her seat to a white rider. Parks refused. The driver then had her arrested.

News of the arrest spread quickly. Members of the Women's Political Council of Montgomery then took a daring step. At the time, African Americans made up about 70 percent of the city's bus riders. What would happen if they all boycotted, or refused to use, the buses on the day when Parks was brought to trial?

**First Day of School**
Elizabeth Eckford is taunted by a mob as she tries to attend school in Little Rock on September 4, 1957. Years later, the woman shown yelling at Eckford apologized to her and they became friends. **Critical Thinking:** *Evaluate Information The day after this photograph was taken, it appeared in newspapers all over the country. How do you think people reacted to it?*

**Main Idea**
In 1955, African Americans in Montgomery, Alabama, organized a protest against segregation laws.

# The Montgomery Bus Boycott

The Montgomery bus boycott began when Rosa Parks decided she was no longer going to accept discrimination. It ended with one of the great victories for civil rights. **Critical Thinking:** *Draw Conclusions* *Why do you think the Montgomery bus boycott succeeded?*

**History** *Interactive*
Learn About the
**Montgomery Bus Boycott**
**Visit:** PHSchool.com
**Web Code:** mvl-9261

Rosa Parks is fingerprinted after ▶ her arrest. A longtime NAACP member, Parks later explained that she was "sick and tired of being sick and tired."

**December 1, 1955**
Rosa Parks is arrested in Montgomery, Alabama, for refusing to give up her bus seat to a white rider.

**December 5, 1955**
Led by Dr. Martin Luther King, Jr., African Americans begin boycott of Montgomery bus system.

As African ▶ Americans carpool to work, an empty city bus passes in the background.

**January 30, 1956**
King's house is bombed.

**March 14, 1956**
Day 100 of bus boycott

**June 22, 1956**
Day 200 of bus boycott

**September 30, 1956**
Day 300 of bus boycott

With the ▶ success of the boycott, these two men no longer have to sit at the back of the bus.

**December 13, 1956**
U.S. Supreme Court outlaws bus segregation.

**December 21, 1956**
Boycott ends as King and other African Americans board Montgomery buses.

Members of the Women's Political Council printed and distributed 52,000 fliers. On Monday morning, December 5, there was not a single African American passenger on the city's buses.

**The Boycott Grows** The protest was originally supposed to last a single day. But that night, some 7,000 people met at a local Baptist church. A young preacher named Martin Luther King, Jr., told the crowd, "There comes a time when people get tired of being trampled over by the iron feet of oppression." At King's urging, the African American community agreed to continue the boycott until the bus segregation laws were taken off the books.

Montgomery's leaders responded to the boycott with outrage. King's home was bombed, and King and others were jailed several times on false charges. But the boycotters <u>persisted</u>. Volunteer drivers transported boycotters between work and home. African Americans walked miles to work or traveled by bicycle. Volunteer chauffeurs drove other protesters between work and home.

The Montgomery bus boycott lasted 381 days. At last, in November 1956, the Supreme Court ruled that segregation on buses was unconstitutional. On December 21, King boarded a bus in Montgomery—and sat in the front seat.

☑**Checkpoint** How did the Montgomery bus boycott end?

☆ **Looking Back and Ahead** One important result of the Montgomery bus boycott was the emergence of Martin Luther King, Jr., as a leader of the civil rights movement. Later, you will explore King's ideas and achievements in more detail.

**Vocabulary** *Builder*
<u>persist</u> (pehr SIHST) *v.* to continue in the face of opposition or difficulty

---

Section 1 | **Check Your Progress**

**Progress Monitoring** ⬤nline
**For:** Self-test with instant help
**Visit:** PHSchool.com
**Web Code:** mva-9261

**Comprehension and Critical Thinking**

1. **(a) Recall** How did the Supreme Court ruling in *Plessy* v. *Ferguson* support segregation laws?
**(b) Analyze Cause and Effect** What effect did the Supreme Court ruling in *Brown* v. *Board of Education* have on *Plessy* v. *Ferguson*?

2. **(a) Describe** What was the Montgomery bus boycott? How did it begin?
**(b) Evaluate Information** Why was a bus boycott an effective tool of protest in Montgomery?

**Reading Skill**

3. **Make Inferences** Reread the text following the subheading "Trouble in Little Rock." What can you infer about President Eisenhower's attitude toward the Supreme Court decision in *Brown* v. *Board of Education*?

**Vocabulary** *Builder*

4. Draw a table with three rows and three columns. In the first column, list the following terms: integration, boycott. In the next column, write the definition of each term. In the last column, make a small illustration that shows the meaning of each term.

**Writing**

5. Choose one of the photographs in this section. Imagine that you were either one of the people who is shown in the photograph or the photographer who took the picture. Write a few sentences describing the moment when the photograph was taken: what was happening, what you were doing, and how you felt at the time.

## Midway
### by Naomi Long Madgett

## Prepare to Read

### Introduction

Naomi Long Madgett began writing as a child and published her first book of poetry at age 17. Many of her poems express her pride in her African American heritage. The poem "Midway" was published in 1956, in response to the Supreme Court decision in *Brown* v. *Board of Education of Topeka*.

### Reading Skill

**Analyze Titles** Some poetry titles describe the subject of the poem. Others are words taken directly from the poem. Still other titles help explain or expand the poem's meaning. As you read this poem, think about what the title "Midway" might mean.

### Vocabulary *Builder*

As you read this literature selection, look for the following underlined words:

**reap** (reep) *v.* to gather a crop

**sow** (soh) *v.* to plant seeds

**abhor** (ahb HOHR) *v.* to turn away from in hatred or disgust

**deride** (dee RĪD) *v.* to ridicule; to make fun of

**Naomi Long Madgett**

### Analyze Titles

What do you think the title "Midway" means? What does it say about events that took place around the time the poem was written? How does the title reflect Madgett's feelings about the future?

If you liked this poem and want to learn more about the early civil rights movement, you might want to read *Rosa Parks: My Story,* by Rosa Parks and James Haskins. Dial Books, 1992.

I've come this far to freedom and I won't turn back.
I'm climbing to the highway from my old dirt track.
   I'm coming and I'm going
    And I'm stretching and I'm growing
And I'll <u>reap</u> what I've been <u>sowing</u> or my skin's not black.

I've prayed and slaved and waited and I've sung my song.
You've bled me and you've starved me but I've still grown strong.
   You've lashed me and you've treed me
    And you've everything but freed me
But in time you'll know you need me and it won't be long.

I've seen the daylight breaking high above the bough.
I've found my destination and I've made my vow,
   So whether you <u>abhor</u> me
    Or <u>deride</u> me or ignore me,
Mighty mountains loom before me and I won't stop now.

From *Star by Star* by Naomi Long Madgett
(Harlo, 1965; Evenill, 1970). Reprinted in *Connected Islands: New and Selected Poems* (Detroit: Lotus Press, 2004).

### *Analyze* **LITERATURE**

Compare this poem to the poem "I, Too" by Langston Hughes. How are the two poems similar? How can you tell Madgett's poem was written at a later time in history?

## Objectives

1. Describe how the U.S. Supreme Court took on a more activist role under Chief Justice Earl Warren.

2. Discover the domestic goals of President Kennedy.

3. Find out how President Johnson's Great Society increased the social role of the federal government.

## Prepare to Read

### 🕥 Reading Skill

**Support Inferences With Text Evidence** As you know, inferences must be supported by evidence stated in the text. One common focus for inferences is as a tool to learn about people in history. Text evidence can help you infer answers to questions, for example, by describing the person or giving examples of his or her actions. Ask: What were they like?

### Vocabulary *Builder*

**High-Use Words**

domestic, p. 883

function, p. 885

**Key Terms and People**

Earl Warren, p. 881

Lyndon Johnson, p. 884

welfare, p. 885

⭐ **Background Knowledge** You have examined the Supreme Court decision in *Brown* v. *Board of Education*. In this section, you will look at other Supreme Court decisions that had a powerful impact on American life. You will also see how two Presidents of the 1960s supported a series of social reforms.

## The Warren Court

In 1953, President Eisenhower appointed former California governor Earl Warren as chief justice of the U.S. Supreme Court. Eisenhower expected the former California governor to keep the Court on its conservative course of respecting past decisions or precedents. Instead, a year later, the Supreme Court broke all precedent with its groundbreaking decision in *Brown* v. *Board of Education of Topeka*.

**Extending Individual Rights** In the 1960s, the Warren Court continued to make decisions with far-reaching effects. In the 1966 case of *Miranda* v. *Arizona*, the Court overturned the guilty verdict of Ernesto Miranda. Miranda had been convicted on the basis of a confession obtained without access to a lawyer. The Court ruled that this violated the Fifth Amendment. As a result of the *Miranda* ruling, the police must now advise arrested persons of their right to remain silent and to have legal counsel. The Court made other rulings to protect the rights of the accused. Many critics argue that such rulings make it more difficult to combat crime.

Another case, *Tinker* v. *Des Moines School District* (1969), expanded the concept of freedom of speech guaranteed in the First Amendment. The Court ruled that school administrators had violated the free speech of students by suspending several of them for wearing black arm bands to protest the war in Vietnam.

**Main Idea**

In the 1960s, the Supreme Court took on an activist role to extend the idea of individual rights.

Police read a suspect his "Miranda rights."

## Key Decisions of the Warren Court

| Case | Decision Based On | Impact |
|------|-------------------|--------|
| *Mapp* v. *Ohio* (1961) | **Fourth Amendment:** Protects "against unreasonable searches and seizures." | Evidence from an illegal search cannot be used in a criminal trial. |
| *Gideon* v. *Wainwright* (1963) | **Sixth Amendment:** Guarantees accused person "the assistance of counsel for his defense." | If a person accused of a crime cannot afford an attorney, the state must provide one. |
| *Miranda* v. *Arizona* (1966) | **Fifth Amendment:** Defendant cannot" be compelled . . . to be a witness against himself." | Before being questioned by police, suspects must be informed of their right to keep silent, as well as to have an attorney. |
| *Tinker* v. *Des Moines School District* (1969) | **First Amendment:** Protects "freedom of speech." | A school cannot interfere with a student's right to free speech unless that speech causes major disruption of the school day. |

**Judicial Activism** Perhaps more important than any individual decision was Warren's approach to the law. Unlike most earlier chief justices, Warren believed that the Constitution must be interpreted flexibly—in light of what the Framers wrote but also in light of what best serves the public interest today. The Warren Court began to strike down laws that the justices regarded as unfair, regardless of past decisions or the exact wording of the Constitution.

This concept of "judicial activism" has stirred controversy. Then and later, critics argue that following their own ideas of fairness gives judges too much power. Only what was written in the Constitution could be written into law, they insist.

☑ Checkpoint  **How did the Supreme Court decision in *Miranda* v. *Arizona* affect law enforcement?**

**Main Idea**
Kennedy pushed programs for social change.

# Kennedy's Brief Presidency

**Election of 1960** In one of the closest presidential elections in history, Kennedy won by about 100,000 of 70 million votes cast. At 43, he became the youngest person ever elected President.

**Mixed Success** In his inaugural address, the young President sounded an idealistic, optimistic note:

> **"**Let the word go forth from this time and place, to friend and foe alike, that the torch has been passed to a new generation of Americans born in this century, tempered by war, discipline by a hard and bitter peace, proud of our ancient heritage—and unwilling to witness or permit the slow undoing of those human rights to which this Nation has always been committed, and to which we are committed today at home and around the world.**"**
>
> —John F. Kennedy, First Inaugural Address

Kennedy had been shocked to learn that one fifth of Americans lived below the poverty line. He called on Congress to take action to end poverty, fight disease, and ensure justice for all Americans. Although Kennedy did win some support for his antipoverty measures, Congress rejected most of his <u>domestic</u> proposals. His most lasting accomplishment was the space program. He set a bold goal: to place a man on the moon by the end of the decade.

Kennedy also became convinced of the need for extensive civil rights legislation. But he did not live to achieve this goal.

**Assassination** On November 22, 1963, Kennedy was in Dallas, Texas, on a political visit. Riding in an open limousine, the President and his wife, Jacqueline, greeted the cheering crowds. Suddenly, shots rang out. Kennedy slumped over. He died shortly afterward.

Within hours, Dallas police arrested Lee Harvey Oswald for the assassination. Two days later, Oswald himself was shot to death while being transferred from one jail to another. Millions of horrified Americans saw the shooting live on television.

**Vocabulary** *Builder*
<u>domestic</u> (doh MEHS tihk) *adj.*
relating to matters within one's own country, rather than to foreign affairs

**The Kennedy Assassination**
Moments after the picture at the left was taken, President Kennedy was shot to death in Dallas. The sign in this New York City store window (right) reflects the nation's shock and grief. **Critical Thinking:** *Make Inferences Why do you think the store owner referred to the assassination as "a national disgrace"?*

## The Great Society

Teacher and students at Head Start program

"Our society will not be great until every young mind is set free to scan the farthest reaches of thought and imagination. We are still far from that goal. Today, 8 million adult Americans . . . have not finished five years of school. . . . We must give every child a place to sit and a teacher to learn from. Poverty must not be a bar to learning, and learning must offer an escape from poverty."

—Lyndon Johnson, "The Great Society," 1964

### Reading Primary Sources
#### Skills Activity

In May 1964, President Lyndon Johnson outlined his vision of what he called the Great Society. In the excerpt here, Johnson discusses his goals for education.

**(a)** **Interpret Primary Sources** What link does Johnson make between education and poverty?

**(b)** **Apply Information** How did Head Start relate to Johnson's goals?

The murder of the young, energetic President stunned the nation. A few months later, a commission headed by Earl Warren concluded that Oswald had acted alone. Still, some people continue to question the conclusions of the Warren Commission.

✓**Checkpoint** What was Kennedy's most lasting success?

## Johnson's Great Society

**Main Idea**
Lyndon Johnson's Great Society was an ambitious attempt to deal with the causes and effects of poverty.

On the day Kennedy was assassinated, Vice President Lyndon Johnson was sworn in as President. The following year, he was elected President in his own right by a landslide.

**Johnson's Background** Lyndon Johnson grew up in a poor family in rural Texas. As a young man, he taught at a school for Mexican Americans. Johnson grew deeply attached to his pupils there and became convinced that something needed to be done to help the nation's poor and oppressed.

An ardent supporter of President Franklin Roosevelt, Johnson was elected to Congress in 1937 on a pro–New Deal platform. He won election to the Senate 11 years later, rising to the powerful position of majority leader. He became Vice President in 1961.

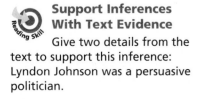

**Support Inferences With Text Evidence**
Give two details from the text to support this inference: Lyndon Johnson was a persuasive politician.

**A Flood of Legislation** As President, Johnson set out to make his mark with an ambitious program of economic and social reforms. Using his political skills, Johnson persuaded Congress to enact more new laws than at any time since the New Deal. One journalist commented, "Johnson had scarcely settled in office before bills were coming out of Congress like candy bars from a slot machine."

At first, he worked to push through legislation that Kennedy had begun, including a major civil rights law. (See Section 3.) Johnson then turned his attention to his own program, which he called the Great Society. Its goal was to expand opportunity and provide a decent standard of living for all Americans.

Much of this legislation was part of what Johnson called his War on Poverty. The Economic Opportunity Act attacked the causes of poverty, such as illiteracy, unemployment, and inadequate public services. Head Start provided preschool education for needy children. Other Great Society programs provided food stamps and welfare to needy families. Welfare is a system in which government agencies make cash payments to the poor. Johnson also created a Department of Housing and Urban Development (HUD) to oversee the building of middle-income and low-income housing.

Perhaps the most important Great Society legislation was Medicare. This act helped citizens 65 years of age or older to pay their medical bills. A companion act, Medicaid, provided money to assist poor people of all ages who were not covered by Medicare.

Like the New Deal, the Great Society greatly expanded the role of the federal government. Critics said providing for people's needs on such a scale was not the proper <u>function</u> of the federal government. They also charged that, though the Great Society programs cost billions of dollars, many were badly run and did not work.

Johnson displays a newly signed antipoverty law.

**Vocabulary** *Builder*
<u>function</u> (FUHNK shuhn) *n.*
purpose; proper use

✓ **Checkpoint**  **Describe two important laws passed during the administration of Lyndon Johnson.**

⭐ **Looking Back and Ahead**  In this section, you saw how Johnson supported social reforms. In the next section, you will see how legislation in the Johnson years advanced civil rights.

---

Section 2 | **Check Your Progress**

**Progress Monitoring** 🌐nline
**For:** Self-test with instant help
**Visit:** PHSchool.com
**Web Code:** mva-9262

**Comprehension and Critical Thinking**

1. **(a) Identify** What were the domestic goals of Kennedy?
   **(b) Evaluate Information** Was Kennedy's program successful or unsuccessful in the long run? Explain.

2. **(a) Describe** Choose and describe two Great Society programs.
   **(b) Draw Conclusions** Do you think the federal government should support expensive social programs? Why or why not?

🎯 **Reading Skill**

3. **Support Inferences With Details** Read the text following the subheading "Johnson's Background." Give two details from the text to support this inference: Lyndon Johnson's sympathy for the poor grew from his own experience.

**Vocabulary** *Builder*

4. Write two definitions of the word welfare—one a formal definition for a teacher, the other an informal definition for a younger child.

**Writing**

5. Imagine that you are one of the following individuals. Write a few sentences explaining your thoughts and feelings.
   • Police officer reacting to the *Miranda* ruling
   • Voter in 1960 choosing between Kennedy and Nixon
   • Resident of Dallas just after Kennedy was shot
   • Poverty-stricken American hearing about Johnson's Great Society program

## Objectives

1. Explore Martin Luther King's use of nonviolent protest to gain equal rights.

2. Find out how new federal legislation helped protect civil rights.

3. Understand why the civil rights movement broke up into several groups.

4. Analyze the achievements and failures of the civil rights movement.

## Prepare to Read

### 🔁 Reading Skill

**Draw Logical Conclusions**
Logic is the cornerstone of drawing conclusions. You must always ask yourself: Does this conclusion make sense? Does it make sense with the evidence in the text? Does it make sense with what I know about these people and their situation? Does it make sense with what I know about the world and how people, in general, act? If the answer to all these questions is yes, you have drawn a logical conclusion.

### Vocabulary *Builder*

**High-Use Words**
**transform**, p. 887
**restore**, p. 888

**Key Terms and People**
civil disobedience, p. 886
sit-in, p. 888
James Meredith, p. 888
Malcolm X, p. 890
Stokely Carmichael, p. 890
ghetto, p. 891
affirmative action, p. 892

⭐ **Background Knowledge** In Section 1, you saw how African Americans won major victories in the fight against segregation during the 1950s. In this section, you will see how the civil rights movement continued and grew in the 1960s. You will also see how the movement divided over goals and methods.

## King's Strategy of Nonviolence

**Main Idea**
Martin Luther King, Jr., urged his followers to use nonviolent protest to resist unjust laws.

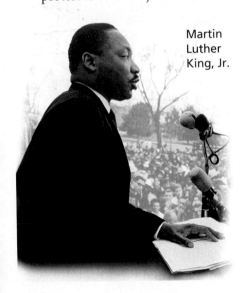

Martin Luther King, Jr.

The Montgomery bus boycott had brought forth a dynamic civil rights leader in Dr. Martin Luther King, Jr. The boycott also provided the first test of King's belief in civil disobedience, or the peaceful refusal to obey unjust laws. As you have read in Chapter 12, the philosophy of civil disobedience had been developed in the 1840s by American writer Henry David Thoreau.

**Sources of King's Ideas** King's belief in nonviolent protest was rooted in Christian teachings. Like his father and grandfather, King was a Baptist minister. Echoing Jesus, King told his followers that they should always meet hate with love.

King also studied the ideas of India's Mohandas Gandhi. Gandhi had led a campaign of nonviolent resistance to win India's freedom from British colonial rule. Like Gandhi, King taught that one should resist injustice even if it meant going to jail or enduring violence.

In addition, King owed much of his thinking to A. Philip Randolph, the prominent African American labor leader. Randolph championed a strategy of nonviolent mass protest.

**SCLC** To build on the momentum of the Montgomery bus boycott, King joined with other African American church leaders to found the Southern Christian Leadership Conference (SCLC) in 1957. The goal of the organization was full equality for African Americans. In their first official statement, SCLC leaders declared their commitment to nonviolent civil disobedience:

> **"**No matter how great the obstacles and suffering, we urge all Negroes to reject segregation. But far beyond this, we call upon them to . . . understand that non-violence is not a symbol of weakness or cowardice, but as Jesus demonstrated, non-violent resistance <u>transforms</u> weakness into strength and breeds courage in face of danger.**"**
>
> —Southern Christian Leadership Conference, "A Statement to the South and to the Nation"

**Vocabulary** *Builder*
<u>transform</u> (trahns FORM) *v.* to change the form, appearance, or nature of something

The SCLC helped shift the base of the civil rights movement. Most early civil rights activity had been dominated by northerners. Now, African American churches in the South took the lead in organizing resistance to injustice. Under King's leadership, the SCLC would be in the forefront of many civil rights protests in the 1960s.

☑**Checkpoint** **Identify three sources of King's philosophy of nonviolent protest.**

# Links Across Time

### Gandhi Preaches Nonviolence

**1930** Mohandas Gandhi of India led a march to protest British laws which forbade Indians from extracting their own salt from seawater. During the Salt March, tens of thousands of peaceful protesters were arrested or beaten. But they refused to give in.

**1955–1968** Inspired by Gandhi's methods, Martin Luther King, Jr., led a series of nonviolent civil rights protests.

### Link to Today  🌐**Online**

**Honoring Gandhi and King** Today, both Gandhi and King are widely honored for their leadership and courage. A federal holiday in January commemorates King's birthday.

**For:** The legacy of Martin Luther King, Jr.
**Visit:** PHSchool.com
**Web Code:** mvc-9263

1930 Gandhi leads the Salt March

**Explore More Video**
To learn more about the civil rights movement, view the video.

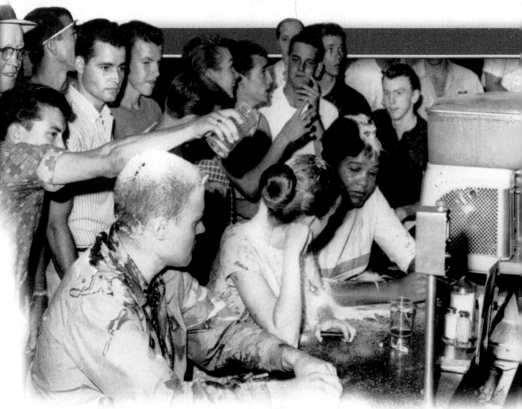

**A Lunch Counter Sit-in** Here, civil rights workers challenge segregation laws by sitting together at a "whites only" lunch counter in Jackson, Mississippi. The three refused to move even when the jeering crowd covered them with ketchup, mustard, and sugar. **Critical Thinking: *Frame Questions*** *Write one question you would like to ask the three protesters and one question you would like to ask the crowd.*

**Main Idea**
Civil rights workers used a variety of tactics, including marches and sit-ins.

**Vocabulary *Builder***
**restore** (ree STOR) *v.* to bring back to a normal state

## Nonviolent Protest Spreads

Nonviolent protest took many forms. In 1960, four African American college students sat down at a "whites only" lunch counter in Greensboro, North Carolina, and ordered coffee. The students refused to move unless they were served. Word of the incident quickly spread. The **sit-in,** a form of protest in which people sit and refuse to leave, became a common tool to protest segregation.

Civil rights leaders organized the first of many Freedom Rides in 1961. Their goal was to test a recent Supreme Court ruling outlawing segregation in interstate travel. Thirteen Freedom Riders—seven black, six white—set out on two buses for a trip through the Deep South. They successfully integrated several bus stations before being violently attacked in Alabama.

In 1962, a federal court ordered the University of Mississippi to admit James Meredith, an African American student. When Meredith arrived on campus, riots broke out. Two people were killed and hundreds more were injured. President Kennedy sent in federal troops to restore order and allow Meredith to register.

**Protests in Birmingham** Early in 1963, the SCLC launched massive demonstrations to protest discrimination in Birmingham, Alabama. Thousands of African Americans, including many children, marched peacefully through Birmingham. Police used dogs, fire hoses, and electric cattle prods against the marchers. Horrified Americans watched the violence unfold on television.

Finally, under intense pressure from business interests in the city, Birmingham authorities agreed to desegregate public facilities. They also agreed to hire African American clerks and salespersons.

**March on Washington** After the events in Birmingham, President Kennedy sent Congress the strongest civil rights bill in the nation's history. To focus attention on the bill, civil rights leaders proposed a march on the nation's capital. The March on Washington took place on August 28, 1963. The sight of nearly 250,000 peacefully assembled citizens stirred more Americans to support civil rights.

Many people, including Christian and Jewish religious leaders, gave speeches that day. But none moved the crowd as did King. His voice rang as he proclaimed, "I have a dream that my four little children will one day live in a nation where they will not be judged by the color of their skins but the content of their character."

☑**Checkpoint**  **How did Freedom Riders protest segregation?**

## Civil Rights Legislation

The civil rights movement now progressed to a new stage. Repelled by the violence against peaceful protesters, Americans pressured their representatives in Congress to take action.

**Civil Rights Act of 1964** Kennedy was assassinated before he could get his civil rights bill through Congress. The new President, Lyndon Johnson, was determined to move the legislation along.

Pushed hard by Johnson, Congress passed the sweeping Civil Rights Act of 1964. It banned discrimination in public facilities and outlawed discrimination in employment. It also provided for faster school desegregation and further protected voting rights.

**Battle for Voting Rights** Still, African Americans in the South continued to face barriers to voting. In 1964, civil rights groups mounted an all-out effort to register African American voters in Mississippi. About a thousand volunteers, mostly college students, answered the call. The project had barely begun when three young volunteers disappeared. They were later found murdered. Other violence included beatings, shootings, and church bombings.

In March 1965, King staged a mass protest in Alabama to draw attention to the issue of voting rights. Hundreds of marchers set out from the city of Selma to Montgomery, the state capital. But state troopers set upon marchers with tear gas, clubs, and whips. Again, Americans witnessed the bloodshed on the evening news. Over the next two days, people in more than 80 cities demonstrated against the violence and demanded passage of a voting rights act.

**Voting Rights Act** In the aftermath of Selma, President Johnson went on national television to support a strong voting rights law. That summer, Congress passed the Voting Rights Act of 1965. It banned literacy tests and other barriers to African American voting.

**Main Idea**

Congress passed the Civil Rights Act and the Voting Rights Act to fight against discrimination.

**March on Washington**

In one of the largest peaceful demonstrations in American history, a quarter of a million people marched on the nation's capital on August 28, 1963. Here, protesters gather around the reflecting pool in front of the Washington Monument. **Critical Thinking: *Apply Information*** *What was the chief goal of the March on Washington?*

The Voting Rights Act also permitted federal officials to register voters directly in states that practiced discrimination. In the next three years, federal voting examiners registered more than 150,000 African Americans in the South.

☑ **Checkpoint**  **What were the goals of the Civil Rights Act of 1964?**

**Main Idea**
Some militant African American leaders grew impatient with gradual change and urged stronger action.

## The Movement Splinters

Some African Americans grew impatient with the gradual pace of the civil rights movement. They turned to more militant leaders.

**Malcolm X**  One of the best known of these leaders was Malcolm X. Born Malcolm Little, he renounced what he called his "slave name" and adopted "X" as a symbol of his lost African name. He embraced the Nation of Islam, a form of Islam whose members were known as Black Muslims.

Malcolm X rejected the goal of integration altogether. "An integrated cup of coffee isn't sufficient pay for four hundred years of slave labor," he insisted. Instead, he called on African Americans to separate completely from white society.

Later, Malcolm X severed his ties with the Nation of Islam. He rejected separatism and spoke instead of an "honest white-black brotherhood." Before he could fully develop these new ideas, he was shot to death in 1965. Three Black Muslims were convicted of the crime.

**Black Power Movement**  Others also grew frustrated with King's nonviolent approach. Stokely Carmichael argued that African Americans should fight back if attacked. Carmichael and others developed a new approach, called "black power." They urged African Americans to achieve economic independence by starting and supporting their own businesses. They also called on African Americans to take pride in their own heritage.

**Militant Voices**
Nonviolence dominated the early stages of the civil rights movement. By the mid-1960s, more-militant voices had emerged. **Critical Thinking: Compare** *How did the ideas of Malcolm X and Stokely Carmichael differ from the ideas of Martin Luther King, Jr.?*

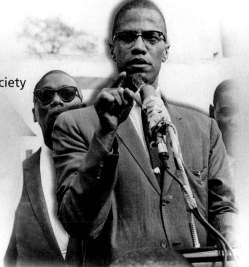

Malcolm X
Called for African Americans to break away from white society

Black power movement
Called for economic independence for African Americans

## Cause and Effect

### CAUSES

- Segregation laws and discrimination lead to the unequal treatment of African Americans.
- The NAACP is formed to fight discrimination.
- African Americans expect equal treatment at home after serving in World War II.

**THE CIVIL RIGHTS MOVEMENT**

### EFFECTS

- *Brown* v. *Board of Education of Topeka* outlaws segregation in schools.
- Martin Luther King, Jr., emerges as a civil rights leader.
- Congress passes Civil Rights Act and Voting Rights Act.
- African Americans make political and economic gains.
- Other groups are inspired to seek equal rights.

**Reading Charts**
**Skills Activity**

The long-term causes of the civil rights movement go as far back as the days of slavery. The long-term effects are still being felt today.

**(a)** Interpret Charts How did World War II help spur the civil rights movement?

**(b)** Analyze Cause and Effect Which effect of the civil rights movement do you consider the most important? Why?

**Protests Turn Violent** The civil rights movement had focused mainly on ending segregation in the South. It had done little to ease the hardships of the millions of African Americans who were crowded into ghettos, or poor run-down neighborhoods, in northern cities.

In August 1965, urban discontent exploded into violence. One of the worst incidents occurred in Watts, a primarily African American area of Los Angeles. Angered by what they saw as an act of brutality by police, residents of Watts burned cars and looted stores. More than 1,000 people were killed or injured.

Over the next two years, dozens of other cities exploded with violence and destruction. A presidential commission appointed to study the situation warned, "Our nation is moving toward two societies, one black, one white—separate and unequal."

**King Is Killed** In 1968, King traveled the country to build support for a Poor People's Campaign to attack economic inequality. On the evening of April 3, King told a gathering in Memphis, Tennessee: "I may not get there with you. But . . . we, as a people, will get to the promised land."

The next day, King was shot to death. A white segregationist was later tried and convicted of the crime. Despite a plea from President Johnson, riots broke out in cities across the nation. With King's death, a major era of the civil rights movement came to an end.

**Draw Logical Conclusions**
Draw a conclusion about the reaction of different Americans to the pace of civil rights change.

✓**Checkpoint** **What was meant by "black power"?**

**Main Idea**

As a result of the civil rights movement, African Americans made a number of political and economic gains.

Justice Thurgood Marshall

# Summing Up the Civil Rights Era

The civil rights movement of the 1960s achieved many important and lasting results. Although it did not end all inequality, it did end legal segregation and it opened education and voting rights to all.

**A Larger Role in Government** As more African Americans participated in the political process, the number of African American elected officials increased. For the first time, African American mayors took office in large cities, such as Atlanta, Cleveland, Detroit, Los Angeles, and Newark.

African Americans made gains in the federal government as well. In 1966, Edward Brooke of Massachusetts became the first African American senator since Reconstruction. A year later, President Johnson appointed Thurgood Marshall to the Supreme Court.

**Affirmative Action** Many gains came as a result of affirmative action programs. Under affirmative action, businesses and schools were encouraged to give preference to members of groups that had been discriminated against in the past.

By the 1970s, thousands of African Americans were attending colleges or entering professions such as medicine or law. Still, a growing number of Americans charged that affirmative action was a form of "reverse discrimination" because it unfairly favored one group of people over another.

✓**Checkpoint** What gains did African Americans make in government?

☆ **Looking Back and Ahead** African Americans made historic gains during the civil rights era. As you will read in the next section, other groups also sought to win equal rights.

---

**Section 3** | **Check Your Progress**

**Progress Monitoring** Online
**For:** Self-test with instant help
**Visit:** PHSchool.com
**Web Code:** mva-9263

## Comprehension and Critical Thinking

1. **(a) Describe** What tactics did Martin Luther King, Jr., favor in the fight for civil rights?
   **(b) Contrast** How did the views of Malcolm X differ from those of King?

2. **(a) Recall** What were the terms of the Voting Rights Act of 1965?
   **(b) Evaluate Information** Why did supporters of the Voting Rights Act favor federal action rather than action on the state level?

## Reading Skill

3. **Draw Logical Conclusions** What can you conclude about the role of television in the civil rights movement?

## Vocabulary *Builder*

Complete each of the following sentences so that the second part further explains the first part and clearly shows your understanding of the key term.

4. In northern cities, poor African Americans often lived in ghettos, _____.

5. Some economic gains came as the result of affirmative action, _____.

6. African Americans who ate at "whites only" lunch counters practiced civil disobedience, _____.

## Writing

7. Use the Internet to gather more background information about one of the people or events discussed in this section. Then, list three important details from the information you found.

## Objectives

1. Discover the gains made by the women's movement.

2. Find out how Mexican Americans struggled to win equal treatment.

3. Explore how Native Americans, older Americans, and the disabled sought fairer treatment.

## Prepare to Read

### Reading Skill

**Support Conclusions With Evidence** Like inferences, conclusions must be supported with evidence. That evidence comes first and foremost from the text but can also come from prior knowledge and personal experience. Identify conclusions that you have made while reading. Then, find the information that led you to that conclusion.

### Vocabulary *Builder*

**High-Use Words**

<u>exert</u>, p. 897
<u>modify</u>, p. 897

**Key Terms and People**

Betty Friedan, p. 893
César Chávez, p. 895
bilingual, p. 895
mandatory retirement, p. 896
Maggie Kuhn, p. 897

⭐ **Background Knowledge** You have seen how African Americans campaigned for equal rights. In this section, you will learn how other groups were inspired by the civil rights movement.

## Women's Rights Movement

By the 1960s, women had won the vote and made other gains. Yet many women believed they still had a long way to go to achieve full equality in jobs and education.

**Main Idea**
In the 1960s, some American women began to call for greater equality.

**Betty Friedan** *The Feminine Mystique*, a 1963 book by Betty Friedan, reignited the women's rights movement. Friedan was a housewife with a degree in psychology. She argued that many women were secretly unhappy with their limited roles in society:

> **❝**The problem lay buried, unspoken, for many years in the minds of American women. It was a strange stirring, a sense of dissatisfaction, a yearning. . . . Each suburban wife struggled with it alone.**❞**
>
> —Betty Friedan, *The Feminine Mystique*

Friedan's book became an instant bestseller. It challenged traditional ideas about the roles of both men and women. It also inspired thousands of women to seek careers outside the home.

In 1966, Friedan helped found the National Organization for Women (NOW). NOW lobbied Congress for laws that would give women greater equality. It demanded that medical schools and law practices train and hire more women. It also campaigned for day-care facilities for the children of mothers who worked outside the home.

Women's rights protesters

## Women in the Workforce, 1950–1975

### Women Working Outside the Home

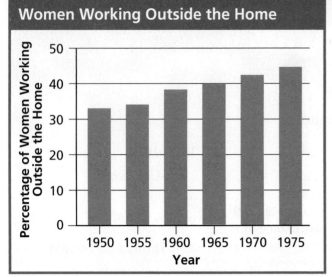

Source: *Historical Statistics of the United States*

### Incomes of Men and Women

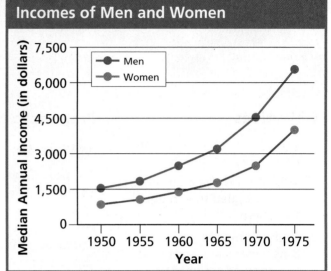

Source: *Historical Statistics of the United States*

### Reading Charts
#### Skills Activity

As the women's rights movement continued, more and more women found work outside the home. Still, their incomes continued to lag behind those of men.

**(a) Interpret Graphs** What percentage of American women worked outside the home in 1950? In 1975?

**(b) Make Predictions** What do you think will happen to the gap between men's incomes and women's incomes in the future?

**The ERA** NOW led a campaign to ratify an Equal Rights Amendment (ERA) to the Constitution. The ERA would forbid any form of sex discrimination. Congress passed the amendment in 1972. To become law, it had to be ratified by 38 states.

The ERA touched off a furious debate. Opponents, both men and women, charged that the amendment would undermine traditional values. They warned that women might lose their rights to alimony or be forced to serve in combat. Critics also claimed that the ERA was unnecessary because several laws already protected women's rights. In the end, the ERA did not receive enough votes for ratification.

**Notable Gains** The women's movement did make notable gains. In 1963, President Kennedy signed the Equal Pay Act, which required equal pay for men and women doing the same jobs. A year later, sex discrimination was included in the Civil Rights Act.

In the workplace, women's salaries continued to lag behind those of men. Still, the number of women working outside the home steadily increased. In addition, more women attended colleges.

Women made gains in the political arena, too. More women were elected to city councils, state legislatures, and the U.S. Congress. In 1969, Shirley Chisholm of New York became the first African American woman elected to Congress. In 1975, Ella Grasso of Connecticut became the first woman elected governor of a state without succeeding her husband.

**Reading Skill**

**Support Conclusions With Evidence**

Give evidence to support the conclusion that some American women responded sympathetically to Betty Friedan's point of view and others did not.

✔**Checkpoint** **What argument did Betty Friedan make?**

# Civil Rights for Mexican Americans

**Main Idea**
Mexican Americans organize to end segregation and win fairer treatment.

While the African American civil rights movement was taking shape, Mexican Americans were waging their own campaign for equal rights. Mexican Americans were not subject to official segregation laws. However, in the Southwest, all-white schools closed their doors to Mexican American children. Instead, they had to attend poorly equipped "Mexican schools." Custom kept Mexican Americans out of many neighborhoods and jobs.

**Organizing for Change** In 1948, Mexican American veterans of World War II formed the American GI Forum. Like the NAACP, the Forum supported legal challenges to discrimination.

In 1954—the same year as *Brown* v. *Board of Education of Topeka*—Mexican Americans also won a major Supreme Court victory. A Mexican American man in Texas had been convicted of murder by an all-white jury. His lawyers argued that the conviction was invalid because Mexican Americans were excluded from serving on Texas juries.

In *Hernández* v. *Texas,* the Supreme Court ruled that excluding Mexican Americans from juries was illegal. Other minority groups would later use the *Hernández* decision to help secure their legal rights.

**Chávez and the UFW** Many Mexican Americans in the Southwest were migrant workers, traveling from farm to farm to pick crops. In 1966, César Chávez helped to form a labor union, the United Farm Workers (UFW). Its goal was to win higher wages and decent working conditions for migrant laborers.

Like King, Chávez favored nonviolent protest. When growers refused to recognize the UFW, he organized a national boycott of California grapes. By 1970, so many Americans had stopped buying grapes that growers agreed to sign a contract with the union.

**Protecting Voting Rights** During this same period, Mexican Americans organized campaigns to win greater rights. As a result, Congress amended the Voting Rights Act in 1975. It required areas with large numbers of foreign-speaking citizens to hold bilingual elections. Bilingual means "in two languages."

Other laws promoted bilingual education in public schools. Supporters of bilingual education said that it would help students keep up with their work as they learned English.

✔**Checkpoint** What did the Supreme Court decide in *Hernández* v. *Texas*?

## Biography Quest

**César Chávez**
**1927–1993**

César Chávez was born into a hard-working Mexican American family. When the Great Depression hit, they were evicted from their land where they had a farm and grocery store. The family saw no choice but to become migrant farmworkers in California and Arizona. Chávez quit elementary school to join his family working in the fields.

**Biography Quest** ⊕**nline**

**When was Chávez awarded the Medal of Honor?**

**For:** The answer to the question about Chávez

**Visit:** PHSchool.com

**Web Code:** mvd-9264

**An Era of Protest**

The demonstrators in these pictures had different goals. However, all of them believed that they could band together to campaign for change. **Critical Thinking:** *Apply Information* How does the Constitution protect the rights of Americans to protest peacefully?

Maggie Kuhn, founder of the Gray Panthers

Protesters in wheelchairs, Washington, D.C.

Member of the American Indian Movement

**Main Idea**

Native Americans, older Americans, and people with disabilities formed groups to work for their interests.

# Organizing for Change

The spirit of reform introduced by the civil rights movement spread into every corner of the nation. More groups began to organize in order to achieve greater protection under the law.

**Native Americans** Indians had long been the poorest segment of the population. They were also subject to shifting federal policy. In the 1960s, activists began to demand change. The National Congress of American Indians sent delegations to Washington to regain land, mineral, and water rights. Increasingly, such efforts succeeded.

The American Indian Movement (AIM) turned to more radical protest. In 1973, armed members of AIM occupied Wounded Knee, South Dakota, for several days. As you have read in Chapter 18, Wounded Knee had been the site of a massacre of Native Americans in 1890. AIM wanted to remind people of the government's long history of unfair dealings with Native Americans.

Not all Native Americans agreed with AIM's militant tactics. But an increasing number showed greater pride in their heritage.

**Older Americans** The number of Americans over the age of 65 has steadily grown. Often, these older citizens had trouble paying for health care and insurance. Many jobs forced **mandatory retirement,** a policy that required people to stop working at a certain age. Most companies set 65 as the mandatory retirement age.

Older people organized to <u>exert</u> their political clout. In 1958, the American Association of Retired Persons (AARP) was founded to promote health insurance for retired Americans. The AARP lobbied for passage of programs such as Medicare. Since then, the AARP has taken a stand on a wide range of issues affecting older Americans.

In 1970, Maggie Kuhn was forced to retire because she had reached age 65. She then organized the Gray Panthers to combat age discrimination. The following year, the Gray Panthers gained national attention by staging a protest in Washington during a White House Conference on Aging. Kuhn defined her vision as "young and old working together for a better world for the young to grow old in."

**Americans With Disabilities** Americans with disabilities also campaigned for equal rights. Disability rights organizations backed laws requiring public buildings to provide access for people with disabilities. As a result, public accommodations were <u>modified</u> to include reserved parking spaces, ramped building entrances, wheelchair lifts on public buses, and Braille buttons on elevators.

Congress also passed laws protecting the educational rights of children with handicaps. The Education for the Handicapped Act of 1975 guaranteed a free education for all children with disabilities. In 1990, Congress passed the Americans With Disabilities Act. It outlawed discrimination in hiring people with physical or mental impairments.

☑**Checkpoint** **How did older Americans work for change?**

☆ **Looking Back and Ahead** The civil rights movement was a time of increasing social upheaval. In the next chapter, you will see how the Vietnam War added to this climate of protest.

Vocabulary *Builder*
<u>exert</u> (ehks ZERT) *v.* to put into action

Vocabulary *Builder*
<u>modify</u> (MAH dih fī) *v.* to make changes to or in; to alter

---

Section 4 | **Check Your Progress**

**Progress Monitoring** ⚫nline
**For:** Self-test with instant help
**Visit:** PHSchool.com
**Web Code:** mva-9264

**Comprehension and Critical Thinking**

1. **(a) Identify** What was the Equal Rights Amendment?
**(b) Detect Points of View** Identify one argument for and one argument against the ERA.

2. **(a) Recall** Explain one way each of the following groups sought better treatment in the 1960s and 1970s: Mexican Americans, Native Americans, older Americans, people with disabilities.
**(b) Compare** How were the efforts of these groups similar?

**Reading Skill**

3. **Support Conclusions With Evidence** Reread the text following the subheading "Civil Rights for Mexican Americans." Give evidence to support the conclusion that many Mexican Americans faced a language barrier.

**Vocabulary *Builder***

Fill in the blank in each question with one of the key terms from this section.

4. _____ ballots were printed in both English and Spanish.

5. Because of _____, many older people had to stop working.

**Writing**

6. Pick one person below. List three details he or she might observe in the circumstances described:
• Woman reentering the work force after raising her children
• Mexican first-grader going to school for the first time in a bilingual class
• Sixty-five-year-old worker deciding to protest mandatory retirement
• Physically disabled person entering a building that has no wheelchair ramp

Decisions involve making choices between alternative courses of action. Understanding the reasons for important historical decisions can help us make decisions in our own lives.

---

In 1962, Fannie Lou Hamer was arrested in Mississippi after she tried to register to vote. Here she describes what happened next.

**Primary Source**  "After we paid the fine among us, we continued on to Ruleville, and Reverend Jeff Sunny carried me four miles in the rural area where I had worked as a timekeeper and sharecropper for eighteen years. I was met there by my children, who told me the plantation owner was angry because I had gone down to try to register.

After they told me, my husband came, and said that the plantation owner was raising Cain because I had tried to register, and before he quit talking the plantation owner came, and said, 'Fannie Lou, do you know—did Pap tell you what I said?'

And I said, 'Yes, sir.'

He said, 'I mean that,' he said. 'If you don't go down and withdraw your registration, you will have to leave . . . because we are not ready for that in Mississippi.'

And I addressed him and told him and said, 'I didn't try to register for you. I tried to register for myself.'

I had to leave that same night."

On the 10th of September, 1962, sixteen bullets was fired into the home of Mr. and Mrs. Robert Tucker for me. . . ."

— Testimony of Fannie Lou Hamer (August 22, 1964)

---

## Learn the Skill

*Use these steps to learn how to make decisions.*

1. **Identify the problem.** What is the issue that must be resolved or the goal that must be achieved?

2. **Understand the options.** What choices are available?

3. **Evaluate consequences.** Understand the pros and cons of each alternative.

4. **Make a decision.** Identify the decision and why it was made.

## Practice the Skill

*Answer the following questions about the primary source on this page.*

1. **Identify the problem.** (a) What did Hamer want to do? (b) What obstacles did she face?

2. **Understand the options.** What choices does Hamer have in this situation?

3. **Evaluate the consequences.** (a) If she does not withdraw her registration, what might happen to Hamer? Why? (b) If she does withdraw her registration, how might she feel?

4. **Make a decision.** What decision does Hamer make? Why?

## Apply the Skill

*See the Review and Assessment at the end of this chapter.*

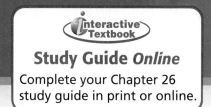

**Study Guide** *Online*
Complete your Chapter 26 study guide in print or online.

## Chapter Summary

### Section 1
### Beginnings of the Civil Rights Movement

- In the early 1900s, the NAACP challenged segregation laws.
- In *Brown* v. *Board of Education of Topeka*, the Supreme Court ruled that segregation in education was unconstitutional.
- African Americans in Montgomery, Alabama, organized a boycott to protest segregation on city buses.

### Section 2
### An Expanding Role for Government

- The Warren Court used judicial activism to protect and extend rights.
- John F. Kennedy favored social reforms, but most stalled in Congress.
- Lyndon Johnson's Great Society attempted to attack the causes of poverty.

### Section 3
### The Civil Rights Movement Continues

- Martin Luther King, Jr., favored nonviolent civil disobedience to achieve civil rights.
- Protests helped persuade Congress to pass civil rights legislation.
- Leaders such as Malcolm X rejected King's approach and supported militant tactics.

### Section 4
### Other Americans Seek Rights

- The women's movement led more women to work outside the home.
- Mexican American groups sought to end segregation and win better conditions for migrant workers.
- Native Americans organized to protect their rights and call attention to injustice.
- Older Americans and people with disabilities organized to support their interests.

## Key Concepts

These notes will help you prepare for questions about key concepts.

### Civil Rights Milestones

**1947:** Jackie Robinson breaks baseball color line
**1948:** Truman desegregates military
**1954:** *Hernández* v. *Texas*; *Brown* v. *Board of Education*
**1955:** Montgomery bus boycott
**1963:** March on Washington; King's "I have a dream" speech
**1964:** Civil Rights Act
**1965:** Voting Rights Act
**1966:** National Organization for Women formed; United Farm Workers formed

### Lyndon Johnson's Great Society

**Economic Opportunity Act:** Attack causes of poverty
**Head Start:** Provide preschool education
**Food stamps and welfare:** Give assistance to the needy
**Medicare:** Help older Americans pay medical bills
**Medicaid:** Provide medical assistance to the poor

### Leaders and Thinkers

**Thurgood Marshall:** Civil rights lawyer; Supreme Court justice
**Rosa Parks:** Challenged segregation on buses
**Martin Luther King, Jr.:** Championed civil disobedience
**Malcolm X:** Favored militant approach and separation
**Stokely Carmichael:** Supported "black power"
**Betty Friedan:** Wrote *Feminine Mystique*; cofounded NOW
**César Chávez:** Organized migrant farmworkers
**Maggie Kuhn:** Founded Gray Panthers

## Vocabulary *Builder*

### Key Terms

Read each sentence below. If the sentence is true, write YES and explain why. If the sentence is not true, write NO and explain why not.

1. As a result of integration, African American and white children attended separate schools.

2. Supporters of civil disobedience were often jailed because they refused to obey laws.

3. César Chávez urged people to boycott grapes in order to increase demand for farm products.

4. Many rural African Americans lived in ghettos.

## Comprehension and Critical Thinking

5. **(a) Summarize** What arguments did Thurgood Marshall use in the case of *Brown* v. *Board of Education of Topeka*?
   **(b) Apply Information** How does the picture below show an effect of the *Brown* case?

6. **(a) Recall** How were the actions of the Warren Court an example of judicial activism?
   **(b) Support a Point of View** Do you agree or disagree with judicial activism? Explain.

7. **(a) Summarize** What approach to civil rights did Martin Luther King, Jr., favor?
   **(b) Apply Information** How were sit-ins and freedom rides examples of King's approach?

8. **(a) Recall** What was the goal of affirmative action programs?
   **(b) Identify Viewpoints** What arguments could be used in favor of affirmative action? What arguments could be used against it?

9. **(a) Recall** What changes in public accommodations did disabled rights groups seek?
   **(b) Analyze Cause and Effect** How would these changes increase economic opportunities for people with disabilities?

## History Reading Skill

10. **Make Inferences and Draw Conclusions** Draw a conclusion about Americans' views about discrimination before and after the civil rights movement.

## Writing

11. **Write one paragraph on the following topic:**
    Explain a problem faced by an individual who is a member of one of the groups discussed in this chapter.

    **Your paragraph should:**
    • describe the individual;
    • identify the time period of the situation you are describing;
    • describe the circumstances of the problem

    When you are finished, exchange papers with another student. Write a brief response to that student's paragraph, looking in particular for details that help create the time period. Revise your own plan in response to your partner's comments.

12. **Write a Narrative:**
    Imagine that you are a young black or white Freedom Rider. Write a letter home explaining why you are going to the South and what problems you face.

## Skills for Life

### Make Decisions

Use the quotation below to answer the questions.

> "The events in Birmingham and elsewhere have so increased the cries for equality that [we cannot] ignore them. . . . We face therefore a moral crisis as a country. . . . It cannot be met by repressive police action. It cannot be left to increased demonstrations in the streets. It cannot be quieted by token moves or talk. . . . I am therefore asking the Congress to enact legislation giving all Americans the right to be served in [public] facilities."
>
> —John F. Kennedy, June 11, 1963

13. **(a)** According to Kennedy, what moral problem faces the United States in 1963? **(b)** What options does he reject?

14. What did Kennedy decide to do? Do you think his decision was correct? Explain.

# Test Yourself

**Refer to the quotation below to answer Question 1.**

> "We shall all be free,"
> We shall all be free,
> We shall all be free some day.
> Oh, deep in my heart,
> I do believe
> We shall overcome some day.
>
> —"We Shall Overcome,"
> civil rights anthem

**1. Who would have been most likely to disagree with the attitude expressed in this song?**

A Malcolm X

B Rosa Parks

C Martin Luther King, Jr.

D Lyndon Johnson

**2. The Voting Rights Act of 1965**

A gave African Americans the right to vote.

B allowed federal officials to register voters.

C required bilingual elections.

D established literacy tests for voting.

**Refer to the symbol below to answer Question 3.**

**3. The above symbol relates to the activities of**

A Maggie Kuhn.    C Earl Warren.

B Betty Friedan.    D César Chávez.

# Document-Based Questions

**Task:** Look at Documents 1 and 2, and answer their accompanying questions. Then, use the documents and your knowledge of history to complete this writing assignment:

> Summarize the main ideas of Chisholm and Schlafly. Then, explain whose viewpoint you agree with and why.

**Document 1:** In May 1969, Representative Shirley Chisholm delivered this speech in Congress. *According to Chisholm, why was the ERA needed?*

> "I wish to introduce . . . a proposal that . . . sooner or later must become part of the basic law of the land— the Equal Rights Amendment.
>
> Let me . . . refute two . . . arguments . . . against this amendment. One is that women are already protected under the law. . . . Existing laws are not adequate to secure equal rights for women. . . Women do not have the opportunities that men do.
>
> A second argument . . . is that [ERA] would eliminate legislation . . . giving special protection to women. . . . Women need no protection that men do not need. What we need are laws to protect working people, to guarantee them fair pay, safe working conditions, protection against sickness and layoffs, and provision for dignified, comfortable retirement. Men and women need these things equally."

**Document 2:** Phyllis Schlafly led the campaign to defeat ERA. In 1986, she summarized her objections. *According to Schlafly, what would have been two negative effects of the ERA?*

> "ERA advocates were unable to show any way that ERA would benefit women or end any discrimination against them. The fact is that women already enjoy every constitutional right that men enjoy. . . .
>
> The opponents of ERA, on the other hand, were able to show many harms that ERA would cause.
> - ERA would take away legal rights that women possessed—*not* confer any new rights on women.
> - ERA would take away women's traditional exemption from military conscription. . . .
> - ERA would make unconstitutional the laws . . . that impose on a husband the obligation to support his wife.
> - ERA would force all schools and colleges, and all the programs and athletics they conduct, to be fully coeducational. . . . ERA would mean the end of single-sex colleges."

# Chapter Preview

When Communists threatened to push into South Vietnam, the United States responded with military aid and military advisers. Gradually, the United States became more involved in the conflict. For nearly 20 years, the United States would be caught in a war it did not win and one that resulted in protest and violence at home.

## ☑ What You Will Learn

Hoping to block the spread of communism, the United States backed South Vietnam with military aid.

An expanding war in Vietnam drew a massive commitment of U.S. forces and sharply divided Americans.

After the United States negotiated peace and withdrew its forces, all of Vietnam came under Communist rule.

President Nixon's accomplishments were overshadowed by the Watergate affair, which led to his resignation.

**U.S. Events**

**1954** Eisenhower starts U.S. military aid to South Vietnam.

**1961** Kennedy sends military advisers to South Vietnam.

**1964** Congress passes Gulf of Tonkin Resolution.

1952    1958    1964

**World Events**

**1954** Vietnam is divided into North Vietnam and South Vietnam.

**1963** President Diem of South Vietnam is assassinated.

**Quick View Video**
View the chapter video for a quick preview of the main ideas.

The Vietnam Veterans Memorial in Washington, D.C., honors the memory of more than 58,000 Americans who died in combat in the Vietnam War.

**1968**
Antiwar demonstrations disrupt Democratic National Convention.

**1973**
Last American troops withdraw from Vietnam.

**1974**
Nixon resigns from office as a result of Watergate scandal.

1964

**1968** Student revolts erupt in France.

1970

**1973** Military leaders oust president of Chile.

1976

**1975** South Vietnam falls to Communist North Vietnam.

**History Reading Skill  Ask Questions**

**Why did some American soldiers have mixed feelings about fighting in Vietnam?**

In this chapter, you will learn what kinds of questions to ask yourself when reading. Read the following account by an American soldier in Vietnam. The side notes highlight ways to ask useful questions.

Many Americans were unsure about the nation's involvement in the Vietnam War. This soldier describes how destroying the village of people who had befriended him made him unsure about America's involvement.

**Primary Source**

What I remember most about the village was this one old woman. We had taken care of her once when she was in great pain. She came back and brought other members of her family, and the third time we were up there she invited me over to their place to eat lunch. So when we'd go up there I'd always have lunch with these people. And now soldiers were taking her and her family and a couple of pigs and their chicken—they didn't have that much—and loading them on a Chinook [helicopter]. She ran up and put her arms around me and wanted me to do something about it. There wasn't anything I could do. And that's when I started having second thoughts about the war. I still can see her face clear as day. I have no idea how her story ended. She reminded me a lot of my mother, always watching out for the kids, scolding, but very loving about it.

—*Everything We Had: An Oral History of the Vietnam War by Thirty-three American Soldiers Who Fought It,* ed. by Al Santoli

> To understand the situation more fully, you might ask: Why did the woman think that the soldier could help her?

> To infer how American views changed, you might ask: What is it about this situation that made the soldier feel uncomfortable?

> To analyze the soldier's reaction, you might ask: How did being reminded of his mother affect the soldier's feelings?

> To learn more, you might ask and research: What happened to Vietnamese families displaced by the war?

**Ask Questions**
- Ask questions in which you infer motivations or reasons for events and attitudes.
- Ask questions that pull many pieces of information together.
- Ask questions that could guide research beyond the text.

**Document-Based Questions**
1. Who is the author of this source?
2. Why did he feel a special attachment to the woman?
3. Why do you think the woman's belongings were being loaded on a helicopter?

# Vocabulary *Builder*

## Previewing High-Use Academic Words

| High-Use Word | Definition | Sample History Sentence |
|---|---|---|
| **fate** (fayt) (Section 1, p. 908) | **n.** outcome; consequence or final result | U.S. leaders said that the <u>fate</u> of many nations depended on how Americans responded to a Communist challenge in Vietnam. |
| **revolt** (ree VOHLT) (Section 1, p. 909) | **n.** uprising; rebellion | The commander was alarmed to hear that some of his troops had staged a <u>revolt</u>. |
| **alter** (AWL ter) (Section 2, p. 911) | **v.** to change in some way; to make different | The hard-won victory greatly <u>altered</u> the soldiers' weary spirits. |
| **sequence** (SEE kwehns) (Section 2, p. 913) | **n.** one thing occurring after another; series of events | In rapid <u>sequence</u>, the legislature passed all of the bills on the President's agenda. |
| **eliminate** (ee LIHM ih nayt) (Section 3, p. 920) | **v.** to remove from consideration | The new regulations <u>eliminated</u> the strictest rules and simplified others. |
| **confer** (kahn FER) (Section 3, p. 920) | **v.** to exchange ideas | Before addressing Congress, the President wanted to <u>confer</u> with the leaders in private. |
| **accommodation** (ak kom moh DAY shuhn) (Section 4, p. 925) | **n.** agreement or change in what is wanted in order to solve a problem | After years of quarreling, the party leaders were at last able to reach an <u>accommodation</u>. |
| **submit** (sahb MIHT) (Section 4, p. 926) | **v.** to give up power or control; to agree to do something | The workers were not willing to <u>submit</u> to management's demands. |

## Previewing Key Terms and People

Ho Chi Minh, p. 906
domino theory, p. 908
Ngo Dinh Diem, p. 908
guerrilla, p. 909
Lyndon B. Johnson, p. 909
escalate, p. 911

napalm, p. 912
hawks, p. 913
doves, p. 913
conscientious objector, p. 915
Richard Nixon, p. 918
Henry Kissinger, p. 920

boat people, p. 923
inflation, p. 924
Gerald Ford, p. 926
Jimmy Carter, p. 927

# The War Begins

## Objectives

1. Explain how Vietnam became a focus of conflict after World War II.

2. Explain why the United States was concerned about developments in Vietnam.

3. Describe how American involvement began to increase under President Kennedy.

## Prepare to Read

###  Reading Skill

**Ask Analytical Questions** As you read about history in this textbook, you may find yourself puzzled at times. *Why* did a particular event happen? *Why* did it have the effect that it did? The text may not answer these analytical questions, but raising them will help you in your reading.

### Vocabulary *Builder*

**High-Use Words**

<u>fate</u>, p. 908
<u>revolt</u>, p. 909

**Key Terms and People**

Ho Chi Minh, p. 906
domino theory, p. 908
Ngo Dinh Diem, p. 908
guerrilla, p. 909
Lyndon B. Johnson, p. 909

---

⭐ **Background Knowledge** In a previous chapter, you learned how, after World War II, the United States and the Soviet Union became locked in a conflict known as the Cold War. In this section, you will learn how the Southeast Asian nation of Vietnam became a major battleground in that struggle.

**Main Idea**
The United States backed France in opposing Vietnamese independence under Ho Chi Minh.

## Origins of the Conflict

The Vietnam War was the longest war that the United States ever fought. Except for the Civil War, it was the most disruptive. While the war was going on, Americans were bitterly divided about the nation's involvement.

The causes of the war go back into Vietnam's history. Vietnam is a tiny land in Southeast Asia, stretching 1,000 miles along the South China Sea. In the 1800s, France seized Vietnam and ruled it for nearly 100 years as part of the colony of Indochina. During World War II, French rule was interrupted when Japan occupied Vietnam.

**Declaring Independence** In August 1945, the Japanese surrendered. Some Vietnamese saw the Japanese defeat as an opportunity to free themselves from French colonial rule. Ho Chi Minh (HOH CHEE MINH), a Communist, organized a revolt to end French colonial rule. Earlier, Ho had asked Americans for help. However, the Americans were suspicious because Ho was a Communist. With his followers, who called themselves Vietminh, Ho occupied Hanoi in North Vietnam. He proclaimed an independent Vietnam.

Ho Chi Minh as newsmaker

**The First Indochina War** The French refused to accept Vietnamese independence, and the two sides were soon at war. The United States threw its support, including large sums of money, behind France's struggle to regain control of its former colony. By helping France, U.S. leaders hoped to block any spread of communism.

Fighting between the French and the Vietminh continued for nearly 8 years. Ho's forces steadily gained strength and popular support. The turning point came in 1954, when the Vietminh forced the French to surrender after a 56-day battle at Dien Bien Phu, in northwestern Vietnam. The defeat was a major blow to the war-weary French, and they agreed to negotiate a settlement. French control over Vietnam was ended.

**Ask Analytical Questions**

Ask an analytical question about the text in this paragraph. You might focus on comparing America's response to the war in Indochina with its response to Communist movements in Latin America. Recall your reading in a previous chapter.

☑**Checkpoint** **Why did the United States support the French side?**

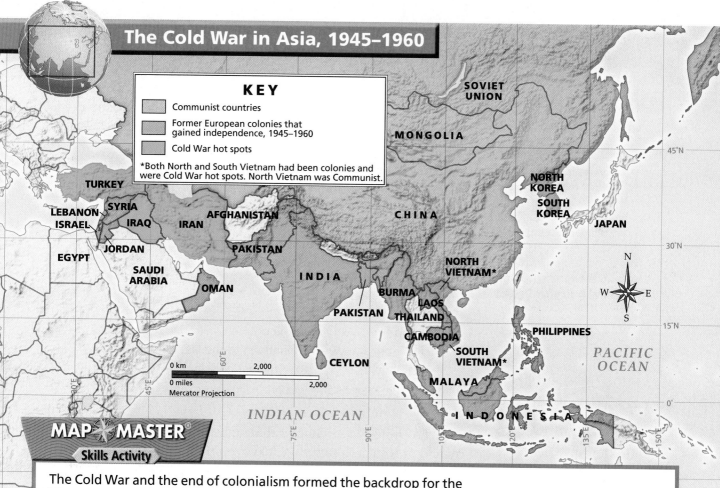

**The Cold War in Asia, 1945–1960**

**KEY**

Communist countries

Former European colonies that gained independence, 1945–1960

Cold War hot spots

*Both North and South Vietnam had been colonies and were Cold War hot spots. North Vietnam was Communist.

SOVIET UNION
MONGOLIA
TURKEY
LEBANON
ISRAEL
SYRIA
IRAQ
IRAN
AFGHANISTAN
JORDAN
EGYPT
SAUDI ARABIA
OMAN
PAKISTAN
INDIA
CHINA
NORTH KOREA
SOUTH KOREA
JAPAN
NORTH VIETNAM*
BURMA
LAOS
THAILAND
PAKISTAN
CAMBODIA
SOUTH VIETNAM*
CEYLON
MALAYA
PHILIPPINES
INDONESIA
PACIFIC OCEAN
INDIAN OCEAN

45°N
30°N
15°N
0°

0 km    2,000
0 miles    2,000
Mercator Projection

**MAP MASTER**
**Skills Activity**

The Cold War and the end of colonialism formed the backdrop for the Vietnam War.

**(a) Interpret Maps** Which Asian countries had Communist governments at the time of the Vietnam War?

**(b) Explain Problems** What problems arose between Communist and non-Communist nations once colonialism ended?

**MapMaster ●nline**

**For:** Interactive map
**Visit:** PHSchool.com
**Web Code:** mvp-9271

**Delicate Balance**

Vietnamese villagers often found themselves in a precarious position during the Vietnam War. **Critical Thinking: *Interpret Photographs*** *In what ways would the war have disrupted these people's lives?*

**Main Idea**

By supporting South Vietnam, U.S. leaders hoped they could keep communism contained.

## The War Spreads

After World War II, U.S. leaders saw the Soviet Union and its system of communism as a threat to world peace. Adding to their fears, China came under Communist rule in 1949. The Korean War began in 1950, when Communist North Korea attacked South Korea.

When Ho Chi Minh defeated the French in 1954, many U.S. political leaders feared a widespread Communist takeover in Southeast Asia. This idea was called the **domino theory.** If one country fell to the Communists, it was thought that neighboring countries would follow. President Dwight D. Eisenhower explained the idea this way:

> **❝**You have a row of dominoes set up. You knock over the first one, and what will happen to the last one is the certainty that it will go over very quickly.**❞**
> —President Eisenhower, press conference remarks, April 7, 1954

The United States hoped that stopping communism in Vietnam would prevent a Communist takeover in Southeast Asia.

**Vietnam Divided** After the French defeat, an international conference in Geneva, Switzerland, determined Vietnam's <u>fate</u>. Under the resulting Geneva Accords, Vietnam was temporarily divided into two states. North Vietnam, with its capital at Hanoi, was under the Communist rule of Ho Chi Minh. South Vietnam, with its capital at Saigon, was governed by Ngo Dinh Diem (noh din dee EHM). The United States pledged to support the South.

*Vocabulary Builder*
<u>fate</u> (fayt) *n.* outcome; consequence or final result

Elections were to unify the country within a few years, but the Diem government blocked them. A South Vietnamese movement organized to oppose Diem. In 1959, the movement launched an armed <u>revolt</u>. Guerrillas, or fighters who carry out hit-and-run attacks, waged a campaign of terror against villages controlled by Diem's officials. Using secret supply lines, the North Vietnamese furnished weapons to the guerrillas, who came to be called the Vietcong.

**The American Role Deepens** President John F. Kennedy continued Eisenhower's policy of support for South Vietnam. Kennedy sent more aid and many more military advisers.

In the meantime, South Vietnam's government was becoming unpopular. President Diem angered many South Vietnamese by imprisoning people who criticized his policies. Many of his handpicked officials were corrupt. U.S. leaders feared that Diem's actions were increasing support for the Vietcong.

In August 1963, when Diem ordered a crackdown against his opponents, Kennedy withdrew his support from Diem. This was a signal for the South Vietnamese military to act. In November 1963, military leaders seized control of the government and assassinated Diem.

Three weeks later, in an action unrelated to Vietnam, Kennedy himself was assassinated. With his death, Vietnam became the problem of the new President, Lyndon B. Johnson.

Missile inspection by President Kennedy

✔**Checkpoint** **What kind of help did the United States give South Vietnam between 1954 and 1963?**

⭐ **Looking Back and Ahead** At first, the United States supplied South Vietnam with money, weapons, and military advisers. In the next section, you will read how hundreds of thousands of U.S. troops became involved in a long, difficult war.

---

Section 1 | **Check Your Progress**

**Progress Monitoring** ⏻nline
**For:** Self-test with instant help
**Visit:** PHSchool.com
**Web Code:** mva-9271

**Comprehension and Critical Thinking**
1. **(a) Recall** After the Japanese surrender in 1945, what happened in Vietnam that led to a new conflict?
**(b) Apply Information** Why do you think Ho Chi Minh gained a strong following in North Vietnam?

2. **(a) Describe** How did Ngo Dinh Diem run South Vietnam?
**(b) Synthesize Information** Why do you think Diem blocked elections during the early years of the government?

**Reading Skill**
3. **Ask Analytical Questions** Reread the text under the heading "The War Spreads." Ask an analytical question about the text. You might focus on the reasons behind the Vietcong fighting style.

**Vocabulary Builder**
Answer the following question in a complete sentence to show your understanding of the key term.
4. How do guerrilla soldiers conduct warfare?

**Writing**
5. Write a paragraph for the place you see in the photograph "Delicate Balance" (on the opposite page). Describe it as if it were a setting for a story in 1958, several years after Vietnam is divided.

# American Involvement Grows

## Objectives

1. Describe how President Johnson widened the war in Vietnam.

2. Explain how the war in Vietnam was different from any previous war in American history.

3. Describe how the Vietnam War divided Americans at home.

## Prepare to Read

### 🎯 Reading Skill

**Ask Inferential Questions**
Inferential questions help you to infer, or figure out, the reasons behind individual actions or the actions of a nation. For example, asking questions such as "Why did people act in a particular way?" will help you understand how events happened and what motivated people's behavior.

### Vocabulary *Builder*

**High-Use Words**
alter, p. 911
sequence, p. 913

**Key Terms**
escalate, p. 911
napalm, p. 912
hawks, p. 913
doves, p. 913
conscientious objector, p. 915

⭐ **Background Knowledge** For more than 100 years, much of Asia had been governed as colonies of the Western powers. In this section, you will learn how Cold War concerns drew the United States deeper and deeper into a war in Vietnam.

## A Wider War

During his first months as President, Lyndon Johnson tried to continue the policies in Southeast Asia that Eisenhower and Kennedy had set in motion. But before long, he began to expand the U.S. commitment.

**Main Idea**
The Gulf of Tonkin incident marked the start of increasing U.S. involvement in Vietnam.

President Johnson meets a soldier in Vietnam

**Growing American Involvement** After the fall of Diem, the government of South Vietnam became increasingly unstable. Military coup followed military coup, with leaders managing to stay in power only a few months. As the ruling generals bickered among themselves, the South Vietnamese military rapidly lost ground to the Vietcong.

Like Eisenhower and Kennedy before him, President Johnson believed in the domino theory. He saw Vietnam as a test of the resolve of the United States to resist the spread of communism. "I am not going to lose Vietnam," Johnson said.

Shortly after taking office, Johnson ordered an increase in economic aid and military advisers to the government and armed forces of South Vietnam. He also authorized a series of secret actions against North Vietnam. In the meanwhile, the Soviet Union and China supported the Vietcong with arms and supplies.

**The Gulf of Tonkin Incident** An event in August of 1964 <u>altered</u> the U.S. role in Vietnam. Reports said North Vietnamese torpedo boats had attacked American destroyers in the Gulf of Tonkin, off the coast of North Vietnam. Details were sketchy. Indeed, the second of two reported attacks may not have taken place at all.

President Johnson, however, was determined to act. He announced that U.S. forces would stage air strikes against North Vietnam. The next day, Johnson asked Congress for the authority to do whatever was needed to resolve, or settle, the conflict. Congress backed the President by passing the Gulf of Tonkin Resolution. It stated:

> **❝** . . . Congress approves and supports the determination of the President . . . to take all necessary measures to repel any armed attack against the forces of the United States and to prevent further aggression. **❞**
> —Gulf of Tonkin Resolution, approved by Congress August 7, 1964

President Johnson began to escalate, or step up, U.S. involvement in the Vietnam War. He cited the resolution as his authority.

☑**Checkpoint** **Why was the Gulf of Tonkin Resolution important?**

# An Unconventional War

The Vietnam War was different from many wars the United States had fought before. Under the Constitution, only Congress can declare war. Although the Gulf of Tonkin Resolution gave the President the authority to use military force, it was not a declaration of war. Many Americans would later question the legality of this "undeclared war."

**A Massive Buildup** Through the fall of 1964, President Johnson was involved in a campaign for reelection, and the United States took limited action in Vietnam. Johnson declared, "We are not about to send American boys . . . to do what Asian boys ought to be doing for themselves." He won the election in a landslide.

Meanwhile, Johnson and his advisers had been working on plans for further actions in Vietnam. Early in 1965, the Vietcong attacked an American base at Pleiku (play KOO), in South Vietnam, killing eight Americans. Johnson responded by ordering a new series of air strikes against North Vietnam. A campaign of sustained U.S. bombing would continue for three years.

U.S. leaders soon realized the need to make plans for an increased commitment of U.S. troops. In March 1965, President Johnson ordered 3,500 marines to protect the American air base in Da Nang—the first American combat troops in Vietnam. Shortly after, he authorized the use of U.S. ground troops for offensive action. Within six weeks, 50,000 American combat troops had arrived in Vietnam; by the end of the year, 184,000 troops were there. In 1968, the figure would reach half a million.

Vocabulary *Builder*
<u>alter</u> (AWL ter) *v.* to change in some way; to make different

**Main Idea**
Despite a massive commitment of U.S. forces, years of fighting did not bring victory in Vietnam.

**Bombing South Vietnam**
U.S. air attacks aimed to kill soldiers and destroy cover.
**Critical Thinking: *Evaluate Information*** *Why was bombing of only limited value in a war against guerrillas?*

**Ask Inferential Questions**

Read the text following the subheading "Search and Destroy." Ask an inferential question. You might focus on how American soldiers interacted with Vietnamese civilians.

**Search and Destroy** American entry into the ground war gave the South Vietnamese government forces a badly needed boost. At the same time, the political situation began to stabilize. A military leader named Nguyen Cao Ky seized power in June 1965 and crushed antigovernment protests by Vietnamese Buddhists. Although Ky's methods were far from democratic, they seemed to be effective in creating a stable government. South Vietnam's government was now able to concentrate on the war against the Vietcong.

The Americans who poured into Vietnam were well trained and equipped with the latest high-tech weapons. They used chemical weapons against the Vietcong. Airplanes dropped bombs containing **napalm,** a jellylike substance that burst into flames, sticking to people's bodies. They also sprayed the herbicide Agent Orange across the Vietnamese countryside. It destroyed crops and vegetation where the enemy might hide. Use of Agent Orange was controversial, with critics blaming it for birth defects, cancer, and other long-term health problems among both U.S. soldiers and Vietnamese. (In 1975, the United States declared that it would never again use herbicides in war unless an enemy did so first.)

The Vietcong dug in and kept fighting. They had some advantages of their own. Familiar with the swamps and jungles of Vietnam, the guerrillas employed hit-and-run attacks. Americans did not know what to expect in this jungle warfare, with no clearly defined battle lines. The situation was more confusing because Americans often could not distinguish between enemy and friend.

The Americans in Vietnam also used other new forms of warfare. Heavily armed helicopters carrying hundreds of American troops would locate an enemy stronghold. After heavy machine-gun fire

**Explore More Video**
To learn more about the soldiers' experiences in the war, view the video.

**Soldiers in Vietnam**

In 1964, President Johnson promised not to send more troops to Vietnam. However, as U.S. involvement increased, Johnson gave in to the request for more troops. **Critical Thinking: Make Predictions** *How do you think Johnson's actions would affect him in the 1968 election?*

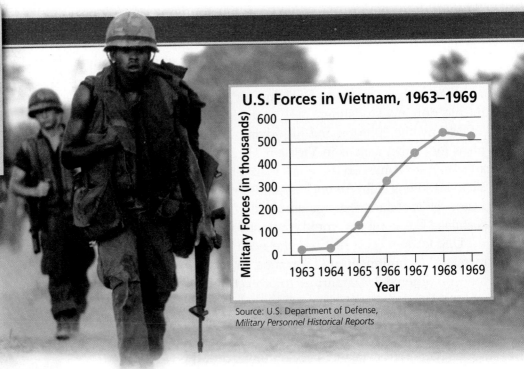

**U.S. Forces in Vietnam, 1963–1969**

Source: U.S. Department of Defense, *Military Personnel Historical Reports*

raked the area, U.S. troops landed and fanned out, searching for Vietcong. The goal of these search-and-destroy missions was not to gain territory but to kill as many of the enemy as possible. American military leaders believed that if they could kill enough Vietcong, sooner or later the enemy would give up.

Chinook helicopter picks up supplies

**The Tet Offensive** On January 31, 1968, the Vietnamese began celebrating Tet, their New Year holiday. Using the celebrations as cover, Vietcong and North Vietnamese soldiers launched attacks on every major city in South Vietnam. In Saigon, they broke through the walls of the American embassy and attacked the presidential palace. Another major assault occurred in the ancient capital of Hue (way). There, the Communists seized the former home of Vietnam's emperors.

Although caught by surprise, American and South Vietnamese forces responded quickly. For weeks, they battled to take back the areas under attack. The Communists fought hard, but in time they yielded to superior U.S. firepower. By February 25, the siege was over. As many as 40,000 North Vietnamese and Vietcong soldiers lost their lives in the fighting.

The Tet offensive set in motion a <u>sequence</u> of events that marked a major turning point of the Vietnam War. On the surface, Tet was a military victory for the United States. But, in fact, Tet dealt a major blow to the U.S. mission in Vietnam. Americans were shocked that enemy forces were capable of such an attack. After Tet, more and more Americans argued that the United States should get out of Vietnam. No matter how many troops the United States sent to Vietnam, they believed, it could never win the war. By now, President Johnson and many of his advisers were also convinced that the United States could not win the war. In addition, the President recognized that support at home for the war was waning.

**Vocabulary Builder**
**sequence** (SEE kwehns) *n.* one thing occurring after another; series of events

☑**Checkpoint** **How did fighting the Vietnam War differ from fighting other wars?**

# A Nation Divided

As the war dragged on, Americans increasingly became divided. They split into two camps: hawks and doves. **Hawks** supported the war in Vietnam. However, many challenged President Johnson's policy of gradual escalation. They said the United States was fighting "with one hand tied behind its back." They wanted the government to mount an all-out military effort that would decisively defeat the Vietcong and North Vietnam. **Doves** believed the Vietnam War could not be won and was morally wrong.

**Main Idea**
The American people were deeply divided over the Vietnam War.

# Vietnam Divides the Nation

Critics of the Vietnam War staged massive protest marches. Supporters of the war were no less eager to publicize their views. **Critical Thinking:** *Detect Points of View* Write a paragraph describing why a person might have joined a demonstration for or against the Vietnam War.

VETERANS FOR PEACE IN VIETNAM

Demonstrators oppose the war and support resistance to the draft. ▼

DON'T DRAFT OUR SONS TO BOMB AND DESTROY!

END THE WAR IN VIETNAM NOW

It was a time of deep divisions among Americans. These demonstrators strongly support the war. ▼

SUPPORT OUR BOYS IN VIETNAM

SUPPORT OUR BOYS IN VIETNAM

BOMB HANOI

NO SURRENDER

TEAMSTERS Nº16

The doves urged withdrawal of U.S. troops. They organized a wide range of protests against the war, including sit-ins and marches.

The U.S. government had long used the draft to select men to serve in the military. During the Vietnam War, about 1.8 million men were drafted. As opposition to the war rose, so did resistance to the draft. Hundreds of young men burned their draft cards to show opposition to the war. Other young men sought recognition as **conscientious objectors,** people who refuse to participate in war because of a strong belief that war is wrong. Some 100,000 Americans fled to Canada to avoid the war.

In 1965 and after, antiwar protests spread across the nation. The antiwar movement included people from every walk of life. Students, college professors, businesspeople, religious leaders, entertainers, and others spoke out against the U.S. role in the war. At first, most antiwar protests were peaceful, using tactics such as petitions and mass marches. But as the war escalated, protesters adopted more dramatic techniques, such as sit-ins and public draft-card burnings. Violent confrontations with police became common.

Meanwhile, television brought the sights and sounds of battle into American living rooms. The graphic images shocked and sometimes sickened viewers. One theory is that the steady diet of blood and horror on TV helped turn Americans against the Vietnam War.

✓**Checkpoint** How did doves protest against the war?

⭐ **Looking Back and Ahead** The commitment of U.S. troops to the Vietnam War in 1965 led to years of warfare. Opposition at home grew as the war dragged on. In the next section, you will read how South Vietnam came under Communist rule.

---

## Section 2 | Check Your Progress

**Progress Monitoring** Online
**For:** Self-test with instant help
**Visit:** PHSchool.com
**Web Code:** mva-9272

**Comprehension and Critical Thinking**

1. **(a) Recall** What event led to the passage of the Gulf of Tonkin Resolution?
   **(b) Summarize** How did President Johnson use the Gulf of Tonkin Resolution?
   **(c) Analyze Cause and Effect** How did the war change after the resolution was passed?

2. **(a) Describe** What happened in Vietnam in 1968 during Tet, the Vietnamese New Year?
   **(b) Apply Information** How did Americans react to those events?

**Reading Skill**

3. **Ask Inferential Questions** Read the text following the subheading "The Gulf of Tonkin Incident." Ask an inferential question. You might focus on why Johnson sought a congressional resolution even though information was sketchy.

**Vocabulary *Builder***

Read each sentence that follows. If the sentence is true, write YES. If the sentence is not true, write NO and explain why.

4. The United States used napalm in South Vietnam to destroy crops and vegetation.

5. Opponents of the Vietnam War adopted the name hawks to show that their cause was wise.

6. A conscientious objector is someone who supports war on religious grounds.

**Writing**

7. Write a paragraph about a peace march protesting the Vietnam War. Describe one of the following phases of the march: as it begins, as it becomes more active, or as it ends. Include details to make the reader aware of what is happening.

# Fighting a Jungle War

American troops faced new challenges in the swamps and jungles of Vietnam. Vietcong guerrillas often used the physical environment to attack—and then flee—American combat patrols. The Vietcong hid in thickets of underbrush to set up a surprise attack. After inflicting damage on unsuspecting American soldiers, the attackers would quickly retreat along hidden paths and tunnels.

American patrols often discovered hidden entrances to Vietcong tunnel systems. Here, soldiers stand guard as an American "tunnel rat" investigates one such entrance. ▶

The Americans had to cut paths through dense jungle foliage in order to fight the Vietcong. Here, American soldiers plunge into a stream while on patrol. ▼

**History Interactive**
**Learn About Jungle War in Vietnam**
**Visit:** PHSchool.com
**Web Code:** mvl-9272

## Understand Effects:
# Search and Destroy

In previous wars, American soldiers fought along defined battle lines. U.S. military planners in Vietnam quickly realized that a jungle environment erased those lines. In order to combat Vietcong hit-and-run attacks, military planners ordered search-and-destroy missions.

▲ U.S. fighter planes dropped chemical explosives like napalm to destroy Vietcong positions. The fighter above dropped a bomb made of another chemical called phosphorus.

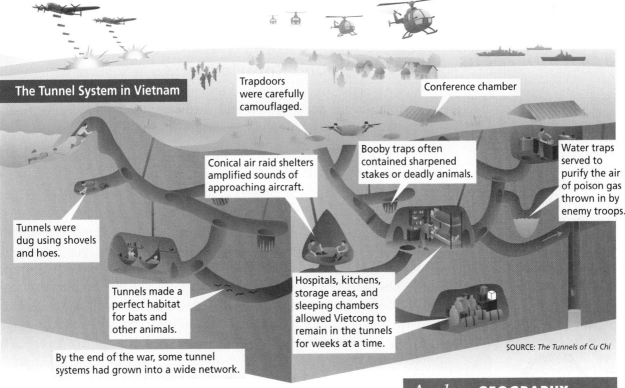

**The Tunnel System in Vietnam**

Trapdoors were carefully camouflaged.

Conference chamber

Conical air raid shelters amplified sounds of approaching aircraft.

Booby traps often contained sharpened stakes or deadly animals.

Water traps served to purify the air of poison gas thrown in by enemy troops.

Tunnels were dug using shovels and hoes.

Tunnels made a perfect habitat for bats and other animals.

Hospitals, kitchens, storage areas, and sleeping chambers allowed Vietcong to remain in the tunnels for weeks at a time.

By the end of the war, some tunnel systems had grown into a wide network.

SOURCE: *The Tunnels of Cu Chi*

▲ Vietcong guerrillas dug large networks of tunnels throughout the countryside. They used the tunnels to hide their movements and to plan hit-and-run attacks on American soldiers.

## Analyze GEOGRAPHY AND HISTORY

How did the Vietcong use the physical environment to wage war against American troops? Write a paragraph explaining how the geography of Vietnam affected the war.

# The War Ends

## Objectives

1. Explain how the Vietnam War affected the election of 1968.

2. Explain how President Nixon decreased U.S. involvement in Vietnam.

3. Describe how the fighting in Vietnam came to an end.

4. Describe the long-term impact of the Vietnam War on Southeast Asia and the United States.

## Prepare to Read

### ⟳ Reading Skill

**Ask Questions That Go Beyond the Text** There is much more to learn and explore about every topic introduced in this textbook. You can explore topics that interest you through research and discussion. Asking questions will help you. Remember to ask questions that focus on *why* or *how*, rather than questions with yes or no answers.

### Vocabulary *Builder*

**High-Use Words**

eliminate, p. 920

confer, p. 920

**Key Terms and People**

Richard Nixon, p. 918

Henry Kissinger, p. 920

boat people, p. 923

---

**Main Idea**
Richard Nixon won the 1968 presidential election for the Republicans.

☆ **Background Knowledge** Despite years of fighting, the United States and its South Vietnamese allies were nowhere near victory. In this section, you will read how the United States finally managed to end its involvement in the Vietnam War.

## Election of 1968

The Vietnam War played a central role in the election of 1968. Heavily criticized by some Democrats for his war policies, President Johnson decided not to seek reelection. Vice President Hubert Humphrey, who backed Johnson's Vietnam policies, then entered the race. The Democrats held their nominating convention in Chicago. Thousands of antiwar demonstrators gathered, too. In what was later deemed a "police riot," officers moved in and struck demonstrators with fists and clubs. Hundreds were injured or arrested.

Inside the hall, the delegates nominated Humphrey. Even as he accepted the nomination, TV cameras cut away to show the chaos in Chicago's streets. Humphrey became the Democratic candidate for President, but the nation was further torn apart.

The Republicans nominated former Vice President Richard Nixon. Nixon promised to restore "law and order" at home and win "peace with honor" in Vietnam. Alabama Governor George Wallace, who had gained national attention by exploiting racial tensions in the South, became a third-party candidate. The election was close, but Nixon won by a small margin.

Nixon campaign button

☑**Checkpoint** What position did Nixon take on the Vietnam War?

## The War Winds Down

Nixon knew that a growing number of Americans believed the war was a mistake. He began looking for a way to get out of Vietnam and still keep his promise of "peace with honor."

**Nixon Pursues a New Course** To begin scaling down American involvement, in June 1969 Nixon announced a policy known as Vietnamization. Under this plan, American troops gradually withdrew from Vietnam and the South Vietnamese assumed responsibility for fighting the war. The first U.S. combat troops left Vietnam the following month, in July 1969. By August, about 25,000 combat troops returned home. By April 1970, nearly 150,000 soldiers left Vietnam.

At the same time, Nixon expanded the war into Vietnam's neighbor, Cambodia. Cambodia had tried to stay neutral, but North Vietnamese soldiers had been carrying arms and supplies along a mountainous route through Laos and Cambodia into South Vietnam. This route was known as the Ho Chi Minh Trail.

In 1969, the United States began bombing Communist bases in Cambodia. American and South Vietnamese forces also attacked bases on the ground. The bases were being used to mount attacks on American troops in Vietnam. Nixon hoped that the American action

**Main Idea**

Using both stepped-up force and negotiation, President Nixon got U.S. troops out of Vietnam.

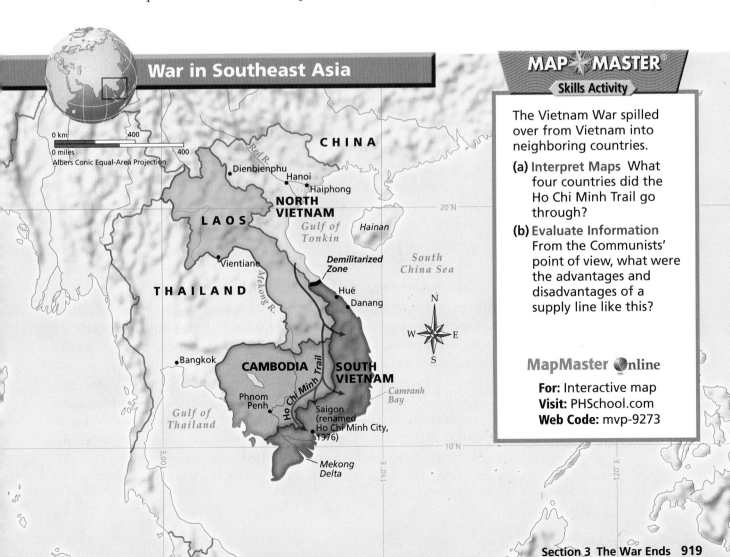

### War in Southeast Asia

### MAP MASTER
### Skills Activity

The Vietnam War spilled over from Vietnam into neighboring countries.

(a) **Interpret Maps** What four countries did the Ho Chi Minh Trail go through?

(b) **Evaluate Information** From the Communists' point of view, what were the advantages and disadvantages of a supply line like this?

**MapMaster Online**

**For:** Interactive map
**Visit:** PHSchool.com
**Web Code:** mvp-9273

## A Nurse Reflects

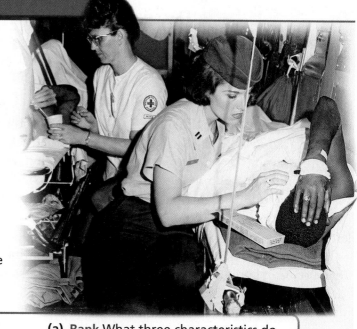

"Those of us who went to Vietnam practiced a lifetime of nursing in one year—our tour of duty there. We were the young, caring for the young. The average age of the wounded soldier in Vietnam was 19.4 years. The average age of the nurse was 23. We quickly learned that the primary reason we were in Vietnam was to get each other home."

—Diane Carlson Evans,
speech, Washington, D.C., 1998

Nurses care for wounded soldiers about to be shipped home.

### Reading Primary Sources
#### Skills Activity

As many as 10,000 women served in uniform with U.S. military forces in the Vietnam War, most as nurses.

**(a) Rank** What three characteristics do you think were most important for a nurse serving in Vietnam?

**(b) Draw Conclusions** What does the speaker mean when she says the main goal was "to get each other home"?

**Vocabulary** *Builder*
<u>eliminate</u> (ee LIHM ih nayt) *v.* to remove from consideration

would <u>eliminate</u> a military threat and pressure North Vietnam to negotiate peace. In fact, the attacks on Cambodia had little effect on the North Vietnamese. The attacks did, however, lead to chaos and civil war in Cambodia.

**A New Round of Protests** The attacks on Cambodia triggered a new storm of protest in the United States. Several antiwar demonstrations ended in tragedy. The worst incident was at Kent State University in Ohio, where nervous National Guardsmen opened fire on a crowd, killing four students. A similar incident at Jackson State College in Jackson, Mississippi, left 2 students dead and 12 injured.

**The Quest for Peace** While the fighting spread, peace talks between the United States and North Vietnam dragged on in Paris. For three years, neither side would budge in its position. Washington wanted all North Vietnamese troops out of South Vietnam. North Vietnam insisted on the withdrawal of U.S. troops from Vietnam. It also demanded that the South Vietnamese government be replaced with a new regime that would include Communist representatives. In 1970, Henry Kissinger, Nixon's national security adviser, began to <u>confer</u> in secret with a North Vietnamese leader. By then, the United States had begun the gradual withdrawal of its troops from Vietnam. In September 1972, only 60,000 remained.

**Vocabulary** *Builder*
<u>confer</u> (kahn FER) *v.* to exchange ideas

In October 1972, just before the U.S. presidential election, Kissinger hinted that an agreement was near. "Peace is at hand," he exclaimed. But his statement proved premature. The South Vietnamese, who had not been consulted, rejected the proposed agreement.

In order to put more pressure on the Communists, President Nixon then ordered new bombings of North Vietnam. After 12 days of concentrated bombing, the North Vietnamese agreed to return to the bargaining table. This time, an accord was reached that all sides accepted. The Paris Peace Accords were signed on January 27, 1973. They closely resembled what had been agreed to in October of the previous year. The last American serviceman to die in combat in Vietnam, Lt. Colonel William B. Nolde, was killed by an artillery shell only 11 hours before a cease-fire went into effect. The last U.S. combat troops were out of Vietnam by March 1973. The longest war in U.S. history was finally over.

> ☑ **Checkpoint** **What was President Nixon's policy of Vietnamization?**

**Ask Questions That Go Beyond the Text**
Ask a possible research question about Nixon's choice to bomb North Vietnam at this time.

## The Final Years of Conflict

Although direct American involvement in the Vietnam War ended in 1973, the struggle between North and South continued for two more years. The Paris Peace Accords allowed North Vietnam to keep some 150,000 troops in the South. Once the Americans were gone, the Communists set out to seize control of the country.

At the end of 1974, the North Vietnamese launched a series of strikes against the South Vietnamese army. The South Vietnamese army tried without success to stop the Communist advance. In March 1975, the North Vietnamese captured the ancient capital of Hue. At the same time, they forced South Vietnamese troops into a retreat from the Central Highlands, along the Cambodian border. Much of the South Vietnamese army was killed or captured, and other soldiers shed their uniforms and fled into the countryside. Thousands of civilians also perished in what became known as the Convoy of Tears.

By April 29, 1975, North Vietnamese forces were nearing Saigon, the capital of South Vietnam. Fearing a blood bath when the Communists entered the city, the United States carried out a dramatic helicopter evacuation of 1,000 American workers and some 5,500 South Vietnamese supporters. At the same time, American ships rescued thousands of South Vietnamese at sea. The Vietnamese had fled the mainland in any vessel they could find, and many of the vessels proved unseaworthy.

**Main Idea**
Two years after the Americans pulled out, North Vietnamese forces took over South Vietnam.

**Fleeing Saigon**
Vietnamese civilians try to climb aboard a U.S. airplane during the hectic evacuation of Saigon in 1975. **Critical Thinking: Analyze Cause and Effect** What was the cause of the evacuation, and what were its effects?

On April 30, North Vietnamese troops entered Saigon. The South Vietnamese government formally surrendered. After decades of fighting, Vietnam was united under a Communist government. And Saigon received a new name: Ho Chi Minh City.

**✓Checkpoint** **What happened in Vietnam after the United States withdrew its combat forces?**

**Main Idea**
The Vietnam War had long-lasting effects on both the United States and Vietnam.

## Vietnam Balance Sheet

The Vietnam War was the first foreign war in which American forces suffered defeat. This failure damaged the nation's pride. It also caused Americans to rethink their role in the world.

**Effect on the United States** The U.S. costs of the war were enormous. More than 58,000 Americans died in combat, and some 300,000 were wounded. On the economic side, the high price tag for the war—around $200 billion—damaged the U.S. economy for years. Unlike veterans of earlier wars, Vietnam vets were not welcomed home with cheering and parades. For many of the survivors, war memories were a nightmare. Many veterans adjusted poorly to civilian life. They suffered high rates of divorce, unemployment, and homelessness.

The Vietnam War undermined the nation's trust in the government and its leaders. In 1971, leading newspapers had published secret government documents known as the Pentagon Papers. They traced the steps by which the United States had committed itself to the Vietnam War and showed that government officials had concealed actions and often misled Americans about their motives.

Two Presidents had sent American troops into battle without a formal declaration of war. Hoping to curb presidential power, Congress passed the War Powers Act in 1973. It declared that a President could not send military forces into action for longer than 60 days without congressional approval.

Another political change resulting from the war was passage in 1971 of the Twenty-sixth Amendment to the Constitution, which lowered the voting age to 18. Supporters of the amendment argued that if 18-year-olds were old enough to fight and die in Vietnam, they were old enough to vote.

**Remembering the Vietnam War** In 1982, the Vietnam Veterans Memorial was completed in Washington, D.C. Known by many simply as "the Wall," it consists of two slabs of black granite sloping into the ground. Etched into the surface are the names of the more than 58,000 Americans who died

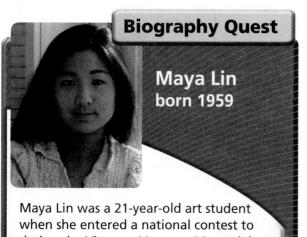

**Biography Quest**

**Maya Lin**
**born 1959**

Maya Lin was a 21-year-old art student when she entered a national contest to design the Vietnam Veterans Memorial. Lin's design for a black granite wall was selected over some 1,400 other entries. Today, the memorial is one of the most visited sites in Washington, D.C.

After that powerful achievement, Lin has gone on to become one of the nation's most respected sculptors and architects.

**Biography Quest**

**Why did Lin's design for the Vietnam Veterans Memorial cause controversy?**

**For:** The answer to the question about Lin
**Visit:** PHSchool.com
**Web Code:** mvd-9273

in Vietnam. In the words of Jack Wheeler, a Vietnam veteran who played a major role in getting the memorial built, "[the Wall] is probably the single most important step in the process of healing."

Vietnamese boat people

**Effect on Vietnam** Vietnamese losses were huge. South Vietnamese battle deaths exceeded 350,000. Estimates of North Vietnamese battle losses range between 500,000 and one million. Millions of civilians also died. The bombing destroyed much of North Vietnam's industry and transportation, but the greatest damage was in South Vietnam. There, 10 million people were left homeless by the war.

At the end of the war, more than a million people fled the new regime. Those who attempted to escape in small boats were called **boat people.** Perhaps 200,000 boat people died at sea or in refugee camps. Eventually, the United Nations acted to relocate the boat people. The United States took in many refugees, as did other nations. Private groups also worked hard to help the refugees from Vietnam.

✓**Checkpoint** How did the Vietnam War affect the people in North Vietnam and in South Vietnam?

☆ **Looking Back and Ahead** The Nixon administration began withdrawing troops from Vietnam and negotiated a peace pact. After U.S. troops left, fighting resumed and North Vietnam overtook South Vietnam and united the country under communism. In the next section, you will read of other issues that affected the United States in this period.

Section 3 | **Check Your Progress**

**Progress Monitoring** ⊙nline
**For:** Self-test with instant help
**Visit:** PHSchool.com
**Web Code:** mva-9273

## Comprehension and Critical Thinking

**1. (a) Recall** What campaign promise did Nixon make regarding the war in Vietnam?
**(b) Apply Information** Why do you think Nixon broke his campaign promise?

**2. (a) Identify** What is the War Powers Act?
**(b) Explain Problems** Why did Congress believe it was necessary to pass the act?

## Reading Skill

**3. Ask Questions That Go Beyond the Text** Ask a possible research question about current Vietnamese views about the war era.

### Vocabulary *Builder*

Read the following sentence. If the sentence is true, write YES. If the sentence is not true, write NO and explain why.
**4.** Henry Kissinger did not feel that the United States should withdraw from Vietnam.

## Writing

**5.** Write a paragraph from the viewpoint of one of the following: (a) a Vietnamese refugee settling in the United States in 1975, (b) an American soldier returning home after the war, or (c) a student protesting the invasion of Cambodia. Give the speaker's opinion of the situation in which he or she is involved. Add details to make the experience seem real.

# A Time of Uncertainty

## Objectives

1. Explain how President Nixon tried to ease Cold War tensions.

2. Describe the impact of the Watergate scandal on the Nixon administration and the nation.

3. Identify the challenges faced by President Gerald Ford.

## Prepare to Read

### ⟳ Reading Skill

**Ask Questions to Synthesize Information** History textbooks contain a great deal of information. Asking questions can help you to reflect on that information and put it into focus. Ask a question that explores the connection between pieces of information, including those from earlier chapters. Answering it will help ensure your understanding of the material.

### Vocabulary *Builder*

**High-Use Words**
accommodation, p. 925
submit, p. 926

**Key Terms and People**
inflation, p. 924
Gerald Ford, p. 926
Jimmy Carter, p. 927

---

☆ **Background Knowledge** With the war in Vietnam as a backdrop, the late 1960s and early 1970s were turbulent times in America. In this section, you will read how the war and other issues affected U.S. domestic and foreign policy during this period.

## Main Idea
President Nixon eased relations with Communist nations while struggling with the economy at home.

Historic moon walk

## Richard Nixon in Office

In running for office, Richard Nixon had criticized the violence and unrest of the Johnson years. The "silent majority," he said, wanted "law and order" and an end to chaos in the streets. Yet, the Nixon years provided their own mix of successes and new troubles.

**Moon Landing** One success was space exploration. President Kennedy had pledged to land an American on the moon before 1970. That goal was achieved by the *Apollo 11* mission. On July 20, 1969, astronaut Neil A. Armstrong descended from the *Apollo*'s *Eagle* landing craft and set foot on the surface of the moon.

**Economic Problems** The economy was in trouble when Nixon came into office. High military spending for the Vietnam War had fed inflation, or a steady rise in prices. At the same time, economic growth had stalled, producing an economic recession and high unemployment. Nixon, like most Republicans, asserted that government involvement in the economy should be limited. But when other methods failed to boost the economy, he shocked his fellow conservatives by ordering a temporary freeze on wages, prices, and rents. His policy, however, met little success, and the freeze was soon lifted.

**Easing Cold War Tensions** Nixon's greatest success as President was in the area of foreign affairs. Through his policies, he helped ease the tensions of the Cold War.

Nixon's most surprising foreign policy move was to open contacts between the United States and Communist China. In 1949, as you have read, Communists led by Mao Zedong won China's civil war by defeating the Nationalists of Chiang Kai-shek. The Nationalists retreated to Taiwan, and the Communists created the People's Republic of China on the mainland. Ever since, the United States had refused to recognize Mao and the Communists as the lawful rulers of China. Instead, the United States treated the Nationalists on Taiwan as China's legitimate rulers. Another reason for hostility between the United States and Communist China was that they had never reached an <u>accommodation</u> after fighting on opposite sides in the Korean War.

Thus, many people were shocked in February 1972 when Nixon announced that he would visit mainland China. Nixon made the trip later that month. He attended banquets with China's Communist leaders. He toured the Great Wall. He met with Chairman Mao Zedong. Nixon said:

> ❝What we have done is simply opened the door, opened the door for travel, opened the door for trade.❞
>
> —Richard Nixon, July 6, 1972

Nixon also smoothed relations with the other great Communist power, the Soviet Union. Several months after visiting China, Nixon went to Moscow. He and Soviet leaders signed the Strategic Arms Limitation Treaty (SALT). SALT restricted the number and type of nuclear warheads and missiles that each nation could build. While it did not end the arms race, SALT showed that the Soviets and Americans were willing to work together to relax tensions.

✓**Checkpoint** Why was Nixon's goal to improve relations with China surprising to many Americans?

**Vocabulary** *Builder*
<u>accommodation</u> (ak kom moh DAY shuhn) *n.* agreement or change in what is wanted in order to solve a problem

**Breakthrough to China**
President Nixon gestures as he stands on the Great Wall of China with Mao Zedong. **Critical Thinking:** *Organize Information Describe the issues that divided the United States and Communist China from 1949 to 1972.*

The tapes

**Main Idea**
President Nixon resigned rather than face impeachment over the Watergate scandal.

**Vocabulary** *Builder*
submit (sahb MIHT) *v.* to give up power or control; to agree to do something

**Ask Questions to Synthesize Information**
Ask a question connecting the Watergate burglary to the House preparations for impeaching the President.

# Watergate Scandal

Nixon was reelected in 1972. But a political scandal would end in his downfall.

During the 1972 election campaign, police arrested five men who broke into Democratic Party offices in the Watergate apartment complex in Washington, D.C. White House officials paid the burglars "hush money" to keep quiet about the illegal activities. However, the story soon came out.

In May 1973, a Senate Committee opened nationally televised hearings into the Watergate affair, as the scandal became known. The star witness was John Dean, former White House counsel. He testified that Nixon himself had approved the coverup.

Another witness revealed that Nixon had secretly taped all conversations in his office. At first, Nixon refused to release the tapes. When a Supreme Court order finally forced him to submit the tapes, they largely confirmed Dean's account. The President had conspired to cover up the Watergate burglary and other misdeeds.

In July 1974, the House of Representatives took steps toward impeaching the President. Realizing that enough votes existed to remove him from office, Nixon resigned on August 9, 1974. Vice President Gerald Ford became President.

**✔Checkpoint** Why did the Watergate affair bring Nixon down?

# The Ford Presidency

**Main Idea**
President Ford dealt with economic problems at home and aftereffects of the war in Vietnam.

On taking office, President Ford tried to restore public confidence in the nation's leaders. But trust in him was badly eroded when he granted Richard Nixon a "full, free, and absolute pardon." Ford had acted, he said, to end the "long nightmare" of Watergate.

The nation faced severe economic problems. President Ford began a program of voluntary wage and price controls called Whip Inflation Now (WIN). They had little effect. In fact, the nation slipped into recession, with the highest unemployment rate in years. At Ford's urging, Congress approved a tax cut to stimulate the economy, but recovery was slow and uncertain.

In foreign affairs, Ford generally followed Nixon's policy of easing Cold War tensions with the Soviet Union and China. Though American involvement in the Vietnam War was over, events in Southeast Asia still demanded attention. The President arranged to airlift more than 50,000 South Vietnamese as Communists swept toward Saigon. In neighboring Cambodia, he sent U.S. marines to free the crew of the *Mayaguez,* an American merchant ship that had been seized by Cambodia's Communists.

Button promoting Ford's voluntary controls

In 1976, the Republicans nominated Ford to run for President in his own right. The Democrats nominated a little known candidate, Jimmy Carter, former governor of Georgia. Carter promised to restore integrity to Washington. In a close election, Carter won.

☑**Checkpoint** **What economic problems did President Ford face?**

⭐ **Looking Back and Ahead** In 1977, Jimmy Carter entered office with high hopes. However, he quickly faced a series of perplexing challenges. In the next chapter, you will see how Carter's troubled presidency helped pave the way for a new era in American politics.

---

Section 4 | **Check Your Progress**

**Progress Monitoring** Online
**For:** Self-test with instant help
**Visit:** PHSchool.com
**Web Code:** mva-9274

## Comprehension and Critical Thinking

**1. (a) List** What were President Nixon's three major actions in foreign affairs?
**(b) Identify Benefits** How did each improve U.S. security in the world?

**2. (a) Recall** What was the Watergate break-in?
**(b) Describe** What did President Nixon do about it?
**(c) Apply Information** How did his actions in the Watergate affair cost him the presidency?

## Reading Skill

**3. Ask Questions to Synthesize Information** Reread the text following the subheading "Easing Cold War Tensions." Ask a question connecting the Vietnam War with Nixon's trips to China and the Soviet Union.

## Vocabulary *Builder*

Answer the following question in a complete sentence that shows your understanding of the key term.
**4.** What happens to prices as a result of inflation?

## Writing

**5.** Write a paragraph describing the viewpoint of one of the following: (a) astronaut Neil Armstrong as his flight to the moon is ready to take off in the summer of 1969 or (b) Richard Nixon during his struggles with the Watergate scandal in 1973.

Synthesizing information enables you to put pieces of evidence together to form conclusions. It often requires analyzing different types of historical information, such as photographs, graphs and charts, and primary sources.

**Primary Source**

The excerpt below is from a speech Robert Kennedy made two days after he announced his candidacy for the Democratic nomination for President.

"The costs of the war's present course far outweighs anything we can reasonably hope to gain by it, for ourselves or for the people of Vietnam. It must be ended, and it can be ended, in a peace of brave men who have fought each other with a terrible fury, each believing that he alone was in the right. We have prayed to different gods, and the prayers of neither have been answered fully. Now, while there is still time for some of them to be partly answered, now is the time to stop."

—Speech by Senator Robert Kennedy, March 18, 1968

**Primary Source**

This excerpt is from a speech made by Eugene V. Rostow, who was in the State Department during Lyndon Johnson's presidency.

"This is what is at stake in Vietnam—the credibility of America's support in Southeast Asia, and, indeed, in the many other areas in whose security we have a national interest. Remove this credibility and we will indeed be placed in the position of becoming world policemen, or captives in a fortress America. In theory, there may be better places to fight than Vietnam; in fact, we have no alternative."

—Speech by Eugene V. Rostow, February 20, 1968

## Learn the Skill

*Use these steps to synthesize information.*

**1** **Identify key facts and main ideas in each piece of evidence.** Look for the most important idea about the subject. Then, find the key facts that support the main idea. If the evidence is a first-person narrative, identify the speaker's point of view or opinion about the subject.

**2** **Compare the pieces of evidence.** Look for similarities and differences in the material to better understand the topic.

**3** **Draw conclusions by synthesizing the evidence.** Use the information from various sources to draw conclusions about the topic.

## Practice the Skill

*Use material on this page and in the chapter to synthesize information.*

**1** **Identify key facts and main ideas in each piece of evidence.** (a) Who gave the speeches excerpted on this page? (b) Study the map in Section 1. Which nations are considered to be the Cold War hot spots? (c) Look at the full-page feature "Vietnam Divides the Nation," in Section 2. What do some of the signs say?

**2** **Compare the pieces of evidence.** (a) What points of view are expressed by Kennedy and Rostow? (b) What do photographs in the feature "Vietnam Divides the Nation" illustrate about public support of the war?

**3** **Draw conclusions by synthesizing the evidence.** What can you conclude about the effect of the Vietnam War on U.S. society from the evidence presented?

### Apply the Skill

*See the Review and Assessment at the end of this chapter.*

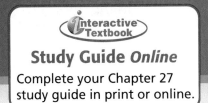

**Study Guide Online**
Complete your Chapter 27 study guide in print or online.

## Chapter Summary

### Section 1
### The War Begins

- Ho Chi Minh and the Vietminh fought for Vietnam's independence from France.
- After the Vietminh defeated the French at Dien Bien Phu in 1954, the Geneva Accords divided Vietnam.
- The United States opposed Ho's Communist government and its attempts to take over South Vietnam.

### Section 2
### American Involvement Grows

- President Johnson sent half a million U.S. combat soldiers to South Vietnam, citing the Gulf of Tonkin Resolution as his authority.
- The U.S. role in the war caused sharp divisions among Americans.
- The Tet offensive in 1968 shocked Americans and undercut support for the war.

### Section 3
### The War Ends

- With Democrats divided over the war, Richard Nixon won the presidency in 1968 and began a policy of Vietnamization.
- The Paris Peace Accords of 1973 led to the withdrawal of U.S. troops from Vietnam.
- The war between the Vietnamese continued until South Vietnam was forced under Communist rule in 1975.

### Section 4
### A Time of Uncertainty

- U.S. astronauts landed on the moon in 1969.
- Nixon's visit to China and a treaty with the Soviet Union eased Cold War tensions.
- Nixon resigned over the Watergate affair, after being forced to reveal evidence that he had conspired to conceal crimes.
- Nixon's successor, Gerald Ford, granted him a pardon.

## Key Concepts

These notes will help you prepare for questions about key concepts.

**The Vietnam War Years**

**1940s**
**1940–1945** Japanese occupy French colony of Indochina, including Vietnam, during World War II.
**1945** Ho Chi Minh takes over the city of Hanoi and declares Vietnam independent.
**1946** French reoccupy Hanoi.

**1950s**
**1954** Vietminh defeat French at Dien Bien Phu. French leave Vietnam.
**1954** Geneva Accords divide Vietnam into two states.

**1955** Ngo Dinh Diem becomes president of South Vietnam. U.S. sends military aid to Diem.
**1959** Vietcong launch armed rebellion against Diem government.

**1960s**
**1963** South Vietnamese military overthrows and kills Diem.
**1964** Congress passes Gulf of Tonkin Resolution. President Johnson launches air attacks on North Vietnam.
**1965** Johnson commits combat troops to war in South Vietnam.
**1968** Tet offensive undercuts support for war in United States.

**1969** Nixon begins policy of Vietnamization.

**1970s**
**1970** Nixon invades Cambodia. Student demonstrators killed at Kent State University, Ohio.
**1973** Paris Peace Accords begin. U.S. troops withdraw from Vietnam.
**1975** South Vietnam is defeated. Vietnam becomes a Communist country.

## Vocabulary *Builder*

### Key Terms

Read each sentence below. If the sentence is true, write YES. If the sentence is not true, write NO and explain why.

1. Hawks were more likely to take part in antiwar demonstrations than were doves.

2. As part of his Vietnamization program, President Nixon began to escalate U.S. military involvement in Vietnam.

3. Guerrillas are people who oppose a government by holding demonstrations.

4. Conscientious objectors believe it is morally wrong to go to war.

5. According to the domino theory, if the United States sent troops to Vietnam to fight the Communists, other countries would then send troops to help.

## Comprehension and Critical Thinking

6. **(a) Describe** What was the South Vietnamese government like under President Diem? What was it like after the fall of Diem?
**(b) Apply Information** How did the nature of the South Vietnamese government hamper the fighting of the war?

7. **(a) Summarize** What was the Tet Offensive?
**(b) Apply Information** How did the events of the Tet Offensive affect the popularity of President Johnson? Explain.

8. **(a) Identify** What was Nixon's policy of Vietnamization?
**(b) Draw Conclusions** How effective was Vietnamization in achieving President Nixon's goal of "peace with honor"?

9. **(a) Classify** Make a table listing the strengths and weaknesses of the American–South Vietnamese side in the Vietnam War.
**(b) Compare** Make a similar table showing the strengths and weaknesses of the Communist side.
**(c) Evaluate Information** Based on an analysis of the information in your tables, why did the Communists eventually succeed?

10. **(a) Describe** What action did President Gerald Ford take to try to restore confidence in the nation's leaders?
**(b) Clarify Problems** How did his action create new problems for his presidency?

## History Reading Skill

11. **Ask Questions** Ask a useful question about what you have read in this chapter. Remember, when possible, to ask questions that examine the text or require learning beyond the text.

## Writing

12. **Write two paragraphs giving an eyewitness view of an event covered in this chapter. Your description should:**
    * identify the eyewitness and the event discussed;
    * indicate why the eyewitness is there;
    * include details appropriate to the time, place, or circumstances of the event;
    * include the eyewitness's description of and response to the event.

13. **Write a Dialogue:**
A Vietnam veteran meets Maya Lin at the Vietnam Veterans Memorial. Think about the veteran's point of view as a soldier having fought in Vietnam. Then, consider Lin's viewpoint as an artist. Write a conversation the two might have about the memorial.

## Skills for Life

### Synthesize Information

Study the excerpt and photograph in Section 3, Reading Primary Sources, "A Nurse Reflects." Then, answer the following questions.

14. Who is the author of the primary source?

15. Compare the photograph and the source. What does each reflect about the role of nurses in the Vietnam War?

16. Based on the photograph and the primary source, what can you conclude about women's roles in the Vietnam War?

# Test Yourself

1. **The killing of four students by National Guardsmen at Kent State University came after which of these events?**

   A the North Vietnamese attack on American destroyers in the Gulf of Tonkin

   B the Tet offensive

   C the U.S. attack on North Vietnamese bases in Cambodia

   D the fall of Saigon to North Vietnamese forces

2. **One foreign policy change of Richard Nixon's term as President was**

   A important summit meetings with leaders of Eastern European nations.

   B the start of better relations with the People's Republic of China.

   C the start of better relations with Cuba.

   D the signing of nuclear arms agreements with Korea.

**Refer to the quotation below to answer Question 3.**

> "We are pursuing our policy . . . on the grounds that a stable peace . . . is difficult to envisage [view] if 800 million people are excluded from a dialogue with the most powerful nation in the world."

3. **The reasons for which event are explained in the quotation above?**

   A the Geneva Accords after the French defeat at Dien Bien Phu

   B the Paris Peace Accords that led to the withdrawal of American forces from Vietnam

   C Nixon's meeting in China with Mao Zedong in 1972

   D the signing of the SALT agreement between the United States and the Soviet Union

# Document-Based Questions

**Task:** Look at Documents 1 and 2, and answer their accompanying questions. Then, use the documents and your knowledge of history to complete this writing assignment:

   Write an essay describing the effects of the Vietnam War.

**Document 1:** More than 47,000 Americans were killed in combat during the Vietnam War. *How does the graph below reflect the pattern of U.S. involvement in Vietnam?*

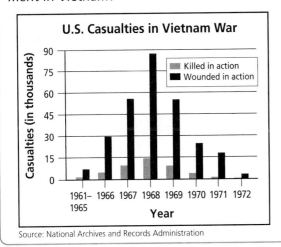

**U.S. Casualties in Vietnam War**

Casualties (in thousands): 90, 75, 60, 45, 30, 15, 0

Killed in action
Wounded in action

Year: 1961–1965, 1966, 1967, 1968, 1969, 1970, 1971, 1972

Source: National Archives and Records Administration

**Document 2:** In a short essay, Mike Murphy, a Vietnam veteran, describes his experience. *How does Murphy view his Vietnam service? Why?*

> "In 1987, I planned a trip to Washington, D.C. I told [my wife] . . . I wanted to see the Museums but the real reason was the Wall. . . . I wanted to see it, . . . but I was also afraid to see it.
>
> On the second day [my wife] asked me where the Vietnam Memorial was; I tell her. . . . As we walk toward the Wall I fall silent, . . . my heart is pounding. . . .
>
> Then I saw the Wall. Black granite half buried in the ground. Half buried like the war, . . . half hidden like the conscience of the country. The tears flowed, I couldn't stop them. . . .
>
> I close my eyes and I am back . . . in Vietnam. I can see it, smell it, touch it and hear it. I quickly open my eyes and I see the Wall. So many names. . . . I close my eyes and let Vietnam flow over me. . . . I cry for the ones that I had known, and for the ones that I did not know. We were all brothers. We went to a land that hated us and came home to a land that hated us. It wasn't supposed to be like that."

## Chapter Preview

In the last decades of the twentieth century, the nation faced major changes at home and overseas. The election of President Ronald Reagan ushered in a new conservative era in government. The collapse of the Soviet Union ended the long Cold War. Increasingly, conflicts in the Middle East came to dominate foreign policy.

**U.S. Events**

**World Events**

**1979**
Militants take 53 Americans hostage in Iran.

**1981**
Ronald Reagan becomes President.

**1987**
United States and Soviet Union agree on arms control treaty.

1977

1983

1989

**1978** Camp David Accords ease Middle East tensions.

**1985** Gorbachev becomes head of Soviet Union.

**1989** China cracks down on pro-democracy demonstrators.

Marines and a marching band parade in front of the U.S. Capitol for the 2001 inauguration of President George W. Bush.

**Discovery SCHOOL**
**Quick View Video**
View the chapter video for a quick preview of the main ideas.

**1991**
United States leads coalition against Iraq in Persian Gulf War.

**1998**
House of Representatives impeaches President Clinton.

**2000**
Supreme Court settles disputed presidential election.

1989

**1991** Soviet Union collapses, ending the Cold War.

1995

**1994** South Africa holds multiracial elections.

**1998** Pakistan and India test nuclear weapons.

2001

## History Reading Skill  Compare and Contrast

**How did President Ronald Reagan feel about the role of religion in America?**

In this chapter, you will practice comparing and contrasting. Read the following speech that President Ronald Reagan gave to a group of religious leaders. The side notes highlight ways to compare and contrast.

> While running for President in 1980, Ronald Reagan expressed his views on the role of religion in American society.

**Primary Source**

This text points to a conclusion that Reagan's views oppose secularism and favor a role for churches in public life.

> This administration is motivated by a political philosophy that sees the greatness of America in you, her people, and in your families, churches, neighborhoods, communities—the institutions that foster and nourish values like concern for others and respect for the role of law under God.

Reagan's views contrast with those of the "prevailing attitude" he mentions. The text underlined in red is a signal.

> Now I don't have to tell you that this puts us in opposition to, or at least out of step with, a prevailing attitude of many who have turned to a modern-day secularism, discarding the tried and time-tested values upon which our very civilization is based.

This text helps you conclude that Reagan thinks both groups are well intentioned.

Reagan contrasts his own value system with that of the other group.

> No matter how well intentioned [it is], their value system is radically different from that of most Americans. . . . Sometimes their voices are louder than ours, but they are not yet a majority.

> —President Ronald Reagan, speech to the National Association of Evangelicals

### Compare and Contrast
- Comparisons and contrasts may not be directly stated. You may need to recall previous text.
- Sometimes you have to make inferences about viewpoints or events before making comparisons and contrasts.
- Compare reasons for historical actions and events. Then, look for what these comparisons tell you about history and its players.

### Document-Based Questions
1. Who is the person quoted in this source?
2. To what group of people is he speaking?
3. How do the speaker's words respond to the concerns of the group being addressed?

# Vocabulary *Builder*

## Previewing High-Use Academic Words

| High-Use Word | Definition | Sample History Sentence |
|---|---|---|
| **violate** (VĪ ah layt) (Section 1, p. 938) | *v.* to break a rule or law; to disrespect; to disturb | The Supreme Court may strike down a law that <u>violates</u> the Constitution. |
| **alter** (AWL ter) (Section 1, p. 939) | *v.* to change in some way; to make different | The President listened carefully to the critics, but refused to <u>alter</u> his policy. |
| **critic** (KRIHT ihk) (Section 2, p. 944) | *n.* someone who makes judgments, especially negative judgments | Some <u>critics</u> argued that the New Deal increased government power too much. |
| **intermediate** (ihn ter MEE dee iht) (Section 2, p. 945) | *adj.* happening in between; part way from one extreme to another | Moderate reformers sought an <u>intermediate</u> position between continued slavery and immediate abolition. |
| **deprive** (dee PRĪV) (Section 3, p. 950) | *v.* to withhold; to take away | Under apartheid, nonwhites in South Africa were <u>deprived</u> of the right to vote. |
| **pursue** (per SYOO) (Section 3, p. 950) | *v.* to follow; to chase; to attempt to gain | President Nixon <u>pursued</u> a policy of détente with the Soviet Union. |
| **confine** (kahn FĪN) (Section 4, p. 955) | *v.* to keep within an area; to shut in or imprison | Under habeas corpus, prisoners cannot be <u>confined</u> for long periods without cause. |
| **crisis** (KRĪ sihs) (Section 4, p. 956) | *n.* turning point or deciding event in history | The attack on Fort Sumter created a <u>crisis</u> in relations between North and South. |

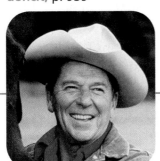

Bill Clinton

## Previewing Key Terms and People

balanced budget, p. 938
Ronald Reagan, p. 938
deregulation, p. 939
deficit, p. 939

George H.W. Bush, p. 939
recession, p. 939
Bill Clinton, p. 940
surplus, p. 940
George W. Bush, p. 941
Mikhail Gorbachev, p. 945
glasnost, p. 945
apartheid, p. 949

sanction, p. 949
Yasir Arafat, p. 955
westernization, p. 956
Ruholla Khomeini, p. 956
Saddam Hussein, p. 956
Norman Schwarzkopf, p. 957
Colin Powell, p. 957

Ronald Reagan

# A Conservative Surge

## Objectives

1. Learn how a growing conservative movement reshaped politics.

2. Compare the policies of five U.S. Presidents.

3. Discover how policymakers dealt with a series of large budget deficits.

## Prepare to Read

### Reading Skill

**Compare and Contrast** You have read about many Presidents in this textbook. One way to remember and to keep track of these many leaders is to compare and contrast their achievements. This also helps you see trends or patterns in American government. As you read this section, recall what you have read about Presidents in earlier chapters. Think about their successes and failures.

### Vocabulary *Builder*

**High-Use Words**

violate, p. 938

alter, p. 939

**Key Terms and People**

balanced budget, p. 938

Ronald Reagan, p. 938

deregulation, p. 939

deficit, p. 939

George H.W. Bush, p. 939

recession, p. 939

Bill Clinton, p. 940

surplus, p. 940

George W. Bush, p. 941

⭐ **Background Knowledge** As you have seen, the New Deal and Great Society increased the size and scope of the federal government. In this section, you will see how later Presidents sought to reverse this trend and bring a conservative approach to government.

**Main Idea**
President Jimmy Carter struggled with problems both at home and abroad.

President Jimmy Carter

## Carter's Troubled Presidency

President Jimmy Carter entered office in 1976 with high hopes. But his inexperience with Washington politics soon proved a disadvantage. During his first year in office, he sent 10 reform bills to Congress. However, he could not get support for any of them.

Carter also faced economic woes. Since the early 1970s, prices had been rising far faster than incomes. The government was unable to slow soaring inflation. By 1979, the annual inflation rate was more than 10 percent. At the same time, taxes were also rising.

Finally, Carter faced an international crisis. In Iran, revolutionaries had overthrown their ruler, the Shah. The Shah had been a long-time ally of the United States. In 1979, Carter allowed the exiled Shah to enter the United States for medical treatment. Angry revolutionaries in Iran seized the American embassy in Tehran and took 53 Americans hostage. The hostage crisis continued for 14 months, eroding Americans' confidence in Carter.

✓**Checkpoint** What troubles plagued President Carter?

# The Conservative Movement

As Carter struggled, a new political movement was gaining strength. This growing conservative movement would reshape American politics.

**What Is a Conservative?** The terms *liberal* and *conservative* have meant different things at different times. By the late 1970s, liberals were generally those who favored federal government action to regulate the economy and solve social problems. Liberals had supported large-scale federal programs such as Franklin Roosevelt's New Deal and Lyndon Johnson's Great Society.

Conservatives fell into two main categories—political conservatives and social conservatives. Political conservatives wanted to shrink "big government," arguing that it had grown too powerful. They felt that more power should be left with state and local governments because these governments were closer to the people. Conservatives also wanted to lower taxes and curb government regulation of business.

Social conservatives were concerned with "traditional values" such as family, patriotism, and religion. One of their leaders was the Reverend Jerry Falwell. In 1979, he created an organization known as the Moral Majority. Falwell stressed the sacredness of marriage and family and the importance of faith in God. The Moral Majority became active in politics. It organized workshops for people who wanted to enter local politics and endorsed like-minded politicians.

**Main Idea**

Riding a conservative tide, Republican Ronald Reagan was elected President in 1980.

**Compare and Contrast**

Compare and contrast the Moral Majority's goals with those of liberals of the 1960s and 1970s. Recall what you have read in earlier chapters.

## The Conservative Movement

❝We [Republicans] see in the sanctity of private property the only durable foundation for constitutional government in a free society. . . . We do not seek to lead anyone's life for him—we seek only to secure his rights and to guarantee him opportunity to strive, with government performing only those needed and constitutionally sanctioned tasks which cannot otherwise be performed. . . . Our towns and cities, then our counties, then our states, then our regional contacts—and only then, the national government. That, let me remind you, is the ladder of liberty.❞

—Barry Goldwater, speech

© 1978 by NEA, Inc.  JIM BERRY ©NEA

"So then Tommy Taxpayer said to the big bully, Godzilla government, 'I am unwilling to pay the bill ...' "

1978 cartoon

### Reading Primary Sources
#### Skills Activity

The modern conservative movement began with Barry Goldwater, Republican candidate for President in 1964. By the late 1970s, conservatives were gaining strength.

**(a) Interpret Primary Sources** According to Goldwater, what is the proper role of the federal government?

**(b) Detect Points of View** Summarize the main point of the cartoon. How does it reflect Goldwater's views?

**Election of 1980** By 1980, conservatives were in control of the Republican Party and had a clear strategy to reach their goals. To shrink government, they planned to slash expensive social programs, cut taxes, and balance the federal budget. With a **balanced budget**, government spends only as much money as it collects. Conservatives also wanted to curb regulation of business. They argued that overregulation <u>violated</u> the principles of free enterprise.

The Republicans nominated an outspoken conservative, former California governor Ronald Reagan, to run against Jimmy Carter. Reagan asked voters if they were better off than they had been when Carter took office. Many Americans agreed that they were not. Reagan won a clear victory. Moreover, the Republicans regained control of the Senate for the first time since the election of Eisenhower in 1952.

☑**Checkpoint** **What changes did conservatives want to make?**

## Reagan's Presidency

Reagan had a unique background among Presidents. He had been a movie star in the 1940s and 1950s. While president of a screen actors' union, he became interested in politics. In the 1960s, he was elected governor of California.

Reagan entered the White House promising to achieve conservative goals at home. In foreign policy, he vowed to strengthen the military to counter the Soviet Union.

**Vocabulary** *Builder*
**violate** (vī ah layt) *v.* to break a rule or law; to disrespect; to disturb

**Main Idea**
President Reagan tried to cut back taxes while shifting spending from social to military programs.

**Explore More Video**
To learn more about President Reagan, view the video.

**The Great Communicator**
President Reagan's open manner and infectious optimism added to his popularity. **Critical Thinking:** *Analyze Cause and Effect How might a career in movies help to prepare someone to be an effective communicator?*

Reagan's skill in presenting ideas in terms that ordinary people could understand gave him great advantages as President. He became known as the Great Communicator. Glowing with optimism, Reagan readily convinced many Americans that he could solve their problems.

**Reducing Government** "Government is not the solution to our problems," Reagan said. "Government is the problem." Reducing government spending and taxes, he argued, would fire up the economy by giving taxpayers more money to spend and businesses more reasons to manufacture and sell. Reagan's economic program became known as Reaganomics.

Reagan began by slicing more than $40 billion from the federal budget. Most of it came from trimming social programs and cutting federal jobs. In 1981, he persuaded Congress to lower taxes by 25 percent. *Time* magazine concluded that he had done more "to alter the economic direction of the country" than any President in 50 years.

Deregulation, scaling back federal rules for businesses, was another way to limit government. Reagan reduced costly antipollution regulations and opened protected federal lands to oil and lumber companies. Such actions brought praise from business leaders and criticism from environmentalists.

**Assessing Reagan** Reagan left the White House in 1989, after two terms, as one of the nation's most popular Presidents. His record was mixed. He did not succeed in balancing the budget. In fact, his tax cuts and increases in military spending had led to record federal deficits. A deficit results when the government spends more money than it collects. Meanwhile, critics charged that cuts in social programs and taxes hurt the poor and favored the rich.

Still, Reagan had made good on his promise to limit government by slowing its growth. His policies helped to expand the economy and shrink inflation. Perhaps most important, he restored faith in the presidency. Reagan also made major breakthroughs in ending the Cold War, as you will read in Section 2.

**Bush Follows Reagan** The victor in the 1988 presidential election was Reagan's Vice President, George H.W. Bush. Bush pledged to continue Reagan's economic policies. "Read my lips," Bush said during the campaign. "No new taxes!"

Facing economic problems, however, Bush broke his promise. As the national debt continued to increase, he concluded that the only way to cut the deficit was to both reduce spending and raise taxes. His call for new taxes outraged many conservatives.

In 1991, the economy fell into a deep recession that lasted more than a year. A recession is a temporary economic slump. Many businesses laid off workers. As unemployment soared, some businesses went bankrupt. Many people blamed the tax hike for causing the recession.

**Checkpoint** How well did President Reagan achieve his goals?

**Vocabulary Builder**
alter (AWL ter) *v.* to change in some way; to make different

This Bush campaign button compares him to earlier Republican Presidents.

## The Clinton Years

By the end of Bush's term, voters were upset with deficits, joblessness, and Washington deadlock. Many were angry with Bush for violating his no-tax pledge.

In the presidential election of 1992, Democrats nominated Arkansas Governor Bill Clinton. The election was a three-way contest. Ross Perot, a Texas billionaire, ran on a third-party platform that promised to bring government closer to the needs of Americans. Clinton won the election with 43 percent of the popular vote. Bush received 38 percent and Perot 19 percent.

**A New Democrat** For the first time in 12 years, a Democrat occupied the White House. Clinton described himself as a "New Democrat" who would steer a middle course between liberalism and conservatism. He vowed to "reinvent" government by slashing its size and its deficits, working with business, and reducing welfare spending. He added that he would not abandon the needy.

President Clinton convinced Congress to raise taxes on higher income groups and reduce some spending. As a result, the deficit was cut in half by 1996. The President also worked with Congress to overhaul welfare. A compromise abolished direct federal spending on welfare and replaced it with grants to states for antipoverty programs. To encourage the jobless to find work, the law limited how long benefits could be paid.

**Prosperity and Scandal** During the Clinton years, the stock market surged to record highs. Unemployment dropped to a 30-year low. Tax receipts from the growing economy produced federal budget surpluses from 1998 through 2001—the first in 29 years. A **surplus** results when the government collects more money than it spends.

Clinton won reelection in 1996, but scandal dogged his second term. The most serious charge involved an improper relationship with a young White House intern. When he was questioned by investigators, Clinton appeared to have lied under oath.

In December 1998, after a bitter debate, the House voted to impeach Clinton. He was only the second President in history to be impeached, after Andrew Johnson in 1868. The Senate did not convict Clinton, so he remained in office. Despite the scandals, he was still popular with many Americans.

✔ **Checkpoint** How was the deficit reduced under Clinton?

**Main Idea**
The economy revived under President Clinton, but scandal marred his second term.

**Clinton Signs a Bill**
Children of minimum-wage earners cluster around President Clinton as he signs a bill to raise the minimum wage. **Critical Thinking: *Apply Information*** *How might a rise in the minimum wage be related to Clinton's efforts to reduce welfare programs?*

Strengthening America's Families
*A New Minimum Wage*

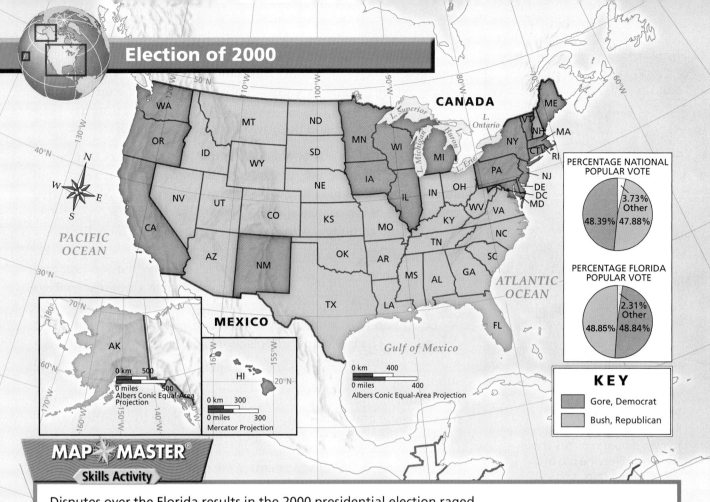

## Election of 2000

CANADA

PERCENTAGE NATIONAL
POPULAR VOTE

3.73%
Other
48.39% 47.88%

PERCENTAGE FLORIDA
POPULAR VOTE

2.31%
Other
48.85% 48.84%

**KEY**

Gore, Democrat

Bush, Republican

PACIFIC OCEAN

ATLANTIC OCEAN

Gulf of Mexico

MEXICO

0 km 500
0 miles 500
Albers Conic Equal-Area Projection

0 km 300
0 miles 300
Mercator Projection

0 km 400
0 miles 400
Albers Conic Equal-Area Projection

**MAP MASTER**
**Skills Activity**

Disputes over the Florida results in the 2000 presidential election raged until the U.S. Supreme Court made a ruling.

**(a) Interpret Charts** What percentage of Florida's votes went to third-party candidates?

**(b) Explain Problems** Why was the result of the Florida election decisive in determining who would become President?

**MapMaster Online**

**For:** Interactive map
**Visit:** PHSchool.com
**Web Code:** mvp-9281

## President George W. Bush

With Clinton's term nearly over, Republicans hoped to win back the White House. The election of 2000 became one of the most controversial in history.

**A Disputed Election** Democrats nominated Vice President Al Gore for President. His running mate was Connecticut Senator Joseph Lieberman, the first Jewish candidate nominated for national office by a major party. Republicans nominated Texas Governor George W. Bush, son of former President George H.W. Bush. He and his running mate, Richard Cheney, promised to support conservative goals and restore integrity to the presidency.

Gore won the popular vote by a paper-thin margin, but Bush led in electoral votes. The key was the state of Florida, where Bush held a tiny advantage. Democrats claimed that the Florida paper ballots were misleading, causing some people to vote for the wrong candidate. They also charged that many votes for Gore had been improperly rejected, especially in heavily African American precincts. They went to court to challenge the Florida results.

**Main Idea**
President George W. Bush pushed through tax cuts and new rules on education.

The Florida Supreme Court ordered a recount. Then, Republicans appealed to the United States Supreme Court. For the first time, the Supreme Court ruled in a presidential election. The court majority held that the Florida justices had overstepped their authority. They stopped the recount, and Bush was declared the winner.

**A Conservative Agenda** After the disputed election, some doubted whether the new President could govern effectively. Bush quickly proved to be a strong leader and a powerful conservative voice. Some of his actions sharply divided the country.

In a time of budget surpluses, tax cuts were high on President Bush's agenda. "The budget surplus is the people's money," the President said. Critics claimed Bush's tax cuts favored the wealthy and would lead to more deficits. After an angry debate, Congress enacted the biggest tax cuts since the Reagan years.

Education was another key issue. Bush signed the No Child Left Behind Act. The law made schools more accountable by using standardized testing to measure student progress. Liberals joined in supporting the law. However, some educators worried that it left little room to do anything but "teach for the test." Critics also pointed out that state and local governments would have to pay the costs of implementing the program.

☑Checkpoint **What arguments were made for and against President Bush's tax cuts?**

⭐ **Looking Back and Ahead** Riding a surge in conservative voting strength, Republican leaders cut taxes and tried to limit government's role in society. Meanwhile, a buildup of U.S. military strength was putting new pressure on the Soviet Union.

**No Child Left Behind**
President George W. Bush spoke to high school students about a law expanding the use of standardized tests. **Critical Thinking:** *Frame Questions Suggest a question that a teacher or school principal might want to ask U.S. leaders about the No Child Left Behind law.*

---

Section 1 | **Check Your Progress**

**Progress Monitoring** Online
**For:** Self-test with instant help
**Visit:** PHSchool.com
**Web Code:** mva-9281

**Comprehension and Critical Thinking**

1. **(a) Describe** How did the conservative movement in 1980 seek to change government?
**(b) Identify Benefits** According to Reagan's supporters, how would his conservative policies benefit businesses and average Americans?

2. **(a) Summarize** How did Republican Presidents after Reagan try to continue his policies?
**(b) Evaluate Information** In general, do you think the conservative movement succeeded in its goals?

**Reading Skill**

3. **Compare and Contrast** Reread the text following the subheading "Assessing Reagan." Compare and contrast the public mood during the Reagan presidency and during the Nixon and Carter presidencies.

**Vocabulary** *Builder*

Answer the following questions in complete sentences that show your understanding of the key terms.
4. How might federal government deregulation affect an industry?
5. What happens to businesses and workers during a recession?

6. How much does a government spend when it wants to keep a balanced budget?
7. What does it mean when a government's budget has a surplus?

**Writing**
8. Create a plot outline for a narrative about the presidential election of 2000. A plot outline includes the following elements: (1) exposition (background information), (2) central conflict or problem, (3) rising action (develops the conflict), (4) climax (high point), and (5) resolution (how things turn out).

## Objectives

1. Learn about Cold War struggles in Afghanistan and Central America.

2. Discover how the Soviet Union responded to President Reagan's arms buildup.

3. Analyze why the Soviet Union dissolved and the Cold War ended.

## Prepare to Read

### ⊙ Reading Skill

**Compare and Contrast Effects** As different Presidents led America and other nations through the years, their actions led to a range of effects. To compare and contrast those effects, you may have to decide which policies or actions caused which effects. Are later effects the same as earlier ones? Are they different?

### Vocabulary *Builder*

**High-Use Words**
critic, p. 944
intermediate, p. 945

**Key Terms and People**
Mikhail Gorbachev, p. 945
glasnost, p. 945

---

⭐ **Background Knowledge** As you have read, President Nixon pursued a policy of détente, easing tensions with the Communist nations. In this section, you will see how the collapse of détente brought new tensions. You will also learn how the Cold War came to an end.

## The End of Détente

At first, President Carter continued the policy of détente. Then, in 1979, the Soviet Union invaded Afghanistan, its mountainous southern neighbor. President Carter joined world opinion in condemning the invasion. In protest, he withdrew from the Senate a pending arms agreement with the Soviet Union. He also pulled the United States from the 1980 Olympic Games in Moscow and imposed restrictions on trade with the Soviet Union. The invasion of Afghanistan ended the era of détente.

**Reagan's Tough Stand** Carter's successor, Ronald Reagan, took an even harder line. He denounced the Soviet Union as an "evil empire." He argued that only a well-armed United States could contain the Soviet empire and halt the spread of communism.

Reagan sent millions of dollars in arms to the government of Afghanistan and the Islamic rebels who were fighting the Soviet Union. The rebels were able to inflict heavy casualties on the Soviets.

One of Reagan's first priorities was to strengthen the military posture of the United States. Accordingly, spending on defense projects jumped by more than 50 percent. One of the key projects was the development of a plane that would be almost invisible to enemy radar. The plane was known as the B-2 stealth bomber.

**Main Idea**
Rejecting the policy of détente, President Reagan took a strong stand against the Soviet Union.

Stealth bomber

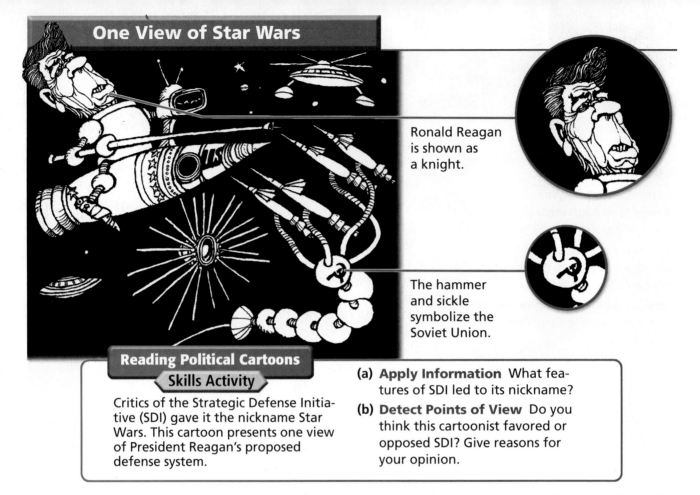

## One View of Star Wars

Ronald Reagan is shown as a knight.

The hammer and sickle symbolize the Soviet Union.

### Reading Political Cartoons
#### Skills Activity

Critics of the Strategic Defense Initiative (SDI) gave it the nickname Star Wars. This cartoon presents one view of President Reagan's proposed defense system.

(a) **Apply Information** What features of SDI led to its nickname?

(b) **Detect Points of View** Do you think this cartoonist favored or opposed SDI? Give reasons for your opinion.

**Vocabulary** *Builder*
<u>critic</u> (KRIHT ihk) *n.* someone who makes judgments, especially negative judgments

Reagan's boldest arms proposal was a laser-guided defense system to shoot down enemy missiles from space. The system, called the Strategic Defense Initiative (SDI), would cost billions. As research began, <u>critics</u> attacked SDI as an expensive fantasy. They called it Star Wars, after the popular science-fiction movie.

**Fighting Leftists in Central America** Reagan's determination to halt the spread of communism led to new U.S. involvements in Central America. In Nicaragua, the United States had long supported dictator Anastasio Somoza because of his strong opposition to communism. In 1979, leftist rebels called Sandinistas overthrew Somoza. They set up a government with close ties to Cuba and the Soviet Union.

Reagan supported the Contras, a guerrilla army made up of anti-Communist opponents of the Sandinistas. Some Americans opposed aid to the Contras, charging them with acts of brutality. However, the President secretly ordered the CIA to train and supply the Contras. Involvement in Central America ignited a heated debate in the United States. When Congress learned of the secret aid, angry lawmakers banned all money and military assistance to the Contras.

Frustration with the ban led to a scandal. In 1985, Iranian-backed militants in Lebanon took seven Americans hostage. Administration officials hatched a complicated plot to free the hostages and, at the same time, secretly send aid to the Contras. The officials agreed to sell arms to Iran. In exchange, Iran pressured the militants into releasing some hostages. Meanwhile, U.S. officials used money from the arms sale to buy weapons for the Contras in Nicaragua.

Americans were stunned when word of this "Iran-Contra deal" leaked out. Eventually, seven government officials were convicted of lying to Congress and destroying evidence. President Reagan said he had no knowledge of the deal. Still, the Iran-Contra affair threw a shadow over Reagan's last years as President.

☑Checkpoint **What was the Iran-Contra scandal?**

## The Soviet Union in Decline

In the 1980s, the Soviet Union was in decline. Its grip on Eastern Europe grew weaker as new movements for democracy sprang up. Within the Soviet Union, opposition to Communist rule was growing.

**Growing Problems** The Afghan war had been a major burden on the Soviet economy. It had also sapped the morale of the Soviet people. In 1989, after 10 years, the Soviet Union accepted defeat and withdrew its troops.

The Soviet Union responded to Reagan's military buildup with a buildup of its own. But heavy military spending weakened the Soviet economy and led to severe shortages at home. When Russians went to stores, they waited in long lines and found shelves nearly empty.

**A Bold New Leader** Mikhail Gorbachev, who became leader of the Soviet Union in 1985, threw his energies into reforming the system. He began to restructure the economy to allow more freedom. He adopted a new policy called glasnost, or speaking openly about Soviet problems. However, Gorbachev's reforms only emboldened the Soviet people to demand more changes.

Gorbachev also tried to improve relations with the West. He realized that a continued arms race could overwhelm the Soviet economy. In 1987, he met with Reagan. The two leaders agreed on a new arms control treaty. Both sides promised to destroy short-range and intermediate-range nuclear missiles. For the first time, the two superpowers agreed to give up entire classes of weapons.

**Compare and Contrast Effects** What was the effect of the Iran-Contra affair on the Reagan presidency? Compare and contrast this with the effect of Watergate on President Nixon's presidency.

**Main Idea**
Economic and military pressures weakened the Soviet Union, and a new Soviet leader introduced reforms.

**Vocabulary** *Builder*
**intermediate** (ihn ter MEE dee iht) *adj.* happening in between; part way from one extreme to another

**Soviet Economic Problems**
Consumers in the Soviet Union often found store shelves empty as the economy went through upheaval in the 1980s and 1990s. **Critical Thinking:** *Identify Costs How were such shortages related to pressures caused by U.S. policies?*

**Eastern Europe Breaks Free** The Soviet Union had long controlled most of the Communist governments of Eastern Europe and kept them in power. In 1956, Soviet troops marched into Hungary and smashed a revolt against its Communist leaders. In 1968, Soviet tanks ended democratic reforms in Czechoslovakia.

Under Gorbachev, the Soviet Union lost interest in supporting unpopular leaders in Eastern Europe. One by one, Communist governments there gave in to demands for democratic change. In Poland, the first free elections since World War II produced a non-Communist government in 1989. Communist regimes in Hungary, Romania, and Czechoslovakia soon crumbled. Communism also fell in Yugoslavia, which the Soviet Union had not dominated.

In November 1989, students and workers in East Germany tore down the Berlin Wall, a bitter symbol of Communist oppression. Berliners danced, exchanged hugs, and battered the Berlin Wall with sledgehammers, pickaxes, and bare hands. Within a year, East and West Germany had reunited as a single nation.

The fall of Communist governments unleashed other forces in Eastern Europe. After 1989, national borders shifted. While Germany reunited, Czechoslovakia split into the Czech Republic and Slovakia. Yugoslavia became several loosely joined republics.

☑**Checkpoint** **How did Gorbachev change Soviet policy?**

# The Cold War Ends

**Main Idea**
The Soviet Union dissolved in 1991, and the Cold War came to an end.

Far-reaching changes affected the Soviet Union, too. It had consisted of 15 republics dominated by a powerful central government in Moscow. As change overtook Eastern Europe, independence movements arose in several Soviet republics.

**The Soviet Union Collapses** In late 1991, the Soviet Union dissolved. Each republic became an independent state. In the biggest state, Russia, a new president, Boris Yeltsin, vowed to continue the drive for democracy and a strong economy.

"Gorbachev knew how to bring us freedom, but he did not know how to make sausage," complained one Russian. Gorbachev's reforms had failed to solve the problems of shortages and shoddy goods. The new Russia also suffered from unemployment and high prices. Crime and corruption thrived. Many Russians began to question whether democracy could make their lives better.

**Unrest in Eastern Europe** In Yugoslavia, the fall of communism led to a civil war. Yugoslavia was made up of several republics, including Croatia, Serbia, and Bosnia-Herzegovina. In 1991, Croatia and Bosnia declared independence. However, Serbs in Croatia and Bosnia wanted to remain part of Yugoslavia. With help from Serbia, they fought to prevent the new governments from splitting away. The civil war lasted for four years. More than 250,000 people died, including many children and teenagers.

# END OF THE COLD WAR

The Cold War had kept international tensions high since the mid-1940s. With the dissolution of the Soviet Union in 1991, the Cold War came to an end. **Critical Thinking:** *Identify Benefits* What benefits might the Soviet people hope for as a result of the collapse of Communist rule?

**History** *Interactive*
Explore the
**End of the Cold War**
**Visit:** PHSchool.com
**Web Code:** mvl-9282

▲ A summit conference between Gorbachev and Reagan in 1988.

**Soviet Reformer**
Soviet ruler Mikhail Gorbachev sought to reform the Soviet system and ease the arms race to relieve pressure on the Soviet economy.

**Too Little, Too Late**
Gorbachev's reforms could not save the Communist system in the Soviet Union. In December 1991, the 15 Soviet republics became independent. Russia began experiments with democratic government and a free-market economy.

**Eastern Europe Abandons Communism**
A surge of pro-democracy movements helped bring down communism in Eastern Europe from 1989 onward.

▲ Demonstrators used sledgehammers to tear down the Berlin Wall in 1989.

Russian ▶ schoolchildren sit on a toppled statue of Stalin.

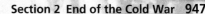

In November 1995, the United States hosted peace talks in Dayton, Ohio. To help enforce the peace, President Clinton sent about 20,000 American troops to Bosnia. Along with Russian and NATO peacekeepers, the troops helped to restore order.

The Dayton Accord did not end trouble in the former Yugoslavia. Ethnic Albanians in Kosovo, a province within Serbia, also sought greater independence. Serbs launched a series of attacks against rebels in Kosovo. Hundreds of thousands of Albanians were killed or forced to flee. President Clinton charged that the attacks fed "the flames of ethnic and religious division." In 1999, American and NATO forces bombed Serbia until Serbian troops left Kosovo.

**Cold War Balance Sheet** The dissolution of the Soviet Union put an end to the 45 years of the Cold War. Americans hailed the emergence of democratic governments in Eastern Europe and the former Soviet Union. U.S. leaders expressed hope that Russia would become a democratic and stable nation.

The United States had paid a heavy price during the Cold War. More than 100,000 Americans died fighting "hot" wars in Korea and Vietnam. Taxpayers spent more than $6 trillion on defense.

The Cold War had often divided the nation, especially during the Vietnam War. Still, from the perspective of the 1990s, Americans hailed the end of the Cold War as an event worthy of celebration.

☑**Checkpoint**  **Why did the Cold War come to an end when it did?**

⭐ **Looking Back and Ahead**  The dissolution of the Soviet Union and the collapse of communism in Eastern Europe brought the Cold War to an end. In the next section, you will read how U.S. policy responded to these changes.

---

Section 2 | **Check Your Progress**

**Progress Monitoring** Online
**For:** Self-test with instant help
**Visit:** PHSchool.com
**Web Code:** mva-9282

**Comprehension and Critical Thinking**

1. **(a) List** What did President Reagan do to strengthen the American military?
**(b) Analyze Cause and Effect** How did his actions contribute to the collapse of the Soviet Union?

2. **(a) Describe** What changes did Mikhail Gorbachev make as leader of the Soviet Union?
**(b) Analyze Cause and Effect** How did his actions help bring about the end of the Soviet Union?

**Reading Skill**

3. **Compare and Contrast Effects** Compare and contrast the effects that Gorbachev hoped to achieve when he took power in the Soviet Union with the actual effects of his leadership.

**Vocabulary** *Builder*

Read the sentence below. If the sentence is true, write YES. If the sentence is not true, write NO and explain why.

4. Under the policy of glasnost, critics of the Soviet government were severely punished.

**Writing**

5. Create a plot outline for an eyewitness narrative of the falling of the Berlin Wall. The plot outline should include the five elements that were listed in the Writing activity in the Section 1 Check Your Progress. Then, write the beginning paragraph of a narrative in which an eyewitness tells about this event.

# A New Role in the World

## Objectives

1. See how U.S. foreign policy developed after the Cold War.

2. Discover how the United States sought to promote change in South Africa, China, and Cuba.

3. Explore efforts to control the spread of nuclear weapons.

## Prepare to Read

### Reading Skill

**Analyze Contrasts** Reading about different times in history can help you draw conclusions about differences between those times. First, identify contrasts between the policies, attitudes, or actions of different time periods. Then, recall the process of drawing conclusions discussed in a previous chapter. Use details in the text and prior knowledge to link the two time periods.

### Vocabulary *Builder*

**High-Use Words**

**deprive**, p. 950

**pursue**, p. 950

**Key Terms**

apartheid, p. 949

sanction, p. 949

⭐ **Background Knowledge** For nearly 50 years, the Cold War had defined U.S. foreign policy. The collapse of the Soviet Union marked the end of that period. In this section, we will look at the changing role of the United States in the world.

## Promoting Democracy and Peace

After the Soviet Union dissolved, the United States was the only remaining superpower. President George H.W. Bush said that the United States faced "the rarest opportunities to shape the world and the deepest responsibility to do it wisely." Under Bush and Clinton, the United States stepped up calls for democracy and peace.

**South Africa** The United States used its influence in many places. In South Africa, a policy of apartheid, or racial separation and inequality, had held democracy in check for decades. The policy barred voting rights for the nonwhite majority.

For years the United States resisted calls for action against South Africa. Then, in 1986, Congress approved economic sanctions over a veto by President Reagan. Sanctions are penalties applied against a country in order to pressure it to change its policies. U.S. companies were forbidden to invest in South Africa or import South African products. Other countries also applied sanctions.

Along with growing protests inside South Africa, the sanctions took a toll. In 1991, South Africa's white government ended apartheid. Nonwhites were allowed full voting rights, and free elections in 1994 put black leaders in office.

**Main Idea**
The United States used its influence to shape developments in other nations.

In 1994, these South African women were able to vote for the first time.

**The Philippines** In the Philippines, the first free election in 14 years ended the rule of dictator Ferdinand Marcos in 1986. Under the banner of "people power," the new government worked to end the corruption and poverty of the Marcos era. The United States sent economic and military aid, as it had to Marcos.

**Northern Ireland** In British-ruled Northern Ireland, years of violence between a Protestant majority and a Catholic minority had left thousands dead. On Good Friday in 1998, the United States helped arrange an agreement for sharing power between the two groups. "We can say to the men of violence and those who disdain democracy: Your way is not the way," declared George Mitchell, the U.S. negotiator.

## Ferment in China

Pro-democracy demonstrations like this were crushed in Tiananmen Square. **Critical Thinking:** *Explain Problems Why did U.S. leaders respond as they did to the Chinese crackdown?*

**China** In China, workers joined students in a campaign to win democratic reforms. Despite limited reforms that opened its economy to private business, China's Communist government allowed no free elections or free speech.

In May 1989, television news showed hundreds of thousands of people demanding democracy in Tiananmen Square in Beijing, China's capital. A week later, the world watched in horror as the Chinese army routed the demonstrators, killing or wounding many.

The brutal crackdown angered many Americans, including President George H.W. Bush. Still, he said it was important to maintain good relations with China. He pursued a policy of persuasion rather than punishment. President Clinton continued this policy. On a visit to China in 1998, Clinton pressed the Chinese on human rights issues while vowing to bring the two nations closer.

**Vocabulary** *Builder*
deprive (dee PRĪV) *v.* to withhold; to take away

**Cuba** In the 1990s, Cuba fell on hard times. Since 1960, the United States had banned trade with Cuba in an effort to oust Communist dictator Fidel Castro. In 1991, the fall of the Soviet Union <u>deprived</u> Cuba of its chief source of trade and economic aid. The Cuban economy stumbled, and 30,000 Cubans fled to the United States.

For a time, Cuban-American relations improved. In 1994, President Clinton allowed more Cubans to enter the United States. U.S. lawmakers began to debate resuming trade with the island nation. However, President George W. Bush <u>pursued</u> a policy of pressure against Cuba. "Well-intentioned ideas about [increasing] trade will only prop up this dictator," Bush said. He refused to relax bans on American trade with and travel to the island nation.

**Vocabulary** *Builder*
pursue (per SYOO) *v.* to follow; to chase; to attempt to gain

**✓Checkpoint** How did the United States seek to promote change in Cuba?

## Easing the Arms Race

In 1972, the United States signed its first arms control treaty with the Soviet Union. The Strategic Arms Limitation Talks (SALT) curbed the number of nuclear warheads and long-range missiles that each side built. Seven years later, the two nations worked out another arms reduction pact (SALT II). But President Carter withdrew the treaty in protest after the Soviet invasion of Afghanistan.

**New Approach** In 1991, Soviet leader Gorbachev and President George H.W. Bush agreed to a path-breaking arms agreement called the Strategic Arms Reduction Treaty (START). Under START, the powers agreed to destroy about 20 percent of their nuclear weapons.

When the Soviet Union dissolved, Russia inherited most of its nuclear arms. In 1993, the United States and Russia negotiated START II. Revised in 1997, the pact required both countries to cut back long-range nuclear weapons by an astounding two thirds.

**Main Idea**
Efforts to control nuclear arms continued after the end of the Cold War.

**Analyze Contrasts**
Contrast START with the original Strategic Arms Limitation Treaty. What can you conclude about the factors influencing arms treaties?

**Nuclear Weapons Status, 2005**

**KEY**
- Nuclear weapon state by 1960
- Nuclear weapon state, 2005
- Suspected of having nuclear weapons programs, 2005

UNITED KINGDOM · RUSSIA · FRANCE · UNITED STATES · ISRAEL · IRAN · CHINA · NORTH KOREA · INDIA · PAKISTAN

ATLANTIC OCEAN · PACIFIC OCEAN · PACIFIC OCEAN · INDIAN OCEAN

0 km 3,000
0 miles 3,000
Mercator Projection

Source: Carnegie Endowment for International Peace

**MAP MASTER**
**Skills Activity**

U.S. leaders want to halt any further spread of nuclear weapons, especially to nations seen as hostile to American interests.

**(a) Interpret Maps** What were the first three nations to acquire nuclear weapons?

**(b) Draw Conclusions** Why was the world so alarmed when both India and Pakistan developed nuclear weapons?

**MapMaster Online**
**For:** Interactive map
**Visit:** PHSchool.com
**Web Code:** mvp-9283

This 1994 magazine cover expresses American fears that North Korea might become a nuclear threat.

**A Continuing Threat** Economic and political instability in the former Soviet Union worried U.S. planners. Russia alone had some 30,000 nuclear weapons; three other republics had some, too. All four pledged to honor existing treaties. In return, Congress sent $400 million per year to help these nations safely store or destroy their nuclear arms.

Another concern was nuclear proliferation—the spread of nuclear arms. Britain, France, and China had long had such weapons, but other nations also sought them. The danger of nuclear war would grow if nuclear weapons spread further.

U.S. intelligence reports said that Israel probably had a nuclear weapon by the late 1960s. Iran, Iraq, and North Korea were also suspected of seeking nuclear arms. South Asia was another problem area. In 1998, feuding neighbors India and Pakistan successfully tested nuclear bombs. The thought that many countries might one day possess nuclear arms was a worrisome one.

✓**Checkpoint** **Why would the United States be worried about nuclear proliferation?**

⭐ **Looking Back and Ahead** After the Cold War ended, the United States turned to issues of democratic change and the dangers posed by the spread of nuclear weapons. In the next section, you will read of American efforts to deal with a tangle of dangerous issues in the Middle East.

---

Section 3 | **Check Your Progress**

**Progress Monitoring** ⬤nline
**For:** Self-test with instant help
**Visit:** PHSchool.com
**Web Code:** mva-9283

**Comprehension and Critical Thinking**

1. **(a) Recall** How did U.S. policy encourage political changes in South Africa and Northern Ireland?
   **(b) Explain Problems** Why do you think the United States was less successful in encouraging change in China?

2. **(a) Describe** How did nuclear weapons spread in the world in the 1990s?
   **(b) Explain Problems** Why is the spread of nuclear weapons considered one of the greatest dangers facing the world?

**Reading Skill**

3. **Compare Causes and Reasons** Reread the text following the subheading "Using American Influence." Compare the reasons for unrest in Northern Ireland and South Africa. Make a generalization about people's views with regard to freedom and self-determination.

**Vocabulary Builder**

Read each sentence below. If the sentence is true, write YES. If the sentence is not true, write NO and explain why.

4. South Africa's policy of apartheid guaranteed that its black citizens could live and work anywhere they wanted to.

5. The U.S. Congress approved sanctions on South Africa that forbade American companies to invest there.

**Writing**

6. Create a plot outline for an eyewitness narrative of the military action against the protesters in Tiananmen Square in China in 1991. Then, list several incidents that might be part of the rising action in this narrative. (Rising action builds on the central conflict and increases tension and suspense.)

# Conflict in the Middle East

## Objectives

1. Learn why the Middle East has been of vital interest to the United States.

2. Examine the causes and effects of Arab-Israeli conflict.

3. Explore U.S. involvement in a series of crises in the Middle East.

## Prepare to Read

### 🔁 Reading Skill

**Compare Causes and Reasons**
Why do events in history take place? Examine events from history and compare their causes and reasons. Then, draw conclusions or make generalizations about what motivates people and nations to feel and act as they do. Remember, generalizations are broad statements that fit many situations.

### Vocabulary *Builder*

**High-Use Words**

<u>confine</u>, p. 955

<u>crisis</u>, p. 956

**Key Terms and People**

Yasir Arafat, p. 955

westernization, p. 956

Ruholla Khomeini, p. 956

Saddam Hussein, p. 956

Norman Schwarzkopf, p. 957

Colin Powell, p. 957

⭐ **Background Knowledge** As you learned, the end of the Cold War did not lessen American involvement in world affairs. In this section, you will see how the United States became increasingly involved in the complex region called the Middle East.

## A Vital Region

The Middle East is a term first used by Europeans to describe Southwest Asia. Often, the term has been extended to include Egypt in northeastern Africa, as well as Afghanistan to the east.

Since ancient times, the Middle East has linked the societies of Europe, Asia, and Africa. Three major religions—Judaism, Christianity, and Islam—arose in the region. Today, Islam is the dominant religion of most Middle Eastern nations. Over the centuries, tensions among various religious groups have often led to conflict.

In recent times, the Middle East has gained world attention because of its vast reserves of petroleum, or oil. Nations such as Saudi Arabia and Kuwait became wealthy selling needed oil to the United States and other industrial nations. Arab nations form the backbone of the Organization of Petroleum Exporting Countries (OPEC). OPEC has become a key player in world affairs by setting the level of oil production and raising or lowering the price of oil.

The United States has had to balance conflicting interests in the Middle East. It strongly supports the Jewish nation of Israel. Yet, it also tries to maintain ties with Arab states that oppose Israel.

**Main Idea**
The oil-rich Middle East is the site of dangerous conflicts among nations and religious groups.

☑**Checkpoint** Why is the Middle East of concern to Americans?

**Main Idea**

A bitter conflict between Arabs and Israelis has dragged on for decades.

**Compare Causes and Reasons**

Compare the reasons that Jews went to Palestine at different times. What can you conclude?

# Arab-Israeli Conflict

Since the late 1800s, Jews from Europe and elsewhere had been migrating to the land long known as Palestine. Joining established Jewish communities, they hoped to create a Jewish state there. This created conflicts with Arabs who already lived on the land. By the mid-1900s, these conflicts had produced cycles of violence.

**A Series of Wars** The rate of Jewish migration increased with the rise of Nazism and then the Holocaust. Against the opposition of neighboring Arab states, Jews formed the state of Israel in 1948. The United States and other nations recognized Israel.

Israelis worked hard to build a prosperous nation, as well as one of the only democracies in the Middle East. However, a number of Arab countries refused to accept the new state and declared war. An Israeli victory in 1948 left more than half a million Palestinian Arabs homeless. They fled to refugee camps in nearby Arab countries.

Further wars followed. In 1956, Israel invaded Egypt but withdrew under pressure from the United Nations and the United States. War broke out in 1967, and again in 1973, when Arab nations launched a surprise attack. In those wars, Israel seized parts of Egypt, Jordan, and Syria. Arabs call these lands the "occupied territories." Tensions rose as Israeli settlers moved into the territories.

**Camp David Accords** In 1977, Egyptian President Anwar el-Sadat attempted to break the cycle of war. He became the first Arab leader to visit Israel in order to seek peace. Still, agreement was not easy to reach.

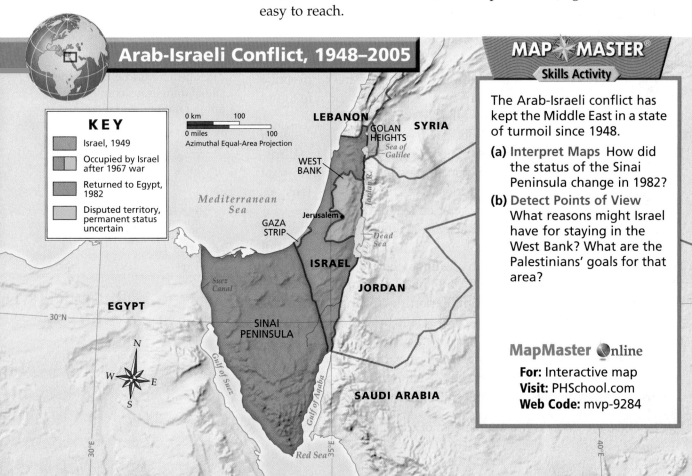

**Arab-Israeli Conflict, 1948–2005**

**MAP MASTER**

**Skills Activity**

**KEY**

- Israel, 1949
- Occupied by Israel after 1967 war
- Returned to Egypt, 1982
- Disputed territory, permanent status uncertain

0 km 100
0 miles 100
Azimuthal Equal-Area Projection

The Arab-Israeli conflict has kept the Middle East in a state of turmoil since 1948.

**(a) Interpret Maps** How did the status of the Sinai Peninsula change in 1982?

**(b) Detect Points of View** What reasons might Israel have for staying in the West Bank? What are the Palestinians' goals for that area?

**MapMaster Online**

**For:** Interactive map
**Visit:** PHSchool.com
**Web Code:** mvp-9284

When peace talks faltered, President Jimmy Carter brought Sadat and Israeli Prime Minister Menachem Begin (muh NAKH uhm BAY gihn) to his Maryland retreat, Camp David. There, the leaders signed the Camp David Accords in 1978. Egypt recognized the state of Israel in exchange for return of the Sinai Peninsula.

**The Palestinian Issue** Palestinian Arabs waged a guerrilla war against Israel. Most Palestinians lived in the occupied territories or in refugee camps outside Israel. Led by Yasir Arafat, the Palestine Liberation Organization (PLO) refused to accept Israel's existence. The PLO claimed the right to an independent state under a Palestinian government in Palestine, including the West Bank and Jerusalem.

In 1987, Palestinians in the occupied territories launched a protest movement or uprising known as the Intifada. The uprising focused world attention on the Palestinian issue.

The United States and other nations tried to broker a peace agreement between the Israelis and Palestinians. In 1993, President Clinton hosted a ceremony in Washington. Israel and the PLO signed a pact providing for limited Palestinian self-rule in the Gaza Strip and part of the West Bank. Arafat promised to give up violence and accept Israel's existence.

Many hoped that the agreement would be the start of a new era. However, new disputes developed. Militant groups on both sides refused to accept the peace process. Arab extremists launched a series of suicide bombings in Israeli cities. Israel responded with military force. Accusing Arafat of secretly supporting the bombers, Israeli troops surrounded his headquarters and <u>confined</u> him there.

Still, moderates on both sides continued to seek a solution. On the twenty-fifth anniversary of the Camp David Accords, former President Carter commented that "peace will come to the Mideast only if two things happen." The first, he said, was for Israel to give up its settlements in the occupied territories. Carter continued:

> **"** The Palestinian national authority and all Arab nations must acknowledge the sovereignty . . . of Israel and its right to live in peace, and must exert their combined effort to control and to prevent any further acts of terrorism or violence by any Palestinian group against the people in Israel.**"**
>
> —Jimmy Carter, speech, September 17, 2003

Contacts picked up after Arafat's death in 2004. The following year, Israel and the new Palestinian leadership announced a cease-fire.

☑**Checkpoint** **Identify the causes of the Israeli-Arab conflict.**

Sadat, Carter, and Begin (left to right) celebrate the Camp David Accords.

**Vocabulary** *Builder*
<u>confine</u> (kahn FĪN) *v.* to keep within an area; to shut in or imprison

## Increasing Tensions

Many Arabs and Muslims have resented American support for Israel. A series of other conflicts increased tensions between the United States and the Muslim world.

**Iran and Lebanon**  As you have read, the United States had long supported the Shah of Iran. The Shah was strongly anti-Communist during the Cold War. However, many Iranians opposed the Shah's harsh, undemocratic rule. Also, devout Muslims opposed his efforts at westernization. Westernization is the adoption of ideas, culture, and technology from Western regions such as the United States and Europe.

In 1979, a revolution forced the Shah to flee. As you have read, the Iranian revolution led to a hostage <u>crisis</u> that contributed to Ronald Reagan's victory over Jimmy Carter.

The United States also became involved in a long, bloody civil war in Lebanon. President Reagan sent American marines as part of a UN peacekeeping force. The forces were later withdrawn after hundreds of American and French troops were killed in suicide bombings in 1983.

**An Extreme Form of Islam** The force behind the Iranian revolution was a Muslim religious leader, Ayatollah Ruholla Khomeini (roo HOH luh koh MAY nee). Khomeini wanted Iran to return to a very strict form of Islam. The new government banned Western books, movies, and music. New laws limited the rights of women.

Over the next decades, extreme forms of Islam gained influence in parts of the Middle East. The followers of these extreme forms were called Islamists. They saw American culture and Western values as threats to their own beliefs. They resented U.S. economic power and the presence of American troops in nations such as Saudi Arabia. Some Muslim extremists encouraged or committed acts of violence against Americans and other westerners.

**Persian Gulf War** The nation of Iraq added to tensions in the region. Iraq had long been ruled by a brutal dictator, Saddam Hussein. In 1990, Hussein sent troops to invade neighboring Kuwait. Kuwait is one of the richest oil-producing nations in the Middle East.

President George H.W. Bush feared the invasion of Kuwait was the start of an Iraqi plan to seize Middle Eastern oil. To block such a move, Bush sent troops to Saudi Arabia. He also persuaded the UN to impose economic sanctions on Iraq.

**Iran Hostage Crisis, 1979**
A poster in Tehran depicts U.S. helplessness during the hostage crisis. **Critical Thinking: *Draw Conclusions*** *Why were many Iranians angry at the United States?*

Bush built a coalition of more than 30 nations, including the Arab nations of Saudi Arabia, Syria, and Egypt. They demanded that Iraq withdraw from Kuwait. When Iraq ignored the demands, the coalition began launching a series of air attacks against the Iraqi capital of Baghdad in January 1991. These were later followed by a ground attack. Military operations were under the command of U.S. General Norman Schwarzkopf and the head of the Joint Chiefs of Staff, Colin Powell.

The Persian Gulf War lasted only six weeks. By February 1991, Hussein was forced to withdraw his troops from Kuwait. The UN then imposed strict economic and military restrictions on Iraq.

Still, Hussein remained in power. Many Americans viewed him as a continuing threat to peace in the Middle East and the world. Of special concern was the suspicion that Hussein was attempting to develop nuclear and biological weapons.

✓**Checkpoint** **What was the outcome of the 1991 Persian Gulf War?**

⭐ **Looking Back and Ahead** Tensions in the Middle East have posed many problems for U.S. foreign policy. After the Persian Gulf War, the United States continued to focus on threats in the region. In the next chapter, you will see how tensions in the Middle East led to a deadly attack within the United States itself.

---

**Section 4 | Check Your Progress**

## Comprehension and Critical Thinking

**1. (a) Recall** What happened in 1948 that increased tensions between Muslims and Jews in the Middle East?
**(b) Draw Inferences** Why do you suppose Jews wanted to create the state of Israel?

**2. (a) Identify** Who was Ruholla Khomeini?
**(b) Clarify Problems** How did his goals clash with those of the United States?

## 🔘 Reading Skill

**3. Compare Causes and Reasons** Reread the text following the subheadings "A Series of Wars" and "Persian Gulf War." Compare U.S. reactions to the many Arab-Israeli wars with the U.S. reaction to Iraq's invasion of Kuwait. Draw a conclusion about why the reactions were different.

## Vocabulary *Builder*

Answer the following question in a complete sentence that shows your understanding of the key term.
**4.** Why might some people see westernization as a threat to traditional Islamic culture?

## Writing

**5.** Write a paragraph that would be part of the rising action of a narrative about one of the following events:
- Camp David Accords of 1978
- Iranian hostage crisis of 1979–1980
- Persian Gulf War in 1991
- Israeli-PLO agreement in 1993

Indicate your narrator's identity and reason for being there. Include concrete details to make the event come to life.

# Global Oil Resources

For millions of years, pools of crude oil collected between rock layers far below the Earth's surface. During the 1850s, people developed technology to drill down to those pools and pump them to the surface for industrial use. Once processed, crude oil becomes petroleum—a resource that has fueled automobiles, energy plants, and everyday products such as bubble gum, crayons, and paint. Although there are oil reserves on nearly every continent, the Middle East rests on a large number of oilfields that make it a vital hub in the global oil network.

Non-OPEC nations also ▶ produce and export their own oil. Russia and Norway are examples of oil exporters outside OPEC ranks. American oil companies drill and pump oil in parts of the United States. However, the United States does not produce enough oil to supply the large U.S. market for gasoline and other products made from oil.

| Top World Oil Exporters | Top World Oil Importers |
| --- | --- |
| 1. Saudi Arabia | 1. United States |
| 2. Russia | 2. Japan |
| 3. Norway | 3. Germany |
| 4. Iran | 4. South Korea |
| 5. United Arab Emirates | 5. China |

Source: *Energy Information Administration*

Venezuela

EQUATOR

MI 0 — 2000
KM 0 — 2000

▲ Venezuelan tanker ships transport oil to bustling ports in South America and across the Pacific Ocean to Asia. Three of the top five oil-importing nations in the world are in East Asia.

## OPEC Controls the Flow

Eleven countries make up OPEC (Organization of the Petroleum Exporting Countries). All but three OPEC nations are located in the Middle East or North Africa. This organization guides the flow and price of a sizeable portion of the planet's oil reserves.

Saudi Arabia produces close to ten million barrels of oil every day. Oil derricks like the one shown here support drill bits that grind through desert sand and bedrock.

## Understand Effects:
# Alternative Energy Sources

Oil is a nonrenewable resource, or a resource that cannot be replaced once it is used. The search for cheap and renewable alternatives to oil is critical to the future of industrialized nations.

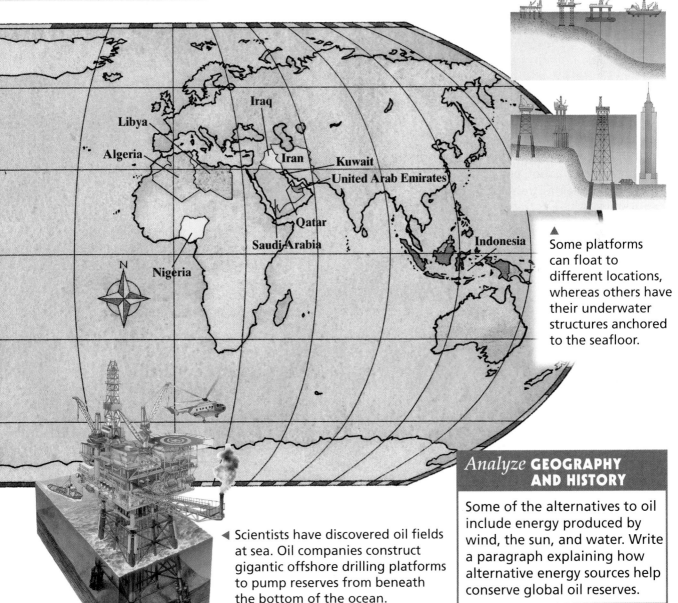

Some platforms can float to different locations, whereas others have their underwater structures anchored to the seafloor.

Scientists have discovered oil fields at sea. Oil companies construct gigantic offshore drilling platforms to pump reserves from beneath the bottom of the ocean.

## Analyze GEOGRAPHY AND HISTORY

Some of the alternatives to oil include energy produced by wind, the sun, and water. Write a paragraph explaining how alternative energy sources help conserve global oil reserves.

A generalization is a broad statement about a person, a group, or an event based on a number of examples and facts. Historians make generalizations to help explain major concepts. Students of history must learn to evaluate the validity of generalizations.

Read the generalization below. Then, use the information below and what you have learned to decide whether or not the generalization is valid.

**Primary Source**

"I think if someone else other than Reagan, someone less of a hardliner, had been in power then the breakthrough in ending the Cold War would not have happened."

—Eduard Shevardnadze, Soviet Union Foreign Minister under Gorbachev

**Primary Source**

"Others hoped, at best, for an uneasy cohabitation [life together] with the Soviet Union; [Ronald Reagan] won the Cold War—not only without firing a shot, but also by inviting enemies out of their fortress and turning them into friends."

—Margaret Thatcher, former Prime Minister of Great Britain in her eulogy for Ronald Reagan

Source: http://homepage.eircom.net/~odyssey/Quotes/History/Cold_Warriors.html

**Generalization:** Ronald Reagan was a driving force behind the end of the Cold War.

| Date | Event |
|------|-------|
| 1948–1949 | ■ Berlin Blockade |
| 1950–1953 | ■ Korean War |
| 1961 | ■ Berlin Wall |
| 1962 | ■ Cuban Missile Crisis |
| 1975 | ■ Communist North Vietnam defeats South Vietnam. |
| 1981 | ■ Ronald Reagan becomes U.S. President. |
| 1985 | ■ Mikhail Gorbachev introduces reform in the Soviet Union. |
| 1989 | ■ The Berlin Wall falls. |
| 1990 | ■ Communist governments in Eastern Europe collapse. |
| 1991 | ■ The Soviet Union collapses. |

## Learn the Skill
*Use these steps to identify valid generalizations.*

**1** **Determine known information.** Read the generalization. Then, study background information and the information provided. Think about what you already know about the topic.

**2** **Identify the relevant facts.** Decide whether the generalization is supported by facts or opinions.

**3** **Check for faulty reasoning.** Generalizations need to be based on sufficient information and draw logical conclusions.

## Practice the Skill
*Answer the following questions.*

**1** **Determine known information.** What information is provided on this page about (a) the Cold War? (b) Ronald Reagan?

**2** **Identify the relevant facts.** (a) What information on the timeline supports the generalization? (b) What information does not?

**3** **Check for faulty reasoning.** Based on the quotes and timeline on this page and what you have learned about the Cold War, does the generalization seem valid? Why or why not?

## Apply the Skill
*See the Review and Assessment at the end of this chapter.*

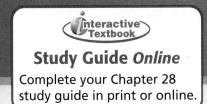

## Chapter Summary

### Section 1
### A Conservative Surge

- President Carter grappled with many domestic and foreign problems.
- Political and social conservatives helped Ronald Reagan win the presidency in 1980.
- Reagan cut domestic spending and taxes.
- Under Bill Clinton, a growing economy produced budget surpluses.
- The election of George W. Bush in 2000 returned conservatives to power.

### Section 2
### End of the Cold War

- President Reagan took a strong stand against the Soviet Union and took steps to build defenses.
- Economic problems and political unrest led to the fall of communism in Eastern Europe, the breakup of the Soviet Union, and the end of the Cold War.

### Section 3
### A New Role in the World

- The United States tried to use its influence to encourage democracy in South Africa, China, and elsewhere.
- The spread of nuclear weapons to other countries became a major concern.

### Section 4
### Conflict in the Middle East

- The Middle East is the site of vast petroleum reserves and bitter conflicts among nations.
- The United States has tried to balance strong support of Israel with close ties to Arab states.
- An Iranian revolution of 1979 signaled the rise of a new, militant form of Islam.
- In the Persian Gulf War, a U.S.-led coalition turned back an Iraqi invasion of oil-rich Kuwait.

## Key Concepts

These notes will help you prepare for questions about key concepts.

### Goals of the Conservative Movement

**Political Conservatives: Limit and Shrink Government**
- Cut government spending
- Lower taxes
- Limit regulation of business
- Balance the federal budget

**Social Conservatives: Preserve Traditional Values**
- Family
- Patriotism
- Religion

### Collapse of Communism

**Reagan Years**
- Reagan takes hard line against Soviet Union
- Military spending weakens the Soviet economy
- Gorbachev begins reforms

**George H.W. Bush Years**
- Soviet troops withdraw from Afghanistan
- Poland elects a non-Communist government
- Berlin Wall comes down
- Soviet Union collapses

### U.S. Involvement in Middle East

**1948** United States recognizes and supports new Jewish state of Israel

**1977** Carter negotiates Camp David Accords

**1979** Iranian revolutionaries take Americans hostage

**1982** Reagan sends peace-keeping force to Lebanon

**1991** Bush leads coalition against Iraq in Persian Gulf War

**1993** Clinton brokers Israeli-Palestinian agreement

## Vocabulary *Builder*

### Key Terms

Fill in the blanks with the correct key terms.

1. Tax cuts and increased spending contributed to a rising budget _____.

2. The introduction of American fashions into the Middle East was an example of _____.

3. To achieve a _____, the government has to spend only as much money as it takes in.

4. By imposing economic _____, the United States tries to influence another nation's policies.

5. Reagan's policy of _____ allowed American businesses to expand more freely.

## Comprehension and Critical Thinking

6. **(a) Identify** What were three goals of the conservative movement?
   **(b) Apply Information** Choose two actions of President Reagan, and explain how each fulfilled one of the three goals.
   **(c) Draw Conclusions** Why do you think many people use the term "the Reagan Revolution" to describe Reagan's impact?

7. **(a) Recall** What was the goal of George W. Bush's No Child Left Behind program?
   **(b) Draw Conclusions** Why do you think many recent Presidents have focused on education as an important issue?

8. **(a) List** Why did the Soviet Union collapse?
   **(b) Identify Costs and Benefits** How did the collapse bring both benefits and drawbacks to people of Eastern Europe and Russia?

9. **(a) Summarize** How did the United States promote democracy around the world?
   **(b) Analyze Cause and Effect** How successful was the United States in supporting democratic movements?

10. **(a) Recall** Why is the Middle East considered a vital region for the United States?

    **(b) Summarize** How was the United States involved in the conflicts of the region?
    **(c) Analyze Cause and Effect** Identify two results of increased American involvement in the Middle East.

## History Reading Skill

11. **Compare and Contrast** Choose any two Presidents discussed in this chapter. Write a paragraph comparing and contrasting their presidencies. Make a generalization based on your comparison.

## Writing

12. **Write an opening and several paragraphs for an eyewitness narrative.**
    Choose one of the narratives that you have been developing in the section activities for this chapter. Use the Internet or library to find more background information about the subject. Then, write two paragraphs describing the rising action for the historical event.
    **Your writing should:**
    - introduce your eyewitness narrator;
    - focus on a historical event covered in this chapter;
    - make the conflict, or central problem, of the narrative clear;
    - create rising action that builds on the conflict with details and actions.

13. **Write a narrative:**
    Imagine that you are an American negotiator at peace talks in the Middle East. Write a letter home explaining what you hope to accomplish and the challenges you face.

## Skills for Life

### Evaluate Generalizations

Evaluate the generalization below using what you have learned about the conservative movement.

> **Generalization:** During the 1980s, most conservatives wanted to increase the size of the federal government.

14. What information about the conservatives is provided in Section 1?

15. **(a)** What facts support the quote?
    **(b)** What facts do not support the quote?

16. Based on what you have learned about the conservatives of the 1980s, does the generalization seem valid? Why or why not?

## Test Yourself

1. **Which action of President Bill Clinton marked a move away from a conservative policy?**

   A slashing the size of government

   B working with business

   C limiting welfare benefits

   D raising taxes on higher income groups

2. **In the 1990s, the United States sent troops to help enforce peace in**

   A Northern Ireland.

   B Bosnia.

   C Iran.

   D South Africa.

**Refer to the map below to answer Question 3.**

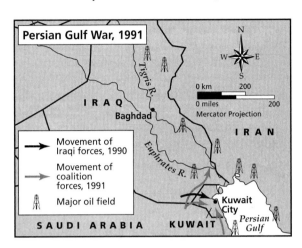

Persian Gulf War, 1991

3. **Based on the map, during the Persian Gulf War, Saudi Arabia**

   A supported Iraq against the U.S.-led coalition.

   B supported the U.S.-led coalition against Iraq.

   C invaded Iraq.

   D was invaded by Iraq.

## Document-Based Questions

**Task:** Look at Documents 1 and 2, and answer their accompanying questions. Then, use the documents and your knowledge of history to complete this writing assignment:

> Write an editorial supporting or criticizing Reaganomics. Be sure to support your arguments with facts.

**Document 1:** Stephen Moore was an economist and adviser in the Reagan administration. *According to Moore, what were Reagan's main economic ideas?*

"Ronald Reagan came to the White House with some simple ideas but they weren't simple-minded ideas. These were ideas to cut tax rates. At that time . . . we had a 70 percent top tax rate. That was really discouraging economic growth. The second big problem . . . was raging inflation. . . . And the third thing was Reagan promised to rebuild the military . . . and to try to bring the Cold War to an end victoriously.

What made Ronald Reagan such a great president . . . was that he came in with these three objectives and was able to accomplish them all."

**Document 2:** Robert Reich was an economist and secretary of labor during the Clinton administration. *According to Reich, what major problem did Reaganomics cause?*

"Reaganomics had some major problems. For one thing, it created a huge deficit. . . . At the start of the Reagan administration the deficit was about 2.5 percent of the national economy. By the end it was about 5 percent of the national economy. . . .

With that kind of deficit, eventually, you've got to pay the piper. There is a day of reckoning, and the day of reckoning came with a huge recession in 1990 and 1991. . . .

The gap between the rich and the poor began to widen during the Reagan administration and has continued to widen since then."

# CHAPTER 29 | Challenges for a New Century
## 1980–Present

## Chapter Preview

As a result of deadly terrorist attacks in 2001, the United States embarked on a global war against terrorism. At the same time, the nation faced many other challenges, including an increasingly global economy, environmental problems, and a changing population.

### ✓ What You Will Learn

The September 11, 2001, terrorist attacks stunned the nation and led to a controversial war in Iraq.

A global economy and growing concern about environmental problems have linked the world.

The computer and other advances in technology and science have transformed modern society.

New immigration and population patterns have led to an increasingly diverse society.

### U.S. Events

### World Events

**1970**
President Nixon forms Environmental Protection Agency (EPA).

**1986**
Congress passes Immigration Reform and Control Act to combat illegal immigration.

1970      1980      1990

**1973** Arab members of OPEC impose oil embargo.

**1989** British scientist proposes World Wide Web.

In 2005, this U.S. Army sergeant was one of the thousands of immigrants who became United States citizens.

**1993**
President Clinton signs North American Free Trade Agreement.

**2001**
Terrorists attack World Trade Center and Pentagon, killing thousands of people.

**2003**
Latinos, or Hispanics, become largest ethnic minority in United States.

1990

2000

2010

**1997** Scientists in Scotland clone a sheep.

**2003** Iraqi dictator Saddam Hussein is captured.

**2005** Terrorists explode bombs in London.

965

**History Reading Skill  Make Generalizations**

## How did Americans react to terrorist attacks?

In this chapter, you will practice drawing conclusions and making generalizations. Read the following article by Anna Quindlen, in which she explores the American character in the wake of the September 11 attacks.

Newspaper columnist Anna Quindlen wrote this article after terrorists flew planes into the World Trade Center and Pentagon, killing several thousand people.

**Primary Source**

One of the things that [the United States] stands for is this vexing notion that a great nation can consist entirely of refugees from other nations, that people of different, even warring religions and cultures can live, if not side by side, then on either side of the country's . . . Avenues. . . . Other countries with such divisions have in fact divided into new nations. . . .

There is a grudging fairness among the citizens of the United States that eventually leads most to admit that . . . new immigrants are not so different from our own parents or grandparents. . . .

When photographs of the faces of all those who died in the World Trade Center destruction are assembled in one place, it will be possible to trace in the skin color, the shape of the eyes and the noses, the texture of the hair, a map of the world. These are the representatives of a . . . nation that somehow, at times like this, has one spirit.

—Anna Quindlen, "A Country and a Conundrum"

> This evidence supports the conclusion that America is unique in the world.

> Specific examples here support Quindlen's generalization that Americans accept diversity.

> You can conclude that America is different from other nations.

> You might use prior knowledge to help you generalize that people come together in difficult times.

## Make Generalizations

- To draw conclusions, use the text and prior knowledge to make a statement about the larger meaning of an event.
- To make generalizations, identify main points or ideas, then restate these in a general way that can apply to many situations.
- Both conclusions and generalizations must be supported by the text.

## Document-Based Questions

1. According to Quindlen, what is unique about the United States?
2. How does Quindlen say Americans respond to crises?

## Vocabulary *Builder*

### Previewing High-Use Academic Words

| High-Use Word | Definition | Sample History Sentence |
|---|---|---|
| **external** (ehks TER nahl) (Section 1, p. 969) | *adj.* on or from the outside | The most important function of the military is to protect the nation from <u>external</u> attack. |
| **consume** (kahn SYOOM) (Section 1, p. 972) | *v.* to use up | Americans <u>consume</u> a large percentage of the world's oil. |
| **provoke** (prah VOHK) (Section 2, p. 977) | *v.* to excite; to cause an action | The Soviet invasion of Afghanistan <u>provoked</u> an angry response from the United States. |
| **fossil** (FAH sihl) (Section 2, p. 980) | *n.* hardened remains of a plant or an animal that lived long ago | Archaeologists have found <u>fossils</u> of large mammals hunted by early Americans. |
| **flexible** (FLEHKS ah bahl) (Section 3, p. 983) | *adj.* easily bent; able to be used in many ways | Some people believe that the meaning of the Constitution is <u>flexible</u> and can change with the times. |
| **distribute** (dihs TRIHB yoot) (Section 3, p. 985) | *v.* to spread in an orderly way | Federal disaster relief programs help <u>distribute</u> food, clothing, and other supplies to victims. |
| **enrich** (ehn RIHCH) (Section 4, p. 987) | *v.* to make richer or fuller; to improve | The writings of Melville, Whitman, and Alcott have <u>enriched</u> American literature. |
| **evident** (EHV ih dehnt) (Section 4, p. 989) | *adj.* clear; obvious | The economic effects of World War II were <u>evident</u> in every American home and factory. |

### Previewing Key Terms and People

terrorism, p. 968
counterterrorism, p. 970
Osama Bin Laden, p. 971
John Kerry, p. 973
globalization, p. 976
trade deficit, p. 976
outsourcing, p. 976

free trade, p. 977
Rachel Carson, p. 978
environmentalist, p. 978
renewable resource, p. 980
global warming, p. 981
e-commerce, p. 983
laser, p. 983

cloning, p. 985
refugee, p. 986
undocumented worker, p. 987
guest worker, p. 987
Condoleezza Rice, p. 989
Sandra Day O'Connor, p. 990

# The Threat of Terrorism

## Objectives

1. Learn about the roots of terrorism.

2. Explore how Americans responded to the terrorist attacks of September 11, 2001.

3. Find out how the United States became involved in wars in Afghanistan and Iraq.

4. Examine the results of the 2004 presidential election.

## Prepare to Read

 **Reading Skill**

**Draw Conclusions** The story of history often includes many apparently separate and small details. When looked at together, however, these details create a picture of an event, a time, or an important person. As you read the final chapter in this textbook, pay careful attention to the many details. Ask yourself what overall picture they create.

### Vocabulary *Builder*

**High-Use Words**
external, p. 969
consume, p. 972

**Key Terms and People**
terrorism, p. 968
counterterrorism, p. 970
Osama Bin Laden, p. 971
John Kerry, p. 973

## Main Idea
In the late 1900s, the use of terrorism as a political tool began to spread.

⭐ **Background Knowledge** You have seen how the United States became involved in conflicts in the Middle East. In 2001, a tragic event brought these conflicts home to Americans.

## Terrorism on the World Stage

In recent decades, terrorism has emerged as a growing threat to world peace and security. Terrorism is the use of violence, often against civilian targets, to force political or social change. Through bombings, hijackings, kidnappings, and other violent acts, terrorists create a climate of fear. Although some attacks are carried out by lone individuals, other terrorists belong to well-organized groups.

**Roots of Terrorism** Terrorism has a long history. During Reconstruction, the Ku Klux Klan used terror tactics to keep African Americans from voting. The assassination that sparked World War I was planned by an organization of Balkan terrorists who sought independence from Austria-Hungary.

More recently, individuals and groups have carried out terrorist attacks in nations from Ireland to Sri Lanka. As you have read, Palestinian terrorists used suicide bombings in their war on Israel. Terrorism has also become a tool of Middle Eastern extremists who seek to eliminate American and Western influence from their lands.

**Abroad and at Home** At first, terrorist attacks against Americans generally occurred abroad. In 1988, an explosion on an airplane over Scotland killed 270 people, including 189 Americans. Between 1996 and 2000, terrorists in Africa and the Middle East launched deadly strikes against American embassies and ships.

In 1993, extremists from the Middle East launched an assault within the United States. A truck bomb exploded beneath one of the twin towers of the World Trade Center, the tallest buildings in New York. Six people were killed and more than 1,000 were injured. Authorities quickly captured most of the terrorists responsible.

The threat of terrorism was not only <u>external</u>. In 1995, a truck bomb destroyed a federal office building in Oklahoma City. The attack killed 168 people, including children in a day-care center. Investigations found that the murders were carried out by three young American men who resented the federal government.

**Vocabulary** *Builder*
<u>external</u> (ehks TER nahl) *adj.* on or from the outside

✓Checkpoint   **Give two early examples of terrorism.**

## The Nation Is Attacked

Despite the spread of terrorism, most Americans still felt secure at home. That sense of security vanished in a single day.

**A Day of Horror** On Tuesday morning, September 11, 2001, Arab terrorists seized four passenger jets that had taken off from Boston. The hijackers crashed two of the planes into the World Trade Center in New York and a third into the Pentagon in Washington, D.C. The fourth jet plummeted into a Pennsylvania field after passengers rushed the terrorists. Many now believe that the intended target of the fourth jet was the White House.

**Main Idea**
After the terrorist attacks of September 11, 2001, the United States took steps to protect its homeland.

# Links Across Time

### Acts of Terrorism

**1920** On September 16, a wagon filled with explosives shattered Wall Street, the heart of New York's financial district. Some 30 people were killed. The bombing was believed to be the work of anarchists, but no one was ever charged.

**1995** On August 19, a truck bomb destroyed a federal office building in Oklahoma City, killing 168 people. A former U.S. soldier was later tried and executed for the crime.

### Link to Today   nline

**Terrorism Today** In 2001, the nation was rocked by even deadlier terrorist attacks. How do these devastating acts affect our lives?

**For:** The impact of terrorism today
**Visit:** PHSchool.com
**Web Code:** mvc-9291

**1995** The Oklahoma City bombing was the worst terrorist attack on U.S. soil up to that time.

Many people escaped from the main towers of the World Trade Center, but fire and searing heat trapped others on upper floors. Firefighters and police rushed into the buildings to aid in the rescue. Then, as millions of dazed people watched on television or from the streets below, the towers collapsed, one by one.

Nearly 3,000 people were killed at the Pentagon, World Trade Center, and on the airplanes. Victims included citizens of some 80 nations and hundreds of rescuers. The mayor of New York later paid tribute to firefighters killed in the line of duty:

> **❝** The New York City firefighters who lost their lives will be remembered among the greatest heroes of American history. Like the brave soldiers who stormed the beaches of Normandy and those who raised the flag over Iwo Jima, our firefighters . . . gave their lives defending our liberty. **❞**
>
> —Rudolph W. Giuliani, *Brotherhood*

**The Nation Reacts** The tragedy of September 11 left Americans stunned, angry, and grief stricken. Yet, they quickly responded to the emergency. Millions lined up to give blood, aid in rescue efforts, or donate money and supplies to help victims and rescuers. Around the nation, Americans flew flags and took part in candlelight vigils. (See the Life at the Time feature in this chapter.) People around the world voiced their sympathy and support.

President George W. Bush expressed the nation's outrage. He vowed to "hunt down and punish those responsible." At the same time, he cautioned Americans not to take out their anger on innocent Arabs and Muslims. "No one should be singled out for unfair treatment or unkind words because of their ethnic background or religious faith," Bush said.

**Defending the Homeland** Bush took steps to protect the nation. He created the Office of Homeland Security to coordinate the country's counterterrorism efforts. Counterterrorism is action taken against terrorism. Counterterrorist goals include identifying and locating terrorists and safeguarding vital transportation, communication, and energy systems.

In December 2001, Bush signed the Patriot Act. It granted authorities sweeping powers to investigate and jail people suspected of having terrorist ties. Under the act, suspects might be held indefinitely without charges being filed and without being allowed to consult a lawyer. The law also enabled investigators to examine library records to see what books people had taken out.

**The Shock of September 11**
The morning after the September 11 terrorist attacks, newspapers across the country and around the world expressed a sense of shock and disbelief.
**Critical Thinking:** *Frame Questions* *What questions do you think Americans were asking immediately after the attacks?*

## Two Views of the Patriot Act

"The terrorists continue to plot against America and the civilized world. . . . We must continue to give homeland security and law enforcement personnel every tool they need to defend us. And one of those essential tools is the Patriot Act, which allows federal law enforcement to better share information, to track terrorists, to disrupt their cells, and to seize their assets."

—George W. Bush, State of the Union address, January 20, 2004

### Reading Primary Sources
#### Skills Activity

In the excerpt above, President Bush explains why he thinks the Patriot Act is necessary. Still, as the cartoon at right shows, many people viewed the new law as a threat to civil liberties.

**(a) Interpret Primary Sources** According to Bush, how does the Patriot Act make the United States safer?

**(b) Detect Points of View** Summarize the main point of the cartoon. How do you think Bush would respond?

The Patriot Act was controversial. Some people felt such strong measures were necessary for national security. Others believed the law was a threat to the liberties guaranteed in the Bill of Rights.

✓**Checkpoint** How did terrorists destroy the World Trade Center?

## The War on Terror

A suspect in the September 11 attacks soon emerged. Osama Bin Laden was a wealthy Saudi Arabian who ran a worldwide terrorist network called al Qaeda (al KĪ duh).

**Invading Afghanistan** Bin Laden took refuge in Afghanistan. There, he was protected by the ruling Taliban, a group of extremists. The Taliban regime was known as one of the most repressive governments in the world. From a mountain hideout, Bin Laden used cell phones and the Internet to run al Qaeda.

The Taliban refused to give up Bin Laden. U.S. troops then attacked Afghanistan in October 2001. The United States quickly toppled the Taliban from power and set up a new government to rebuild Afghanistan. However, Bin Laden escaped capture.

**War in Iraq** Bush next targeted Iraq as a threat. The Persian Gulf War of 1991 had not removed Iraqi dictator Saddam Hussein from power. Bush accused Hussein of having ties with Bin Laden. He also claimed that Hussein was developing weapons of mass destruction (WMDs), such as nuclear and chemical weapons.

**Main Idea**
Not all Americans agreed when President Bush ordered an attack on Iraq as part of a global war on terrorism.

## The War in Iraq

At left, an American soldier guards a checkpoint in Baghdad, Iraq, shortly after a deadly car bombing. Despite the continuing violence, millions of Iraqi citizens went to the polls on January 30, 2005, in the nation's first free election in 50 years. **Critical Thinking:** *Analyze Cause and Effect Describe a cause-and-effect link between these two photographs.*

**Vocabulary** *Builder*
<u>consume</u> (kahn SYOOM) *v.* to use up

Bush argued that the United States was justified in attacking another country it judged to be a threat, even if that country had not attacked first. This policy caused a rift between the United States and some of its key European allies, such as France and Germany. Other nations, such as Britain, pledged their support.

In March 2003, the United States led a coalition of about 30 nations in an attack on Iraq. Using advanced weapons, coalition forces smashed Iraq's defenses in six weeks. On May 1, Bush announced the end of major combat operations.

Rebuilding Iraq proved difficult. Militants and supporters of Hussein killed American troops and Iraqis. Attacks continued even after Hussein was captured late in 2003. Meanwhile, no WMDs were found, nor was any link to Bin Laden proved.

**Americans Divided** Most Americans supported the Iraq War. Bush's strong actions, they said, toppled a brutal dictator and promoted democracy. They hoped that free elections in 2005 would stabilize Iraq and provide a model for other Middle Eastern nations.

An outspoken minority criticized Bush's actions. They felt Iraq had not posed an immediate threat. Some even accused Bush of deceiving Americans about Iraqi WMDs. Other critics charged that the war <u>consumed</u> money, supplies, and troops that were needed to pursue Bin Laden and combat terrorism.

✓**Checkpoint**   Why did President Bush consider Saddam Hussein a threat?

# Election of 2004

The controversy over Iraq proved a major issue in the 2004 presidential election. Many Democrats were confident of victory. Polls seemed to indicate that a growing number of Americans were dissatisfied with the progress of the war in Iraq. In addition, tax cuts and spending on military and domestic programs had created a huge budget deficit.

The Democrats nominated Senator John Kerry of Massachusetts, a decorated Vietnam War veteran. The hard-fought campaign indicated how deeply Americans were divided over key issues. Kerry accused Bush of mishandling the war in Iraq. Bush charged that Kerry lacked the determination to fight terrorism.

On election day, Bush won the clear-cut victory in popular and electoral votes that had eluded him in 2000. Republicans also won expanded majorities in both houses of Congress.

During his second term, Bush turned to domestic issues, such as reforming Social Security. Still, by the summer of 2005, polls again indicated that Bush was losing support. A growing number of Americans were disturbed by the continued losses in Iraq and asked Bush to set a timetable for withdrawing U.S. troops. In response, Bush vowed to continue the war against terrorists. "We will fight them there, we will fight them across the world, and we will stay in the fight until the fight is won," he said.

**☑ Checkpoint** How did Bush and Kerry disagree over Iraq?

⭐ **Looking Back and Ahead** The global war on terrorism showed how events around the world had a powerful impact on Americans. In the next section, you will examine the role of the United States in a growing world economy.

**Main Idea**
The war in Iraq was a major issue in the presidential election of 2004.

**Draw Conclusions**
Draw a conclusion about whether Americans generally accepted or opposed the decision to send troops into Iraq.

---

| Section 1 | **Check Your Progress** |

**Progress Monitoring Online**
**For:** Self-test with instant help
**Visit:** PHSchool.com
**Web Code:** mva-9291

## Comprehension and Critical Thinking

**1. (a) Summarize** How did the United States respond to the terrorist attacks of September 11, 2001?

**(b) Apply Information** Agree or disagree with the following statement: The battle between the United States and terrorism did not begin on September 11. Give reasons for your answer.

**2. (a) Describe** Why did President Bush send troops into Afghanistan and Iraq?

**(b) Detect Points of View** Summarize one argument for the war in Iraq and one argument against it.

## Reading Skill

**3. Draw Conclusions** Based on your reading of this section, draw a conclusion to describe how a terrorist differs from a soldier.

## Vocabulary *Builder*

**4.** Write definitions of the key terms terrorism and counterterrorism. Then, based on those definitions, define the prefix *counter-*.

## Writing

**5.** Write a paragraph ending a narrative by someone who was in New York City or in Washington, D.C., on September 11, 2001. The paragraph should sum up the narrator's reactions to the events of that day. It should also explain the long-term effects of September 11 on his or her life.

# 9/11: Courage and Remembrance

September 11, 2001, has been called "the day that changed America." In the days following the terrorist attacks, Americans responded with sorrow, anger, hard work, and a renewed sense of unity and patriotism.

### ◀ Rescue and Recovery ▲

The place where the twin towers of the World Trade Center collapsed became known as Ground Zero. For the first few days, rescue teams used specially trained dogs to search for survivors in the rubble. Recovery and clearance efforts went on for many months more.

**Explore More Video**

To learn more about the September 11 terrorist attacks, view the video.

## Coming Together ▲

All over the country, Americans gathered for candlelight vigils.

▶

A rescue worker and a relative of a victim embrace during a memorial service at Yankee Stadium.

## ◀ Remembering the Victims

Americans vowed never to forget the people killed in the attacks. In New York, Washington, and Pennsylvania, people left notes, pictures, flowers, and flags to honor the victims.

### *Analyze* LIFE AT THE TIME

Choose two of the photographs on these pages. For each photograph, write a caption that describes the emotions of the people shown. Then, describe your own feelings as you look at those pictures.

# Economy and the Environment

## Objectives

1. Explore the role of the United States in the new global economy.
2. Understand the goals of the environmental movement.
3. Learn about the problem of energy and possible solutions.

## Prepare to Read

### 🔁 Reading Skill

**Support Conclusions With Evidence** Remember that any conclusions you draw must be supported with evidence. To find this evidence, first read the text carefully. What does it say? What conclusion do you think can be drawn? Then, look back at the text details. What details support your instinctive conclusion? Is there evidence from outside the text, such as from your personal knowledge, that can help you support the conclusion? Add up the evidence and adjust your conclusion if necessary.

### Vocabulary *Builder*

**High-Use Words**

<u>provoke</u>, p. 977
<u>fossil</u>, p. 980

**Key Terms and People**

globalization, p. 976
trade deficit, p. 976
outsourcing, p. 976
free trade, p. 977
Rachel Carson, p. 978
environmentalist, p. 978
renewable resource, p. 980
global warming, p. 981

☆ **Background Knowledge** Since colonial times, Americans have traded with other parts of the world. In recent years, foreign economic ties have grown even stronger. In this section, you will explore how economic and environmental issues link the world.

## A World Linked by Trade

Since 1970, trade between the United States and other nations has more than doubled. Today, foreign trade accounts for about 25 percent of the American economy. This trend is part of the increasing globalization of the economy. Globalization is the process of creating an international network.

**Trade Deficits** American manufacturers face a disadvantage in the global economy. Workers in Latin America, Eastern Europe, and Asia are generally paid less than American workers. As a result, many foreign goods are cheaper to produce and can be sold at lower prices. Competition with low-priced foreign goods has led to trade deficits. A trade deficit occurs when a country buys more from other nations than it sells to them. In 2003, the U.S. trade deficit reached almost $500 billion.

In response, more American companies have turned to outsourcing, or having work done in other countries. By building

**Main Idea**
The elimination of trade barriers between nations led to growth but also caused controversy.

American sneaker factory in Vietnam

factories in places such as Mexico and Southeast Asia, American manufacturers can take advantage of cheap labor. But critics charge that outsourcing hurts American workers.

**Tariffs or Free Trade?** Foreign competition has <u>provoked</u> heated debate. Some argue that the United States should protect American profits and jobs by raising tariffs on foreign goods. Others say that tariffs spark expensive "trade wars," leading other nations to raise tariffs on American goods. Instead, opponents of tariffs favor free trade, or the removal of trade barriers. Free trade, they claim, increases business and creates new jobs around the world.

In 1993, President Clinton signed the North American Free Trade Agreement (NAFTA). The treaty removed trade barriers among the United States, Mexico, and Canada. Clinton said:

> ❝We know that it's not just the United States, no wealthy country in the world today can create new jobs without expanding trade. It cannot be done.❞
>
> —Bill Clinton, Speech, October 20, 1993

Most experts agree that NAFTA, along with global trade regulators such as the World Trade Organization (WTO), has increased trade and generated jobs.

Vocabulary *Builder*
**provoke** (prah VOHK) *v.* to excite; to cause an action

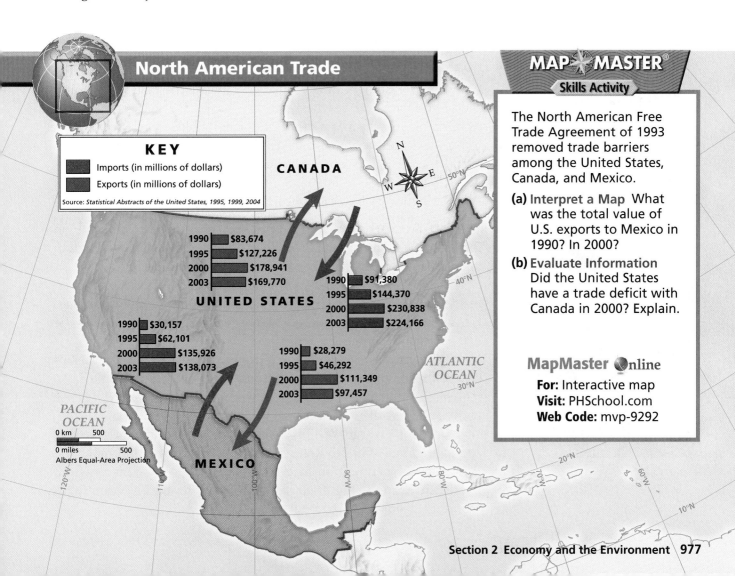

**North American Trade**

**MAP MASTER®**

**Skills Activity**

KEY

▬ Imports (in millions of dollars)

▬ Exports (in millions of dollars)

Source: *Statistical Abstracts of the United States, 1995, 1999, 2004*

**CANADA**

1990 | $83,674
1995 | $127,226
2000 | $178,941
2003 | $169,770

**UNITED STATES**

1990 | $91,380
1995 | $144,370
2000 | $230,838
2003 | $224,166

1990 | $30,157
1995 | $62,101
2000 | $135,926
2003 | $138,073

1990 | $28,279
1995 | $46,292
2000 | $111,349
2003 | $97,457

*PACIFIC OCEAN*

0 km 500
0 miles 500
Albers Equal-Area Projection

**MEXICO**

*ATLANTIC OCEAN*

The North American Free Trade Agreement of 1993 removed trade barriers among the United States, Canada, and Mexico.

**(a) Interpret a Map** What was the total value of U.S. exports to Mexico in 1990? In 2000?

**(b) Evaluate Information** Did the United States have a trade deficit with Canada in 2000? Explain.

**MapMaster ●nline**

**For:** Interactive map
**Visit:** PHSchool.com
**Web Code:** mvp-9292

Still, opponents of free trade charge that trade agreements weaken efforts to safeguard workers' rights and the environment. NAFTA, for example, has led American makers of auto parts to move to Mexico, where labor and antipollution laws are less strict.

Meetings of the WTO and other trade organizations have drawn thousands of angry demonstrators. In 2001 alone, protesters tried to disrupt international trade meetings in Canada, Sweden, and Italy.

☑**Checkpoint**  **How did NAFTA encourage free trade?**

## The Environment

The environment is tied to the global economy. Polluted air or water in one country affects the people and economies of other countries. Natural disasters such as hurricanes, tornadoes, and earthquakes destroy lives and property and change the landscape. Individuals and nations differ over how to solve the problems.

**The Environmental Movement** The modern environmental movement began with Rachel Carson. Carson, a marine biologist, published *Silent Spring* in 1962. The book warned that DDT, a chemical used by farmers to kill insects, remained in the environment, killing birds and fish, and might eventually contaminate human food supplies. As a result of *Silent Spring,* Congress passed a law restricting the use of the chemical DDT.

A series of environmental disasters increased public alarm. In 1969, an oil spill fouled the ocean for hundreds of miles along the California coastline. Smog blanketed cities across the nation, and sewage washed onto beaches.

Organizations such as the Sierra Club lobbied Congress for laws to protect the environment. In April 1970, environmentalists organized the first Earth Day. An **environmentalist** is a reformer who seeks to protect the environment. Some 20 million Americans massed across the country to voice concern over threats to the environment.

**Taking Action** Under public pressure, the Nixon administration formed the Environmental Protection Agency (EPA). New legislation targeted auto emissions, lakes, and rivers for cleanup.

Local governments also took action. Many communities required residents to recycle glass, paper, and aluminum. Recycling reduces the amount of garbage that must be buried or burned and slows the rate at which resources are consumed.

The environmental movement has spawned controversy. Critics charge that environmental regulations are costly. For example, laws requiring automakers to add pollution control devices to cars are costly and raise the price of cars.

President George W. Bush called for oil drilling in Alaska's Arctic National Wildlife Refuge to reduce fuel prices and make the nation less dependent on foreign oil. Environmentalists resisted, but Bush argued that their concerns had to be balanced with economic needs.

**Main Idea**
In recent years, more people have become concerned about threats to the world's physical environment.

Rachel Carson

**The Wrath of Katrina** Natural disasters can cause great distress to the environment and the economy. On August 29, 2005, Hurricane Katrina swirled out of the Gulf of Mexico and tore into Louisiana, Mississippi, and Alabama, smashing an area as big as Great Britain. Winds of up to 175 miles per hour blew down buildings, ripped up roads, snapped power lines, and drove as many as one million people from their homes. Levees, or protective embankments, were washed away. The city of New Orleans lay defenseless against surging floodwaters. "The world we know is no more," said a survivor. It was one of the worst natural disasters in U.S. history.

For days, stranded victims wandered the flooded streets of New Orleans in search of food and clean water. Tens of thousands sought shelter in the Superdome, a large sports arena. But the arena was inadequate for the massive numbers of evacuees.

While the federal government began its response, people helped people. Within days, private contributions reached a record $200 million. Cities as far away as Detroit promised free hotel rooms to those with no place to live. Families, friends, and strangers opened their doors to survivors. In Texas, the Houston Astrodome took in thousands and fed them three meals a day prepared by local churches and charities. More than 20 countries, including Afghanistan and Honduras, pledged aid.

Early estimates put losses at a staggering $100 billion. The port of New Orleans, the busiest in the nation, shut down. One fourth of U.S. oil output and 10 percent of its refined oil come from the Gulf Coast. When these operations shut down, energy costs spiked upward. In the wake of Katrina, the Gulf Coast states and the nation started on the long road to recovery.

**Hurricane Katrina**
With winds of up to 175 miles per hour, Hurricane Katrina caused severe damage to coastal communities along the Gulf of Mexico. Here, a helicopter rescues people trapped on the roof of their house. **Critical Thinking: Analyze Cause and Effect** *What were some of the social and economic effects of the storm?*

☑**Checkpoint** **What steps did the federal government take to protect the environment?**

# The Energy Supply

The disrupted oil production after Hurricane Katrina underlined the importance of energy conservation. Accounting for less than 5 percent of the world's population, the United States uses over 25 percent of the world's energy supplies.

**Oil Embargo** In 1973, Arab members of OPEC voted to cut off oil supplies to the United States. The oil embargo deprived the United States of Middle Eastern oil for a year. The price of a barrel of oil quadrupled, from $3 to $12. Oil shortages became severe. Motorists sometimes waited hours for a few gallons of gasoline.

**Main Idea**
Growing dependence on foreign oil has led many Americans to seek other sources of energy.

## Sources of Energy

| Energy Source | Advantages | Disadvantages |
|---|---|---|
| Oil | ■ Easy to extract and transport<br>■ Efficient source of energy | ■ Produces air pollution<br>■ A few countries control the supply of oil<br>■ Nonrenewable source |
| Coal | ■ Inexpensive<br>■ Large amounts exist in the United States | ■ Produces air pollution<br>■ Nonrenewable source |
| Wind | ■ Free if available<br>■ Renewable source | ■ Varies by place<br>■ Can affect endangered birds |
| Solar | ■ Produces no waste or pollution<br>■ Renewable source | ■ Requires large equipment<br>■ Availability depends on the weather |
| Nuclear | ■ Almost limitless energy<br>■ No air pollution | ■ Produces long-lasting radioactive wastes<br>■ Possible radiation leak |

### Reading Charts
#### Skills Activity

Americans have explored a variety of alternative energy sources.

**(a) Interpret Charts** What is one advantage of solar power? What is one drawback?

**(b) Evaluate Information** Do you think the advantages of nuclear power outweigh the disadvantages? Why or why not?

**Vocabulary** *Builder*
**fossil** (FAH sihl) *n.* hardened remains of a plant or an animal that lived long ago

**Support Conclusions With Evidence**
Find evidence to support the following conclusion: For now, the United States continues to be dependent on foreign oil.

In response to the oil shortage, Americans tried to conserve oil. New legislation ordered car makers to improve fuel efficiency. The government created an oil reserve to guard against future boycotts. People lowered the settings on their thermostats, insulated their attics to save heating oil, and bought smaller cars that used less gas.

**Alternative Energy Sources** The OPEC oil embargo also increased pressure to find alternative sources of energy. Each alternative offers both drawbacks and advantages.

The United States has plentiful supplies of coal. However, fossil fuels, such as petroleum and coal, take thousands of years to form and are not easily replaced. Environmentalists encourage the use of **renewable resources,** or energy sources that are more easily restored by nature.

Water, solar energy, and wind are renewable resources that can each be turned into electricity. However, water power is available only in areas with plentiful rivers. The equipment for collecting solar energy takes up too much space to be used on a large scale. Wind does not blow steadily, so the energy collected varies widely.

Nuclear power plants hold out the hope of near-limitless energy. However, nuclear plants are costly and produce radioactive waste that lasts for thousands of years. In 1979, an accident at the Three-Mile Island nuclear power plant in Pennsylvania raised the threat of radiation leaks. Leaking radiation has led to environmental and health problems across Europe.

☑**Checkpoint**　What is a major disadvantage of fossil fuels?

# The Question of Global Warming

Environmentalists have become concerned about the possibility of global warming, or a worldwide rise in temperatures. Since the late 1800s, scientists have recorded a general rise in world temperatures. Many blamed this trend on "greenhouse gases," such as carbon dioxide, emitted by cars, factories, and homes. According to the Environmental Protection Agency, "There is no doubt" that human activities are rapidly adding greenhouse gases to the atmosphere, and that these gases "tend to warm our planet."

Still, there was disagreement about the possible danger of global warming. Environmentalists warned that shifting temperatures could turn green fields into deserts and threaten the existence of many plants and animals. But some scientists pointed out that Earth had gone through many cold and warm periods in the past. The EPA noted, "The fundamental scientific uncertainties are these: How much more warming will occur? How fast will this warming occur? And what are the potential adverse and beneficial effects?"

In an effort to deal with the possibility of global warming, the United States signed the Kyoto Protocol in 1997. In this agreement, industrialized nations pledged to reduce carbon dioxide emissions. However, President Bush rejected the Kyoto Protocol in 2001. He argued that the evidence for global warming was not enough to justify the cost for American businesses.

**☑ Checkpoint** **Why does global warming concern many scientists?**

⭐ **Looking Back and Ahead** Although technology is blamed for many environmental problems, it may also hold the key to solving these problems. In the next section, you will explore other ways science and technology have changed the world.

**Main Idea**
Many environmentalists fear that rising temperatures may someday threaten life on Earth.

Satellite image of Earth

---

Section 2 | **Check Your Progress**

**Progress Monitoring** Online
**For:** Self-test with instant help
**Visit:** PHSchool.com
**Web Code:** mva-9292

## Comprehension and Critical Thinking

**1. (a) Explain** Why did the United States experience a trade deficit in the late 1900s?
**(b) Identify Alternatives** Suggest two ways that the United States might reduce its trade deficit.

**2. (a) Recall** What role did Rachel Carson play in the modern environmental movement?
**(b) Compare** Recall what you learned about the Progressive Era. How was Carson's role similar to that of muckrakers?

## 🔁 Reading Skill

**3. Support Conclusions With Evidence** Give two examples from Section 2 to support the following conclusion: The goal of protecting the environment sometimes conflicts with the goal of expanding the economy.

## Vocabulary *Builder*

Complete each of the following sentences so that the second part further explains the first part and clearly shows your understanding of the key term.
**4.** Solar and water power are renewable resources, _____.

**5.** Reducing tariffs are one way of encouraging free trade, _____.
**6.** Many companies reduced costs by outsourcing, _____.

## Writing

**7.** Rewrite the following sentences to make the time sequence more clear: During the 1950s, gasoline cost about 27 cents per gallon. During the Arab oil embargo, the price more than doubled. In 1925, you could buy a full tank of gas for less than a dollar. Now, more than 30 years later, that 1974 price of 57 cents per gallon looks good!

# Science and Technology

## Objectives

1. Explore the ways in which computers have transformed American life.

2. Discover some of the recent achievements of medical science.

## Prepare to Read

###  Reading Skill

**Make Generalizations** A generalization is a broad statement that can be applied to a variety of situations. To make a generalization, identify the main points or ideas. Then, develop a general principle or statement that applies to all of the points or ideas. You may need to include main points or ideas from earlier readings or from your own knowledge.

### Vocabulary *Builder*

**High-Use Words**
flexible, p. 983
distribute, p. 985

**Key Terms**
e-commerce, p. 983
laser, p. 983
cloning, p. 985

⭐ **Background Knowledge** You have seen many examples of the powerful impact of technology, from the Industrial Revolution of the early 1800s to the invention of the telephone and automobile to the development of deadly new weapons of war. In this section, you will explore advances in science and technology.

## Main Idea

The development of computers led to an information revolution.

## The Computer Age

Perhaps no recent technology has revolutionized daily life as much as the computer. With computers, vast amounts of information can be stored, analyzed, and shared in a flash.

**Rapid Advances** Before the 1970s, machines called mainframes did most of the computing. These costly mainframes weighed tons and filled whole rooms. They were used chiefly by governments, universities, and big businesses.

The invention of transistors, circuits on tiny silicon chips, led to the development of smaller computers. In 1977, a new company, Apple, introduced the first computer for home use. Four years later, International Business Machines (IBM) marketed its own personal computer.

Computer hardware became smaller, and software became easier to use. In the 1970s, Bill Gates, a young Harvard dropout, began developing software that would let ordinary people run computers. Gates cofounded Microsoft, which became one of the world's most successful businesses. By 1990, Americans were buying more than nine million computers every year for their homes, offices, and schools.

Mainframe computer, 1950

**An Information Revolution** In 1969, the Department of Defense began to link its computers with those in a number of American universities. This electronic network formed the basis of the Internet.

The Internet helped to create an information revolution. In 1989, British scientist Tim Berners-Lee proposed the World Wide Web, a visual presentation of information that was easy to use. By 2003, more than half of all Americans used the Internet to find information and communicate.

**E-commerce,** or buying and selling online, is growing rapidly as companies use the Internet to advertise and conduct business. More people are using the Internet to manage bank accounts, pay bills, and buy airline tickets and other items.

The development of satellite technology has added to the information revolution. Telecommunications satellites orbiting Earth carry millions of radio and television signals.

**Difficult Issues** Like all the other technological advances, the information revolution has draw-backs. Today, computers keep records about almost everything we do. As a result, "hackers" who tap into computers can threaten our privacy. Computer hacking has contributed to the spread of a new crime, identity theft. People also fear that telecommunications systems might become a target for terrorists seeking to disrupt our lives and economy.

Cellular phones, introduced in 1973, may be another threat to privacy. Many Americans favor a ban on the use of cell phones in public places, such as restaurants and airplanes. They argue that people have a right to sit in peace and quiet without being forced to listen to other people's conversations. Cell phone use has also been blamed for many auto accidents. Many states now allow people to use only hands-free cell phones while driving.

**✔Checkpoint** How did computers become smaller?

## Biography Quest

### Bill Gates
### born 1955

Computer software made Bill Gates the richest American of his time. He has also given away more money than any American of his time.

In 2004, Gates pledged $1 billion to send minority students to college. Close to 1,000 African American, Latino, Native American, and Asian students will be eligible for these scholarships. Gates has also promised $15 million to help improve educational standards in high schools.

**Biography Quest**

**What did Gates do to promote world health?**

**For:** The answer to the question about Gates

**Visit:** PHSchool.com

**Web Code:** myd-9293

## Medical Advances

New technology has aided doctors in the detection and treatment of many medical problems. For example, lasers, or powerful beams of focused light, have become a critical tool for surgeons. Beams of laser light are more <u>flexible</u> than scalpels and can be focused on a much smaller area. Using lasers, doctors can now perform delicate eye and skin surgery. Researchers are studying how lasers might be used to treat one of the nation's leading killers, heart disease.

**Main Idea**
Technology helps detect and treat medical problems.

**Vocabulary *Builder***
<u>flexible</u> (FLEHKS ah bahl) *adj.* easily bent; able to be used in many ways

# Technology of Modern Medicine

Thanks to modern technology, doctors today can diagnose illnesses more accurately than ever before. They can also make repairs to the human body that earlier doctors could only dream of. **Critical Thinking:** *Apply Information Based on what you have seen or heard, identify one other type of technology used by doctors today.*

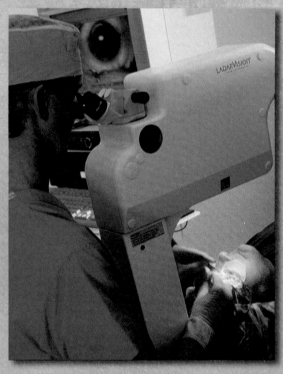

**Laser Surgery ▶**
This doctor is using a laser to change the shape of a patient's cornea. This type of surgery, known as LASIK, can reduce or eliminate a person's need for eyeglasses. Lasers are also used for many other types of microsurgery.

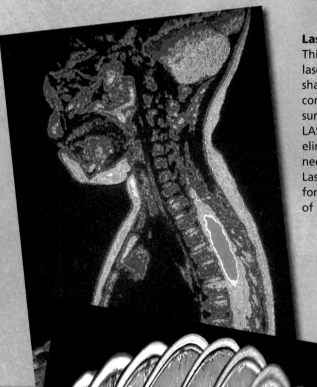

**Bionics**
Bionics is the design of replacement body parts. The man here lost his hand in a train accident. His bionic hand works so well ▼ that he can even use it to play the keyboard. ▼

▲
**Magnetic Resonance Imaging**
The MRI gives doctors an incredible look inside the human body. Top: The red area indicates a spinal tumor. Bottom: MRI "slices" give a cross section of the brain of a healthy 16-year-old boy.

Another new medical tool, magnetic resonance imaging (MRI), provides an accurate view of internal organs and systems. Using MRIs helps doctors identify injuries or signs of illness while reducing the need for surgery.

**The AIDS Epidemic** In recent decades, new diseases have challenged medical science. Perhaps the most deadly is Acquired Immune Deficiency Syndrome (AIDS). Since it began in the 1980s, the AIDS epidemic has killed millions of people in the United States and around the globe. In some African countries, over 20 percent of the population is infected with the virus causing AIDS.

New drugs have extended the lives of many sufferers, but the drugs are too expensive for most people in developing countries. In 2003, President Bush promised a $15 billion program to <u>distribute</u> these medicines in a bold "assault on the global AIDS pandemic."

**Cloning** One of the most controversial areas of medical research involves cloning. Cloning is the process of making a genetic double of a plant or an animal. Cloning made headlines in 1997 when a Scottish researcher cloned a sheep named "Dolly." In 2004, South Korean scientists cloned a human embryo.

Many people worry about the biological and ethical dangers of cloning human beings. In 1997, President Clinton prohibited federal funding of human cloning. Still, many believe that cloning research may help find cures for people with serious medical conditions.

✓**Checkpoint** **How has AIDS affected the world?**

☆ **Looking Back and Ahead** In this section, you have seen how technology has transformed our lives. In the next section, you will examine other ways that American society has changed.

**Vocabulary *Builder***
**distribute** (dihs TRIHB yoot) *v.* to spread in an orderly way

**Make Generalizations**
Make a generalization about the relationship between science and ethics.

---

Section 3 | **Check Your Progress**

**Progress Monitoring** ⊕nline
**For:** Self-test with instant help
**Visit:** PHSchool.com
**Web Code:** mva-9293

**Comprehension and Critical Thinking**

1. **(a) Summarize** Describe the development of the computer.
**(b) Make Inferences** Do you think computers would have had the same impact on society without the development of the semiconductor?

2. **(a) Recall** What new technologies have aided medical research?
**(b) Detect Points of View** How has technology transformed our lives?

**Reading Skill**

3. **Make Generalizations** Make a generalization about the impact of computers and cellular telephones on American society.

**Vocabulary *Builder***

4. Draw a table with three rows and three columns. In the first column, list the following terms: e-commerce, laser, cloning. In the next column, write the definition of each word. In the last column, make a small illustration that shows the meaning of the word.

**Writing**

5. Revise the following paragraph to improve the style and create a consistent tone: I remember the first time I tried to use a mouse. I was in a computer store in the early 1980s looking at a display for the new computer. I was used to arrow keys. They made the cursor go up and down, back and forth. I was just fine with them. The mouse seemed harder to control. So I gave up and walked away. Who'd've thought I'd be comfortable today?

**Section 3 Science and Technology 985**

# A Changing Society

## Objectives

1. Learn how immigration and population patterns have changed in recent decades.

2. Discover how progress toward equal rights has continued for many Americans.

3. Explore issues that affect American schools and families.

## Prepare to Read

### Reading Skill

**Support Generalizations With Evidence** It is important when making generalizations to support them with evidence. Otherwise they can become overstatements or even statements of bias. As you read Section 4, look for evidence to support the generalizations offered.

### Vocabulary *Builder*

**High-Use Words**

enrich, p. 987

evident, p. 989

**Key Terms and People**

refugee, p. 986

undocumented worker, p. 987

guest worker, p. 987

Condoleezza Rice, p. 989

Sandra Day O'Connor, p. 990

**Main Idea**
As immigration has increased, Americans have become concerned about illegal immigration.

⭐ **Background Knowledge** As you have learned, from its earliest years, the United States attracted immigrants from around the world. In this section, you will learn how immigration is just one factor that continues to change and challenge American society.

## Changing Immigration Patterns

Today, more immigrants enter the United States every year than at any time since the early 1900s. As in the past, many newcomers are seeking economic opportunities. Others are refugees, people who flee war or persecution in their own countries.

**Sources of Immigration** As you have read, immigration laws of the 1920s set up a quota system that favored immigrants from Northern Europe. In 1965, President Lyndon Johnson signed a new immigration law. It ended decades of limits on non-Europeans who wanted to enter the country. As a result, immigration patterns underwent a radical change.

No immigrant group has grown more rapidly than Asians. Many refugees fled war or political oppression in countries such as Vietnam and China. The lure of education and jobs has drawn a growing number of people from India, Korea, and the Philippines.

Latin America has continued to be the largest source of immigration. Many refugees fled dictatorships in Cuba and Chile or civil wars in El Salvador, Guatemala, and Nicaragua. Poverty drove much immigration from Mexico, Central America, and the Caribbean.

Immigration from Europe has continued as well. Since the end of the Cold War, many newcomers have come from Eastern Europe and the former Soviet Union.

New citizens from Ethiopia and India

Many Americans welcome the newcomers as hardworking people whose diverse cultures <u>enrich</u> American life. Others claim that cheap immigrant labor drives down wages and that immigrants drain funds for education, health care, and welfare.

**Changing Policies** Much of the resentment has focused on **undocumented workers,** laborers who enter the country without legal permission. The Immigration Reform and Control Act of 1986 imposed stiff penalties on employers who hired undocumented workers. At the same time, the law permitted illegal immigrants who came before 1982 to apply for citizenship.

The terrorist attacks of September 11, 2001, raised new concerns about immigration. The attacks had been carried out by terrorists from the Middle East. Federal officials feared that other immigrants might be linked to terrorist groups. They monitored foreign-born college students and professors, as well as other immigrants.

In 2004, President Bush proposed a policy allowing more **guest workers,** or temporary immigrant workers, to enter the country. The goal, he said, was "to match willing foreign workers with willing employers when no Americans can be found to fill the job." Still, debate continues over how best to address illegal immigration.

✓**Checkpoint** **Why are many Americans concerned about increased immigration?**

**Vocabulary** *Builder*
enrich (ehn RIHCH) *v.* to make richer or fuller; to improve

**Support Generalizations With Evidence**

Find evidence in the text to support this generalization: People become less welcoming when their economic security or sense of safety is threatened.

**History** *Interactive*

**Explore Trends in Immigration**
**Visit:** PHSchool.com
**Web Code:** mvl-9294

## Changing Immigration Patterns

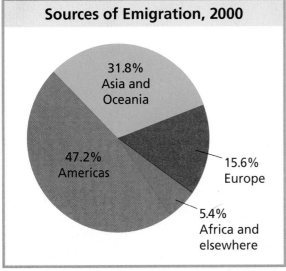

**Sources of Emigration, 2000**

31.8% Asia and Oceania

47.2% Americas

15.6% Europe

5.4% Africa and elsewhere

Source: *Statistical Yearbook of the Immigration and Naturalization Service*

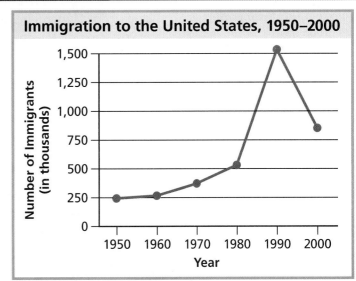

**Immigration to the United States, 1950–2000**

Source: *Yearbook of Immigration Statistics, 2003*

**Reading Charts**
**Skills Activity**

In the 1960s, new laws ended many restrictions on immigration. Since then, immigration has increased. The places immigrants come from have also changed.

**(a) Interpret Charts** How much did yearly immigration rates increase between 1950 and 2000?

**(b) Contrast** Compare these graphs to the ones in a previous chapter. How have immigration patterns changed since the early 1900s?

Recent changes to the American population have included great diversity, an increase in the number of older Americans, and a shift in population to the South and West.

# A Changing Population

Immigration has contributed to shifts in the nation's population. For example, the nation has grown more diverse in terms of religion. While the vast majority of Americans classify themselves as Christian, growing numbers are Muslim, Hindu, or Buddhist.

**Latinos: The Largest Minority** In 2003, Latinos, or Hispanics, became the largest ethnic minority in the United States, making up 12.5 percent of the total population. The terms *Latino* and *Hispanic* refer to people of Latin American birth or descent, as well as to people who speak Spanish as their primary language.

The impact of this shift has been dramatic. In the 1990s, Miami, Florida, became the first major U.S. city with a Latino majority. The political and economic influence of the Latino community has also grown. By 2003, Latinos boasted 23 members of the House of Representatives. The number of Latino-owned businesses grew four times in 20 years.

Still, many Latinos continue to struggle. Nearly four Latino children in ten lived in poverty in 2003. Unemployment rates for Latinos was greater than that of the national average.

**Asian Americans** By 2000, 11 million Americans were of Asian descent. A large number enjoyed economic success, due, in part, to a high level of education. The average incomes of Japanese and South Asians in the United States were above the national average.

Still, in cities with large Asian populations, more Asians than whites work in low-paying jobs. Some Asian immigrants who were doctors or lawyers in their own countries have been unable to obtain licenses to practice their professions in the United States.

**A Growing Population**

Latino neighborhoods like this one are now a vital part of most large American cities. The pie graph below shows the varied origins of the nation's growing Latino population. **Critical Thinking:** *Apply Information In which group shown on the pie chart are the people American citizens from birth?*

## Latinos by Region of Origin, 2000

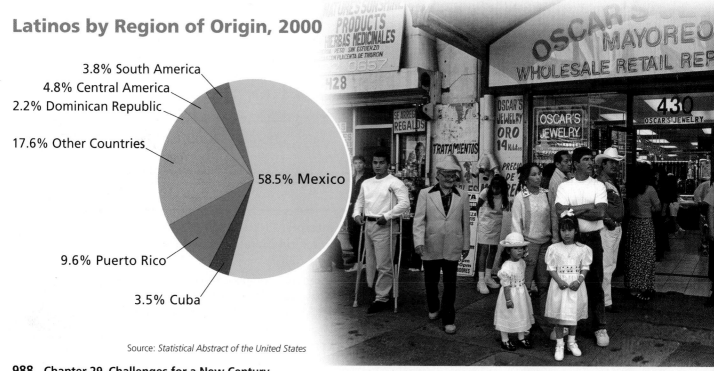

3.8% South America
4.8% Central America
2.2% Dominican Republic
17.6% Other Countries
58.5% Mexico
9.6% Puerto Rico
3.5% Cuba

Source: *Statistical Abstract of the United States*

**An Aging Population** In recent decades, birthrates have been declining. In addition, thanks to improved medical care, people live longer than ever before. As a result, the percentage of older Americans is far greater than it was 50 years ago. The 2000 census indicated that 12.4 percent of the population was over the age of 65. Older Americans have gained political strength because the percentage of older people who vote is larger than that of younger people.

The aging population has raised concern about issues such as health care and Social Security. Many worry that the number of people collecting Social Security will rise faster than the number of people paying Social Security taxes. By 2005, the future of Social Security was one of the most hotly debated domestic issues.

**People on the Move** Centers of population have also shifted. More people and industries have moved from the colder states of the Northeast and Midwest to the warmer climates of the South and Southwest, nicknamed the Sunbelt. The 2000 census showed that sunny Nevada was the fastest growing state in the union.

The political consequences of this population shift have been evident. As their populations increased, Sunbelt states have won more representation in Congress and more electoral votes.

☑Checkpoint **What is the nation's largest ethnic minority?**

Vocabulary *Builder*
<u>evident</u> (EHV ih dehnt) *adj.* clear; obvious

# Expanding Opportunities

In Chapter 26, you learned about the civil rights movement of the 1950s and 1960s. Since then, many groups continued to make progress toward equal rights and opportunities.

**African Americans** The civil rights movement produced economic and political gains for African Americans. Employment rose and the African American middle class expanded. By 2000, more African Americans were earning college degrees and fewer were living in poverty.

Over 10,000 African Americans held public office. In the presidency of George W. Bush, African Americans achieved two key firsts. Colin Powell became the first African American secretary of state, while Condoleezza Rice served as national security adviser. Rice later succeeded Powell as secretary of state.

Despite such advances, problems persisted. In 2003, unemployment for African Americans stood at twice that for whites. The number of African American children living below the poverty level was more than three times that of white children.

**Women** By 2000, six of ten American women worked outside of the home. Many held jobs once closed to them, such as firefighter, airline pilot, and police officer. Growing numbers have become lawyers, professors, stockbrokers, and doctors.

**Main Idea**
African Americans, women, and Native Americans have made economic progress but still face challenges.

Secretary of State Condoleezza Rice meets with the president of Mexico

Still, women often faced economic challenges. Top jobs in management often go to men. Women generally earn less than men, and they continue to head most single-parent households.

Women have expanded their role in government. In 1981, President Reagan appointed Sandra Day O'Connor the first woman to sit on the Supreme Court. An increasing number of women have served in the Cabinet, in Congress, and as governors.

**Native Americans** In the 2000 census, more than four million people identified themselves as American Indian, or Native American. Only a third of modern-day Indians live on reservations. Over half live in cities. High rates of unemployment, poverty, and juvenile delinquency continue to plague Indian communities.

Still, Indians have made progress as tribes won greater power. In 1978, the American Indian Religious Freedom Act prohibited the government from interfering with Indian religious customs. On reservations, businesses such as banks, factories, and gambling casinos are strengthening tribal economies.

✓**Checkpoint** **What economic advances have women made?**

# Challenges for the Young

Younger Americans face difficult challenges in the twenty-first century. One agonizing problem has been the outbreak of violence in American schools. Between 1996 and 2003, hundreds of students were killed or wounded in armed attacks on school grounds. Often, the attackers were students themselves. Schools began to install metal detectors, enlist police in patrolling halls, and train students and teachers in resolving conflicts peacefully.

Illegal drug use has also been a problem. One study showed that half of all high school students knew where to buy drugs. Some schools have used random drug testing to identify students who use illegal drugs. But a debate rages over whether to treat drug abuse as a criminal problem that deserves stiff penalties or as a social problem best addressed through therapy.

Another type of drug problem has recently gained attention. In 2005, Congress investigated the illegal use of steroids, chemicals that increased muscle size, by professional athletes. Steroid use also increased among high school students. Health experts warn that steroid use can lead to physical and emotional problems, such as cancer, depression, and an increase in aggressive behavior. Many people also worry that steroid use encourages cheating.

✓**Checkpoint** **How have schools tried to combat violence?**

**Main Idea**
Young Americans are deeply affected by issues such as violence and drug use.

**War on Drugs**
These students are taking part in Red Ribbon Week, a national campaign in which young people wear red ribbons to call attention to the fight against illegal drugs. **Critical Thinking: *Draw Conclusions*** *Why do you think many antidrug messages are aimed at people your age or younger?*

# Looking Back and Ahead

**Main Idea**
Shared values help bind Americans together despite their differences.

How can Americans best meet the challenges of a new century? For many, the answer to that question lies in the enduring ideals on which the country was founded.

When Arnold Schwarzenegger, an Austrian immigrant, became governor of California in 2003, he spoke of the American past and how it can serve as a model for the future:

> **"**For guidance, let's look back in history to a period I studied when I became a citizen. The summer of 1787. Delegates of the original 13 states were meeting in Philadelphia. . . . Divisions were deep. Merchant against farmer. Big states against small. North against South. . . . What happened in that summer of 1787 is that they put their differences aside—and produced the blueprint for our government: our Constitution.**"**
>
> —Arnold Schwarzenegger, inaugural address, November 17, 2003

Since that time, the United States has continued to face difficult crises and deep divisions. During the Civil War, these divisions nearly tore the union apart. Yet, an American identity has sprung from shared values: faith in democracy, respect for individual rights, tolerance for different viewpoints, the opportunity to build a better future. These ideals define us as a nation and as a people.

☑**Checkpoint** **Identify two values that most Americans share.**

Americans visiting Mount Rushmore National Memorial in South Dakota

---

## Section 4 | Check Your Progress

**Progress Monitoring** ●nline
**For:** Self-test with instant help
**Visit:** PHSchool.com
**Web Code:** mva-9294

### Comprehension and Critical Thinking

**1. (a) Recall** How have immigration patterns changed since the 1960s?
**(b) Draw Conclusions** Why do you think people are still eager to come to the United States?

**2. (a) Explain** Why has the American population gotten older?
**(b) Evaluate Information** Agree or disagree with the following statement and give reasons for your answer: Younger Americans should be concerned about issues affecting older Americans.

### ● Reading Skill

**3. Support Generalizations With Evidence** Find evidence in the section text to support this generalization: Opportunities for many Americans have improved since the civil rights era.

### Vocabulary *Builder*

Read each sentence below. If the sentence is true, write YES and explain why. If the sentence is not true, write NO and explain why not.

**4.** Most Americans were eager to let undocumented workers enter the country.

**5.** Refugees choose to leave their homes in order to find work.

**6.** President Bush's plan would allow guest workers to enter the country on a temporary basis.

### Writing

**7.** Revise the following paragraph to correct spelling and punctuation errors: I remeber watching the mickey Mouse club show I mean the ariginal one in the 1950s not the one with Britney Spears Sumtimes the announcer woud say to all of we kids in the tV audience You the leaders of the 21th century. That always sent a chill down my back. And now its really the 21th century!

To predict consequences, or results, you must analyze what has happened in the past and compare it to the present situation. The data below show demographic, or population, trends. Demographic data help social scientists, as well as town and city planners, form a more complete picture of a certain population and establish trends over a period of time.

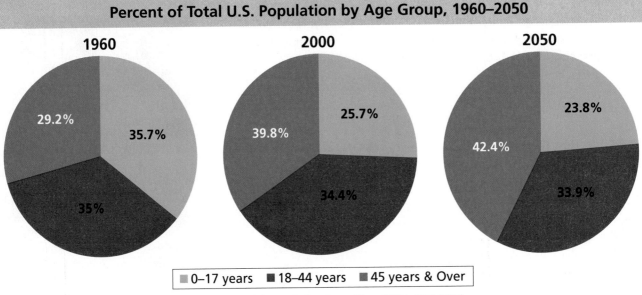

**Percent of Total U.S. Population by Age Group, 1960–2050**

**1960**
- 29.2%
- 35.7%
- 35%

**2000**
- 39.8%
- 25.7%
- 34.4%

**2050**
- 42.4%
- 23.8%
- 33.9%

Legend: ■ 0–17 years ■ 18–44 years ■ 45 years & Over

Source: U.S. Bureau of the Census, *Projections of the Population of the U.S., by Age, Sex, and Race: 1995 to 2050* (2002)

## Learn the Skill

*Use these steps to make predictions.*

**1 Identify the subject of the data.** Read the graph or chart title to understand what is being measured. Always look for the source of the data.

**2 Analyze the data.** Study the data to see trends or patterns. Remember, information can be presented in different ways: tables, graphs, charts, or as text. Data may appear as percentages or in thousands or millions.

**3 Predict possible future developments.** Draw conclusions or make generalizations based on the data on the chart.

## Practice the Skill

*Answer the following questions about the data on this page.*

**1 Identify the subject of the data.** (a) What is the title of the pie graphs? (b) What years are shown on the graphs? (c) What is the source of the data?

**2 Analyze the data.** (a) What percentage of the population was between 0 and 17 years of age in 1960? (b) Which age group shows the most growth between 1960 and 2050? (c) Which group decreases the most?

**3 Predict possible future developments.** (a) How do you think changes in the population will affect the construction of schools and houses built between 2000 and 2005? (b) What advice would you offer to hospitals and health care facilities based on this data?

## Apply the Skill

*See the Review and Assessment at the end of this chapter.*

## Chapter Summary

### Section 1
### The Threat of Terrorism

- On September 11, 2001, terrorists attacked the World Trade Center and the Pentagon, killing thousands of people.
- In response to the terrorist attacks, the United States took steps to protect the homeland and fight terrorism worldwide.
- Not all Americans agreed when President Bush sent American troops into Iraq.

### Section 2
### Economy and the Environment

- In response to growing trade deficits, the United States promoted free trade.
- Environmentalists called attention to problems such as air and water pollution.
- In order to reduce dependence on foreign oil, Americans have explored alternative sources of energy.

### Section 3
### Science and Technology

- The development of computers led to an information revolution.
- Medical science has developed new ways to detect and combat diseases but also faces challenges such as the AIDS epidemic.

### Section 4
### A Changing Society

- Immigration has increased from regions such as Asia and Latin America.
- The population of the United States has grown more diverse, and the average age of the American people has increased.
- Women and African Americans have made some major economic and political gains.
- School violence and illegal drug use strongly affect younger Americans.

## Key Concepts

These notes will help you prepare for questions about key concepts.

### Effects of September 11 Terrorist Attack

- Almost 3,000 people are killed at the Pentagon and World Trade Center.
- Office of Homeland Security is formed.
- President Bush signs Patriot Act.
- Bush declares global war on terrorism and orders invasion of Afghanistan.
- United States invades Iraq and topples Saddam Hussein.

### Key Economic Issues

**Trade Deficits**
- United States buys more from other countries than it sells to them.
- American companies lower costs by outsourcing.

**Free Trade**
- Supporters say free trade increases business and creates new jobs.
- Opponents say free trade threatens American jobs and weakens workers' rights.

### A Changing Population

- Immigration increases from Asia and Latin America
- Ethnic and religious diversity grows
- Latinos become nation's largest ethnic minority
- Average age of the population increases
- Population shifts from Northeast and Midwest to South and Southwest (Sunbelt)
- More women enter the workforce
- More African Americans and Latinos move into middle class

## Vocabulary *Builder*

### Key Terms

Fill in the blanks with the correct key terms.

1. A _____ occurs when a nation imports more than it exports.

2. Water, wind, and solar power are _____.

3. Many _____ came to the United States to escape wars in Asia, Africa, or Central America.

4. One goal of _____ is to protect the nation from bombings and other attacks.

5. Immigration laws impose punishments on companies that hire _____.

6. As a result of _____, many American products are manufactured overseas.

## Comprehension and Critical Thinking

7. **(a) Summarize** How did Americans respond to the terrorist attacks of September 11, 2001?
   **(b) Compare** How was this reaction similar to the reaction of Americans to the bombing of Pearl Harbor in December 1941?

8. **(a) Describe** What was the effect of the North American Free Trade Agreement (NAFTA)?
   **(b) Detect Points of View** Explain how you think each of the following might feel about NAFTA: the president of an American automobile company; a member of an American auto workers union; a Mexican worker.

9. **(a) List** Identify three actions the government took to protect the environment.
   **(b) Evaluate Information** Why did some business leaders oppose increased environmental regulations?
   **(c) Make Decisions** Would you be willing to pay higher prices for products in order to protect the environment? Why or why not?

10. **(a) Recall** How did immigration laws change in the 1960s? What were the effects of this change?
    **(b) Identify Alternatives** What steps has the government taken to control illegal immigration?

11. **(a) Recall** What actions have American schools taken to solve the problems of violence?
    **(b) Identify Alternatives** Suggest one additional action or approach that might help solve this problem.

## History Reading Skill

12. **Draw Conclusions and Make Generalizations** Using information from this chapter, draw a conclusion or make a generalization about the challenges that Americans face for the future. Explain the evidence you used to support your conclusion or generalization.

## Writing

13. **Write four paragraphs of an eyewitness account of an event or situation described in this chapter.**
    **Your account should:**
    - identify the eyewitness,
    - include details about the event or situation,
    - describe the eyewitness's thoughts and feelings.

    When you are finished, exchange papers with another student. List one element that you like and one element that you think could be improved. Revise your narrative in response to your partner's list.

14. **Write a Letter to the Future:**
    Write a letter to a student your age studying American history 25 years from now. Describe your feelings about our nation's history and your hopes for the nation's future.

## Skills for Life

### Make Predictions

Use the graph below to answer the questions.

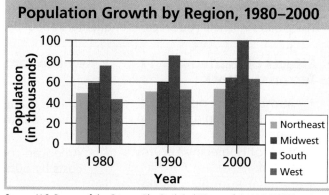

**Population Growth by Region, 1980–2000**

Source: U.S. Bureau of the Census, *The Statistical History of the U.S.* (1976) and 2000 Census of the U.S. www.census.gov

15. What is being measured by the data?

16. **(a)** In 1980, how many people lived in the Northeast? **(b)** What happened to the population of the South from 1980 to 2000?

17. Make a prediction about how this graph might look in 2020.

# Test Yourself

1. **One reason that President George W. Bush gave for sending troops into Iraq in 2003 was that**

   **A** Iraq had invaded Kuwait.

   **B** terrorist leader Osama Bin Laden was hiding in Iraq.

   **C** Iraq was developing weapons of mass destruction.

   **D** Iraq had imposed an oil embargo against the United States.

2. **Which of the following statements accurately describes one reason the population of the United States has gotten older?**

   **A** Couples are marrying earlier and having more children.

   **B** More older people are immigrating to the United States.

   **C** Science and technology have led to improved medical care.

   **D** More people have moved to the Sunbelt.

Refer to the quotation below to answer Question 3.

> "It was a spring without voices. On the mornings that had once throbbed with the dawn chorus of robins, catbirds, doves, jays, wrens . . . there was now no sound; only silence lay over the fields and woods and marsh."
>
> —Rachel Carson, *Silent Spring*

3. **The above passage describes a possible effect of**

   **A** chemical pesticides.

   **B** solar power.

   **C** terrorism.

   **D** cloning.

4. **Companies practice outsourcing in order to**

   **A** reduce unemployment.

   **B** increase trade deficits.

   **C** cut labor costs.

   **D** create more jobs for women.

# Document-Based Questions

**Task:** Look at Documents 1 and 2, and answer their accompanying questions. Then, use the documents and your knowledge of history to complete this writing assignment:

> Write a brief essay comparing the views of technology presented by the two documents. Using specific details, explain which document better represents your view of technology.

**Document 1:** In testimony before Congress in 1998, journalist Stewart Alsop described great advances that computers have made possible. *What does Alsop mean when he says that computers have "personally empowered" him?*

> "I am constantly amazed by what the software industry has delivered to me and to people like me. I am amazed that I can use computers to communicate, produce, calculate, entertain, research, and discover in ways that were not available to people, to my parents and their generation. I have been personally empowered by the technology developed by the software industry and am thankful to have lived in the time when this technology became available."

**Document 2:** Some people wonder whether computers have really improved our lives. In this cartoon, a "techie" is overwhelmed by his beeping and whirring machines. *How does this cartoon present a negative view of the computer age?*

"ALL THIS TECHNOLOGY... IT'S SO LIBERATING!"

# Writing Workshop

## Narrative Essay
## Historical Narrative

### ▶ Introduction

In a historical narrative, you tell about a historical event, blending facts with imagined characters and situations. When you write a historical narrative, you combine fiction with nonfiction. Like nonfiction, a historical narrative describes people who actually lived and events that actually happened. However, a historical narrative also includes fictional people and details imagined by the writer. A historical narrative should have the following characteristics:

- accurate historic events and details of actual places
- one person's point of view
- some characters and circumstances invented by the writer
- chronological organization

**Assignment** On the following pages, you will learn how to write a historical narrative. You will get step-by-step instructions. Each step will include an example from a historical narrative in which a cameraman in the television studio recalls the first Kennedy-Nixon presidential debate in 1960.

Read the instructions and the examples. Then, follow each step to plan and write a 300-to-400-word historical narrative on this topic:

> **Write a historical narrative about Martin Luther King's march on Washington in 1963.**

For a review of the steps in the writing process, see the **Historian's Toolkit, *Write Like a Historian.***

### ▶ Prewriting

**Choose a historical event and a central character.** Begin by deciding on the historical event you will narrate. Then, choose a real or fictional person to place at the center of your narrative. Ask the questions in the chart to help you make this decision.

**Brainstorm for and research background details about the historical event.** In order to write a convincing historical narrative, you need to learn as much as you can about the event you are relating.

| Choosing Events and Characters: Guiding Questions | |
|---|---|
| **For real people** | • What individuals were actually involved in this historical event? |
| | • In what way was each involved? |
| **For fictional characters** | • What other types of people might have participated in or witnessed the event? |
| **For fictional and real** | • Of all these people—real and fictional—who would have the most interesting perspective on the story? |
| | • Which one would I most enjoy writing about? |

Use libraries and the Internet to gather information. Use the points highlighted in the chart to guide your research.

**Describe your central character and his or her surroundings.** Write a few sentences in which your central character describes himself or herself in the first person ("I," "me," "my," etc.). Then, have your central character describe the setting of the historical event, the time and place in which he or she lives.

**Chart your narrative's sequence.** Most historical narratives use chronological organization. Decide at what point your narrative will start and when it will end. Then, list the series of events that you want to cover.

| Researching a Historical Narrative: Guiding Questions | |
|---|---|
| **Historical event** | • What exactly happened?<br>• Why, when, and where did it happen?<br>• Were the surroundings urban or rural?<br>• What did the scene of the event look like?<br>• What details about the event are known? |
| **Current event** | • What year is it?<br>• What was happening at home and abroad? |
| **Values** | • What did people of that time and culture believe in?<br>• What were they concerned about? |
| **Economics** | • What was it like to be a wealthy person?<br>• What was it like to be poor?<br>• What kinds of jobs did people have? |
| **Daily life/Culture** | • How did people dress?<br>• What did they eat?<br>• How were they entertained?<br>• What did they read? |
| **Imagine yourself living in that time and place** | • How do you think you would have fit into that world? Would *you* have liked living then and there? Why or why not? |

## ▶ Drafting

**Open the narrative.** In the first paragraphs of your narrative, introduce your main character and his or her world to your readers. As you write, think about the following questions:

• What details root this person in a particular time and place?

• How does he or she feel about the historical event?

• Why is this story being told? Is your storyteller relating this narrative to a friend? Talking to a group of strangers?

**Develop the narrative.** After you have introduced your storyteller and setting, relate the series of events that make up the narrative. Keep the narrative in the first person. Use transitions—such as *first, before, later on, after, the next day,* and so on—to help your audience keep track of time.

The narrative should progress until it reaches a high point. As you build up to that point, increase your reader's interest. Use powerful and vivid language to intensify the storyteller's emotions and to show his or her reaction to what happens.

**Close the narrative.** The final paragraphs of your historical narrative should wind down the action.

> **Sample description:**
> Normally my job is pretty routine, but I think I saw something tonight that I'll remember for a long time. I'm a cameraman, and tonight I worked at WBBM Studios in Chicago, where the first presidential debate took place.

# Writing Workshop *continued*

## ► Model Narrative

Read the following model of a historical narrative about the presidential debate in 1960, between John F. Kennedy and Richard M. Nixon. Notice that it includes the characteristics you have learned.

### The First Televised Presidential Debate

The central character describes his surroundings.

Normally my job is pretty routine, but I saw something tonight that I'll remember for a long time. I'm a cameraman, and tonight I worked at WBBM Studios in Chicago, where the first presidential debate took place between Vice President Nixon and Senator Kennedy.

This first debate has turned into a big deal. The whole setup for the debate was really brand new, since the television networks all gave an hour of free time—no commercials. President Eisenhower even signed a special law to allow it. So it was definitely a *very* big deal.

The writer included historical events in the narrative.

When I got to the station late this afternoon, everyone seemed pretty keyed up. I was too—I was really worried about not making any mistakes. I was really excited when the two candidates arrived. Vice President Nixon got there first, with a Secret Service man. Nixon wore a baggy-looking gray suit that made him blend into the back wall. Not good. His shirt collar looked too big, and I remember that he'd had some kind of bad leg injury a few weeks before, so maybe he lost weight in the hospital. Also not good.

The writer blends fiction and nonfiction to create the narrative.

Then Senator Kennedy came. Kennedy seemed younger than Nixon and was definitely healthier looking — all tanned. His suit was dark blue, which contrasted well with the gray wall. Kennedy wore a white shirt, which looked great with his dark suit and tan. But white is terrible on television, since it starts to glow. Someone had to get him a light-blue shirt. The director offered the candidates makeup. The Vice President said "No" (bad idea, since he was pretty pale). But the senator, who was already tanned, thought he wanted some (smart—it keeps your face from showing sweat).

# ► Revising

After completing your draft, read it again carefully to find ways to make your writing better. Here are some questions to ask yourself:

**Revise for clarity.**
- Is the event portrayed accurately and clearly, with detail?
- Does the narrative establish a clear impression of the storyteller and his or her world?
- Does the narrative include transitions to help the reader?

**Revise for tone and style.**
- Does your storyteller's language sound convincing?
- What impression of the storyteller does your writing create?
- Does your narrative convey the emotion you wanted?

**Revise to meet written English-language conventions.**
- Are all sentences complete, with a subject and a verb?
- Are all the words spelled correctly?
- Are all proper nouns capitalized?
- Are all sentences punctuated correctly?

# ► Rubric for Self-Assessment

*Evaluate your historical narrative using the following rating scale:*

| | Score 4 | Score 3 | Score 2 | Score 1 |
|---|---|---|---|---|
| **Organization** | Develops the narrative clearly in chronological order; includes all necessary explanations and interesting details; does not lose track of the main event in the story | Follows chronological order but may be missing some important explanations; could use more interesting details | Roughly follows chronological order but skips around several times; is missing some vital explanations; occasionally loses track of the main event | Shows lack of organizational strategy |
| **Presentation** | Includes first-person narration of a historic event by an actual or fictional character; storyteller's role is well developed; smoothly incorporates factual information and maintains reader interest | Is usually first-person narration with a few inconsistencies; storyteller's character seems undeveloped at times; uses good factual information but is sometimes awkward in incorporating it; occasionally loses reader interest | Shifts between first-person and third-person narration; storyteller's character is not developed; includes some factual information but awkwardly incorporated; there are also several inaccuracies; loses reader interest | Does not use first-person narration; there is no sense of a storyteller at all; barely uses any factual information; there are many inaccuracies; confuses reader |
| **Use of Language** | Varies sentence structure and vocabulary successfully; includes almost no mechanical errors | Uses some variety in sentence structure and vocabulary; includes several mechanical errors | Uses the same types of sentences without varying them; repeats words; includes many mechanical errors | Writes incomplete sentences; uses language poorly; sounds confused; includes many mechanical errors |

# Reference Section

## Table of Contents

# Presidents of the United States

**1** George Washington (1732–1799)

**Years in office:**
1789–1797
**Party:**
none
**Elected from:**
Virginia
**Vice President:**
John Adams

**2** John Adams (1735–1826)

**Years in office:**
1797–1801
**Party:**
Federalist
**Elected from:**
Massachusetts
**Vice President:**
Thomas
  Jefferson

**3** Thomas Jefferson (1743–1826)

**Years in office:**
1801–1809
**Party:**
Democratic
  Republican
**Elected from:**
Virginia
**Vice President:**
1) Aaron Burr,
2) George Clinton

**4** James Madison (1751–1836)

**Years in office:**
1809–1817
**Party:**
Democratic
  Republican
**Elected from:**
Virginia
**Vice President:**
1) George Clinton,
2) Elbridge Gerry

**5** James Monroe (1758–1831)

**Years in office:**
1817–1825
**Party:**
Democratic
  Republican
**Elected from:**
Virginia
**Vice President:**
Daniel Tompkins

**6** John Quincy Adams (1767–1848)

**Years in office:**
1825–1829
**Party:**
National
  Republican
**Elected from:**
Massachusetts
**Vice President:**
John Calhoun

**7** Andrew Jackson (1767–1845)

**Years in office:**
1829–1837
**Party:**
Democratic
**Elected from:**
Tennessee
**Vice President:**
1) John Calhoun,
2) Martin Van
  Buren

**8** Martin Van Buren (1782–1862)

**Years in office:**
1837–1841
**Party:**
Democratic
**Elected from:**
New York
**Vice President:**
Richard Johnson

**9** William Henry Harrison* (1773–1841)

**Years in office:**
1841
**Party:**
Whig
**Elected from:**
Ohio
**Vice President:**
John Tyler

**10** John Tyler (1790–1862)

**Years in office:**
1841–1845
**Party:**
Whig
**Elected from:**
Virginia
**Vice President:**
none

**11** James K. Polk (1795–1849)

**Years in office:**
1845–1849
**Party:**
Democratic
**Elected from:**
Tennessee
**Vice President:**
George Dallas

**12** Zachary Taylor* (1784–1850)

**Years in office:**
1849–1850
**Party:**
Whig
**Elected from:**
Louisiana
**Vice President:**
Millard Fillmore

*Died in office

**13 Millard Fillmore** (1800–1874)

**Years in office:**
1850–1853
**Party:**
Whig
**Elected from:**
New York
**Vice President:**
none

**14 Franklin Pierce** (1804–1869)

**Years in office:**
1853–1857
**Party:**
Democratic
**Elected from:**
New Hampshire
**Vice President:**
William King

**15 James Buchanan** (1791–1868)

**Years in office:**
1857–1861
**Party:**
Democratic
**Elected from:**
Pennsylvania
**Vice President:**
John Breckinridge

**16 Abraham Lincoln**\*\* (1809–1865)

**Years in office:**
1861–1865
**Party:**
Republican
**Elected from:**
Illinois
**Vice President:**
1) Hannibal Hamlin,
2) Andrew Johnson

**17 Andrew Johnson** (1808–1875)

**Years in office:**
1865–1869
**Party:**
Republican
**Elected from:**
Tennessee
**Vice President:**
none

**18 Ulysses S. Grant** (1822–1885)

**Years in office:**
1869–1877
**Party:**
Republican
**Elected from:**
Illinois
**Vice President:**
1) Schuyler Colfax,
2) Henry Wilson

**19 Rutherford B. Hayes** (1822–1893)

**Years in office:**
1877–1881
**Party:**
Republican
**Elected from:**
Ohio
**Vice President:**
William Wheeler

**20 James A. Garfield**\*\* (1831–1881)

**Years in office:**
1881
**Party:**
Republican
**Elected from:**
Ohio
**Vice President:**
Chester A. Arthur

**21 Chester A. Arthur** (1829–1886)

**Years in office:**
1881–1885
**Party:**
Republican
**Elected from:**
New York
**Vice President:**
none

**22 Grover Cleveland** (1837–1908)

**Years in office:**
1885–1889
**Party:**
Democratic
**Elected from:**
New York
**Vice President:**
Thomas Hendricks

**23 Benjamin Harrison** (1833–1901)

**Years in office:**
1889–1893
**Party:**
Republican
**Elected from:**
Indiana
**Vice President:**
Levi Morton

**24 Grover Cleveland** (1837–1908)

**Years in office:**
1893–1897
**Party:**
Democratic
**Elected from:**
New York
**Vice President:**
Adlai Stevenson

\*\*Assassinated

## 25 William McKinley** (1843–1901)

**Years in office:**
1897–1901
**Party:**
Republican
**Elected from:**
Ohio
**Vice President:**
1) Garret Hobart,
2) Theodore
   Roosevelt

## 26 Theodore Roosevelt (1858–1919)

**Years in office:**
1901–1909
**Party:**
Republican
**Elected from:**
New York
**Vice President:**
Charles Fairbanks

## 27 William Howard Taft (1857–1930)

**Years in office:**
1909–1913
**Party:**
Republican
**Elected from:**
Ohio
**Vice President:**
James Sherman

## 28 Woodrow Wilson (1856–1924)

**Years in office:**
1913–1921
**Party:**
Democratic
**Elected from:**
New Jersey
**Vice President:**
Thomas Marshall

## 29 Warren G. Harding* (1865–1923)

**Years in office:**
1921–1923
**Party:**
Republican
**Elected from:**
Ohio
**Vice President:**
Calvin Coolidge

## 30 Calvin Coolidge (1872–1933)

**Years in office:**
1923–1929
**Party:**
Republican
**Elected from:**
Massachusetts
**Vice President:**
Charles Dawes

## 31 Herbert C. Hoover (1874–1964)

**Years in office:**
1929–1933
**Party:**
Republican
**Elected from:**
California
**Vice President:**
Charles Curtis

## 32 Franklin D. Roosevelt* (1882–1945)

**Years in office:**
1933–1945
**Party:**
Democratic
**Elected from:**
New York
**Vice President:**
1) John Garner,
2) Henry Wallace,
3) Harry S Truman

## 33 Harry S Truman (1884–1972)

**Years in office:**
1945–1953
**Party:**
Democratic
**Elected from:**
Missouri
**Vice President:**
Alben Barkley

## 34 Dwight D. Eisenhower (1890–1969)

**Years in office:**
1953–1961
**Party:**
Republican
**Elected from:**
New York
**Vice President:**
Richard M. Nixon

## 35 John F. Kennedy** (1917–1963)

**Years in office:**
1961–1963
**Party:**
Democratic
**Elected from:**
Massachusetts
**Vice President:**
Lyndon B.
Johnson

## 36 Lyndon B. Johnson (1908–1973)

**Years in office:**
1963–1969
**Party:**
Democratic
**Elected from:**
Texas
**Vice President:**
Hubert Humphrey

*Died in office
**Assassinated

 **37** **Richard M. Nixon*** (1913–1994)

**Years in office:**
1969–1974
**Party:**
Republican
**Elected from:**
New York
**Vice President:**
1) Spiro Agnew,
2) Gerald R. Ford

 **38** **Gerald R. Ford** (b. 1913)

**Years in office:**
1974–1977
**Party:**
Republican
**Appointed from:**
Michigan
**Vice President:**
Nelson
    Rockefeller

 **39** **Jimmy Carter** (b. 1924)

**Years in office:**
1977–1981
**Party:**
Democratic
**Elected from:**
Georgia
**Vice President:**
Walter Mondale

 **40** **Ronald W. Reagan** (b. 1911–2004)

**Years in office:**
1981–1989
**Party:**
Republican
**Elected from:**
California
**Vice President:**
George H.W.
    Bush

 **41** **George H.W. Bush** (b. 1924)

**Years in office:**
1989–1993
**Party:**
Republican
**Elected from:**
Texas
**Vice President:**
J. Danforth
    Quayle

 **42** **William J. Clinton** (b. 1946)

**Years in office:**
1993–2001
**Party:**
Democratic
**Elected from:**
Arkansas
**Vice President:**
Albert Gore, Jr.

 **43** **George W. Bush** (b. 1946)

**Years in office:**
2001–
**Party:**
Republican
**Elected from:**
Texas
**Vice President:**
Richard Cheney

***Resigned

# The Fifty States

| State | Date of Entry to Union (Order of Entry) | Land Area in Square Miles | Population (In Thousands) | Number of Representatives in House* | Capital | Largest City |
|---|---|---|---|---|---|---|
| Alabama | 1819 (22) | 50,750 | 4,447 | 7 | Montgomery | Birmingham |
| Alaska | 1959 (49) | 570,374 | 627 | 1 | Juneau | Anchorage |
| Arizona | 1912 (48) | 113,642 | 5,131 | 8 | Phoenix | Phoenix |
| Arkansas | 1836 (25) | 52,075 | 2,673 | 4 | Little Rock | Little Rock |
| California | 1850 (31) | 155,973 | 33,872 | 53 | Sacramento | Los Angeles |
| Colorado | 1876 (38) | 103,730 | 4,301 | 7 | Denver | Denver |
| Connecticut | 1788 (5) | 4,845 | 3,406 | 5 | Hartford | Bridgeport |
| Delaware | 1787 (1) | 1,955 | 784 | 1 | Dover | Wilmington |
| Florida | 1845 (27) | 53,997 | 15,982 | 25 | Tallahassee | Jacksonville |
| Georgia | 1788 (4) | 57,919 | 8,186 | 13 | Atlanta | Atlanta |
| Hawaii | 1959 (50) | 6,423 | 1,212 | 2 | Honolulu | Honolulu |
| Idaho | 1890 (43) | 82,751 | 1,294 | 2 | Boise | Boise |
| Illinois | 1818 (21) | 55,593 | 12,419 | 19 | Springfield | Chicago |
| Indiana | 1816 (19) | 35,870 | 6,080 | 9 | Indianapolis | Indianapolis |
| Iowa | 1846 (29) | 55,875 | 2,926 | 5 | Des Moines | Des Moines |
| Kansas | 1861 (34) | 81,823 | 2,688 | 4 | Topeka | Wichita |
| Kentucky | 1792 (15) | 39,732 | 4,042 | 6 | Frankfort | Louisville |
| Louisiana | 1812 (18) | 43,566 | 4,469 | 7 | Baton Rouge | New Orleans |
| Maine | 1820 (23) | 30,865 | 1,275 | 2 | Augusta | Portland |
| Maryland | 1788 (7) | 9,775 | 5,296 | 8 | Annapolis | Baltimore |
| Massachusetts | 1788 (6) | 7,838 | 6,349 | 10 | Boston | Boston |
| Michigan | 1837 (26) | 56,809 | 9,938 | 15 | Lansing | Detroit |
| Minnesota | 1858 (32) | 79,617 | 4,919 | 8 | St. Paul | Minneapolis |
| Mississippi | 1817 (20) | 46,914 | 2,845 | 4 | Jackson | Jackson |
| Missouri | 1821 (24) | 68,898 | 5,595 | 9 | Jefferson City | Kansas City |
| Montana | 1889 (41) | 145,556 | 902 | 1 | Helena | Billings |
| Nebraska | 1867 (37) | 76,878 | 1,711 | 3 | Lincoln | Omaha |
| Nevada | 1864 (36) | 109,806 | 1,998 | 3 | Carson City | Las Vegas |
| New Hampshire | 1788 (9) | 8,969 | 1,236 | 2 | Concord | Manchester |
| New Jersey | 1787 (3) | 7,419 | 8,414 | 13 | Trenton | Newark |
| New Mexico | 1912 (47) | 121,365 | 1,819 | 3 | Santa Fe | Albuquerque |
| New York | 1788 (11) | 47,224 | 18,976 | 29 | Albany | New York |
| North Carolina | 1789 (12) | 48,718 | 8,049 | 13 | Raleigh | Charlotte |
| North Dakota | 1889 (39) | 68,994 | 642 | 1 | Bismarck | Fargo |
| Ohio | 1803 (17) | 40,953 | 11,353 | 18 | Columbus | Columbus |
| Oklahoma | 1907 (46) | 68,679 | 3,451 | 5 | Oklahoma City | Oklahoma City |
| Oregon | 1859 (33) | 96,003 | 3,421 | 5 | Salem | Portland |
| Pennsylvania | 1787 (2) | 44,820 | 12,281 | 19 | Harrisburg | Philadelphia |
| Rhode Island | 1790 (13) | 1,045 | 1,048 | 2 | Providence | Providence |
| South Carolina | 1788 (8) | 30,111 | 4,012 | 6 | Columbia | Columbia |
| South Dakota | 1889 (40) | 75,898 | 755 | 1 | Pierre | Sioux Falls |
| Tennessee | 1796 (16) | 41,220 | 5,689 | 9 | Nashville | Memphis |
| Texas | 1845 (28) | 261,914 | 20,852 | 32 | Austin | Houston |
| Utah | 1896 (45) | 82,168 | 2,233 | 3 | Salt Lake City | Salt Lake City |
| Vermont | 1791 (14) | 9,249 | 609 | 1 | Montpelier | Burlington |
| Virginia | 1788 (10) | 39,598 | 7,079 | 11 | Richmond | Virginia Beach |
| Washington | 1889 (42) | 66,582 | 5,894 | 9 | Olympia | Seattle |
| West Virginia | 1863 (35) | 24,087 | 1,808 | 3 | Charleston | Charleston |
| Wisconsin | 1848 (30) | 54,314 | 5,364 | 8 | Madison | Milwaukee |
| Wyoming | 1890 (44) | 97,105 | 494 | 1 | Cheyenne | Cheyenne |
| District of Columbia | | 61 | 572 | 1 (nonvoting) | | |

| Self-Governing Areas, Possessions, and Dependencies | Land Area in Square Miles | Population (In Thousands) | Capital |
|---|---|---|---|
| Puerto Rico | 3,515 | 809 | San Juan |
| Guam | 209 | 155 | Agana |
| U.S. Virgin Islands | 132 | 121 | Charlotte Amalie |
| American Samoa | 77 | 65 | Pago Pago |

Sources: Department of Commerce, Bureau of the Census

*As of 108th Congress.

| Alabama | Alaska | Arizona | Arkansas | California |
|---|---|---|---|---|

| Colorado | Connecticut | Delaware | Florida | Georgia |
|---|---|---|---|---|

| Hawaii | Idaho | Illinois | Indiana | Iowa |
|---|---|---|---|---|

| Kansas | Kentucky | Louisiana | Maine | Maryland |
|---|---|---|---|---|

| Massachusetts | Michigan | Minnesota | Mississippi | Missouri |
|---|---|---|---|---|

| Montana | Nebraska | Nevada | New Hampshire | New Jersey |
|---|---|---|---|---|

| New Mexico | New York | North Carolina | North Dakota | Ohio |
|---|---|---|---|---|

| Oklahoma | Oregon | Pennsylvania | Rhode Island | South Carolina |
|---|---|---|---|---|

| South Dakota | Tennessee | Texas | Utah | Vermont |
|---|---|---|---|---|

| Virginia | Washington | West Virginia | Wisconsin | Wyoming |
|---|---|---|---|---|

# English and Spanish Glossary

The glossary defines all high-use words and many key historical words and terms. The high-use words appear underlined the first time that they are used in the text. The key words and terms appear in blue type the first time that they are used. Each word in the glossary is defined in both English and Spanish. The page number(s) after the English definition refers to the page(s) on which the word or phrase is defined in the text. For other references, see the index.

## Pronunciation Key

When difficult names or terms first appear in the text, they are respelled to help you with pronunciation. A syllable printed in small capital letters receives the greatest stress. The pronunciation key below lists the letters and symbols that will help you pronounce the word. It also includes examples of words using each of the sounds and shows how each word would be pronounced.

| Symbol | Example | Respelling |
|---|---|---|
| a | hat | (hat) |
| ay | pay, late | (pay), (layt) |
| ah | star, hot | (stahr), (haht) |
| ai | air, dare | (air), (dair) |
| aw | law, all | (law), (awl) |
| eh | met | (meht) |
| ee | bee, eat | (bee), (eet) |
| er | learn, sir, fur | (lern), (ser), (fer) |
| ih | fit | (fiht) |
| ī | mile | (mīl) |
| ir | ear | (ir) |
| oh | no | (noh) |
| oi | soil, boy | (soil), (boi) |
| oo | root, rule | (root), (rool) |
| or | born, door | (born), (dor) |
| ow | plow, out | (plow), (owt) |

| Symbol | Example | Respelling |
|---|---|---|
| u | put, book | (put), (buk) |
| uh | fun | (fuhn) |
| yoo | few, use | (fyoo), (yooz) |
| ch | chill, reach | (chihl), (reech) |
| g | go, dig | (goh), (dihg) |
| j | jet, gently bridge | (jeht), (JEHNT lee), (brihj) |
| k | kite, cup | (kīt), (kuhp) |
| ks | mix | (mihks) |
| kw | quick | (kwihk) |
| ng | bring | (brihng) |
| s | say, cent | (say), (sehnt) |
| sh | she, crash | (shee), (krash) |
| th | three | (three) |
| y | yet, onion | (yeht), (UHN yuhn) |
| z | zip, always | (zihp), (AWL wayz) |
| zh | treasure | (TREH zher) |

## A

**abolitionist** (a boh LIH shuhn ihst) person who wanted to end slavery (p. 423)
*abolicionista* persona que quería abolir la esclavitud

**accelerate** (ak SEL er ayt) to increase in speed (p. 621)
*acelerar* aumentar la velocidad

**accommodation** (ak kom moh DAY shuhn) adjustment; adaptation (pp. 501, 925)
*acomodo* ajuste; adaptación

**accumulate** (uh KYOOM yoo layt) to collect slowly; to increase in amount over time (pp. 81, 753)
*acumular* reunir lentamente; aumentar una cantidad con el tiempo

**adobe** (uh DOH bee) sun-dried, unburned brick made of clay and straw (p. 12)
*adobe* seco al sol, ladrillo no quemado hecho de arcilla y paja

**affirmative action** (uh FERM uh tihv AK shuhn) program to provide more job and education opportunities for people who faced discrimination in the past (p. 892)
*acción afirmativa* programa diseñado para proporcionar más oportunidades de trabajo y educación a la gente que sufrió discriminación en el pasado

**aggression** (uh GREHSH uhn) warlike act by one country against another without cause (p. 804)
*agresión* acto de guerra de un país en contra de otro sin causa alguna

**airlift** (AIR lihft) emergency shipment of supplies sent via airplane (p. 838)
*puente aéreo* envío de mercancía de emergencia por avión

**alien** (AY lee ihn) outsider; someone from another country (pp. 298, 392)
*extranjero* persona que no pertenence a un grupo; persona de otro país

**alliance** (ah LĪ ans) agreement between countries to aid and support one another (pp. 57, 141, 183)
*alianza* convenio entre países por el que se comprometen a ayudarse y apoyarse mutuamente

**alter** (AWL ter) to change; to make different (pp. 315, 613, 911, 939)
*alterar* cambiar; hacer algo diferente

**amend** (ah MEHND) to change or revise (p. 264)
*enmendar* cambiar o revisar

**amendment** (ah MEHND mehnt) revision or addition to a bill, law, or constitution (p. 221)
*enmienda* revisión o adición a un proyecto de ley, ley o constitución

**amnesty** (AM nehs tee) government pardon (p. 547)
*amnistía* indulto que otorga el gobierno

**analyze** (AN ah līz) to examine something in detail in order to determine its nature (p. 750)
*analizar* examinar algo en detalle para establecer su naturaleza

**anarchist** (AN ahr kehst) person who opposes all forms of government (pp. 629, 739)
*anarquista* persona que se opone a todas las formas de gobierno

**annex** (an NEHKS) to add on or take over (p. 456)
*anexar* agregar o apoderarse de algo

**anti-Semitism** (an tee SEH mih tihz uhm) prejudice against Jews (p. 665)
*antisemitismo* prejuicio contra los judíos

**apartheid** (uh PAHR tayt) in South Africa, policy of strict racial segregation (p. 949)
*apartheid* en Sudáfrica, política de estricta segregación racial

**appeal** (ah PEEL) to ask that a court decision be reviewed by a higher court (p. 262)
*apelar* pedir que una decisión de un tribunal sea revisada por un tribunal superior

**appeasement** (uh PEEZ mehnt) policy of giving into aggression in order to avoid war (p. 804)
*apaciguamiento* política de consentir la agresión para evitar la guerra

**apprentice** (uh PREHN tihs) person who learns a trade or craft from a master (p. 110)
*aprendiz* persona que aprende un oficio o destreza de un maestro

**arms race** (ahrmz rays) contest in which nations compete to build more and more powerful weapons (p. 855)
*carrera armamentista* lucha en la cual las naciones compiten por construir armas cada vez más potentes

**assembly line** (ah SEHM blee līn) manufacturing method in which a product is put together as it moves along a conveyor belt (p. 613)
*línea de montaje* método de manufactura por el cual se arma un producto a medida que se desplaza en una banda transportadora

**assimilation** (ah sih mih LAY shuhn) process of becoming part of another culture (p. 627)
*asimilación* proceso de convertirse en parte de otra cultura

# B

**baby boom** (BAY bee boom) large increase in the birthrate from the late 1940s through the early 1960s (p. 845)
*baby boom* gran aumento de la tasa de natalidad entre la segunda mitad de la década de 1940 y la primera mitad de la década de 1960

**backcountry** (bak KUHN tree) frontier region located along the eastern slope of the Appalachian Mountains (p. 81)
*backcountry* región fronteriza ubicada a lo largo de la ladera oriental de los montes Apalaches

**balanced budget** (BAL ehnst BUHJ iht) condition that exists when a government spends only as much as it collects (p. 938)
*presupuesto equilibrado* condición que existe cuando un gobierno gasta sólo tanto como lo que recibe

**bankruptcy** (BANK ruhpt see) financial failure caused by an inability to pay one's debts (p. 772)
*quiebra* fracaso financiero causado por la incapacidad para pagar las deudas

**barrio** (BAHR ree oh) Latino neighborhood in the United States (p. 663)
*barrio* vecindario latino de Estados Unidos

**bilingual** (bī LIHNG gwuhl) in two languages; describing a person that has the ability to speak two languages fluently (p. 895)
*bilingüe* en dos idiomas; descripción de una persona que tiene la habilidad para hablar dos idiomas con fluidez

**bill** (bihl) proposed law (p. 259)
*proyecto de ley* ley propuesta

**bill of rights** (bihl uhv rīts) written list of freedoms that a government promises to protect (pp. 103, 205)
*declaración de derechos* lista escrita de las libertades que un gobierno se compromete a proteger

**black codes** (blak kohds) southern laws that severely limited the rights of African Americans after the Civil War (p. 553)
*códigos negros* leyes sureñas que limitaron severamente los derechos de los afroamericanos después de la Guerra Civil

**blockade** (BLAHK ayd) shutting a port or roadway to prevent people or supplies from coming into or leaving an area (pp. 161, 328, 515)
*bloqueo* cierre de un puerto o camino para impedir que entren o salgan personas o provisiones en cierta zona

**boat people** (boht PEE puhl) after the Vietnam War, refugees who escaped from Vietnam in small boats (p. 923)
*balseros* después de la Guerra de Vietnam, refugiados que huyeron de Vietnam a bordo de botes pequeños

**bond** (bahnd) certificate issued by a government for a certain amount of money that the government promises to pay back with interest (p. 284)
*bono* certificado emitido por un gobierno por cierta cantidad de dinero que el gobierno promete devolver con intereses

**bonus** (BOH nuhs) additional sum of money (p. 775)
*bono* suma de dinero adicional

**bootlegger** (BOOT lehg uhr) person who smuggled liquor into the United States during Prohibition (p. 741)
*contrabandista de alcohol* persona que contrabandeaba alcohol a Estados Unidos durante el período de la Prohibición

**borderland** (BOR der land) land along a frontier (p. 90)
*tierra limítrofe* tierra a lo largo de una frontera

**border state** (BOR der stayt) slave state that remained in the Union during the Civil War (p. 513)
*estado fronterizo* estado esclavista que permaneció en la Unión durante la Guerra Civil

**boycott** (BOI kaht) organized campaign to refuse to buy or use certain goods and services (pp. 147, 879)
*boicot* campaña organizada para rehusar comprar o usar ciertos bienes y servicios

**bracero** (bruh SER oh) Mexican laborer (p. 820)
*bracero* trabajador mexicano

**bull market** (bool MAHR kiht) period of increased stock trading and rising stock prices (p. 752)
*mercado alcista* período de aumento en la transacción de acciones y aumento de sus precios

**buying on margin** (BĪ ihng ahn MAHR jihn) borrowing money in order to buy stocks (p. 753)
*comprar sobre la base de margen* pedir prestado dinero para poder comprar acciones

# C

**canal** (kah NAHL) artificial waterway dug across land to improve transportation (p. 403)
*canal* vía navegable artificial excavada a lo largo de un terreno para mejorar el transporte

**capitalism** (KA piht ahl ihz uhm) economic system in which people put money, or capital, into a business or project in order to make a profit later on; economic system in which privately owned businesses compete in a free market (p. 344)
*capitalismo* sistema económico en el que las personas invierten dinero (capital) en un negocio o proyecto para obtener ganancias más adelante; sistema económico en el que los negocios de propiedad privada compiten en un mercado libre

**capitalist** (KA piht ahl ihst) person who invests capital, or money, in a business to earn a profit (p. 383)
*capitalista* persona que invierte capital (dinero) en un negocio para obtener ganancias

**carpetbagger** (KAHR peht BAG er) uncomplimentary nickname for a northern white who went to the South after the Civil War to start a business or pursue a political career (p. 555)
*carpetbagger* sobrenombre despreciativo dado a los norteños blancos que se mudaron al Sur después de la Guerra Civil para emprender un negocio o seguir una carrera política

**casualty** (KA su ahl tee) military term for a person killed, wounded, or missing in action (p. 520)
*baja* término militar que describe a una persona muerta, herida o desaparecida en combate

**cattle drive** (KAT tl drīv) herding and moving of cattle over long distances, usually to railroads (p. 590)
*arreo de ganado* conducción y traslado de ganado a grandes distancias, por lo regular hacia los ferrocarriles

**cattle kingdom** (KAT tl KING duhm) region dominated by the cattle industry and its ranches, trails, and cow towns (p. 593)
*región ganadera* región donde predomina la industria ganadera y sus ranchos, sendas y pueblos vaqueros

**caucus** (KAW kuhs) private meeting of members of a political party (p. 352)
*reunión de comité* encuentro privado de los integrantes de un partido político

**cavalry** (KAV uhl ree) units of troops on horseback (p. 183)
*caballería* unidades de tropas a caballo

**cease** (sees) to stop; to come to an end (pp. 296, 313, 388)
*cesar* detenerse; llegar a su fin

**cede** (seed) to give up (pp. 144, 345, 457)
*ceder* entregar

**censorship** (SEHN sor shihp) the power to review, change, or prevent the publication of news (p. 267)
*censura* poder de revisar, cambiar o evitar la publicación de noticias

**censure** (SEHN sher) to officially condemn (p. 854)
*censura* condenar oficialmente

**charter** (CHAHR ter) official document that gives certain rights to an individual or a group (pp. 67, 342)
*carta de privilegio* documento oficial que confiere ciertos derechos a un individuo o grupo

**checks and balances** (chehks and BAL an sez) a principle of the U.S. Constitution that gives each branch of government the power to check, or limit, the actions of the other branches (p. 257)
*control y equilibrio* principio de la Constitución de Estados Unidos que otorga a cada rama del gobierno el poder de controlar o limitar las acciones de las otras ramas

**circuit** (SIR kuht) route repeatedly traveled; circular trip around an area (pp. 340, 633)
*circuito* trayecto que se recorre una y otra vez; un recorrido circular en torno a un área

**circumnavigate** (ser kuhm NAV ih gayt) to travel all the way around Earth (p. 40)
*circunnavegar* hacer un recorrido completo alrededor de la Tierra

**citizen** (SIHT ih zehn) person who owes loyalty to a particular nation and is entitled to all its rights and protections (p. 270)
*ciudadano* persona que debe lealtad a una determinada nación y que tiene derecho a recibir todos sus derechos y protecciones

**civil disobedience** (SIHV ihl dih soh BEE dee ehns) idea based on nonviolence that people have a right to disobey a law they consider unjust, if their consciences demand it (pp. 433, 886)
*desobediencia civil* idea de que las personas tienen derecho, sin usar la violencia, a desobedecer una ley que consideren injusta, si su conciencia así lo exige

**civil rights** (SIHV uhl rīts) rights guaranteed in the Constitution, especially voting and equal treatment under the law (p. 784)
*derechos civiles* derechos garantizados en la Constitución, especialmente el derecho a voto y el trato igualitario ante la ley

**civil service** (SIHV ihl SER vihs) system that includes most government jobs, except elected positions, the judiciary, and the military (p. 645)
*administración pública* sistema que incluye a la mayoría de los trabajos del gobierno, excepto a los cargos elegidos, a los judiciales y a los militares

**civil war** (SIHV ihl wor) war between people of the same country (p. 503)
*guerra civil* guerra entre habitantes de un mismo país

**civilian** (suh VIHL yuhn) person not in the military (p. 187)
*civil* persona que no pertenece a las fuerzas armadas

**civilization** (sihv uh luh ZAY shuhn) advanced culture in which people have developed cities, science, and industries (p. 8)
*civilización* cultura avanzada en la cual la gente ha desarrollado ciudades, la ciencia y la industria

**clan** (klan) group of families that are related to one another (p. 15)
*clan* grupo de familias que están relacionadas entre sí

**clarify** (KLAIR ih fī) to make the meaning of something clear (p. 497)
*aclarar* explicar el significado de algo

**clause** (klawz) part of a law, treaty, or other written agreement (p. 430)
*cláusula* parte de una ley, tratado u otro acuerdo escrito

**clinic** (KLIHN ihk) place where people receive medical treatment, often for free or for a small fee (p. 622)
*clínica* lugar donde las personas reciben asistencia médica, en muchos casos gratuitamente o a cambio de un pago reducido

**cloning** (KLOHN ihng) process of making a genetic double of a plant or an animal (p. 985)
*clonar* proceso de hacer una duplicación genética de una planta o animal

**closed shop** (klohzd shahp) workplace in which only union members can be hired (p. 843)
*plantilla de sindicación obligatoria* lugar de trabajo en el cual sólo se puede contratar a trabajadores sindicalizados

**collective bargaining** (koh LEHK tihv BAHR gehn ing) negotiation between company management and a union representing a group of workers about wages, benefits, and working conditions (pp. 618, 791)
*negociación colectiva* negociación entre un sindicato que representa a un grupo de trabajadores y la dirección de una compañía acerca de los salarios, prestaciones y condiciones de trabajo

**collide** (koh LĪD) to come together with great force or violence; to crash (pp. 140, 715)
*colisionar* encontrarse con gran fuerza o violencia; chocar

**commit** (kuh MIHT) to make a pledge or a promise (pp. 491, 658)
*comprometerse* hacer un voto o una promesa

**communism** (KAHM yoo nihz uhm) economic and political system in which the state owns the means of production and a single party rules (p. 738)
*comunismo* sistema económico y político en el que el estado es dueño de los medios de producción y gobierna un partido único

**compromise** (KAHM proh mīz) agreement in which each side gives up part of what it wants to end a disagreement (p. 214)
*acuerdo* compromiso por el que cada una de las partes renuncia a una parte de lo que desea con el fin de acabar con una desavenencia

**compulsory education** (kuhm PUHL sor ee ehd jyoo KAY shuhn) requirement that children attend school up to a certain age (p. 632)
*educación obligatoria* exigencia de que los niños asistan a la escuela hasta una edad determinada

**confer** (kuhn FER) to exchange ideas with someone (pp. 783, 920)
*conferir* intercambiar ideas con alguien

**confine** (kuhn FĪN) to keep within certain limits; to shut or imprison (pp. 188, 955)
*confinar* mantener dentro de ciertos límites; encerrar o encarcelar

**conquistador** (kahn KWIHS tuh dor) conqueror, especially one of the sixteenth-century Spanish soldiers who defeated the Indian civilizations of Mexico, Central America, or Peru (p. 44)
*conquistador* persona que conquista, especialmente uno de los soldados españoles del siglo XVI que derrotaron a las civilizaciones indígenas de México y América Central o Perú

**conscientious objector** (kahn shee EHN shuhs ahb JEHK tehr) person who refuses to take part in war because of a strong belief that war is wrong (p. 915)
*objetor de conciencia* persona que rehúsa participar en la guerra debido a su fuerte creencia de que la guerra es algo erróneo

**conservation** (kahn ser VAY shuhn) protection of natural resources (p. 651)
*conservación* protección de los recursos

**constitution** (kahn stih TYOO shuhn) document in which the laws, principles, organization, and processes of a government are established (p. 204)
*constitución* documento que establece las leyes, principios, organización y procedimientos de un gobierno

**consume** (kuhn SYOOM) to use up (p. 972)
*consumir* usar

**containment** (kuhn TAYN muhnt) policy of limiting the expansion or influence of a hostile power; America's method to limit Soviet expansion during the Cold War (p. 838)
*contención* política de limitar la expansión o influencia de una potencia hostil; método de EE.UU. de limitar la expansión soviética durante la Guerra Fría

**continental** (kahn tihn EHN tuhl) form of paper money printed during the American Revolution (p. 188)
*continental* forma de papel moneda impreso durante la Guerra de la Independencia

**continental divide** (kahn tihn EHN tuhl dih VĪD) mountain ridge that separates river systems flowing toward opposite sides of a continent (p. 318)

*divisoria continental* cadena montañosa que separa sistemas fluviales que corren hacia lados opuestos de un continente

**contract** (KAHN trakt) agreement between two or more parties that can be enforced by law (p. 346)
*contrato* convenio entre dos o más partes que se puede hacer valer por ley

**contrast** (KAHN trast) difference shown between things when compared (pp. 89, 214)
*contraste* diferencia que se manifiesta entre dos cosas cuando son comparadas

**convert** (kuhn VERT) to change from one purpose or function to another; to change from one political party or religion to another (pp. 91, 357, 415, 816)
*convertir* cambiar de un propósito o función a otro; cambiar de un partido político o de una religión a otra

**Copperhead** (KAHP er hehd) northerner who opposed using force to keep the southern states in the Union (p. 531)
*Copperhead* norteño que se oponía al uso de la fuerza para mantener a los estados sureños dentro de la Unión

**corduroy road** (KOR der oi rohd) road made of sawed-off logs, laid side by side (p. 403)
*camino de troncos* camino hecho de troncos aserrados y colocados uno al lado de otro

**corollary** (KOR oh lair ee) a logical extension of a doctrine or proposition (p. 696)
*corolario* una extensión lógica de una doctrina o proposición

**corporation** (kor por AY shuhn) business owned by many investors (p. 614)
*compañía* empresa que es propiedad de muchos inversionistas

**cotton gin** (KAHT tuhn jihn) machine that used a spiked wooden cylinder to remove seeds from cotton fibers (p. 396)
*despepitadora de algodón* máquina que servía para quitar las semillas a las fibras de algodón por medio de un cilindro de madera con púas

**counterterrorism** (kownt er TEHR ehr ihz uhm) action taken against terrorism (p. 968)
*contraterrorismo* acción tomada en contra del terrorismo

**coureur de bois** (koo REHR duh BWAH) French term for "runner of the wood" (p. 54)
**coureur de bois** término francés para "corredor del bosque" o contrabandista de pieles

**cow town** (kow town) settlement at the end of a cattle trail (p. 592)
**pueblo vaquero** asentamiento situado al final de una ruta de ganado

**crisis** (KRĪ sihs) turning point or deciding event; situation involving great risk (pp. 156, 315, 484, 664, 956)
**crisis** momento crucial o acontecimiento decisivo; una situación que implica un gran riesgo

**critic** (KRIHT ihk) someone who makes judgments about objects or actions (pp. 331, 553, 681, 749, 944)
**crítico** persona que hace juicios sobre objetos o acciones

**culture** (KUHL cher) way of life (p. 10)
**cultura** forma de vida

**culture area** (KUHL cher AIR ee uh) region in which groups of people have a similar way of life (p. 11)
**área cultural** región en la cual grupos de personas tienen una forma de vida similar

**currency** (KER rehn see) money used to make purchases (pp. 11, 531)
**moneda** dinero que se usa para realizar compras

# D

**dame school** (daym skool) school run by a woman, usually in her own home (p. 119)
**escuela de señoritas** escuela administrada por una mujer, generalmente en su propia casa

**debtor** (DEH tor) person who cannot pay his or her debts (p. 87)
**deudor** persona que no puede pagar sus deudas

**decline** (dee KLĪN) to lose strength or power over a period of time (pp. 54, 324, 770)
**decaer** perder fuerza o poder a lo largo de cierto tiempo

**default** (dee FAWLT) failure to repay loans (p. 772)
**no pago** incumplimiento del pago de los préstamos

**deficit** (DEHF uh siht) debt that results when more money is spent than earned (p. 939)
**déficit** deuda que resulta de gastar más dinero del que se gana

**deficit spending** (DEHF uh siht SPEHND ihng) government practice of spending more money than is taken in from taxes (p. 792)
**déficit presupuestario** práctica gubernamental de gastar más dinero del que se recauda con los impuestos

**demilitarized zone** (DMZ) (dee MIHL uh tuh rīzd zohn) area from which military forces are prohibited (p. 852)
**zona desmilitarizada** área en la que se prohíbe la entrada a fuerzas militares

**deport** (dee PORT) to expel from a country (p. 739)
**deportar** expulsar de un país

**deprive** (dee PRĪV) to keep from happening; to take away something needed by force or intent (pp. 7, 487, 950)
**privar** impedir que suceda; tomar por la fuerza o con intención algo que se necesita

**deregulation** (dee rehg yuh LAY shuhn) reduction of federal or state restrictions on businesses (p. 939)
**desregulación** reducción de las restricciones federales o estatales sobre los negocios

**devise** (dee VĪZ) to carefully think out; to invent (pp. 206, 657)
**idear** hacer planes cuidadosamente; inventar

**devote** (dee VOHT) to commit; to apply time and energy (p. 397)
**dedicar** comprometer; destinar tiempo y energía

**dictatorship** (dihk TAY tor shihp) government in which one person or a small group holds complete authority (pp. 252, 455)
**dictadura** gobierno en el que una persona o un grupo pequeño ejerce una autoridad total

**dimension** (duh MEHN shuhn) size or extent; length, width, or height (p. 821)
**dimensión** tamaño o alcance; longitud, anchura o altura

**direct democracy** (dir EHKT deh MAH kra see) system of government in which ordinary citizens have the power to govern (p. 24)
***democracia directa*** sistema de gobierno en el que los ciudadanos comunes tienen poder para gobernar

**disarmament** (dihs AHR muh mehnt) reduction or limitation of armed forces and military weapons (p. 738)
***desarme*** reducción o limitación de las fuerzas armadas o armas militares

**discrimination** (dihs krihm ihn AY shuhn) denial of equal rights or equal treatment to certain groups of people (p. 395)
***discriminación*** negación de igualdad de derechos o de un tratamiento igualitario a ciertos grupos de personas

**dissent** (dihs SEHNT) disagreement (p. 267)
***disensión*** desacuerdo

**distinct** (dihs TIHNKT) clear or definite; clearly different in its quality (pp. 12, 466, 514)
***distinto*** claro o definido; que difiere claramente en cuanto a su calidad

**distribute** (dihs TRIHB yoot) to spread in an orderly way (p. 985)
***distribuir*** diseminar de manera ordenada

**divine right** (dih VĪN rīt) belief that a ruler's authority comes directly from God (p. 122)
***derecho divino*** creencia en que la autoridad de un gobernante proviene directamente de Dios

**dollar diplomacy** (DAHL er dih PLOH mah see) idea that economic ties were the best way to expand American influence (p. 696)
***diplomacia del dólar*** idea de que los lazos económicos eran el mejor recurso para expandir la influencia estadounidense

**domestic** (doh MEHS tihk) having to do with the home or household; pertaining to a country's internal affairs (pp. 108, 736, 782, 883)
***doméstico*** relacionado con la casa o el hogar; relativo a los asuntos internos de un país

**domino theory** (DAHM uh noh THEER ee) idea that if one country fell to communism, neighboring countries would follow (p. 908)
***teoría del efecto domino*** idea de que si un país caía bajo control comunista, los países vecinos lo seguirían

**doves** (duhvz) those who oppose war (p. 913)
***palomas*** quienes se oponen a la guerra

**draft** (draft) system of required military service (p. 530)
***leva*** sistema del servicio militar obligatorio

**dumping** (DUHMP ing) selling goods in another country at very low prices (p. 342)
***inundación de mercado*** venta de productos en otro país a precios muy bajos

**duty** (DOOT ee) import tax (p. 146)
***aranceles*** impuestos a las importaciones

# E

**e-commerce** (ee KAHM ers) business and trade over the Internet (p. 983)
***comercio electrónico*** negocio y comercio a través de Internet

**economic depression** (eh koh NAH mihk dee PREH shuhn) period when business activity slows, prices and wages drop, and unemployment rises (p. 208)
***depresión económica*** período en el que la actividad comercial disminuye, los precios y los salarios bajan y el desempleo aumenta

**economy** (ee KAHN uh mee) system governing the production, use, and distribution of goods; system of business and personal transactions by which people in a region or nation earn their livings (p. 404)
***economía*** sistema que gobierna la producción, el uso y la distribución de bienes; sistema de transacciones comerciales y personales mediante las cuales los habitantes de una región o país se ganan la vida

**efficient** (ee FISH ehnt) acting effectively, without wasted cost or effort (pp. 191, 386, 463, 650, 826)
***eficiente*** que actúa con eficacia, sin desperdiciar costos ni esfuerzos

**eliminate** (ee LIHM ih nayt) to get rid of (pp. 422, 615, 920)
***eliminar*** deshacerse de algo

**emancipate** (ee MAN sih payt) to set free (p. 524)
***emancipar*** liberar

**embargo** (ehm BAHR goh) government order that forbids foreign trade (p. 324)
*embargo* orden gubernamental que prohíbe el comercio exterior

**embrace** (ehm BRAYS) to accept; to hold tight to; to readily accept (p. 496)
*abrazar* aceptar; aferrarse a; aceptar sin dificultad

**emotion** (ee MOH shuhn) strong feeling such as sadness, anger, or love (pp. 214, 432)
*emoción* sentimiento intenso; por ejemplo, tristeza, ira o amor

**emotional** (ee MOH shuh nuhl) appealing to the emotions, or feelings, of people (p. 147)
*emocional* relativo a las emociones o sentimientos de la gente

**emphasize** (EHM fah sīz) to stress; to make more important (pp. 389, 809)
*recalcar* destacar; dar más importancia

**encomienda** (ehn koh mih EHN dah) land granted to Spanish settlers that included the right to demand labor or taxes from Native Americans (p. 147)
*encomienda* terreno otorgado a los colonos españoles, que incluía el derecho a exigir trabajo o impuestos de los indígenas americanos

**encounter** (ehn KOWN ter) battle or fight (p. 859)
*encuentro* batalla o lucha

**encounter** (ehn KOWN ter) to meet in an unexpected way; to experience (pp. 534, 859)
*tropezar con* encontrar de modo inesperado; experimentar

**enlightened** (ehn LĪT ehnd) to be freed from the superstitions and ignorance of the Middle Ages and embrace reason and experience (p. 4)
*ilustrado* liberado de las supersticiones e ignorancia de la Edad Media y que ha abrazado la razón y la experiencia

**enlist** (ehn LIHST) to sign up for military duty (p. 187)
*enlistarse* inscribirse para el servicio militar

**enrich** (ehn RIHCH) to make wealthy; to improve or increase in quality or wealth (pp. 362, 644, 987)
*enriquecer* hacer rico; mejorar o aumentar en cuanto a calidad o riqueza

**entrepreneur** (ahn treh preh NEWR) someone who sets up new businesses to make a profit (p. 614)
*empresario* persona que establece negocios nuevos para obtener ganancias

**environmentalist** (ehn vī ruhn MEHNT uhl ihst) person who works to protect the environment (p. 978)
*ambientalista* persona que trabaja para proteger el medio ambiente

**escalate** (EHS kuh layt) to increase or expand (p. 911)
*escalar* aumentar o ampliar

**evident** (EHV ih dehnt) clear; easy to understand; obvious (p. 989)
*evidente* claro; fácil de entender; obvio

**exceed** (ehks SEED) to go beyond what is expected; to outdo or be greater than what was planned (pp. 535, 842)
*exceder* ir más allá de lo esperado; superar lo proyectado

**excise tax** (EHKS īz tax) tax placed on the making of or use of a product (p. 379)
*impuesto sobre consumos* impuesto que se aplica a la manufactura o uso de un producto

**exclude** (ehks KLOOD) to keep out or expel; to reject or not be considered (pp. 428, 629, 684)
*excluir* mantener fuera o expulsar; rechazar o no considerar

**executive** (ehks ZEHK yoo tihv) in government, person who runs the government and sees that the laws are carried out (p. 205)
*ejecutivo* en un gobierno, persona que dirige el gobierno y hace cumplir las leyes

**exert** (ehks ZERT) to use; to put into action (pp. 645, 897)
*ejercer* utilizar; poner en acción

**expansion** (ehks PAN shuhn) extending of a nation beyond its existing borders (p. 447)
*expansión* acto de extender un país más allá de sus fronteras existentes

**expedition** (ehks peh DIH shuhn) journey undertaken by a group of people with an objective (p. 317)
*expedición* viaje que emprende un grupo de personas con un objetivo concreto

**extended family** (ehks TEHN dehd  FAM ih lee) close-knit family group that includes parents, children, grandparents, aunts, uncles, and cousins (pp. 107, 400)
*familia extensa* grupo familiar unido que incluye a los padres, hijos, abuelos, tías, tíos y primos

**external** (ehk STER nuhl) from the outside; having to do with foreign countries (p. 969)
*externo* de afuera; relacionado con países extranjeros

# F

**faction** (FAK shuhn) organized political group (pp. 290, 382)
*facción* grupo político organizado

**factor** (FAK tor) condition or quality that causes something else to happen (pp. 45, 558, 608)
*factor* condición o cualidad que provoca que ocurra algo distinto

**factory system** (FAK tor ee  SIHS tehm) methods of production that bring workers and machinery together in one place (p. 383)
*sistema de fábricas* métodos de producción que reúnen trabajadores y maquinaria en un mismo lugar

**famine** (FAM ihn) widespread starvation (p. 394)
*hambruna* escasez generalizada de alimentos

**farm cooperative** (fahrm  koh AH per at ihv) group of farmers who pool their money to make large purchases of tools, seeds, and other supplies at a discount (p. 598)
*cooperativa agrícola* grupo de agricultores que forman un fondo común con su dinero para hacer compras grandes de herramientas, semillas y otras provisiones a precio con descuento

**fascism** (FASH ihz uhm) political system based on militarism, extreme nationalism, and blind loyalty to the state and its leader (p. 803)
*fascismo* sistema político basado en el militarismo, en el nacionalismo extremo y en la lealtad ciega al estado y su líder

**fate** (fayt) outcome; consequence or final result (p. 908)
*destino* resultado; consecuencia o resultado final

**federalism** (FEHD er uhl ihz uhm) principle of the U.S. Constitution that establishes the division of power between the federal government and the states (p. 257)
*federalismo* principio de la Constitución de Estados Unidos que establece la división de poderes entre el gobierno federal y los estados

**feudalism** (FYOOD uhl ihz uhm) system in which a ruler grants parts of his land to lords in exchange for military service and financial assistance (p. 25)
*feudalismo* sistema en el cual el gobernante otorga parte de su tierra a los señores a cambio de servicio militar y ayuda financiera

**finance** (FĪ nans) to pay for; to supply with money (p. 120)
*financiar* pagar por algo; proveer dinero

**fireside chat** (FĪR sīd chat) informal radio speech first given by President Franklin D. Roosevelt while in office (p. 777)
*charla informal* discurso radial informal dado inicialmente por el presidente Franklin D. Roosevelt mientras estaba en el cargo

**flexible** (FLEHKS ah bahl) capable of change (pp. 221, 983)
*flexible* capaz de cambiar

**forty-niner** (FOR tee  NĪ ner) person who came to California in search of gold (p. 464)
*los del cuarenta y nueve* personas que vinieron a California en busca de oro

**fossil** (FAHS uhl) hardened remains of a plant or animal that lived long ago (p. 980)
*fósil* restos endurecidos de una planta o animal que vivió hace mucho tiempo

**fragment** (FRAG mehnt) broken part or piece; small section of something (p. 501)
*fragmento* parte rota o pieza de algo; sección pequeña de algo

**free enterprise** (free  EHN ter prīz) economic system in which each privately owned business decides what to produce, how much to produce, and what prices to charge (p. 616)
*libre empresa* sistema económico en el que cada empresa de propiedad privada decide qué producir, cuánto producir y qué precios cobrar

**free trade** (free trayd) agreement between countries to buy and sell without quotas or tariffs on imports or exports (p. 977)
*libre comercio* acuerdo entre países para vender y comprar sin cupos o aranceles sobre las importaciones o exportaciones

**freedmen** (FREED mehn) men and women who were legally freed from slavery after the Civil War (p. 548)
*libertos* hombres y mujeres liberados jurídicamente de la esclavitud después de la Guerra Civil

**freedom of the press** (FREE duhm  uhv  thuh  prehs) right of newspapers and other public media to publish articles believed to be accurate (p. 105)
*libertad de prensa* derecho de los diarios y otros medios públicos de comunicación a publicar artículos cuyo contenido consideran como cierto

**frontier** (fruhn TIR) land that forms the furthest extent of a nation's settled regions (p. 444)
*frontera* territorio que constituye la extensión más lejana de las regiones establecidas de un país

**fugitive** (FYOO jih tihv) runaway (p. 484)
*fugitivo* persona que huye

**function** (FUHNK shuhn) purpose; proper use; official duty (pp. 90, 885)
*función* propósito; uso adecuado; responsabilidades que conlleva un cargo

**fundamental** (fuhn duh MEHN tahl) most important part; foundation of an idea or action; the essential quality (pp. 78, 293, 385, 793)
*fundamental* lo más importante; la base de una idea o acción; la cualidad esencial

# G

**genocide** (JEHN uh sīd) deliberate attempt to kill or destroy an entire nation or group of people (p. 826)
*genocidio* intento deliberado de matar o destruir a toda una nación o grupo de personas

**gentry** (JEHN tree) upper class of colonial society (p. 110)
*alta burguesía* clase alta de la sociedad colonial

**ghetto** (GEHT oh) poor run-down neighborhood where one group of people live due to poverty or prejudice (p. 891)
*gueto* vecindario pobre y decadente donde vive un grupo de gente por motivos de pobreza o prejuicios

**glacier** (GLAY sher) thick sheet of ice (p. 6)
*glaciar* gruesa capa de hielo

**glastnost** (GLAHS nawst) policy in the Soviet Union of speaking openly about society's problems (p. 945)
*glastnost (apertura)* política de la Unión Soviética de hablar abiertamente sobre los problemas de la sociedad

**global warming** (GLOH buhl WAWRM ihng) slow but steady worldwide rise in temperatures (p. 981)
*calentamiento global* aumento lento, pero constante, de las temperaturas en el mundo

**globalization** (gloh buhl ī ZAY shuhn) process of creating an international network of trade, communication, and culture (p. 976)
*globalización* proceso de crear una red internacional de comercio, comunicación y cultura

**graduated income tax** (GRAD yoo ay tehd IHN kuhm  taks) tax on earning that charges different rates for different income levels (p. 647)
*impuesto sobre la renta escalonado* impuesto sobre las ganancias que aplica tasas diferentes a los distintos niveles de ingreso

**grandfather clause** (GRAND fah ther  klawz) law that excused a voter from a literacy test if his father or grandfather had been eligible to vote on January 1, 1867 (p. 560)
*cláusula del abuelo* ley que eximía a un votante de la prueba de alfabetización si su padre o abuelo había tenido derecho a votar el 1 de enero de 1867

**grange** (graynj) group of farmers who met for lectures, sewing bees, and other events (p. 598)
*grange* grupo de agricultores que se reunían para participar en conferencias, círculos de costura y otras actividades

**grievance** (GREE vans) formal complaint (p. 172)
*querella* queja formal

**guerrilla** (guh RIHL uh) fighter who works as part of a small band to make hit-and-run attacks (pp. 191, 909)
*guerrillero* combatiente dentro de un pequeño grupo que realiza ataques relámpago

**guest worker** (gehst WER ker) temporary immigrant worker (p. 987)
*trabajador visitante* trabajador inmigrante temporero

# H

**habeas corpus** (HAY bee ihs KOR puhs) the right not to be held in prison without first being charged with a specific crime; constitutional protection against unlawful imprisonment (pp. 104, 252, 529)
*habeas corpus* derecho a no ser encarcelado sin antes haber sido acusado de un delito específico; protección constitucional contra el encarcelamiento ilegal

**hawks** (hawks) those who support, or are in favor of, a particular war (p. 913)
*halcones* personas que apoyan o están a favor de una guerra específica

**homesteader** (HOHM steh der) settler who acquired free land offered by the government (p. 595)
*finquero* colono que adquirió tierras gratis ofrecidas por el gobierno

**hostile** (HAHS tihl) unfriendly; intending to do harm (pp. 291, 383, 450, 688, 837)
*hostil* poco amistoso; que se propone hacer daño

# I

**immigrate** (IHM mah grayt) to move into a foreign region or country (p. 581)
*inmigrar* mudarse a una región o país extranjero

**impeachment** (ihm PEECH mehnt) process of bringing formal charges against a public official (p. 556)
*juicio político* proceso que consiste en presentar una acusación formal contra un funcionario público

**imperialism** (ihm PIR ee uhl ihz uhm) building empires by imposing outside rule on peoples around the world (p. 681)
*imperialismo* construcción de imperios imponiendo un gobierno extranjero a pueblos de otras partes del mundo

**impose** (ihm POHZ) to place a burden on something or someone (pp. 66, 285, 490, 555, 738)
*imponer* colocar una carga sobre algo o alguien

**impressment** (ihm PREHS mehnt) act of forcing a person into service; practice of seizing sailors on American ships and forcing them to serve in the British navy (pp. 296, 388)
*leva* práctica de obligar a una persona a prestar servicio militar; captura de marineros de navíos estadounidenses para obligarlos a servir en la armada británica

**impulse** (IHM puhls) sudden push or driving force; sudden action; driving force behind an action (p. 415)
*impulso* empujón repentino o fuerza motriz; acción repentina; la fuerza motriz detrás de una acción

**inauguration** (ihn awg er AY shuhn) ceremony in which the President officially takes the oath of office (pp. 282, 374)
*toma de mando* ceremonia en la que el presidente hace el juramento propio de su cargo

**income tax** (IHN kuhm taks) tax on the money people earn (p. 531)
*impuesto a los ingresos* impuesto sobre el dinero que la gente gana

**indentured servant** (ihn DEHN cherd SER vehnt) person who signs a contract to work for a set number of years in exchange for ocean passage to the colonies (p. 111)
*sirviente contratado* persona que firma un contrato para trabajar durante un número determinado de años a cambio de un pasaje oceánico a las colonias

**individualism** (ihn dih VIHD yoo uhl ihz uhm) concept that stresses the importance of each individual (p. 432)
*individualismo* concepto que hace hincapié en la importancia de cada individuo

**Industrial Revolution** (ihn DUHS tree uhl rehv oh LYOO shuhn) gradual replacement of many hand tools by machines (p. 382)
*Revolución Industrial* sustitución gradual de muchas herramientas manuales por máquinas

**inferior** (ihn FIR ee uhr) less worthy; less valuable; of lower rank; of poorer quality (pp. 395, 561, 803)
*inferior* menos digno; menos valioso; de categoría más baja; de menor calidad

**inflation** (ihn FLAY shuhn) general rise in prices (pp. 531, 599, 924)
*inflación* aumento generalizado de los precios

**infrastructure** (IHN frah struhk cher) basic public works needed for a society to function, including the systems of roads, bridges, and tunnels (p. 343, 778)
*infraestructura* obras públicas básicas necesarias para el funcionamiento de una sociedad, como los sistemas de carreteras, puentes y túneles

**initiative** (ihn IH shee ah tihv) process that allows voters to put a bill before a state legislature (p. 647)
*iniciativa* procedimiento que permite a los votantes presentar un proyecto de ley ante una legislatura estatal

**inner city** (IHN er SIHT ee) center of an older city (p. 847)
*centro urbano* la zona centro de una ciudad con bastantes años

**installment buying** (ihn STAWL mehnt BĪ ihng) buying on credit (p. 752)
*compra a plazos* compra por medio de crédito

**integrate** (IHN teh grayt) to bring together; to join parts so they become a whole; to bring together individuals of different races to achieve equality (p. 60)
*integrar* reunir; juntar partes para que formen un todo; reunir individuos de diferentes razas para lograr igualdad

**integration** (ihn tuh GRAY shuhn) mixing of different racial groups (p. 875)
*integración* mezcla de diferentes grupos raciales

**interchangeable parts** (ihn ter CHAYNJ ah buhl pahrts) identical pieces that can be assembled quickly by unskilled workers (p. 386)
*partes intercambiables* piezas idénticas que pueden ser ensambladas con rapidez por trabajadores no calificados

**interest group** (IHN trehst groop) organization that represents the concerns of a particular group (p. 271)
*grupo de intereses* organización que representa los asuntos que conciernen a un grupo en particular

**intermediate** (ihn ter MEE dee iht) happening in between; in the middle (p. 945)
*intermedio* que ocurre entre determinadas cosas; en medio

**intern** (IHN tern) to temporarily imprison so as to keep from leaving a country (p. 818)
*recluir* encarcelar temporalmente con el fin de evitar la huida del país

**interstate commerce** (IHN ter stayt KAHM mers) trade between two or more states (p. 344)
*comercio interestatal* intercambio comercial entre dos o más estados

**invest** (ihn VEHST) to purchase something with money with the hope that its value will grow; to supply money for a project in order to make a profit (pp. 284, 383, 696)
*invertir* adquirir algo a cambio de dinero con la esperanza de que su valor aumente; facilitar dinero para un proyecto para que dé ganacias

**iron curtain** (Ī ern KERT uhn) barrier of secrecy and censorship that keeps a country isolated from the rest of the world (p. 837)
*telón de acero* barrera de secretismo y censura que mantiene a un país aislado del resto del mundo

**ironclad** (Ī ern klad) warship covered with protective iron plates (p. 518)
*acorazado* barco de guerra cubierto con placas protectoras de hierro

**irrigate** (IR uh gayt) to water crops by channeling water from rivers or streams (p. 7)
*irrigar* regar los cultivos canalizando el agua de los ríos o arroyos

**island hopping** (Ī luhnd HAHP ihng) Allied strategy used during World War II to gain control of the Pacific Islands (p. 824)
*salto de isla a isla* estrategia aliada usada durante la Segunda Guerra Mundial para obtener el control de las islas del Pacífico

**isolate** (Ī soh layt) to set apart; to separate (pp. 403, 503, 627, 743)
*aislar* apartar; separar

**isolated** (ī soh lay tehd) set apart; separated (p. 449)
**aislado** apartado; separado

**isolationism** (ī soh LAY shuhn ihz uhm) avoiding involvement in other countries' affairs (p. 675)
**aislacionismo** práctica de evitar la participación en los asuntos de otros países

**isthmus** (IHS muhs) narrow strip of land having water on each side and joining two larger areas of land (p. 687)
**istmo** franja estrecha de tierra con agua a ambos lados y que une dos extensiones de tierra más grandes

# J

**jazz** (jaz) original style of music that combined rhythms from West Africa and the Caribbean, work chants and spirituals from the rural South, and harmonies from Europe (p. 747)
**jazz** estilo original de música que combina ritmos de África occidental y el Caribe, cantos laborales y religiosos del sur rural estadounidense y harmonías de Europa

**joint resolution** (joint  reh soh LYOO shuhn) agreement approved by a majority of members in both houses (p. 458)
**resolución conjunta** convenio aprobado por una mayoría de los integrantes de las dos cámaras

**judicial branch** (jyoo DIH shuhl  branch) system of courts to settle disputes involving national issues (p. 213)
**poder judicial** sistema de tribunales para dirimir pleitos referentes a cuestiones nacionales

**judicial review** (jyoo DIH shuhl  ree VYOO) principle that the Supreme Court has the right to decide whether acts of Congress are constitutional or not (p. 313)
**revisión judicial** principio según el cual la Corte Suprema tiene derecho a decidir si los actos del Congreso son constitucionales

**jurisdiction** (jer ihs DIHK shuhn) power of a court to hear and decide cases (p. 262)
**jurisdicción** potestad de un tribunal para conocer y resolver sobre casos

**justify** (JUHS tih fī) to give good reason for an action (p. 616)

**justificar** dar buenas razones para una acción

# K

**kamikaze** (kah muh KAH zee) World War II Japanese pilot trained to make a suicidal crash attack, usually upon a ship (p. 824)
**kamikaze** piloto japonés de la Segunda Guerra Mundial entrenado para realizar ataques suicidas, estrellándose generalmente sobre un barco

**kayak** (KĪ ak) boat consisting of a light wooden frame covered with watertight skins except for a single or double opening in the center, and propelled by a double-bladed paddle (p. 12)
**kayac** bote que consta de una ligera estructura de madera cubierta de pieles impermeables a excepción de una única o doble abertura en el centro, y que se impulsa por medio de un remo de dos paletas

# L

**laissez faire** (LAY seh  fair) idea that government should not interfere in the economy (p. 311)
**laissez faire** idea de que el gobierno no debe entrometerse en la economía

**land grant** (land  grant) government gift of land (p. 446)
**concesión de tierras** donación de tierras por parte del gobierno

**laser** (LAY zer) device that sends out a powerful beam of focused light (p. 983)
**láser** dispositivo que emite un potente haz de luz concentrada

**legislature** (LEHJ ihs lay cher) part of a government that makes laws (pp. 103, 205)
**legislatura** parte de un gobierno que se encarga de elaborar leyes

**levy** (LEHV ee) to impose a tax by law; to force to be paid (pp. 102, 454, 531)
**gravar** imponer una contribución por ley; obligar a que se pague

**libel** (LĪ behl) publishing of false statements that unjustly damage a person's reputation (pp. 105, 267)
**libelo** publicación de afirmaciones falsas que dañan injustamente la reputación de una persona

**limited government** (LIHM ih tehd GUHV ern mehnt) the principle that the government has only the powers that the Constitution gives it (p. 256)
*gobierno limitado* el principio de que el gobierno tiene únicamente los poderes que la Constitución le otorga

**literacy test** (LIH ter ah see tehst) examination to see if a person can read and write; used in the past to restrict voting rights (p. 560)
*prueba de alfabetización* examen para establecer si una persona sabe leer y escribir, se usaba en el pasado para restringir el derecho al voto

**lode** (lohd) large deposit of precious metal that reaches from deep underground toward the surface (p. 466)
*filón* depósito grande de un metal precioso que se extiende desde un punto profundo bajo tierra hacia la superficie

**logic** (LAH jihk) reason; good sense; careful thought (p. 171)
*lógica* razón; buen juicio; reflexión cuidadosa

**lynching** (LIHNCH ihng) when a mob illegally seizes and executes someone (p. 661)
*linchamiento* cuando una multitud captura y ejecuta ilegalmente a una persona

# M

**mandatory retirement** (MAN duh tawr ee ree TĪR mehnt) policy that requires people to stop working at a certain age (p. 896)
*jubilación obligatoria* política que obliga a la gente a dejar de trabajar a cierta edad

**manual** (MAN yoo ahl) involving work done by hand (pp. 444, 581)
*manual* referente al trabajo que se hace con las manos

**martial law** (MAHR shuhl law) type of rule in which the military is in charge and citizens' rights are suspended (p. 513)
*ley marcial* tipo de gobierno en el que los militares están al mando y se suspenden los derechos de los ciudadanos

**mass production** (mas proh DUHK shuhn) manufacturing of large numbers of identical products quickly and cheaply (pp. 386, 612)

*producción en masa* manufactura rápida y a bajo costo de un gran número de productos idénticos

**maximum** (MAK suh muhm) largest; highest; greatest (p. 113)
*máximo* el más extenso; más alto; mayor o mejor

**mercantilism** (MER kan tihl ihz uhm) economic policy that held that a nation prospered by exporting more goods to foreign nations than it imported from them (p. 50)
*mercantilismo* principio económico según el cual una nación prospera exportando más bienes a países extranjeros que los que importa de ellos

**mercenary** (MER sehn air ee) soldier who fights merely for pay, often for a foreign country (pp. 161, 181)
*mercenario* soldado que combate tan sólo por una paga, casi siempre en favor de un país extranjero

**middle class** (MIHD uhl klas) in the 13 colonies, a portion of the colonial population that included small planters, independent farmers, and skilled craftsworkers (p. 111)
*clase media* en las 13 colonias, parte de la población colonial que incluía a los pequeños cultivadores, a los granjeros independientes y a los artesanos

**migrant worker** (MĪ grehnt WER ker) person who moves from one region to another in search of work (p. 784)
*trabajador migrante* persona que se muda de una región a otra en busca de trabajo

**militarism** (MIHL uh tuh rihz uhm) glorification of the military (p. 706)
*militarismo* glorificación de los militares

**militia** (mih LIH shah) organized body of armed volunteers (p. 140)
*milicia* cuerpo organizado de voluntarios armados

**minimize** (MIHN ah mīz) to reduce to the lowest possible amount (p. 204)
*reducir al mínimo* disminuir a la cantidad más pequeña posible

**minimum** (MIHN ah muhm) smallest amount possible or allowed (pp. 146, 632, 791)
*mínimo* cantidad más pequeña posible o permitida

**minuteman** (MIHN uht man) colonial militia volunteer who was prepared to fight at a minute's notice (p. 152)
*miliciano de la Guerra de Independencia* voluntario de la milicia colonial que estaba siempre preparado para luchar

**mission** (MIHSH uhn) religious settlement run by Catholic priests and friars; settlement that aims to spread a religion into a new area (p. 47)
*misión* colonia religiosa administrada por sacerdotes católicos y frailes; asentamiento cuya finalidad es diseminar la religión en una nueva zona

**modify** (MAHD ih fī) to change to or in (p. 897)
*modificar* cambiar a algo o en algo

**monopoly** (muhn AH poh lee) company that controls all or nearly all business in a particular industry (pp. 150, 615)
*monopolio* compañía que controla toda o casi toda la actividad de una industria en particular

**monotheism** (MAHN oh thee ihz uhm) belief that there is only one god (p. 22)
*monoteísmo* creencia de que solamente hay un dios

**motive** (MOH tihv) thought or feeling behind an action (p. 55)
*motivo* pensamiento o sentimiento detrás de una acción

**mountain man** (MOWN tehn man) fur trapper of the Northwest (p. 449)
*hombre de montaña* cazador de pieles del Noroeste

**muckraker** (MUHK rak er) crusading journalist (p. 648)
*muckraker* periodista que busca poner en evidencia las ruindades de las personas

**mutualista** (myoo chew LEES tah) Mexican American mutual aid group (p. 663)
*mutualista* grupo de ayuda mutua de los estadounidenses de origen mexicano

**myth** (mihth) story or legend; imaginary object; invented story (pp. 37, 593)

*mito* cuento o leyenda; objeto imaginario; relato inventado

# N

**napalm** (NAY pahm) explosive, jelly-like substance that would burst into flames and stick to peoples' bodies, causing severe burns (p. 912)
*napalm* sustancia explosiva de tipo gelatinosa que estalla en llamas y se pega a la piel de las personas, causando severas quemaduras

**national park** (NA shuhn uhl pahrk) natural area protected and managed by the federal government (p. 651)
*parque nacional* extensión natural protegida y administrada por el gobierno federal

**nationalism** (NA shuhn uhl ihz uhm) devotion to the interests of one's own country; pride in one's own nation or ethnic group (pp. 327, 693)
*nacionalismo* lealtad a los intereses del propio país; orgullo respecto a la propia nación o grupo étnico

**nativist** (NAY tihv ihst) person who wanted to preserve the United States for white, American-born Protestants and who was opposed to immigration (p. 394)
*nativista* persona que buscaba reservar Estados Unidos para los protestantes blancos nacidos en el país, y que se oponía a la inmigración

**natural rights** (NA cher uhl rīts) rights that belong to every human being from birth (p. 122)
*derechos naturales* derechos de los que goza todo ser humano desde el momento de su nacimiento

**naturalization** (na cher uhl ih ZAY shuhn) legal process guaranteeing citizenship (p. 270)
*naturalización* procedimiento jurídico que garantiza la ciudadanía

**navigation** (nav uh GAY shuhn) science of locating the position and plotting the course of ships (p. 19)
*navegación* ciencia de ubicar la posición y de trazar el trayecto de los barcos

**negative** (NEHG ah tihv) in opposition to an idea; not positive (pp. 41, 846)
*negativo* opuesto a una idea; no positivo

**neutral** (NEW truhl) not favoring either side in a dispute (pp. 295, 387, 513)
*neutral* que no favorece a ninguna de las partes en un pleito

**nominating convention** (NAHM ih nay ting kuhn VEHN shuhn) large meeting of party delegates to choose candidates for office (p. 352)
*convención de postulación* gran encuentro de delegados de un partido para elegir candidatos a un cargo

**northwest passage** (NORTH wehst PAS saj) water route through or around North America (p. 51)
*paso del noroeste* ruta navegable a través o alrededor de América del Norte

**nullification** (nuhl ih fih KAY shuhn) idea that a state has the right to nullify, or cancel, a federal law that the state leaders consider to be unconstitutional (p. 364)
*anulación* idea de que un estado tiene derecho a anular o cancelar una ley federal que los dirigentes del estado consideran inconstitucional

**nullify** (NUHL ih fī) to cancel a federal law; to deprive of legal force (pp. 301, 393)
*anular* cancelar una ley federal; privar de fuerza jurídica

## O

**open range** (OH pehn raynj) unfenced land (p. 590)
*campo abierto* terreno no cercado

**option** (AHP shuhn) choice; possible course of action (p. 192)
*opción* elección; posible manera de actuación

**outsourcing** (OWT sors ihng) having work done in other countries; sending out work to an outside provider or manufacturer in order to cut costs (p. 976)
*subcontratación* realizar el trabajo en otros países; enviar el trabajo a un proveedor o manufacturero exterior con el fin de recortar costes

**overproduction** (oh ver proh DUHK shuhn) situation in which the supply of manufactured goods exceeds the demand (p. 771)
*superproducción* situación en la cual la oferta de bienes manufacturados excede la demanda

**override** (OH ver rīd) set aside; disregard; overrule; replace (pp. 259, 553)
*invalidar* dejar de lado; no tener en cuenta; no admitir; sustituir

## P

**parochial school** (pah ROH kee uhl skool) school sponsored by a church (p. 665)
*escuela parroquial* escuela auspiciada por una iglesia

**participate** (pahr TIHS ah payt) to take part in; to share in an activity (pp. 24, 349, 754)
*participar* tomar parte en algo; compartir una actividad

**patent** (PAT ehnt) document that gives someone the sole right to make and to sell an invention (p. 610)
*patente* documento que otorga a una persona el derecho exclusivo a fabricar y vender un invento

**payroll tax** (PAY rohl tax) money the government is authorized to remove from a worker's salary and used to help support the government (p. 790)
*impuestos sobre sueldos* cantidad de dinero que el gobierno está autorizado a retirar del salario de los trabajadores y que se usa para el mantenimiento del gobierno

**pendulum** (PEHN jah luhm) hanging weight that swings from side to side in a steady rhythm (p. 811)
*péndulo* peso que cuelga y que oscila de lado a lado a ritmo constante

*peninsular* (peh nihn suh LAR) Spanish colonist who was born in Spain (p. 48)
*peninsular* colono español nacido en España

**pension** (PEHN shuhn) sum of money paid regularly as a retirement benefit (p. 781)
*pensión* cantidad de dinero pagada regularmente como beneficio o prestación de jubilación

**persecute** (PER suh kyoot) to mistreat due to one's religion, race, or political beliefs (p. 69)
*perseguir* maltratar a alguien por razón de su religión, raza o creencias políticas

**persist** (per SIHST) to endure; to continue in the face of difficulty (pp. 591, 879)
*resistir* soportar; continuar a pesar de la dificultad

**petition** (peh TIH shuhn) formal written request to someone in authority that is signed by a group of people (p. 147)
*petición* solicitud formal por escrito, firmada por un grupo de personas y dirigida a una autoridad

**pilgrim** (PIHL gruhm) person who takes a religious journey (p. 69)
*peregrino* persona que emprende un viaje religioso

**plantation** (plan TAY shuhn) large estate farmed by many workers (pp. 47, 87)
*plantación* finca grande cultivada por muchos trabajadores

**poll tax** (pohl taks) personal tax to be paid before voting (p. 560)
*impuesto al voto* impuesto personal que debía pagarse para poder votar

**polygamy** (poh LIHG ah mee) practice of having more than one wife at a time (p. 463)
*poligamia* práctica de tener más de una esposa al mismo tiempo

**pool** (pool) agreement to divide up business in an area and fix rates at a high level (p. 609)
*mancomunidad* convenio para dividirse el negocio de una zona y fijar tarifas altas

**popular sovereignty** (PAH pyoo lahr SAH ver ehn tee) the idea that the people are the key source of a government's authority; right of people in a territory or state to vote directly on issues rather than have their elected representatives decide (pp. 256, 483)
*soberanía popular* la idea de que la gente es la fuente clave de la autoridad del gobierno; derecho de los habitantes de un territorio o estado a votar directamente sobre ciertas cuestiones en vez de que sus representantes electos decidan

**potlatch** (PAHT lach) ceremony held by some Native American groups at which the hosts showered their guests with gifts such as woven cloth, baskets, canoes, and furs (p. 12)

*potlach* ceremonia realizada por algunos grupos de indígenas americanos en la cual los anfitriones agasajaban a sus huéspedes con regalos como tejidos, cestas, canoas y pieles

**preamble** (PREE am buhl) introduction to a declaration, constitution, or other official document (p. 172)
*preámbulo* introducción a una declaración, constitución u otro documento oficial

**precedent** (PREH seh dehnt) example to be followed by others in the future (pp. 283, 375)
*precedente* ejemplo a seguir por otros en el futuro

**precise** (pree SĪS) exact; accurate (p. 27)
*preciso* exacto; acertado, certero

**predestination** (pree dehs tihn AY shuhn) idea that God decides the fate of a person's soul even before birth (p. 415)
*predestinación* idea de que Dios decide el destino del alma de una persona incluso antes de su nacimiento

**presidio** (prih SIHD ee oh) military post where soldiers lived in the Spanish colonies (p. 92)
*presidio* puesto militar donde vivían los soldados en las colonias españolas

**primary** (PRĪ mair ee) election in which voters, rather than party leaders, choose their party's candidate for an election (p. 646)
*primaria* elección donde los votantes, y no los dirigentes de un partido, eligen el candidato de su partido para una elección

**prior** (PRĪ or) preceding in time; earlier; former (p. 150)
*previo* que precede en tiempo; anteriormente; antiguo

**private property** (PRĪ veht PRAH per tee) property owned by an individual (p. 252)
*propiedad privada* propiedad que pertenece a una persona

**privateer** (prī vuh TEER) armed civilian ship that had the government's permission to attack enemy ships and keep goods seized (p. 190)
*corsario* barco civil armado con el permiso del gobierno para atacar a los barcos enemigos y quedarse con los bienes capturados

**productivity** (proh duhk TIHV uh tee) rate at which workers produce goods (p. 845)
*productividad* índice de producción de bienes de los trabajadores

**prohibition** (proh ih BIH shuhn) total ban on the sale and consumption of alcohol (pp. 416, 659, 741)
*ley seca* prohibición total de la venta y consumo de alcohol

**propaganda** (prah peh GAN dah) false or misleading information that is spread to further a cause; information used to sway public opinion (p. 488)
*propaganda* información falsa o engañosa que se difunde para apoyar una causa; información usada para influir en la opinión pública

**proprietary colony** (proh PRĪ eh tair ee  KAHL uhn ee) English colony in which the king gave land to one or more proprietors, or owners, in exchange for a yearly payment (p. 78)
*colonia de propietarios* colonia inglesa donde el rey concedía tierras a uno o más propietarios o dueños a cambio de un pago anual

**proprietor** (proh PRĪ ah tor) owner of a business or colony (p. 86)
*propietario* dueño de una empresa o colonia

**prospect** (PRAHS pehkt) expectation; something to look forward to happening (pp. 110, 170, 310, 464, 684)
*prospecto* expectativa; algo que se desea que ocurra

**protectorate** (proh TEHK tor ayt) independent country whose policies are controlled by an outside power (p. 692)
*protectorado* país independiente cuya dirección está bajo el control de una potencia extranjera

**province** (PRAHV ahns) governmental division of a country, similar to a state (pp. 51, 346)
*provincia* división gubernamental de un país, semejante a un estado

**provoke** (prah VOHK) to cause to anger; to excite; to cause an action (pp. 301, 393, 457, 977)
*provocar* incitar al enojo; excitar; dar lugar a una acción

**public school** (PUHB lihk  skool) school supported by taxes (pp. 118, 417)
*escuela pública* escuela financiada con impuestos

**pueblo** (PWEHB loh) town in the Spanish colonies; Anasazi village (p. 93)
*pueblo* asentamiento en las colonias españolas; aldea anasazi

**pursue** (per SYOO) to chase after; to try to capture (pp. 331, 402, 851, 950)
*perseguir* ir tras de algo; tratar de capturar

# Q

**quote** (kwoht) to repeat the exact words spoken or written (p. 357)
*citar* repetir las palabras exactas habladas o escritas

# R

**racism** (RAY sihz uhm) belief that one race is superior or inferior to another (p. 116)
*racismo* creencia de que una raza es superior o inferior a otra

**ranchero** (ran CHAIR oh) owner of a ranch (p. 446)
*ranchero* dueño de un rancho

**ratify** (RAT ih fī) to approve (pp. 218, 264)
*ratificar* aprobar

**rationing** (RASH uhn ihng) limits set on the amount of certain goods people can buy (p. 817)
*racionar* establecer límites sobre la cantidad de ciertos bienes que la gente puede comprar

**react** (ree AKT) to act in response to an action; to respond (pp. 152, 298, 350, 390)
*reaccionar* actuar en respuesta a una acción; responder

**realist** (REE uhl ihst) writer or artist who tries to show life as it is (p. 634)
*realista* escritor o artista que intenta mostrar la vida tal como es

**recall** (REE kawl) process by which voters can remove an elected official from office (p. 647)
*destitución* proceso por el cual los votantes pueden retirar de su cargo a un funcionario electo

**recession** (rih SEHSH uhn) temporary economic slump that is milder than a depression (p. 939)
*recesión* descenso económico temporal menos grave que una depresión

**reconcentration** (ree kahn sehn TRAY shuhn) forced movement of large numbers of people into detention camps for military or political reason (p. 682)
*reconcentración* traslado de un gran número de personas a campos de confinamiento por motivos militares o políticos

**referendum** (reh fer EHN duhm) process by which citizens vote directly on a bill (p. 647)
*referéndum* procedimiento por el cual los ciudadanos votan directamente respecto a un proyecto de ley

**refugee** (REHF yoo jee) person who flees his or her homeland to seek safety elsewhere (p. 986)
*refugiado* persona que escapa de su país de origen en busca de seguridad en otro lugar

**reign** (rayn) period of dominance or rule (p. 393)
*reinado* período de dominación o gobierno

**reinforce** (ree ihn FORS) to make stronger; to strengthen; to make more effective (pp. 122, 328, 519, 875)
*reforzar* hacer más fuerte; fortalecer; hacer más eficaz

**rendezvous** (RAHN day voo) yearly meeting where trappers would trade furs for supplies (p. 449)
*rendezvous* encuentro anual en el que los tramperos intercambiaban pieles por provisiones

**renewable resource** (rih NOO uh buhl REE sors) energy source that can be quickly restored by nature (p. 980)
*recurso renovable* fuente energética que puede ser restablecida rápidamente por la naturaleza

**repeal** (ree PEEL) to cancel (pp. 152, 255)
*revocar* cancelar

**representative government** (reh pree SEHN tah tihv GUHV ern mehnt) political system in which voters elect others to make laws (p. 69)
*gobierno representativo* sistema político en el que los votantes eligen a otras personas para que elaboren las leyes

**reproduce** (ree prah DOOS) to make a copy (p. 435)
*reproducir* hacer una copia

**republic** (ree PUHB lihk) system of government in which the people choose representatives to govern them (pp. 25, 252)
*república* sistema de gobierno en el que la gente elige representantes que los gobernarán

**reservation** (reh zer VAY shuhn) area set aside by the government for Native Americans to live on (p. 586)
*reservación* territorio que el gobierno destina a ser habitado por indígenas americanos

**reside** (ree ZĪD) to live in; to dwell for a while; to exist in (pp. 8, 595)
*residir* vivir en algún lugar; habitar por un tiempo; existir

**resolution** (rehz uh LOO shuhn) formal statement of opinion or policy (p. 171)
*resolución* declaración formal de una opinión o política

**resolve** (ree SAHLV) to decide; to solve (pp. 143, 364, 548, 853)
*resolver* decidir; dar solución

**resource** (REE sors) supply of something to meet a particular need (pp. 188, 514)
*recurso* abasto de algo que satisface una necesidad en particular

**restore** (ree STOR) to bring back to a normal state; to put back; to reestablish (p. 50, 188, 326, 524, 888)
*restaurar* devolver a una condición normal; reponer; restablecer

**restrict** (ree STRIHKT) to confine; to keep within a certain boundary or limit; to place limitations on something or somebody (pp. 75, 742)
*restringir* confinar; mantener dentro de ciertas fronteras o límites; poner limitaciones a algo o alguien

**retain** (rih TAYN) to keep (p. 103)
*retener* mantener

**revival** (ree VĪ vuhl) huge outdoor religious meeting (p. 415)
*reunión evangelista* encuentro religioso de grandes proporciones al aire libre

**revolt** (ree VOHLT) uprising; rebellion; to rebel (pp. 116, 400, 682, 858, 909)
*revuelta* sublevación; rebelión

**rigid** (RIH jihd) strict; not easily bent or changed (pp. 48, 653)
*rígido* estricto; que no se dobla o cambia con facilidad

**rock-and-roll** (RAHK and rohl) style of music derived from rhythm and blues and country music (p. 846)
*rocanrol* estilo de música derivada del rhythm-and-blues y country (p. 846)

**royal colony** (ROI uhl KAHL uh nee) colony under direct control of the English crown (p. 78)
*colonia real* colonia bajo control directo de la corona inglesa

# S

**sachem** (SAY chuhm) member of the tribal chief council in the League of the Iroquois (p. 15)
*sachem (representante en tiempo de paz)* miembro del consejo del jefe tribal de la Liga de los iroqueses

**salvation** (sal VAY shuhn) in Christianity, the means for saving one from evil; everlasting afterlife (p. 23)
*salvación* en la cristiandad, la manera para librarse del mal; la vida eterna

**sanction** (SANK shuhn) penalty applied against a country in order to pressure it to change its policies (p. 949)
*sanción* castigo aplicado a un país con el fin de presionarlo para que cambie su política

**satellite** (SAT uhl īt) nation that is dominated politically and economically by a more powerful nation (p. 837)
*satélite* nación dominada política y económica-mente por otra más poderosa

**scalawag** (SKAL eh wag) southern white who opposed secession (p. 555)
*scalawag* blanco sureño que se oponía a la secesión

**secede** (seh SEED) to withdraw from membership in a group (pp. 331, 484)
*separarse* retirarse como miembro de un grupo

**sedition** (seh DIH shuhn) stirring up of rebellion against a government (pp. 300, 392)
*sedición* acto de fomentar la rebelión contra un gobierno

**segregation** (sehg reh GAY shuhn) enforced separation of races (p. 560)
*segregación* separación obligada de dos razas

**self-government** (sehlf GUHV ern mehnt) right of people to rule themselves independently (p. 348)
*autogobierno* derecho de las personas a gobernarse a sí mismas de forma independiente

**separation of powers** (seh pahr AY shuhn uhv POW ers) principle by which the powers of government are divided among separate branches (pp. 123, 253)
*separación de poderes* principio por el cual los poderes del gobierno se dividen entre sus distintas ramas

**sequence** (SEE kwehns) one thing occurring after another; series of events (p. 913)
*secuencia* cuando una cosa ocurre después de otra; serie de acontecimientos

**settlement house** (SEHT ehl mehnt hows) center offering help to the urban poor (p. 622)
*centro comunitario* centro que ofrece ayuda a los habitantes pobres de una ciudad

**sharecropper** (SHAIR krah per) person who rents a plot of land and farms it in exchange for a share of the crop (p. 561)
*aparcero* persona que alquila un terreno y lo cultiva a cambio de una parte de la cosecha

**siege** (seej) military blockade or bombardment of an enemy town or position in order to force it to surrender (pp. 455, 535)
*sitio* cerco militar o bombardeo de una población o posición enemiga a fin de obligarla a rendirse

**sit-down strike** (SIHT down strīk) form of protest in which workers remain in the workplace, but refuse to work until a settlement is reached (p. 791)
**huelga de brazos caídos** forma de protesta en la que los trabajadores permanecen en el lugar de trabajo, pero en la que rechazan trabajar hasta que se consiga un acuerdo

**sit-in** (SIHT ihn) form of protest in which people sit and refuse to leave (p. 888)
**sentada** forma de protesta en la cual la gente se sienta y se niega a irse

**slave code** (slayv kohd) one of a group of laws that controlled every aspect of enslaved African Americans' lives and denied them basic rights (pp. 116, 399)
**código de la esclavitud** una de un grupo de leyes que regulaban la vida de los esclavos afroamericanos y les negaban los derechos fundamentales

**smuggling** (SMUH glihng) act of illegally importing or exporting goods (p. 324)
**contrabando** importación o exportación ilegal de mercancías

**social reform** (SOH shuhl ree FORM) organized attempts to improve conditions of life (p. 414)
**reforma social** intentos organizados de mejorar las condiciones de vida

**sod** (sahd) soil held together by the tangled roots of grasses (p. 596)
**tepe** pedazo de tierra sujetado por las raíces enmarañadas del pasto

**sodbuster** (SAHD buhs ter) farmer on the Great Plains in the late 1800s (p. 596)
**sodbuster** granjero de las Grandes Llanuras de la segunda mitad del siglo XIX

**sooner** (SOO ner) person who sneaked onto the land before the start of the Oklahoma land rush (p. 598)
**sooner** persona que se introdujo a escondidas en las tierras antes de que comenzara la carrera por las tierras de Oklahoma

**speakeasy** (SPEEK ee zee) illegal tavern that served liquor during Prohibition (p. 741)
**taberna clandestina** taberna ilegal donde se servían bebidas alcohólicas durante la Prohibición

**specify** (SPEHS uh fī) to describe or to point out in detail (pp. 73, 777)
**especificar** describir o señalar en detalle

**speculator** (SPEHK yoo lay tor) person who invests in a risky venture in the hope of making a large profit (p. 284)
**especulador** persona que invierte en una empresa arriesgada con la esperanza de tener grandes ganancias

**sphere** (sfeer) rounded shape; area of interest or influence (pp. 17, 837)
**esfera** figura redondeada; zona de interés o influencia

**sphere of influence** (sfir uhv IHN floo ehns) area of one nation where another nation had special economic and political control (p. 678)
**esfera de influencia** zona de una nación donde otra ejercía un control económico y político

**spirituals** (SPIR ih chyoolz) religious folk songs that blended biblical themes with the realities of slavery (p. 400)
**canto espiritual** canto religioso tradicional que combinaba temas bíblicos con las realidades de la esclavitud

**spoils system** (spoilz SIHS tehm) act of replacing government officials with supporters of a newly elected President (p. 354)
**sistema de sinecuras** sustitución de funcionarios gubernamentales por partidarios del presidente recién electo

**stalemate** (STAYL mayt) situation in which neither side wins (p. 851)
**estancamiento** situación en la que ningún contendiente gana

**standard of living** (STAN derd uhv LIHV ihng) index based on the amount of goods, services, and leisure time people have (p. 845)
**nivel de vida** índice basado en la cantidad de bienes, servicios y tiempo de ocio que posee la gente

**states' rights** (stayts rīts) the right of states to limit the power of the federal government (pp. 301, 393)
**derechos de los estados** derecho de los estados a limitar el poder del gobierno federal

**steerage** (STIR ihj) large compartments of ships that usually held cattle (p. 626)
*tercera clase* grandes compartimientos de los barcos en los que normalmente se transportaba ganado

**stock** (stahk) share of ownership in a corporation (p. 614)
*acción* participación en la propiedad de una compañía

**stockpile** (STAHK pīl) to collect (p. 856)
*almacenar* hacer acopio o acumular

**strait** (strayt) narrow passage that connects two large bodies of water (p. 40)
*estrecho* travesía estrecha que conecta dos grandes masas de agua

**submit** (suhb MIHT) to give up power and control (pp. 661, 925)
*someterse* ceder el poder y el control

**subsidy** (SUHB sih dee) grant of land or money (p. 580)
*subsidio* concesión de tierras o dinero

**suffrage** (SUH frihj) right to vote (p. 351)
*sufragio* derecho al voto

**suffragist** (SUH frihj ihst) person who worked for women's right to vote (p. 657)
*sufragista* persona que luchaba por el derecho al voto de las mujeres

**superior** (suh PIR ee er) of greater importance or value; above average in quality; higher in position or rank (pp. 519, 803)
*superior* de mayor importancia o valor; por encima del promedio en cuanto a calidad; que ocupa una posición o categoría más alta

**superpower** (SOO per pow er) country with the military, political, and economic strength to influence events worldwide (p. 855)
*superpotencia* país con la fuerza militar, política y económica para influir en los acontecimientos a nivel mundial

**surplus** (SER pluhs) excess; quantity that is left over (pp. 7, 598, 940)
*superávit* excedente; cantidad sobrante

**survey** (ser VAY) to measure an area using special instruments and the techniques of mathematics (p. 84)
*medir* estudiar y medir una zona por medio de instrumentos especiales y técnicas matemáticas

**sustain** (suh STAYN) to keep going; to support as just (pp. 68, 525)
*sostener* mantener en marcha; apoyar como justo

# T

**tariff** (TAIR ihf) tax placed on goods entering a country from another country (pp. 286, 379)
*arancel* impuesto con que se gravan las mercancías que entran en un país provenientes de otro

**telegraph** (TEHL eh graf) invention that allows messages to be sent quickly over long distances by sending electrical signals along a wire (p. 391)
*telégrafo* invento que permite enviar mensajes rápidamente a grandes distancias por medio de señales eléctricas que viajan por un cable

**temperance movement** (TEHM per ehns MOOV mehnt) organized effort to end alcohol consumption (p. 416)
*movimiento por la temperancia* esfuerzo organizado en contra del consumo de alcohol

**tenement** (TEHN eh mehnt) building divided into many tiny apartments (p. 622)
*conventillo* un edificio dividido en muchos apartamentos pequeños

**tepee** (TEE pee) portable tent made of buffalo skins (p. 584)
*tipi* tienda portátil construida con pieles de búfalo

**terrorism** (TEHR er ihz uhm) deliberate use of violence, often against civilian targets, to achieve political or social goals (p. 968)
*terrorismo* uso deliberado de la violencia, a menudo en contra de objetivos civiles, con el fin de alcanzar objetivos políticos o sociales

**toleration** (tahl er AY shuhn) recognition that other people have the right to different opinions (p. 73)
*tolerancia* reconocimiento de que otras personas tienen el derecho de mantener opiniones distintas

**total war** (TOH tuhl  wor) all-out attacks aimed at destroying not only an enemy's army but also its resources and its people's will to fight (pp. 536, 811)
**guerra total** ataques masivos encaminados a destruir no sólo al ejército enemigo, sino también sus recursos y la voluntad de luchar de la población

**totalitarian state** (toh tal uh TER ee uhn stayt) nation in which a single party controls the government and every aspect of people's lives (p. 802)
**estado totalitario** país en el que un sólo partido político controla el gobierno y todos los aspectos de la vida de las personas

**town meeting** (town MEET ing) meeting in colonial New England during which settlers discussed and voted on issues; form of direct democracy in which residents meet to make decisions for the community (p. 75)
**cabildo abierto** reunión en la Nueva Inglaterra colonial donde los colonos discutían y votaban sobre sus asuntos; forma de democracia directa en la que los residentes se reúnen para tomar decisiones que conciernen a la comunidad

**trade deficit** (trayd DEHF uh siht) occurs when a country buys more from other nations than it sells to them; an excess of imports over exports (p. 976)
**déficit comercial** hecho que ocurre cuando un país compra a otras naciones más de lo que les vende; exceso de importaciones sobre las exportaciones

**traitor** (TRAY ter) person who betrays his or her country (p. 192)
**traidor** persona que traiciona a su país

**transcendentalism** (trans sehn DEHN tuhl ihz uhm) movement that sought to explore the relationship between humans and nature through emotions rather than through reason (p. 432)
**trascendentalismo** movimiento que se proponía explorar la relación entre los seres humanos y la naturaleza mediante las emociones en vez de la razón

**transcontinental railroad** (trans kahn tihn EHN tuhl RAYL rohd) rail line that spans the continent (p. 581)
**ferrocarril transcontinental** sistema ferroviario que cruza un continente de costa a costa

**transform** (trans FORM) to change in appearance or form; to change the condition of something (pp. 183, 584, 887)
**transformar** cambiar la apariencia o la forma; cambiar la condición de algo

**transmit** (trans MIHT) to pass along; to send (p. 16)
**trasmitir** pasar, circular; enviar

**travois** (trav OI) small sled (p. 584)
**travois** trineo pequeño

**triangular trade** (trī ANG yuh ler trayd) three-way colonial trade route between the colonies, the islands of the Caribbean, and Africa (p. 115)
**comercio triangular** ruta de comercio colonial a tres bandas entre las colonias, las islas del Caribe y África

**tribute** (TRIH byoot) money paid by one country to another in return for protection (p. 295)
**tributo** dinero que un país paga a otro a cambio de protección

**trust** (truhst) group of corporations run by a single board of directors (p. 615)
**trust** grupo de compañías dirigidas por un solo consejo directivo

**trustbuster** (TRUHST buhs ter) person who worked to destroy monopolies and trusts (p. 650)
**trustbuster** persona que lucha para destruir los monopolios y trusts

**turnpike** (TERN pīk) road built by a private company that charges a toll to use it (p. 492)
**camino de peaje** camino construido por una compañía privada que cobra una cuota por su uso

# U

**unconstitutional** (uhn kahn stih TOO shuhn uhl) contrary to what is permitted by the U.S. Constitution (pp. 263, 285)
**inconstitucional** contrario a lo que permite la Constitución de Estados Unidos

**undocumented worker** (uhn DAHK yuh mehnt īhd WER ker) laborers who enter the country without legal permission (p. 987)
***trabajador indocumentado*** obreros o jornaleros que entran en el país sin permiso legal

**urbanization** (er ban ihz AY shuhn) movement of large numbers of people from rural areas to cities; rapid growth of city populations (pp. 390, 620)
***urbanización*** desplazamiento de un gran número de personas de las zonas rurales a las ciudades; crecimiento rápido de la población de las ciudades

# V

**vague** (vayg) uncertain; not precise or exact (p. 819)
***vago*** incierto; no preciso o exacto

**vaquero** (vah KAIR oh) Spanish word for cowboy (p. 592)
***vaquero*** término que se aplica a los ganaderos mexicanos o hispanos

**veto** (VEE toh) to reject, as when the President rejects a law passed by Congress (p. 259, 840)
***vetar*** rechazar, como cuando el Presidente rechaza una ley aprobada por el Congreso

**via** (VEE ah) by way of (p. 424)
***vía*** paso por algún lugar

**vigilante** (vihj ihl AN tee) self-appointed law enforcer (pp. 465, 580)
***vigilante*** persona que se designa a sí misma para hacer cumplir la ley

**violate** (VĪ ah layt) to break a rule or law; to disrespect; to disturb (pp. 589, 938)
***violar*** no cumplir una regla o ley; ofender; molestar

**vital** (VĪ tuhl) necessary for life; of great importance; spirited; lively (pp. 183, 482)
***vital*** necesario para la vida; de gran importancia; lleno de vida; animado

**voluntary** (VAHL ahn tair ee) not forced; done of one's free will (pp. 357, 547, 775)
***voluntario*** no forzado; hecho por voluntad propia

# W

**war crime** (wor crīm) wartime act of cruelty and brutality that is judged to be beyond the accepted rules of war and human behavior (p. 827)
***crimen de guerra*** acto cruel y brutal realizado en tiempo de guerra que sobrepasa las reglas establecidas para la guerra y el comportamiento humano

**war hawk** (wor hawk) one of the members of Congress from the South and the West who called for war with Britain prior to the War of 1812 (p. 327)
***halcón de guerra*** uno de los miembros del Congreso de representantes del Sur y del Oeste que instaban a la guerra con Gran Bretaña antes de la guerra de 1812

**water rights** (WAW ter rīts) legal right to use water from a river, stream, or other body for a purpose (p. 464)
***derecho de aguas*** derecho jurídico a utilizar el agua de un río, arroyo u otra masa de agua con un fin determinado

**welfare** (WEHL fair) system in which government agencies make cash payments to the poor (p. 885)
***asistencia social*** sistema en el cual las agencias gubernamentales efectúan pagos en efectivo a las personas pobres (p.885)

**westernization** (wehs tern ih ZAY shuhn) adoption of ideas, culture, and technology from Western regions such as the United States and Europe (p. 956)
***occidentalización*** adopción de ideas, cultura y tecnología de las regiones occidentales como de los Estados Unidos y Europa (p. 956)

**women's rights movement** (WOO mehns rīts MOOV mehnt) organized campaign to win property, education, and other rights for women (p. 429)
***movimiento por los derechos femeninos*** campaña organizada para obtener el derecho a la propiedad, a la educación y otros derechos para la mujer

**women's suffrage** (WOO mehns SUH frihj) right of women to vote (p. 428)
**sufragio femenino** derecho de las mujeres a votar

**writ of assistance** (riht uhv uh SIHS tehns) court order that allowed officials to make searches without saying for what they were searching (p. 148)
**auto de asistencia** orden judicial que permitía a determinados funcionarios a realizar registros sin tener que revelar lo que andaban buscando

**Y**

**yellow journalism** (YEHL oh JER nahl ihz uhm) style of reporting and displaying news in a sensational way that distorts the truth (p. 635)
**periodismo amarillista** estilo de reseñar y presentar noticias de un modo sensacionalista que deforma la verdad

# Primary Sources

## The Magna Carta

### Background

King John ruled England from 1199 to 1216. During his troubled reign, he found himself in conflict with England's feudal barons. The nobles especially resented John's attempts to tax them heavily.

In 1215, the barons forced John to sign the Magna Carta, or Great Charter. Most of this document was intended to protect the rights of the barons.

However, over time, the document came to guarantee some basic rights of English citizens. When English colonists came to North America, they brought these ideas with them. Eight of the 63 clauses of the Magna Carta are printed here.

### Vocabulary *Builder*

**counsel** (KOWN suhl) *n.* advice; consent

**bailiff** (BAY lihf) *n.* tax collector in medieval England

**credible** (KREHD uh buhl) *adj.* believable

**peer** (peer) *n.* person of equal rank

**realm** (rehlm) *n.* kingdom

**enjoin** (ehn JOIN) *v.* to order; to enforce

12. No [tax] nor aid shall be imposed on our kingdom, unless by common <u>counsel</u> of our kingdom, except for ransoming our person, for making our eldest son a knight, and for once marrying our eldest daughter; and for these there shall not be levied more than a reasonable aid. . . .

30. No sheriff or <u>bailiff</u> of ours, or other person, shall take the horses or carts of any freeman for transport duty, against the will of the said freeman.

31. Neither we nor our bailiffs shall take, for our castles or for any other work of ours, wood which is not ours, against the will of the owner of that wood. . . .

38. No bailiff for the future shall, upon his own unsupported complaint, put any one to his "law," without <u>credible</u> witnesses brought for this purpose.

39. No freeman shall be taken or imprisoned . . . or exiled or in any way destroyed, nor will we go upon him nor send upon him, except by the lawful judgment of his <u>peers</u> or by the law of the land.

40. To no one will we sell, to no one will we refuse or delay, right or justice. . . .

45. We will appoint as justices, constables, sheriffs, or bailiffs only such as know the law of the <u>realm</u> and mean to observe it well. . . .

63. Wherefore it is our will, and we firmly <u>enjoin</u>, that the English Church be free, and that the men in our kingdom have and hold all the aforesaid liberties, rights, and concessions, well and peaceably, freely and quietly, fully and wholly, for themselves and their heirs, of us and our heirs, in all respects and in all places for ever, as is aforesaid.

The Magna Carta, in *Source Problems in English History,* ed. White and Notestein

### Comprehension and Critical Thinking

1. Which clauses of the Magna Carta listed here protect the right of people to their own private property?

2. What promise is made in clause 12?

3. **Critical Thinking: *Link Past and Present*** How do the principles expressed in clauses 38–40 apply to the United States today?

# Primary Sources

## Patrick Henry, *Speech in the House of Burgesses*

### Background

Patrick Henry was born in Virginia in 1735. Trained as an attorney while a young man, he became known for his speaking skills. Henry was elected to the Virginia House of Burgesses in 1765 and strongly opposed the Stamp Act. In a speech related to the crisis, he spoke against Parliament and the king, declaring, "If this be treason, make the most of it." Bitter criticism from delegates forced him to apologize for the statement and affirm his loyalty to the king.

In March 1775, Henry made the following speech, which became his best known. Some credit this speech with being the deciding act in gaining Virginia's troops for the Revolutionary cause. At the end of the speech, members of the assembly jumped from their seats and shouted, "To Arm! To Arms!"

### Vocabulary Builder

**adversary** (AD vehr sayr ee) *n.* enemy; opponent

**irresolution** (ih rehz oh LOO shuhn) *n.* uncertainty on how to act

**supine** (soo PĪN) *adj.* lying on one's back

**delusive** (dih LOOS ihv) *adj.* unreal; misleading

**vigilant** (VIHJ uh lehnt) *adj.* on the alert for danger

**extenuate** (ihk STEHN yuh wayt) *v.* to excuse; to make light of

---

They tell us, sir, that we are weak; unable to cope with so formidable an <u>adversary</u>. But when shall we be stronger? Will it be the next week, or the next year? Will it be when we are totally disarmed, and when a British guard shall be stationed in every house? Shall we gather strength by <u>irresolution</u> and inaction? Shall we acquire the means of effectual resistance by lying <u>supinely</u> on our backs and hugging the <u>delusive</u> phantom of hope, until our enemies shall have bound us hand and foot?

Sir, we are not weak if we make a proper use of those means which the God of nature hath placed in our power. Three millions of people armed in the holy cause of liberty, and in such a country as that which we possess, are invincible by any force which our enemy can send against us. . . . The battle, sir, is not to the strong alone; it is to the <u>vigilant</u>, the active, the brave.

Besides, sir, we have no election. If we were base enough to desire it, it is now too late to retire from the contest. There is no retreat but in submission and slavery! Our chains are forged! Their clanking may be heard on the plains of Boston! The war is inevitable—and let it come! I repeat, sir, let it come!

It is vain, sir, to <u>extenuate</u> the matter. The gentlemen may cry, Peace, peace! But there is no peace. The war has actually begun! The next gale that sweeps from the north will bring to our ears the clash of resounding arms! Our brethren are already in the field! Why stand we here idle? What is it that gentlemen wish? What would they have? Is life so dear or peace so sweet as to be purchased at the price of chains and slavery? Forbid it, almighty God. I know not what course others may take, but as for me, give me liberty or give me death!

—Patrick Henry, speech to the Virginia Assembly, March 23, 1775

### Comprehension and Critical Thinking

1. According to Henry, why would the Americans be difficult to defeat?

2. Why does Henry think the Americans have no "election," or choice, but to fight?

3. **Critical Thinking: *Detect Points of View*** How do you think a colonist who did not want to break away from Britain might respond to Henry's argument?

# Thomas Paine, *Common Sense*

## Background

Thomas Paine was born in England in 1737. He failed and left school at the age of 12. Later, he unsuccessfully tried a variety of careers, from sailor to tax collector. Then, he met Benjamin Franklin in London. Franklin helped Paine come to the American colonies and find work as a journalist.

Two years later, in 1776, Paine published *Common Sense* in order to stir up support for American independence. In different parts of the pamphlet, Paine gives political, military, and moral arguments for breaking away from Britain. In the excerpt below, Paine discusses economic reasons.

## Vocabulary *Builder*

**advocate** (AD vuh kiht) *n.* person who speaks in favor of something

**reconciliation** (rehk uhn sihl ee AY shuhn) *n.* making peace after a disagreement

**renounce** (ree NOWNS) *v.* to promise to give up

**variance** (VAIR ee uhns) *n.* quarrel; dispute

**contention** (kuhn TEHN shun) n. disagreement; conflict

I challenge the warmest <u>advocate</u> for <u>reconciliation</u>, to show a single advantage that this continent can reap, by being connected with Great Britain. I repeat the challenge, not a single advantage is derived. Our corn will fetch its price in any market in Europe, and our imported goods must be paid for, buy them where we will.

But the injuries and disadvantages we sustain by that connection, are without number; and our duty to mankind at large, as well as to ourselves, instruct us to <u>renounce</u> the alliance: Because, any submission to, or dependence on Great Britain, tends directly to involve this continent in European wars and quarrels; and sets us at <u>variance</u> with nations, who would otherwise seek our friendship, and against whom, we have neither anger nor complaint. As Europe is our market for trade, we ought to form no partial connection with any part of it. It is the true interest of America to steer clear of European <u>contentions</u>. . . .

Europe is too thickly planted with kingdoms to be long at peace, and whenever a war breaks out between England and any foreign power, the trade of America goes to ruin, because of her connection with Britain.

Thomas Paine, *Common Sense*

**Thomas Paine**

## Comprehension and Critical Thinking

1. According to Paine, what advantages can the colonies gain by remaining connected with Britain?

2. What effect does Paine say Britain has on American trade?

3. Critical Thinking: *Evaluate Information* Paine's purpose was to persuade colonists to support independence. Which colonists do you think would be most persuaded by the arguments given above?

## James Madison, *The Federalist, No. 39*

### Background

The *Federalist Papers* is a name given to a series of 85 essays written in 1787 by Alexander Hamilton, James Madison, and John Jay. Their goal was to win support for the Constitution.

Originally, the three authors did not sign the essays with their own names. Instead, they used the Roman name *Publius*, from the Latin word for "public." Using such pen names was a common practice in political writing of the time. It indicated the great respect the early leaders of the United States had for the ancient Roman Republic.

The following excerpt is from *The Federalist* No. 39. Here, James Madison shows that the government formed by the Constitution is a republic.

### Vocabulary *Builder*

**bestow** (bee STOH) *v.* to give

**inconsiderable** (ihn kuhn SIHD uh buhl) *adj.* small; unimportant

**standard** (STAN duhrd) *n.* something against which other things are judged

**conformable** (kuhn FORM uh buhl) *adj.* in harmony or agreement

**magistrate** (MAJ ihs trayt) *n.* official who enforces the law

We may define a republic to be, or at least may <u>bestow</u> that name on, a government which derives all its powers directly or indirectly from the great body of the people, and is administered by persons holding their offices during pleasure, for a limited period, or during good behavior. It is ESSENTIAL to such a government that it be derived from the great body of the society, not from an <u>inconsiderable</u> proportion, or a favored class of it. . . .

On comparing the Constitution planned by the convention with the <u>standard</u> here fixed, we perceive at once that it is, in the most rigid sense, <u>conformable</u> to it. The House of Representatives, like that of one branch at least of all the State legislatures, is elected immediately by the great body of the people. The Senate, like the present Congress, and the Senate of Maryland, derives its appointment indirectly from the people. The President is indirectly derived from the choice of the people, according to the example in most of the States. . . . The Senate is elective, for the period of six years; which is but one year more than the period of the Senate of Maryland, and but two more than that of the Senates of New York and Virginia. The President is to continue in office for the period of four years; as in New York and Delaware, the chief <u>magistrate</u> is elected for three years, and in South Carolina for two years.

James Madison, *The Federalist* No. 39

**James Madison**

### Comprehension and Critical Thinking

1. What does Madison consider to be the most important quality of a republic?

2. Describe two examples Madison uses to show that the government under the Constitution fits the definition of a republic.

3. Critical Thinking: *Draw Inferences* Why do you think Madison tries to show that the proposed new government has many similarities to the state governments?

# George Washington, *Farewell Address*

## Background

As he prepared to leave office, President George Washington made a speech describing his vision of the nation's future. The speech became known as Washington's Farewell Address.

The speech deals with a wide range of topics, from the need to keep down the nation's debt to the importance of education. Washington also warns against the dangers of forming political parties, which began during his presidency.

The following excerpt from Washington's Farewell Address deals with relations between the United States and other countries. Washington's ideas about foreign relations influenced American foreign policy for generations.

## Vocabulary *Builder*

**commercial** (KUH MER shuhl) *adj.* relating to trade

**caprice** (kuh PREES) *n.* sudden change

**patronize** (PAY truh nīz) *v.* to support

**infidelity** (ihn fuh DEHL uh tee) *n.* disloyalty; unfaithfulness

**maxim** (MAK sihm) *n.* wise saying

The great rule of conduct for us in regard to foreign nations is, in extending our <u>commercial</u> relations, to have with them as little political connection as possible. So far as we have already formed engagements, let them be fulfilled with perfect good faith. Here let us stop. Europe has a set of primary interests which to us have none; or a very remote relation. Hence she must be engaged in frequent controversies, the causes of which are essentially foreign to our concerns. . . . Why, by interweaving our destiny with that of any part of Europe, entangle our peace and prosperity in the toils of European ambition, rivalship, interest, humor or <u>caprice</u>?

It is our true policy to steer clear of permanent alliances with any portion of the foreign world; so far, I mean, as we are now at liberty to do it; for let me not be understood as capable of <u>patronizing</u> <u>infidelity</u> to existing engagements. I hold the <u>maxim</u> no less applicable to public than to private affairs, that honesty is always the best policy. I repeat, therefore, let those engagements be observed in their genuine sense. But, in my opinion, it is unnecessary and would be unwise to extend them.

George Washington, Farewell Address

**George Washington**

## Comprehension and Critical Thinking

1. Restate the main point of the first sentence of the excerpt in your own words.

2. How does Washington think the United States should deal with agreements that it has already made with other nations?

3. Critical Thinking: *Identify Costs* Based on the above, what is one way the United States might suffer from forming permanent alliances with a European country?

# Primary Sources

## Francis Scott Key, *The Star-Spangled Banner*

### Background

The War of 1812 gave birth to an enduring American tradition. On September 13, 1814, British ships bombarded Fort McHenry near Baltimore. A young lawyer, Francis Scott Key, waited anxiously to find out if the fort would fall. The next morning, Key was relieved to see the American flag still flying over the fort.

Key described his feelings in the poem "The Star-Spangled Banner." The poem was then set to a traditional English tune and quickly became popular. In 1889, it was officially chosen to be played at all military flag raisings. The tradition of performing the song at Major League baseball games began in 1918. Finally, in 1931, Congress adopted "The Star-Spangled Banner" as the national anthem of the United States.

### Vocabulary Builder

**twilight** (TWĪ līt) *n.* dim light between sunset and dark

**perilous** (PEHR uh luhs) *adj.* dangerous

**rampart** (RAM pahrt) *n.* defensive wall

**haughty** (HAWT ee) *adj.* overly proud

**repose** (ree POHZ) *v.* to rest

**fitful** (FIHT ful) *adj.* at irregular intervals

---

Oh, say, can you see by the dawn's early light
  What so proudly we hailed at the <u>twilight</u>'s last gleaming,
Whose broad stripes and bright stars through the <u>perilous</u> fight,
  O'er the <u>ramparts</u> we watched were so gallantly streaming?
And the rockets' red glare, the bombs bursting in air,
  Gave proof through the night that our flag was still there.
Oh, say, does that star-spangled banner yet wave
O'er the land of the free and the home of
  the brave?

On the shore, dimly seen through the mists of the deep,
  Where the foe's <u>haughty</u> host in dread silence <u>reposes</u>,
What is that which the breeze, o'er the towering steep,
  As it <u>fitfully</u> blows, half conceals, half discloses?
Now it catches the gleam of the morning's first beam,
  In full glory reflected, now shines on the stream.
'Tis the star-spangled banner; oh long may it wave
O'er the land of the free and the home of the brave!

Francis Scott Key, "The Star-Spangled Banner"

**The flag as it was in 1812**

### Comprehension and Critical Thinking

1. How did Key know that Fort McHenry had not fallen to the British?

2. What words does Key use to describe the people of the United States?

3. **Critical Thinking:** *Apply Information* Based on what you have read, why would Key have been concerned about the safety of Fort McHenry?

# Ralph Waldo Emerson, *Self-Reliance*

## Background

Ralph Waldo Emerson was not only the most influential thinker of the transcendentalist movement, he was also one of the most admired Americans of his day. His essays and poems won a wide readership. In his lifetime, Emerson was best known for his popular lectures. He traveled across the country, especially the Northeast, addressing large crowds on a wide variety of topics. His early training as a minister helped make him a powerful speaker—especially when he was speaking out against slavery.

In one of his most important essays, *Self-Reliance,* Emerson warned against conformity, or blind following of standards set by others. Instead, he argued in favor of individualism.

### Vocabulary *Builder*

**envy** (EHN vee) *n.* desire for or resentment of what others have

**bestow** (bee STOH) *v.* to give as a gift

**integrity** (ihn TEHG ruh tee) *n.* state of being true and sincere

**arduous** (AHR joo uhs) *adj.* very difficult

**solitude** (SOL uh tood) *n.* state of being alone

There is a time in every man's education when he arrives at the conviction that <u>envy</u> is ignorance; that imitation is suicide; that he must take himself for better for worse as his portion; that though the wide universe is full of good, no kernel of nourishing corn can come to him but through his toil <u>bestowed</u> on that plot of ground which is given to him to till. . . .

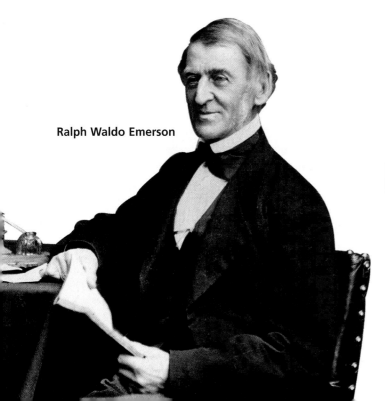

**Ralph Waldo Emerson**

Trust thyself: every heart vibrates to that iron string. . . . Nothing is at last sacred but the <u>integrity</u> of your own mind. . . .

What I must do is all that concerns me, not what the people think. This rule, equally <u>arduous</u> in actual and in intellectual life, may serve for the whole distinction between greatness and meanness. It is the harder because you will always find those who think they know what is your duty better than you know it. It is easy in the world to live after the world's opinion; it is easy in <u>solitude</u> to live after our own; but the great man is he who in the midst of the crowd keeps with perfect sweetness the independence of solitude.

Ralph Waldo Emerson, *Self-Reliance*

### Comprehension and Critical Thinking

1. According to Emerson, who has the right to judge a person's actions?

2. How does Emerson define greatness?

3. Critical Thinking: *Apply Information* If you were designing a T-shirt devoted to the idea of individualism, what words from *Self-Reliance* would you put on it? Why?

## Frederick Douglass, *What the Black Man Wants*

### Background

Frederick Douglass was born into slavery in Maryland in 1817. Escaping to the North, he became a leading abolitionist. He spoke at antislavery conventions, published the antislavery newspaper the *North Star*, and wrote a best-selling autobiography that awakened many people to the injustices of slavery. In addition, Douglass was a delegate to the 1848 women's rights convention at Seneca Falls.

Only a few days after the end of the Civil War, Douglass addressed the annual meeting of the Massachusetts Anti-Slavery Society. He discussed one of the key issues of Reconstruction: the enfranchisement of, or giving the vote to, African Americans. This is an excerpt from that speech.

### Vocabulary *Builder*

**unconditional** (uhn kuhn DIHSH uhn uhl) *adj.* without limits or reservations

**mockery** (MAHK uhr ee) *n.* false imitation

**sufficient** (suh FIHSH uhnt) *adj.* enough

**deprivation** (deh prih VAY shuhn) *n.* act of taking something away

**incapacity** (ihn kuh PAS ih tee) *n.* lack of ability

I am for the "immediate, <u>unconditional</u>, and universal" enfranchisement of the black man, in every State in the Union. Without this, his liberty is a <u>mockery</u>; without this, you might as well almost retain the old name of slavery for his condition; for in fact, if he is not the slave of the individual master, he is the slave of society, and holds his liberty as a privilege, not as a right. He is at the mercy of the mob, and has no means of protecting himself. . . .

It may be asked, "Why do you want it? Some men have got along very well without it. Women have not this right." Shall we justify one wrong by another? This is the <u>sufficient</u> answer. Shall we at this moment justify the <u>deprivation</u> of the Negro of the right to vote, because some one else is deprived of that privilege? I hold that women, as well as men, have the right to vote, and my heart and voice go with the movement to extend suffrage to woman; but that question rests upon another basis than which our right rests.

We may be asked, I say, why we want it. I will tell you why we want it. We want it because it is our right, first of all. No class of men can, without insulting their own nature, be content with any deprivation of their rights. We want it again, as a means for educating our race. Men are so constituted that they derive their conviction of their own possibilities largely by the estimate formed of them by others. If nothing is expected of a people, that people will find it difficult to contradict that expectation. By depriving us of suffrage, you affirm our <u>incapacity</u> to form an intelligent judgment respecting public men and public measures; you declare before the world that we are unfit to exercise the elective franchise, and by this means lead us to undervalue ourselves.

Frederick Douglass, *What the Black Man Wants*

### Comprehension and Critical Thinking

1. According to Douglass, when should the government grant African Americans the right to vote? Under what conditions?

2. What is Douglass's view of women's suffrage?

3. Critical Thinking: *Evaluate Information* Summarize one argument Douglass uses in favor of granting the vote to African Americans. Explain whether you find that argument persuasive and why.

# Index

*Italicized* page number followed by *c* refers to chart; *g*, graph; *m*, map; *i*, illustration; *p*, photo; *q*, quotation.

## A

**abolitionists**
in antislavery movement, 423–426, *425i, 436q, 437c*
during Civil War, 524–525, 527
emblem of, *377i*
leading slave revolt, 497–498
*See also* antislavery movement
**Acquired Immune Deficiency Syndrome (AIDS)**, 985
**Act of Union of 1841 (Canada)**, 348
**Adams, John,** *139i, 1001i*
on colonial rights, 149, 170
at Continental Congress, 152
as second President, 293, 298–301, *303c, 305q*
at Treaty of Paris signing, 193
as Vice President, 220
**Adams, John Quincy**
on antislavery, 424, 426
as President, 350–351, *351q, 1001i*
as secretary of state, 347
**Adams, Samuel,** 149, *149i,* 152
**Adams-Onís Treaty of 1819,** 345
**Addams, Jane,** 622, 661, 713, 875
**adobe,** 12
**affirmative action,** 892
**Afghanistan,** 943, 944, 971
**AFL.** *See* American Federation of Labor (AFL)
**Africa**
countering communism in, 857, *861c*
pirates from Northern, 322–323
policies toward South, 949
terrorists in, 968
trade in humans from, 48, 69, *69i*
trade networks of, 16–18, *20–21m*
voyages of slaves from, *114q, 129i, 129q*
after World War I, 724
World War II in Northern, 811–812, *812m*
**African Americans**
as abolitionists, 423–424, *425i, 436q,* 497–498, 527
and American Revolution, 186–187, *187i,* 205, 215, *215c*
and Civil War, *187i,* 352, 395, 398–400, 495, 526–527, *526i*
in colonial times, 90, 104, 112, 117
during Depression, 783–784
during early 1900s, 658, 660–662, 745, 750
education of, 119, 419, *543i,* 548, *551i,* 662

elected/appointed, 555, 892, 989
in Korean War, *187i*
in literature/arts, 434, 634
music by, 435, 747, *748p*
and Native Americans, 345, 355, 586
and Reconstruction, *477i,* 553–557, 560–563, *564m, 565c*
in sports, 624
in 2000s, 989
in the West, 317, 467, 597
and World War I, 713, *713p,* 714
and World War II, 809, 819
*See also* civil rights movement; racial conflict/violence; slave trade/labor
**African Methodist Episcopal Church (PA),** 395, 662
**age discrimination,** 897
**Age of Jackson**
democracy in, *337i, 351g,* 352–354, *369c*
length/influence of, 349, 366
reforms of, 414, 418
**Agent Orange,** 912
**aggression,** 804
**aging population,** 790, 896–897, 989
**agriculture**
advances in, 392, 396, 399, *407c*
during Depression, 770, 778–779
during Reconstruction, 562–563
during World War I, 714, *716p*
**Aguinaldo, Emilio,** 690, 692, *692p*
**aid.** *See* charities; government aid
**Aid to Dependent Children (ADC),** 790
**AIDS epidemic,** 985
**air flight, firsts in,** *612p,* 747
**airlifts, massive,** *765p,* 838, *839p,* 921, *921p,* 927
**airplanes**
in Gulf War, 957
in Vietnam War, *911p,* 912, *917i*
in World War I, 708, *709p*
in World War II, 809–811, 813, *814–815q,* 824–825
**Alabama,** 877–879, *878p,* 888–889
**Alamo,** 455, *455i*
**Alaska,** 680–681, *699c,* 978
**Albanians,** 948
**Albany Congress,** 141–142
**alcoholic beverages.** *See* prohibition
**Alcott, Louisa May,** 434
**Aldrin, Buzz,** *317p*
**Alger, Horatio,** 634
**Alien Act of 1798,** 299–300
**Allen, Ethan,** 158, *158i*
**alliance,** 57, 141, 183
**alliance systems,** 706, *729c,* 972
**Allies**
in World War I, 706, 709–710, 718–722, *719m,* 724

in World War II, 811, *812m,* 821–822, *823m,* 824
**Alsop, Stewart,** *995q*
**alternative energy resources,** 959, 980, *980c*
**Amendments, Constitutional**
First, 221, *240q,* 266, 881, *882c*
Second, 221, *240q*
Third, 221, *240q*
Fourth, 221, *241q, 882c*
Fifth, 221, *241q,* 881, *882c*
Sixth, 221, *241q, 265c, 882c*
Seventh, 221, *242q*
Eighth, 221, *242q*
Ninth, 221, *242q,* 271
Tenth, 221, *242q*
Eleventh, *242q*
Twelfth, *243q,* 310
Thirteenth, *243q, 255p,* 552, *565c*
Fourteenth, *244q,* 553–554, *565c,* 875
Fifteenth, *245q,* 556–557, *565c*
Sixteenth, *245q,* 647, *667c*
Seventeenth, *245q,* 647, *667c*
Eighteenth, *246q, 255p,* 659, *667c*
Nineteenth, *246q, 255p,* 657–658, *667c,* 713
Twentieth, *246–247q*
Twenty-first, *247q,* 742
Twenty-second, *248q*
Twenty-third, *248q*
Twenty-fourth, *248q*
Twenty-fifth, *249q*
Twenty-sixth, *250q, 255p,* 922
Twenty-seventh, *250q*
Equal Rights Amendment (ERA), 894, *901q*
*See also* Constitution
**American Anti-Slavery Society,** 423
**American Association of Retired Persons (AARP),** 271, 897
**American Colonization Society,** 422
**American Federation of Labor (AFL),** 618, 791
**American Fur Company,** 448–449
**American GI Forum,** 895
**American Indian Movement (AIM),** 896
**American Indian Religious Freedom Act of 1978,** 990
**American Protective League,** 715
**American Revolution**
arguments supporting, *202q*
beginning of, *137i,* 152–153, 156–161, 1778–1781, *168q,* 191–192, *193m,* 1776–1778, 170–185, *180m*
events leading to, *138q, 152c, 163c*
impact of, 195, 284
key figures of, *197c*
overseas help in, 183, 186–190
reasons for success of, *194i*
talks/treaty after, 195

## Index (continued)

**land,** *238q, 241q,* 357
**land bridge theory,** 6
**land grants,** 446
**land grids.** *See* township grids
**Land Ordinance of 1785,** 207, *210–211m*
**Land Ordinance of 1787,** 207, *210–211m*
**Land Rush in Oklahoma,** 597
**Lange, Dorothea,** 787
**language classes (1800s),** 627
**Laos,** 919, *919m*
**Larcom, Lucy,** *388–389q*
**Las Casas, Bartolomé de,** 47–48
**laser-guided defense system,** 944
**lasers in medicine,** 983, *984p*
*Last of the Mohicans* **(Cooper),** 431
**Latin America**
  and the Cold War, 858–859, *861c*
  immigrants from, 784–785, 986, 988
  independence of, 195, 346, *346m*
  and Monroe Doctrine, 347, *347c*
  policies toward, *677i,* 693–697, *698m, 699c,* 806
  war with Spain in, 690, *691m*
  *See also* Central America; Mexico; South America
**Latinos,** 988, *988g*
**League of Iroquois,** *4q*
**League of Nations,** 724, 725, *726i,* 804
*Leaves of Grass* **(Whitman),** 434
**Lebanon,** 944, 956
**Lee, Richard Henry,** 171
**Lee, Robert E.,** 497, 514, 519, 534–537
**"leeverites,"** 451
**"Legend of Sleepy Hollow" (Irving),** 431
**legislative branch,** 213, *228–234q, 256–257c,* 258–259
  *See also* Congress
**legislative process,** *231q*
**legislature,** 103, 214, *228q*
**Leif Eriksson,** 36
**leisure activities.** *See* entertainment; sports
**Lend-Lease Act of 1940,** 808
**Lenin, Vladimir,** 719
*Letters of a Loyalist* **(Hulton),** *138q*
**Lewis, John L.,** 791
**Lewis, Meriwether,** *308q, 316m,* 317–319, *318i, 320–321i*
**Lewis, Sinclair,** *749q*
**Lexington (MA),** 153
**libel,** 105
**liberals,** 780–781, 937, 942
*Liberator* **(Garrison),** *423q*
**Liberia,** 422
**Liberty Bonds,** 715, *730i*
**libraries (late 1800s),** 633
**Lieberman, Joseph,** 941

**Life at the Time**
  Arts of Early American, *288i*
  Danger at Sea, *42–43i*
  Going to School, *420–421i*
  Growing Up in the 1950s, *848–849p, 717p*
  Immigrant's Journey, *630–631p*
  9/11: Courage and Remembrance, *974–975p*
  On the Home Front (World War I), 716
  South After the Civil War, *550–551i*
  Spirit of Protest, *154–155i*
**light bulb,** 610
**Liliuokalani,** *679p,* 683, *683p*
**Lin, Maya,** *922p*
**Lincoln, Abraham,** *476p, 495i, 501p, 545i, 1002p*
  assassination of, *548i,* 549
  during Civil War, *503q,* 512, 519, 520, 529, 535
  on Dred Scott decision, *495q*
  on emancipation, 524–526
  Gettysburg Address by, *535q, 538q*
  on Mexican land dispute, 457, *471q*
  as President, 499–503, *501q,* 536, 537
  during Reconstruction, 546–547
**Lincoln University (PA),** 419
**Lincoln-Douglas debates,** 496–497, *496c*
**Lindbergh, Charles,** 747
**Links Across Time**
  African American Soldiers, *187i*
  Beyond the Monroe Doctrine, *347c*
  Civil Rights for Native Americans, *588p*
  Elections and the Media, *496p*
  Exploration, *317p*
  Fighting for Civil Rights, *562p*
  Gandhi Preaches Nonviolence, *887p*
  Holocaust and Genocide, *826p*
  Honoring Veterans, *721p*
  Korea, *852c*
  Making State Laws, *104c*
  Political Parties Then and Now, *292i*
  Public education, *418p*
  Republican Government, *25p*
  Slavery and the Constitution, *215c*
  Technology and Work, *385p*
  Terrorism in the United States, *969p*
  Wall Street, *56p*
  Water Rights in the West, *465p*
**literacy test,** 560
**literature**
  of 1800s, 433–434, 634
  of 1920s, 749–750, *757c*
  in the colonies, 120
  influences on, 431–432
**Literature (feature)**

*Dauntless: A Novel of Midway and Guadalcanal* **(Tillman),** *814–815q*
"How I Became a Printer" (Franklin), *124–125q*
"I, Too" (Hughes), *751q*
*The Jungle* (Sinclair), *654–655q*
"Midway" (Madgett), *880q*
"Mill Workers" (Larcom), *388–389q*
*Sequoyah and the Cherokee Alphabet* (Cwiklik), *360–361q*
*Uncle Tom's Cabin* (Stowe), *492 493q*
*Valley Forge* (Anderson), *185q*
**Little Rock (AR),** 877
*Little Women* **(Alcott),** 434
**Livingston, Robert,** 315
**Locke, John,** 122, 172, 253, *253p*
**locomotive, steam,** 393
**Lodge, Henry Cabot,** 725–726, *726q*
**London, Jack,** 634
**Long, Huey,** 781, *781p*
**Longfellow, Henry Wadsworth,** 434
**Los Angeles (CA),** *465p,* 663, 891
**Louis XVI, King of France,** *296i*
**Louisiana,** 979
**Louisiana Purchase,** *277i,* 315–316, *316m, 320–321i*
**L'Ouverture, Toussaint,** 315, *315i*
**Lowell, Francis Cabot,** 384–385
**"Lowell girls,"** 385, *388–389q, 389i*
**Loyalists,** 157, 170, 191
*Lusitania* **(British),** 709–710, *710i*
**Luther, Martin,** 26
**lynching,** 661–662, *662q,* 665, 784
**Lyon, Mary,** 429

# M

**MacArthur, Douglas,** 812, 824, *824p,* 850–851
**machine-gun warfare,** 708, *709p*
**Madgett, Naomi Long,** *880p, 880q*
**Madison, Dolly,** 330
**Madison, James**
  on Alien and Sedition acts, 301
  at Constitutional Convention, 213, *214i*
  as Federalist, 218, 220
  on political factions, *290q*
  as President, *301i,* 325, *1001i*
  *See also Marbury* v. *Madison*
**Magellan, Ferdinand,** *38–39m,* 40
*Maggie: A Girl of the Streets* **(Crane),** 634
**Magna Carta,** *102q,* 172, 252
**magnetic resonance imaging (MRI),** *984p,* 985
**Mahan, Alfred T,** 682
**mah-jongg,** 746, *746p*
*Maine* **(ship),** 689, *689i*
**Maine (state),** 71, 161
**Malcolm X,** 890

Mount Rushmore (SD), *991p*
mountain men, 449, *449i*
movies. *See* motion picture industry
Mt. Vernon (VA), *279i*
muckraker, 648, 652
Muhammad, 16
Muir, John, *651p*
multimedia research report, 864–867
Munich Pact, 804–805, *828q*
Murrow, Edward R., *827q*
music
 of 1800s, 435, 623
 of 1900s (early), 747, *748p*, 749,
  *757c*
 of 1950s, 846–847, *848–849p*
 early American, *289i*, 330
musket, *182p*
Muslims, 16–19, 956–957, 970
Mussolini, Benito, 802–803, *803p*
mutualista, *663p*
*My Soul Is Rested* (Hamer), *872q*,
 *898q*

**N**

Nagasaki (Japan), 825
Naismith, James, 624
napalm, 912, *917p*
Napoleon Bonaparte, 299, 315, *324i*,
 330
narrative essay, HT 21, 372–375,
 996–999
Nast, Thomas, *556i*, 646
Nation, Carrie, 659
Nation of Islam, 890
National Aeronautics and Space
 Administration (NASA), 856
National Association for the
 Advancement of Colored People
 (NAACP), 661, 819, 875
National Association of Colored
 Graduate Nurses, 819
National Association of Colored
 Women, 658
National Defense Education, 856
*National Gazette*, 292
National Grange, 598
National Guardsmen, 920
National Labor Relations Act of
 1935, 791
National Labor Relations Board, 791
National League of Professional
 Baseball Clubs, 624
National Organization for Women
 (NOW), 893
National Recovery Act of 1933, *785p*
National Recovery Administration
 (NRA), 778
National Rifle Association, 271
National Road, *402m*, 403

National Woman Suffrage
 Association (NWSA), 429, 656
nationalism, 327, 706, *729c*
Native American resistance
 Britain supporting, 327–330
 to English colonies, 76, 85, 145–146
 during Mexican revolution in 1810,
  346
 in North and South, 330
 and Tecumseh's death, *330i*
 to western settlers, 294–295, 325
  326, 327, 453, 586–588
Native Americans
 and American Revolution, 188–189
 art depicting, 435
 during Depression, 785, *785p*
 early cultures of, *3q*, *4q*, 10–11,
  12–15
 effects of colonization on, 41,
  47–48, *47i*, 57, *61g*, 91
 and English colonists, 67–68, 70,
  73, 79, *79i*, *94q*
 and French/British wars, 140–144
 land taken from, *325m*
 and Lewis & Clark expedition,
  317–318
 removed to Indian Territory,
  355–359, *356m*
 rights of, 104, 553–554, *588p*, 896
 at Spanish missions, 93, 446
 in 2000s, 990
 and War of 1812, 327–331
 and western settlements, 325, 446,
  453, 464, 467, 584–589, *587m*, *601c*
 in World War I, 713
 *See also specific people/nation*
nativists, 394, *628i*, 629
NATO. *See* North Atlantic Treaty
 Organization (NATO)
natural rights, 122, *122c*, 172
naturalization, 270
Navajo Nation, 587, 824
navigation, 19, 27, *42–43i*
Navigation Acts of 1651, 106, 115
Navy, United States
 and foreign trade, *674i*, 682–683
 in Mexican-American War, *461i*,
  *691m*
 in War of 1812, 328, *328i*
 women in (World War I), *712p*
 *See also* Continental army/navy;
  military
Nazi Party, 803, 826–827
Nazi-Soviet Pact of 1939, 806
NBC (National Broadcasting
 Company), 743
Nebraska, 489
Netherlands, 56, 69, 78, 151, 183
Neutrality Act of 1935, 805–806
neutrality in disputes, 295, 513, 689,
 708–709
Nevada, 91, 989

New Deal, 776–781, 790–793,
 884–885
New England Anti-Slavery Society,
 423
New England Colonies, 69–70,
 71–76, *74m*, *88c*
*New England Girlhood, A* (Larcom),
 *388–389q*
*New England Primer*, 119
New Freedom program, 653
New Hampshire, 71, 72–73, 75, *88c*
New Harmony (IN), 416
New Jersey, 77–78, *88c*, 180
New Jersey Plan, 214
New Mexico, 91
New Netherland, 56
New Orleans (LA), 747, 979
*New York Considered and Improved,
 1695* (Miller), *64q*
New York (NY)
 in 1800s (late), *605p*, 620–621,
  *622p*, *631p*, *636q*
 in 1920s, 646, *733p*
 as nation's capital, 282
 terrorists attacks in, 969–970, 974
  *975p*
New York (state), 56, 77–78, *88c*,
 179–183
New York Stock Exchange, *56p*
*New York World*, 635
newspapers (1800s), 635
Nez Percés Nation, 587
Ngo Dinh Diem, 908–909
Nguyen Cao Ky, 912
Nicaragua, 738, 944–945
Nicholas II of Russia, 711
9/11. *See* September 11, 2001
Nisei Regimental Combat Team,
 **442nd**, 819
Nixon, Richard M.
 campaigning, *496p*, *918p*
 on EPA, 978
 foreign policy of, 925, *925p*, 943
 as President, 918, 924, *1004p*
 on Vietnam War, 919–921
 and Watergate, 926, *926i*
No Child Left Behind Act of 2002,
 942, *942p*
"no man's land," 707
Nolde, William B., 921
nominating conventions, 352
nonviolence, 886–889, *887p*
Normandy (France), 821–822
North (northern states)
 discrimination in (1960s), 874
 dividing South and, *380q*, 482–485,
  486–491, 494–498
 divisions within, 529
 growth/change of, 390–395
 slavery ends in, 422
 South at war with, 499–503
 *See also* Union

# Acknowledgments

## Staff Credits

The people who made up the *America: History of Our Nation* team—representing design services, editorial, editorial services, education technology, manufacturing and inventory planning, market research, marketing services, planning and budgeting, product planning, production services, publishing processes, and rights and permissions—are listed below. Boldface type denotes the core team members.

**Mary Aldridge, Helene Avraham, Renée Beach,** Kerry Lyn Buckley, **Libby Forsyth, Joe Galka, Holly Gordon,** Barbara Hall, **Monduane Harris,** John Kingston, Marian Manners, Kathleen Mercandetti, **Xavier Niz, Carrie O'Connor, Kim Ortell,** Ryan Richards, Kirsten Richert, **Laura Ross,** Colleen Searson, Donna Schindler, **Frank Tangredi,** Rachel Winter

## Additional Credits

Penny Baker, Claudio Barriga, Lois Brown, Pradeep Byram, Rui Camarinha, Sarah Carroll, Jennifer Ciccone, Jim Doris, Doreen Galbraith, Beth Hyslip, Daniela Mastria, Michael McLaughlin, Karen Mancinelli Paige, John McClure, Mark O'Malley, Lesley Pierson, Matt Raycroft, Maureen Raymond, Andrew Roney, Rose Sievers, Mildred Schulte, Ann Shea

## Map and Art Credits

**Maps:** Mapping Specialists Limited, except where noted and with additional type set by Justin Contursi

**Illustrated Maps:** Anthony Morse: **20, 82, 210, 320–321, 425, 460–461, 582, 686, 788** with additional type set by Artur Mkrtchyan

**Illustrations:** Kevin Jones Associates: **13, 451;** Justin Contursi: Atlas design and photo treatments for Skills Activities; gdps: **200–203, 278–281, 302, 305, 306–309, 332, 336–339, 364, 378–381, 410–413, 436, 440–443, 468, 478–481, 504, 507, 508–511, 538, 542–545, 574–577, 604–607, 636, 640–643, 667, 676–679;** Brainworx: **210–211, 216, 286, 288–289, 320–321, 341, 420–421, 425, 432–433, 450–451, 460–461, 502, 522–523, 550–551, 582–583, 596–597, 610–611, 630–631, 686–687**

## Photo Credits

Photo Research: Omni-Photo Communications, Inc.; **Cover** K.C. DenDooven; **A1** Getty Images, Inc.; A2 Esbin/Anderson/Omni-Photo Communications, Inc.; **A3 b.** Dallas and John Heaton/CORBIS; **A3 t.** AP/Wide World Photos; **A4** Tom & Susan Bean; **A5** Julie Habel/CORBIS; **A5** Marvin Newman; **A6** Grant Heilman Photography; **A7** Bill Ross/CORBIS; **A7** Giancarlo de Bellis/Omni-Photo Communications, Inc.; **A10** Larry Downing/Reuters/CORBIS; **A11** CORBIS; **A12 m.** Connie Ricca/CORBIS; **A12 t.** Smithsonian American Art Museum, Washington, DC/Art Resource, NY; **A12 b.** Bettmann/CORBIS; **13 t.** Bettmann/CORBIS; **A13 b.** Jay Dorin/Omni-Photo Communications, Inc.; **A15 l.** Anaheim Public Library; **A15 r.** D. Boone/CORBIS; **A16 backgrnd** ©Royalty-Free/Corbis; **A16** CORBIS; **i** K.C. DenDooven; **ii** Jamestown-Yorktown Educational Trust, VA, USA/The Bridgeman Art Library, London/New York; **iv–v** John Guthrie, Guthrie Studios; **vii** The Granger Collection, New York; **viii** Courtesy National Archives, photo no. ( ); **ix** O.C. Seltzer, *Lewis and Clark with Sacagawea, at the Great Falls of the Missouri River*, #0137.871. From the Collection of Gilcrease Museum, Tulsa, Oklahoma; **x** Collection of The New-York Historical Society, negative no. 26280; **xi** AP/Wide World Photos; **xii** The Granger Collection, New York; **xiii** Bettmann/ CORBIS; **xiv** ©Bettmann/CORBIS; **xv** AP/Wide World Photos; **xviii** Courtesy of the Library of Congress; **HT 1** Omni-Photo Communications, Inc.; **HT 2 l.** Courtesy National Archives; **HT 2 r.** Omni-Photo Communications, Inc.; **HT 3** Lawrence Migdale/Pix; **HT 4** CORBIS/Bettmann; **HT 5** © David Young-Wolff/PhotoEdit inc.; **HT 8 l.** David Stoecklein/CORBIS; HT **8 r.** Sime s.a.s./eStock/PictureQuest; **HT 12** Copyright ©North Wind/North Wind Picture Archives; **HT 13** CC Lockwood/Animals Animals; **HT 14** Mary Evans Picture Library; **HT 15** The Granger Collection, New York; **HT 19** KAL/The Baltimore Sun/CartoonArts International/CWS; **HT 21** Brand X Pictures/PictureQuest; **HT 22** © Jeff Greenberg/PhotoEdit Inc.; **1 t.r.** Jamestown-Yorktown Educational Trust, VA, USA/The Bridgeman Art Library, London/New York; **1 t.l.** Hair Comb (Seneca Iroquois) late 17th century, carved moose antler, 4 1/2" H (11.4 cm.). From the collections of the Rochester Museum & Science Center, Rochester, New York (RM 2932).; **1 b.** CORBIS/Bettmann; **2–3** Tom Bean/CORBIS; **5 l.** Tinglit kayak (wood), Inuit School (19th century)/Private Collection, Boltin Picture Library/Bridgeman Art Library; **5 r.** IND 123 0784502/2 Vasco da Gama (c.1469–1525) Portuguese navigator, Spanish School, (16th century)/Private Collection, Index;/www.bridgeman.co.uk; **6** Jonathan Blair/CORBIS; **8** Charles & Josette Lenars/CORBIS; **8 inset** The Granger Collection, New York; **9** Jorge Ianiszewski/Art Resource, NY; **10** Werner Forman/Art Resource, NY; **11 r.** The Granger Collection, New York; **11 l.** Michel Zabe/© Dorling Kindersley; **11 m.** Michel Zabe/© Dorling Kindersley; **13 r.** Stock Montage, Inc.; **13 b.l.** PhotoDisc, Inc./Getty Images; **13 t.l.** Andy Deering/Omni-Photo Communications, Inc.; **14** Hair Comb (Seneca Iroquois) late 17th century, carved moose antler, 4 1/2" H (11.4 cm.). From the collections of the Rochester Museum & Science Center, Rochester, New York (RM 2932).; **15** The Art Archive/Cherokee Indian Museum North Carolina/Mireille Vautier; **17 l.** Courtesy of the Freer Gallery of Art, Smithsonian Institution, Washington, D.C.: Purchase, F1946.12, f. 38b; **17 t.r.** Peter Chadwick/© Dorling Kindersley; **17 b.r.** Roger Phillips/© Dorling Kindersley; **17 m.r.** Philip Dowell© Dorling Kindersley; **18** Giraudon/Art Resource, NY; **19** Figure of Shou Lao (jade), Chinese School, (17th century)/Fitzwilliam Museum, University of Cambridge, UK/Bridgeman Art Library; **20 l.** photolibrary.com; **20 r.** © Tom Stoddart/Woodfin Camp & Associates; **21 r.** The Granger Collection, New York; **21 t.l.** © Markus Matzel/Peter Arnold, Inc.; **21 b.l.** Philip Dowell© Dorling Kindersley; **23** Tissot, James Jacques Joseph (1836–1902) *Moses and the 10 Commandments* c. 1896–1902. Gouache on board. 10 11/16 x 5 5/8". Gift of the Heirs of Jacob Schiff, x1952-190. Photo by John Parnell. The Jewish Museum, New York, NY, U.S.A./Art Resource, NY; **24** Bildarchiv Preussischer Kulturbesitz/Art Resource, NY; **25** AP/Wide World Photos; **26** The Granger Collection, New York; **29** Bildarchiv Preussischer Kulturbesitz/Art Resource, NY; **30** Figure of Shou Lao (jade), Chinese School, (17th century) /Fitzwilliam Museum, University of Cambridge, UK/ Bridgeman Art Library; **31** © Royalty-Free/CORBIS; **32–33** Amos Zemer/Omni-Photo Communications, Inc.; **36** The Granger Collection, New York; **37** Ridolfo Ghirlandaio (1483–1561) *Christopher Columbus.* Museo Navale di Pegli, Genoa, Italy. Scala/Art Resource, NY.; **38** Astrolabe, copper, by Ahmad Ibn Khalaf an Iraqi Arab, 9th century, NO_DATA/Bibliotheque Nationale de Cartes et Plans, Paris, France/ Bridgeman Art Library; **39 t.** John Cabot (c. 1450–c. 1499), Genoese navigator. Image Select/Art Resource, NY; **39 b.** The Art Archive/Museo de la Torre del Oro Seville/Dagli Orti/The Picture Desk; **40 t.l.** Corel Professional Photos CD-ROM™; **40 b.r.** Corel Professional Photos CD-ROM™; **40 m.l.** Corel Professional Photos CD-ROM™; **40 t.r.** Corel Professional Photos CD-ROM™; **40 b.l.** Corel Professional Photos CD-ROM™; **40 m.r.** Roger Phillips/© Dorling Kindersley; **42 b.** National Gallery Collection; by kind permission of the Trustees of the National Gallery, London/CORBIS; **42 t.** Copyright © North Wind/North Wind Picture Archives—All rights reserved.; **43 t.l.** Mary Evans Picture Library; **43 t.r.** The Granger Collection, New York; **43 b.** James Stevenson/© National Maritime Museum, London,© Dorling Kindersley; **45** The Granger Collection, New York; **47** The Granger Collection, New York; **49** *Portrait of Henry VIII* (1491–1547), Holbein, Hans the Younger (1497/8–1543)/ Belvoir Castle, Leicestershire, UK/Bridgeman Art Library; **50 r.** Peter M. Fisher/Corbis; **50 t.** © Dorling Kindersley; **50 b.** Bettmann/CORBIS; **51** *Queen Elizabeth I playing the lute* (miniature, Hilliard, Nicholas (1547–1619)/Berkeley Castle, Gloucestershire, UK/ Bridgeman Art Library; **52** Tate Gallery, London / Art Resource, NY; **55** The Granger Collection, New York; **56** ©Monica Graff/The Image Works; **57** The Granger Collection, New York; **60** Copyright © North Wind/North Wind Picture Archives—All rights reserved.; **62–63** CORBIS/Bettmann; **68** State Capitol, Commonwealth of Virginia. Courtesy The Library of Virginia.; **69** Courtesy of the Library of Congress. Art © Romare Bearden Foundation/Licensed by VAGA, New York, NY; **70** Head of Squanto (d.1622), an American Indian of the Pawtuxet tribe who became a good friend to the Pilgrims (wood),

# Acknowledgments

American School, (17th century)/Private Collection/Bridgeman Art Library; **71** T11999 *The Spermaceti Whale,* DETAIL, engraved by William Home Lizars (1788–1859) plate 10 from Vol 12 of Sir William Jardine's 'Naturalist's Library', pub. 1833–45 (hand-coloured engraving), Stewart, James (1791–1863) (after)/Natural History Museum, London, UK,/Bridgeman Art Library; **72 t.l.** Courtesy, American Antiquarian Society; **72 b.l.** CORBIS; **72–73** Courtesy of The Salem Witch Museum, Salem, Massachusetts; **75** Courtesy of the Library of Congress; **76** Mary Evans Picture Library; **79** The Granger Collection, New York; **83 t.** Roy Rainford/Robert Harding World Imagery; **83 m.** © Charles E. Rotkin/CORBIS; **83 b.** © Philip Gould/CORBIS; **84** Courtesy of the Library of Congress; **85** The Granger Collection, New York; **87** *Portrait of General James Edward Oglethorpe (1696–1785) founder of the State of Georgia,* copy of original portrait in Atlanta, c.1932 (oil on canvas), Ravenet, Simon Francois (1706/21-74) (after)/Corpus Christi College, Oxford, UK/ Bridgeman Art Library; **89** Hulton Archive/Getty Images Inc.; **90** Everett C. Johnson/eStock Photography, LLC; **92** *Tumacacori Mission,* 1855 (oil on canvas), Pratt, Henry Cheever (1803-80)/© Phoenix Art Museum, Arizona, Francis Hover Stanley and Carolanne Smurthwaite/Bridgeman Art Library; **92** inset Jack Dykinga /Getty Images; **96** The Granger Collection, New York; **98–99** Embroidered by: Eunice Bourne, Massachusetts (Barnstable), 1732—before 1781. Overmantel (detail). American, Colonial, mid-18th century. Plain weave linen embroidered with wool, silk and metallic yarns, glass beads, and wood frame with glass. 63 x 129 cm (24 13/16 x 50 13/16 in) (including frame). Museum of Fine Arts, Boston. Seth K. Sweetser Fund, 21.2233. Photograph © 2006 Museum of Fine Arts, Boston.; **101** CORBIS; **103** The Granger Collection, New York; **105 r.** The New York Public Library, Rare Book Division/Art Resource;**105 l.** Copyright © North Wind/North Wind Picture Archives—All rights reserved. ;**106** Courtesy of the Library of Congress; **107 m.** Geoff Brightling (c) Dorling Kindersley, Courtesy of the Museum of English Rural Life, The University of Reading; **107 r.** Andy Crawford (c) Dorling Kindersley, Courtesy of the Museum of the Revolution, Moscow; **107 l.** Geoff Dann (c) Dorling Kindersley, Courtesy of the Barleylands Farm Museum and Animal Centre, Billericay; **109 b.r.** CORBIS/Bettmann; **109 b.l.** © Richard T. Nowitz/CORBIS; **109 t.l.** The Granger Collection, New York;**109 t.r.** Colonial Williamsburg Foundation, gift of Frances Matthews.; **109** Corel Professional Photos CD-ROM™; **110 r.** Victoria & Albert Museum, London/Art Resource, NY; **110 l.** Wenham Museum; **111** The Granger Collection, New York; **112** The Granger Collection, New York; **115** The Granger Collection, New York; **116** *Slaves preparing tobacco, Virginia, America,* c.1790, from 'Le Costume Ancien et Moderne', Volume II, plate 50, by Jules Ferrario, engraved by Angelo Biasioli (1790–1830), published c.1820s–30s (colour litho), Bramati, G. (19th century) (after)/Private Collection, The Stapleton Collection/Bridgeman Art Library; **117** CORBIS; **119 b.** CORBIS/Bettmann; **119 t.l.** The Granger Collection, New York; **119 t.r.** The Granger Collection, New York; **120** Schomburg Center/Art Resource, NY; 121 Copyright © North Wind/North Wind Picture Archives—All rights reserved.; **123** Archivo Icongrafico, S.A/CORBIS; **125 t.** Collection of The New-York Historical Society (1938.312); **125 b.** Pearson Education/PH School Division; **128** The Granger Collection, New York; **129** The Granger Collection, New York; **134 t.** Tony Freeman /PhotoEdit; **134–35 b.** Courtesy National Archives.; **134–35 t.** The Granger Collection, New York; **135 b.r.** Copyright © North Wind/North Wind Picture Archives—All rights reserved.; **136–37** *The Fight on Lexington Common, April 19, 1775,* from 'The Story of the Revolution' by Woodrow Wilson (1856–1924), published in Scribner's Magazine, January 3, 1898 (oil on canvas), Pyle, Howard (1853–1911)/© Delaware Art Museum, Wilmington, USA, Howard Pyle Collection;/Bridgeman Art Library; **139 r.** CORBIS; **139 l.** CORBIS/Bettmann; **141** The Granger Collection, New York; **143** Robert Griffing/Paramount Press, Inc.; **144** Mary Evans Picture Library; **147** Copyright © North Wind/North Wind Picture Archives—All rights reserved.; **148** The Granger Collection, New York; **149** The Granger Collection, New York; **151 r.** The Granger Collection, New York; **151 l.** Boston Tea Party tea leaves in a glass bottle, collected by T.M. Harris, Dorchester Neck, December 1773, American School, (18th century)/© Massachusetts Historical Society, Boston, MA, USA/Bridgeman Art Library; **151 m.** Courtesy, American Antiquarian Society; **153** Jim Conaty/Omni-Photo Communications, Inc.;

**154 t.** Courtesy of the Library of Congress; **154 b.l.** John Singleton Copley (American, 1738–1815), *Mrs. James Warren (Mercy Otis)* ca.1763. Oil on canvas. 49 5/8 x 39 1/2 in. (126 x 100.3 cm). Bequest of Winslow Warren. Courtesy, Museum of Fine Arts, Boston. Reproduced with permission. (c)2000 Museum of Fine Arts, Boston. All Rights Reserved. Photograph © 2006 Museum of Fine Arts, Boston.; **154 b.r.** Jim Barber/StockRep, Inc.; **154 m.** The Granger Collection, New York; **155** The Granger Collection, New York; **157** The Granger Collection, New York; **158** Fort Ticonderoga Museum; **159** Fort Ticonderoga Museum; **160 t.r.** Copyright © North Wind/North Wind Picture Archives—All rights reserved.; **160 b.** Copyright © North Wind/North Wind Picture Archives—All rights reserved.; **160 t.l.** American 18th Century, *Attack on Bunker's Hill, with the Burning of Charles Town,* oil on canvas, .533 x .708 (21 x 27 7/8); framed: .603 x .774 x .038 (23 3/4 x 30 1/2 x 1 1/2). Gift of Edgar Williams and Bernice Chrysler Garbisch, Photograph (c) 2000 Board of Trustees, National Gallery of Art, Washington, 1783 or after, oil on canvas.; **166–67** Corel Professional Photos CD-ROM™; **171** Bettmann/ CORBIS; **172** The Granger Collection, New York; **173** Maryland Historical Society, Baltimore; **174** Courtesy National Archives and Records Administration, College Park, Maryland, photo no. (USH001TF 011 004); 175 Index Stock Imagery, Inc.; **179** The Granger Collection, New York; **181** The Granger Collection, New York; **182 l.** Uniforms of the American Revolution: 1777 Private Field Dress from the 1st Georgia Continental Infantry (gouache & w/c on paper), Lefferts, Charles MacKubin (1873–1923)/© New-York Historical Society, New York, USA/Bridgeman Art Library; **182 t.r.** Colonial Williamsburg Foundation; **182 b.r.** Courtesy National Park Service, Museum Management Program and Valley Forge National Historical Park. Rifle, 1760–1770, Pennsylvania "Mountain" flintlock rifle. Steel, iron, wood. L 137.8 Barrel L 99.7 cm. The George C. Neumann Collection, Valley Forge National Historical Park, VAFO 172.; **182 m.r.** The Connecticut Historical Society Museum, Hartford, Connecticut; **183** The Granger Collection, New York; **184** PhotoDisc, Inc./Getty Images; **185** Pearson Education/PH School Division; **187** CORBIS/Bettman; **188** The Granger Collection, New York; **19** The Granger Collection, New York; **192** Copyright © North Wind/North Wind Picture Archives—All rights reserved.; **194 t.** The Granger Collection, New York; **194 b.** The Granger Collection, New York; **194 m.** The Granger Collection, New York; **197** PhotoDisc, Inc./Getty Images; **198** Corel Professional Photos CD-ROM™; **200** Jon Feingersh/Stock, Boston; **200-01** Fenimore Art Museum, Cooperstown, New York. Photo credit: Richard Walker.; **203 r.** *James Wilson (1742–1798) American Revolutionary Statesman,* 1792 by Jean Pierre Henri Louis.(1755–1799) Watercolor on ivory, 6.7 x 5.2 cm., detail, Smithsonian American Art Museum, Washington, D.C./Art Resource, NY; **203 l.** Art Resource, NY; **205** Virginia Tourism Corp.; **208** The Granger Collection, New York; **211 b.** Richard Hamilton Smith/CORBIS; **211 t.** Raymond Bial; **213 r.** Gary Randall/Getty Images, Inc.—Taxi; **213 l.** Bob Krist/CORBIS; **214** *James Wilson (1742–1798) American Revolutionary Statesman,* 1792 by Jean Pierre Henri Louis.(1755–1799) Watercolor on ivory, 6.7 x 5.2 cm., detail, Smithsonian American Art Museum, Washington, D.C./Art Resource, NY; **216 m.** Courtesy National Archives; **216 m.b.** CORBIS/Bettmann; **216 t.l.** Art Resource, NY; **216 b.l.** CORBIS/Bettmann; **216 t.r.** CORBIS/Bettmann; **216 b.r.** Jon Feingersh/Stock, Boston; **219** CORBIS; **220** (c) Courtesy, American Antiquarian Society; **225** Courtesy of the Library of Congress; **227** Donovan Reese/Getty Images - Photodisc-; **228** Donovan Reese/Getty Images - Photodisc-; **244** Corbis Royalty Free; **250** Photograph by Robin Miller, 2001. Independence Hilstorical Park Corbis/Bettmann; **251** Bettmann/CORBIS; **252** CORBIS/Bettmann; **253 t.r.** CORBIS/Bettmann; **253 b.r.** © Archivo Iconografico, S.A./CORBIS; **253 l.** CORBIS is all caps; **254** Steve Bronstein/Getty Images; **255 t.r.** Courtesy of the Library of Congress; **255 b.r.** Drug Enforcement Administration; **255 b.l.** Tony Freeman/PhotoEdit; **255 t.l.** California Historical Society, San Francisco; **258** © Joseph Sohm; ChromoSohm, Inc./CORBIS; **263** Supreme Court Historical Society; **265** Jeff Cadge/Getty Images; **266** The Granger Collection, New York; **267 l.** Jeff Greenberg/Omni-Photo Communications, Inc.; **267 r.** Nick Ut /AP/Wide World Photos; **268** The Granger Collection, New York; **269** © Michael S. Yamashita/CORBIS; **270** Paul Sakuma/AP/Wide World Photos; **271** ©Paul Conklin/PhotoEdit;

# Acknowledgments

*Abraham Lincoln* (1809–1865), Sixteenth US President. Watercolor on ivory, c. 1860. National Portrait Gallery, Smithsonian Institution/Art Resource, NY. (detail); **496** CORBIS/Bettmann; **497** Kansas State Historical Society; **498** The Granger Collection, New York; **499** National Portrait Gallery, Smithsonian Institution/ Art Resource, NY (NPG.71.29); **501** Hulton-Deutsch Collection/CORBIS; **502 m.** The Granger Collection, New York; **502 b.** United States Department of the Interior; **502 t.** Courtesy of the Library of Congress, Geography and Map Division; **506** Kansas State Historical Society; **507** The Granger Collection, New York; **508–09** David Muench/Muench Photography Inc.; **515 l.** Omni-Photo Communications, Inc.; **515 r.** Omni-Photo Communications, Inc.; **516** Courtesy Beverley R. Robinson Collection, US Naval Academy Museum; **517** Dave King / Dorling Kindersley (c) Confederate Memorial Hall, New Orleans; **519** Bettmann/CORBIS; **519** inset Steve Helber/AP/Wide World Photos; **522–23** from Great Battles of the Civil War by kind permission of Marshall Editions Ltd; **523 l.** Publisher's Press, Inc.; **523 r.** Collection of Picture Research Consultants, Inc. Photo © Collection of David and Kevin Kyle; **525** Collection of the personal papers of General Robert H. Milroy, Courtesy of the Jasper County Public Library, Rensselaer, Indiana (detail); **526** AP/Wide World Photos; 529 The Granger Collection, New York; **530 r.** The Granger Collection, New York; **530 l.** Getty Images Inc.—Hulton Archive Photos; **532** AP/Wide World Photos; **533** Courtesy National Archives and Records Administration, College Park, Maryland, photo no. (NWDNS-111-B-326); 535 Courtesy of the Library of Congress; **541** The Granger Collection, New York; **542** Antique Textile Resource; **542–43** CORBIS; **545 m.** Courtesy of the Library of Congress; **545 r.** The Granger Collection, New York; **545 l.** John Henry Brown, *Abraham Lincoln* (1809–1865), Sixteenth US President. Watercolor on ivory, c. 1860. National Portrait Gallery, Smithsonian Institution/Art Resource, NY.; **547** CORBIS/Bettmann; **548 r.** CORBIS/BETTMANN; **548 l.** Getty Images—Hulton Archive Photos; **550 m.** The Charleston Museum; **550 b.** The Granger Collection, New York; **550 t.** Dave King/ Dorling Kindersley © Confederate Memorial Hall, New Orleans; **551 t.l.** Copyright © North Wind/North Wind Picture Archives—All rights reserved.; **551 m.** Douglas Mudd, National Numismatic Collection, The Smithsonian Institution; **551 t.r.** neg. #86-113-74, Rudolf Eickmeyer, National Museum of American History, Smithsonian Institution; **551 b.** The Museum of the Confederacy, Richmond, Virginia, Photography by KATHERINE WETZEL; **552** Courtesy of the Library of Congress; **553 l.** The Granger Collection, New York; **553 r.** Courtesy of the Library of Congress; **554 r.** Courtesy of the Library of Congress; **554 l.** Courtesy of the Library of Congress; **555** The Granger Collection, New York; **556** The Granger Collection, New York; **557 t.** Old Court House Museum, Vicksburg, Photo by Bob Pickett; **557 b.** Collection of Mississippi State Historical Museum/Mississippi Department of Archives and History; **560 l.** Courtesy of the Library of Congress; **560–61** CORBIS; **562** CORBIS/Bettmann; **563** CORBIS; **565** CORBIS; **566** *His First Vote,* 1868 (oil on canvas), Wood, Thomas Waterman (1823–1903)/Private Collection, Christie's Images/www.bridgeman.co.uk/The Bridgeman Art Library, London/New York; **567** The Granger Collection, New York; **572 t.** Solomon D. Butcher Collection, Nebraska State Historical Society; **572 b.l.** Corbis-Bettmann; **573 t.l.** Copyright © North Wind/North Wind Picture Archives—All rights reserved.; **573 b.** From the Collections of The Henry Ford; **573 t.r.** Courtesy of State Museum Resource Center, California State Parks; **574–75** Tim Cox, *Ahead of the Storm* 1989, oil, 12" x16". Courtesy of Eagle Creek Enterprises; **577** Courtesy of the Library of Congress; **579** Pearson Education; **583 b.l.** Union Pacific Historical Collection; **583 b.r.** California State Capitol Museum; **583 t.** CORBIS / Bettmann; **585 l.** Lynton Gardiner (c) Dorling Kindersley, Courtesy of The American Museum of Natural History; **585 r.** Robe, possibly Roan Eagle, Oglala Sioux, 1870s, Denver Art Museum Collection: Evans Indian Fund, 1931.28. Photo by the Denver Art Museum. All rights reserved.; **585 m.** Corel Professional Photos CD-ROM™; **586** Courtesy of the Library of Congress; **588** © Wally McNamee/CORBIS; **592 t.** History Collections, Los Angeles County Natural History Museum; **592 b.** Panhandle-Plains Historical Museum, Canyon TX; **592 m.** Art Archive/Bill Manns; **593** Frederic Remington/SuperStock; **594** Ken Cole/Animals Animals; **596 l.** The Granger Collection, New York;

**596 r.** Joel Sartore/Grant Heilman Photography—All rights reserved.; **597 l.** Solomon D. Butcher Collection, Nebraska State Historical Society; **597 r.** Kansas State Historical Society, Topeka; **599** Courtesy of the Library of Congress; **603** Solomon D. Butcher Collection, Nebraska State Historical Society; **604–05** Everett Longley Warner (American, 1877–1963), *Along the River Front, New York,* 1912, oil on canvas, 32 x 40 in. (81.2 x 101.6 cm), Toledo Museum of Art, Museum Purchase Fund, 1914.109; **610 l.** The Granger Collection, New York; **610 r.** The Granger Collection, New York; **610 m.** The Granger Collection, New York; **611 l.** The Granger Collection, New York; **611 r.** Hulton-Deutsch Collection/CORBIS; **611 m.r.** The Granger Collection, New York; **611 m.l.** Lynn Historical Society; **612** CORBIS; **615** Bettmann/CORBIS; **616** Bettmann/CORBIS; **617** Snark/Art Resource, NY; **617** Snark/Art Resource, NY; **618** The Granger Collection, New York; **619** CORBIS/Bettmann; **621** Underwood & Underwood/CORBIS; **622** Jessie Tarbox Beals, *Room in a Tenement flat,* 1910, detail, Reprinted by permission of the Museum of the City of New York, The Jacob A. Riis Collection; **624 b.** Christie's Images; **624 t.** National Baseball Hall of Fame Library, Cooperstown, N.Y.; **625** Bettmann/CORBIS; **627** Omni-Photo Communications, Inc.; **628** The Granger Collection, New York; **630 b.** Bettmann/CORBIS; **630 m.** Bettmann/CORBIS; **630 t.** Bettmann/CORBIS; **631 t.** Hulton Archive/Getty Images; **631 b.** Bettmann/Corbis; **634 r.** The Granger Collection, New York; **634 l.** The Granger Collection, New York; **635** Syracuse University Library, Department of Special Collections.; **637** Bettmann/CORBIS; **640–41** © Bettmann/CORBIS; **643** Stock Montage, Inc./Historical Pictures Collection; **645** The Granger Collection, New York; **646** The Granger Collection, New York; **649** The Museum of American Political Life, University of Hartford; **651** Amos Zezmer/Omni-Photo Communications, Inc.; **651** inset Courtesy of the Library of Congress; **652** The Granger Collection, New York; **653** Stock Montage, Inc./Historical Pictures Collection; **655 t.l.** CORBIS; **655 t.r.** Chicago Historical Society, G1978.154.4; **655 b.** Pearson Education/PH School Division; **658** Underwood and Underwood photo. Courtesy of the Library of Congress; **659** Corbis/Bettmann; **661 l.** Getty Images Inc. — Hulton Archive Photos; **661 r.** Schomburg Center for Research in Black Culture/Art Resource; **662** Corbis/Bettmann; **663 l.** Courtesy, Los Mineros Photograph Collection, Chicano Research Collection, Arizona State University Libraries; **663 r.** UT Institute of Texan Cultures, 98–949; **664** Courtesy of State Museum Resource Center, California State Parks; **666 r.** Courtesy of the Library of Congress; **666 l.** Reprinted by permission of the Museum of the City of New York; **668** Snark/Art Resource, NY; **674 t.** CORBIS; **674 b.** The Granger Collection, New York; **674–75** backgrnd The Granger Collection, New York; **675 t.l.** Courtesy National Archives and Records Administration, College Park, Maryland.; **675 t.r.** Chris Forsey/© Dorling Kindersley; **675 b.** Courtesy of The Advertising Archives; **676–77** The Granger Collection, New York; **679 r.** The Granger Collection, New York; **679 l.** The Granger Collection, New York; **680** National Portrait Gallery, Smithsonian Institution/Art Resource, NY; **681** The Granger Collection, New York; **683** The Granger Collection, New York; **684** Courtesy of the Library of Congress; **686** The Art Archive, The Picture Desk/Kobal Collection; **687 t.l.** 2004 © Anchorage Museum/AlaskaStock.com; **687 t.r.** The Granger Collection, New York; **687 b.r.** Corel Professional Photos CD-ROM™; **687 b.l.** © Dorling Kindersley; **689 r.** Chicago Historical Society; **689 t.l.** (c) Collection of The New-York Historical Society; **689 b.l.** Collection of The New-York Historical Society, New York City; **690** Getty Images Inc. - Hulton Archive Photos; **692** The Granger Collection, New York; **695 t.** CORBIS; **695 b.** Joe Viesti/Viesti Associates; **697** Culver Pictures, Inc.; **699** Getty Images Inc. - Hulton Archive Photos; **700** The Granger Collection, New York; **701** The Granger Collection, New York; **702–03** Courtesy National Archives and Records Administration, College Park, Maryland.; **705 r.** Courtesy National Archives, photo no. W&C 490; **705 l.** CORBIS; **708 l.** Getty Images; **708–09** Hulton Archive/Getty Images Inc.; **708 r.** West Point Museum Collection, United States Military Academy; **709 t.** © Bettmann/ CORBIS; **709 b.** The Art Archive/Culver Pictures; **710 r.** © SuperStock, Inc / Superstock; **710 l.** © Bettmann/ CORBIS; **711** Culver Pictures, Inc.; **712** CORBIS; **713** West Point Museum Art Collection, United States Military Academy; **714** Courtesy of the Library of Congress; **716 t.l.** © David Pollack/ CORBIS;

**716 b.** © Bettmann/CORBIS; **716 t.r.** Nebraska State Historical Society Photograph Collections; **717 t.l.** © Bettmann/CORBIS; **717 m.** 'Our Boys Need Sox, Knit Your Bit', American Red Cross 1st World War poster (colour litho), American School, (20th century)/Private Collection, Barbara Singer;/Bridgeman Art Library; **717 b.** © Schenectady Museum; Hall of Electrical History Foundation/CORBIS; **717 t.r.** © Swim Ink 2, LLC/CORBIS; **720** AP/Wide World Photos; **721** © royalty-free/ CORBIS; **722** The Granger Collection, New York; **724** © Bettmann/ CORBIS; **726** Mary Evans Picture Library; **727** Hulton Archive/Getty Images Inc.; **728** CORBIS/ Bettmann; **730** © Swim Ink 2, LLC/CORBIS; **732–33** *The Great White Way—Times Square,* New York by Howard Thain, 1925; oil on canvas, 30 x 36 inches; accession #1963.150. Collection of The New-York Historical Society, detail; **737** The Granger Collection, New York; **738** Courtesy of the Library of Congress; **739** Shahn, Ben. *Bartolomeo Vanzetti and Nicola Sacco* from the Sacco-Vanzeti series of twenty-three paintings. (1931–32). Tempera on paper over composition board, 10 1/2 x 14 1/2" (26.7 x 36.8 cm). The Museum of Modern Art/Licensed by Scala-Art Resource, NY. Gift of Abby Aldrich Rockefeller. Digital Image. (c) The Museum of Modern Art/Licensed by SCALA/Art Resource, NY. The Museum of Modern Art, New York, N.Y., U.S.A. Art © Estate of Ben Shahn/Licensed by VAGA, New York, NY; **740** © Bettmann/ CORBIS; **741** © CORBIS; **742** CORBIS/Bettmann; **743** © Underwood & Underwood/ CORBIS; **744** The Granger Collection, New York; **745** Courtesy of the Library of Congress; **746** © Bettmann/ CORBIS; **746 inset** Collection of Ines and Gerald A. Lynas; **747** AP/Wide World Photos; **748 l.** Frank Driggs Collection; **748 b.** Bettmann/ CORBIS; **748 t.** © MaxJazz/ Lebrecht; **748 m.r.** The Granger Collection, New York; **748 border** istockphoto.com; **749** The Granger Collection, New York; **750** Photo by A.M. Rivera; **751 l.** The Amistad Research Center; **751 r.** Pearson Education/PH School Division; **752** The Granger Collection, New York; **754** The Granger Collection, New York; **755 b.** Ron Wade Buttons; **755 t.** Ron Wade Buttons; **758** Shahn, Ben. *Bartolomeo Vanzetti and Nicola Sacco* from the Sacco-Vanzeti series of twenty-three paintings. (1931–32). Tempera on paper over composition board, 10 1/2 x 14 1/2" (26.7 x 36.8 cm). The Museum of Modern Art/Licensed by Scala-Art Resource, NY. Gift of Abby Aldrich Rockefeller. Digital Image. (c) The Museum of Modern Art/Licensed by SCALA/Art Resource, NY. The Museum of Modern Art, New York, N.Y., U.S.A.. Art © Estate of Ben Shahn/Licensed by VAGA, New York, NY; **764 b.** CORBIS; **764 t.** © CORBIS; **764 m.** ©Bettmann/CORBIS; **764–65** b. Walter Sanders/ Time Life Pictures/Getty Images; **765 t.** The Granger Collection, New York; **766–67** Courtesy of the Library of Congress. Art © Estate of Ben Shahn/Licensed by VAGA, New York, NY; **769** © Hulton-Deutsch Collection/CORBIS; **771 r.** Hulton Archive/Getty Images Inc.; **771 l.** UPI/CORBIS-BETTMANN; **773 b.** CORBIS/Bettmann; **773 t.r.** Popperfoto/Retrofile; **773 t.l.** AP/Wide World Photos; **774** Courtesy of the Library of Congress; **776** Franklin Delano Roosevelt Library, Hyde Park, NY; **777 r.** Courtesy of the Library of Congress; **777 l.** The Granger Collection, New York; **778b.** © CORBIS; **778 t.** © David J. & Janice L. Frent Collection/CORBIS; **780** The Granger Collection, New York; **781** CORBIS; **783 l.** ©Underwood & Underwood/ CORBIS; **783 r.** ©Bettmann/ CORBIS; **783 m.** CORBIS; **784** Detail. National Portrait Gallery, Smithsonian Institution/ Art Resource, NY; **785** © Bettmann/CORBIS; **786** (Detail) National Museum of American Art, Washington, DC, U.S.A./ Art Resource, NY; **787** Courtesy Everett Collection; **788** © CORBIS; **789** © CORBIS; **789 inset** Smithsonian American Art Museum, Washington, DC/Art Resource, NY; **790** Courtesy of the Library of Congress; **791** CORBIS/Bettmann; **793** © Bettmann/CORBIS; **794** *Unemployed,* 1938 (tempera on paper), Shahn, Ben (1898–1969)/Private Collection, Christie's Images;/Bridgeman Art Library. Art © Estate of Ben Shahn/Licensed by VAGA, New York, NY; **795** © Bettmann/CORBIS; **796** Popperfoto/Retrofile; **798–99** © Bettmann/CORBIS; **801** AP/Wide World Photos; **802** The Granger Collection, New York; **803 r.** CORBIS/Bettman; **803 l.** AKG London Ltd; **804** Hulton Archive/Getty Images; **806** Popperfoto/Retrofile; **808** (c) Judith Miller / Dorling Kindersley / Hope and Glory**809** © Bettmann/CORBIS; **810 b.** Courtesy of the Library of Congress; **810 r.** Terra Foundation for American Art, Chicago/ Art Resource, NY; **810 l.** Hulton Archive/Getty Images Inc.; **813** © CORBIS; **815 t.** Naval Historical Foundation Photo Service; **817 r.** CORBIS; **817 l.** Courtesy of the Library of Congress; **817 l.** Courtesy of the Library of Congress; **818** The Art Archive/ National Archives Washington DC; **819** Courtesy of the Library of Congress; **820** © Bettmann/CORBIS; **822** AP/Wide World Photos/ U.S. Army; **824** Hulton Archive/Getty Images Inc.; **826** CORBIS; **827** © Molly Riley/Reuters/CORBIS; **829** CORBIS; **830** Terra Foundation for American Art, Chicago/ Art Resource, NY; **831** Courtesy National Archives.; **832–33** Richard Ward © Dorling Kindersley; **833** Courtesy of the Library of Congress, reproduced with permission from the Marcus Family; **837** CORBIS/Bettmann; 839 b. Walter Sanders/ Time Life Pictures/Getty Images; **839 t.l.** Courtesy of the Library of Congress; **839 t.r.** Hulton Archive/Getty Images Inc.; **841** UPI/CORBIS/Bettman; **843** Time Life Pictures/Getty Images; **844** CORBIS/Bettmann; **845** Kim Mould/Omni-Photo Communications, Inc.; **846 r.** H. Armstrong Roberts/Retrofile; 846 l. George Cohen; **848 b.r.** © Bettmann/CORBIS; **848 t.** Lambert/Hulton Archive/Getty Images Inc.; **848 b.l.** Michael Ochs Archives.com; **849 m.l.** Michael Ochs Archives.com; **849 t.** Getty Images; **849 inset** Courtesy Everett Collection; **849 b.l.** Michael Ochs Archives.com; **849 b.r.** Courtesy Everett Collection; **853** "It's Okay — We're Hunting Communists". From "Herblock Special Report (W.W. Norton, 1974). Reprinted by permission of the Herb Block Foundation.; **854** AP/Wide World Photos; **855** Alan Band/Hulton Archive/Getty Images Inc.; **856** NASA; **857 t.** Courtesy of The Peace Corps; **857 b.** Courtesy of The Peace Corps; **858 t.l.** CORBIS/Bettmann; **858 t.r.** CORBIS/Bettmann; **858 b.** MPI/Hulton Archive/Getty Images Inc.; **863** CORBIS/Bettmann; **868 t.** Bettmann/CORBIS; **868–69 backgrnd** AP/Wide World Photos; **869 b.** ©Peter Bono/Images.com; **869 t.r.** David Brauchli/Reuters/CORBIS; **869 t.l.** AP/Wide World Photos; **870–71** Bettmann/CORBIS; **875 r.** ©Constantine Manos/ Magnum Photos; **875 l.** CORBIS; **876** The Granger Collection, New York; **877** © Bettmann/CORBIS; **878 m.** Don Cravens/ Time Life Pictures/Getty Images; **878 b.** AP/Wide World Photos; **878 t.** AP/Wide World Photos; **880 t.** Courtesy of Detroit Free Press; **881** Michael Newman/PhotoEdit Inc.; **883 l.** © Walt Cisco/CORBIS; **883 r.** ©Bettmann/CORBIS; **884** Paul S. Conklin/PhotoEdit Inc.; **885** Hulton Archive/Getty Images Inc.; **886** ©Bob Adelman/ Magnum Photos; **887** ImageQuest; **888** AP/Wide World Photos; **889** AP/Wide World Photos; **890 r.** AP/Wide World Photos; **890 l.** © David J. & Janice L. Frent Collection/CORBIS; **892** CORBIS/Bettmann; **893** John Olsen/Time Life Pictures/ Getty Images; **895** © Najlah Feanny/CORBIS; **896 r.** Ernst Haas/Hulton Archive/Getty Images Inc.; **896 l.** AP/Wide World Photos; **896 m.** © Bettmann/CORBIS; **900** Bettmann/CORBIS; **901** Silver Burdett Ginn; **902–03** © Wally McNamee/CORBIS; **905** AP/Wide World Photos; **906** Time Life Pictures/ Getty Images; **908** © Michael S. Yamashita/CORBIS; **909** © Bettmann/CORBIS; **910** © Yoichi Okamoto/CORBIS; **911** Charles Bonnay/Black Star; **912** Robert Ellison/Black Star; **913** © Bettmann/CORBIS; **914 t.r.** © Wally McNamee/CORBIS; **914 m.t.** © Bettmann/CORBIS; **914 t.l.** © David J. & Janice L. Frent Collection/CORBIS; **914 m.b.** Hulton Archive/Getty Images Inc.; **914 b.l.** Herbert Orth/Time Life Pictures/Getty Images; **914 b.r.** © Leif Skoogfors/CORBIS; **916 b.** AP/Wide World Photos; **916 t.** ©Henri Bureau/CORBIS SYGMA; **917 t.** Larry Burrrows/Time Life Pictures/Getty Images; **918** Terry Ashe/Time Life Pictures/Getty Images; **920** © Bettmann/CORBIS; **921** CORBIS/Bettmann; **922** Richard Howard/Time Life Pictures/Getty Images; **923** AP/Wide World Photos; **924** Digital Vision; **925** © CORBIS; **927** Pearson Education/PH School Division; **932–33** Shawn Thew/AFP/Getty Images; **935 r.** D.B. Owen/Black Star; **935 l.** Courtesy Ronald Reagan Library; **936** Courtesy: Jimmy Carter Library; **937** Jim Berry/NEA INC NORTHERN ELECTRONICS AUTOMATION; **938 l.** © Bettmann/ CORBIS; **938 r.** Courtesy Ronald Reagan Library; **939** The Political Bandwagon; **940** AP/Wide World Photos; **942** AP/Wide World Photos; **943** U.S. Air Force photo; **944** EWK, CartoonArts International/CWS; **945** © Novosti/Sovfoto; **947 b.** AP/Wide World Photos; **947 t.** AP/Wide World Photos; **947 m.** David Brauchli/Reuters/CORBIS; **949** AP/Wide World Photos; **950** © Peter Turnley/CORBIS; **952** Time Life Pictures/Getty Images; **955** © Wally McNamee/CORBIS; **956 t.** AP/Wide World Photos; **956 b.** CORBIS/ Bettmann; **957** Helene C. Stikkel/ U.S. Department of Defense Visual Information Center; **958** Andrew Alvarez/AFP/Getty Images; **959 t.** Robert Azzi/Woodfin Camp & Associates; **959 b.** Luciano Corbella/© Dorling Kindersley; **962** AP/Wide World Photos; **964–65** Karl